A Blueprint for Implementing Best Practice Procedures in a Digital Forensic Laboratory

Meeting the Requirements of ISO Standards and Other Best Practices

A Blueprint for Implementing Best Practice Procedures in a Digital Forensic Laboratory

Meeting the Requirements of ISO Standards and Other Best Practices

Second Edition

David Lilburn Watson
Head of Forensic Computing Ltd, Ryde, United Kingdom

Andrew Jones
Professor at the Universities of Suffolk, Hertfordshire and South Wales, Ipswich, United Kingdom

ACADEMIC PRESS

An imprint of Elsevier

ELSEVIER

Academic Press is an imprint of Elsevier
125 London Wall, London EC2Y 5AS, United Kingdom
525 B Street, Suite 1650, San Diego, CA 92101, United States
50 Hampshire Street, 5th Floor, Cambridge, MA 02139, United States
The Boulevard, Langford Lane, Kidlington, Oxford OX5 1GB, United Kingdom

Notices
Knowledge and best practice in this field are constantly changing. As new research and experience broaden our understanding, changes in research methods, professional practices, or medical treatment may become necessary.

Practitioners and researchers must always rely on their own experience and knowledge in evaluating and using any information, methods, compounds, or experiments described herein. In using such information or methods they should be mindful of their own safety and the safety of others, including parties for whom they have a professional responsibility.

To the fullest extent of the law, neither the Publisher nor the authors, contributors, or editors, assume any liability for any injury and/or damage to persons or property as a matter of products liability, negligence or otherwise, or from any use or operation of any methods, products, instructions, or ideas contained in the material herein.

ISBN 978-0-12-819479-9

For information on all Academic Press publications
visit our website at https://www.elsevier.com/books-and-journals

Publisher: Stacy Masucci
Acquisitions Editor: Elizabeth A. Brown
Editorial Project Manager: Joshua Mearns
Production Project Manager: Fahmida Sultana
Cover Designer: Matthew Limbert

Typeset by STRAIVE, India

Contents

4. The integrated management system

8. Incident response

9. Case processing

10. Forensic case management

11. Forensic case evidence presentation

12. Secure working practices

13. Ensuring continuity of operations

14. Managing business relationships

15. Effective records management

19. Accreditation and Certification for a digital forensic laboratory

About the authors

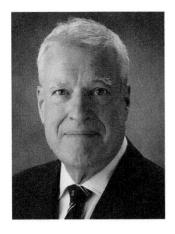

David Lilburn Watson heads up Forensic Computing Ltd., a specialist digital forensic recovery and investigation company. He is responsible for the coordination and efficient delivery of the digital forensic evidence recovery services and digital investigations and provides support for a broad range of investigative, information security and risk consulting assignments. He holds the following certifications and degrees:

Certificate in Governance of Enterprise IT Systems (CGEIT);
Certificate of Cloud Security Knowledge (CCSK);
Certified Computer Crime Investigator (CCCI);
Certified Computer Forensics Technician—Advanced (CCFT);
Certified Fraud Examiner (CFE);
Certified Identity Risk Manager (CIRM);
Certified in Risk and Information System Control (CRISC);
Certified Information Forensics Investigator (CIFI);
Certified Information Security Manager (CISM);
Certified Information System Security Professional (CISSP);
Certified Information Systems Auditor (CISA);
Chartered Fellow (BCS—United Kingdom);
Chartered IT Professional (BCS—United Kingdom);
MSc—Distributed Computer Networks (University of Greenwich);
MSc—IT Security (University of Westminster)—Distinction;
MSc—Fraud Risk Management (Nottingham Trent University)—Distinction.

David has also led many organisations to certification against ISO 9001, ISO 22301, and ISO/IEC 27001. Forensic Computing Ltd. (FCL) complies with ISO 17020 and ISO 17025 but has not sought accreditation.

Amongst other achievements, David was the HTCIA Chapter President in the United Kingdom and a member of the Metropolitan Police Computer Crime Unit—Expert Advisors Panel.

Andrew Jones served for 25 years in the British Army's Intelligence Corps. After this he became a manager and a researcher and analyst in the area of information warfare and computer crime at a defence research establishment. In 2002, he left the defence environment to take up a post as a principal lecturer at the University of Glamorgan in the subjects of network security and computer crime and as a researcher on the threats to information systems and computer forensics. At the university, he developed and managed a well-equipped computer forensics laboratory and took the lead on a large number of computer investigations and data recovery tasks. In January 2005, he joined the Security Research Centre at BT where he became a chief researcher and the head of information security research. From BT, he went on sabbatical to Khalifa University in the United Arab Emirates to establish a postgraduate programme in information security and computer crime and to create a research capability. He then took up a post of the Head of the Cyber Security Research Laboratory at the University of Hertfordshire. Andy has an MSc in information security and computer crime and a PhD in the area of threats to information systems. He currently holds posts as a visiting professor at the University of Suffolk, the University of Hertfordshire, and the University of Derby.

Acknowledgements

The writing of this book has been an epic endeavour that went far beyond what was originally conceived. A large number of people have either knowingly or unknowingly helped and provided knowledge, inspiration, support, coffee, and sympathy at the right time.

To this end, we particularly thank the following individuals who have helped us achieve our goal:

Clive Blake, Late Met Police Computer Crime Unit
Clive Hudson, NZ Serious Fraud Office
Edward P Gibson, Public Arbitrator-FINRA; J.D.-U.S.; Solicitor-U.K, FBI Supervisory Special Agent (Ret.)
James Arthur, Grant Thornton
Josh Dinsdale, Dataswift Ltd.
Jung Son, NZ Serious Fraud Office
Luke Jeffries, Dataswift Ltd.
Shane Mannix, NZ Serious Fraud Office
Urooje Sheikh, Grant Thornton, Late Met Police Computer Crime Unit
Vadim Lugovets, Lugovets Associates
Vijay Rathour, Grant Thornton

We also thank the project team and the publishing professionals at Elsevier—Elizabeth Brown and Joshua Mears—for their patience and support during the rather lengthy process.

In addition, we acknowledge our wives, Kath Jones and Patricia Watson, for their ongoing tolerance as well as editorial and inspirational support when the writing (and sometimes the authors) became difficult and sometimes very difficult!

Finally, we thank all of you that have taken the trouble to use this book. We hope that the information that we have provided contributes to the smooth running of your digital forensic laboratory.

Chapter 1

Introduction

1.1 Introduction

1.1.1 Rationale for the second edition

This is the second edition of this book which was first written in 2013. The second edition has been produced because, in the intervening period, almost all of the standards that it refers to and addresses have been updated and the whole discipline of digital forensics have progressed alongside the existing technologies and new concepts such as the Internet of Things (IoT), integration of Operational Technology (OT) into Information Technology (IT), and the application of Artificial Intelligence (AI).

Whilst some of the book is generic guidance aimed at any digital forensic laboratory, the policies, procedures, and checklists are those that are actually implemented in the FCL IMS.

1.1.2 What is digital forensics

Digital forensics is a highly specialised and fast-growing field of forensic science relating to the recovery of evidence from digital storage media. Digital forensics applies traditional forensics processes and procedures to this new evidential source.

It can also be referred to as computer forensics, but technically speaking, the term only relates to recovery of evidence from a computer, and not the whole range of digital storage devices that may store digital data to be used as evidence. Computer and digital forensics is also often referred to as cyber forensics.

In this book, as in the case of the FCL Forensic Laboratory (FCL), the term digital forensics is used.

Digital forensics can be used in civil and criminal cases or any other area of dispute. Each has its own set of handling requirements relevant to the jurisdiction in which the case is being investigated.

Typically, digital forensics involves the recovery of data from digital storage media that may have been lost, hidden, or otherwise concealed or after an incident that has affected the operation of an information processing system. This could be an accidental or deliberate act, carried out by an employee or outsider, or after a malware attack of any type.

No matter what the specific details of the case, the overview of processing a digital forensic case by FCL follows the same series of processes, interpreted for the jurisdiction according to case requirements. The processes are as follows:

- preserving the evidence;
- identifying the evidence;
- extracting the evidence;
- documenting the evidence recovered and how it was recovered;
- interpreting the evidence; and
- presenting the evidence (either to the client or a court).

Inspection of numerous sources gives differing definitions of 'digital (computer or cyber) forensics', depending on the organisation and its jurisdiction. They all contain some or all of the elements mentioned above (explicitly defined or implied). FCL uses the following definition:

The use of scientifically derived, proved, traceable, and repeatable methods for:

- preserving the evidence;
- identifying the evidence;
- extracting the evidence;
- documenting the evidence recovered and how it was recovered;
- interpreting the evidence; and
- presenting the evidence.

to reconstruct relevant events relating to a given case.

A Blueprint for Implementing Best Practice Procedures in a Digital Forensic Laboratory. https://doi.org/10.1016/B978-0-12-819479-9.00018-6

The same processes and techniques are used for any media, whether it is a hard disk drive, a SIM card from a mobile device, digital music players, digital image recording devices, or any other digital media.

Details of handling different types of cases are given in Chapter 9. A list of typical types of cases where FCL has been involved is given in Appendix 1.

1.1.3 The need for digital forensics

The world population, in 2022, exceeded 8,000,000, and the number of Internet users reported in 2022 is estimated to be 4,950,000,000,[a] some 62% of the population. This is an increase of 1355% since the year 2000.[b]

As the world increasingly embraces information processing systems and the Internet, there are more data being held on digital media. At the same time, an individual country's Gross Domestic Product (GDPs) is being boosted by an increasing Internet-based component. Alongside the growth in the number of internet users has come a massive increase in the value of the internet in terms of business, which makes it an increasingly attractive target for criminals. The value of ecommerce in 2021 has continued to grow dramatically, and the market was estimated to be worth US$ 13 Trillion in 2021 and be worth US$843 billion in the United States and to reach approximately £169 billion in the United Kingdom.

At the same time as the Internet economy has been growing, the size of local digital storage for personal computers has grown. IBM likes to think that they produced the first personal computer (the 'PC' or Model 5150) on 12 August 1981; there were a number of personal computers in operation for years prior to this, including Tandy TRS, Apple, Nascom, Commodore PET, Texas Instruments, Atari, and a variety of CP/M machines, as well as those running proprietary operating systems. A random view of digital storage growth is given in Appendix 2.

Whilst this table shows disks available for personal computer users, those available to corporate users or those with mainframes or, as an increasing number of organisations are, using the cloud, can have considerably larger capacities. Details of disk size nomenclature are given in Appendix 3.

The amount of data produced has, according to Statistica in June 2021,[c] 79 zettabytes and is estimated to reach 180 zettabytes by 2025.

At the same time, information processing systems of all types are being used to perpetrate or assist in criminal acts or civil disputes as well as just holding evidence relating to the matter. This rapidly changing technology has spawned a completely new range of crimes such as hacking (unauthorised access to a computer system or unauthorised modification to or disclosure of information contained in it) or distributed denial of service attacks. It can be argued that there are no new crimes just variations of old ones, but that legislation needs to be amended to handle new types of execution of offenses.[d]

Whatever the outcome of this argument, more and more information processing devices are used in the commission of criminal acts or are assisting in their execution. There are no fixed statistics for the total number of crimes committed where an information processing device is involved, but there are many 'guesstimates'. All show increasing use. At the same time, corporate use of information processing devices and digital storage is increasing rapidly.

Given the rapid expansion of both information processing systems and stored data on digital media, it is not difficult to see that digital forensics, with its ability to search through vast quantities of data in a thorough, efficient, traceable, and repeatable manner, in any language, is essential. This allows material to be recovered from digital media and presented as evidence that may not otherwise be recoverable and presentable in a court.

At this stage, the needs of the corporate world and that of law enforcement (LE) differ on a number of levels:

- LE works under more restrictive legislation and regulations that their counterparts in the corporate world;
- The burden of proof is typically more stringent in criminal cases than in civil cases; and
- Each is governed by the 'good practices' defined by their various governing bodies, and these often differ (e.g. LE relates to the criminal process in the jurisdiction, and corporates are more focused on implementation of information security and security incident management).

Corporates are often loathe to involve LE in any incident for a variety of reasons, but legislation now exists in some jurisdictions to report any security incident that discloses personal information or that makes nominated individuals personally liable for breaches or other information security failures. In cases such as this, digital forensics may be called on not

---

a. https://wearesocial.com/us/blog/2022/01/digital-2022/.
b. From Internet World Stats http://www.internetworldstats.com/stats.htm.
c. https://www.statista.com/statistics/871513/worldwide-data-created/.
d. A Decade of Financial Crime on the Internet (1992–2002) New Technology-New Crimes?, David Lilburn Watson, MSc Dissertation, University of Westminster, 2004.

only to determine how the breach occurred but also to determine the effectiveness of the risk treatment (typically controls) in place to minimise the risk of unauthorised access or disclosure.

1.1.4 The purpose of this book

This book has been produced to provide as close as possible to a one stop shop for a set of policies, procedures, and checklists that meet industry good practice and international standards for handling digital evidence through its complete lifecycle. These encompass the needs of groups from 'First Responders', digital forensic laboratories, individual employees, and management whether they are LE, other government, or civilian. The procedures are distilled from international standards, government procedures, corporate practices and procedures, police and LE procedures, and generally accepted good practice. The procedures are jurisdiction independent and should be reviewed for specific jurisdictions.

If digital evidence can be handled properly from the start of its lifecycle for an investigation using standard operating procedures based on good practice to meet relevant standards, then there will be consistent handling throughout the industry and the many cases that fail on account of evidence contamination at the outset, or at some point during its processing, will be avoided.

Anyone that has been involved in working in, or managing, a digital forensics laboratory will be aware of the large number of processes and procedures that are essential for the efficient and safe running of the laboratory. If a digital forensic laboratory also aspires to achieve an accreditation from one of the accreditation bodies such as the International Standards Organization (ISO), then additional processes and procedures have to be implemented and followed.

This book has been written as a follow-on from the book 'Building a Digital Forensic Laboratory', which as the name suggests was aimed at providing guidance for creating and building a digital forensic laboratory. When that book was written, the aim was to guide the user through the issues that needed to be addressed when a digital forensic laboratory was created and to give guidance on the issues of building and managing it. This book is written to provide the reader with guidance on the policies and procedures that should be adopted and maintained in order to run a forensic laboratory in an efficient and professional manner and also to allow the digital forensic laboratory to be compliant with the numerous standards that apply to a digital forensic laboratory. The book has not been designed to address the legal issues of any specific region, but instead to provide advice and guidance on good practice in the broader aspects of laboratory management. It also does not address the use of any specific tools or deal with handling any specific hardware or software in a forensic laboratory; there are many other books and documents dealing with this.

1.1.5 Book structure

As part of this book, a large number of templates and checklists have been included to provide a 'one stop shop' for the reader. These, in themselves, have been produced as the result of good practice and an understanding of the requirements imposed by various standards. The policies and procedures that are covered in this book are covered in a great deal of detail in some areas where it is considered necessary and in other areas where it is not, less so.

This book is divided into three logical areas: policies and procedures for setting up a forensic laboratory, policies and procedures that will be required during the normal running of a forensic laboratory, and the policies that are required for gaining and maintaining accreditation and/or certification.

As the requirements for the running of a digital forensic laboratory develop, the policies and procedures will inevitably need to change to meet new requirements.

1.1.6 Who should use this book?

The anticipated audience for this book is anyone that is involved in the teaching, conduct, or management of any aspect of the digital forensics lifecycle. This will include the following:

- **academics:** who are educating the next generation of practitioners and managers;
- **practitioners:** who are conducting investigations; and
- **managers:** of forensic laboratories and facilities.

For the academics, it is important not only that they teach the tools and techniques that the Forensic Analyst and Investigator should be able to carry out investigations but also the principles, rules of evidence, and appropriate standards to ensure that the evidence that their students will recover is acceptable in the courts and has been collected, preserved, and analysed in a scientifically sound manner.

For the Forensic Analyst and Investigator, it is intended to be an aide memoire of the procedures and standards that they should follow and also a repository of the forms that they will need in their everyday jobs. Some of these they will use every day and be very familiar with, others they will only use occasionally or rarely.

For the Forensic Laboratory Manager, this book covers all of the standards and procedures for all aspects of an investigation or a digital forensic laboratory. In the United Kingdom, the Forensic Regulator has now mandated that all Law Enforcement Laboratories must be certified to ISO/IEC 17025 and it is hoped that this book will assist managers of such laboratories in achieving this.

Anyone who is, or wants to become, a Forensic Analyst can benefit from this book. It will also assist Forensic Laboratory Managers who wish to submit to, and pass, relevant ISO standards certification or accreditation, as appropriate.

It contains cross references from relevant ISO standards to this book and the procedures in it that can be amended to suit working practices in the jurisdiction whilst still meeting the relevant ISO requirements.

1.1.7 The need for procedures in digital forensics

In order to understand the need for procedures in digital forensics, we must first be clear on what we mean by digital forensics. The term, 'digital forensics' was defined at the Digital Forensic Research Workshop in 2001 as "The use of scientifically derived and proven methods toward the preservation, collection, validation, identification, analysis, interpretation, documentation and presentation of digital evidence derived from digital sources for the purpose of facilitating or furthering the reconstruction of events found to be criminal, or helping to anticipate unauthorized actions shown to be disruptive to planned operations."[e,f] The use of scientifically derived and proven methods means that there is a requirement for a high level of consistency, traceability and repeatability. This is commonly represented as meaning that any other skilled practitioner should, given the data available, be able to reproduce the results obtained. In the United States, two cases have defined the acceptability of evidence for courts and the findings have been widely accepted around the world.

The first was a federal case, Frye v. United States[g] in 1923, a federal case that was decided by the District of Columbia (DC) Circuit. In Frye, the DC Circuit considered the admissibility of testimony based on the systolic blood pressure test, a precursor of the modem polygraph. The court stated that any novel scientific technique "must be sufficiently established to have gained general acceptance in the particular field in which it belongs." The court found that in this case, the systolic blood test had "not yet gained such standing and scientific recognition among physiological and psychological authorities." As a result of this, under the Frye standard, it is not sufficient that a qualified individual expert or even a group of experts testify that a particular technique is valid. Under the Frye standard, scientific evidence will only be allowed into the courtroom if it is generally accepted within the relevant scientific community. Frye imposes the burden that the relevant scientific community must 'generally' accept the technique. The Frye standard has now been abandoned by many of the states and the federal courts in favour of the Daubert standard, but it is still law in some states in the United States.

The second case was that of Daubert v. Merrell Dow[h] in 1993. In this case, the US Supreme Court rejected the Frye test with regard to the admissibility of scientific evidence. Instead of the 'general acceptance' in the scientific community standard stipulated in Frye, under Daubert the new test required an independent judicial assessment of reliability. Under the Daubert ruling, to be admissible in a court in the United States, evidence must be both relevant and reliable. The reliability of scientific evidence, which includes the output from a digital forensics tool, is determined by the Judge (as opposed to a jury) in a pretrial 'Daubert hearing'. The responsibility of a judge in a Daubert hearing is to determine whether the underlying methodology and techniques that have been used to isolate the evidence are sound, and whether as a result, the evidence is reliable. The Daubert process identifies four general categories that are used as guidelines when a procedure is assessed:

- **testing:** Can and has the procedure been tested?
- **error rate:** Is there a known error rate for this procedure?
- **publication:** Has the procedure been published and subject to peer review?
- **acceptance:** Is the procedure generally accepted in the relevant scientific community?

---

e. Digital Forensic Research Workshop (DFRWS) 2001, DFRWS Technical Report, DTR-TOOl-01 Final, A Road Map for Digital Forensic Research http://old.dfrws.org/2001/dfrws-rm-final.pdf.

f. As can be seen, this only relates to criminal or "unauthorised actions shown to be disruptive to planned operations." The definition used by FCL in Section 1.1 overcomes this hurdle.

g. A Simplified Guide to Forensic Evidence Admissibility & Expert Witnesses, http://www.forensicsciencesimplified.org/legal/frye.html.

h. Daubert v. Merrell Dow Pharmaceuticals, Inc. https://caselaw.findlaw.com/us-supreme-court/509/579.html.

As a result of this, the 'Daubert Test' replaced the 'Frye Standard' with regard to the admissibility of scientific evidence. Prior to this, under the 'Frye Standard', the courts placed responsibility of determining acceptable procedures within the scientific community through the use of peer-reviewed journals. The shortcoming of this approach was that not every area of science, and particularly the 'newer' areas, has peer-reviewed journals. Digital (or computer/cyber) forensics, with its short history and rapidly changing environment, clearly falls into this category. The adoption of the Daubert Test provides the opportunity for additional methods to be used to test the quality of evidence.

In ensuring that potential evidence in the field of digital forensics is handled in a manner that complies with the legal and regulatory requirements and that it will be in a condition that allows it to be presented in a court of law, it is important to know what to do and what not to do. What should or should not be done will vary from incident to incident, the approach taken by an individual or group and the laws in effect in the relevant jurisdiction(s). If it is left to decisions by individual organisations or people, the outcome will inevitably be a range of interpretations of the requirements and the situations. This does not align with the standards required for repeatability and consistency for scientific processes. In order to reduce the potential for this happening, the industry has adopted good practices, processes, and procedures. In addition to this, there have been numerous standards introduced for forensic laboratories, including accreditation, as well as a range of certifications for individual Forensic Analysts. This is covered in detail in Chapter 19 and Chapter 6, Appendix 24, respectively.

In addition to the obvious benefits across the whole community of developing a consistent approach to all aspects of the digital forensic process, there are also significant potential business advantages of gaining certification or accreditation, whether for the individual to demonstrate a level of skill or for a forensic laboratory to demonstrate that they have achieved a level of competency and compliance with a range of industry and international standards. For LE agencies, compliance with standards gives an external validation that the processes and procedures being used are appropriate and of a suitable quality and, if the procedures have been followed, will make challenges to them in the court more difficult. In commercial organisations, compliance with, and maintenance of, standards gives a quality mark that gives confidence to potential clients.

There are a number of good practices and standards that have been developed to ensure that both within a region and also globally, the way in which the processes of digital forensics are conducted are in a manner that is acceptable to the relevant court. The applicable standards cover a far wider spectrum than just the area of digital forensics and encompass health and safety, quality, and security.

When we talk of good practices and standards, there is a presumption that there will only be one that applies to a particular aspect of a process. Unfortunately, this is rarely true, so whilst we can be compliant with a standard, it does not mean that it can be assumed that other organisations or laboratories that are also 'compliant' will be adhering to the same standard. It is also likely that at any given time there will be a number of standards that a forensic laboratory will be expected to meet. For example, in FCL just a few of the standards that are relevant include the current versions of the following:

- **ISO 900x**—Quality management systems series;
- **ISO 45001**—Occupational health and safety management systems—Requirements with guidance for use;
- **ISO/IEC 27xxx**—Information technology—Security techniques—Information security management systems series;
- **ISO 31000**—Risk management-principles and guidelines series;
- **ISO/IEC 17020**—Conformity assessment—requirements for the operation of various types of bodies performing inspection;
- **ISO/IEC 17025**—General requirements for the competence of testing and calibration laboratories; and
- **ISO 22301**—Security and resilience—business continuity management systems—requirements

In addition to this, there are a range of relevant good practice guides that include the following:

- **UK ACPO**—Good Practice Guide for Computer-Based Electronic Evidence;
- **US-DOJ**—Electronic Crime Scene Investigation: A Guide for First Responders;
- **US-DOJ**—Searching and seizing computers and obtaining electronic evidence in criminal investigations;
- **IOCE**—Guidelines for best practice in the forensic examination of digital technology;
- **RFC 3227**—Guidelines for evidence collection and archiving;
- **GS**—Digital Evidence Principles; and
- **CTOSE**—Cyber Tools On-Line Search for Evidence.

The scope of the procedures that are covered in this book has been made as wide as is reasonably possible. The intention of this book is to aid the user in the whole spectrum of policies and procedures that they should be aware of when they are operating in the digital forensics arena.

1.1.8 Problems with digital evidence

The various articles of literature refer to computer evidence, digital evidence and electronic evidence. For consistency throughout this book, we will use the term 'digital evidence'.

All stages of the process of digital evidence are potentially prone to problems. These result from a number of causes:

- the first is of the rapid developments that are continuing to take place in technology which cause the need for the development of new tools, techniques, and procedures and the need for them to be validated and tested;
- the second is the fact that digital evidence cannot be seen with the naked eye and as a result is difficult for a nontechnologist to conceive;
- the third is that the general public and a large proportion of the judiciary do not understand the technologies, the way in which digital evidence is recovered, or the relevance of the evidence; and
- the fourth is that laws take a long time to bring into effect and by their nature need to be relatively generic, which means that the technology has moved on by the time they are in use.

To give some ideas of the problems faced, the major findings of a now somewhat dated, but still relevant 2015 report, stated that:

- There is uncertainty and apprehension about the impact of rapidly changing digital technology on the administration of justice. There is also concern that the law is not keeping up with technology. *Ninety-three percent of respondents agreed with the statement that the law must be continuously monitored in order to stay current with advances in digital technology. Concerns about electronic fraud or forgery were on the minds of sixty-seven percent of respondents, followed by fifty-eight percent who were concerned about the introduction of new forms of digital evidence;*
- How to deal with digital evidence is an emerging issue for those concerned with the administration of justice. *Sixty percent of respondents have encountered issues of identification, admissibility or weight of digital evidence;*
- Issues with digital evidence are encountered most often in discovery, disclosure of evidence or other proceedings before trial. Civil trials and, to a lesser extent, criminal trials also raise issues of digital evidence. *Fifty-five percent of respondents have faced issues with digital evidence on discovery or disclosure. Another thirty-eight percent have faced such issues in other pre-trial proceedings. Sixty percent of respondents have faced digital evidence issues in a civil trial. Digital evidence in criminal trials was an issue for thirty-two percent of respondents; and*
- Email and social media are the types of digital evidence in which issues are most frequently encountered in litigation. *In legal proceedings, sixty-eight percent of respondents encountered issues with email as digital evidence, followed closely by social media at sixty-one percent. Survey respondents also experienced issues in litigation with text messages (56%) and digital photographs (46%).*

In some ways, digital evidence is the same as any other evidence. In many ways, it is no different from a gun that is seized in a murder case or a knife that is seized in a domestic dispute case. For evidence to be admissible in a Court of Law, it must have been legally obtained. In a Civil Case, the organisation's policies and procedures must have been followed fully and with care. If the organisation has an incident response plan, then this should be followed. It is always prudent to ensure that in all cases, whether criminal or civil, the relevant laws related to search and seizure are followed as what is initially thought to be a civil case may, as evidence is recovered, become a criminal matter. In either type of case, the evidence must have been:

- **legally obtained**—the evidence must have been collected in accordance with the scope and instructions of the search warrant or in accordance with the incident response plan. For digital evidence to be admissible, it must conform to current laws, which will depend on the legal system in force in the jurisdiction, and this may be a problem if it has been collected in another jurisdiction. It must also be the evidence which the trial judge finds useful and which cannot be objected to on the basis that it is irrelevant, immaterial, or violates the rules against hearsay and other objections. If it does not, in reality, you may as well not have spent the effort in collecting it, as it will be of no value;
- **relevant**—'relevant evidence' means evidence having any tendency to make the existence of any fact that is of consequence to the determination of the action more probably or less probably than it would be without evidence. The question of relevance is thus different from whether evidence is sufficient to prove a point;
- **complete**—to satisfy the concept of completeness, the storey that the material purports to tell must be complete. Consideration must also be given to other storeys that the material may tell that might have a bearing on the case. In other words, the evidence that is collected must not only include evidence that can prove the suspect's actions (inculpatory) but also evidence that could prove their innocence (exculpatory);

- **reliable**—the evidence must remain unchanged from its original. Following accepted procedures and good practice will help in ensuring that fragile and potentially volatile digital evidence does not get modified in any way or deleted. Ensuring that the chain of custody is maintained will help to ensure that evidence remains reliable;
- **authentic**—for digital evidence to be authentic, it must explicitly link the data to physical person and must be self-sustained. This is one of the fundamental problems of digital forensics. The Forensic Analyst or Investigator can often associate the evidence to a specific computer or device, but the problem is then to associate the user with that device. To achieve this, it may be possible to use supporting evidence from access control systems, audit logs, or other supporting or collateral evidence, such as CCTV;
- **accurate**—for digital evidence to be accurate it should be free from any reasonable doubt about the quality of procedures used to collect the material, analyze the material if that is appropriate and necessary, and finally to introduce it into Court and produced by someone who can explain what has been done. In the case of exhibits which themselves contain statements—a letter or other document, for example 'accuracy' must also encompass accuracy of content; and that normally requires the documents originator to make a Witness Statement or Deposition and be available for cross examination[i]; and
- **believable**—a jury and/or a judge in a criminal case or the Corporate Managers and Auditors in a civil case need to be able to understand and be convinced by the evidence.

The term 'chain of custody' refers to the process used by the First Responder or the digital forensics specialists to preserve the scene of a crime. This can include the collection and preservation of data stored on computers, storage devices, or even the computer logs on the hard drive of a network server. Each step in the process has to be carefully documented so that, if the case is taken to Court, it can be shown that the digital records were not altered during the investigation process.

Maintaining the chain of custody is a fundamental requirement for all investigations, whether the evidence is physical or logical. A definition of the chain of custody from a legal dictionary[j] states that, "A proper chain of custody requires three types of testimony:

- that a piece of evidence is what it purports to be (for example, a litigant's blood sample);
- of continuous possession by each individual who has had possession of the evidence from the time it is seized until the time it is presented in Court; and
- and by each person who has had possession that the particular piece of evidence remained in substantially the same condition from the moment one person took possession until the moment that person released the evidence into the custody of another (for example, testimony that the evidence was stored in a secure location where no one but the person in charge of custody had access to it)."

Proving the chain of custody is necessary to 'lay a foundation' for the evidence in question, by showing the absence of alteration, substitution, or change of condition. Specifically, foundation testimony for tangible evidence requires that exhibits be identified as being in substantially the same condition as they were at the time the evidence was seized, and that the exhibit has remained in that condition through an unbroken chain of custody. For example, suppose that in a prosecution for possession of illegal narcotics, Police Sergeant A recovers drugs from the defendant; he gives Police Officer B the drugs; B then gives the drugs to Police Scientist C, who conducts an analysis of the drugs; C gives the drugs to Detective D, who brings the drugs to Court. The testimony of A, B, C, and D constitutes a 'chain of custody' for the drugs, and the prosecution would need to offer testimony by each person in the chain to establish both the condition and identification of the evidence, unless the defendant stipulated as to the chain of custody in order to save time.[k]

An article in the Observer newspaper[l] in October 2021 reported that Defence lawyers have warned the Court system in England and Wales is at breaking point as figures reveal a rising number of cases collapsing because of Police and prosecution failures to disclose key evidence.

In the year to 30 June 2021, 1648 cases collapsed over disclosure failures—more than double the number in 2015/16, according to Crown Prosecution Service figures.

Experts say the official figure may be the tip of the iceberg because of concerns that disclosure failures are not always properly recorded.

---

i. Sommer P., Intrusion Detection Systems as Evidence, RAID 98 Conference, 1998.

j. Lehman J., Phelps S., West's Encyclopaedia of American law: Volume 2.

k. http://legal-dictionary.thefreedictionary.com/chain+of+.

l. https://www.theguardian.com/law/2021/oct/31/courts-are-close-to-collapse-over-police-disclosure-failures.

In October 2021, the BBC reported[m] that a £3m diamond fraud trial at Southwark crown court involving 'The Only Way is Essex' star Lewis Bloor collapsed after the Crown Prosecution Service admitted it had failed to disclose some evidence that could have been helpful to Bloor and his codefendants.

Also in October 2021, it was reported[n] that a Specialist Fraud Division and HMRC 5-year operation into a £34M alleged international money laundering operation involving money service bureaus and foreign exchange services had collapsed at Snaresbrook Crown court. The lead counsel for the main defendant, Zacharias Miah argued there had been 'catastrophic disclosure failures' on the part of the Crown forcing the prosecution to accept they had not prepared their case properly. The trial Judge accepted the submissions of Mr. Miah and refused an adjournment.

In the United Kingdom in 2018, there was a report[o] that a rape trial has collapsed after the UK Crown Prosecution Service offered no evidence when it emerged that images from the defendant's phone of him in bed with his alleged victim had not been disclosed. The failure of the case is another example of crucial digital evidence contained on a mobile either not being found or not being handed over to defence solicitors.

The lawyers for Samson Makele, who had been under investigation for 18 months, said that if they had not recovered the photographs themselves the trial could have resulted in a miscarriage of justice. Scotland Yard was already in the process of conducting an urgent review of similar problems after another rape case from December 2017 under similar circumstances when phone messages between the man and woman cast doubt on the prosecution's version of events.

In a 2017 article in Computerworld,[p] it was reported that the Police in Cockrell Hill, Southwest Dallas, admitted to losing digital evidence from as far back as 2009 after the department's server was compromised with ransomware. The Cockrell Hill Police Department stated that, "As a result, all bodycam video, some photos, some in-car video, and some police department surveillance videos were lost."

A July 2018 report from Myanmar[q] on a case that recently went to trial against the jailed Reuters journalists Wa Lone and Kyaw Soe Oo that revolved around alleged physical documents in their possession, the seizure of their phones has also raised serious questions about the handling of digital evidence.

Defence lawyers say that the material that was submitted to the court is only a fraction of what was extracted from the phones. To date, all that has been submitted as phone evidence in the Reuters case have been printed copies of 21 documents, containing "allegedly confidential government letters and plans for the development of an island off Myanmar's west coast for tourism," according to Reuters.

Defence requests for digital copies of the documents and communication records prior to the reporters' 12 December arrest have been rejected by Judge Ye Lwin. The reason given was that prosecution witness and IT expert, Police Major Aung Kyaw San, had already shown that the process had been 'systematically' conducted.

Whilst the makers of the software used, Cellebrite, claim that the integrity of digital evidence can be maintained in part through the use of radio frequency-shielded bags upon seizure, this measure was apparently not taken in the case of the Reuters journalists.

Defence lawyer Khin Maung Zaw told the court on 29 May that Wa Lone's phone had been used to send a single WhatsApp message—'OK'—after the reporters' arrest. The defence also claims that the location of the phones whilst in transit from Yangon to Nay Pyi Taw after being seized by police could be easily tracked online, meaning there is no guarantee they were not tampered with remotely or in-person following the arrest.

Police Major Aung Kyaw San said he was not aware of the WhatsApp exchange, or of anybody having access to the phones who was not designated as part of the investigation, according to Reuters.

Myanmar ICT for Development Organisation (MIDO) executive director Htaike Htaike Aung, who attended several hearings as a Court Observer, noted that there is a lack of legal framework in Myanmar for the use of these powerful tools in criminal investigations.

With regard to the issue of warrants in the Reuters case, Police Major Aung Kyaw San told the court in a 28 May hearing that this did not apply to the data extraction due to charges being brought under the Official Secrets Act.

---

m. https://www.bbc.co.uk/news/uk-england-essex-58927034.

n. https://www.9bedfordrow.co.uk/our-news-views/latest-news/massive-34m-money-laundering-case-collapses-after-legal-arguments-led-by-zacharias-miah/.

o. Bowcott O, Guardian, London rape trial collapses after phone images undermine case. https://www.theguardian.com/law/2018/jan/15/london-rape-trial-collapses-after-phone-images-undermine-case.

p. Storm D., Computerworld, Police lost 8 years of evidence in ransomware attack, https://www.computerworld.com/article/3163046/security/police-lost-8-years-of-evidence-in-ransomware-attack.html.

q. Erickson E., Mizzima, Use of digital forensics raises questions in Reuters case, http://mizzima.com/news-domestic/use-digital-forensics-raises-questions-reuters-case.

If found guilty of violating the Official Secrets Act, Wa Lone and Kyaw Soe Oo will face a maximum sentence of 14 years in prison and contradictory testimony concerning an alleged plot to entrap the reporters could make digital evidence a deciding factor.

Another example of a failure to handle digital evidence correctly is that of the CD Universe case, in which three companies, Network Associates, Kroll O'Gara, and Infowar.com, failed to establish a proper chain of custody.[r] This case related to 'Maxim' (or 'Maxus' depending on which report you read) claimed to be a 19-year-old Russian male, who broke into the computers of Internet retailer CD Universe and stole details of 300,000 credit cards. Whilst the investigation was ongoing, an FBI source commented that "The chain of custody was not established properly," and that this had virtually eliminated the possibility of a prosecution.

In contrast to a written document, because digital evidence cannot be seen with the naked eye, it has to be presented with an accurate interpretation, which identifies its significance in the context of where it was found. The hard disk of a computer will contain raw binary data which may be encoded in a simple binary form or as binary-coded decimal or as hexadecimal data. Even dates and times can be encoded in a number of ways including both the 'big endian' and 'little endian' approach. If there is doubt on the interpretation of a piece of evidence, it can often be supported with other evidence such as the Internet history, logs files, link files, and a range of other information sources.

Having said earlier in this chapter that there are many similarities between physical and digital evidence, there are also many potential differences from other types of evidence because digital evidence:

- can be changed during the process of evidence collection;
- can be duplicated exactly. This means that it is possible to examine a copy and avoid the risk of damaging or altering the original;
- can be easily altered without trace;
- can change from moment to moment both whilst within a computer and whilst being transmitted;
- is not human readable and cannot always be 'read' or 'touched'. It may need to be printed out;
- is relatively difficult to destroy and can be recovered even if it has been 'deleted'. When an attempt is made to destroy digital evidence, it is common for copies of that evidence to remain stored in other locations of which the user is unaware;
- may be created by a computer (and not the user) as well as recorded on it;
- may be encrypted; and
- may be stored on a number of computers and devices in more than one jurisdiction.

There are any numbers of issues that may cause problems in each stage of the process. Through every step of the process, it is crucial to develop and to maintain the chain of custody. It is vitally important to accurately record and document everything that is done and every tool and process and procedure that is used. This ensures that the process is repeatable. Unfortunately, this can be a tedious and difficult task and is probably the single biggest cause of failure in court for cases involving digital evidence. Looking at each of the phases of the digital evidence process, a few examples of issues in each of the phases of the process are detailed in the next section.

In the collection phase, the data must have been searched and seized in a manner consistent with the law. The acquisition processes and the procedures that were used must be adequate and the relevant rules of evidence have been followed. The tools and techniques that are used must also be acceptable. Care must be taken to stay within the scope of the search warrant or Court Order. The chain of custody process and documentation must be initiated and adequate. Care must also be taken with the packing and the transportation of the evidence. For example, did the equipment need to be shielded from radio emissions and were steps taken to ensure that batteries did not become exhausted? Once the material has arrived at the digital forensic laboratory, has it been documented and stored in an appropriate manner?

The search and seizure of digital evidence is the first process that is often disputed. If it can be shown that this step was not completed properly, the evidence may not be admitted. If the search and seizure was not legal or the methodology that was used during the search and seizure was not an accepted practice, then the evidence obtained may be rejected. Whilst there is a long history of the precedent for the search and seizure of physical evidence, the relative short history of digital devices and the rapid development of hardware and software has meant that in the area of digital evidence, there are few precedents that apply. To date there are few standards that apply to search and seizure and as highlighted above, the guidelines and recommendations differ between LE entities depending on the jurisdiction.

---

r. http://www.zdnet.com/news/cd-universe-evidence-compromised/96132.

In April 2021, ComputerWeekly published an article[s] on the Post Office Horizon scandal which started in 2009, that had forced the government to consider fast-tracking changes to the rules on the use of digital evidence in court. The Post Office Horizon scandal saw hundreds of people who own and run Post Office branches prosecuted, with some sent to prison based on computer evidence that has since been proved to be wrong.

In another case reported in 2017,[t] Judge Alison J. Nathan of the Federal District Court in Manhattan delivered a stern warning to prosecutors when she granted a motion by Benjamin Wey, a New York City financier, to suppress everything seized during searches of his office and home in 2012. The New York Times reported that the ruling, if upheld, could deal a significant blow to proving charges filed in 2015 accusing him of stock manipulation and laundering the proceeds from selling shares, because it is unclear what other documentary evidence the government has.

The report stated that the challenge in white-collar-crime investigations is to draught a warrant that is not so broad that it empowers agents to seize virtually any document or search every computer file because it might be related to nebulous misconduct. The Fourth Amendment requires that a warrant 'particularly' describes the place to be searched and things seized. This requirement was a response to the aversion of the framers of the Constitution to so-called general warrants, used by the British before the American Revolution to conduct broad searches for goods imported without payment of the proper duties.

In a 2013 report in the Portland Press Herald,[u] it was stated that Maine State Police officers who searched the home and business of Mark Strong Sr. in 2012 in the investigation of the Kennebunk prostitution case briefly lost custody of a piece of evidence that was now central to Strong's defence. A computer hard drive that Strong claims contained all the information he had compiled as a private investigator looking into unprofessional conduct in the Kennebunk Police Department fell into the hands of an officer Strong was investigating, Audra Presby.

State police Sgt. Mark Holmquist testified on the third day of Strong's trial in York County Superior Court. Strong, 57, of Thomaston, is charged with conspiring with Alexis Wright to run a prostitution business from Wright's Zumba studio in Kennebunk.

Holmquist, who works in the state police Major Crimes Unit, coordinated the raids in conjunction with Kennebunk police. He testified that all computer evidence seized from Strong's home and business on 10 July was supposed to remain in the state police evidence locker. All other evidence was supposed to be stored at the Kennebunk Police Department. "We simply overlooked that one piece of evidence," Holmquist said of the hard drive. "It went into (Presby's) trunk instead of our barracks." When Presby delivered the hard drive to the state police Computer Crimes Unit in Vassalboro 2 days later, the serial number of the hard drive was not in evidence records there, he said.

Lilley, the attorney for Strong, asked Holmquist why evidence seized in police investigations must be documented correctly and recorded every time a piece changes hands and Holmquist replied that "It's important that everything is documented and gone through methodically because cases usually live or die by the evidence."

When transporting the evidence back to the secure evidence store in a forensic laboratory, there are a number of precautions that must be taken. Good practice in the preparation of a computer or other type of electronic device for transport includes:

- making sure that the evidence is not exposed to any magnetic sources such as police radios;
- creating and maintaining the chain of custody;
- ensuring that the digital evidence is kept in the possession of one of the Investigators at all times and making sure that they do not stop anywhere on the way back to the forensic laboratory from the crime scene;
- ensuring that the computers or mobile devices that have been seized are not used;
- placing tape over all the drive slots and other openings of computers;
- the evidence tag should be created and the manufacturer, make, model, and serial number of the equipment should be recorded; and
- the Evidence Custodian must log each piece of evidence in an evidence log.

In the preservation phase, the evidence that is found must be preserved in a state that is as close as possible to its original state. Any changes that are made to the state of the evidence during this phase must be documented and justified. All procedures that are used in the examination should be auditable, that is, a suitably qualified independent expert appointed by the other side of a case should be able to track all the investigations carried out by the prosecution's experts and produce the same results.

---

s. https://www.computerweekly.com/news/252498901/Demands-for-changes-to-barmy-rules-on-digital-evidence-have-governments-ear.

t. Henning P. J., New York Times, Mishandle a Fraud Search, and All That Fine Evidence Could Be for Nothing, https://www.nytimes.com/2017/06/26/business/dealbook/mishandle-a-fraud-search-and-all-that-fine-evidence-could-be-for-nothing.html.

u. Detective: Evidence mishandled in Kennebunkprostitution case.

Full details of handling of different types of physical evidence and their transportation to FCL are given in Chapter 8.

In the analysis phase, once the potential evidence has been collected and preserved, it must then be analysed to extract the relevant information and recreate the chain of events. Care must be taken to ensuring that the tools that are used are appropriate and that any results obtained can be reproduced. It is also essential that all of the relevant evidence is obtained, including exculpatory evidence. Problems that can occur in the analysis phase include dealing with the volume of data that may be involved. It is common for a desktop computer to contain between 1 and 2 Tb of storage and for servers to contain from tens of terabytes to petabytes of storage. Sifting through this can be extremely time consuming, but there is a duty to find all of the evidence relevant to a case. Increasingly, there are tools available to assist the Forensic Analyst, but the use of these can create its own set of problems such as can the results that have been obtained be replicated using other tools or techniques. Have the tools been tested and validated? Full details of case processing for different types of physical evidence in FCL are given in Chapter 9.

In the presentation phase, it is essential to ensure that the method of presentation is appropriate for the audience for which it will be used. Communicating the meaning of the evidence is essential, otherwise it has no value. The presentation must be clear and also represent all of the facts. The problems in this phase of the process are all about communication of the findings but not every Forensic Analyst or Investigator is highly skilled in this area. When presenting digital evidence to a tribunal, a jury, or a judge, it has to be presented in a form that can be understood and which is convincing. This may entail significant additional effort to creating the evidence in a form such as a slide show, PowerPoint presentation, or an animation to represent a timeline of events that is outside the normal skills of the Forensic Analyst or Investigator.

Another issue that has to be considered in every stage of the process is that of spoliation, which is the destruction or significant alteration of evidence or the failure to preserve the property for another's use as evidence in pending or reasonably foreseeable litigation.[v] In law, the spoliation of evidence can be either as the result of an intentional act or through negligence and may be caused by the withholding, hiding, altering, or destroying of evidence relevant to a legal proceeding.

There are two possible consequences that will result from spoliation:

- in jurisdictions where the intentional act is criminal by statute, it may result in fines and/or imprisonment; and
- in jurisdictions where relevant case law precedent has been established, proceedings possibly altered by spoliation may be interpreted under a spoliation inference.

This means it may be considered that a negative evidentiary inference can be drawn from the destruction of a document or other object that is relevant to ongoing or reasonably foreseeable civil or criminal proceedings. There are many examples of the spoliation of digital evidence. For example, it may simply be electronically deleted or the media that the information had been stored on can be physically destroyed. Another example is that the digital information may also have its attributes, such as the date, modified which could mean that evidence has been created after the event or modified after the event. It is also possible that the metadata[w] may have been modified.

One of the most significant spoliation decisions from the digital information arena is the opinions that came from the Zubulake v. UBS Warburg[x] case, in which sanctions were sought for a failure to preserve digital evidence. In the Zubulake vs UBS Warburg case, the Court first imposed sanctions of redepositions for failure to preserve all relevant backup tapes, and then, in a follow-on decision, imposed the sanction of adverse inference instruction to be given for wilful destruction (deletion) of relevant email.

1.1.9 The principles of digital evidence

In digital forensics, there are a number of underpinning principles that have been generally accepted throughout the community. One of the most widely used explanations of these principles can be found in the UK Association of Chief Officers

---

v. West v. Goodyear Tire & Rubber Co., 67 F.3d 776, 779 (2d Cir.1998).

w. Metadata describes other data. It provides information about a certain item's content. For example, an image may include metadata that describes how large the picture is, the colour depth, the image resolution, when the image was created, and other data. A text document's metadata may contain information about how long the document is, who the author is, when the document was written, and a short summary of the document. Web pages often include metadata in the form of meta tags. Description and key words meta tags are commonly used to describe the Web page's content. Most search engines use this data when adding pages to their search index. (From http://www.techterms.com/definition/metadata.)

x. Zubulake v. UBS Warburg, LLC, 229 F.R.D. 422 (S.D.N.Y. 2004) ("Zubulake V"), http://www.ediscoverylaw.com/2004/12/articles/case-summaries/zubulake-v-court.

(ACPO) Good Practice Guide for Computer-Based Electronic Evidence.[y] The guide defines four principles that have been widely accepted as the basic principles for the handling of electronic evidence:

- **principle 1:** No action taken by LE agencies or their agents should change data held on a computer or storage media which may subsequently be relied upon in court;
- **principle 2:** In circumstances where a person finds it necessary to access original data held on a computer or on storage media, that person must be competent to do so and be able to give evidence explaining the relevance and the implications of their actions;
- **principle 3:** An audit trail or other record of all processes applied to computer-based electronic evidence should be created and preserved. An independent third party should be able to examine those processes and achieve the same result; and
- **principle 4:** The person in charge of the investigation (the Case Officer) has overall responsibility for ensuring that the law and these principles are adhered to.

Whilst these principles provide an excellent base from which to start, there are some limitations. The principles apply primarily to investigations that have a single source of evidence and network, cloud-based evidence, or real-time investigations may cause problems. Consideration should also be given to whether or not Locard's Exchange Principle applies.

Locard's exchange principle[z] is the underlying principle for all forensic science and when applied to a crime scene, says that the perpetrator(s) of the crime will both bring something into the scene and take away something from the scene when they leave. Kirk[aa] interprets Locard's exchange principle as: "Wherever he steps, whatever he touches, whatever he leaves, even unconsciously, will serve as a silent witness against him. Not only his fingerprints or his footprints, but his hair, the fibres from his clothes, the glass he breaks, the tool mark he leaves, the paint he scratches, the blood or semen he deposits or collects. All of these and more, bear mute witness against him. This is evidence that does not forget. It is not confused by the excitement of the moment. It is not absent because human witnesses are. It is factual evidence. Physical evidence cannot be wrong, it cannot perjure itself, and it cannot be wholly absent. Only human failure to find it, study and understand it, can diminish its value."

Whilst this interpretation applies to potential physical traces, the same principle equally applies to the digital world. In the following chapters, the procedures that are needed to support all phases of an investigation and also the wider management of an efficient digital forensics laboratory are given in more depth.

Appendix 1—Some types of cases involving digital forensics

Some types of cases that FCL has dealt with include the following:

Criminal cases

- abduction;
- auction fraud;
- burglary;
- cyber stalking;
- deliberate circumvention of information processing security system measures;
- denial of service attacks;
- drugs;
- digital vandalism;
- forgery;
- fraud achieved by the manipulation of computer records;
- identity theft (and subsequent exploitation of the theft of identity);
- industrial espionage (which could include unauthorised access or theft of equipment);
- information warfare;
- intellectual property theft, including software piracy;

---

y. https://www.npcc.police.uk/documents/crime/2014/Revised%20Good%20Practice%20Guide%20for%20Digital%20Evidence_Vers%205_Oct%202011_Website.pdf.

z. Dr. Edmond Locard of Lyon, France, formulated the basic principle of forensic science: "Every contact leaves a trace."

aa Kirk, P., L. Crime investigation: physical evidence and the police laboratory, 1953, Interscience Publishers, Inc.: New York.

- murder;
- paedophilia (creating it and distributing it);
- phishing (and its variants);
- rape;
- release of malware of any kind (e.g. a virus, Trojan horse, worm, etc.);
- sexual crimes;
- spamming (if it is illegal in the jurisdiction);
- terrorism;
- theft;
- unauthorised access to information (often called hacking); and
- unauthorised modification of data or software.

Civil cases

- allegations of breaches of duty of care;
- asset recovery;
- breach of contract;
- copyright issues;
- defamation;
- employee disputes;
- questioned documents;
- theft of corporate resources for private gain;
- to avoid charges of breach of contract;
- to meet requirements of discovery in civil claims;
- tort;
- to support a variety of civil claims; and
- unauthorised access by employees.

Note

In some cases, cases may be pursued through the civil and criminal courts, either simultaneously or consecutively, depending on the legislation and practices within the jurisdiction. Examples may include, but are not limited to, copyright issues, defamation, unauthorised access.

Appendix 2—Growth of hard disk drives

Year	Capacity	Details
Pre 1981	Various	8″ floppy disks or cassette tapes
1981	360 Kb	IBM PC-one or two 5 1/4″ floppy drives
1983	10 Mb	IBM XT
1984	20/1.2 Mb	IBM AT 6 MHz hard disk and floppy disk. They also had a 360 Kb floppy disk drive
1986	30 Mb	IBM AT 8 MHz
1986	720 Kb	IBM Convertible-3 1/2″ floppy disks
1987	20/1.44 Mb	IBM PS/2-PS/2s also had the capability to utilise 2.88 Mb floppy disks
1989	30 Mb	IBM PS/2
1991	60–130 Mb	Available range of hard disk drives, but not all fitted to a PC as standard
1996	1.6–6.4 Gb	Available range of hard disk drives, but not all fitted to a PC as standard

Continued

Year	Capacity	Details
1998	3.2–16.8 Gb	Available range of hard disk drives, but not all fitted to a PC as standard
2003	20–80 Gb	Available range of hard disk drives, but not all fitted to a PC as standard
2005	200–500 Gb	Available range of hard disk drives, but not all fitted to a PC as standard
2006	750 Gb	First 750 Gb drive available
2007	1 Tb	First 1 Tb drive available
2008	1.5 Tb	First 1.5 Tb drive available
2009	2 Tb	First 2 Tb drive available
201 0	3 Tb	First 3 Tb drive available
2011	4 Tb	First 4 Tb drive available
2014	10 Tb	First 10 Tb drive available
2018	16 Tb	First 16 Tb drive announced
2021	20 Tb	First 20 Tb HAMR drive available

Appendix 3—Disk drive size nomenclature

Name	Binary	Number of bytes	Equal to
Byte (B)		1	
Kilobyte (KB)	2^{10}	1024	1024 B
Megabyte (MB)	2^{20}	1,048,576	1024 KB
Gigabyte (GB)	2^{30}	1,073,741,824	1024 MB
Terabyte (TB)	2^{40}	1,099,511,627,776	1024 GB
Petabyte (PB)	2^{50}	1,125,899,906,842,624	1024 TB
Exabyte (EB)	2^{60}	1,152,921,504,606,846,976	1024 PB
Zettabyte (ZB)	2^{70}	1,180,591,620,717,411,303,424	1024 EB
Yottabyte (YB)	2^{80}	1,208,925,819,614,629,174,706,176	1024 ZB
Brontobyte (BB)	2^{90}	1,237,940,039,285,380,274,899,124,224	1024 YB
Geopbyte	2^{100}	1,267,650,600,228,229,401,496,703,205,376	1024 BB

Note

A typical page of A4 requires between 2 and 5 Kb for storage. A low-resolution photograph is about 100 Kb.

Chapter 2

The building

2.1 The building

2.1.1 General

In general terms, it is unlikely that many forensic laboratories will have the luxury of being able to be built from the 'ground up'. More likely, it will be housed in an existing building, and this will have to be adapted to meet the requirements of a forensic laboratory.

In most cases, it will be necessary to develop some sort of business case, even if an existing building is to be converted and some degree of conversion is needed to make it an efficient forensic laboratory.

This chapter assumes that a forensic laboratory is being built from scratch with all current good practice included, and it is being built as a data centre with additional workspace for all necessary office or forensic laboratory purposes.

2.1.2 Business case

It is worth starting with the business case that is needed to justify the expenditure (which may be considerable) and to establish the requirements for the type of accommodation and the square footage that is needed for a forensic laboratory. Experience shows that there are a number of factors that should be considered when designing the layout of a forensic laboratory. The first of these is that, however modest or comprehensive the requirements are for a forensic laboratory, it will inevitably be too small. The factors that affect the size and design of a forensic laboratory include the following:

- estimation of the space needed for each work area;
- the role of the forensic laboratory and the range of tasks that it will undertake;
- size reduction during the costing and management approval process; and
- underestimating the space required for evidence and consumable storage.

In LE or government, it is often thought that one or more of these factors are not relevant, but for the most part this is a mistake. Although it may not require a full business case to be developed, it is almost certain that there will have to be some sort of justification and plan, with costs, for the creation or the development of a forensic laboratory. In reality, whatever it is called, it is the outline justification and costing for the development of a forensic laboratory. Developing a business case will always be a subjective affair, and there is considerable advice and examples of good practice available to assist in this task. Additionally, there may be accepted and documented ways of preparing a business case within an organisation. As with any document that senior management is to review and absorb to achieve a successful outcome, there should be an executive summary at the front explaining briefly what the document is about and giving them the 'elevator pitch' level of information that they are required to approve.

The business case outline that was successfully used for the establishment of the FCL Laboratory is defined in Appendix 1.

There are two main options when selecting the building in which a forensic laboratory will be located. The options are to either take over space in an existing building or to have a new build forensic laboratory. There are advantages and disadvantages to both options.

A new building has the advantage that it will be built to the forensic laboratory's specifications and should have a low maintenance bill for the first few years of operation. It will also be possible to have the latest technology built into the infrastructure. Some of the disadvantages of a new building are the time it will take to get it through the design, approval, and build phases and the cost.

When taking over space in an existing building, some of the advantages are that much of the infrastructure that is required may already be in place and that the time scale is likely to be much shorter. The disadvantages include the fact that the space will have to be adapted and may not meet all of the forensic laboratory's requirements. The ultimate choice for the location of a forensic laboratory may well be decided by a higher authority or dictated by the requirements for it to be in a specific area.

A Blueprint for Implementing Best Practice Procedures in a Digital Forensic Laboratory. https://doi.org/10.1016/B978-0-12-819479-9.00021-6

Issues that should be considered, and that are often overlooked, include that of vehicular access and parking, good communication and transport links, and proximity to the area which the forensic laboratory will serve. If any of these are missing, whilst the building being considered may appear to be ideal for a forensic laboratory, it may not be as effective as it could have been and employees will have pressures put upon them that they do not need.

The location of a forensic laboratory will be dictated by a number of factors, some of which are within the forensic laboratory's control and some of them will not. The location may be dictated by the need to be close to other parts of the organisation or to be central to an area of operations. The cost of real estate in different areas may also have some influence. In reality, if the location is not fixed because it is going to be sited in a building that is already owned or in use by the organisation, it is usual to end up with a trade-off between some or all of the other influences.

Within a building, careful consideration should be given to the exact location of the forensic laboratory. There are plenty of arguments from a security perspective for it to be located in the basement (no windows, control of access, thick walls, and a host of other factors), but this should be balanced against the fact that electricity and water do not mix well and the fact that water flows downhill. This may seem a bit obvious, but this is just one of the many considerations and compromises that will have to be made.

The size of a forensic laboratory will be determined, in part, by the scope of the services that have been defined in the business case and the predicted volume of throughput. Another factor that will affect the size of a forensic laboratory is issues such as health and safety regulations. One issue that is often underestimated when planning a forensic laboratory is the space that will be required for the storage of evidence. Remember that secure storage will be needed not only for cases in progress (or to be processed) but also for past cases. The length of time that evidence should be retained will vary from jurisdiction to jurisdiction but may be as long as for 75 years (currently required in Australia and being considered in the United Kingdom).

2.1.3   Standards

Depending on the jurisdiction, there are a number of standards that are applicable to the creation of a forensic laboratory. These include, but are not limited to, the following:

- ISO—amended as required and have a 5–10-year update cycle;
- TIA—reviewed, amended, or rescinded on a 5-year cycle;
- IEEE—remain current until a change is needed; and
- Local/national standards vary.

The most important thing for anyone setting up a forensic laboratory is to ensure that the relevant standards are checked for the jurisdiction and that all current revisions are considered.

2.2   Protecting against external and environmental threats

Note

More detailed information security aspects of protection against external and environmental threats are defined in Chapter 12, Sections 12.3 and 12.4.

When deciding on the location of a forensic laboratory, consideration should be given to minimising the risk from external and environmental threats. This section lists necessary conditions for the operations of a forensic laboratory to be protected against external and environmental threats.

When choosing a building where a forensic laboratory operates, the following should be considered:

- risk from fire;
- risk from flood;
- risk from civil unrest;
- risk from other facilities in the locality; and
- risks from any other relevant manmade or natural sources.

Determination of recovery times based on risk profiles, including business continuity planning, is defined in Chapter 13, Section 13.4.

When storing any hazardous material on site, they shall be securely and safely stored, preferably away from the main forensic laboratory area.

Appropriate fire and water detection systems shall be put in place, preferably connected to an annunciator panel at a centralised manned station.

The installed burglar alarm shall be connected to a centralised manned station.

Appropriate fire quenching materials shall be made available with forensic laboratory employees trained in their use and an appropriate number of Fire Wardens present.

Where appropriate polythene sheeting or similar shall be held in storage to protect the forensic laboratory's assets from any water leakage from above.

Consideration shall be given to complete environmental monitoring, if thought to be appropriate.

The forensic laboratory backup systems and media store shall be at a secure location that cannot be affected by any disaster affecting the main forensic laboratory area.

The ongoing requirement for 'green computing' and environmental control in the management of digital forensic cases.

2.3   Utilities and services

Note 1

More detailed information security aspects relating to utilities and services are defined in Chapter 12, Section 12.3.14.5.4.

Note 2

It is assumed that all utilities supplied to any forensic laboratory are under the control of the utility companies, and the forensic laboratory is dependent on these and has no control over their supply.

When setting up a forensic laboratory, whether in a new build site or in a conversion to an existing building, it will be necessary to have a number of utilities and services supplied and operational.

2.3.1   Power and cabling

A forensic laboratory is a high-tech facility and will therefore have above average requirements for power supply to keep equipment operational and within operational tolerances defined by the manufacturer.

When determining the power requirements for a forensic laboratory, the following should be considered:

- lighting;
- air conditioning;
- building infrastructure requirements;
- forensic and information-processing equipment; and
- other equipment that may be present, such as photocopiers, kettles, water coolers, fridges, etc.

Whilst considering power requirements, it is essential to consider future growth and ensure that there is sufficient capacity to accommodate future demands.

Forensic and information-processing equipment falls into two specific categories:

- LAN/WAN infrastructure; and
- Forensic Analyst's workspace.

The LAN/WAN infrastructure may be in a dedicated and purpose-built server room or in a secure room used as a server and communications room. If a dedicated server room is to be used, design standards exist from a variety of standards bodies. These include, but are not limited to;

- **TIA/EIA 942**—Telecommunications Infrastructure Standard for Data Centers (plus the Addenda);
- **ANSI/BICSI 002-2019**—Data Center Design and Implementation Best Practices;
- **CENELEC, EN 50173-5**—Information technology—Generic cabling systems—Part 5: Data centres; and
- **ISO/IEC 11801-5:2017**—Information technology—Generic cabling for customer premises—Part 5: Data centres.

The LAN/WAN infrastructure will depend on operational requirements.

Note

In the FCL, there shall be two separate and distinct LANs, one for business operations and one for forensic examination support. Each shall be physically and logically separated. Both LANs shall need careful planning and provision of appropriate power and cabling requirements, which are typically different.

The Forensic Analyst's workspace will be different to that of a 'standard corporate' environment. In the corporate environment, the user will typically have a PC, two monitors, and maybe one or two peripherals attached (e.g. a local scanner or printer). In the FCL Laboratory workspace for Forensic Analysts may have a number of different cases running at any one time and a variety of different technology running at any one time. Additionally, the Forensic Analyst's equipment is usually in an 'always on' state as it is often performing overnight operations (e.g. searches or indexing). The workspace will also require numerous electrical outlets for all equipment that may be in use, as opposed to those required in the 'normal' business environment. Even taking a simple operation of cloning a disk will require at least five electrical sockets:

- forensic workstation;
- monitors;
- power to disk to be cloned;
- write blocker; and
- power to target disk.

and the Forensic Analyst may be running numerous operations simultaneously.

Note

In FCL it was found that there were never too many electrical sockets.

Electrical sockets should be ergonomically sited, as no Forensic Analyst likes to be crawling under their desk every time they want to power up or power down some electrical equipment! A backup power system, typically dual routing from different suppliers, Uninterruptible Power Supply (UPS), and a generator shall be considered.

An UPS shall be installed to protect all relevant information-processing equipment that is able to take the load of that equipment, perform a graceful close down if required, and seamlessly integrate with the generator (if installed). Significant losses of processed data can occur due to power failures or power surges. All relevant equipment shall be subject to UPS, and this should be regularly tested and maintained. Details of required maintenance and testing are defined in Chapter 7, Section 7.5.4.

If backup power cannot be arranged, a secure alternate location for undertaking forensic processing shall be considered for those occasions when there is a loss of power. All power and telecommunications cabling used by a forensic laboratory shall be safeguarded from interception or damage to minimise security risks and protect against loss of data.

Whilst a forensic laboratory may not implement TIA/EIA 942 Telecommunications Infrastructure Standard for Data Centers (plus the Addenda), an explanation of the requirements is given in https://www.accu-tech.com/hs-fs/hub/54495/file-15894024-pdf/docs/102264ae.pdf.

In addition to main power, the risks of static electricity and electromagnetic interference shall be considered. Static electricity is countered by the use of antistatic equipment on an individual basis and is covered by the requirements of personal protective equipment (PPE) as defined in Chapter 17, Section 17.5.1.5.

2.3.2   Heating, ventilation, and air conditioning

Most equipment has a manufacturer's recommended operating temperature and humidity range. It is essential that the operation of equipment in a forensic laboratory is within this range. Careful consideration of the local environment (e.g. location, elevation, and building construction) is essential as these may materially affect requirements for heating, ventilation, and air conditioning (HVAC). Forensic laboratory employees also will want to work in comfortable working temperature and humidity ranges, and in some jurisdictions, the acceptable range of working environment conditions is mandated by law.

The HVAC system shall have adequate capacity for all of the current and foreseeable future requirements. It will need to be an effective system that is reliable and has a high level of availability. A backup plan or spare or redundant capacity for the HVAC systems shall be considered. This may include the use of portable HVAC units.

It may be necessary to instal shielding in the ducting to ensure that the system is not acting as an antenna into and out of the forensic laboratory. It may also be necessary to consider grilles in the ducts to prevent unauthorised access.

2.3.3 Communications

Communications for a forensic laboratory will primarily consist of the phone system and internet access. The type of phone system to be used will depend on the numbers of employees in a forensic laboratory but will typically have the following minimum functionality:

- automatic call back;
- busy extension diversion;
- call hold;
- call transfer;
- conference calling;
- group pickup;
- save and use number dialled;
- system short code dialling; and
- voice mail functionality.

In addition to the landline capability, a number of corporate mobile phones or Bring Your Own Device (BYOD) may be used. These shall all have the capability of being remotely managed and wiped in case of loss. They will be used for forensic laboratory business purposes and may include additional functionality in addition to standard telephony. Security requirements for these devices are defined in Chapter 12, Section 12.3.9 and 12.3.10.

Internet access will be dependent on the local Internet Service Providers (ISPs). In general terms, the bigger the internet pipe available, the better. Each ISP local to a forensic laboratory will have broadly similar services. It may also be sensible to have the ISP host the forensic laboratory web site so long as there is no confidential or customer information located on it.

2.3.4 Water

Water services are required for building management services as well as the supply of a potable drinking source and sewage purposes. In some locations, mains water should not be used for drinking purposes so that a bottled supply or water coolers shall be used.

Water pipes should not be located above the server room if possible. Water detection and portable pumps may be required depending on specific circumstances.

2.4 Physical security

Note

More detailed information security aspects relating to utilities and services are defined in Chapter 12, Section 12.4.

2.4.1 General

As part of the selection of a location for a forensic laboratory, physical security shall be an underpinning consideration in the selection of the location and design. Physical security shall be designed in layers to meet the requirements for a forensic laboratory and its working practices.

Depending on the type of building in which the forensic laboratory is housed, this may start with the area outside the forensic laboratory itself and include the following:

- fences or walls;
- barriers;
- alarms;

- sensors;
- CCTV systems; and
- guard forces.

    Inside the building, there shall be:

- access control systems;
- security doors;
- alarms;
- sensors;
- CCTV systems; and
- guard forces.

    Within the laboratory itself, there shall be:

- physical and logical access control systems;
- security doors;
- alarms;
- sensors;
- CCTV systems; and
- encryption of data.

The issue here that is often missed is that if all of the separate security measures are not integrated and used as a single system, then they may not be optimally effective and there may be gaps or overlaps in the security systems. For example, if the guard force cannot respond in time to an incident that is captured on the CCTV, then there is little point in having them. If the CCTV cameras do not cover all of the access points and any potential weaknesses in the perimeter defences, then again there is little point in spending money on them. The bad guys will spend time identifying the flaws in the systems.

Physical security of a forensic laboratory premises is the first step in the process of securing the forensic laboratory's information-processing systems. It is essential that appropriate physical security is in place for all of the forensic laboratory premises. The Forensic Laboratory Physical Security Policy is defined in Appendix 2.

2.4.2   Signage

There is always a trade-off between the school of thought that requires that there is no external signage to advise the function of the building and having signs to guide visitors to the forensic laboratory (directional signs) and then when they arrive there, information signs. The directional signs are optional and if present, they will need to comply with the organisational scheme, if appropriate. If, when operating the forensic laboratory, there is a need determined not to advertise its presence, then appropriate 'dummy' signage to provide a passable explanation of what the space is being used for will be required (people get curious when they see people entering and leaving an area that has no advertised reason to exist).

The information signs will serve a number of functions, and they may be on the outside the forensic laboratory or within the access controlled area. These signs are intended to advise who can enter the relevant parts of a forensic laboratory (do they have the requisite clearances and the need to enter?) and if they are allowed to enter, under what conditions (escorted, equipment that they are not allowed to bring in, etc), and the first line health and safety notices (fire escape, hazardous materials, etc.).

Once inside a forensic laboratory, signs may be needed for the different areas or zones of the forensic laboratory, emergency exits, health and safety and hazardous materials, access limitation, and a range of other purposes.

2.4.3   Building infrastructure

Both at the external interface to the rest of the building and within a forensic laboratory, any walls will have to be of an appropriate thickness and to the full height (all the way to the fixed ceiling and into subfloor plenum spaces).

Doors shall be to a specification that protects against both physical assault and fire.

If there are windows, they shall be secured not only from break-ins but also from being opened. It is desirable to avoid things being blown or thrown out of an open window, as well as the possibility of someone monitoring activity within a forensic laboratory from outside (even with a telescope).

Air conditioning vents shall be secured with grilles through the ducting that are fixed to the walls where they enter and leave the area.

If the services that are being offered require it, then the installation of a Faraday Cage or Room will need to be planned with all of the commensurate issues that this will cause. In addition, the space that is allocated for evidence and other equipment storage shall meet both health and safety and security requirements as well as being placed in a location that makes it as convenient as possible for the anticipated level of traffic.

2.4.4   Access control

When implementing an access control system in a forensic laboratory, it shall, if possible and practical, be integrated into the building or organisational access control system. This helps in providing defence in depth (layers of security). Integration will also make any postincident access violation investigation easier, as the logs can be centrally accessed.

The access control system shall also be comprehensive, effective, managed, and regularly tested. The choice of type of access control system will depend on:

- budget;
- contractual requirements;
- existing installations;
- relevant standards and good practice; and
- the highest security or sensitivity level of the material being processed.

The system shall be as state of the art as possible, whilst still a tested and proven system with a low false alarm and failure rate. There will always be a trade-off between these two sets of requirements, and, at the end, it will be a decision based on a risk assessment. Whatever system is implemented, it shall be practical and meet the forensic laboratory's needs. A good example of what may not suit a forensic laboratory is the use of security interlock systems. This is a revolving tube system, just large enough for a person, which is fine for controlling people in and out of the environment but makes the movement of equipment very difficult.

To maintain a secure infrastructure in a forensic laboratory, the layered physical security implementation shall cover the following:

- access to the forensic laboratory building;
- access to the forensic laboratory forensics processing areas;
- access to the server room;
- access by visitors; and
- deliveries to, and collections from, the forensic laboratory.

Procedures for access controls are defined in Chapter 12, Section 12.4.2 and 12.4.3.

Failure to control access to a forensic laboratory, or any part of it by appropriately authorised employees or visitors, could leave a forensic laboratory open to challenge over maintaining the 'chain of custody'.

2.4.5   Fire detection and quenching

With the range of equipment that will be in use in a forensic laboratory, effective fire detection and quenching systems are essential. If the accommodation is located in a larger building, the fire detection system shall be tied into the building management system. The fire detection system shall cover all rooms, as well as any ceiling voids and subfloor plenum gaps.

Fire detection is usually controlled by standards, regulations, and legislative requirements in most jurisdictions. In whatever environment the forensic laboratory is located, the alarm system shall be connected to a manned control point and shall have a centralised annunciator panel.

Fire classes are not universally used and vary from location to location. The most common ones are given below:

American	European	Australian/Asian	Fuel/heat source
Class A	Class A	Class A	Ordinary combustibles
Class B	Class B	Class B	Flammable liquids
	Class C	Class C	Flammable gasses
Class C	Class F/D	Class E	Electrical equipment
Class D	Class D	Class D	Combustible metals
Class K	Class F	Class F	Cooking oil or fat

The most likely fire classes encountered in a forensic laboratory will be:

- ordinary combustibles; and
- electrical equipment.

Detection systems fall into three different types:

- smoke detectors;
- heat detectors; and
- flame detectors.

Careful consideration of the correct types of detection devices shall be undertaken by a competent authority, often in conjunction with the local fire service. As well as automatic detection devices, there shall be a range of manual alarms installed.

The main types of fire quenching systems are:

- wet pipe;
- dry pipe;
- inert gas;
- foam; and
- dry chemical.

As can be seen, there are a range of fire quenching devices and again, careful consideration of the correct types of quenching devices shall be undertaken by a competent authority, often in conjunction with the local fire service/department. In addition to the automated quenching systems, there are always a range of hand-held quenching devices available for the different classes of fire identified above.

2.4.6 Close circuit television and burglar alarms

Issues that need to be considered with close circuit television (CCTV) and alarm systems include the resolution and placement of the cameras. The resolution and the placement of the cameras shall be such that individuals can be identified, but a decision will need to be made as to whether the cameras are capable of capturing the contents of any monitors that they overlook (is it a requirement to be able to see what was on the screen at any time or are there other security systems in place that will identify what activity was taking place?).

Consideration shall also be given to whether it is a requirement to have continuous monitoring or whether the cameras should be motion activated. Another issue shall be whether there is a requirement for low-light cameras. The output from the cameras shall be saved to a digital store within the forensic laboratory (assuming that the forensic laboratory has a modem digital rather than an analogue system). The volume of data that will need to be stored will depend on the number of cameras and period that the data needs to be stored, and this shall be taken into consideration at the planning stage. In a number of jurisdictions, there are legislative requirements for the retention periods for CCTV output.

CCTV shall be used to cover all entry and exit points in the forensic laboratory (inside and out), as well as access to and egress from any restricted area. The legislation with regard to the use of CCTV will vary depending on the jurisdiction. In the United Kingdom, there are three main pieces of legislation that affect the use of CCTV. These are:

- The Protection of Freedoms Act 2012,
- The Surveillance Camera Code of Practice 2013 (the 'SCCOP'), and
- The General Data Protection Regulation (GDPR) and associated Data Protection Act 2018 (the 'DPA').

The Protection of Freedom Act of 2012, in Part 2 (Regulation of Surveillance), Chapter 1, gives details of the Regulation of CCTV and other surveillance camera technology. The SCCOP legislation is designed to balance the need for CCTV cameras with the public's right to privacy. Some of the SCCOP only applies to CCTV for commercial use. GDPR and the DPA give individuals the right to see information held about them, including CCTV recordings.

2.4.7 Clean room

The first question that should be answered is 'is a clean room needed?'

They are expensive to set up and also to maintain. If the services that a forensic laboratory is to offer include the disassembly of disks, then a clean room facility may be needed. However, depending on the number of disks to be disassembled, it may be that a positive pressure table or compartment will be sufficient.

The final decision will depend on the expected role of a forensic laboratory and also the anticipated level of use. No provision has been made for a clean room in the layout suggested in Section 2.5 as FCL does not have one, or expect to need, one. A clean room can be included if needed. There are a number of standards relating to the implementation of clean rooms and these include the following:

- ISO 14644:2015—cleanrooms and associated controlled environments;
- ISO 14644-1:2015—this specifies the classification of air cleanliness in terms of concentration of airborne particles in cleanrooms and clean zones; and separative devices as defined in ISO 14644-7; and
- EU Good Manufacturing Process (EU GMP).

2.4.8 On-site secure evidence storage

Secure evidence storage is dedicated storage space for the sole purpose of securely storing evidence relating to any forensic cases that a forensic laboratory may process or has processed. The secure evidence storage facility is the physical embodiment of the chain of custody, supported by robust procedures for management of evidence. Evidential storage shall be the most secure area of storage in a forensic laboratory and the most rigorously controlled area with full CCTV and alarm coverage. All access to it shall be controlled and access regularly reviewed and restricted to the minimum possible number of employees.

The secure evidence storage facility shall be constructed so that it can defeat any forced or otherwise unauthorised entry as well as being resistant to any environmental threats. Depending on requirements, the secure evidence storage may require physical protection such as electromagnetic shielding. All access and egress to and from the secure evidence store shall be logged and have an available audit trail.

Note

Within FCL, a single evidence custodian (with an alternate) has been appointed.

2.4.9 Fire safes

In addition to the evidence storage space requirements, there will always be the requirement for protecting some material in the event of a fire. This may require the installation of fire safes within a forensic laboratory or alternatively, access to a fire safe in another location or part of the organisation. In the planning phase, consideration shall be given to the size required and the location of the safe as well as the quality of fire resistance required. One thing that is often overlooked is the floor loading required for a fire safe, and on account of this they are usually located on the ground floor if of any significant size.

The most common standards for these are those operated by the Underwriters' Laboratory which has a number of different classes for protection of the safe's contents.

2.4.10 Secure off-site storage

All IT operations require a secure off-site capability to store backup media and other operational necessities to be used in case of a disaster at the main processing site. All media storing forensic laboratory information shall be stored in accordance with the manufacturer's recommendations. Details of this are defined in Chapter 12, Section 12.3.12.

A forensic laboratory may use an off-site storage service provider, rather than having its own remote site. If considering a dedicated and owned secure off-site location, then the following shall be considered:

- ease of access to the storage facility;
- the distance from the forensic laboratory;
- logistics of storing and recovering off-site material; and
- security; and
- cost.

2.5 Layout of a forensic laboratory

There are a number of issues that need to be considered when setting up the internal layout of a forensic laboratory. If the square footage of floor that was required in the initial plans is achieved, then some of the issues detailed below may not be relevant. Unfortunately, this is often not the case and the premises that are acquired for a forensic laboratory will usually be a compromise in one way or another. The main issues to be considered when designing a forensic laboratory include the following.

2.5.1 Separation of space for specific roles and tasks

This will be influenced by the scope of the tasks that a forensic laboratory will undertake. The wider the range of tasks that a forensic laboratory will undertake, the more effort and consideration will need to go into working out how to organise the available space so that each task can be carried out in an appropriate environment and in a sensible ergonomic order.

The main issue is that a number of separated areas need to be in a specific order from the entrance. From the entrance door, an 'air lock' shall be implemented so that people entering the forensic laboratory can enter the environment and seal the outer door before they are allowed to move on into the working parts of the forensic laboratory. In this space, anyone entering the forensic laboratory shall be properly identified and authorised prior to entry. This area will also be used to manage any visitors and employees as well as for storage of any electronic equipment (phones, radios, laptops) that is not allowed in the forensic laboratory.

FCL has a secure viewing area in an isolated room where visitors can view cases without being given access to the working areas in FCL (e.g. other experts, Lawyers, clients, etc.). Controlled access to this area shall also be implemented from the working areas in FCL.

Once in the working space of a forensic laboratory, then the available space should be divided into a number of functional areas. These may include the following:

- analysis and report writing area;
- bathrooms;
- kitchen/rest area;
- locker space;
- equipment storage;
- hard disk imaging area;
- mobile device imaging area (Faraday Room);
- office space;
- research area;
- secure evidence storage area;
- server room;
- evidence viewing area;
- isolation room (for quarantined material); and
- unpacking and disassembly area.

A possible layout for a forensic laboratory is given in Fig. 2.1.

The need to segregate duties and operations in the same area is another area often overlooked, and there will inevitably be a number of investigations taking place in a forensic laboratory at any one time and these may be of differing sensitivities. It may be worth organising the space so that each of the workstations has a degree of privacy, so that the work being undertaken on one workstation cannot be seen from the others. It may also be worth considering, in the design of the laboratory, creating an environment that clearly separates out the areas by role.

Security requirements for equipment siting are defined in Chapter 7, Section 7.3.4.

2.5.2 Ergonomics

An often overlooked area of the design of a forensic laboratory is the ergonomics of processing a case. Ergonomics are an important consideration when designing a forensic laboratory. Ergonomics is defined by the free dictionary as:

Design factors, as for the workplace, intended to maximize productivity by minimizing operator fatigue and discomfort.

In terms of a forensic laboratory, this relates to the arrangement of the work areas to enable the work to 'flow' through a forensic laboratory. For example, the disassembly area will be at one end of a forensic laboratory, and next to it would be the disk imaging area, then the analysis area, etc. Whilst it may seem trivial and is often not achievable, it should be considered and implemented wherever possible. It makes sense and will save on movement back and forward within a forensic laboratory.

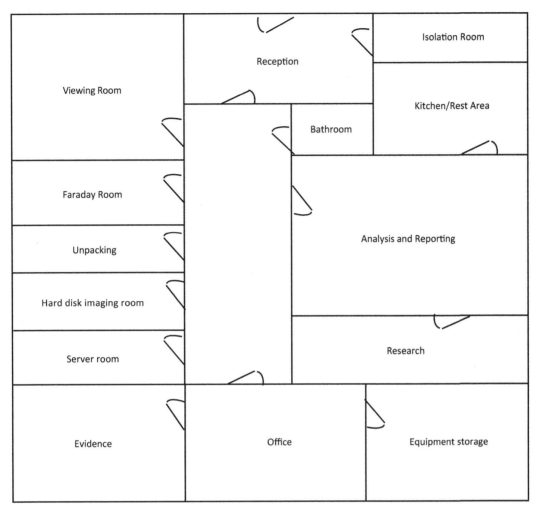

FIG. 2.1 Laboratory layout.

2.5.3 Personal workspace

Each Forensic Analyst will require a significant work area to enable them to carry out all of the tasks that they are expected to perform. Their workspace is in effect a personalised miniature forensic laboratory completely equipped to allow them to perform all their assigned forensic tasks as well as perform necessary business functions. This will require two separate information-processing systems, the forensic workstation and the business system necessary for day-to-day nonforensic operations.

There will be the need for a number of common area operations, rather than replicating all forensic operations for all Forensic Analysts. The scope of shared resources will vary depending on the tasks that the forensic laboratory undertakes but would include business as well as forensic equipment such as:

- dedicated media copiers;
- dedicated media production equipment;
- disk duplication equipment;
- printers; and
- scanners.

2.5.4 Size estimating

When estimating the square footage needed, a good rule of thumb is to double the size of the original estimate. There is nothing worse that discovering a year after moving into new premises that it has run out of space and that a move to a larger building is needed.

2.5.5 Infrastructure rooms

Depending on how a forensic laboratory is set up (dedicated or part of a shared building), there will be the need for a number of specific areas, that may, or may not be dedicated to the forensic laboratory, and may be in the building containing the forensic laboratory, these include the following:

- battery room;
- electrical power rooms;
- HVAC control room;
- switch room; and
- UPS room.

Appendix 1—Sample outline for a business case

An executive summary.

1. An outline of the business proposal
   - the nature of the digital forensic service offering;
   - the scope of the digital forensic service; and
   - business strategy for the parent organisation vis-a-vis digital forensics.
2. Product, customers, markets, channels, brand, and pricing for digital forensics services
   The need for a digital forensics service
   - customers;
   - markets;
   - channels; and
   - pricing.
3. Competitive strength of the digital forensic service
   - competitor analysis;
   - differentiators; and
   - unique selling points (USPs).
4. Key business issues for the parent organisation vis-a-vis digital forensics
5. Summary of compelling business proposition for the parent Organisation
6. Organisation of the digital forensic service
   - key staff for the digital forensic service;
   - interfaces and dependencies;
   - resources;
   - location and facilities;
   - intellectual capital;
   - intellectual property for the digital forensic service;
   - knowledge of the digital forensic service;
   - financial approach; and
   - anticipated revenues and costs for the digital forensic service.
7. Formation costs for a forensic laboratory
   - legal and regulatory issues affecting the digital forensic service;
   - benefits to the parent organisation, if appropriate;
   - financial; and
   - nonfinancial.
8. Risks and critical success factors (CSFs) for the digital forensic service(s)
9. Set-up phase
10. Product liability
11. Market development
12. Management and service delivery
    - financial; and
    - legal.

13. Exit plan for the parent organisation
- responsibilities for exit management; and
- distribution of assets and liabilities.

Appendix 2—The physical security policy

Introduction

Physical security of FCL's premises is the first step in the process of securing the FCL's information-processing systems. Appropriate physical security shall be implemented in FCL.

Purpose

This policy provides rules for anyone wanting to access FCL's premises.

Effective implementation of this policy will minimise unauthorised access to the forensic laboratory and provides more effective auditing of physical access controls.

Scope

This policy applies to all FCL premises, including the Server Room and Disaster Recovery (DR) site.

Audience

This policy applies to all employees.

Policy statements

It is the FCL policy that:

- access cards shall be granted to employees according to their rights;
- access cards shall not be shared between employees;
- employees shall not be permitted entry into the FCL premises outside the time permitted by their access cards;
- employees with personal offices shall lock them when not in use;
- all employees shall wear their access cards in a visible manner when on FCL premises;
- employees who forget their access cards shall obtain a visitor badge for the day;
- employees who lose their access cards shall report the loss to the Information Security Manager immediately on discovering their loss;
- access to the Server Room and DR site shall be restricted to named employees and service engineers with a justified 'need to access', and authorised by the IT Manager or his nominated alternate;
- emergency 'out of hours' access for employees shall only be granted as an exception and subject to next day review by the employee's Line Manager. All visitors shall be authorised in advance of their visit and authenticated on arrival;
- all visitors shall be accompanied at all times by their Escort till they leave FCL's premises;
- all visitors shall clearly display their visitor badges whilst on site at all times; and
- all access to FCL premises shall be logged and regularly reviewed.

Responsibilities

The following responsibilities are defined in this policy:

- **Host:** to ensure that a visitor is preauthorised for their visit;
- **Escort:** to accompany a visitor at all times and ensure that he/she signs out and leaves the forensic laboratory premises;
- **IT Manager (or alternate):** to authorise access to the Server Room or DR site;
- **Employees:** to comply with this policy and report any breaches of it to the Information Security Manager; and
- **Information Security Manager:** to manage the access control system, review access, and act on being advised of any breach of this policy.

Ownership

This policy is owned by the Information Security Manager.

Enforcement, monitoring, and breaches

All employees are responsible for monitoring and enforcing this policy.

Breaches of this policy by employees shall be dealt with under the Disciplinary rules. Visitors and third-party employees breaching this policy shall have appropriate action taken.

Review and maintenance

The policy shall be effective from the date of approval and shall be reviewed at least annually, after any significant breach or on influencing change.

Approval

This policy has been approved by Top Management.

Chapter 3

Setting up a forensic laboratory

3.1 Setting up a digital forensic laboratory

This chapter is the summary of many small elements, each of which gives guidance on areas that shall be considered from the planning stage onwards. All of the elements discussed below shall be addressed both for good management and for preparation for the accreditation and certification for a forensic laboratory, if this is required—otherwise to meet good practice.

When initially setting up a forensic laboratory, there are a number of issues that need to be considered. Many of these are touched on in other chapters, and some are expanded here. Once the business case (or the equivalent if in government or law enforcement) has been developed, a range of issues shall be addressed and these shall be documented to describe the fundamental basis on which the forensic laboratory is being established and on which it will be run. The first issue that shall be clearly documented is that of the forensic laboratory's terms of reference (ToR). There will also normally be a ToR for the project to develop and deliver the forensic laboratory, but the concepts that are defined below hold good for both cases.

3.1.1 Laboratory terms of reference

The ToR is the document that serves as the basis of the relationship between the organisation that owns the forensic laboratory and the team responsible for carrying out the work. It describes the purpose and structure of a forensic laboratory and shows how the scope of the forensic laboratory will be defined and verified. It shall also provide the yardstick against which the success of the forensic laboratory will be measured. It provides a documented basis for future decisions and for a common understanding of the scope among the interested parties.

The ToR sets out a clear path for the operation of a forensic laboratory by stating what needs to be achieved, by whom and when. It identifies the set of deliverables that satisfy the requirements and the scope and any constraints shall be set out in this document. The ToR for the operation of a forensic laboratory shall be created during the earliest stages of the project for the establishment of a forensic laboratory and immediately after the business case has been approved. Once the ToR has been approved, there is a clear definition of the scope of the forensic laboratory. The ToR shall also identify the success factors, risks, and boundaries. The ToR shall be written in some detail and shall include the following:

- vision;
- scope and objectives;
- deliverables;
- boundaries, risks, and limitations;
- roles, responsibilities, authority, accountability, and reporting requirements;
- interested parties;
- the regulatory framework;
- resources available;
- work breakdown structure and schedule;
- success factors; and
- intervention strategies.

A description of the ToR used to set up FCL's Laboratory is defined in Appendix 1.

Once the ToR has been developed and agreed, a range of other elements that outline how FCL shall develop and manage its forensic laboratory and structure it.

3.1.2 The status of the FCL laboratory

There shall be a clear statement of the status of the forensic laboratory. This shall define the ownership, the services that it will offer, the structure of the forensic laboratory, the standards that it will work to, and the expected customers. This shall be prepared in some detail as it will be the foundation for future decisions.

A Blueprint for Implementing Best Practice Procedures in a Digital Forensic Laboratory. https://doi.org/10.1016/B978-0-12-819479-9.00004-6

3.1.3 The FCL laboratory principles

The FCL Laboratory has adopted the following principles for its operation.

3.1.3.1 Responsibilities

The FCL Laboratory relies upon the Laboratory Manager to develop and maintain an efficient, high-quality forensic laboratory.

3.1.3.2 Integrity

The FCL Forensic Team shall be honest and truthful with their peers, supervisors, and subordinates. They shall also be trustworthy and honest when representing the FCL Laboratory to outside organisations.

3.1.3.3 Efficiency

FCL Managers and employees shall ensure that FCL's products and services are provided in a manner which maximises organisational efficiency and ensures an economical expenditure of resources and personnel.

3.1.3.4 Productivity

The Laboratory Manager shall establish reasonable goals for the production of forensic casework in a timely fashion. Highest priority shall be defined to cases which have a potentially productive outcome and which could, if successfully concluded, have an effective impact on the enforcement or adjudication process.

3.1.3.5 Meet organisational expectations

The Laboratory Manager shall implement and enforce the relevant organisational policies and procedures and shall establish additional internal procedures designed to meet the ever-changing needs of forensic case processing.

3.1.3.6 Health and safety

The Laboratory Manager shall be responsible for planning and maintaining systems that reasonably assure safety in FCL as well as when the First Response Team are in the field. Such systems shall include mechanisms for input by the First Response Team, maintenance of records of injuries, and routine safety inspections as defined by existing health and safety procedures. FCL shall comply with the requirements of ISO 45001, which has replaced OHSAS 18001.

3.1.3.7 Information security

The Laboratory Manager shall be responsible for planning and maintaining the security of the laboratory. Security measures shall include control of access both during and after normal business hours. FCL shall comply with the requirements of the current version of ISO/IEC 27001 and the supporting standards in the series.

3.1.3.8 Management information systems

The Laboratory Manager shall be responsible for developing management information systems. These systems shall provide information in a timely manner regarding current and past work carried out by FCL.

3.1.3.9 Qualifications

The Laboratory Manager shall only hire employees of sufficient academic qualifications or competence to provide them with the fundamental scientific principles for work in FCL and shall be assured that they are honest, forthright, and ethical in their personal and professional life.

3.1.3.10 Training and development

The Laboratory Manager shall provide training in the principles and the details of forensic science as it applies to FCL's.

Training shall also include handling and preserving the integrity of physical evidence. Before analysis and case work are performed, specific training for the processes and procedures as well as for the specific tools to be utilised shall be undertaken. A full training programme for all Forensic Analysts and Investigators shall be developed.

3.1.3.11 Maintaining employee competency

The Laboratory Manager shall monitor the skills and proficiency of the Forensic Analysts on a continuing basis as well as on an annual basis as required by HR procedures. FCL shall have an ongoing programme of training, awareness, and competency.

3.1.3.12 Environment

The Laboratory Manager shall ensure that a safe and functional work environment is provided with adequate space to support all the work activities required by FCL. Facilities shall be adequate so that evidence under FCL's control shall be protected from contamination, tampering, or theft.

3.1.3.13 Supervision

The Laboratory Manager shall provide the Forensic Analysts and Investigators with adequate supervisory review to ensure the quality of their work product. The Laboratory Manager shall be held accountable for the performance of the Forensic Analysts and Investigators and the enforcement of clear and enforceable processes and procedures. The Forensic Analysts and Investigators shall be held to realistic performance goals which take into account reasonable workload standards.

The Laboratory Manager shall ensure that the Forensic Analysts and Investigators are not pressured to perform substandard work through case load pressure or unnecessary outside influence. FCL shall have in place a performance evaluation process.

3.1.3.14 Conflicts of interest

The Laboratory Manager, the Forensic Analysts, and the Investigators shall avoid any activity, interest, or association that interferes or appears to interfere with their independent exercise of professional judgment. The Conflict of Interest Policy is defined in Appendix 3.

3.1.3.15 Legal compliance

The Laboratory Manager shall establish and publish, with appropriate training, operational procedures in order to meet good procedural, legislative, and good practice requirements relating to digital evidence in the jurisdictions of operations.

3.1.3.16 Accountability

The Laboratory Manager and the Lead Forensic Analyst shall be accountable for their decisions and actions. These decisions and actions shall be supported by appropriate documentation and be open to legitimate scrutiny.

3.1.3.17 Disclosure and discovery

FCL's records shall be open for reasonable access when legitimate requests are made by Officers of the Court or other legitimate requesters. Specific requirements are necessary for the release of unlawful material.

3.1.3.18 Work quality

The Laboratory Manager shall establish a quality assurance program. The Forensic Analysts and Investigators shall accept responsibility for evidence integrity and security; validated, reliable methods; and casework documentation and reporting. FCL shall comply with the requirements of the current version of ISO 9001 and ISO/IEC 17025.

3.1.3.19 Accreditation and certification

The Laboratory Manager shall achieve and maintain whichever certifications and accreditations that the Top Management deem necessary.

3.1.3.20 Membership of appropriate organisations

The Laboratory Manager shall ensure that Forensic Analysts join appropriate professional organisations and that they are encouraged to obtain the highest professional membership grade possible.

3.1.3.21   Obtain appropriate personal certifications

The Laboratory Manager shall ensure that the Forensic Analysts achieves appropriate certifications of both generic and tool-specific types to demonstrate their skill levels.

3.1.4   Laboratory service level agreements

A service level agreement (SLA) is a part of a service contract where the level of service that will be provided by a forensic laboratory is formally defined. The SLA is sometimes used to refer to the contracted delivery time for the services offered by FCL (usually called the 'Turn Round Time') or the quality of the work.

The SLA shall be considered from the start of the planning and development process to ensure that a forensic laboratory will be structured to the appropriate level. Service providers normally include SLAs within the terms of their contracts with customers to define the level of service that is being provided in plain language using easily understood terms. Any metrics included in an SLA shall be measurable and shall be tested on a regular basis. The SLA shall also normally outline the remedial action and any penalties that shall take effect if the delivered service falls below the defined standard. The SLA forms an essential element of the legal contract between the forensic laboratory and the customer. The actual structure of the SLA will be dependent on the services offered by FCL, but the general structure of the agreement is as follows:

- contract;
- amendments;
- service description;
- service availability;
- management information;
- reliability;
- customer support;
- service performance;
- change management procedures;
- security;
- service reviews;
- glossary; and
- amendment sheet.

If a forensic laboratory takes services from either an external supplier (e.g. Internet Access or utility supplier) or from the owning organisation (e.g. human resources or logistics), then suitable SLAs shall be agreed with these service providers.

Note

It shall be up to each forensic laboratory to determine its requirements.

3.1.5   Impartiality and Independence

In order to obtain and retain accreditation to the current version of ISO/IEC17025 (General requirements for the competence of testing and calibration laboratories), there is a requirement for a forensic laboratory to be able to show evidence that its work and results are 'free from undue influence or pressure from customers or other interested parties' and that 'laboratories working within larger organisations where influence could be applied (such as police laboratories) are free from such influence and are producing objective and valid results.'

3.1.6   Codes of practice and conduct

In the United Kingdom, the Forensic Science Regulator has produced Codes of Practice and Conduct[a] for forensic science providers and practitioners in the Criminal Justice System. These Codes of Practice and Conduct were the first stage in the development of a single quality standards framework for digital forensic science for use in the Criminal Justice System to

---

a. Forensic Science Regulator, Codes of Practice and Conduct for forensic science providers and practitioners in the Criminal Justice System, https://assets.publishing.service.gov.uk/government/uploads/system/uploads/attachment_data/file/651966/100_-_2017_10_09_-_The_Codes_of_Practice_and_Conduct_-_Issue_4_final_web_web_pdf__2_.pdf.

replace the ad hoc approach to standards that had been used in the past. These Codes of Practice and Conduct were built on the internationally recognised good practice of the current version of ISO/IEC 17025 as the preferred standard for digital forensic science laboratories. In the UK, the Forensic Regulator has now mandated that all digital forensic laboratories in the Criminal Justice System shall be accredited to the current version of ISO/IEC 17025.

An appendix to these Codes of Practice and Conduct provides guidance to deal with the specific requirements for the providers of forensic science services at scenes of incidents based on ISO/IEC 17020 (Conformity assessment—Requirements for the operation of various types of bodies performing inspection). This standard for inspection bodies is gradually being adopted across Europe as the most appropriate standard for crime scene investigations.

The requirements that are described in the Codes of Practice and Conduct and the associated appendices are targeted at three levels:

- **the organisation**: to outline what is required of it, particularly from the management, with regard to quality assurance and compliance. Most forensic services are supplied by people working in organisations and the organisational culture with regard to quality is a major factor. Accountability for quality rests with the management, and each organisation is required to nominate a senior manager as the 'accountable person';
- **the practitioner**: to outline the professional standards to which they are expected to perform; and
- **the scientific methodology**: to ensure that the methodology is robust and will reliably produce, and continue to produce, valid results.

These Codes of Practice and Conduct were developed so that they were be applied to all organisations and practitioners whose primary role is the provision of forensic services into the Criminal Justice System in England and Wales. While these Codes of Practice and Conduct were designed for the UK community, they are based on sound principles and international standards, are a good guideline and a basis for codes of practice for other regions, and have been adopted by FCL.

3.1.7 Quality standards

Quality standards in forensic science are essential to ensure that the highest possible standards are maintained by FCL as a supplier of forensic services. This shall include resourcing, training, equipment, processes, and integrity benchmarks such as accreditation and certification. Unless these standards are maintained, there is an increased possibility that those guilty of crimes may not be brought to justice or that those who are innocent may be convicted.

Quality standards in forensic science are best attained through accreditation to the current version of international standard ISO/IEC 17025, which builds on the current version of ISO 9001 standard. However, on its own, ISO/IEC 17025 will not guarantee quality, as it does not cover areas such as setting of FCL strategy for a case, or the interpretation of the results, or the presentation of the evidence in the Court. A cross reference between the current version of ISO 9001 and ISO/IEC 17025 is defined in Appendix 2. This clearly shows a close correlation, but the current version of ISO/IEC 17025 has more technical requirements in it than the current version of ISO 9001.

Note

FCL has not sought ISO 17025 accredited certification.

3.1.8 Objectivity

A professional Forensic Analyst or Investigator, when providing any service, shall determine whether there are any threats to compliance with the fundamental principle of objectivity. These threats will normally result from the Forensic Analyst, Investigator (or the forensic laboratory itself) having interests in, or a relationship with any member of the client organisation or some aspect of the case being investigated. An example of a familiarity threat to objectivity could be created from a family or close personal or business relationship. Independence of thought is necessary to enable the professional Forensic Analyst or Investigator to express a conclusion, without bias, conflict of interest, or undue influence from others.

The existence of threats to objectivity when providing any professional service will depend upon the specific circumstances of the engagement and the nature of the work. A professional Forensic Analyst or Investigator shall evaluate the significance of any threats and, when necessary, ensure that suitable measures are taken to eliminate threats or reduce them to an acceptable level. Examples of the types of measures that may be considered include the following:

- advising FCL management of the potential threat;
- the Forensic Analyst or Investigator removing themselves from the case;

- FCL shall have in place suitable peer review and supervisory procedures; and
- terminating the relationship that gives rise to the threat.

If the measures that have been put in place to eliminate or reduce FCL's threats to an acceptable level are not effective, they shall either decline or terminate the contract with the customer.

3.1.9 Management requirements

There are many ways in which FCL management requirements shall be implemented using an Integrated Management System (IMS) based on the commonality between management systems (Specifically Annex L). Full details of the IMS are defined in Chapter 4.

This approach has allowed FCL to implement the relevant parts of following current ISO and local standards, including but not limited to:

- ISO 15489—Information and documentation-Records management;
- ISO/IEC 17020—Conformity assessment—Requirements for the operation of various types of bodies performing inspection;
- ISO/IEC 17025—General requirements for the competence of testing and calibration laboratories;
- ISO 22301—Societal security—Business continuity management systems;
- ISO/IEC 27001—Information technology—Security techniques-Information security management systems-Requirements;
- ISO 9001—Quality management systems—Requirements;
- ISO 45001—Occupational health and safety;
- The Forensic Science Regulators Codes of Practice and Conduct for forensic science providers and practitioners in the Criminal Justice System;
- Modules in a Forensic Science Process, ILAC G19;
- Relevant requirements from the American Society of Crime Laboratory Directors (ASCLD);
- In-house digital forensic procedures.

3.1.10 Forensic laboratory policies and procedures

In order to assure the integrity of their results, the forensic laboratory shall have appropriate policies and supporting procedures in place. The implementation of these policies will be in the form of practices and procedures that define how FCL shall operate to meet the relevant good practice and forensic science and quality standards. The constant developments in technology mean that there is an ongoing need to update the policies and their supporting procedures in order to meet changing laws and regulations in order to prevent unfairness and wrongful conviction. The forensic laboratory policies and their supporting procedures shall ensure the integrity of any results produced.

The main purpose of policies and procedures within the forensic laboratory is to assure the integrity of results, to provide a repeatable and transparent process, and to prevent miscarriages of justice. There are many examples of mistakes within forensic laboratories. One well publicised example is the analysis of the data in the Casey Anthony trial in July 2011, when the number of times that she had accessed the internet to search for the word 'Chloroform' was initially reported as 84 times but was later found to be only one time.[b] Another example is the CD Universe case where the evidence was compromised because the chain of custody was not properly established.[c] Policies and procedures are also necessary within FCL to ensure that the employees receive and are able to maintain a suitable level of training and certification, and they shall also address funding levels and the policy on investigation of allegations of misconduct or negligence. The policies and procedures shall also contain sections on the code of ethics and the relevant standards and regulations.

3.1.11 Documentation requirements

The relevant standards implemented within FCL shall dictate much of the required documentation for everyday operations. Documented procedures are included in the relevant chapters in this book.

---

b. Forensic Data Recovery, Digital Evidence Discrepancies—Casey Anthony Trial, July 11, 2011, https://www.digital-detective.net/digital-evidence-discrepancies-casey-anthony-trial/ The State v. Casey Anthony: Analysis of Evidence from the Case, July 18, 2011, http://statevcasey.wordpress.com/tag/digital-forensics/.

c. CD Universe evidence compromised, https://www.zdnet.com/article/cd-universe-evidence-compromised/.

3.1.12   Competence, awareness, and training

All management standards have requirements for competence, awareness, and training. All employees shall also be aware of client requirements and the relevance of their activities. They shall understand how their actions contribute to achieving the forensic laboratory's quality policy and objectives. This is normally achieved by awareness training, performance reviews, and employee participation in internal audit processes. Top management shall define the necessary skills, experience, and training required for each role and identify the records of education, training, skills, and experience that need to be maintained. The quality policy is defined in Appendix 4.

3.1.13   Planning

There are a number of actions that need to be taken throughout the planning process. These include the following:

3.1.13.1   Risk assessment and management

A fundamental element of the planning process is the risk assessment. The objective of the risk assessment is to discover and document the current risks and threats to the business and to identify and implement measures to mitigate or reduce the risks that carry the highest probability of occurring or the highest impact. The risk assessment document shall give guidance on how to conduct the risk assessment and also how to evaluate and analyse the information that is collected.

It shall also contain guidance for the organisation on how to implement strategies to manage the potential risks.

Risk management in FCL is covered in Chapter 5.

3.1.13.2   Business impact analysis

The risk assessment is only one part of an overall business assessment. The business assessment is divided into two parts, the risk assessment and a business impact analysis (BIA). The risk assessment is intended to measure the present risks and vulnerabilities to the business's environment, while the BIA evaluates the probable losses that could occur as a result of an incident. To maximise the value of a risk assessment, a BIA shall also be completed. A BIA is an essential element of an organisation's business continuity plan. The BIA shall include an assessment of any vulnerabilities and plans for the development of strategies to minimise risk. The BIA describes the potential risks to the organisation studied and shall identify the interdependencies between the different parts of the organisation and which are the critical elements. For example, a forensic laboratory may be able to continue to operate more or less normally if the air conditioning system failed but would not be able to function if the network failed.

As part of a business continuity plan, the FCL BIA shall identify the probable costs associated with failures, such as loss of cash flow, cost of facility repair, cost of equipment replacement, overtime payments to address the backlog of work, loss of profits, etc. A BIA report shall quantify the importance of the individual elements of FCL's business operations and suggest appropriate levels of funding for measures to protect them. Potential failures shall be assessed in terms of the financial cost and the impact on legal compliance, quality assurance, and safety. Business continuity is covered in Chapter 13.

3.1.13.3   Legal and regulatory considerations

The investigation of crimes involving digital media and the examination of that digital media in most countries are covered by both national and international legislation. In criminal investigations, national laws normally restrict how much information can be seized and under what circumstances it can be seized. For example, in the United Kingdom, the seizure of evidence by law enforcement officers is governed by the Police and Criminal Evidence Act (1984) and the Regulation of Investigatory Powers Act (2000) (RIPA). The Computer Misuse Act (1990) provides legislation regarding unauthorised access to computer material, and this can affect the Investigator as well as the criminal and is a particular concern for civil investigators who have more limitations on what they are allowed to do than law enforcement officers.

In the United States, one of the pieces of legislation that the Investigator shall be aware of is the rights of the individual under the Fourth Amendment, which limits the ability of government agents to search for and seize evidence without a warrant. The Fourth Amendment states: 'The right of the people to be secure in their persons, houses, papers, and effects, against unreasonable searches and seizures, shall not be violated, and no Warrants shall issue, but upon probable cause, supported by Oath or affirmation, and particularly describing the place to be searched, and the persons or things to be seized.' According to the Office of Legal Education (OLE),[d] the Supreme Court stated that a 'seizure of property occurs when there

---

d. Hagen E., Searching and Seizing Computers and Obtaining Electronic Evidence in Criminal Investigations Computer Crime and Intellectual Property Section Criminal Division Published by Office of Legal Education, Executive Office for United States Attorneys.

is some meaningful interference with an individual's possessory interests in that property,' United States v. Jacobsen, 466 U.S. 109, 113 (1984), and the Court has also characterised the interception of intangible communications as a seizure. See Berger v. New York, 388 U.S. 41, 59–60 (1967). Furthermore, the Court has held that a 'search occurs when an expectation of privacy that society is prepared to consider reasonable is infringed.' Jacobsen, 466 U.S. at 113.

OLE goes on to state that 'A search is constitutional if it does not violate a person's 'reasonable' or 'legitimate' expectation of privacy. Katz v. United States, 389 U.S. 347, 361 (1967) (Harlan, J., concurring).'

Another piece of legislation in the United States is the Patriot Act, which provides law enforcement agents with an increased ability to use surveillance tools such as roving wiretaps. The Patriot Act introduced important changes that have increased the prosecutorial power in fighting computer crimes. The Patriot Act references the Computer Fraud and Abuse Act (18 U.S.C. § 1030) with both procedural and substantive changes. There were also changes to make it easier for law enforcement to investigate computer crimes.

Also relevant in the United States is a piece of legislation with regard to border searches. According to the Supreme Court, routine searches at the border do not require a warrant, probable cause, or even reasonable suspicion that the search may uncover contraband or evidence.

Similar to the UK's RIPA, since 1968, in the United States, the Wiretap Statute (Title III), 18 U.S.C. §§ 2510-2522 has been the statutory framework used to control the real-time electronic surveillance of communications. When law enforcement officers want to place a wiretap on a suspect's phone or monitor a hacker breaking into a computer system, they have to do so in compliance with the requirements of Title III. The statute prohibits the use of electronic, mechanical, or other devices to intercept a private wire, an oral, or electronic communication between two parties unless one of a number of statutory exceptions applies. Title III basically prohibits eavesdropping (subject to certain exceptions and interstate requirements) by anyone, everywhere in the United States.

In the United States, the Electronic Communications Privacy Act (ECPA) places limitations on the ability of Investigators to intercept and access potential evidence. In Europe, Article 5 of the European Convention on Human Rights (ECHR) gives similar privacy limitations to the ECPA and limits the processing and sharing of personal data both within the EU and with other countries outside the EU.

The Convention on Cybercrime (ETS No. 185), also known as the Budapest Convention on Cybercrime, is an international treaty that was created to try to address the harmonisation of national laws relating to computer crime and Internet crimes in order to improve the investigative techniques and increase cooperation between nations. The Convention was adopted by the Committee of Ministers of the Council of Europe on November 8, 2001, and was opened for signature in Budapest, later that month. The convention entered into force on July 1, 2004, and by the end of 2018, 62 states had signed, ratified, and acceded to the convention. These included Canada, Japan, the United States, and the Republic of South Africa. A further four countries have also signed the convention but not yet ratified it. The Convention is the only binding international instrument dealing with cybercrime.

The 'International Organisation on Computer Evidence (IOCE)' is an organisation that was established in 1999 and has been working to establish compatible international standards for the seizure of evidence to guarantee the ability to use digital evidence collected by one state in the Courts of another state.

In civil investigations, the relevant laws of many countries restrict the actions that the investigator can undertake in an examination. Regulations that are in place with regard to network monitoring and the accessing of personal communications or data stored in the network exist in many countries, and the rights of an individual to privacy is still an area which is still subject to decisions in the Courts.

This is intended only to highlight the range of laws and regulations that the Investigator will need to be aware of and that the forensic laboratory will need to ensure that have been taken into account when developing the guidelines for operational processes and procedures.

3.1.14 Insurance

FCL shall regularly review its insurance coverage to ensure that it is appropriate for the types of insurance required in the jurisdiction and at a level commensurate with the business undertaken, specific contractual requirements, and the number of employees.

3.1.15 Contingency planning

This is activity that is undertaken to ensure that suitable and immediate steps can be taken by management and staff in the event of an emergency. The main objectives of contingency planning are to ensure the containment of the incident and to limit any damage, injury, or loss and to ensure the continuity of key operations. The contingency plan identifies the immediate actions that shall be taken and also the longer-term measures for responding to incidents. The process of developing the contingency plan involves the identification of critical resources and functions and the establishment of a recovery plan that is based on the length of time that FCL can operate without specific functions. The plan shall be a 'living document' and needs to be continuously updated to keep pace with changes in regulations, the environment, and the work taking place within the forensic laboratory. The contingency plan shall be documented in straightforward terms and exercised at regular intervals to ensure that it is effective and that all of the parties involved understand their roles and responsibilities. Contingency plans are part of business continuity planning. Business continuity is covered in Chapter 13.

3.1.16 Roles and responsibilities

The roles of all employees shall be defined together with the responsibilities that are related to that role. Specific job roles are defined in the relevant chapters relating to the implemented IMS.

3.1.17 Business objectives

It is common for business objectives to be set in financial terms; however, not all objectives have to be expressed in these terms. Ideally, objectives shall adhere to the SMART acronym, which describes five characteristics:

- S-Specific;
- M-Measurable;
- A-Achievable;
- R-Realistic; and
- T-Time Bound.

    Objectives could include the following:

- desired throughput and profit levels;
- amount of income generated;
- value of the business or dividends paid to shareholders;
- quality of customer service; and
- innovation.

3.1.18 Laboratory accreditation and certification

Accreditation is something that a forensic laboratory may aspire to achieve at the earliest opportunity and may be a requirement within the jurisdiction. The most widely recognised accreditation is ISO 17025. Once accreditation has been achieved, the activities of the forensic laboratory shall be monitored on a periodic basis by the relevant accreditation body. Once it has been achieved, the forensic laboratory shall comply with specific criteria relating to the digital forensic laboratory's management and operations, personnel, and physical plant in order to maintain its accreditation. The criteria and standards address the areas of the digital forensic laboratory administrative practices, procedures, training, evidence handling, quality control, analysis protocols, testimony, proficiency testing, personnel qualifications, space allocation, security, and a number of other topics. The issue of digital forensic laboratory accreditation and certification is dealt with in much greater detail in Chapter 19.

3.1.19 Policies

A digital forensic laboratory shall develop policies that contain clear statements covering all of the major digital forensic issues, including, but not limited to:

- subcontracting;
- contacting law enforcement;
- carrying out monitoring; and
- conducting regular reviews of policies, guidelines, and procedures.

At the top level, a forensic laboratory's policies shall only allow authorised personnel to carry out tasks which may include monitoring systems and networks and performing investigations. A forensic laboratory may also need a separate policy to cover incident handlers and other digital forensic roles. There is a requirement for the policies to be reviewed and updated at frequent intervals because of changes in technology or changes to laws and regulations, as well as to take account of new court rulings. A forensic laboratory case handling policies shall also be consistent with other policies, including policies related to privacy.

3.1.20 Guidelines and procedures

A digital forensic laboratory shall develop and maintain guidelines and procedures for carrying out all tasks relating to processing digital forensic cases and management systems. The forensic laboratory's forensic guidelines shall include general guidelines for investigations and shall also include step-by-step procedures for performing the routine tasks, such as the imaging of a hard disk or the capturing of volatile data from live systems.

The reason for developing these guidelines and procedures is that they shall ensure that there is consistency in the way in which material is processed. This will lead to good practices and a consistent approach to tasks within the forensic laboratory and will ensure that the cases are all processed to the same standard whether it is anticipated that they will go to the Court or not. It shall also ensure that evidence collected, for example, for a case that starts off as an internal disciplinary action into computer misuse, can be used if it discovered that there was a more serious crime that may lead to a prosecution. By using guidelines and policies to ensure consistency, the integrity of any data that is used or results that are created can be demonstrated. The guidelines and procedures shall support the admissibility of any evidence produced in the laboratory into legal proceedings.

If tasks are outsourced to external third parties, the way in which the forensic laboratory engages with the third party and the material that is provided to them and recovered from them shall be described in the guidelines and policies. Normally, when a third party carries out work on behalf of a forensic laboratory, the contract with the third party shall require that they adhere to the forensic laboratory's handling and processing standards.

The process of outsourcing is covered in Chapter 14. Once the guidelines and procedures have been developed, it is important that they are regularly reviewed and maintained so that they remain accurate and represent the current laws, technology, and good practice. The frequency with which they are reviewed and updated shall be determined by top management and shall be regular but this may also be influenced by changes in the relevant laws or technologies. The second edition has been produced because, in the intervening period, almost all of the standards that it refers to and addresses have been updated and the whole discipline of digital forensics has progressed alongside the existing technologies and new concepts such as the Internet of Things (IoT), integration of Operational Technology (OT) into information technology (IT), and the application of Artificial Intelligence (AI).

Appendix 1—The laboratory terms of reference (TOR)

The vision

A short statement, normally of one or two paragraphs, which explains the mandate defined to the team and defines the reason for the FCL Forensic Laboratory's creation and its purpose.

Scope and objectives

It is essential to define the scope of the work that is to be conducted by FCL. The ToR shall specify the work to be undertaken and the types of deliverables from this work. It shall also give timescales for the production of deliverables.

Deliverables

FCL's deliverables shall be defined. This shall not only include the outcome of the investigations but also the internal deliverables such as accounts, audits, and test results and reports.

Boundaries, risks, and limitations

This section describes where FCL's process/system /operation starts and ends. A statement of the authority delegated to FCL to implement change and any powers defined to it shall be included. It is in this section that the systems, policies, procedures, relevant legislation, etc., shall be mentioned. The risks shall also be detailed.

Roles, responsibilities, authorities, accountability, and reporting requirements

FCL policies shall clearly define the roles and responsibilities of all employees, supported by specific job descriptions. They shall detail the roles, responsibilities, and functions of each employee and clearly define the authority that is associated with each of the roles. It shall also define the accountability associated with each of the roles and the reporting requirements for each role and task. It shall include the actions to be performed during both routine work activities and an incident. The policy shall clearly indicate who is responsible for and authorised to contact which internal teams and external organisations and under what circumstances.

Interested parties

It is important to identify the main interested parties and their interests, roles, and responsibilities. The interested parties will include the representatives of the owning organisation, employees, clients and will extend to other parties who have an interest in the efficient running of FCL.

Regulatory framework

The legal, institutional, and contractual framework for the operation of the FCL Laboratory shall be stated. This shall include regulations of regional bodies such as the European Union, Federal (National), State (Provincial), or Municipal Governments, and any legislation or policies and practices that pertain to parent corporations, partnerships, etc.

Resources

The resources identified shall include real estate, employees, equipment, and support services. The elements that need to be considered will include the following:

- administrative support;
- available budget;
- employees;
- materials and supplies;
- other supporting functions (e.g. security);
- resources available and how they are to be accessed;
- information processing equipment (business and forensic); and
- training requirements and how this will be provided.

Work breakdown structure and schedule

The work breakdown structure is a list of tasks that require action. When the individual tasks are considered together with relevant dependencies and timelines are introduced, then the schedule shall be created. The work that is to be undertaken by FCL shall be broken down into smaller and smaller tasks that eventually become the work breakdown structure. Additional details of task durations and dependencies shall be required to aid in the building of the schedule.

Success factors

Success factors (SFs), also sometimes referred to as critical success factors (CSFs), are the measure of those factors or activities required for ensuring FCL's success. They shall be used to identify a small number of key factors that FCL shall focus on to be successful. SFs are important as they are things that are capable of being measured and because of this they get done more often than things that are not measured. Each SF shall be measurable and associated with a target goal. Primary measures that shall be included are aspects such as success levels for areas such as the number of jobs processed in the month and number of hours spent on each task. SFs shall be identified for any of the aspects of the business that are identified as vital for defined targets to be reached and maintained. SFs are normally identified in such areas as laboratory processes, employee and organisation skills, tools, techniques, and technologies. CSFs may change over time if the business undertaken by FCL changes.

Intervention strategies

These shall cover the contingency plans for any emergency and shall define what constitutes an emergency.

Appendix 2—Cross reference between ISO 9001:2015 and ISO/IEC 17025:2017

This table gives a high-level cross reference between the current version of ISO 9001 and ISO/IEC 17025. Not all controls are included, as this is at a high level.

ISO 9001	ISO 17025
Clause 0	Not present
Clause 1	Clause 1
Clause 2	Clause 2
Clause 3	Clause 3
4.1	Not present
4.2	4.1, 4.2, 7.2.2.3, 7.9
4.3	Annex B2
4.4	Annex B
5.1.1	8.2.3
5.1.2	5.4, 8.6.2
5.2.1	Not present
5.2.2	8.3.2, 6.6.3
5.3	5.2, 5.4, 5.6, 6.2.4, 8.2.5
6.1.1	8.5.1
6.1.2	8.5.2
6.2	8.2.1, 8.5.1, 8.6.1, 8.9.1, 8.9.2
6.3	5.7 b)
7.1.1	6.1
7.1.2	6.2
7.1.3	6.3
7.1.4	6.3
7.1.5	6.1, 6.5
7.1.6	6.2.2
7.2	6.2.1, 6.2.2, 6.2.3, 6.2.5, 7.1.3, 8.2.2
7.3	6.2.4
7.4	5.7 a), 6.2.4, 6.6.3, 7.9.6
7.5	5.5 c), 6.2.2, 7.2.1.2, 7.5, 7.8.6.1, 8.1.1, 8.2, 8.3, 8.4
8.1	7.1
8.2	7.1, 7.2, 7.4, 7.7, 7.8
8.3	7.2, 7.6, 7.7, 7.8
8.4	6.6, 7.1.1 c), 7.11.4
8.5	6.3, 6.4, 6.5, 7.1–7.8
8.6	7.8
8.7	7.9, 7.10
9.1	6.2.3, 7.7, 7.9, 8.6

ISO 9001	ISO 17025
9.2	8.8
9.3	8.9
10.1	8.6
10.2	7.9, 7.10, 8.7
10.3	8.2.3, 8.6, 8.9

There are a number of ISO/IEC 17025 specific controls that are only applicable to a forensic laboratory that are not in ISO 9001. These include 5.4 (meeting regulatory authorities and organisations providing recognition, 6.2.3 (evaluation of significance of deviations, 6.2.6 authorise personnel for laboratory activities, 6.3.1 (suitable facilities for laboratory activities), etc.

Appendix 3—Conflict of interest policy

This policy describes the Conflict of Interest Policy for all work undertaken, including digital forensics, general management consultancy, and regulatory work.

There is no right or wrong approach to handling potential conflicts of interest. Ultimately, the issue is about the application of common sense within a legislative, regulatory, contractual, or ethical framework. The key principles to any effective policy are as follows:

- **Define a conflict of interest**: Would there have to be some personal financial or other interest for an employee for a conflict of interest to be considered, or would historical connection to the beneficiary of a decision be sufficient to trigger the procedures.
- **Consider the future likelihood of such conflicts**: Is the conflict of interest likely to be exceptional in which case the employee's membership of the decision-making body is unproblematic, or would it be so frequent that it might be best to consider alternative membership of the council.
- **Agree the method of declaring an interest**: This may be a written declaration completed annually or before undertaking a task (project, case, etc.) or may be prior to a meeting, etc.
- **Agree the method of addressing the conflict**: Again, there are numerous ways of addressing a conflict of interest. The employee in question might absent themselves completely from all consideration or they may participate in the discussion but not the decision. Each case shall be decided on the factors involved.

It is the FCL's policy to have an open, transparent, fair, objective, customer-focused, yet accountable process for any possible conflict of interest. FCL owes contractual duties, as well as a duty of care, to all of its clients and this shall be observed and complied with, as well as being seen to be observed and complied with;

This policy shall be implemented to protect FCL and all employees from the appearance of an impropriety.

At the start of any forensic case or assignment, the employees involved shall consider the scope of the assignment and consider if they have now, in the past, or in the foreseeable future, any possible conflicts of interest relating to the assignment. These may arise from such issues as:

- personal, or familial involvement, with someone who is involved in the management of the contract of the assignment;
- personal, or familial involvement, with someone who is the subject of a forensic case or assignment;
- a breach of the code of ethics of any professional organisation of the organisation that any employee on the case or assignment may belong to or be bound by;
- the offer (or acceptance) of any inducement, hospitality, or gift that may impair, limit the extent, rigor, or objectivity in the performance of the assignment, case, or project;
- having a financial interest in the outcome of the case or assignment;
- impaired decisions or actions that may not be in the best interest of FCL's client or the Court; and
- a perception that FCL or its employees are acting improperly because of a perceived conflict of interest.

Where a possible conflict is identified after the start of any assignment, it shall be brought to the attention of the Laboratory Manager, who has accountability and responsibility for Compliance and Governance, as soon as is practicably possible, and within 24 h at the maximum. As soon as the conflict is identified, the employee shall excuse themselves from any decision taking until the conflict has been resolved. In some cases, it will be necessary for the employee to excuse themselves from any work on the case or assignment. This is specifically the case for forensic work and may be applicable in other assignments, as identified.

In some cases, a 'Declaration of Interest Form' shall be required to be executed before each assignment, and in other cases, an annual (or regular) declaration will be required.

Where a conflict is declared to the Laboratory Manager, they shall take such action as they see fit to both declare and resolve the conflict. This may (and probably will) involve communication with the other parties in the case or assignment. All discussions and decisions shall be regarded as records, be retained, and secured appropriately.

All possible or actual conflicts of interest shall be investigated thoroughly, quickly, impartially, and all relevant parties shall be advised of the outcome.

A review of all conflicts and possible conflicts shall be undertaken at Management Reviews.

This policy is issued and maintained by the Laboratory Manager, who also provides advice and guidance on its implementation and ensures compliance.

All employees shall comply with this policy.

Appendix 4—Quality policy

FCL is committed to good quality practice. The objective for all employees is to perform their activities in accordance with FCL standards to ensure that all the products and services provided meet those standards and meet or preferably exceed the client's expectations.

Management strives to underline this approach in all their day-to-day activities.

Quality in FCL shall be measured by Key Performance Indicators (designated as quality objectives) which top management review and set each year to ensure that FCL and its employees attain quality standards, and to ensure continuous improvement of the defined quality objectives.

Quality is the responsibility of all employees. Each employee shall ensure that they are familiar with those aspects of FCL's policies and procedures that relate to their day-to-day work and understand how their contribution affects the FCL's products and services.

The Key Performance Indicators which define FCL quality objectives are set out in Planning within the Business in Chapter 6, Section 6.2.2.1. The scope of the quality system implemented in FCL is the whole of the digital forensics operations undertaken.

It is the FCL's policy to:

- only purchase from approved suppliers, who shall be regularly audited, this includes all outsourcing partners (as defined in Chapter 14);
- handle all client feedback, including complaints, in an effective and efficient manner and use them as input to continuously improve the FCL's products and services (as defined in Chapter 6, Section 6.14);
- ensure that all agreed client requirements are met;
- implement a process of continuous improvement (as defined in Chapter 4, Section 4.10 and Appendix 24);
- ensure that all employee training needs are identified at a Training Needs Analysis as part of the employee's annual appraisal process or as required (as defined in Chapter 4, Section 4.7.3 and Chapter 18, Section 2.2).

Where a client requests that FCL conforms to their own quality system, FCL shall apply this system as defined in Chapter 6.

This policy is issued and maintained by the Quality Manager who also provides advice and guidance on its implementation and ensures compliance.

All employees shall comply with this policy.

Chapter 4

The integrated management system

4.1 Introduction

Note

This chapter is heavily based on what has been implemented in FCL. Each forensic laboratory must make its own decisions as to what it wants to include in its integrated management system (IMS).

In order to manage processes and procedures cohesively and consistently across the organisation, FCL originally implemented an IMS based on PAS 99. PAS 99 was the world's first IMS requirements specification based on the six common requirements of ISO Guide 72, which was a standard for writing management system standards (MSSs). This approach gave one holistic approach to manage all processes and procedures within FCL in a single cohesive management system and ensured continuous improvement, while eliminating duplication and increasing efficiently.

With multiple different structures in the different management systems that FCL was using, the implementation of an IMS based on PAS 99 was still a difficult task.

Since the original PAS 99 system was implemented, the International Standards Organisation (ISO) agreed that ISO Guide 83 (high-level structure and identical text for management system standards and common core management system terms and definitions), in 2010 tries to resolve some of these issues and provides a common and consistent approach. This tried to overcome the issue of an organisation implementing multiple MSSs where, while the standards had common principles and aims, the technical and administrative details in them meant that it was possible to have a common IMS that may pass the requirements for one standard but yet fail another. This was compounded by the interpretation of the standard's requirements and the approach of different Conformance Assessment Bodies. As such, Guide 83 was not a standard but a guide to writing management system standards.

While this was a 'Guide,' Annex SL was formally adopted in 2011 with the familiar 10 clauses, based on W Edwards Deming's PDCA (Plan, Do, Check, Act) cycle; now also referred to as the PDSA (Plan, Do, Study, Act cycle)—though not all standards mandate or use this (e.g. ISO/IEC 27001):

1. Scope;
2. Normative references;
3. Terms and definitions;
4. Context of the organisation;
5. Leadership;
6. Planning;
7. Support;
8. Operation;
9. Performance evaluation; and
10. Improvement.

Note

As of 2019, Annex SL has been renamed 'Annex L' in the ISO/IEC Directives Part 1.

All new and revised MSSs ('Type A'—Requirements, and where appropriate 'Type B—Guidelines') shall adopt this structure to ensure a common language and structure is used and eliminate inconsistencies and incompatibilities. Annex L has 45 mandatory requirements ('Shalls'), resulting in 84 specific requirements, with each individual standard having its own requirements in addition to these core requirements.

A Blueprint for Implementing Best Practice Procedures in a Digital Forensic Laboratory. https://doi.org/10.1016/B978-0-12-819479-9.00024-1

FCL has adopted the Annex L approach to replace its PAS 99 approach and has used this for all management standards in use as well as all other procedures in use.

Annex L has provided the template for all of the Type A MSSs in use in FCL. These include (either fully or partially implemented in FCL), but are not limited to:

- ISO 9001—Quality management systems—Requirements;
- ISO 14001—Environmental management systems;
- ISO 20000—Information technology—Service management;
- ISO 22301—Societal security—Business continuity management systems;
- ISO 45001—Occupational Health and Safety Management Systems—Requirements with guidance for use;
- ISO/IEC 27001—Information technology—Security techniques—Information security management systems—Requirements; and
- Other members of the ISO/IEC 27xxx, ISO 291xx and ISO 223xx family of standards as appropriate.

Type B MSSs are guidelines, and some of these currently follow Annex L, but many do not. The IMS has aligned all of the standards and procedures in use with Annex L. These include (either fully or partially implemented in FCL), but are not limited to:

- ISO 10002—Quality management—Customer satisfaction—Guidelines for complaints handling in organisations;
- ISO 10003—Quality management—Customer satisfaction—Guidelines for dispute resolution external to organisations;
- ISO 15489—Information and documentation—Records management;
- ISO/IEC 17020—Conformity assessment—Requirements for the operation of various types of bodies performing inspection;
- ISO/IEC 17025—General requirements for the competence of testing and calibration laboratories;
- ISO 19011—Guidelines for auditing management systems;
- ISO 19600—Compliance management systems—Guidelines;
- ISO 26000—Guidance on social responsibility;
- ISO/IEC 27036 Parts 1, 2 and 3—Supplier relationships;
- ISO/IEC 27036 Part 4—Information technology—Security techniques—Information security for supplier relationships;
- ISO/IEC 27701—Security techniques—Extension to ISO/IEC 27001 and ISO/IEC 27002 for privacy information management—Requirements and guidelines
- ISO 31000—Risk management—guidelines;
- ISO 37002—Whistleblowing management systems—Guidelines;
- ISO 37500—Guidance on outsourcing; and
- In house digital forensic procedures.

All are managed through the same consistent and common IMS.

This allows FCL to concentrate its efforts on the discipline specific requirements of the relevant MSSs implemented, typically in S6—Planning and S8—Operation.

A glossary of terms relating to Annex L is defined in Appendix 1.

4.2 Benefits

FCL has found the following benefits in adopting the single IMS based on Annex L to manage all of its processes and procedures:

- **reduced costs**—by avoiding duplication in internal audits, document control, training, and administration, adopting future MSSs and procedures will be much more effective and efficient;
- **time savings**—by having the ability to have combined management reviews and integrated and combined internal audits;
- **a holistic approach to managing business risks**—by ensuring that all consequences of any action are considered, including how they affect each other and their associated risks, across all MSSs managed by the IMS;
- **reduced duplication and bureaucracy**—by having one set of core MSS processes ensures the requirements of the specific standards are co-ordinated, workloads streamlined, and disparate systems avoided;
- **less conflict between systems and departments**—by avoiding separate 'empires' or 'silos' for the requirements of different systems and defining responsibilities clearly from the outset within the IMS;

- **improved communication, both internal and external**—by having one common set of objectives (one for each MSS), a team approach culture can thrive and improve communication. Using one communication channel for all MSSs consistently ensures that all employees are made aware of updates and changes for all MSSs, as required;
- **enhanced business focus**—by having one IMS linked to FCL's strategic business objectives, the IMS contributes to the overall continual improvement process within FCL;
- **improved employee morale and motivation**—by involving and linking roles and responsibilities to objectives, it makes change and new initiatives easier to implement and makes FCL more dynamic, efficient and able to adopt change; and
- **optimised internal and external audits**—by minimising the number of audits required by undertaking integrated and combined audits and maximising resource usage.

4.3 The IMS

There are an increasing number of standards, national and international, that follow the W Edwards Deming (or Plan, Do, Check, Act—PDCA) Cycle. Historically, these have been stand-alone systems and this has led to:

- duplication of effort;
- conflict between different management systems;
- increased bureaucracy; and
- multiple audits of systems.

FCL has adopted the approach outlined in Annex L and has created an IMS for all of its business processes that are either Legislative, Regulatory or contractual requirements, standards requirements, good practice requirements or internal process requirements. This allows one single view of FCL's operation to be seen by top management and so:

- provide improved business focus;
- provide a more holistic approach to risk management;
- reduce conflict between management systems and other integrated procedures;
- reduce bureaucracy;
- reduce duplication of effort;
- provide a streamlined audit and management review process;
- have a common continuous improvement process; and
- provide total management oversight.

The mapping of the requirements of Annex L and how they are met in this book is defined in Appendix 2.

4.3.1 General requirements

FCL has implemented this process for all of the management systems and other procedures that are implemented.

4.3.1.1 Overview

If FCL is not continually improving the way that they provide services and products to their clients, it is losing competitive advantage.

FCL's core values require it, their work environment need it, and their clients demand it.

PDCA is FCL's methodology for conducting all process improvement projects. Regardless of position or role in FCL, if the PDCA method is followed, whether in a project team or for a complete management system, it has found that the opportunity of success is increased. The PDCA method is made up of eight simple steps (or questions):

4.3.1.2 Plan

1. **Goal statement**—What is trying to be achieved? In clear terms, define the purpose and goal of the project or management system. Usually this is to increase a desirable effect or decrease an undesirable one. The Goal Statement sets the scope and alignment for rest of the project or management system's actions. FCL's Goal Statement is defined in Appendix 3.
2. **Cause analysis**—What are the significant causes keeping FCL from achieving the Goal Statement, and how are the significant causes defined? Causes are usually a brainstormed list, but their significance (impact) is validated with data.

3. **Baseline measure**—What is/are the baseline measure(s) of the Goal Statement? FCL's baseline measures are defined in the Appendix 4.
4. **Solution development**—What are the proposed fixes (changes in processes) that, when properly implemented, will make a dramatic impact toward achieving the Goal Statement?
5. **Implementation planning**—What are the detailed plans that will successfully implement the proposed solution into the work environment? These plans shall address the people, process, technology, products, services and equipment/facility changes needed to transition from the current way to the proposed way.

4.3.1.3 Do

Implement the solution that was planned—If possible, implement the solution in a proof of concept (manageable) fashion before rolling it out in its entirety. During implementation, adjustments are made to refine the proposed solution to match reality.

4.3.1.4 Check

Measure of improvement—What is the measured improvement of the Goal Statement? This is measured by evaluation of the meeting of the management system's objectives using performance evaluation and SMART metrics and KPIs as defined in Chapter 3, Section 3.1.17.

4.3.1.5 Act

How will the solution be sustained over time? What are FCL's plans to measure and adjust the solution in order keep its gains from degrading over time? This is a combination of performance evaluation and corrective action (as defined in Sections 4.9 and 4.10).

4.4 FCL context

Note

The following sections (4–10) reflect the same sections in Annex L and show how FCL meets them.

FCL is a digital forensic laboratory based in the UK dealing with UK based digital forensic cases and works across all industry sectors.

The context of the IMS is the business environment or ecosystem in which FCL operates which is a combination of external and internal contexts (i.e. factors, conditions, investment and the needs and expectations of interested parties) that will have an effect on the delivery of FCL' products and services.

4.4.1 Understanding FCL and its context

4.4.1.1 External context

External context is anything outside the FCL's control that may influence business objectives and achieving them. These include:

- **Investors**: These are the FCLs financial backers and their requirements;
- **Market forces**: This includes competitors and the requirements to ensure that current technology is appropriate and works correctly to support the business, delivering the correct products and services to clients in a timely manner to the expected level of quality;
- **Suppliers**: These include the third-party suppliers that support FCL. These cover hardware, software, infrastructure, office services, office suppliers, etc. and their contractual obligations and assured delivery of products and services to FCL;
- **Supplier culture**: Not only are there contractual relationships in place with third-party suppliers, but they also have their own cultures and standards that shall be considered as part of the relationship between FCL and these third-party suppliers;
- **Politics**: There are no known political issues in addition to the Legislative, Regulatory and contractual requirements as defined in Chapter 12 Section 12.3.13.1;

- **Economic**: There are no known issues;
- **Sociological**: The increased use of technology and social media are managed by aggressive risk management that is subject to regular review. There is demonstrable top management support for managing the multiple management systems and procedures implemented in the IMS;
- **Technological**: New technology and the requirements to meet new Legislative requirements is managed through the risk assessment and management process deriving the Statement of Applicability (for ISO/IEC 27001), which is under regular review. As the pace of technology changes (as does the drive for antiforensics), it is essential that FCL remains abreast of these developments and is able to manage client cases effectively and efficiently with ever evolving technological challenges;
- **Environmental**: FCL accepts their corporate social responsibilities and tries, wherever possible, to reduce the impact that it has on the environment. FCL has also adopted the requirements of the EU Sustainable Finance Disclosure Regulation (SFDR);
- **Risks**: evaluation of risks to the delivery of products and services to internal and external clients and the risk treatment to reduce these risks to an acceptable level in line with the FCL Risk Appetite (as defined in Chapter 5, Section 5.5.9.1) or that they are knowingly accepted and reviewed on a regular basis; and
- **Legislation**: A variety of Legislation is applicable to FCL for the products and services it provides. While the Legislation is international and national and applicable to many organisations, contractual terms are specific to the contracting parties. One of the most important changes in recent years is the GDPR and the associated UK Data Protection Act 2018 (DPA 2018), which was then amended on Brexit to be UK centric and a list of applicable Legislation, Regulation, and contractual obligations is defined in Chapter 12, Section 12.3.13.1,

4.4.1.2 Internal context

FCL's internal context is the internal environment in which they seek to achieve their defined business objectives, as defined in Appendix 5.

The internal context is anything that can influence the way that FCL manages the risks to their success. A forensic laboratory shall establish their internal context because:

- risk management within the forensic laboratory shall take place in the context of the business objectives; and
- it is necessary not only to measure and manage the 'downside' of risk but also to recognise opportunities to achieve the forensic laboratory's business objectives as this will affect ongoing commitment, credibility, trust, and value.

FCL's internal context is governed its requirements and is finely tuned to the specific requirements of their business. These include, but not be limited to:

- governance, corporate structure, roles, and accountabilities;
- policies, objectives, and the strategies that are in place to achieve them;
- products and services activities, resources, supply chain assurance, and the relationships with the interested parties;
- future opportunities and business priorities;
- capabilities, understood in terms of resources and knowledge (e.g. capital, time, people, processes, systems, competencies, and technologies);
- protection of internal and client information based on aggressively managed risk management with a low risk appetite;
- close management of third-party suppliers, including regular Service Level Review meetings and a regular planned schedule of second party audits;
- information systems, information flows and decision-making processes (both formal and informal);
- identification of the interested parties within the forensic laboratory, as well as outside it, and understanding their needs and expectations as defined in Section 4.2;
- the forensic laboratory 's organisational values, mission, vision, policies and objectives expressed in its culture;
- the forensic laboratory 's culture of creativity and openness but in a controlled and managed secure environment;
- standards, guidelines, and models adopted by the forensic laboratory; and
- details of contractual relationships.

4.4.2 Needs and expectations of interested parties

The needs and expectations of the interested parties are best summarised as the safe and secure delivery of FCL's products and services defined in the scope statement to internal and external clients and the specific needs and expectations as defined in Appendix 6.

4.4.3 Purpose and scope of the IMS

The purpose of the IMS is to provide a common management framework for managing all of the MSSs and the included procedures to provide a secure and resilient infrastructure to support FCL operations to reduce risks of an adverse event occurring. If an adverse event occurs, that affects the delivery of those products and services, then there is a tried and tested incident management and business continuity management process in place to ensure timely recovery and resumption of products and services to clients.

The scope of the IMS is divided into four sections as below:

4.4.3.1 Organisation

Note 1

Different forensic laboratories will have different organisational set ups. Therefore, no FCL organisational chart has been supplied. This is a matter for all forensic laboratories to determine and implement as they see fit for their business purposes.

Note 2

Job descriptions for specific roles for the relevant management systems are defined in different chapters in this book, as appropriate.

Note 3

Basic human resources controls such as employee screening) (as defined in Appendix 30), segregation of duties (as defined in Chapter 12, Sections 12.3.5 and 12.3.6), training, awareness, and development and maintenance of competencies (as defined in Chapter 12, Section 12.3.2) are included in FCL's procedures.

All employees have a duty to:

- safeguard FCL and client information and assets in their care;
- comply with all of the relevant IMS policies and supporting procedures;
- comply with FCL business process procedures; and
- report any suspected or actual information security incidents to their line management.

4.4.3.2 Location

This will depend on the specifics of a forensic laboratory and where it operates.

4.4.3.3 Assets

The assets that come under the scrutiny of the IMS are as follows.

- **Information**—of all types relevant to the FCL and their clients and is held in the Configuration Management Database (CMDB) as part of the Service Desk;
- **Software**—details of all software is held in the Configuration Management Database (CMDB) as part of the Service Desk;
- **Hardware**—details of all hardware is held in Configuration Management Database (CMDB) as part of the Service Desk;

- **People**—employees;
- **Services**—includes gas, water, electricity, telephone, internet, public services, and third-party suppliers; and
- **Image and reputation**—FCL's image and reputation is a huge asset. Any compromise of information that compromises this asset will have a major effect on FCL's business.

4.4.3.4 Technology

The technology in use is defined as the products and services in use in FCL to deliver products and services to internal and external clients and includes, but is not limited to the following:

- backup and replication;
- business continuity;
- change management;
- disaster recovery;
- Email;
- infrastructure management;
- IT service contract management;
- managing 'starters, movers and leavers';
- network management;
- outsourced services to support delivery of products and services to internal and external clients;
- secure network file systems;
- secure networking including Wi-Fi;
- secure printing;
- service desk;
- service provision reporting;
- software licence management;
- software patching and maintenance;
- standard desktop;
- telephony (mobile and desktop);
- VPN access; and
- vulnerability management.

4.4.3.5 The IMS

The IMS comprises a number of management systems, partial or full implementations of various MSSs (Type A and B) as well as other internal procedures that can be managed by the IMS. A forensic laboratory can integrate any processes it has within an IMS and each forensic laboratory will be different, typically with a number of common standards but different procedures supporting them.

4.5 Leadership

4.5.1 Leadership and commitment

FCL top management is fully committed to the implementation of a business-driven IMS based on risk management for their information processing facilities, their information, and their client's information. Specifically, this includes their commitment to the:

- ownership;
- establishment;
- implementation;
- operation;
- monitoring;
- review;
- maintenance; and
- improvement.

of the IMS, the policies and procedures that it contains, this includes:

- ownership of the IMS;
- establishment and approval of relevant IMS policies and procedures;
- complying with applicable Legislation, Regulation, contractual terms, and other requirements relevant to the delivery of FCL's products and services to clients, as defined in Chapter 12, Section 13.3.13.1;
- defining the FCL business-driven IMS objectives, as defined in Section 4.6.2;
- ensuring that the requirements of the IMS are all integrated and embedded into all FCL work (including projects) at every stage;
- appoint a suitable employee to perform the role of Information Security Manager, as defined in Section 4.5.3;
- appoint a suitable employee to perform the role of Business Continuity Manager, as defined in Section 4.5.3;
- appoint a suitable employee to perform the role of Quality Manager, as defined in Section 4.5.3;
- appoint a suitable employee to perform the role of Laboratory Manager, as defined in Section 4.5.3;
- establishing appropriate roles and responsibilities to support the IMS and document them with appropriate job descriptions and competencies;
- ensuring that these roles are established with suitable authority and responsibility and that the post holders have the appropriate resources, including budget and funding, to perform their roles;
- providing oversight of the IMS by the relevant management committees;
- ensuring that relevant issues from these management committees are escalated to the FCL Board;
- assigning appropriate numbers of competent employees to support the IMS and its supporting business processes;
- communicating, to all employees, and relevant third parties, the importance of the IMS and its supporting business processes;
- communicating, to all employees, and relevant third parties, the importance of the continuous improvement of the IMS and its supporting business processes;
- communicating, to all employees, the importance of compliance with the relative Legislation, Regulations, and contractual terms relating to the IMS and its supporting business processes;
- evaluating the effectiveness of the IMS in achieving its stated objectives using appropriate performance evaluation, as defined in Section 9, and where this is not fulfilled, applying appropriate corrective action to address the shortfall, as defined in Section 10;
- ensuring that client requirements are determined and met with the aim of improving client (internal or external) satisfaction;
- determining risk levels within FCL;
- managing those risks appropriately;
- determining and setting the FCL risk appetite;
- ensuring that a schedule of internal (first party) audits, supplier (second party) audits, external (third party) audits, technical assessments, self-assessments, exercises, tests, and management reviews are carried out to ensure continued suitability, adequacy, and effectiveness of the IMS;
- actively being engaged in relevant exercises and testing of relevant aspects of the IMS;
- ensuring that top management receives reports relating to the performance of the IMS via the management reviews;
- embedding continuous improvement for all meeting the defined objectives in all IMS processes; and
- providing demonstrable leadership support to all aspects of the IMS.

4.5.1.1 Management committees

To provide and support an overarching governance process in FCL, the following management committees, with associated Terms of Reference, exist and meet regularly to discharge their duties:

- Audit Committee (Appendix 7);
- Business Continuity Committee (Appendix 8);
- Environment Committee (Appendix 9);
- Health and Safety Committee (Appendix 10);
- Information Security Committee (Appendix 11);
- Quality Committee (Appendix 12);
- Risk Committee (Appendix 13); and
- Service Delivery Committee (Appendix 14).

Each Terms of Reference is under regular review.

4.5.2 Policies

FCL has a number of policies that are integral to FCL's business processes.

Note

Some of these are specific to the Legislation within the jurisdiction, they are not reproduced in the Appendix, but mentioned in passing only.

4.5.2.1 Legislative

There will be the need for a number of policies that are specific to the Legislation in the jurisdiction. These can cover issues such as:

- disability;
- discrimination;
- equal opportunities;
- data privacy and protection (more recently GDPR and DPA 2018);
- etc.

4.5.2.2 ISO high-level policy documents

The following high-level policy documents based on ISO Standards are implemented in FCL:

- Quality Management Policy (ISO 9001) (Chapter 3, Appendix 4);
- Environmental Management Policy (ISO 14001) (Appendix 16);
- Health and Safety Policy (ISO 45001) (Appendix 17);
- Service Management Policy (ISO 20000) (Appendix 18);
- Business Continuity Policy (ISO 22301) (Appendix 19); and
- Information Security Policy (ISO/IEC 27001) (Appendix 20).

Note

The relevant standards follow the policy named above.

4.5.2.3 ISO detailed policy documents

The following detailed policy documents based on ISO Standards are implemented in FCL:

- Access Control Policy (ISO/IEC 27001) (Appendix 21);
- Change or Termination of Employment Policy (ISO/IEC 27001) (Appendix 22);
- Clear Desk and Clear Screen Policy (ISO/IEC 27001 & ISO 20000) (Appendix 23);
- Continuous Improvement Policy (all standards) (Appendix 24);
- Cryptographic Control Policy (ISO/IEC 27001) (Appendix 25)
- Document Retention Policy (all standards) (Appendix 26);
- Financial Management Policy (ISO 20000) (Appendix 27);
- Mobile Device Policy (ISO/IEC 27001) (Appendix 28);
- Network Services Policy (ISO/IEC 27001) (Appendix 29);
- Personnel Screening Policy (ISO/IEC 27001) (Appendix 30);
- Relationship Management Policy (ISO 20000) (Appendix 31);
- Release Management Policy (ISO 20000) (Appendix 32);
- Service Reporting Policy (ISO 20000) (Appendix 18);
- Service Management Policy (ISO 20000) (Appendix 33); and
- Third Party Access Control Policy (ISO/IEC 27001) (Appendix 34).

4.5.2.4 Specific policy documents

The following specific policy documents are implemented:

- Acceptable Use Policy (Appendix 35); and
- Conflict of Interest Policy (Chapter 3, Appendix 3);

4.5.2.5 Review of management system documents

FCL performs reviews of their Management System documentation, typically policies, procedures, and other relevant documentation to:

- assess the continuing suitability, adequacy, and effectiveness of the documentation; and
- identify and manage improvements to the documentation.

Reviews of the MSS documentation shall take place regularly (ideally at least once a year) or on influencing change and are the responsibility of the relevant MSS Owner. Reviews of the MSS documentation may take place in parallel with the management review of the MSSs, or as the subject of a separate review process as needed (Fig. 4.1).

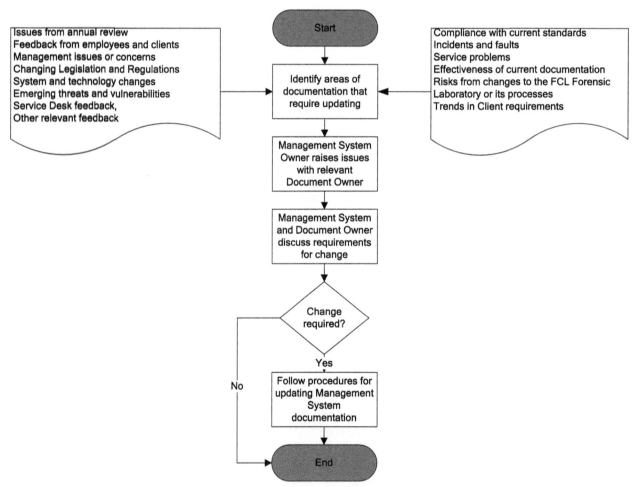

FIG. 4.1 MSS documentation review.

The relevant Management System Owner identifies areas of the management system documents that require a review or update, based on:

- issues arising from the annual review of the management system (including feedback from independent audits of the system);
- any feedback from employees concerning the effectiveness of the management system documentation;

- management issues concerning the management system documentation;
- compliance with the relevant standard;
- changes in risk profile;
- changes to systems and infrastructure that have been, or are about to be implemented;
- changes to risks arising from changes to FCL's technology, its products and services, and which may impact on management system objectives
- incidents and faults;
- complaints;
- client feedback;
- service problems;
- risks arising from organisational changes and technology and service processes;
- emerging threats and vulnerabilities;
- emerging Legislation and Regulation changes;
- emerging trends in client's requirements; and
- the continuing effectiveness of the current documentation.

The Management System Owner raises the document issues with the Document Owner as defined in Section 4.7.5.

The Management System Owner and the Document Owner discuss the issues and the possible requirements for the further development of the document.

If the document is to be updated the procedure in Section 4.7.5.4 is followed.

If it is not to be updated, the document control is updated to reflect the review has taken place and the document reissued.

4.5.3   Organisational roles, responsibilities and authorities

The relevant Management System Owner has overall ownership and responsibility for ensuring that 'their' part of the IMS exists, is resourced and is subject to continuous improvement to meet strategic business objectives and for ensuring that the IMS and its supporting documentation policies, procedures, and work instructions meets the requirements of the relevant standards implemented.

The following roles, responsibilities, and authorities are defined within the IMS:

4.5.3.1   General roles and responsibilities

General roles, responsibilities, and authorities for all employees are defined in:

- the Scope Statement for the IMS; and
- various documentations within the IMS.

4.5.3.2   Specific roles, responsibilities and authorities

Specific roles and responsibilities for jobs and tasks are defined in the:

- FCL Management generic roles and responsibilities as defined in Section 4.5.3 and Appendix 36;
- The Quality Manager as defined in Chapter 6, Appendix 4;
- The Information Security Manager as defined in Chapter 12, Appendix 16;
- The Business Continuity Manager as defined in Chapter 13, Appendix 3;
- Laboratory Manager as defined in Chapter 6, Appendix 21;
- Asset Owners as defined in Appendix 37;
- Risk Owners as defined in Appendix 38; and
- Custodians as defined in Appendix 39.

4.5.4   Roles and responsibilities for third parties employed by FCL

Where third parties are employed by FCL to perform specific tasks, they will be advised of their specific responsibilities by the following means, where appropriate:

- Contractual terms.

4.6 Planning

FCL is committed to planning its management systems and business processes to ensure that they are appropriate and effective and meet the needs of the interested parties, as defined in Section 4.5.2. It achieves this by adopting the following.

4.6.1 Actions to address risks and opportunities

4.6.1.1 Identification and evaluation of aspects, impacts, and risks

Top management is committed to a process of continuous improvement of its IMS and business processes. And this is evidenced by:

- defining various policies to support the IMS as defined in Section 4.5.2;
- defining the scope of the IMS as defined in Section 4.4.3;
- business processes have been identified as part of the ISO 9001 process for those processes that affect quality of outputs (i.e. deliverables) to all clients (internal and external) as defined in Chapter 6;
- making available resources to implement, operate, and monitor the IMS and business processes as defined in this chapter, Section 4.7.1;
- ensuring that employees who implement, operate, and monitor the IMS and other business processes are competent as defined in Section 4.7.2;
- identifying, evaluating, and treating business risk by managing a various risk registers. The FCL risk assessment and risk treatment process is covered in detail in Chapter 5.
- identifying relevant Legislation, Regulation, and contractual obligations that can affect the management systems and business processes implemented as defined in Section 4.6.1.2 and Chapter 12, Section 12.3.13;
- maintaining fault logs and fault reporting and actioning processes as defined in Chapter 7, Section 7.4.10.6;
- maintaining problem logs and problem reporting and actioning processes as defined in Chapter 7, Section 7.4.2.2;
- maintaining incident logs and incident reporting and actioning processes as defined in Chapter 7, Section 7.2.

4.6.1.2 Identification of legislative, regulatory, and contractual requirements

Identification of Legislative, Regulatory, and contractual requirements that may affect the relevant management systems is part of the remit of the various Management System Owners. This is also part of the management review process, and the agenda is defined in Section 4.9.3 and Appendix 40.

Management System, Business Process, and Project Owners are responsible for ensuring that all Legislative, Regulatory, contractual, and other requirements are considered as part of the normal business processes for managing their risks through the corporate risk register or providing them as interested party input to the management review process.

The current list of Legislative, Regulatory, contractual, and other requirements for FCL is defined in Chapter 12, Section 12.3.13.

4.6.1.3 Contingency planning

Not all of the management systems require a contingency planning process, but ISO 9001 (Section 8.7.1 refers to 'nonconforming outputs' and that 'appropriate action based on the nature of the nonconformity and its effect on the conformity of products and services. This shall also apply to nonconforming products and services detected after delivery of products, during or after the provision of services.'). ISO/IEC 27001 has a major clause relating to 'Information security aspects of business continuity management'. ISO 22301 is a standard that exclusively addresses business continuity, and it is this standard on which FCL has based their contingency planning. Early notice of the possible invocation of contingency plans is provided through:

- training and awareness of employees and any third parties working for them;
- fault reporting and management of the fault log;
- problem reporting and management of the problem log; and
- incident reporting and management of the incident log.

A Business Continuity Manager has been appointed in FCL, and their specific job description is defined in Chapter 13, Appendix 3. All relevant employees are trained in contingency issues, and records of this training are maintained by HR.

The risk of needing to invoke the contingency plans is reduced through the risk management process and the application of appropriate controls to lessen the likelihood of occurrence and so the need to invoke the plan(s).

Business continuity is fully covered in Chapter 13.

4.6.2 Objectives

FCL has a set of business objectives agreed by the Board. FCL sets a variety of management system objectives in various business processes and within the IMS. Where possible, metrics have been set and these are measurable as defined in Section 4.9.1.

Specific management system objectives have been defined as below:

- Business continuity—as defined in Chapter 13, Section 13.1.5;
- Health and safety—as defined in Chapter 12, Section 12.3.7 and Appendix 5;
- Information security—as defined in Chapter 12, Appendix 6; and
- Quality—as defined in Chapter 6, Appendix 5.

Each of the management systems implemented is responsible for meeting these objectives. These are measured and reviewed through:

- internal audits;
- external audits;
- self-assessment;
- test and exercises;
- complaints;
- client feedback;
- the management review; and
- the continuous improvement process.

4.6.3 Organisational structures, roles, responsibilities, and authorities

The organisation chart for FCL is specific to its own operations alone, and every forensic laboratory will work in a slightly different manner.

Roles, responsibilities, and authorities shall be defined in relevant job descriptions. A number of FCL' Role Descriptions are defined in Appendices 37, 38, and 39 and the Appendices in Chapter 18. These are under constant review by HR.

4.7 Support

Each management system and business process has differing requirements, but there are a number of common ones as defined in Annex L. Where there are specific requirements for a management system or business process exist (mainly in Section 6 Planning and Section 8 Operations), they are covered in the procedures for each management system and business process individually.

4.7.1 Management of resources

FCL shall ensure that they provide appropriate resources (employees, technology, services, etc.) for each management system and business process to:

- identify the Legislative requirements for the relevant management systems and business processes implemented in FCL;
- address the Regulatory requirements for the relevant management systems and business processes implemented in FCL;
- meet the contractual requirements for the relevant management systems and business processes implemented in FCL;
- implement the relevant management systems and business processes implemented in FCL;
- operate the relevant management systems and business processes implemented in FCL;
- monitor the relevant management systems and business processes implemented in FCL;
- review the relevant management systems and business processes implemented in FCL;
- maintain the relevant management systems and business processes implemented in FCL;
- implement appropriate controls to manage the relevant management systems and business processes implemented in FCL;
- continually improve the effectiveness of the relevant management systems and business processes implemented in the forensic laboratory by ensuring that internal audits, external audits, self-assessments, exercises, tests, and management reviews are carried out to ensure continued suitability, adequacy, and effectiveness of the relevant management systems and business processes;

- enhance client satisfaction by meeting, and where possible exceeding, client requirements; and
- manage the relevant management systems and business processes in FCL.

Top management is committed supporting this IMS and its supported processes and procedures.

4.7.2 Competence

FCL is committed to ensuring that all employees receive appropriate training for the tasks that they are required to perform to ensure their competence.

All employees shall be suitably trained and competent to provide the products and services that FCL and its clients require, based on:

- education;
- skills;
- training;
- experience;
- their own levels of requirement; and
- their own levels of ability.

There are corporate development programs for all employees and some specific training requirements, these are classed as:

- general HR training;
- project specific training; and
- management system specific training.

Records of training and competence matched against identified competence requirements are held by HR.

Initially all training is discussed between the employee and their Line Manager. This will agree initial personal development standards for the year and these are, when agreed, submitted to the HR for action. Ongoing discussion throughout the year between employees and their Line Managers may identify further training or development needs and objectives.

FCL shall ensure that there is equal opportunity for all employees to have access to appropriate training and personal development to meet their personal objectives.

All employees shall have annual appraisals as defined in Chapter 18, Section 18.2.4, to monitor their performance and provide an avenue for dialogue between the employee and their Line Managers and permit constructive feedback leading continuous improvement of the employee's competence.

Employees who show exceptional competence or excellence shall be recognised for their effort by the top management. This shall be in an appropriate manner as decided by the top management.

4.7.3 Training and awareness

4.7.3.1 General HRs training

Through HR, FCL shall:

- determine necessary competences for all employees in association with the relevant Line Managers;
- produce job descriptions for all posts;
- identify, through training needs analysis (TNA), the training requirements for all employees working for FCL as defined in Chapter 18, Section 18.2.2;
- provide training to achieve and maintain these competences;
- encourage all employees to take vocational training;
- evaluate effectiveness of training;
- ensure that all employees understand the relevance and importance of conforming with the requirements of the relevant business processes and management systems in FCL;
- ensure that all employees understand the relevance and importance of their contribution to FCL's success;
- ensure that all employees understand the benefits to FCL of their personal performance in conforming with the requirements of the relevant business processes and management systems in FCL;
- ensure that all employees understand the potential consequences (actual or potential) that could occur in FCL if they do not conform to the requirements of the relevant business processes and management systems in FCL;

- ensure that all employees understand the emergency procedures and contingency plans in place, should they be needed, for supporting the relevant business processes and management systems in FCL;
- book employees on external training course;
- arrange in-house training courses;
- ensure that those employees not undertaking mandatory training are forced to take it by appropriate means;
- maintain records of all training undertaken by all employees; and
- ensure that those employees appointed to manage the relevant business processes and management systems have appropriate skills, competence, and experience.

Training needs and competencies shall be regularly reviewed by HR.

4.7.3.2 Project training

At the planning stage of a new project, employees may require specific training to enable them to effectively contribute on being assigned to the project.

An employee identifies training they would like to receive and seeks approval from their Line Manager to attend a course.

If training is required, HR shall arrange suitable in-house training or contact external training organisations to assess and then book a place on a training course.

4.7.3.3 Management system specific training

Each individual management system has its own requirements for training, and each is covered within the requirements for that specific management system.

4.7.3.4 Training records

All employees have their CVs (Resumes) held by HR.

FCL encourages all of its employees to maintain Continual Professional Development or Continuous Professional Education (CPD or CPE) logs for their relevant professional organisations. The records of these are held by the individual employee and HR.

4.7.3.5 Infrastructure

FCL shall determine, provide, and maintain the work infrastructure to ensure that it is suitable for all employees to achieve the requirements of the implemented business processes and management standards. Infrastructure includes:

- buildings, offices, and workspace equipment;
- technology;
- finance;
- competent employees; and
- services.

4.7.3.6 Environment

FCL shall determine and manage the work environment to ensure that it is suitable for all employees to achieve the requirements of the business processes and management standards implemented in FCL.

4.7.4 Communication

FCL has put in place procedures and processes to ensure that effective internal, and where appropriate external, distribution of communication of the contents of the management systems, and business processes takes place. These take the form of:

- the in-house IMS as a repository of procedures and records;
- email for alerting employees of updates to this intranet system;
- competence, training, and awareness programmes;
- feedback to interested parties from internal audits;
- feedback to interested parties from external audits;
- feedback to interested parties from self-assessments;

- feedback to interested parties from exercises and other tests;
- feedback to interested parties from management reviews; and
- relevant committees for the management systems installed in FCL, as defined in Section 4.5.1.1.

4.7.5 Documented information

Note 1

Documentation may be created and maintained in Microsoft Office documents in stand-alone format or may be deposited in a Wiki, intranet, or in SharePoint. This section has been written for a manual system.

Note 2

If a document management system is used, it may automatically provide workflow capabilities, an audit trail, automated document review reporting and controlled access. This section will require amendment based on the document system in use in another forensic laboratory.

FCL maintains strict control over its documentation, as is shown below:

4.7.5.1 General

The IMS comprises:

- management system policies for each MSS implemented in FCL as defined in Chapter 3, Appendices 3 and 4 as well as various Appendices in this Chapter;
- manuals, where appropriate, to support the relevant management systems and business processes implemented in FCL;
- documented procedures to support the relevant management systems and business processes implemented in FCL;
- documented procedures to support the effective and efficient planning, implementation, operation, and management of the management systems and business processes implemented in FCL; and
- records required by the relevant management systems and business processes implemented in FCL to provide proof of the effective and efficient operation of the IMS.

  Documented procedures are crucial to the day-to-day operations in FCL as they:

- act as a repository of information to assist with Legislative, Regulatory and contractual obligations, as well as compliance, with FCL's own internal objectives;
- formally document and accurately reflect the current processes and practices implemented in FCL;
- present all of the IMS documentation in a consistent and usable style and therefore make documents easier to maintain;
- extract knowledge from key and experienced employees;
- act as a training tool for new employees and provide a first point of reference for problem-solving;
- help employees identify roles and responsibilities, and help reduce misunderstanding; and
- improve the quality of service to internal and external clients.

4.7.5.2 System documentation

For all FCL management systems and business processes, the following are defined, where relevant:

- management system policies;
- a scope statement for the management systems;
- justifications for the exclusion and inclusion of clauses or controls from the relevant management system, where appropriate;
- documented procedures for the various FCL systems;
- manuals, where appropriate, for the management systems; and
- records generated by the relevant management systems and business processes.

Documentation will typically comprise a number of different document types that reflect their use. These include, but are not limited to, the following document types:

- policies;
- procedures;
- manuals;
- work instructions;
- technical documents;
- forms;
- terms of reference;
- records required by the relevant standard, management system or business process;
- plans;
- service level agreements (SLAs); and
- etc.

These documents are all controlled within FCL and are subject to strict change control.

All documents in FCL are in HTML, Microsoft Office, or Adobe PDF format.

4.7.5.3 Control of documents

When drafting, editing, and issuing of all documentation that are generated by employees shall comply with the following responsibilities.

4.7.5.3.1 Roles and responsibilities

For those employees involved in the production of documentation, the following responsibilities are defined:

4.7.5.3.1.1 Document Owner responsibilities

The Document Owner is the relevant management system or business process owner who has management responsibility for the management system and all of the management system documentation within FCL, and is responsible for:

- appointing a Document Author as required;
- investigation and planning of a document where required;
- monitoring the research for a document;
- managing the writing/updating a document;
- circulating documents for review;
- approving the document after final review;
- issuing a 'live' version of the document.

Note

A Document Owner may write/update a document for which they have management responsibility or delegate the writing to a Document Author.

4.7.5.3.1.2 Document Author responsibilities

A Document Author is any employee who has the responsibility to research and write or update a document, and is responsible for:

- investigation and planning of a document;
- researching a document;
- writing/updating a document;
- reporting to the Document Owner on the progress of the work on a document;
- issuing draft revisions of a document for review;
- checking comments from the reviewers in conjunction with the Document Owner;
- implementing comments made by reviewers for a document;
- archiving all previous versions of a document through the Document Registrar.

4.7.5.3.1.3 Reviewer responsibilities

The Document Reviewer(s) is/are the employee(s) who is/are appointed by the Document Owner to review a document, using their specific knowledge, and they are responsible for:

- reviewing the document content using their specific knowledge;
- making comments/suggestions as appropriate for the document;
- returning comments and/or edits to the Document Owner.

4.7.5.3.1.4 Quality manager responsibilities

The Quality Manager shall be a 'sign off' for documents produced in FCL as part of the workflow for document review and updating, or may audit documents produced as part of standard internal audits to ensure that:

- the document has been properly reviewed by the Reviewer(s) appointed by the Document Owner;
- the requirements of the Document Control Checklist have been met, as defined in Appendix 41;
- metadata entered into all documents is appropriate and that a full version history is maintained as defined in Appendix 42;
- other tasks as the Quality Assurance Manager determines are appropriate, dependant on the document being reviewed.

4.7.5.3.1.5 Site owners responsibilities

Note

This relates to any location where the IMS may be stored. This could be in a Wiki, intranet, SharePoint, or a set of directories used for the IMS.

A Site Owner is any employee who is responsible for the management of all or part of the IMS, these responsibilities shall include:

- copy, move, or delete files;
- create new libraries, lists, sub sites, etc.;
- ensure that current documents are the only ones available to authorised employees;
- ensure that records are available, as required;
- ensure that obsolete documents are archived;
- give appropriate access to the site for all employees;
- make sure all classified documents are available to all authorised employees;
- optionally appoint a Custodian to undertake regular site maintenance on their behalf;
- regularly review access rights to their site; and
- the overall structure and content of their site.

4.7.5.3.1.6 Document Registrar responsibilities

The Document Registrar is the employee who has the responsibility for issuing and tracking documents. They are independent from the Document Owner and Document Author and shall be responsible for:

- maintaining the Document Register;
- controlling documents during the writing and approval process;
- generating PDF versions of issued documents for publication, as applicable;
- withdrawing and marking up obsolete documents; and
- regularly auditing the Document Register.

4.7.5.4 Writing and updating documents

When a Document Owner (or delegated Document Author) writes a new document or updates an existing document, a standard process shall be followed in FCL. This ensures that there is a standard methodology for the whole document lifecycle for all. The process involves:

4.7.5.4.1 Generating a request

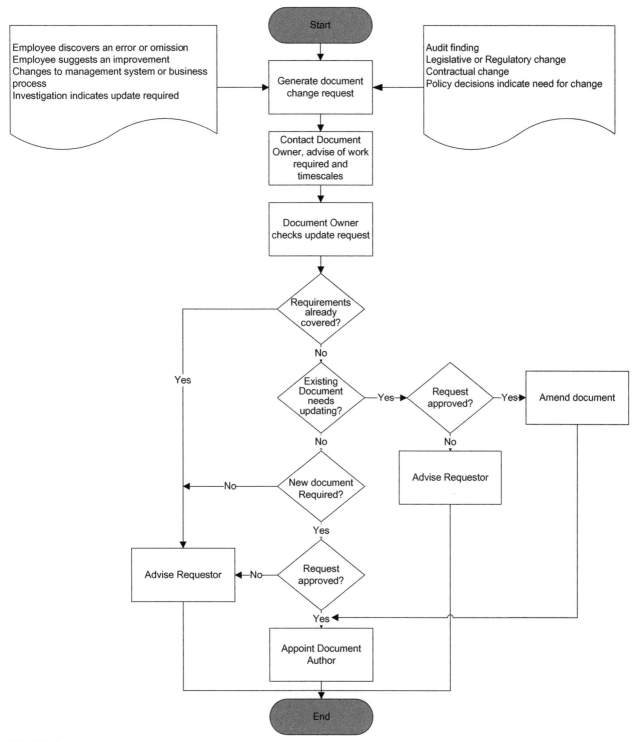

FIG. 4.2 Document request generation.

The tasks that shall be performed to request a document are (Fig. 4.2):

1. An employee identifies a need for a new document, or an update to an existing document. Typically, this may happen when:
   - an employee is working and discovers errors or lack of information within an existing document;
   - an employee suggests an improvement to a document;

- the management system or business process changes and implementation necessitate an update to a document;
- an audit highlights an area that is not adequately covered by a documented procedure;
- Legislation affects FCL's working practices; and
- policy decisions by FCL require a change in management system operations or business processes.

2. The employee contacts the Document Owner and advises them of the following:
   - the nature of work that requires documenting;
   - a risk assessment, if required; and
   - estimated writing and issuing timescales for the document.

3. The Document Owner checks the request and determines whether:
   - the requirements are already covered in other documents;
   - an existing document should be amended to reflect the additional requirements; or
   - a completely new document is required.

4. The Document Owner does either of the following:
   - if a request is approved—appoints a Document Author to write or update the document; or
   - if a request is not approved—informs the Requestor and takes no further action.

Note

Where a Document Owner does not exist (i.e. a new document is required), the person performing the role of Document Owner is the relevant management system or business process owner.

If the document is controlled, it is subject to the Document Change Management process and all changes to the document shall be approved before final approval and issue.

4.7.5.4.2 Researching and writing/updating a document

The Document Author shall research the document requirements as follows (Fig. 4.3):

1. Plan changes to the document by considering the following:
   - assess the requirements for the area to be documented;
   - assess existing work methods;
   - scope the amount of work involved; and
   - decide timescales;
   - arrange information-gathering meetings where required.

2. Gather the information required to write or amend the document as required, issues to consider are:
   - decide what is covered by the document in terms of scope—what to include and what to exclude;
   - produce a simple list of the main steps in the document from a normal start point to a normal end point, making sure that any monitoring tasks are covered, if appropriate;
   - for each step identified in the document, decide:
     - why is the step performed?
     - what is an input to the step?
     - what happens during the step?
     - what is an output from the step?
     - who performs tasks during the step?
     - what evidence exists that the step has been performed?
   - identify any areas where reviews/signoffs are performed and note the:
     - review method;
     - feedback and update loops;
     - authorisation required; and
     - documentary evidence of the review.
   - identify other employees or external organisations that have input to the document;
   - identify the risk areas in the work; and
   - compile a set of documents, forms, checklists, and reports that provide more information. Remember to highlight the areas that are relevant.

3. Create a new document or obtain the current issued version from the Document Registrar.

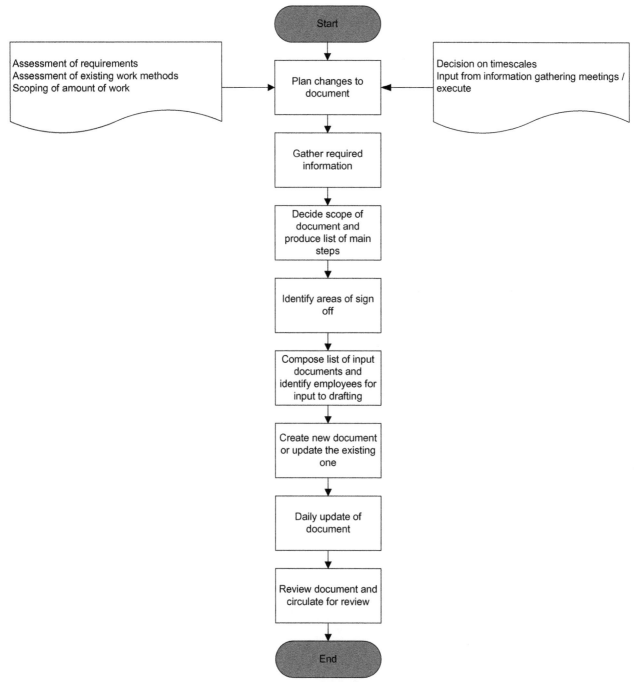

FIG. 4.3 Document creation or amendment.

4. Write or update the draft document as required by:
   - creating/modifying text and graphics, as required;
   - creating/modifying process flowcharts, as required; and
   - formatting the document, as required.
5. Every day, the document name shall be updated according to the file naming convention, as defined in Appendix 43. This allows the reversion to any previous version of a document.

6. Review the document and check it for:
   - content;
   - style and structure;
   - spelling and grammar; and
   - layout.
7. Trial the document in a real situation, then review and refine the text and rewrite it as required.
8. Generate an Acrobat PDF file of the document for circulation and formal review, if appropriate.

4.7.5.4.3 Reviewing a document and implementing edits

All draft documents produced by a Document Author shall be reviewed and edited, where necessary. The Document Owner shall ensure that reviews are properly conducted as follows (Fig. 4.4):

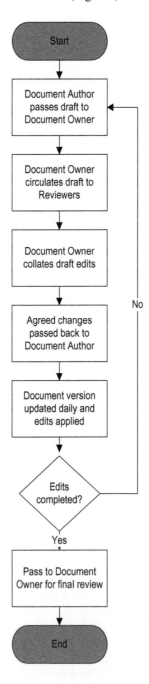

FIG. 4.4 Document review and edit.

1. The document author shall pass the draft document to document owner

---

Note

In this case, the Document Owner will be the employee who owns the business process that the document relates to.

---

2. The Document Owner shall circulate copies of the draft document to the relevant employees for review, using the document review process ensuring that the following is stated:
   - that this is a draft of the document by ensuring that is suitably watermarked. Watermarks in use in the Forensic Laboratory are defined in Appendix 44;
   - that the document shall be printed and all edits required shall be written on the printed copy or using the Document Review Form; and
   - a date by when all comments shall be received.
3. The Document Owner shall collate all returned edits. These are:
   - evaluated;
   - discussed with the Reviewer, if appropriate; and
   - agreed by the Document Owner for inclusion in the document.
4. The Document Owner shall the agreed changes to the Document Author.
5. Every day, the document name shall be updated according to the file naming standards. This allows the reversion to any previous version of a document.
6. Update the date and version information in the document control section.
7. Perform the required edits to the text and graphics.
8. Save the document.
9. Repeat steps 1–8 until no further comments on the document are received.
10. Generate an Acrobat PDF file of the document for circulation and final review, if appropriate.
11. File the marked up printed copies of the reviewed document.

Note 1

Where a Document Owner does not exist (i.e. a new document is required), the person performing the role of Document Owner shall be the relevant management system or business process owner.

Note 2

Typically, no longer than a week (5 working days) shall be allowed for return of review comments.

Note 3

The Document Review Form used defined in Appendix 45.

Note 4

An alternative to the manual process of edits shall use the 'Track Changes' option in Microsoft Word, however, care shall be taken when collating differing review points to ensure that they are all included.

4.7.5.4.4 Issuing a document

Note

When an updated document is issued, and where practical, the new text shall be identified in the new document. If the changes are significant, consideration of additional training for those the changes affect shall be given.

Once a document has passed through the edit process, it shall be issued for use, the Document Author performs the following tasks:

4.7.5.4.4.1 *Word documents*
1. Open the Word document and save the file as the first/next release version according to the file naming standards.
2. Generate an Acrobat PDF file of the document, if appropriate.
3. Send all versions of the Word documents to the Document Registrar for archive purposes.
4. E-mails the PDF to the Document Registrar for publishing.
5. The Document Registrar shall e-mail all relevant employees indicating that a new document exists. The e-mail shall invite comment from all recipients.

4.7.5.4.4.2 *HTML documents*
1. Open the HTML document and save the file as the first/next release version according to FCL's file naming standards.
2. Send all versions of the HTML documents to the Document Registrar for archive purposes.
3. E-mails the HTML document(s) to the Document Registrar for publishing.
4. The Document Registrar shall e-mail all relevant employees indicating that a new document exists. The e-mail shall invite comment from all recipients.

4.7.6 Control of records

FCL shall record and maintain records to provide evidence of conformity and the effective operation of their management systems and business processes.

FCL shall ensure that these remain:

- legible;
- readily identifiable; and
- retrievable.

FCL shall have procedures in place to:

- identify;
- store;
- protect;
- retrieve;
- set retention times; and
- securely dispose of;

records.

4.8 Operation

During IMS operation, FCL shall actively plan, resource, implement, and operate the processes, policies, and procedures that are required to ensure that the IMS is operated in a secure manner that meets the relevant management systems, good practices, and its contractual requirements.

This includes FCL management of third party and outsource service suppliers.

FCL shall set a number of management system objectives that support the FCL business objectives, and the effectiveness of the implementation of the risk treatment plan to achieve these objectives is under constant monitoring, measurement, and corrective action, where necessary.

Any changes to existing business processes, information processing systems, policies and procedures are all subject to a formalised and rigid Change Management procedures that shall ensure that no unauthorised changes are made and that all changes to be implemented are fully assessed and tested prior to implementation, and that documentation is updated, where appropriate.

Records of all changes to, and operation of, the IMS shall be retained according to the Document Retention Policy and associated schedule.

Operation of the various parts of the IMS will depend on the specific requirements of the management system, and these are articulated in the relevant parts of this book as all have different specific requirement.

4.9   Performance evaluation

To ensure that FCL is able to continuously improve its management systems and all associated procedures, FCL shall monitor and measure how well the applicable requirements from those management systems are being met.

4.9.1   Monitoring, measurement, analysis, and evaluation

This shall be carried out using a mix of the following:

- examination of fault logs;
- examination of incident reports;
- examination of problem reports;
- exercise feedback;
- external audits;
- internal audits;
- complaints;
- client feedback;
- whistleblowing concerns raised;
- Management reviews;
- penetration testing;
- self-assessments;
- such other processes as top management sees fit; and
- trend analysis.

The scope, frequency, aims, and objectives of these tests shall be defined and be agreed with the Audit Committee. Records of these monitoring and measurement processes shall be maintained with associated Corrective Action Requests (CARs).

The results of these tests and any associated CARs shall be communicated to relevant interested parties, as appropriate.

Where an incident results in the invocation of the business continuity plan, a post incident review shall take place.

The results of the monitoring and measurement processes above shall be used to evaluate the level of compliance that FCL has for the aims and objectives of its management systems, other governing processes and Legislative requirements.

A formal report of these evaluations shall be maintained and presented, with their supporting records, to the relevant Management Committee(s).

At a high-level, metrics shall be quantifiable measurements of some aspect of a management system. For a management system, there are some identifiable attributes that collectively characterise the level of compliance of the management system to the MSS. This is a quantitative measure of how much of that attribute the management system is meeting and can be built from lower-level physical measures that are the outcome of monitoring and measurement.

The following types of metrics shall be identified and studied:

- **Process metrics**—Specific metrics that serves as quantitative or qualitative evidence of the level of maturity for a particular management system that serve as a binary indication of the presence or absence of a mature process.
- **Management system metrics**—A measurable attribute of the result of a capability maturity process that serves as evidence of its effectiveness. A metric may be objective or subjective, and quantitative or qualitative.

The first type of metric shall provide information about the processes themselves. The second type of metric shall provide information on the results of those processes and what they can tell the interested parties about how effective use of the processes has been in achieving an acceptable outcome. These metrics categories shall tailor their own metrics program to measure their progress against defined objectives.

There are a number of capability maturity models that can be used to evaluate compliance levels and that are recognised worldwide These include, but are not limited to:

- Building in Security Maturity Model (BSIMM);
- Capability Maturity Model (CMM) for quality;
- CMM for business continuity;
- CMM for health and safety;
- CMM for information security;
- CMM for IT services;
- CMM for people;
- CMM for portfolio, program and project management;
- CMM for service integration;
- CMM for services;
- CMM for System Security Engineering (this has since become ISO/IEC 21827:2008);
- Cybersecurity Capability Maturity Model (C2M2);
- Security & Privacy Capability Maturity Model (SP-CMM)

It is up to each forensic laboratory to determine how it wants to measure maturity of its management systems.

4.9.2 Internal auditing

Note

This section on auditing has been written assuming that a paper-based system is in place. This is to show the processes, checklists, and supporting forms. In practice, any number of auditing applications can be used that will electronically uses these forms and checklists, capture objective evidence and produce reports. The choice if paper vs. application is up to each forensic laboratory as is the application that they choose to use.

4.9.2.1 Overview

Note

The performing of internal audits is applicable to all FCL management systems, and this includes:

- internal processes;
- Legislative processes;
- management systems;
- Regulatory systems;
- forensic case processing; and
- other systems or processes as required.

FCL shall undertake regular planned audits of their management systems to:

- determine whether activities covered by the management systems are performing as expected;
- review controls, procedures, processes, and the management systems documentation;
- review the level of risk based on changes to FCL's organisation, technology, business objectives and processes, and identified threats;
- review the scope of the management systems; and
- identify improvements to management systems processes.

The key points about an internal audit are:

- they shall involve a systematic approach;
- they shall be carried out, where possible, by independent Auditors who are competent to perform the audit of the management systems;

- they shall be conducted in accordance with a documented audit procedure; and
- their outcome is a documented audit report.

All audits and tests within FCL shall be carried out according to a defined schedule, called the 'IMS Calendar', unless circumstances require an audit or test to be carried out that is not on the schedule (e.g. post incident, nonconformity identified, client feedback, complaint, whistleblowing concern, client requirement, etc).

While every forensic laboratory will undertake audits, exercises and tests according to their own requirements, the outline of the types of tests and audits undertaken in FCL's IMS Calendar are defined in Appendix 46.

The IMS Calendar shall ensure a rolling series of audits, exercises, and tests are carried out throughout the year and that all relevant areas of operation are covered at least annually or as required by top management.

4.9.2.2 Audit responsibilities
4.9.2.2.1 Owners

The Management System or Business Process Owner to be audited shall be responsible for the following aspects of internal audits:

- arranging audits and management reviews of their management systems or business processes;
- ensuring that the audits and management reviews of the management systems or business processes are performed;
- providing the resources needed by the Auditor to ensure that the audit is conducted effectively;
- cooperating with the Auditor when an audit is performed to ensure that the audit is conducted effectively;
- recording recommended improvements to the relevant management system or business process;
- identifying, with the Auditor and other relevant interested parties, and agreeing improvements to the relevant management system or business process;
- ensuring ongoing compliance with the relevant management standard(s);
- generating, processing and tracking CARs to implement recommended improvements to the relevant system;
- verifying that remedial action has been performed within the agreed timescales; and
- reviewing the relevant management system documentation on an annual basis or after influencing change.

4.9.2.2.2 Auditors

The Auditor shall be responsible for the following aspects of relevant system audits:

- defining the requirements of an audit;
- planning an audit;
- reviewing documentation for the area of operation being audited;
- auditing the area of operation;
- reporting any critical nonconformity during the audit to the Auditee immediately;
- reporting any nonconformity during the audit to the Auditee;
- recording CARs to the management system or business process;
- reporting the audit results to the auditee and top management;
- verifying the effectiveness of remedial actions within a timescales agreed with the auditee;
- collating and filing all audit documentation; and
- being suitably qualified and competent to perform the audit.

4.9.2.2.3 Auditees

Note

The term 'Auditee' can refer to the organisation being audited or the actual individual being audited. In this case, the term is used to indicate the individual.

The Auditee shall be responsible for the following aspects of relevant system audits:

- liaising with the Auditor to arrange for an audit of their area of operation;
- providing all resources needed by the Auditor to ensure that the audit is conducted effectively;

- co-operating with the Auditor when an audit is performed to ensure that the audit is conducted effectively;
- providing evidential material and other records when asked by the Auditor; and
- determining and initiating remedial action based on the findings in the Audit report.

4.9.2.3 Auditing management system(s)

Note

The performing of internal audits is applicable to all the management systems, this includes:

- internal processes;
- Legislative processes;
- management systems;
- Regulatory systems;
- other systems or business processes as required.

  FCL shall undertake regular planned audits of their management systems to:

- determine whether activities covered by the management system are performing as expected;
- review controls, procedures, processes, and the management systems documentation;
- review the level of risk based on changes to the organisation, technology, business objectives and processes, and identified threats;
- review the scope of the management systems; and
- identify improvements to management systems processes.

4.9.2.4 Audit planning charts

To assist in the audit planning process FCL shall use audit planning charts to effectively plan an annual cycle of audits to ensure that all controls are audited at least once through the 'audit year.'

An audit planning chart is typically a list of requirements of a management system or business process and assigning an auditee to be audited on that specific part of the management system or business process.

The charts have a list of requirements as rows and auditees (or months for the audit action to take place) as the columns. The applicability is marked by a 'tick' so, at a glance, the referential integrity of the annual audit plan can be seen to ensure that all controls are covered or the specific requirements for planning for an individual Auditee.

4.9.2.5 Audit nonconformity definitions

A nonconformity shall be recorded whenever the Auditor discovers that the documented procedures are inadequate to prevent breaches of the system requirements, or they are adequate but are not being followed correctly.

4.9.2.5.1 Nonconformity

The nonfulfilment of a requirement.

4.9.2.5.2 Major nonconformity

4.9.2.5.2.1 *Definition*

A failure to implement or comply to one or more of the applicable control requirements, such that it raises significant doubts as to the adequacy of measures to comply with the requirements of the audit and/or represents an unacceptable risk as would be perceived by the relevant interested parties and/or affects the capability of the management system to achieve the intended results.

4.9.2.5.2.2 *Examples*

Nonconformities could be classified as 'Major' in the following circumstances:

- if there is a significant doubt that effective process control is in place, or that products or services will meet specified requirements;
- ongoing and systemic breaches of the requirements have been found.

Note

A number of minor nonconformities associated with the same requirement or issue could demonstrate a systemic failure and thus constitute a major nonconformity.

4.9.2.5.3   Minor nonconformity

4.9.2.5.3.1   Definition

An isolated situation in which some aspect of an applicable control requirement has not been fulfilled, such that it raises some doubts as to the adequacy of measures to comply with the requirements of the audit and/or represents a minor risk as would be perceived by the interested parties but that does not affect the capability of the management system to achieve the intended results.

4.9.2.5.3.2   Examples

These occur when one off breaches of the requirements have been found, usually caused by human error.

Note

A number of minor nonconformities associated with the same requirement or issue could demonstrate a systemic failure and thus constitute a major nonconformity.

4.9.2.5.4   Opportunity for improvement (OFI)

An OFI is a statement of fact made by an Auditor during an audit, and substantiated by objective evidence, referring to a weakness or potential deficiency in a management system which if not improved may lead to a nonconformity in the future.

Organisations are free to identify corrective actions to OFIs as they wish, but Auditors shall take note of previous OFI raised when performing their audits and look for signs of improvement.

Note

Conformance Assessment Bodies may provide generic information about industrial best practices but no specific solution shall be provided as a part of an opportunity for improvement. They have to ensure that they do not give 'consultancy advice'; however, this is not applicable for first or second party audits carried out.

4.9.2.6   Planning an internal audit

The first stage in performing an internal audit is to plan the audit.

Initial considerations that shall be considered as input to the audit planning stage include:

- CARs which have been implemented in the management system being audited;
- previous audits performed on the system;
- system changes that have been, or are about to be, implemented;
- occurrence of security breaches/incidents;
- complaints;
- client feedback;
- whistleblowing concerns raised;
- risks arising from changes to the FCL's organisation, its technology and business processes;
- ensuring that all areas of the management system are audited at least once in any 'audit year'; and
- any outstanding issues from previous management reviews, audits or tests.

To plan an audit the appointed Auditor performs the following tasks (Fig. 4.5):

1. Check the IMS Calendar and determine which area within FCL requires an audit. The IMS Calendar shows the proposed:
   - BCP exercises;
   - external audits;
   - internal audits;

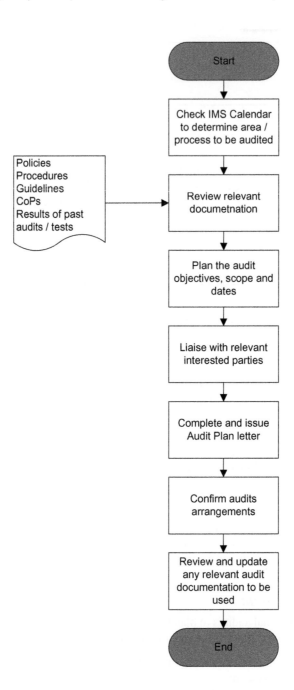

FIG. 4.5 Audit planning.

- Management reviews;
- penetration tests;
- self-assessment tests;
- other evaluations of management systems and business processes.

Planned for the year. This shall be agreed at the management review.

2. Review the relevant documentation for the area to be audited. This may include, but not be limited to, the following documents:
    - **policies**—copies of the policies relevant to the scope of the audit;
    - **procedures**—in-house procedures that provide detailed step-by-step instructions to employees on how to deal with the specific requirements of the systems within the scope of the audit;

- **guidelines**—in-house guidance or training materials that has produced to increase employee awareness for the scope of the audit;
- **codes of practice**—any industry or sector-specific codes of practice that regulate how FCL operates within the scope of the audit; and
- **results of past audits, exercises and tests**—any audits, exercises, tests, self-assessments undertaken since the last audit of the area with the results of remediation and remediation status;

3. Plan for the audit:
   - define the objectives and scope;
   - identify the employees (Auditees) that have responsibilities within the area of operation;
   - identify a suitable date and time for the audit, based on the IMS Calendar;
   - identify the time and duration of each major audit activity;
   - liaise with the Audit Committee, as appropriate;
   - liaise with the relevant management system committee, as appropriate; and
   - confirm timescales for the delivery of the audit report.
4. Complete the Audit Plan and issue it to the Auditees. The Auditee can comment on the proposed audit if necessary. The Template Audit Plan Letter is defined in Appendix 47.
5. Confirm the arrangements with the Auditee to conduct the audit using the Audit Plan Letter.
6. Review and amend the standard Audit Work Programmes (AWPs) for use during the audit, as required. The AWPs shall be used to assist in the evaluation of compliance and are merely the requirements of an MSS or business process turned into a list of questions and requirements for records to support any audit finding.

Note

It is also a good idea to examine what happens when systems are under pressure rather than functioning as normal, for example what happens:

- when a lot of employees are off sick or on holiday;
- at the end of the month or the financial year;
- when the computer system breaks down;
- when work levels are abnormally high.

4.9.2.7   Conducting an internal audit

The second stage of an audit is to conduct the audit itself to determine whether an area of operation complies with the requirements of the audit for the scope.

When conducting an audit, the Auditor shall:

- remain within the audit scope;
- exercise objectivity;
- collect and analyse evidence that is relevant and sufficient to draw conclusions regarding the scope of the audit;
- remain alert for indications of areas that may require further examination; and
- question thoroughly all employees involved in the area of operation.

To conduct an audit the appointed Auditor performs the following tasks (Fig. 4.6):

1. Collate all the resources that are needed to perform the audit, including:
   - copy of the management system documentation for the area being audited;
   - audit plan;
   - the AWP;
   - outstanding CARs;
   - CARs completed since the last audit;
   - any audits, test results, or self-assessments undertaken since the since the last audit;
   - audit reporting forms, as defined in Appendix 48;
   - CAR forms, as defined in Appendix 49; and
   - any other documentation that the Auditor feels relevant to the scope of the audit.

FIG. 4.6 Conducting and audit.

2. Hold an opening meeting with the Auditee in the area to be audited. The opening meeting agenda is defined in the Appendix 50. At the meeting outline the following:
   - inform employees of the purpose of the audit;
   - confirm which functions will be involved in the audit;
   - confirm which employees within the area will be involved in the audit;
   - confirm the schedule for the Auditor which employees will be involved at each stage, i.e. supply a copy of the Audit Plan;
   - confirm the time and location of the closing meeting and establish who will be present;
   - confirm the format of written/oral feedback that will be presented at the closing meeting, i.e. the Audit Report with associated CARs; and
   - discuss the arrangements for any potential follow-up audits to confirm that any required corrective action has been taken.

3. The Auditor works their way through their AWP, remembering to concentrate on the processes and the procedures that form the scope of the audit.
4. For each question on the AWP, the Auditor works through the following sequence:
   - **Ask**: Ask the question to establish the facts;
   - **Verify**: Listen to the auditee's answer and verify where necessary the understanding of the actual situation;
   - **Check**: Confirm that what the Auditee says corresponds with what the system being audited actually says should occur. Also check that any associated records and logs are correct and up to date; and
   - **Record**: Write down the audit findings.

   It is important that the Auditor is prepared to change the order of questions from those drawn up in the AWP or to add/remove questions. This is to encourage the flow of information from the Auditee and so obtain the required information faster.

5. Note details on the AWP as follows:
   - **Evidence (documents) examined**: Record details of the evidence presented in answer to the question. In the case of documents, reference numbers that uniquely identify them should be recorded such as procedure reference, etc. Where possible borrow a copy of the evidence if a full Audit Report is to be written so that full details can be recorded.
   - **Findings and observations**: Record the assessment of how well the evidence presented demonstrates conformity with the requirements of the system being audited and its documented policies and procedures;
   - **Assessment**: Grade the answer for each requirement:
     - **Pass**: The evidence demonstrates full conformity;
     - **Major**: The evidence demonstrates a Major Nonconformity;
     - **Minor**: The evidence demonstrates a Minor Nonconformity; and
     - **OFI**: No nonconformity was found but an OFI about potential problems and how improvements could be made has been made.

   Audit Marking definitions are defined in Section 4.9.2.5.

6. Review the marked up AWP following the audit and document:
   - Nonconformities and OFIs found using the Audit Reporting Form.
7. Hold a closing meeting with the Auditee. A closing meeting agenda is defined in the Appendix 51 At the meeting the following shall be covered:
   - thank the auditees and top management for their assistance, co-operation, and hospitality;
   - emphasise that the auditing process can only sample the system that forms the scope of the audit at the time of the audit; and
   - present the detailed findings which involves:
     - confirm each nonconformity found;
     - agree suitable corrective action for each nonconformity;
     - indicate the timescales for completion of corrective action;
     - present an Audit summary including a judgement of the level of conformity achieved by the area/process being audited; and
     - invite questions for clarification and provide immediate answers wherever possible.
8. Obtain sign-off from the Auditee on the CAR Forms.

4.9.2.8 Preparing the Audit report

1. The Auditor shall produce a draft Audit Report using the Audit Report Template that documents the findings and observations of the audit. The Audit Report Template is defined in Appendix 52. The report shall reflect accurately the content of the audit and include as a minimum (Fig. 4.7):
   - objectives and scope of the audit;
   - an objective assessment of whether the area/process being audited is conformant with the Audit Criteria (MSS or other documentation);
   - an objective assessment of the effectiveness of the area of operation;
   - an objective assessment of the management system's ability to achieve its stated objectives;
   - recommendations for improvements to the management system based on objective assessments of the documentation and operation, and the ability of the management system or business process to achieve its objectives;
   - recommendations on how improvements are to be implemented;

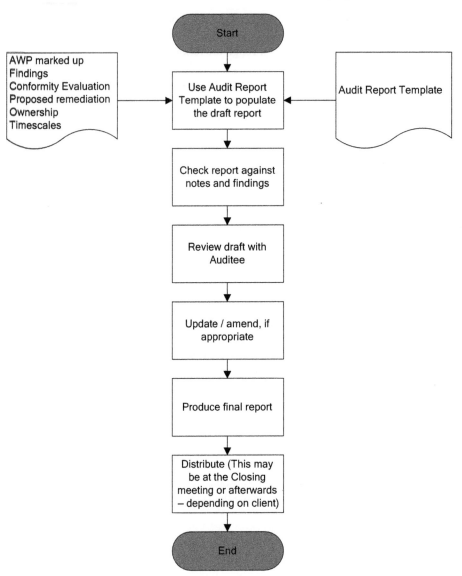

FIG. 4.7   Preparing the Audit report.

- timeframe for completion of actions in the CARs; and
- responsibility for performing those actions.

2. The Auditor checks the draft report against notes, findings, and recommendations.
3. The Auditor checks the draft report for factual accuracy and practicality of remediation with the Auditee, updating as appropriate;
4. The Auditor prints, dates, and signs the report.
5. The report is then sent to the Auditee for action and a copy sent to the relevant Audit Committee and the Chairman of the relevant management standard committee.

4.9.2.9   Completing the Audit

1. At the end of the audit the Auditor collates all documentation that formed the audit including (Fig. 4.8):
   - their own working notes;
   - their audit plan;
   - their audit report;

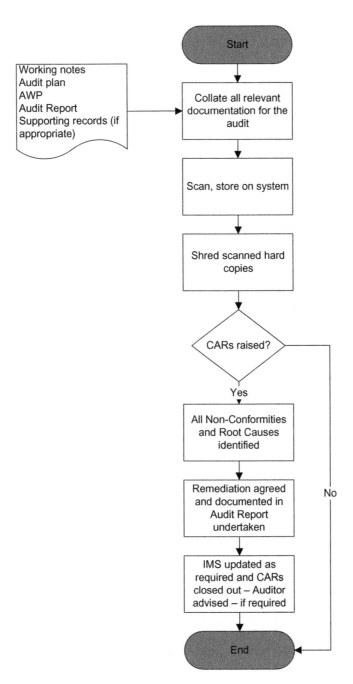

FIG. 4.8 Completing the Audit.

- their marked up AWP;
- supporting records.
2. All relevant documentation is scanned by the Auditor and then stored in the Internal Audit virtual folder.
3. The paper documentation is shredded and then securely disposed of.
4. If there are corrective actions, the Auditor sets a deadline/follow-up date with the Auditee for corrective actions to have been completed. Corrective action is performed as follows:
    - all nonconformities and their causes are identified from the audit report;
    - feedback from any management reviews should also be considered (where relevant) for purposes of taking preventative action;
    - for operational nonconformities, corrective action is proposed by the Auditee and discussed and agreed with the Auditor;

- all agreed action is documented in the relevant audit report; and
- the Auditee updates the management systems in accordance with the agreed action.

If there are no corrective actions (or when all further action from an audit is complete), the Auditor informs the relevant Management System Owner that the audit is complete.

4.9.3 Management reviews

Reviews of the management systems shall take place at least once a year (and more often if required—such as on influencing change or after a major incident), to ensure the continued suitability, adequacy and effectiveness of the relevant management systems. The provision of details for the management review is the responsibility of the relevant Management System Owner.

While the provision of the details of the management review remains the responsibility of the relevant Management System Owner, the review shall be carried out by top management with the Management System Owner and such employees as they see fit to include.

- the management review shall include assessing opportunities for improvement and the need for changes to the relevant management system(s), including their supporting policies, procedures, supporting documentation and objectives; and
- the results (i.e. records) of management reviews shall be clearly documented and records shall be maintained of the meeting in the form of minutes and CARs.

4.9.4 Review input

The input to a management review will depend on the management system being reviewed, the agenda for the management review for:

- ISO 9001;
- ISO 22301;
- ISO/IEC 27001;
- ISO 45001.

Note

Not all management systems are reviewed at the management review. The ones above are deemed critical to operations, while other standards implementations are complied with, where appropriate, and not subject to the management review (e.g. ISO 14001).

Management reviews shall include, where appropriate:

- any changes that could affect the management systems, including Regulatory and legal issues;
- approvals needed (operate, residual risk acceptance, etc.,);
- client (or any other interested parties) feedback;
- financial effects of management system related activities;
- management systems performance and effectiveness;
- marketplace evaluation and strategies;
- other opportunities for improvement not covered by the above;
- performance and status of suppliers and strategic partners;
- recommendations for improvement to the management systems;
- results of management systems audits, management systems reviews, penetration tests, benchmarking, other audits, or self-assessments of the management systems;
- results of reviews of the management system documentation;
- review of all external third-party documents in IMS to ensure they are up to date;
- review of KPIs and annual review of business;
- security issues, faults, and incidents reported of note;
- status and follow-up of management review action items;
- status and results of management systems objectives and management system improvement activities;
- status of corrective actions;

- techniques, products, or procedures, which could be used in FCL to improve the management systems; and
- vulnerabilities or threats not adequately addressed in the previous risk assessment.

These inputs, and others as appropriate, shall comprise the agenda of the management review which shall be based on the required inputs from each management standard or an agenda based on the above.

These agendas may be used for a management review of a single management system or for a review of multiple management systems. Where used for a single management system, the details related only to that management system are considered. Where used for multiple management systems, the details related to all of the management systems being reviewed are considered.

4.9.5 Review output

The output from the management review shall include any decisions and actions related to the following, where appropriate.

- amended resource needs;
- continuous improvement of the effectiveness of the management systems;
- corrective actions identified;
- financial or budgetary requirements;
- formally agreed minutes of the management review by the interested parties;
- improvement of client deliverability;
- improvement of the effectiveness of controls is being measured;
- modification of procedures and controls that affect the management systems, as necessary, to respond to internal or external events that may impact on the management systems, including changes to:
  - business processes affected by changes in technology;
  - business requirements and objectives;
  - contractual obligations;
  - increased resilience requirements from the business and/or clients;
  - levels of risk and/or criteria for accepting risks;
  - management system requirements;
  - Regulatory or Legal requirements; and
  - supporting documentation.
- revised performance objectives;
- update of the business impact analysis, risk assessment, and risk treatment plan for the relevant management systems;
- updated approvals (risk acceptance, approval to operate, etc.,);
- updated management system policies, if appropriate; and
- variation of the scope of the management system.

Actions shall be articulated in the form of CARs and shall be managed to completion through the relevant Line Managers and Management System Owners.

Reviews of the management system shall take place at least once a year (and ideally more often as required) and are the responsibility of the relevant Management System Owner.

4.10 Improvement

FCL is committed to a program of continuous improvement of their management systems and business processes. This process covers all of the management systems and business processes implemented, and the Continuous Improvement Policy has been approved by top management.

Top management shall ensure that there are regular audits and management reviews of the management systems and business processes with a view to continuous improvement, and focus on:

- how the services supported by the management systems and their supporting activities are performing (in particular whether any activities are not performing as expected);
- the effectiveness of system controls, policies, and procedures;
- the level of risk to FCL based on changes to technology, business objectives and processes, and potential threats;
- the scope of the management systems, and whether they require changing; and
- potential improvements to management systems processes.

4.10.1 Handling of nonconformities

Where nonconformities have been identified either from:

- **External Audit finding**—Any adverse finding in the management system found and reported by External Auditors;
- **Incident**—any incident identified and reported that affects the expected outcome of the management system and may lead to corrective action;
- **Internal Audit finding**—Any adverse finding in the management system found and reported by Internal Auditors;
- **Management review finding**—Any adverse finding in the management system found and reported by a management review of the management system; and
- **Preventive action**—The processing of ideas or suggestions for product and/or service improvement within the management systems.

They shall be reviewed to determine action to be taken, based on the root cause of the nonconformity occurring. While there may be any number of root causes for nonconformity, the most common are defined in Appendix 53. Often the root cause is not obvious and therefore a careful analysis of all possible causes is required.

In some cases, the response to an Audit Report may suffice, but if action is needed it shall be raised as a CAR and communicated to all relevant interested parties as appropriate.

In FCL a Corrective Action and Preventive Action (CAPA) database system is used although a paper-based system could be used.

Note

Not all management systems now refer to 'Preventive Action' as it is judged by some to be made obsolete by risk assessment and management. FCL has retained both processes.

4.10.2 Planning and implementing corrective actions

Corrective action stems from either an audit nonconformity or an incident leading to the identification of a weakness or fault that requires corrective action.

FCL also uses trend analysis for identification of persistent nonconformities, incidents, or faults.

If an immediate corrective action is required to protect FCL from suffering a serious security breach or failure of a product or service, this shall be treated as an emergency change for implementation. The relevant Management System Owner can determine the appropriate implementation actions as required in conjunction with specialist employees. Following the implementation, all supporting documentation and approvals shall be obtained.

Depending on the nature and severity of the nonconformity, the employee identifying the nonconformity shall do one the following:

- report it using the normal incident management process as defined in Chapter 7, Section 7.4.1;
- report it to their Line Manager;
- report it to the relevant Management System Owner; or
- report it to top management.

Depending on the nature and severity of the nonconformity it shall be discussed at the next relevant management system meeting. In exceptional circumstances an emergency meeting can be, and may be, called. It shall:

- determine the root cause of the nonconformity; and
- evaluate the corrective action needed to be taken to ensure that triage is carried out and that the nonconformity does not recur;

The nonconformity shall be actioned and tracked. The resulting action may be:

- a change in policy or working practices that shall then be documented and publicised. Changes to documented procedures or work instructions resulting from corrective action shall be performed as described in the Document Control Procedures;
- to reinforce the application and compliance with an existing policy or practice;
- to post advice through email or on the corporate intranet;

- to make operational changes to the infrastructure; and
- to consider, but reject, any change.

4.10.3 Corrective action requests

Once a corrective has been identified, it shall be recorded, have appropriate resources assigned to it, be managed to a satisfactory conclusion and be monitored by management during the time between the identification and closure of the corrective action. All CARs shall be subject to Post Implementation Review (PIR), with the results reported to the relevant Management System Owner or other Process Owner as required.

4.10.4 Corrective action ownership

Corrective action shall be owned by the relevant Management System Owner, as below:

- ISO 9001—Quality Manager;
- ISO/IEC 17025—Laboratory Manager;
- ISO 20000—Service Level Manager;
- ISO 22301—Business Continuity Manager;
- ISO 45001—Health and Safety Manager;
- ISO/IEC 27001—Information Security Manager.

Job descriptions are defined for each role in the Appendices in the relevant chapters of this book.

4.10.5 Corrective action oversight

Oversight of the relevant CARs shall be performed by:

- ISO 9001—Quality Committee;
- ISO 14001—Environment Committee;
- ISO/IEC 17025—Quality Committee;
- ISO 20000—Service Delivery Committee;
- ISO 22301—Business Continuity Committee;
- ISO 45001—Health and Safety Committee;
- ISO/IEC 27001—Information Security Committee.

In addition, there are the following committees:

- Audit Committee;
- Risk Committee.

Terms of reference for the committees above are defined in Appendices 7 and 13 respectively.

Appendix 1—Definition of core terms in Annex L

Note 1

The numbers in brackets after (or as part of) the definition refers to other terms in this Appendix.

Note 2

Where a definition includes 'XXX', this refers to the specific management system.

Note 3

At the time of writing Annex L definitions are undergoing a review and revision. Where possible, these changes have been adopted in the table below or notes applied.

Clause	Term	Definition
3.1	Organisation	Person or group of people that has its own functions with responsibilities, authorities and relationships to achieve its objectives (3.8) Note 1 to entry: The concept of organisation includes, but is not limited to sole-trader, company, corporation, firm, enterprise, authority, partnership, charity or institution, or part or combination thereof, whether incorporated or not, public or private Note 2 to entry: If the organisation is part of a larger entity, the term 'organisation' refers only to the part of the larger entity that is within the scope of the XXX management system
3.2	Interested party (preferred term) Interested party (admitted term)	Person or organisation (3.1) that can affect, be affected by, or perceive itself to be affected by a decision or activity
3.3	Requirement	Need or expectation that is stated, generally implied or obligatory Note 1 to entry: 'Generally implied' means that it is custom or common practice for the organisation and interested parties that the need or expectation under consideration is implied Note 2 to entry: A specified requirement is one that is stated, e.g. in documented information
3.4	Management system	Set of interrelated or interacting elements of an organisation (3.1) to establish policies (3.7), objectives (3.8), and processes (3.12) to achieve those objectives Note 1 to entry: A management system can address a single discipline or several disciplines Note 2 to entry: The management system elements include the organisation's structure, roles and responsibilities, planning, and operation Note 3 to entry: The scope of a management system can include the whole of the organisation, specific and identified functions of the organisation, specific and identified sections of the organisation, or one or more functions across a group of organisations
3.5	Top management	person or group of people who directs and controls an organisation (3.1) at the highest level Note 1 to entry: Top management has the power to delegate authority and provide resources within the organisation Note 2 to entry: If the scope of the management system (3.4) covers only part of an organisation, then top management refers to those who direct and control that part of the organisation
3.6	Effectiveness	Extent to which planned activities are realised and planned results are achieved
3.7	Policy	Intentions and direction of an organisation (3.1), as formally expressed by its top management (3.5)
3.8	Objective	Result to be achieved Note 1 to entry: An objective can be strategic, tactical, or operational Note 2 to entry: Objectives can relate to different disciplines (such as finance, health and safety, and environment) and can apply at different levels (such as strategic, organisation-wide, project, product and process (3.12)) Note 3 to entry: An objective can be expressed in other ways, e.g. as an intended result, a purpose, an operational criterion, as an XXX objective, or by the use of other words with similar meaning (e.g. aim, goal, or target) Note 4 to entry: In the context of XXX management systems, XXX objectives are set by the organisation, consistent with the XXX policy, to achieve specific results
3.9	Risk	Effect of uncertainty Note 1 to entry: An effect is a deviation from the expected—positive or negative Note 2 to entry: Uncertainty is the state, even partial, of deficiency of information related to, understanding or knowledge of, an event, its consequence, or likelihood Note 3 to entry: Risk is often characterised by reference to potential 'events' (as defined in ISO Guide 73) and 'consequences' (as defined in ISO Guide 73), or a combination of these Note 4 to entry: Risk is often expressed in terms of a combination of the consequences of an event (including changes in circumstances) and the associated 'likelihood' (as defined in ISO Guide 73) of occurrence

Clause	Term	Definition
3.10	Competence	Ability to apply knowledge and skills to achieve intended results
3.11	Documented information	Information required to be controlled and maintained by an organisation (3.1) and the medium on which it is contained Note 1 to entry: Documented information can be in any format and media, and from any source Note 2 to entry: Documented information can refer to: – the management system (3.4), including related processes (3.12); – information created in order for the organisation to operate (documentation); – evidence of results achieved (records)
3.12	Process	Set of interrelated or interacting activities that uses or transforms inputs delivering results
3.13	Performance	Measurable result Note 1 to entry: Performance can relate either to quantitative or qualitative findings Note 2 to entry: Performance can relate to managing activities, processes (3.12), products, services, systems, or organisations (3.1)
3.14	Outsource (verb)	Make an arrangement where an external organisation (3.1) performs part of an organisation's function or process (3.12) Note 1 to entry: An external organisation is outside the scope of the management system (3.4), although the outsourced function or process is within the scope
3.xx	Provider	Supplier organisation that provides a product or a service EXAMPLE Producer, distributor, retailer, or vendor of a product or a service Note 1 to entry: A provider can be internal or external to the organisation Note 2 to entry: In a contractual situation, a provider is sometimes called 'contractor'
3.xx	External provider	External supplier provider that is not part of the organisation EXAMPLE Producer, distributor, retailer or vendor of a product or a service Note 1 to entry: An external provider is outside the scope of the management system, although the externally provided function or process may be within the scope
3.15	Monitoring	Determining the status of a system, a process (3.12) or an activity Note 1 to entry: To determine the status, there can be a need to check, supervise or critically observe
3.16	Measurement	Process (3.12) to determine a value
3.17	Audit	Systematic, independent, and documented process (3.12) for obtaining objective evidence and evaluating it objectively to determine the extent to which the audit criteria are fulfilled Note 1 to entry: An audit can be an internal audit (first party) or an external audit (second party or third party), and it can be a combined audit (combining two or more disciplines) Note 2 to entry: An internal audit is conducted by the organisation itself, or by an external party on its behalf Note 3 to entry: 'Audit evidence' and 'audit criteria' are defined in ISO 19011
3.18	Conformity	Fulfilment of a requirement (3.3)
3.19	Nonconformity	Nonfulfilment of a requirement (3.3)
3.20	Corrective action	Action to eliminate the cause(s) of a nonconformity (3.19) and to prevent recurrence
3.21	Continual improvement	Recurring activity to enhance performance (3.13)

Appendix 2—Meeting the core requirements of Annex L

This section contains the mapping of Annex L to the procedures developed to implement the standard in FCL.

Note 1

Where a definition includes 'XXX', this refers to the specific management system.

Annex L	Control	Procedure(s)
4	Context of the organisation	Section 4.4—FCL Context
4.1	Understanding the organisation and its context	Section 4.4.1—Understanding FCL and Its Context
4.2	Understanding the needs and expectations of interested parties	Section 4.4.2—Needs and Expectations of Interested Parties
4.3	Determining the scope of the XXX management system	Section 4.4.3—Purpose and Section Cope of the IMS
4.4	XXX management system	The whole of the IMS
5	Leadership	Section 4.5—Leadership
5.1	Leadership and commitment	Section 4.5.1—Leadership and Commitment
5.2	XXX policy	Section 4.5.2—Policies
5.3	Roles, responsibilities and authorities	Section 4.5.3—Organisational Roles, Responsibilities and Authorities Section 4.5.4—Role and Responsibilities for Third Parties Employed by FCL Section 4.6.3—Organisational Structures, Roles, Responsibilities and Authorities
6	Planning	Section 4.6—Planning
6.1	Actions to address risks and opportunities	Section 4.6.1—Actions to address risks and opportunities
6.2	XXX objectives and planning to achieve them	Section 4.6.2—Objectives
6.3	Planning of changes	Chapter 7, Section 7.4.3—Change management Chapter 15, Section 15.8.1.9—Managing changes to supplier services
7	Support	Section 4.7—Support
7.1	Resources	Section 4.7.1—Management of Resources
7.2	Competence	Section 4.7.2—Competence
7.3	Awareness	Section 4.7.3—Training and Awareness
7.4	Communication	Section 4.7.4—Communication
7.5	Documented information.	Section 4.7.5—Documented Information
8	Operation	Section 4.8—Operation
8.1	Operational planning and control	Section 4.8—Operation
9	Performance evaluation	Section 4.9—Performance Evaluation
9.1	Analysis and evaluation	Section 4.9.1—Monitoring, Measurement, Analysis and Evaluation
9.2	Internal audit	Section 4.9.2—Internal Auditing
9.3	Management review	Section 4.9.3—Management Reviews Section 4.9.4—Review Input Section 4.9.5—Review Output
10	Improvement	Section 4.10—Improvement
10.1	Continual improvement	Section 4.10—Improvement

Annex L	Control	Procedure(s)
10.2	Nonconformity and corrective action	Section 4.10.1—Handling of Nonconformities Section 4.10.2—Planning and Implementing Corrective Actions Section 4.10.3—Corrective Action Requests Section 4.10.4—Corrective Action Ownership Section 4.10.5—Corrective Ownership Oversight

Appendix 3—The Goal Statement

The Goal Statement is to:

- create a high-performance client-facing organisation;
- enhance the operational value from our existing portfolio;
- expand our portfolio profitably;
- meet or exceed client expectations;
- comply with all Legislative, Regulatory, contractual obligations, and accepted good practice including ethical considerations; and
- be known as a digital forensic centre of excellence.

Appendix 4—The Baseline Measures

The Baseline Measures to support the Goal Statement are to:

- minimise complaints;
- achieve or exceed Service Level Agreements, specifically turn round times (TRTs);
- achieve an average of over 4 (out of 5) for all client feedback;
- speak at relevant major conferences with competent FCL speakers;
- publish in relevant learned journals/magazines;
- increase repeat business from existing clients;
- increase new business; and
- minimise any adverse incidents or 'near misses'.

Note

FCL has figures for these measures as KPIs, but these are not repeated here as this shall be a business-based decision for any other forensic laboratory to make. Additionally, another forensic laboratory may choose to add or remove baseline measures from this list according to its specific business requirements.

Appendix 5—The business objectives

Note

Different forensic laboratories may (and probably will) set different business objectives.

FCL has set a number of business objectives that it is to achieve, these are defined below:

Financial objectives

FCL has the following financial objectives:

- grow shareholder value;
- grow earnings per share;
- increase revenue by winning new business and starting new businesses;

- manage cost;
- balance the budget;
- ensure financial sustainability; and
- maintain profitability.

Client objectives

FCL has the following client objectives:

- provide best value for the cost;
- provide a broad product and service offering across all industry sectors;
- provide reliable and consistent products and services;
- cross-sell more products across industry sectors;
- increase share of market;
- understand client needs and ensure that they know this;
- partner with clients to provide solutions;
- meet and exceed all client contractual obligations;
- minimise re-work and/or complaints from clients; and
- provide best of breed service to all clients.

Internal objectives

FCL has the following internal objectives:

- innovate and invest in innovation;
- differentiate FCL products and services from opposition offerings;
- grow sales from each innovated product or service or by winning new business;
- acquire new clients from innovated products or services;
- provide exemplary client service that is subject to continuous improvement and provides improved client satisfaction;
- invest in client management;
- partner with clients to develop innovative products and services;
- ensure client retention and manage existing clients to achieve this;
- ensure that FCL provides the products and services required internally to support internal and external clients; and
- provide secure information processing facilities to protect client information.

Operational excellence

FCL has the following operational excellence objectives:

- regularly reduce costs, waste, and need to redo work for all client on an annual basis;
- implement appropriate standards to increase efficiency, quality, effectiveness and information security;
- implement a culture of continuous improvement and reduce error rates in product and service delivery;
- ensure continuity of service to all clients in the event of any adverse incident affecting deliverability of products and services;
- ensure all Legislative, Regulatory, and contractual requirements are met;
- ensure that internal governance, as appropriate to business needs including control frameworks, internal and external auditing and Management reviews, is implemented, monitored and managed;
- ensure that all employees are competent with plans in place to maintain and improve competence;
- implement tools and processes to improve operational excellence;
- attract and retain the best employees; and
- build high-performing teams.

Appendix 6—Specific needs and expectations of interested parties

Note

Different forensic laboratories may (and probably will) have different needs and expectations of their interested parties.

The needs and expectations of FCL's interested parties are defined below:

Interested party	Need/Expectation
Investors	A profitable business that provides return on investment
The market and clients	Products and services that meet their needs and expectations when they need them and at an appropriate price according to contractual requirements Clients also expect state of the art technology and the facility of fast and reliable communications with FCL They also expect that their information processed and stored by FCL is held in a secure and resilient environment, and increasingly are requiring proof of compliance with, or certification to relevant, national and/or international standards
Suppliers	Need a contract for services or products to supply their products or services to FCL
Top Management	Top management set direction for FCL and manage employees according to FCL's corporate vision, mission, objectives, policies, and procedures
Employees	Employees require a safe and secure place to work with a well-structured working environment
Government Agencies	FCL shall comply with relevant governmental requirements
Compliance	It is required that FCL shall comply with all relevant Legislation, Regulation, and contractual terms within the jurisdiction of operations
Trade Bodies	FCL shall comply with the relevant standards and Codes of Practice from various trade bodies to which FCL subscribes or is bound by
Emergency Services	The emergency services are needed in any adverse event that affects the delivery of FCL's products and services to internal or external clients
Utilities	FCL relies on a variety of utility suppliers to enable them to provide their products and services to their internal and external clients
IT Service Availability	All of FCL's products and services depend on the IT Department to a great degree. The IT Department is required to meet these requirements in terms of confidentiality, integrity, and availability (including resilience)—and recovery in case of any adverse incident that affects the delivery of those products and services
Insurers	FCL's insurers expect FCL to manage their business is a safe and secure manner to minimise adverse incidents that could give rise to an insurance claim
Media	FCL relies on good media exposure to establish and grow their reputation and the level of trust that their clients have in them

Note

Each of these needs and expectations is aggressively managed by regular risk reviews and planned first-, second-, and third-party audits.

Appendix 7—The FCL audit committee

Title

The title of this committee shall be:
    'The FCL Audit Committee'.

Constitution

The FCL Audit Committee (the 'Committee') is constituted as a Committee of the Management Board, with a remit to oversee and coordinate all audit and management review activities in FCL.

The Committee's terms of reference may be amended at any time by the Management Board.

Authority

The Committee is authorised by the Management Board to review or investigate any activity within its terms of reference.

The Committee is authorised by the Management Board to require from the Executive such additional information to support audit and management review activities and/or corrective action as it deems appropriate.

Membership

The Committee shall be appointed by the Management Board from among its members and shall consist of not less than three members.

The Chairman of the Committee shall be the Laboratory Manager.

Appointments to the Committee shall be for a period of 1 year and reviewed at the annual Management Board meeting.

Nominations for the Committee shall be submitted to the Management Board by the Laboratory Manager.

The Laboratory Manager shall appoint the Secretary to the Committee.

Agenda and minutes

Agendas shall be distributed to all members of the Committee at least 5 working days before the meeting. Any relevant attachments shall be attached to the agenda (typically this may include updated risk registers, risk reports, etc.) as agreed by the Chairman of the Committee.

Minutes of the meeting shall be distributed within 10 working days of the meeting.

Attendance at meetings

The quorum necessary for the transaction of the business of the Committee shall be a simple majority of the Committee members.

Meetings that are inquorate cannot pass formal resolutions but can undertake business and make recommendation for consideration at the next meeting.

Other Management Board members may attend meetings of the Committee.

At the request of the Committee any members of senior management shall attend meetings.

Frequency of meetings

Meetings shall be held at least once a quarter or more often if required.

Additional meetings may be called by the Management Board, or the Chairman of the Management Board acting for the Management Board, or by the Chairman of the Committee.

Responsibilities

The Audit Committee has a number of responsibilities:

Financial reporting

The Committee shall monitor the integrity of FCL financial statements, including its annual and interim reports, preliminary results, announcements, and any other formal announcement relating to its financial performance, reviewing significant financial reporting issues and judgements which they contain. The Committee shall also review summary financial statements, significant financial returns to Regulators and any financial information contained in certain other documents, such as announcements of a price sensitive nature.

The Committee shall review and challenge where necessary:

- the consistency of, and any changes to, accounting policies both on a year on year basis and across FCL;
- the methods used to account for significant or unusual transactions where different approaches are possible;
- whether FCL has followed appropriate accounting standards and made appropriate estimates and judgements, considering the views of the external Auditor;
- the clarity of disclosure in FCL's financial reports and the context in which statements are made;
- all material information presented with the financial statements, such as the operating and financial review and the corporate governance statement.
- The Committee shall review the annual financial statements of the pension funds which are not reviewed by the Management Board as a whole, if appropriate.

Internal controls and management systems

The Committee shall:

- keep under review the effectiveness of FCL's internal controls, risk management systems, and management systems in association with the Risk Committee and each of the Management System Committees;
- review and approve the statements to be included in the Annual Report concerning internal controls, risk management, and management systems (unless this is done by the Management Board as a whole).

Whistleblowing and the code of conduct

The Committee shall review FCL's arrangements for its employees to raise concerns, in confidence, about possible wrongdoing in financial reporting or other matters through a Whistleblowing Policy as defined in Appendix 15. The Committee shall ensure that these arrangements allow proportionate and independent investigation of such matters and appropriate follow up action. It shall also review FCL's arrangements for ensuring its employees are made aware of what is expected of their behaviour and business conduct.

Internal Audit

The Committee shall:

- monitor and review the effectiveness of FCL's internal audit function in the context of FCL's overall risk management system;
- approve the appointment and removal of the Internal Audit Manager;
- consider and approve the remit of the internal audit function and ensure it has adequate resources and appropriate access to information to enable it to perform its function effectively and in accordance with the relevant professional standards. The Committee shall also ensure the function has adequate standing and is free from management interference or other restrictions;
- review and assess the annual internal audit plan and management review plan;
- review promptly all reports on FCL from the internal and external Auditors;
- review and monitor top management's responsiveness to the findings and recommendations of the internal and external Auditors;
- meet the Internal Audit Manager at least once a year, without management being present, to discuss their remit and any issues arising from the internal audits carried out. In addition, the Internal Audit Manager shall be given the right of direct access to the Chairman of the Management Board and to the Committee.

External Audit

The Committee shall:

- consider and make recommendations to the Management Board, to be put to the relevant interested parties for approval, in relation to the appointment, re-appointment and removal of FCL's external Auditor. The Committee shall oversee the selection process for new Auditors and if an Auditor resigns, the Committee shall investigate the issues leading to this and decide whether any action is required;

- oversee the relationship with the external Auditor including, but not limited to:
  - ➤ approval of their remuneration, whether fees for audit or nonaudit services and that the level of fees are appropriate to enable an adequate audit to be conducted or nonaudit services to be delivered;
  - ➤ approval of their terms of engagement, including any engagement letter issued at the start of each audit and the scope of the audit;
  - ➤ assessing annually their independence and objectivity taking to account relevant professional and Regulatory requirements and the relationship with the Auditor as a whole, including the provision of any nonaudit services;
  - ➤ satisfying itself that there are no relationships (such as family, employment, investment, financial, or business) between the Auditor and FCL (other than in the ordinary course of business);
  - ➤ agreeing with the Management Board a policy on the employment of former employees of FCL's Auditor, then monitoring the implementation of this policy;
  - ➤ monitoring the Auditor's compliance with relevant ethical and professional guidance on the rotation of audit partners; and
  - ➤ assessing annually their qualifications, expertise and resources and the effectiveness of the audit process which shall include a report from the external Auditor on their own internal quality procedures.
- meet regularly with the External Auditor, including once at the planning stage before the audit and once after the audit at the reporting stage. The Committee shall meet the External Auditor at least once a year, without management being present, to discuss their remit and any issues arising from the audit;
- review and approve the annual audit plan and ensure that it is consistent with the scope of the audit engagement;
- review the findings of the audit with the external Auditor. This shall include, but not be limited to, the following;
  - ➤ a discussion of any major issues which arose during the audit;
  - ➤ any accounting and audit judgements; and
  - ➤ levels of errors identified during the audit.
- review any representation letter(s) requested by the external Auditor before they are signed by top management;
- review the management letter and top management's response to the Auditor's findings and recommendations; and
- develop and implement a policy on the supply of nonaudit services by the external Auditor, considering any relevant ethical guidance on the matter.

Other

- be responsible for co-ordination of the internal and external Auditors;
- oversee any investigation of activities which are within its terms of reference and act as a 'Court of the last resort';
- at least once a year, review its own performance, constitution, and terms of reference to ensure it is operating at maximum effectiveness and recommend any changes it considers necessary to the Management Board for approval.
- review the effectiveness of the internal audit, external audit, management review and other testing processes; and
- approve the text of the section of FCL annual review dealing with corporate governance issues and the Committee.

Reporting procedures

The minutes of the Committee shall normally be considered at the Management Board meeting following the Committee meeting.

Where this proves to be impractical, the minutes shall be circulated to all members of the Management Board as soon as possible.

Review of terms of reference

These terms of reference shall be reviewed on an annual basis by the Committee with input from all interested parties.

Appendix 8—The FCL business continuity committee

Title

The title of this committee shall be:
'The FCL Business Continuity Committee'.

Constitution

The FCL Business Continuity Committee (the 'Committee') is constituted as a Committee of the Management Board, with a remit to oversee the continuity of business services within FCL both to internal and external clients.

The Committee's terms of reference may be amended at any time by the Management Board.

Authority

The Committee is authorised by the Management Board to review or investigate any activity within its terms of reference.

The Committee is authorised by the Management Board to require of the Executive such additional business continuity audits, tests, exercises, or management reviews and/or corrective action as it deems appropriate.

Membership

The Committee shall be appointed by the Management Board from among its members and shall consist of not less than three members.

The Chairman of the Committee shall be the Business Continuity Manager.

Appointments to the Committee shall be for a period of 1 year and reviewed at the annual Management Board meeting.

Nominations for the Committee shall be submitted to the Management Board by the Business Continuity Manager.

The Business Continuity Manager shall appoint the Secretary to the Committee.

Agenda and minutes

Agendas shall be distributed to all members of the Committee at least 5 working days before the meeting. Any relevant attachments shall be attached to the agenda (typically this may include audit reports, incident reports, exercise test results, etc. as agreed by the Chairman of the Committee.

Minutes of the meeting shall be distributed within 10 working days of the meeting.

Attendance at meetings

The quorum necessary for the transaction of the business of the Committee shall be a simple majority of the Committee members.

Meetings that are inquorate cannot pass formal resolutions but can undertake business and make recommendation for consideration at the next meeting.

Other Management Board members may attend meetings of the Committee.

At the request of the Committee any members of senior management shall attend meetings.

Any Independent Assessors may also be invited to attend.

Frequency of meetings

Meetings shall be held at least twice a year or more if required.

Additional meetings may be called by the Management Board, or the Chairman of the Management Board acting for the Management Board, or by the Chairman of the Committee.

Responsibilities

To keep under review FCL's business continuity and resilience procedures and systems, ensuring that they meet FCL's requirements and reflect good practice.

To receive and consider, on a regular basis, reports about, where relevant:

- updates of Legislation, Regulation, or good practice that may affect the IMS;
- results of management system audits and reviews;

- results of performance reviews;
- results of audits of key suppliers, outsourcing partners, and other associated third parties;
- feedback from interested parties (including any complaints about the service);
- any relevant whistleblowing concerns raised;
- techniques, products, or procedures, which could be used in FCL to improve the IMS' performance and effectiveness;
- status of corrective actions;
- vulnerabilities or threats not adequately addressed in the previous risk assessments (where appropriate);
- review of the level of risk present against the risk appetite;
- results from effectiveness measurements and any testing carried out;
- incidents or other nonconformities;
- follow-up actions from previous management reviews;
- any changes that could affect the IMS;
- feedback from awareness and similar training;
- feedback from any line manager affected by the management system;
- feedback from the management system owner, including adequacy of resources (financial, personnel, material);
- lessons learned from any incidents, testing, or similar events;
- lessons learned from similar organisations; and
- recommendations for improvement.

To receive and consider six-monthly reports from the Independent Assessor, where an Independent Assessor is appointed.

In conjunction with the Audit Committee, to commission and/or review internal audit reports, results of other tests and exercises pertaining to business continuity matters within FCL and the management responses to the recommendations.

To approve the text of the section of FCL annual review dealing with business continuity matters and the Committee.

Reporting procedures

The minutes of the Committee shall normally be considered at the Management Board meeting following the Committee meeting.

Where this proves to be impractical, the minutes shall be circulated to all members of the Management Board as soon as possible.

Review of terms of reference

These terms of reference shall be reviewed on an annual basis by the Committee with input from all interested parties.

Appendix 9—The FCL environment committee

Title

The title of this committee shall be:
'The FCL Environment Committee'.

Constitution

The FCL Environment Committee (the 'Committee') is constituted as a Committee of the Management Board, with a remit to oversee the environmental protection activities within FCL.

The Committee's terms of reference may be amended at any time by the Management Board.

Authority

The Committee is authorised by the Management Board to review or investigate any activity within its terms of reference.

The Committee is authorised by the Management Board to require of the Executive such additional environmental audits or management reviews and/or corrective action as it deems appropriate.

Membership

The Committee shall be appointed by the Management Board from among its members and shall consist of not less than three members.

The Chairman of the Committee shall be the Environment Manager.

Appointments to the Committee shall be for a period of one year and reviewed at the annual Management Board meeting.

Nominations for the Committee shall be submitted to the Management Board by the Environment Manager.

The Environment Manager shall appoint the Secretary to the Committee.

Agenda and minutes

Agendas shall be distributed to all members of the Committee at least 5 working days before the meeting. Any relevant attachments shall be attached to the agenda (typically this may include audit reports, incident reports, etc. as agreed by the Chairman of the Committee).

Minutes of the meeting shall be distributed within 10 working days of the meeting.

Attendance at meetings

The quorum necessary for the transaction of the business of the Committee shall be a simple majority of the Committee members.

Meetings that are inquorate cannot pass formal resolutions but can undertake business and make recommendation for consideration at the next meeting.

Other Management Board members may attend meetings of the Committee.

At the request of the Committee any members of senior management shall attend meetings.

Any Independent Assessors may also be invited to attend.

Frequency of meetings

Meetings shall be held at least twice a year or more if required.

Additional meetings may be called by the Management Board, or the Chairman of the Management Board acting for the Management Board, or by the Chairman of the Committee.

Responsibilities

To keep under review FCL's environmental protection procedures and systems, now also including Environmental, Social and Governance (ESG) requirements, ensuring that they meet FCL's requirements and reflect good practice.

To receive, and consider, on a regular basis, reports about, where relevant:

- updates of Legislation, Regulation, or good practice that may affect the IMS;
- results of management systems audits and reviews;
- results of performance reviews;
- results of audits of key suppliers, outsourcing partners, and other associated third parties;
- feedback from interested parties (including any complaints about the service);
- techniques, products, or procedures, which could be used in FCL to improve the management systems performance and effectiveness;
- status of corrective actions;
- vulnerabilities or threats not adequately addressed in the previous risk assessments (where appropriate);
- review of the level of risk present against the risk appetite;
- results from effectiveness measurements and any testing carried out;
- incidents or other nonconformities;

- any changes that could affect the management system;
- feedback from awareness and similar training;
- feedback from any line manager affected by the management system;
- feedback from the management system owner, including adequacy of resources (financial, personnel, material);
- lessons learned from any incidents, testing, or similar events;
- lessons learned from similar organisations; and
- recommendations for improvement.

To receive and consider six-monthly reports from the Independent Assessor, where an Independent Assessor is appointed.

In conjunction with the Audit Committee, to commission and/or review internal audit reports, results of other tests, and exercises pertaining to environmental protection and ESG within FCL and the top management responses to the recommendations.

To approve the text of the section of FCL annual review dealing with environmental protection matters and the Committee.

Reporting procedures

The minutes of the Committee shall normally be considered at the Management Board meeting following the Committee meeting.

Where this proves to be impractical, the minutes shall be circulated to all members of the Management Board as soon as possible.

Review of terms of reference

These terms of reference shall be reviewed on an annual basis by the Committee with input from all interested parties.

Appendix 10—The FCL health and safety committee

Title

The title of this committee shall be:
'The FCL Health and Safety Committee'.

Constitution

The FCL Health and Safety Committee (the 'Committee') is constituted as a Committee of the Management Board, with a remit to oversee the health and safety activities within FCL.

The Committee's terms of reference may be amended at any time by the Management Board.

Authority

The Committee is authorised by the Management Board to review or investigate any activity within its terms of reference.

The Committee is authorised by the Management Board to require of the Executive such additional health and safety audits or management reviews and/or corrective action as it deems appropriate.

Membership

The Committee shall be appointed by the Management Board from among its members and shall consist of not less than three members.

The Chairman of the Committee shall be the Health and Safety Manager.

Appointments to the Committee shall be for a period of 1 year and reviewed at the annual Management Board meeting.

Nominations for the Committee shall be submitted to the Management Board by the Health and Safety Manager.

The Health and Safety Manager shall appoint the Secretary to the Committee.

Agenda and minutes

Agendas shall be distributed to all members of the Committee at least 5 working days before the meeting. Any relevant attachments shall be attached to the agenda (typically this may include audit reports, incident reports, 'near misses', etc.) as agreed by the Chairman of the Committee.

Minutes of the meeting shall be distributed within 10 working days of the meeting.

Attendance at meetings

The quorum necessary for the transaction of the business of the Committee shall be a simple majority of the Committee members.

Meetings that are inquorate cannot pass formal resolutions but can undertake business and make recommendations for consideration at the next meeting.

Other Management Board members may attend meetings of the Committee.

At the request of the Committee any members of senior management shall attend meetings.

Any Independent Assessors may also be invited to attend.

Frequency of meetings

Meetings shall be held at least twice a year or more if required.

Additional meetings may be called by the Management Board, or the Chairman of the Management Board acting for the Management Board, or by the Chairman of the Committee.

Responsibilities

To keep under review FCL's health and safety procedures and systems, ensuring that they meet FCL's requirements and reflect good practice.

To act as a focus for joint participation between FCL and health and safety representatives.

To receive, and consider, on a regular basis, reports about, where relevant:

- updates of Legislation, Regulation, or good practice that may affect the IMS;
- results of management systems audits and reviews;
- results of performance reviews;
- results of audits of key suppliers, outsourcing partners, and other associated third parties;
- feedback from interested parties (including any complaints about the service);
- techniques, products or procedures, which could be used in FCL to improve the management system performance and effectiveness;
- status of corrective actions;
- vulnerabilities or threats not adequately addressed in the previous risk assessments (where appropriate);
- review of the level of risk present against the risk appetite;
- results from effectiveness measurements and any testing carried out;
- incidents or other nonconformities;
- follow-up actions from previous management reviews;
- any changes that could affect the management systems;
- feedback from awareness and similar training;
- feedback from any line manager affected by the management system;
- feedback from the management system owner, including adequacy of resources (financial, personnel, material);
- lessons learned from any incidents, testing, or similar events;
- lessons learned from similar organisations; and
- recommendations for improvement.

To receive and consider six-monthly reports from the Independent Assessor, where an Independent Assessor is appointed.

In conjunction with the Audit Committee, to commission and/or review internal audit reports, results of other tests and exercises pertaining to health and safety matters within FCL and the top management responses to the recommendations.

To approve the text of the section of FCL annual review dealing with health and safety matters and the Committee.

Reporting procedures

The minutes of the Committee shall normally be considered at the Management Board meeting following the Committee meeting.

Where this proves to be impractical, the minutes shall be circulated to all members of the Management Board as soon as possible.

Review of terms of reference

These terms of reference shall be reviewed on an annual basis by the Committee with input from all interested parties.

Appendix 11—The FCL information security committee

Title

The title of this committee shall be:
    'The FCL Information Security Committee'.

Constitution

The FCL Information Security Committee (the 'Committee') is constituted as a Committee of the Management Board, with a remit to oversee the information security activities within FCL both to internal and external clients.

The Committee's terms of reference may be amended at any time by the Management Board.

Authority

The Committee is authorised by the Management Board to review or investigate any activity within its terms of reference.

The Committee is authorised by the Management Board to require of the Executive such additional information security audits, tests or management reviews and/or corrective action as it deems appropriate.

Membership

The Committee shall be appointed by the Management Board from among its members and shall consist of not less than three members.

The Chairman of the Committee shall be the Information Security Manager.

Appointments to the Committee shall be for a period of 1 year and reviewed at the annual Management Board meeting.

Nominations for the Committee shall be submitted to the Management Board by the Information Security Manager.

The Information Security Manager shall appoint the Secretary to the Committee.

Agenda and minutes

Agendas shall be distributed to all members of the Committee at least 5 working days before the meeting. Any relevant attachments shall be attached to the agenda (typically this may include audit reports, incident reports, penetration tests, exercise test results, etc. as agreed by the Chairman of the Committee.

Minutes of the meeting shall be distributed within 10 working days of the meeting.

Attendance at meetings

The quorum necessary for the transaction of the business of the Committee shall be a simple majority of the Committee members.

Meetings that are inquorate cannot pass formal resolutions but can undertake business and make recommendation for consideration at the next meeting.

Other Management Board members may attend meetings of the Committee.

At the request of the Committee any members of senior management shall attend meetings.

Any Independent Assessors may also be invited to attend.

Frequency of meetings

Meetings shall be held at least twice a year or more if required.

Additional meetings may be called by the Management Board, or the Chairman of the Management Board acting for the Management Board, or by the Chairman of the Committee.

Responsibilities

To keep under review FCL's information security procedures and systems, ensuring that they meet FCL's requirements and reflect good practice.

To receive, and consider, on a regular basis, reports about, where relevant:

- updates of Legislation, Regulation, or good practice that may affect the IMS;
- results of management systems audits and reviews;
- results of performance reviews;
- results of audits of key suppliers, outsourcing partners, and other associated third parties;
- feedback from interested parties (including any complaints about the service);
- techniques, products, or procedures, which could be used in FCL to improve the management systems performance and effectiveness;
- status of corrective actions;
- vulnerabilities or threats not adequately addressed in the previous risk assessments (where appropriate);
- review of the level of risk present against the risk appetite;
- results from effectiveness measurements and any testing carried out;
- incidents or other nonconformities;
- follow-up actions from previous management reviews;
- any changes that could affect the management systems;
- feedback from awareness and similar training;
- feedback from any line manager affected by the management system;
- feedback from the management system owner, including adequacy of resources (financial, personnel, material);
- lessons learned from any incidents, testing, or similar events;
- lessons learned from similar organisations; and
- recommendations for improvement.

To receive and consider six-monthly reports from the Independent Assessor, where an Independent Assessor is appointed.

In conjunction with the Audit Committee, to commission and/or review internal audit reports, results of other tests and exercises pertaining to information security matters within FCL and the top management responses to the recommendations.

To approve the text of the section of FCL annual review dealing with information security matters and the Committee.

Reporting procedures

The minutes of the Committee shall normally be considered at the Management Board meeting following the Committee meeting.

Where this proves to be impractical, the minutes shall be circulated to all members of the Management Board as soon as possible.

Review of terms of reference

These terms of reference shall be reviewed on an annual basis by the Committee with input from all interested parties.

Appendix 12—The FCL quality committee

Title

The title of this committee shall be:

'The FCL Quality Committee'.

Constitution

The FCL Quality Committee (the 'Committee') is constituted as a Committee of the Management Board, with a remit to oversee the quality assurance activities within FCL.

The Committee's terms of reference may be amended at any time by the Management Board.

Authority

The Committee is authorised by the Management Board to review or investigate any activity within its terms of reference.

The Committee is authorised by the Management Board to require of the Executive such additional quality assurance audits or management reviews and/or corrective action as it deems appropriate.

Membership

The Committee shall be appointed by the Management Board from among its members and shall consist of not less than three members.

The Chairman of the Committee shall be the Quality Manager.

Appointments to the Committee shall be for a period of 1 year and reviewed at the annual Management Board meeting.

Nominations for the Committee shall be submitted to the Management Board by the Quality Manager.

The Quality Manager shall appoint the Secretary to the Committee.

Agenda and minutes

Agendas shall be distributed to all members of the Committee at least 5 working days before the meeting. Any relevant attachments shall be attached to the agenda (typically this may include audit reports, incident reports etc. as agreed by the Chairman of the Committee.

Minutes of the meeting shall be distributed within 10 working days of the meeting.

Attendance at meetings

The quorum necessary for the transaction of the business of the Committee shall be a simple majority of the Committee members.

Meetings that are inquorate cannot pass formal resolutions but can undertake business and make recommendation for consideration at the next meeting.

Other Management Board members may attend meetings of the Committee.

At the request of the Committee any members of senior management shall attend meetings.

Any Independent Assessors may also be invited to attend.

Frequency of meetings

Meetings shall be held at least twice a year or more if required.

Additional meetings may be called by the Management Board, or the Chairman of the Management Board acting for the Management Board, or by the Chairman of the Committee.

Responsibilities

Note

The Quality Committee remit is not only ISO 9001 but includes ISO/IEC 17020 and 17025.

To keep under review FCL's quality assurance procedures and systems, ensuring that they meet FCL's requirements and reflect good practice.

To receive, and consider, on a regular basis, reports about, where relevant:

- updates of Legislation, Regulation, or good practice that may affect the IMS;
- results of management systems audits and reviews;
- results of performance reviews;
- results of audits of key suppliers, outsourcing partners, and other associated third parties;
- feedback from interested parties (including any complaints about the service);
- techniques, products, or procedures, which could be used in FCL to improve the management systems performance and effectiveness;
- status of corrective actions;
- vulnerabilities or threats not adequately addressed in the previous risk assessments (where appropriate);
- review of the level of risk present against the risk appetite;
- results from effectiveness measurements and any testing carried out;
- incidents or other nonconformities;
- follow-up actions from previous management reviews;
- any changes that could affect the management systems;
- feedback from awareness and similar training;
- feedback from any line manager affected by the management system;
- feedback from the management system owner, including adequacy of resources (financial, personnel, material);
- lessons learned from any incidents, testing, or similar events;
- lessons learned from similar organisations; and
- recommendations for improvement.

To receive and consider six-monthly reports from the Independent Assessor, where an Independent Assessor is appointed.

In conjunction with the Audit Committee, to commission and/or review internal audit reports, results of other tests and exercises pertaining to quality within FCL and the management responses to the recommendations.

To approve the text of the section of FCL annual review dealing with quality matters and the Committee.

Reporting procedures

The minutes of the Committee shall normally be considered at the Management Board meeting following the Committee meeting.

Where this proves to be impractical, the minutes shall be circulated to all members of the Management Board as soon as possible.

Review of terms of reference

These terms of reference shall be reviewed on an annual basis by the Committee with input from all interested parties.

Appendix 13—The FCL risk committee

Title

The title of this committee shall be:
'The FCL Risk Committee'.

Constitution

The FCL Risk Committee (the 'Committee') is constituted as a Committee of the Management Board, with a remit to oversee and coordinate risk management activities to identify, evaluate, and manage all of the key business and technical risks in FCL.

The Committee's terms of reference may be amended at any time by the Management Board.

Authority

The Committee is authorised by the Management Board to review or investigate any activity within its terms of reference.

The Committee is authorised by the Management Board to require of the Executive such additional information to support risk management activities and/or corrective action as it deems appropriate.

Membership

The Committee shall be appointed by the Management Board from among its members and shall consist of not less than three members.

The Chairman of the Committee shall be the Risk Owner.

Appointments to the Committee shall be for a period of 1 year and reviewed at the annual Management Board meeting.

Nominations for the Committee shall be submitted to the Management Board by the Risk Owner.

The Risk Owner shall appoint the Secretary to the Committee.

Agenda and minutes

Agendas shall be distributed to all members of the Committee at least 5 working days before the meeting. Any relevant attachments shall be attached to the agenda (typically this may include updated risk registers, risk reports, etc.) as agreed by the Chairman of the Committee.

Minutes of the meeting shall be distributed within 10 working days of the meeting.

Attendance at meetings

The quorum necessary for the transaction of the business of the Committee shall be a simple majority of the Committee members.

Meetings that are inquorate cannot pass formal resolutions but can undertake business and make recommendation for consideration at the next meeting.

Other Management Board members may attend meetings of the Committee.

At the request of the Committee any members of senior management shall attend meetings.

Frequency of meetings

Meetings shall be held at least once a quarter or more if required.

Additional meetings may be called by the Management Board, or the Chairman of the Management Board acting for the Management Board, or by the Chairman of the Committee.

Responsibilities

The committee focuses on the risk management process with the following responsibilities:

- approve methodologies and processes for managing all types of risk in FCL, e.g. risk assessment, risk management, risk treatment, risk appetite, information classification;
- identify significant threat changes and exposure of information and information processing facilities to internal and external risks, deliberate or accidental;
- raise the level of management awareness and accountability for the business risks experienced by FCL;
- develop risk management as part of FCL's culture;
- provide a mechanism for risk management issues to be discussed and disseminated to all areas of FCL;
- co-ordinate activities to obtain a more effective risk management process from existing resources;
- prioritise and accelerate those risk management strategies that are critical to the achievement of corporate objectives.
- assess the adequacy and co-ordinate the implementation of risk treatment; and
- manage and oversee the management of all of the risk registers within FCL.

In conjunction with the Audit Committee, to commission and/or review internal audit reports, results of other tests and exercises pertaining to risk related issues within FCL and the management responses to the recommendations.

To approve the text of the section of FCL's annual review dealing with risk management issues and the Committee.

Reporting procedures

The minutes of the Committee shall normally be considered at the Management Board meeting following the Committee meeting.

Where this proves to be impractical, the minutes shall be circulated to all members of the Management Board as soon as possible.

Review of terms of reference

These terms of reference shall be reviewed on an annual basis by the Committee with input from all interested parties.

Appendix 14—The FCL service delivery committee

Title

The title of this committee shall be:
'The FCL Service Delivery Committee'.

Constitution

The FCL Service Delivery Committee (the 'Committee') is constituted as a Committee of the Management Board, with a remit to oversee the service delivery within FCL both to internal and external clients.

The Committee's terms of reference may be amended at any time by the Management Board.

Authority

The Committee is authorised by the Management Board to review or investigate any activity within its terms of reference.

The Committee is authorised by the Management Board to require of the Executive such additional service delivery audits or management reviews and/or corrective action as it deems appropriate.

Membership

The Committee shall be appointed by the Management Board from among its members and shall consist of not less than three members.

The Chairman of the Committee shall be the Service Level Manager.

Appointments to the Committee shall be for a period of 1 year and reviewed at the annual Management Board meeting.

Nominations for the Committee shall be submitted to the Management Board by the Service Delivery Manager.

The Service Delivery Manager shall appoint the Secretary to the Committee.

Agenda and minutes

Agendas shall be distributed to all members of the Committee at least 5 working days before the meeting. Any relevant attachments shall be attached to the agenda (typically this may include audit reports, incident reports, etc. as agreed by the Chairman of the Committee.

Minutes of the meeting shall be distributed within 10 working days of the meeting.

Attendance at meetings

The quorum necessary for the transaction of the business of the Committee shall be a simple majority of the Committee members.

Meetings that are inquorate cannot pass formal resolutions but can undertake business and make recommendation for consideration at the next meeting.

Other Management Board members may attend meetings of the Committee.

At the request of the Committee any members of senior management shall attend meetings.

Any Independent Assessors may also be invited to attend.

Frequency of meetings

Meetings shall be held at least twice a year or more if required.

Additional meetings may be called by the Management Board, or the Chairman of the Management Board acting for the Management Board, or by the Chairman of the Committee.

Responsibilities

To keep under review FCL's service delivery procedures and systems, ensuring that they meet FCL's requirements and reflect good practice.

To receive, and consider, on a regular basis, reports about, where relevant:

- updates of Legislation, Regulation, or good practice that may affect the IMS;
- results of management systems audits and reviews;
- results of performance reviews;
- results of audits of key suppliers, outsourcing partners, and other associated third parties;
- feedback from interested parties (including any complaints about the service);
- techniques, products, or procedures, which could be used in FCL to improve the management system's performance and effectiveness;
- status of corrective actions;
- results from effectiveness measurements and any testing carried out;
- incidents or other nonconformities;
- any changes that could affect the management system;
- feedback from awareness and similar training;
- feedback from any line manager affected by the management system;
- feedback from the management system owner, including adequacy of resources (financial, personnel, material);
- lessons learned from any incidents, testing, or similar events;
- lessons learned from similar organisations; and
- recommendations for improvement.

To receive and consider six-monthly reports from the Independent Assessor, where an independent assessor is appointed.

In conjunction with the Audit Committee, to commission and/or review internal audit reports, results of other tests and exercises pertaining to service delivery matters within FCL and the management responses to the recommendations.

To approve the text of the section of FCL's annual review dealing with service delivery matters and the Committee.

Reporting procedures

The minutes of the Committee shall normally be considered at the Management Board meeting following the Committee meeting.

Where this proves to be impractical, the minutes shall be circulated to all members of the Management Board as soon as possible.

Review of terms of reference

These terms of reference shall be reviewed on an annual basis by the Committee with input from all interested parties.

Appendix 15—The FCL whistleblowing policy

Internal whistleblowing encourages and enables employees to raise serious concerns within FCL rather than overlooking a problem or 'blowing the whistle' outside.

Employees are often the first to realise that there is something seriously wrong within FCL or relating the FCL's operations. However, they may not express their concerns as they feel that speaking up would be disloyal to their colleagues or to FCL or that they may be victimised because of raising their concerns.

FCL is committed to the highest possible standards of openness, probity and accountability. In line with that commitment employees, who have serious concerns about any aspect of FCL's work are encouraged to come forward and voice those concerns.

This policy has been developed to:

- encourage employees to feel confident in raising concerns and to question and act upon concerns about any aspect of FCL's business;
- provide avenues for raising concerns in confidence and receive feedback on any action taken;
- ensure that any concerns are acknowledged and how to pursue them if any employee is not satisfied with the actions taken by FCL's top management; and
- reassure employees that they will be protected from possible reprisals or victimisation if they have a reasonable belief that the disclosure has been made in good faith.

The types of concern that can be raised include, but are not limited to:

- actions which are unprofessional, inappropriate, or conflict with a general understanding of what is right and wrong;
- conduct which is an offence or a breach of Legislation or Regulation within the jurisdiction;
- damage to the environment;
- disclosures related to miscarriages of justice;
- failure to comply with a legal obligation in the jurisdiction;
- health and safety risks, including risks to the public as well as other employees;
- other unethical conduct;
- possible fraud and corruption;
- sexual, physical, or other abuse of clients or other employees;
- the unauthorised use of corporate funds; and
- undeclared conflicts of interest.

FCL recognises that the decision to report a concern can be a difficult one for an employee to make. If the concerns raised are true, they should have nothing to fear because, by raising these concerns, the employee is doing their duty to both FCL and to any client to whom FCL provides a product or service.

FCL will not tolerate any harassment or victimisation (including informal pressures) and will take appropriate action to protect any employee who raises a concern in good faith.

All concerns shall be treated in confidence and every effort will be made not to reveal the employees identity, but it shall be recognised that the employee may need to come forward as a witness.

Prior to raising a concern, the employee shall:

- disclose the information in good faith;
- believe it to be substantially true;
- not act maliciously or make false allegations; and
- not seek any personal gain.

As a first step, any employee with a concern shall normally raise the concern with their immediate Line Manager or their superior. This may depend, however, on the seriousness and sensitivity of the issues involved and who is suspected of the malpractice.

This policy is issued and maintained by the Information Security Manager in association with various employees and external legal counsel, who also provides advice and guidance on its implementation and ensure compliance.

All employees shall comply with this policy.

Appendix 16—The FCL environment policy

All employees shall be committed to the care of the environment and the prevention of pollution.

FCL ensures that all its activities are carried out in conformance with the relevant environmental Legislation.

FCL shall:

- create as little waste as possible and disposing of waste responsibly;
- recycle waste, where possible;
- use recycled materials where recycling alternatives are available;
- encourage the use of electronic media to lessen the amount of paper used;
- ensure the energy-efficiency of the equipment is used;
- switch off equipment when not in use, where possible;

- encourage employees to make use of public transport where possible;
- where practical, use fair traded products;
- use low energy lighting where possible, with dimmers and timers where appropriate;
- ensure a 'No Smoking' office; and
- train employees to understand their environmental responsibilities and encourages new ideas on improving our environmental performance.

An essential feature of the environmental management system is a commitment to improving environmental performance. This is achieved by setting annual environmental improvement objectives and targets which are regularly monitored and reviewed. The objectives and targets shall be publicised throughout FCL organisation, and all employees are committed to their achievement.

In order to ensure the achievement of the above commitments, FCL has implemented an environmental management system which satisfies the requirements of ISO 14001.

This policy and the obligations and responsibilities required by the environmental management system have been communicated to all employees.

The policy is available to the public on request.

This policy is issued and maintained by the Environment Manager, who also provides advice and guidance on its implementation and ensure compliance.

All employees shall comply with this policy.

Appendix 17—The FCL health and safety policy

FCL shall provide a safe and healthy working environment in accordance with the relevant Health and Safety Legislation and other requirements to which FCL subscribes.

The responsibility for health, safety, and welfare within FCL is placed with top management. At the heart of this commitment to health and safety are the seven core safety principles that all employees are required to embrace and which will facilitate this commitment to continual improvement of health and safety performance. These are:

1. all injuries can be prevented;
2. employee involvement is essential;
3. management is responsible for preventing injuries;
4. working safely and contributing to safety improvements is a condition of employment;
5. all operating exposures can be safeguarded;
6. training employees to work safely is essential; and
7. prevention of personal injury is good business sense.

Top management, through the various business streams and line management, shall ensure that all employees on FCL's premises, or on site, fulfil these commitments by:

- pursuing the deployment of FCL's safety strategy and the goal of zero injuries;
- ensuring that arrangements and resources exist to support this policy;
- effective management of health and safety;
- recognising the risks inherent in a consultancy and service management organisation;
- conducting and maintaining risk assessments and safe systems of work;
- meeting the requirements of ISO 45001, the Health and Safety Management requirements specification;
- ensuring that they meet all Legislative and Regulatory requirements relating to health and safety;
- setting, reviewing, and agreeing Health and Safety Objectives at the management review;
- ensuring that management set an example for all employees in the areas of health and safety;
- ensuring that there are appropriate financial, technical, and human resources present to implement, manage, and continuously improve FCL's Health and Safety Management System;
- ensuring that all relevant health and safety issues are taken into consideration when influencing changes are made to business processes;
- providing advice, training, and support for all FCL's employees to maintain a safe and healthy workplace;
- ensuring that any corrective actions required by the performance assessments process are fully implemented on time to reduce risk to an acceptable level;
- ensuring that documented risk assessments are maintained and that a risk register of all hazards and controls is maintained;

- ensuring that any identified hazards and their controls are communicated to all relevant employees;
- ensuring that a regular schedule of internal audits for health and safety are undertaken; and
- undertaking management reviews of FCL's health and safety processes in accordance with the requirements of ISO 45001 and ISO/IEC 17020.

FCL shall continue to invest in health and safety improvements on a progressive basis, setting objectives and targets in the annual health and safety programmes.

FCL shall engage and involve all employees in creating and maintaining a safe working environment.

This policy is issued, reviewed, and maintained by the Health and Safety Manager, who shall provide advice and guidance on its implementation and ensure compliance.

All employees shall comply with this policy.

Appendix 18—The FCL service management policy

The provision of a secure, stable, and well-managed IT infrastructure has a critical role in ensuring that the products and services provided to FCL's clients are well designed, implemented, and managed.

FCL shall:

- ensure that a full-service management system is planned and implemented so that FCL can meet their client's requirements;
- design all products and services in consultation with FCL's clients and ensure that the appropriate service operation objectives are agreed;
- perform continuous improvement activities to ensure that all products and services are monitored and improved where necessary and that FCL meets, and exceeds, client's expectations;
- provide the appropriate resources to ensure that the products and services required by FCL's clients are maintained at the correct level to meet their business needs; and
- ensure that all employees are aware of their responsibility to adhere to this policy and ensure that high-quality services are maintained for all of FCL's clients.

The Service Desk Manager shall be responsible for the co-ordination and management of services within FCL.

All relevant FCL managers shall be directly responsible for implementing the policy within their operational area, and for its adherence by all employees.

A service management system provides the framework for the implementation of this policy within FCL and shall be supported by a comprehensive set of policies and procedures. This system shall be regularly reviewed to ensure that it remains valid.

This policy is issued and maintained by the Service Level Manager, who shall provide advice and guidance on its implementation and ensure compliance.

All employees shall comply with this policy.

Appendix 19—The FCL business continuity policy

The business success of FCL is reliant upon the preservation of its critical business activities to ensure that products and services are delivered internally to employees and externally to clients.

This policy sets out the framework for how FCL responds to business disruptions in its business activities, how FCL manages the continuation of these activities, and how FCL manages their subsequent restoration.

The scope of business continuity at FCL is to provide resilience for its business activities through the implementation of controls that minimise the impact of a disruption on its business products, services, employees, and infrastructure located in all FCL offices.

FCL shall:

- regard business continuity and resilience as a key organisational activity and maintain a comprehensive business continuity programme to implement and manage this;
- identify the critical business activities in FCL through business impact analysis on the events that could cause significant business disruption;
- implement an appropriate business continuity and resilience strategy that meets FCL's needs;
- develop and implement plans to manage business disruptions that cover FCL's information systems, business processes, business premises, and employees;

- regularly exercise and test business continuity plans to ensure that they:
  - ➤ maintain or rapidly recover critical activities;
  - ➤ maintain the availability of key resources to support critical activities; and
  - ➤ prevent or limit the disruption to employees and clients;
- define the responsibilities of all employees involved in business continuity and resilience activities and provide training to ensure that these responsibilities can be carried out successfully;
- provide training to raise employee awareness of business continuity and resilience; and
- regularly review FCL's business continuity and resilience activities, policies, plans, tests, and responsibilities to ensure that the business continuity strategy remains appropriate to FCL's needs.

This policy, and the subordinate policies, processes, and procedures to this document, provides a clear statement of FCL's commitment to ensure that critical FCL business activities can be maintained during a disruption. This policy is subordinate to the FCL Information Security Policy which also gives further guidance on risk management and information assurance.

FCL has implemented ISO 22301 to manage its business continuity operations, and this is managed by this IMS.

The Business Continuity Management System (BCMS) provides the framework for the implementation of this policy within FCL and shall be supported by a comprehensive set of processes and procedures. This system shall be regularly reviewed to ensure it remains effective and that all critical business activities are covered.

This policy is issued and maintained by the Business Continuity Manager, who shall provide advice and guidance on its implementation and ensure compliance.

All employees shall comply with this policy.

Appendix 20—The FCL information security policy

FCL owes its success, and its excellent reputation, to its high-quality and professional service.

FCL's ability to maintain this reputation, and the levels of service to their clients, depends on the highest standards of professionalism and integrity. It is paramount that these standards include the way in which FCL uses and protects information and information systems. Any loss of confidence in FCL's ability to provide these products and services could cause the business to suffer. New technology exposes FCL to new and potentially greater risks because much greater reliance is placed on automated systems, and because of the extensive use of networked computers. FCL wants to reap the benefits of the new technology but shall not take unacceptable risks to do so.

It is FCL policy to secure information and systems in a manner which meets or exceeds accepted good practice. FCL shall ensure the continuity of their business operations and manage business damage by the implementation of controls to minimise the impact of security incidents.

FCL shall ensure that:

- all client data is appropriately protected and is not divulged to any third party without authorisation;
- all business premises are protected by suitable physical security and environmental controls, and where appropriate, access is restricted to authorised employees;
- confidentiality, integrity, and availability of all information is maintained;
- information is accessible to all employees according to business need and is protected against unauthorised access;
- access to FCL data and personal data is appropriately controlled;
- contractual, Regulatory, and Legislative requirements are all met;
- all in house systems development is appropriately controlled and tested before live implementation;
- all employees are provided with training in information security awareness and individual responsibilities are defined; and
- all employees are aware of their responsibility to adhere to the policy and ensure that all breaches of information security, actual or suspected are reported to and investigated by the Information Security Manager.

This policy provides a clear statement of FCL's commitment to protect all information assets from threats internal and external, intentional, or accidental.

The information security management system provides the framework for the implementation of this policy within FCL and is supported by a comprehensive set of procedures. This system is regularly reviewed via a risk management process to ensure that all identified risks are treated.

This policy is issued and maintained by the Information Security Manager, who shall provide advice and guidance on its implementation and ensure compliance.

All employees shall comply with this policy.

Appendix 21—The FCL access control policy

This policy defines the principles, standards, guidelines, and responsibilities related to accessing FCL information processing systems. This policy shall support information security by preventing unauthorised access to information processing facilities and the information that they contain.

New technologies and more automation are increasing opportunities for information sharing, meaning that FCL shall seek a balance between the need to protect information resources and allowing greater access to data and applications. Several factors affect how FCL controls access to its computers, networks, and data—this includes evaluation of risk and consequences of unauthorised access.

The primary objectives of the access control policy are to:

- communicate the need for access control;
- establish specific requirements for protecting against unauthorised access; and
- create an infrastructure that will foster information sharing without sacrificing security of information resources.

Access control protects information by managing access to all entry and exit (or end) points, both logical and physical. Adequate perimeter security and logical security measures shall protect against unauthorised access to sensitive information on FCL information processing systems. These measures shall ensure that only authorised users have access to specific computer resources, networks, data, and applications and include:

- FCL security administration activity regarding access control breaches or incidents shall be reported via the standard incident management process;
- applications used in FCL shall incorporate controls for managing access to selected information and functions;
- FCL systems shall authenticate functions that are consistent with the level of confidentially or sensitively of the information they contain and process. Identification is unique for each user of the system and the system provides a method to accurately identify the user through a directory system, passphrases, smart tokens, smart cards, or other means;

Note

Some system accounts are generic (therefore shared). These accounts shall be authorised, reviewed at least annually on a risk-based approach and records of review shall be kept.

- the authorities to read, write, modify, update, or delete information from automated files or databases shall be established by the Owner(s) of the information. Individuals may be granted a specific combination of authorities. Individuals shall not to be given any authority beyond their needs. Access rules or profiles shall be established in a manner that restricts users from performing incompatible functions or functions beyond their responsibility and enforces a separation of duties;
- FCL computer operations which support sensitive information operate in accordance with procedures approved by the information owner(s) and shall ensure that:
  - information cannot be modified or destroyed except in accordance with procedures;
  - operating programs prohibit unauthorised access or changes to, or destruction of, records;
  - operating programs are used to detect and store all unauthorised attempts to penetrate the system; and
  - special requirements, including all contractual, Regulatory and Legislative obligations are all met.
- access to FCL network shall be subject to the security policies and procedures of the network;
- passphrases shall be used (not passwords) and shall be confidential and at least 16 alphanumeric characters long. Passphrases shall not be a single dictionary word, repeating character strings, or identifying information that is linked to the user;
- strong passphrases are automatically forced on the user by the operating system, so there is no account expiration requiring a passphrases change.

Note

FCL took the view that it is better to have one strong passphrase to remember than to keep changing them. Given that there are so few employees and the level of physical security, the top management have accepted this risk;

- for forensic workstations, all access shall be controlled by biometric fingerprint scanners for additional security;
- employees with broad access to data in sensitive positions shall undergo appropriate screening checks as a condition of employment;
- security shall be required not only for software and information, but also for physical security of equipment which shall include at least the following:
  - restrict physical access to information processing facilities where continued operation is essential or where sensitive or confidential data are stored online;
  - restrict access to computer facilities to employees who need such access to perform assigned work duties; and
  - restrict access to software documentation and data storage to employees who need such access to perform assigned work duties.
- FCL shall revoke access to the network to ensure the confidentiality, integrity, and availability of the network to other users;
- all FCL users shall be made aware of workstation security:
  - sensitive or confidential information shall not be stored on the workstation hard drive for security and business reasons. Most workstations pose a risk of unauthorised access because the drives are accessible;
  - reasonable efforts shall be made to safeguard individual workstations to protect against unauthorised access to the workstation, network, or information;
  - passphrases for workstation logon should not be built into the logon script for auto-sign on;
  - mobile device users shall follow FCL guidelines to protect against the theft, destruction, or loss of equipment and information;
  - users shall log off when the system will be left inactive or unattended; and
  - a clear desk and clear screen policy shall operate throughout FCL.

This policy is issued and maintained by the Information Security Manager, who shall provide advice and guidance on its implementation and ensure compliance.

All employees shall comply with this policy.

Appendix 22—The FCL change or termination of employment policy

FCL pursues an active policy of promoting awareness of information security to ensure that security issues are addressed when all employees terminate or change employment.

Consideration of security during termination and change of employment shall reinforce FCL's commitment to information security by ensuring that all employees are properly managed, that all relevant issues concerning information security are properly addressed, and that issues concerning the removal of all employee's access rights are fully resolved.

FCL policies and procedures for termination and changes to employment shall be controlled and maintained by HR.

FCL policy for managing security during termination and change of employment is:

- all employment termination and changes (permanent, temporary, and third-party) shall be managed in accordance with HR policies and procedures for managing termination and changes to employment;
- FCL managers shall work in accordance with HR policy and procedures when terminating employment as defined in the HR Termination Checklist for Line Managers—it is the responsibility of the relevant Line Manager to ensure they comply with requisite policy and procedures;
- all security considerations outlined in HR Termination Checklist for Line Managers—both information and physical—shall be addressed and resolved when an employee leaves FCL, or changes employment within FCL;
- termination or changes to employment roles with specific information security tasks or activities shall be managed appropriately by either the relevant business manager and/or HR;
- all employees shall return any FCL assets which are in their possession on termination;
- all access rights to information and information processing facilities (both physical and virtual) shall be removed on termination or change of employment, as appropriate;
- removal of access rights to FCL information-processing and network facilities shall be performed in accordance with FCL procedures for managing user accounts;
- removal and review of access privileges to FCL information processing facilities shall be performed in accordance with FCL procedures for managing system access.

This policy is issued and maintained by the Information Security Manager and the HR Manager, who shall provide advice and guidance on its implementation and ensure compliance.

All employees shall comply with this policy.

Appendix 23—The FCL clear desk and clear screen policy

Clear desk policy

FCL shall operate a clear desk policy to reduce risks from unauthorised access, loss, and damage to classified paper and storage media.

FCL shall ensure that:

- all employees shall maintain a clear desk for classified information when leaving their work area for a significant period of time (including lunch breaks, and at the end of each working day) or be locked away at the least;
- all classified information shall be properly stored in secure file cabinets, closets, or storage rooms after use;
- classified information that is not to be used or archived shall be shredded;
- all printed documents (print outputs, photocopies) shall be collected from the relevant output devices (and then either used, shredded, or archived);
- where possible secure printing shall be implemented having two factor authentication to access print queues;
- printers and photocopiers shall be checked regularly (at least every day after business hours) for prints outs that are not collected (the items should be secured until the proper owners of the documents are available), even where 'follow me' printing is used; and
- all information on whiteboards, work boards, etc. shall be wiped after use.

Clear screen policy

FCL shall operate a clear screen policy to reduce risks from unauthorised access, loss, and damage to information held in FCL information processing systems.

FCL shall ensure that:

- no system which is available via a workstation shall be accessible if the workstation is left temporarily unattended;
- workstations that are left temporarily unattended (up to 60 min for desktops, 5 min for portable devices and 30 min for servers) shall have access temporarily blocked using either:
  - a manual, passphrase-protected keyboard lock facility initiated by a user before leaving their workstation; and
  - an automatic, passphrase-protected screen saver which shall be activated after 60 min inactivity for desktops, 5 min for portable devices, and 30 min for servers.
- personnel shall not stick attachments (e.g. post-it notes or similar) to workstation screens (particularly sensitive information such as client data or passphrases).

This policy is issued and maintained by the Information Security Manager, who shall provide advice and guidance on its implementation and ensure compliance.

All employees shall comply with this policy.

Appendix 24—The FCL continuous improvement policy

FCL is committed to operating efficiently and effectively in order to meet the needs of its clients. Continuous improvement in all activities is vital for FCL's continued success.

FCL shall undertake ongoing quality control and evaluation of all its products and services to ensure maintenance of standards appropriate to the expectations of its clients.

Continuous improvement within FCL shall be based on adherence to the following principles:

- a commitment by all employees to continuous improvement of products and services and their management;
- input and involvement of all employees in identifying and implementing improvements to products and services and their management; and
- systematic use of qualitative and quantitative feedback as the basis for identifying and prioritising improvement opportunities.

Continuous improvement shall be carried out through:

- monitoring and reviewing of FCL processes and procedures;
- professional development of employees;
- monitoring and implementation of standards;
- client satisfaction surveys;
- responding to unsolicited feedback on the products, services, or operations;
- review of any whistleblowing concerns raised;
- ad hoc continuous improvement working parties;
- internal and external audits; and
- Management reviews on services and operations.

All suggested improvements shall be assessed, authorised, and implemented via an authorised continuous improvement plan.

Implemented corrective actions shall be subject to a Post Implementation Review (PIR) to ensure that the implemented measures meet the required outcome.

All improvement activities shall be monitored on an ongoing basis.

This policy is issued and maintained by the Quality Manager, in association with other Management System Managers, who shall provide advice and guidance on its implementation and ensure compliance.

All employees shall comply with this policy.

Appendix 25—cryptographic control policy

Cryptographic controls shall be implemented by FCL to provide additional safeguards against the compromise of data transmitted across the public network infrastructure as follows:

- the Information Security Manager shall be the authority responsible for the management of all cryptographic controls within FCL;
- all cryptographic keys used shall be secret keys;
- the same cryptographic keys shall be used on all equipment;
- cryptographic keys shall be stored as part of an equipment's configuration and shall be backed up;
- the use of cryptographic keys shall be reviewed at least annually or influencing change and shall be changed on an as needed basis; and
- the management of cryptographic keys shall be restricted to the Information Security Manager and the Network Manager.

This policy is issued and maintained by the Information Security Manager, who shall provide advice and guidance on its implementation and ensure compliance.

All employees shall comply with this policy.

Appendix 26—The FCL document retention policy

Note

Different jurisdictions will have differing document retention requirements. Below are some areas to consider for document retention without values being inserted.

To prevent unauthorised or accidental disclosure of the information, it is important to protect its security and confidentiality during storage, transportation, handling, and destruction.

All employees have a responsibility to consider safety and security when handling information in the course of their work. Consideration shall be given to the nature of the information involved (how sensitive is it?), and the format in which it is held.

FCL shall have procedures appropriate to the information held and processed by them and ensure that all employees are aware of those procedures. In addition, a record of retention and disposal may be required to be maintained by Legislation or Regulation.

Legislation, Regulation, and good practice shall be used to define retention periods within the jurisdiction of operations.

Note

This will vary for differing forensic laboratories, and as such FCL retention periods are not shown as it is up to each forensic laboratory to identify and implement their specific requirements.

FCL 'records' mean any data recorded in any form, including (but not limited to):

- paper files;
- computer files;
- audio tapes;
- video tapes;
- film and microfiche; and
- any other data maintained by employees in the course of their employment.

The following controls shall be in place in FCL:

- no record shall be destroyed without authorisation by the Information Security Manager or a business stream manager (if there is any doubt about the need for authorisation in a specific case, employees shall consult their Line Managers);
- when records are disposed of, on-site or off, methods shall be used to prohibit future use or reconstruction;
- paper records containing personal information shall be shredded, not simply thrown out with other rubbish or general records;
- special care shall be taken with electronic records, which can be reconstructed from deleted information;
- similarly, erasing or reformatting computer disks or personal computers with hard drives which once contained personal information is not enough. Software tools shall be used which securely remove all data from the medium so that it cannot be reconstructed. Removable media shall be physically destroyed, wherever possible;
- a disposal record shall be maintained indicating what records have been destroyed, when, by whom, and using what method of destruction; and
- records which have been kept or archived shall also be tracked. The record may consist of a simple list on paper or be part of an electronic records management system.

Record types, retention periods, and approved destruction methods are unique to each forensic laboratory and should be defined by them to meet their needs to comply with relevant legislation, regulation, contractual terms, and business requirements.

Appendix 27—The FCL financial management policy

This policy describes the financial practices used within FCL to manage budgets.

FCL shall:

- agree budgets based upon the products services that FCL provide to their clients;
- maintain effective financial management programmes and systems;
- conduct a continuous programme of monitoring to improve financial operations and systems and to identify more efficient methods of operations regarding budgeting, accounting, financial reporting, and auditing;
- be responsive to FCL's management needs; and
- be responsive to the financial reporting and other FCL top management requirements.

Budget holders shall ensure that:

- initial budget planning for their operational area is performed;
- their operational area budgets are monitored at least each month; and
- the correct allocation of budgets from their operational area is performed.

This policy is issued and maintained by the Finance Director, who shall provide advice and guidance on its implementation and ensure compliance. All FCL budget holders are directly responsible for implementing and complying with this policy.

All employees shall comply with this policy.

Appendix 28—The FCL mobile device policy

With the increasing use of mobile devices, comes the increase of the risk to the safety and security of the hardware used and more importantly the information held on it. Information held, whether it be FCL's own data or that belonging to someone else for which FCL is responsible (i.e. clients) shall be protected against unauthorised access modification, erasure, and disclosure.

This policy describes the mobile device policy for FCL.

Users

- shall accept the conditions of use contained within this policy;
- shall not attach unauthorised equipment to FCL computer network, including Bring Your Own Device (BYOD);
- shall not share passphrases to anyone. Passphrases shall not be written down and attached to mobile devices;
- only those who have specific authorisation from FCL shall connect to the network using a mobile device;
- shall not connect any laptop equipment that is not under the direct supervision of the IT department.
- shall be responsible for 'their' FCL mobile devices which are connected to the IT infrastructure, and for ensuring that they are in good working condition;
- shall ensure the physical protection of 'their' FCL computing equipment (including risks from theft, and leaving equipment unattended);
- shall ensure that no business-critical data is **only** stored locally on 'their' FCL mobile device;
- shall not allow 'their' FCL mobile device to act as a server of any kind;
- shall exercise particular care when using mobile devices in public places to:
  - avoid disclosure or information stored locally on a mobile device; and
  - avoid overlooking by unauthorised persons.

Visitors

- where visitors require a connection to the FCL network, they shall seek approval from the IT Department prior to connection and only use the 'Guest' network which is a physically separate network from FCL production networks.

FCL

- shall develop, maintain, and update the mobile device policy and security standards;
- shall resolve mobile communication problems;
- shall enable mobile connections to FCL production network following a request from a Line Manager or Department Head;
- shall monitor performance and security when necessary;
- shall monitor the development of new mobile device technology and security and evaluate and implement where necessary;
- shall safeguard the security of FCL information and information processing facilities; and
- shall ensure that system administrators and users understand the security implications and performance limitations of mobile device technology.

USB devices

USB devices, including memory sticks, shall not be connected to any networked desktop or laptop computer if:

- the device has not been authorised for use by the user's Line Manager and the Information Security Manager;
- does not store information in an encrypted form; and
- the device has not been registered with the IT Department.

Protection of data

To protect data from unauthorised use or access, the following shall apply:

- only FCL mobile devices shall be permitted to be used in FCL;
- mobile devices shall only be used by employees for legitimate business purposes;
- mobile devices shall not be loaned to any other user;

- the registered Owner shall be responsible for all data held on any mobile devices, including ensuring that data is fully backed up; and
- passphrases shall protect (when necessary) any personal data that is kept on a mobile devices.

Warning The use of passphrase protection on documents is at the user's own risk. If the passphrase is forgotten, the document may not be able to be accessed.

General information

- FCL has overall responsibility for the IT computer infrastructure, and shall be responsible for the deployment, management and support of all mobile computing;
- business proposals which may require a resource of mobile devices shall be discussed with relevant employees (e.g. IT Manager, Information Security Manager, etc.);
- FCL shall not accept responsibility or liability for any damage or loss of personal data to any mobile device while in transit or connected to the network; and
- traffic on the network shall be monitored by FCL to secure effective operation, and for other lawful purposes.

FCL shall suspend access to the network via a mobile device for any user found in breach of this or any other FCL security policy.

This policy is issued and maintained by the Information Security Manager in association with the HR Manager, who shall provide advice and guidance on its implementation and ensure compliance.

All employees shall comply with this policy.

Appendix 29—The FCL network service policy

This policy defines the principles, standards, guidelines, and responsibilities related to connections to FCL network system. This policy shall support information security by reducing the opportunity for unauthorised access to FCL information processing facilities and information.

The primary objectives of the networked services policy are that:

- users shall be provided with direct access to the services that they have been specifically authorised to use;
- users shall only be able to access the network and network services which they are allowed to access;
- users shall be authorised to access networks and networked services via their job role and function; and
- controls and procedures shall protect access to network connections and network services.

The following guidelines shall apply:

- network devices shall only be connected to FCL network from approved connection points;
- only approved devices shall be connected to FCL network;
- all devices connected to the network shall comply with FCL naming conventions and IP address schemes;
- the IT Manager shall take appropriate steps to protect FCL network if a network device, desktop computer, mobile device, or server exhibits characteristics that could be regarded as a threat to FCL network, this includes:
  - a device that imposes an exceptional load on a service;
  - a device that exhibits a pattern of malicious network traffic associated with scanning or attacking others;
  - a device that exhibits behaviour consistent with host compromise; and
  - a device that exhibits behaviour consistent with illegal activity.
- all devices that connect to FCL network shall meet the prevailing security standards as defined by the Information Security Manager and the IT Manager, including:
  - installation of malware protection and endpoint security software and updated definition files on all computers; and
  - installation of security patches on the system as soon as practical.
- additional protection shall be provided for systems with sensitive and personal data that complies with relevant Legislation;
- the IT Manager shall be responsible for reliable network services and shall give approval to any individual or department that may want to run its own particular service to ensure that this service does not interfere with the functioning of centrally provided services. This shall include:
  - IP address assignment (i.e. Dynamic Host Configuration Protocol (DHCP) servers), Domain Name System (DNS), or other management services for networking;
  - e-mail services shall not be provided by any other departments, unless warranted by exceptional circumstances, and if required and authorised shall first be reviewed and approved to ensure that they are secure and that they interface properly with other services;

- provision of authorised user accounts to access network services;
- the IT Manager and the Information Security Manager shall reserve the right to restrict certain types of traffic coming into and across FCL network; and
- the Information Security Manager shall undertake risk assessments, where appropriate, to determine risks and controls to treat them.

This policy is issued and maintained by the Information Security Manager in association with the IT Manager, who shall provide advice and guidance on its implementation and ensure compliance.

All employees shall comply with this policy.

Appendix 30—The FCL personnel screening policy

This policy describes the FCL personnel screening policy.

Screening employees at recruitment stage

Successful job applicant screening and verification shall be a routine process in FCL which helps to minimise risks from theft, fraud, and misuse of facilities. All job applicants at FCL shall be subject to screening and verification checks, particularly new recruits who require access to sensitive data.

FCL screening policy for applicants of permanent employment is:

- all potential permanent employees shall be screened in accordance with FCL policy for screening job applicants as outlined in this policy;
- responsibility for performing screening checks lies with the HR Manager and the Information Security Manager;
- any failures or issues that arise as a consequence of a screening check and which may affect information security, shall be reported by the HR Manager to the Information Security Manager;
- verification checks shall be performed on all applicants for permanent employment as follows:
  - employee applications, CV details, experience, and qualifications shall be matched against a job description to verify the potential suitability of the applicant;
  - interviews shall be conducted on an individual basis to verify suitability. Formal offers of employment may only be made to an individual subject to the following checks being made by the HR Manager:
  - character and professional references shall be confirmed by obtaining two employer references;
  - academic and professional qualifications shall be confirmed by requesting original printed copies (certified copies will suffice if originals are not available) of the most relevant qualifications;
  - an applicant's identity shall be verified via a passport or a driving licence; and
  - the right to work in the jurisdiction shall be checked.
- a criminal record check shall be performed (if available) on all new employees immediately after an individual commences employment (the check is initiated and monitored by the HR Manager) credit checks shall be performed by, and at the discretion of, the HR Manager under the following circumstances; and
- during application for employment by an individual who may have access to sensitive data or financial information periodically, for senior management and/or employees with access to financial data.

Temporary and contract staff

All screening of temporary and contract employees shall be performed by the preferred recruitment agency in accordance with these screening requirements:

- character and professional references shall be obtained via a minimum of two employer references;
  - where relevant, academic, and professional qualifications shall be confirmed;
  - an applicant's identity shall be verified via a passport or a driving licence;
  - the HR Manager shall be responsible for notifying the agency of FCL's screening requirements for temporary or contract employees; and
- the HR Manager shall confirm with the recruitment agency that employee screening has been completed and verify the results.

If the recruitment agency does not perform these tasks, the HR Manager shall arrange for them to be carried out.

Third party screening service providers

FCL has not the resources or competence to carry out screening checking in house. In the UK, FCL shall use third-party screening service providers who are using the current version of BS 7858—Security screening of individuals employed in a security environment. Code of Practice.

This policy is issued and maintained by the HR Manager, who shall provide advice and guidance on its implementation and ensure compliance.

All employees shall comply with this policy.

Appendix 31—The FCL relationship management policy

FCL shall:

- enable FCL to provide better information processing services to its clients;
- enable FCL to better serve clients through the introduction of reliable processes and procedures for interacting with both clients and suppliers;
- improve the quality of products and services provided by FCL;
- simplify client-related and supplier-related processes, and enhance relationships;
- provide a mechanism for identifying potential problems with FCL products and services on a proactive basis;
- provide a means of registering and resolving formal client complaints;
- provide a mechanism for identifying and correcting service deficiencies;
- allow FCL to better understand their client's requirements, so that they can identify how clients define quality and thus design a product and service strategy which is tailored to their needs; and
- involve client and supplier relationship management in all aspects of service level management at FCL.

This policy is issued and maintained by the Quality Manager, who shall provide advice and guidance on its implementation and ensure compliance.

All employees shall comply with this policy.

Appendix 32—The FCL release management policy

Release Management is the process of planning, building, testing, deploying hardware/software and the version control and storage of software. Its purpose is to ensure that a consistent method of deployment is followed. It reduces the likelihood of incidents as a result of rollouts and ensures that only tested and accepted versions of hardware and software are installed at any time.

To ensure that all releases are performed to a consistent standard and in a timely manner, FCL shall implement a release management policy to govern releases at a high level. Additional release management documentation in the service management system shall provide further guidance on planning and implementing releases.

FCL shall:

- ensure that all types of release, major, minor, and emergency, including hardware and software, are performed in a controlled manner;
- ensure that all releases are performed at the time agreed with business clients to minimise service disruption but in line with FCL's operational situation;
- ensure that releases can only be performed following full approval through FCL change management system;
- ensure that all releases are planned and documented by the Release Manager in conjunction with business clients (where appropriate), are uniquely identified and contain full descriptions of what is contained in the release;
- ensure that a release can only be approved for implementation by the Release Manager after all planning and implementation activities are agreed within FCL and business clients (where appropriate);
- ensure that, where appropriate, several releases can be grouped into a single or reduced number of releases to minimise service disruption;
- ensure that the processes and procedures for building, testing and distributing releases are fully documented and agreed; and
- ensure that the success of a release is verified and confirmed by the Release Manager and employees and is accepted by business clients.

This release policy shall be reviewed and revised or extended when FCL's IT infrastructure is changed.

This policy is issued and maintained by the Release Manager in association with the IT Manager and the Change Manager, who shall provide advice and guidance on its implementation and ensure compliance.

All employees shall comply with this policy.

Appendix 33—The FCL service reporting policy

Timely and accurate reporting is the key to supporting and improving service management. This reporting enables FCL management and business clients to assess the state of products and services being provided and provides a sound basis for decision making.

FCL shall:

- agree all reporting requirements during service management planning with a business client;
- document all reporting requirements in Service Level Agreements (SLAs) including report types, frequency, and responsibilities for production for all third party suppliers;
- provide timely and accurate service reports for internal management and business clients;
- provide reporting that covers all measurable aspects of a service that details both current and historical analysis;
- use appropriate reporting tools to ensure that the information within reports is comprehensive, accurate, and has clear presentation; and
- use service reporting as an input into the service review and improvement programme.

All FCL Managers shall be responsible for producing reports in their operational area.

The Service Level Manager shall be responsible for producing reports on third party supplier performance.

This policy is issued and maintained by the Service Level Manager, who shall provide advice and guidance on its implementation and ensure compliance.

All employees shall comply with this policy.

Appendix 34—The FCL third party access control policy

This policy describes the requirements for third-party access control within FCL:

- unescorted access to the server or networking equipment shall only be granted to employees that require routine physical access to this equipment in order to perform their primary job functions and who are on the access list. (All others will be classified as 'Third-Party');
- the access list for authorised and unescorted persons shall be held by the IT Manager;
- exceptions can be made, when warranted, but only by top management, the Information Security Manager and the IT Manager;
- all those not on the authorised access list shall require an escort anytime access is required;
- the individual providing escort (the 'host') shall remain with the individual requiring escort until their access requirement is finished;
- former employees shall not be permitted access to server or networking equipment whether with or without an escort;
- server and networking equipment shall remain secured at all times. Only those individuals with unescorted access rights shall be authorised to access it unless escorted continuously by their host;
- all requests for unescorted access rights shall be made in writing to the IT Manager and authorised by the Information Security manager; and
- the relevant employee shall any requests for access.

This policy is issued and maintained by the Information Security Manager in association with the IT Manager, who shall provide advice and guidance on its implementation and ensure compliance.

All employees shall comply with this policy.

Appendix 35—The FCL acceptable use policy

General

FCL encourages the use of electronic communications to share information and knowledge in support of their goals and to conduct their business. To this end, FCL supports and provides interactive electronic communications services and facilities such as:

- telephones;
- voicemail;
- teleconferencing;
- video teleconferencing;
- electronic mail;
- list servers;
- newsgroups;
- electronic publishing services such as the World Wide Web;
- electronic broadcasting services such as Web radio and Webcasting.

These communications services rely on underlying voice, video, and data networks delivered over both physical and wireless infrastructures. Digital technologies are unifying these communications functions and services, blurring traditional boundaries. This policy recognises this convergence and establishes an overall policy framework for all electronic communications.

This policy clarifies the applicability of Law and other FCL policies relating to electronic communications. It also establishes new policies and procedures where existing policies do not specifically address issues particular to the use of electronic communications. Where there are no such particular issues, this policy defers to other FCL policies.

An integrated policy cannot anticipate all the new issues that might arise in electronic communications. One purpose of this policy is to provide a framework within which these new issues can be resolved and that recognises the inter-related legal, corporate, and individual interests involved.

All FCL information processing facilities shall be provided to support FCL's business and administrative activities. The information held on the network forms part of its critical assets and are susceptible to security breaches that may compromise confidential information and expose FCL to losses and other legal risks.

These FCL policies and procedures change from time to time, therefore users shall refer to online versions of this and other FCL policies in the IMS.

Any infringement of this policy may be subject to penalties under civil or criminal law, and such law may be invoked by FCL. Any infringement of this policy shall constitute a disciplinary offence or a contractual breach and may be treated as such regardless of legal proceedings.

This policy shall be regularly reviewed by the Information Security Manager who shall provide any assistance in interpreting this policy.

Purpose

This policy shall:

- provide guidelines for the conditions of acceptance and the appropriate use of FCL's information processing facilities;
- provide mechanisms for responding to external complaints about actual or perceived abuses originating from FCL's information processing facilities;
- protect the privacy and integrity of information stored on FCL's information processing facilities;
- mitigate the risks and losses from security threats to computer and network resources such as malware attacks and compromises of FCL's information processing facilities;
- reduce interruptions and ensure a high availability of an efficient infrastructure essential for sustaining FCL's business; and
- encourage users to understand their own responsibility for protecting FCL's information processing facilities.

Applicability

This policy shall apply to:
- users using FCL provided equipment connected locally or remotely to FCL's information processing facilities;

Note

Throughout this policy, the word 'user' shall be used collectively to refer to all such individuals or groups.

- all equipment connected (locally or remotely) to FCL's information processing facilities;
- information processing facilities owned by and/or administered by FCL;
- connections made to external networks through FCL's information processing facilities; and
- to all external entities that have executed contractual agreements with FCL for use of FCL's information processing facilities.

FCL's information processing facilities shall only be used for business purposes in serving FCL's interests, its users in the course of normal operations.

Any information processing equipment or electronic communications address, site, number, account, or other identifier associated with FCL or assigned by FCL to users, shall remain the property of FCL.

FCL's information processing records relating to their business shall be considered FCL records whether or not FCL owns the information processing facilities, systems, or services used to create, send, forward, reply to, transmit, store, hold, copy, download, display, view, read, print, or otherwise record them. This shall be consistent with the current data protection and data privacy legislation.

All of FCL's information processing facilities shall have nominated Owners and optionally Custodians.

This policy is owned by the Information Security Manager.

Responsibilities

Holders of user accounts or owners of information processing facilities connected to FCL's information processing facilities shall be responsible for all actions associated with the user account or information processing facilities that is assigned to them.

Users shall ensure that they use all reasonable means to protect their equipment and (if applicable) their account details and passphrases.

Engaging in any activities referred to in the 'unacceptable use' section is prohibited and shall result in disciplinary action or contractual action being taken, as appropriate.

Users shall assist IT and Information Security employees with investigations into suspected information security incidents.

Acceptable use

FCL's information processing facilities shall be provided to support FCL's business mission, its users and clients. The use of these facilities constitutes acceptance of this policy and is subject to the following limitations, necessary for the reliable operation of the electronic communication systems and services:

- users shall comply with all applicable Legislation within the jurisdiction of operations;
- FCL's information processing facilities shall be used for the purpose for which they are intended;
- users shall respect the rights, privacy, and property of others;
- users shall adhere to the confidentiality rules governing the use of passphrases and accounts and details of which shall not be shared;
- passphrases shall not be disclosed to anyone even if the recipient is a member of the IT Department. Temporary passphrases provided by the IT Department to users shall be changed immediately following a successful login;

Note

It is noted that some passphrases may, no matter what, be known by IT employees (e.g. Service Accounts), however, wherever possible, users shall input their own passphrases. Where this is not possible, it shall be ensured that IT employees are subject to confidentiality clauses in their contract or NDAs as appropriate.

- FCL's information processing facilities shall only be used for work which complies with this policy and the requirements of the IMS; and
- where FCL's information processing facilities are used to access other networks, any abuses against that network will be regarded as an unacceptable use of FCL's information processing facilities and a breach of this policy and shall result in disciplinary action or contractual action being taken, as appropriate.

Personal use

FCL's information processing facilities may be used for incidental personal purposes provided that:

- the purposes are of a private nature not for financial gain and do not contravene any other FCL policies and procedures;
- such use does not cause noticeable or unavoidable cost to FCL;
- such use does not inappropriately interfere with any FCL official business; and
- such use does not include any actions defined in the unacceptable use section below.

Unacceptable use

FCL's information processing facilities shall not be provided to users or third parties where such services do not support the mission of FCL or are not in the commercial interest of FCL.

Any misuse of FCL's information processing facilities shall result disciplinary action or contractual action being taken, as appropriate. This may also include legal action, depending on the policy breach.

FCL's information processing facilities shall not be used for the following activities:

- the creation, dissemination, storage, and display of obscene or pornographic material;
- the creation, dissemination, storage, and display of indecent images of children;
- the creation, dissemination, storage, and display of hate literature;
- the creation, dissemination, storage, and display of defamatory materials or materials likely to cause offence to others;
- the creation, dissemination, storage, and display of any data that is illegal;
- the downloading, storage, and disseminating of copyrighted materials including software and all forms of electronic information without the permission of the holder of the copyright or under the terms of the licences held by FCL;
- initiating spam emails and sending them or forwarding other types of spam email, included, but not limited to, chain letters, etc.
- any activities which do not conform to the law in the relevant jurisdiction and other FCL guidelines and policies regarding the protection of intellectual property and data. Specific emphasis is placed on the downloading and copying of both music and video files through the internet using peer-to-peer file sharing utilities;
- the deliberate interference with or gaining illegal access to user accounts and data including viewing, modifying, destroying, or corrupting the data belonging to other users;
- use of a username and passphrases belonging to another user;
- attempts to crack, capture passphrases, or decode encrypted data;
- any other use that may bring the name of FCL into disrepute or expose FCL to the risk of civil or criminal action;
- intentional creation, execution, forwarding, or introduction of any malware or software code designed to damage, self-replicate, or hinder the performance of FCL network;
- deliberate actions that might reduce the effectiveness of any antimalware, endpoint protection software, or other information security management precautions installed by authorised employees;
- attempts to penetrate information security measures (hacking) whether or not this results in a corruption or loss of data;
- purposefully scanning internal or external machines in an attempt to discover or exploit known computer software or network vulnerabilities, except for those employees who are authorised to perform this as part of their job;
- engaging in commercial activities that are not under the auspices of FCL. Third-party employees shall declare all other commercial activities at engagement time or during their employment to ensure that they are not in conflict with FCL's objectives;
- intentionally using computing resources (CPU, time, disk space, bandwidth) in such a way that it causes excessive strain on the computer systems or disrupts, denies, or create problems for other authorised FCL users; and
- connecting any computer device to FCL's information processing facilities without authorisation.

Email policy

FCL shall provide electronic mail services ('email') to support the business and administrative objective of FCL for use by authorised users.

Email is a critical means of communication and many official FCL communications are transmitted between employees and to clients using email.

This policy shall apply to authorised users and has been established to provide guidelines for the acceptable use of the email service.

Email between computers connected to FCL's information processing facilities and the Internet shall be relayed via the FCL email gateway.

Any FCL mail server shall not accept mail to external addresses sent from an address, which is itself external to FCL.

FCL mail server shall not accept mail sent from a computer which has not been properly registered with an authorised network address.

All email communication from FCL shall contain any legally required disclaimers and other required information, as well the full contact details of the sender.

All official FCL email communication to employees shall be delivered to their FCL account and shall not be automatically forwarded to external email accounts.

All email transmissions shall have the ability to be encrypted where the content classification requires it.

Users of FCL's information processing facilities shall not give the impression that they are representing, giving opinions, or otherwise making statements on behalf of FCL unless appropriately authorised (explicitly or implicitly) to do so. While it is permissible to indicate one's affiliation with FCL, unless it is clear from the context that the author is not representing FCL an explicit disclaimer shall be included.

Users of FCL's information processing facilities shall only send unsolicited mass communications in support of FCL's business where this meets legal and regulatory requirements and is approved by the Head of Marketing and Communications. Individual users shall not send mass unsolicited marketing or other similar materials.

In general, FCL shall not, and does not wish to, be the arbiter of the contents of electronic communications. Neither can FCL, in general, protect users from receiving electronic communications they might find offensive.

Users of FCL's information processing facilities shall be required to use the same personal and professional courtesies and considerations in emails as they would in other forms of communication.

Video conferencing

FCL shall provide video conferencing facilities to support the business and administrative objective of FCL for use by authorised users.

Video conferencing may be recorded for business purposes.

Video conferencing shall be encrypted for transmission.

Loss and damage

Save as set out below, FCL accepts no liability to users (whether in contract, tort (including negligence), breach of statutory duty, restitution or otherwise) for:

- any loss or damage incurred by a user as a result of personal use of FCL's information processing facilities. Users shall not rely on personal use of FCL's information processing facilities for communications that might be sensitive with regard to timing, financial effect, privacy or confidentiality;
- the malfunctioning of any FCL information processing facilities, or for the loss of any data or software, or the failure of any security or privacy mechanism, whether caused by any defect in FCL's information processing facilities or by any act or neglect by FCL;
- the acts or omissions of other providers of telecommunications services or for faults in or failures of their networks and equipment; or
- any injury, death, damage, or direct, indirect or consequential loss (all three of which terms include, without limitation, pure economic loss, loss of profits, loss of business, loss of data, loss of opportunity, depletion of goodwill and like loss) howsoever caused arising out of or in connection with the use of FCL's information processing facilities.

FCL shall not exclude its liability under this policy (if any) to users for:

- personal injury or death resulting from FCL's negligence;
- for any matter which it would be illegal for FCL to exclude or to attempt to exclude its liability; or
- for fraudulent misrepresentation.

Users shall agree not to cause any form of damage to FCL information processing facilities, or to any accommodation associated with them. Should such damage arise, FCL shall be entitled to recover from such user, by way of indemnity, any and all losses, costs, damages, and/or expenses that FCL incurs or suffers as a result of such damage.

Deletion of data

Users should be aware that data deleted from local disks by the users, may still be accessible in some cases, via certain system tools.

Newsgroup articles, contributions to social media, non-FCL owned mailing lists and emails that once sent are stored on machines outside the jurisdiction of FCL and in these cases withdrawal or deletion of these messages or emails may not be possible.

Back-up services

FCL information processing facilities shall be backed up to protect system reliability and integrity, and to prevent potential loss of data.

The back-up process results in the copying of information on FCL's information processing facilities onto storage media that might be retained for periods of time and in locations unknown to the originator or recipient of the information.

The practice and frequency of back-ups and the retention of back-up copies vary from system to system and are detailed in FCL backup procedures.

Information can sometimes be susceptible to corruption due to hardware or software failure and users are encouraged to keep regular backups of their data on the server. The IT Department shall make reasonable attempts to recover data, if the back-up becomes corrupted, however it might not be possible to provide this in all situations.

Software and hardware auditing

FCL has an obligation to ensure that only legal software is used on FCL information processing facilities and to support this, appropriate technology shall be used to audit FCL owned software on FCL owned equipment or mobile devices without an employee's permission.

Note

While FCL has control over their own employees and information processing facilities, they cannot necessarily control third party employees and information processing facilities to the same level. This may mean that these employees have non-FCL software on their systems. This shall be excluded from any audits.

Top management shall be notified of any illegal or unlicensed software discovered as part of the audit process.

Removal of equipment

No FCL information processing facilities may be borrowed, removed or moved from a designated location, without the explicit permission of the IT Manager or designated Owner, as appropriate.

For permission to be granted the necessary forms detailing the purpose of the removal of the equipment and the equipment details shall be filled in by the applicant and countersigned by the appropriate Line Manager, IT Manager, Information Security Manager, or designated Owner as mentioned above.

Telephone systems

In some jurisdictions, legislation protects the privacy of telephone conversations. Without Court approval in many jurisdictions, it is illegal to record or monitor audio or visual telephone conversations without advising the participants that the call is being monitored or recorded.

Monitoring and recording of telecommunications by employers for the purpose of evaluating client service, measuring workload, or other business reasons is permitted by law but requires that participants be informed that the call is being monitored or recorded.

The use of FCL telephone equipment creates transaction records (which include the number called and the time and length of the call) that shall be reviewed by FCL management as part of routine accounting procedures.

Employees who use FCL telephones including mobile devices for personal or other purposes should be aware that Line Managers have access to records of all calls made from FCL telephones assigned to their use and that such records shall be used for administrative purposes.

Access by third parties

Third parties with access to FCL information processing facilities who have executed contractual agreements with FCL may access appropriate resources and shall comply with FCL's guidelines and policies.

All requests from third parties that have responsibilities for accessing FCL information processing facilities shall submit a request via the Service Desk and include, but not be limited to the following:

- date;
- name of individual requesting access;
- organisation;
- address and telephone number of person requesting access;
- name of FCL systems contact;
- resources required;
- IP address of internal machine to be accessed;
- IP address of external company;
- port number and service required;
- operating system;
- application software required; and
- length of time access required for (maximum 12 months).

The Information Security Manager shall review and determine the level of risk associated with each request. Additional security controls may be required prior to access being granted. The Service Desk shall contact the Requester with the account and access information if access is granted.

Third parties may access FCL information processing facilities to gain access to their home site however, they shall comply with any published rules for their use.

The employer of external contractors or companies shall be held jointly liable for any actions on their part or that of their employees, agents or subcontractors that violate the FCL's Acceptable Use Policy.

Any external visitors that have been authorised to use FCL information processing facilities shall be bound by FCL's procedures and are liable for the actions of the attendees.

Investigation of information security incidents

FCL has an obligation to protect the confidentiality, integrity and availability of FCL information processing facilities by ensuring that the resources are available, secure, and accessible.

To meet this obligation, the Information Security Manager shall monitor and respond to network breaches as they occur.

FCL recognises that principles of freedom of speech and privacy of personal information hold important implications for the use of electronic communications. FCL affords privacy protections to electronic communications comparable to those it traditionally affords paper mail and telephone conversations. This policy reflects these firmly held principles within the context of FCL's legal and other obligations.

FCL policy prohibits its employees from seeking out, using, or disclosing personal information without authorisation, and requires them to take necessary precautions to protect the confidentiality of personal information encountered in the performance of their duties or otherwise. This prohibition applies to all types of electronic communications.

Incidents and information security breaches shall be advised to the Information Security Manager either directly or via the Service Desk, via internal or external complaints, the intrusion detection system or discovered in the normal course of business.

The actions taken after a breach of this policy or any supporting FCL procedures shall be dependent on the particular circumstances.

The Information Security Manager shall:

- determine the impact of the alleged breach and take, without notice, any necessary action if FCL or client information, resources, and services are adversely affected to prevent immediate and further damage to FCL network. Such actions may include:
  - suspension of an account;
  - disconnection of systems or disable network ports;
  - termination of running processes and programs; and
  - any other actions deemed necessary to restore network services.

- gather evidence and provide information as required to comply with any internal investigation. In some cases, the users may not be notified first or it may be required by law to provide the information without notifying the user;
- determine if FCL is legally obliged to report the incident to the authorities;
- investigate and address any complaint. Such investigation may involve examining systems and network activity logs and transaction logs. Contents of emails and other files shall not be examined as part of a routine except in the following circumstances without the holder being notified:
  - a court order requires that the content be examined and disclosed; or
  - the Information Security Manager is instructed in writing by top management as part of an internal investigation.

The Information Security Manager or the IT Manager may have to conduct an internal investigation relating to systems performance or problems which require that user files to be examined to identify a cause. In this case, guidance shall be sought from top management prior to the work being undertaken. During such investigations if any illegal activity is discovered, then the investigation will be referred immediately to the Information Security Manager.

If the breach does not prevent other users from accessing network computer resources or result in disciplinary action or contractual action being taken, as appropriate, being instigated, the Information Security Manager shall notify the IT Manager of the activities causing the breach. The matter shall result in disciplinary action or contractual penalties if the user refuses to comply.

Network access may be terminated immediately if the breach has been caused by a third party with a contractual agreement with FCL while the breach is investigated.

Users should be aware that, during the performance of their duties, employees who operate and support FCL information processing facilities shall need, from time to time, to monitor transmissions or observe certain transactional information to ensure proper functioning of FCL's information processing facilities and services. On these and other occasions, they might inadvertently observe the contents of emails.

Except as provided elsewhere in this policy or by law, they are not permitted to:

- hear, see, or read the contents intentionally;
- observe transactional information where not germane to the foregoing purpose; and
- disclose or otherwise use what they have seen, heard, or read.

Disciplinary action shall be taken against any IT employees observed intentionally gaining access to user data which has no relevance to the investigation.

One exception to the foregoing paragraph is the need for systems personnel to inspect the contents of electronic communications and transactional records when redirecting or disposing of otherwise undeliverable email or other quarantined electronic communications.

Such unavoidable inspection of email or other electronic communications shall be limited to the least invasive level of inspection required to perform such duties. This exception does not exempt IT employees from the prohibition against disclosure of personal and confidential information, except insofar as such disclosure equates with good faith attempts to route the otherwise undeliverable email or other electronic communication to its intended recipients.

Re-routed email and other electronic communications normally shall be accompanied by notification to the recipient that the email or other electronic communication has been inspected for such purposes.

Except as provided above, IT employees shall not intentionally search email, other electronic communications records or transactional information for breaches of law or policy but shall report breaches discovered inadvertently in the course of their duties.

Reporting information security incidents

All users of FCL's information processing facilities shall be required to note and report any observed or suspected information security incident, security weaknesses in or threats to those systems and services.

Appendix 36—Management roles and responsibilities

FCL management level employees shall be responsible for the following with regard to employees:

- on-boarding employees in accordance with the relevant FCL recruitment procedures;
- defining requirement specifications for new employees;
- ensuring that all employees have the necessary skills sets and personal qualities to perform their role in attainment of the IMS objectives;

- assigning appropriate team mentors to new employees;
- ensuring that employees observe appropriate IMS policies and procedures;
- performing employee appraisals, and determining/initiating action based on the findings of appraisals;
- identifying opportunities for employee training, and determining requirements for the ongoing employee development;
- providing authorisation for employee training;
- updating employee records following an appraisal; and
- ensuring that their employees, and relevant third parties under their control, comply with the requirements of the IMS.

Specific managers shall have individual job descriptions for their delegated roles.

Appendix 37—Asset owners

Objective and role

Asset Owners are existing employees who have this responsibility in addition to their job description. This is not a full-time job, but an additional role that the employee undertakes as part of their 'normal' job.

Note

The Asset Owner is often the Risk Owner.

Problems and challenges

The Asset Owner is faced with assessing the value of an asset to the organisation and then classifying it to determine how labelling and handling of that asset shall be carried out for its lifecycle in FCL. Over classification can add additional cost and bureaucracy to the asset handling and information security controls required, while under classification can leave an asset at risk from threat actors as it has not been properly classified and therefore may not have an appropriate level of information security applied to it.

Asset owners shall ensure that their assets are only accessed by authorised users and in the manner authorised and shall regularly review the access rights to the assets that they own.

Role and responsibilities

An Asset Owner is an employee who has responsibility for a predetermined set of assets or processes (referred to collectively as 'assets') and who is therefore personably accountable and responsible for the integrity, availability, confidentiality, auditability and accountability of the asset. An Asset Owner shall also be accountable for the consequences of the actions of users of these assets.

The Asset Owner is usually a senior employee who is responsible for the control and supervision of one or more specific assets, the asset may be:

- hardware;
- software;
- information;
- an information processing system;
- part of an information processing system;
- a business process;
- a building; or
- any component that supports the processing of FCL or client information.

The Asset Owner shall authorise access to, or use of, the asset and collaborates with the Information Security Manager to classify the asset and appointing Custodians to act on their behalf in their duties.

Asset Ownership shall convey authority and responsibility for, but not limited to:

- judging the asset's value and importance to FCL, in association with the Information Security Manager and/or Business Continuity Manager;

- defining the classification review schedule, in association with the Information Security Manager;
- assisting in the Business Impact Analysis (BIA) process with the Business Continuity Manager;
- classifying the asset and reviewing control and classification decisions;
- ensuring that information asset security and application system controls are in place;
- reviewing classifications and ensuring they are current;
- authorising and revoking access to the asset;
- assigning Custodian(s) to act on their behalf;
- communicating control and protection requirements to suppliers of services and users;
- reviewing service delivery for their asset(s) against service level agreements (SLAs);
- acting where service delivery does not meet the contractual SLA;
- participating in the risk assessment and risk acceptance process;
- ensuring that backup data is available in the event of any destruction or other computer centre outage;
- responsible for the implementation of adequate physical and local security safeguards for information that they own; and
- be competent to make decisions relating to the assets that they own.

Asset Owners shall be responsible for the classification of all of their assets to ensure that the correct levels of security and monitoring procedures are set up and maintained. The FCL Information Security Policy and its supporting procedures specify the minimum requirements that should be in place.

For practical purposes, it is likely that responsibility for implementing the security measures required shall be delegated to the Custodian. Irrespective of this delegation, the Asset Owners shall retain personal accountability.

Note 1

Within this document, reference normally is made to the Asset Owner, but it should be borne in mind that the tasks might have been delegated to the Custodian.

Note 2

Where FCL assets are held or controlled by a third party, the same level of responsibility of the Asset Owner remains, however, the Custodian may be a third-party employee. Additional details of responsibilities for an Asset Owner who owns assets held or controlled by a third party are defined in Supplier Relationships in Chapter 7, Section 7.4.10.1.2.

Authority

The Asset Owner shall have the authority to:

- classify assets that they own (indicating security controls to be in place);
- review access rights their 'their assets' and manage accordingly;
- review and comment on asset classification; and
- appoint Custodians to perform some of their tasks, while still retaining accountability and responsibility for the Custodian's actions.

Contacts

Internal

Within FCL to all relevant employees.

External

Relevant third-party suppliers.

Reports to

Normal reporting line for the post holder in their Job Description.

Appendix 38—Risk owners

Objective and role

Risk Owners are existing employees who have this responsibility in addition to their job description. This is not a full-time job, but an additional role that the employee undertakes as part of their 'normal' job.

Note

The Risk Owner is often the Asset Owner.

Problems and challenges

The Risk Owner is faced with identifying risks to their assets and being able to assess the risks to them and managing these risks in association with assistance from the Information Security Manager and other members of FCL. Cost effective and efficient solutions shall be determined, implemented, managed, and monitored that do not restrict work but allow it to continue in a safe and secure manner.

Role and responsibilities

A Risk Owner is an employee who has responsibility for undertaking risk assessments and defining risk treatment for a predetermined set of assets.

Risk Ownership shall convey authority and responsibility for, but not limited to:

- reviewing classifications and ensuring they are current with the Asset Owner and Information Security Manager;
- undertaking the risk assessment and risk acceptance process;
- determining, with the relevant Asset Owners, the controls to be implemented;
- maintaining the risk register;
- regularly reviewing the risk register; and
- be competent to make risk decisions relating to assets.

Risk Owners shall be responsible for the determining the risks to all of assets for which they are responsible to ensure that the correct levels of security and monitoring procedures are set up and maintained. The FCL Information Security Policy and its supporting procedures specify the minimum requirements that should be in place.

For practical purposes, it is likely that responsibility for implementing the security measures required shall be delegated to the Custodian. Irrespective of this delegation, overall, the Risk Owners retain personal accountability for risk assessment and risk treatment of 'their assets' with input from the Asset Owner and the Information Security Manager.

Note

Where FCL assets are held or controlled by a third party, the same level of responsibility of the Risk Owner remains, however, the Custodian may be a third-party employee. Additional details of responsibilities for a Risk Owner who owns assets held or controlled by a third party are defined in Chapter 5, Section 5.2.1.

Authority

The Risk Owner shall have the authority to:

- review and comment on asset classification;
- undertake risk assessments for assets, in association with the Asset Owner, Information Security Manager and other relevant Employees;
- determine risk treatment plans for assets, in association with the Asset Owner, Information Security Manager, and other relevant Employees;
- ensure that risk treatment plans are implemented for assets, in association with the Asset Owner, Information Security Manager, and other relevant employees;

- manage risks to assets on an ongoing basis; and
- report risk status to the relevant management committees.

Contacts

Internal

Within FCL to all relevant employees.

External

Relevant third-party suppliers.

Reports to

Normal reporting line for the post holder in their Job Description.
For this role, additionally to the Risk Committee.

Appendix 39—Custodian

Objective and role

Custodians may be appointed to take on the day to day operations of an Asset Owner or a Risk Owner. While they may carry these out for the relevant Owner, the relevant Owner shall still retain accountability and responsibility for the asset or risk. This shall still be the case if the Custodian is a third party.

Problems and challenges

The Custodian shall be responsible for carrying out the relevant Owner's requirements, and these may well be in conflict with the operational requirements of the department where the Custodian is located, and so these shall be managed. Where the Custodian is a third party, there are often management and reporting issues as well as cultural ones that shall be overcome to ensure a successful outcome.

Role and responsibilities

The Custodian shall often be (but not always) a member of the IT Department. Depending on whether they are the Custodian for an Asset Owner or a Risk Owner, the tasks are slightly different.
Custodian responsibilities shall include:

- complying with the requirements set by the Asset or Risk Owner;
- working closely with the Asset or Risk Owner to gain a better understanding of their requirements;
- documenting what security controls have been implemented and where gaps exist in current controls. This documentation shall be made available to the relevant Asset or Risk Owner;
- ensuring the availability of the Asset Owners information for processing on a continuing basis;
- monitoring, with the System Administrators, any access breaches;
- reporting all breaches to the relevant reporting point and the Information Security Manager, where relevant;
- undertaking tasks that should normally be undertaken by the Asset Owner but are more easily completed by the Custodian (e.g. technical IT monitoring and reporting);
- provision and de-provision access rights as authorised by the Asset Owner (i.e. the Information Owner);
- ensure that all relevant technical and physical security policies and procedures shall be implemented with appropriate tools to protect the confidentiality, availability, integrity, auditability, accountability, and nonrepudiation (where needed) of the information for which they are Custodians;
- document all of their processes and procedures for approval by the Asset Owner;
- understand the risks to information and information processing facilities and advise the Asset Owner of suitable risk treatment;
- providing alerts and reports to the Asset or Risk Owner, as required;

- maintaining their competence to undertake tasks for which they are the Custodian undertaking those tasks on behalf of the relevant Owner; and
- undertaking any other tasks as required.

Note

A Custodian may be a third-party employee who is acting on behalf of FCL Asset or Risk Owner. The Custodian still shall comply with the relevant Owner's requirements and maintain communications with them about any event that may affect any FCL or client information or information processing systems.

Authority

The Custodian shall have the authority to:
- perform tasks as agreed with the relevant Owner.

Contacts

Internal

Within FCL to all relevant employees.

External

Relevant third-party suppliers.

Reports to

Normal reporting line for the post holder in their Job Description.
    As a Custodian, to the relevant Owner that appointed them.

Appendix 40—Management review agenda

Item no.	Description	ISO 9001[a]	ISO 22301	ISO/IEC 27001	ISO 45001
1	Apologies for absence	✓			
2	Approval of previous minutes	✓			
3	Matters Arising	✓			
4	Status of actions from previous management reviews	9.3.2 a)	9.3 a)	9.3 a)	9.3 a)
5	Changes in external and internal issues that are relevant to the management system[b]	9.3.2 b)	9.3 b)	9.3 b)	9.3 b)
	Information on the performance and effectiveness of the quality management system, including trends in:	9.3.2 c)		9.3 c)	
6	Customer satisfaction and feedback from relevant interested parties	9.3.2. c) 1)		9.3 d)	
7	The extent to which quality objectives have been met	9.3.2. c) 2)			
8	Process performance and conformity of products and services	9.3.2. c) 3)			
9	Nonconformities and corrective actions and continuous improvement	9.3.2. c) 4)	9.3 c) 1	9.3 c) 1)	9.3 d) 1)

Item no.	Description	ISO 9001[a]	ISO 22301	ISO/IEC 27001	ISO 45001
10	Monitoring and measurement results	9.3.2. c) 5)	9.3 c) 2)	9.3 c) 2)	9.3 d) 2)
11	Audit results	9.3.2. c) 6)	9.3 c) 3)	9.3 c) 3	9.3 d) 4)
12	The performance of external providers	9.3.2. c) 7)			
13	The adequacy of resources	9.3.2 d)			9.3 e)
14	The effectiveness of actions taken to address risks and opportunities	9.3.2 e)		9.3 e)	9.3 b) 3) and 9.3 d) 6)
15	Opportunities for improvement	9.3.2 f)	9.3 d)	9.3 f)	9.3 g)
16	Fulfilment of information security objectives			9.3 c) 4)	
17	Changes in the needs and expectations of interested parties				9.3 b) 1)
18	Changes in legal and other requirements				9.3 b) 2)
19	Extent to which management system objectives have been met				9.3 c)
20	Results of evaluation of compliance with legal and other requirements				9.3 d) 3)
21	Consultation and participation of workers				9.3 d) 5)
22	Relevant communications with interested parties				9.3 f)
23	Other opportunities for improvement not covered by the above	✓			
24	Any other business	✓			
25	Date, place and time of next meeting	✓			

[a] *ISO/IEC 17025 has the same requirements for a management review as ISO 9001, but uses a different standards numbering system, which is not reproduced above. ISO/IEC 17025 does not mandate inputs and outputs, as is the case in some other management standards. ISO 17025 requires that the management review 'shall take account of' the items listed under ISO 9001 above.*

[b]*This applies to the different management systems, Quality, Information Security, Health and Safety.*

Appendix 41—Document control checklist

Digital forensics procedures

The following checklist shall be filled in for all documents produced in FCL and shall be retained for audit.

Requirement	Completed on (dd/mm/yyyy)	Completed By (sign)[a]
Requirements of FCL Document and Record Control Procedures shall be met		
References to other documents shall not refer to a version but the document title		
No names shall be referred to—only job titles, apart from the Document Author in the document control section for reports and procedures. All Owners and Reviewers shall be referred to by job role		
The correct and current FCL template shall be used for the document		
All document control metadata shall be entered as required by the template on document creation		
Tables of content shall be regenerated using <f9> (Function Key F9) or References | Update Table		
The Copyright notice shall always be present and appropriate. It shall never be removed		

Continued

Requirement	Completed on (dd/mm/yyyy)	Completed By (sign)[a]
All documents shall be written in the third person. However, gender should not be used (i.e. 'he' and 'she' etc. should not be used)		
All tables and figures shall have appropriate captions appropriately underneath them. A list of figures shall be produced after the table of contents		
Where acronyms are used, they shall be defined in full on first use, followed by the acronym. The acronym should then be used in the text. A glossary shall be inserted at the end of the document as an Appendix		
Tense use shall be consistent throughout and always in the present tense		
In FCL documents, the following words shall be used to define requirements: 'shall' indicates a requirement; 'should' indicates a recommendation; 'may' is used to indicate that something is permitted; 'can' is used to indicate that something is possible, for example, that an organisation or individual is able to do something		
Short sentences shall be used		
Wordiness shall be avoided		
Jargon shall be avoided		
Visio and other diagrams shall be embedded in the text so that they can be edited in the document (Insert | Object | Create from File)		
Footnote and endnote use should be kept to a minimum		
Formatting shall be correct and consistent		
Spell checking shall be undertaken using word (<f7>—Function Key F7) as well as a visual check		
All documents shall be peer reviewed prior to release		

[a] *Whilst this is a checklist for document production, the auditing and signing process is optional. It helps to prove that the document has gone through the processes on the check list.*

Appendix 42—Document metadata

Note

The metadata below shall be used in FCL, other forensic laboratories will use their own internal standards for metadata.

Document metadata shall be entered on the first page of any report produced by FCL. HTML pages in the IMS do not use this process, as defined in this Appendix, as below:

Header

The header is as below.

CLASSIFICATION	
FCL Logo	Subject

Classification

This is the classification of the report, as defined by FCL's classification process.

- alignment centre;
- font Arial 14, bold;

- paragraph spacing before 12 pt.;
- paragraph spacing after 12 pt.;
- tables 1 in., left.

Logo

FCL Logo.

Subject

This is the Subject from Word Properties:

- alignment left;
- font Arial 7;
- paragraph spacing before 3 pt.;
- paragraph spacing after 3 pt.;
- tables 1 in., left.

Note

The box surround is not visible.

Document details table

The document details table is as below:

Title			
Subject			
Synopsis	:	Synopsis	
Authors	:	Author(s)	
Keywords	:	Keywords	
Issue	:	Issue	
Release Date	:	Date of Release	
File Name	:	File name	
Status	:	Status	
Deliverability	:	Original	File
	:	Copy 1	Recipient 1
	:	Copy 2	Recipient 2
Page Count	:	number of pages	
Signed	:		
Proposal Wording if appropriate			

Title

This is the Title from Word Properties.

Subject

This is the Subject from Word Properties.
The Title and Subject are both:

- alignment centre;
- font Arial 16, bold;
- paragraph spacing before 12 pt.;
- paragraph spacing after 12 pt.;
- tables 1 in., left.

Note

All of the following are:
- alignment Left;
- font Arial 12, normal;
- paragraph spacing before 6 pt.;
- paragraph spacing after 6 pt.;
- tables 1 in., left.

Synopsis

A synopsis of the document in two or three paragraphs.

Author(s)

Name of author(s) from Word Properties.

Keywords

Tags from Word Properties.

Issue

The version number of the document.

Release date

The date the document was released to the recipient.

File name

The name of the file.

Status

The status of the document (Draft or Issued).

Deliverability

To whom the document is issued. Typically, original is to file and copies are numbered.

Page count

Pages in document from Word Properties.

Signature

Signature of the Document Owner.

Proposal wording

Where the document is a proposal, the following text shall be added:

This proposal contains information that is commercially confidential to client. It is supplied to client on the understanding that it will not be communicated to any third party, either in whole or in part, and that it will be used solely in connection with the evaluation of the commercial bid contained herein.

Footer

The footer is as below.

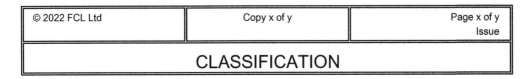

© 2022 FCL Ltd	Copy x of y	Page x of y Issue
CLASSIFICATION		

Copyright

This is standard text

- alignment left;
- font Arial 7;
- paragraph spacing before 3 pt.;
- paragraph spacing after 3 pt.;
- tables 1 in., left.

Copy number

This is in the form 'Copy x of y'

- alignment right;
- font Arial 7;
- paragraph spacing before 3 pt.;
- paragraph spacing after 3 pt.;
- tables 1 in., left.

Note

This is an optional field, depending on the classification of the document.

Page number

This is in the form 'Page x of y' and is from Word Properties

- alignment right;
- font Arial 7;
- paragraph spacing before 3 pt.;

- paragraph spacing after 3 pt.;
- tables 1 in., left.

Classification

This is the classification of the report, as defined by FCL's classification process.

- alignment centre;
- font Arial 14, bold;
- paragraph spacing before 12 pt.;
- paragraph spacing after 12 pt.;
- tables 1 in., left.

Note

The box surround is not visible.

Second and subsequent pages

The second and subsequent pages shall only contain the header and footer as defined above.

Appendix 43—File naming standards

Note

The file naming below shall be used in FCL, other forensic laboratories will use their own internal standards for file naming.

Documents and records

Files shall all be named as follows:

<date><name><version><author's initials>.<extension>

The date shall be inserted in 'yymmdd' order so that the most recent version an always be 'sorted' to the top of the directory listing.

Draft documents

Draft documents are those documents that have not been formally issued. These documents are still in draft and shall undergo several review phases before they are issued.

Documents typically shall pass through a number of draft stages, typically three which are identified by the version numbers 0.1, 0.2, etc.

Version	Description
0.1	First draft of a document. It shall include an employee's own edit pass of the document. The version number can increment to 0.11, 0.12, 0.13, etc., until the Document Author is sure the document is ready for an internal review
0.2	Second draft of a document. It shall include the implemented edits from the Reviewer(s). The version number can increment to 0.21, 0.22, 0.23, etc., until the Document Author is sure the document is ready to be issued for an internal or external review
0.3	Third draft of a document. It shall include the implemented edits from the internal or external review. The version number can increment to 0.31, 0.32, 0.33, etc., until the Document Author is sure the document is ready to be issued for release

As illustrated within each main draft stage, version numbers can increment (e.g. to 0.21 and 0.22) if the document progresses without moving on to the next stage. This allows for the fact that editing is an iterative process and enables an employee to identify different versions of a document when it is at any one draft stage.

For example:

220101 Proposal V0.1 DLW.doc

Indicating that the file was created on 1 January 2022, it is a client proposal first draft (v0.1), was created or updated by DLW and is a Word document.

File names shall be made as meaningful as possible and kept as short as practical.

Every day that the document is worked on, the date shall be updated and if appropriate the author's initials and version. Where the document is worked on or reviewed by the same person a number of times in the day after it has been worked on or reviewed by someone else, the days data shall be suffixed by an 'a', 'b', 'c', etc. as required.

For example:

220101a Proposal V0.1 DLW.doc

Indicating that the file was created on January 1, 2022, this is the second time that DLW has worked on this document after someone else has worked on it during January 1, 2022, it is a client proposal first draft (v0.1), was created or updated by DLW and is a Word document.

Files of different types such as flowcharts, presentations, spreadsheets, etc. shall follow the same principles and always begin at document number V0.1 with appropriate file extensions.

Issued documents

Issued documents are those documents that have passed through the draft review process internally. These documents are no longer in draft and are issued for use (i.e. are live).

The first issued version of a document shall be version 1.0.

For example:

220111 Proposal V1.0 DLW.doc

Indicating that the file was created on January 11, 2022, it is a client proposal released (v1.0), was updated by DLW and is a Word document.

The second issued version of the document shall be version 2.0.

For example:

220111 Proposal V2.0 DLW.doc

Indicating that the file was created on January 11, 2022, it is the second version of the client proposal released (v2.0), was updated by DLW and is a Word document.

If only a small change is required to an issued document, the Document Author shall consider an intermediate increment for the document number. For example, if only one paragraph is changed in the proposal above, the updated issued version could be:

220111 Proposal V1.1 DLW.doc

Indicating that the file was created on January 11, 2022, it is an updated client proposal released (v1.1), was updated by DLW and is a Word document.

All documents shall be retained for an indefinite period from the date of issue, but they may be archived.

The IMS

Note

All documents shall conform to this standard apart from those that form part of the IMS (apart from records). The logic for this is that the manual maintenance of links between a large number of files that comprise the IMS means that where the system is updated there would be disproportionate effort in checking the linkages. Therefore, HTML files and forms used in the IMS shall be named as below:

<name>.<extension>

Naming is as above.

The version number of all documents is that set at the change control page.

Appendix 44—Watermarks in use in FCL

Note

The watermarks below shall be used in FCL, other forensic laboratories will use their own internal standards for watermarks.

The following watermarks are in use:

- Draft—for Comment;
- Issued;
- Not authorised for Release;
- Uncontrolled Copy when Printed.

  These are applied in Word using Design | Watermark | Custom Watermark.

Note 1

'Uncontrolled copy when Printed' is used for all copies of procedures printed from the IMS and is used to ensure that the integrity of the document control system is enforced. However, occasionally IMS documented procedures may be released outside FCL, and it is essential that they are marked with this watermark.

Note 2

When released outside FCL this fact shall be recorded with the relevant recipient, date of issue and version, so that updates can be transmitted when available to ensure the third party always has the current version.

Appendix 45—Document review form

Note

The document review form below shall be used in FCL, other forensic laboratories will use their own internal document review form.

Review the attached document(s) and then sign and return this form together with one fully marked up copy of the document(s).

- project, client, business process, or Management System name;
- document name;
- version;
- Document Author name;
- Reviewer name;
- date sent;
- return by date; and
- comments.

  Please mark up all edits on the attached printed document. Write any overall comments in this space.

- reviewed by:
- signature;
- position; and
- date.

  Please note that our continuing ISO 9001 quality system compliance relies upon this form being returned.

Appendix 46—IMS calendar

The IMS calendar shall contain sample details of the following types of audits and tests to be carried out during the year on a month by month basis. The can include but not be limited to:

- 1st party (internal) audits—case processing;
- 1st party (internal) audits—management systems;
- 2nd party (supplier) audits;
- access reviews (physical access);
- account rights and access reviews (logical access);
- business continuity (BCP) exercises and tests;
- calibration tests;
- CAPA audits and PIR reviews;
- clear screen and clear desk inspections;
- contract reviews;
- due diligence reviews;
- external and internal penetration testing;
- evacuation testing for FCL;
- firewall audits;
- internal penetration and vulnerability tests for the network;
- maintenance audits;
- Management reviews;
- management system committee meetings;
- perimeter scans for open ports;
- physical asset audits;
- PIRs for new equipment or processes;
- produce metrics for management system objectives;
- refresher training for all employees;
- regular management system refresher training;
- UPS testing;
- vulnerability scanning for servers, workstations, mobile devices and network devices; and
- workstation scans.

Note 1

All audits and test results are regarded as records within FCL shall be filed in the Electronic Records Management System (ERMS). CAPAs are raised and followed through to conclusion.

Note 2

Audits of management system may be structured according to the relevant management standard or be process based, following a process through from start to finish for representative samples to determine that relevant procedures have been followed. Forensic case processing shall always follow this approach for sample cases to be audited.

Appendix 47—Audit plan letter

Note 1

The details of the audit need to be filled in as appropriate where <DEFINE> is shown in the text below.

Note 2

Depending on whether the audit is of an area (e.g. HR) or a process (e.g. Change Management), delete 'area' or 'process' below as appropriate.

This document is a plan for the internal audit of <DEFINE>.

Objectives of the audit

The objectives of this audit are to:

- determine the conformity or nonconformity of the <DEFINE> area/process;
- determine the effectiveness of the implementation of the management system in the area/process;
- fulfil the requirements of <DEFINE> regarding the regular auditing of procedures;
- fulfil the requirements of the relevant Legislation, MSS, other standard or business process for the ongoing auditing of <DEFINE>;
- ensure that <DEFINE> is continuously monitored, managed, and improved.

Scope of the audit

This audit covers all activities within the area/process.
   The basis of the audit will be the procedure and associated files within the <DEFINE>.
   The Auditor is <NAME>.
   The Auditee is <NAME>.

Audit schedule

The audit will take place at <DEFINE> at <NAME> on <DD/MM/YY>.

Audit report

An audit report shall be produced following the audit, to be issued on <DD/MM/YY>.

Appendix 48—Audit reporting form

- department;

Reference

- area;
- audit date;
- details of the nonconformity;
- nonconformity category (Major, Minor, or OFI);
- Auditee function;
- Auditee name;
- Auditee signature;
- Audit date;
- Auditor name; and
- follow-up date.

Appendix 49—Corrective action request (CAR) form

- CAR number;
- Auditor name;
- date;
- business area;
- contact;
- phone;
- email;
- issue requiring corrective action;
- source (e.g. Management review, internal audit, external audit, self-assessment test, etc.);

- source reference (detail the actual origin—i.e. audit document reference, etc.);
- standard (e.g. ISO 9001, ISO 14001, ISO/IEC 17020, ISO/IEC 17025, ISO 45001, ISO 20000, ISO/IEC 27001, other—define);
- Audit marking (Major Nonconformity/Minor Nonconformity/Opportunity for Improvement (OFI);
- what is the nonconformity/OFI/Issue to be addressed;
- details of where the evidence of this is to be found (Document reference, system, or procedure);
- what is the impact of this on FCL;
- action to be taken (what—e.g. Change xyz document, Change Procedure 'Procedure name,' etc.);
- where is the Action to be taken (define location);
- action owner (name);
- date for completion;
- action owner (signature);
- agreed CAR Owner (name);
- date agreed;
- agreed CAR Owner (signature);
- CAR action is approved/rejected;
- what further is required and by whom (if CAR is rejected);
- CAR action agreed (name);
- date agreed;
- CAR action agreed (signature);
- CAR action referred to (name);
- date;
- CAR PIR carried out by (name);
- date;
- what further is required and by whom (if appropriate)
- CAR action referred to (name);
- date;
- CAR PIR agreed (signature); and
- date.

Appendix 50—Opening meeting agenda

The Lead Auditor shall:

- introduce auditing staff and the Auditee shall introduces their employees;
- confirm the statement of confidentiality and ensure that the auditee is aware of the security procedures for retaining the auditee's sensitive information and how this will be cared for during the audit, if appropriate;
- enquires if there are any secure facilities that can be used during the audit for securing sensitive information when the Auditor(s) is/are off site;
- confirms the standard against which the audit will be performed is <Define Standard(s)>;
- confirms the Statement of Applicability is up to date, if appropriate;
- confirms the scope of the audit;
- explains how the audit will proceed;
- describes method of nonconformity reporting;
- provides definitions of nonconformity (Major and Minor) and Opportunities for Improvement (OFIs);
- explains how corrective actions relating to nonconformities should be undertaken;
- confirms the Audit Plan (interviews and dates/times);
- identifies any problems (employee absences, etc.);
- obtains any documentation that was not submitted in advance and requested (for whatever reason);
- ensures that other employees are aware of the visit (where necessary);
- ensures management approval is in place for asking sensitive questions, viewing sensitive documents, or accessing sensitive areas;
- confirms that 'Guides' are available to assist Auditors;
- confirms availability of office services (desk, etc.—as agreed);

- confirms start and finish times and lunch arrangements;
- answers any questions from Auditee;
- thank them all for their assistance;
- finalises plan for audit—last minute issues; and
- starts the audit.

Appendix 51—Closing meeting agenda

The Lead Auditor shall:

- thank the auditee for their hospitality, assistance and co-operation;
- re-confirm confidentiality undertaking, if appropriate;
- re-confirm the standard against which the audit was performed;
- re-confirm the scope of the audit;
- inform auditee of the overall outcome of the audit;
- provide definitions of nonconformity (Major and Minor)—if required;
- summarise any nonconformities and Opportunities for Improvement (OFIs)—if required;
- invite the auditee to comment on the nonconformities and/or OFIs—if required;
- explain the required corrective actions and invite the auditee to comment them—if required;
- obtain auditee signature on all reports;
- inform the auditee of the requirement to maintain the systems and advise FCL of any changes to the system that may affect FCL management system, if appropriate;
- return any paperwork to the Auditee that is not to be taken off site as part of the audit file; and
- thank the auditee again, pack up, and leave.

Appendix 52—Audit report template

- executive summary;

Introduction

- audit objective;
- Major nonconformities summary;
- Minor nonconformities summary;
- OFIs and other tasks;
- follow-up;
- 1 audit overview;
- 1.1 introduction;
- 1.2 audit objectives;
- 1.3 audit scope;
- 1.4 audit criteria;
- 1.5 audit logistics;
- 1.6 approach;
- 1.7 purpose;
- 1.8 distribution;
- 2 summary of findings;
- 2.1 Major nonconformities;
- 2.2 Minor nonconformities;
- 2.3 OFIs and other tasks;
- Appendix A—Auditees;
- Appendix B—Audit Team;
- Appendix C—Distribution list;
- Appendix D—Audit Markings;
- Document control.

Appendix 53—Root causes for nonconformity

- an isolated incident;
- architectural weakness;
- client requirements changed without advising FCL;
- communications failure;
- component failure (e.g. media);
- defined procedure is not complete;
- defined procedure not followed;
- deliberate act;
- equipment failure;
- failure to comply with Legislation, Regulations, Standards, or Contractual Terms;
- failure to follow procedure;
- failure to integrate security into the business and projects;
- failure to manage assets;
- failure to manage suppliers;
- inadequate BCP/DRP process;
- inadequate incident response procedures;
- inadequate testing;
- inconsistent setting of baseline;
- incorrect baseline set;
- incorrect policy or procedure;
- incorrect training/education;
- insufficient monitoring;
- insufficient patch management;
- insufficient risk management;
- insufficient threat management;
- lack of clear ownership;
- lack of consistent use of policies and procedures across enterprise;
- lack of due diligence (HR);
- lack of due diligence (Suppliers);
- lack of enforcement of existing Legislation, Regulations, Standards, or Contractual Terms;
- lack of procedures;
- lack of resource;
- lack of tools;
- lack of training/education;
- management failure;
- missing policy or procedure;
- no defined procedure;
- no one accepts responsibility;
- operator error;
- poor design;
- poor project management;
- process changed, but procedure not updated;
- records that should be kept are not being kept;
- security requirements not defined;
- supplier failure;
- tool failure;
- trying to meet unrealistic deadlines.

Chapter 5

Information risk management

5.1   A short history of risk management

Note 1

This chapter is heavily based on what has been implemented in FCL. Each forensic laboratory must make its own decisions as to how to manage risk and what tools to use.

Note 2

FCL uses the term information security to cover cyber security as well as it regards cyber security as a subset of information security; therefore, information security covers the whole of securing information.

Risk management has been used by man since the dawn of time on a personal basis. Typically, it was used then for personal survival, is it safe to walk through the jungle? It is safe to attack this animal for food, etc.? This was individual responsibility and accountability.

One of the greatest moves from individual responsibility and accountability was when Chancellor Otto von Bismarck started the 'social insurance' schemes in Germany in 1881. This signalled a move from individual responsibility and accountability to corporate and governmental. This spread throughout much of the world over the next 50 years.

The 1920s saw British Petroleum setting up the Tanker Insurance Company which was a 'captive', emphasising internal financing of risk. Historically, insurance had always, where it existed, been to a third party. The 1920s also saw Frank Knight published '*Risk, Uncertainty and Profit*', separating risk from uncertainty. John Maynard Keynes published '*A Treatise on Probability*', where he emphasised the importance of relative perception and judgement when determining probabilities of events.

The 1950s saw Life Insurance companies determining mortality rates for smokers and how they could affect premiums. In 1956, Dr. Wayne Snider of the University of Pennsylvania suggested that the 'professional insurance manager shall be a risk manager'.

1965 saw Ralph Nader published '*Unsafe at any Speed*'—unmasking the faults in the Corvair. This heralded the birth of the consumer movement and turned caveat emptor to *caveat vendor*.

1980 saw the birth of the Society for Risk Analysis in the United States, and in 1986, the Institute for Risk Management was formed in London.

In 1992, the Cadbury Committee in the United Kingdom suggested that organisational governing boards are responsible for setting risk management policy, assuring that a forensic laboratory understands the risk it faces and accepting oversight for the risk management process. This was later followed by other countries following this lead, and there were successor committees set up in the United Kingdom (Greenbury 1995, Hempel 1998, Turnbull 1999 and a review of Turnbull in 2004).

In 1993, the title 'Chief Risk Officer' was used in GE Capital.

1995 saw the fall of Barings, precipitated by Nick Leeson. The failures leading up to this reignited interest in risk management. 1995 also saw the development of the first risk management standard—AS/NZS 4360. Since then, there have been many risk-based initiatives and the risk management culture is becoming firmly embedded in corporate culture.

The current history of information risk management standards used in FCL is based on:

- SP 800-30 March 2011—Guide for Conducting Risk Assessments—National Institute of Standards and Technology;
- SP 800-39 September 2012—Managing Information Security Risk—National Institute of Standards and Technology;

A Blueprint for Implementing Best Practice Procedures in a Digital Forensic Laboratory. https://doi.org/10.1016/B978-0-12-819479-9.00002-2

- ISO/IEC 27001: 2022 Information technology—Security techniques—Information security management systems—Requirements;
- ISO 27005: 2018 Information technology—Security Techniques—Information Security Risk Management; and
- ISO 31000:2018—Risk management—Guidelines on principles and implementation of risk management.

In addition to these standards, there are a number of well-established risk management methodologies that can be used to manage information security risk in a forensic laboratory. These include:

- EBIOS (France);
- IRAM (United Kingdom);
- MARION (France);
- MEHARI (France);
- OCTAVE (United States); and
- Österreichisches IT-Sicherheitshandbuch (Austria).

Even if it has deeper foundations, risk management, as it is practiced today, is a post-1960s phenomenon rather than relying on purchasing third-party insurance policies.

Whilst FCL holds appropriate insurance for its areas of operations and to meet the legislative requirements in its jurisdiction of operations, it also uses risk management for managing its business, covering its information security risk, business continuity risk, data protection and privacy risk, environmental risk, and health and safety risk. This chapter focuses on information security risk and not business opportunity risk, business continuity risk, data protection and privacy risk, environmental risk, and health and safety risk though the same processes shall be used for them all.

5.2 An information security risk management framework

5.2.1 Some definitions

- A **Resource** is defined as a physical asset or an element or component of an information system, manual, or computerised. It could be the process itself, a part of the process, data, hardware or software, data files, paper files, transaction profiles, terminals, terminal input/output, disk/tape volumes, user IDs and programmes;
- An **Owner** is the person who has responsibility for a predetermined set of resources and who is therefore accountable for the integrity, availability, confidentiality, auditability, and accountability of the resources. In FCL, the term 'Resource Owner' refers to an Asset or Risk Owner who is also accountable for the consequences of the actions of users of these resources; and
- A **Custodian** may be appointed by the Resource Owner to undertake day-to-day tasks and decision making on the data, on their behalf.

5.2.2 Overview

The loss of confidentiality, integrity, availability, accountability, auditability, authenticity, and reliability of FCL's information and related services can have a severe, if not catastrophic, impact. FCL shall appropriately secure information and information processing systems that it owns or has in its custody.

The provision of effective, unobtrusive, and affordable information security has always been a major organisational challenge. This is becoming increasingly critical with the increase in system connectivity, information and data processing systems, the amount of information and data being processed, and the distributed nature of the processing. Too often the provision of appropriate security measures is secondary to the provision of functionality and is often a 'bolt on' afterthought.

Protecting information processing assets is an essential organisational goal and shall be achieved by:

- establishing and implementing a comprehensive and systematic programme for information security risk management; and
- recognising that management of information security risk is an integral part of the risk management process.

FCL has adopted a multitiered risk management process as defined by the US National Institute of Standards and Technology Special Publication (NIST SP) 800-39.

This approach addresses risk at three levels:

- Organisational;
- Mission/business process; and
- Information system level (Fig. 5.1).

FIG. 5.1 Multitiered risk management process.

Tier 1 provides a prioritisation of mission/business functions which in turn drives investment strategies and funding decisions thus affecting the development of an enterprise-wide enterprise architecture that embeds information security at Tier 2 and the allocation and deployment of management, operational and technical security controls at Tier 3.

FCL shall capture these risks in the high-level corporate risk register.

Tier 2 addresses risk from a mission/business process perspective and is driven by decisions at Tier 1. Tier 2 risk management activities include:

- defining the mission/business processes needed to support FCL's missions and business functions;
- prioritising the mission/business processes with respect to the strategic goals and FCL's business objectives;
- defining the types of information needed to successfully execute FCL's mission/business processes, the criticality/ sensitivity of the information, and FCL's internal and external information flows;
- incorporating information security requirements into the mission/business processes; and
- establishing an enterprise architecture with an embedded information security architecture that promotes cost-effective and efficient information technology solutions consistent with FCL's strategic goals and objectives and performance evaluation and continuous improvement as defined in Chapter 4, Sections 4.6.2, 4.9.1, and 4.10.

Tier 2 activities directly affect the activities carried out at Tier 3. The risk assessment and management process in FCL derives the Statement of Applicability (SoA) as defined in Section 5.5.10.

FCL uses the activities carried out at Tier 2 to provide feedback to Tier 1 and may lead to changes in Tier 1 processes or findings.

FCL captures these risks in the individual business unit risk registers.

Tier 3 addresses risk from an information system perspective and is guided by the risk context, risk decisions, and risk activities at Tiers 1 and 2.

Tier 3 risk management activities include:

- identification of information assets;
- identifying information Resource Owners;
- classifying information assets;
- identifying, assessing, and managing risks to the identified information assets;
- deriving the SoA from selections from ISO/IEC 27001 Annex A and elsewhere; and
- managing the implementation, assessment, authorisation, and ongoing monitoring of information security controls in the SoA.

FCL shall capture these risks in the information security risk register.

The risk management framework used in FCL is shown below, and it can be applied to all, or any, part of a forensic laboratory.

It shall be remembered that risk management is not a 'fire and forget' process, and it is a process of continuous improvement and as a forensic laboratory's risk profile changes as its business processes, or the environment in which it operates, change.

ISO/IEC 27001:2005 (not 2022), ISO/IEC 27005, and ISO 31000, along with other management standards, imply, recommend, or mandate a Plan-Do-Check-Act (PDCA) process as shown in Fig. 5.2.

FIG. 5.2 Plan, Do, Check, Act process.

Plan—establish the context, develop risk treatment plan, define risk acceptance criteria, etc.;
Do—implement the risk treatment plan;
Check—assess and where possible measure conformity, reporting results to top management for review;
Act—take corrective action for continuous improvement.

This has been implemented in FCL, as shown in Fig. 5.3.

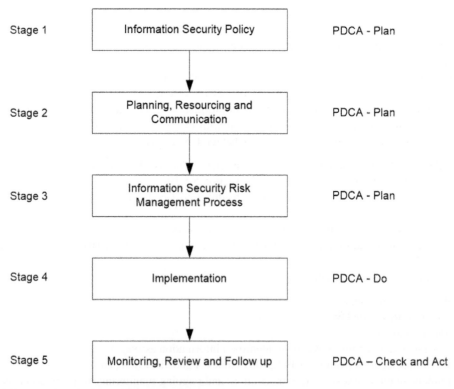

FIG. 5.3 The FCL Information Security System Management Framework.

Each of the stages in the diagram is described briefly below and in depth later in this chapter. The relevant part of the PDCA process is identified on the right of the diagram above for reference:

- **stage 1**—the starting point for implementing appropriate information security based on risk management is to define the scope or context of the information security management system (ISMS). Once this process has been completed, an Information Security Policy appropriate for the scope or context is developed based on the scope or context defined. The FCL Information Security Policy is defined in Chapter 4, Appendix 20;
- **stage 2**—to effectively implement the Information Security Policy, roles and responsibilities shall be identified and adequate resources allocated. It is also essential that there is effective communication with all internal and external interested parties as appropriate at each stage of the risk management process and concerning the process as a whole. A communication and consultation plan shall be developed. The template for the Communication Plan is defined in Appendix 1;
- **stage 3**—the assets within the scope or context identified shall be considered in terms of risks that they face and impacts to FCL should a risk crystallise. Controls to reduce the likelihood or impact of the risk shall be identified and agreed with the Resource Owners and residual risk shall be agreed with them. The outcome of this step is an Information Security Plan or Risk Treatment Plan (RTP) and the SoA. The Resource Owner formally accepts the residual risk;
- **stage 4**—the Information Security Plan or RTP shall be implemented with an appropriate security awareness and training programme; and
- **stage 5**—to ensure that implemented controls work effectively, monitoring, and reviewing of their effectiveness shall be undertaken. This will include follow-up activities for continuous improvement.

5.2.3 Critical success factors

The successful implementation of information security shall depend on a number of factors, such as:

- a clear understanding of the security requirements and risks facing FCL or the assets within the scope or context;
- an approach to implementing security that is consistent with FCL's culture;
- appropriate communication of comprehensive guidance on the Information Security Policy, standards, and procedures to all employees;
- appropriate training, awareness, and education;
- effective selling and marketing of information security to all employees;
- establishing an effective Information Security Incident Management process as defined in Chapter 7, Section 7.4.3;
- implementing an appropriate process for measuring the effectiveness of the implemented controls for treating the risks within the scope or context as defined in Chapter 4, Section 4.9;
- knowledge of all relevant Legislative and Regulatory requirements as defined in all implemented management standards in the IMS, specifically as defined in Chapter 4, Section 4.5.2 and evaluated at the management reviews. The management review agenda is defined in Chapter 4, Appendix 40;
- security policy, objectives, and activities being based on business objectives; and
- a visible and demonstrable support and commitment from top management as defined in all implemented management standards.

5.2.4 Information security risk components

5.2.4.1 The components

There are a number of component parts to the information security risk process. Each is briefly described below:

- legal, statutory, and contractual requirements with which FCL shall comply;
- policies, principles, objectives, and requirements to support its business operations at FCL;
- unique security risks which could result in significant losses if they occur;
- **Information security risk**—an information security risk is the potential that a given threat will exploit a vulnerability to cause loss or damage to an asset or group of assets, and directly or indirectly affect FCL. The information security risk level is determined from the combination of the asset values, levels of threats to, and associated vulnerabilities of, an asset and their impact values;

- **Threats**—a threat is something that could cause a risk to happen. They can come from the natural environment or from human action (accidental or deliberate). Some examples of security threats are defined in Appendix 8; and
- **Vulnerabilities**—a flaw or weakness in a system that could be exploited by one or more threats. A vulnerability that cannot be exploited by a threat is not harmful to the asset. Some examples of security vulnerabilities are defined in Appendix 9;

5.2.4.2   Relationship between the components

The relationship between the components was clearly described in BS 7799 and is shown in Fig. 5.4.

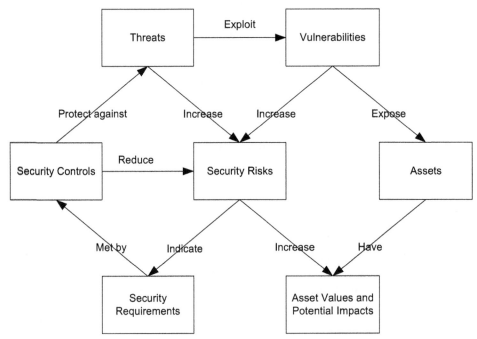

FIG. 5.4   Relationship between the components.

Note

This diagram is not in ISO/IEC 27001, BS 7799's successor.

5.3   Framework stage 1—Information security policy

5.3.1   Overview

As part of the risk management process, FCL shall develop and implement a Risk Management Policy. This policy shall include the objectives for, and management commitment to, information security risk management. It shall be aligned with the FCL goals and objectives. The FCL Risk Management Policy is defined in Appendix 10.

Top management shall set a clear direction and demonstrate their support for and commitment to the Information Security Management System (ISMS) by issuing a formally agreed and documented Information Security Policy across FCL. Top management shall approve the policy.

However, before a policy can be prepared for a forensic laboratory, the scope or context of the ISMS shall be defined. It may be the entire organisation but could be a single site or a particular system or service. The FCL's IMS and ISMS Scope Statement is defined in Appendix 11.

The FCL Information Security Policy serves as the foundation of the ISMS programme and the basis for adopting specific procedures and technical controls. It is the first step in establishing an information security culture that strives to make all employees aware of the need for information security and the role they personally have to play.

Note

This stage follows the process defined in Chapter 4, Section 4.7.3.

5.3.2 Establish the context and scope

This process occurs within the framework of FCL's strategic, organisational, and risk management context. This shall be established to define the basic parameters within which risks shall be managed and to provide guidance for decisions within more detailed risk management studies. This sets the context and scope for the rest of the risk management process and defines the boundaries for the FCL Information Security Policy.

5.3.2.1 External context

This involves defining FCL's relationship to its environment, identifying the strengths, weaknesses, opportunities and threats. The context can include FCL's financial, operational, competitive, political, social, client, cultural, and legal aspects. FCL shall identify both internal and external interested parties and also consider their perceptions and establish communication strategies with these parties. This step is focused on the environment in which FCL operates.

5.3.2.2 Internal context

Before the process can be undertaken FCL's and its capabilities, as well as its goals and objectives and the strategies to achieve them. Areas to be considered shall include, but not be limited to:

- any projects and their relationship to FCL;
- costs of activities, both direct and indirect;
- intangibles (reputation, goodwill, etc.);
- legal context;
- FCL's capabilities;
- FCL's missions and goals;
- revenue and entitlements, budgets;
- the criticality of operations; and
- FCL's structure.

5.3.2.3 Establish the scope

Setting the scope and boundaries of the IMS that has assets to be protected shall involve defining the:

- assets in the scope;
- extent of the risk management activities to be carried out in the defined area;
- extent of the risk management project in time and location;
- roles and responsibilities for supporting risk management and information security management in the defined area;
- physical location, its boundaries, the project or activity and establishing their goals and objectives;
- relationships across the boundaries of the defined scope area; and
- technology in use in the defined area.

ISO/IEC 27001:2005 recommended defining the scope as a minimum using the following four headings:

- assets;
- location;
- organisation; and
- technology.

However, this has not been carried forward to ISO/IEC 27001:2022.

5.3.2.4 Risk evaluation criteria

FCL shall decide and agree the criteria against which the risks are to be evaluated. Decisions concerning risk acceptability and risk treatment may be based on operational, technical, financial, legal, social, or other criteria. These shall depend on FCL's policies, goals, and objectives and the interests of interested parties.

The risk criteria shall assist in determining a tolerable level of risk for management, aspects, and activities that are critical to the outputs, functions, and activities.

Defining risk criteria shall assist in:

- identifying the more important risks,
- preparing appropriate treatments and/or counter measures; and
- providing a benchmark against which the success of the action plan can be measured.

Criticality ratings are defined in Appendix 12.

5.3.3 Information security policy content and format

A well-written and appropriate Information Security Policy is the cornerstone of, and the first regular step in, implementing appropriate information security and good corporate governance in any organisation. It informs and gives directions to employees that have access to a forensic laboratory's or client's information or information processing facilities.

Policies vary widely in their scope, detail, and content, but they all establish the overall management intention and outcomes.

Typically, a policy document is short and high level. In a forensic laboratory, there may be a single document or a set of documents depending on the size of the forensic laboratory, its requirements, and circumstances.

Within its scope, an effective Information Security Policy shall be:

- achievable with clearly defined responsibilities for all employees and users;
- enforceable and enforced both procedurally and technically, and with sanctions when breaches occur;
- implementable through processes, procedures, technical controls, or other methods; and
- support legislative, regulatory contractual obligations, and other business requirements.

There are no defined rules for the format or content of an Information Security Policy. However, a structure of the policy using four main headings may be useful.

5.3.3.1 Statement of executive intent

This is a short statement in the Information Security Policy setting the scene for the forensic laboratory and the required executive outcomes. It includes:

- a definition of information security, its overall objectives, and scope within the forensic laboratory; and
- emphasis on why information and information processing facilities need to be protected.

5.3.3.2 Responsibilities and accountabilities

This covers direction on the responsibilities and accountabilities of individual employees having access to a forensic laboratory's information or information processing facilities. This shall be explicit, enforceable, enforced and shall focus on the proper and authorised use of information and information processing facilities. Typically, it will refer to detailed requirements found in the contract of employment (or service provision for third parties), the employee handbook and job descriptions. A variety of job descriptions are defined in the Appendices of various chapters in this book that relate specifically to the IMS.

5.3.3.3 General direction

There are a number of areas of general direction that may be covered in the policy and these include, but are not limited to:

- auditing and monitoring and review requirements;
- business continuity, disaster recovery, and resilience planning;
- information handling;
- information security incident management;
- information security requirements derived from legal and regulatory sources;
- information security training and awareness; and
- the method of risk assessment and criteria for the acceptability of risks.

Inspection of FCL's Information Security Policy shows that all of these elements are present.

5.3.3.4 Policy review and ownership

All IMS policies shall be owned and regularly reviewed.

The owner of the FCL Information Security Policy is the Information Security Manager and their delegated authority comes from top management who shall endorse all IMS policies.

Policies shall be reviewed on an annual or regular basis unless any influencing changes affect this regular review. This is defined in all of the policies in the Appendices in Chapters 3, 4 and this chapter.

5.3.4 Information security policy communication

Once the FCL Information Security Policy has been developed and endorsed by the top management, it shall be distributed, understood, implemented, and maintained by appropriate means to all employees. This shall include:

- ensuring that as revisions occur the training, awareness, and contractual measures are updated as defined in Chapter 4, Sections 4.7.2 and 4.7.3;
- including the FCL Information Security Policy as part of the contract for all third-party service providers;
- including the FCL Information Security Policy, or at least a reference to conformity with it and all other policies and procedures as part of the contract of employment for employees;
- including the FCL Information Security Policy as part of the induction and ongoing awareness training, where records shall be kept of all attendees, as defined in Chapter 4, Sections 4.7.2 and 4.7.3; and
- where appropriate, making employees sign two copies of the FCL Information Security Policy, where HR and the employee each retain a copy.

A forensic laboratory will have to choose how they achieve this requirement, but the ones listed above are the most common. Further guidance is defined in Chapter 4, Section 4.7.4.

5.4 Framework stage 2—Planning, resourcing and communication

5.4.1 Management commitment

According to the ISMS International User Group, one of the key factors for successful information security in any organisation is the:

- visible and demonstrable support and commitment from all levels of management starting with the Chief Executive Officer or equivalent;

Demonstrable and visible top management direction on, and commitment to, information security, shall positively influence FCL's information security culture throughout the organisation.

Top management's commitment to information security shall be demonstrated by ensuring that:

- an ISMS shall be established, as part of the IMS, implemented and maintained in accordance with internal requirements and relevant international standards as appropriate;
- appropriate resources shall be allocated to information security as defined in Chapter 4, Section 4.7.1;
- there shall be a process of evaluating the performance of the ISMS in place and that the results of the evaluation are reported to management for review and shall be used as a basis for continuous improvement as defined in Chapter 4, Section 4.10.

Note

Each forensic laboratory should define their own metrics to determine if the information security objectives required by ISO/IEC 27001 6.2 are being met and how continuous improvement is being implemented; and

---

- this is reflected in the FCL Information Security Policy.

5.4.2 Planning

Information security planning is the product of the ISMS scope, the FCL Information Security Policy and information security risk management processes. Some of the outputs of the planning process may affect the FCL Information Security

Policy and scope and vice versa. This may lead to iteration between planning and policy as organisational and resourcing issues are resolved. It may also be that the development of SoA also requires further iterative work.

Any new information processing system, changes in existing information processing system or take on of work that may affect existing information processing systems shall ensure that information security requirements, based on risk management, are addressed throughout the project from the initiation to the Post Implementation Review (PIR).

After developing the draught FCL Information Security Policy, preparations for the subsequent stages in the framework shall include:

- defining IMS and ISMS responsibilities. Specific ones are defined in Job Descriptions in the Appendices in this book;
- defining physical security responsibilities based on the Physical Security Policy, defined in Chapter 2, Appendix 2;
- determining and implementing interactions between IT and information security;
- establishing an effective risk management structure; and
- establishing an effective IMS and ISMS management structure.

There may be other plans to consider, and these shall depend on a forensic laboratory's specific requirements, but those above are the minimum set for any organisation and are used in FCL.

5.4.3 Responsibility and authority

The responsibilities, authorities, and interactions of the employees who manage the IMS and the ISMS shall be defined and documented. This is specifically important where cross departmental boundary actions have to be taken, such as:

- any problem areas for the management of risk;
- areas where information security risks need to be managed;
- areas that may need further treatment of risks until the level of risk becomes acceptable according to the agreed risk appetite;
- areas that will need appropriate cross functional business continuity plans developed, documented, and exercised;
- areas where incident management processes may affect the different departments in FCL;
- areas where risk treatment solutions may have to be recommended, initiated, installed, maintained, and monitored; and
- internal and external communication channels to all levels of employees.

5.4.3.1 Cross functional fora

A number of committees to oversee all aspects of the IMS, including risk management, shall be defined with their terms of reference defined in the Appendices in Chapter 4.

5.4.3.2 Information Security Manager (ISM)

Depending on the size of a forensic laboratory, it may appoint a full or part time ISM, with or without a team to support them. The ISM may have a functional reporting path to any department but shall have a 'dotted line' responsibility to top management and relevant Management Committees, as needed.

The ISM shall direct, coordinate, plan, and organise information security activities throughout FCL. The ISM shall act as the focal point for all communications related to information security with employees, including clients and suppliers. The ISM shall work with a wide variety of employees from different departments, bringing them together to implement controls that reflect workable compromises as well as proactive responses to current and future information security risks.

The ISM shall be responsible for defining and implementing the controls needed to protect FCL information as well as information that has been entrusted to it by any client or other third party. The position shall involve overall responsibility for information security regardless of the form that the information takes (paper, digital, optical, magnetic media, audio tape, embedded in products or processes, etc.), the information handling technology employed (servers, desktops, laptops, mobile devices, telephones, local area networks, file cabinets, etc.), or the people involved (employees, vendors, outsourcing firms, etc.).

Threats to information and information processing systems addressed by the ISM include, but are not limited to:

- information unavailability;
- information corruption;
- unauthorised information destruction;

- unauthorised information modification;
- unauthorised information access;
- unauthorised information usage; and
- unauthorised information disclosure.

These threats to information and information processing systems include consideration of physical security matters only if a certain level of physical security is necessary to achieve the required level of information security (e.g. as is necessary to prevent theft of mobile devices).

A job description for the ISM is defined in the Chapter 12, Appendix 15.

5.4.3.3 Information Security Management Team

A forensic laboratory may have an ISM supported by an Information Security Management Team who shall undertake the following:

- assist in developing, implementing and monitoring information security matters, including risk management;
- assist HR in areas of information security, including training and awareness;
- assist in managing and monitoring information security incidents;
- supporting operational management and monitoring of control systems;
- performing internal audits and technical testing of information security controls;
- provision of advice on information security matters to projects and trading partners, as appropriate; and
- undertaking business continuity management responsibilities.

This is not an exhaustive list but is the minimum set of requirements for an Information Security Management Team tasking.

5.4.3.4 Resource owners

Resource ownership conveys authority and responsibility for the tasks defined in Chapter 4, Appendix 38.

Resource Owners shall be registered with the ISM with details of the resources which they own.

Note

Even if a Custodian is appointed, the Resource Owner retains personal accountability and responsibility for the resource(s) that they 'own'.

5.4.3.5 Custodians

The Resource Owner may appoint a Custodian to undertake day-to-day tasks and decision making on the data, on behalf of the Resource Owner.

The Custodian is usually a member of the IT Department.

Custodian authority and responsibility is defined in Chapter 4, Appendix 39.

Custodians shall be registered with the ISM with details of the resources that they manage on behalf of the Risk Owner(s).

5.4.3.6 Information users

The success of security in practice depends on the performance of the users. An information user is an individual user, who has permission from the Resource Owner to access and use the Resource Owner's information, information processing facilities or resources. An information user may well be a Resource Owner of their own information, or someone else's.

Information user responsibilities shall include:

- being responsible and accountable for all access to information processing systems made by their user identity;
- bringing security exposures, misuse, or nonconformity situations to management and the ISM in a timely manner;
- complying with all security controls designated by either the Resource Owner, the ISM or top management;
- complying with information asset security and application system controls as specified by the Resource Owner and any relevant third-party service supplier;
- effectively using control facilities and capabilities;
- ensuring that their system, information, and application passphrases meet specified requirements;

- ensuring that their passphrases are not shared and are properly protected at all times;
- not disclosing any information to anyone without the consent of the Resource Owner, or their Line Manager; and
- using information processing systems only when authorised and only for approved purposes.

5.4.4 Resourcing

Resourcing requirements within a forensic laboratory will depend on the implementation, management, and monitoring requirements for information security within the forensic laboratory and the size and complexity of the organisation.

In FCL, top management shall make available the appropriate resources to implement, manage, and maintain the ISMS programme. These resources shall have appropriate skills and a planned training agenda to ensure that their skills are maintained and match FCL's requirements as defined in Chapter 4, Section 4.7.1.

A simple Information Security Management Team structure showing its place in FCL is defined in Fig. 5.5.

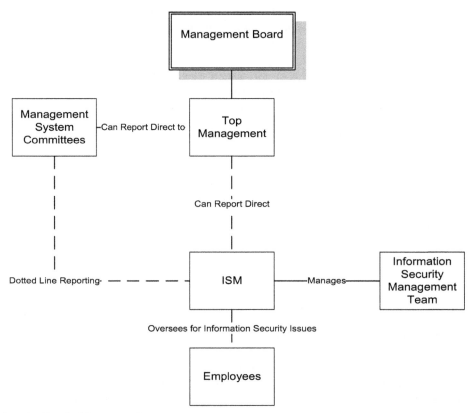

FIG. 5.5 FCL Information Security Management Team structure.

5.4.5 Communications and consultation

5.4.5.1 Communications

Throughout the process of designing, implementing, maintaining, monitoring, and improving information security within FCL, appropriate communication with the target audience shall be undertaken.

There is no 'one size fits all', but the messages to be sent shall be tailored for the specific intended audience.

A communication plan shall be developed at the earliest stages of the process therefore ensuring that both internal and external interested parties are aware of the issues relating to both the risk itself and the process to manage it.

Appropriate communication shall:

- ensure that all interested parties are aware of their roles and responsibilities;
- ensure that the varied views of interested parties are considered; and
- improve understanding of risk and the risk management process.

Security communications are defined as an interactive process of exchange of information and opinion, involving multiple messages about the nature of risk and risk management. Inappropriate communication can lead to a breakdown in trust by interested parties or poor information security implementation.

These requirements are in addition to the requirements defined in Chapter 4, Section 4.7.4.

5.4.5.2 Consultation

Consultation is a process of informed communication between interested parties and FCL on an issue prior to the making of a decision or a determination. It can be characterised as:

- a process not an outcome;
- focusing on inputs to decision making not necessarily joint decision making; and
- impacting on a decision through influence not power.

Note

More detailed guidance on Communication and Consultation for risk management is defined in Section 5.5.5.

5.5 Framework stage 3—Information security risk management process

5.5.1 Overview

Information Security Risk Management is the systematic application of management policies, procedures, and practices to the task of establishing the context, identifying, analysing, evaluating, treating, monitoring, and communicating information security risks.

Information security management can be successfully implemented with an effective information security risk management process. There are a number of national and international standards that specify risk approaches, and a forensic laboratory can choose which it wishes to adopt. A list of some of these are defined in Section 5.1.

The FCL ISMS is a documented system that shall describe the information assets to be protected, FCL's approach to risk management, the control objectives and controls, and the degree of assurance required.

Note

An ISMS can be applied to a specific system, components of a system or to a forensic laboratory as a whole.

5.5.2 Benefits of risk management

As with all processes, there are a number of benefits from expending effort on implementing, managing and monitoring risk management with associated resource costs, and these include, but are not limited to:

- a move from reactive to proactive management;
- awareness of the need to identify, quantify, and treat risk;
- compliance with relevant legal, regulatory, and contractual requirements;
- confident decision making based on a rigorous risk management process;
- effective allocation and use of resources in the risk management process;
- enhanced safety and security;
- improved financial reporting;
- improved identification of threats and opportunities;
- improved incident management and prevention;
- improved operational effectiveness and efficiency;
- improved interested party confidence and trust; and
- loss reduction.

5.5.3 Principles for managing risks

ISO 31000 gives a number of principles for the management of risk that FCL adheres to and these are:

- risk management shall be an integral part of decision making;
- risk management shall be based on best available information;
- risk management shall be capable of continuous improvement and enhancement;
- risk management shall be dynamic, iterative, and responsive to change;
- risk management shall be integrated into business processes;
- risk management shall be structured and systematic;
- risk management shall be tailored to business needs;
- risk management shall be transparent and inclusive;
- risk management shall create value in one or more areas of the business;
- risk management shall explicitly address uncertainty; and
- risk management shall consider human factors.

5.5.4 The FCL approach to risk management

Note

FCL has based their approach to risk on NIST 800-30, NIST 800-39, ISO 31000, and ISO/IEC 27001 and 27005.

The FCL model is defined below based on good practice and combining common areas from well-known standards. Each of the steps below is dealt with in the subsequent sections of this chapter.

A forensic laboratory will need to determine what steps can be combined or omitted (Fig. 5.6).

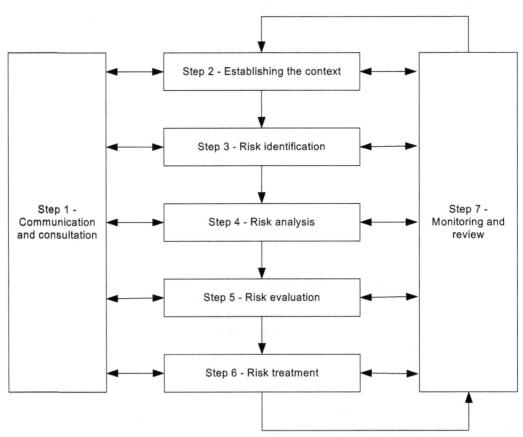

FIG. 5.6 FCL approach to risk management.

- **Step 1**—Communication and consultation—with internal and external interested parties as appropriate at each stage of the risk management process and concerning the process as a whole. A communication and consultation plan shall be developed early in the process;
- **Step 2**—Establishing the context—this involves the establishment of the strategic, organisational and risk management context in which the rest of the process will take place. Risk evaluation criteria against which risk will be evaluated shall be established and agreed. The risk analysis process shall be defined. The resources and assets within the scope also shall be identified so that the risks to them can be analysed and managed.
- **Step 3**—Risk identification—identifying the risks that are relevant to the assets and resources identified in the last step. This shall determine what can happen and how it can happen. Some common types of risks that may be considered are defined in Appendices 6 and 7.
- **Step 4**—Risk analysis—determine the existing controls and analyse risks in terms of consequence and likelihood in the context of those controls. The analysis shall consider the range of potential consequences and how likely those consequences are to occur. Consequence and likelihood may be combined to produce an estimated level of risk. A consequences table is defined in Appendix 5, and the likelihood table is defined in Appendix 13.
- **Step 5**—Evaluate the risk—compare the estimated levels of risk against the preestablished criteria. This enables risks to be ranked so as to identify management priorities. If the levels of risk established are low, then risks may fall into an acceptable category and risk treatment may not be required. FCL's risk appetite is defined in Appendix 14.
- **Step 6**—Treat the risk—accept and monitor the low priority risks. For those above the tolerable level of risk set by the risk appetite, a specific RTP shall be developed and implemented with a management plan which includes consideration of funding. ISO/IEC 27001 requires the use of the controls in Annex A, and those not included shall have their reasons for exclusion defined.

Note

There is nothing to say that other controls cannot be used. CObIT 2019 can provide business aligned information controls and these are defined in Appendix 15. Other frameworks, such as NIST may be used, the choice will depend on what a forensic laboratory wants to use.

- **Step 7**—Monitor and review—the performance of the risk management system and changes which might affect it.

  Each of the steps is defined below.

5.5.5 Step 1—Communication and consultation

Note

This section is specifically aimed at communication and consultation relating to risk management. It is in addition to Chapter 4, Section 4.7.4.

5.5.5.1 Overview

At each step of the risk management process, it is important to consider communication and consultation with all interested parties. A communication plan shall be developed at the earliest stages of the process therefore ensuring that both internal and external interested parties are aware of the issues relating to both the risk itself and the process to manage it.

5.5.5.2 Defining risk communication and consultation

'Risk communication' is defined as an interactive process of exchange of information and opinion, involving multiple messages about the nature of risk and risk management.[a]

Consultation is a process of informed communication between the interested parties on an issue prior to the making of a decision or a determination about risk management.

---

a. National Research Council, 1989. Improving risk communication.

5.5.5.3 The importance of risk communication and consultation

The identification of interested parties and key players shall assist in the consideration of their needs and views.

Good communication is essential in the development of a risk culture. Communication about the risks faced shall establish a positive attitude towards risk management.

Involving others is an essential and crucial ingredient of an effective approach to risk management.

Other benefits shall include:

- **adding value to FCL**—the sharing of information and perspectives on risk shall help to create coherence. It shall identify crucial areas of joint achievement and strategies for FCL and any involved interested party;
- **integrating multiple perspectives**—those involved within FCL and relevant interested parties shall make judgements about risk based on their perceptions. These perceptions can be varied by a number of factors such as, values, beliefs, assumptions, experiences, needs, and concerns. It is important to document these perceptions of identified risks and the understanding of the reasons for them;
- perceptions also vary between technical experts and other interested parties. It is essential to effectively communicate the level of risk if informed decisions are to be made and implemented;
- decisions about acceptability of risk are often based on a range of factors including:
- the degree of personal control that can be exercised;
- the potential for an event to result in catastrophic consequences;
- the distribution of the risks and benefits amongst those affected;
- the degree to which exposure is voluntary; and
- the degree of familiarity with, or understanding of, the activity being assessed.
- there is less understanding of risks where the respondent has little control over them; and
- **making risk management explicit and relevant**—risk is considered implicitly in decision making and thinking. By discussing each step with other relevant interested parties, it shall become a conscious and formal discipline and provide a mechanism to help ensure that past lessons are considered.

5.5.5.4 Developing trust

Communication between FCL and its interested parties shall allow it to develop an association with its 'community of interest' and to establish relationships based on trust.

5.5.5.5 Developing a process of risk communication and consultation

5.5.5.5.1 Interested party identification

Interested parties can be internal or external and are those who may affect, be affected by, or perceive themselves to be affected by the risk management processes.

Interested parties shall be identified. If an interested party is initially overlooked, it is possible that they will be identified later but the benefits of early consultation will have been missed.

Note

It is important to realise that a forensic laboratory does not pick the interested parties, they choose themselves.

5.5.5.5.2 The risk communication and consultation plan

The extent of risk communication and consultation shall depend on the situation and this varies from situation to situation. For example, risk management in the course of local and operational decision-making entails a less formal communication process than strategic risk management.

The essential elements of a risk communication and consultation plan shall include:

- the Risk Communication and Consultation Plan shall be influenced by what it is trying to achieve. It shall:
  - build awareness and understanding about risk within FCL's area of operations;
  - learn about perceived risk from interested parties;
  - influence the target audience;
  - obtain a better understanding of the context, the criteria, the risks faced, or the effectiveness of the risk treatment;
  - achieve an attitude or behaviour shift; or
  - a combination of the above.

- the communication and consultation methods to be used (this may vary throughout the risk management cycle);
- the objectives of the communication and consultation;
- the participants who need to be included (i.e. the interested parties, risk experts, and others as the situation requires); and
- the perspectives of all participants that need to be taken into consideration.

5.5.6 Step 2—Define the approach to risk assessment

The scope and the parameters of the IMS and ISMS shall be clearly defined at the beginning of the process, building on the work in the previous step. This sets the framework for the rest of the process within which risks shall be managed and provides guidance for making decisions. A definition of the boundaries avoids unnecessary work and improves the quality of risk management within a forensic laboratory.

This step shall clarify the following:

- the information and resources that need to be protected;
- the information security requirements;
- the issues that need to be considered in assessing information security risks; and
- the parts of FCL that rely on the accuracy, integrity, or availability of information for essential decisions.

The key components in the scoping of the IMS and ISMS for risk management shall be to:

- define the information assets;
- define the risk activity structure;
- develop risk evaluation criteria;
- establish the laboratory context;
- establish the risk management context; and
- establish the strategic context.

5.5.6.1 Establish the strategic context

Any decisions regarding the management of information security risk shall be consistent with FCL's environment.

This component is focused on the environment in which FCL operates. FCL shall determine the crucial elements that might support or impair its ability to manage its information security risks. The FCL Information Security Policy created at Stage 1 in Section 5.3.3 is one of the inputs at this stage.

FCL shall understand the following:

- its internal and external interested parties, considering their objectives and perceptions;
- its strengths, weaknesses, opportunities, and threats (SWOT analysis); and
- the financial, operational, competitive, political (public perceptions/image), social, client, cultural, and legal aspects of FCL's functions. FCL risk tools such as the PESTLE (Political, Economic, Social, Technological, Legal, and Environmental) approach shall be used for this.

There shall be a close inter-relationship between information security risk management and FCL's strategic business objectives.

5.5.6.2 Establish the organisational context

This component requires an understanding of FCL, its organisation, its capabilities, goals, objectives and the strategies that are in place to achieve them. This shall be used to define the criteria to determine whether a risk is acceptable or not and form the basis of controls and risk treatment options. The general nature of FCL's information assets in broad terms of their tangible and intangible value shall form part of the organisational context.

Failure to achieve FCL's objectives for a specific business activity or project may be partially due to poorly managed information security risks.

5.5.6.3 Establish the risk management context

This component determines the scope and depth of the review of information security risks. This shall involve:

- defining the information security risk management review project and establishing its goals and objectives. This could be a review for the whole of FCL, a specific department, or a specific case or project. The assets within the scope of the review shall be identified;

- defining the resources required to conduct the information security risk management review. The review could be conducted by internal employees or external third-party suppliers. The scope of the review shall determine the need for employee input both for the review team and their respondents. The respondents chosen shall be those best able to answer the relevant questions and also be available. The tools to be used shall also be made available for the review; and
- defining the timeframe and locations to be covered by the information security risk management review project, the time allocated to the review shall be defined and understood so the review team can work towards this goal.

5.5.6.4 Develop risk evaluation criteria

In order to assess the risks, impacts, consequences, and the selection of controls, the quantitative and/or qualitative criteria to be used shall be defined. FCL's risk appetite shall be considered as part of this process.

The development of the detailed risk criteria shall be influenced by a number of factors such as:

- expectations of interested parties and specifically clients;
- legal and regulatory requirements; and
- FCL' goals and objectives.

Appropriate risk criteria shall be determined at the outset of the risk assessment and shall be continually reviewed throughout the risk assessment process. Risk criteria may be further developed and refined to ensure that risk criteria remain current and appropriate.

Decisions concerning risk acceptability and the subsequent risk treatment may be based on the operational, technical, financial, legal, social, humanitarian, other criteria, or a combination of these.

When defining risk criteria, factors to be considered shall include, but not be limited to:

- how likelihood will be defined;
- how the level of risk is to be determined as defined in Appendices 5 and 13;
- nature and types of consequences that may occur and how they will be measured, this shall not just be based on financial loss, but other consequences as appropriate;
- the level where the risk becomes acceptable;
- the timeframe of the likelihood or consequence; and
- what level of risk shall require treatment?

When considering consequence, the following areas shall be considered:

- availability breach;
- confidentiality breach;
- integrity breach;
- regulatory or legislative breach; and
- reputational and employee's morale loss.

Each of which is considered in the consequences table.

5.5.6.5 Define the information assets

An asset is something which FCL finds useful or valuable and therefore requires protection. In the identification of assets, information shall be considered in the wider context than just the IT system(s) within FCL and its associated hardware and software. Hence, FCL shall structure its risk activity based on the categories of assets at risk, as defined in ISO/IEC 27005 Annex B for identification of Primary and Supporting Assets.

All assets within the risk management context shall be identified and recorded to an appropriate level of detail. Any assets to be excluded from the context, for whatever reason, may need to be assigned to another review to ensure that they are not forgotten or overlooked and that all Primary and relevant Supporting Assets shall be accounted for.

The Asset Inventory shall include the following information, as a minimum:

- asset identification number;
- asset description;
- asset classification (if appropriate);
- asset Custodian (if appropriate);

- asset location;
- Resource Owner;
- asset category; and
- date the asset was last audited.

The FCL high-level asset categorisation is defined in Appendix 3.

5.5.6.6 *Information classification and labelling*

To provide a consistent basis for determining the level of protection required, information (whether electronic, paper, or on any other media) and related information processing equipment shall be labelled in accordance with security classification.

FCL's information classification system is defined in Appendix 16. Associated with the classifications will be a minimum level of security that shall be applied to the classified asset, these are defined in Chapter 12, Section 12.3.14.6.

Note

Information classifications will vary between forensic laboratories; different governments have different classification schemes for all government classified information and commercial enterprises will also vary.

5.5.6.7 *Outputs*

This step shall produce the following deliverables:

- information and resources required for the information security risk management review;
- risk evaluation criteria;
- the asset listing for those assets within the scope and context of the information security risk management review;
- the scope and structure of the information security risk management review; and
- the strategic and organisational context that is the subject of the information security risk management review.

All the above information shall be included in a project plan, which shall be endorsed by top management and/or the relevant Resource Owner(s).

5.5.7 Step 3—Undertake a risk assessment

There are a number of different tools and methodologies for undertaking a risk assessment. These range from a paper-based checklist-based approach to a fully functional integrated software tool. Different digital forensics laboratories will adopt different tools and methodologies depending on their own unique requirements.

Whatever standard, tool, or methodology is chosen, all broadly follow the same framework approach. Specialised risk management tools can be used for a detailed or specialised risk assessment in addition to a general one, if needed. Whatever approach is chosen, it shall be used consistently so that a comparison for 'risk on risk' evaluations can be undertaken.

FCL still uses a manual process with spreadsheets as no tools were identified that had the breadth of coverage required to manage all IMS risks in the same tool.

The output from the process shall be captured in the relevant risk register(s) where it can be managed. The risk register structure for FCL is defined in Appendix 17.

5.5.7.1 *Risk identification*

Risk identification seeks to identify, classify, and list all the risks, vulnerabilities, or threats that may affect information assets identified in Section 5.5.6.5 above. This shall produce a comprehensive list of risks that may enhance, prevent, degrade, or delay the achievement of FCL's objectives.

A well-structured systematic approach shall be used to ensure a comprehensive identification of risks. This identification shall include all risks whether they can be controlled by FCL or not. Potential risks not identified at this stage shall be excluded from further analysis, until they are identified and included.

It is not uncommon that certain risks, vulnerabilities, or threats may affect more than one of the aspects of information security (integrity, confidentiality, availability, accountability, auditability, authenticity, and reliability). Risks, vulnerabilities, the threat landscape, and threat actors are continually changing.

The focus shall be on the nature and source of the risk, such as:

- who or what can be harmed?
- what could happen or go wrong?
- where can it happen?
- when can it happen?
- why can it happen?
- how could it happen?

The sources of risk shall be evaluated from the perspective of all interested parties, whether internal or external.

In identifying risks, risks associated with not pursuing an opportunity shall also be considered, remembering that risk also encompasses opportunities.

5.5.7.2 Risk analysis

Risk analysis shall separate the minor acceptable risks from the major risks and provide data for the evaluation and treatment of risks. It shall involve the determination of the consequences arising from an undesirable event and the likelihood of the risk occurring. The level of risk shall be determined by the combination of asset values, likelihood, and consequence assessments in the context of the existing risk treatment.

In determining the existing risk treatment present, various methods may be used including audit, inspection of records, or self-assessment processes for the relevant employees. If a control does exist, it does not mean that it is being used effectively or efficiently. This shall also be assessed and objective evidence that it is being used effectively and efficiently shall be sought.

The risk analysis may be qualitative or quantitative, and some details of the difference between the two methods are defined in Appendix 18. The decision whether to use qualitative or quantitative risk management is an individual choice based on circumstance. FCL has found it easier to use qualitative risk.

- the asset valuation used in FCL is defined in Appendix 4;
- examples of some generic risks found in FCL are defined in Appendices 6 and 7;
- examples of some common threats found in FCL are defined in Appendix 8;
- examples of some common vulnerabilities found in FCL are defined in Appendix 9;
- the consequences of risks crystallising are defined in Appendix 5;
- the likelihood of a risk crystallising. FCL uses a 5-level table, though a 10-level one can be used if more granularity is needed; and
- the risk evaluation process used in FCL and its risk appetite.

Each of the above can be adjusted to suit differing requirements, but consistency shall be maintained once a method has been chosen.

There are a number of published sources that can assist in assessing consequences and likelihoods of risks, these include:

- benchmarks and statistics;
- expert and specialist judgements;
- historical records;
- industry practice and experience;
- past recorded experience; and
- research and studies.

5.5.7.3 Recommended approach

Risk analysis can be both time consuming and resource hungry. The optimum method for conducting a risk analysis is to perform an initial high-level risk analysis of the assets to identify risks that are common and for which there is an established set of baseline controls to treat them and, at the same time, identify risks that need more investigation.

These are risks that are potentially serious and a detailed risk analysis shall be undertaken. This approach has the advantage of treating the majority of risks quickly with a baseline approach and allows time for the detailed risk analysis focusing on the potentially serious risks.

5.5.7.3.1 High-level risk analysis

This high-level risk analysis considers the business values of FCL's information processing systems and the information it handles, and the risks from a business point of view. The following shall be considered in determining which risks require further analysis:

- the business objectives of the information processing system;
- the level of importance of the information processing system and its information;
- the value of the investment to the information processing system; and
- the value to FCL of the information produced by the information processing system.

However, if the business objectives of the information processing system are important to FCL's business objectives, the system replacement costs are high or if the values of the assets are at high risk, then a detailed risk analysis shall be undertaken. Any one of these conditions may be enough to justify conducting a detailed risk analysis.

The 'rule of thumb' for high-level and detailed information security risk assessment is that:

- if a lack of information security can result in significant harm or damage to FCL, its business processes or its assets, then a detailed risk analysis shall be undertaken to identify suitable risk treatment options; or
- otherwise, a baseline approach to risk treatment is appropriate.

5.5.7.3.2 Interdependencies

There may well be information processing systems that are interdependent. In this case, an insignificant system that feeds critical data to another information processing system may well affect the risk analysis results.

These interdependencies shall be examined and where necessary detailed explanations defined for the risk analysis results.

5.5.7.3.3 Detailed risk analysis

For assets that require a detailed risk analysis, this shall involve an asset valuation, a threat, and vulnerability assessment, similar to the high-level risk analysis described in Section 5.5.7.3.1. In this case, however, a more detailed or granular approach shall be used and include specialised tools.

5.5.7.4 Risk evaluation

Once the assets, their values, the vulnerabilities, and threats that may exploit them, their likelihood and consequences have been identified and assessed the risks shall be prioritised.

At this point, the risk is 'gross', in that it has not had any existing controls factored into the gross score to produce the 'net' risk values. As has been said earlier the effective or efficient use of risk treatment shall be evaluated and factored in to reduce the gross risk score appropriately.

This process will produce a list of risks that shall be sorted into a prioritised listing in the relevant risk register so that it is possible to determine the risks that are acceptable and those that are not. This will also:

- assist the top management in deciding the allocation of resources to support risk treatment;
- assist Resource Owners to prioritise risk treatment;
- give an overview of the general level and pattern of risk in FCL; and
- identify the higher risk items.

Some reasons for accepting a risk can include but not be limited to:

- the level of risk is so low that risk treatment is not appropriate;
- the risk is controlled outside of FCL (but a forensic laboratory could choose to avoid the risk); and
- the total cost of the risk treatment (implementation and management) exceeds the benefits.

5.5.7.5 Outputs

This step shall produce the following deliverables:

- a list of assets and their values relative to integrity, confidentiality, availability, accountability, auditability, authenticity, and reliability and replacement costs;

- a list of assets and their asset values mapped to the threats and vulnerabilities and the likelihood and the consequences of the threat occurring;
- a list of assets for which a baseline approach is appropriate;
- a list of assets for which further analysis is required and the results of that detailed risk analysis; and
- a prioritised list of risks for determining risk treatment.

5.5.8 Step 4—Manage the risk

5.5.8.1 Managing the risk

FCL shall manage risks and safeguard its operations to effectively protect its information processing systems, its own information or information entrusted to it by any third parties. Part of this is understanding how to treat the risks to those assets appropriately and realise that risk can never be eliminated, unless the activity that gave rise to it is avoided but can be reduced to an acceptable level. This is the process of managing the risk to the assets.

Risk treatment options shall include:

- reduce the consequences—by implementing controls to reduce the threats and vulnerabilities or by modifying the assets at risk in some way;
- reduce the likelihood of the risk occurring—by implementing controls to reduce the threats and vulnerabilities;
- retain the risk;
- risk avoidance—by deciding not to go ahead with an activity likely to generate risk;
- risk transfer—by arranging for another party to bear part or all of the risk, e.g. insurers; and
- sharing the risk with another party or parties.

These options may be used on their own or in association with one or more other options.
When selecting appropriate risk treatment options, the following shall be borne in mind:

- the current risk treatment in place;
- the effectiveness of the treatment in managing risks, if implemented and operated correctly;
- the fit of the proposed treatment with the current implemented treatments and architecture;
- the resources needed for implementation and management (i.e. employees, funds, equipment); and
- the risk treatment needed to reduce risk to an acceptable level.

5.5.8.2 Outputs

This step shall produce the following deliverables:

- a list of knowingly accepted risks. These may well be affected by the treatment options addressing other risks. Additionally, the Resource Owner shall approve the accepted residual risks; and
- a list of treatment options for the unacceptable risks identified.

5.5.9 Step 5—Select controls

Having identified risk treatment options for the risks identified and had them approved by the Resource Owner, suitable controls to reduce the risks to an acceptable level in line with the risk appetite shall be identified. In FCL, these shall be selected with a cost–benefit analysis (CBA).

Existing and planned controls shall have been considered already for the risk evaluation process. These may be considered at this stage for application to other risks than they were implemented or planned for. It shall be emphasised that unnecessary duplication of controls shall be avoided. It is also possible that an existing or planned control may no longer be justified and may need to be removed, replaced by a more suitable control, or remain implemented due to cost reasons.

When considering controls to be selected, experience dictates that the function of the control shall be identified. Typical functions of controls are:

- **detection**—identify the occurrence of an undesired event;
- **deterrence**—avoid or prevent the occurrence of an undesired event;
- **protection**—protect assets from the occurrence or consequences of undesired events;
- **response**—react to or counter the occurrence of an undesired event; and
- **recovery**—restore the assets to their correct state following the occurrence of an undesired event.

Many protective controls can serve multiple functions. It is usually more cost effective to select protective controls that can serve multiple functions. A well-designed security regime provides 'defence in depth' by using controls that provide a mixture of these functions.

Using the clauses in ISO/IEC 27001, Annex A, these types of controls can be deployed in the following areas:

- A.5 Organisational Controls;
- A.6 People Controls;
- A.7 Physical Controls; and
- A.8 Technological Controls.

5.5.9.1   Risk appetite

Once controls have been selected, the remaining risk shall be evaluated to ensure that it is either within the risk appetite or, if not, additional controls are selected until they are. If this is not possible, the Resource Owner shall knowingly accept the risk.

5.5.9.2   Baseline approach

A baseline approach to risk treatment requires the establishment of a minimum set of controls to safeguard against the most common threats. These baseline controls are compared with existing or planned controls for the scope or context being considered, this shall be done by use of a gap analysis exercise. Those that are not in place are implemented, if applicable.

The risk of the baseline approach is that there may be unidentified assets, threats, or vulnerabilities that are missed by the baseline approach or gap analysis that may seriously prejudice assets in the event of an undesired event. To overcome this, FCL shall set its own baseline of controls to be implemented.

Note

ISO/IEC 27001 requires the risk management process is carried out and not use the baseline approach. However, this does not preclude using a baseline approach combined with a detailed risk management process for assets that fall outside the baseline.

There are a number of sources that can be used for the selection of baseline controls, these include, but are not limited to:

- ISO/IEC 27001 and other standards in the ISO/IEC 27xxx family of standards;
- NIST 800-xxx series provides a number of different documents that can provide baselines,[b] and
- CobIT 2019[c]

5.5.9.3   Factors influencing control selection

There are a number of factors that shall be considered when selecting controls for implementation, and these shall include, but not be limited to:

- compatibility with existing controls;
- compatibility with existing security architecture;
- cost of control to manage over time;
- cost of control to purchase;
- ease of use of the control;
- external mandatory requirements (legislative, governmental, or contractual);
- in house skill to support the control(s);
- proximity of control to asset requiring protection;
- user transparency; and
- where using assured products, the assurance level.

---

b. International Standards are chargeable whilst the NIST 800-xxx series are free downloads from www.nist.gov.
c. CobIT is free to members of ISACA, but otherwise chargeable.

5.5.9.4 Outputs

This step shall produce the following deliverables:

- the Information Security Plan based on the outputs of the risk review.

Whilst no two plans are ever the same, the FCL template is defined in Appendix 2.

5.5.10 Step 6—Prepare statement of applicability

The SoA documents the control objectives and controls for each risk where treatment is considered necessary as well as the mandatory controls defined in Sections 4–10 of the standard.

The decision to select (or reject) particular controls within ISO/IEC 27001 shall be recorded and explained. In some cases, this explanation can be very brief, but in other cases where the choice is complex or has a significant impact on risks more detail shall be provided.

The risk treatment process may also indicate that controls not found in ISO/IEC 27001 are included. These shall also be documented in the SoA.

The SoA Template is defined in Appendix 19.

5.5.11 Step 7—Management approval

The final step in the planning phase is to obtain management approval for the residual risks and for a programme to develop, to operate the ISMS, and implement the RTP. Budgetary cycles may require that an initial RTP be developed and costed at this step.

Approval shall be given at the management review to accept residual risks, though the Resource Owner can accept residual risks and implement an RTP at any time through the Risk Management Committee.

5.5.12 Records and documentation

Documenting each step of the information risk management process and maintaining records (i.e. proof of having performed a task) shall be undertaken for the following reasons:

- it demonstrates that the process has been carried out correctly;
- it facilitates continuing monitoring and review;
- it facilitates sharing information and communication;
- it provides an accountability mechanism;
- it provides an audit trail; and
- it provides evidence of decisions made and approvals given.

The level of records required shall depend on the requirements and complexity of the risk assessment undertaken and shall be retained for later audit or reference.

5.6 Framework stage 4—Implementation and operational procedures

5.6.1 Implementation of the RTP

The RTP shall be produced from the deliverables created during the planning phases of the risk management process defined above. The correct implementation of security controls relies on a well-structured and documented RTP. When the RTP is completed, the Resource Owner's approval shall be obtained for the implementation of the security controls for their risks and/or assets. Top management approval may also be required for all risks as their implementation will have resource and financial implications.

The main elements of the RTP shall include, but not be limited to:

- information security training;
- performance measures;
- proposed actions, priorities, and time plans;
- reporting and monitoring requirements;
- resource requirements; and
- roles and responsibilities of all parties involved in the proposed actions.

Day-to-day management of IMS and ISMS operations and resources shall also be required.

5.6.2 Implementation of controls

Whilst the Resource Owner shall be accountable and responsible for the protection of their assets at risk, it may not be them that are responsible for the actual implementation of the agreed security controls. A senior manager may be given responsibility for the implementation of the RTP. Whoever shall implement the RTP, they shall ensure that the priorities and the schedule(s) outlined in the RTP are followed and the plan is fully implemented.

The RTP and supporting documentation, specifically risk information, can be very sensitive and shall be protected against unauthorised access, modification, disclosure, or erasure.

5.6.3 Training

In addition to the information security awareness and training programme, which shall apply to all employees, specialist training shall be provided for those with specific risk management responsibilities. These may include those who:

- are Resource Owners or Custodians;
- perform risk management;
- undertake audits and security reviews; and
- develop and implement risk treatment.

5.7 Framework stage 5—Follow up procedures

5.7.1 Follow-up

Implemented controls can only work effectively if they are used correctly, properly managed, monitored, and any changes or breaches are detected and dealt with appropriately and in a timely manner.

Over time, there is the real possibility that performance of the RTP will deteriorate if there is no follow up or monitoring.

The management of information security shall be an ongoing process that continues after the implementation of the RTP. All aspects of it shall be audited on a regular basis and at least annually.

Follow-up shall include:

- conformity checking;
- configuration management;
- incident management;
- maintenance; and
- monitoring.

5.7.1.1 Conformity checking

Conformity checking is the process of review and analysis of the implemented controls to check whether the implemented controls, and their output, meet the security requirements documented in the RTP. Conformity checks are sometimes called internal or external audits, Risk and Control Self Assessments (RCSAs), technical testing, management reviews or ongoing checking, and they shall be used to check the conformity of:

- existing information processing systems if changes to the implemented controls have been made, to see which adjustments are necessary to maintain the required security level;
- existing information processing systems if there are influencing changes that may affect the risk profile;
- existing information processing systems on a regular basis to ensure they are still meeting their documented objectives; and
- new information processing systems as part of their implementation and after they have been implemented as part of their PIR.

The controls protecting the information processing systems shall be checked by:

- conducting a planned series of internal or external audits or reviews as defined in Chapter 4, Section 4.9.2 for internal audits and Chapter 12, Sections 12.3.13.2 for external audits;
- conducting periodic planned inspections and tests as defined in Chapter 12, Section 12.3.14.4 and Chapter 13, Section 13.6 for BCP exercising and testing;
- conducting periodic planned management reviews as defined Chapter 4, Section 4.9.3;
- conducting periodic unplanned inspections, exercises, and tests;
- conducting spot checks;

- monitoring operational performance against actual incidents occurring;
- reviewing the continuous improvement process as defined in Chapter 4, Section 4.10; and
- technical testing on an ongoing basis as defined in Chapter 12, Section 12.3.13.2.

Conformity checking shall be based on the agreed controls from the risk analysis results for the scope or context as well as security operating procedures which the top management shall approve. The objectives shall be to ascertain whether controls are implemented and working correctly and are fit for purpose.

5.7.1.2 Configuration management

Information systems and the environment in which they operate are constantly changing. Changes can result in new risks, threats, and vulnerabilities.

Changes to information systems may include, but not be limited to:

- new locations where FCL operates (buildings or countries);
- new or updated connections or interconnectivity;
- new or updated equipment;
- new or updated features;
- new or updated procedures; and
- new or updated software (application or operating system).

When a change to an information processing system occurs or is planned it shall be managed within the configuration and change management process as defined in Chapter 12, Section 12.9.4.2.1. The impact the change will have on the security of the existing information processing systems shall be determined. For major changes that involve the purchase of new hardware, software, or services, an updated risk assessment shall be required to determine additional controls needed to treat the risks identified. Minor changes may not require any additional risk assessments. Whether a risk assessment is required or not is a management decision made by the Resource Owner.

5.7.1.3 Information security incident handling

No information security system works perfectly all the time and information security incidents do occur. ISO/IEC 27001 and 27002 have clauses dedicated to information security incidents (Clauses A.5.24–28). This refers to ISO/IEC 27035 Information technology—Security techniques—Information security incident management that covers this in more detail.

Employees shall be educated to know what to report and where to report it in the case of an information security incident. FCL shall have the capability to analyse the incidents reported, take appropriate action if needed and collect forensic evidence if required.

Information security incident analysis shall:

- assist in the prevention of incidents;
- improve risk analysis and management reviews;
- learn from their experiences;
- raise the level of awareness of information security related issues; and
- understand the main areas of risk that FCL faces.

Information security incident management is fully covered in Chapter 7, Section 7.4.1.

5.7.1.4 Maintenance

Most equipment and controls require maintenance and administrative support to ensure that they continue to function correctly and meet evolving business needs. The cost of maintenance and administration of the controls shall have been considered when selecting the relevant equipment and controls. This is because costs can vary from one control to another.

Maintenance activities shall include, but not be limited to:

- addressing identified vulnerabilities;
- checking of log files;
- installing new versions of software;
- modifying configuration and parameters to reflect changes and additions;
- replacing obsolete or ineffective hardware, software, applications, and controls; and
- undertaking regular preventive maintenance.

Modifications may require changes to documentation, which shall be under formal document change control and configuration management.

Maintenance of IT equipment is fully covered in Chapter 7, Section 7.5.4.

5.7.1.5 Monitoring

Once controls are implemented, they shall be monitored and measured to determine the effectiveness of the controls implemented. Whilst traditional auditing and management reviews check that the controls are in place and operate according to the documented requirements, it is difficult to determine the effectiveness of the controls. This requires the implementation of Information Security Metrics.

Like business objectives, they shall be SMART, as defined in Chapter 3, Section 3.1.17.

Information Security Metrics are an effective and valuable tool for ISMs to discern the effectiveness of various components of their information security programmes. Metrics shall assist in identifying levels of risk in not taking a given action, and so provide guidance in prioritisation of corrective actions. The results of security metrics shall be published to be used in awareness training. Given the feedback from metrics, ISMs shall be able to justify return on investment and answer top management's questions, such as:

- are we getting value for money?
- are we more secure today than we were before?
- are we secure enough?
- how do we compare to others in the same industry sector?
- where are our major problems so that they can be addressed?

There are few standards for security metrics; however, the following exist:

- ISO/IEC 27004—Information technology—Security techniques—Information security management—Monitoring, measurement, analysis and evaluation; and
- SP 800-55—Performance Measurement Guide for Information Security.

To implement a security metrics plan, the top-level steps shall be to:

- create a corrective action plan and implement it;
- determine what security metrics will demonstrate meeting the agreed information security objectives;
- decide which security metrics are important and so the ones to generate;
- define the security metrics programme goal(s) and objectives;
- determine the security metrics reporting process, media and audience;
- develop strategies for generating the security metrics;
- establish a continuous improvement process; and
- establish benchmarks and targets.

The security metrics used by FCL are defined in Appendix 20.

A forensic laboratory should develop its own security metrics and reporting process to support their defined information security objectives.

Appendix 1—FCL communication plan

No two communications plans are the same, but the FCL high-level template is defined below:

- capture all current thoughts from interested parties about communications for this initiative, e.g. ideas, concerns, options, barriers;
- determine the best possible outcomes for this initiative;
- how might you reach these targets?
- what are the outcomes that are most acceptable?
- what is the timetable?
- what monitoring and evaluation system is going to be used for the communications?
- what sorts of messages are to be conveyed?
- who are the internal 'targets' of the information security message and what particular issues are there that might motivate or worry them?
- who are the key external 'targets' for each of these objectives?
- update process; and
- feedback process.

Appendix 2—FCL information security plan

There is no single template for an information security plan, but the FCL high-level template is defined below:

Describe the asset

For each asset within the scope or context:

- name and details of all Resource Owners;
- description and purpose of the information asset;
- description of the information flow for the information asset from input to output;
- who are the users of the information asset;
- what hardware, software, and communications equipment are needed for the asset; and
- what interrelationships are there between this information asset and other information assets?

Information security requirements

The information security requirements shall be defined in terms of the aspects of information. For each of the clauses, it shall categorise the requirement. The level of requirements shall be defined, currently they are:

- very high;
- high;
- medium or moderate;
- low; and
- very low.

   In addition to the risk level, any security drivers such as legislation or regulations that may affect the assets shall be defined.

Note

there is now a move to a four-layer model to ensure that there are not so many 'medium' or 'moderate' risks.

Risk assessment methodology

The risk assessment methodology shall be defined. This is a requirement of ISO/IEC 27001 6.1.2.

Review of security controls

Have any independent security reviews or tests recently been conducted on the information asset and if so—list them with their results.

Threats and vulnerabilities

Summarise the threats and vulnerabilities identified and the consequences and impacts arising from these.

Value of assets

The value of the assets within the scope shall be identified. This may be the whole asset or its components. Briefly summarise the value of the asset or the component of the asset, if applicable, and the basis for the valuation.

Level of protection required

The level of protection required for the asset shall be defined.

Acceptable level of risk

The criteria for the acceptance of the residual risk shall be defined. This shall include a high-level matrix of the controls mapped to the threats identified.

   The controls implemented or planned for the information asset shall be defined for the scope or context.

Organisational and management controls

ISO/IEC 27001 Annex A and ISO/IEC 27002 provided guidance in this area, it has four clauses:

- A.5 Organisational Controls;
- A.6 People Controls;
- A.7 Physical Controls; and
- A.8 Technological Controls.

These are a sound basis the implementation of management controls.

Appendix 3—Asset type examples

Based on ISO/IEC 27705, the following asset types are defined in FCL:

Primary assets

Primary assets are usually the core processes and information of the activity in the scope. Other primary assets such as other processes shall also be considered, which will be more appropriate for drawing up an Information Security Policy or a business continuity plan. To be effective, asset identification boundaries shall be limited to the scope of the IMS and be at a suitable level of detail that is fit for purpose.

Primary assets are of two types:

Business processes

Business processes (or subprocesses) and activities include, but are not limited to:

- processes whose loss or degradation make it impossible to carry out FCL's business operations;
- processes that contain classified processes or processes involving proprietary technology;
- processes that, if modified, can greatly affect the accomplishment FCL's business objectives; and
- processes that are necessary for FCL to comply with contractual, legal, or regulatory requirements.

Primary information

Primary information includes, but is not limited to:

- vital information for FCL's business operations;
- personally identifiable information (PII), as defined specifically in the sense of the national laws regarding privacy (and specifically special categories of PII);
- strategic information required for achieving objectives determined by the business objectives;
- high-cost information whose gathering, storage, processing, and transmission require a long lead time and/or involve a high acquisition cost.

Supporting assets

Secondary assets are those that have vulnerabilities that are exploitable by threats aiming to impair the primary assets of the scope (i.e. business processes and primary information). They comprise various types of assets, including, but not limited to:

- **hardware**—any information processing system hardware required for processing FCL information (e.g. desktop computers, mobile devices, servers of any type/size, peripherals of any kind, electronic, and physical storage media);
- **software**—any software that is necessary for processing FCL or client information (e.g. operating system software, COTS, specifically written software to manage FCL information, forensic case processing software, utilities and tools);
- **network equipment**—equipment used to provide communications between multiple disparate sites or offices (e.g. routers, switches, firewalls, cabling, data communications lines, wireless communications equipment, telephone equipment including POTS, etc.);
- **employees**—the employees who have a number of different specialised and general roles in FCL;
- **location**—the location and facilities where FCL assets are located (e.g. location of a facility, the building itself, location/area/zone within a building, services and utilities needed to operate the building or facility. This will also include remote and fallback facilities);
- **third-party support**—any third party supplying products and services that are required to perform FCL activities.

Note 1

Any asset may need to be exploded into its component parts to get a clearer understanding of the risks that FCL faces relating to the specific asset identified.

Note 2

All assets shall have a documented Asset Owner recorded in the relevant Asset Register. The names of Asset Owners shall be maintained.

Appendix 4—Asset values

Note 1

These are the values set by FCL, other forensic laboratories should set their own valuation levels.

Value	Description	Interpretation
5	Very high	Value to FCL of over £1,000,000
4	High	Value to FCL of between £500,000 and £1,000,000
3	Medium	Value to FCL of between £250,000 and £500,000
2	Low	Value to FCL of between £50,000 and £250,000
1	Very low	Value to FCL of less than £50,000

In this case, the asset value for information shall be chosen based on value range where it is located in the table above. Values could be calculated by a number of ways, such as:

- cost to create;
- cost to recreate (if possible);
- value to a competitor; and
- cost of lost sales due to information being unavailable.

Appendix 5—Consequences table

Note 1

These are the values set by FCL, other forensic laboratories should set their own values.

		Confidentiality		Integrity		Availability	
Value	**Type of effect; severity**	**Disclosure of information**	**Personal Privacy Infringement**	**Corruption of data**	**Published outside organisation**	**Disruption to activities (£)**	**Nonavailability of systems**
1	Very low	Unauthorised disclosure of one or two records	Unauthorised disclosure of one or two sets of personal details	Very small corruption, easily recoverable	No	Up to 50k	Less than half a day
2	Low	Unauthorised disclosure of a few records	Unauthorised disclosure of a few sets of personal details	Small corruption, easily recoverable	No	50k–250k	Less than a day
3	Medium	Unauthorised disclosure of many records	Unauthorised disclosure of many sets of personal details	Medium-sized corruption can be recovered, large effort	Yes	250k–500k	Between a day and 2 days

		Confidentiality		Integrity		Availability	
Value	Type of effect; severity	Disclosure of information	Personal Privacy Infringement	Corruption of data	Published outside organisation	Disruption to activities (£)	Nonavailability of systems
4	High	Unauthorised disclosure of a large number of records	Large number of personal details revealed and/or compromised	Major corruption may be recovered, very considerable effort	Yes	500k–1m	Between 2 days and a week
5	Very high	Unauthorised disclosure of a very large number of records	All personal details revealed and/or compromised	Major corruption may be recovered, major effort	Yes	Above 1m	More than a week

Appendix 6—Some common business risks

- a delay in one task causes cascading delays in dependent tasks;
- accidental disclosure of data;
- acquisition of required employees takes longer than expected;
- actions not taken by all in a timely manner;
- additional requirements are added;
- backup failures (i.e. failure to recover from backup tapes);
- budget cuts;
- budgeting failures due to unclear priorities;
- cannot build a product of the size specified in the time allocated;
- capacity of information processing systems;
- cash flow inwards;
- client finds products and services to be unsatisfactory;
- client introduces new requirements after agreed upon requirements specification is complete;
- client review/decision cycles are slower than expected;
- communication failure between departments;
- components developed separately cannot be integrated easily;
- conflicts between team members;
- conflicts between team objectives;
- contractor delivers components of unacceptably low quality, and time shall be added to improve quality;
- contractor does not deliver components when promised;
- contractor does not provide the level of domain expertise needed;
- contractor does not provide the level of technical expertise needed;
- corrupted data (held);
- corrupted data (received);
- critical dependency on third parties;
- critical dependency on a technology that is new or still under development;
- critical dependency on key suppliers;
- critical employee loss;
- data conversion activities are underestimated or are ignored;
- database failure;
- design fails to address major issues;
- design requires unnecessary and unproductive implementation overhead;
- developers unfamiliar with development tools;
- development environment structure, policies, procedures are not clearly defined;
- development in an unfamiliar or unproved hardware environment;
- development in an unfamiliar or unproved software environment;

- development of extra software functions that are not required extends the schedule;
- development of flawed software functions requires redesign and implementation;
- development of flawed user interface results in redesign and implementation;
- disaster recovery failure to recover in time;
- effort is greater than estimated (per line of code, function point, module, case, etc.);
- employee's assignments do not match their strengths;
- employees need extra time to learn unfamiliar hardware environment;
- employees need extra time to learn unfamiliar tools or operating systems;
- employees with critical skills needed for the project cannot be found;
- excessive schedule pressure;
- facilities are available but inadequate (e.g. no phones, network wiring, furniture, office supplies, etc.);
- facilities are crowded, noisy, or disruptive;
- facilities are not available on time;
- failure of disaster recovery site to mirror the production site;
- failure of utilities supplying the FCL office(s);
- failure to comply with legislative, regulatory, and contractual requirements;
- failure to consistently use documented processes;
- failure to detect and respond to security incidents in a timely manner;
- failure to enhance contracts as contract life progresses;
- failure to follow processes/procedures;
- failure to have and communicate long-term plans (strategic planning);
- failure to have and use a capacity plan;
- failure to manage contracts properly;
- failure to meet customer needs;
- failure to meet disaster recovery service level agreement;
- failure to meet financial objectives;
- failure to monitor contract performance;
- failure to monitor, measure, and manage systems for service level agreement reporting automatically;
- failure to process cases in a timely manner;
- failure to provide clear operational budgets;
- failure to respond to business changes in operational delivery;
- failure to test business continuity plans, as appropriate;
- failure to test changes properly;
- failures leading to reputation loss;
- flawed design;
- fraudulent manipulation of data (external sources);
- fraudulent manipulation of data (internal employees);
- having the wrong contract in place;
- human error;
- impact of planned outages;
- impact of unplanned outages;
- improper infrastructure, design, and implementation of solutions;
- improper management of service level agreements (suppliers);
- inability of the information processing systems to scale to customer needs;
- inaccurate progress tracking;
- inaccurate status reporting;
- inappropriate change and configuration management;
- inappropriate incident and problem management;
- inappropriate privileges on information processing systems according to job function;
- inappropriate TRTs;
- incomplete data (held);
- incomplete data (received);
- inconsistent data (held);
- inconsistent data (received);

- inconsistent management direction;
- inefficient team structure reduces productivity;
- information processing system/infrastructure failure;
- infrastructure is not resilient;
- key employees are available only part time;
- key software or hardware components become unavailable, unsupported or are unexpectedly scheduled for de-support;
- lack of appropriate business continuity planning;
- lack of continuous innovation;
- lack of information classification and so protection;
- lack of needed specialisation (includes technical and domain knowledge) increases defects and rework;
- lack of office space and facilities;
- lack of spares on site;
- lack of specific technical expertise;
- lack of tools for managing and monitoring operational systems;
- lack of tools to manage and monitor information processing systems and business processes;
- layoffs and cutbacks reduce the Forensic Team's capacity;
- long decision-making process;
- loss of customers;
- management review/decision cycle is slower than expected;
- marketing objectives not clear;
- meeting product's size or speed constraints requires more time than expected, including time for redesign and re-implementation;
- multiple interested parties outside the normal department chain of command;
- necessary functionality cannot be implemented using the selected methods and tools;
- new development personnel are added late in the project, and additional training and communications overhead reduces existing team members' effectiveness;
- nontechnical third-party tasks take longer than expected (control agency approvals, procurement, equipment purchase, legal reviews, etc.);
- payment failures to suppliers;
- poor external vendor support;
- poor planning;
- poor quality administrative support;
- poor quality assurance;
- poor quality software delivered;
- premises and facilities failures (space, parking, etc);
- pressure of work on the Forensic Team;
- pricing wrong;
- problem team members are not removed from the Forensic Team;
- procurement failures;
- re-estimation in response to schedule slips does not occur, or is overly optimistic or ignores project history;
- requirement to operate under multiple operating systems takes longer to satisfy than expected;
- requirements are poorly defined, and further definition expands the scope of the case or assignment;
- requirements have been base lined but continue to change;
- schedule is optimistic, 'best case', rather than realistic, 'expected case';
- schedule savings from productivity enhancing tools are overestimated;
- service level agreement failure;
- supplier failure;
- system availability;
- task prerequisites (e.g. training, completion of other cases or tasks) cannot be completed on time;
- too little formality (lack of adherence to policies and procedures);
- too much formality (bureaucratic adherence to policies and procedures);
- tools are not in place by the desired time;
- tools do not provide the planned productivity;
- tools do not work as expected developers need time to create workarounds or to switch to new tools;

- unacceptable performance;
- unplanned turnover of key employees;
- upstream quality-assurance activities are limited or cut short;
- use of unfamiliar methodology;
- weak risk management fails to detect major risks; and
- wrong technology in place.

Appendix 7—Some common project risks

Digital forensic cases can be regarded as projects and may suffer from some of the project risks below:

- a contingency plan has not been identified for the appropriate risks;
- adequate competent employees have not been identified and allocated to the project or case;
- all external interfaces are not under FCL's control;
- all key players have not lived up to their accountabilities and responsibilities and this has not been addressed;
- all known management and technical risks have not been assessed and are few mitigation strategies in place for all identified risks;
- all the contingency plans have not been documented and do not include anticipated cost and effort;
- an adequate business case analysis has not been performed;
- budget may not cover project or case;
- business case is not based on the full cost of the project or case;
- changes in scope are not being managed;
- clearly defined, documented, and understood responsibilities, accountabilities, and authorities do not exist for each of the major players in this project or case;
- costs are not allocated in accordance with work breakdown structures;
- each risk has not been assigned a loss (impact) if risk occurs;
- each risk has not been assigned a probability of occurrence;
- failure to get interviews scheduled;
- failure to review draughts and return without prejudicing timetable;
- for any risk exceeding defined trigger values, the appropriate level of management has not approved the implementation of the contingency plan;
- for each risk rated high, no specific risk mitigation has been documented;
- for each risk to be mitigated, an effort and/or cost has not been estimated for the mitigation action plan;
- hidden agenda;
- in the event of serious problems, decisive actions are often not taken;
- inadequate employees allocated to the scheduled tasks at the scheduled time;
- independent review of this project or project been not conducted;
- lack of documentary proof available;
- lack of employee training;
- lack of power and authority of Project Manager or Lead Forensic Analyst;
- management not committed;
- mandated to interview wrong people;
- necessary information not always available to support decisive action;
- no clear escalation path documented;
- no formal mechanisms and tools in place to monitor the project or case schedule and costs;
- Project Manager and Sponsor cannot list the current top project or case risks;
- project or case specifications are not precisely defined;
- project or case specifications have changed significantly, these changes have not been well documented and approved by the appropriate interested parties;
- relevant risks have not been rated;
- resource conflicts;
- status/progress meetings do not occur regularly;
- the client commitment level is passive and hard to engage;
- the client demonstrates a poor understanding of the requirements;
- the project or case is not on time or budget;

- the project or case justification is not based on a return on investment with an attractive projected return;
- the risks have not been ranked in order of exposure and agreed to by the Laboratory Manager or top management, as appropriate;
- the technology being used is not well tested and employees do not have sufficient experience and knowledge in using it;
- there is dependence on facilities not under control of the employees on this project or case; and
- there was no formal process used to break down the work and estimate task duration.

Appendix 8—Security threat examples

Some of the most common security threats include, but are not limited to:

- abduction;
- accidental disclosure of sensitive material via waste;
- acts of omission,
- acts of war;
- adverse media coverage;
- air conditioning failure;
- alcohol abuse;
- angry or hostile clients;
- animals;
- armed hold-up;
- assault—mental;
- assault—verbal;
- blackmail;
- bomb threats;
- break and enter to the office;
- bribery;
- building structural collapse;
- chemical/biological hazards;
- civil unrest;
- commercial espionage;
- communication problems;
- communication system exploitation;
- communications interception;
- communications services failure (phones or computers);
- communications system or cabling damage;
- competitors;
- compromise;
- computer malfunction;
- contamination;
- corrupt employees;
- criminal acts by employees;
- criminal acts by partners or suppliers;
- currency fluctuations;
- cyclone;
- deliberate disclosure of data by employees;
- demonstrations;
- denial of services;
- design error;
- deterioration of storage media;
- disaffected groups;
- disgruntled clients;
- disgruntled employees;
- drought;
- drug abuse;

- dust or similar;
- earthquake;
- eavesdropping (electronic or physical);
- embezzlement;
- employee death from industrial accident or disease;
- employee pilfering/theft;
- employee sabotage;
- employee shortage;
- environmental contamination;
- errors and omissions;
- espionage;
- extortion;
- extreme of temperature/humidity;
- fire;
- flood;
- foreign intelligence services activity;
- fraud—external;
- fraud—internal;
- hacking of computer system;
- hardware failure;
- health and safety issues to employees or clients;
- hostage situations;
- hurricane;
- illegal import/export of software;
- illegal use of software;
- incompetent employees;
- incompetent management;
- industrial accidents;
- industrial action;
- industrial espionage;
- injury to employees or clients through accidents;
- internal security problems;
- issue motivated groups;
- kidnapping;
- lightning;
- litigation by clients or suppliers;
- loss of data and records;
- loss of key employees;
- loss of physical and infrastructure support;
- maintenance error;
- major price undercutting by competitors;
- malicious code;
- malicious hacking, e.g. through masquerading;
- malicious rumour mongering by competitors;
- maverick acts;
- misrouting or re-routing of messages;
- misuse of resources;
- money laundering;
- network failure;
- nonpaying clients;
- operations error (of any type);
- organised crime—any sort;
- phreaking (breaking into phone/comms systems);
- political upheaval;

- politically motivated violence;
- pollution;
- power loss/failure/cut-off;
- ransomware;
- religious objections;
- repudiation (service/transaction/receipt/delivery);
- sabotage;
- siege;
- sit-ins;
- smuggling;
- software failure;
- spamming (multi/large messages to email);
- sting operations;
- structural faults;
- subornment;
- substandard quality control;
- subversion;
- terrorist act; and
- theft.

Appendix 9—Common security vulnerabilities

There are a number of vulnerabilities that can be exploited by threats. These are some of the vulnerabilities that have been identified—there are many others. Each vulnerability shall be considered in relation to the threat that may exploit it.

A number of headings are defined, and some vulnerabilities are given for each.

Some common security vulnerabilities are:

Communications

- ease of access to communications cabinets and equipment;
- inadequate network management;
- lack of identification and authentication of sender and receiver;
- lack of proof of sending or receiving a message;
- poor cable jointing;
- transfer of passphrases in clear;
- unprotected communication lines;
- unprotected public network connections; and
- unprotected sensitive traffic.

Documents

- inappropriate disposal;
- inappropriate storage; and
- uncontrolled copying.

Environment and infrastructure

- building in location which is a terrorist target;
- inappropriate access control to buildings, rooms;
- lack of evacuation procedures;
- lack of physical protection of the building, doors, and windows;
- location in an area susceptible to flood;
- poor building design—unable to absorb shock; and
- uncertainty of utility supply.

Generally applying vulnerabilities

- inadequate service maintenance response;
- inappropriate or no business continuity plan; and
- single points of failure.

Hardware

- ineffective configuration or change control;
- insufficient maintenance/faulty installation;
- lack of maintenance or upgrades;
- lack of replacement or upgrade of storage media;
- susceptibility to environment;
- susceptibility to temperature variations; and
- susceptibility to voltage variations.

Human resources

- absence or shortage of competent employees;
- inadequate recruitment procedures;
- incorrect use of software and hardware;
- insufficient security training;
- lack of monitoring mechanisms;
- lack of security awareness;
- susceptibility of employees to environmental contamination; and
- unsupervised work by employees.

Software and system management

- complicated user interface;
- failure to have appropriate system and data backups;
- failure to log off when leaving the workstation;
- inadequate audit trail;
- inadequate work instruction;
- inappropriate identification and authentication mechanisms;
- ineffective configuration or change control;
- insufficient software testing;
- poor or incomplete documentation;
- poor passphrase management;
- uncontrolled downloading and using unauthorised software;
- unprotected passphrase tables;
- well-known flaws in the software; and
- wrong allocation of access rights.

    This is not an exhaustive list.

Appendix 10—The FCL risk management policy

Risk management is about managing threats and opportunities to FCL.

By managing risk effectively, FCL shall be in a stronger position to meet its business objectives. By managing opportunities well, FCL shall be in a better position to provide improved products and services and offer better value for money.

In this policy and its supporting management framework, risk is defined as something happening that may have an impact on the achievement of business objectives. When management of the risks is effective, it often remains unnoticed. When it fails, however, the consequences can be significant and high profile. Effective risk management is needed to prevent such failures and capitalise on successes.

This policy is supported by a complete risk management framework and this supports the business objectives. There are a number of specific requirements for different legislation, regulations, contractual obligations, management systems, and business processes. These specific requirements shall be addressed in the correct part of the IMS, but the central core of risk management is this Risk Management Policy and its supporting management framework.

This risk management framework describes the processes that FCL shall put in place and linked together to identify, assess, treat, review, and report on the identified risks and their status. This policy and its supporting risk management framework shall be used for the management of risk across the whole of FCL.

Overall, the goals of FCL Risk Management Policy and its supporting framework shall be to have procedures in place to:

- clearly identify risk exposures;
- ensure conscious and properly evaluated risk decisions;
- fully document major threats and opportunities;
- identify a risk management and treatment process that fits into FCL's culture;
- implement cost-effective actions to reduce risks;
- integrate risk management into FCL's culture; and
- manage risk in accordance with good practice.

This policy is issued and maintained by the Information Security Manager, who shall provide advice and guidance on its implementation and ensure compliance.

All FCL employees shall comply with this policy.

Appendix 11—The FCL IMS and ISMS scope statement

The FCL IMS is based on the common standard on Annex L (for details of Annex L—see Chapter 4, Section 4.3 and Appendix 2).

The IMS is common for all of the standards, and the specific requirements for each standard are defined below:

ISO/IEC 27001:2005 was the only standard that defines the components of a scope statement, and this is the one used as the basis for the IMS. It requires this to be defined in terms of:

- organisation;
- location;
- assets; and
- technology.

Note 1

This is no longer in ISO/IEC 27001:2022.

Note 2

Different forensic laboratories will have different technology and organisational structures in place.

Overview of FCL

The overview of FCL, its products, and services shall be given here.

Organisation

The organisation of FCL shall be defined here, with an organogram to show how the component parts all fit together. It also may have a link to the relevant job descriptions in the IMS.

Location

The FCL office location(s) shall be defined here. If there is more than one, those within the scope of the IMS shall be defined here.

Assets

The assets that come under the scrutiny of the IMS shall include:

- **information**—Details of all databases are held in the Asset Register. All case processing files are held in the virtual files on the corporate business or forensic network. The information stored is a mixture of structured and unstructured information (e.g. email, Office documents, etc.);
- **software**—Details of all software are held in the Asset Register;
- **hardware**—Details of all hardware are held in the Asset Register;
- **people**—All employees;
- **services**—All services to the FCL office(s) and includes, but is not limited to, gas, water, electricity, telephone, internet, local and national government services and supplier; and
- **image and reputation**—FCL's image and reputation is a huge asset. Any mishandling of information that compromises this asset will have a major effect on company business.

Technology
Hardware
Computers

Business and forensic hardware shall be defined here.

Network equipment

Network equipment shall be defined here.

Servers

Servers shall be defined here.

Printers

Printers shall be defined here.

Other peripherals

Other peripherals shall be defined here.

Operating systems
Desktop

Operating systems in place on workstations and mobile devices shall be defined here.

Server

Operating systems in place on servers shall be defined here.

Network operating system

Network operating systems shall be defined here.

Desktop applications

Desktop applications (i.e. nonforensic tools) shall be defined here.

Forensic tools

Forensic tools in use shall be defined here. This is ever changing and so no complete list of tools shall be defined, only the major/core applications.

Diagrams

Physical layout diagrams and network diagrams to support the scope statement shall be defined here.

Scope statement

The agreed scope statement for the management system standards that are included in this IMS is:

The provision of forensic case processing and forensic consultancy services.

Appendix 12—Criticality ratings

The criticality rating of an asset or function is determined from an analysis of the *consequences* of its loss, compromise, destruction and is shown below:

- **vital:** loss or compromise will result in the possible abandonment or long-term cessation of FCL's business capability and/or functions;
- **major:** loss or compromise will necessitate a major change in FCL's practices and activities and will have a major impact on operations and/or reputation;
- **significant:** loss or compromise will have a significant impact on FCL's practices, activities, and financial position;
- **low:** loss or compromise will be covered by usual business practices; and
- **unknown:** insufficient data is available for evaluation.

Appendix 13—Likelihood of occurrence

Below is a 5-level likelihood table and a 10-level likelihood table, alternates, such as a 3-level or 4-level table can be used.

Five-level likelihood table

Value	Description	Interpretation
1	Very low	Infrequently (yearly or less frequently)
2	Low	Occasionally (two or three times a year)
3	Medium	Sometimes (monthly)
4	High	Frequently (weekly)
5	Very high	Frequently (daily)

Ten-level likelihood table

Value	Description	Interpretation
1	Negligible	Once every 1000 years or less
2	Extremely unlikely	Once every 200 years
3	Very unlikely	Once every 50 years
4	Unlikely	Once every 20 years
5	Feasible	Once every 5 years

Continued

Value	Description	Interpretation
6	Probable	Annually
7	Very probable	Quarterly
8	Expected	Monthly
9	Confidently expected	Weekly
10	Certain	Daily

Very approximately each one is four times more likely than the previous one, which covers the range 'once in 1000 years' to 'daily' in a range of 1–10.

Appendix 14—Risk appetite

FCL has established levels of risk that it is prepared to accept and those that shall be treated. Using its five levels of likelihood for its five levels of severity of impact if the risk crystallises gives a 5×5 matrix as shown below:

FCL has established levels of risk that it is prepared to accept and those that shall be treated. Using its five levels of likelihood for its five levels of severity of impact if the risk crystallises gives a 5×5 matrix as shown below:

		Likelihood				
		1 (Very Low)	2 (Low)	3 (Medium)	4 (High)	5 (Very High)
Severity of Impact	1 (Very Low)	1	2	4	7	11
	2 (Low)	3	5	8	12	16
	3 (Medium)	6	9	13	17	20
	4 (High)	10	14	18	21	23
	5 (Very High)	15	19	22	24	25

This gives a risk level of between 1 and 25.

Note

The values are representative of the levels and no more.

The risk level is banded as:

Exposure level	Risk Level
1 – 5	Very Low
6 – 10	Low
11 – 15	Medium
16 – 20	High
20 – 25	Very High

Where the risk levels are defined as:

- **Very low risk** is a condition where risk is identified as having minimal effects on the identified FCL assets; the probability of occurrence is sufficiently low to cause only minimal concern. These risks shall be reviewed on an annual basis.

- **Low risk** is a condition where risk is identified as having minor effects on the shall be defined here. FCL assets; the probability of occurrence is sufficiently low to cause only minor concern. These risks shall be reviewed on a 6-monthly basis.
- **Medium risk** is a condition where risk is identified as one that could affect the identified FCL assets. The probability of occurrence is high enough to require close control of all contributing factors. These risks shall be reviewed on a 3-monthly basis.
- **High risk** is the condition where risk is identified as having a high probability of occurrence and the consequence would affect the identified FCL assets. The probability of occurrence is high enough to require close control of all contributing factors, the establishment of risk actions, and an acceptable fallback position. These risks shall be reviewed on a monthly basis.
- **Very high risk** is the condition where risk is identified as having a very high probability of occurrence and the consequence would affect the identified FCL assets. The probability of occurrence is so high as to require very close control of all contributing factors, the establishment of risk actions, and an acceptable fallback position. These risks shall be reviewed on a 2-weekly basis, or more frequently, if appropriate.

Note 1

The target level is to reduce all risks to the green (Very low or Low) level.

Note 2

Where this cannot be achieved by application of appropriate risk treatment, the Resource Owner shall knowingly accept the risk.

Note 3

Risks shall be reviewed as defined above, unless an incident occurs involving them or there is some other influencing change, in which case they shall be reviewed more frequently.

Appendix 15—Security controls from COBIT 2019

Note

A number of the controls below, in fact many of them, are mappable to those in ISO/IEC 27001, but there are a number of them that are not and these may be considered for risk treatment, especially as CObIT 2019 aligns the business, IT, and information security strategies.

CObIT controls

CObIT 2019 is based around a core model of 40 management objectives in 5 categories.
Evaluate, Direct, and Monitor

- EDM01—Ensured Governance Framework Setting and Maintenance
- EDM02—Ensured Benefits Delivery
- EDM03—Ensured Risk Optimisation
- EDM04—Ensured Resource Optimisation
- EDM05—Ensured Stakeholder Engagement

Align, Plan, and Organise

- APO01—Managed I&T Management Framework
- APO02—Managed Strategy

- APO03—Managed Enterprise Architecture
- APO04—Managed Innovation
- APO05—Managed Portfolio
- APO06—Managed Budget and Costs
- APO07—Managed Human Resources
- APO08—Managed Relationships
- APO09—Managed Service Agreements
- APO10—Managed Vendors
- APO11—Managed Quality
- APO12—Managed Risk
- APO13—Managed Security
- APO014—Managed Data

Build, Acquire, and Implement

- BAI01—Managed Programs
- BAI02—Managed Requirements Definition
- BAI03—Managed Solutions Identification and Build
- BAI04—Managed Availability and Capacity
- BAI05—Managed Organisational Change
- BAI06—Managed IT Changes
- BAI07—Managed IT Change Acceptance and Transitioning
- BAI08—Managed Knowledge
- BAI09—Managed Assets
- BAI10—Managed Configuration
- BAI11—Managed Projects

Deliver, Service, and Support

- DSS01—Managed Operations
- DSS02—Managed Service Requests and Incidents
- DSS03—Managed Problems
- DSS04—Managed Continuity
- DSS05—Managed Security Services
- DSS06—Managed Business Process Controls

Monitor, Evaluate, and Assess

- MEA01—Managed Performance and Conformance Monitoring
- MEA02—Managed System of Internal Control
- MEA03—Managed Compliance with External Requirements
- MEA04—Managed Assurance

Appendix 16—Information classification

Information held or created by FCL shall be evaluated against the following criteria and classified accordingly:

Public

'Public' information is information that can be disclosed to anyone without violating an individual's right to privacy or prejudice FCL in any way, including financial loss, embarrassment, or jeopardising the security of any assets.

Internal use only

'Internal Use Only' information is information that, due to technical or business sensitivity, is limited to FCL employees and relevant third-party suppliers. It is intended for use only within FCL. Unauthorised disclosure, compromise, or destruction shall not have a significant impact on FCL or its employees.

Confidential

'Confidential' information is information that FCL and its employees have a legal, regulatory, contractual, or social obligation to protect. It is intended for use solely within defined groups in FCL. Unauthorised disclosure, compromise, or destruction would adversely impact FCL or its employees.

Strictly confidential

'Strictly Confidential' information, the highest level of classification in FCL, is information whose unauthorised disclosure, compromise, or destruction could result in severe damage, provide significant advantage to a competitor, or incur serious financial impact to FCL or its employees. It is intended solely for named individuals within FCL and shall be limited to those with an explicit, predetermined 'need to know'.

Appendix 17—The risk register template

The contents of FCL risk registers are shown below:

- risk number;
- risk;
- business process;
- value;
- probability;
- impact;
- gross exposure;
- gross risk level;
- consequence;
- gross total risk;
- mitigation (treatment);
- risk owner;
- residual probability;
- residual exposure;
- residual risk level;
- residual total risk;
- design effectiveness;
- operating efficiency;
- last reviewed;
- date for next review; and
- days overdue.

Appendix 18—Comparison between qualitative and quantitative methods

Both qualitative and quantitative approaches to security risk management have their advantages and disadvantages. Certain situations may adopt the quantitative approach, others will find the qualitative approach much more to their liking. The following table summarises some of the benefits and drawbacks of each approach:

	Quantitative	Qualitative
Benefits	Risks are prioritised by financial impact; assets are prioritised by financial values. Results facilitate management of risk by return on security investment. Results can be expressed in management-specific terminology (e.g. monetary values and probability expressed as a specific percentage). Accuracy tends to increase over time as the organisation builds historic record of data whilst gaining experience.	Enables visibility and understanding of risk ranking. Easier to reach consensus. Not necessary to quantify threat frequency. Not necessary to determine exact financial values of assets. Easier to involve people who are not experts on security or computers.

Continued

	Quantitative	Qualitative
Drawbacks	Impact values assigned to risks are based on subjective opinions of participants. Process to reach credible results and consensus is very time consuming. Calculations can be complex and time consuming. Results are presented in monetary terms only, and they may be difficult for nontechnical people to interpret. Process requires expertise, so participants cannot be easily coached through it.	Insufficient differentiation between important risks. Difficult to justify investing in control implementation because there is no basis for a cost–benefit analysis. Results are dependent upon the quality of the risk management team that is created.

In years past, the quantitative approaches dominated security risk management and this is still prevalent in some countries. This has changed recently as an increasing number of practitioners have admitted that strictly following quantitative risk management processes typically results in difficult, long-running projects that see few tangible benefits. This has led to the favouring of qualitative or hybrid risk assessment.

Appendix 19—FCL SOA template

The ISMS is split into two specific parts, the mandatory management part from ISO/IEC 27001 Sections 4–8 and the controls derived from the risk assessment from ISO/IEC 27001 Annex A. It may also have a third part where controls not listed in ISO/IEC 27001 Annex A are indicated by the risk treatment process.

Below is the template in use in FCL.

Note 1

This only shows a few entries to demonstrate how the three parts are implemented in FCL's SoA.

Note 2

FCL has included the mandatory Sections 4–10, which is not absolutely necessary. This is because the right hand column showing how the requirement is met has the document or record linked to the IMS allowing one to move directly from the SoA to the relevant document or record.

Mandatory SoA

Control section	Management components	
4	Context of the organisation	
4.1	Understanding the organisation and its context	
	Requirement	Interpretation
	The organisation shall determine external and internal issues that are relevant to its purpose and that affect its ability to achieve the intended outcome(s) of its information security management system.	The internal and external contexts are defined in context.html

Annex A

This SoA assumes that a risk management tool was used as well as a business risk workshop, to define which of the controls in Annex A are indicated, as currently performed in FCL.

ISO 27001 clause	Organisational control	Control	Include	Exclude	RA tool	Workshop	Notes
A.5.1	Policies for information security	Information Security Policy and topic-specific policies shall be defined, approved by management, published, communicated to and acknowledged by relevant personnel and relevant interested parties, and reviewed at planned intervals and if significant changes occur.	✓		✓		The index for all policies in the IMS is IMS Policy Index. html. Each IMS policy is accessible here either as an HTML file or a PDF for download. The procedures for policy review IMS Document Review. html is also located here All policies shall be approved by top management and appropriately published to all employees, with records held of distribution so updates can be issued

Controls not in Annex A

Control	Include	Exclude	RA tool	Workshop	Notes
All employees shall be forced to take their annual holiday entitlement	✓		✓		Indicted by risk assessment and reduces the opportunity for insider fraud and will enforce segregation of duties. Integrated into HR procedures outside the IMS

Appendix 20—FCL's security metrics template

The table below shows metrics for the reporting period to support the agreed Security Objectives, which are defined in Chapter 12, Appendix 6. All of the metrics below support objectives 1 and 4 and so this is not shown in the right-hand column.

Note

This template shows a sample of metrics used in FCL, it will be up to each forensic laboratory to determine its own metrics to support its agreed metrics.

ISO 27001 control	Control	Metric	Description	How calculated	Responsible for collection (Owner)[a]	Target	Score	Cross reference to security objective(s)
6.1.2	Identify the risks	Number of risk register reviews per month	Number of risk register reviews per month	Count of risk register review meetings		1		3, 4, 6, 7, 8, 10, 12, 13
6.1.2	Assess and evaluate risks	% of risks in FCL by category	Numbers of risks in the risk register in each of the high and medium risk categories	From risk register		VH=0 H=0 M≤20		3, 6, 7
6.1.2	Identify and evaluate risk treatment options	% of risks accepted	Number of identified risks identified that are knowingly accepted without treatment	The number of accepted risks that have not been treated as a percentage of all risks identified. As in the current risk register		VH=0 H=0 M≤5%		3, 6, 7
6.1.2	Management approval for residual risks	Last time residual risk were accepted	Last date of residual risk acceptance	From management review minutes or form		≤365 days		3, 6, 7
6.1.3	Statement of applicability	% of controls in Annex A implemented	Number of controls in Annex A that are implemented in FCL	The number of controls in the SoA as a percentage of those in Annex A.		≥90%		2, 3, 5, 6, 7, 8, 9, 10, 11, 12, 13, 14, 15
7.1	Resource management—provision of resources	% of budget assigned to information security	The percentage of FCL's budget spent on information security information security	Percentage of IT budget assigned		3%		3, 7, 10, 15
7.1	Resource management—provision of resources	Full time support for maintaining ISO 27001 certification	Number of full time equivalent employees that are dedicated to maintaining ISO 27001 certification	Head count of dedicated information security professionals employed		2		1, 2, 3, 5, 6, 7, 8, 9, 10, 11, 12, 13, 14, 15
9.2	Internal ISMS audits	% of audits completed on time	The number of audits completed on time in FCL measured against those planned	The number of audits completed on time as a percentage of those planned		≥95%		3, 5, 6, 7, 8, 9, 10, 11, 12, 13, 14, 15
9.3	Review input	Number of mandatory inputs not covered at management review	The number of mandatory agenda items that were not covered at the last management review	Inspection of minutes		0%		3, 5, 6, 7, 8, 9, 10, 11, 12, 13, 14, 15
9.3	Review output	% of actions completed	Number of actions raised at the management review that have been converted into CAPAs	The number of actions from management reviews that have been raised as CAPAs as a percentage of all management review Actions.		≥95%		3, 5, 6, 7, 8, 9, 10, 11, 12, 13, 14, 15

					Target	Ref.
10.1	Corrective action	% of corrective actions completed on time (including PIRs)	Number of corrective actions completed on time in FCL measured against all corrective actions opened in the time period	The number of corrective actions completed on time as a percentage of those opened in the quarter	≥95%	3, 5, 6, 7, 8, 9, 10, 11, 12, 13, 14, 15
A.5.1	Review of the Information Security Policy	Last time information policy document was reviewed	Last date of Information Security Policy review	From management review minutes or policy	≤365 days	5
A.5.2	Allocation of information security responsibilities	% of JDs with security responsibilities defined	All JDs shall have all security responsibilities defined	Numbers of JDs with security responsibilities defined in them as a percentage of all FCL JDs	100%	5
A.5.4	Resource management—training, awareness and competence	% of new employees undergoing induction training within 31 days of joining FCL	Number of new employees, and third parties working for FCL, that have undergone induction training within 31 days of joining that have stated in the reporting period	Number new employees, and third parties working for FCL, that have undergone induction training within 31 days of joining that have started in the reporting period as a percentage of new starters	≥95%	3, 5
A.5.4	Resource management—training, awareness and competence	% of new employees undergoing information security training	Number of new employees, and third parties working for FCL, that have undergone information security training that have stated in the reporting period	Number new employees, and third parties working for FCL, that have undergone information security training in the reporting period as a percentage of new starters	≥95%	3, 5
A.5.4	Resource management—training, awareness and competence	% of new all employees undergoing information security refresher training	Number of employees, and third parties working for FCL, that have undergone information security refresher training that have stated in the reporting period	Number new employees, and third parties working for FCL, that have undergone information security refresher training as a percentage of all employees and third parties working for FCL	≥20%	3, 5
A.5.9	Ownership of assets	% of Asset Owners who understand responsibilities	The percentage of Asset Owners who both understand their responsibilities and implement them	The number of Asset Owners understanding and implementing duties as a percentage of all Asset Owners.	≥95%	3, 5, 6
A.5.9	Ownership of assets	% of assets without owners	The percentage of assets that are without Asset Owners	The number of assets without Owners as a percentage of all assets	≤5%	3, 5, 6
A.5.12	Classification guidelines	% of assets that are unclassified	The percentage of assets that have not been classified	The number of assets that are unclassified as a percentage of all assets	≤5%	5, 6, 13

[a] Where the person responsible for collection is also the owner, only one name is given. If someone other than the owner collects the results, then their name is given with the Owner in (brackets).

Appendix 21—Risk glossary

The following terms are related to risk and have been extracted from various standards:

Note

As can be seen, the same term can have different definitions in different standards

---

Term	Definition
Acceptable risk	A concern that is acceptable to responsible management for a system or process due to the cost and magnitude of implementing security controls.
Accountability	The property that ensures that the actions of an entity may be traced uniquely to that entity. [ISO 7498-2:1989]
AIRMIC	Association of Insurance and Risk Managers.
ALE	Annual loss expectancy.
Annual loss expectancy	The total amount of money that an organisation will lose in a year if nothing is done to mitigate the risk.
Annual rate of occurrence	The number of times one might reasonably expect a risk to occur in a year.
ARO	Annual rate of occurrence.
Asset	A useful or valuable thing or person. A property owned by a person or organisation.
AV	Asset value.
Availability	Property of being accessible and usable upon demand by an authorised entity. [ISO IEC 13335-1:2004]
Best practice	A technique or methodology that, through experience and research, has proven to reliably lead to a desired result.
BS	British Standard.
BSI	British Standards Institute.
Business risk	The risk that external factors can result in unexpected loss (typically financial loss). Business risk, if managed well, can also result in a competitive advantage being gained.
CMM	Capability Maturity Level.
Communication and consultation	A continual and iterative processes that an organisation conducts to provide, share or obtain information and to engage in dialogue with stakeholders and others regarding the management of risk. [ISO Guide 73:2009]
Confidentiality	Property that information is not made available or disclosed to unauthorised individuals, entities, or processes. [ISO IEC 13335-1:2004]
Consequence	The outcome of an event affecting objectives. [ISO Guide 73:2009]
Control	A measure that is modifying risk. [ISO Guide 73:2009]
Corporate risk	A category of risk management that looks at ensuring an organisation meets its corporate governance responsibilities takes appropriate actions when required and identifies and manages emerging risks.
EF	Exposure factor
Establishing the context	Defining the external and internal parameters to be taken into account when managing risk and setting the scope and risk criteria for the risk management policy. [ISO Guide 73:2009]
Event	The occurrence or change of a particular set of circumstances. [ISO Guide 73:2009]
Expected loss	The average financial loss or impact that can be anticipated for a particular loss event or risk. It is usually calculated based on experience and historical information. It is normally given as the average annual loss amount.

Term	Definition
Exposure	The susceptibility to loss, or the vulnerability to a particular risk.
Exposure factor	The exposure factor represents the percentage of loss that a realised threat could have on a certain asset.
External context	The external environment in which the organisation seeks to achieve its objectives. [ISO Guide 73:2009]
Frequency	A measure of the number of occurrences per unit of time
Harm	Physical injury or damage to health, property of the environment.
Hazard	Source of potential harm or a situation with a potential for harm.
Impact	A noticeable effect or influence.
Incident	An event.
Information security	Preservation of confidentiality, integrity and availability of information; in addition, other properties, such as authenticity, accountability, nonrepudiation, and reliability can also be involved.
Inherent risk	The possibility that some activity or natural event will have an adverse effect on a legal entities asset(s) and which cannot be managed, assigned or transferred away.
Insurance	A contract to finance the cost of a given risk. Should a specified loss (a risk event) occur, the insurance contract (or policy) will pay the holder the agreed amount.
Integrated risk management	A process where risk is managed in an integrated way across the whole of an organisation.
Integrity	Property of safeguarding the accuracy and completeness of assets. [ISO IEC 13335-1:2004]
Internal context	The internal environment in which the organisation seeks to achieve its objectives. [ISO Guide 73:2009]
ISO	International Standards Organisation.
Legal entity	Any individual, partnership, corporation, association or other organisation that has, in the eyes of the law, the capacity to make a contract or an agreement and the abilities to assume an obligation and to pay off its debts. A legal entity, under the law, is responsible for its actions and can be sued for damages.
Level of risk	The magnitude of a risk, expressed in terms of the combination of consequences and their likelihood. [ISO Guide 73:2009]
Likelihood	Used as a general description of probability or frequency. Chance of something happening. [ISO Guide 73:2009]
Management of risk	See Risk management.
Management of risk framework	See Risk management framework.
Management of risk owner	See Risk owner.
Management of risk policy	See Risk management policy.
Maturity level	A well-defined evolutionary plateau towards achieving a mature process. The traditional five levels are: • Initial; • Repeatable; • Defined; • Quantitative; • Optimising. These are from the Capability Maturity Model (CMM) from the Carnegie Mellon SEI.
Mitigation	The process of limiting a negative impact or consequence of an event.
Monitoring	The continual checking, supervising, critically observing, or determining the status in order to identify change from the performance level required or expected. [ISO Guide 73:2009]
Near miss	A situation or event that has been averted due to chance or conscious action and whose potential impact can be quantified.

Continued

Term	Definition
Operational risk	The category of risk where deficiencies in information systems or internal controls will result in unexpected loss. The risk is usually associated with human error, system failures, and inadequate procedures and controls affecting the continuity of business services.
Opportunity	A future event that, should it occur, would have a favourable impact.
Organisation	A formal group of people with one or more shared goals.
Organisation risk management	A process where both current and emerging risks are managed in an integrated way throughout the organisation.
Owner	An Owner is the person who has responsibility for a predetermined set of resources and who is therefore accountable for the integrity, availability, confidentiality, auditability, and accountability of the resources. An Owner is also accountable for the consequences of the actions of users of these resources. It does not mean that the asset 'belongs' to the owner in a legal sense.
Probability	The likelihood of an event occurring.
Problem	Something that is difficult to deal with or understand.
Project risk	The category of risks that are concerned with stopping the successful completion of a project. Typically, these risks include: • Personnel; • Technical issues; • Costs • Scheduling; • Resourcing; • Operational support; • Quality; • Supplier issues.
Protective measure	The means used to reduce risk.
Qualitative risk assessment	A form of risk assessment that analyses the general structures and systems currently in place. This is a descriptive methodology, which typically involves risk mapping and risk matrices. These assessments do not involve any detailed measurements. (See: Quantitative risk assessment.)
Quantification	The objective measure of the seriousness of risk or impact. This is often measured in financial, legislative, or regulatory terms.
Quantitative risk assessment	A form of risk assessment that analyses the actual numbers and values involved. This type of methodology typically applies mathematical and statistical techniques and modelling. (See: Qualitative risk assessment.)
Recoverable loss	Financial losses due to an event that may be reclaimed in the future, e.g. through insurance or litigation.
Residual risk	The level of uncontrolled risk remaining after all cost-effective actions (i.e. risk treatment) has been taken to lessen the impact and probability of a specific risk or group of risks, subject to the legal entities risk appetite. The risk that remains after countermeasures have been applied. [RFC 2828] The risk remaining after risk treatment. [ISO Guide 73:2009]
Resource	A Resource is defined as an element or component of an information processing system. It could be information, hardware, software, services needed to keep the information processing system operating, staff, knowledge, or intangible assets such as reputation.
Review	The activity undertaken to determine the suitability, adequacy, and effectiveness of the subject matter to achieve established objectives [ISO Guide 73:2009]
RFC	Request for comment
Risk	Combination of the probability of an event and its consequence [BS 7799:3, ISO Guide 73, and ISO 31000]. Effect of uncertainty on objectives [ISO 31000] The combination of the probability of harm and the severity of that harm [ISO Guide 51] The chance of something happening that will have an impact on objectives [AS/NZS 4360: 2004]. Something that might happen and its effect(s) on the achievement of objectives [BS 31100]. The net mission impact considering (1) the probability that a particular threat source will exercise (accidentally trigger or intentionally exploit) a particular system vulnerability and (2) the resulting impact if this should occur. [NIST 800-30].

Term	Definition
	Combination of the probability of an event and its outcome. The chance of something happening, measured in terms of probability and consequences. The consequence may be either positive or negative. The threat of an action or inaction that will prevent an organisation's ability to achieve its business objectives. The results of a risk occurring are defined by the impact. The uncertainty of outcome (whether positive opportunity or negative threat).
Risk acceptance	The informed decision made to accept a risk.
Risk analysis	The systematic process of identifying the nature and causes of risks to which an organisation could be exposed and assessing the likely impact and probability of those risks occurring. The systematic use of information to identify: • Threats; • Probability of occurrence; • Severity of the impact. To evaluate this data and provide information to management so that risk mitigation decisions can be taken. The process to comprehend the nature of risk and to determine the level of risk. [ISO Guide 73:2009]
Risk appetite	The willingness of an organisation to accept a defined level of risk in order to conduct its business cost-effectively. Different legal entities at different stages of their existence will have different risk appetites. The amount and type of risk that an organisation is prepared to pursue, retain or take. [ISO Guide 73:2009]
Risk assessment	The process of risk identification, analysis, and evaluation. Process of analysing threats to and vulnerabilities to a system and the potential impact resulting from the loss of information or capabilities of a system. This analysis is used as a basis for identifying appropriate and cost-effective security countermeasures (Risk treatment). Synonymous with risk analysis. The overall process of risk identification, risk analysis, and risk evaluation. [ISO Guide 73:2009]
Risk attitude	An organisation's approach to assess and eventually pursue, retain, take, or turn away from risk [ISO Guide 73:2009]
Risk aversion	Attitude to turn away from risk [ISO Guide 73:2009]
Risk avoidance	An informed decision not to become involved in a risk situation.
Risk based auditing	Audits that focus on risk and risk management as the audit objective.
Risk categories	Risks of similar types are grouped together under key headings, otherwise known as 'risk categories'. These categories can include: • Reputation; • Strategy; • Financial; • Investments; • Operational infrastructure; • Business; • Regulatory compliance; • People; • Technology and knowledge.
Risk communication	The exchange of communications between stakeholders (or others) about risk.
Risk concentration	The risks associated with having Mission Critical Activities and/or their dependencies, systemic processes, and people located either in the same building or close geographical proximity (zone), that are not reproduced elsewhere, i.e. a single point of failure and lack of organisational resilience.
Risk context	The environment in which risks exist. This can be broken down into the strategic context such as the relationship between the organisation and the external business environment, and the organisation context such as: • Goals; • Objectives; • Capabilities; • Resources; • Culture; • Strategies.

Continued

Term	Definition
Risk control	Actions implementing risk management. That part of risk management which involves the implementation of policies, standards, procedures, and physical changes to eliminate or minimise adverse risks.
Risk criteria	The terms of reference against which the significance of a risk is evaluated. [ISO Guide 73:2009]
Risk estimation	The process of assigning values to the probability and consequences of a risk.
Risk evaluation	The process of comparing actual risk levels with previously established risk criteria. From this risks can be prioritised for further action. The assessment of probability and impact of an individual risk, taking into account predetermined standards, target risk levels, interdependencies, and other relevant factors. The process of comparing the results of risk analysis with risk criteria to determine whether the risk and/or its magnitude is acceptable or tolerable. [ISO Guide 73:2009]
Risk event	An event that could potentially lead to an adverse impact on the business or function. The manifestation of a risk into a reality.
Risk financing	The application of techniques to fund the treatment and consequences of risk (e.g. using insurance). A means of accounting for potential loss exposures. Examples include various types of risk retention (e.g. internal contingency funds) and risk transfer techniques (e.g. insurance contracts, self-insurance, etc.).
Risk identification	The process of identifying what can happen, why and how. Determination of what could pose a risk. A process to describe and list sources of risk (threats). The process of finding, recognising, and describing risks and involves the identification of risk sources, events, their causes, and their potential consequences. [ISO Guide 73:2009]
Risk level	See: Risk profile.
Risk log	See: Risk register
Risk management	The systematic identifying, analysing, evaluating, treating, reviewing, and monitoring risk to provide an environment for proactive and infirmed decision making. The processes put in place to effectively manage potential opportunities and adverse effects. As it is not possible or desirable to eliminate all risk, the objective is to implement cost effective processes that reduce risks to an acceptable level by appropriate risk treatment and rejection of unacceptable risks. The task of ensuring that the organisation makes cost-effective use of risk processes. Risk management requires: • Access to reliable up to date information about risk; • Processes in place to monitor risks; • The right balance of control to treat those risks; • Decision making processes supported by a framework of risk analysis and evaluation. Coordinated activities to direct and control an organisation with regard to risk [ISO Guide 73:2009]
Risk management framework	A framework in which risks are managed, in terms of how they will be: • Identified; • Analysed; • Controlled; • Monitored; • Reviewed. It must be consistent and comprehensive with processes that are embedded in management activities throughout the organisation.
Risk management plan	A scheme within the risk management framework specifying the approach, the management components, and resources to be applied to the management of risk. [ISO Guide 73:2009]
Risk management policy	The documentation that governs how the management of risk framework will be adopted within a given context (i.e. for an organisation, a specific project, etc.). Statement of the overall intentions and direction of an organisation related to risk management. [ISO Guide 73:2009]

Term	Definition
Risk management process	The systematic and documented process of clarifying the risk context and identifying, analysing, evaluating, treating, monitoring, communicating, and consulting on risks. The systematic application of management policies, procedures, and practices to the activities of communicating, consulting, establishing the context, and identifying, analysing, evaluating, treating, monitoring, and reviewing risk. [ISO Guide 73:2009]
Risk mitigation	Measure taken to reduce exposures to risks. See: Risk reduction.
Risk on security investment	The ALE before risk treatment minus the ALE after risk treatment minus the annual cost of the risk treatment applied.
Risk optimisation	A process to minimise the negative and maximise the positive consequences of a risk and their probabilities.
Risk owner	An accountable and named individual responsible for the treatment of risk for a specific risk or area of the organisation and the acceptance of residual risk. A person or entity with the accountability and authority to manage the risk. [ISO Guide 73:2009]
Risk perception	Value or concern with which stakeholders view a particular risk. Stakeholders view risks differently; this is usually related to their attitude to risk (i.e. whether they are a risk taker or are risk averse).
Risk policy	See: Risk management policy.
Risk prioritisation	The relation of acceptable levels of risks amongst alternatives. See: Risk ranking.
Risk profile	The combined result of consequence and probability. See: Risk level. The description of any set of risks [ISO Guide 73:2009]
Risk profiling	The systematic method by which all the risks and associated controls relating to an entity are identified, assessed, and documented using risk management tools.
Risk ranking	The prioritisation of the risks in various alternatives, projects, or units. See: Risk prioritisation.
Risk reduction	A selective application of appropriate techniques and management principles to reduce or mitigate either likelihood of an occurrence or its consequences, or both. See: Risk mitigation
Risk register	A product used to maintain information on all the identified risks pertaining to a particular activity (project or programme).
Risk response	Actions that may be taken to bring the situation to a level where the exposure to risk is acceptable to the organisation. Individual risk responses can be to: • Accept a risk; • Avoid a risk; • Transfer a risk (or some aspects of it); • Treat a risk. See: Risk treatment
Risk retention	Intentional (or unintentional) retaining of responsibility for loss or risk financing within the organisation.
Risk scenarios	A method of identifying and classifying risks through application of probabilistic events and their consequences. The process is used to simulate 'what might happen'. This can be achieved through various techniques (e.g. brainstorming) or through the mathematical and statistical techniques and modelling (e.g. fault tree or event tree analysis).
Risk sharing	Sharing the loss or gain from a particular risk with another party.
Risk source	An element which alone or in combination has the intrinsic potential to give rise to risk. [ISO Guide 73:2009]

Continued

Term	Definition
Risk standards	Various Risk Standards have been published around the world providing guidance for business on managing risk. Some examples are: • AIRMIC—A Risk Management Standard • AS/NZS 3931 1998: Risk analysis of technological systems—Application guide • AS/NZS 4360: 2004 Risk Management; • BS 31100 Code of practice for risk management; • BS 7799 Part 3: 3006 Information Security Management Systems. Part 3: Guidelines for information risk management; • HB 436: 2004 Risk Management Guidelines; • ISO 13335—Part 3: Information Security—Guidelines for the management of IT security part 3: Techniques for the management of IT security; • ISO 31000 Risk management—Guidelines on principles and implementation of risk management; • ISO Guide 51: Safety aspects—Guidelines for their inclusion in standards; • ISO Guide 73 Risk management—Vocabulary—Guidelines for use in standards; • NIST 800-30 Risk Management Guidelines for Information Technology Systems.
Risk tolerance line	A line drawn on the Summary Risk Profile. Risks which appear above this line are those which cannot be accepted without referring them to a higher authority. For a project, the Project Manager would refer these to the SRO.
Risk transfer	A series of techniques describing the various means of addressing risk through insurance and similar products. This includes recent developments such as the securitisation of risk and creation of, for example, catastrophe bonds.
Risk treatment	The selection and implementation of relevant options for managing risk. The options are: • Acceptance—risks are retained by the organisation; • Avoidance—deciding not to carry on with the proposed activities due to the risk being unacceptable or finding another alternative that is more acceptable; • Treatment—reducing the likelihood and/or consequence of the risk; • Transfer—transferring the risk in part or in totality to another. Insurance is an example of risk transfer. The process to modify risk [ISO Guide 73:2009]
Role	A set of responsibilities, activities, and authorisations, which can be assigned to someone.
ROSI	Risk on Security Investment.
Safeguard	Protection implemented to counteract a known or expected condition. A countermeasure or set of countermeasures.
Security	See information security.
SEI	Software Engineering Institute (Part of Carnegie Mellon University).
Self-insurance	The decision to bear the losses that could result from a risk crystallising rather than take out an insurance policy to cover the risk.
Senior responsible owner	The single individual with overall personal responsibility for ensuring that a project or programme meets its objectives and delivers the projected benefits.
Severity of risk	The degree to which the risk could affect a situation.
Single loss expectancy	The total amount of revenue lost from a single occurrence of a risk.
SLE	Single loss expectancy
Source	Something (i.e. an event, activity or asset) that has the potential for a consequence.
Source identification	The process of identifying, listing, and defining sources.
SRO	Senior responsible owner.
Stakeholder	A person or organisation that can affect or be affected by a risk. Those with an interest in an organisation's achievements (e.g. customers, partners, employees, suppliers, shareholders, owners, government, regulators). [BS 25999 2006] A person or organisation that can affect, be affected by, or perceive themselves to be affected by a decision or activity [ISO Guide 73:2009]

Term	Definition
Standard	Documented agreements containing technical specifications or other precise data to be consistently used as rules, guidelines, or definitions or characteristics to ensure that materials, products, processes, and services are fit for their purpose. [ISO IEC 2382]
Strategic risk	Risk concerned with where the organisation wants to go, how it plans to get there, and how it can ensure survival and growth.
Summary risk profile	A tool to increase visibility of risks. It is a graphical representation of information normally found on an existing risk register.
System	A composite entity of any level of complexity that contains: • Personnel; • Procedures; • Physical assets; • Facilities; • Intangible assets; • Equipment; • Materials.
Systemic risk	The risk that the failure of one participant or part of a process, system, industry, or market to meet its obligations will cause other participants to be unable to meet their obligations when due causing significant problems thereby threatening the stability of the whole process, system, industry, or market.
Threat	A factor that could lead to a risk occurring (i.e. a cause of a risk). An action or event that could prejudice security.
Threat agent	A method used to exploit a vulnerability in a system, operation, or facility.
Threat analysis	The examination of all actions and events that might adversely affect a system or operation.
Threat monitoring	The analysis, assessment, and review of audit trails and other data collected for the purpose of searching out system events that may constitute violations or attempted violations of system security.
Threat source	The intent and method targeted at the intentional exploitation. The situation and method that may accidentally trigger a vulnerability.
Unexpected loss	The worst-case financial loss or impact that a business could incur due to a particular loss or risk.
Vulnerability	A flaw or weakness in a system that could be exploited by one or more threats.

Chapter 6

Quality in FCL

6.1 Quality and good laboratory practice

Every forensic laboratory, in every discipline, throughout the world should strive to achieve good practice and meet, or preferably exceed, their client's expectations by producing a quality product or service.

To achieve this, a number of organisations have produced good guidance documentation (guidance, standards, or procedures) for advising a forensic laboratory how to achieve this. A number of these are general in their nature, and some are sector specific. Some of the general ones are applicable to all forensic laboratories, and these include:

- ISO 9000—Quality management systems series; and
- ISO/IEC 17025—General requirements for the competence of testing and calibration laboratories.

Others are specifically defined for digital forensic laboratories, and some of these include, but are not limited to:

- Scientific Working Group on Digital Evidence (SWGDE), Establishing a Quality Management System for a Digital and Multimedia Organization under ISO-IEC 17025 or 17020 Version: 2.0 (17 June 2021)
- SWGDE Technical Overview for Reverse Projection Photogrammetry v1.0, 13 January 2022;
- SWGDE Guideline for Low Light Crime Scene Photography v1.0, 13 January 2022;
- SWGDE Guidance for DME Labs on Addressing ANABs 2020 Update on Field Sampling v1.0, 13 January 2022;
- SWGDE Best Practices for Vehicle Infotainment and Telematics Systems v3.0, 13 January 2022;
- SWGDE Best Practices for the Forensic Use of Photogrammetry v1.2, 13 January 2022;
- SWGDE Best Practices for Obtaining Google Reverse Location Data for Investigative Purposes v1.1, 13 January 2022;
- SWGDE Best Practices for Drone Forensics v1.0, 13 January 2022;
- SWGDE Best Practices for Acquiring Online Content v1.0, 13 January 2022;
- NIST Handbook 150, National Voluntary Laboratory Accreditation program, Procedures and General Requirements, 2016;
- European Network of Forensic Science Institutes (ENFSI), Best Practice Manual for the Forensic Examination of Digital Technology, Version 1, 2015; and
- UK Forensic Science Regulator (FSR), forensic science providers: codes of practice and conduct, 2021, issue 7, March 2021.

As can be imagined, there is a large degree of overlap between these documents.

This chapter concentrates on the requirements of ISO 9001 certification if it is to be achieved by a forensic laboratory and the requirements for ISO/IEC 17025 accreditation. The mapping of ISO 9001 and ISO/IEC 17025 requirements to the procedures in the FCL IMS is defined in Appendix 1 and Appendix 2, respectively.

The specific requirements of the FSR relating to quality processes in FCL have been mapped to FCL's IMS procedures in Appendix 3.

6.2 Management requirements for operating FCL

Having physically set up FCL as defined in Chapters 2 and 3, a large number of management processes shall be set up to operate FCL. Some of these relate to quality processes and others to everyday operations. This is not meant to be a primer on running a business but to identify some issues relevant to operating a forensic laboratory, specifically FCL.

6.2.1 Forensic laboratory organisation

6.2.1.1 Legal status

FCL has been set up according to its own requirements and in line with the legislative and regulatory requirements of the jurisdiction(s) in which it operates. This will ensure that it is a 'legal person' within the jurisdiction(s) of operations and can be legally responsible for its actions.

A Blueprint for Implementing Best Practice Procedures in a Digital Forensic Laboratory. https://doi.org/10.1016/B978-0-12-819479-9.00010-1

FCL is an independent forensic laboratory processing digital evidence to resolve client's evidential requirements on a commercial basis.

6.2.1.2   Ownership

FCL's ownership shall be clearly defined and made public, if required, for the jurisdiction(s) where it operates. The shareholder details shall be recorded in the relevant business register.

If FCL becomes part of a larger organisation, then this shall be clearly stated and the whole organisational structure shall be clearly documented. This shall include the organisational structure of FCL, its position in the parent organisation's structure, and all relationships between other parts of the organisation, including operations, support, and management.

Where a forensic laboratory is part of a larger organisation that performs activities other than digital forensic services, the clear delineation of roles and responsibilities shall be clearly defined so that any potential conflicts of interest can be identified and addressed at the earliest possible opportunity. No employee of any other part of the organisation should be able exert any undue influence on the forensic laboratory, its employees, or clients.

6.2.1.3   Organisation

Whilst the actual FCL organisation chart is not reproduced, a generic forensic laboratory organisational chart is shown in Fig. 6.1.

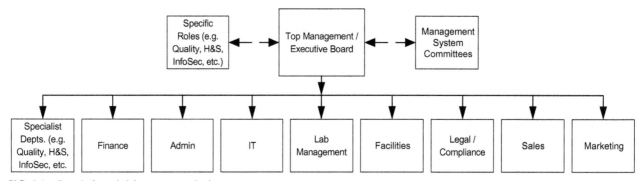

FIG. 6.1   Generic forensic laboratory organisation.

Details of the Management System Committees are defined in Chapter 4, Section 4.5.1.1 and their terms of Reference in Chapter 4, Appendices 7–14.

6.2.1.4   Job descriptions

Within FCL, all jobs shall have defined general job descriptions as defined by HR in Chapter 18, Section 18.1.5.

Top management shall appoint a Quality Manager who has appropriate authority and responsibility to carry out their duties and to ensure that FCL's quality system is implemented, monitored, and continuously improved.

The Quality Manager's job description is defined in Appendix 4. There are a number of specialist roles that have detailed job descriptions relevant to the IMS (e.g. health and safety, information security, service delivery, change management, etc.), and these are defined in the relevant chapters in the rest of this book.

Note

Depending on the size of a forensic laboratory, full-time appointees to these specialised roles may not be possible in a small to medium sized forensic laboratory. In this case, it may be necessary to have a single employee undertake a number of roles, so long as segregation of duties can be maintained as far as possible, as defined in Chapter 12, Sections 12.3.5 and 12.3.6. In a large forensic laboratory, deputies for these roles should be appointed.

6.2.1.5   Authorities and responsibilities

It is FCL's duty to meet all legislative, regulatory, and other relevant requirements.

Specific authorities, responsibilities, reporting procedures, and taskings for all employees shall be contained in their job descriptions. Those that are relevant to the IMS are defined in this book, whilst generic job descriptions are the remit of HR and relevant Line Managers.

6.2.1.6 Impartiality and independence

Impartiality and independence have been mentioned in Chapter 3, Section 3.1.5; however, if a forensic laboratory is part of a larger organisation, it may have problems demonstrating this to any third party.

To demonstrate this and that its employees are free from any undue commercial, financial, and other influences which might affect their technical judgement, the Conflict of Interest Policy is implemented as defined in Chapter 3, Section 3.1.3.14.

Whilst the Conflict of Interest Policy primarily applies to individuals, top management shall ensure that FCL does not undertake any work that may endanger the client and public trust in its perceived impartiality, independence and integrity in relation to its provision of digital forensic services.

6.2.1.7 Finances

FCL shall ensure that its accounting and financial procedures meet the requirements of the jurisdiction. Appropriate reporting and public disclosure shall be implemented.

6.2.1.8 Insurance

The provision of appropriate insurance cover has been covered in Chapter 3, Section 3.1.14.

6.2.1.9 Accreditation and certification

Accreditation for a forensic laboratory is covered in Chapter 3, Section 3.1.18, and the relevant chapters in this book specific to the relevant accreditations and certifications that a forensic laboratory wishes to achieve.

Mappings between the requirements of the relevant standards to the procedures in the IMS are also given in the relevant chapters in this book. This will assist any forensic laboratory to choose those that are relevant to their business model and implement the relevant procedures.

6.2.2 Operations

6.2.2.1 Business planning within FCL

The main planning tool is FCL's business plan and the template that FCL uses for all business plans is defined in Appendix 5.

Reviews of the plan shall be performed on a regular basis by top management, as follows:

- a monthly review of the business, financial, and forensic case processing metrics and key performance indicators (KPIs) shall be undertaken to check whether the business is performing in-line with expectations and meeting its objectives, and
- an annual review of the entire business plan shall be undertaken to assess its status and to plan for the next financial year—this involves reviewing the services, market, financial forecasts, and resources and then generating a new or revised plan. This is typically carried out as part of the management review.

6.2.2.2 Managing FCL

FCL operates in an effective and efficient manner by following the processes and procedures embedded in the IMS and ensuring that all employees are aware of their responsibilities and the opportunities available. Employee meetings within departments occur on a regular and frequent basis to discuss, as applicable to each department, the following types of matters:

- **development of the business**—financial performance, client news, new business, etc.;
- **forensic cases**—progress on forensic cases, problems encountered, timescales, changes to requirements, new possibilities, meetings arranged, etc.; and
- **design developments**—new ways of working to improve the levels of service to clients including new methodologies and tools, new or revised standards, training opportunities, technological developments in the field, etc.

Formal meetings shall all have agendas and be minuted, and their minutes shall be kept as records in the IMS as defined in Chapter 4, Section 4.7.6.

Some information exchange also occurs on an informal basis through informal meetings, telephone conversations, and email between individuals and is not always formally documented.

At the end of each forensic case, a formal audit shall be performed on the forensic case that covers the business and technical aspects of the forensic case and the training and development aspects of the employees involved in the forensic case. Any gaps or areas where improvements could be achieved, such as a change in a procedure, additional employee training, additional tools, or any other relevant matter, shall be assessed and appropriate action is taken. This is defined Chapter 4, Section 4.9, and the results shall be fed into the continuous improvement process defined in Chapter 4, Section 4.10.

6.2.2.3 Service to clients

FCL's raison d'être is to provide digital forensic products and services to its clients in line with the requirements of its in-house procedures defined in the IMS, based on current good practice It is FCL's responsibility to ensure that **all** products and services supplied to the client shall satisfy legislative, regulatory, and in-house requirements. Meeting legal, regulatory, and client requirements is a primary goal for FCL.

6.2.2.4 Management system (the IMS)

The IMS covers all activities carried out by FCL, wherever they may be performed (the office, client site, scene of crime, or other locations as appropriate). The IMS is a 'one stop shop' for all policies, processes, procedures, work instructions, forms and checklists used in FCL. Regular training and updating of all employees on its contents shall be undertaken and records of this training shall be maintained as formal records, as defined in Chapter 18, Section 18.2.1.8.

6.2.2.5 Applicability of the IMS

The IMS shall apply to all employees for all tasks performed by FCL in the provision of products and services to their clients.

6.2.2.6 Confidentiality of information

FCL shall ensure the confidentiality of all information entrusted to it (either its own information or information trusted to it by a client or other third party) for the duration it is under FCL's control. Details of how confidentiality of forensic case files shall be maintained is defined in Section 6.11 and uses the processes defined in Chapter 12.

6.3 ISO 9001 in FCL

6.3.1 Goal

The goal of FCL is to be known and recognised as a reputable forensic laboratory that is highly regarded for the quality of its products, services, and employee skills by a stable and varied set of clients. FCL's goal statement is defined in Chapter 4, Appendix 3.

To achieve this, FCL shall comply with ISO 9001.

6.3.2 Quality policy

FCL quality policy is defined in Chapter 3, Appendix 4. It shall be endorsed by top management, as have all other management system policies defined in Chapter 4, Section 4.1.

6.3.3 Quality policy statements

Top management shall endorse the following quality statements:

- FCL is committed to good quality working practice in all tasks relating to its products and services for delivery to its clients;
- all employees shall always perform their activities in accordance with policies, procedures, and standards documented in the IMS and to ensure that all products and services provided meet, and exceed, client expectations;

- all forensic case processing shall meet the requirements of the IMS, be scientifically sound, repeatable, and provide the client with reliable results;
- all employees shall undergo appropriate training to ensure that they are competent to perform their tasks;
- quality shall be measured by 'Key Performance Indicators' (designated as quality objectives) which top management shall review and set each year to ensure that all employees attain quality standards, and to ensure continuous improvement of quality and other objectives. 'Key Performance Indicators' are defined in Section 6.2.2.1;
- all employees shall ensure that they are familiar with those aspects of all policies and procedures in the IMS that relate to their day-to-day work;
- FCL is committed to a process of continuous improvement in all of its products and services as defined in Chapter 4, Section 4.10; and
- quality is the responsibility of all employees.

6.3.4 Scope of the quality management system (QMS)

The QMS is a part of the IMS and they share a common scope which is defined in Chapter 5, Appendix 11. This also includes the scope statement for all of the management standards in the IMS.

6.3.5 Using a client's QMS

FCL may occasionally be required to use and conform to a client's QMS and procedures as a condition of performing work for that client.

FCL's QMS may not match the client's QMS, in a number of areas. In the event that a situation such as this arises, attempts shall be made to conform to as much as possible to the client's QMS within the constraints imposed by the client's QMS.

Ideally, at the proposal stage of work with a client, the Account Manager shall ascertain whether FCL's QMS is acceptable to the client.

If the client decides not to accept FCL's QMS and requires that FCL conforms to its QMS, the Account Manager shall document and agree the differences between FCL's and the client's QMS and confirm to the client the following items, in writing:

- those aspects of FCL QMS that will be followed;
- those aspects of the client QMS that will be followed; and
- areas where no provision is identified or agreed. This may be subject to later agreement and updated documentation.

FCL will then proceed with the forensic case using the identified 'hybrid' QMS or top management may consider excluding the forensic case from FCL's QMS.

6.3.6 Benefits of ISO 9001

Some of the benefits of ISO 9001 include, but are not limited to:

- communicating a positive message about commitment to quality to employees and clients;
- constantly monitoring the quality of products and services;
- defining all quality responsibilities;
- enhancing image and reputation of FCL's products and services;
- having an independent audit by an Accredited Conformance Assessment Body will demonstrate independently assessed commitment to quality processes and continuous improvement, if appropriate;
- having well-defined and documented procedures improves the consistency of products and services delivered to clients;
- identifying nonconforming products and services early in the production cycle and continuously improving production processes to address failures;
- improving efficiency;
- improving employee attitudes to 'right, first time, every time';
- improving focus on client needs;
- international acceptability;
- lessening reliance on key individuals by having all processes documented as well as facilitating new employee take on

- moving from being in 'detection mode' to 'prevention mode';
- providing a basis for adding new management systems to the IMS as the QMS models the business processes and is the ideal start point;
- providing consistent training for all employees;
- providing continuous assessment and improvement;
- providing top management with an efficient management process and improved business oversight;
- proving marketing opportunities;
- reducing costs; and
- reducing waste and re-work, as client requirements are confirmed and there is continuous client communication in place.

6.4 FCL's QMS

FCL shall establish, document, implement, and maintain a QMS as part of its IMS. This QMS, like the other management systems in the IMS, shall share a common set of procedures for a number of requirements, as defined in Chapter 4.
FCL shall:

- identify the business processes to be included in the QMS;
- identify the sequence and interaction of these processes;
- determine criteria and methods needed to ensure the operation and control of these processes is, and remains, effective;
- document appropriate policies and procedures to ensure that all products and services are delivered to meet, and exceed client expectations and all external drivers;
- ensure that management responsibilities to establish, document, implement and maintain the QMS exist and are effective, as defined in Section 6.5;
- ensure the availability of resources and information necessary for the operation and monitoring of these processes. Management of resources is covered in Chapter 4, Section 4.7.1;
- undertake regular audits of the QMS as defined in Chapter 4, Section 4.9.3;
- undertake management reviews on a regular basis as defined in Chapter 4, Section 4.9.3; and
- implement actions necessary for continuous improvement of these processes, as defined in Chapter 4, Section 4.10.

Note 1

Where FCL outsources services to a third party, FCL shall ensure that the outsourcing supplier complies with the requirements of the IMS and that it maintains control over the provision of these products and services as defined in Chapter 10.

Note 2

FCL developed its original Quality Plan in 2003 for the original requirements for a QMS. The QMS was the first management standard to be implemented and since then, the IMS has grown, but this plan is still appropriate and demonstrates the original requirements. The outline for the plan is defined in Appendix 7.

6.5 Responsibilities in the QMS

There are a number of specific responsibilities within the QMS for top management and all employees, and these shall include demonstrating commitment to ensuring that all of their products and services are of a suitable quality for both internal and external clients and that:

- this requirement has been communicated to all employees as defined in Chapter 4, Section 4.7.4 and forms part of the induction process for all new employees. The induction checklist is defined in Appendix 8;
- a Quality Policy has been developed and implemented which is included in the induction process as defined in Chapter 3, Appendix 4;
- regular management reviews are carried out for the QMS as part of the IMS management review process, as defined in Chapter 4, Section 4.9.3;
- appropriate resources shall be made available for the efficient and effective operation and management of this IMS and specifically the QMS, as defined in Chapter 4, Section 4.7.1 and Section 6.4;
- a Quality Manager whose job description is defined in Appendix 4 shall be appointed and trained;

- up-to-date QMS policies, procedures, and other associated documentation shall be present for all processes covered by the IMS; and
- regular audits shall be undertaken as part of the continuous improvement process for this IMS as defined in Chapter 4, Section 4.9.2 and specifically for forensic case processing in Section 6.13.3.

Products and services shall always be client focused whether they are for internal or external clients. To ensure that this is the case, the following processes shall be implemented:

- client requirements shall be carefully collated and documented as part of the sales cycle as defined in Section 6.6;
- these requirements are captured in the proposal to the client. The table of contents of a standard proposal are defined in Appendix 10; and
- when the proposal has been internally reviewed, it is reviewed with the client to ensure that it meets their requirements and where necessary, it is amended and approved prior to formal release to the client.

Note 1

In some cases, just a quotation is required for a job (typically, this is where a contractual business relationship already exists and the client requires a quotation for an additional forensic case). The table of contents of a standard quotation for processing a forensic case are defined in Appendix 12.

Note 2

The standard Terms and Conditions for forensic case processing are defined in Appendix 13.

A quality management policy shall be developed and implemented as defined in Chapter 3, Appendix 4 that is appropriate to its business that:

- has been endorsed by top management;
- ensures that the supporting QMS is continuously monitored and improved as part of the IMS performance assessment as defined in Chapter 4, Section 4.9.1 and Section 6.13 as well as the continuous improvement process defined in Chapter 4, Section 4.10;
- provides a framework to establish and review KPIs (quality objectives). Details of KPIs are defined in Appendix 6;
- is communicated to all employees as part of their induction process; and
- is regularly reviewed during the management review process for continued suitability within FCL as defined in Chapter 4, Section 4.9.3 and Chapter 4, Appendix 46.

The QMS shall be defined and implemented so that it is appropriate to the way that top management operate and this shall include:

- ensuring that all changes to the IMS and specifically the QMS, are subject to Change Management System as defined in Chapter 7, Section 7.4.3; and
- ensuring that all changes to the IMS and specifically the QMS are communicated appropriately to all employees as defined in Chapter 4, Section 4.7.4.

All responsibilities in the IMS shall be defined and shall be documented in:

- the IMS scope statement (at a high level) as defined in Chapter 5, Appendix 11;
- defined job descriptions for all employees are defined in various chapters in this book;
- the appointment of a Quality Manager with defined responsibilities and authority;
- the ongoing internal audit process as defined in Chapter 4, Section 4.9.2 and specifically in Section 6.13.3 for auditing forensic case processing;
- the management review process as defined in Chapter 4, Section 4.9.3;
- the continuous improvement process as defined in Chapter 4, Section 4.10; and
- the internal communication process as defined in Chapter 4, Section 4.7.4.

Appropriate resources shall be provided to implement, operate, manage, and monitor the QMS. This shall be evidenced by:

- managing the resources available in the optimal manner to support the QMS as defined in Chapter 4, Section 4.7.1;
- appointing employees to specific roles and documenting these in their job descriptions;
- regularly auditing the QMS;
- undertaking regular management reviews of the QMS;
- enhancing client satisfaction by ensuring that proposals, products, and services meet, and hopefully exceed, the client's expectation;
- obtaining, where appropriate and possible, feedback on work performed for clients using the forensic case feedback process defined in Chapter 14, Section 14.2.1.4 and Chapter 16, Section 16.2.6; and
- taking action on any client complaints to ensure continuous improvement as defined in Section 6.14.

6.6   Managing sales

The sales cycle is the start of the 'Client Engagement' process. This covers two specific situations:

- new business; and
- repeat business.

New business is where a new client is taken on for forensic case processing and requires the 'full treatment' including marketing material and a formal proposal. Whilst basic details about FCL are supplied to a prospective client either as part of a marketing campaign or with a proposal, a client may request additional details. The details defined in Section 6.6.2.1, assuming they contain no confidential information, shall be supplied to the client, as well as any references to support the quality of the products and services to be provided that are relevant to the prospective client.

Repeat business is where an existing client is already under a blanket contract and requires one or more additional forensic cases to be processed.

6.6.1   Handling a sales enquiry

A contact from an existing or potential new client is received by:

- telephone;
- post;
- email;
- face to face at a conference or similar (Fig. 6.2).

All contact from existing clients shall be handled by the Account Manager who currently services their needs.

Prospective new clients shall be handled by an Account Manager with the appropriate skill set or experience. This contact shall establish the client's:

- name;
- job title;
- company name;
- telephone number;
- email address;
- initial work requirements; and
- timescales.

Initial work requirements are only ever accepted as required outcomes rather than a series of prescribed sets of tasks that may not agree with the in-house procedures, methodologies or approach. Some issues to consider when taking on a forensic case for a new or existing client are defined in Appendix 11.

Whenever a query from a potential client is received by FCL, the objective is to secure a meeting where the proposed work is discussed and the result of the meeting is to obtain go-ahead for the presentation of a proposal.

Where an existing client requires additional work and is subject to an existing contract, a quotation shall be submitted to the client for their consideration, as defined in Appendix 12.

There may be invitations to bid on a contract (e.g. an invitation to tender (ITT), request for proposal (RFP), or similar). In these situations, a decision shall be made as to whether to proceed according to the terms set. If so, then the required documentation to bid on the invitation shall be submitted.

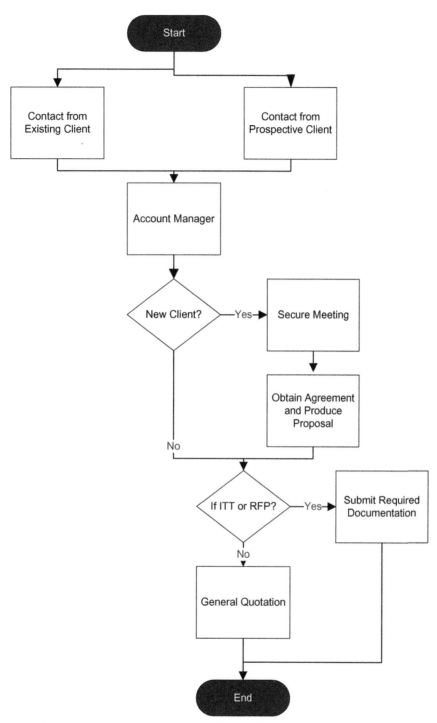

FIG. 6.2 Handling a sales enquiry.

6.6.2 A new client

6.6.2.1 *Attending an initial meeting for a new client*

The relevant Account Manager, with other employees, as appropriate, attends an initial meeting with the potential client.

At the meeting work methods shall be described, the skills that can be brought to the client shall be outlined and the required conclusion of the meeting shall be to determine how to proceed with the proposed work. Agreement shall be reached on the next step and when contact shall be made between the parties again.

The Account Manager shall write to the potential client within 5 working days of the meeting, summarising the discussions and highlighting the actions they shall now take and the next steps that were agreed at the meeting.

6.6.2.2 Setting up a client virtual file

Where a meeting with a potential client is to be attended, records of this shall be retained. These shall be stored in the client's virtual file, which shall be set up at this point. Assuming the proposed work goes ahead, the client's virtual file shall contain all documentation relating to the client relationship. If the proposed work does not proceed, then the client virtual file shall be filed with other 'Failed Proposals', in case of later need. To set up a client's virtual file, the Account Manager shall (Fig. 6.3):

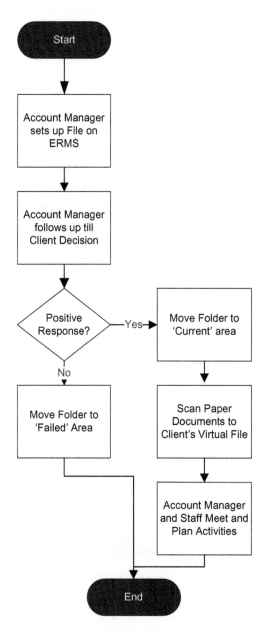

FIG. 6.3 Setting up a client virtual file.

1. Create a folder on the relevant area of the server in the Electronic Records Management System (ERMS). This shall contain all documentation relating to the client. There are four different areas for client matters in the ERMS, these are defined in Appendix 14.

2. Follow-up as required until notification of the client's decision is received.
3. Where a positive response is received from the client, the Account Manager shall move the client's virtual file into the 'current' area.
4. Scan any paper correspondence and notes made into the client virtual file. The paper documents shall be shredded and then disposed of appropriately.
5. Meet with any other relevant employees to discuss the project and plan the production of the relevant response to scope the work.
6. On many occasions, an order for work will initially be a verbal request that shall be followed later by written confirmation.
7. Where a negative response is received from the prospective client, the Account Manager shall move the client's virtual file to the 'failed' area and call a meeting with the relevant employees to determine the reasons for the negative response and how to improve the sales process from the lessons learned. Any outcomes from this meeting shall be formally recorded as records and filed in the client's virtual file. Any paper correspondence and notes made shall be scanned into the client virtual file. The paper documents shall be shredded and then disposed of appropriately.

6.6.2.3 The proposal creation lifecycle

A proposal shall be produced for requested work for a new client. The proposal is a thorough scoping exercise which shall include a detailed fixed-price cost based upon an agreed set of deliverables, although 'time and materials' based forensic cases may be undertaken.

Note 1

There are circumstances when a proposal is not produced for a client, for example a letter may be produced that details costs that is subsequently used as the basis for a project or a quotation for a forensic case is requested.

Note 2

All documents, including proposals, shall follow the document control process in Chapter 4, Section 4.7.5.3. In the case of the production of a proposal, the Account Manager is the Document Owner, may be the Document Author or may appoint one.

The responsibilities for producing the proposal shall lie with the client's Account Manager. The proposal production process is shown below:

6.6.2.3.1 Planning for the information gathering meeting

Ideally, a clarification or information gathering meeting between the parties shall take place. This shall be attended by the Account Manager, such other employees, as appropriate and the client's representative(s).

An internal information gathering meeting is the first stage in this process. The Document Author shall check all information about the client before the meeting so that pertinent questions can be asked. The steps for gathering information for the meeting shall be:

- gather all relevant information from the original sales meeting and other meetings with the client;
- research past forensic cases with similar content or structure, and review the methods used and work produced for these;
- prepare a list of questions for the information gathering meeting; and
- collect items to take to the information gathering meeting, such as samples, brochures, case studies, white papers, etc.

Note

As early as possible (at least 2 working days) before an information gathering meeting the Account Manager and the Laboratory Manager shall discuss and agree the objective for the meeting and any additional issues.

6.6.2.3.2 Attending an information gathering meeting

The Account Manager shall attend the information gathering meeting with any other appropriate employees. Every meeting is different, but there shall always be the following stages:

- introduction session with the client employees;
- confirmation of the plans and objectives for the meeting;
- information gathering session that includes:
- interviewing client employees;
- reading client documents;
- presentations from client employees;
- shadowing client employees; and
- closing session with the client employees.

During the information gathering, the Account Manager and other attending employees shall:

- project a professional image;
- demonstrate relevant expertise—discuss examples of past work;
- obtain a walk-through of the forensic case—from which the work is scoped;
- understand the forensic case and requirements fully—so that accurate time and cost estimates can be produced;
- cover all relevant topics—referring to their question list; and
- take full notes—to help when writing the proposal.

Note

When discussing past clients, ensure that the existing confidentiality agreements in force are not breached.

The Document Author shall arrange a date for when the proposal is to be reviewed with the client. This is typically 1–2 weeks after the submission of the proposal.

6.6.2.3.3 Writing the first draught of the proposal

Unless they are the same person, the Document Author and the Account Manager shall meet to discuss the proposed content of the proposal following the information gathering meeting. At this meeting they shall ensure they agree on the:

- deliverables to be produced;
- sections to include in the proposal;
- approach for the forensic case; and
- time scales for the forensic case (the turn round time required).

To save time, the Document Author may base a proposal on a previous one. To do this, the Document Author shall select a previous proposal on which the current one can be based. The Document Author may need to look through all client virtual files in the ERMS to find a similar proposal. The Document Author shall select one that is fairly recent (within a year) that reflects any new developments in work practice, including any lessons learned if a proposal from the 'Failed' area is chosen.

The Document Author shall make a copy of a proposal from the relevant client virtual file or creates a new one using FCL proposal template. The usual tool for writing a proposal is Microsoft Word. The new proposal shall be saved into the new client virtual file. If the Document Author uses an existing proposal on which to base the new one, then all references to the original recipient of the proposal shall be removed. Just using the 'search and replace' function in a word processor is not enough to perform this task. This task shall be performed manually and remove all references to the original recipient of any type that exist. It is for this reason that it is preferred that the proposal template is used rather than editing an existing one, but time pressures do not always allow this. Checking for references to past clients shall include, but not be limited to the following areas of the documents:

- all the text;
- document properties;
- headers and footers;
- information on any sample screen shots;
- metadata in the document;
- text on diagrams; and

- text on flowcharts;

  The Document Author shall write the proposal and:

- pay close attention to their notes from the information gathering meeting;
- not be tempted to include text from the copied proposal if it is not absolutely relevant;
- not be afraid to vary the headings in the proposal template, if necessary—the proposal shall be adapted to address the client's concerns and requirements;
- estimate the time and cost of the forensic case. Costs shall be calculated according to the number of days required per deliverable, as well as materials required based upon past experience. To assist in this a forensic case costing spreadsheet is used as defined in Appendix 15. These may be confirmed by the Laboratory Manager; and
- follow document control requirements defined in Chapter 4, Section 4.7.5.3 and the proposal template.

6.6.2.3.4 Internally reviewing the proposal

1. The Laboratory Manager shall review the proposal and provide comment on the changes as required. Particular attention shall be made to the project costs. All comments shall be stored in the client virtual file in the ERMS (Fig. 6.4).

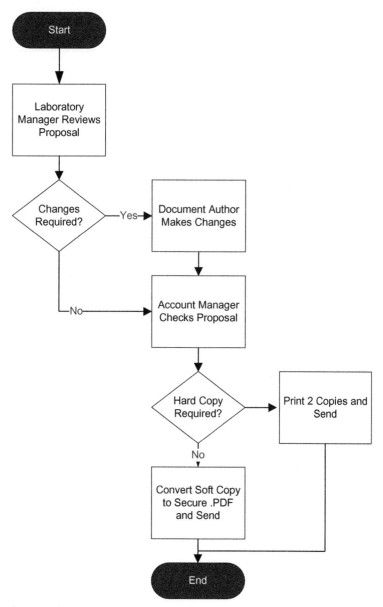

FIG. 6.4 Internally reviewing the proposal.

2. The Document Author shall check all comments received and judges which comments to implement. The Document Author shall consult with the Account Manager and/or Laboratory Manager when in doubt as to the validity of comments and ask for explanations of these comments.
3. The Document Author shall amend the proposal in accordance with the Writing and Updating Documents procedures in Chapter 4, Section 4.7.5.4.
4. The Account Manager shall double-check the proposal to ensure that edits have been implemented correctly and that no new errors have been introduced. This is the version to be issued to the client for review.
5. If a hard copy is required, then the Document Author shall print two copies of the proposal:
   - one for the client; and
   - one for the client file.
6. If a soft copy is to be sent to the client, then it shall be converted to 'secured' PDF format and sent by email with a receipt request.
7. Depending on the information classification of the proposal, as defined in Chapter 5, Appendix 16, appropriate means of protection of the proposal shall be applied according to the controls defined in Chapter 12, Section 12.3.14.

Note

Extra copies can, of course, be produced if necessary. The client can circulate their copy of the proposal if additional people need to see it at the client site, but FCL has no control over this process.

6.6.2.3.5 Issuing the proposal

The Document Author shall write to the client enclosing the proposal. The normal delivery method is post, but if time is short and it is essential that the proposal arrives on the following day, it shall be sent by courier or emailed.

The method of transmission shall also ensure that data handling procedures for the classification for the proposal are met, as defined in Chapter 12, Section 12.3.14.

6.6.2.4 *The proposal review lifecycle*

Note

For simplicity, the 'team' attending the review have been referred to as the 'Document Author' irrespective of who actually attends.

Once a proposal has been produced and sent to a client, the Document Author shall liaise with the client to discuss it and to arrange a review of the proposal.

It is not always required to hold a formal review meeting with a client to discuss a proposal. Sometimes a telephone call or an email can suffice, particularly when the work required is straight-forward. In all cases however, the proposal shall be discussed and agreed with the client.

The Account Manager shall be responsible for planning and holding a review with the client. It may well be that the Laboratory Manager or another employee shall attend the review process with the Document Author.

6.6.2.4.1 Planning the review

The Document Author's major objectives of the review shall be to agree with the client the:

- deliverables covered in the proposal;
- production schedule for the deliverables;
- costs, including a payment schedule; and
- start date for the forensic case.

The Document Author shall ask the client to confirm any order in writing and send a purchase order for the forensic case.

6.6.2.4.2 Reviewing the proposal with the client

The client shall review their copy of the proposal sent by the Document Author. This may be a meeting or can be telephone or email based.

The Document Author shall answer any client questions on the proposal and resolve any issues that remain. Any negotiations on cost and content of the work usually take place at this stage. The Document Author shall take full notes to ensure that an updated proposal can be produced after the meeting that contains all the necessary information and reflects the client's view. The notes shall be added to the client virtual file in the ERMS.

The proposal is updated as required.

6.6.2.4.3 Approving the case

If the client is proceeding with the forensic case, the Document Author shall arrange the following:

- confirmation from the client of the forensic case going ahead, preferably with a purchase order or at least with a letter of intent;
- a forensic case start date when the work can begin;
- the signing of the contract; and
- updated proposal, if required.

Under no circumstances shall work on the forensic case be started until a signed contract is received from the client. This shall also ensure that Professional Indemnity insurance applies to all work performed.

6.6.2.4.4 Following up the review

The Document Author shall confirm in writing to the client the outcome of the review:

- if the project is going ahead as planned—confirm the start date, costs and what the client can expect to happen next;
- if the project is not going ahead—confirm the outcome of the meeting and arrange any follow-up meetings as necessary, including moving the virtual client file to 'Failed Proposals';
- if the project is not going ahead, the Document Author (and any other interested parties) shall hold a debrief to determine the cause of the failure to proceed, and promulgate any lessons learned for future sales;
- if there is another way forward—shall confirm the tasks required on both sides, arrange any follow-up meetings; and
- If there are many changes to a proposal, the Document Author shall update the proposal and the Account Manager shall check that the proposal has been updated as required.

When signed-off by the client, unless there are further changes to the forensic case, the proposal shall be the terms of reference for the project.

The Document Author sends version V1.0 of the proposal, if required, to the client with a covering letter.

The Document Author shall file all documentation relating to the proposal in the client virtual file in the ERMS.

The next stage in the project lifecycle is for work to begin on the forensic case.

6.6.3 An existing client

Where the client is already and existing one, the same process shall be followed as above if an existing contract does not exist.

If it exists, the quotation route shall be followed, with a new quotation supplied under the existing contract as defined in Appendix 12.

Part of the above process shall be carried out by the Account Manager, as appropriate.

6.7 Provision of products and services

Note

ISO 9001:2015 now refers to 'provision of products and services' whilst ISO 10005 still refers to 'product realisation'. This book refers to 'products and services' as its generic term for deliverables of any sort so the standard can be adopted and adapted universally. This term has been used throughout the book as it is the term used in ISO 9001.

Products and services are usually documents of one type or another and the type of document varies depending on the client requirements. Due to the varied nature of the forensic cases undertaken, it is not possible to provide exact procedures for the whole provision of product and service process, in some cases these are only guidelines that shall be interpreted in the context of the specific forensic case. That having been said, there are a number of procedures that shall be followed and guidelines interpreted to ensure that the provision of product or service is effective.

6.7.1 Planning of provision of products and services

The provision of products and services process is the process needed to identify, create, and supply the required product or service (usually a forensic case report and supporting evidence) to a client. This shall be made up of the following processes (Fig. 6.5):

- identification of the products and services required by the client during the sales process;
- agreeing the deliverables with the client in an agreed proposal as defined in Section 6.6.2.3;

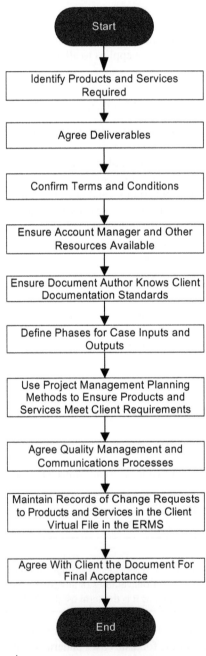

FIG. 6.5 Planning of provision of products and services.

- confirming the terms and conditions of delivery in a contract for the products and services to be provided as defined in Appendix 13;
- ensuring that the Account Manager and other competent resources are available to deliver the products and services to the client, as required; and
- ensuring that the relevant Document Authors are aware of the standards for producing documents for delivery to the client, as defined in Chapter 4, Section 4.7.5 and in Section 6.6.2.3.

Typically, forensic cases are split into a number of phases and their inputs, tasks, and outputs defined.

Standard project planning methods shall be used to ensure that delivery of the products and services meets the client's requirements. This shall use Microsoft Project as the project management tool.

At this stage, the quality assurance and communication process shall be agreed in the proposal to the client by the Quality Manager.

Records of all changes requested to any product or service to be delivered shall be recorded in the client virtual file in the ERMS. These shall be agreed between the parties in writing.

As part of the proposal, the documentation for final acceptance of the products and services defined in the proposal shall be agreed. Typically, this is a signed copy of the contract, quotation, or other similar and acceptable document.

6.7.2 Client-related processes

A number of client-related processes shall be implemented to ensure that product realisation is achieved. These shall include, but not be limited to:

- the production of proposals for internal review, as defined in Section 6.6.2.3.4;
- the client review of the draught proposal to permit any feedback for amending the proposal to ensure that the proposal meets the client's requirements, as defined in Section 6.6.2.4;
- knowledge of applicable legislation or regulation applicable to the product or service to be supplied either based on the client's stated requirements or knowledge and experience of similar projects as defined in Chapter 12, Section 12.3.13.1;
- ensuring that there are sufficient resources available to meet the client's requirements, as defined in Chapter 4, Section 4.7.1;
- ensuring that the resources are suitably skilled with appropriate training and competence, as defined in Chapter 4, Section 4.7.3;
- ensuring that all documentation (marked up proposals and draught reviews) shall be maintained in the client's virtual file folder in the ERMS, as defined in Chapter 15;
- ensuring that any changes to the requirements shall be documented and included in the proposal as part of the internal or client review process, as defined in Sections 6.6.2.3 and 6.6.2.4;
- where changes occur after the project has started, to ensure that any changes are agreed between the parties in writing and shall be catered for in the proposal and/or contract;
- communication with the client at all relevant stages of the forensic case;
- handling of complaints, as defined in Section 6.14;
- formal signoff of deliverables, if applicable; and
- feedback from the client, as defined in Chapter 16, Section 16.2.6.

6.7.3 Design and development

One-off solutions shall be provided to all clients, as each forensic case is different. Each of these is subject to an individual proposal, or where a contract is already present, a quotation or purchase order for additional forensic cases to be processed. This process shall:

- determine the client need and articulate it in a proposal, as defined in Section 6.6.2.3;
- review the proposal internally prior to submission to the client, as defined in Section 6.6.2.3.4;
- review the proposal with the client to ensure that the proposal is correct, making amendments where appropriate, as defined in Section 6.6.2.4.2;
- arrange for suitable resources to be available to ensure that the client requirements are met, as defined in Chapter 4, Section 4.7.1;
- have knowledge of applicable legislation or regulation applicable to the products and services to be supplied either based on the client's stated requirements or knowledge and experience of similar projects; and
- ensure that each iteration of the proposal is archived, with documented annotations of changes required.

At the point of product and service planning, changes to documentation, products, or services shall not be subject to the Change Management Process.

6.7.4   Purchasing

General purchases or Commercial off the Shelf (COTS) items are from suppliers approved by the Finance Department, who maintain a list of approved suppliers.

The use of consumables shall be controlled for their lifecycle in forensic case processing, where appropriate (e.g. hard disks and other media used for forensic case processing but not paper and stationery).

All products received shall be checked for appropriateness and that they are fit for purpose, according to the asset management procedures, as defined in Chapter 12, Section 12.3.14. Records of all deliveries and inspection of incoming material shall be retained.

Annual reviews of suppliers shall be carried out. Key suppliers shall be subject to second party audits on a risk-based approach, others may be subject to formal second party audits or informal reviews, as defined in Chapter 14, Section 14.8.2.3. The measure of their acceptance shall be their continued use.

Third parties may be employed on contract when there are not ether the skills or the capacity to fulfil a client's requirements. All deliverables from these third shall be reviewed as if they were from employees. Where there is a shortfall, they shall either undergo the appraisal process or have their contracts terminated. Managing outsourcing suppliers is defined in Chapter 14, Section 14.8.

6.7.5   Product and service provision

Product and service delivery (typically a forensic case report with supporting evidence or a statement) for a client shall be maintained by:

- use of a virtual file for each client, as defined in Section 6.2.2 and Appendix 14;
- the collection or delivery of exhibits to be processed to produce the required forensic case report or statement, as defined in Chapter 9, Section 9.1.2;
- ensuring that the appropriate resources are available to the Laboratory Manager to produce the required deliverables, as defined in Chapter 4, Section 4.7.1
- work is carried out for clients according to:
- the agreed contract;
- the agreed proposal that defines the deliverables;
- good practice for the delivery of the forensic case report or statement;
- the relevant legislation or regulation that affects the delivery of the document; and
- any changes to the requirements based on feedback or other reasons from the client.
- once a draught deliverable has been created, it shall be reviewed internally, as defined in Section 6.8.1;
- when considered suitable for release the deliverable shall be issued to the client, as defined in Section 6.8.3;
- the deliverable shall be reviewed with the client, as defined in Section 6.8.4;
- the document shall be edited accordingly and reviewed again internally;
- the document shall be released again to the client;
- this process shall continue until the final draught is issued to the client as the deliverable;
- if this document is the final deliverable for the client, the forensic case is signed off as defined in Section 6.9;
- the forensic case and all matters relating to it shall be archived when the forensic case is concluded according to the retention schedule, as defined in Chapter 4, Appendix 26 and Section 6.10. This may involve archiving just a specific forensic case, or the whole client virtual file if there is no other forensic case processing required for the client;
- If there are any complaints, these shall be resolved using the complaint procedure, as defined in Section 6.14; and
- during the whole case lifecycle all client information shall be handled according to its classification, as defined in Chapter 5, Appendix 16 and Section 6.11, so that client confidentiality is maintained.

6.8   Reviewing deliverables

All deliverables produced for a client shall be reviewed and edited at several stages in the project lifecycle, as can be seen from the previous sections. This ensures that any deliverable that is sent to a client for their review shall:

- conform to the document production standards as defined in Chapter 4, Section 47.5 and Sections 6.6.2.3, 6.6.2.4, and 6.8;
- conform to the quality assurance process as defined in this chapter;
- conform to the deliverables identified by the proposal and/or quotation as defined in Section 6.6.2.3; and
- been reviewed internally and externally and achieved the required level of quality to be sent to a client as defined Section 6.8.

Typical deliverables include an interim report, a final report and any other documentation that the client may require including relevant objective evidence.

The Document Author, the relevant Account Manager and optionally the client shall be responsible for reviewing all forensic case deliverables.

The process for reviewing deliverables is:

6.8.1   Reviewing the document internally

The Document Author shall perform final checks on the document including:

- spell-checking the document;
- regenerating any contents list;
- checking fonts and layouts;
- checking formatting;
- ensuring that the document meets the requirements set by the client; and
- setting the correct version number.

The Document Author shall print a copy of the document for review and complete a Draught Review Form, as defined in Appendix 16, with the correct details, and attach it to the printed copy of the document and send it to the Account Manager. One elapsed week shall be allowed for the return of comments.

Note

This process may be implemented by a forensic laboratory using an Electronic Document Management System (EDMS) with in-built workflow, rather than a paper process.

The Account Manager shall review the document and provide comment on the changes as required. The Account Manager shall:

- check for consistency and ambiguities;
- check for structure and layout; and
- check that the content complies with the client's requirements.

The Account Manager shall write all comments on the printed document and then signs the Draught Review form and return the document and the Draught Review Form to the Document Author.

The Document Author shall check all comments received and judge which comments to implement. The Document Author shall consult the Account Manager when in doubt as to the validity of comments and asks for explanations on their comments.

Note

The document may well be sent to more than the Account Manager for review, the reviewers shall be determined by the Account Manager and the Laboratory Manager.

6.8.2   Implementing edits internally

The Document Author shall implement comments received on the document as follows:

- scan the marked up document and Draught Review form for storage in the client virtual file, securely shredding the original paper versions;
- rename the original file according to the document control procedure;

- update the version information in the document;
- perform the required edits;
- save the document;
- perform final checks on the document including:
  - ○ spell-checking the document;
  - ○ regenerating any contents list;
  - ○ checking fonts and layouts;
  - ○ checking formatting; and
  - ○ setting the correct version number.
- prints a copy of the document for final check by the Account Manager;
- the Account Manager shall perform a review of the document and returns it to the Document Author;
- the Document Author shall repeat the steps above until the document is agreed as ready to release to the client;
- records of all reviews undertaken, including the date, Reviewer and any relevant feedback shall be added to the Draught Review Form and stored in the client virtual file in the ERMS;
- the document is now ready for issue to the client;
- if a soft copy is to be sent to the client, then it shall be converted to 'secured' PDF format; and
- depending on the information classification of the deliverable, as defined in Chapter 5, Appendix 26 and Section 6.11, appropriate means of protection of the proposal shall be applied as defined in Chapter 12, Section 12.3.14.

Note

Extra copies can, of course, be produced if necessary. The client can circulate their copy of the deliverable if additional people need to see it at the client site.

6.8.3 Issuing the document

The Document Author writes to the client enclosing the deliverable. The normal delivery method is post, but if time is short and it is essential that the deliverable arrives on the following day, it shall be sent by courier or emailed with a delivery and read receipt request.

The method of transmission shall also ensure that data handling procedures for the classification for the proposal are met as defined in Chapter 12, Section 12.3.14.

6.8.4 Reviewing the document with the client

Once a document has been produced and sent to a client, the Document Author shall liaise with the client to discuss the document.

It is not always required to hold a formal review meeting with a client to discuss a document. Sometimes a telephone call or an email can suffice, particularly when the work required is straight-forward. In most cases, however, the document shall be discussed with the client.

The Document Author shall be responsible for planning and holding a document review with a client, assisted by the relevant Account Manager. It may well be that the Account Manager or another employee attends the review process with the Document Author.

The Document Author's major objective of the review shall be to ensure that there are no changes to the deliverables, or if there are they are discovered early enough that they can be addressed without wasting time and effort.

The client shall review their copy of the document(s) sent by the Document Author. This may be a meeting or can be telephone, email, or internet (i.e. Zoom, Teams, or similar) based. Where there have been amendments to the client's original instructions, these shall be recorded in the client's virtual forensic case file and reviewed at this point.

The Document Author shall answer any client questions on the document and resolve any issues that remain. The Document Author shall take full notes to ensure that an updated document can be produced after the meeting that contains all the necessary information and reflects the client's view.

The document shall be edited as required, as defined in Section 6.8.2.

6.8.5 Following up the review

The Document Author shall return the updated document to the client within the agreed timescale. If no timescale is agreed, then this shall be within 5 working days.

The Document Author shall issue the updated version of the document to the client as defined in Section 6.8.2.

The Document Author shall file all documentation relating to the update in the client virtual file in the ERMS.

Note

The review process may occur more than once, if required.

6.9 Signing off a forensic case

Once all work on a forensic case has been completed, the client shall check the work and then sign it off as completed. The sign off process also provides an opportunity for the Account Manager and the client to review the forensic case to ensure that it has met, or preferably exceeded, client expectations. The sign off form is defined in Appendix 17.

The Account Manager shall be responsible for ensuring that the client signs off a forensic case, though in practice this may be performed by the Forensic Analyst undertaking the client's forensic case.

The Account Manager shall send the signoff form to the client.

The Account Manager shall telephone or email the client to arrange a sign-off meeting.

The Account Manager and any other relevant employees shall attend the sign-off meeting at the appointed time, chairs the meeting, and:

- provides an overview of the forensic case;
- works through the deliverables produced for the client and requests confirmation that each has been completed to their satisfaction; and
- obtains any lessons learned for continuous improvement.

The Account Manager shall receive the signed sign off form.

The Account Manager shall file all correspondence and meeting minutes in the client's virtual forensic case file in the ERMS.

6.10 Archiving a forensic case

After all work on a forensic case has been completed and the client has signed off the forensic case, all forensic case material shall be considered for archiving according to the Document Retention Schedule as defined in Chapter 4, Appendix 26.

The Account Manager shall be responsible for ensuring the forensic case is archived.

The Account Manager shall archive a forensic case by moving the entire forensic case folder from the 'current' area to the 'finished' area in the ERMS. The Account Manager may have to create a new client folder within the 'finished' area if the forensic case is the first one completed for a client.

All data on the servers shall be backed up according to the current backup procedures defined in Chapter 7, Section 7.7.4.

6.11 Maintaining client confidentiality

During work on a forensic case, authorised employees may be issued with a great deal of information about the forensic case. Much of this information is confidential.

This information shall be kept confidential by:

- signing confidentiality agreements with client, if requested;
- safeguarding all material issued by a client whether in paper or electronic form;
- returning material to a client, if requested or contractually agreed; and
- securely disposing of client material when no longer required by appropriate secure disposal methods according to the type of media and its classification, as defined in Chapter 5, Appendix 16.

Top management shall be responsible for ensuring that client confidentiality is maintained, though in practice it may be Account Manager that undertakes all tasks relating to confidentiality of client information.

6.12   Technical requirements

6.12.1   General

Whilst ISO 9001 concentrates on management requirements for quality, ISO/IEC 17025 has management requirements as well as technical requirements. Much of the management requirement defined in ISO/IEC 17025 duplicate the requirements in ISO 9001. International Laboratory Accreditation Cooperation (ILAC) G19—Guidelines for Forensic Laboratories clarifies the application of ISO/IEC 17025 in a forensic laboratory context. The cross referencing between ISO 9001 and ISO/IEC 17025 is defined in Chapter 3, Appendix 2.

Note

Accreditation to ISO/IEC 17025 by an accreditation service demonstrates that a forensic laboratory not only operates a quality management system, but they are 'technically competent and are able to generate technically valid results' and it 'specifies the requirements for the competence to carry out tests and/or calibrations including sampling'.

There are a number of factors that can affect the correctness and reliability of results for forensic case processing performed by FCL. These can vary, but shall include such issues as:

- accuracy of documented procedures;
- all employees following documented procedures in the IMS;
- employee training and awareness;
- ensuring continual improvement;
- environmental and accommodation conditions present;
- hardware, software, and tools in use; and
- traceability, auditing, and sampling.

Some of these are covered by ISO 9001 and other by ISO/IEC 17025. Those not covered above in ISO 9001 are covered below as part of ISO/IEC 17025 quality procedures.

6.12.2   Benefits of ISO/IEC 17025

In addition to the benefits of ISO 9001, the benefits of ISO/IEC 17025 accreditation include:

- allows for the comparable quality of evidence produced in cross border forensic cases;
- demonstrable proof of competent employees performing forensic case processing;
- demonstration of continuing technical competence; and
- demonstration of impartiality.

6.12.3   The Laboratory Manager

The Laboratory Manager is in charge of the technical management of forensic case processing. This role is distinctly different from that of the Quality Manager, even though the Laboratory Manger has a duty of care to ensure that all technical forensic case processing meets the quality requirements set by the Quality Manager. The Laboratory Manager shall be responsible for all first response, forensic case processing and evidence presentation, and their job description is defined in Appendix 21.

6.12.4   Key questions—ISO/IEC 17025 answers

For any specific forensic case that has been processed, from initial contact to evidence presentation, it can be demonstrated that:

- the forensic case processing, from initial contact to evidence presentation, was performed by a competent and properly qualified Forensic Analyst who has been trained in the tools and methodologies that they used in processing the forensic case and had access to all information necessary for processing the forensic case;

- the methods and tools used to process the forensic case were technically sound and appropriate to the client's requirements;
- all tools, hardware, and software used in processing the forensic case were properly maintained and licenced during their use on the forensic case;
- the forensic case results were thoroughly reviewed prior to delivery and met the client's requirements;
- that any nonconformity identified during forensic case processing was addressed in a timely manner that it was effective;
- that documented procedures exist for all aspects of forensic case processing; and
- that records exist in the client virtual forensic case file in the ERMS to support this.

6.12.5 Technical qualifications

In addition to the management system training, ISO/IEC 17025 requires that all employees shall be competent and have records to support this competence. Job descriptions shall be reviewed every year to ensure that they remain current as part of the employee's annual appraisal process as defined in Chapter 18, Section 18.2.4.

For each role, a job description is defined by HR, details of specific job descriptions relating to the management of implemented management systems and forensic case processing are defined in the various Appendices in other chapters of this book. The job description for a Forensic Analyst is defined in Appendix 22. This job description is a generic one for any employee performing forensic case processing and includes all levels of Forensic Analysts.

All training requirements for forensic case processing employees shall be agreed with the Laboratory Manager, and where appropriate, the Quality Manager. This shall start with employee induction training. Management system training and refresher training shall carry on for the duration that the employee remains employed. Whilst new entrants may have considerable experience, they shall be trained in the methods and tools used by FCL. This is not a reflection on their competence, but a requirement that they know, understand, and use FCL's processes and procedures.

All new employees shall undergo induction training when starting their employment; this includes any employees of outsourcing partners. Ongoing refresher training shall be mandatory for all employees.

An example of the requirements of the training for Forensic Analysts for their initial training process is defined in Appendix 23, though it is expected that most inductees will have completed part of the training prior to employment. The requirements of undertaking a Training Needs Analysis (TNA) as part of annual appraisals is defined in Chapter 18, Section 18.2.2. After this level of training, any further training shall depend on specialisms sought, types of forensic cases to be processed or other relevant matters.

Note

Identification of training needs should be focused on forensic case processing rather than desires of an individual employee, as this is what a forensic laboratory is to be accredited against—and not the individual Forensic Analyst.

All employees shall have records of all training undertaken during their employment filed with their personnel files. This shall include feedback on all training, internal and external, that the employee undertakes. Training records shall provide evidence that an employee is competent to perform one or more tasks or use one or more digital forensic tools and records shall be used to provide an audit trail to prove this. Copies of all certifications and qualifications gained during employment shall be held on the employee's personnel file.

When an employee claims a new competence, the Laboratory Manager must be satisfied that the employee is technically competent to carry out forensic case processing using the new competence. This shall be carried out using reference material (e.g. a reference forensic case with known outcomes).

Employee competence shall be regularly reviewed and reassessed, as required. Identification for the need for reassessment may also come from a client or as the result of presentation of evidence produced to Court or Tribunal, where the Forensic Analyst's findings are successfully challenged. In this case, the Laboratory Manager shall take action as appropriate, which may include withdrawing authorisation to use specific tools or methodologies used within the forensic laboratory.

Individual Forensic Analysts shall be encouraged to obtain specialised certifications relevant to forensic case processing, in addition to those given in Appendix 23, and a list of some of the better known individual certifications are defined in Appendix 24. Many of these require the certification holder to undergo reassessment on an annual basis and the submission of supporting statements, copies of qualifications, and evidence of Continuing Professional Development/Education (CPD and CPE, respectively).

In addition to retaining a comprehensive digital forensic library of relevant manuals, books, and journals (hard copy or online subscriptions), FCL shall maintain documentation relating to the digital forensic qualifications and their exams as referred to, but not limited to, those defined in Appendix 24.

6.12.6 Accommodation and environmental conditions

The general requirements for accommodation and environment are defined in Chapters 2 and 3. General security requirements for the accommodation and environment are defined in Chapter 12. This section is related to the requirements for accommodation and environment for testing, calibration and forensic case processing. Accommodation and the environment used for forensic case processing shall be configured so that it shall not impact the correct performance of any test, calibration, or forensic case processing.

6.12.6.1 Accommodation

Access levels and authorisations are defined in Chapter 4, Appendix 21. The levels of access control shall be based on confidentiality of forensic cases being processed, the 'need to know' principle, the 'need to access principle', the need to protect the integrity of forensic case processing, and the requirements for segregation of duties (Chapter 12, Sections 12.3.5 and 12.3.6).

Areas where segregation of duties or tasks are required shall have appropriate access control (e.g. restricted access to the secure evidence store to ensure continuity of evidence). Physical security is defined in Chapter 12, Section 12.4.

6.12.6.2 Environment

There is the specific need to protect against environmental conditions that may affect the processing of forensic cases. A number of these have been covered in previous chapters and include:

- electrical power fluctuations;
- electromagnetic disturbances;
- all Forensic Analysts shall have appropriate ergonomic conditions in their workspace to perform their forensic case processing duties. This shall include, but not be limited to furniture settings, lighting and computer equipment positioning. In some jurisdictions, the ergonomic settings of a workspace are legislative requirements (e.g. The Health and Safety (Display Screen Equipment) Regulations 1992, for the EU); and
- temperature and humidity controls to ensure that evidence (typically digital media) remains within manufacturer's recommended limits.

The first and fourth items shall be subject to automatic monitoring and reporting to a central annunciator panel and/or a control workstation. These shall be recorded either to paper printouts (that shall be regularly changed and stored as records or retained as computer files, according to the retention schedule defined in Chapter 4, Appendix 26). The second one is dependent on Forensic Analysts ensuring that they follow the procedures laid down for evidence handling defined in Chapter 8, Section 8.6.9.

6.12.6.3 Health and safety

Whilst ISO/IEC 17025 does not explicitly define health and safety requirements, the requirements of ISO 45001, as defined in Chapter 17 shall be implemented.

6.12.6.4 Off site issues

Where off site forensic case processing is performed (e.g. on a client site or a crime scene), all Forensic Analysts shall ensure that the procedures used internally are used as closely as possible 'off site'. This shall include both First Response, as defined in Chapter 8, and outsourcing, as defined in Chapter 14, Section 14.8.

6.12.6.5 Other issues

Whilst other types of forensic laboratories may have other specific requirements (e.g. control of chemicals or equipment used in testing nondigital samples), FCL does not have these direct requirements, though they may be secondary (e.g. further testing by different forensic laboratories of evidence under FCL's control).

6.12.7 Test methods and validation

During the proposal stage of negotiations, as defined in Sections 6.6.2.3 and 6.6.2.4, the client shall define their required outcomes. If a specific process or methodology that is required by the client is needed, then the methods or process required shall be evaluated to ensure that they are internationally acceptable, either by reference to standards, or recognised benchmarking (e.g. NIST Computer Forensic Tool Testing Program).

In general terms, forensic case processing software is provided by the developer as 'fit for purpose'. Usage amongst the digital forensic fraternity shall rapidly discover where this is not the case, and it is usual that this is made public in relevant journals or on the internet.

In many cases, the use of digital forensic tools has been accepted in a court and having results that are repeatable by any other competent Forensic Analyst provides this evidence. These are defined as standard methods for forensic case processing, as they follow the processes defined in the tool's instruction manual, accepted validated processes, or relevant standards, and these shall be used wherever possible.

Nonstandard methods shall be avoided in forensic case processing as reliance on tried and tested methods shall be used in all possible situations. Before going live, all new tools shall go through the Change Management Process. Part of this process is testing expected output using reference forensic cases and/or dual tool verification, where the 'other' tool has already been validated. Should a nonstandard method be required by the client or proposed for processing the client's forensic case, this shall be covered in the proposal or quotation, as appropriate.

The handling and transport of items for forensic case processing is covered in Chapter 8, Section 8.7. Instruction manuals for digital forensic hardware and software tools shall be accepted as 'definitive use' documents. However, a 'watching brief' shall be kept on their use in relevant forensic cases, to ensure that their use is not discredited in any way. Any variations from the client's outcome requirements, including tool and methodology usage, shall be both agreed with the client and documented. Should a tool, method, or process required to be used by the client be deemed as inappropriate for any valid reason, then the client shall be advised. The records of this shall be added to the client's virtual file in the ERMS.

Where internal methodologies and processes are developed for forensic case processing, they shall be only developed and used by competent employees. Before use for processing any client forensic cases, any such methods shall be validated by an appropriate method. The process for validating, and revalidating a tool where appropriate, is defined in Chapter 7, Section 7.5.5. Assuming they are successful, all relevant documentation shall be updated and relevant employees trained to use the new process. All records of training shall be updated to show competence of the employees using the new method or procedure.

Existing tools and technologies (e.g. basic forensic case processing tools such as Encase, FTK, Cellebrite UFED, Graykey, XRY, and Paraben), that are accepted by the Courts, have detailed procedural manuals, provide training in their use and additional certification of competence shall be used (some of these certifications are defined in Appendix 24). The maintenance of the hardware on which they operate is covered in Chapter 7, Section 7.5.

Where output from any forensic tools is produced in a report or statement for a client, the origin of that data shall be defined. This shall include the tool name, version number, and any other relevant details so that the tests can be reproduced by any other competent Forensic Analyst.

For general office software (e.g. COTS products, such as Microsoft office), these are regarded as validated products, even given the alarming level of security and other patches being released.

ISO/IEC 17025 requires that there shall be "instructions on the use and operation of all relevant equipment, and on the handling and preparation of items for testing and/or calibration, or both, where the absence of such instructions could jeopardise the results of tests and/or calibrations." Each forensic case is different, but the competence of the Forensic Analysts, the use of the forensic case processing forms as used in Chapter 9 and the manuals for tool usage are seen as meeting this requirement.

Validation of methods of forensic case processing is not really practical after each change to the Forensic Analysts workstation, given the number of patches that are required for the operating system. However, where a new tool is installed or a new version of an existing tool is installed, the known reference forensic case shall be run and the output compared to ensure that the same results are achieved as from the previous version of the tool, for existing tools, and from a similar outcome from a different tool for new tools. There is the problem introduced that the assumption is that the original output that is used as a baseline measure is correct. This is also the case where new technology is to be examined. As forensic case evidence is almost always contested, another competent Forensic Analyst working for the 'other side' will have run their own tests, and discrepancies between the findings shall be investigated and resolved. This may require the updating of procedures used in the IMS.

For this reason, dual tool verification of results shall be undertaken, as required. The decision for performing dual tool verification shall rest with the Laboratory Manager.

6.12.8   Equipment

FCL contains all equipment (hardware, software, procedures, and infrastructure), needed to satisfy client requirements for forensic case processing. If a need for additional equipment is needed, it can be purchased using the process defined in Chapter 12, Section 12.3.14.2. Where external resources are required, they shall be managed in accordance with the requirements in Chapter 14. Annual second party audits of all suppliers shall be undertaken in accordance with the requirements defined in Chapter 4, Section 4.4.1 and Chapter 4, Section 4.5.1.1.

All equipment (assets) valued above the 'de minimus' level (i.e. fixed assets) shall be recorded in the asset register maintained by the Finance Department. The asset purchasing process is defined in Chapter 12, Section 12.3.14. All IT assets, including any equipment for forensic case processing, shall be recorded in the IT Service Desk system, however this shall exclude consumables. The contents of the IT asset register in the Service Desk system are defined in Chapter 12, Appendix 8. This shall cover hardware as well as software in use and contains the whole life history of the equipment from its receipt to its eventual disposal and records all employees that have 'owned' it, as defined in Chapter 12, Section 12.3.14.

After receipt and checking for completeness and correctness of any equipment, it shall only be commissioned into service through the Change Management Process. Where this includes equipment used for forensic case processing, the known reference forensic case shall be used to ensure that expected results are produced. This shall not be performed for business related or infrastructure equipment. The results of the running of the reference forensic case shall be retained as records for the equipment in question and associated with the equipment record in the IT Service Desk. All equipment shall be given its own unique asset tag that is securely affixed to it and is readily visible. This asset tag shall remain with the equipment for its 'life'. ISO/IEC 17025 mandates that records of all equipment in use shall be held and gives a recommendation for a minimum set of data to be retained. This is defined in Appendix 25, with locations for the procedures implemented or locations where the records are stored, to meet these requirements.

Where forensic case processing is carried out off site by Forensic Analysts, all equipment shall be transported to and from the remote site securely, according to the procedures in Chapter 8, Section 8.7.

Where any forensic case processing is outsourced to any third party, these procedures and the requirements of the rest of the IMS shall be met and regular second party audits shall confirm this.

A random sample of all equipment used in FCL shall be undertaken. This shall occur on receipt and after any significant or influencing changes (e.g. new software upgrades, hardware replacements, etc.).

6.12.9   Measurement traceability

There are rarely national metrology laboratories that can be used by a digital forensic laboratory that holds the standards for all measurements in forensic case processing or any traceability to the International System of Units (SI). As this is the case the use of standard reference forensic case(s) shall be used to ensure that equipment performs consistently by running the relevant reference standard reference forensic case for all new hardware or software upgrades. Use of recognised forensic tool providers with the ability to have results challenged in a Court, Tribunal, or similar, shall provide assurance of the methods in use. All its Forensic Analysts shall be shown to be technically competent on the tools that they use in forensic case processing. This shall include relevant training courses from the manufacturer and obtaining and maintaining relevant individual certifications, where possible.

Records of this testing shall be maintained in the ERMS to provide an audit trail of measurement and testing. In addition to this, forensic acquisition tools usually provide evidence of successful acquisition by use of hashing techniques. Dual tool verification shall ensure that the same result is achieved by two different forensic case processing tools from the same source evidence.

6.12.10   Administration of forensic case work and sampling

Before starting any forensic case processing, the proposal and contract review process defined in Sections 6.6.2 and 6.6.3 shall have been completed, in addition to ensuring that appropriate competent resources shall be in place to process the forensic case.

The Laboratory Manager shall oversee all forensic cases from the initial receipt of an exhibit to be processed (whether delivered by the client, collected from the client or seized as part of a first response). On receipt, or recovery, it shall be recorded as an exhibit. The Laboratory Manager shall appoint the relevant forensic team process the client's forensic case, but only if the relevant preconditions have been met.

On receipt of an exhibit, the exhibit shall be inspected and securely stored in the secure evidence store as defined in Chapter 9, Section 9.6.1. If it is to be rejected for any reason, then the procedure in Chapter 9. Section 9.6.1 shall be followed, including the advising of the client. On receipt, all exhibits shall be uniquely identified using the exhibit naming procedures. This may well be in addition to other naming conventions used for the exhibit.

When all relevant details are present, the Laboratory Manager shall allocate the forensic case to the relevant Forensic Analyst(s), based on the forensic case requirements and the Forensic Analyst's competence and workload. This is usually in the form of the documented requirements from the client or those defined by the Account Manager after consultation with the client as part of the contract negotiations as defined in Sections 6.6.2 and 6.6.3. After the forensic case has been processed, the deliverable (typically a report, statement, or deposition) shall be produced. This shall contain all relevant document control information, as defined in Chapter 9, Sections 9.13, 9.15, and 9.16. All reports shall go through though the deliverable review process defined in this Section 6.8, prior to final delivery to the client. This shall ensure that the deliverable is meeting internal standards as well as the original client expectations.

Post forensic case processing retention and disposal of forensic case material is covered in Chapter 9, Section 9.18.

All documents relating to a specific forensic case shall be recorded in the client's virtual forensic case file in the ERMS.

6.12.11 Assuring technical quality of products and services

The majority of products and services provided to clients are reports or statements relating to forensic case processing. Much of the quality process is covered by the requirements of ISO 9001; however, this does not cover technical quality of the results.

There is no available CRM for forensic case processing, and there are reference forensic case(s) that shall be used whenever a hardware or software upgrade is performed as part of its Change Management Process. The details of this reference forensic case test results are defined in Appendix 26; however, more reference results can be added as required for new tools and methods. However, as discussed above, this is based on the assumption that the original reference material results are correct.

The principles used in ISO Guide 35, Reference materials—General and statistical principles for certification, contain much advice that was used for the production of in house reference forensic case material. Due to the sensitivity of forensic cases processed and the need to maintain client confidentiality, as defined in Section 6.11, it is not really possible to undertake interlaboratory proficiency or comparison exercises apart from those that the derived results are actually are challenged in a Court of competent jurisdiction. Dual tool validation shall be used wherever there is any doubt as to the veracity of results produced.

Should any results produced be challenged and be proved to be incorrect they shall be treated through the nonconforming product route as defined in Section 6.13.2. This may come from a challenge from the client themselves, via their feedback as defined in Chapter 16, Section 16.2.6, or from a public challenge in a Court or Tribunal. This shall ensure that the root cause is determined and appropriate corrective action is undertaken. This may include advising other clients of possible nonconforming products and services (i.e. forensic case reports or statement) recall. The results of any challenge or negative feedback shall be treated as records and stored in the relevant client's virtual forensic case file. The corrective action undertaken shall be recorded in the CAPA database.

Whilst almost all forensic case processing shall follow the steps provided in the relevant tool instruction manual, there may be occasions where an in-house method is required. In this case, all steps undertaken will be recorded in Examination Record, as defined in Chapter 9, Appendix 9. This shall allow for both traceability of actions as well as providing for repeatability by another competent Forensic Analyst. Any deviations from established practice or development of in house methods shall be formally authorised by the Laboratory Manager, and records of this shall be recorded in the client's virtual file. This may also require an update to the forensic reference forensic case(s) and their results. Where a nonstandard method is to be used or developed, it is prudent, and mandatory, to involve the client in the process and obtain their consent. Again, records of meetings with the client, actions arising from them and formal consent shall be stored in the client's virtual forensic case file.

6.12.12 Case processing reports

ISO/IEC 17025 is quite specific about what information shall be present in a report, which shall also include the client's requirements, as defined in Sections 6.6.2.4 and 6.8.4. The requirements defined by ISO 170125 are defined in Appendix

27. Whilst ISO/IEC 17025 allows the relaxation of these requirements with agreement of the client, they shall be readily available, so the standard report format includes them, as defined in Appendix 28.

Whilst reports or statements shall be issued based on recoverable facts and these should be repeatable by any other competent Forensic Analyst, Clients can require a second opinion or interpretation to be made based on recovered digital forensic evidence. In these cases, it shall be possible to show that these opinions and interpretations are made based on sound judgement by competent Forensic Analysts who have the relevant competence to back up and validate their results. In all cases, opinions, or interpretations shall be endorsed by the Laboratory Manager as part of the document review process, as defined in Chapter 4, Section 4.7.5.4.

All reports and statements (i.e. deliverables for a client) shall go through the review process defined in Section 6.8, prior to release to the client. Where appropriate, changes shall be made to meet client requirements or where results are challenged. All versions of any deliverables shall be retained within the ERMS in the relevant client virtual file. Records of reviews and authorisation for release shall be retained, in the client virtual file in the ERMS.

All authorised reports for a client shall be issued in the Adobe Portable Document Format (PDF) format that is secured. These shall be protected against unauthorised modification and, where the classification requires it, be numbered copies issued on an individual recipient basis. This shall be based on the classification of the report as defined in Chapter 5, Section 5.5.6.6, and be agreed by the client as part of the proposal, as defined in Section 6.11.

All records of issue and receipt of any client deliverables shall be retained and added to the client virtual file in the ERMS, whether it is issued by email, post, email, or hand-to-hand, along with the agreed recipient.

Where any amendment of a client deliverable is required, the process defined in Section 6.8 shall be followed and all copies of previous versions of the deliverable retained in the client's virtual forensic case file, allowing reversion to any previous version of the deliverable.

6.13   Measurement, analysis, and improvement

Appropriate measurement, analysis and improvement processes shall be in place for all products and services. Measurement of the suitability of products and services is the only way to determine if FCL is 'getting it right'. The analysis of feedback provides inputs to the improvement process to ensure that FCL gets it right, first time, every time.

Monitoring, measurement, analysis, and continuous improvement processes shall be planned and implemented that are appropriate for the products and services (primarily forensic case processing reports and expert testimony) provided to clients.

To achieve this, the following processes shall be employed:

6.13.1   Monitoring and measurement

At relevant stages of a forensic case being processed, feedback shall be obtained from the client to ensure that the deliverable(s) meet their expectations, as defined in this Sections 6.6 and 6.8.

6.13.2   Control of nonconforming product

No nonconforming products shall be delivered to a client. It is the objective of the management system to ensure that this is so. As the client is involved in the complete forensic case processing life cycle, it is likely that this will be the case.

Where appropriate, the client shall be advised of any nonconformities discovered and this may require the recall of material delivered to the client. This will require the repeating of the deliverables.

6.13.3   Case processing audits

Audits covering all aspects of forensic case processing (e.g. casework, research, training, etc.) shall be conducted at least once a year by the Quality Manager or the Laboratory Manager, whichever is appropriate. All internal audits shall be conducted in line with the requirements of Chapter 4, Section 4.9.2.

Where client forensic case files are reviewed in audits, they shall be chosen randomly taking into account any sensitive issues related to the forensic case. This shall include, but not limited to its profile, any negative feedback received, work of a specific Forensic Analyst where there is any question about their competence, etc.

Records of each audit shall be kept and stored in the ERMS. Where nonconformities are identified, they shall be tracked through to completion in FCL CAPA database.

6.13.4 Analysis of data

The IMS (and the QMS that forms part of it) shall be evaluated to ensure that it is suitable and effective for its declared purposes. This process shall take input from a variety of sources and use it to continuously improve its products and services to its clients.

6.13.5 Continuous improvement

Continuous improvement of delivery of products and services to internal and external clients is the goal. To achieve this, the following processes shall be employed:

- complying with the quality management policy as defined in Chapter 3, Appendix 4;
- reviewing deliverables as defined in Section 6.8;
- reviewing and acting on client complaints as defined in Section 6.14;
- handling nonconformities as defined in Section 6.13.2;
- undertaking internal audit as defined in Chapter 4, Section 4.9.2;
- ensuring forensic case processing signoff as defined in Section 6.9;
- undertaking management reviews as defined in Chapter 4, Section 4.9.3; and
- ensuring continuous improvement for all products and services as defined in Chapter 4, Section 4.10.

6.14 Managing client complaints

The complaints policy shall ensure all complaints relating to the quality of results or the level of products and services provided to clients are fully investigated and reported promptly. Lessons shall be learned from any complaints made and ensure that corrective action addresses them.

Complaints may be made by internal or external clients concerning any aspect of a service that is provided.

A complaint is defined as a written or verbal expression of dissatisfaction by a client about products or services provided to a client that requires investigation, response, and closure.

A complaint may be raised at any point in the relationship between the parties and not just at the sign off and feedback form at the end of a forensic case.

Managing complaints effectively shall be just one method of continuously improving the products and services provided to clients.

A client only needs to know three things about a complaint:

- where to complain;
- how to complain; and
- to feel confident that the complaint shall be handled effectively and efficiently.

Top management shall commit to make the complaints management process highly visible and accessible to all clients. Complaints can be made using the following methods:

- email;
- face to face;
- letter;
- phone;
- signoff and Feedback Forms; and
- web site.

As a complaint may be made to any employee, the complaint handling process is covered as part of the employee's induction training.

The information that is required for recording a complaint is defined in Appendix 18.

6.14.1 Responsibilities for managing client complaints

There are a number of responsibilities in the client complaint process, these are as defined below:

6.14.1.1 Laboratory Manager

The Laboratory Manager shall be the person with overall responsibility for the complaint management process, and for ensuring that complaints received from internal and external clients about products and services shall be resolved promptly and to the client's satisfaction. For external clients, this shall be via the relevant client Account Manager, and for internal complaints, via the relevant Line Manager, where it is a forensic case processing issue.

Responsibilities shall include:

- monitoring the progress of formal complaints;
- assisting with complaint investigation and resolution if required;
- acting as a contact point for the client for complaints relating to products and services, unless this has been devolved to the relevant Account Manager; and
- collating reports of complaints, their progress, and their resolution as necessary to relevant interested parties, these shall include the client and any relevant mandatory reporting bodied (e.g. Regulators);

Note

Should a complaint be critical, it shall be escalated directly to top management.

6.14.1.2 Service Desk

The Service Desk shall be responsible for recording and tracking of any complaints from clients concerning any supplied products and services.

Responsibilities of the Service Desk shall include:

- recording and tracking all complaints in the Service Desk system in accordance with the procedures for incident management;
- escalating a complaint to the appropriate person for investigation and resolution;
- closing a formal complaint in the Service Desk system on advice from the relevant Account Manager, Line Manager, or Laboratory Manager; and
- maintaining and providing reports recorded in the complaint process.

6.14.1.3 Client complaint process

Note

The incident reporting process shall be used for recording complaints, as complaints are regarded as a type of incident in FCL.

The process by which complaints shall be managed from a client about products and services provided to them, is:

1. A complaint may be received about an aspect of a product or service that a client receives. Sources of complaints may include:
   - by any of the methods defined in Chapter 14; or
   - directly from a client via the Service Desk.

Note

Any complaints about the products and services which are received informally at top management level shall be referred to the Service Desk so that they can initiate the formal complaint process.

---

2. The Service Desk shall initiate the complaint process by logging the complaint in the Service Desk system.
3. When a complaint is registered by the Service Desk:
   - the complaint shall be registered in accordance with these procedures;
   - complaints shall always be assigned a high priority response;

- the person registering the complaint shall be notified in accordance with the procedure for managing incidents, as defined in Chapter 7, Section 7.4.1; and
- the Laboratory Manager shall automatically be notified of the complaint registration and details (the Laboratory Manager may choose to notify the top management and other relevant interested parties or employees if the complaint is of a serious nature).

4. The Service Desk shall send the details of the complaint to the appropriate employee for action. For external clients, this is usually the relevant Account Manager and for internal clients, the relevant Line Manager.
5. The person who has been delegated to deal with the complaint shall receive the complaint. If necessary, they shall contact the client to:
- obtain further information as required; and
- confirm the issues that are to be investigated.

Any additional information shall be recorded, and this allows the tracking of the complaint through its whole lifecycle from initial receipt through to final resolution.

The complaint shall be acknowledged and the complainant formally advised accordingly.

When a complaint has been received, it shall be assessed as soon as is practically possible to see if it requires immediate action, is a known problem, has an impact on the FCL's reputation and other relevant factors.

The complaint shall be investigated, and guidance taken on the actions that are required to resolve it to the client's satisfaction.

Corrective actions shall be determined and agreed to resolve the complaint.

The relevant Account Manager, Line Manager, or the Laboratory Manager, as appropriate, shall contact the client to outline and confirm the proposed resolution action. Once agreed, the remediation is carried out.

Note

Any changes to product and service provision or the IT infrastructure shall be performed in accordance with the Change Management Process.

The relevant Account Manager, Line Manager, or the Laboratory Manager, as appropriate, shall contact the client to confirm the remediation action has been performed.

Details shall be logged in the Service Desk system in accordance with the procedures for recording and managing incidents, as defined in Chapter 7, Section 7.4.1, and the Laboratory Manager shall be notified.

The relevant Account Manager, Line Manager or the Laboratory Manager, as appropriate, shall contact the client to confirm their satisfaction with the resolution (100% of external clients who register complaints shall be contacted to confirm their satisfaction with the remediation).

If the client is satisfied with the remediation, the complaint shall be closed in the Service Desk system, and the Laboratory Manager notified.

If the client is not satisfied with the remediation, the complaint is escalated in accordance with the procedure for managing and escalating incidents, as defined in Chapter 7, Section 7.4.1, and the Laboratory Manager shall be notified. Depending on the client and the complaint, top management may also be advised.

Appendix 1—Mapping ISO 9001 to IMS procedures

ISO 9001 section	Control	Procedure(s)
4	Context of the organisation	
4.1	Understanding the organisation and its context	Chapter 4, Section 4.4
4.2	Understanding the needs and expectations of interested parties	Chapter 4, Section 4.4.1 Chapter 4, Section 4.4.2
4.3	Determining the scope of the quality management system	Chapter 4, Section 4.4.3 Chapter 5, Appendix 11
4.4	Quality management system and its processes	Chapter 4
5	Leadership	

Continued

ISO 9001 section	Control	Procedure(s)
5.1	Leadership and commitment	Chapter 3, Appendix 4 Chapter 4, Section 4.5.1 Appendix 4
5.1.1	General	Chapter 3, Appendix 4 Chapter 4, Section 4.5.1 Appendix 4
5.1.2	Customer focus	Section 6 Chapter 16
5.1	Policy	Chapter 3, Appendix 4
5.2.1	Developing the quality policy	Chapter 3, Appendix 4
5.2.2	Communicating the quality policy	Chapter 4, Sections 4.7.4
5.3	Organisational roles, responsibilities and authorities	Chapter 3, Section 3.1.16 Chapter 4, Section 4.5.3 Section 5
6	Planning	
6.1	Actions to address risks and opportunities	Chapter 4, Section 4.6.1
6.2	Quality objectives and planning to achieve them	Chapter 4, Section 4.6.2
6.3	Planning of changes	Chapter 7, Section 7.4.3
7	Support	
7.1	Resources	Chapter 4, Section 4.7.1
7.1.1	General	Chapter 4, Section 4.7.1
7.1.2	People	Chapter 4, Section 4.7.1
7.1.3	Infrastructure	Chapter 4, Section 4.7.1 Chapter 5, Appendix 11
7.1.4	Environment for the operation of processes	Chapter 4, Section 4.7.1
7.1.5	Monitoring and measuring resources	Chapter 4, Section 4.9.1
7.1.6	Organisational knowledge	The whole IMS
7.2	Competence	Chapter 4, Section 4.7.2
7.3	Awareness	Chapter 4, Section 4.7.3
7.4	Communication	Chapter 4, Section 4.7.4
7.5	Documented Information	Chapter 4, Sections 4.7.5
7.5.1	General	Chapter 4, Section 4.7.5.1
7.5.2	Creating and updating	Chapter 4, Section 4.7.5.4
7.5.3	Control of documented information	Chapter 4, Section 4.7.5.3
8	Operation	
8.1	Operational planning and control	Chapter 4, Section 4.8
8.2	Requirements for products and services	This chapter, Section 7
8.2.1	Customer communication	This chapter, Section 6
8.2.2	Determining the requirements related to products and services	This chapter, Section 6
8.2.3	Review of requirements related to products and services	This chapter, Section 7
8.2.4	Changes to requirements for products and services	This chapter, Section 7
8.3	Design and development of products and services	This chapter, Section 7.3

ISO 9001 section	Control	Procedure(s)
8.3.1	General	
8.3.2	Design and development planning	This chapter, Section 7.1
8.3.3	Design and development inputs	This chapter, Section 7
8.3.4	Design and development controls	This chapter, Section 7
8.3.5	Design and development outputs	This chapter, Section 7
8.3.6	Design and development changes	This chapter, Section 7
8.4	Control of externally provided processes, products and services	This chapter, Section 7.4
8.4.1	General	This chapter, Section 7.4
8.4.2	Type and extent of control	This chapter, Section 7.4 Chapter 12, Section 12.3.14
8.4.3	Information for external providers	This chapter, Section 7.4 Chapter 12, Section 12.3.14
8.5	Production and service provision	This chapter, Section 7 Chapter 8 Chapter 9
8.5.1	Control of production and service provision	This chapter, Section 7 Chapter 7, Section 7.4
8.5.2	Identification and traceability	This chapter, Section 7
8.5.3	Property belonging to customers or external providers	This chapter, Section 7
8.5.4	Preservation	This chapter., Section 7
8.5.5	Postdelivery activities	This chapter, Sections 7 and 14
8.5.6	Control of changes	This chapter, Section 7
8.6	Release of products and services	This chapter, Section 7
8.7	Control of nonconforming outputs	This chapter, Section 7
9	Performance evaluation	
9.1	Monitoring, measurement, analysis, and evaluation	Chapter 4, Section 4.9.1
9.1.1	General	Chapter 4, Section 4.9.1
9.1.2	Customer satisfaction	Chapter 4, Section 4.9.1 Section 14
9.1.3	Analysis and evaluation	Chapter 4, Section 4.9.1
9.2	Internal audit	Chapter 4, Section 4.9.2
9.3	Management review	Chapter 4, Section 4.9.3
9.3.1	General	Chapter 4, Section 4.9.3
9.3.2	Management review inputs	Chapter 4, Section 4.9.4
9.3.3	Management review outputs	Chapter 4, Section 4.9.5
10	Improvement	
10.1	General	Chapter 4, Section 4.10
10.2	Nonconformity and corrective action	Chapter 4, Section 4.10.2 Chapter 4, Section 4.10.3 Chapter 4, Section 4.10.4 Chapter 4, Section 4.10.5
10.3	Continual improvement	Chapter 4, Section 4.10

Appendix 2—Mapping ISO/IEC 17025 to IMS procedures

ISO/IEC 17025 section	Control	Procedure(s)
4	General requirements	
4.1	Impartiality	Chapter 3, Section 3.1.3.14 Chapter 3, Section 3.1.5 Chapter 3, Appendix 3 Section 6.2.1.6
4.2	Confidentiality	Chapter 4, Appendix 20 Section 6.2.2.6
5	Structural requirements	Chapter 3, Section 3.1.2 Chapter 3, Section 3.1.3.1 Chapter 3, Section 3.1.16 Chapter 4, Section 4.5
6	Resource requirements	Chapter 3, Section 3.1.12 Chapter 4, Section 4.7.1 Chapter 4, Section 4.7.2
6.1	General	Chapter 3
6.2	Personnel	Chapter 4, Section 4.7.1 Chapter 4, Section 4.7.2
6.3	Facilities and environmental conditions	Chapter 2, Section 2.2 Chapter 4, Appendix 9 Chapter 4, Appendix 16 Chapter 4, Appendix 17 Section 6.12.6
6.4	Equipment	Section 6.12.8 Chapter 7, Section 7.1.4 Chapter 7, Section 7.3.1 Chapter 7, Section 7.5 Chapter 7, Appendix 2 Chapter 7, Appendix 26
6.5	Metrological traceability	Section 6.12.9
6.6	Externally provided products and services	Chapter 14
7	Process requirements	
7.1	Review of requests, tenders, and contracts	Section 6.6.2.4
7.2	Selection, verification, and validation of methods	Section 12.7
7.2.1	Selection and verification of methods	Section 12.7
7.2.2	Validation of methods	Section 12.7
7.3	Sampling	Not appropriate to FCL
7.4	Handling of test or calibration items	Not appropriate to FCL
7.5	Technical records	
7.6	Evaluation of measurement uncertainty	Section 12.7
7.7	Ensuring the validity of results	Section 12.7
7.8	Reporting of results	Section 12.7
7.8.1	General	
7.8.2	Common requirements for reports (test, calibration, or sampling)	Section 12.7

ISO/IEC 17025 section	Control	Procedure(s)
7.8.3	Specific requirements for test reports	Section 6.12.12 Appendix 27 Appendix 28
7.8.4	Specific requirements for calibration certificates	Not appropriate to FCL
7.8.5	Reporting sampling—specific requirements	Not appropriate to FCL
7.8.6	Reporting statements of conformity	Section 6.12.12
7.8.7	Reporting opinions and interpretations	Section 6.12.12
7.8.8	Amendments to reports	Section 6.12.12
7.9	Complaints	Section 6.14 and Appendices 18, 19 and 20
7.10	Nonconforming work	Section 13.2
7.11	Control of data and information management	The IMS Chapter 7, Section 7.7 Chapter 12, Section 12.6
8	Management system requirements	
8.1	Options	The IMS
8.1.1	General	The IMS
8.1.2	Option A	The IMS
8.1.3	Option B	The IMS
8.2	Management system documentation (Option A)	The IMS
8.3	Control of management system documents (Option A)	Chapter 4, Section 4.7.5
8.4	Control of records (Option A)	Chapter 4, Section 4.7.6
8.5	Actions to address risks and opportunities (Option A)	Chapter 5
8.6	Improvement (Option A)	Chapter 4, Section 4.10
8.7	Corrective actions (Option A)	Chapter 4, Section 4.10.2 Chapter 4, Section 4.10.3 Chapter 4, Section 4.10.4 Chapter 4, Section 4.10.5
8.8	Internal audits (Option A)	Chapter 4, Section 4.9.2
8.9	Management reviews (Option A)	Chapter 4, Section 4.9.3

Appendix 3—Mapping FSR quality requirements to IMS procedures

FSR section	Control	Procedure(s)
6	Management requirements	Appendix 7
7	Business continuity	Chapter 3, Section 3.1.15 Chapter 13
8	Independence, impartiality and integrity	Chapter 3, Section 3.1.5 Chapter 3, Appendix 3 Section 6.2.1.6
9	Confidentiality	Chapter 4, Appendix 20 Chapter 5, Appendix 16 Section 11 Chapter 12, Section 12.3.3.3
10	Document control	Chapter 4, Section 4.7.5.3

Continued

FSR section	Control	Procedure(s)
11	Review of requests, tenders, and contracts	Appendix 16
12	Subcontracting	Chapter 14
13	Packaging and general chemicals and materials	Not applicable to FCL
14	Complaints	Section 6.14 and Appendices 18, 19 and 20
15	Control of nonconforming testing	Chapter 4, Section 4.9.2 Section 6.13.2
16	Control of records	Chapter 12, Section 12.3.13 Chapter 12, Section 12.3.14
16.1	General	Chapter 4, Section 4.7.5 Chapter 5, Appendix 16 Section 6.11 Chapter 12, Section 12.3.14
16.2	Technical records	Chapter 8, Section 8.6.15 Chapter 9
16.3	Checking and review	Section 8 and Appendix 16
17	Internal audits	Chapter 4, Section 4.9.2, Appendix 52 Section 6.13.3 Chapter 7, Section 7.4.3
18	Technical requirements	Section 6.12
18.1	Personnel	Chapter 18, Sections 18.1.3 and 18.1.4
18.2	Code of conduct	There are a number of codes of conduct—examples are from the relevant individual certifications Chapter 3, Section 3.1.6
18.3	Training	Chapter 4, Section 4.7.3 Chapter 18, Section 18.2.1
19	Competence	Chapter 4, Section 4.7.2 Appendix 24 Chapter 18, Section 18.2.5
20	Accommodation and environmental conditions	Chapter 2 Chapter 3 Section 6.12.6 Chapter 12, Sections 12.3.8, 12.3.14.10, and 12.4
20.1	Laboratory/examination facilities	Chapter 2
20.2	Contamination avoidance, monitoring and detection	Chapter 5 Chapter 8, Sections 8.2, 8.3 and 8.7 Chapter 12, Sections 12.4.4 and 12.6
21	Test methods and method validation	Section 12.7 Chapter 7, Section 7.5.5
21.1	Selection of methods	Sections 6.6.2.3, 6.6.2.4, 6.12.7 and Appendix 11
21.2	Validation of methods	Section 12.7 Chapter 7, Section 7.5.5
21.2	Determining the end-user's requirements	Sections 6 and 8 and Appendices 11, 12 and 13 Chapter 12, Section 12.9.6
21.2	Determining the specification	Section 6 Section 8 and Appendices 11, 12 and 13 Chapter 12, Section 12.9.6
21.2	Risk assessment of the method	Chapter 5 Chapter 7, Section 7.5.5

FSR section	Control	Procedure(s)
21.2	Review of the end-user's requirements	Sections 6 and 8
21.2	The acceptance criteria	Sections 6 and 8
21.2	The validation plan	Section 12.7
21.2	Validation of measurement-based methods	Not applicable to the forensic laboratory
21.2	Validation of interpretive methods	Section 12.7 Chapter 7, Section 7.5.5
21.2	Verification of the validation of adopted methods	Section 12.7 Chapter 7, Section 7.5.5
21.2	Minor changes in methods	Section 12.7 Chapter 7, Section 7.4.3
21.2	Infrequently used methods	Section 12.7 Chapter 7, Section 7.5.5
21.2	Validation outcomes	Section.12.7 Chapter 7, Section 7.5.5
21.2	Assessment of acceptance criteria compliance	Section 12.7 Chapter 7, Section 7.5.5
21.2	Validation report	Section 12.7 Chapter 7, Section 7.5.5
21.2	A statement of validation completion	Section 12.7 Chapter 7, Section 7.5.5
21.2	Validation library	Section 12.7 Chapter 7, Section 7.5.5
21.2	Implementation plan and any constraints	Section 12.7 Chapter 7, Sections 7.4.3 and 7.5.5
22	Estimation of uncertainty	Section 12.7 Chapter 7, Section 7.5.5
23	Control of data	Section 12.7 Chapter 12
23.1	General	Section 12.7 Chapter 12
23.2	Electronic information capture, storage, transfer, retrieval, and disposal	Chapter 12
23.3	Electronic information security	Chapter 12
23.3	Access control to electronic information	Chapter 12, Section 12.4.4
23.3	The section, use, and management of passwords	Chapter 12, Section 12.6
23.3	Protection against malware	Chapter 4, Appendix 29
23.3	Management of removable storage media	Chapter 12, Section 12.3.12
23.3	The segregation of Forensic Networks	Chapter 12, Section 12.9.10
23.3	Backups, recovery, and business continuity	Chapter 7, Section 7.7.4 Chapter 12, Section 12.3.14 Chapter 13
23.3	Network security and mobile working	Chapter 12, Sections 12.3.9 and 12.6
23.3	Use of cloud-based services	FCL does not use cloud services for storing information and keeps all information on premises. Should a forensic laboratory use cloud services they shall comply with this requirement

Continued

FSR section	Control	Procedure(s)
23.3	Security monitoring and situational awareness	Chapter 5 Chapter 12, Section 12.6.7
23.4	Reference collections and databases	Not applicable in the forensic laboratory
24	Equipment	Section 6.12.8 Chapter 7, Section 7.4.3 Chapter 7, Section 7.5.5
24.1	Computers and automated equipment	Section 12.8 Chapter 7, Section 7.4.3 Chapter 7, Section 7.5.5 Chapter 7, Section 7.1 Chapter 12, Section 12.3.13.1.2 Chapter 12, Section 12.3.14
25	Measurement traceability—immediate checks	Section 12.9 Chapter 7, Section 7.5.5
26	Handling of Test items	Section 12.9 and Appendix 26
26.1	Receipt of cases and exhibits at the laboratory	Chapter 9, Section 9.6
26.2	Case assessment and prioritisation	Chapter 9, Section 9.7
26.3	Exhibit handling, protection, and storage	Chapter 8, Section 8.6.9 Chapter 8, Section 8.6.10 Chapter 8, Section 8.6.11 Chapter 8, Section 8.6.13 Chapter 8, Section 8.6.14 Chapter 8, Section 8.6.15 Chapter 9, Section 9.7 Chapter 12, Section 12.3.14
26.4	Exhibit return and disposal	Chapter 9, Section 9.6 Chapter 9, Section 9.20 Chapter 12, Section 12.3.14.10
27	Assuring the quality of test results	Sections 8 and 13
27.1	Interlaboratory comparisons (proficiency tests and collaborative exercises)	Not applicable to FCL
28	Reporting the results	Section 6.12.12 and Appendix 28 Chapter 12, Section 12.3.14.8 Chapter 12, Section 12.3.14.9
28.1	General	Chapter 4, Appendix 26 Section 12.12 Chapter 18, Sections 18.2.5 and 18.2.6
28.2	Declarations of compliance and noncompliance with required standards	Appendix 28
28.3	Reports and statements to the CJS	Section 6.6 Section 12.12 and Appendix 28 Chapter 9, Sections 9.13 Chapter 9, Sections 9.15
28.4	Reporting competencies	Chapter 3, Section 3.1.12 Chapter 4, Section 4.7.2
28.5	Retention, recording, revelation and prosecution disclosure	Specific to Legislation in jurisdictions of operations
25.6	Defence examinations	Specific to Legislation in jurisdictions of operations
28.7	Opinions and interpretations	Section 12.12 and Appendix 28 Chapter 9, Section 9.16

Appendix 4—Quality Manager, job description

Objective and role

The Quality Manager shall be responsible for establishing and monitoring adherence to ISO 9001 and other quality standards. Quality shall include both the qualitative and quantitative measures. This shall include complying with all mandated requirements including maintaining ISO 9001 and ISO/IEC 17025 compliance.

Problems and challenges

The primary challenge for the Quality Manager is establishing a good working relationship with all employees that encourage cooperation and teamwork instead of conflict and avoidance. The Quality Manager shall work all employees to ensure that quality is built into all products and services to all clients from the beginning.

Principal accountabilities

The Quality Manager shall:

- promote quality achievement and performance improvement for all products and services;
- set Quality Assurance compliance objectives and ensure that targets are achieved;
- maintain awareness of the business context and company profitability, including budgetary control issues;
- assess product and service specifications and their suppliers, and comparing them with client requirements;
- work with purchasing employees to establish quality requirements from external suppliers;
- ensure compliance with relevant international and national standards and legislation, this also specifically includes the requirements of ISO 9001 and ISO/IEC 17025;
- consider the application of environmental and health and safety standards;
- agree standards and establish clearly defined quality methods for all employees to apply to their products and service offerings to their clients;
- define quality procedures in conjunction with relevant FCL business units;
- set up and maintain controls and documentation procedures in the IMS;
- identify relevant quality-related training needs and deliver relevant training;
- collate and analyse performance data and charts against defined quality parameters;
- ensure quality tests and procedures are properly understood, carried out, and evaluated and that product modifications are investigated, if necessary;
- supervise technical employees in carrying out quality tests and checks;
- write relevant technical and management systems reports;
- brings together employees of different disciplines to plan, formulate, and agree comprehensive quality procedures;
- persuade reluctant employees to change their way of working to incorporate quality methods;
- liaise with clients' auditors and ensures the execution of corrective action and compliance with clients' specifications;
- establish standards of service, in association with relevant departments for all clients;
- prepare clear explanatory quality documents;
- monitor performance by gathering relevant quality data and producing statistical reports;
- maintain ISO 9001 compliance;
- ensure that quality systems are continuously improved;
- ensure that all corrective actions are completed in a timely manner;
- develop plans for migration of quality management policies and procedures to support future directions;
- develop long range quality management strategy;
- participate in international, national, and local SIG presentations, and publishes management approved articles describing FCL's quality management initiatives and how they relate to the business;
- develop and manage effective working relationships with all appropriate internal and external interested parties;
- maintain external links to other forensic laboratories to gain competitive assessments and share information, where appropriate;
- identify the emerging technologies to be assimilated, integrated and introduced into the IMS, which could significantly impact product and service offering SLAs;

- interface with external industrial and academic organisations in order to maintain state-of-the-art knowledge in emerging quality management issues and to enhance FCL's image as a first-class solution provider utilising the latest thinking in this field;
- adheres to all established policies, standards, and procedures; and
- perform all responsibilities in accordance with, or in excess of, the requirements of the Integrated Management System.

Authority

The Quality Manager shall have the authority to:

- monitor product and service offerings for adherence to quality standards;
- monitor internal processes and procedures for adherence to quality standards;
- monitor Service Level Agreements and their associated metrics; and
- take appropriate action to ensure that quality is maintained and continuously improved in the IMS and for all of its product and service offerings.

Contacts

Internal

Contacts throughout the whole organisation.

External

Appropriate Special Interest Groups (SIGs), other Quality professionals and organisations such as the Chartered Quality Institute (CQI), the Institute of Quality Assurance (IQS), etc.

Reports to

The Quality Manager shall report to top management.

Appendix 5—Business plan template

Executive summary

- business overview;
- the market for products and services;
- the business potential; and
- forecast profit.

Description of the business

- a brief description of the business;
- business history and its ownership;
- legal status;
- location of provision of products and services;
- a description of products and services offered to clients;
- unique selling points;
- competitor analysis—by size, location, market share, ownership, pricing structure, services offered;
- a description of proposed new products and services;
- intangible assets and how assets are protected;
- current size and expected growth of the market;
- analysis of market by segments;
- identification of new markets segments;
- existing and potential clients;

- routes to market; and
- management team.

Situational audit (current situation)

This is based on metrics from the business, including sales and marketing information and shall:

- identify competitive advantages;
- Identify strengths, weaknesses, opportunities and threats (SWOT);
- prioritise new opportunities to pursue (from the risk register—as defined in Chapter 5); and
- provide accurate details for business planning and strategy development.

Aims and objectives (target situation)

- overview of a '5 years plan'; and
- SMART[a] objectives—quantitative goals.

Strategy and tactics (how to get there)

- the strategic approach to achieving the objectives; and
- the tactics refer to the details of the strategy.

Note

The details will be contained in subordinate departmental plans.

Marketing plan

- brand development;
- customer service strategy;
- market research;
- pricing strategy;
- segmentation and targeting of clients; and
- unique selling points.

 The marketing plan shall answer the following questions:

- how is the digital forensics market segmented?
- what are FCL's competitive advantages?
- what is special about the FCL products and services?
- what is FCL's marketing strategy?
- what is the size and growth rate of the digital forensics market?
- who are FCL's competitors?
- who are FCL's customers?

Operations plan

- capacity—current and potential with current employees;
- implementation plans—with departmental breakdowns, accountabilities, budgets, and target delivery dates;
- IT strategy;
- key suppliers and alternates

---

a. SMART has been defined in Chapter 3, Section 3.1.17.

- purchasing arrangements;
- quality control plans; and
- research and development.

Management, staffing, and organisation

- corporate governance requirements;
- key employees;
- organisational chart (current and proposed);
- recruitment strategy;
- remuneration (salaries and bonuses);
- senior management details;
- employee screening requirements; and
- training.

Financial plan

- details of any financing required (internal or external);
- financial ratios required;
- forecast balance sheet;
- forecast cash flow;
- forecast profit and loss; and
- forecast sales.

Note 1

Any assumptions made for any forecast shall be included.

Note 2

Forecasts should be a month by month basis for a minimum of 3 years.

Appendix 6—Business KPIS

The following business KPIs shall be used:

- **financial governance compliance**—ensuring that financial returns are made on time and are correct;
- **legislative governance**—ensuring that all relevant legislative requirements are met in the jurisdiction of operations;
- **profit levels**—the current profit levels shall be checked against forecasts on a monthly basis;
- **repeat business**—50% of clients place one repeat order (where possible since some clients require only a single piece of work) which shall be checked against the accounts system;
- **accreditation and certification**—successful gaining and maintaining of any relevant organisational or personal accreditations and certifications, if required; and
- **audits (internal and external)**—passing all audits with no nonconformities. If a nonconformity is raised that it shall be remediated in the agreed time.

Note

There are other metrics and KPIs embedded within the management systems standards in the IMS, but these are not reproduced here.

Appendix 7—Quality plan contents

Below is the table of contents of the quality plan to meet the requirements of ISO 9001 and ISO/IEC 17025. ISO 9001 was the first management system implemented in any forensic laboratory as it maps the business processes, and all other management systems can flow from that.

- table of contents;
- introduction;
- overview;
- quality system scope;
- quality system structure;
- quality manual structure;
- document retention;
- ISO 9001 and ISO/IEC 17025 mapping;
- quality manual format;
- auditing;
- proposed development and certification timescales;
- initial list of required quality procedures; and
- document control.

Appendix 8—Induction checklist contents

All inductees shall go through the HR induction process and the checklist for shall include:

Prior to inductee starting

- confirm start date and time;
- confirm reporting location and any special requirements;
- book welcome meeting with Line Manager and others, as appropriate;
- submit new user form to IT Department to set up access to information processing systems, as appropriate and authorised; and
- advise relevant employees and inductees of start details.

On the first day

Company and role details

Introduction

These are details processes and procedures given to the inductee by HR. The inductee signs to confirm that they have received them.

- corporate overview;
- values;
- products and services;
- meeting internal and external expectations;
- business planning and development;
- clients and partners;
- finance; and
- communications.

Role details

These are details of the inductee's role and responsibilities given to the inductee by HR. The inductee shall sign to confirm that they have received them.

- introduction to Line Manager, mentor, and colleagues;
- management structure as applicable to inductee;

- responsibility and accountability;
- key goals and targets;
- training and development; and
- facilities.

General

- issue temporary ID card if permanent one not available;
- identify location of toilets and refreshment facilities;
- explain first aid procedures and identify First Aiders;
- explain emergency evacuation procedures, identify emergency exit, and Fire Wardens;
- if disabled, identify 'emergency buddy';
- explain telephone system;
- explain building security and out of hours working procedures;
- explain car parking facilities;
- explain procedures for reporting sickness;
- explain on site health and safety procedures, including accident and 'near miss' reporting;
- explain pay and expense claim process; and
- explain or demonstrate any other relevant issues to the inductee.

Information capture

Ensure that the following information is already captured, verify it or capture it on the first day the inductee starts work:

Personal details

- full name;
- title,
- date of birth;
- marital status;
- home address;
- home telephone number;
- mobile telephone number;
- personal email address; and
- social security (or equivalent) number.

Work details

- start date;
- probation period;
- department;
- Line Manager;
- position;
- term (permanent, contract, etc.);
- status (full time, part time, etc.);
- salary; and
- grade.

Bank details

- bank name;
- branch name;
- branch address;
- account number;
- account name;

- branch code;
- IBAN; and
- BIC.

Next of kin details

- full name;
- relationship;
- address;
- home telephone number;
- work telephone number; and
- email address.

Comments

- e.g. special needs (e.g. disability);
- e.g. languages; and
- e.g. training requirements.

Employee number and identity

- employee number issued;
- employee photo identity badge issued (will require photo)—unless already issued;
- printed name;
- signature; and
- date.

Documentation

Received

All documents shall be signed for by the inductee and any relevant comments added:

- signed contract;
- tax documents;
- evidence of right to work in the country;
- signed information security policy;
- induction feedback form, as defined in Appendix 9; and
- qualifications.

Issued

All documents and items issued shall be signed for by the inductee and any relevant comments added:

- policies, as applicable to the inductee (specify);
- employee handbook;
- keys/access codes (specify); and
- other (specify).

Training

General training

This is details of any initial training given to the inductee by HR or others, the date is recorded and the inductee's signature is recorded against each of the training programmes attended.

- induction; and
- others—define.

Management system training

This is the detail of all relevant management system training given to the inductee by the Management System Owner(s).

- understanding the management system;
- objectives;
- policies and procedures;
- inductee responsibilities;
- metrics; and
- using the management system.

Note 1

Responsibilities for completing the induction process are defined in Chapter 18, Section 18.1.7.

Note 2

For all of the items on the checklist, the date they were performed and the signature of the person managing the induction shall be required. In some cases, countersignature by the inductee shall be required to signify that the action has taken place.

Appendix 9—Induction feedback

The inductee's feedback on the induction process shall be sought after induction training has finished. This is a confidential process and shall answer the following questions:

- does the inductee understand their responsibilities?
- does the inductee understand how they fit into FCL?
- does the inductee understand how their input affects FCL's products and services?
- does the inductee understand the opportunities available?
- were documents easy to understand and relevant?
- was there anything missed from the induction process?
- any other issues that could improve the induction experience?

The answers shall be used for continuous improvement of the induction process.

Appendix 10—Standard proposal template

Below is the standard proposal template, it shall be amended according to client requirements, as needed. It gives details about:

- FCL;
- FCL organisation;
- the benefits to the client of using FCL;
- the terms of reference;
- general;
- scope;
- detailed deliverables statements;
- proposed methodology;
- general approach;
- phase life cycle;
- quality assurance;
- assumptions;
- risks;
- terms and conditions;
- CVs/resumes of employees working for the client; and
- document control.

Note

Within FCL, the proposal forms part of the contract.

Appendix 11—Issues to consider for forensic case processing

There are a number of evaluation criteria and points to agree that shall be considered prior to final acceptance of a forensic case. These shall include, in no particular order, but not be limited to:

- are there the required skills in house (or via trusted partner) to deliver the forensic case on time?
- are there any special requirements or precautions to be taken to preserve the evidence?
- are there jurisdictional issues?
- do any conflicts of interest exist?
- does the client want to use a method or process that is out of date, unacceptable or discredited in some other way?
- is there capacity to deliver to client TRT?
- does the client want, or need, to use a nonstandard method—if so, the client shall be advised and approve this as part of the proposal;
- how is transfer of the evidence to be undertaken (collection by client, delivery to client or delivery to a third party)?
- how is acceptance of the evidence to be undertaken (on site acquisition, collection from client or delivery by client)?
- how will the forensic case be assessed and what is the strategy for production of the required deliverables?
- if an expert witness needed—is one available?
- is it legally permissible?
- is their required price (where stated) feasible?
- what is the classification/sensitivity of the forensic case?
- is there anything about the forensic case that could bring FCL into disrepute or affect its reputation negatively?
- retention and disposal requirements?
- the financial status of client (regarding past payments);
- what exactly is the required deliverable(s)?
- what is the reporting format type required?
- what items are to be examined and are there any risks related to them that shall be considered?
- what will be the sequence of the examination process—is this a client requirement or will it follow standard IMS methods?
- will taking on the specific client cause a key risk?

Note

If any of the issues above, or any other relevant issues, are raised for a specific forensic case, these shall be raised with the client and resolved prior to proceeding with the forensic case.

Appendix 12—Standard quotation contents

Quotations may vary on client requirements, but the standard contents shall include:

- instructing client details
- client reference;
- hardware to be processed;
- outcomes required;
- specific methodologies to be used, if appropriate;
- report type required;
- any other deliverables required;
- turn round time required;
- delivery and collection details;
- what is to be done with the original material supplied by the client at the end of the forensic case; and
- price.

Appendix 13—Standard terms and conditions

The standard terms and conditions for any forensic laboratory will depend on the jurisdiction, but the one used by FCL contains the basic requirements, and is reproduced below:

- hourly rate for forensic case processing;
- hourly rate for travelling;
- travel class (planes and trains);
- hourly rate for attending courts/tribunals whether evidence is given or not;
- miscellaneous expenses charging;
- tax on fees;
- terms of payment;
- penalties for late payment;
- requirement for full written instructions;
- communication for forensic case processing;
- acceptance of only written instructions by authorised representatives;
- use of best ability to assist client;
- legislation for agreement; and
- dispute resolution.

Appendix 14—ERMS client areas

Within the ERMS, the area relating to client matters shall be separated into four distinct areas. These relate to the status of the client (or prospective client) in their relationship lifecycle. The four areas are:

- **prospects**—where the virtual file is initially opened and shall contain all correspondence relating to the prospective client until the 'stop/go' decision relating to the proposed work is received;
- **current**—where the virtual file is moved if there is a positive outcome from the initial meeting and the proposed work proceeds. All forensic case processing files shall be stored in this file along with any other matters relating to the client. The virtual file shall stay in this area until the client terminates their relationship;
- **failed**—where the virtual file is moved if the initial proposal is rejected by the client. If there is a further possibility of working with the client, the virtual file shall be moved back to the prospects area; and
- **finished**—where the virtual file is moved for archive purposes when the relationship with the client is finished. Should the client restart their relationship with the client, the virtual file shall be returned to the 'current' area.

Note

Virtual files shall be retained in the 'Failed' and 'Finished' areas for a set period of time until they are considered for archive or disposal according to the document retention policy in force, as defined in Chapter 4, Appendix 26.

Appendix 15—Cost estimation spreadsheet

The cost per item of the items below shall be evaluated and also the hourly rate for the employee's time spent on a forensic case and an estimate for the hours to be spent. The spreadsheet shall include the following:

Forensic case start up

- cost of collection (driver hourly rate);
- booking in exhibit and checking it;
- photographing and describing it;
- examination, labelling, and writing up;
- performing backups to disk/tape/cloud (if appropriate); and
- forensic case administration—virtual and paper file setup, etc.

Forensic case processing

- backup to disk—two copies (original evidence);
- backup to tape (original evidence);
- backup to server (original evidence—if appropriate);
- working disk(s);
- disk for backup images;
- disk for backup of forensic case;
- tape for backup of forensic case;
- caddies to hold hard disks;
- performing forensic case processing;
- report production (paper);
- report (binder);
- report (dividers);
- report (packaging);
- media for output (CD/DVD/thumb drive) as per client choice; and
- cost of delivery (driver hourly rate).

Note

Some of these are hard costs (e.g. the cost of consumables), whilst others will depend on time estimations (e.g. forensic case processing or collection/delivery). Therefore, if a fixed price is to be offered, it is essential that estimates are accurate.

Maintaining forensic cases after processing has finished

- disks;
- tapes; and
- overheads for storage.

Note

the length of time, and possibly the conditions under which storage shall take place, may well be dictated by legislation or regulation in the jurisdiction.

Appendix 16—Draught review form

Whilst a draught review form is used in FCL, other forensic laboratories may use an electronic document management system (EDMS) with inbuilt workflow to manage document control and other reviews. Where a draught review form is used, it shall contain the following:

- project name;
- client name;
- document name(s);
- version(s);
- author name;
- reviewer name;
- date sent;
- return by date;
- comments;
- reviewed by;
- signature;
- position; and
- date.

Note 1

It is up to each forensic laboratory whether they use a paper based or electronic system for document review.

Note 2

FCL is evaluating EDMS' for transition from a paper-based system.

Appendix 17—Client sign off and feedback form

Forensic case details

- Forensic Case No;
- Forensic Case Name; and
- client details.

Feedback

Feedback shall be requested on the following aspects of how the forensic case was handled:

- communication;
- speed of delivering results;
- quality of results;
- timeliness of delivery;
- quality of deliverables;
- understandability of the deliverables; and
- meeting requirements (as defined).

    The above are all marked as follows:

1. Very poor;
2. Poor;
3. Good;
4. Very good;
5. Excellent.

Forensic case result

What was the result of the forensic case/investigation that this recovered evidence was used to support (Did the recovered evidence play a pivotal role)?

Sign off

- confirmation of signoff of the forensic case;
- signed;
- date; and
- name.

Appendix 18—Information required for registering a complaint

- complaint number;
- date of complaint
- time of complaint;
- name of complainant;

- complainant's details;
- details of complaint;
- action taken from initial action chronologically recorded till closure;
- was the complaint justified?
- root cause identified as;
- date closed;
- time closed; and
- closed by.

Appendix 19—Complaint resolution timescales

Action	Target time
Complaint received	Start to investigate immediately
Refer to Line Manager/client Account Manager/Laboratory Manager	2 h
Enter complaint into Service Desk System	When advised
Attempt to resolve	Within 24 h
Acknowledge complaint	Within 1 working day
Find resolution	Within 5 working days
Present report on complaint to top management, if applicable	Within 10 working days
Present complaints summary report	Management review agenda item and regular management information (MI) reports.

Appendix 20—Complaint metrics

Metrics for complaint reporting shall include:

- complaints received;
- complaints regarded as justified (as a percentage of all complaints as well as numbers);
- complaints resolved at source;
- complaints incorrectly prioritised;
- complaints incorrectly categorised;
- complaints not acknowledged within target time;
- repeat complaints;
- complaints not justified;
- complaints not resolved within target time; and
- complaint reports not presented to management within target time.

Appendix 21—Laboratory Manager, job description

Objective and role

The Laboratory Manager shall be responsible for establishing and monitoring adherence to ISO 9001 and ISO/IEC 17025 from a technical requirements viewpoint. This shall include complying with all mandated requirements including maintaining ISO/IEC 17025 compliance and assisting the Quality Manager in maintaining ISO 9001 compliance.

Problems and challenges

The primary challenge for the Laboratory Manager shall be to ensure competent employees are in place who can produce consistent forensic case processing results that meet client's requirements. As digital forensic technology is a rapid changing area, it is essential that the Laboratory Manager shall keep up to date with all relevant developments in this area. Depending on the number of forensic cases being processed at any one time, the ability to manage resources to meet client requirements can be problematic. Often, forensic cases are required to be processed in a rush, and the Laboratory Manager shall ensure that this is achieved, but without sacrificing quality of deliverables to the client.

Principal accountabilities

The Laboratory Manager shall:

- promote quality achievement and technical performance improvement;
- set technical competence and forensic case processing objectives and ensuring that targets are achieved;
- maintain awareness of the business context and company profitability, including budgetary control issues;
- assess product and service specifications and their suppliers, and comparing them with client requirements;
- ensure compliance with relevant international and national standards and legislation, this also specifically includes the requirements for ISO/IEC 17025 and ISO 9001;
- define technical quality procedures for forensic case processing;
- set up and maintains technical documentation procedures in the IMS;
- identify relevant competence training needs and deliver relevant training;
- collate and analyse forensic case performance data and chart against defined performance parameters;
- ensure calibration, tests, and procedures are properly understood, carried out and evaluated;
- supervise all employees in carrying out all aspects of forensic case processing, including first response and evidential recovery from client sites or crime scenes;
- manage multiple concurrent forensic cases;
- writes relevant technical and management systems reports;
- establishes standards of service for forensic case processing, and seeks to continuously improve them;
- administer and/or conduct test and examinations, evaluating test results and making recommendations based on those results;
- manage the process of evidence presentation for forensic cases to clients or the relevant Court or Tribunal;
- prepare clear explanatory technical documents;
- monitor performance by gathering relevant forensic case processing and producing statistical reports;
- maintain ISO/IEC 17025 compliance and assist the Quality Manager in maintaining ISO 9001 compliance relating to forensic case processing;
- ensure that all corrective actions are completed in a timely manner;
- develop plans for technical delivery to support future directions;
- develop long-range forensic case processing management strategy;
- participate in international, national and local SIG presentations, and publishes management approved articles describing FCL's forensic case processing capabilities;
- develops and manages effective working relationships with all appropriate internal and external interested parties;
- ensuring that all Forensic Analysts have access to counselling, if required, after handling disturbing forensic cases;
- maintain external links to other forensic laboratories to gain competitive assessments and share information, where appropriate;
- identify the emerging technologies to be assimilated, integrated and introduced within FCL, which could significantly impact FCL's product and service offering SLAs;
- interfaces with external industrial and academic organisations in order to maintain state-of-the-art knowledge in emerging forensic case processing issues and to enhance FCL's image as a first-class solution provider utilising the latest thinking in this field;
- adheres to all established policies, standards, and procedures; and
- performs all responsibilities in accordance with, or in excess of, the requirements of FCL Integrated Management System.

Authority

The Laboratory Manager shall have the authority to:

- monitor product and service offerings for adherence to technical and quality standards;
- manage Forensic Analysts and all other employees relating to forensic case processing;

- monitor Service Level Agreements and turn round times and their associated metrics; and
- take appropriate action to ensure that client deliverability for forensic case processing is maintained and continuously improved.

Contacts

Internal

Contacts throughout the whole organisation.

External

Those external will be with appropriate Special Interest Groups (SIGs), other technical forensic case processing for a, such as the High Tech Crime Investigation Association (HTCIA), International Association of Computer Investigative Specialists (IACIS), Association of Digital forensics, Security and Law (ADFSL), etc.

Reports to

The Laboratory Manager shall report to top management.

Appendix 22—Forensic Analyst, job description

Note

This job description relates to all those involved in forensic case processing and refers to both Forensic Analysts as well as their Supervisors. The only difference is that the Supervisors shall have supervisory experience that the Forensic Analysts will not have, marked with an '*' below.

Objective and role

The Forensic Analyst shall be responsible for all stages of forensic case processing. This can start with first response for on-site evidence collection, through to presentation of evidence to the client, a Court or Tribunal. The exact tasks shall depend on the requirements of the forensic case and the Forensic Analyst's competence.

Problems and challenges

The primary challenge for the Forensic Analyst is the rate of change of the technology and the varying technologies that they may be called upon to examine. The Forensic Analyst shall keep up to date with all relevant developments in this area. Depending on the number of forensic cases being processed at any one time, the ability to process forensic cases to meet client requirements without sacrificing quality of deliverables.

Principal accountabilities

The Forensic Analyst shall:

- conduct forensic examinations on a range of information processing systems;
- physically disassemble hardware and examine it;
- use software tools to analyse recovered evidence;
- make forensic images of media, where appropriate
- maintain the chain of custody of any evidence under their control;
- attend incident or crime scenes to recover evidence, as required;
- examine digital and optical media to recover evidence;
- record all actions taken on all forensic cases they are processing and producing reports and statements relating to the forensic case;

- give oral and written evidence, as required;
- research and develop new methodologies of forensic case processing, as required;
- consult with external agencies and clients, as required;
- analyse and interpret evidence;
- collect, label, transport, and secure evidence from incident or crime scenes and/or during processing;
- know and understand relevant legislation relating to forensic case processing in the jurisdiction;
- understand relevant hardware, standard software and network processing, relevant to forensic cases that they are processing;
- prioritise forensic case processing to meet client turn round times;
- perform forensic case processing to a high degree of accuracy;
- ensure compliance with relevant international and national standards and legislation, this also specifically includes the requirements for ISO/IEC 17025 and ISO 9001;
- manage multiple concurrent forensic cases;
- prepare clear explanatory technical documents;
- manages employees that report to them to achieve forensic case processing requirements;
- participate in international, national, and local SIG presentations, and publishes management approved articles describing FCL's forensic case processing capabilities;
- develop and manage effective working relationships with all appropriate internal and external interested parties;
- identify the emerging technologies which could be assimilated, integrated, and introduced within FCL;
- interface with external industrial and academic organisations in order to maintain state-of-the-art knowledge in emerging forensic case processing issues and to enhance FCL's image as a first-class solution provider utilising the latest thinking in this field;
- adhere to all established policies, standards, and procedures; and
- perform all responsibilities in accordance with, or in excess of, the requirements of the Integrated Management System.

Authority

The Forensic Analyst shall have the authority to undertake forensic case processing, as required.

Contacts

Internal

Contacts are throughout the whole organisation.

External

Those external will be with appropriate Special Interest Groups (SIGs), other technical forensic case processing for a, such as the High Tech Crime Investigation Association (HTCIA), International Association of Computer Investigative Specialists (IACIS), Association of Digital Forensics, Security and Law (ADFSL), etc.

Reports to

The Forensic Analyst shall report to the Laboratory Manager.

Appendix 23—Training agenda

The following chart is a recommended approach to the technical training requirements.[b]

---

b. This is taken from ACPO guidance—but appears universally applicable.

Digital evidence recovery staff

Months 1–6	Months 6–12	Months 12–24	Months 24–36
Understanding equipment in the forensics Laboratory	Forensic computing foundation course	Introduction to Linux forensics course	Forensic Internet course
Hardware qualification such as A+	Introductory training on secondary forensic tool	Intermediate Internet forensics course	Intermediate Linux forensics course
Core data recovery and analysis skills	Other specialised training as required depending on case work	Network foundation course	Advanced training on forensic laboratory primary forensic tool
Introductory training on forensic laboratory primary forensic tool		Intermediate training on forensic laboratory primary forensic tool	Intermediate and/or advanced court, evidence requirements and report writing skills course
		Introduction to court, evidence requirements and report writing skills course	Other specialised training as required depending on case work
		Other specialised training as required depending on case work	

Network investigators

Months 1–6	Months 6–12	Months 12–24	Months 24–36
Core network investigator skills	Hands on Linux training	Advanced network investigation	Covert Internet investigation course
Researching, identifying and tracing the electronic suspect	Introductory and/or intermediate training on the forensic laboratory primary forensic tool (cross training)	Consider product specific certification courses, e.g. Cisco CCNA, etc. (depending on environment)	Consider further product specific certification courses, e.g. Cisco CCNA, etc. (depending on environment)
Open-source intelligence research	Other specialised training as required depending on case work	Network intrusion, hacking or penetration testing courses (leading to certification?)	Advanced training on the forensic laboratory primary forensic tool (cross training)
Introductory training on the forensic laboratory primary forensic tool		Introduction to court, evidence requirements, and report writing skills course	Intermediate and/or advanced court, evidence requirements, and report writing skills course
		Other specialised training as required depending on case work	Other specialised training as required depending on case work

Appendix 24—Some individual forensic certifications

Some current certifications that may be considered by employees are listed below:

Postnominals	Certification	Specifically forensic
	MSAB. XRY certification	Yes
	CompTIA A+ certification	
ACE	AccessData Certified Examiner	Yes
CCCI	Certified Computer Crime Investigator	Yes
CCFT	Certified Computer Forensic Technician	Yes

Continued

Postnominals	Certification	Specifically forensic
CFCE	Certified Forensic Computer Examiner	Yes
CCE	Certified Computer Examiner	Yes
CDFE	Certified Digital Forensics Examiner	Yes
CDFP	Certified Digital Forensics Professional	Yes
CEDS	Certified E-Discovery Specialist	Yes
CFE	Certified Fraud Examiner	
CFIP	Certified Forensic Investigation Practitioner	Yes
CHFI	Computer Hacking Forensic Investigator	Yes
CIFI	Certified Information Forensics Investigator	Yes
CISM	Certified Information System Manager	
CISSP	Certified Information System Security Professional	
CMFS	Certified Mac Forensics Specialist	Yes
CMI	Certified MalWare Investigator	
CSFA	CyberSecurity Forensic Analyst	Yes
DSMO	Paraben DSMO Mobile Operator Certification	Yes
EnCE	EnCase Certified Examiner	Yes
EnCEP	Encase Certified e-Discovery Practitioner	Yes
GASF	GIAC Advanced Smartphone Forensics	Yes
GCFA	GIAC Certified Forensics Analyst	Yes
GCFE	GIAC Certified Forensics Examiner	Yes
GCTI	GIAC Cyber Threat Intelligence	
GIME	GIAC iOS and MacOS Examiner	Yes
GNFA	GIAC Network Forensic Analyst	Yes
GREM	GIAC Reverse Engineering Malware	
SSCP	System Security Certified Practitioner	
UFED	Cellebrite UFED Pro certificate	Yes

Note 1
Some of these are only available to Law Enforcement or have other specific requirements associated with them that may preclude some employees from applying for them.

Note 2
There are also a number of universities that offer undergraduate and postgraduate digital forensics focused courses.

Appendix 25—Minimum equipment records required by ISO/IEC 17025

ISO/IEC 17025/IEC, Section 6.4.13 mandates the following minimum records for all equipment:

- the identity of equipment, including software and firmware version as defined in Chapter 12, Appendix 8;
- the manufacturer's name, type identification, and serial number or other unique identification as defined in Chapter 12, Appendix 8;

- evidence of verification that equipment conforms with specified requirements as defined in Chapter 12, Appendix 8;
- the current location as defined in Chapter 12, Appendix 8;
- calibration dates, results of calibrations, adjustments, acceptance criteria, and the due date of the next calibration or the calibration interval as defined in Chapter 12, Appendix 8,
- documentation of reference materials, results, acceptance criteria, relevant dates and the period of validity as defined in Chapter 7, Section 7.5.5;
- the maintenance plan and maintenance carried out to date, where relevant to the performance of the equipment as defined in Chapter 7, Section 7.5; and
- details of any damage, malfunction, modification to, or repair of, the equipment as defined in Chapter 7, Section 7.4.

Appendix 26—Reference forensic case tests

The reference forensic case tests include the following standard tests and results:

- acquisition testing (usually by hashing);
- documents and settings (Windows);
- extracted files by document type;
- favourites (Windows);
- hash analysis of defined files;
- Internet history;
- link parser;
- recent (Windows);
- recovered files;
- searches by keyword;
- signature analysis; and
- unique email addresses.

Note 1

These are standard tests, and any others can be added according to the client's requirements. They shall be regression tested to ensure they are robust.

Note 2

Dual tool verification shall also be used.

Appendix 27—ISO/IEC 17025 reporting requirements

ISO/IEC 17025 Section 7.8.2 requires the following:

- a title (e.g. 'Test Report', 'Calibration Certificate', or 'Report of Sampling');
- the name and address of the laboratory;
- the location of performance of the laboratory activities, including when performed at a customer facility or at sites away from the laboratory's permanent facilities, or in associated temporary or mobile facilities;
- unique identification that all its components are recognised as a portion of a complete report and a clear identification of the end;
- the name and contact information of the customer;
- identification of the method used;
- a description, unambiguous identification, and, when necessary, the condition of the item;
- the date of receipt of the test or calibration item(s), and the date of sampling, where this is critical to the validity and application of the results;
- the date(s) of performance of the laboratory activity;
- the date of issue of the report;

- reference to the sampling plan and sampling method used by the laboratory or other bodies where these are relevant to the validity or application of the results;
- a statement to the effect that the results relate only to the items tested, calibrated, or sampled;
- the results with, where appropriate, the units of measurement;
- additions to, deviations, or exclusions from the method;
- identification of the person(s) authorising the report;
- clear identification when results are from external providers.

Note 1

Hard copies of test reports and calibration certificates shall also include the page number and total number of pages.

Appendix 28—Standard forensic laboratory report

The report format below is used for a Windows forensic case processing report and is the most commonly used template. Other operating systems or devices shall have variations of this, as appropriate to the client's instructions, and the content of the forensic case. In the right hand column is a cross reference back to Appendix 27, to show how this meets the requirements defined in ISO/IEC 17025.

Report contents	ISO/IEC 17025 7.8.2.1
Front page	
Title of Report—defining the evidence examined, usually the client's reference number (assuming it exists)	(a)
Client details	(e)
FCL details	(b)
Protective Marking—front page classification of report as defined in Chapter 4, Appendix 48 and Chapter 5, Appendix 16	
Every page	
Title of Report in header—typically using the unique exhibit number(s) processed	(a)
Copyright notice in footer	
Pagination in footer (page x of y) to show the report is complete	Note 1
Version details in footer, according to FCL's document control defined in Chapter 4, Section 4.7.5	
Protective Marking—front page classification of report as defined in Chapter 4, Appendix 48 and Chapter 5, Appendix 16	
Document control page	
Review History—part of FCL's document control system, showing the history of the document and its updates	(j)
Issue Status—draught or issued	(j)
Document authors, reviewers, owners and authoriser	(o)
Table of contents	
Table of contents	
Body of report	
client instructions	
Location of forensic case processing (all defined from seizure to report production)	(b)

Report contents	ISO/IEC 17025 7.8.2.1
Receipt and identification of exhibits to be processed, including photographs as appropriate clearly showing identification of each exhibit. If part of a first response operation, the location where they were each recovered. This will also include all movements of the exhibit(s) as recorded in FCL Exhibit log, as defined in Chapter 8, Appendix 7 and the Exhibit Movement Forms, as defined in Chapter 8, Appendix 17.	(g)
Initial physical examination of exhibit(s)	(d)
Action summary	(e)
Detailed findings matched to the client's requirements. This includes tools used, version numbers of software, screenshots of results, if appropriate, and details of methods used from the Examination record, as defined in Chapter 9, Sections 9.9 and 9.10 and Appendix 9. And the identity and competence of the Forensic Analysts performing the forensic case processing. The report structure is: ● acquisition details including hash verification; ● file integrity; ● PC details; ● hard disk details; ● BIOS details; ● Registry information; ● files identified and found; ● Profiles; ● Desktop; ● Favourites; ● Links; ● Media; ● Recent; ● My Documents; ● Email addresses; ● Internet history; ● FTK view of evidence (dual tool verification) ● recovered files; ● HTML carver; ● answers to specific questions raised by the client; ● text search results.	(f) (h) (i) (m) (n) (o)
Details of any third party involved in the forensic case processing and their input to the report	(p)
Statement of results achieved against evidence	(l)
Appendices	
The appendices will vary depending on the specifics of a forensic case, but would typically include: ● malware reports from more than one tool—to counter the Trojan Defence; ● EnCase case summary; ● recovered files, where relevant ● recovered email, where relevant; ● search hits; ● additional tasks; ● instructions for using the forensic case report (held on a DVD and how to access the DVD); ● details of the Forensic Analyst's qualifications	

Chapter 7

IT infrastructure

7.1 Hardware

Within FCL, there are different types of hardware used for different processes. These include, but are not limited to:

- desktop workstations;
- mobile devices;
- networking equipment;
- desktop forensic workstations;
- mobile forensic workstations;
- specialised forensic hardware;
- servers;
- storage area network (SAN); and
- peripherals.

The choice of hardware shall be driven by a number of factors, including:

- budget;
- equipment available and maintainable in the location of operations;
- local and regional preferences;
- past experience of the Forensic Analysts selecting the hardware;
- being the optimum hardware for the tasks to be performed;
- tools that the Forensic Analysts have been trained on; and
- type of work that is expected to be undertaken.

Note

The rule of thumb for forensic case processing hardware is that one buys the fastest workstations with the most memory that you can afford and hardware for a specific purpose.

7.1.1 Accommodation

All hardware, and all assets, shall be appropriately protected against unauthorised access and loss. The first layer of security shall be the building security, as defined in Chapter 12, Section 12.3.14. In the building, there shall be areas segregated according to business role, with strict access control enforced between different operating areas. Servers shall be stored in the server room where access is further restricted to authorised members of the IT Department. The general business area shall house the relevant desktop, laptop, mobile devices, and peripherals that relate to nonforensic case processing.

The forensic case processing network shall be secured within the laboratory itself. This shall contain all components for the forensic case processing network, including all cabling, network devices, and infrastructure. The Forensic Analysts shall have their own 'personal' workspace for forensic case processing. Peripherals and specialised hardware and tools for forensic case processing shall be located in the dedicated secure area, so access shall be restricted to only the authorised Forensic Analysts. Forensic Analysts shall also require some access to the business network; however, all forensic case processing shall be carried out on the forensic network. These two networks are physically, not logically, separated.

A Blueprint for Implementing Best Practice Procedures in a Digital Forensic Laboratory. https://doi.org/10.1016/B978-0-12-819479-9.00006-X

7.1.2 Desktop workstations

Desktop workstations shall be commercially purchased, and their specification depends on the capacity plan and the specific requirements of the department where they are used. FCL decided that it would use thin client technology to support its security model. While this is known as a possible single point of failure (SPoF), by building a resilient business network, the risk of this was reduced to an acceptable level. Local departmental variations include multiple screen requirements and some specialised local peripherals.

7.1.3 Mobile devices

Mobile devices are becoming more prevalent and, in some cases, de facto, and these shall be used where the requirement is identified and the business case justifies it. There are many different types of mobile devices available, and mobile device security is defined in Chapter 12, Section 12.3.9.

FCL does not subscribe to the fashion for bring your own device (BYOD) for security and support reasons.

7.1.4 Networking equipment

Appropriate networking equipment shall be used on both networks and this shall include:

- firewalls;
- routers;
- smart cabling; and
- switches.

These are all purchased commercially and are 'best of breed' COTS networking equipment.

7.1.5 Desktop forensic workstations

There are a number of suppliers who can supply 'off the shelf' forensic workstations. This is an ever changing list as technology evolves and so no details are given here.

The Forensic Analysts build and validate their own forensic workstations, as defined in Section 7.5.5.

While technology is changing all the time, the following shall be the base set of requirements for a forensic case processing workstation:

- fastest processor(s) available—typically quad processors currently;
- maximum RAM;
- maximum disk capacity—typically now SATA drives;
- hot swappable disk drives;
- best video card available;
- sound card and speakers;
- at least two, and often four, monitors;
- support for a variety of 32 and 64 bit operating systems;
- modular PCI ports;
- USB interface support;
- modular Firewire ports; and
- DVD burner.

COTS workstations shall not be used in forensic case processing, this gives flexibility for Forensic Analysts who understand the hardware that they use and they will encounter in forensic case processing instead of just 'using a box'. In many forensic cases, the hardware makeup of a forensic workstation is reconfigured and with in-house built forensic workstations, this is usually easier to perform than with some COTS products.

At the end of the day, it is up to a forensic laboratory to decide what hardware and tools they want to use to meet the client's requirements, though these will be agreed by the client.

7.1.6 Mobile forensic workstations

Mobile forensic workstations shall have all the capabilities required for forensic case processing outside the laboratory as the desktop equivalents, where possible (i.e. on site and first response situations).

Some of the requirements for desktop workstations are defined in Section 7.1.2 are relevant to mobile forensic workstations, but some are evidently not (e.g. multiple monitors). In addition to these requirements, a portable forensic workstation shall also include, but not be limited to, the following functionality:

- ability to bypass hard disk passwords;
- compact and transportable—preferably able to fit on an aircraft as 'carry on' luggage;
- disk imaging capability;
- easy to use;
- hot swappable capability;
- multiple hard disk type connectivity;
- multiple interfaces;
- preview capability for onsite working;
- safe and robust casing;
- technical support available in case of need while on site;
- theoretical unlimited capacity—a modular disk capability (this could also include tape capacity); and
- write blocking built in or as an external device.

These shall be purchased from relevant specialised authorised suppliers.

7.1.7 Specialised forensic hardware

Specialised forensic hardware shall be used, based on specific forensic case requirements. This can range from mobile devices to specialised hardware for a specific forensic case.

There are a number of dedicated forensic hardware devices used in the laboratory, these include, but are not limited to:

- Cellebrite UFEDs;
- XRY hardware;
- dedicated malware 'sheep dip' workstation;
- dedicated standalone imaging workstations;
- degausser;
- forensic workstation on a USB stick;
- multiple disk copiers;
- standalone internet access workstation;
- various adapters; and
- various cables.

7.1.8 Servers

Business servers shall be commercially purchased and their specification depends on the capacity plan, as defined in Section 7.4.6.

The laboratory server farm shall be capable of storing huge amounts of data and processing it for the Forensic Analysts. Given that a home user can currently buy laptops with one Terabyte disk and desktops can contain multiple multiterabyte hard disks of various sizes or have multiple external multiple Terabyte hard disks attached, servers shall ensure they have the capacity to store (or archive) this amount of data according to its record retention requirements, as defined in Chapter 4, Section 4.7.6 or specific client SLAs.

Note

At the time of writing the largest hard disk drive is 20Tb, the largest SSD is 16TB and home computers can have multiple disks in them in removable disk caddies or local NAS boxes. The Drobo 8 which includes the new 'Intelligent Volume Technology' allows one to create storage volumes as large as 128TB. Storage capacity will only increase with time.

A conscious top management decision was made that FCL would not use cloud computing, apart from encrypted backups, as this risk was not accepted and in-house control of on-site assets was an acceptable risk. Use of a Cloud Service

Provider (CSP) introduced a number of risks for forensic case processing and these include, but are not limited to, depending on specifics of the forensic case being processed and jurisdictional issues:

- data location—this may breach contractual agreements or legislation without FCL being aware of it;
- having the right to audit a CSP to ensure that legislative, contractual and other requirements are met;
- how backups are managed to meet legislative, regulatory, and contractual requirements, and how these are regularly tested for recoverability in case of need;
- how the CSP can guarantee service continuity;
- how the CSP screens its employees;
- how the CSP undertakes a forensic investigation in the cloud;
- the ability to prove compliance to a third party;
- the eventual responsibility in case of an information security incident or personal data breach;
- the possibility of unequal contracting parties; and
- enforcement of access rights to tenant information (i.e. who else can access the FCLs information (and so client data).

7.1.9 Storage Area Network

FCL shall implement a local Storage Area Network (SAN) on-site that is expandable based on client and forensic case processing needs.

7.1.10 Peripherals

Centralised departmental peripherals shall be used wherever possible, although some departments shall have specialised local processing needs. Centralised peripherals used shall include the following functionality:

- printing;
- scanning;
- photocopying; and
- faxing (where still required).

Where a single device can provide the functionality above, they are known as multifunction peripherals (MFP) or all in one (AIO) devices. Access to their functionality shall be restricted by use of the employee's access control card, allowing monitoring of use, security of use, access to specified print queues and functionality, and correct departmental chargeback.

The laboratory shall use the same peripherals as the rest of the business, as defined above, but they shall be located within the secure forensic laboratory environment. Some Forensic Analysts may have specialised peripherals attached to their workstations, and these will vary on the requirements of specific forensic cases.

7.1.11 Building forensic workstations

As has been said above, Forensic Analysts shall build their own workstations from a variety of components as needed for a specific forensic case. Some of the reasons for this decision included, but were not limited to:

- the ability to build a forensic workstation to specific requirements for a forensic case, which is often not possible from COTS products;
- the ability to choose best of breed components;
- the ability to explain the operation of a forensic workstation by a Forensic Analyst, if offering expert testimony;
- the ability to upgrade a component as required, rather than need to replace the whole workstation;
- building and retaining in-house knowledge of hardware and components; and
- cost considerations.

Having made the decision to build in-house forensic workstations, a standard baseline build shall be developed for all forensic workstations, but this can be amended as required by a Forensic Analyst for processing a specific forensic case. Technology and components are constantly changing, so there is no point in defining the specific builds used as it would be soon out of date.

7.2   Software

As with hardware, the choice of software shall be driven by many of the same factors that apply to the hardware, including but not limited to:

- budget;
- certification, training. and experience that the Forensic Analysts have obtained;
- experience of the Forensic Analysts selecting the software;
- hardware in use in forensic workstations;
- local, regional or client preferences;
- software and its support available in the region; and
- type of work that is expected to be undertaken.

7.2.1   Operating systems

The operating system that is selected may be dependent on the hardware that has been selected, the software that is required for the tasks to be undertaken on a specific forensic case or the equipment that was selected.

Note

The selection of the hardware, operating system, and tools is not sequential (i.e. firstly selecting the hardware then the operating system, then the tools). It may be that the tools that are to be used will dictate the operating system and that this will dictate the type of hardware.

Various versions of the following operating systems shall be available for use:

- Android;
- BSD;
- Helix;
- iOS;
- Knoppix;
- Linux;
- OSX;
- Slackware;
- Ubuntu; and
- Windows.

Depending on the specific forensic case, other less common operating systems or previous versions of common operating systems may be required.

7.2.2   Desktop applications

On the business network, the Forensic Analysts shall have access to the following:

- Adobe products;
- email;
- malware detection;
- Microsoft office applications;
- other applications that may be necessary;
- the ERMS—but for nonforensic case processing files; and
- the internet.

Any software to be added shall be supportable by the IT Department, be legally licensed, as defined in Chapter 12, Section 12.9 and only installed by the IT Department after being submitted to, and approved by, the Change Advisory Board (CAB), as defined in Section 7.4.3.5.

7.2.3   Forensic tools

A variety of forensic tools shall be used but as this is ever changing with changes in technology, it is pointless to list them as the list would soon become out of date. Suffice it to say the major tools are in use but supported by specific tools to do dedicated forensic tasks, as required by the Forensic Analysts for forensic case processing.

7.2.4   VM ware

The concept of a Virtual Machine (VM) is that of a virtual computer running inside a physical computer. One host computer may be capable of running multiple VMs at the same time and VMs have been created to run on most of the major operating systems. The benefit of VMs is that they allow the Forensic Analysts to run forensic tools in a controlled environment (allowing states to be saved and restored at will) or to recreate a replica of a suspect's 'computer' in a virtual environment. Forensic Analysts shall use VMs where required.

7.2.5   Open source tools

There are a number of open-source forensic case processing tools available, and often forensic laboratories use them for pure economic reasons. The issue that has to be considered with open-source software is whether or not they are producing scientifically sound tools and that the results are consistent and repeatable.

FCL has made the decision not to use open-source tools for forensic case processing.

If this were to change, then FCL shall ensure that the source of the tool is carefully selected (a trusted source), the tool package shall then be verified (normally by checking the MD5 hash of the file) to ensure that it has not been tampered with and that it undergoes full validation, as defined in Section 7.5.5.

7.2.6   Updates

Operating system software, business tools and forensic case processing tools will have updates released that often add new functionality as well as fix flaws (bugs) and vulnerabilities. The process used for managing technical vulnerabilities is covered in Section 7.6.2.

Updates shall only be released into the live environment after full testing, as defined in Chapter 12, Section 12.9 and then formal approval by the CAB as part of the Change Management Process, as defined in Section 7.4.3.

7.2.7   Upgrades

A software upgrade is when a newer version of software, whether a forensic tool, an application, or operating system that is being used, is brought into use. The reasons for upgrading the software may be that it has more features, is more efficient or that the provider is no longer willing to support the existing version.

FCL shall not run unsupported software of any type.

Release of upgrades is handled in the same manner as updates, as defined in Section 7.2.6.

7.3   Infrastructure

The network infrastructure shall be split into two separate parts, the business infrastructure and the physically separated forensic case processing infrastructure.

The forensic case processing network shall be a totally closed network in that it shall have no external links permitted.

The business network shall also be a closed network but with access to the internet, but this shall be strictly controlled by using firewalls.

Wireless access to any of its resources shall not be permitted.

Security of the network connections is covered in Chapter 12, Section 12.9.

7.3.1   Equipment

The network infrastructure for both the business and the forensic case processing networks comprise the following components:

- firewalls;
- routers;

- smart cabling; and
- switches.

The networks shall be built and maintained by the IT Department, as required.

7.3.2   Security of cabling

Cabling is used to connect all IT equipment and FCL has made the conscious decision not to permit wireless connections on account of the material it processes and the possible risks of wireless networking. The FCL Policy for Securing IT Cabling is defined in Appendix 1.

7.3.2.1   Procedure for siting and protecting IT cabling

When installing new or upgraded IT cabling, all possible steps shall be taken to protect it from physical risks, to protect information from security threats, and to minimise possible risks from environmental hazards. The following steps shall be undertaken:

1. A need is identified for installation of new IT cabling replacement or repair of existing cabling.
2. The IT Manager, the Information Security Manager (ISM), and the Laboratory Manager (if appropriate) shall perform an assessment to:
   - consider the requirements of installation of the cabling;
   - consider all physical and environmental issues;
   - consider all security issues regarding the physical location of cabling, including all cable runs;
   - consider all security issues regarding the information carried on the cabling and its classification;
   - determine where the cabling is best routed, and where any associated equipment is best located; and
   - during this assessment the IT Manager, the ISM and the Laboratory Manager (if appropriate) may:
     o consult other employees as required (e.g. IT, or non-IT employees or Managers who may be using or located near to the new cabling and associated equipment;
     o consider all issues outlined in the Policy for Securing IT Cabling;
     o consider isolation of the equipment, if required and defined in Section 7.3.3; and
     o consider the impact of an adverse event or disaster in nearby premises.
3. The IT Manager, in association with the ISM and the Laboratory Manager (if appropriate), shall make a decision as to where the new cabling and any associated equipment is to be located with associated cable runs.
4. The IT Manager shall communicate with all interested parties as needed to:
   - outline the decision regarding the routing of the new cabling, and the location of any associated equipment;
   - outline the reasons for the decision; and
   - invite further comments (if required).
5. Solutions to any issues that arise at this stage shall be agreed and confirmed before the new cabling is installed.
6. The cabling shall be installed in accordance with the agreed conditions.
7. The IT Manager, the ISM, and the Laboratory Manager (if appropriate) shall perform a review to:
   - ensure that the new cabling has been routed in accordance with the agreed conditions;
   - ensure that the new cabling has been afforded the best possible protection from all identified potential security threats; and
   - address any issues which may have become evident after installation.
8. In the event that changes are required, the IT Manager shall communicate with the relevant interested parties to outline proposed changes, and the changes shall be implemented in accordance with standard Change Management Process.

Note

In the United States, much of this is dictated by the National Fire Protection Association publication #70 (NFPA 70): National Electrical Code (NEC), which is the benchmark for safe electrical design, installation, and inspection to protect people and property from electrical hazards. Other jurisdictions may have similar requirements, and these shall be followed as applicable.

7.3.3 Isolating sensitive systems

In the event that a client requires a dedicated computing environment that is physically and logically segregated from other systems holding less critical information or information belonging to other clients, the following guidelines shall be followed for a dedicated computing environment:

- apply operating system and applications hardening procedures where possible;
- logical segregation via VLANs;
- physically segregation via separate rooms, dedicated servers, or computers;
- use of physical access control mechanisms;
- use of strong authentication methods for access by only nominated individuals; and
- when a sensitive application is to run in a shared environment, employ strict resource, file or object share, or permission controls.

7.3.4 Siting and protecting IT equipment

IT equipment often has specific needs in addition to the baseline physical security implemented. All information processing equipment and information under the control of the IT Department shall be carefully sited to physically protect that information processing equipment and information from security threats, and to minimise potential risks from environmental hazards. The Policy for Siting and Protecting IT Equipment is defined in Appendix 2.

7.3.4.1 Procedure for siting and protecting IT equipment

The following procedures shall be in place to determine how new information processing equipment is to be installed in order to physically protect it from security threats, and to minimise possible risks from environmental hazards.

1. A need is identified for installation of a new item of IT equipment.
2. The IT Manager, in association with the ISM and the Laboratory Manager (if appropriate), shall perform a risk assessment to:
   - consider all usage requirements;
   - consider all security issues regarding the equipment's usage and location;
   - determine where the equipment is best located;
   - during this assessment the IT Manager, in association with the ISM and the Laboratory Manager (if appropriate) shall:
     - o consult with other employees as required (e.g. members of the IT Department, other business users and/or Managers who may be using or sited near to the new equipment); and
     - o consider all issues outlined in the Policy for Siting and Protecting IT Equipment.
   - additional items which shall warrant consideration for particular items of equipment that may require special protection are:
     - o isolation of the equipment; and;
     - o consider the impact of an adverse event or disaster in nearby premises.
3. The IT Manager, in association with the ISM and the Laboratory Manager (if appropriate), shall make a decision as to where the new equipment is to be sited to afford it the best protection possible.
4. The IT Manager shall e-mail all interested parties as needed to:
   - outline the decision regarding the siting of the new equipment;
   - outline the reasons for the decision/proposed location; and
   - invite further comments (if required).
5. Any issues that arise at this stage shall be agreed and confirmed before the new equipment is installed.
6. The new equipment shall be installed in accordance with the agreed conditions after being approved by the CAB, as part of Change Management Process.
7. The IT Manager shall perform a review to:
   - ensure that the new equipment has been sited in accordance with the agreed conditions;
   - ensure that the new equipment cabling has been afforded the best possible protection from all potential security threats; and
   - address any issues which may have become evident after installation.

7.3.5 Securing supporting utilities

The IT Manager shall control the security of information processing equipment and information in terms of supporting utilities in order to minimise loss and damage to the business.

Special controls shall be implemented to safeguard supporting utilities for information processing equipment and information processing facilities. These shall include but not be limited to:

- a generator or other alternate power supplies is available and is maintained and regularly tested;
- all of the utilities shall be monitored to determine if thresholds are breached at which point alerts shall be raised. This shall include:
  - water detection;
  - power failure or variation;
  - UPS battery life and stability;
  - air conditioning;
  - humidity;
  - heat; and
  - smoke.
- all servers shall be dual power sourced from different sources;
- an UPS shall be available on all critical servers, telephone switches and other critical infrastructure, and shall be regularly tested according to the manufacturer's recommendations;
- basic safeguards shall be used, i.e. health and safety best practice;
- CAT 5 or Cat 6 cabling and mains electrical cabling shall be separated and not use the same ducting;
- emergency power off switches shall be available near the exit doors of the Server Room;
- fire detection and fire quenching shall be appropriate and in place, as defined in Chapter 2, Section 2.2;
- air conditioning shall have sufficient redundancy to allow for a single failure and have enough power to keep the area at the appropriate temperature; and
- the water supply shall be stable and adequate for fire suppression purposes.

All of the above shall be monitored using a centralised building management system and alerts raised and sent to the appropriate Managers and third parties, as appropriate. The building Facilities Manager shall always be alerted for all threshold breaches.

Note

All other utilities in the building are normally under the control of the utility companies, and FCL will be dependent on these and have little or no control over their supply.

7.4 Process management

A number of these processes meet the requirements of ISO 20000-1, Information technology—Service management—Part 1: Service management system, requirements and where they do, they are mapped to ISO 20000-1 in Appendix 3.

Note

FCL has not implemented all of ISO 20000-1 and does not intend to, so there will be a number of controls in the mapping in Appendix 3 that have no corresponding section in this chapter or elsewhere in the book.

7.4.1 Information security incident management

The primary goal of information security incident management is to restore normal service operations as quickly as possible and to minimise the adverse impact on business operations, thus ensuring that the optimum levels of service quality and availability are maintained for all clients.

An information security incident is defined in this book as:

- 'any event which is not part of the standard operation of a service and which causes, or may cause, an interruption to, or a reduction in, the quality of that service'.

Note

Information security incidents may be IT related or a business (non-IT) incident (e.g. sanctions being applied, a pandemic, inclement weather, etc.).

Examples of an information security incident include but are not limited to:

- a business service is not available;
- an application bug is preventing work being carried out;
- a system is down;
- a printer is not printing;
- a service request;
- a request for a change (all changes at the IT Department shall be performed in accordance with the Change Management Process);
- any disruption to service provision to internal clients; or
- any disruption to service provision to external clients.

Information security incidents are related to problems. In terms of Information Security Incident Management, however, a 'problem' is an unknown underlying cause of one or more incidents (not the difficulty that a client is experiencing).

7.4.1.1   Role of the Service Desk

The Service Desk is central to the provision of an effective information security incident management service, with the following functionality:

- the Service Desk shall be operational 24/7 (either by email or phone);
- the Service Desk shall be the first point of contact for all client-related problems and queries regarding the services;
- calls registered by the Service Desk shall be categorised as:
  - a client request for a service or information;
  - a client reporting a difficulty with IT hardware, software, or a service; or
  - an information security incident or weakness.
- all requests and incidents to the Service Desk shall be registered in the Service Desk system;
- the Service Desk provides first-line support and shall attempt to provide solutions for all information security incidents reported;
- incidents shall be escalated from the Service Desk to 2nd line and 3rd line IT Department Support as necessary (e.g. to PC Support, Technical Support, Management System Manager(s), etc.);
- critical information security incidents that require additional support because of their critical nature shall follow the normal information security incident management process but with additional investigation, communication, and reporting, as defined in Section 7.4.1.5; and
- information security incidents shall only be closed when a resolution is provided, and to the satisfaction of the client.

7.4.1.2   Classification of information security incidents and resolution times

Normal business service and operations or a workaround solution shall be provided to all information security incidents and service requests according to their classification. Information security incident classifications, and target resolution times for each incident classification, shall be defined for clients in their specific SLAs for individual services where required.

7.4.1.3   Information security incident management responsibilities

Within the incident management process, there shall be a number of defined roles, these include, but are not limited to:

- Service Desk;
- Service Desk Manager (as defined in Appendix 4);
- Management System Manager(s);
- IT Department;
- other specialist employees;
- employees; and
- clients.

7.4.1.3.1 Information Security Incident Manager

The Information Security Incident Manager shall be the ISM. Responsibilities shall include:

- leading the information security incident response team (IRT);
- maintaining information security incident response procedures including scenario-based playbooks for information security incident response;
- ensuing that the IRT members are all trained and competent;
- ensuring that regular exercising of the information security response is undertaken;
- providing management information to relevant committees on information security incident issues; and
- reviewing, developing, and maintaining the information security incident management process.

The Information Security Incident Managers job description is defined in Appendix 5.

7.4.1.3.2 Service Desk

The Service Desk is the body that shall act as a first point of contact for all clients that use the products and services that they provide, and they shall provide first-line IT Department support to resolve all information security incidents and service requests. The responsibilities of the Service Desk shall include, but not be limited to:

- receiving calls, categorising information security incidents and service requests and raising a security incident;
- first-line client liaison;
- recording and tracking all information security incidents and service requests;
- making an initial assessment of an information security incident or service request, and attempting to resolve it or referring it to 2nd or 3rd line support;
- monitoring information security incidents and service requests and escalating them when necessary;
- confirming an information security incident or service request resolution, and confirming client satisfaction with a resolution (this task is normally the responsibility of the Service Desk Manager but may be delegated to other Service Desk employees, as necessary); and
- closing information security incidents and service requests that have been satisfactorily resolved (as required by the Service Desk Manager).

7.4.1.3.3 Service Desk Manager

The Service Desk Manager has managerial responsibility for the Service Desk and its employees. The responsibilities of this role with respect to information security incident management shall include, but not be limited to:

- managing the work of the Service Desk (information security incident and service request recording, classification and first-line IT Department response);
- acting as a contact point between the IT Department, the relevant business streams and clients for management level activity relating to information security incidents and service requests;
- monitoring information security incidents and their appropriate escalation to other specialist employees, as appropriate;
- liaising with relevant third parties;
- confirming 100% of resolved information security incidents are completed to the customer's satisfaction (this task may be designated to other Service Desk employees as necessary);
- closing information security incidents and service requests that have been confirmed as satisfactorily resolved (this task may be designated to other Service Desk employees);
- managing critical information security incidents through to resolution in association with other IT management; and
- generating statistics and reports on information security incident management for input to clients and the Management Review, as defined in Chapter 4, Section 4.9.3.

Note

The Service Desk Manager shall assist the Information Security Incident Manager for all incidents and is assigned as the Deputy Information Security Incident Manager.

The Service Desk Manager's and Information Security Incident Manager's job description is defined in Appendices 4 and 5 respectively.

7.4.1.3.4 Management System Manager(s)

The relevant **Management System Manager** has managerial responsibility for managing the resolution of information security incidents and disruptions to their management systems or disruptions to the services that they provide, and for reviewing the information security incidents or disruptions, identifying trends and recommending continuous improvement to 'their' Management Systems. The responsibilities of this role shall include, but not be limited to:

- categorising, with the Service Desk, information security incidents and disruptions;
- liaising with management and specialist employees on incidents and disruptions;
- determining initial investigations;
- assigning specialist employees for information security incident or disruption resolution;
- communicating with employees during information security incident resolution;
- communicating with clients during information security incident resolution;
- monitoring investigation and resolution activities;
- approving information security incident resolution;
- invoking a BCP response, if appropriate;
- reviewing information security incidents and disruptions to identify trends; and
- creating and monitoring CAPAs to resolution, as appropriate.

7.4.1.3.5 IT Department

As well as managing day-to-day IT operations, the IT Department mainly provide 2nd or 3rd line response to resolve information security incidents and service requests, for example, PC support or technical support. Responsibilities of the IT Department shall include, but not be limited to:

- documenting resolutions and workarounds for resolved information security incidents and service requests in the Service Desk system;
- escalating information security incidents to third-party organisations where required, additional reporting to relevant business units may be required;
- information security incident investigation and diagnosis (including resolution where possible); and
- providing 2nd and 3rd line response for information security incidents and service requests that cannot be resolved on receipt or initial investigation by the Service Desk.

7.4.1.3.6 Other specialist employees

Other specialist employees shall be responsible for the following:

- conducting response and recovery actions as directed by the Business Continuity Manager and management, according to the BCP response procedures, if applicable;
- determining resolution actions within their competence;
- implementing, or assisting the implementation of resolution activities; and
- investigating information security incidents and disruptions to determine a diagnosis, as directed.

7.4.1.3.7 Employees

Employees shall be responsible for the following:

- identifying information security incidents and weaknesses in the Management Systems;
- reporting information security incidents and weaknesses to the Service Desk and/or the relevant Management System Manager;
- reporting service disruptions (either internally or from clients) to the Service Desk and/or the relevant Management System Manager; and
- responding to information security incidents or disruptions as directed by the relevant Management System Manager or the Information Security Incident Manager.

7.4.1.3.8 Clients

Clients are the internal or external users of products and services. Their responsibilities shall include:

- agreeing SLAs and TRTs for their services;
- reporting information security incidents in a timely manner to the Service Desk;

- requesting services via the Service Desk;
- assisting the Service Desk or other employees in closing their information security incidents; and
- confirming closure of their incidents.

7.4.1.4 *Information security incident management procedures*

7.4.1.4.1 Receiving and categorising an information security incident

A client or employee contacts the Service Desk to report an information security incident, or to place a service request. Contact with the Service Desk may be made via:

- telephone call;
- fax;
- e-mail;
- self-service request into the Service Desk system; or
- a visit in person.

The Service Desk shall receive and process the information security incident or service request as follows (Fig. 7.1):

1. The Service Desk shall use the Service Desk system to locate and confirm the client's or employee's details, as recorded in the system. These details shall include:
   - caller's name;
   - job role;
   - client name;
   - client location;
   - client cost centre; and
   - client contact details.

Note

The caller may be an internal or external client. For ease both have been referred to as 'clients'.

---

2. The Service Desk shall create a Service Desk Request (SDR) in the Service Desk system (the client or employee details are automatically transferred into the new SDR).
3. The information security incident or service request details are recorded, and the SDR is automatically assigned a status of 'Open'.

   Details of information security incident status levels are defined in Appendix 6.
4. The Service Desk shall agree a Priority level for the SDR with the client based on the following:
   - priority—the effect that the information security incident or the service request has on the businesses capability to function normally; and
   - impact—the number of clients affected by the information security incident/service request.

Note

Priority levels and Impact are defined in the individual client's SLA or TRT.

Details of information security incident priority levels are defined in Appendix 7.

If the Priority of the incident is 1, the Service Desk shall contact the ISM immediately and a decision shall be made on the immediate measures to begin response actions in accordance with the procedure for Managing Critical Information Security Incidents, as defined in Section 7.4.1.5.

5. The Service Desk shall complete and save the details of the information security incident or service request. An SDR number shall be automatically generated and the status of the SDR shall be changed to 'Current' in the Service Desk system.

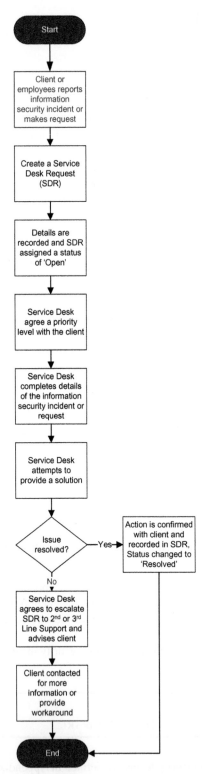

FIG. 7.1 Receiving and categorising an information security incident.

6. The Service Desk shall attempt to provide a solution to the request or the information security incident, if possible (they may already know a resolution, or may search the Service Desk system to try and find a matching information security incident and a solution).

7. If the Service Desk resolve the incident:
   - all action(s) taken shall be recorded in the SDR;
   - the action shall be confirmed with the client;
   - the SDR status shall be changed to 'Resolved';
   - the incident shall be closed as described in Section 7.4.1.4.4.

8. If the Service Desk cannot resolve the information security incident, or if the information security incident is a service request that needs to be performed by some other employee, the Service Desk shall assign the incident to 2nd or 3rd line Support (this may be a technical expert, a Forensic Analyst or a Management System Manager).

Note

2nd Line Support is the IT Department, 3rd Line Support may be the IT Department or external resources.

---

9. To do this the Service Desk shall:
   - informs the client that the information security incident or service request shall be assigned to 2nd or 3rd line Support for resolution;
   - informs the client that 2nd or 3rd line IT Department will contact them for either information, or to agree a resolution or workaround;
   - assign the SDR to 2nd or 3rd line Support, as appropriate;
   - the incident is now progressed as described Section 7.4.1.4.2.

Note

The Service Desk may also telephone the 2nd or 3rd line Support to inform them that a new information security incident has been assigned to them.

7.4.1.4.2 Investigating an information security incident

If an information security incident or service request that is received and logged cannot be resolved at the Service Desk, it shall be assigned to 2nd or 3rd line Support. An incident investigation shall then be performed as follows (Fig. 7.2):

1. The 2nd or 3rd line Support shall open the SDR in the relevant queue in the Service Desk system (new information security incidents which have been assigned to them may also be confirmed verbally by the Service Desk).

2. The 2nd or 3rd line Support shall check the SDR details displayed for the information security incident and determines whether further information is required from the client.

3. If additional information is required, the assigned 2nd or 3rd line Support shall contact the client and obtain the required information. All actions performed by the 2nd or 3rd line Support shall be recorded in the SDR log in the Service Desk system.

4. If the information security incident has been assigned to the wrong person, the 2nd or 3rd line Support shall reassign it to the appropriate person using the Service Desk system.

5. The 2nd or 3rd line IT Support shall investigate the information security incident to identify all possible means of resolving it, both procedural and technical, and this shall include:
   - determining possible solutions or workarounds;
   - examining courses of actions that require further investigation; and
   - testing possible solutions or workarounds before implementing the most suitable one.

6. If a solution cannot be obtained 2nd line Support they shall reassign the incident to 3rd line Support, as necessary.

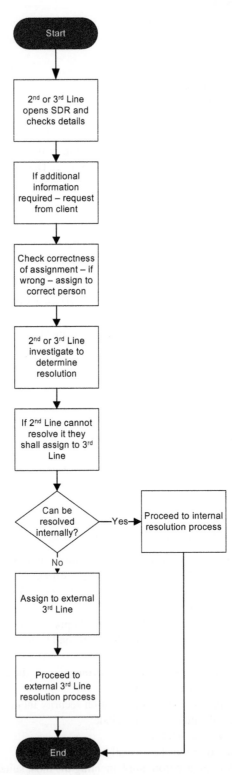

FIG. 7.2 Investigating an information security incident.

7. Where a resolution is not possible internally, Support shall assign the information security incident to the appropriate third party for resolution as follows:
   - contact the Service Desk Manager and brief them on the progress on the information security incident;
   - contact the required third party for resolution using the appropriate method;
   - monitor the third party, and co-ordinate any resolution activity; and
   - record all activity in the SDR log.
8. The 3rd party should deliver a fix or a workaround to the information security incident within an agreed timescale. If a fix or a workaround is not delivered within the agreed timescale, the information security incident is escalated to the Service Desk Manager.

Note

All evidence collected during investigation work shall be handled in accordance with the procedures for evidence collection, as defined in Section 7.4.1.7, in case of later need, to ensure that the evidence is not contaminated.

7.4.1.4.3   Resolving an information security incident

1. When an information security incident or service request has been investigated and a solution or workaround has been discovered, the resolution shall be applied as follows:
   - 2nd or 3rd line Support shall perform the required resolution, and test that the resolution works correctly; and
   - 2nd or 3rd line Support shall contact the client to discuss the resolution, and to confirm that the resolution is satisfactory.
2. In the event that a solution to an information security incident cannot be provided, Support shall discuss possible courses of action with the Incident Manager and other Managers as required. These shall include:
   - reassigning the information security incident to a different employee for further investigation and attempted resolution;
   - suspending the information security incident, if it is certain that a solution cannot currently be provided, or is outside the scope of 2nd or 3rd line Support internally, examples include:
     - o delaying investigation of an information security incident with the agreement of the client (e.g. to resume investigation in 24 h, 7 days, etc.)—in which case the Service Desk auto wake-up function shall be used to automatically notify Service Desk and/or 2nd or 3rd Line Support when investigation is to be resumed;
     - o known errors such as a bug fix for application software; or
     - o seeking the involvement of a third-party supplier.
   - closing the information security incident with the agreement of the client;
   - the 2nd or 3rd line Support shall enter full and comprehensive information about the solution to the information security incident into the Service Desk system; and
   - the Service Desk shall change the status of the information security incident to 'Resolved'.
3. This reassigns the SDR to the call closure queue in the Service Desk system for closure by the Service Desk Manager.

7.4.1.4.4   Closing an information security incident

1. Information security incidents and service requests shall be closed by the Service Desk Manager in the following circumstances only:
   - a solution or workaround has been provided;
   - the client agrees that a solution is not required—that is the information security incident is not important;
   - all required information about an information security incident has been entered into the Service Desk system; and
   - all required information for changed configuration items relating to an information security incident has been entered into the Configuration Management Database (CMDB), as defined in Section 7.7.4.5.
2. If the resolution to an information security incident involves a change to the IT infrastructure, a request or incident shall not be closed until the change has been formally approved and signed-off through the Change Management Process.

3. It is Service Desk policy to perform a quality control check on 25% of all SDRs which are recorded in the Service Desk system. The client feedback form for the Service Desk is defined in Appendix 8. Normally this check is performed by the Service Desk Manager (but may be delegated to other Service Desk staff) to:
   - confirm that an information security incident has been resolved;
   - confirm that a client is satisfied with the resolution; and
   - allow the SDR to be closed.
     Warning: Information security incidents shall only be closed by the Service Desk Manager after confirmation by the client. Service Desk employees shall not be able to close information security incidents.
4. The Service Desk accesses the SDR in the Service Desk system call closure queue and shall:
   - review the progress of the information security incident or service request since the SDR was first logged;
   - confirm that Support has fully documented the information security incident or request solution; and
   - confirm that Support has resolved all actions generated during the resolution process.
5. For a random sample of 25% of SDRs with a status of 'Resolved', the Service Desk Manager (or some other designated person) shall contact the client to:
   - confirm that a solution or a workaround has been implemented;
   - confirm that the information security incident or the request is successfully resolved;
   - confirm that the client is satisfied with the resolution or workaround; and
   - confirm that the SDR can be closed in the Service Desk system.
6. If the client is not satisfied with the solution or workaround that has been provided, the Service Desk shall:
   - obtain further details from the client about the continuing issues or problem;
   - inform that client that the information security incident will be reassigned for further investigation;
   - reassign the incident to 2nd or 3rd line Support as necessary (the SDR status is changed to 'Re-opened');
   - update the SDR details in the Service Desk system.
7. If the resolution of the information security incident is not satisfactory and 3rd party supplier has been used, the Service Desk Manager shall contact the 3rd party and request a different solution or workaround. As a minimum requirement, a new fix or workaround shall be received and successfully implemented;
8. The Service Desk Manager shall close the incident or service request in the Service Desk system.

7.4.1.5 Critical information security incident management

A business-critical information security incident is defined as one that causes serious disruption to the delivery of products and/or services, either for internal or external clients. These critical information security incidents are those information security incidents which need greater management input that for normal information security incidents, to ensure that a resolution is provided as soon as possible (Fig. 7.3).

To manage a critical information security incident:

1. The Service Desk shall log a critical information security incident and contacts the Information Security Incident Manager immediately.

Note

A critical information security incident may also be raised during the analysis, investigation, or resolution phase of a normal information security incident. In this case the information security incident is already logged in the Service Desk system, and the information security incident category and priority shall be updated.

---

2. The Information Security Incident Manager shall escalate the critical information security incident to the top management to alert relevant key client management to the critical information security incident so they can initiate the response.
3. Top management may involve other the employees, as appropriate, including the Management System Manager(s).
4. The Information Security Incident Manager and IT Department initiate and manage the response to the critical information security incident through to successful resolution. All actions performed during the critical information security incident investigation and resolution shall be recorded in the Service Desk system.
5. The Information Security Incident Manager shall initiate immediate actions to start the resolution process. These actions shall vary depending upon the critical information security incident.

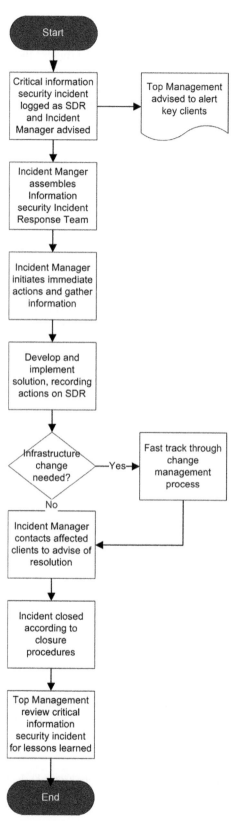

FIG. 7.3 Critical information security incident management.

6. During the resolution process the Incident Manager shall:
   - determine whether to initiate standby solutions;
   - ensure that affected business clients are kept informed of progress throughout the critical information security incident resolution process on a regular basis (e.g. telephone, e-mail, discussion etc.) via the established communications process;
   - obtain business stream agreement, as needed, to any actions affecting service levels;
   - document all actions in the Service Desk system;
   - keep the Service Desk system updated with details of significant events in the resolution process as they occur; and
   - ensure that all interested parties informed of progress as required.
7. The Information Security Incident Manager and IT Department shall gather information to assist in resolving the critical information security incident and:
   - confirm the true cause by testing, fixing, and checking results—this may require third-party assistance;
   - identify possible causes of the critical information security incident—in many cases this may be obvious and this step in the process may be minimal, but in all cases, it is essential that the root cause of the critical information security incident shall be identified before any actions are taken. Standard root causes are defined in Chapter 4, Appendix 53. These are not the only root causes possible and others shall be defined as needed; and
   - plan employee involvement—who does what, and when, where and how.
8. The IT Department develop a solution to the critical information security incident, and then implement it.
9. If the resolution to the critical information security incident involves a change to the IT infrastructure, the change can be fast-tracked through the Change Management Process for immediate resolution.
10. The Information Security Incident Manager shall contact the Account Managers of the business clients who are affected to agree that the critical information security incident has been resolved, and the agreed level of service has been restored.
11. The Information Security Incident Manager shall agree to closure of the critical information security incident with the Service desk Manager in accordance with the closure procedure, as defined in Section 7.4.1.4.4.
12. Top management shall review the critical information security incident with a view to future provision and improvement of services.

Note

Any infrastructure or service improvement changes which arise from the review shall implemented in accordance with the relevant the processes, including the Change Management Process.

7.4.1.6 *Reviewing information security incidents*

As part of the information security incident management improvement process, regular reviews of information security incidents, weaknesses and disruptions shall be carried out to:

- evaluate and continually improve the information security incident management responses and processes;
- improve the systems, products and services in order to minimise disruption to the business;
- learn and identify trends; and
- review business critical information security incidents.

Management System Managers shall perform monitoring and trend analysis as part of their ongoing role to review causes and outcomes of all information security incidents, especially those that cause service disruptions.

Note

Business critical information security incidents classed as 'Priority 1' (or 'Critical') shall always be reviewed by the top management immediately following their successful resolution.

The information security incident management review process shall be as follows:

1. Information security incidents shall always be reviewed at the next Management Review meeting unless a critical information security incident requires a specific meeting to discuss it. The relevant Management System Manager shall also

be also present at the meeting and optionally the employees involved in specific information security incident investigation or resolution activities (as required).

2. Information security incidents shall be discussed at the meeting with a view to identifying improvements to the infrastructure, management systems, product, and service offerings to clients and the information security incident management system itself. Inputs to the discussion shall include, but not be limited to:

   - future projects;
   - outcomes from business continuity response and recovery;
   - outcomes from information security incident investigation and resolution (including outcomes from a business critical information security incident);
   - outcomes from previous information security incident management reviews and improvement activities;
   - planned upgrades or changes to the information systems, processes or services; and
   - reports from the employees relating to information security incidents, weaknesses, or disruptions reported to the Service Desk; and
   - trend analysis by the relevant Management System Manager(s).

3. The Management System Manager shall provide recommendations on possible actions for agreement by the top management. This may include:

   - changes and improvements to the systems and infrastructure;
   - changes and improvements to the operating practises; or
   - changes to BCPs.

Note

Outcomes and agreed actions shall be documented in the meeting minutes and raised as CAPAs.

---

4. The relevant Management System Manager shall oversee the agreed actions for:

   - changes to Information Security Incident Management Plans and Business Continuity Plans to be developed and/or updated in accordance with the procedures for developing and implementing a BCM response, as defined in Chapter 13;
   - changes to the infrastructure shall be conducted in accordance with the Change Management Process; and
   - changes to working practises which impact on documented procedures shall be developed and updated in accordance with the procedures for document control, as defined in Chapter 4, Section 4.7.5.

7.4.1.7   Evidence collection

Where evidence needs to be collected, either for internal disciplinary proceedings or for a forensic case, the Forensic Incident Response procedures shall be followed, as defined in Chapter 8, Section 8.3.

7.4.2   Problem management

Problem management is the process whereby the underlying causes of information security incidents shall be identified and remediated.

The primary goals of problem management shall be to:

- determine the root cause of information security incidents;
- identify information security incident trends;
- minimise the effect on the business of incidents and problems caused by errors in the infrastructure, the products, or services supplied by the to its clients;
- prevent the recurrence of information security incidents related to problems; and
- proactively prevent the occurrence of information security incidents and problems, and to reduce their severity.

A problem is the unknown underlying cause of one or more information security incidents (or one or more *potential* information security incidents). Examples of problems shall include:

- a problem interpreting evidence in a forensic case due to software issues or incompatibilities between the image and the available tools;
- a problem with imaging a forensic case;

- a server capacity issue that causes degraded performance of a service;
- a software bug; or
- an intermittent hardware fault.

A 'known error' is a problem for which a root cause has been diagnosed, and for which a solution or workaround (temporary or permanent) can be provided.

The Service Desk shall act as the repository for all information concerning problems and known errors including the tool for recording, monitoring, and closing of all problems and known errors. The Service Desk system shall record the following information:

- all problems and known errors;
- classification of problems;
- details of known error solutions, fixes, and workarounds; and
- results of problem investigation, diagnosis, and resolution.

The Service Desk is critical to the provision of an effective problem management process and ensure that:

- all problems identified shall be registered by the Service Desk and classified appropriately;
- problems shall be escalated by the Service Desk for investigation, diagnosis, and resolution;
- problems shall only be closed in the Service Desk after a resolution has been implemented and all associated information security incidents are closed; and
- the Service Desk shall be the first point of contact for all problems.

7.4.2.1 Responsibilities

7.4.2.1.1 Problem Manager

The Problem Manager is the member of the IT Department who shall have managerial responsibility for the problem management process. Responsibilities shall include, but not be limited to:

- allocating resources for problem support efforts;
- ensuring the effectiveness of the problem management process and for successful diagnosis of problems, and resolution of known errors;
- generating statistics and reports on problem management for review;
- managing problem support, or third parties acting on their behalf;
- monitoring all problem and known error activity, and their appropriate escalation to other employees; and
- reviewing, developing, and maintaining the problem management process.

The Problem Manager's job description is defined in Appendix 9.

7.4.2.1.2 Service Desk

The Service Desk is the body that acts as a first point of contact for all clients that use the products and services. The responsibilities of the Service Desk with regard to problem management shall include, but not be limited to:

- recording and classifying problems;
- 1st line client liaison;
- monitoring and tracking all problems through the Service Desk system;
- resolving problems, if possible; and
- escalating problems as necessary.

7.4.2.1.3 IT Department

The IT Department shall provide support for investigation, diagnosis, and resolution of problems and known errors. Responsibilities of IT Department with respect to problem management shall include, but not be limited to:

- identifying problems (by analysing incident information, for example);
- investigating problems, according to impact, through to resolution or error identification;
- implementing solutions to known errors (where possible);
- escalating problems or known errors to external 3rd line Support for diagnosis and/or resolution as required; and

- documenting resolutions and workarounds for known problems and known errors in the Service Desk system (and advising other the employees of such).

The procedure to manage a problem shall involve these key stages:

- recording and classifying a problem;
- investigating and diagnosing a problem; and
- resolving a problem.

Note 1

The process for processing problems through the Service Desk is very similar to the process for recording, monitoring, and progressing information security incidents.

Note 2

On account of this, no flowchart is provided.

7.4.2.2 Recording and classifying a problem

1. A problem is identified, typically by:
   - an analysis of information security incidents received at the Service Desk;
   - routine monitoring of systems across the network;
   - information provided by any relevant third party; and
   - activity by management or IT Department.
2. The problem shall be recorded in the Service Desk system in accordance with the procedure for recording an information security incident, as defined in Section 7.4.1.4.1. During this stage, the Service Desk shall:
   - receive details about a problem;
   - enter the details;
   - agree a Priority level with the client; and
   - relate the problem to other information security incidents and/or problems recorded in the Service Desk system.
3. If the problem is a known error, the Service Desk shall inform the client that a permanent or temporary solution is available. Possible courses of action are:
   - if a solution or workaround is easily performed for the client, the Service Desk shall provide the details, and then change the status of the problem in the Service Desk system to 'Resolved'. This reassigns the problem report to the call closure queue in the Service Desk system for closure by the Service Desk Manager;
   - if a solution needs to be implemented by the IT Department, the Service Desk shall assign the problem to IT Department and the problem shall be progressed to resolution; or
   - if a solution needs to be implemented via change management, the Service Desk shall assign the resolution to the Problem Manager for progression through the Change Management Process.
4. If the problem is not a known error, the Service Desk shall assign the problem to IT Department for investigation and diagnosis. To do this the Service Desk shall:
   - inform the client that the problem request is to be assigned to another employee for further investigation; and
   - assign the problem to the relevant IT Department employee.
5. The problem shall be progressed by the relevant IT Department employee(s).

7.4.2.3 Investigating and diagnosing a problem

If a problem is logged by the Service Desk that is not a known error, it shall be assigned to IT Department and investigation and diagnosis shall then performed as follows:

1. IT Department shall investigate the problem to identify all possible causes, this shall include:
   - determining possible causes;
   - examining courses of action; and
   - testing solutions.

2. If a solution cannot be obtained, the IT Department may reassign the problem to other IT Department employees, or third parties acting on their behalf, as necessary for diagnosis and development of a solution as follows:
   - contact the Problem Manager and brief them on the progress;
   - contact the appropriate third party for problem diagnosis using the appropriate method;
   - monitor the third party, and co-ordinate any solution activity; and
   - record all activity in the Service Desk system.
3. The third party shall deliver a fix or a workaround to the problem within an agreed timescale. If a fix or a workaround is not delivered within the agreed timescale, the issue shall be escalated to the Problem Manager.
4. IT Department implement a fix or a workaround (permanent or temporary), this includes:
   - determining possible solutions or workarounds; or
   - testing solutions/workarounds to establish the most suitable.
5. All activity shall be recorded in the SDR, and the Problem Manager shall be kept informed of progress.
6. In the event that a fix or workaround cannot be provided, the IT Department shall discuss possible courses of action with the Problem Manager (and other Managers as required). Options may include:
   - further investigation;
   - suspending the problem; or
   - seeking the involvement of a different third-party supplier.
7. A problem for which a fix or workaround is successfully developed (or made available by a third party) shall be reclassified as a 'known error', and full details of the error and resolution shall be recorded in the Service Desk system.

7.4.2.4   Resolving a problem

1. When a problem has been diagnosed and a solution or workaround has been discovered, a resolution shall be applied as follows:
   - where a solution or fix can be implemented without the need for a formal change:
     o IT Department performs the required resolution, and tests that the resolution works correctly;
     o IT Department contacts the client to discuss the resolution, and to confirm that the resolution is satisfactory; and
     o IT Department records the activity in the SDR so that the problem and any associated incidents can be closed.
2. Where a solution to a known error can only be implemented via change management, the resolution shall be progressed in accordance with the Change Management Process. The Problem Manager shall be responsible for progressing all known errors through the Change Management Process (though this task may be delegated as necessary).

7.4.2.5   Closing a problem

When a problem has been resolved it can be closed. The process shall be that the Service Desk Manager closes all related information security incidents, in accordance with the information security incident closure procedure, as defined in Section 7.4.1.4.4.

7.4.2.6   Reviewing problems

As part of the problem management improvement process, the Problem Manager shall regularly review problems to:

- determine actions for improvement in problem management;
- determine if problem management activities are performing as expected; and
- review outstanding or resolved problems and known errors.
  1. The Problem Manager shall identify areas of the problem management system that require review based upon:
     o occurrences of problems, known errors, and information security incidents;
     o effectiveness of problem resolution;
     o planned changes to the organisation, technology, and business processes; and
     o inputs from clients and employees.
  2. The Problem Manager shall plan the review and:
     o define the objectives and scope of the review;
     o identify the inputs to the review, which shall include, but not be limited to, reports and statistics from the Service Desk system on information security incidents, problems and known errors; and
     o identify a suitable date and time for the review.
  3. The Problem Manager shall prepare a brief outline review plan describing the above details. The plan shall be issued to all relevant employees, and relevant external 3rd Line Support, involved in the review (they may comment on the plan and suitable amendments shall be made, if appropriate).

4. The Problem Manager, and any other relevant interested parties, shall review the problem management system and discuss:
   o availability of information to Incident Management;
   o how problem management activities are performing (in particular whether any activities are not performing as expected);
   o outstanding problems and known errors;
   o the effectiveness of problem resolutions; and
   o the effectiveness of the problem management process.
5. Improvements may be identified, and where possible agreed. These may include possible changes for inclusion in the Service Improvement Plan (SIP). The standard contents of a SIP are defined in Appendix 10.
6. The Problem Manager shall email all relevant interested parties, with the results of the review and any agreed follow-up actions. Follow-up actions shall then be implemented, as appropriate, via the CAPA process.

7.4.3 Change management

Controlling changes to the IT infrastructure is crucial for the provision of products and services to all clients. The purpose of change management is to ensure that:

- change processes are properly planned and managed;
- communication channels are in place to inform the management and all interested parties of changes, the effect on the provision of products and services, and the progress of change implementation (where appropriate);
- resources to implement a change are identified and made available;
- risks associated with a change are identified and minimised;
- standard methods and procedures allow efficient and prompt handling of all changes to the IT Infrastructure (or services for clients dependent on the IT Infrastructure);
- the impact of any changes made on the whole IT infrastructure is considered; and
- the impact on the business of implementing a change is minimised.

7.4.3.1 General

Change management enables operational systems (hardware, software, documented procedures, and the products and services that they deliver) to be modified in a planned, controlled, and methodical manner. The purpose of change management is not to block or hinder changes, but to ensure the effective communications between all relevant interested parties and minimise the risk of failure while increasing the chances of successful implementation for improved products and services.

Change management shall be applied to the provision of new elements, and changes to existing elements within the processes, infrastructure, systems, computers, and applications which affect the products and services provided to internal and external clients.

7.4.3.2 Types of change

Changes are typically to the IT infrastructure but can include other parts of operational processes such as documentation, products, or services provided to internal and external clients. Three types of change are defined:

- Standard—a change that is predefined, and proved as reliable, which is not processed through the normal Change Management Process but which shall be logged and processed by the relevant department, typically the IT Department. Standard changes have no downtime. This shall include some documentation changes;
- Normal—a change that is processed through the normal Change Management Process. This shall include critical documentation changes;
- Emergency—a change that is implemented, and then processed retrospectively through the Change Management Process.

The categories of change and the service levels that apply are defined in Appendix 11.

7.4.3.3 Change status

During the Change Management Process, a change shall be assigned a status which shall be updated at each stage of the lifecycle of the change. The timeline for submitting a change shall be as follows:

- Day −1—the final time by which a change can be submitted for review at the weekly CAB meeting;
- day 0—the CAB meeting to approve a change; and
- day 5—implementation of change.

7.4.3.4 Change management responsibilities

Note

If a forensic laboratory is a small organisation, some of the roles within the Change Management Process may be undertaken by one person, however the process of maintaining segregation of duties shall be strictly enforced so that no one personal can control the whole Change Management Process, wherever possible.

Within the Change Management Process, there are a number of defined roles, these are:

7.4.3.4.1 Change Manager

The Change Manager shall control the Change Management Process. The Deputy Change Manager is the person who shall act as the Change Manager in the event of their absence.

Responsibilities of the Change Manager shall include, but not be limited to:

- assessing and approving business critical, noncomplex, or minimal impact requests for change according to risk exposure;
- establishing and maintaining a schedule of planned and proposed requests for change (RsfC), including changes that require IT action (e.g. updating the infrastructure);
- informing clients of RsfC, the effect of these changes, and the progress of change implementation (where appropriate);
- liaising with Requestors to ensure RsfC are fully documented and that all necessary agreements are in place before a CAB meeting takes place;
- organising and leading CAB meetings;
- recording and filing all RsfCs submitted;
- reviewing submitted RsfCs and establishing their category (emergency, normal, or standard); and
- supporting the review of the Change Management Process through feedback from Requestors to ensure that the process remains effective.

The Change Manager may need to involve the top management in some RsfC, for example emergency changes, which may have a serious impact on service delivery.

The Change Manager's job description is defined in Appendix 12.

7.4.3.4.2 Requestor

A Requestor is a person who owns a request for change (RfC) in the Change Management Process, and whose responsibilities shall include, but not be limited to:

- attending CAB meetings, as required, to support a submitted RfC;
- consulting all teams involved in, or affected by, an RfC and have agreed to the proposed approach, including resource demands, and have confirmed this in writing or by e-mail;
- fully testing, or arranging for fully testing, of an RfC;
- leading the change process for a particular RfC from inception to completion;
- leading the implementation of an RfC;
- performing an initial evaluation of an RfC covering risk assessment and impact analysis;
- producing sufficient and accurate documentation to successfully implement an RfC; and
- testing implementation and back out plans;

Note 1

The Requestor may originate from a business stream or the IT Department.

Note 2

The information needed for an RfC may change between different types of change, but the standard requirements for an RfC are defined in Appendix 13.

7.4.3.4.3 Change Advisory Board (CAB)

The CAB is the body who approve or reject an RfC.

The CAB is not a technical discussion forum but shall be formed from interested parties that will be affected by the proposed RfC who meet to ensure that the appropriate management processes have been fully addressed in planning the RfC. The responsibilities of the CAB shall include, but not be limited to:

- approving or rejecting an RfC;
- assessing a change based upon a submitted RfC;
- assessing an RfC based upon risk to the business at critical production periods;
- conducting reviews of RsfC that have failed;
- providing a forum for shared learning gained from particular RsfC and the change process overall; and
- requesting further information regarding an RfC to assist in making a decision.

CAB meetings shall occur on a regular basis. The Requestor, or their representative, shall be present at these meetings to ensure that the RfC is discussed. If the Requestor or their representative is not present, the RfC can be automatically rejected. These meetings shall:

- discuss any RsfC taking place during the coming period;
- prepare for upcoming RsfC; and
- review RsfC that have been implemented during the period.

CAB meetings are primarily used to identify all proposed RsfC that will impact upon live services. All issues concerning an RfC shall be documented using the RfC process and discussed in these meetings.

7.4.3.4.4 The IT Department

The IT Department is assigned responsibility for assisting with or implementing an RfC, and whose responsibilities shall include, but not be limited to:

- assessing change requirements based upon a submitted a RfC;
- logging details in the configuration management database of any new assets installed when a standard RfC is performed;
- logging details of standard RfC requests;
- maintaining a store of completed RfCs; and
- marking changes which have been performed as 'Complete' in the change management system.

7.4.3.5 Managing a standard change

The procedure for requesting and implementing a standard category RfC is (Fig. 7.4):

1. An employee identifies a need for a change.
2. They contact their Line Manager to informally discuss the change. The Manager shall be designated the Requestor.
3. The Requestor shall contact the Service Desk and outline the requirements of the RfC.
4. The Service Desk shall:
   - check whether the RfC is on the Standard Change list. If so, the process shall continue via the Service Desk. If the change is not listed, the Normal Change process shall be followed; and
   - advise the Requestor of the appropriate procedure required to progress the RfC.
5. The Requestor shall complete the RfC process, the following information shall be included:
   - service requested—the services required and those that may be affected by the RfC;
   - originator information—Requestor name, business stream, contact details, and authorisation;
   - application access requests—the application required; and
   - user information for access requests—information about the users affected by the RfC.

The following information may additionally need to be provided depending on the type of RfC:

- purchased items—details of hardware, and software;
- software installation details—for any device and/or location for intended use;
- software transfer information—if moving products between devices;
- equipment loan information—if loaning devices; and
- equipment relocation details—details of assets being moved, current location, and intended destination.

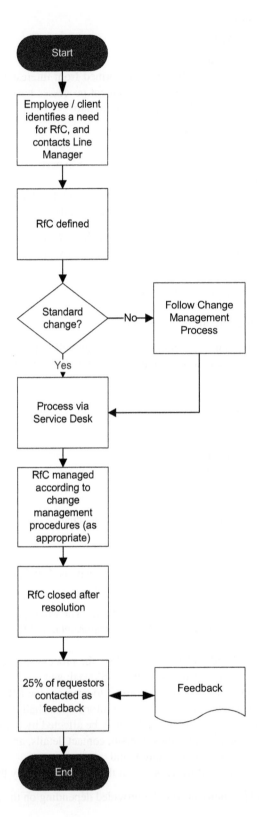

FIG. 7.4 Managing a standard change.

Note

All relevant sections of the RfC process shall be completed and:

- the Requestor shall submit the completed RfC to the Change Manager;
- the Change Manager shall log details of the change in the change system using the information provided on the RfC;
- the Change Manager shall assign the RfC for implementation after being authorised by the CAB;
- the RfC shall be actioned by the IT Department; and
- the IT Department shall obtain sign off from the Requestor on an Installation Sheet to confirm that the RfC has been successfully implemented.

6. If any new assets have been installed as part of the RfC, details of these shall be logged on the Installation Sheet. The IT Department shall submit the Installation Sheet to the Service Desk, who shall:
   - mark the RfC as complete in the Service Desk system;
   - log details of any new assets in the configuration management database and update the asset register, if appropriate, as defined in Section 7.4.5 and Chapter 12, Appendix 8 respectively;
7. The Service Desk Manager shall close the change request in accordance with standard call logging procedures.
8. In line with standard call closure procedures, the Service Desk Manager shall contact a sample of 25% of users who request standard changes to confirm that:
   - the change has been successfully performed; and
   - the RfC can be closed.

7.4.3.6 Managing a normal change

The procedure for requesting and implementing a normal change to the IT Department IT systems and services is (Fig. 7.5):

1. An employee identifies a need for a change.
2. They contact their Line Manager to informally discuss the RfC. The Line Manager is designated the Requestor.
3. The Requestor shall contact the Service Desk and outline the requirements of the RfC.
4. The Service Desk shall:
   - check whether the RfC is on the Standard Change list. If so, the Standard Change process shall be followed. If the RfC is not listed, the Normal Change process continues; and
   - advise the Requestor of the appropriate procedure required to progress the RfC.
5. The Requestor shall complete the RfC process, the following information shall be included, together with an initial impact assessment:
   - Requestor's name, business stream, and contact details;
   - IT applications or services which are involved in the RfC;
   - business case for implementing the RfC(s)—the reasons for the RFC(s), and all associated costs including equipment and staff time as relevant;
   - business impact—including the date by which the RFC(s) needs to be implemented; and
   - signature for budgetary authorisation for all associated costs.
6. The Requestor shall submit the RfC (together with any relevant supporting documentation) to the Change Manager.
7. The Change Manager shall allocate the RfC to a relevant member(s) of the IT Department to:
   - investigate the technicalities of preparing and implementing the change;
   - complete the technical sections of the RfC process; and
   - submit the RfC and all associated documentation to the Requestor.
8. The IT Department, in conjunction with the Requestor and any other relevant IT or business staff, shall prepare details about the RfC for formal submission. These details shall be documented in the technical sections of the RfC form and shall include, where appropriate:
   - environments—the environments in which the RfC(s) are to be implemented (Staging, Production, Products, Services, etc.);
   - implementation plan—a description about how the RfC(s) will be implemented including timescales and schedule, system downtime, and resource deployment and risk analysis;

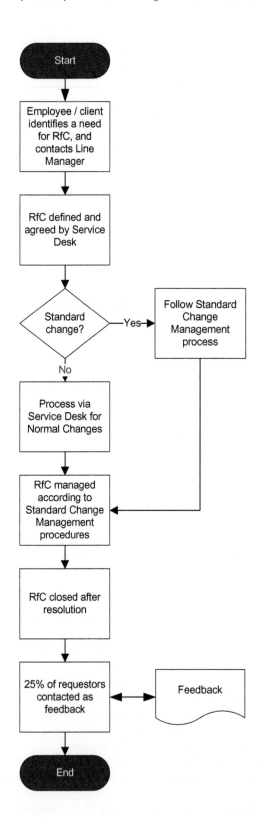

FIG. 7.5 Managing a normal change.

- test pack—a set of documents that describes how the RfC shall be tested to ensure that it has been implemented successfully (this test pack may cover a test plan, details of test results expected and/or achieved, and test sign-off, as appropriate);
- back out plan—a description and procedure describing how the RfC can be reversed if a problem occurs during implementation.

Note

Individual employees may be tasked with investigating particular aspects of a change to enable a full report to be included with the formal change submission.

---

9. The Requestor and the IT Department shall submit the RfC and all associated documentation to the Change Manager.
10. The RfC shall be submitted in accordance with the user notification requirements associated with a normal change type (5 working days).
11. The Change Manager shall review the RfC and associated documentation and determine whether the RfC can be approved without being submitted to the CAB. The following types of RfC shall be approved without being discussed in advance by the CAB:
    - changes that are not complex (of a nonroutine nature); or
    - changes that have a minimal impact upon users and systems.
12. If the Change Manager assesses the RfC as one that can be approved without consultation by the CAB, authorisation shall be provided to the Requestor. The CAB shall be informed of the approval. The Requestor shall be accountable for the success of the change, and for reporting its closure to the Change Manager.
13. If the Change Manager assesses the RfC as one that requires discussion in the CAB, it shall be formally submitted for review.
14. If the Change Manager decides that the RfC requires further investigation work, the RfC shall be rejected at this time.
15. The CAB shall meet at the regular time. During the meeting, the submitted change shall be assessed to ensure:
    - full consultation/communication with all interested parties has occurred either on an informal basis or though formal committee meetings, as appropriate depending on the impact of the RfC;
    - risks and impact have been fully addressed;
    - full consultation within the IT Department and the business has occurred;
    - appropriate scheduling is considered; and
    - an effective back out plan is available.

Note

If an RfC is particularly complicated, or additional factors need to be considered, the Change Manager may request further details about an RfC or may talk to the Requestor to clarify areas of concern before a decision on the change can be made.

---

16. The CAB shall approve or reject the RfC:
    - if the RfC is approved:
      - o the status of the RfC shall be amended to 'Approved';
      - o the Change Manager shall authorise the RfC using the Approvals section of the RfC Form; and
      - o the RfC can be implemented at the scheduled time.
    - if the RfC is rejected:
      - o the status of the RfC shall be amended to 'Rejected';
      - o the Change Manager shall detail the rejection using the Rejection Summary section of the RfC Form; and
      - o no further work shall be performed on the change.
17. The RfC Form and any associated documentation shall be filed by the Change Manager.

Note 1

If the RfC is rejected in its current form but is still required, the CAB may opt to convert the change status to 'Pending' until further clarification and investigation work is performed. The change shall be re-submitted to the CAB.

Note 2

In cases where CAB is unable to agree, the Change Manager shall escalate to top management.

Note 3

If a Pending RfC is not resubmitted within 5 working days, the RfC shall be automatically rejected and all work on the RfC stopped.

Note 4

The Release Team shall perform the change. During the implementation of the change, all interested parties involved in supporting applications and services prior to any change shall be informed on progress, so any failed changes can be managed.

Note 5

It is important that all employees involved carefully monitor the change as it is implemented so that any perceived risk is immediately brought to the attention of the Release Manager, the Requestor, and the Change Manager.

---

18. The Release Manager shall check whether the implementation has been performed successfully against the success criteria agreed:
    - if the implementation has been successfully performed, the Release Manager shall:
      - o report the successful outcome to the Change Manager (and other relevant employees as needed);
      - o obtain sign off from the Requestor; and
      - o ensure that all relevant documentation is updated to reflect the impact of the change.
    - if the implementation has not been successfully performed, the Release Team shall initiate the back out plan to return the systems to their previous state. The Change Manager shall be informed of the failure, whether the back out plan was successful, and any follow-up actions that are required.
19. In addition, if IT services to users are affected, the Service Desk shall also be informed so that users can be kept fully up to date. The status of the change shall be amended to 'Failed'. The Requestor shall assess the reasons for the failure and after investigation shall resubmits the change to the CAB and reports back the reasons for the failure.
20. If any new assets have been installed as part of the change, details of these shall be logged on the Installation Sheet.
21. The Release Manager shall submit the Installation Sheet to the Service Desk Manager, who shall:
    - mark the change as 'Resolved' in the Service Desk system; and
    - log details of any new assets in the configuration management database and updates the asset register, if appropriate, as defined in Section 7.4.5 and Chapter 12, Appendix 8 respectively.
22. The Service Desk Manager shall close the change request in accordance with standard call logging procedures.
23. In line with standard call closure procedures, the Service Desk Manager shall contact a sample of 25% of users who request standard changes to confirm that:
    - the change has been successfully performed; and
    - the change request can be closed.

7.4.3.7　Managing an emergency change

Emergency changes are those designated as top priority, which shall be implemented immediately to prevent or rectify a serious service failure within the systems. The Emergency Change policy is defined in Appendix 14.

7.4.3.7.1 Managing an emergency change

The procedure for implementing an emergency change to the information processing systems and services shall be (Fig. 7.6):

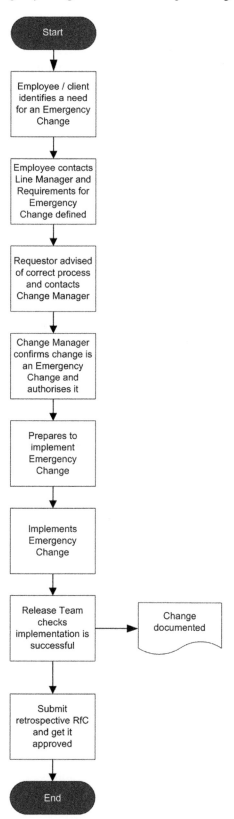

FIG. 7.6 Managing an emergency change.

1. An employee identifies a need for an emergency change, for example:
   - prevention or fix of business critical system failure;
   - elimination or fix of a major security breach; or
   - for reasons of health and safety.
2. The employee shall contact their Line Manager to inform them of the need for the change. The Line Manager shall be designated the Requestor.
3. The Requestor shall contact the Service Desk and outline the need for the change.
4. The Service Desk shall advise the Requestor of the appropriate procedure required to progress the change.
5. The Requestor shall contact the Change Manager (or a nominated deputy in the Change Manager's absence) to notify them of the circumstances of the emergency change request.
6. The Change Manager shall:
   - confirm that the change is an emergency;
   - authorise the change; and
   - allocate the change to a relevant member of the IT Department for implementation.

Note

If the Change Manager decides that the change is not an emergency change, the change shall be passed back to the Service Desk for processing as a standard change.

---

7. The IT Department Team, in conjunction with the Requestor and any other relevant employees, shall prepare to implement the change:
   - individual employees shall be tasked with investigating particular aspects of change implementation as required;
   - the change shall be implemented;
   - during the implementation of the change, employees involved in supporting applications, and services prior to any change shall be kept informed on progress, so any problems can be managed.

Note

All employees involved in the change shall carefully monitor the change as it is implemented so that any perceived risk is immediately brought to the attention of the Release Manager, the Requestor, and the Change Manager.

---

8. The Release Team performing the change shall check whether the implementation has been performed successfully:
   - if the implementation has been successfully performed:
     - o the Release Manager shall report the successful outcome to the Change Manager and the Requestor (and other relevant interested parties as needed); and
     - o the Release Manager shall obtain sign off from the Requestor.
   - if the implementation has not been successfully performed, the Release Manager shall continue until the change is performed successfully.
9. The change shall be fully documented via an RfC form and any other supporting documentation which shall then be processed retrospectively through the standard Change Management Process, via the Change Manager and the CAB, before the change can be closed.
10. The Requestor and the Release Manager shall be responsible for progressing the retrospective change submission.

7.4.3.8 Managing changes to third-party services

There will be occasions when there are changes required to third-party services, these may be on account of, but not limited to:

- addressing weaknesses or addressing security incidents;
- change of vendor or vendor takeover/merge;
- changes needed to reflect changing business needs;
- changes of medium that the services are being delivered by;
- changes to physical locations where services are being delivered;
- improving and upgrading existing services;

- maintaining existing services;
- provision of new services or features for existing services; or
- use of new technologies.

Where changes are to be made to the services supplied to the laboratory by a third party they shall all go through the Change Management Process.

Any unauthorised changes to services supplied by the third party shall be dealt with contractually.

7.4.3.9 Managing changes to forensic workstations

Most forensic workstations shall be connected to the dedicated forensic network, which is primarily used to provide information storage and printing facilities.

Where appropriate, Forensic Analysts shall have a separate workstation that is on the main business network.

A number of standalone workstations shall also exist in the laboratory for Forensic Analysts, these shall be for dedicated processes (e.g. forensic imaging, malware testing, multiple media copying devices, standalone internet access, etc.).

Forensic workstations are frequently rebuilt, upgraded for a specific forensic case, or have specific hardware added to them.

Changes to these forensic workstations shall not need to go through any change control process as the Forensic Analysts are all competent to make changes to their workstations as required. If the change is considered a risk, a standalone workstation shall be used.

7.4.3.10 Outsource providers

Where backend services are outsourced, the outsource provider shall undertake these actions. Any outsource providers shall be audited as 2nd party suppliers to ensure that they have appropriate processes and procedures in place using the Audit process, as defined in Chapter 4, Section 4.9.2 on a risk based assessment. The provision of outsourcing providers is covered in detail in Chapter 14, Section 14.8.

7.4.4 Release Management

Release Management is the process of planning, building, testing, deploying hardware/software and the version control and storage of software. Its purpose is to ensure that a consistent method of deployment is followed. It reduces the likelihood of incidents as a result of rollouts and ensures that only tested and accepted versions of hardware and software are installed at any time.

To ensure that all releases are performed to a consistent standard and in a timely manner, a Release Policy has been developed and implemented to govern releases at a high level, as defined in Appendix 15.

There are three types of release:

- major software releases and hardware upgrades—normally containing large areas of new functionality, some of which may make intervening fixes to problems redundant. A major upgrade or release usually supersedes all preceding minor upgrades, releases and emergency fixes;
- minor software releases and hardware upgrades—normally containing small enhancements and fixes, some of which may have already been issued as emergency changes. A minor upgrade or release usually supersedes all preceding emergency changes; and
- emergency software and hardware fixes—normally containing the corrections to a small number of known problems.

Release Management is proactive technical support focused on the planning and preparation of new services. Some of the benefits include:

- the opportunity to plan expenditure and resource requirements in advance;
- a structured approach to rolling out all new software or hardware, which is efficient and effective;
- changes to software are 'bundled' together for one release, which minimises the impact of changes on users;
- testing before rollout, which minimises possible information security incidents affecting users and requires less reactive support;
- an opportunity for users to accept functionality of software before it is fully implemented;
- training in advance of rollout, which means that users do not experience system downtime while learning new features; and

- version control and central storage of software, ensuring that correct versions are installed at all times, which minimises incidents and the need for reinstallation.

The Release Management process works by providing a consistent framework for defining and creating new products and services and ensuring that the correct versions of tested and approved software are implemented on a day-to-day basis (i.e. after initial rollout).

Release Management links with the Change Management process to enable implementation and to the Configuration Management process to maintain configuration records as defined in Section 7.4.5.

7.4.4.1 Roles and responsibilities

The following responsibilities are defined in the release management system.

7.4.4.1.1 Release Manager

The Release Manager is the person who controls the release management process within the laboratory. The Release Manager's job description is defined in Appendix 16. The Release Manager's deputy is the person who acts as the Release Manager in the event of their absence.

Responsibilities of the Release Manager shall include, but not be limited to:

- ensuring that the release management process is followed;
- developing release policies, plans, and operational procedures;
- ordering hardware and software for use in a release;
- providing a management interface to the change management and configuration management processes;
- supervising a release and managing the Release Team; and
- leading a review of the release process and managing the implementation of changes if required.

7.4.4.1.2 Release Team

The Release Team are members of the IT Department responsible for building and implementing a release.
Responsibilities of the Release Team shall include, but not be limited to:

- assembling all hardware and software required for a release;
- creating a release build;
- testing the stability of a build and resolving any issues relating to the release;
- testing the impact of new services on existing components of the build and resolving any issues relating to the release;
- creating build procedures for all new hardware and software installation;
- testing the functionality of new hardware and software from the user perspective and determining whether the product does what it was intended to do;
- preparing a suitable build environment for testing;
- implementing a release using the agreed installation procedure; and
- reviewing of the release process and managing the implementation of changes, if required.

7.4.4.1.3 Users

Users are employees or third-party employees with authorised access to information or information processing resources, who are responsible for testing and approving a release.
Responsibilities of users shall include, but not be limited to:

- agreeing test criteria with the Release Team;
- performing full testing on a release build; and
- signing off a release.

7.4.4.2 Managing a release

All releases shall be managed by the Release Manager and implemented by the Release Team (Fig. 7.7).
To manage a release:

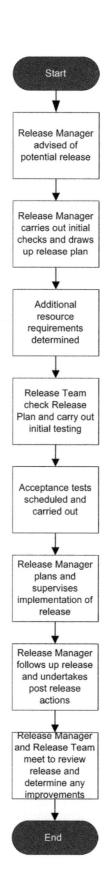

FIG. 7.7 Managing a release.

1. The Release Manager is informed about a potential release from one of the following sources:
   - the Change Manager via an approved or potential change; or
   - the Helpdesk via a user request.
2. The Release Manager shall perform initial checks on the requirements for the release and may need to develop a specific policy for the release. A specific release policy shall reflect the overall release policy but shall include specific details for the release in hand. The policy developed shall include the following:
   - release naming and numbering conventions;
   - identification of business-critical times to avoid for the implementations;
   - expected deliverables for the release;
   - the policy on the production and degree of testing of back-out plans; and
   - descriptions of the release control process (e.g. review meetings, progress assessments, escalation, impact analysis, etc.).
3. The Release Manager shall discuss the details of the release with the relevant members of the IT Department and then draw up a release plan. The content of the plan shall vary depending upon the type of release.

Note

A release plan is not mandatory but for anything more than a small release it is recommended that a plan is produced.

The release plan shall include, where appropriate:
- resources required for the release including IT Department and other employees, hardware, and software;
- detailed quotes and negotiating with suppliers for new hardware, software or installation services;
- acceptance criteria for the IT Department and users;
- roles and responsibilities of all employees and any third-party employees involved in the release;
- procedures for building and implementing the release;
- details about tools to support the release of hardware and software into the live environment, e.g. software distribution;
- training of IT Department employees and users before and after the release;
- outline release schedules;
- template documents to assist with the planning of the releases;
- the build and test environments for the release are available;
- the correct release mechanisms within IT are in place; and
- back-out plans for reversing the release.

4. The Release Manager, in conjunction with relevant members of the IT Department, shall determine the additional hardware requirements for the release and shall place an order for them by following the IT purchasing procedures, as defined in Chapter 6, Section 6.7.4 and Chapter 12, Appendix 8.
5. The Release Manager, in conjunction with relevant members of the IT Department, shall determine the additional software requirements for the release and place an order for them.

Note

If bespoke software development is required, additional work shall be performed to prepare system design documents and put the development work out to tender, if required.

---

6. The Release Team shall check the release plan and obtain all the relevant hardware and software and build the release according to the requirements. The build process shall include, but not be limited to:
   - building and configuring hardware;
   - developing, installing, and configuring software;
   - developing installation packages;
   - producing a test plan; and
   - developing test criteria in conjunction with users.

7. The Release Team shall perform initial testing on the release and confirm that the release is performing as expected. For areas not performing as expected the build shall be reviewed and corrected, as appropriate.

8. The Release Team shall schedule and manage a full IT and user acceptance test of the release. The testing shall be performed in a controlled test environment that matches the existing live infrastructure as closely as possible so that known configurations of both software and hardware can be easily reinstated. The testing shall cover:
   - installation procedures and the functional integrity;
   - system hardware and software together with network infrastructure;
   - updated IT support procedures; and
   - back-out procedures.

   The Release Manager shall obtain sign-off of each activity within the test.

   If the testing is not successful, the Release Team shall investigate the failed items, perform another build and then repeat the test, until it is successful.

Note

All unsuccessful releases shall be tracked and reported through Change Management as failed changes. Failed releases and their impact on operations shall be monitored.

If the testing is successful, the Release Manager shall sign off the test. The release implementation shall be planned and scheduled.

9. The Release Manager shall plan the implementation of the release ensuring that the following shall include, but not be limited to:
   - producing an implementation timetable that outlines all actions, resources and staff assigned;
   - listing all configuration items to instal and decommission;
   - producing release notes, where appropriate;
   - planning communications between all involved parties including regular formal updates from the Service Desk to users;
   - acquiring the hardware and software for the implementation including procedures for secure storage prior to rollout and asset tagging during deployment;
   - scheduling meetings for managing the release and all those involved in it or affected by it; and
   - listing all training and support documentation that is required to support the release.

   The release is now ready for implementation.

10. The Release Manager shall supervise the Release Team during the implementation.

11. The Release Team shall perform the required implementation actions. If the implementation has been successfully performed, the Release Manager shall:
    - report the successful outcome to all parties including the Change Manager and affected users (via the Service Desk).

    If the implementation has not been successfully performed, the Release Manager shall initiate the back out plan for the Release Team to return the systems to their previous state. The Change Manager shall be informed of the failure, whether the back out plan was successful, and any follow-up actions that are required.

    In addition, if IT services to users are affected, the Service Desk shall also be informed so that users can be kept fully up to date. The Release Manager shall assess the reasons for the failure and after investigation shall report to the CAB the reasons for the failure.

12. **The Release Manager shall follow up the successful implementation and shall:**
    - collate all CI information and pass this to the Configuration Manager to enable an update of the CMDB;
    - store all decommissioned configuration items prior to recycling or disposal;
    - store all software in the definitive software library;
    - ensure that all relevant systems and operations documentation is updated to reflect the impact of the release;
    - confirm the release details with the Service Manager to enable an SLA update if required; and
    - confirm the release details with the Business Continuity Manager to enable an update of the business continuity plan, if required.

13. The Release Manager and Release Team shall meet to review the planning and implementation of the release, and discuss:

- the effectiveness of the release process including all planning, build, testing and implementation activities;
- communications and relationship links between all parties involved in the release including the business and users; and
- possible improvements to the release process.

14. The Release Manager shall identify improvements to the release process and implement them.

7.4.5 Configuration management

Configuration management is a major component of successful service delivery. Without effective configuration management, the integrity of assets and the ability to report on the status and configuration of the assets are jeopardised.

Configuration management establishes a consistent method for formally identifying and controlling configuration items (CIs). It is an integral function in delivering IT services because it facilitates the protection of project assets and communicates changes that have been made to them. Configuration management, effectively planned and executed, protects assets and contributes to production of high quality products and services, with the avoidance of rework. The configuration management system is designed to:

- account for all the IT assets and configurations;
- provide accurate information on configurations and their documentation to support all the other Service Management processes;
- provide a sound basis for Incident Management, Problem Management, Change Management, and Release Management; and
- verify the configuration records against the infrastructure and correct any exceptions.

In addition, information security asset classification shall be applied to elements of configuration management to ensure that assets and information are suitably protected.

The Configuration Management Plan serves as the core planning tool describing the overall planning efforts for implementing and executing configuration management on everyday operations and on a project basis if needed. The template used is defined in Appendix 17. It provides visibility and control of assets including hardware, software, user interfaces, project documentation, and system documentation. Configuration management facilitates orderly management of information about, and changes to, developmental baseline assets that need to be controlled.

Configuration management consists of four basic functions as follows:

- identification—identifying and specifying all components which go to make up the infrastructure (including assets such as software, desktop systems, servers);
- control—agreeing and baselining configuration items and then making changes only with the agreement of appropriate authorities (this includes controlling product releases);
- status accounting—the recording and reporting of all current and historical data concerned with each CI; and
- verification—reviewing and auditing to ensure that there is conformity between all configuration items and the authorised configuration record.

Configuration management and components are defined as follows:

- configuration—the complete technical description required to build, test, accept, install, operate, maintain, and support a system (including all relevant documentation relating to the system as well as the system itself);
- Configuration Item (CI)—a component of a configuration that has a defined function and is designated for configuration management. CIs may vary widely in complexity, size, and type from a complete system including all hardware, software, and documentation to a single module or a minor hardware component. A complete system is a top level CI that can be broken down into components that are themselves CIs and so on;
- Configuration Management Data Base (CMDB)—a repository that holds details of all CIs. It can include the CI name, description, owner, serial and licence numbers, file reference, purpose, location, author, version number, etc.

The configuration management process is closely aligned with the change and release processes, as defined in Section 7.4.4. Change and release management are tasked with providing component change information to configuration management, which then records the information in the CMDB. The Configuration Management Policy is defined in Appendix 18.

Configuration management shall be monitored and maintained by the Configuration Manager. The Configuration Manager shall ensure that:

- all assets both physical and electronic are identified and classified and the appropriate controls applied;
- all CIs are identified and baselined;
- changes to CIs are only performed with the agreement of appropriate authorities via the correct processes (including change management and release management);
- regular reporting is performed on current and historical data for CIs;
- regular reviews and audits are performed to ensure that there is conformity between all CIs and the authorised configuration record; and
- all members of the IT Department are aware of configuration management and follow the implemented configuration management system using the guidance and procedures provided.

The full job description for the Configuration Manager is defined in Appendix 19.

7.4.5.1 Configuration management and information security

To ensure that assets (both physical and electronic) are suitably protected, a classification of the asset shall be applied to the asset according to its sensitivity and value in a consistent and uniform manner, as defined in Chapter 5, Appendix 16 and Chapter 12, Appendix 8. This enables risks to be managed so that CIs and information shall be protected in a consistent and cost effective way.

These classifications shall be applied to all classified assets including electronically stored information, paper, films, recordings, magnetic tapes, disks/diskettes, and microfilm. Data held in other forms such as shorthand notebooks shall also be classified. The classification process shall also include data from any third party transferred to FCL, in the course of normal business dealings.

There are four categories of assets that shall be classified:

- information assets;
- software assets;
- physical assets; and
- services.

7.4.5.1.1 Information assets

These shall include, but are not limited to:

- information—this is information has been collected, classified, organised and stored in various forms;
- databases—information about clients, employees, production, sales, marketing, finances. This information is critical for the business. It's confidentiality, integrity, and availability are of utmost importance;
- data files—transactional data giving up-to-date information about each event;
- operational and support procedures—these have been developed over the years and provide detailed instructions on how to perform various activities;
- archived information—old information that may be required to be maintained by law or client contracts;
- case processing files—client deliverables; and
- IT Service Continuity plans, fallback arrangements—these are developed to overcome any adverse event or disruptive incident and maintain the continuity of business.

7.4.5.1.2 Software assets

These shall include, but are not limited to:

- application software—application software implements business rules of the organisation. Creation of application software is a time consuming task. Integrity of application software is very important. Any flaw in the application software could impact the business adversely, especially when using forensic tools for processing client's cases;
- system software—packaged software programs like operating systems, DBMS, development tools and utilities, software packages, office productivity suites etc. Most of the software under this category is available off the shelf unless the software is obsolete or nonstandard; and
- forensic tools—specific software used in forensic case processing.

All software shall be stored in the Definitive Software Library.

7.4.5.1.3 Physical assets

These shall include, but are not limited to:

- computer equipment—servers, desktops, and mobile computing devices;
- communication equipment—modems, routers, switches, PABXs, and (still) fax machines;
- specialised equipment—CCTV, specialised forensic case processing hardware/tools;
- storage media—network attached storage, magnetic tapes, disks, and other removable media;
- technical equipment—power supplies, air conditioners; and
- furniture and fixtures.

7.4.5.1.4 Services

These shall include, but are not limited to:

- computing services—internal systems managed by the IT Department managed services from a third party for which negotiated contracts are in place;
- communication services—voice communication, data communication, value added services, wide area network, local area network, etc.; and
- environmental conditioning services—heating, lighting, water, air conditioning, power.

7.4.5.2 Roles and responsibilities

7.4.5.2.1 Resource Owner

The duties of a Resource Owner are defined in Chapter 5, Section 5.4.3.4.

7.4.5.2.2 Custodian

The duties of a Custodian are defined in Chapter 5, Section 5.4.3.5.

7.4.5.2.3 Configuration Manager

The Configuration Manager shall be responsible for the configuration process, and to act as sponsor for all configuration issues. The responsibilities of this role shall include:

- producing and maintaining a Configuration Management Plan, as defined in Appendix 17;
- liaising with other resource owners and Line Managers to implement consistent change management, configuration management, and release management;
- identifying, managing, and controlling CIs;
- ensuring consistency of the CMDB, Definitive Software Library (DSL) and the Definitive Hardware Library (DHL) so that the authorised state of the infrastructure is properly reflected;
- maintaining control of hardware, technical standards, and all relevant documentation;
- providing supporting services (such as registration and checking) of releases delivered by third parties;
- producing regular reports on the configuration database and all CI status;
- promoting the awareness of configuration management processes and procedures appropriate to employee's work;
- managing the configuration audit process and monitor exceptions and implement corrective actions; and
- providing advice and guidance on configuration management issues.

7.4.5.2.4 Configuration Librarian

The Configuration Librarian shall be responsible for maintaining the CMDB. The responsibilities shall include:

- storing, retrieving and maintaining CIs in the CMDB;
- maintaining an audit trail of changes to a CI (revision history);
- deleting CIs as directed by the Configuration Manager; and
- producing regular reports on the CMDB and the status of all CIs.

7.4.5.3 Producing a configuration management plan

To ensure that a configuration management system is implemented and maintained successfully on an organisational and project level, the Configuration Manager shall produce a Configuration Management Plan, as defined in Appendix 17.

This plan shall describe the actions for assuring that the configuration management process has adequate control over all items necessary for creating or supporting the deliverables.

The Configuration Management Plan shall be developed in coordination with, and be accessible by, all affected employees and any relevant clients. All scheduled and work plan activities and roles and responsibilities required for execution of this plan shall be integrated into any project or organisational plan.

1. The Configuration Manager shall meet with other relevant Managers to discuss configuration management. This discussion shall cover:
   - the scope of configuration management and how it is defined; and
   - roles and responsibilities of all parties.

   This meeting shall be minuted, and the minutes shall form the basis for the requirements of configuration management. These shall be stored in the ERMS as records of the meeting.
2. The Configuration Manager shall produce a draft configuration management plan. This plan shall contain the information defined in Appendix 17 and any other relevant information for the release.
3. The Configuration Manager shall circulate the plan to all relevant Managers, affected clients, and third parties for comment.
4. The Managers, affected clients, and third parties shall review the plan and ensure that all items raised are satisfactory. All comments shall be passed back to the Configuration Manager.
5. The Configuration Manager shall review and then implement the comments, as appropriate.
6. Once the plan has been accepted, configuration management implementation shall be undertaken.

7.4.5.4 Implementing configuration management

Once the configuration management plan has been agreed, the next stage shall be to implement the provisions of the plan.

1. The Configuration Manager shall arrange for a meeting with all relevant Managers, affected clients and third parties and request that they review the configuration management plan and prepare further details for input to the meeting.
2. The Configuration Manager, relevant Managers, affected clients, and relevant third parties shall meet to discuss the implementation of the plan.

   The following details shall be confirmed during the discussion:
   - the allocation of funds and budgets for each aspect of the plan;
   - the allocation of roles and responsibilities for overall implementation of each aspect of the plan;
   - provision for documenting and maintaining the policies, plans, procedures and definitions for each process or set of processes;
   - the management of the teams including the Service Desk and operations; and
   - the process for reporting progress against the plans.

   The outcome of the meeting (or meetings, if required) shall be a series of implementation documents or resource plans to implement service management. These shall be stored in the ERMS.

3. The Configuration Manager shall implement the plan according to the service management plan, regularly reporting to the IT Manager on the progress of the implementation.
4. The IT Manager shall report regularly on the progress of implementation and then confirm that configuration management is now successfully running.

The maintenance and auditing of configuration management shall then be performed.

7.4.5.5 Maintaining CIs

The Configuration Manager and the Configuration Librarian shall ensure that the CMDB is regularly updated and maintained. This shall include:

- adding a new CI
- changing a CI; and
- deleting a CI.

7.4.5.5.1 Adding a new CI

1. The Configuration Manager receives details of a new CI.
2. The Configuration Manager shall check the details of the CI and confirm that all the relevant information is available. If information is missing the Configuration Manager shall contact the provider and request the outstanding details.
3. The Configuration Manager shall pass the details to Configuration Librarian to enter into the CMDB.
4. The Configuration Librarian shall create a new record in the CMDB and enter the relevant details. A check shall be performed to ensure that all required information has been entered.

Note

It is important that all items are entered correctly using the appropriate CI categories and codes.

At the end of each month, the Configuration Manager shall produce a report that details all new CIs added to the CMDB.

7.4.5.5.2 Changing a configuration item

1. The Configuration Manager receives details of a change to a CI, for example:
   - a change, e.g. a replacement hardware or software item is installed;
   - a configuration move; or
   - as a result of a configuration audit.
2. The Configuration Manager shall check the details of the CI and confirm that all the relevant information is available. If information is missing the Configuration Manager shall contact the provider and request the outstanding details.
3. The Configuration Manager shall pass the details to Configuration Librarian to update the existing CI in the CMDB.
4. The Configuration Librarian shall open the existing CI record in the CMDB and update it with changed details. A check shall be performed to ensure that all required information has been entered.

At the end of each month, the Configuration Manager shall produce a report that details all CIs that have changed in the database.

7.4.5.5.3 Deleting a configuration item

1. The Configuration Manager receives details of a CI that is no longer needed. Typically, this is when a CI is disposed of.
2. The Configuration Manager checks the details of the CI and confirms that it can be deleted from the configuration database.
3. The Configuration Manager passes the details to Configuration Librarian to delete the configuration item.
4. The Configuration Librarian opens the existing CI record in the CMDB and deletes it. A check is performed to ensure that all associated CI information is also deleted or retained as appropriate.

At the end of each month, the Configuration Manager produces a report that details all CI that have been deleted from the CMDB.

7.4.5.6 Maintaining the definitive libraries

All information processing equipment purchased shall be recorded in the CMDB. The information recorded for hardware and software is defined in Appendix 20.

7.4.5.7 Auditing configuration items

The Configuration Manager shall undertake a programme of configuration audits to:

- ensure that the configuration management system remains effective;
- ensure that the baseline is correctly identified and properly versioned;
- ensure that the baseline is complete (i.e. it contains the proper versions of the proper configuration items);
- determine whether operational activities are performing as expected; and
- determine actions that need to be taken to resolve configuration item breaches.

All audits shall be performed by the Configuration Manager or his nominee.

1. The Configuration Manager shall schedule an area of the configuration system to audit based upon:
   - any outstanding issues from a previous audit;
   - configuration changes that have been or are about to be implemented;
   - occurrence of errors in the configuration database; and
   - a regular audit as recorded in the IMS calendar of audits.
2. The Configuration Manager shall appoint an Auditor to perform the review on the identified area of the management system. The Auditor shall not have any management responsibility for the area being audited.
3. The Configuration Manager shall produce a report of all CIs for the area to be audited and passes this to the Auditor.
4. The Auditor shall perform a floor check on all CIs and notes whether the correct CIs are present. This shall include all items that make up the baseline.
5. The Auditor shall collate the results of the audit and produce a configuration audit report that details configuration defects that require correction.
6. The Configuration Manager shall task the Configuration Librarian to apply corrections to CIs in the CMDB that were identified in the report.
7. The Configuration Manager shall circulate a copy of the report to the IT Manager for reference.

7.4.5.8 Producing configuration reports

The Configuration Manager shall regularly produce reports on the CIs in the CMDB. The following configuration reports shall be produced:

- CI detailed status report;
- CI change history;
- released items report;
- product baseline status report; and
- results of audits.

7.4.6   Capacity management

The IT Department shall ensure that information processing facilities meet anticipated capacity requirements through proper capacity planning and management. This covers:

7.4.6.1   Roles and responsibilities

7.4.6.1.1   Capacity Manager

The Capacity Manager shall be responsible for the following aspects of capacity planning and management:

- creating the yearly capacity plan in coordination with relevant internal and external clients; and
- ensuring that the capacity plan is up to date.

Note

The Capacity Manager Job Description is given Appendix 21.

7.4.6.1.2   IT Manager

The IT Manager shall be responsible for the following aspects of capacity planning and management:

- conducting a monthly system capacity review in coordination with the Capacity Manager and other relevant interested parties;
- providing trending and analysis information relating to capacity, as required;
- reviewing any incidents raised at the Service Desk that relate to capacity issues;
- determining anticipated capacity requirements for all new systems to be implemented in the laboratory;
- reporting these new capacity requirements to the Capacity Manager;
- updating the IT Department capacity plan with the Capacity Manager; and
- authorising changes to information systems for enhanced capacity purposes.

7.4.6.2   Scope of capacity planning

Capacity planning at the includes, but is not limited to, the following:

- Data Centre requirements (e.g. temperature, space);
- electrical requirements;
- email capacity;
- human resources requirements;
- network and security systems capacity (e.g. ports, processors, memory);
- network internal and external link bandwidth;
- servers capacity (e.g. CPU, memory, storage);
- software licences; and
- storage space requirements.

7.4.6.3   Monitoring system capacity

System capacity shall be monitored through the use of utilisation reports that document the use of information processing capability.

Software-specific monitors shall be used to capture utilisation measurements for processors, channels and secondary storage media such as disk and tape drives.

Depending on the operating system, resource utilisation for multiuser computing environments shall not reach 75% with allowances for utilisation that occasionally reach 100% and may, at times, fall below 70%. Trends provided by utilisation reports shall be used by the Capacity Manager and the IT Manager to predict where more or fewer processing resources are required.

If utilisation is routinely above the 95% level, the IT Manager shall consider:

- reviewing user and application patterns to free up space; and
- upgrading computer hardware and/or investigating where savings can be made by eliminating nonessential processing or moving less critical processing to less demanding periods (such as during the night).

If the utilisation is routinely below 75%, the IT Manager shall determine whether hardware exceeds processing requirements.

7.4.6.4   Reviewing system capacity

As part of the overall IT planning process the Capacity Manager shall review existing system capacity on an annual basis. The findings of the review shall be documented in a plan to ensure that cost-justifiable capacity always exists to:

- process the agreed workloads; and
- provide the required performance quality and quantity.

The template for the Capacity Plan is defined in Appendix 22.
The system capacity review procedure is as follows:

1. At least once a year the Capacity Manager shall convene a meeting to review system capacity, this shall include:
   - the IT Manager;
   - the ISM; and
   - other relevant interested parties.
2. System, physical, and resource capacity shall be discussed with a view to the IT Department and other interested parties being able to provide capacity for processing anticipated workloads. Inputs to the discussion shall include:
   - results of capacity monitoring activity;
   - trend analysis;
   - reports regarding system capacity;
   - planned upgrades or changes to information systems;
   - business-based capacity planning requirements based on sales information projected and actual; and
   - future projects.
3. The meeting shall agree any action required.
4. The Capacity Manager shall document the agreed actions with recommendations for processing agreed workloads.

Note

Changes to the IT infrastructure shall be conducted in accordance with the Change Management Process.

7.4.7 Service management

Service management covers:

- planning for service management through reviews and discussions with clients (internal and external);
- implementing service management through action plans;
- monitoring service management through audits and client contact, as defined in Chapter 4, Section 4.9.2 and Chapter 6, Sections 6.6 and 6.8; and
- improving service management via a policy of continuous service improvement using feedback, improvement plans, and service actions. The Continuous Improvement Policy is defined in Chapter 4, Appendix 24. The Client Feedback forms are defined in Chapter 6, Appendix 17.

7.4.7.1 Planning for service management

To ensure that service management is implemented effectively, the relevant Management System Owner(s) shall define and produce service management plans. These plans shall cover all the required aspects of implementing services by management.

1. Relevant Account Managers shall meet to discuss service management requirements. This discussion shall cover:
   - the scope of service management and how it is defined, for example by location and service;
   - the products and services that internal and external clients require;
   - the products and services that can be provided; and
   - roles and responsibilities of all parties.

Note

This meeting shall be minuted, and the minutes shall form a basis for the requirements of service management and shall be stored in the ERMS.

---

2. Relevant Managers shall meet to review the meeting held with Business Managers and prepare a draft service management plan. This plan shall reflect the requirements of the business and also the capability of the to provide the required products and services.

   The IT Manager shall lead the meeting and take responsibility for producing a draft service management plan. The plan shall contain the following information:
   - the scope of service management within the business based upon the agreed outline with relevant Account Managers and internal Managers;
   - the objectives that are to be achieved by implementing service management;
   - an outline of the resources and facilities necessary to meet the defined objectives;
   - an outline of management roles and responsibilities for implementing service management, including the management of third-party suppliers;
   - the interfaces between service management processes and the manner in which processes are to be coordinated;
   - the approach taken in identifying, assessing, and managing risks so the defined objectives are achieved;
   - a resource schedule showing when financial resources, employee (and any third-party suppliers) skills, and equipment resources are available;
   - the approach to changing the plan and the services defined by the plan; and
   - the approach to continuing quality control through interim audits.

   The service management plan shall include provisions to cater for service management process and service changes triggered by events such as:
   - o service improvement;
   - o service changes;
   - o infrastructure standardisation;

  o changes to legislation; and

  o regulatory changes, e.g. changes in the exam system.

3. The IT Manager shall draft the plan and then circulate it to all relevant Managers for comment.

4. Several elements of the plan can be delegated to the relevant Managers for production and return to the IT Manager, for example, roles and responsibilities, or resource requirements within particular area of operation. If processes already exist for sections of the plan, for example an auditing or risk identification and management process, these shall be referenced.

5. Managers shall review the service management plan and ensure that all items raised are satisfactory. All comments shall be passed back to the IT Manager.

6. The IT Manager shall review and then implement the comments as appropriate.

7. The plan shall be circulated again to the relevant Managers as a final draft. At this stage, the IT Manager shall only require confirmation from all parties that the plan is suitable and acceptable.

8. The IT Manager shall forward the plan to the relevant Account Manager(s) and arrange a meeting with them to review it.

9. The IT Manager and relevant Account Manager(s) shall meet to discuss the plan. If additional or detailed information is required, relevant or third-party employees shall present this at the meeting for prepare further information for input to the plan. The goal at this stage shall be to obtain management approval for the approach of service management within the business streams.

10. Top management and relevant business management confirm that the plan is acceptable.

11. The next stage is to implement the plan within the laboratory.

7.4.7.2 Implementing service management

Once a service management plan has been agreed, the next stage shall be to implement the provisions of the plan.

1. The IT Manager shall arrange for a meeting with all relevant Managers and request that they review the service management plan and prepare further details for input to the meeting.

2. The IT Manager and other relevant Managers shall meet to discuss the implementation of the plan.
   The following details shall be confirmed during the discussion:
   - provision for documenting and maintaining the policies, plans, procedures and definitions for each process or set of processes;
   - the allocation of funds and budgets for each aspect of the plan;
   - the allocation of roles and responsibilities for overall implementation and each aspect of the plan;
   - the co-ordination of service management processes as they are implemented;
   - the identification and management of risks to the services defined in the plan;
   - the identification of the managing teams for the services, for example recruiting and developing appropriate employees or relevant third-party employees;
   - the management of facilities and budget;
   - the management of the teams including the Service Desk and operations; and
   - the process for reporting progress against the plans.

   The outcome of the meeting (or meetings, if required) shall be series of implementation documents or resource plans to implement service management.

3. The Managers for the operational areas shall implement service management according to the service management plan. They shall report regularly to the IT Manager on the progress of the implementation.

4. The IT Manager shall review the progress of implementation and then confirm it to top management and the relevant Business Managers that service management is now successfully running.

5. The planning, implementation, and review of services shall now be performed within the framework of service management. Service management shall be reviewed at least each year.

7.4.7.3 Monitoring and reviewing service management

The monitoring and reviewing of service management shall be performed regularly.

 A formal review shall be performed at least each year and when a significant change is required to the service management system. The review shall determine whether service management:

- conforms with the service management plan;
- conforms to the relevant parts of ISO 20000; and
- is effectively implemented and maintained.

Procedures for performance measurement, including internal audits on the management system are defined in Chapter 4, Section 4.9.

7.4.8 Managing service improvement

A programme of service improvement to improve the client satisfaction levels via the continuous improvement of the products and services it provides shall be implemented.

7.4.8.1 Planning and implementing service improvements

Once service management is implemented and being measured, opportunities shall arise for improvements. These improvements shall be planned and controlled to achieve effective change.

1. On a regular basis, relevant Managers shall collect performance information on the delivery of products and services to clients (internal and external). This information shall come from a variety of sources including, but not limited to:
   - management meetings;
   - account management meetings;
   - client meetings;
   - incident follow-up calls for customer satisfaction;
   - system management metrics; and
   - forensic case feedback analysis.
2. The relevant managers shall meet to assess the collected information at the monthly service management meeting. The discussion shall include:
   - trends in service provision;
   - assessment on whether the figures meet the agreed baseline or other targets (e.g. Turn Round Times); and
   - identification of products, services and areas of the business that require improvement.
3. The relevant Managers shall draft an improvement plan for their respective service area. The plan shall cover the resources, communications, and documentation needed to implement the required improvements.

   New targets for improvements in quality, costs and resource utilisation shall be included, in addition to details on the predicted improvement measures, to assess the effectiveness of the change.

Note

If the plans require input from the business streams, the relevant Managers shall arrange for this input via meetings etc.

---

4. The plan shall be circulated to the relevant Managers, including top management, for comment.
5. The Managers shall meet to discuss the various improvement plans. Relevant inputs about improvements from all service management processes should be considered. Any relevant comments and feedback are incorporated into the plan.
6. The Managers shall prepare for the implementation of the service improvement in their service area, including:
   - communicating the service improvements to all affected employees and relevant third parties; and
   - revising all affected service management policies, plans, and procedures.
7. The relevant Managers shall implement the service improvement in their service areas.

Note

All improvements affecting a service shall be implemented using the Change Management Process.

Initial additional measuring and reporting shall be undertaken by the relevant Managers to ensure that the improvements are achieving their intended objectives. Comparisons shall be made against the baseline and predicted improvements to assess the effectiveness of the change.

7.4.9 Service reporting

Timely and accurate reporting is key to supporting and improving service management. Reporting shall enable management and all clients to assess the state of products and services being provided and provide a sound basis for decision making. The Service Management and Reporting Policy is defined in Appendices 23 and 25.

All Managers shall be responsible for producing reports in their operational areas. The Service Level Manager job description is defined in Appendix 24.

7.4.9.1 Producing service reports

Service reports shall be produced by Managers on a regular basis as specified in service level agreements.

1. For the reporting period, the Manager shall collate information about a service for inclusion in their report.
2. The Manager shall use various reporting tools to generate report information as agreed.
3. The Service Level Manager shall combine these reports into a single report across all business lines.
4. Reports shall be reviewed at the relevant oversight committees, as defined in Chapter 4, Section 4.5.1, or other business streams, as appropriate.
5. Where needed, corrective action shall be taken, as defined in Chapter 4, Section 4.10.

7.4.10 Managing logs

All activities on information and information processing facilities shall be logged and the logs for audit trails of actions undertaken with individual accountability as all user IDs shall be uniquely assigned to an individual (apart from service accounts), as defined in Chapter 12, Section 12.6.4.

A log consolidation tool shall be implemented to permit reporting across multiple audit logs to a central point so that log management is simplified.

7.4.10.1 Roles and responsibilities

7.4.10.1.1 Information security manager (ISM)

The ISM shall be responsible for:

- investigation into suspicious or anomalous activity identified by the log reports;
- performing the risk assessment to identify the type and level of audit logging and monitoring that might be required for each individual information asset; and
- undertaking regular reporting from logs.

7.4.10.1.2 Asset owners

Asset owners shall be responsible for:
- identifying and agreeing with the ISM on logging and monitoring capabilities of the assets they own and for having them configured to meet the requirements of the risk assessment. Detailed requirements of Owners are defined in Chapter 5, Section 5.4.3.5.

7.4.10.1.3 IT Department

The IT Department shall be responsible for configuring the information systems to meet the logging requirements.

7.4.10.2 Audit, operator, and administrator logging guidelines

- a list of all systems for which user activity audit logging is configured, together with the audit log requirements shall be maintained; and
- this list shall be reviewed at least annually by the ISM, the Service Level Manager, relevant Account Managers, and the relevant System Owners. However, some logs shall be reviewed on a more frequent basis for the Risk Committee, as defined by the risk exposure identified or as part of an information security incident investigation.

Note

The list of systems with their audit log requirements and the audit log reports shall be classified as 'CONFIDENTIAL' information and shall be handled in line with the requirements for handling confidential information, as defined in Chapter 12, Section 12.3.14.6.

- system administrators shall be prohibited from erasing or de-activating logs of their own activities;
- all logs shall be archived and available for later independent audit according to the Retention Schedule, as defined in Chapter 4, Appendix 26; and
- operator and administrator activity which shall be recorded in each log event shall include, but not be limited to:
  - date and time of operator activity;
  - name of operator or administrator;
  - description of activity; and
  - error handling details or resolution.

7.4.10.3   Checking operator and administrator logs procedure

The process for checks of operator and administrator logs shall be as follows:

1. The logs shall be monitored 24/7 by the ISM and the Security Operations Centre (SOC).
2. The ISM shall regularly check the operator and administrator logs for completeness, ensuring that the relevant information is being recorded:
   - date and time of operator activity;
   - name of operator or administrator;
   - description of activity; and
   - error handling details or resolution.
3. If some information is missing:
   - the Service Desk shall create a new incident in the Service Desk system and assign the incident to the relevant IT Department member and mark it as an information security incident, as defined in Section 7.4.1;
   - after the relevant IT Department member completes their investigation, the information security incident shall be updated in the Service Desk system; and
   - the Service Desk shall close the incident.

7.4.10.4   Reviewing event logs

Event logging shall be reviewed on an ongoing basis using the event log consolidation software.

Reviews shall be organised by the ISM with system owners and the process shall be as follows:

1. The ISM shall receive regular reports of suspicious activity from the event log correlation software.
2. On a planned basis, according to the IMS Calendar, specific reports shall be run and investigated. These shall include, but not be limited to:
   - administration level access;
   - access to sensitive systems; and
   - access to forensic case files.
3. At the review session, the following shall be discussed:
   - outcomes and outstanding actions from the previous review;
   - types of events which are logged, and methods by which logging needs to be changed;
   - additional needs for tools for automated event logging and event log correlation;
   - risk factors (e.g. the value of information, the extent of the network, past experience of infiltration, etc.);
   - trends which may indicate potential security risks;
   - security of the logging facility from potential tampering; and
   - further action required (which is agreed by all attending the review). These shall be raised as CAPAs, as appropriate.
4. The ISM shall document the findings of the review, the CAPAs raised, and responsibilities for clearing them.

7.4.10.5   Protection of log information

The general guideline by which logs shall be protected is as follows:

- Administrators shall be prohibited from disabling logging activity; disabling audit logs or tampering with audit log information;
- controls shall be implemented to ensure that the log files are protected against:
  - alterations to the message types that are recorded;
  - log files being edited or deleted; and
  - storage capacity of log files being exceeded.
- log files that are required to be retained for legislative or contractual reasons shall be written to archive and retained as required.

7.4.10.6   Managing fault logs

The IT Department shall manage fault logging to record faults and ensure that appropriate corrective and preventive action is performed.

7.4.10.6.1   Guidelines for fault logging

The following guidelines shall be in place for fault logging with the information processing and communication systems:

- the IT Department shall log all reports of errors or problems with information processing or communication systems; and
- all error or problem logs shall be recorded in the Service Desk system in accordance with the IT procedures for managing incidents and managing problems, as defined in Sections 7.4.1 and 7.4.2 respectively.

Fault logs shall include details of the following; however, this is a minimum part of the required input to the Service Desk System:

- name of person reporting fault;
- date/time of fault;
- description of error/problem/fault;
- description of initial Service Desk response;
- description of problem resolution (if known), or action taken; and
- date/time of resolution.

7.4.10.6.2   Resolving faults

All faults which are logged by the IT Department in the Service Desk system shall be resolved in accordance with the IT procedures for managing incidents and managing problems.

7.4.10.6.3   Reviewing faults

All faults which are logged by the IT Department shall be reviewed on a regular basis to ensure resolution. This shall include, but not be limited to:

- open incidents or problems shall remain open until satisfactorily resolved;
- all fault logs shall be stored in the Service Desk ticketing system; and
- the Service Desk Manager shall review fault progress on a daily basis, taking action, as appropriate.

7.4.10.6.4   Checking fault logs

The general process by which fault logs shall be checked is as follows:

1. The Service Desk Manager shall check the logs from all monitoring systems. This shall include all automatic network monitoring logs.
2. The Service Desk Manager shall check the logs for completeness, ensuring that the relevant information is being recorded, such as user, date, time, etc.

3. If there are any issues found in the fault logs, the Service Desk Manager shall pass details to the relevant or third-party employee for investigation and completion:
   - the Service Desk shall create a new incident in the Service Desk ticketing system and assign the incident, as appropriate;
   - the incident shall be updated in the Service Desk ticketing system; and
   - resolution of the incident shall be undertaken in accordance with the processes for incident management.

7.5 Hardware management

7.5.1 Servicing and maintaining equipment

All equipment, including IT equipment, shall be maintained and serviced according to the manufacturer's specifications in order to meet their requirements and minimise loss and damage in case of equipment failure.

All information processing equipment owned or used, including infrastructure, shall be subject to these policies and procedures. Proper maintenance of IT equipment and any supporting infrastructure is essential to ensure continued availability and integrity.

7.5.1.1 Servicing and maintaining equipment

When equipment is to be serviced or maintained, the following procedures shall be followed to enable continued availability and integrity (Fig. 7.8):

1. A need for equipment servicing or maintenance is identified, for example:
   - a member of the IT Department identifies a need for equipment service or maintenance as part of the IT Department's routine servicing and maintenance schedule;
   - a member of the IT Department identifies a need for equipment servicing or maintenance as a consequence of an incident investigation;
   - an Engineer arranges a visit as part of service or maintenance contract;
   - a call to the Service Desk reports a fault; or
   - a call to the Service Desk requests for an item of equipment to be serviced or which needs maintenance;
2. If the need for equipment service or maintenance is identified via a call to the Service Desk, the request shall be logged in the Service Desk system, and the call shall be assigned to an IT Department specialist.
3. A member of IT Department (either the person who identified the need for equipment service or maintenance, or the person who is assigned to an incident by the Service Desk) shall assess the requirements for the equipment service or maintenance. The options are:
   - on-site service or maintenance by the IT Department—in which case the maintenance activity may be performed either at the location of the equipment, or at some other location within the premises (e.g. a designated equipment build/maintenance room);
   - on-site service or maintenance by a service engineer from an approved and authorised third party (either a routine visit as part of an agreed service or maintenance contract, or an arranged visit initiated at the request of the IT Department); or
   - off-site service or maintenance by an approved and authorised third party.
4. If the service or maintenance operation involves internal service or maintenance within IT:
   - the member of IT who is performing the service or maintenance shall plan the activity as required (plans may not be considered necessary for routine servicing of equipment, for example cleaning of printers). Planning activities shall include, where appropriate:
     o scheduling of the service or maintenance activity;
     o informing the business users of a temporary reduction in, or loss of, service;
     o ordering of parts in accordance with the appropriate the procedure, as defined in Chapter 6, Section 6.7.4 and relevant Finance Department procedures in force.
     o arranging for equipment to be transferred to a designated build/maintenance area if it cannot be serviced at its permanent location; and
     o involving other IT Department members.
   - at the scheduled time, the member of the IT Department shall perform the necessary equipment service or maintenance;

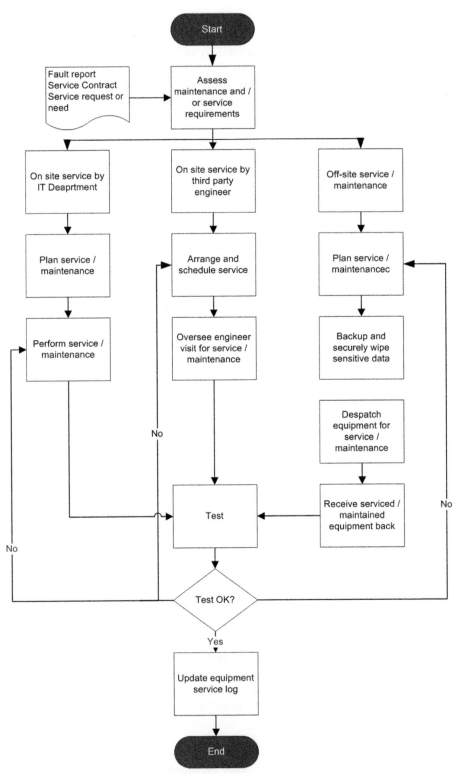

FIG. 7.8 Servicing and maintaining equipment.

- the member of the IT Department who performs the service or maintenance activity shall test the equipment to confirm:
  - o the necessary service or maintenance has been performed correctly; and
  - o the equipment is fully operational.
- the member of the IT Department who performs the service or maintenance activity shall complete any other activities as required, for example:
  - o transfer equipment back to its permanent location (and then confirm through testing that the equipment is operating correctly); and
  - o inform the business users of a resumption of a service.

5. If the service or maintenance operation involves on-site service or maintenance by a service engineer:
   - the member of the IT Department who is responsible for the equipment service or maintenance shall contact an approved and authorised third party to arrange and schedule a visit from a service engineer. If relevant, the member of the IT Department shall inform the business users that the maintenance will/may cause a temporary reduction of, or loss in, service.

Note

If required, the member of the IT Department shall ensure that they first obtain the necessary authorisation from the IT Manager.

   - the service engineer shall perform the necessary equipment service or maintenance at the arranged time;

6. The visit by the engineer shall be hosted by the member of the IT Department who is responsible for the equipment service or maintenance and in accordance with the procedure for hosting visitors and service engineers, as defined in Chapter 12, Section 12.4.2;
   - the member of the IT Department who is responsible for the equipment service or maintenance shall ensure that the equipment is tested to confirm that the service or maintenance activity has been performed, and that the equipment is fully operational. Testing shall be performed by either the service engineer (in the presence of the member of the IT Department), or by the member of the IT Department.

Note

Equipment shall be tested to the satisfaction of the IT Department before the engineer leaves the premises.

---

7. If the service or maintenance operation involves off-site service or maintenance:
   - the member of the IT Department who is responsible for the service or maintenance shall plan the activity, as required. This shall include:
     - o seeking authorisation from the IT Manager, or the Laboratory Manager, if appropriate, for the off-site service or maintenance;
     - o contacting an approved and authorised third party to arrange and schedule service or maintenance of the equipment;
     - o informing relevant business users of a planned temporary reduction in, or loss of, service (if relevant);
     - o scheduling a swap-in of equipment to offset a service loss (or arranging some other service), if appropriate; and
     - o assessing risks to the security of any information held on the equipment.
   - if the equipment holds sensitive (i.e. highly classified or PII) information, the member of IT responsible for the equipment service or maintenance shall perform the following (as required) immediately prior to sending the equipment off-site:
     - o back up any critical information held on the equipment;
     - o securely wiping any sensitive information from the equipment or removing the media containing it—so long as this does not affect the service or maintenance activity; and
     - o send the equipment off-site for service or maintenance, and in accordance with the procedures for securing IT equipment off-site, as defined in Chapter 12, Section 12.3.10.
   - the member of the IT Department who arranges the equipment service or maintenance shall update the service log for the equipment. Details to be recorded shall include, but not be limited to:
     - o date and time of log entry;
     - o reasons for service or maintenance; and
     - o service or maintenance activity details (including information securely wiped, date restored, etc.).

- the equipment shall be returned and received in accordance with the IT procedures for isolating deliveries from operational areas, as defined in Chapter 12, Section 12.3.13.4.1;
- the member of the IT Department who is responsible for the equipment service or maintenance shall ensure that the equipment shall be tested to confirm that the necessary service or maintenance activity has been performed, and that the equipment is fully operational. If necessary, testing may be performed in a development or test environment; and
- the member of the IT Department who performs the service or maintenance activity shall complete any other activities as required, for example:
  - restoration of information;
  - transfer equipment back to its permanent location (and then confirm, through testing, that the equipment is operating correctly); and
  - inform the business users of a resumption of a service.
8. The member of IT who performs or arranges the equipment service or maintenance shall update the service log for the equipment item. Information recorded in a service or maintenance log shall always include:
  - date and time of log entry;
  - service or maintenance activity details (including any parts replaced, information wiped, date restored, etc.);
  - details of persons who performed the service or maintenance activity (including any necessary management authorisations where required); and
  - additionally, a service or maintenance log may include:
    - date of next scheduled service or maintenance;
    - details of faults (actual and suspected); and
    - fault prevention and correction actions.
9. If the service or maintenance activity has been initiated via a call to the Service Desk, the call shall be closed by the Service Desk Manager.

7.5.2 Managing voice communications

As well as ensuring that appropriate security shall be applied to information processing systems, all voice communications shall be secured against the same threats of unauthorised access, disclosure, modification or deletion.

7.5.2.1 Guidelines for voice communications

It is essential that all employees, and third parties working for the Laboratory, are conscious of disclosing business confidential or strictly confidential information during conversations with other the employees or third parties. When there is a business need to discuss the information:

- employees or third parties shall not discuss business information in public places; and
- employees or third parties shall not leave business information (particularly confidential or strictly confidential information) in voicemails or on answer phones/voice mail.

If maintenance of the corporate telephone system is fully outsourced and this shall be monitored by the IT Department as follows:

1. The service provider shall maintain records of key voice facilities e.g. PBX configurations and settings, and an inventory of telephones and associated wiring and cables.
2. Changes to the configuration settings for the voice communications shall only be performed by authorised third-party service provider personnel and shall be approved by the IT Manager and processed through the Change Management Process.
3. The performance of voice communications services shall be monitored by the IT Manager to ensure capacity is sufficient to meet target levels of service.
4. The IT Manager shall ensure the service provider has taken specific resilience measures to provide continuity of service to the users.
5. Invoices for telecommunications services shall be reviewed to identify errors, misuse, or fraud.

7.5.2.2 Reviewing voice communications security

The process for the reviews of voice communications security shall be as follows:

1. The IT Manager receives details about changes to the voice communications systems from the supplier or from internal managers.

2. The IT Manager shall assess the requirements from a security perspective, taking particular notice of changes in configuration settings and access by third-party suppliers.
3. The IT Manager shall send an email outlining his findings to the ISM, together with any recommendations, as appropriate.
4. The ISM shall check the findings and determine whether the voice communications requirements can be approved. Additional discussions shall be held by the ISM and any other relevant interested parties to clarify any of the findings or recommendations.
5. The ISM shall confirm the decisions as follows:
   - if approved, the ISM shall send an email to the IT Manager confirming that the request can be implemented (subject to any changes to the configuration etc. that are recommended).

Note

The request is not granted on a permanent basis. A review of the request shall be scheduled by the ISM and the IT Manager within 12 months to ensure that the request remains valid.

   - if rejected, the ISM shall send an email to the IT Manager outlining the reasons for rejection.
6. The IT Manager shall implement the change to the voice communications system.
7. At the appointed time according to the review schedule, the voice communications system shall be assessed again to check whether it remains valid using the above procedure.

7.5.2.3 Voice recording system

If it is allowed within the jurisdiction a voice recording system shall be implemented to record all external calls, the system shall be effectively managed to protect the exchange of information and ensure the quality of the services:

7.5.2.4 Voice recording system guidelines

- all calls relating to forensic case files shall be associated with the relevant forensic case in the ERMS and retained for the duration that the virtual forensic case file is retained; and
- all other recorded calls shall be available and retrievable for a minimum of 3 months.

7.5.2.5 Procedures for retrieving calls

Where a call is to be retrieved either for a forensic case by an authorised employee, the following process shall be followed:

1. An authorised the Line Manager shall send a request to the IT Manager and the ISM to retrieve a call. The request shall include:
   - time of call;
   - telephone extension;
   - justification; and
   - authorisation.
2. The IT Manager shall log on to the voice recording system or the ERMS, as appropriate, copy the file, and send it to the Requester.
3. If the call contains disclosure of confidential, strictly confidential information or PII, or it shows misbehaviour from an employee towards a client, the employee shall become subject to disciplinary actions, as defined in Chapter 18, Section 18.3.4.1.

7.5.3 Managing the video surveillance system

If it is allowed within the jurisdiction, a closed circuit television (CCTV) system shall be implemented to monitor entrances, exits, and secure areas. These cameras shall operate continuously and be linked to a recording system.

A policy supported by a number of guidelines and procedures shall be developed and implemented for managing the CCTV system along with the video recording system to protect the information and provide legally admissible evidence in incident investigations when needed.

Note 1

Some jurisdictions may require warning or other signage to alert people that are under video surveillance.

Note 2

All legislation and regulation relating to the use of CCTV, including compliance with data protection and privacy legislation shall be met.

7.5.3.1   Roles and responsibilities

7.5.3.1.1   Information security manager

The ISM shall be responsible for:

- ownership of the CCTV system and video recording;
- annual review, service, and maintenance of both systems;
- detecting any abnormal behaviour through the regular review of the CCTV records; and
- retrieving video recordings of approved requests.

7.5.3.1.2   IT Department

The IT Department shall be responsible for:

- the CCTV and video recording systems maintenance; and
- technical support for the systems.

7.5.3.2   Video surveillance system guidelines

- all video monitoring activities shall be available and retrievable for a minimum of 3 months, where permissible within the jurisdiction; and
- the video surveillance system is part of the physical security controls and shall be subject to the physical security audits, as defined in Chapter 4, Section 4.9.2 and Chapter 12, Section 12.3.13.2.2.

7.5.3.3   Procedures for retrieving video recordings

Where a video recording is to be retrieved by an authorised employee or an authorised third party:

1. An authorised Line Manager shall send a request to the IT Manager and the ISM to retrieve a video recording. The request shall include:
   - time and day of recording;
   - location of recording (camera);
   - justification; and
   - authorisation.
2. The ISM shall log on to the video recording system and arranges to show it to the Requestor.
3. If authorised and appropriate, a copy shall be shown to the Requestor and may be provided to the Requestor.

Note

Care shall be taken to comply with all relevant data protection and privacy legislation within the jurisdiction.

7.5.4   Equipment service or maintenance

Proper service or maintenance of information processing equipment is essential to ensure its continued availability and integrity. The Policy for Maintaining and Servicing IT Equipment is defined in Appendix 26.

The following guidelines shall be in place for information processing equipment:

- information processing equipment shall only be serviced or maintenance by either an appropriately trained and competent member of the IT Department, or by an authorised and competent service engineer;
- information processing equipment service or maintenance shall only be performed in accordance with the manufacturer's recommended service intervals and specifications;
- all information processing equipment faults shall be recorded by the Service Desk as an incident;
- all information processing equipment service or maintenance by service engineers or other third parties shall be undertaken in accordance with the procedures for hosting visits by third parties, as defined in Chapter 12, Section 12.4.2;
- a record of all information processing equipment service or maintenance shall be maintained which records:
  - all information processing equipment service or maintenance performed by competent employees (including corrective and preventative action); and
  - all information processing equipment service or maintenance performed by service engineers and third parties.
- Information processing equipment which needs to be sent off-site for maintenance shall be subject to the following controls:
  - equipment may only be sent for off-site service or maintenance to an approved and authorised third party;
  - the IT Manager shall be responsible for coordinating all off-site service or maintenance;
  - where possible all information processing equipment that is sent off-site for repair shall be wiped or media holding information removed; and
  - all off-site maintenance shall be recorded.

7.5.5 Tool validation

7.5.5.1 Requirements

With the rapid growth of digital forensics, the validation of operations of the technology and software associated with conducting digital forensic examinations is increasingly important.

According to the National Institute of Standards and Technology (NIST), results of tests shall be both *repeatable* and *reproducible* for them to be considered admissible as electronic evidence. NIST defines these terms as follows:

- **Repeatability** refers to obtaining the same results when using the same method on identical test items in the same laboratory by the same operator using the same equipment within short intervals of time; and
- **Reproducibility** refers to obtaining the same results being obtained when using the same method on identical test items in different laboratories with different operators utilising different equipment.

In addition to this, a result of the *Daubert v. Merrell Dow Pharmaceuticals Inc.* ruling in the United States was defined by the courts of scientific methodology as:

the process of formulating hypotheses and then conducting experiments to prove or falsify the hypothesis.

The Daubert Standard allows for new and novel tests to be admitted into Court, as long as they meet a number of criteria. The criteria listed below were identified as being necessary to determine the reliability of a particular scientific technique:

- has the method in question undergone empirical testing?
- has the method been subjected to peer review?
- does the method have a known or potential error rate?
- do standards exist for the control of the technique's operation?
- has the method received general acceptance in the relevant scientific community?

While the Daubert Standard is not a legal requirement in all jurisdictions, it has been adopted as a criteria for forensic case processing by many forensic laboratories.

7.5.5.2 Benefits of independent validation and testing

The benefits to the of independent testing and validation include, but are not limited to:

- using a tested tool means users can be assured of its capabilities;
- limitations of the tool are known;
- clients can be advised if their required tool is not 'fit for purpose' based on objective evidence;
- when validating tools, the tools capabilities are known, much of the validation will then just be confirmation that they perform as expected on forensic workstations; and

- independent testing and validation by a recognised body, such as NIST, is usually accepted without question in a Court or Tribunal. The currently tested tools list is maintained by NIST in the Computer Forensics Tool Testing programme (CFTT) at http://www.cftt.nist.gov/tool_catalog/index.php. The current tool testing web page is correct at the time of writing, as November 15, 2022.

Tools tested by NIST fall under the following categories:

- disk imaging;
- forensic media;
- software write block;
- hardware write block;
- deleted file recovery;
- mobile devices;
- forensic file carving;
- forensic string search;
- MS Windows registry tools; and
- SQLite.

The CFTT Raw Test files and reports are available at https://www.nist.gov/itl/ssd/software-quality-group/computer-forensics-tool-testing-program-cftt/cftt-technical/cftt-raw.

7.5.5.3 Tool testing and validation

The forensic network shall be segregated into the three traditional domains that should be present in all properly run IT Departments, namely:

- Development;
- Production; and
- Test.

How these are created, managed, and used is defined in Chapter 12, Section 12.8.

Forensic tools shall be tested and validated prior to them being used for any forensic case processing activities where their results support the evidence and findings presented to the client. While independent testing, such as NIST's CFTT programme gives generally accepted results, there are three major drawbacks to just accepting these tests 'carte blanche' and this represents an unacceptable risk. The reasons for this are:

- many of the tests undertaken are for noncurrent versions of the software, whereas the current versions may not have been tested;
- many of the tools used have never been tested or validated by the CFTT Programme;
- the amount of time taken for independent testing and validation may not fit in with the client's requirements; and
- the tests performed were not undertaken in the specific environment uses (e.g. different hardware or operating system versions).

Therefore, in-house validation and testing shall always be used, where appropriate. This shall be performed by the Forensic Analyst on a clients' forensic case, and the results shall be reviewed by the Laboratory Manager and approved if the tests are successful. This shall allow the Laboratory Manager and the Forensic Analyst to testify to having authorised the tool's use after testing and validation that they personally had carried out and that spoliation of the evidence did not occur.

Testing and validation shall be undertaken to demonstrate and provide documented proof that tools and methods used in processing a forensic case preserved the integrity of the evidence delivered for forensic case processing.

There are other tool validation tests available, such as:

- http://www.cfreds.nist.gov/

7.5.5.4 Roles and responsibilities

7.5.5.4.1 Laboratory Manager

The Laboratory Manager shall:

- agree the testing and validation process proposed by the Forensic Analyst or define it themselves;
- authorise the Forensic Analyst to undertake the relevant testing and validation;
- review the results of the testing and validation;

- authorise the use of the tool or method for the forensic case;
- ensure that records of the test and its results are stored securely in the client virtual forensic case file in the ERMS; and
- advises the client, if appropriate.

7.5.5.4.2   Forensic Analyst

The Forensic Analyst shall:

- define the testing and validation process needed for the forensic case, alternatively, the Laboratory Manager may direct a specific test to be undertaken;
- undertake the agreed testing and validation;
- produce the results and documents them for review by the Laboratory Manager;
- assuming they are acceptable, use the tested, and validated tool and or method;
- if they are not acceptable, identify an alternative and advise the Laboratory Manager. The alternative solution shall be tested and validated as above; and
- use the authorised tool and or method for processing the forensic case.

7.5.5.5   *Planning for validation and testing*

The method, tool, and client requirements shall determine the actual tests to be undertaken for validation of a tool or method. Standard test forensic cases shall be used for all testing.

Forensic tool testing and validation shall consist of a number of well-defined stages, as follows:

- identify the method or tool to be tested;
- Identify the requirements for the test;
- develop test assertions based on the requirements;
- amend the standard test forensic case to cater for these requirements, if necessary;
- develop test method and any supporting procedures;
- undertake test(s);
- produce test results;
- review results with Laboratory Manager; and
- file results in the client virtual file in the ERMS.

The test method documentation required for any nonstandard test is defined by ISO 17025, Clause 7.2.2.1, reproduced in Appendix 27. This shall form the basis for all nonstandard method testing and validation.

Most of the testing required has already been built into the standard test forensic case, and this shall be the standard test case used. If the requirements of the of the test to be undertaken are not met by the existing standard test forensic case, then additional evidence shall be added to it to ensure that the test can be carried out. Any additions to the standard test forensic case shall be approved by the Laboratory Manager and formally authorised, with records kept of the additional evidence and expected tested test results. The new forensic case shall then be hashed, and the hash shall be recorded with the new standard test forensic case in the ERMS. The standard tests used are defined in Appendix 28. While this is the base set of tests, not all may be required for the testing of a specific tool.

Use shall be formally authorised for use by the Laboratory Manager and a record of the authorisation shall be added to the ERMS.

7.5.5.6   *Testing and validating procedure*

The following procedure shall be performed for all testing and validation (Fig. 7.9):

1. A 'clean' disk shall be prepared by securely wiping it and validating the deletion.
2. A copy of the current standard test forensic case, authorised by the Manager, shall be copied to the 'clean disk'.
3. The forensic test case shall be hashed to ensure that it is not corrupted in any way prior to use and records of the 'correct' state of the standard test forensic case shall be recorded in the ERMS.
4. Perform the relevant tests on the standard test forensic case.
5. Create a forensic image of the forensic case.
6. Ensure that the image is correct by hashing it.
7. Analyse the image with the tool or method being tested and ensure that that the results meet expected outcome. If they do not, then the Laboratory Manager shall take appropriate action.

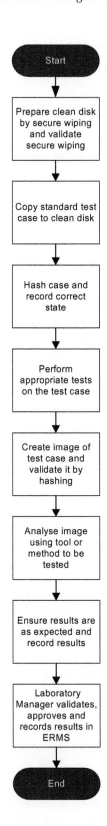

FIG. 7.9   Testing and validation.

8. Results of the test or validation shall be created; the test report template is defined in Appendix 29.

9. The Laboratory Manager shall approve the test, expected outcomes and results assuming it is a success.

10. The results of the test or validation shall be stored in the ERMS.

Note 1

In processing forensic cases and as part of the validation process, dual tool verification shall be used, where appropriate.

Note 2

While the above is the practical testing procedure, the requirements of ISO 17025, Clause 7.2.2.1, given in Appendix 27 shall also be met.

7.5.5.7   Review, retesting, and revalidating

The ongoing testing, and retesting, of methods and tools shall provide an audit trail of testing and validation that the tools and methods in use are repeatable and reproducible, the documented audit trail shall be stored in the ERMS.

When installing a test bed for testing and validation, all installed software shall be hashed and tested against the known file filter (KFF) to ensure that the installed software is of known provenance. On an ongoing basis, a file integrity checker shall be used to ensure the integrity of the test bed.

This process shall also be used for all forensic workstations and is regarded as good practice.

7.6   Software management

7.6.1   Controlling malicious software

Malicious software (Malware) is the generic term used to describe any software that may affect information or information processing facilities by disrupting operations, corrupting information, or allowing unauthorised access to it. All information and information processing facilities shall be protected against all malware.

Malware includes, but is not limited to:

- adware;
- backdoors;
- computer viruses;
- ransomware;
- root kits;
- spyware;
- Trojan horses;
- worms; and
- other malicious programmes.

7.6.1.1   An overview of malicious software control

Since new and mutant viruses are appearing with increasing frequency, antimalware software and identification files shall be frequently updated to counter attacks, and these procedures shall be regularly reviewed to ensure that the processes are suitable for containing and removing viruses.

The malware protection system shall be implemented as follows:

- all workstations, servers, and gateways shall be protected against known viruses;
- shall be installed on servers, network workstations, stand-alone computers, laptops, and mobile devices, where available;
- on mail servers, malware software shall be configured to scan for viruses on inbound and outbound emails;
- antimalware software shall be installed on the gateways and configured to scan for viruses on inbound and outbound files and e-mails;

- antispam and internet site blacklisting shall be performed;
- blocking rules shall be applied to all incoming files to filter unwanted content;
- checks for updated virus identification files shall be automatically performed each hour and downloaded and distributed to all relevant information processing devices, where appropriate;
- mobile computing devices shall be automatically updated following a virus identification file distribution when a connection is made to the network(s), where possible;
- antimalware software updates shall be done automatically via the internet;
- antimalware software patches shall be implemented via automatic updates to the implemented antimalware software;
- real-time scanning on disks shall be performed regularly on email and file servers and on workstations;
- the gateways shall be setup to:
  - automatically stop executable, batch, and script files and offensive material where it can be identified;
  - check that web requests are valid;
  - check the origination of an email to reduce spoofing; and
  - check for spam emails.
- antimalware notification services, such as CERTs and vendor notifications shall be subscribed to and their integrity shall be checked when received by the ISM and the IT Manager.

Note 1

All employees shall be trained on malware and how to deal with it during their security induction.

Note 2

Exemptions to the application of antimalware software shall be made for certain software tools as many of the tools that are used in forensic case processing for tasks such as breaking passwords are considered 'malware' by many antimalware products. This shall be carried out on standalone dedicated forensic workstations.

Email malware and content validation checks shall be performed at the following points:

- all gateways;
- all servers;
- all workstations;
- email incoming;
- email outgoing; and
- where possible, all mobile devices.

Internet access malware scanning and address validation checks shall be performed at the following points:

- content returned;
- website access request against blacklist; and
- website access request for validity.

7.6.1.2 Roles and responsibilities

7.6.1.2.1 Service Desk

The Service Desk shall act as a first point of contact for users with malware problems. The responsibilities of this role shall include receiving calls and first-line user liaison for malware information.

7.6.1.2.2 IT Department

The IT Department shall act as 2nd line Support for malware control. The responsibilities of this role shall include:

- checking that antimalware update files are successfully downloaded and propagated to the systems;
- maintaining website blacklist and spam listings;
- manually downloading and updating antimalware software, if required; and
- responding to malware incidents.

7.6.1.2.3 IT Manager

The IT Manager shall be the central authority for malware control implementation in association with the ISM. The responsibilities of this role shall include:

- ensuring that adequate malware controls are in place; and
- managing response to malware incidents with the ISM.

7.6.1.3 Maintaining malware protection

The antimalware software shall be automatically updated daily, where appropriate. Regular manual checks shall be performed by the IT Department Team.

7.6.1.4 Handling a malware outbreak

If a malware outbreak occurs, the following shall occur:

1. The Service Desk is advised of an information security incident by email or telephone alerts.
2. The Service Desk shall raise an information security incident at the Service Desk, as defined in Section 7.4.1.3.2.
3. The IT Manager and the ISM shall organise a short review meeting with the IT Department to determine how the malware entered the systems and decide response actions. These actions may include:
   - obtaining updated antimalware files;
   - scanning systems to detect and remove the malware;
   - checking the automatic update system;
   - reviewing current antimalware procedures;
   - e-mailing all relevant the users to inform them about the malware incident; and
   - invoking the relevant BCP in the event of a serious outbreak, as defined in Chapter 13.
4. The IT Manager shall email all relevant members of the IT Department summarising the review meeting and confirming the actions required.
5. The relevant members of the IT Department shall implement the required actions.
6. The relevant members of the IT Department shall review the outbreak with the IT Manager and the ISM. Any changes which can be applied to the IT infrastructure to avoid similar malware outbreaks shall be implemented in accordance with the Change Management Process.
7. The information security incident shall be closed at the Service Desk, as defined in Section 7.4.1.4.4.

7.6.1.5 Processing bounced emails

Emails and file requests that meet the criteria as a malware or a spam attack shall be automatically 'bounced' into a quarantine area. This area shall be checked by the IT Department, on a regular basis or when required.

In general, the criterion for bouncing emails shall be to ensure that as much material as possible is allowed onto the network without additional work being placed on the IT Department to deal with trivial emails.

There are occasions when a user is expecting material via an email that has been bounced. The user shall contact the IT Department and request that a bounced email is released. The IT Department shall open the quarantine area and check the items. If the item does not contain malware or is not spam, it shall be released to the user. If an item is malware or spam it shall be deleted.

At regular intervals, and at least each month, a review shall be performed of the bounced material to review the types of emails being bounced. If the review determines that a certain type of previously blacklisted email is acceptable then it shall be removed from the malware/spam listings.

7.6.1.6 Maintaining blacklists and greylists

All incoming emails, and internal website requests, shall be checked against rules within the SMTP Gateway Server. If the file or request breaks these rules, the file shall be blocked and the request is denied. A log of these shall be retained within gateway logs.

The IT Department shall add in additional specific blacklist items, such as email subjects containing links to graphics files or inappropriate wordings.

The IT Department shall create, maintain, and view blocking rules and blacklists and greylists via the SMTP Console.

7.6.1.7 Information leakage

Information leakage may occur, and opportunities for this shall be prevented. Often this occurs through malicious software such as 'Trojan Horses', through 'covert channels' or through employee action.

As a minimum, the following shall be implemented to reduce the chances of information leakage:

- scanning of outbound media and communications for hidden information;
- monitoring of personnel and system activities;
- monitoring resource usage in computer systems;
- using tools to reduce the likelihood of Trojan Horse infections;
- use of key features and benefits of the firewalls, for example the blocking of unnecessary outgoing ports on a physical firewall;
- comprehensive high-availability solution for subsecond failover between interfaces or devices;
- full mesh configurations to allow for redundant physical paths in the network, thereby providing maximum resilience;
- virtual system support to allow partitioning into multiple security domains, each with a unique set of administrators, policies, VPNs, and address books;
- interface flexibility for varying network-connectivity requirements and future growth requirements;
- virtual router support to map internal, private, or overlapped IP addresses to a new IP address, providing an alternate route to the final destination and concealing it from public view;
- customisable security zones to increase interface density without additional hardware expenditures, lower policy-creation costs, contain unauthorised users and attacks, and simplify management of firewall/VPNs;
- transparent mode to allow the device to function as a Layer 2 IP security bridge, providing firewall, VPN, and DoS protections, with minimal change to the existing network;
- management through central management consoles;
- policy-based management to allow centralised, end-to-end life-cycle management;
- implementation of customisable data loss prevention (DLP) tools to address the risk of employee action leading to information leakage as well as reinforcing defences against external threat actors.

7.6.2 Control of technical vulnerabilities

Technical vulnerability management shall be implemented in an effective, systematic and repeatable way with measurement taken to confirm its effectiveness. These considerations shall include operating systems, and any applications in use.

7.6.2.1 Roles and responsibilities

7.6.2.1.1 IT Department

The IT Department shall be responsible for:
- monitoring vulnerabilities and vendors' releases of patches and fixes and installing operational software updates, patches, and fixes on the operational systems.

7.6.2.1.2 Information security manager

The ISM shall be responsible for vulnerability risk assessments.

7.6.2.2 Evaluation of assets at risk

The following guidelines shall be in place for evaluation of assets at risk within the laboratory:

- all assets shall be recorded in the software asset register and/or CMDB with details of owners;
- details in the software asset register shall include:
  - vendor; and
  - version number.
- assets shall be continuously reviewed by the Asset Owner to ensure that they are maintained at the correct technical level.

7.6.2.3 Vulnerability management process

The following processes shall be implemented to address technical vulnerabilities:

- vulnerability monitoring from such sources as vendors, CERTs etc.;
- coordination of responsibilities within the IT Department and the business for patching;

- a timeline shall be set for reacting to vulnerability notifications;
- a suitable risk assessment process to determine risks and countermeasures, as defined in Chapter 12;
- required controls shall be implemented through the Change Management Process;
- vulnerability control decisions shall be tracked (and shall be audited) through either the Change Management Process or the incident management procedure;
- the patch testing and evaluation process shall be followed; and
- the Information Security Committee shall receive reports on vulnerability management, including information about the number of identified vulnerabilities, what additional controls are in place, what outstanding issues there are, and updates on previous issues on a regular basis for their meetings.

7.6.3 Implementing software patches and updates

The update of software shall include responses to specific security alerts that have been received from software vendors or other reputable sources. This shall include:

- firmware;
- network equipment;
- operating systems; and
- applications.

7.6.3.1 An overview of software patches and updates

The software patch and update system shall be implemented as follows (Fig. 7.10):

- updates and patches shall be implemented manually on servers;
- if a patch is available, the risks associated with installing the patch shall be assessed (the risks posed by the vulnerability shall be compared with the risk of installing the patch);
- updates and patches shall be automatically implemented on networked workstations and laptops;
- updates and patches hall be implemented manually on all stand-alone workstations;
- automatic scanning shall be used to scan all information processing devices for building the patch list regularly.

7.6.3.2 Roles and responsibilities

7.6.3.2.1 IT Department

The IT Department is the primary instigator of patches and updates. The responsibilities of this role shall include:

- checking vendor sites for patches and updates on a regular basis;
- implementing patches and updates on servers using Azure Update Management;
- configuring Microsoft Intune for patching desktops and laptops;
- checking application patches, which shall also be implemented using Microsoft Intune;
- checking for firmware patches, as appropriate;
- ensuring that the patching process works properly;
- checking reports to confirm implementation;
- liaising with the IT Manager for updates and patches on critical servers; and
- determining update implementation schedules.

7.6.3.2.2 IT Manager

The IT Manager is the central authority for patches and updates. The responsibilities of this role shall include:

- ensuring that adequate patch and update controls are in place;
- liaising with Service Level Manager about changes to critical servers or changes that have a major impact on services.

7.6.3.3 Implementing patches and updates on servers

Most servers on the business network are of a standard configuration and therefore patches required for one will also be needed for several others. The forensic network servers shall be similar.

Patches and updates implemented on servers shall be managed via the Change Management Process.

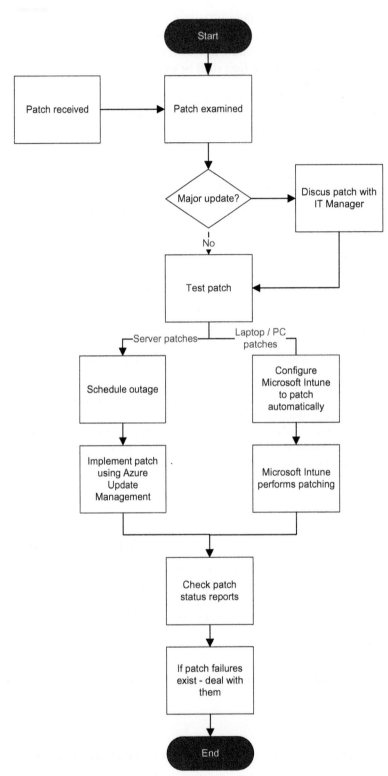

FIG. 7.10 An overview of patching and updating.

1. The IT Department shall identify the patch required for a server. This shall be determined via a range of sources that include the vendor alerts, security alerts, software upgrade programs etc.
2. The IT Department shall check the details of the patch available and evaluate it. If it is determined that the patch has a minor impact on the server or the services provided by it, the IT Department shall schedule the update. If it is determined that the patch has a major impact on the server or the services provided by it, the IT Department shall discuss the installation of the patch with the IT Manager and the ISM and confirm appropriate actions in an email.

Note

In all circumstances for both minor and major patches, no critical server shall have a patch or update installed without the patch or update first being installed on a noncritical server.

---

3. The IT Department shall test the patch on a suitable test machine in the IT Department.
4. The IT Department shall schedule an outage of the relevant server via the Service Desk. Scheduled outages shall take place at time of low user activity such as at weekends or overnight.
5. The IT Department shall log on to the relevant server and then update the server software by either:
   - using Azure update management;
   - downloading and manually running the relevant patch(es);
   - inserting a DVD if received from the software vendor and installing the update using the installation program;
   - manually running an update to select the patch(es) required and instal them;
   - running a previously downloaded patch.
6. Once the patch or update is installed by whatever method, the IT Department shall check to ensure that the patch or update has been successfully installed.
7. Where a patch or update is determined as missing, appropriate action shall be taken to implement it.

7.6.3.4 Implementing patches and updates on workstations, PCs, and laptops

Most workstations, PCs, and laptops are of a standard configuration, apart from those that are used as forensic workstations, and therefore patches and updates required for one will also be needed for multiple others.

Patches and updates implemented on workstations, PCs, and laptops shall be managed using Microsoft Intune.

1. The IT Department shall configure Microsoft Intune to automatically perform patching and updating on workstations, PCs, and laptops for all relevant patches.
2. Patching shall be carried out automatically.
3. Once the patch or update is installed by whatever method, the IT Department shall check to ensure that the patch or update has been successfully installed.
4. Where a patch or update is determined as missing, appropriate action shall be taken to implement it.

Note 1

Intune can also perform automatic patching on some software, and this is also configured in Intune.

Note 2

If the application is in the Microsoft App store, auto-updating takes place.

7.7 Network management

7.7.1 Managing network security

The Network Services Policy is defined in Chapter 4, Appendix 29.

7.7.1.1 Guidelines for network management

Information security is highly dependent on network operations and management functions, and therefore, specific measures shall be taken to ensure security is not compromised by network failures or information security breaches of the network.

For security purposes, network management arrangements shall include, where possible, the following:

- establish service level agreements (SLAs) with users and third-party service providers and develop connection rules, as defined in Chapter 12, Section 12.5;
- segregate the duties within the IT Department of those who are running the network from those developing/designing the network, as defined in Chapter 12, Section 12.3.5;
- reduce dependence on key individuals by automating key tasks, ensuring complete and accurate documentation of operational procedures, and arranging alternative cover for key positions;
- closely control activities of Network Administrators, by supervision and logging of activity, as defined in Chapter 12, Section 12.3.5;
- fully screen applicants for positions that involve running the network, as defined in Chapter 18, Appendix 2;
- use awareness and training programs to ensure that all employees are aware of the existence and importance of information and network security controls, as defined in Chapter 12, Section 12.3.2;
- all Network Administrators shall be competent to run the network under normal and peak conditions, as defined in Chapter 4, Section 4.6.1.1; and
- all Network Administrators shall be competent to deal with error, exception and emergency conditions and shall be required to report faults and other disruptive events.

7.7.1.2 Network design

The design of the network shall be based on sound design principles so that it:

- has security functionality built-in;
- is designed to be compatible with other networks;
- can cope with foreseeable developments in information technology, including capacity planning, as defined in Section 7.4.6.
- coherent technical standards shall be used to support consistent naming conventions, and to comply with legislative, regulatory, contractual and industry requirements;
- proper capacity planning shall ensure growth and interconnection with other networks is possible if needed (based upon known and projected bandwidth requirements) and to ensure that the network technologies selected can cope with the existing volume of traffic and are capable of accommodating growth and changing requirements, as defined in Section 7.4.6;
- a combination of static and dynamic routing methods shall be used to ensure easier administration and build resistance to the introduction of routing errors;
- the physical topography shall attempt to avoid areas that are prone to disruption (e.g. areas where building work is likely to take place);
- guidelines on the depth of burial and the physical protection requirements of cables (e.g. armoured conduit) shall be clearly documented in the design;
- where possible, key devices shall perform only one major function and all other services and functions that are not required shall be disabled or removed according to the defined hardened builds;
- distinct subnetworks shall be used, protected by rule-based traffic filtering;
- common servers shall be centralised to enable better management of network traffic;
- switched networks shall be used where possible (as opposed to slower shared networks);
- the number of entry points into the network shall be limited, and each entry point shall serve a valid business purpose;
- strong authentication mechanisms shall be used; and
- network management reports and audit trails shall be maintained.

7.7.1.3 Network resilience

Communications facilities and devices are critical to the continuity of network services, and specific measures shall be taken to:

- reduce the risk of malfunction of critical communications equipment, software, links, and services;
- minimises single points of failure by:

- automatic re-routing of communications should critical nodes or links fail;
- rerouting in the event of a network failure or changes in the network topology;
- all critical network devices shall be reachable via more than one path, use of network traffic load balancing, and redundancy of key devices; and
- duplicate devices shall be provided where necessary.
- risks of malfunctions with critical communication equipment, software, and links shall be minimised by:
  - giving high priority to reliability, compatibility, and capacity in the acquisition process;
  - using only proven products, keeping them up-to-date, and in good working order;
  - ensuring that key network components can be replaced quickly or that spares are held on site;
  - using modern protocols that can be updated quickly and withstand high capacity to ensure that the network is supported by a robust and reliable set of hardware and software; and
  - maintaining network system devices according to vendor standards.

7.7.1.4   Network documentation

Accurate, up-to-date, documentation to support network operations shall be maintained, which is consistent with security requirements. Accurate documentation (in paper or electronic form) shall be maintained for the configuration of the network (internal and external), including all nodes and connections, communications equipment, software, links, and services (including up-to-date inventories and labelling of equipment), and in-house cabling (including identification of cable runs and labelling of cables). The documentation shall be readily accessible to authorised personnel, subject to supervisory review and checked periodically to ensure that no unauthorised changes have been made.

The network documentation shall cover:

- network hardware and software manuals, and operating procedures covering, network devices, test equipment, network management software, and network monitoring software;
- recovery and continuity plans, specifying the requirements for holding network documentation in secure off site locations networking roles and responsibilities;
- descriptions of the network (network topology diagrams);
- circuits;
- devices; and
- cabling.

7.7.1.5   Traffic management and control

All-important network devices shall be properly configured and network-filtering methods applied across all internal and external networked services. This shall ensure that networks are protected against undesirable network traffic and prevent unauthorised users gaining access.

All internal and external network connections shall be compliant with the Access Control Policy, as defined in Chapter 4, Appendix 21 the procedures for controlling network access as defined in Section 7.7.2 and the procedures for controlling remote access as defined in Section 7.7.3. Elements of the network that may be accessed, and the authorisation procedure for gaining access, shall be determined on the rules and rights of users or groups of users, which shall be driven by business requirements.

Access to the network shall be controlled via the use of enforced paths, user or node authentication, segregation of networks and network connections, routing, and filtering controls.

The minimum acceptable authentication requirements for all users wishing to access information resources via the network shall be by means of a unique User ID and passphrase, while access to the forensic network shall be by two factor authentication.

The internal network addressing scheme shall not be visible to external connections to keep threat actors or other unauthorised external parties from easily gaining information about the structure of the network and its information processing systems.

7.7.1.6   Device configuration

All-important network devices (network servers, routers, front-end processors, bridges, switches, firewalls, and IDS/IPS) shall be properly configured to:

- comply with a standard technical build where undesirable and inessential services shall always be disabled;

- ensure they function as required and do not compromise the security of the network; and
- highlight overload or exception conditions, where possible.

  The following guidelines shall be adopted:

- all changes to the network shall go through the Change Management Process;
- all network devices shall log events in a form suitable for review via the security incident and event management (SIEM) solution in place, as defined in Section 7.4.10;
- all network devices shall be tested after the build to ensure the device is working correctly;
- build and configuration settings shall be documented;
- log events shall be reviewed regularly and appropriate action taken where anomalies are found, as defined in Section 7.4.10.4.
- logging shall alert Network Administrators of changes;
- measures shall be taken to prevent unauthorised or incorrect updates to network devices;
- network devices shall be built to a standard hardened build, where possible;
- network services on systems shall be disabled, unless a specific business reason for the service is needed;
- new patches and updates shall, where possible, be thoroughly tested before being applied, as defined in Section 7.6.3;
- passphrases (and privileges) shall be set up on all network devices (e.g. firewalls, routers, IDS, etc.) for all means of connection that are required (e.g. directly, via the network, via dial-up link, or via console connection); and
- passphrases shall be changed on a periodic basis where this is practical (e.g. it is not always practical to change some hard-coded passwords on legacy systems) or are strong passphrases as defined in Chapter 12, Section 12.6.3.1.

7.7.1.7 Traffic filtering

Traffic filtering shall be deployed to ensure unauthorised or undesirable network traffic is not allowed to gain access to specified parts of the network. Network filtering devices shall be configured to filter specific types of traffic, to block or otherwise restrict particular types or sources of traffic.

Filtering of traffic shall be based on predefined, documented and signed-off rules or tables based on the principle of 'least access' (i.e. that which is not expressly permitted is denied). These rules and tables shall be developed by the ISM with the Network Administrators and shall be subject to operational review by the IT Manager and relevant Resource Owners as defined in Chapter 12, Sections 12.7.4 and 12.7.5.

Network filtering devices (i.e. firewalls) shall be implemented to ensure that they cannot be bypassed, are fully resilient, and shall only be accessed from designated workstations or network addresses. Any failure or vulnerabilities identified shall be raised as an information security incident at the Service Desk.

While filtering devices are used to detect inbound attacks upon the network, measures shall be taken to detect and prevent outbound attacks upon external networks. This shall prevent employees using the internal network as a launch pad to attack the networks of other organisations. If the source of attacks upon an external organisation can be clearly identified it may be possible for the victim to seek legal redress, i.e. the organisation from which the attack originated may be regarded as liable for the malicious act.

Protection against outbound attacks shall be achieved by ensuring connection to the Internet only occurs via a proxy server or with the appropriate placement of intrusion detection sensors combined with proper logging and monitoring of outbound traffic.

7.7.1.8 Monitoring the network

Network monitoring shall be performed by the Network Administrators to assess the performance of the network, to reduce the likelihood of network overload, and to detect potential or actual malicious intrusions:

- routine monitoring shall include current and projected volumes of network traffic, utilisation of network facilities, and identification of any potential bottlenecks or overloads; and
- firewall activity shall be monitored via separate system logs.

7.7.1.9 Reviewing and assessing network security

The procedures for reviewing and assessing network access and security shall be as follows:

1. The Network Administrators shall be responsible for managing network security and reviewing network security. They shall also receive authorised requests from network users to change aspects of the network security system via the Service Desk.

2. The Network Administrators shall assess the requirements (or the existing setup for a review) and shall take particular notice of:
   - network design—determine whether the requirements have security built-in;
   - network resilience—determine whether the requirements reduce single points of failure and/or reduce the risk of malfunction of critical communications equipment, software, links, and services;
   - network documentation—determine the changes needed in network documentation to ensure it is current;
   - traffic management and control—determine whether the requirements affect network traffic to ensure that the network is protected against undesirable network traffic and prevent unauthorised users gaining access;
   - device configuration—determine whether the requirements affect network device configuration (network servers, routers, front-end processors, bridges, switches, firewalls, and IDS/IPS);
   - traffic filtering—determine whether the requirements affect network-filtering method; and
   - monitoring the network—determine whether the requirements affect the performance of the network; reduce the likelihood of network overload, and to detect potential or actual malicious intrusions.
3. The Network Administrators shall send an email outlining their findings to the IT Manager and the ISM, together with any recommendations, as appropriate.
4. The IT Manager checks the findings and determines whether the requirements can be approved. Additional discussions shall be held with the ISM and Network Administrators to clarify any of the findings or recommendations.
5. The IT Manager shall confirm the decisions as follows:
   - if approved, the IT Manager shall send an email to the Network Administrators and the ISM confirming that the request can be implemented (subject to any changes to the configuration etc. that are recommended);

Note

The request shall not be granted on a permanent basis. A review of the request shall be scheduled by the Network Administration Team Leader within 12 months to ensure that the request remains valid.

---

6. If rejected, the IT Manager shall send an email to the Network Administration Team Leader and the ISM outlining the reasons for rejection.
7. The Network Administrators shall implement the changes to the network as required.
8. At the appointed time, according to the review schedule, the network shall be assessed again to check whether it remains valid using the above procedures.

7.7.2 Controlling network access

Network access control is essential to implement and shall be implemented using a variety of controls, as below:

7.7.2.1 Segregation in networks

The network shall be divided into distinct domains to provide additional security. The following controls are in place:

- Active Directory shall be utilised to create domain divisions and shall be used to manage issues such as passphrase limits and logon retries via the Active Directory's Group Policy Object (GPO); and
- domains shall serve as containers for security policies and administrative assignments.

7.7.2.2 Network connection control

Unauthorised or undesirable network traffic shall not be allowed to gain access to any part of the network.
The controls that shall be in place to achieve this shall include, but not be limited to:

- filtering of traffic shall be based on predefined rules and tables based on the principle of 'least access' (i.e. that which is not expressly permitted is denied). These rules and tables shall be developed and maintained by the IT Department;
- internal connection to the internet shall occurs via a proxy server to protect against outbound attacks;
- network filtering devices (i.e. firewalls) shall be implemented to ensure they cannot be bypassed;
- network filtering devices shall be configured to filter specific types of traffic (e.g. IP address, ports etc.) block or otherwise restrict particular types or sources of traffic, such as those that can be used to execute 'denial of service' attacks and limit the use of communications that are prone to abuse;

- network filtering devices shall limit information about the network (and its hosts) being divulged; and
- network traffic shall be routed through an effective filtering device, such as intelligent routers, application proxies, or firewalls prior to being allowed access to the network.

7.7.2.3 Network routing control

Network routing controls shall ensure that computer connections and information flows do not breach the Access Control Policy.

The following controls shall apply:

- access rules shall be added as business needs arise;
- access rules shall be reviewed as defined in Chapter 12, Section 12.6;
- all routers connected to the network shall be operated and managed by the IT Department;
- no local user accounts shall be configured on routers;
- router passphrases shall be kept in a secure encrypted form on all routers. The router shall have the 'enable password' set to the current production passphrase, if possible; and
- standardised SNMP community strings shall be used on routers and switches and shall be changed from the defaults of 'public' and 'private'.

7.7.2.4 Reviewing and assessing network access controls

The procedures for reviewing and assessing network access control shall be as follows:

1. The Network Administrators shall be responsible for managing the access review or receive requests from IT users to change aspects of network access.
2. The Network Administrators shall assess the requirements (or the existing setup for a review) from a security perspective, taking particular notice of:
   - segregation in networks—determine whether the network or the new requirements have sufficient segregation to provide additional security;
   - network connection control—determine whether the network or new requirements ensure that unauthorised or undesirable network traffic is not allowed to gain access; and
   - network routing control—determine that existing or new computer connections and information flows do not breach the Access Control Policy.
3. The Network Administrators shall send an email outlining their findings to the IT Manager and the ISM, together with any recommendations as appropriate.
4. The IT Manager shall check the findings and determine whether the requirements can be approved. Additional discussions shall be held with the ISM and the Network Administrators to clarify any of the findings or recommendations.
5. The IT Manager shall confirm the decisions as follows:
   - if approved, the IT Manager shall send an email to the Network Administration Team Leader and the ISM confirming that the request shall be implemented (subject to any changes to the configuration etc. that are recommended).

Note

The request shall not be granted on a permanent basis. A review of the request shall be scheduled by the Network Administration Team and the ISM within 12 months to ensure that the request remains valid.

   - if rejected, the IT Manager shall send an email to the Network Administration Team Leader and the ISM outlining the reasons for rejection.

6. The Network Administration Team shall implement the changes to the environments as required.
7. At the appointed time according to the review schedule, the network access controls shall be assessed again to check whether they remain valid using the above procedure.

7.7.3 Remote connections

The network shall be protected from any remote host, untrusted host, and remote network.

This shall apply to remote access connections, including but not limited to, reading or sending email and viewing intranet web resources. The remote access implementations that shall be covered by this shall include, but are not limited to, DSL, VPN, SSH, SLIP, SASE, ZTNA, and cable modems, etc.

7.7.3.1 Guidelines for remote connections

The guidelines that apply shall be:

- access to diagnostic ports shall be restricted and controlled by the IT Department;
- all hosts that are connected to the internal networks via remote access technologies shall use the most up-to-date anti-malware software, as defined in Section 7.6.1;
- at no time shall any the employee provide his or her login or email passphrase to anyone, business, IT Department, or family;
- remote access shall be approved and managed by the IT Manager and the ISM; and
- secure remote access shall be strictly controlled and is enforced via two factor authentication.

7.7.3.2 Managing remote connections

The procedures for managing remote connection access shall be as follows:

1. A request for a remote connection is received from a user at the Service Desk. The user shall complete the Service Access Request form and shall be approved by the user's Line Manager before it can be processed further.
2. If it is not authorised by the Line Manager, then the Service Desk shall return it to the Requestor.
3. The Service Desk shall assign the request to the relevant member of the IT Department for processing.
4. The IT Manager and the ISM shall assess the requirements (or the existing connection for a review) and take particular notice of:
   - the remote connection standards that apply;
   - the actual business need for the connection;
   - security implications of using the connection; and
   - period for which the connection is required.
5. Additional discussions shall be held with the IT Manager, the ISM and the Requestor to clarify any of the findings or recommendations.
6. The IT Manager shall confirm the decisions as follows:
   - if approved, the IT Manager shall send an email to the Requestor and the ISM confirming that the request shall be implemented (subject to any changes to the configuration etc. that are recommended);

Note

The request shall not be granted on a permanent basis. A review of the request shall be scheduled by the ISM with the IT Manager for the end of the requested period or within 12 months to ensure that the request remains valid.

---

7. If rejected, the IT Manager shall send an email to the Requestor and the ISM outlining the reasons for rejection. This email shall be passed on to the Requestor.
8. The IT Department shall implement the new connection and test it before enabling user access. The Service Desk shall be informed that the connection is ready.
9. The Service Desk shall email the user and the Requestor and confirms that the connection is available.
10. At the appointed time according to the review schedule, the connection shall be assessed again to check whether it remains valid using the above procedure.

7.7.3.3 Managing third-party remote access

There are a number of third parties that may have legitimate access to the information and information processing facilities. It is essential that these connections shall be properly managed and do not allow unauthorised access.

Specific third-party support groups may also be given remote access to secure systems.

The procedures for this shall include, but not be limited to:

- access rights shall be restricted via the login account;
- all access shall be by a named individual using an account to the network, i.e. there shall be no sharing of user IDs by a third party. This shall be a contractual requirement;
- multifactor authentication shall be used to provide secure authentication; and
- requests for remote access shall be initiated by business Line Managers for a specific and justified need.

7.7.3.3.1 Roles and responsibilities

7.7.3.3.1.1 Service Desk The Service Desk shall act as first-line IT Department for remote access user group maintenance. The responsibilities of this role shall include:

- establishing accounts for remote access;
- periodically monitoring remote access; and
- revoking remote access.

7.7.3.3.1.2 IT Manager The IT Manager shall be the central authority for managing remote access. The responsibilities of this role shall include:

- ensuring that adequate remote access controls are in place;
- performing risk assessments, in association with the ISM; and
- reviewing remote access rights for third parties.

7.7.3.3.1.3 Information security manager The ISM shall be the central authority for approving remote access. The responsibilities of this role shall include:

- ensuring that adequate remote access controls are in place;
- performing 2nd party audits on suppliers who have remote access, as defined in Chapter 4, Section 4.9.2.
- performing risk assessments, in association with the IT Manager; and
- reviewing all remote access rights for continued business need on a regular basis.

7.7.3.4 Granting remote access

The procedures for granting remote access shall be as follows:

1. A Line Manager sends a request for remote access to the Service Desk, with the details after they have filled in the Account Management Form.
2. The Service Desk shall check the request to ensure that all the required details are available including the expiry date of the needed access, log it in the Service Desk system, and then advise the IT Manager.
3. The IT Manager and the ISM shall assess the requirements of the remote access and grant or refuse access. If appropriate a risk assessment shall be performed—this shall be based on the extent of remote access required and the sensitivity of information accessible.
4. The IT Manager shall confirm the decision to the Service Desk. Any additional details, such as the risk assessment shall also be recorded.
5. The Service Desk shall log the decision in Service Desk system and email the Requestor. If access is granted, the IT Department shall implement the relevant access process. If appropriate, the change shall be processed through the Change Management Process.

   Warning: Contracts or Non-Disclosure Agreements (NDAs) for third parties and Confidentiality Agreements for employees shall be in place before remote access is enabled.
6. The Service Desk shall add the new remote access user to the authorised remote access list.

7.7.3.5 Reviewing and revoking remote access

The procedures for reviewing and revoking remote access shall be as follows:

1. Every 3 months, or at any time when required for operational reasons, the IT Manager and the ISM shall check the remote access list to determine whether remote access is still required (e.g. if a third-party support contract has expired, or an employee with remote access leaves, or there is no longer a business need for the access, then the remote access shall be revoked).
2. The IT Manager shall email the Service Desk and confirms those remote access accounts that are no longer required.
3. The Service Desk shall log the details in Service Desk system and then blocks access to secure systems for the identified user(s). The user shall be removed from the remote access list.
4. The removal shall be confirmed to the original Requestor.

7.7.4 Managing backups

The IT Department shall be responsible for ensuring that servers are properly backed up, are recoverable, and the information is safeguarded.

7.7.4.1 An overview of backups

All information in the laboratory shall be stored on relevant dedicated servers, whether this is in the ERMS or other dedicated information repositories. In the case of laptops, data shall be stored locally until it can be uploaded to the relevant server as a manual or automated process.

Cloud storage shall only be used where the data stored in the cloud is encrypted with the encryption being approved by the ISM.

Servers shall be backed up as below:

- Cloud backup shall be used where approved by the ISM and the IT Manager; for current and archived forensic cases and other operational data;
- physical backup media shall be cycled off site to a location remote from the office to ensure that any event that affects the site shall not also affect the remote location;
- closed forensic cases and business data shall be considered for archival according to the Document Retention Policy, as defined in Chapter 4, Appendix 26;
- daily backups of all work directories shall be taken overnight on every weekday and on the weekend;
- redirection of users' home directories, and the use of online synchronisation shall be implemented as this ensures that the users' files are on the appropriate server(s), and shall be backed up automatically when the server is backed up;
- the backup types are all full backups;
- where possible, laptops and other mobile devices shall use local cached file copies, and be automatically synchronised when attached to the local network; and
- where possible, no business critical data shall be only stored on local hard drives, as these shall not be backed up by the centralised backup system. Those using laptops or other nonoffice based information processing resources shall ensure that all of their information is uploaded to the centralised information processing resources so that it can be included in the overnight backup process. However, to overcome the possibility of this process failing, technology shall be used to back up all local drives on laptops to a third party where they shall be securely stored in an encrypted format.

7.7.4.2 Roles and responsibilities

7.7.4.2.1 IT Manager

The IT Manager shall be the central authority for backups. The responsibilities of this role shall include, but not be limited to:

- analysing the failure of overnight backup jobs and implementing appropriate resolution actions;
- authorising the secure destruction of damaged backup media, as defined in Chapter 12, Section 12.3.14.10;
- checking the completion of overnight backup jobs;
- ensuring that adequate server access controls are in place; and
- liaising with the Information Asset Owners and Custodians about backup requirements.

7.7.4.2.2 IT Department

The IT Department shall carry out all backup, restoration, and associated backup tasks.

7.7.4.2.3 Information Asset Owners

The Information Asset Owner (or their Custodian) shall have ownership responsibility for backups, as defined in Chapter 12, Section 12.3.14.7. The responsibilities of this role shall include:

- determining the value of their business information;
- determining, in conjunction with the IT Manager, the backup requirements;
- reviewing the backup processes for continued business need; and
- requesting changes to the backup process as required.

7.7.4.3 Checking daily backups

Each workday morning the IT Manager (or their nominated deputy) shall check the overnight backups to see whether any backup jobs have failed or have not fully completed.

Causes for any job to fail shall be determined and logged as an incident in the Service Desk.

Any jobs that have to be re-run shall be re-run, otherwise the IT Manager may decide to abandon the backup for the day.

The Daily Backup checklist shall be updated by the IT Department and signed off by the IT Manager (or their nominated deputy) and filed, where appropriate. Where records are retained on the server, the full detail of the manual process is not required. The Overnight Backup Checklist is defined in the Appendix 30.

7.7.4.4 Performing restores from a backup

The procedures for restoring files from a backup shall be as follows:

1. An employee contacts the Service Desk and requests a restore.
2. The Service Desk shall discuss the request with the user and determines the date on which the data was last available.
3. The Service Desk shall assign the restore job to a member of the IT Department.
4. The relevant backup media shall be recovered and mounted unless it is easier and faster to restore from the Cloud backup.
5. The relevant files shall be recovered and the employee advised.
6. The backup media shall be returned to store, if appropriate, and the job closed.

7.7.4.5 Disposing of damaged backup media

During the backup process, backup media are occasionally damaged and cannot be used again. Any damaged backup media shall be securely destroyed by the ISM, as defined in Chapter 12, Section 12.3.14.10.

7.7.4.6 Tape cleaning and re-tensioning

Tape cleaning and re-tensioning shall be carried out according to the manufacturers' instructions. A record of this shall be recorded on the Overnight Backup Checklist as defined in Appendix 30.

7.7.5 Synchronising system clocks

Using synchronised clocks is essential for assisting with system problem diagnosis and resolution and ensure reliable event logging, automatic software updates, and other time-related security activities. If clocks are not synchronised and accurate, security investigations will probably be hampered, and the evidence uncovered may be unreliable, and therefore unusable as evidence for disciplinary action or prosecution.

The Network Time Protocol (NTP) protocol with a time source, obtained from the NASA or the US Navy NTP servers and distributed via a specified server shall be used to ensure synchronised time is implemented across the estate. The following controls shall be in place:

- a periodic resynchronisation shall be performed to correct system clock drifts from NASA NTP Server.
- all clocks on the servers, workstations, laptops, PCs, CCTV, access control systems, and any other device that contains a clock that is used as part of operations shall be automatically set to UTC standard time.
- clocks shall be reset following a system crash, a power outage, an operating system upgrade, or some other event that might affect the clocks, where appropriate.

The procedures for checking system clocks shall be as follows:

1. The IT Department check (or set) the system clock as follows:
   - when installing a new device that contains a clock, the system clock shall be set to the correct time;
   - on a system failure that affects operations a check shall be performed to reset the clock to the correct time, if required.
   - The IT Department shall email details of any synchronisation failures, and the corrective action taken, to the IT Manager. If there is a failure it shall be raised as an information security incident in the Service Desk.
   - The ISM shall review system clocks as part of the internal audits, as defined in the IMS calendar.

Appendix 1—Policy for securing IT cabling

All power and telecommunications cabling used shall be safeguarded from interception or damage to minimise security risks and protect against loss of information and information processing facilities. The following standard controls shall be implemented to secure IT cabling:

- all IT cabling shall be CAT 5 or Cat 6 certified;
- all wiring cabinets shall be physically secured, and access shall only be provided to authorised IT Department employees, where necessary, or possible. They shall be defined as secure areas within the laboratory;
- cabling shall be routed through secure ducting;
- cabling that passes through public areas shall be secured to as great a degree as is possible (e.g. fibre or secure ducting). Passing through public areas shall be avoided if at all possible;
- fibre cabling shall be used, when possible;
- network elements shall be sited to maximise access protection, where necessary or possible;
- no CAT 5 or Cat 6 cabling shall be no greater than 100 m in length;
- power cabling shall be physically segregated from communications cabling; and
- underground ducting shall be used where possible.

For sensitive or critical systems further controls to consider shall include:

- consideration of TEMPEST shielding;
- initiation of technical sweeps and physical inspections for unauthorised devices being attached to the cables;
- use of alternative routings and/or transmission media providing appropriate security; and
- use of electromagnetic shielding to protect the cables.

This policy is issued and maintained by the IT Manager. All Managers shall be directly responsible for implementing the policy within their operational area, and for its adherence by their employees.

This policy shall be regularly reviewed to ensure that it remains valid.

This policy has been approved by the top management.

All employees shall comply with this policy.

Appendix 2—Policy for siting and protecting IT equipment

The following rules shall govern the physical positioning of IT equipment:

- all information processing equipment shall always be placed in an environmentally controlled location;
- all information processing equipment shall always be stored in secure locations with restricted access to authorised employees and authorised visitors only; and
- printers or other output devices which are used for handling sensitive information shall always be stored in a secure location.

Physical positioning of IT equipment shall be determined by many factors; however, the IT Department shall always follow these guidelines when determining the location of equipment and information:

- always minimise potential damage from electrical or electromagnetic interference;
- equipment and information shall always be sited so that unnecessary access to a work area is minimised;
- equipment siting shall always be located to minimise risks of theft or misuse;
- potential security risks from employees and visitors shall always be considered in ensuring that those with no 'need to access' have no access rights to information or information processing facilities; and
- when considering risks from fire, flooding, humidity, and other potential environmental hazards, equipment shall be sited to minimise those risks, consider implementing environmental monitoring devices, where appropriate.

This policy is issued and maintained by the IT Manager. All Managers shall be directly responsible for implementing the policy within their operational area, and for its adherence by their employees.

This policy shall be regularly reviewed to ensure that it remains valid.

This policy has been approved by the top management.

All employees shall comply with this policy.

Appendix 3—ISO 20000-1 mapping

Note

Not all controls in ISO 20000-1 have been implemented in FCL. The mapping below identifies the controls that have been implemented in FCL.

ISO 20000-1 Section	Control	Procedure(s)
4	Context of the organisation	
4.1	Understanding the organisation and its context	Chapter 4, Section 4.4.1
4.2	Understanding the needs and expectations of interested parties	Chapter 4, Section 4.4.2
4.3	Determining the scope of the service management system	Chapter 4, Section 4.4.3
4.4	Service management system	Covered in part by multiple separate sections in each chapter
		Section 7.4.7.1
		Section 7.4.7.2
		Section 7.4.7.3
		Section 7.4.8
		Section 7.4.9
5	Leadership	
5.1	Leadership and commitment	Chapter 4, Section 4.5.1
5.2	Policy	Chapter 4, Section 4.5.2
5.2.1	Establishing the service management policy	Chapter 4, Appendix 18
5.2.2	Communicating the service management policy	Chapter 4, Section 4.7.4
5.3	Organisational roles, responsibilities, and authorities	Chapter 4, Section 4.5.4
		Appendix 4
		Appendix 24
		Appendix 25
		Appendix 26
		Appendix 27
6	Planning	
6.1	Actions to address risks and opportunities	Chapter 4, Section 4.6.1.1
6.2	Service management objectives and planning to achieve them	Not implemented in FCL
6.2.1	Establish objectives	Not implemented in FCL
6.2.2	Plan to achieve objectives	Not implemented in FCL
6.3	Plan the service management system	Chapter 4, Section 4.6.2
7	Support of the service management system	
7.1	Resources	Chapter 4, Section 4.7.1
7.2	Competence	Chapter 4, Section 4.7.2
7.3	Awareness	Chapter 4, Section 4.7.3

ISO 20000-1 Section	Control	Procedure(s)
7.4	Communication	Chapter 4, Section 4.7.4
7.5	Documented information	Chapter 4, Section 4.7.5
7.5.1	General	Chapter 4, Section 4.7.5.1
7.5.2	Creating and updating documented information	Chapter 4, Section 4.7.5.3
7.5.3	Control of documented information	Chapter 4, Section 4.7.5.3
7.5.4	Service management system documented information	This Chapter, Section 7.5 The IMS
7.6	Knowledge	Not implemented in FCL
8	Operation of the service management system	
8.1	Operational planning and control	Not implemented in FCL
8.2	Service portfolio	Not implemented in FCL
8.2.1	Service delivery	Not implemented in FCL
8.2.2	Plan the services	Not implemented in FCL
8.2.3	Control of parties involved in the service lifecycle	Not implemented in FCL
8.2.4	Service catalogue management	Not implemented in FCL
8.2.5	Asset management	Chapter 12, Section 12.3.14
8.2.6	Configuration management	Section 7.4.5 Appendix 17 Appendix 18 Appendix 19
8.3	Relationship and agreement	Chapter 14, Section 14.2.1
8.3.1	General	Chapter 14, Section 14.2.1
8.3.2	Business relationship management	Chapter 14, Sections 14.2.1, 14.5 and 14.6
8.3.3	Service level management	Chapter 14, Section 14.4 Chapter 14, Section 14.4
8.3.4	Supplier management	Chapter 14, Section 14.4, Sections 14.5 and 14.6 Chapter 14
8.4	Supply and demand	
8.4.1	Budgeting and accounting for services	Not implemented in FCL
8.4.2	Demand management	Not implemented in FCL
8.4.3	Capacity management	Section 7.4.6 Appendix 21 Appendix 22
8.5	Service design, build and transition	Not implemented in FCL
8.5.1	Change management	Section 7.4.3
8.5.2	Service design and transition	Not implemented in FCL

Continued

ISO 20000-1 Section	Control	Procedure(s)
8.5.3	Release and deployment management	Section 7.4.4
		Appendix 14
		Appendix 15
		Appendix 16
8.6	Resolution and fulfilment	Not implemented in FCL
8.6.1	Incident management	Section 7.4.1
		Appendix 5
		Appendix 6
		Appendix 7
		Appendix 8
8.6.2	Service request management	Not implemented in FCL
8.6.3	Problem management	Section 7.4.2
		Appendix 9
8.7	Service assurance	
8.7.1	Service availability management	Chapter 13
8.7.2	Service continuity management	Chapter 13
8.7.3	Information security management	Chapter 12
9	Performance evaluation	
9.1	Monitoring, measurement, analysis, and evaluation	Chapter 4, Section 4.9.1
		Chapter 16, Section 16.2.1
9.2	Internal audit	Chapter 4, Section 4.9.2
		Chapter 16, Section 16.2.5
9.3	Management review	Chapter 4, Section 4.9.3
		Chapter 16, Section 16.2.9
9.4	Service reporting	Chapter 14, Section 14.4.2
		Chapter 14, Section 14.5.3
		Chapter 16
10	Improvement	
10.1	Nonconformity and corrective action	Chapter 4, Section 4.10.1
		Chapter 4, Section 4.10.2
		Chapter 4, Section 4.10.3
		Chapter 4, Section 4.10.4
		Chapter 4, Section 4.10.5
10.2	Continual improvement	Chapter 4, Section 4.10
		Chapter 4, Appendix 24

Appendix 4—Service Desk Manager, job description

Objective and role

The role of the Service Desk Manager (SDM) shall be to provide service support for all users of IT technology within the laboratory and for clients. This scope of responsibility is to capture, log, and provide immediate first line support to all users and coordinate all other issues relating to products and services within the laboratory. Regular reporting of all calls (incidents, problems, complaints, service requests, and service level reporting) shall be produced from the Service Desk to assist in the continuous improvement process. Liaison internally with 2nd line Support and external 3rd line Support shall be undertaken.

Problems and challenges

The SDM faces the challenge of meeting client demand and service levels with limited resources in a rapidly changing environment. As new systems and applications are implemented, the SDM shall ensure that the Service Desk is properly trained to handle all calls.

The SDM shall be able to communicate effectively with all levels of employees, third-party vendors, and clients.

Principal accountabilities

The SDM shall:

- identify and initiate resolutions to all client service issues and concerns associated with all IT applications, computer equipment, hardware, software, and service requests to the client's satisfaction;
- plan and coordinate the training for installation and implementation of desktops, client servers, hardware, and software according to the IT Department standards and procedures;
- assist HR in analysing the training needs of users, developing user curricula, providing quality individual and group training programs designed to ensure maximum utilisation of IT within the laboratory;
- maintains software and hardware versions, maintenance levels, registration and inventory to provide upgrades as necessary and ensure appropriate security levels are maintained;
- maintain current technical expertise in the rapidly changing technology and utilise state-of-the-art techniques when implementing any IT-related solutions;
- prepare daily, weekly, monthly, and quarterly status reports quantitatively reporting results of relevant Service Desk activities;
- recognise and identify potential areas where existing policies and procedures require change, or where new ones need to be developed, especially regarding future business expansion;
- fulfil business requirements in terms of providing work coverage and administrative notification at all times;
- train, supervise, assign projects to evaluate and be responsible for hiring/termination of Service Desk employees to maintain optimum performance of the Service Desk;
- interface with external industrial and academic organisations in order to maintain state-of-the-art knowledge in emerging service management issues and to enhance FCL's image as a first-class solution provider utilising the latest thinking in this field;
- adhere to established policies, standards, and procedures; and
- perform all responsibilities in accordance with, or in excess of, the requirements of the Integrated Management System.

Authority

The SDM shall have the authority to:

- resolve problems with all products and services;
- resolve all client related issues reported to the Service Desk;
- plan and coordinate implementation of all internal IT hardware, software, and infrastructure;
- carry out relevant training for internal users on relevant IT issues;
- assist HR in identifying training needs and possible solutions;
- work with all users and with external vendors;

- identify potential service level problems before they occur and implement solutions; and
- schedule and prioritise work to accommodate business requirements and client needs while minimising impact on current projects and service delivery.

Contacts

Internal

Contacts with those in the operational areas that directly affect service delivery. This will include a variety of employees and clients.

External

Suppliers of hardware, software, other relevant services and clients that the Service Desk supports.

Reports to

The Service Desk Manager shall report to:
- The IT Manager.

Appendix 5—Incident Manager, job description

Objective and role

The Incident Manager (IM) shall be responsible for ensuring that normal service in the laboratory is restored as soon as possible, after an information security incident that affects the provision of products and service(s).

Failure to provide appropriate services is defined as failing to meet an agreed Service Level Agreement for clients.

The role is closely integrated with the Business Continuity Manager (BCM) and the Service Desk Manager (SDM).

Problems and challenges

Information security incident management is an absolutely critical function of everyday business operations. For this responsibility, there is no substitute for advanced planning.

The IM faces the challenge of developing ever-current response plans to a volatile set of possible information security incidents, and ever changing threat landscape and an ever changing array of threat actors that may affect service delivery. These can be internal, external, via the client or via the supply chain.

Principal accountabilities

The IM shall:

- establish procedures and priorities for the incident management process;
- respond to all reported information security incidents;
- log, categorise and prioritise information security incidents;
- provide initial information security incident support;
- respond to and record actions, as appropriate, relating to the information security incident, including the invocation of Business Continuity Plans (BCPs);
- undertake information security incident investigation and diagnosis;
- implement information security incident resolution or recovery using workarounds;
- close information security incidents after confirmation from affected clients;
- provide input to the BCP for critical information security incident handling;
- evaluate information security incidents to determine if they are problems to be referred to the Problem Manager;
- ensure adherence to the relevant SLAs, even during information security incidents;
- produce regular information security incident management reports as required to all interested parties;
- provide input to the Service Improvement Plan (SIP);
- ensure that all information security incident management procedures are documented and maintained;

- perform risk assessments and implement risk management to reduce risk to an acceptable level to reduce the likelihood of service interruptions, where practical and cost justifiable;
- assess changes submitted to the Change Advisory Board (CAB) for impact on the service provisions;
- attend the CAB, as appropriate;
- define direction of in-house technical training seminars to improve overall employee awareness, response time, and ability to look into future business continuity and business recovery requirements;
- participate in international, national and local SIG presentations, and publish articles describing FCL's activities and assessments of incident management and business recovery and how they relate to the business;
- develop and manage effective working relationships with all appropriate internal and external interested parties;
- maintain external links to other companies in the industry to gain competitive assessments and share information, where appropriate;
- identify the emerging information technologies to be assimilated, integrated and introduced which could significantly impact FCL's information security incident management and business recovery ability;
- interface with external industrial and academic organisations in order to maintain state-of-the-art knowledge in emerging information security incident management and business recovery issues and to enhance FCL's image as a first-class solution provider utilising the latest thinking in this field;
- adhere to established policies, standards, and procedures; and
- perform all responsibilities in accordance with, or in excess of, the requirements of the Integrated Management System.

Authority

The IM shall have the authority to:

- attend the CAB and comment on proposed changes;
- develop, maintain, and implement, if necessary, the incident response procedures and processes; and
- provide improvements to the SIP.

Contacts

Internal

This position requires contact with all levels of employees to determine business recovery and deal with information security incidents.

External

Externally, the IM shall maintain contacts with suppliers and vendors, as required. Additionally, contact shall be maintained with clients to determine their requirements as well as insurers to ensure that insurance coverage is appropriate.

Reports to

The IM shall report to:
- The IT Manager and top management, as required.

Appendix 6—Information security incident status levels

The following status levels shall be used for information security incidents:

Status	Description
Opened	When no action has been taken on an information security incident (usually when the incident has been logged)
In Progress	Move into this status when actively working on the information security incident (if started working on another incident, then this status remains current)
Pending	Move into this status when working on the ticket but not actively working on (e.g. request for a meeting room setup/desk move/started a virus scan on a machine and have moved onto another ticket)

Continued

Status	Description
Contact Made	Move into this status when attempts to contact the user via phone or email and by leaving an information security incident comment explaining attempted contact have been made for further information (if the user does not respond within 3 days the ticket shall be automatically closed)
Response Made	This is a system generated status. When an information security incident contact has been made and the user responds via email the system shall move the status into 'Response Made'
Need More Info	Move into this status when the user has not provided enough information. This shall always be followed up by a call and a comment in the ticket stating that a request for more information has been made
Awaiting 3rd Party	Move into this status when the information security incident has been escalated to external 3rd line Support and are awaiting further communication from them
Ordered Awaiting Delivery	Move into this status once product has been received and the job number for implementation is available
Re-opened	This is a system generated status. When an information security incident is closed and the user emails back about the information security incident, it will re-open a closed information security incident and this is moved to this status
Escalated	This is a system generated status. When an information security incident has passed the required time agreed to act on an incident, the system moves this into this status and emails an escalation email
Resolved	Move to this status when the Service Desk think that they have resolved the information security incident, but still need client approval to close the information security incident
Closed	Move to this status when the information security incident is closed and the client confirms satisfaction with the resolution

Appendix 7—Information security incident priority levels

FCL shall correct, restore normal business service and operations or provide a workaround solution, to all information security incidents and service requests according to their classification. Information security incident classifications, and target resolution times for each information security incident classification, are defined for clients in their specific SLAs for individual services where required, but the standard ones used are defined below:

Priority	Category	Status	Resources affected	Example	Target response time	Target resolution time (h)
1	Critical	Business critical failure (critical incident)	All or most clients, business severely disrupted	Failure of central IT systems and services	Immediate	1
2	High	Serious incident	Most (or a high proportion) of clients affected to a fairly serious degree, or a smaller number of important clients severely affected	ADSL line failure, failure of service from third-party supplier, service performance severely degraded	10 min	4
3	Medium	Moderate incident	Most slightly affected, or a fewer number of clients are more seriously affected, but business operational	New users, new equipment, new minor changes to offices, upgrades to equipment and software, telecoms installations, moves, additions and changes	1 h	8
4	Low	Low level incident	Minimal impact on the client's day-to-day business		1 day	24

Appendix 8—Service Desk feedback form

The following details are included on the feedback form to evaluate the Service Desk's performance:

- overall service received from the Service Desk;
- initial information received on contacting the Service Desk;
- desk side service received (if applicable);
- accuracy and completeness of technical information (if applicable);
- product knowledge relating to the call (if applicable);
- courtesy and professionalism;
- availability of resources to complete service request; and
- timeliness of closure.

The above are all scored as follows:

0—not applicable.
1—extremely dissatisfied.
2—dissatisfied.
3—neither dissatisfied nor satisfied.
4—satisfied.
5—extremely satisfied.

This provides quantitative feedback while there is a text box to allow for any recommendations for improvement that provides for qualitative feedback.

Appendix 9—Problem Manager, job description

Objective and role

To minimise the adverse effects of incidents and problems on the and its internal and external clients caused by errors within the IT infrastructure and prevent the recurrence of information security incidents related to those problems.

Problems and challenges

The Problem Manager (PM) is challenged by having to identify problems from information security incidents and fault reports and then take action to resolve them and prevent their reoccurrence.

Principal accountabilities

The PM shall:

- develop, maintain, review efficiency, and effectiveness of the problem management process;
- review the effectiveness and efficiency of proactive problem management activities;
- manage all problems;
- prevent information security incidents from happening, where possible;
- minimise the effect of information security incidents that do occur;
- determine root causes for information security incidents and uses this as input to the problem solving process;
- maintain information about known errors and workarounds;
- provide workarounds, where available, to the Incident Manager while developing final solutions for known errors;
- maintain, in association with the Service Desk, trending information for the early identification of problems;
- log, categorise, and prioritise problem resolution;
- provide initial problem support;
- investigate and diagnose problems;
- close problems;
- maintain the known error database (KEDB);
- ensure adherence to the relevant Service Level Agreements (SLAs);
- produce management information;
- allocate resources for problem resolution internally or externally, as required;

- raise Requests for Change (RsfC) where appropriate;
- assess changes submitted to the Change Advisory Board (CAB) for impact on the service provisions;
- attend the CAB, as appropriate;
- assist in handling major information security incidents, if required;
- prevent problems from recurring, where possible;
- develop plans for migration of problem management policies and procedures to support future business direction;
- develop the long-range problem management strategy;
- participate in international, national, and local SIG presentations, and publishes articles describing FCL's problem management initiatives and how they relate to the business;
- develop and manage effective working relationships with all appropriate internal and external interested parties;
- maintain external links to other companies in the industry to gain competitive assessments and share information, where appropriate;
- identify the emerging information technologies to be assimilated, integrated, and introduced within FCL which could significantly impact FCL's product and service offering SLAs;
- interface with external industrial and academic organisations in order to maintain state-of-the-art knowledge in emerging problem management issues and to enhance FCL's image as a first-class solution provider utilising the latest thinking in this field;
- adhere to established policies, standards, and procedures; and
- perform all responsibilities in accordance with, or in excess of, the requirements of the Integrated Management System.

Authority

The PM shall have the authority to:

- be the central focus for all problem management issues;
- utilise appropriate resources to assist in problem resolution;
- monitor all operational processes for trend analysis for incidents and problems; and
- establish and make decisions about management reporting methods, and outputs.

Contacts

Internal

Contacts shall be throughout the whole business who have reported faults or issues that turn out to be problems. Close cooperation with the Incident Manager, the Service Desk and the ISM will be routine and contact with other managers will be as required.

External

Appropriate Special Interest Groups (SIGs), other Problem Managers, external vendors, and service providers.

Reports to

The PM shall report to:
- the IT Manager.

Appendix 10—Contents of the SIP

While a SIP can relate to internal initiatives (e.g. optimise resource usage) or client driven ones (e.g. reviewing SLAs that are no longer achievable), the following template shall be used as the basis of all SIPs. It shall be amended as required based on the specific SIP being implemented:

- process or service to be improved;
- process or service Owner;
- SIP owner (who may or may not be the process or service owner);
- management approval;

- SIP priority—agreed by top management;
- description of the SIP;
- source of the requirement being defined (e.g. internal review, internal audit, client feedback etc.);
- business case, including:
  - expected outcome of the initiative;
  - cost estimate; and
  - desired result of the SIP (e.g. a specific decrease in cost for providing a service to clients, a new service for clients, etc.)
- implementation schedule, and for each milestone:
  - description of the deliverable to be completed;
  - key deliverables;
  - owner of each milestone; and
  - target delivery date;
- monitoring and reporting; and
- training requirements.

Note

SIPs are typically IT Infrastructure Library (ITIL) based, but they shall also be used as part of the continuous improvement process for non-IT improvement in the Plan, Do, Check, Act (PDCA) (W Edwards Deming) cycle.

Appendix 11—Change categories

The following change categories shall be used with their notification times:

Category	Description	Minimum notification time to clients
Emergency	A top priority change that needs to be implemented immediately to prevent or rectify a serious service failure within the laboratory	Immediately
Normal	A change which could cause an impact on services to users, multiple areas or business groups. Typical examples are software upgrades, changes to critical applications, infrastructure upgrades, router moves, new service provision	5 working days
Standard	A change that potentially has minimal effect on users. Typical examples include user moves, printer additions, documentation	None

Appendix 12—Change Manager, job description

Objective and role

The Change Manager (CM) shall be responsible for managing the quality of the production environment by implementing and overseeing a Change Management Process for promoting products and services from the test environment to the production environment. This shall result in high-quality systems, thus providing internal and external clients with quality products and services.

The CM shall also define 'standard changes'.

Problems and challenges

The challenges facing the CM involve facilitating a 'zero defect' environment for all production and operational systems. This shall involve managing the review of new or modified products and services, keeping abreast of the continuous flow of changes within the volatile development environment, controlling access to source and object code, and overseeing the airtight methodology for running and documenting nonstandard or one-time tasks.

Principal accountabilities

The CM shall:

- manage the change control system and procedures for the movement of systems and documents into the production environment;
- maintain or develop change control procedures as needed;
- receive, log, and allocate priorities to all Requests for Change (RsfC), and reject impractical RsfC;
- ensure that all RsfC have been fully completed as required by the Change Management Process and its supporting forms;
- categorise received RsfC;
- define and manage duties of Change Advisory Board (CAB);
- table all RsfC for CAB meetings where appropriate;
- issue agenda and issue all RsfC to CAB members in advance of CAB meetings to allow prior consideration;
- decide who will attend meetings depending on nature of the RsfC;
- convene CAB or emergency CAB (ECAB) meetings for urgent RsfC;
- chair all CAB and ECAB meetings;
- authorise accepted changes;
- produce and distribute via the Service Desk, a Forward Schedule of Changes (FSC);
- coordinate all change building, testing, and implementations;
- own and maintain all change logs;
- manage all actions to correct problems and feedback to Service Improvement Plan (SIP);
- review all changes to ensure compliance to objectives, appropriately referring all failures and back outs;
- review all RsfC awaiting consideration and action;
- analyse change records to determine trends and apparent problems, and feedback to appropriate parties;
- closes RsfC;
- produce regular and accurate management reports on changes to the operational the systems;
- assure the integrity of all Code Management System (CMS) libraries. This shall involve overseeing a system of organisation for these libraries;
- maintain training and awareness for employees and third-party suppliers acting on their behalf, on the importance and impact of maintaining stringent controls;
- manage the Post Implementation Review (PIR) process;
- participate in international, national and local SIG presentations, and publishes articles describing FCL's change management system how it relates to the business;
- develop and manage effective working relationships with all appropriate internal and external interested parties;
- maintain external links to other companies in the industry to gain competitive assessments and share information, where appropriate;
- identify the emerging information technologies to be assimilated, integrated and introduced within FCL, which could significantly impact FCL's Change Management Processes;
- interfaces with external industrial and academic organisations in order to maintain state-of-the-art knowledge in emerging change management issues and to enhance FCL's image as a first-class solution provider utilising the latest thinking in this field;
- adheres to established policies, standards, and procedures; and
- performs all responsibilities in accordance with, or in excess of, the requirements of the Integrated Management System.

Authority

The CM shall have the authority to:

- determine the categorisation of changes submitted via the RfC process;
- ensure that the appropriate level of authorisation is present for each RfC submitted;
- establish and make decisions about the Change Management Process;
- establish the CAB;
- make changes to the Change Management Process as required; and
- manage the CAB process with the ability to co-opt required employees for CAB meetings.

Contacts

Internal contacts

This position requires contact with the business, Project Teams and their Project Managers, and the IT Department.

External contacts

The primary external contacts shall be with contract service providers, clients, vendors, and industry peers. Contact with information technology product and service companies shall also made on a periodic basis.

Reports to

The CM shall report to:
- the IT Manager.

Appendix 13—Standard requirements of a request for change (RfC)

The following are the standard template for requirements for an RfC:

- change name;
- date created;
- date required;
- change owner name;
- change owner contact details;
- description of change;
- reason for change;
- location of change;
- change type;
- whom the change will affect and to what level;
- products and services affected by the change
- duration of the change;
- duration of impact to users of affected products and services;
- support resources required;
- change category;
- change window;
- impact to users of the 's products and services;
- impact if the change is not carried out;
- risk assessment;
- change status;
- reason for rejection, if appropriate;
- details of the configuration of the change;
- communications plan;
- period of notification prior to the change;
- testing results and test packs;
- UAT sign off by the business, if appropriate;
- back out plan;
- prerequisites and dependencies;
- change review decision;
- change progress and actions;
- change outcome;
- reason for failure, if appropriate;
- results of post implementation review;
- approvals; and
- closure date.

Appendix 14—Emergency change policy

The IT Department shall operate a strict policy for emergency changes. The policy is:

- no standard change (of any priority) shall be implemented via the emergency change process;
- only changes that prevent or rectify a serious service failure within the business shall be classed as an emergency;
- only changes designated as 'Emergency' by the Change Manager shall be implemented immediately;
- all clients (Internal and External) that may be affected by an emergency change shall be informed about downtime, when practical, during an emergency change; and
- all emergency changes shall be fully documented and then processed retrospectively through the standard Change Management Process.

This policy is issued and maintained by the IT Manager. All Managers shall be directly responsible for implementing the policy within their operational area, and for its adherence by their employees.

This system shall be regularly reviewed to ensure that it remains valid.

This policy has been approved by the top management.

All employees shall comply with this policy.

Appendix 15—Release Management Policy

The Release Management Policy shall:

- ensure that all types of release, standard, normal, and emergency, including hardware and software are performed in a controlled manner;
- ensure that all releases are performed at the time agreed with clients to minimise service disruption but in line with the laboratory operational situation;
- ensure that releases shall only be performed following full approval through the change management system;
- ensure that all releases planned and documented by the Release Manager, in conjunction with external clients where appropriate, shall be uniquely identified and contain full descriptions of what is contained in the release;
- ensure that a release shall only be approved for implementation by the Release Manager after all planning and implementation activities are agreed within the and clients, where appropriate;
- ensure that, where appropriate, several releases shall be grouped into a single or reduced number of releases to minimise service disruption;
- ensure that the processes and procedures for building, testing, and distributing releases shall be fully documented and agreed; and
- ensure that the success of a release is verified and confirmed by the Release Manager and is accepted by internal and external clients, as appropriate.

This policy is issued and maintained by the Release Manager. All Managers shall be directly responsible for implementing the policy within their operational area, and for its adherence by their employees.

This system shall be regularly reviewed to ensure that it remains valid.

This policy has been approved by the top management.

All employees shall comply with this policy.

Appendix 16—Release Manager, job description

Objective and role

The Release Manager's (RM) role shall be to plan and oversee the successful rollout of all software, hardware, and changes into the production environment. This shall include:

- planning the test environment;
- planning the actual releases;
- testing the release packages;
- testing the deployment environment;
- managing the release and deployment; and
- post implementation reviews (PIRs).

Problems and challenges

The RM is challenged with ensuring that only approved releases are promoted to the production environment.

Principal accountabilities

The RM shall:

- design and implement an effective Release Policy;
- plan and manage all software and hardware rollouts;
- manage extensive testing of planned releases to predefined acceptance criteria, including:
  - scope of release;
  - effectiveness of release with third-party suppliers;
  - planning rollback models;
  - planning building of tests;
  - planning pilot test phases in test environment;
  - service operation test;
  - service operation readiness test;
  - implementing the pilot;
  - verification of implemented deployment.
- sign off releases that pass acceptance testing for release implementation.
- ensure accurate audits performed prior to and following implementation of changes to Configuration Items (CIs).
- builds, maintains and manages the Definitive Software Library (DSL) and Definitive Hardware Library (DHL).
- design, verify, and test appropriate Release Back-Out Plan (RBOP).
- identifies appropriate resources required to support the RBOP;
- plan the release and delivery;
- manage the resources needed for the release, testing and deployment;
- create the release packages;
- manage the deployment team;
- develop plans for migration of release management policies and procedures to support future business direction;
- transfer and deployment of the release;
- remove of old, obsolete, or superfluous deployments;
- ensure that users can actually use the deployed service as required/expected;
- develop the long range release management strategy;
- make recommendations to the Service Improvement Plan (SIP);
- participate in international, national, and local SIG presentations, and publishes articles describing FCL's release management initiatives and how they relate to the business;
- develop and manage effective working relationships with all appropriate internal and external interested parties;
- maintain external links to other companies in the industry to gain competitive assessments and share information, where appropriate;
- identify the emerging information technologies to be assimilated, integrated and introduced within FCL which could significantly impact its service offering SLAs;
- interface with external industrial and academic organisations in order to maintain state-of-the-art knowledge in emerging release management issues and to enhance FCL's image as a first-class solution provider utilising the latest thinking in this field;
- adhere to established policies, standards, and procedures; and
- perform all responsibilities in accordance with, or in excess of, the requirements of the Integrated Management System.

Authority

The RM shall have the authority to:

- be the central focus for all release management issues;
- define the planning and timing of all releases and deployments;
- control all releases into, and changes to, the production environment;

- define tools, processes and procedures for release and deployment;
- manage all resources for testing and deploying the release; and
- establish and make decisions about management reporting methods, and outputs.

Contacts

Internal

Contacts are with personnel in the operational areas which are directly affected by release management. This will specifically include the Configuration Manager and the Change Manager but may include a variety of other employees.

External

Those external shall be clients and their employees, who determine requirements for products and services.

Reports to

The RM shall report to:
- The IT Manager.

Appendix 17—Configuration management plan contents

The following is the basic plan template used in the laboratory, but it can be amended as required, depending on the specific requirements of a release.

- plan approval;
- introduction;
  - scope;
  - purpose;
  - system overview;
  - roles and responsibilities;
  - points of contact; and
  - resource requirements;
- configuration control;
  - Change Advisory Board;
  - configuration items;
  - baseline identification;
  - Configuration Management Data base (CMDB); and
  - the various configuration libraries and their maintenance.
- change control;
- configuration status accounting;
- configuration auditing;
- configuration management libraries;
- release management;
- tools;
- training;
- references; and
- acronyms and key terms.

Appendix 18—Configuration Management Policy

Configuration management is a set of techniques and procedures that provide the mechanism to manage configuration items.

The Configuration Management Policy shall ensure:

- control the versions of configuration items (CIs) in use, and maintain information on their status, ownership, and relationships;

- manage CIs by ensuring changes shall only be made with the agreement of appropriate authorities;
- audit the record of CIs to ensure it is accurate and relevant.
- ensure there is one configuration management process;
- represent the actual known state of the IT environment in the Configuration Management Database (CMDB);
- ensure each CI has an Owner responsible for ensuring CI data is complete, accurate and current;
- ensure that changes to the CMDB are authorised and implemented by authorised members of the IT Department;
- maintain configuration records in a timely manner; and
- regularly undertake exception reporting and formal CMDB audits;

Configuration management shall provide the assurance of product and service integrity and allow for a coherent set of information on configuration items to be held and maintained.

This policy is issued and maintained by the Configuration Manager. All Managers shall be directly responsible for implementing the policy within their operational area, and for its adherence by their employees.

The configuration management system shall provide the framework for the implementation of this policy and shall be supported by a comprehensive set of policies and procedures.

This policy shall be regularly reviewed to ensure that it remains valid.

This policy has been approved by the top management.

All employees shall comply with this policy.

Appendix 19—Configuration Manager, job description

Objective and role

The Configuration Manager (CfM) shall be responsible for ensuring that the Configuration Management Database (CMDB) is maintained for all Configuration Items (CIs) through the Change Management Process.

Problems and challenges

The CfM is challenged with having to maintain the CMDB with all CIs for all internal and external operations and clients.

Principal accountabilities

The CfM shall:

- produce and maintain Configuration Management Plan;
- populates and manage the CMDB;
- identify, manage, and control CIs;
- ensure consistency and accuracy of the CMDB so that the authorised state of the IT Infrastructure is properly reflected;
- implement consistent Change Management, Configuration Management and Release Management Processes;
- maintain control of hardware, technical standards, and all documents;
- provide supporting services (such as registration and checking) of releases delivered by 3rd parties;
- produce regular reports on the CMDB and all CI status;
- make recommendations to the Service Improvement Plan (SIP);
- ensure that the Configuration Management System (CMS) is aware of, and capable of coping with, future workloads and growth;
- ensure that all members of the IT Department are aware of and familiar with the CMS process and procedures appropriate to their work;
- define status accounting requirements to support all Service Management processes;
- aid with audit process, monitor exceptions and implement corrective actions;
- investigate problems caused by poor control and recommend remedial action;
- provide advice where release components should be located on infrastructure;
- advise internal and external projects on what to include in the Configuration Management System and Release Plans to ensure successful transfer to final service;
- develop plans for migration of configuration management policies and procedures to support future business direction;
- develop the long range configuration management strategy;

- define direction of in-house technical training seminars to improve overall employee awareness, response time, and ability to look into future configuration management requirements;
- participate in international, national, and local SIG presentations, and publishes articles describing FCL's configuration management activities and how they relate to the business;
- develop and manages effective working relationships with all appropriate internal and external interested parties;
- maintain external links to other companies in the industry to gain competitive assessments and share information, where appropriate;
- identify the emerging information technologies to be assimilated, integrated and introduced within FCL, which could significantly impact configuration demands;
- interface with external industrial and academic organisations in order to maintain state-of-the-art knowledge in emerging configuration management and to enhance FCL's image as a first-class solution provider utilising the latest thinking in this field;
- adhere to established policies, standards, and procedures; and
- perform all responsibilities in accordance with, or in excess of, the requirements of the Integrated Management System.

Authority

The CfM shall:

- be the central focus for all configuration management issues;
- define the requirements for the CMDB and the CMS; and
- establish and make decisions about configuration management reporting methods, and outputs.

Contacts

Internal contacts

This position requires contact with business and IT support personnel within the laboratory. This will specifically include the Release Manager and the Change Manager but may include a variety of employees.

External contacts

The primary external contacts are with clients, contract service providers, clients, vendors, and industry peers. Contact with information technology product and service companies is also made on a periodic basis.

Reports to

The CfM reports to:
- the IT Manager.

Appendix 20—Information stored in the DHL and DSL

Definitive Hardware Library

- site—where the equipment is installed;
- business stream—business stream which owns the equipment;
- group—the group within the business stream;
- name—name of the owner of the equipment;
- asset number—asset number of the equipment;
- item type—what the equipment is, i.e. workstation, server, printer etc.
- make/model—make and model of the equipment;
- processor—for workstations and servers, this fields records the processor type and speed;
- RAM—for workstations, servers, and some printers, this shows the amount of memory installed;
- hard disks—for workstations, servers, and some printers, this shows the size of the hard disk drives installed;
- monitor type—for workstations and servers, this shows the type of monitor the system has;
- monitor serial number—serial number of the screen associated with the workstation or server;

- operating system—operating system of the workstation or server;
- serial number—serial number of the device;
- MAC address—MAC address of the device;
- mobile number—for cell phones, his field records the mobile phone number of the unit;
- purchase date—date on the purchase order against which the goods were ordered;
- purchase order—the purchase order number for purchasing the device;
- install date—date when the unit was installed for the users;
- last health check—the date of the last health check carried out on the device;
- outside supplier—the supplier supporting the equipment in the event of a hardware failure;
- Service Desk ticket—the ticket against which the device was installed (this will be the change request ticket number for installation);
- modified by—the user ID of the last person to update the current record;
- modified date—the date when the record was last updated;
- comments—a free text field to record any additional information as required;
- software profile—a subtable, shown only for workstations and servers, detailing which items of software are installed; and
- audit trail—of all changes made to the record.

Definitive Software Library

- supplier name—the name of the supplier from whom the software was purchased;
- order date—the date recorded on the purchase order against which the software was purchased;
- software ID—the ID number associated with the software in question;
- software description—name of the software;
- purchased copies—number of licences purchased on this particular order;
- additional details—free text field to record any additional information about the software;
- purchase order number—the number of the purchase order against which the software was purchased;
- Service Desk reference—the service desk ticket number used to request the purchase;
- business stream—the business stream which purchased the software;
- site—site from where the purchase request originated;
- licence reference number—not always applicable, but if there is a reference number for the software it is recorded here;
- licence key—if the software has a licence key it is recorded here;
- licence date—date when the licence was received;
- modified by—the user ID of the last person to update the current record;
- modified date—the date when the record was last updated;
- comments—a free text field to record any additional information as required; and
- audit trail—of all changes made to the record.

Appendix 21—Capacity Manager, job description

Objective and role

The Capacity Manager (CaM) shall be responsible for initiating the capacity planning process and developing capacity planning for the technical and operational functions of IT in the future in a cost effective manner.

The CaM shall also be responsible for long-range capacity planning to provide the highest level of client service possible in the future and for developing and maintaining a management reporting system. This shall include the prediction of future demands from clients in association with the Sales Team and other employees, as appropriate. These future demands shall be used as input to capacity planning.

Problems and challenges

The CaM is challenged with having the vision to plan for future information processing (not just IT equipment but all resources) capacity needs, determine future requirements from clients, as well as developing a comprehensive and useful management reporting system, according to budgetary criteria.

Principal accountabilities

The CaM shall:

- determine future business needs for capacity;
- provide capacity planning services to the relevant employees, including the Sales Team, the IT and HR Departments, and relevant business teams. This shall include performance related issues, if appropriate;
- produce the Capacity Plan, reflecting current and future capacity needs to service its clients;
- ensure cost-justified capacity exists to process the agreed workloads;
- provide the required performance quality and quantity agreed in the Service Level Agreements (SLAs);
- assist in fault and problem resolution, where appropriate and relevant;
- assess changes submitted to the Change Advisory Board (CAB) for impact on the demand and capacity requirements and the need to revise the Capacity Plan, if appropriate;
- attend the CAB, as appropriate;
- recommend proactive measures to improve performance, where relevant and cost effective;
- determine the need for upgrades to systems to maintain or improve capacity requirements;
- provide long-range planning for operational areas;
- serve as a 'futurist' for demand and capacity issues;
- develop, implement, and update the Capacity Management System (CMS);
- monitor the IT services used, the products and services provided, checking performance levels experienced are as agreed in the SLAs, recommending corrective action where deviations exist by feedback to the Service Level Manager (SLM);
- work to ensure quality client service levels through capacity planning functions;
- work closely with the Business Continuity Manager (BCM) to ensure that the Business Continuity Plans (BCPs) are updated appropriately;
- assist in developing and maintaining SLAs with clients;
- ensure that capacity is used to its optimum, and where underutilisation exists recommend methods of spreading workloads;
- manage the inputs and outputs of the CMS through performance, workload, resources, demands, modelling;
- ensure maximum utilisation of all Configuration Items (CIs);
- develop plans for migration of capacity planning policies and procedures to support the future business direction;
- develop the long-range capacity management strategy;
- define direction of in-house technical training seminars to improve overall employee awareness, response time, and ability to look into future demand and capacity requirements;
- participate in international, national, and local SIG presentations, and publishes articles describing FCL's capacity planning and management activities and how they relate to the business;
- develop and manage effective working relationships with all appropriate internal and external interested parties;
- maintain external links to other companies in the industry to gain competitive assessments and share information, where appropriate;
- identify the emerging information technologies to be assimilated, integrated and introduced within FCL, which could significantly impact FCL's capacity demands;
- Interface with external industrial and academic organisations in order to maintain state-of-the-art knowledge in emerging capacity planning and management and to enhance FCL's image as a first-class solution provider utilising the latest thinking in this field;
- adhere to established policies, standards, and procedures; and
- perform all responsibilities in accordance with, or in excess of, the requirements of the Integrated Management System.

Authority

The CaM shall have the authority to:

- develop long-term demand requirements for clients;
- develop long-range budget estimation and capacity estimates; and
- establish and make decisions about capacity management reporting methods, and outputs.

Contacts

Internal contacts

This position requires contact with all interested parties, including Asset Owners, the IT and HR Departments, and all business streams.

External contacts

The primary external contacts are with clients, contract service providers, clients, vendors, and industry peers. Contact with information technology product and service companies shall also be made on a periodic basis.

Reports to

The CaM shall report to:
- the IT Manager.

Appendix 22—Capacity management plan

The capacity plan template is defined below.

Note

All capacity requirements are dependent on client requirements so monitoring capacity in real time shall be undertaken, providing input for updating Capacity Plans.

The Capacity Plan shall contain the following:

- current requirements;
- projected, as known now, requirements; and
- future desires.

These shall cover, but are not limited to:

- ability to meet TRTs;
- capability requirements in Forensic Analysts;
- capacity (storage requirements);
- processing requirements for forensic case processing tools; and
- other requirements as required.

Appendix 23—Service Management Policy

It is the Service Management Policy to:

- ensure that a full service management system shall be planned and implemented so that client requirements are met, if not exceeded;
- design all services, in consultation with clients, and ensure that the appropriate service operations objectives shall be agreed;
- perform continuous improvement activities to ensure that all products and services are monitored and improved where necessary and that client requirements shall be met, if not exceeded;
- provide the appropriate resources to ensure that the products and services required by clients shall be maintained at the correct level to meet their business needs; and
- ensure that all employees are aware of their responsibility to adhere to this policy and ensure that high-quality services shall be maintained for all clients.

The Service Level Manager shall be responsible for the co-ordination and management of services.

This policy is issued and maintained by the Service Manager. All Managers are directly responsible for implementing the policy within their operational area, and for its adherence by their employees.

The service management system shall provide the framework for the implementation of this policy and shall be supported by a comprehensive set of policies and procedures.

This policy shall be regularly reviewed to ensure that it remains valid.

This policy has been approved by the top management.

All employees shall comply with this policy.

Appendix 24—Service Level Manager, job description

Objective and role

The role of the Service Level Manager (SLM) shall be to define, agree, record, and manage levels of service offered to all clients and ensure that the mandated service levels as defined in the Service Level Agreements (SLAs) are met for both new and existing products and services.

Problems and challenges

The SLM is challenged with ensuring that the services offered to the client meets or exceeds the SLA while managing the internal resources to meet the SLAs. This will involve a delicate balancing act between resources and deliverables. The ability to define the offered services in financial terms may cause variety as it is often viewed differently by different clients. The production of differentiation information will vary between clients.

Principal accountabilities

The SLM shall:

- evaluate service offerings for value definitions;
- analyse existing services for cost cutting options;
- create business value while managing the service risk;
- define the services in the Service Catalogue in terms of value;
- formulate, agree and maintain an appropriate Service Level Management (SLM) structure to include:
  - the Service Level Agreement (SLA) structure.
  - all Operation Level Agreements (OLAs);
  - Underpinning Contracts (UCs); and
  - accommodating the Service Improvement Plan (SIP) within the SLM process.
- negotiate, agree, and maintain SLAs, OLAs, and UCs;
- negotiate and agree with clients the SLAs for new and developing products and services;
- analyse and review service performance against SLAs, OLAs, and UCs;
- measure service delivery against SLAs;
- produce regular reports on performance against SLAs, OLAs, and UCs to internal and external clients and relevant third parties, as required;
- develop a service measurement and reporting model;
- organise and maintain regular Service Level Reviews with internal and external clients and relevant 3rd Parties to cover:
  - outstanding actions from previous reviews;
  - current performance;
  - Service Level targets;
  - agree appropriate action to maintain/improve service levels;
  - initiate actions to maintain and improve Service Levels.
- conduct the Annual Review of the entire service offering to internal and external clients;
- agree and co-ordinate temporary amendments to SLAs;
- make recommendations to the Service Improvement Plan (SIP);
- assist in developing the long range service strategy;
- participate in international, national, and local SIG presentations, and publishes articles describing FCL's service management initiatives and how they relate to the business;
- develop and manage effective working relationships with all appropriate internal and external interested parties;
- maintain external links to other companies in the industry to gain competitive assessments and share information, where appropriate;

- identify the emerging information technologies to be assimilated, integrated and introduced within FCL which could significantly impact FCL's product and service offerings;
- interface with external industrial and academic organisations in order to maintain state-of-the-art knowledge in emerging service management issues and to enhance FCL's image as a first-class solution provider utilising the latest thinking in this field;
- adhere to established policies, standards, and procedures; and
- perform all responsibilities in accordance with, or in excess of, the requirements of the Integrated Management System.

Authority

The Service Level Manager shall have the authority to:

- define the level of services provided, as authorised by top management;
- design tools and technology required to produce the SLAs;
- design SLA models with predefined activities. Any changes to these activities shall be transitioned;
- identify potential service level problems before they occur and implement solutions;
- evaluate operating advantages and cost benefits of proposed and existing SLAs;
- arrange for systems reviews against SLAs and evaluate the results;
- schedule and prioritise work to accommodate internal and external client needs while minimising impact on current projects; and
- monitor and report on services offering and compare them with the SLA. Where appropriate, make changes to the service offering to improve them for the client.

Contacts

Internal

Contacts shall be with employees in the operational areas which directly affect service delivery. This will include a variety of employees.

Close cooperation with the Service Desk, Sales Team, Project Managers, and other Managers shall be as required.

External

Those external shall include appropriate Special Interest Groups (SIGs), clients, external vendors, and service providers.

Reports to

The Service Level Manager shall report to:
- Top management.

Appendix 25—Service Reporting policy

The Service Reporting policy shall:

- agree all reporting requirements during service management planning with all clients, internal and external;
- document all reporting requirements in Service Level Agreements including report types, frequency, and responsibilities for production;
- provide timely and accurate service reports for internal and external clients;
- provide reporting that covers all measurable aspects of a product or service that details both current and historical analysis;
- use appropriate reporting tools to ensure that the information within reports is comprehensive, accurate, and has clear presentation; and
- use service reporting as an input into the service review and the continuous improvement process.

This policy is issued and maintained by the Service Manager. All Managers shall be directly responsible for implementing the policy within their operational area, and for its adherence by their employees.

This policy shall be regularly reviewed to ensure that it remains valid.

This policy has been approved by the top management.

All employees shall comply with this policy.

Appendix 26—Policy for Maintaining and Servicing IT Equipment

The Policy for Maintaining and Servicing IT Equipment shall ensure that:

- IT equipment shall only be maintained by either an appropriately competent member of the IT Department, or by an appropriate service engineer or third party;
- IT equipment maintenance shall only be performed in accordance with the manufacturer's recommended service intervals and specifications;
- all IT equipment faults shall be recorded by the Service Desk as an incident;
- all IT equipment maintenance by service engineers or other third parties shall be undertaken in accordance with the guidelines for hosting visits;
- a record of all IT equipment maintenance shall be maintained which records:
  - all IT equipment maintenance performed by the IT Department (including corrective and preventive action);
  - all IT equipment maintenance performed by service engineers and third parties.
- IT equipment which needs to be sent off-site for maintenance shall be subject to the following controls:
  - equipment shall only be sent for off-site maintenance to an approved and authorised third party;
  - the IT Department is responsible for coordinating all off-site maintenance; and
  - all off-site maintenance shall be recorded.

Note

Where possible all equipment that is sent off-site for repair shall be securely wiped or the media removed. If this is not possible and the equipment contains any classified data, there are only two options:

- ensure maintenance is carried out on site; or
- dispose of the equipment securely.

Note

The option chosen shall be agreed by the ISM and the owner of the information on the equipment, based on a risk assessment.

This policy is issued and maintained by the IT Manager. All Managers shall be directly responsible for implementing the policy within their operational area, and for its adherence by their employees.

This policy shall be regularly reviewed to ensure that it remains valid.

This policy has been approved by the top management.

All employees shall comply with this policy.

Appendix 27—ISO 17025 tool test method documentation

The following shall be documented for tool testing:

- appropriate identification;
- scope;
- description of the type of item to be tested or calibrated;
- parameters or quantities and ranges to be determined;
- apparatus and equipment, including technical performance requirements;
- reference standards and reference materials required;
- environmental conditions required and any stabilisation period needed;
- description of the procedure, including:
  - affixing of identification marks, handling, transporting, storing, and preparation of items;
  - checks to be made before the work is started;
  - checks that the equipment is working properly and, where required, calibration and adjustment of the equipment before each use;
  - the method of recording the observations and results; and
  - any safety measures to be observed;

- criteria and/or requirements for approval/rejection;
- data to be recorded and method of analysis and presentation; and
- the uncertainty or the procedure for estimating uncertainty.

Appendix 28—Standard forensic tool tests

The following are the basic tests undertaken for a new forensic tool, an upgrade to an existing tool or a new operating environment:

- acquisition hashing;
- recovery of deleted files;
- recovery of deleted folders;
- recovery of deleted partitions;
- text searches;
- internet history searches;
- detection of bad file names from signature analysis;
- identification of 'known files';
- image recovery;
- text and social media recovery;
- email address recovery;
- specific artefact recovery; and
- other tests as appropriate to either the specific forensic case or tool.

Appendix 29—Forensic tool test report template

The standard template used in the for testing nonstandard methods or tools is:

- title defining product tested;
- the location of performance of the laboratory activities, including when performed at a customer facility or at remote sites away from the laboratory or in associated temporary or mobile facilities;
- test environment, including hardware and software;
- details of the product vendor;
- unambiguous identification of the product tested including version, patches, etc.;
- details of the condition of the tool being tested, if appropriate;
- test criteria;
- details of standard test forensic case relevant to this test;
- the date of receipt of the test item(s);
- the date(s) of testing;
- test results;
- if the testing also included any third party, the identification of the third party(ies) and the role they performed;
- a statement to the effect that the results relate only to the specific item(s) tested;
- details of the Forensic Analyst performing testing, including qualifications;
- where appropriate and needed, opinions and interpretations;
- any other pertinent matters relevant to the test;
- details of Laboratory Manager reviewing the results and authorising the product use;
- signatures of the Forensic Analyst and Laboratory Manager, with dates; and
- the date of issue of the report.

In addition to this the requirements for document control, as defined in Section 7.6.3 shall be met along with the report's classification, as defined in Chapter 5, Appendix 16.

Appendix 30—Overnight backup checklist

For each server, a backup checklist shall be maintained on paper in the server room as well as in the backup software log. This shall ensure that the member of the IT Department who checks the backups actually signs the checklist to show the task has been performed. The checklist shall contain the following information.

- day of week;
- date;
- tape ID;
- success?
- tape cleaned, if appropriate?
- tape re-tensioned, if appropriate?
- tape replaced, if appropriate?
- comments;
- signature;
- name;
- incident number if a failure occurs.

Each checklist for a server shall be for a month, and when completed, they shall be scanned and added to the ERMS as records of the backup process.

Chapter 8

Incident response

8.1 General

Note 1

Whilst many books refer to the scene to be investigated as a 'crime scene' or a 'locus of a crime', this book refers to the scenes as an 'incident scene' as it is not always certain that a crime has been committed.

Note 2

This chapter only deals with the actual seizure of evidence from an incident scene and its transportation back to the laboratory for case processing, actual processing of the evidence, rather than the incident scene, is covered in Chapter 9.

8.1.1 Overview

FCL may be asked to act as a First Responder in the following situations:

- as part of a planned seizure operation for a client;
- as an advisor 'after the event';
- as an attendee in any relevant role at a crime scene.

Only trained First Responders that are competent and have received the relevant training shall attend as a First Responder. Other members of the team may comprise qualified Forensic Technicians or Analysts.

ISO 17020—General criteria for the operation of various types of bodies performing inspection shall be applied to crime scene investigation. Depending on the actual services a forensic laboratory supplies, it may be an 'A', 'B', or a type 'C' inspection body. The mapping of the FCL procedures to ISO 17020 is defined in Appendix 1. EA 5/03—Guidance for the implementation of ISO 17020 in the field of crime scene investigation and IAF/ILAC-A4: 2004 Guidance on the application of ISO/IEC 17020 provide additional guidance for the implementation of ISO 17020.

The work of the Forensic Response team attending an incident where first response is required shall be to:

- plan the initial response for attending the scene based on facts available (Plan);
- assess the scene, on arrival (Do);
- revise and update as appropriate, the examination and seizure strategy (Check and Act);
- examine the scene and collect evidence using the relevant recovery procedures for exhibit identification and seizure, as required (Do);
- remove evidence from the scene securely, if appropriate (Do);
- document all findings both contemporaneously and as part of the final report, if requested (Do); and
- review the results and rework if appropriate (Check and Act).

This process is basically the PDCA cycle, as shown above.

8.1.2 Legislative considerations

All incident scenes are unique and any legislative requirements and other relevant issues shall all be considered in any First Response attendance. Where appropriate, these generic procedures shall be amended to ensure compliance with the requirements of the relevant jurisdiction.

There may be any number of legislative considerations that apply to the collection of electronic evidence for the specific jurisdiction.

A Blueprint for Implementing Best Practice Procedures in a Digital Forensic Laboratory. https://doi.org/10.1016/B978-0-12-819479-9.00019-8

These may dictate actions to be undertaken, orders of actions or additional requirements. The First Response Team Leader shall understand the generic procedures and be competent and able to adapt them for the incorporation of local requirements for the jurisdiction as the situation dictates.

As part of the planning process for the seizure or attending a possible crime scene, the First Response Team Leader shall ensure that these requirements have been identified and that all members of the First Response Team are aware of them and that they are met.

The First Response briefing shall cover the specific requirements and the First Response Briefing Agenda template is defined in Appendix 2.

The First Response Team shall use caution when seizing any electronic or digital evidence, as improper seizure may not only prejudice any legal proceedings but may also be illegal.

Before collecting any electronic or digital evidence, the First Response Team leader shall ensure that legal authority exists for seizure of the evidence. No one wants to have the doctrine of 'fruits of the poison tree' applied to any evidence that they seize as all subsequent information derived from illegally seized physical evidence is inadmissible in a court of law and cannot be used to support the findings in any case.

8.1.3 Work standards

There may be forensic First Response or evidence collection work standards that are mandated for the collection of electronic evidence for the specific jurisdiction. When dealing with electronic or digital evidence the basic principles that the First Response Team shall adhere to include, but are not limited to, are:

- the process of identifying, collecting, securing, and transporting electronic or digital evidence shall not change the original evidence, and this shall be provable;
- in specific circumstances where the First Response Team need to access original data, rather than a forensically produced image, they shall be both competent to perform the actions and be able to give evidence explaining the relevance and the implications of their actions;
- electronic or digital evidence shall only be seized or examined by competent Forensic Analysts;
- an audit trail of any actions relating to the search for, seizure of, transportation of, and booking in of electronic or digital evidence shall be supported by a contemporaneous audit trail. The audit trail shall be fully documented, securely preserved and available for later examination;
- any independent third party should be able to examine the source evidence, the processes and procedures involved, and if competent, produce the same results; and
- the instructing client (Law Enforcement or Corporate) who is in charge of the forensic case has ultimate responsibility to ensure compliance with all relevant legislation, regulation and accepted working practices within the jurisdiction and be personally accountable for compliance.

Note

The Health and Safety of the First Response Team and any others shall remain the primary responsibility and concern of the First Response Team Leader.

8.1.4 Health and safety issues

Compliance with health and safety legislation is essential in all of the work carried out by the First Response Team during all stages of the First Response process.

As part of the planning process for the seizure or attending a possible crime scene, the First Response Team Leader shall ensure that the relevant health and safety requirements have been identified, that all members of the First Response Team are aware of them and the requirements that these places on them for every aspect of the first response process and that these requirements are met.

Details of generic Health and Safety requirements are given in Chapter 17. However, specific requirements for the First Response Team include:

- a health and safety briefing should be held prior to the First Response Team departing to the incident scene. The briefing may indicate the need for Personal Protective Equipment (PPE) to be used by the First Response Team on site;
- where appropriate, a Health and Safety Risk Assessment shall be carried out on site by the First Response Team Leader or other competent authority;

- all First Response Team members shall wear protective latex gloves for all searching and seizing operations on site. This is to both protect the First Response Team and preserve any fingerprints that may be required to be recovered at a later date;
- gloves should only be used once and then disposed of in appropriate containers or returned to the laboratory for disposal;
- care shall be taken in handling computer hardware and it is the responsibility of the First Response Team Leader to ensure that any member of the First Response Team who may lift heavy equipment have been given appropriate 'manual handling' training, as defined in Chapter 17, Section 17.3.4.1.8;
- additionally, all grab bags shall contain a full medical first aid kit for minor injuries such as cuts from sharp edges on equipment, etc.;
- any such injuries shall be recorded in the FCL accident book in accordance with the health and safety policy and supporting procedures.

8.1.5 Competence

The First Response Team shall all be competent to perform their tasks. No-one at the incident scene shall attempt to explore the contents of evidence or recover information from an information processing or storage device, with the exception of recording what is on screen or in the location of the evidence to be seized unless they are competent to perform the tasks.

The successful seizure of evidence at the scene is the 'making or breaking' of any forensic case. No matter how rigorous the investigation of recovered evidence is after seizure, it is worthless if the seizure itself was flawed or inappropriately carried out. In many cases, where the First Response Team attend, they shall be under the guidance of a third party (often Law Enforcement) and will have to operate under their rules, but they shall provide specialist experience in the seizure and recovery of digital evidence and information processing equipment.

The First Response Team shall be comprised of competent employees and that this can be demonstrated as required.

8.1.6 Consent

There may be times that the suspect is present and that their consent is required to obtain forensic evidence and also that consent is given.

In cases such as this, appropriate forms for the jurisdiction shall be used and these shall be carried in the forensic grab bag. Sample contents of the forensic grab bag are defined in Appendix 3.

These shall be used and distributed according to the requirements of the legislation in force in the jurisdiction.

8.2 Forensic evidence

Forensic evidence at the incident scene can take many forms and may be readily visible or may require later analysis to recover it. The value of physical evidence in any case:

- may be the deciding factor is determining guilt or innocence;
- can corroborate other evidence discovered;
- can establish the key elements in a case;
- may exonerate those under suspicion, where appropriate;
- may be used for the identification of the person or persons responsible;
- can link together a chain of circumstantial evidence;
- can test the statements or assertions of others in the case, e.g. witnesses or suspects; and
- can verifying that an event occurred.

In digital forensic cases, the evidence may be easy to find or steps may have been taken to try hide or delete it.

The 'best evidence rule' states that the best evidence is the original exhibit, rather than a copy. However, with hashing techniques it is possible that no more, or no less, is present at the time of acquisition and that the copy made is as good as the original exhibit.

There is rarely a second chance to obtain evidence at the scene so it is essential that the incident scene shall be properly and methodically processed. The First Response Team may fail to do this for a number of reasons, and of these may include, but not be limited to:

- external pressure to reach a certain conclusion;
- external pressure to reach results;
- failure to seize potential physical evidence at the scene;

- poor communication in the First Response Team;
- poor instructions from the client or at briefing time;
- potential evidence destroyed at the scene by accident;
- potential evidence destroyed at the scene by carelessness or sloppy work practices;
- potential evidence destroyed at the scene on purpose;
- preconceived ideas;
- premature conclusions;
- time constraints; or
- volatility of evidence.

It is therefore essential that first response shall be carried out in a slow, methodical, and thorough manner.

RFC 3227, Evidence Collecting and Archiving, states that evidence needs to be:

- **admissible:** it shall conform to certain legal rules before it can be put before a Court;
- **authentic:** it shall be possible to positively tie evidentiary material to the incident;
- **complete:** it shall tell the whole story and not just a particular perspective;
- **reliable:** there shall be nothing about how the evidence was collected and subsequently handled that casts doubt about its authenticity and veracity; and
- **believable:** it shall be readily believable and understandable by a Court.

Physical evidence shall be handled as little as possible to avoid any possible contamination.

8.3 Incident response as a process

Incident scene investigation shall be carried out as a process and it is generally accepted that there are seven stages of processing a scene, and these are:

- assessment;
- control;
- examination;
- interpretation;
- recording;
- collection; and
- case management.

Whilst these are the ideal steps, they may not be what actually happens in fact, as the first responders may be local management not trained in crime scene processing.

The objectives of processing an incident scene shall be:

- safety of those at the scene, specifically the First Response Team;
- preservation and recovery of evidence and intelligence;
- minimisation of contamination;
- maximising the potential to detect and solve crime;
- maximising the potential to apprehend offenders and exonerate the innocent; and
- meet the client's other legal requirements, as agreed and if possible.

8.4 Initial contact

Depending on the exact scenario of the deployment of the First Response Team, the method of first contact and how the case develops cannot be predicted.

As soon as a new forensic case to be processed is identified, a 'New Case' form shall be filled in containing the initial data captured from the client. All forensic cases shall start with this initial data capture, and the information required for this is defined in Appendix 4. Whilst reference is to paper forms in the book, these are all duplicated in the Case Management System (MARS).

Where the incident is a planned seizure, more information may be available as opposed to the First Response Team being invited to attend an existing incident.

The procedures for starting a new forensic case shall be (Fig. 8.1):

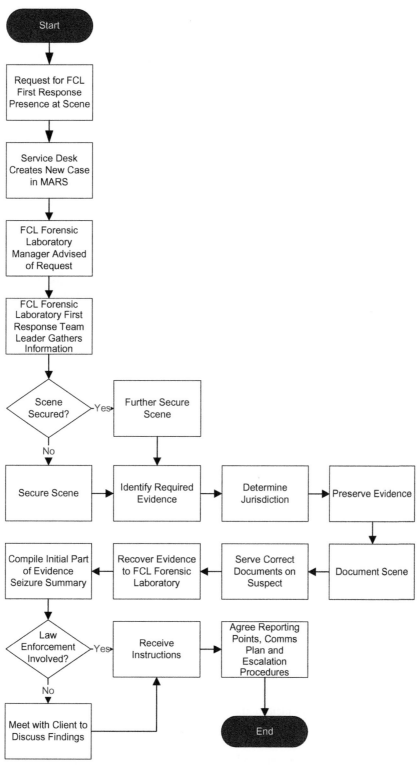

FIG. 8.1 Starting a new case.

1. A request is made to for a First Response presence by phone, email, personal attendance, etc. to the Service Desk.
2. The Service Desk shall create a new forensic case in the MARS system and fill in as much as they know of the details on the new forensic case form.
3. The Laboratory Manager shall be advised of the request and assigns one or more Forensic Analysts to the First Response Team, as appropriate, based on the forensic case requirements and the competencies of the Forensic Analysts.
4. The First Response Team Leader shall be briefed on the known information about the incident, typically this shall include as a minimum, if available:
   - description of incident;
   - instructing client's details;
   - name of the onsite Incident Manager running the incident, if applicable;
   - case name/title for the incident;
   - location of incident;
   - what jurisdiction the case and/or seizure is to be performed under;
   - details of what is to be seized (make, model, location, ID, etc.);
   - other work to be performed at the scene (e.g. full search, evidence required, etc.);
   - whether the search and seizure is to be overt or covert and whether local management are to know; and
   - whether local law enforcement agencies are involved, and if so which ones.
5. When the First Response Team is invited to an incident, then it may be that someone local to the incident has secured the scene, stopped anyone contaminating the scene, even pulled the power to the relevant computer(s) and made basic notes of their findings. In this case, the First Response Team shall be invited to provide assistance in some, or all of the following areas:
   - (further) securing the scene;
   - identifying the required evidence;
   - determining the jurisdiction and ensuring that the work is carried out in accordance with the requirements of the jurisdiction;
   - preserving the required evidence according to the First Responder procedures, as amended for the jurisdiction;
   - documenting the scene;
   - maybe undertaking an initial interview with the suspect;
   - ensuring that the correct paperwork has been served on the suspect; and
   - recovering the evidence to the laboratory for investigation or performing recovery work on site.
6. Once the initial information has been captured requiring the First Response Team to attend the site, the initial part of the Evidence Seizure Summary form shall be filled in for the forensic case. The details for the seizure summary log are defined in Appendix 5.
7. Where the client is Law Enforcement, the legislation within the jurisdiction is usually well known and specific instructions for the jurisdiction can be expected to be received from the client to allow a proposal to be prepared in accordance with the requirements of Chapter 6, Section 6.6.
8. Where the client is corporate and the matter relates to an internal issue (which may become a tribunal or become the subject of a court case), the client shall be advised to contact their own Legal Counsel and Human Resources Department (HR), where appropriate, for advice and guidance. This may take the form of written instructions or requests for meeting or a mixture of both. Issues to be discussed shall include, but are not limited to:
   - employee privacy issues;
   - employee use of client assets;
   - employee conduct at work;
   - relevant client policies and procedures relating to the incident; and
   - other issues relating to the incident as identified.

   The outcome of any meetings, and any written instructions shall be used to finalise the proposal and shall all be filed in the client's virtual case file in the ERMS as records for the case.
9. Reporting points, a communications plan and escalation procedures shall be agreed between the client and the First Response team.

8.5 Types of first response

First response to an incident may involve three different groups of people, and each will have differing skills and need to carry out differing tasks based in the circumstance of the incident.

The three groups are:

- client System Administrators;
- client management; and
- a competent first response team.

Each is dealt with in turn below:

8.5.1 First response for system administrators

The role of a System Administrator is vital in ensuring all aspects of network security and maintenance, but this individual also plays the most important role in the event a computer is used in, or is subject to, an information security incident. The System Administrator will most likely be the primary point of contact for individuals wishing to make a report of computer use violations after the incident has been reported to the Service Desk. In addition, a System Administrator may come across a violation during the normal course of their duties.

The actions taken by the System Administrator after discovery of a potential computer violation shall play a vital role in the investigation, forensic evaluation of the computer system, and potential prosecution or administrative actions.

From a forensic standpoint, the ideal situation is to isolate the computer from additional use or tampering. However, many of the systems that may be compromised can be of critical importance to the business and isolation of the system may not be possible or feasible.

A suspected computer violation will result in difficult decisions in weighing the loss of potential evidence to the inability to utilise a computer system tied to the network. It is essential that top management in the victim organisation is in a position to make decisions knowingly about the immediate actions to be taken and the implications of any action undertaken.

After the System Administrator is either alerted to a possible incident, or becomes aware of it through their own observations, it is essential that the Systems Administrator shall take appropriate action.

This could include doing nothing until full instructions are received from top management unless immediate actions are needed to minimise the effect of the breach or incident. If any actions are taken, then the System Administrator shall make full and contemporaneous notes of all actions undertaken for later records and possible action.

Depending on the actual incident, some or all of the following actions shall be undertaken by the System Administrator:

- call in the in-house first response team, if there is one;
- record what is on screen and what is happening;
- try to take copies of any system logs onto clean media; and
- if the computer is switched on and the screen display is on:
- make records of what happened from initial discovery of incident;
- seek top management direction, especially if there is an ongoing attack or the business may be prejudiced prior to powering any systems down;
- seek top management approval to get competent and qualified help, if it is not available in house;
- ensure that the area surrounding the information processing systems that are linked to the incident are kept secure and that no unauthorised, or unneeded, person has access to them; and
- keep a watching brief until qualified assistance arrives, recording anything that happens that is relevant to the incident.

The Systems Administrator shall wait for the arrival of qualified first responders or direction from top management.

8.5.2 First response by client management

Typically, this will be the case where one of the client's management or some other nonforensic expert will be on site with the suspect or victim and/or their information processing system and they need to secure the scene.

Once initial perimeter security has been established, the scene shall not be left unattended or unsecured for any reason until the processing of the scene by the competent internal first responder team or an external first response team is completed. Instructions shall be provided to any individuals securing the scene concerning access. Only individuals with a direct need for access relating to the incident shall be allowed to enter the incident scene and the numbers of individuals involved in working in the incident scene shall be kept at a minimum. Detailed contemporaneous notes shall be maintained regarding how perimeter and scene security was established to include the identification of all security and other personnel involved.

Detailed notes shall be maintained during all aspects of the scene processing. This not only includes the usual:

- who;
- what;
- when;
- why; and
- how[a]

but overall observations of the scene.

Notes and/or photographs/videos shall record exactly what the scene looked like upon arrival. This shall include items of furniture within the scene and their locations, the condition of the room (clean, dirty, etc.), locations of any information processing equipment, disks, tapes, USBs, etc., along with the locations and descriptions of any potential evidence.

During initial observations, a determination shall be made concerning the possibility that potential evidence is at immediate risk of destruction or exposure (i.e. disk format or upload of information in progress). This may require an immediate decision to disconnect the power supply. All factors, such as the potential loss of data, shall be taken into consideration when making this decision, but it shall be made quickly and in association with local management and the relevant competent first response team.

When dealing with PCs and mobile processing devices, this shall include, but not be limited to, the following tasks:

- not letting the suspect or anyone else touch the computer or any other items relating to the incident;
- photographing (if possible) or drawing a sketch map of the computer and/or media and how it is connected;
- recording what is on screen if the computer is switched on and the screen display is on;
- if the screen appears blank—move the mouse to see if there is a screen saver and if so, continue as defined in Appendix 10—if the screen restores, record what is on the screen as above;
- if the system is a server—wait until qualified help arrives;
- record whether the computer is connected to a network; and
- check for wireless connectivity.

Client management shall then wait for qualified assistance to arrive without undertaking any other actions.

Whilst the above are the ideal situations, this rarely happens and the level of information available at an incident scene can vary greatly.

8.5.3 First response team

Whilst the client's management may be the first attendees at an incident, it may also be their first response team (if they have one) or a competent external first response team. The procedures below are for the First Response Team but will also be applicable to any in house first response team.

Once the target information processing system, office or location for seizure has been identified, determination shall be made as to whether the seizure shall be overt or covert. This may depend on a number of factors such as nature of the incident or position of the suspect or victim in the client's organisation.

The procedures below shall be relevant to either type of seizure, but covert seizures are typically carried out during the 'quiet hours'. This may have some impacts on office services such as removal of wastepaper bins—this shall be addressed at this stage.

At this point, it should also be possible to identify what hardware is to be seized, where it is located and possibly what ancillary equipment may need to be seized. It may well be that the local management have already seized this equipment as a precaution.

---

a. These are Kipling's 6 'friends'!

Given this, the First Response Team should be able to plan what resources and equipment will be needed to affect the required seizure. Contact with the local management or other investigative teams at this point shall be undertaken and to gain other local knowledge as required.

On arrival at the incident scene, the First Response Team, depending on their tasking, shall undertake some or all of the following tasks (Fig. 8.2):

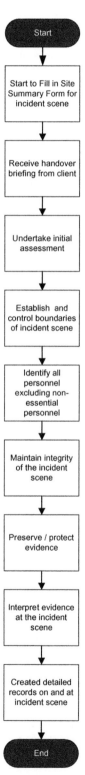

FIG. 8.2 Initial tasks on arrival.

On arrival at the incident scene., the First Response Team shall:

1. Start to fill in a Site Summary Form, given in Appendix 6.
2. Receive the handover briefing from the client when they arrive and take over the scene:
   - obtain assistance as required from any client or third party employees; and
   - obtain transfer of control of notes or other information relating to the incident scene.

Note

Much of this will depend on the actual incident, but circumstances will dictate the actions to be taken.

---

3. Undertake an initial assessment to include:
   - assess health and safety risks and take adequate safety precondition; and
   - ascertain any new information regarding the incident scene and confirm the information already held.
4. Establish and preserve incident scene boundaries:
   - establish incident scene boundaries by identifying the focal point(s) of the incident scene and extending outward;
   - set up physical barrier(s), using appropriate means (e.g. locking doors, tape, or similar);
   - control the flow of personnel and animals, if appropriate, entering and exiting the scene and document all people entering and exiting the scene;
   - maintain integrity of the scene;
   - preserve/protect evidence at the scene;
   - document the original location of the suspect/victim(s) or objects at the scene that were observed being moved; and
   - follow jurisdictional laws related to search and seizure, if known. If they are not known, then do not attempt any search or seizure.
5. Control the incident scene and all persons at the scene:
   - restrict movement of persons at the scene;
   - define an access and exit path for the scene and ensure all attending the scene use them;
   - prevent persons from altering physical or logical evidence;
   - prevent persons from destroying physical or logical evidence;
   - continue to maintain safety at the scene;
   - restrict areas of movement within the scene; and
   - continue to control the scene by maintaining a client Management presence.
6. Identify all persons at the scene.

Note

Identify means to obtain verifiable personal information.

   - identify victims/suspects and keep them secure and separate;
   - identify witnesses and keep them secure and separate where possible;
   - instruct the witnesses not to discuss the incident if they cannot be separated, as this may distort each other's impressions by suggestion;
   - identify bystanders and others not intimately related to the incident and remove them from the incident scene;
   - identify suspects/victims/family members/friends and keep them under control whilst showing compassion—if appropriate; and
   - identify medical and assisting personnel, if appropriate.
7. Exclude unauthorised/nonessential personnel from the incident scene, including:
   - other client staff, or third parties acting on their behalf, that are not involved in the incident; and
   - other nonessential personnel (e.g. any persons not performing investigative or safety functions at the scene).

Note

Should the First Response Team feel threatened or considers there is a danger to them performing their duties, then they shall take immediate action that may include increasing their physical security protection to immediately leaving the incident scene.

---

8. Maintain integrity of the scene by ensuring that an appropriate communication plan is in place and that all communications shall be through authorised channels.

9. Preserve/protect evidence at the scene;
   - protect evidence from environmental elements, if possible;
   - identify and apply an appropriate search pattern;
   - accurately record the scene as it is being processed. Photographs of the scene and exhibits in situ shall be taken, and a video of the whole scene, if possible, as defined in Section 8.6.6. Sketches of the scene may also be made as defined in Section 8.6.7. The exhibits and photographs shall all be appropriately 'tagged and bagged' with a unique reference number as defined in Section 8.6.10;
   - make detailed records of the incident scene including photographs of the scene and exhibits in situ and photographs of electronic devices and peripherals in situ;
   - locate all relevant evidence relating to the incident;
   - make appropriate arrangements for evidence collection; and
   - obtain advice and assistance from other specialists, including the client's employees as required.

10. **Interpret the evidence at the incident:**
    - establish possible significance of the evidence;
    - establish the possible sequence of events, if appropriate; and
    - document all actions.

8.5.4 Planning the next steps

Whilst it may be possible to obtain some information regarding the incident, it is not usually possible to plan the actions to be taken, with the exception of site security or site takeover, without detailed investigation. Even with an agreed proposal in place, this will define required outcomes rather than detailed work plans. Once the scene has been taken over, or initial response secures the scene, the First Response Team Leader shall plan the next steps in detail. This will require detailed examination of the scene as well as interviews with a number of the client's employees or their suppliers.

The time spent in planning at this stage shall be allocated to ensure plans are developed in appropriate detail, as an unstructured 'wild goose chase' without any detailed and cohesive plan is frustrating for all concerned, wastes the client's money, wastes resources and does not present a professional approach to the processing of the scene. At this stage, the First Response Team Leader shall determine whether the client's required outcomes are realistic and achievable and any final amendments to the resourcing, costing and proposal shall be made based on the new information determined from the scene. The following shall be performed by the First Response Team Leader:

Develop a detailed plan for undertaking the scene processing, whilst it is accepted that all incidents are different, the procedure for processing the incident scene, as shown above.

A checklist for the process is defined in Appendix 20.

The procedures for processing an incident scene shall include, but not be limited to the following:

1. Revise the proposal and agree it with the client, including the Plan.
2. Identify any additional resources, whether internal, client employees or third parties and ensure their availability.
3. Collect the evidence relating to the incident in a manner that precludes contamination and ensures integrity of the evidence. This shall include ensuring that sanitised media is used for onsite evidence collection by competent staff, electrostatic and other protection measures shall be in place to prevent contamination, including write blockers.
4. Ensure that only those items covered by the Search Warrant, consent or other authority to seize shall be examined. If there is any doubt with regard to an item, it may be necessary to carry out a forensic preview of the item, as defined in Section 8.6.16.
5. Review the collected evidence for any anomalies or fresh leads that may indicate the requirement for other evidence to be seized, so long as it is within the terms of the legal authority in 4 above. If other evidence is authorised for collection, then steps 2–4 above shall be repeated until all relevant evidence has been collected.
6. Depending on circumstances, time constraints may affect this process, but shortcuts shall not be taken.
7. Ensure the chain of custody is in place for all exhibits and that appropriate security is in place, until they are securely logged in the Secure Property Store.

In addition to the above, any of the following may be of interest to the First Response Team and shall, where possible, be collected for later evaluation, so long as they are legally obtained:

- handwritten notes;
- other computers, external and internal hard drives, flash drives, and mobile devices, together with peripheral equipment such as chargers and power cables;
- any and all computer or data processing software or data, including hard disks or transient storage device(s);
- access password(s), and pattern lock code(s) (PIN codes) for any computer system, mobile devices, software, databases, and data storage devices;
- other data storage devices to provide access to information necessary to access that data;
- the contents of wastepaper bins.

In addition, the First Response Team shall:

- locate and secure any backup storage media relating to the incident. In some instances, files that are deleted from the hard drive will be present within the backup on the backup storage media;
- contact the relevant communications support point or communications supplier and attempt to obtain the phone numbers dialled from the incident scene and also the mobile phone details for the users located in the incident scene;
- possibly conduct interviews of individuals with access to the system or network, if appropriate;
- determine the type and information security classification of the work normally performed on the suspect/victim's system. If classified information may have been breached, the impact of this shall be evaluated. If personal data is involved there may legislative requirements for reporting the breach to either a Regulator or the individuals whose personal information has been compromised. Contractual requirements may also require the organisation to advise their clients of any possible incidents or breaches affecting their information;
- determine the identity of all individuals that have both physical and logical access to the information processing system involved; and
- determine if the information processing system is part of a network and the type of network system involved, as well as the furthest reach that any possible attacker may have exploited and caused damage.

The First Response Team shall fill in, to the best of their ability, all of the other details found on Site Summary Form, defined in Appendix 6, covering the details above including topology, operating systems as well as other occupancy of the incident scene and details of any personal effects found there.

This form shall be countersigned by the victim/suspect (or if this is refused or not possible, the fact annotated on the form).

8.6 The incident scene

Any location could be the scene of an incident, and every incident shall be regarded as a possible crime scene and it shall be processed accordingly so that the same procedures are used whether the case ends up in court or not. This shall ensure that rigorous procedures are applied at the start of a case, rather than having to 'back track'.

The primary scene is the location where the incident was reported and is being investigated by the First Response Team. This investigation may, in turn lead to a secondary scene (e.g. an employee's workplace is the primary scene and their home becomes the second scene). Both may need investigation and evidence seizure.

8.6.1 First response team taking over an incident scene

When the First Response Team arrives at a scene that has been secured by local management, they shall address or perform the following:

1. The manner in which the information processing equipment and storage media is secured after a suspected incident is reported will be dependent on the situation, the facilities available and the information processing system involved. In some instances, it may be impractical to seize the computer as in the case of a networked mail server, but it may be more appropriate to seize the back-up media or to make a backup at the time of the event and perform remote forensics or perform real time forensics on site. However, the forensic examination of backup media means that there are typically only files available and there is no access to such information areas as defined in 'Other Areas' in Appendix 8. It also precludes any volatile information that may have been present on the original evidence.

2. If appropriate, undertake a review of the volatile data on systems that are running, noting any anomalies regarding running processes, open ports, etc. If the forensic case warrants it, a RAM dump shall be conducted.

Note

Contrary to the old best practice guidance, it is now considered to be best to acquire the hard disk drive first and to undertake the basic triage **before** capturing the RAM. Also, it is important to capture virtual memory such as pagefile.sys and swapfile.sys. The reason for this is that with the recent update to Windows 10 and 11 operating systems, the RAM Capturing software (especially FTK Imager) will cause a blue screen of death. If that happens, and if the computer is BitLocker encrypted, access to the data will be lost. Hence, the First Response Team shall conduct a logical acquisition, perform triage and **then** do the RAM dump, documenting all actions.

---

3. In many instances, systems are backed up on a daily basis. If the victim or the individual suspected in an incident attempts to delete files from the primary storage device (e.g. a hard drive), these files could/should still remain on the backup storage media.

4. The ideal situation would call for the System Administrator to ensure no destructive programmes are in operation, secure the scene and have security personnel trained in the seizure of computer systems respond to process the workstation. Sadly, there are few situations that are ideal, and advice on less than ideal situations is defined below:

- in addition to these immediate actions and taking control of the incident site, the First Response Team shall liaise with local management and undertake a full handover from the local management team to First Response Team. This shall include a full briefing and transfer of all notes and documentation relating to the incident;

Note

Some items may have already been seized by the local management in the victim/suspect's area and already been documented.

- once the handover has been completed, the local management team shall be stood down unless specialised local information is needed.

8.6.2 Physical security of the scene

When the First Response Team takes over an incident scene, they shall immediately reassess the security of the scene. It is essential in any incident scene processing to be able to prove that the scene was secured, that security was maintained and documented whilst the First Response Team was on site and that the chain of custody was maintained. The objective of securing the incident scene shall be to:

- prevent evidence being destroyed or contaminated;
- control release of information and ensure that proper communication channels are maintained;
- ensure chain of custody is maintained and documented for each item of evidence handled and recovered;
- ensure that the minimum number of people is present at the incident scene. The more people present, the greater the likelihood of evidence contamination and it may also inhibit the processing of the scene; and
- ensure that all relevant evidence for the case has been recovered, recorded, and securely transported to the laboratory for further examination.

Physical security at the scene shall be provided by:

- physically locking or sealing rooms;
- posting guards;
- use of barrier tape or rope; and
- other processes/methods that are appropriate for the incident scene.

8.6.3 Health and safety at the scene

The safety of the First Response Team and anyone else present, is the primary responsibility of the First Response Team Leader. The issue of Health and Safety at scene is covered in Chapter 17; however, there are some incident scene concerns that are raised here. The First Response Team Leader shall be aware of the safety and wellbeing of their team, this shall include appropriate use of PPE as well as fatigue or other stress issues. Breaks and refreshments shall be considered, if appropriate. Typical PPE that is used at incident scenes shall include protection for:

- eyes;
- hands—also to preclude the First Responder leaving their own fingerprints and contaminating the scene;
- feet;
- antistatic—also to prevent contamination or destruction of the evidence; and
- other PPE may be indicated, depending on the specifics of the incident scene.

Secure areas shall be defined and protected (e.g. for temporary storage of exhibits prior to transportation) and areas where refreshments can be taken, if on site for a prolonged period. Health and safety issues shall be covered at the initial briefing, as defined in Appendix 2.

In addition to the physical health and safety of the First Response Team, it is often possible that the risks encountered are mental rather than physical (e.g. dealing with child abuse). Details for assessment for psychological risks are given in Chapter 17, Section 17.4.1.13.

8.6.4 The chain of custody

1. If more than one device is to be seized, consideration shall be given to the appointing of an Evidence Custodian who shall hold all seized evidence in a secure area prior to being transported to the laboratory.
2. If a single device is to be seized then the Forensic Analyst shall be their own Evidence Custodian and hand carry the evidence back to the laboratory where it shall be signed into the Secure Property Store.
3. The 'Chain of Custody' refers to a written account of individuals who have had sole physical custody of a piece of evidence from the time it was seized until the end of the case.
4. By becoming a 'link' in the 'Chain of Custody' and taking possession for a piece of evidence, an individual shall be responsible for securing it in a manner which can later stand legal scrutiny in case there are later claims raised that the evidence was tampered with.
5. A piece of evidence shall only be as good as the Chain of Custody accompanying it. An item could be seized which has great evidentiary value, but unless the manner it was secured and accounted for can be articulated and proven, it may be worthless in legal or administrative proceedings.
6. An employee who assumes physical possession of a piece of evidence shall be responsible for the security of it. Evidence shall be secured in a manner where only the employee who has signed for it can gain access to it, though it is noted that this is not always possible.
7. The use of a Secure Property Store with a single Evidence Custodian able to access the exhibits shall be the preferred manner of handling exhibits.
8. Signing for evidence and becoming a 'link' in the chain of custody shall not to be taken lightly by any employee, who shall ensure that they can fulfil their duties in the Chain of Custody before committing to becoming the link.

8.6.5 Searches and recovery

No matter where or why the FCL are involved, a search of the incident scene of the alleged incident shall be required, whether it is for the victim or the suspect. Whilst each case requires separate and different handling, many of the common issues are below.

Once the First Response Team has arrived at the scene and unloaded their equipment, they shall move to the incident scene.

The isolation of an information processing system (whether it is a workstation, network server, mobile device, or complete network) or other forms of media that can contain digital evidence so evidence will not be lost is of utmost importance.

Some of these may have already been seized by the local management in the suspect's area and documented them already.

The manner in which the exhibits shall be secured after a suspected incident is reported shall be dependent on the facilities available and the exhibits involved. In some instances, it may be impractical to seize the information processing device (e.g. a corporate networked mail server), but it shall be more appropriate to seize the back-up media or to make a backup at the time of the event, perform remote forensics or perform real time forensics on site.

A search may have been done by the local management. This initial search and seizure conducted within an information processing related scene is much like any traditional crime scene. The area of primary importance shall be the location and identification of any fragile or volatile evidence that could be altered or lost if not immediately collected.

In many instances, systems are backed up on a daily basis. If the individual suspected in the incident attempts to delete files from the primary storage device (hard drive), these files could still remain on the backup storage media.

A formal handover of the scene from local Management who have maintained the security of the scene to the First Response Team Leader shall take place and this shall be fully documented.

Copies of the notes regarding the actions undertaken and notes that local management made shall be provided to the First Response Team Leader—the originals shall be retained by local management in case a formal statement is needed—based on the notes.

8.6.6 Photographing the scene

The old adage of incident scene processing, 'you cannot take too many pictures' is also true when processing a scene where digital evidence is involved. Photographing the scene shall be one of the first steps taken by the Forensic Team on arrival. This shall accurately depict the condition of the scene prior to any evidence collection or disruption that will occur during processing (unless a local management search or seizure has been carried out).

The order photographs are taken shall be carried out in a manner that will not corrupt the scene. The ideal situation is to first take several photographs that shall establish the location of the scene (i.e. building, office number, etc.), followed by an entry photograph (what is seen as one enters the room), followed by a series of '360 degree' photographs.

'360 degree' photographs are simply overlapping photographs depicting the entire crime scene. The key to remember in crime scene photography is to go from the overall scene down to the smallest piece of evidence. This photography shall be completed prior to any evidence collection taking place or the scene being disturbed in any manner. At this point there shall be no attempt to search the contents of desks or any other containers within the scene (unless a local management search or seizure has been carried out). The initial set of photographs shall depict exactly the condition of the scene as the Forensic Team found it.

If the target information processing equipment is/are operational on arrival, photographs shall be taken of the monitor screen depicting what is currently displayed.

In the event a 'screen saver' is being utilised, press the 'down arrow' key or move the mouse (assuming one is present) to redisplay the open file or the password protected login screen.

Other than touching that one key or moving the mouse, no other keystrokes shall be pressed and the computer shall not be turned off unless a self-destruct programme is running.

Each information processing equipment shall be photographed in situ, allocated a unique exhibit identifier and removed from the site.

The setup of the information processing equipment and any attached peripherals shall be photographed from the 'big picture' view followed by close ups.

Photographs shall also be taken of the immediate work area involved in the incident to include information processing devices, handwritten notes, diaries, digital media.

Photographs shall also be taken of the rear of the information processing equipment (where appropriate) to accurately display how the cables are connected. If this cannot be done in situ, then all cables shall be labelled and the information processing equipment reconnected back at the laboratory to be photographed.

Even if information processing or other equipment is not to be seized and it is present at the incident scene, it shall be photographed.

Digital cameras shall be used that record Exif metadata and these shall be recorded in the seizure log given in Appendix 7. The photographs shall all be added to the client's virtual case file held in the ERMS. The metadata shall be extracted from the series of pictures taken and added to the case file.

8.6.7 Sketching the scene

An incident scene sketch shall be prepared which details the overall scene. This shall include the locations of items within the incident area. Again, the rule of thumb for incident scene sketching is to go from the overall scene to the smallest piece of evidence. This may require several sketches to accurately depict the scene. An overall sketch shall be completed, followed by a sketch of the (for example) top of a desk detailing where items of evidence are present, followed by a projection sketch of the rear of the information processing equipment detailing where different cables are plugged in.

Measurements showing the location of all evidence seized shall be taken and the measurements are always taken from at least two nonmoveable items, such as windows, doors, walls, etc.

In the event that the incident scene is information processing equipment within a large office area or in an office where more than one individual has access, consideration shall be given to the preparation of a sketch detailing the location of the scene in relation to other offices or information processing equipment in the vicinity of the incident scene.

This shall support the photographs taken or be instead of them if photographs are not possible.

Even if equipment is not to be seized and is present at the incident scene, it shall be located on the sketches. This shall also include network access points.

In addition, the client shall be asked for any:

- cabling plans;
- floor plans; and
- network diagrams.

That relate to the incident scene. It should be determined that these are not only up to date, but accurate.

8.6.8   Initial interviews

It may be that the First Response Team requires answers from a suspect, if present. It may be that the First Response Team assists at the interview or supplies questions for the interviewer to ask.

Note

The First Response Team shall never undertake interviews on their own unless qualified to interview and a witness is present.

The process for interviews shall be:

1. If the suspect is present at the search and seizure time, the First Response Team Leader may consider asking some questions of the suspect, but these shall comply with the relevant Human Resources or legislative guidelines for the jurisdiction.
2. At initial interviews the suspect often has little time to concoct any alibis, etc., and often when asked questions they answer truthfully to such questions like 'what are the passwords for the account', etc. Typical questions could include:
   - are there any keys—some computer cases and server racks have physical key locks;
   - what are the user IDs and passwords for the computer; and
   - what email addresses are in use and what are the user IDs and passwords for them?

   This is not a complete list—circumstances shall dictate.

8.6.9   Evidence collection

This section contains the overview of evidence collection by the First Response Team.

As the Forensic Team complete their search of the incident area, there shall be a number of items that may be regarded as evidence that need to be seized.

The scene shall be searched in a circular motion with the concept of the target information processing equipment being at the centre of the circle. Items of evidence, as located, shall be photographed, sketched, identified, and documented within notes and then collected. Whilst the Forensic Team shall use the circular (or spiral) approach to searching an incident scene, the other options are using the:

- 'strip';
- 'grid';
- 'quadrant'; or
- 'zone'.

approaches. All of these are valid, and it is really up to the First Response Team Leader to define the optimum approach, based on the specifics of the scene. All searching shall be methodically and diligently carried out following whichever search pattern is appropriate to the incident scene.

Evidence shall be identified, recorded, seized, bagged, and tagged on site with no attempts to determine contents or status. This may be different for some information processing equipment that need to maintain charge or systems that show evidence that is volatile and that the evidence will be lost if the equipment is powered off.

As items that need to be evaluated as evidence are collected, care shall be taken to note their position at the time of processing and to ensure they are not altered from their original state.

This deals primarily with any information processing equipment or storage media (USBs, disks, tapes, etc.) that are identified during processing. They shall be collected in the state they are found with no attempts to determine contents or status—unless an onsite preview or processing is required.

When processing a scene where information processing equipment is suspected to have played a part in a security incident or criminal act, the natural instinct is to seize the relevant information processing equipment as the first item of evidence.

In reality, due to the time involved and the number of items involved in seizing any information processing equipment, this shall be one of the last items removed from the scene.

Entries within the seizure log shall contain a description of the item (to include model and serial number if the item is a piece of hardware), the evidence log number and the location from where it was seized. The contents of the seizure log for each item seized are defined in Appendix 7.

8.6.10   Exhibit numbering

All evidence collected shall be marked as exhibits so they can be easily identified at a later date. All exhibits and possible exhibits (i.e. anything removed from an incident scene in this case) shall be properly seized, labelled, transported, and handled for evidence recovery purposes. The following naming convention shall be used for all evidence seized or created during forensic evidence processing:

aaa / ddmmyyyy / nnnn

where:

- aaa are the initials of the First Response Team member (or other person) seizing the equipment;
- dd/mm/yyyy is the date of the seizure;
- nnnn is the sequential number of the exhibits seized by aaa—starting with 001 and going to nnnn;

The labels shall be affixed as appropriate to all equipment that is being seized, typically on dedicated evidence bags.

Note 1

There may be other types of evidence obtainable from seized or examined evidence that can corroborate digital forensic evidence recovered (e.g. fingerprints, DNA, etc.).

Note 2

All information processing equipment on a network shall have network identification information to allow them to be addressed on the network.

Note 3

All information processing equipment, and many component parts (e.g. other devices inserted into the information processing devices) shall have serial numbers that can often be traced from the location that they were seized back to the manufacturer and possibly all intervening stages in the purchasing cycle.

Note 4

All software and manuals relating to any information processing equipment or the software and applications that they run shall also be seized.

8.6.11 What to take?

In a word, all of the items that are covered by the Search Warrant, consent or other authority to seize! Every case is different and needs to be viewed on its merits. It may well be that the items seized shall be limited by a search warrant of other issues (e.g. business imperatives for maintaining operations). In an ideal world, everything that may relate to the incident shall be seized and examined, as there are usually no second chances for seizure.

Note

Whilst the First Responder Team is competent in recovery and processing of digital forensic evidence, they are not experts in all forensic fields. There may well be other latent evidence present at the scene that should be preserved. The First Response Team shall ensure that they do not compromise nondigital evidence and this may involve other experts or Law Enforcement.

Increasingly, the information processing equipment and mobile phones are encrypted. If the situation allows, then the encryption key shall be obtained and associated with any evidence that is recovered. If it is not possible to obtain the encryption key then a 'live' acquisition shall be undertaken, if possible.

Each different item to be seized shall be handled differently and guidance for this is defined below:

8.6.11.1 Cloud storage

8.6.11.1.1 Description

Cloud computing refers to network services that can be interacted with over the network. This may mean that the work is done by a server at a location that may not be owned by the organisation, on the Internet, which may be backed up by physical or virtual hardware. There has been a significant increase in the use of virtualised environments, which makes it likely that the cloud service is running somewhere in a virtualised environment.

8.6.11.1.2 Primary use

Cloud Services are typically used for processing and storing data. These manage all file management processes, email use, and I/O services for all of the users on the system to ensure that there are no conflicts and to ensure that all users have appropriate access to these services.

8.6.11.1.3 Potential evidence obtainable

Different types of evidence shall be needed for different case types, and some of these are given in Appendix 9.

8.6.11.1.4 Possible issues with the evidence

1. Because the cloud environment may not be under the control of the organisation, the geographical location of the Cloud Service Provider (CSP), Service Level Agreements (SLAs) and the technical issues involved in the capturing of data from the cloud environment, shall require specific tools and processes to be adopted.
2. In some cases, the physical amount of data that has to be processed shall preclude in depth investigation.

8.6.11.1.5 Process of seizing the evidence

Note

A cloud environment may hold multiple terabytes or even petabytes of data and if it is to be imaged, then a suitably sized system to contain this volume of data must be available. If a Cloud instance is to be seized, the following steps shall be undertaken:

- Capturing memory in a shared environment requires a method of capture on a per-instance basis. To acquire running memory of instances shall require separate tools, whether remote or local (e.g. Rekall from Google).
- Hibernating a workload is another method for creating a memory capture on the disk volume in some cloud environments, such as AWS. In the Google Cloud Platform (GCP), a RAM disk shall be generated for in-memory data. There are also many third-party, agent-based tools that have been adapted to work in cloud environments.
- Network forensics is made possible in most cloud environments with emerging network traffic mirroring and packet capture capabilities. Flow log data shall be used to build network traffic behavioural models.

- Additionally, VPC Traffic Mirroring in AWS and GCP Packet Mirroring are available to any clients. These services enable the investigator to automatically copy traffic to a Network Intrusion Detection System (NIDS) or storage location for forensic analysis. The Azure virtual network Terminal Access Point (vTAP) can also copy traffic to a selected destination. Network detection and response tools are also widely available for leading cloud provider environments.
- The client organisation shall enable write-once storage that is owned and controlled solely by the First Response Team. They shall also need to ensure that the identity and access management policy is documented and a least privilege access model is in place.
- Evidence acquisition and evidence storage location activities shall also be fully logged. This shall be done with storage logging, as well as general cloud control plane logging (e.g. AWS CloudTrail, Azure Monitor, and GCP's operations suite);
- Seizure records shall be updated.

8.6.11.2 Servers

8.6.11.2.1 Description

The main processing device used on a system by multiple users, typically through a network.

8.6.11.2.2 Primary use

Servers are typically used for processing data and providing file and print services. These manage all file management processes, email use, and I/O services for all of the users on the system to ensure that there are no conflicts and to ensure that all users have appropriate access to these services. The file and print service engine is the main workhorse of all networks.

Any computer, including a laptop, can be configured as a server.

8.6.11.2.3 Potential evidence obtainable

1. There are a number of areas on a computer where evidence may be found, some of these are given in Appendix 8.
2. Different types of evidence will be needed for different case types, and some of these are given in Appendix 9.

8.6.11.2.4 Possible issues with the evidence

1. Because of their size and business criticality, it is unlikely that a server can be seized.
2. In some cases, the physical amount of data that has to be processed will preclude in depth investigation.

8.6.11.2.5 Process of seizing the evidence

Note

A server may hold multiple terabytes or even petabytes of data and if it is to be imaged, then a suitably sized system to contain this volume of data shall be available. If a server is to be seized, the following steps shall be undertaken:

- photograph the server in place, including all components;
- using adhesive labels, label each of the server's connections (ports);
- using adhesive labels, label each of the cables connected to the server with numbers or letters corresponding to the server connection they were attached to;
- seal the power plug connector and 'power on' switch on the device with tape so that inadvertent powering up does not happen and a conscious decision to remove the 'do not power up' label has to be made;
- seal any disk drives or removable media bays with tape to ensure that nothing can fall out or be inserted without removing the tape. If there is any removable media in the drives, it should be recorded on the seizure form;
- depending if the device is powered on or off and is to be seized or not follow the 'On/Off Rules' given in Appendix 10;
- assuming it is to be seized and the 'On/Off Rules' has been followed, disconnect all the cables from the server;
- mark as evidence and place items in evidence bags and seal. Record the details of the evidence bag and on the front of the evidence bag record the details of the contents;
- pack in original packaging, if possible. If not possible, ensure that the server is protected from accidental damage during transit;
- update seizure records.

Note

if the server cannot be removed then consideration should be given to what data it contains that may be relevant to the investigation and a selective acquisition of that data shall be undertaken.

8.6.11.3   Desktop computers

8.6.11.3.1   Description

A device for processing data for a user.

8.6.11.3.2   Primary use

These are primary devices for a user to interact with a network or other devices on the network. In other cases, they may be standalone devices just connected to local peripherals (e.g. scanner, printer, etc.).

8.6.11.3.3   Potential evidence obtainable

1. There are a number of areas on a computer where evidence may be found, some of these are given in Appendix 8.
2. Different types of evidence will be needed for different case types, and some of these are given in Appendix 9.

8.6.11.3.4   Possible issues with the evidence

1. Some desktops may be critical to operations and business reasons may preclude them from being removed for investigative purposes.
2. In some cases, the amount of data that has to be processed will preclude an onsite investigation.
3. There are a number of different operating systems that may be encountered, and this may also cause problems for onsite investigation, in cases where there are no appropriate tools in the First Response Kit.
4. Some hardware (e.g. Apple equipment) may need to have all equipment related to the desktop computer seized to ensure proper operation (e.g. integral screens, keyboards, and mice). Therefore, it is essential that the hardware is understood and that all relevant hardware for proper in depth investigation shall be seized.

8.6.11.3.5   Process of seizing the evidence

- photograph the computer in place, including all components;
- using adhesive labels, label each of the computer connections (ports);
- using adhesive labels, label each of the cables connected to the computer with numbers or letters corresponding to the computer connection they were attached to;
- disconnect all the cables from the computer;
- seal the power plug connector and 'power on' switch on the device with tape so that inadvertent powering up does not happen and a conscious decision to remove the 'do not power up' label has to be made;
- seal any disk drives or removable media bays with tape to ensure that nothing can fall out or be inserted without removing the tape. If there is any removable media in the drives, it should be recorded on the Seizure Form;
- mark as evidence and place in evidence bag and seal. Record the details of the evidence bag and on the front of the evidence bag record the details of the contents;
- pack in original packaging, if possible. If not possible, ensure that the computer is protected from accidental damage during transit;
- update seizure records.

8.6.11.4   Laptop computers and tablet computers

8.6.11.4.1   Description

A device for processing data for a user, really a mobile desktop computer.

8.6.11.4.2   Primary use

The same as a desktop, but that can be transported and used outside the office.

8.6.11.4.3 Potential evidence obtainable

The same as a desktop.

8.6.11.4.4 Possible issues with the evidence

1. Similar issues relate to laptops as to desktops.
2. However, the use of hibernation files and ensuring that the battery is disconnected to ensure that there is not accidental power up occurring.

Note

Some laptops may be powered up by opening the lid. Beware of laptops in hibernation mode and deal with them accordingly.

8.6.11.4.5 Process of seizing the evidence

- photograph the computer in place, including all components;
- using adhesive labels, label each of the computer connections (ports);
- using adhesive labels, label each of the cables connected to the computer with numbers or letters corresponding to the computer connection they were attached to;
- disconnect all the cables from the computer;
- seal the power plug connector and 'power on' switch on the device with tape so that inadvertent powering up does not happen and a conscious decision to remove the 'do not power up' label has to be made;
- seal any disk drives or removable media bays with tape to ensure that nothing can fall out or be inserted without removing the tape. If there is any removable media in the drives, it should be recorded on the Seizure Form;
- remove the battery and store with the laptop and any charger recovered;
- mark as evidence and place in evidence bag and seal. Record the details of the evidence bag and on the front of the evidence bag record the details of the contents;
- pack in original packaging, if possible. If not possible, ensure that the computer is protected from accidental damage during transit;
- update seizure records.

8.6.11.5 External storage media

8.6.11.5.1 Description

An external drive is usually a sealed container holding one or more hard disks that are used to boost storage, either for a desktop computer, a laptop, or a server. At the time of writing there are drives available that can contain many Terabytes of data. There are a number of technologies that provide external disk storage such as Network Attached Storage (NAS) systems.

8.6.11.5.2 Primary use

The only use of external drives is for storage of information in any form.

8.6.11.5.3 Potential evidence obtainable

Any evidence may be recovered from these devices.

8.6.11.5.4 Possible issues with the evidence

1. Some external drive systems may be critical to operations and business reasons may preclude them from being removed for investigative purposes.
2. In some cases, the physical amount of data that has to be processed will preclude an onsite investigation;
3. There are a number of different operating systems that may be encountered, and this may also cause problems for onsite investigation, in case there are no appropriate tools in the First Response Kit;

8.6.11.5.5 Process of seizing the evidence

Note

A variety of different external drives may be encountered. These can include USB drives, hard disk drives or any size or type, CD and DVD drives, removable drives as well as tape drives or any type or others may all be encountered. Each drive (except USB drives, hard disks, or solid state drives) will have media associated with it. This may be in the drive, close to it or stored in some remote location. Media for all such devices shall be seized along with any relevant software and manuals relating to their operation:

- if the external drive has removable cables, attach hand numbered adhesive labels to the cables and their associated connecting points;
- seal the power plug connector on the device with tape so that inadvertent powering up does not happen and a conscious decision to remove the 'do not power up' label has to be made;
- there are a number of different types of external drives. If the external drive uses removable media, the media shall be removed (if possible) prior to packaging the drive for shipping;
- mark as evidence and place in evidence bag and seal, Record the details of the evidence bag and on the front of the evidence bag record the details of the contents;
- any media that was removed from the device shall be marked as evidence, placed in a static free container and notes generated indicating it was removed from the external drive;
- pack in original packaging, if possible. If not possible, ensure that the external drive is protected from accidental damage during transit;
- update seizure records.

8.6.11.6 Printers

8.6.11.6.1 Description

A method for printing hard copy images. Types can include:

- inkjet;
- laser;
- thermal; and
- impact.

  All are either connected to a computer system through a cable, or a wireless connection, typically:

- serial cables;
- parallel cables;
- USB connectors;
- Firewire connectors;
- Wi-Fi; or
- Infrared ports or wireless connections.

8.6.11.6.2 Primary use

The primary use of a printer is to print documents of any type (text, images, etc.) from a computer system to hard copy media, which typically could be:

- paper; or
- transparencies.

8.6.11.6.3 Potential evidence obtainable

1. In some cases, it may be possible to identify the specific printer that produced a hard copy document (e.g. by marks on the output). Therefore, printers may need to be seized.
2. There can often be printer output of note, in the printer output tray, beside it or in a bin close by—all of these areas shall be searched.

3. Some printers contain a memory buffer, allowing them to receive and store multiple page documents whilst they are spooling their print prior to actually printing it. Often printer artefacts can be found on a hard disk on the computer that was linked to the computer.
4. Some printers may also contain a hard drive.
5. Printers may maintain usage logs, time and date information, and, if attached to a network, they may store network identity information.
6. Some printers may display unique characteristics that may allow for positive identification of a specific printer (e.g. printing a serial number or other unique watermarking device as well as intrinsic or extrinsic signatures that can uniquely identify a printer).
7. Some printers may use ribbons from which it is possible to recover details of documents printed.
8. In more modern printers it is often a requirement that the user logs into the printer to receive their printout, and so this is recorded in the printer log.

8.6.11.6.4 Possible issues with the evidence

It may not be possible to determine who has printed out hard copy to a specific printer, especially if it is a network printer. In some cases, it is possible to identify when a printer was installed on a computer.

8.6.11.6.5 Process of seizing the evidence

- allow the printer to finish printing, you never know what it will reveal;
- if the printer has removable cables, attach hand numbered adhesive labels to the cables and their associated connecting points;
- seal the power plug connector and 'power on' switch on the device with tape so that inadvertent powering up does not happen and a conscious decision to remove the 'do not power up' label has to be made;
- mark as evidence and place in evidence bag and seal. Record the details of the evidence bag and on the front of the evidence bag record the details of the contents;
- pack in original packaging, if possible. If not possible, ensure that the printer is protected from accidental damage during transit;
- update seizure records.

8.6.11.7 Scanners

8.6.11.7.1 Description

An optical device that can take a physical image and convert it into a digital form. This may comprise copies of hard copy documents or biometric images used for access control purposes.

8.6.11.7.2 Primary use

Scanners provide a method of:

1. converting hard copy (e.g. documents) into a digital form that can be made into a searchable database or provide space saving for documents being scanned and then disposed of after scanning verification. Images created by a scanner can also be manipulated by specialised software and transmitted to other users over an internal network or over the internet.
2. providing a trial template for checking against a reference template in biometric terms to authenticate a person using the service that the biometric authorisation provides access to.

8.6.11.7.3 Potential evidence obtainable

1. Often there are hard copy documents that are either on the scanner or in its vicinity, that have either been scanned or are waiting to be scanned. In addition, there are the scanned images themselves. These could be any type of document;
2. scanners can be used in a variety of crimes, including but not limited to:
    - paedophilia;
    - identity theft;
    - counterfeiting;
    - forgery; and
    - IPR theft.

In addition to the above, evidence can be gained from the device itself, be it from fingerprints or DNA or from its dates of installation, and possibly installer, on a system.

Depending on the scanner, it may be possible to link an image to a specific scanner where there are imperfections or scratches on the glass or in the scanning device itself. In addition to this, it intrinsic and extrinsic signatures can uniquely identify a scanner.

In some cases, it is possible to identify when a scanner was installed.

8.6.11.7.4 Possible issues with the evidence

Biometric scanners may be hard wired into the infrastructure and it may not be possible to seize them, especially in building access control systems. However, it should be possible to produce a variety of access control reports from their records.

8.6.11.7.5 Process of seizing the evidence

- if the scanner is removable and has removable cables, attach hand numbered adhesive labels to the cables and their associated connecting points. This can include scanners used for creating soft copy images from hard copy ones as well as authentication scanners;
- seal the power plug connector and 'power on' switch on the device with tape so that inadvertent powering up does not happen and a conscious decision to remove the 'do not power up' label has to be made;
- care shall be exercised when handling scanners. If the owner's manual for the scanner is available, determine the proper way to prepare the scanner for shipping. Mark as evidence and place in evidence bag and seal, and record the details of the evidence bag and on the front of the evidence bag record the details of the contents;
- pack in original packaging, if possible. If not possible, ensure that the scanner is protected from accidental damage during transit;
- update seizure records.

8.6.11.8 Fax machines

8.6.11.8.1 Description

Whilst no longer in common use, there are a number of organisations that are still using these legacy devices. The fax is a device that can send an electronic copy (a facsimile—hence 'fax') of a document from one phone number to any other phone number in the world that has a corresponding fax machine to receive the transmission or over the internet. The fax machine may be standalone device or be a part of a network or connected to other information processing equipment.

8.6.11.8.2 Primary use

Transmitting electronic images of hard copy documents from one location to another.

8.6.11.8.3 Potential evidence obtainable

1. Often there are hard copy documents that are either on the fax scanner or in its vicinity, that have been sent to a recipient.
2. Phone numbers that have been stored in the fax machine indicating possible recipients of faxes.
3. The send/receive fax log indicating details of the source and destination of faxes linked to the fax machine. Additionally, phone records can be sought to collaborate the fax log.
4. Most fax machines have a facility for storing received faxes prior to them being printed, as well as storage prior to transmission. Some fax machines can allow preprogramming of printing or transmitting of faxes. In some fax machines, many hundreds of pages can be stored, and forensically recovered.
5. Usually, fax machines have a speed dial facility which is used to store frequently used numbers for fax destinations.
6. Typically, a fax will have a header set indicating ownership (or origin of the fax) details. This can contain owner name, address, contact details, or any other details the owner wishes to enter.
7. In some cases, especially if a computer is used, images of the faxes sent or received can be stored in the fax system itself.
8. in more modern fax machines, it is often a requirement that the user logs into the fax machine to send or receive a fax, and so this is recorded in the fax log.

In addition to the above, evidence can be gained from the device itself, be it from fingerprints or DNA or from its dates of installation, and possibly installer.

8.6.11.8.4   Possible issues with the evidence

1. Often, with fax machines in an open office, there is no accountability for action with 'open' faxes and so it may not be possible to identify the sender or intended recipient of a specific fax.
2. Fax machines usually have their own clocks and this may not be correct, so the variation between the 'real' time and the time on the fax machine shall be calculated and be factored into any investigations.
3. It is not possible to determine whether the date and time of the clock has been changed (and possibly changed back) and by whom.
4. Powering off a switched on fax may lose any volatile data present.

8.6.11.8.5   Process of seizing the evidence

- if the fax is a standalone fax machine and has removable cables, attach hand numbered adhesive labels to the cables and their associated connecting points;
- seal the power plug connector and 'power on' switch on the device with tape so that inadvertent powering up does not happen and a conscious decision to remove the 'do not power up' label has to be made;
- if the fax is integral to any information processing equipment, handle as per computers above;
- record the phone number that the fax machine is connected to;
- if the owner's manual for the scanner is available, determine the proper way to prepare the scanner for shipping. Mark as evidence and place in evidence bag and seal, if possible, record the details of the evidence bag and on the front of the evidence bag record the details of the contents;
- pack in original packaging, if possible. If not possible, ensure that the fax is protected from accidental damage during transit;
- update seizure records.

8.6.11.9   Copiers

8.6.11.9.1   Description

A copier is usually a device that is used to copy paper documents and produce one or more hard copies of the original document. These days it is most common for a printer to include this capability, but there are still legacy copiers in use. Whilst the primary output of a copier is paper, a variety of hard copy media can be used.

8.6.11.9.2   Primary use

Their primary use is making hard copies of original documents.

8.6.11.9.3   Potential evidence obtainable

1. Often there are hard copy documents that are either on the copier or in any waste bins located close by.
2. In more modern copiers, it is often a requirement that the user logs into the copier to make copies, and so this information is recorded in the copier log.
3. In some cases, especially if the copier contains a hard disk, images of copies made may be stored and so be recoverable.

8.6.11.9.4   Possible issues with the evidence

1. With copiers in an open office and no logging facility, it may not be possible to determine who has made a specific copy or when it was made.
2. On account of their criticality of business operations, it may not be possible to seize a copier.

8.6.11.9.5   Process of seizing the evidence

- if the copier is a standalone device and has removable cables, attach hand numbered adhesive labels to the cables and their associated connecting points;
- seal the power plug connector and 'power on' switch on the device with tape so that inadvertent powering up does not happen and a conscious decision to remove the 'do not power up' label has to be made;

- if the owner's manual for the copier is available, determine the proper way to prepare the copier for shipping. Mark as evidence and place in evidence bag and seal, if possible, record the details of the evidence bag and on the front of the evidence bag record the details of the contents;
- pack in original packaging, if possible. If not possible, ensure that the copier is protected from accidental damage during transit;
- update seizure records.

8.6.11.10   Multifunction devices

8.6.11.10.1   Description

Multifunction devices are typically printers, scanners, and copiers all combined into one device.

8.6.11.10.2   Primary use

Their primary use is a combination of the uses of the three individual devices and often used to save spare or reduce costs.

8.6.11.10.3   Potential evidence obtainable

The evidence available from a multifunction device is the same as the evidence from each of the individual devices.

8.6.11.10.4   Possible issues with the evidence

The issues with evidence for a multifunction device will be the same as the combined issues with the individual devices.

8.6.11.10.5   Process of seizing the evidence

The seizure process for a multifunction device is the same as the process for all of the individual devices, where appropriate.

8.6.11.11   Access control devices

8.6.11.11.1   Description

There are a number of devices that can be used in the access control process. These include, but are not limited to:

- biometric scanners;
- smart cards; or
- dongles.

8.6.11.11.2   Primary use

Smart cards are small handheld devices that contain a microprocessor that can contain an encryption key or authentication information (password), digital certificate, or other information used for authentication purposes. Smart cards also can be used for storing a monetary value (e.g. a digital wallet), or any other electronic files. They often resemble a credit card.

A dongle is a small device that plugs into a computer port that contains types of information similar to information on a smart card that is used for authorising access to specific items of hardware or software.

8.6.11.11.3   Potential evidence obtainable

1. Where a smart card is used for storing access credentials, these can be recoverable from the card. Likewise, any encryption keys can be recovered to allow access to any documents that have been encrypted using the keys.
2. Where a smart card is used for authentication and access management, it will give details of the access rights relating to the user that the card is assigned to. Some cards may also store access log details.
3. Where a smart card is used only for storage, the files stored on it will be available for investigation.
4. Where a dongle has been used, it may show what the user has been able to access and allow the Forensic Analysts to have access to the same resources as the user who has been assigned the dongle.
5. Often, there will be a smart card reader or device for writing data to it, with connecting cables, in the vicinity of any smart cards found. Additionally, there may be software, manuals, and other associated materials related to a smart card. These shall also be seized.

8.6.11.11.4 Possible issues with the evidence

Smart cards and dongles are small devices and may not always be available at the information processing equipment where they are used. Typically, they are retained by the user and they may be overlooked in the seizure process if they are not immediately identified.

Data held on a smart card or dongle may be encrypted and shall be decrypted before it can be processed.

8.6.11.11.5 Process of seizing the evidence

- a smart card or dongle shall be identified and its use and contents determined. The user shall be asked, at the time of seizure for any relevant passwords and what the device is used for. If this is not done at the time of seizure the opportunity of determining these details may be lost forever. All details shall be documented and enclosed in the evidence bag with the smart card or dongle;
- take the smart card or dongle and mark as evidence and place in evidence bag and seal, if possible, record the details of the evidence bag and on the front of the evidence bag record the details of the contents;
- pack in original packaging, if possible. If not possible, ensure that the smart card or dongle is protected from accidental damage during transit;
- update seizure records.

8.6.11.12 Photographic recording devices

8.6.11.12.1 Description

There are two main types of photographic recording devices that may be encountered in everyday seizure:

- still image capture devices (e.g. cameras or mobile devices);
- moving image capture devices (e.g. videos or still cameras or other devices with the ability to capture moving images).

The difference between the two types of device is blurring with increased functionality and storage space. Additionally, mobile phones and devices other than cameras that can capture both still and moving images and the differentiation between device types is also blurring.

In addition to the standard still or video cameras, there are a number of specialised image recording devices that may be encountered. These include, but are not limited to:

- web cameras, capturing images to an image processing device;
- close circuit TV cameras (CCTV), capturing images to an image processing device;
- video conferencing systems, capturing images to an image processing device; and
- other specialised image capturing devices—which will vary according to a range of different requirements.

8.6.11.12.2 Primary use

The primary use of a camera or video recorder is the capture of still or video images. Whether the device is the standard digital one or one that uses the older type of traditional film or tape is irrelevant for seizure purposes but will be significant in the investigation process.

Once captured, an image can be stored, modified, or transmitted to others.

8.6.11.12.3 Potential evidence obtainable

Depending on the type of image capturing device to be seized, there may be a range of evidence available, and this will depend on the device and circumstance. This will include, but not be limited to:

1. In the case of traditional film and storage cartridges from still or video cameras, the film is in a cartridge and may be available. However, it may need to be developed and printed (or converted to digital images), for further processing. The chain of custody and maintaining the integrity of the evidence in these cases is essential.
2. From any type of image recording equipment, the actual image(s) themselves shall be recovered. Where captured, sound may also be present.
3. With images recorded by a digital process, there is usually metadata associated with them. However, this will depend on the operator having set the correct parameters. Some of the possible metadata associated with images is defined in Appendix 11.

8.6.11.12.4 Possible issues with the evidence

1. With traditional image recording devices that use physical film, it may not be possible to determine the date and time that an image was created or any of the other metadata that may be recoverable from a digital image recording device.
2. Where a digital recording device is seized, the metadata on the device may be wrong or never have been entered. This may seriously impact the credibility of the evidence produced from such devices.
3. Digital devices, after being stored for a period of time, may lose their battery charge. In cases such as this, it may not be possible to determine the time difference between 'local' time at the point of seizure and the time recorded in the device.
4. A digital device can have its clock reset during the sequence of images stored on it thus possibly 'confusing the evidence trail'. It is essential that all images recovered are 'time lined' to identify any such anomalies.

8.6.11.12.5 Process of seizing the evidence

- other than mobile phones, few, if any, standard image recording devices have password protected access to them; however, the user shall be asked, at the time of seizure for any relevant passwords or PINs and what the device is used for. If this is not done at the time of seizure the opportunity of determining these details may be lost forever. All details shall be documented and enclosed in the evidence bag with the device;
- take the image recording device and mark as evidence and place in an evidence bag and seal, if possible. Record the details of the evidence bag and on the front of the evidence bag record the details of the contents;
- pack in original packaging, if possible. If not possible, ensure that the image recording device is protected from accidental damage during transit;
- update seizure records.

8.6.11.13 Close circuit television

8.6.11.13.1 Description
Close Circuit Television (CCTV) is often in place in a client location that is the incident scene. The CCTV system should record all activity carried out in the area(s) that the CCTV system covers.

8.6.11.13.2 Primary use
The primary use of a CCTV system is the recording of actions taken that are covered by the CCTV camera.
   Once captured, the CCTV image is normally stored and can be made available to those investigating an incident.

8.6.11.13.3 Potential evidence obtainable
The evident obtained from a CCTV system will cover all actions taken where the CCTV camera(a) are pointing.

8.6.11.13.4 Possible issues with the evidence

1. The time and date of the CCTV cameras may be incorrectly set.
2. The CCTV camera may not include evidence required and may include evidence that is neither required nor helpful for the case.
3. The CCTV images may have been wiped so the storage media can be reused.

8.6.11.13.5 Process of seizing the evidence
Different requirements will be present in different jurisdictions, and these shall be met; however, the following guidelines shall be used:

- all details of the CCTV system (including all cameras) shall be recorded;
- photographs of their location shall be taken and their location recorded on the sketch of the incident scene;
- the current system settings shall be recorded including differences in time and date settings;
- determine the cameras for which images are required and the time period, then request them;
- preferably copy the CCTV images to write only media (e.g. CD/DVD) for later analysis or seize the original equipment with all of the backups (though this is usually impossible);
- the copy made shall be at the same resolution as the original, rather than applying compression algorithms to it;

- if a proprietary format is used, a copy of the software needed to view it shall be acquired;
- check the image to see that it is a match for the original, though this shall be carried out on equipment other than the original recording equipment;
- ensure that the CCTV equipment is working properly after the seizure;
- take the image and mark as evidence and place in an evidence bag and seal, if possible. Record the details of the evidence bag and on the front of the evidence bag record the details of the contents;
- pack in original packaging, if possible. If not possible, ensure that the image is protected from accidental damage during transit;
- update seizure records.

8.6.11.14   Removable media

8.6.11.14.1   Description

Removable media is a term used to describe any media that is easily and habitually removed from any information processing equipment that stores information in any form. Typical forms of information that can be stored on removable media are:

- computer programmes;
- text files;
- digital images;
- multimedia files;
- spreadsheets;
- presentations;
- databases; and
- output from specific programmes.

Typical media types used for removable storage include, but are not limited to:

- floppy disks;
- high capacity removable drives (e.g. Jazz and Zip drives);
- CDs and DVDs;
- external hard drives;
- tape and cartridge storage; and
- USB devices (e.g. thumb drives or memory sticks).

Note

Floppy disks and high capacity removable drives are now legacy devices but may still be encountered.

The unique thing about removable media is that the information written to the removable media is not 'lost' or deleted when the power to them is removed.

Additionally, it is usually possible to recover deleted information from removable media after it has been 'deleted'.

As technology changes there will be newer and different types of removable media that can hold information in different formats.

8.6.11.14.2   Primary use

The primary use of removable media is to store data. Typically, this is for backup or information exchange purposes.

8.6.11.14.3   Potential evidence obtainable

The types of evidence that can be recovered from removable media will be similar to, if not the same as, that which can be recovered from any type of information processing equipment, as it is almost always created by some form of information processing equipment.

8.6.11.14.4   Possible issues with the evidence

1. Removable media are usually small devices and may not always be available at the information processing equipment or in their vicinity. Typically, they are retained by the user and they may be overlooked in the seizure process if they are not immediately identified and recovered.

2. Data held on a removable device may be encrypted and shall be decrypted before it can be processed.

3. There are a large number of possible removable devices, and it is essential that Forensic Analysts keep up to date with this fast changing area of information storage.

4. On account of the fact that removable devices are, by their very nature, removable, there can be issues in determining who has written information to a removable device and more importantly (in some cases) who has accessed or copied that information.

8.6.11.14.5 Process of seizing the evidence

Note 1

Removable media require special attention during the evidence collection phase. The media can be found in a variety of locations at an incident scene or remote from it. The location where it is found shall be recorded and other pertinent information about the collection of removable media. If removable media are stored in the case, box, or other storage container, it is recommended that the media remain in the storage container when it is seized.

Note 2

Some removable media (e.g. diskettes and backup tapes) comprise fragile magnetic media. If they are packed loosely and allowed to strike each other repeatedly during transit, the media could be damaged. A magnetic field may also destroy information held on magnetic media.

To protect this type of media, the following procedures shall be undertaken:

- **USB Drives**—mark initials, time and date on the case, using a permanent marker or Dymo label. Apply any write protection devices present on the media, if present;
- **CDs and DVDs (including Blu-Ray)**—Mark with initials, time, date on corners using a permanent marker or Dymo label;
- **Floppy disks**—write protect 3½ in. disks by placing the write protect tab in the open position. Mark with initials, date on corners using a permanent marker or Dymo label;
- **Cassette Tape**—write protect cassette tapes by removing the record tab. Mark with time, date and initials on plastic surface of tape case using a permanent marker or Dymo label;
- **Disk Cartridges**—write protect disk cartridges (removable hard drives) by placing tape over notch. Mark with time, date, and initials with a permanent marker or Dymo label;
- **Cartridge Tapes**—write protect cartridge tapes by turning the dial until arrow is aligned with 'safe' mark or white dot is facing out. Mark initials, time and date on plastic surface or cartridge case using a permanent marker or Dymo label; and
- **Other media**—secure according to manufacturer's guidance and Mark initials, time, and date on plastic surface or cartridge case using a permanent marker or Dymo label.

Once marked, the media shall be placed, where possible in an antistatic bag to protect against magnetic fields and then placed in an evidence bag and sealed as normal.

- pack in original packaging, if possible. If not possible, ensure that the removable media is protected from accidental damage during transit;
- update seizure records.

8.6.11.15 Network management devices

8.6.11.15.1 Description

Whilst individual users can use dedicated information processing equipment for their own use, many first response situations encountered by the First Response Team will encounter networked systems, where a number of users will use shared information processing equipment.

These will have a number of network management devices that may need to be investigated as part of a first response capability and this could include, but not be limited to, the following types of devices:

- network interface cards;
- routers;

- bridges;
- hubs;
- switches;
- firewalls;
- wireless connection devices (WAPs); and
- hard wired cables.

8.6.11.15.2 Primary use

The primary use of network management devices is to facilitate the sharing of resources and exchange of information across a network by connecting them.

8.6.11.15.3 Potential evidence obtainable

Note

The types of evidence that network management devices can contain will depend on the actual device itself, however some types of evidence that may be recovered include:

1. The device itself, and the functionality it provides.
2. The configuration tables, where appropriate.
3. The address of the device, this is typically a Media Access Control (MAC) address. The address may also be referred to as an Ethernet Hardware Address (EHA), hardware address or physical address. Devices may have more than one Network Interface Card (NIC), and each one will have its own MAC.
4. A network node may have multiple NICs and will then have one unique MAC address per NIC.

8.6.11.15.4 Possible issues with the evidence

1. Data travelling across a network is volatile and is lost after transmission if the power is lost.
2. Interpreting core dumps or other output from network devices requires specialised tools for the specific device in a number of cases or there may not be tools that can easily perform analysis of output from network devices.
3. Volatile information may not contain the evidence needed for the forensic case.
4. Where volatile evidence is seized, especially where it is a covert investigation or where there are tight time constraints, the First Response Team may not have the right tools for undertaking the evidence capture.

8.6.11.15.5 Process of seizing the evidence

Note

There are two different types of evidence seizure for network devices, these are for the volatile information as it is passing through the device and for 'burned in' information.

- volatile information shall be seized in real time using appropriate tools. Typically, this will be written to forensically 'clean media';
- devices where the evidence is obtained shall be photographed and all of their device information (make, model, serial number, etc.) shall be recorded;
- where the device is located on the network (both logically and physically) shall have its location recorded. This may be recorded by the Forensic Analyst or by using the client's own network diagram(s); with verification of physical location
- seal the power plug connector and 'power on' switch on the device with tape so that inadvertent powering up does not happen and a conscious decision to remove the 'do not power up' label has to be made;
- the media on which the evidence has been recorded shall be treated as an exhibit and be marked as evidence and placed in an evidence bag and sealed. Record the details of the evidence bag and on the front of the evidence bag record the details of the contents;
- ensure the media is protected against any possible contamination by electric or magnetic fields;
- where a physical network device is to be seized, take the device and mark it as evidence and place it in an evidence bag and seal, if possible. Record the details of the evidence bag and on the front of the evidence bag record the details of the contents;

- pack in original packaging, if possible. If not possible, ensure that the network management devices is protected from accidental damage during transit;
- update seizure records.

8.6.11.16 Telephones

8.6.11.16.1 Description

Telephones come in four generic types, each with their own issues for evidential recovery, these are:

- **cell (or mobile phones)**—a wireless handset on its own that draws its power from its own integral battery that is charged when connected to a charging source (computer or electrical outlet). These are still used in some cases and so can still be encountered;
- **smart phones**—typically a smart phone is a cellular phone with the ability to run applications and have internet access;
- **cordless**—a handset that usually resides in a remote base station that draws its power from an internal battery that is permanently charging when the handset is located in its base station and is connected to a landline;
- **landline**—that is permanently connected to the telephone system and the power for the telephone is taken directly from the telephone system itself.

Telephones come in a variety of colours and shapes. Depending on the country, different phone connections are used for landline systems. A list of countries with different phone connections is defined in Appendix 12.

8.6.11.16.2 Primary use

The primary use of a telephone is to have multiway communication between two or more communicants. Communication can be over the following media:

- dedicated land lines;
- radio transmission; or
- cellular transmission.

Transmissions may use a combination of the above.

Note

Some telephones have integral message taking capability (e.g. answer phone or voicemail).

8.6.11.16.3 Potential evidence obtainable

Depending on the telephone type, make and model, a range of evidence may be recoverable from any telephone seized. Possible recovered evidence may include:

- browser bookmarks;
- browser URLs (Uniform Resource Locator) visited,
- caller ID for incoming calls;
- chat logs;
- contact list;
- cookies and passwords for site access;
- databases;
- email addresses for emails sent or received;
- emails sent and received;
- map locations;
- messages, if a voicemail service is used;
- numbers called or calling the phone;
- numbers stored for speed dial;
- phone book, giving names, addresses and phone numbers;
- photographs and other images;

- SMS (Short Message Service) messages sent and received;
- social networking information (e.g. Facebook, Twitter, MySpace, etc.);
- stored files in folders;
- task list;
- the calendar;
- the carrier the phone uses;
- the device number;
- the image on the start-up screen;
- the IMEI (International Mobile Station Equipment Identity)
- the make and mode of the phone;
- the phone's serial number;
- the SIM (Subscriber Identity Module);
- the software and version for installed applications;
- user dictionary of words added for spell checking purposes;
- user entered data, such as the user's name;
- voice mail;
- voicemail or other messages left on the phone; and
- web sites visited.

8.6.11.16.4 Possible issues with the evidence

- depending on the phone type, it is possible to remotely manipulate the phone, including deleting all information on it. Care shall be taken to ensure that the remote access service cannot connect to the phone;
- as mobile phone batteries have a finite life, evidence may be lost if the batteries fail. This is why all chargers shall also be seized to overcome the issue of loss of battery power;
- consideration shall be given to charging the device on a regular basis or immediate investigation shall be undertaken to overcome this issue;
- the use of Faraday Cages or bags and other shielding devices shall be considered, however, phone jamming devices may be illegal within the jurisdiction. As an alternative, the developing best practice is to access the device and put it into 'airplane mode'.
- care shall be taken if the phone is to be switched off as this may activate the password lockout feature;
- where a phone is password protected, unless the First Response Team have the password, incorrect password entry may erase all of the information on the phone;
- in some cases, there may not be the appropriate tools in the First Responder Kit, so seizure shall be undertaken; and
- whilst there are few issues with corporately owned phones, those that are privately owned may cause legal issues for search and seizure. Ideally, this issue shall be resolved prior to attending the incident site.

8.6.11.16.5 Process of seizing the evidence

Note

There is usually little point in seizing land lines that are hard wired in an office and the impracticality of this usually precludes it. It is usual that the phones that are seized are cellular, or smart.

- PIN numbers shall be sought if possible and recorded in the Seizure Form. It may be that these are written down on loose paper or often in the back of a diary;
- where a cellular or smart phone is seized, all associated manuals and charging equipment shall be seized;
- in some cases, on site imaging shall be undertaken, especially if the phone has no charger, to ensure that the battery remains in operation. If on site imaging is undertaken, then the phone shall be packed after imaging has been undertaken;
- pack in original packaging, if possible. If not possible, ensure that the phone is protected from accidental damage during transit;
- update seizure records.

8.6.11.17 Pagers

8.6.11.17.1 Description

Whilst now, for the most part, pagers re a legacy device, there are still a number of organisations that use them, particularly in the healthcare sector. A pager is a handheld, portable electronic device that can contain volatile evidence (telephone numbers, voice mail, email messages). Early pagers only produced a sound, but more modern ones can send and receive messages and email. Cell phones and smart phones can also be used as paging devices.

8.6.11.17.2 Primary use

The primary use of a pager is to send and receive electronic messages, which can be numeric (phone numbers, etc.) and alphanumeric (text, often including email).

8.6.11.17.3 Potential evidence obtainable

1. text messages;
2. email messages; and
3. phone numbers.

8.6.11.17.4 Possible issues with the evidence

- As pagers are battery powered, volatile memory may be lost when the battery power is lost.

8.6.11.17.5 Process of seizing the evidence

- where a pager is seized, all associated manuals and charging equipment shall be seized, if available;
- pack in original packaging, if possible. If not possible, ensure that the phone is protected from accidental damage during transit;
- update seizure records.

8.6.11.18 Satellite navigation systems (SATNAV)

8.6.11.18.1 Description

A SATNAV is a device that allows a user to navigate between locations using radio signals to indicate current position and directions to the planned destination. SATNAVs can be standalone devices and any modern cars are now fitted with integral SATNAV systems.

8.6.11.18.2 Primary use

The primary use of a SATNAV is navigation between the current location and the planned destination.

8.6.11.18.3 Potential evidence obtainable

- favourite destinations;
- home location;
- previous journeys undertaken;
- previous routes;
- travel logs; and
- way points.

8.6.11.18.4 Possible issues with the evidence

Note

Smart phones often have SATNAV capability.

- As SATNAV devices that are not integral to a vehicle are battery powered, volatile memory may be lost when the battery power is lost. Therefore, it is essential that all manuals, chargers and cabling are seized.
- If the SATNAV is in a car, access to the car will be needed and the ability to start the engine may be required.

8.6.11.18.5   Process of seizing the evidence

- where a dedicated standalone SATNAV device is seized, all associated manuals and charging equipment shall be seized;
- seal the power plug connector and 'power on' switch on the device with tape so that inadvertent powering up does not happen and a conscious decision to remove the 'do not power up' label has to be made;
- pack in original packaging, if possible. If not possible, ensure that the SATNAV is protected from accidental damage during transit;
- update seizure records.

8.6.11.19   Audio devices

8.6.11.19.1   Description

Audio devices come in a variety of forms, by the four most common are:

- A **dedicated media player** is typically a device that can store and play audio files in a variety of different recording formats. Usually this relates to music or video files but can be any recorded audio file. Because this is digital storage, other types of files and programmes may be stored on these devices.
- A **mobile phone** can play a variety of stored files or access them from the internet and play them;
- A **dictating machine** is used to store a message for later transcription to a document or as a memo. Typically, it is a portable device and used by an individual user; and
- An **answering machine** is usually in a telephone but can be a standalone device attached to a telephone and is dedicated to taking messages specifically for the phone to which it is attached.

Note 1

There are a number of different devices that have the ability to record or play audio files.

Note 2

Older audio devices used physical media to record data, typically cassettes or cartridges.

8.6.11.19.2   Primary use

Audio devices are primarily used for recording and/or playing audio and video files. They can be dedicated or general purpose devices.

8.6.11.19.3   Potential evidence obtainable

- the contents of the audio file or the media containing the recording;
- time and date of the recording;
- with files created by a computer, a variety of metadata can be recovered; and
- answering machines can also store call subscriber information, as well as caller information.

8.6.11.19.4   Possible issues with the evidence

This will depend on the device.

8.6.11.19.5   Process of seizing the evidence

- where an audio device is seized, all associated manuals and charging equipment shall be seized;
- seal the power plug connector on the device with tape so that inadvertent powering up does not happen and a conscious decision to remove the 'do not power up' label has to be made;
- pack in original packaging, if possible. If not possible, ensure that the audio device is protected from accidental damage during transit;
- update seizure records.

8.6.11.20 Other devices

8.6.11.20.1 Description

There is a variety of other devices that may be encountered by the First Response Team. It is impossible to provide a comprehensive list of devices that may be encountered, as there are so many possibilities.

8.6.11.20.2 Primary use

This will depend on the device.

8.6.11.20.3 Potential evidence obtainable

This will depend on the device.

8.6.11.20.4 Possible issues with the evidence

This will depend on the device.

8.6.11.20.5 Process of seizing the evidence

It is not possible to provide hard and fast procedures for handling other devices that may be encountered, but the advice given above should be used as a basis for handling any other device.

8.6.11.21 Seizing paperwork

8.6.11.21.1 Description

There are a variety of different types of paperwork that may be considered for seizure. This can include handwritten notes, manuals, and books as well as diaries, printer output, and the contents of wastepaper baskets.

8.6.11.21.2 Primary use

This will depend on the paperwork seized.

8.6.11.21.3 Potential evidence obtainable

This will depend on the paperwork seized.

8.6.11.21.4 Possible issues with the evidence

This will depend on the paperwork seized.

8.6.11.21.5 Process of seizing the evidence

1. The search team shall concentrate on the recovery of the following types of evidence:
   - passwords or IP addresses written on paper (check in the drawers, back of diaries, under blotters, mouse pads, etc.);
   - address books;
   - diaries;
   - items of interest in the bins;
   - computer keys; and
   - manuals for hardware or software seized.
2. Where found and thought to be relevant and deserving of later evaluation, these items shall be 'tagged and bagged' as follows:
   - photograph the items being seized in situ;
   - place the items in an evidence bag and seal. Insert the exhibit number; and
   - update seizure records.

8.6.12 Interviews

Where appropriate, the suspect or the victim may be present at the site and may be available for interview. Interviews shall only be undertaken by competent interviewers, and this may not be a member of the First Response Team, but a member of law enforcement. If questions are asked of a victim or suspect a witness shall be present.

Whilst the information to be determined at interview will depend on the specifics of the forensic case, the standard list of questions that are used a basis for interviews are defined in Appendix 13.

8.6.13   Evidence bags

Appropriate evidence bags shall be used for the different types and sizes of evidence.

It is essential that all parts of an exhibit are enclosed in the sealed evidence bag (e.g. power supplies for portables or mobile phones.) unless they need to be accessible (e.g. to maintain charge for batteries) or are too big to fit in an evidence bag (e.g. a photocopier).

8.6.14   Faraday bags and boxes

For battery-powered devices that use wireless communications, such as smart phones and tablets, it may be necessary to isolate them from the networks or from wireless signals to ensure that the evidence is not changed by incoming calls or signals that take place once the device has been seized. This is normally achieved by the use of Faraday bags or boxes that isolate the device from the radio frequency environment. Again, current practice is increasingly to access the device and place it in 'airplane mode'.

8.6.15   Seizure records

Scanned copies of all records shall be added to the client's virtual case file held in the ERMS, as defined in Chapter 15.

8.6.15.1   Personal notebooks

1. All Forensic Analysts shall keep personal notebooks recording actions taken on any given First Forensic Response and forensic case. These are preferred for offsite working as they have a better audit trail with numbered pages than the traditional case work forms used for laboratory work.
2. These notes shall be contemporaneous.
3. The following rules shall apply to all forensic notebooks:
   - pocketbooks shall be pocket sized with all pages numbered so as to refute claims of evidence tampering;
   - pocketbooks shall be issued on an individual basis;
   - once filled, pocketbooks shall be securely stored by the Laboratory Manager;
   - blank parts of pages shall have a line through them and initialled; and
   - no pages shall be ripped out or otherwise removed from the notebook.
4. When filling in a notebook, the following shall be on all pages:
   - case no;
   - date;
   - time;
   - actions; and
   - initialled by the notebook holder—countersigned if appropriate.
5. All notebooks shall be audited on a regular basis by the Laboratory Manager.

Note

When a Forensic Analyst leaves FCL, their pocketbooks shall be handed over to the Laboratory Manager, who shall securely store them.

8.6.15.2   Evidence bag contents list

The panel on the front of evidence bags shall be filled in with at least the following details:

- date and time of seizure;
- seized by;
- exhibit number;
- where seized from; and
- details of the contents of the evidence bag.

8.6.15.3 Seizure records

1. The Seizure Record Forms for each item seized shall be filled in and the Seizure Summary Form updated as the search/ seizure progresses.
2. All details required on the form shall be filled in and the form signed and dated by the First Responder completing the form.

8.6.15.4 Witness signature

Depending in the legislation in the jurisdiction a signature (or two) may or may not be required to certify collection of evidence.

1. Typically, where one is required, this is the Forensic responder or Law Enforcement Officer performing the seizure.
2. Where two are required, guidance shall be sought to determine who the second signature shall be. Whoever it is will need to understand what they are doing and may be called upon to provide a witness statement or attend court.

8.6.15.5 Evidence bags and tags

Depending on circumstances, either preprinted evidence bags or evidence tags to be affixed to the exhibit shall be used. The type used will depend on the physical makeup of the exhibit, availability of correct size of bags, local custom within the jurisdiction or the client's own standards (e.g. a Law Enforcement Agency).

Whichever is used, the minimum information that shall be recorded on the tag or the bag is defined in Appendix 14.

8.6.16 Forensic previewing

There are occasions when forensic previewing of evidence shall be undertaken to determine whether the information processing equipment contains evidence relevant to the forensic case. Previewing can identify, but is not limited to:

- examinations that may require experience outside the First Response team's competence;
- exhibits requiring prioritised investigation (depending on the forensic case parameters);
- investigation strategy where more detailed investigation is needed; and
- media likely to contain evidence.

To do this:

1. Forensic previewing shall be performed if the Laboratory Manager or the Incident Manager requires and authorises it.
2. Typically, previewing shall be used to determine if there are grounds for seizing a particular system:
    - a portable acquisition write blocking device or portable forensic workstation with suitable write blocker shall be used and the preview function of EnCase or similar tools shall be used with no image made;
    - the Laboratory Manager or the Incident Manager shall be advised of any results as soon as possible; and
    - if previewing is to be undertaken, then the Forensic Preview Form shall be used. This has been designed to be used with Encase as this is one of the tools of choice. The form is defined in Appendix 15. Should another tool be used, then the form may need to be amended.

8.6.17 Onsite imaging

Onsite imaging shall be carried out in specific situations:

- if client's management require a copy;
- if the First Response Team Leader believes that there are insufficient grounds for seizing a particular system but that there are grounds for obtaining a copy;
- If the First Response Team Leader believes that there are grounds for seizing a system but that this would result in unacceptable loss or hardship to the suspect or the organisation where the evidence is located; or
- normal procedures for imaging shall be followed—but on site rather than in the laboratory. The process for imaging is defined in Chapter 9, Section 9.9.

8.6.17.1 Performing imaging on site with dedicated hardware

1. Imaging can be performed on site using dedicated forensic acquisition hardware so long as it is used by trained and qualified Forensic Analysts or First Responders. The acquired image shall have its hash values checked against the original to ensure that the two images are identical.
2. Once the image is captured in this way, appropriate backups of it shall be made and shall be hashed to ensure that they also have matching hashes.

8.6.17.2 Performing imaging on site with a travelling laboratory

1. It is possible to use a portable PC with a copy of forensic imaging software to capture the required images from a suspect machine if required. The process to be followed shall be the same as that which is carried out in the laboratory but on site with a portable PC. If this is to be carried out, appropriate equipment shall be carried in the grab bag, as defined in Appendix 3.
2. The specification for the travelling laboratory system is defined in Appendix 16.

8.6.18 Direct data access and live acquisition

This shall be considered in the same circumstances as 'on site imaging' but with the additional difficulty that even shutting down the system concerned for a short period may result in unacceptable loss or hardship or that traditional 'pulling the plug' was not an appropriate approach to securing relevant evidence.

8.6.18.1 The need for live acquisition

The need for live acquisition is being driven by rapid changes in technology and the computing environment, including, but not limited to:

- applications can be installed from external media and then virtualised into RAM, leaving no trace on a hard disk;
- data in RAM is lost when the device is rebooted, powered off or when an open session or shell is closed;
- dedicated software can be used to 'scrub' a disk and delete the audit trail and history of actions on closedown;
- hidden areas of a hard disk are often used, that are not visible to the standard operating system;
- malware that is fully RAM resident and may have no trace on a hard disk;
- root kits are designed to remain 'hidden' to the operating system so trusted tools are required;
- software, and specifically web browsers, have evidence eradication processes that delete the audit trail or history when the browser is closed;
- some parts of a suspect information processing equipment at the incident scene may have 'booby trapped' software that may trigger Trojans, time bombs, or other destructive programmes; and
- web-based email does not leave trace evidence on a hard disk, as with traditional email clients like Microsoft Outlook or Mozilla.

8.6.18.2 The order of volatility

Live forensic acquisition shall provide for digital evidence collection in the order that acknowledges the volatility of the evidence and collects it in the order of volatility to maximise the preservation of evidence. The order of volatility within information processing equipment and supporting storage media can range from nanoseconds cache memory to tens of years (CDs, DVDs, paper output).

The order of volatility (OOV) is:

- CPU, memory cache, and the registers;
- routing tables;
- ARP cache;
- process state and processes running;
- kernel modules and statistics;
- main memory (RAM);
- temporary system files;
- swap files;

- network configuration and connections;
- system settings;
- command history;
- open files, clipboard data, logged on users; and
- the file system.

Appropriate tools shall be used for live capture.

8.6.18.3 Procedure for remote acquisition

The term Remote Forensics (also identified as Network Forensics or Online Forensics by some organisations) is used most commonly to refer to performing digital forensics remotely in an enterprise environment. It is comprised of the collection, examination, and reporting of digital evidence from a connected, operating computer on a live network.

The primary benefit of Remote Forensics tools is that it will provide a response capability and a method for First Response teams to capture an image of information processing equipment when it is not possible to gain physical access to it. Most Remote Forensic tools use a servlet, a piece of software installed onto the information processing equipment that allows the First Responder or a Forensic Analyst to access and analyze the information processing equipment remotely.

The process for remote acquisition is defined in Chapter 9, Section 9.9.3.

8.6.18.4 Procedure for live capture

The process for live capture is similar to that of remote acquisition with the following differences (Fig. 8.3).

1. The Laboratory Manager, the Incident Manager, the First Response Team Leader and the relevant Business Manager shall be informed of the potential consequences of obtaining evidence in this manner and authorise the process in writing.
2. The acquisition shall either done by the employees on site or remotely from the laboratory.
3. Network traffic dumps shall be taken, as this can reveal important information about the machine to be processed, especially if it is accessed remotely or across a network. This information can influence the next steps.
4. Evidence shall be collected according to the order of volatility (OOV), starting with the most volatile evidence and then capturing other evidence as required by the specifics of the forensic case.
5. A dedicated hardware capture device or the First Response Team or Forensic Analyst's portable forensic laboratory shall be used for this.
6. Evidence shall then be processed as normal.
7. If the physical evidence is to remain on site, then this process shall be followed without the physical seizure.

Live capture shall only be attempted when the conditions listed in the relevant forensic guidance for the jurisdiction can clearly be shown to have been complied with, particularly with reference to the competence of the First Responder or Forensic Analyst concerned.

In addition, with the use of malware software detection, the ability to deny the 'Trojan Horse Defence' shall be considered.

Note

Live capture in an intrusion detection situation may alert the intruder whilst either monitoring the system or acquiring evidence.

8.6.19 Secondary search of scene

Once all evidence has been collected, a secondary search of the incident scene shall be conducted. In the event additional evidence is located during this second search, it shall be noted, photographed and collected following the procedures used for the initial search.

All paperwork relating to the incident scene shall be reviewed and at least two people shall perform the search, if possible, to ensure completeness and that the chances of anything being overlooked are minimised.

8.6.20 Release of the incident scene

1. Prior to release of the incident scene when the secondary or final search has been carried out, photographs of the incident scene shall be made showing its final condition.

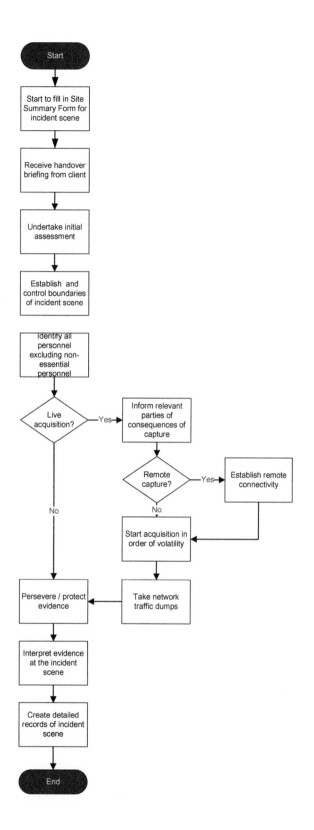

FIG. 8.3 Live forensics.

2. The First Response Team Leader shall undertake a post incident team debriefing to check that the incident scene processing has been completed and all post incident scene processing responsibilities have been fulfilled. The attendees at the debriefing shall comprise the relevant employees (First Response Team, Forensic Analysts (if used) and other specialists used—e.g. photographer, artist, etc.), the first client employees at the scene (if available) and other interested parties as required. This debriefing shall:
   - determine what evidence was collected;
   - discuss and agree required outcomes and how the evidence recovered shall support this;
   - discuss and agree the proposed processing to be undertaken;
   - discuss and agree the sequence and prioritisation of tasks;
   - ensure that all outstanding actions from the crime scene processing have been assigned and tracked through to completion; and
   - establish post incident scene processing responsibilities for all attendees, if appropriate.
3. Upon completion of processing, the incident scene shall be released, after checking:
   - all areas of the incident scene have been inspected and checked;
   - all evidence collected is accounted for and is securely packed for transportation to the laboratory;
   - all equipment and material is packed for transportation back to the laboratory;
   - all documentation from the scene has been completed; and
   - the incident scene shall be released in accordance with requirements in the jurisdiction, if appropriate.
4. The scene shall be released to the System Administrator or supervisor for the incident scene. The scene shall only be released by the First Response Team Leader.
5. A copy of the evidence/property documents listing items removed from the scene shall be provided to the person who 'owns' the incident scene.
6. Ensuring that all relevant evidence has been identified and processed cannot be overstressed. As has been said before it is rare that a second visit to the incident scene is possible and that may require a new warrant or other permission.
7. Undertake a post incident scene review to understand lessons learned and the opportunities for continuous improvement.

8.7 Transportation to the laboratory

8.7.1 Minimum handling of exhibits

There shall be a minimum number of employees handling the exhibits from securing the incident scene until they are safely and securely locked in the Secure Property Store.

The reason for this is simple:

The fewer people handling the evidence, the fewer statements shall be required, the fewer people shall have to testify and the less likely mistakes will occur with handling and continuity.

8.7.2 Packing

1. Evidence to be recovered from the scene of the incident to the Secure Property Store shall be properly packed, recorded and labelled prior to despatch.
   - seizure records shall be checked off against physical evidence bags; and
   - evidence bags shall be checked to ensure that they have been properly and completely filled in;
2. Any containers used shall be appropriate for the job and be properly labelled.
3. Information processing equipment and media shall be handled gently during packing and covered in protective material.
4. The condition of the equipment is not known when it is seized. Any disturbance could result in connections coming loose. In addition, not all fixed magnetic media is self-parking. Head parking moves the electromagnetic equipment inside a disk away from the electromechanical magnetic media. The 'parking' of the heads provides some protection but shall never be substituted for careful handling. It shall always be assumed that the heads are not parked. Any significant trauma to the computer could result in hard drive failure.
5. The ideal packing material for any information processing equipment is the original factory container. If this cannot be located, then bubble wrap shall be used if it available, it this is not possible, the information processing equipment shall be packed and carried as it was set up.
6. If possible, information processing equipment shall be packed in antistatic containers.

7. Differing jurisdictions do not always use plastic evidence bags but prefer paper ones so that there is no risk from condensation or humidity contamination.
8. Smart phones, mobile phones and similar devices shall be packed in Faraday isolation bags or boxes or radio frequency shielded material to prevent messages being sent or received after seizure.

8.7.3 Transport

1. If the Forensic Analyst or First Responder are their own Evidence Custodian, then they will hand carry or escort the evidence back to the Secure Property Store. The evidence shall be hand carried/escorted and not leave the Forensic Analyst or First Responder until it is signed into the Secure Property Store. This means that it shall be carried on any aeroplane as hand baggage and not be put in the hold or the 'Chain of Custody'; is lost.
2. If evidence cannot be hand carried, then a car or other vehicle shall be used for transporting it back to the Secure Property Store.
3. Where possible, avoid turning a computer upside down or laying it on its side during transport.
4. When transporting information processing equipment, it shall not be placed in the boot (trunk) or any other area of the vehicle where there is the possibility of possible dramatic temperature and humidity changes.
5. In a vehicle, the ideal place for transport shall be on the rear seat, placed in a manner where it will not fall during a sudden stop or quick manoeuvre.
6. All evidence shall be protected from any magnetic sources or similar sources of power that could affect the integrity of the electronic evidence.
7. Couriers shall be avoided unless they can guarantee hand to hand contact (i.e. evidence is not left in a 'hub' overnight or similar). In this case, the 'Chain of Custody' shall be signed by the Courier, who may need to provide a statement supporting this. This is one good reason to avoid couriers.
8. Postal services for conveying evidence are not acceptable and shall not be used.

8.7.4 Movement records

When any exhibit is moved, the Movement Record form for the exhibit shall be updated. This shows the complete movement of any exhibit from initial receipt or seizure to final return to the client or disposal.

The content of the Movement Form is defined in Appendix 17.

8.8 Incident scene and seizure reports

Often a First Response action as part of overall case processing, rather than a standalone seizure operation. In this case, contemporaneous notes shall be used as input to the final case report and shall contain:

- client instructions;
- initial response documentation;
- entry/exit documentation;
- photographs/videos;
- crime scene sketches/diagrams and plans;
- evidence documentation;
- new case form;
- First Responder seizure summary log;
- site summary form;
- seizure log;
- forensic preview forms;
- movement forms;
- other responders' documentation; and
- record of consent form(s) or search warrant(s).

Where a specific report type is needed for an incident scene report, it will depend on what specifically the client requires, and this may have been agreed as part of the proposal, as defined in Chapter 6, Section 6.6. The Incident Response Report template is defined in Appendix 18.

The report shall be factual, not contain any interpretations and meet the requirements of the document control requirements, as defined in Chapter 4, Section 4.7.5, classified according to the classifications defined in Chapter 5, Appendix 16 and handled in accordance with Chapter 12, Section 12.3.14.9.

8.9 Post incident review

One of the most important parts of the Deming Cycle is continuous improvement, and all too often this is overlooked. This shall be built into the Integrated Management System (IMS), as defined in Chapter 4, Sections 4.3.1.5, 4.7, 4.8, and 4.9 and Chapter 6, Section 6.13.5.

The First Response Teams shall constantly keep up with new technologies, new tools, and methods and the recommendations for improvements that come from client feedback and internal audits and reviews.

Post incident reviews shall be held soon after the incident and preferably after the incident response report has been completed. They shall be attended by the First Response Team, relevant Forensic Analysts, other employees attending and any relevant client Management staff. Depending on the incident itself; this may be a long meeting (if a major incident) or a short one for an isolated incident.

A standard agenda template for Post Incident Reviews is defined in Appendix 19.

All actions raised at the meeting shall be tracked through the CAPA database to completion. How the client deals with them is a matter for the client.

Appendix 1—Mapping ISO 17020 to IMS procedures

ISO 17020 section	Control	Procedure(s)
4	General requirements	
4.1	Impartiality and independence	Chapter 3, Section 3.1.5
		Chapter 3, Appendix 3
		Chapter 4, Section 4.5.1
		Chapter 5
		Chapter 6, Section 6.2.1.6
4.2	Confidentiality	Chapter 6, Section 6.11
5	Structural requirements	
5.1	Administrative requirements	Chapter 3, Section 3.1.2
		Chapter 3, Section 3.1.4
		Chapter 6, Section 6.2.11
		Chapter 6, Section 6.2.1.2
		Chapter 6, Section 6.1.3
5.2	Organisation and management	Chapter 4, Section 4.5.3
		Chapter 4, Section 4.6.3
		Chapter 6, Section 6.2.1.3
		Section 8.1.5
		Chapter 18, Section 18.1.5 and job descriptions are in various appendices in the book

ISO 17020 section	Control	Procedure(s)
6	Resource requirements	
6.1	Personnel	Chapter 3, Section 3.1.3.10
		Chapter 3, Section 3.1.5
		Chapter 3, Section 3.1.12
		Chapter 3, Appendix 3
		Chapter 4, Section 4.5.1
		Chapter 5
		Chapter 6, Section 6.2.1.6
		Chapter 4, Section 4.6.3
		Chapter 4, Section 4.7.1
		Chapter 4, Section 4.7.2
		Chapter 4, Section 4.7.3
		Chapter 6, Section 6.11
		Chapter 6, Appendix 8
		Chapter 6, Appendix 23
		Chapter 18, Section 18.2.1
		Chapter 18, Section 18.2.2
6.2	Facilities and equipment	Chapter 2
		Chapter 3
		Chapter 4, Section 4.6.2.2
		Chapter 4, Section 4.6.2.4
		Chapter 4, Section 4.6.2.5
		Chapter 6, Section 6.7.4
		Chapter 6, Section 6.12
		Chapter 7
		Sections 8.6.2, 8.6.3, and 8.6.4
		Chapter 12, Section 12.3.8
		Chapter 12, Section 12.4.4
		Chapter 12, Section 12.6
		Chapter 7, Section 7.5.4
		Chapter 6, Section 6.7.4
		Chapter 12, Section 12.3.14
		Chapter 14
6.3	Subcontracting	Chapter 15

Continued

ISO 17020 section	Control	Procedure(s)
7	Process requirements	
7.1	Inspection methods and procedures	Chapter 4, Section 4.6.2.2
		Chapter 4, Section 4.6.3
		Chapter 4, Section 4.9.1
		Chapter 5, Appendix 16
		Chapter 6, Section 6.6
		Chapter 6, Section 6.7.1
		Chapter 6, Section 6.8
		Chapter 6, Section 6.11
		Chapter 6, Section 6.13.1
		Chapter 6, Appendix 14
		Chapter 6, Appendix 20
		Chapter 7, Section 7.5.5
		Section 8.6.3
		Chapter 9, Section 9.10.2.13
		Chapter 9, Section 9.13
		Chapter 9, Section 9.15
		Chapter 12, Sections 12.8.3.2 and 12.8.4
		Chapter 17
7.2	Handling inspection items and samples	Section 8.6.10
		Each section in Section 8.6.11.4 for protection of each piece of evidence seized
		Section 8.6.13
		Section 8.6.14
		Section 8.6.15
		Section 8.7
		Section 8.8
		Appendix 14
7.3	Inspection records	The ERMS and contents of the virtual forensic case file for each client/forensic case
7.4	Inspection reports and inspection certificates	Chapter 6, Section 6.12
		Chapter 6, Appendix 27
		Chapter 6, Appendix 28
		Appendix 18
7.5	Complaints and appeals	Chapter 6, Section 6.14
		Chapter 16, Section 16.2.7
		Chapter 6, Appendix 18
		Chapter 6, Appendix 19
		Chapter 6, Appendix 20
		Chapter 14, Section 14.2.1.3
		Chapter 16, Section 2.8

ISO 17020 section	Control	Procedure(s)
7.6	Complaints and appeals process	Chapter 6, Section 6.14
		Chapter 16, Section 16.2.7
		Chapter 6, Appendix 18
		Chapter 6, Appendix 19
		Chapter 6, Appendix 20
		Chapter 14, Section 14.2.1.3
		Chapter 16, Section 2.8
8	Management system requirements	
8.1	Options	**The IMS**
8.2	Management system documentation (Option A)	Chapter 4, Section 4.7.5
8.3	Control of documents (Option A)	Chapter 4, Section 4.7.5.3
8.4	Control of records (Option A)	Chapter 4, Section 4.7.6
8.5	Management review (Option A)	Chapter 4, Section 4.9.3
		Chapter 4, Section 4.9.4
		Chapter 4, Section 4.9.5
8.6	Internal audits (Option A)	Chapter 4, Section 4.9.2
8.7	Corrective actions (Option A)	Chapter 4, Section 4.10
8.8	Preventive actions (Option A)	Chapter 4, Section 4.10

Appendix 2—First response briefing agenda

There are many different situations where a first response presence shall be required. It is not possible to give a detailed agenda for an initial briefing meeting, as these shall vary based on who else is attending, the specifics of the incident, location, etc. However, the following is the framework that is used in FCL and is amended as required for the specific circumstances of the incident where a response is required:

- **status report on the incident**—what is known about the situation to date;
- **other parties involved**—what third parties are involved (client, law enforcement, others);
- **roles and responsibilities**—of all of those involved in the incident;
- **location**—of the incident with all details relating to accessing the site;
- **health and safety**—any concerns about attending the incident scene. This shall include any specific equipment health and safety issues known in advance, and shall include any laser type equipment, dangerous emissions (e.g. microwave transmissions) or any equipment that may retain a charge after unplugging it. The First Response Team shall be advised of any equipment that poses a health and safety risk discovered during the first response;
- **secure areas**—for temporary storage;
- **smoking, eating, and refreshments facilities and locations**;
- **legal considerations**—jurisdictional issues, law enforcement liaison, relevant contractual issues;
- **use of other facilities on site**—e.g. toilets, phones, etc.;
- **timings and mobilisation**—who is to go where and when and time constraints, if any;
- **immediate actions**—if the scene needs to be secured or if any triage needs to be undertaken on the client's systems;
- **evidence required**—what is to be proved and where it may be found (if known);
- **searching protocols**—what can be removed and what cannot;

- **business continuity**—ensuring the client's business can continue, as far as is reasonably practicable;
- **on site forensic operations**—will on site imaging, previewing, or real-time forensics be required?
- **records**—to be made of the client site and identity of the evidence of the Evidence Custodian(s);
- **progress meetings**—if they are to take place, who shall attend and when they are to be held;
- **site handover**—checklists for formally handing the scene back to the client;
- **post attendance meeting**—details of the post incident response meeting, discussing issues and next actions—including lessons learned for continuous improvement; and
- **any other issues**—that are not covered in the above briefing agenda.

Appendix 3—Contents of the grab bag

Different members of First Response Teams usually tailor their grab bags for the equipment that they find most useful at an incident. Below are the standard grab bag contents:

Essential kit

- consent to search forms;
- evidence seizure forms;
- business cards;
- crime scene barricade tape;
- first-aid kit;
- international phone connectors;
- list of contact telephone numbers for assistance;
- mobile telephones;
- personal protective equipment (PPE), as required by the briefing, however, standard equipment includes latex gloves, goggles, and electrostatic protection; and
- spare batteries.

Search kit

- case processing forms;
- A4 Paper in clipboards;
- cutting instruments (knife, scissors clippers);
- digital camera (still and video) with flash/spare memory/tripod and charger for camera battery;
- envelopes;
- evidence collection bags (various sizes);
- evidence identifier labels;
- evidence seals/tape;
- Label writer;
- latex gloves;
- magnifying glass;
- measuring tape;
- evidential notebooks;
- pens and highlighters;
- permanent markers;
- photographic scale (a ruler);
- plastic bags;
- rubber bands;
- sketch paper;
- label writer spare cartridge and batteries;
- tape recorder;
- tweezers/forceps; and
- small torches and extra batteries.

Imaging kit

Note

If multiple systems are to be imaged then the items marked with an asterisk * will need to be increased to ensure that all systems can be imaged.

- *large hard disk for containing image of suspect device;
- assorted hard disk adaptors;
- Multipoint power adaptor;
- adjustable spanner;
- antistatic wrist band;
- assorted instructions, driver CDs, etc.;
- assorted SCSI device adaptors;
- forensic imaging software[b];
- clean booting USB device;
- forensic investigation software;
- dongles (as required by the software deployed);
- ethernet card;
- extension cables;
- write blockers[c];
- various external cables (including USB, network RJ45, FireWire, etc.);
- hard disk bay keys;
- hex-nut drivers;
- modem cable;
- mouse;
- multicard reader;
- PDA and mobile device recovery kit;
- Parallel cable;
- PC internal power cables;
- pliers, various;
- power adaptors;
- roll of labels;
- rolls of tape;
- screwdriver bits;
- screwdrivers—various heads (Phillips, flat head, posidrive, torx, etc.);
- secure-bit drivers;
- portable media reader and cards;
- specialised manufacturer specific screwdrivers (manufacturer-specific, e.g. Compaq, Macintosh);
- star-type nut drivers;
- TV connectors;
- tweezers, grabbers, etc.;
- wire strippers/cutters; and
- yellow 'crossover' Cat 5 cable.

8.9.1 Package and transport supplies

- antistatic bags;
- antistatic bubble wrap;
- faraday bags/boxes;
- cable ties;

---

b. A range of tools including Encase, FTK and dd.
c. Write clockers such as the FastBloc, Tableau or others according to the First Responder's choice.

- evidence bags;
- evidence tape;
- packing materials (avoid materials that can produce static electricity such as Styrofoam or Styrofoam peanuts);
- packing tape; and
- sturdy boxes of various sizes.

Appendix 4—New forensic case form

Note

Depending on the forensic case, not all of this information may be relevant.

The following details shall be recorded for the start of any new forensic case:

- case name, if known;
- case number, generated by the Case Management System, in sequence of the form yyyy/nnnn (where yyyy is the year and nnnn is a sequential case number for the year (yyyy) starting with 0001 and going to 9999);
- client contact details;
- client reference;
- client;
- Forensic Analyst(s) assigned to the case;
- jurisdiction;
- on site contact details;
- other agencies or organisations involved;
- seizure type (overt or covert);
- details of seizure requirements, if known;
- summary of evidence requested;
- summary of the actions so far;
- incident type;
- how was the incident discovered;
- is the incident still ongoing?
- is there network surveillance or IDS in place?
- has the system been taken offline?
- if so, who authorised it?
- If not, who authorised it to remain attached to the network?
- physical security at site;
- who has access to the system since the incident started?
- who else knows about the incident;
- what is the logical security for the system;
- is the source IP of the attack?
- what investigative steps have been undertaken to date?
- what are the results?

Other forms shall be completed, as appropriate, during the progress of the case.

Appendix 5—First responder seizure summary log

The following details shall be captured in the First Responder Log. Some of this will be copied onto the form from the New Forensic Case Form, and the rest shall be filled in as the case progresses and the facts become known.

- case no;
- case name;
- location of seizure:
  - room no;
  - building name;
  - address line 1;

- address line 2;
- address line 3;
- address line 4;
- post/zip code;
- details of incident;
- incident manager on site;
- contact details;
- first on scene;
- contact details;
- is scene secured? (yes/no);
- if secured, by whom?
- contact details;
- legislative jurisdiction;
- local client contact;
- contact details;
- overt or covert operation?
- description of incident;
- evidence required;
- Forensic Analyst(s) assigned; and
- Evidence Custodian.

Appendix 6—Site summary form

The following details shall be captured on the Site Summary Form. Some of this will be copied onto the forms from the New Forensic Case Form, and the rest shall be filled in as the case progresses and the facts become known.

- case no;
- case name;
- location of seizure:
  - room no;
  - building name;
  - address line 1;
  - address line 2;
  - address line 3;
  - address line 4;
  - post/zip code;
- details of incident;
- incident manager on site;
- contact details;
- first on scene;
- contact details;
- name and address details of all present at the scene and those removed from the scene;
- date and time of arrival at the scene;
- actions taken since discovery of the incident;
- assessed health and safety hazards and their treatments;
- records of PPE used;
- incident site boundaries;
- identified entry and exit point to the scene;
- maintain records of all actions and observations;
- taken appropriate photographs;
- drawn appropriate plans and sketches;
- collected the relevant evidence (separate evidence logs are maintained);
- labelled all exhibits according to the naming standard in place;
- updated paper forms, notebooks, and the Case Management System as appropriate;

- date and time of scene release;
- released to;
- released by; and
- signatures.

Appendix 7—Seizure log

For any item seized during a forensic case, the full chain of custody shall be maintained. To assist in this process, a seizure log shall be used for each item seized. The forms used shall contain the following information:

Case details

- case no;
- case name;
- location of seizure:
  - room no;
  - building name;
  - address line 1;
  - address line 2;
  - address line 3;
  - address line 4;
  - post/zip code.

Details of evidence seized

- type of evidence seized (e.g. computer, disk, mobile device, paper, etc.);
- location;
- make;
- model;
- serial number;
- evidence bag number;
- acquisition details of how the exhibit was seized;
- passwords recovered from the owner (Y/N)?
- if 'Yes'—details;
- was the seized equipment connected to a network/internet/phone when seized (Y/N)?
- if 'Yes'—details;
- was the equipment switched on at the time of seizure (Y/N)?
- if 'Yes'—details;
- has the equipment been switched on since seizure (Y/N)?
- if 'Yes'—details;
- if yes to above, state the reason and the details of the person who switched it on (including. Date, time, reason competence);
- photo(s) of exhibit(s) taken (Y/N)?
- if 'Yes'—attach them;
- who took them—name;
- photographer's signature;
- sketch(es) of exhibit(s) taken (Y/N)?
- if 'Yes'—attach them;
- who drew them—name;
- artist's signature;
- witness signature (Forensic Analyst making seizure):
  - full name;
  - title;

- phone number;
- address;
- date;
- time.
- signature of person from whom seizure made:
  - full name;
  - title;
  - phone number;
  - address;
  - date;
  - time.
- witness signature (second one—if needed in jurisdiction):
  - full name;
  - title;
  - phone number;
  - address;
  - date;
  - time.
- signature of Evidence Custodian:
  - full name;
  - title;
  - phone number;
  - address;
  - date; and
  - time.

Appendix 8—Evidence locations in devices and media

There are a variety of information processing devices and other information storage in use today that the Forensic Analyst may encounter. The actual information shall vary from forensic case to forensic case as well as from device to device. Some shall be general purpose devices and may contain evidence as described below, and others (e.g. a dedicated computer chip such as found in a washing machine, car engine management system or shop till) shall only contain specific evidence relating to the use of the device in which they are found.

Note 1

It is also possible to subvert the original intended use of a device, and this shall always be borne in mind when dealing with forensic case evidence recovery. The subversions will depend on the case and can vary greatly, but an example is the use of a game console or a digital video recorder (DVR) to store paedophile material.

Some of the types of potential evidence that shall be recovered include, but not be limited to:

Computer files

User created files

A user can create any number of different files and file types on an information processing device that contain evidence relevant to an incident or a forensic case.

The content of the files will depend on what the user has been doing and the case type.

The file types will typically be dependent on the software that is on the information processing device (or has been removed from it). User created files can be created for one application using other software (e.g. a text editor).

Some common types of files that can be recovered as evidence shall include, but be not limited to:

- address books;
- audio files;
- calendars;

- correspondence or other word processed files;
- database files;
- documents;
- email correspondence;
- images or graphics files;
- internet bookmarks;
- internet favourites;
- metadata;
- other correspondence media conversations;
- photographs;
- presentations;
- spreadsheets; and
- video files.

User protected files

All users have the opportunity to hide or otherwise protect evidence in a variety of different ways using a variety of different tools (some of which are freely available for download on the internet).

A user may want to protect sensitive files for perfectly valid reasons or there may be slightly more suspicious reasons for protecting files on a computer.

Typical methods of protecting files include:

- compressed files;
- encryption;
- hidden files;
- incorrectly named files (e.g. those with a bad file extension);
- password protection of files using a third-party product;
- password protection of files using the file's creation software facilities;
- simple hiding of files (e.g. a jpg file embedded into a spreadsheet); and
- steganography.

Computer created files

In any forensic case processing, evidence can also be found in files and other data areas created as a routine function of the information processing device's operating system and applications and often the user is unaware of this. The sorts of information that may get written to the storage media without the user knowing includes, but is not limited to:

- Alternate Data Streams (ADSs);
- auto-complete history files;
- backup files;
- browser histories;
- configuration files;
- cookie information;
- cookies;
- date, time, and other creation modification and deletion dates as metadata in files;
- hibernation files (showing a snapshot of RAM);
- hidden files;
- history files;
- index.dat (in windows);
- internet activity;
- location bar history;
- log files showing detailed actions undertaken by all user IDs with time and date details;
- log files;
- media player and similar file listings;
- metadata;

- open and save history files;
- other details depending on the operating system;
- passwords;
- plug-ins from downloaded files;
- printer spool files;
- recent documents;
- recycle bin;
- search history files;
- start-up menus;
- swap files;
- swap files;
- system files;
- temporary backup files;
- temporary files or caches; and
- temporary internet files.

Other data areas

In addition to files created by the operating system, there are a number of other areas in storage media or in memory, in addition to the files above, that may contain evidence and these include, but are not limited to:

- bad clusters;
- deleted files;
- free space;
- hidden partitions;
- lost clusters;
- metadata;
- other partitions;
- reserved areas;
- reserved system areas;
- slack space;
- software registration within an application or the operating system; and
- unallocated space.

Other devices

Information processing devices other than a desktop/laptop or server may contain a variety of possible evidence source, and some of these include, but are not limited to:

Device or media	Potential evidence
Cell phones/smart phones	Similar to computer files above
Copiers	Similar to computer files above for copiers containing hard disks and hard copy evidence, use logs
Digital cameras	Images, metadata, audio files
Digital video recorders (DVRs)	Similar to computer files above
Fax machines	Messages, message logs, phone numbers
Firewalls	MAC address, logs, configuration information
Games consoles	Similar to computer files above
Satellite Navigation System (SATNAV)	Route information, home, and destination details
Intrusion Detection System (IDS)	Intruder detection logs
Memory cards	Similar to computer files above

Continued

Device or media	Potential evidence
MP3 players	Files, video and audio recordings
Network sniffers	Logs
Printers	Similar to computer files above, hard copy output, use logs
Routers	Logs, ACLs, routing tables
Smart cards	ID credentials
Switches	MAC address, logs
USB storage devices	Similar to computer files above

Appendix 9—Types of evidence typically needed for a forensic case

Whilst there are no hard and fast rules about what evidence is needed for a specific forensic case, the following provide some guidance on the types of evidence that could be required for a forensic case type. Each forensic case shall be judged on its merits and on the client's specific requirements; however, the list below provides a 'starter for ten':

- alternate data streams;
- databases;
- deleted files;
- document files (e.g. word processing files or spreadsheets);
- emails;
- encrypted files;
- images;
- internet history;
- link files;
- metadata;
- password protected files;
- the recycle bin;
- the registry.

Appendix 10—The on/off rule

General

During the evidential seizure process, it is usually necessary to seize some information processing equipment or forensically examine it on site. The information processing equipment will be either:

- switched on;
- switched off.

When the First Response Team arrives, decisions as to the next steps shall be taken by the First Response Team Leader to ensure that the evidence shall not become contaminated, based on the circumstances in which it is found, the client's requirements and the First Response Team's competence. The issues to be faced with possible solutions are given below with reasoning for each action. However, this shall not be regarded as hard and fast rules, merely guidance that shall be considered for all situations before an onsite decision is made.

Note

There may be changes in digital forensic thinking that will mean that this rule may be changed.

The issues

The first fact to establish is whether the information processing equipment is currently powered on or powered off.

When dealing with a powered on and running information processing device,

STOP and THINK.

The necessity for considered action arises from the fact that there is no standard step-by-step procedure for maintaining the integrity of any information processing equipment that is applicable in every situation. Every situation encountered shall require careful consideration of the nature of the forensic case and the information processing equipment in question. What may be a sensible set of actions for maintaining the integrity of one piece of information processing equipment may in fact lead to loss of evidence for another.

The issues to be considered are numerous and shall include, but not be limited to:

- based on the nature of the incident and the status of the information processing equipment found at the incident scene, where is crucial evidence likely to be located?
- which component or components of the information processing equipment shall have their integrity maintained to ensure that the evidence is not contaminated at the scene; and
- whether key evidence likely to be on the hard drive(s) or in memory?

In the past, the majority of digital forensic investigations involved the analysis of hard disk drives or solid state memory devices that had been either separated from their host or were examined in situ (e.g. mobile phones).

This made sense in the past as the vast majority of information contained within an information processing device was usually be found on the hard drive, rather than in memory and there were few tools available to examined volatile memory (RAM or flash memory).

However, the contents of RAM and flash memory in an active information processing device undoubtedly hold some information relevant to the evidence in the case and often this can be vitally important to a case. Examples of this can include, but not be limited to:

- information that may be encrypted on disk but may be unencrypted in memory;
- processes running at the time of seizure may need to be identified or examined;
- investigation of root kits and malware (thus addressing the 'malware defence');
- crash dump files;
- registry information;
- hibernation information; and
- other volatile memory that has not been written to disk.

Any such information in memory shall almost certainly be lost when the power supply to the information processing equipment is turned off. The standard operating procedures for the First Responder shall have a documented and proven set of procedures to guard against the loss of this critical information that is held in memory.

If unable to determine power state

There may be occasions when the First Responder is unable to determine the power state easily. If this is the case, then the following should be undertaken:

- check for any LEDs showing activity;
- check for disks spinning;
- check for fans running;
- other signs of activity; and
- whether any connected output or input devices show any activity.

The results of the above should give an indication of power state. If still unsure, then a value judgement shall be made, and the equipment handled accordingly.

If unsure of activity status

There will be occasions when information processing equipment is seen to be powered on, but there is nothing on the screen to indicate any activity. If is the case, then press the 'down arrow' key or move the mouse to redisplay the open file or the password protected login screen, as defined in Section 8.6.6.

If the screen is displayed, the following shall be checked:

- evidence of any encryption in place, which may cause potential evidence to become inaccessible if the device is powered off;
- evidence of any other type of communication between the device and any other device;
- evidence of any remote access being undertaken; and
- signs of evidence deletion software being run.

Should any of these types of process be active, a value judgement shall be made as to what to do. Typically, the power shall be pulled if any processes running could be considered to interfere with the evidence.

If the screen is locked, then attempts shall be made to discover the password to access it. If this is not possible, then a value judgement as to how to deal with it shall be taken and then process it accordingly.

Options

Traditionally, when information processing equipment was located in a powered off state the best practice was to leave it powered off. This was achieved by unplugging the power directly from the back of any relevant information processing equipment (not from the wall socket). The traditional approach required the First Responder to ensure the information processing equipment was truly off, not just appearing to be off as it could be in hibernation or sleep mode. The best practice to do this was to either move the mouse or hit the shift key on the keyboard.

The rationale behind leaving the information processing equipment powered off was the fact that turning it on would introduce changes to the data. These changes could be in the form of last shutdown time, last logged on time, etc. The rationale behind the traditional approach remains relevant today. However, changes in technology have forced a rethink of this approach. The traditional golden rules of digital forensics best practice are that it comes down to what the First Response Team is after, or if legislation allows then to perform that action.

The topic of best practice in the current and developing environment is discussed further in Chapter 20 where the existing best practice and the current reality are compared.

Appendix 11—Some types of metadata that may be recoverable from digital images

There are a variety of standards dealing with metadata for digital images. Some cameras allow the user to enter personal data into the camera (e.g. owner name). The majority of metadata is calculated and recorded by the camera with little input from the user, apart from taking the picture itself. Typical information recorded includes, but may vary between camera makes and models:

- compressed bits per pixel;
- current date and time;
- date and time of picture;
- Exif version;
- exposure bias;
- exposure time;
- F number;
- flash;
- focal length;
- Global Positioning System (GPS) information (but only for some cameras);
- manufacturer;
- maximum aperture value;
- model;
- owner name and other details;
- resolution unit;
- software version;
- type of compression;
- unique number of each picture taken auto increments;
- x-resolution;
- YcbCr Positioning; and
- y-resolution.

Appendix 12—Countries with different fixed line telephone connections

Below is a list of some of the countries that have different telephone connectors:

- Australia;
- Austria;
- Belgium;
- Brazil;
- Czech Republic;
- Denmark;
- Finland and Norway;
- France;
- Germany;
- Greece;
- Holland;
- Hungary;
- India;
- Japan;
- Kuwait, Jordan, Iran, and Iraq;
- Russia and Poland;
- South Africa;
- South Korea;
- Sweden;
- Switzerland;
- Turkey; and
- United Kingdom.

Note 1

This is not a complete list, but a list of those connectors that have connection adaptor kits commercially available for them.

Note 2

Some countries may have more than one type of connector.

Note 3

The grab bag shall contain a set of telephone connectors appropriate for all jurisdictions.

Appendix 13—Some interview questions

Note 1

Not all of these questions will necessarily be relevant to the case.

Note 2

These questions may be asked only by a competent First Responder of other competent person (e.g. client HR or Law enforcement). The list is provided as an 'aide memoir' for whomever is asking the questions.

Below are a range of questions that could be asked from a suspect or victim at the incident scene. This is not meant to be a complete list but provides the basic set of questions that can be developed based on the specifics of the case.

The individual

The following shall be ascertained:

- name;
- address;
- contact details;
- nicknames used;
- background information, including job and computing competence.

System administrators and management

- is there anything particularly sensitive about the system;
- what security mechanisms are in place?
- are there any personnel/personal issues that may affect the incident?
- have you noticed any suspicious activity recently, apart from the incident itself?
- how many people have root or administrator access?
- what remote access mechanisms exist and how are they controlled
- what logging facilities exist and how are they managed?
- what are the current security mechanisms in place?
- how are they managed?
- what have you done since the incident was discovered?
- what were the results?

Basic information

- what is the computer specification?
- where was it purchased?
- when was it purchased?
- have you had it from new?
- is it always under your control?
- who else may have had access to it (full details)?
- do they have their own user accounts?
- who set up these accounts?
- details of all accounts and known passwords?
- what is the operating system?
- what applications are on it?
- what do you use it for?
- what applications do you use most?
- who loaded the applications onto it?
- where was the software purchased?
- what antivirus software do you use?
- how is it configured—scanning and updating?
- have you had any malware incidents?
- how was this handled—details, dates, type, etc.?
- who installed and configured it?
- do you have a firewall?
- how is it configured?
- who installed and configured it?
- do you use encryption?
- what type/products?
- why do you use it?
- details of all keys?
- do you use any software to cover your tracks on the internet or browse anonymously?
- what do you use?
- why?

Network information

Obviously if not networked, this section can be omitted:

- how are the different computers networked?
- do you use wireless connectivity?
- who set this up?
- how is security configured?
- what is the password and user ID for setting up the router?
- how is the router configured?
- how is remote access configured?
- who set it up?
- IP addresses in use?

Storing information

- where do you store information?
- do you use external hard disk storage?
- do you use external USB or memory stick drives?
- do you use and other external storage devices?
- do you use any remote storage locations (e.g. in the cloud or elsewhere)?

Other peripherals

- what other peripherals are attached to your computer?
- what do you use them for?
- how often do you use them?
- where do you store the information recorded by the peripherals?
- who installed them?

Internet access

- do you have internet access?
- who is your supplier (ISP)?
- how do you pay for it?
- what services do you receive?
- how do you connect to the internet?
- what do you use the internet for?
- how often do you use it?
- what user IDs and passwords do you use for internet access?
- what software do you use for internet access and web browsing?
- what search engines do you use?
- do you create favourites?
- how are favourites organised?
- where do you store favourites?
- do you use any addons for Internet access?
- have you created any web sites?
- if so—details including hosters, user accounts, and passwords?
- where do you save files you download from the Internet?
- have you paid to download files from the internet?
- if so—details?
- have you accessed and downloaded files from password protected web sites or those that require you to register?
- if so details?
- do you use newsgroups?

- if so details?
- what do you use them for?
- how do you access them?
- do you use any file sharing or Peer to Peer (P2P) software?
- if so—what?
- what for?
- where do you store these files?
- what have you uploaded for sharing?
- What social network sites do you use (Facebook, Twitter, MySpace, etc.)?
- what for?
- details of all accounts and known passwords?

Email

- do you use email?
- if so—what email addresses do you use and what are the passwords?
- what software do you use to access your email?
- who set it up?
- does anyone else use your computer to access email—if so who and user accounts and passwords?

Messaging and chatting

- do you use any messaging or chatting tools (WhatsApp, Signal, etc.)?
- do you use instant messaging?
- do you use any other communications services?
- details of all user accounts and passwords?
- what chat rooms do you use?
- how do you arrange offline, private messaging, or private chats?
- what nicknames or user IDs do you use?
- do you use a webcam whilst messaging or chatting?
- have you exchanged files with anyone whilst chatting, private messaging, or using other similar programmes?

Other

Depending on the specifics of the incident and whether the interviewee is a suspect or a victim, other questions shall be asked. It is the skill of the interviewer that will determine what they are.

Appendix 14—Evidence labelling

The following is the minimum information that shall be attached to any exhibit that is seized at an incident. The information may be integral to the evidence bag or attached as a label.

- exhibit number;
- case number;
- client;
- description;
- seized from—location;
- seized from—person;
- date and time seized;
- seized by;
- signature;
- signatures of other witnesses (e.g. Evidence Custodian);
- a statement of certification of seizure.

The evidence label may also include details of chain of custody details attached to the evidence.

Note

If a new evidence bag is to be used after removing the exhibit from the original one, the original evidence bag or tag shall be enclosed in the new exhibit bag or attached to the exhibit.

Appendix 15—Forensic preview forms

- case number;
- exhibit reference number;
- reason for preview;
- location of seizure:
  - room no;
  - building name;
  - address line 1;
  - address line 2;
  - address line 3;
  - address line 4;
  - post/zip code.
- owner;
- owner aware (Y/N);
- owner present (Y/N);
- examination details:
  - start time;
  - end time;
  - BIOS keystroke(s);
  - boot sequence;
  - BIOS password (Y/N);
  - Password;
  - BIOS time;
  - BIOS date;
  - actual time;
  - actual date;
  - how connected;
- Encase boot details:
  - number of hard disks;
  - number of partitions:
  - total number of images identified in gallery mode;
  - approximate number of indecent child images in gallery mode;
  - approximate number of adult pornographic images in gallery mode;
- additional Information and/or checks;
- Forensic Analyst name;
- date;
- signature.

Appendix 16—A travelling forensic laboratory

The minimum specification for the Laptop PC that is the portable laboratory shall be:

Laptop

- dual boot Windows and Linux/Helix or similar;
- Wi-Fi, network, IDE, and SCSI cards;

- maximum memory available;
- maximum CPU available;
- external disk drives;
- ethernet hub, cables.

Software

- forensic examination software;
- other software as required (preferably a full copy of a laboratory PC).

Note

The laptop PC shall be validated before use, and records of the validation shall be held in the client's virtual case file.

Appendix 17—Movement form

The Movement Form shall contain, for each exhibit:

- forensic case number;
- client/case name;
- exhibit reference number;
- reason for movement/comment;
- unique exhibit number;
- evidence seal number;
- date;
- time;
- examiner or person receiving the exhibit;
- signature of recipient.

Appendix 18—Incident response report

Note 1

Not all parts of the template shall be used for every forensic case, only those relevant.

Note 2

This report shall only cover the processing of the incident scene to obtain the evidence. The actual processing of the evidence is defined in Chapter 9.

If an incident response report is required then the standard Incident Response Report template shall be used. If this has not been agreed by the client in advance, then the following headings shall be used:

- Front page:
  - Title of report—defining the evidence examined, usually the client's reference number (assuming it exists);
  - client details;
  - FCL details; and
  - Protective marking—front page classification of report as defined in Chapter 5, Appendix 16.
- Every Page:
  - Title of report in header—typically using the unique exhibit number(s) processed;
  - Copyright notice in footer;
  - Pagination in footer (page x of y) to show the report is complete;
  - Version details in footer, according to the document control defined in Chapter 4, Section 4.7.5; and
  - Protective Marking—front page classification of report as defined in Chapter 5, Appendix 16.

- Document Control Page:
  - Review history—part of the document control system, showing the history of the document and its updates; and
  - Issue status—draught or issued.
- Table of contents;
- Client Instructions;
- Details of the incident:
  - Date (incident discovered and date reported);
  - Type of incident;
  - Contact information of person detecting incident;
  - Location of incident;
  - Physical security at site and how it is managed;
  - How the incident was detected;
  - Other resources affected;
  - Who has accessed the system since the incident was discovered?
  - Who else knows about the incident?
  - What investigative steps have been taken to date?
  - What the results of the investigation produced; and
  - Details of First Responder(s) (employees and/or third parties).
- Information processing equipment details (for each device):
  - Make and model;
  - Operating system;
  - Primary user of the system;
  - Systems administrator(s) of the system;
  - Network/IP addresses of the system;
  - Critical information on the system (with copy of risk assessment if available); and
  - Other relevant system information.
- Seizure Details:
  - Details of the seizure—including all of the forms used in this chapter. This will include the details of processing the incident scene;
  - Evidence collected; and
  - Chain of custody for all evidence seized.
- Packaging;
- Transportation to the laboratory;
- Incident Containment:
  - Whether the incident is ongoing;
  - Whether network monitoring is in place;
  - Whether the system is still connected to the network and who authorised it;
  - If not—who authorised it;
  - Any logging in place and how the logs are being secured; and
  - Other steps taken to contain the incident.
- Next Steps Recommended:
  - Summary of recommendations for risk reduction; and
  - Timescales for actions.
- Lessons Learned:
  - Results of the post incident review; and
  - Recommendations for continuous improvement.

Appendix 19—Post incident review agenda

- introduction to all attendees and their roles;
- a detailed timeline of the incident;
- client instructions;
- the incident scene;
- what security was in place?

- did it work?
- did the client employees follow their own procedures?
- First Response Team performance;
- were the First Response Team procedures followed?
- were they adequate?
- what information was needed sooner?
- were there any actions undertaken by anyone that could have prejudiced the integrity of the scene or any further evidence processing?
- what should be done differently in processing the scene for any future incidents?
- what corrective actions does FCL need to undertake?
- what preventive actions does the client need to undertake?
- what corrective actions does the client need to undertake?
- any other lessons learned?

Appendix 20—Incident processing checklist

The following checklist shall be used for incident scene processing. It shall be amended as required for each forensic case. This shall develop into the Forensic Plan for any incident scene that needs processing.

- Planning:
  - initial contact and start-up:
    - intent and scope of the incident;
    - incident details;
    - does the client have its own first response capability?
    - What have they done?
    - Arrangements for locating at the site including domestic and travel and other relevant arrangements;
    - Sort out the initial meeting with relevant client personnel (HR? Legal? IT, others).
  - legal considerations:
    - jurisdiction;
    - overt or covert?
    - law enforcement involved?
    - employee privacy concerns;
    - other legal considerations—client Legal Counsel.
  - scope of First Responder Team authority:
    - authority to seize?
    - authority to interview client employees?
    - authority to take down production systems?
  - client requirements:
    - proposal to the client;
    - client required outcome?
    - internal matter or criminal?
    - has a price been agreed?
    - does the client understand that scope and cost can vary?
    - reporting process;
    - escalation process;
    - access to top management;
    - main client contact.
  - Resourcing:
    - have the First Response Team access to competent employees?
    - agree First Response Team and Team Leader;
    - are outsourcing partners needed?
    - what support will client provide;
    - timeframe required for completion
    - is budget agreed?
  - situation report (SitRep):
    - document known facts with timeline;
    - obtain organisation chart;
    - obtain all documents to date;
    - identify all people involved in the incident—including third parties, if appropriate.

- determining approach:
  - confirm facts:
    - interview schedule;
    - confirm respondent availability.
  - health and safety:
    - determine health and safety risks;
    - ensure appropriate PPE available.
  - risks to investigation and mitigation:
    - can suspect(s) still access the system?
    - if so, how?
    - what sort of remote access is there?
    - how is it controlled?
    - are files likely to be protected (encryption, passwords, etc.)?
    - any suspects?
    - details of suspect(s);
    - access to passwords, encryption keys?
    - what client security is in place?
    - does it work properly?
    - last audit report?
    - specialised equipment to evidence recovery and incident processing.
  - Interviews:
    - define interview questions for respondents according to their role.
  - case processing:
    - determine evidence seizure approach;
    - location(s);
    - technology;
    - ensure that First Response Team has competences required;
    - identify workarounds if competence shortfall.
- identification and preservation of the scene:
  - locations for processing:
    - sketches;
    - photographs;
    - incident scene security and maintaining it;
    - identification of entries and exits;
    - access control methods in use and their management.
  - evidence identification:
    - is this all identified?
    - is all evidence covered by due legal process?
    - If not—what is there a legal workaround.
  - evidence seizure:
    - information processing devices to be seized;
    - information processing devices to be imaged;
    - information processing devices to undergo live acquisition;
    - information processing devices to be previewed;
    - updating of logs, notebooks and forms for all seizure activities.
  - review the site for completeness of seizure;
  - undertake secondary search;
  - release scene.
- packing and transportation:
  - appropriate packing for evidence;
  - checking out evidence from the incident site;
  - ensure appropriate transportation.
- post incident review:
  - identify attendees;
  - issue agenda;
  - undertake meeting
  - produce report and recommendations;
  - raise and follow through CAPAs, as required.

Chapter 9

Case processing

9.1 Introduction to case processing

Note

FCL shall always use tools that are validated and are in general use. This overcomes challenges in later Court or Tribunal Cases.

9.1.1 General

The previous chapter dealt with evidence seizure and not evidential processing, except for forensic previewing as defined in Chapter 8, Section 8.6.16, some on-site imaging as defined in Chapter 8, Section 8.6.17 and the need for direct data access and live acquisition as defined in Chapter 8, Section 8.6.18.

This chapter deals with the actual processing of the data captured from seized evidence, as defined in Chapter 8 and the processes in the paragraph above.

A forensic laboratory will only undertake forensic case processing where it is both competent to undertake the work and it is legally permitted so to do. Therefore, it may not perform all of the actions defined in this chapter that can be performed by FCL. This chapter describes all of the processes that it undertakes, and each forensic laboratory should adopt them as they see fit, have the required competence, and be legally permitted to perform them.

9.1.2 Case processing overview

There is a well-defined four-step forensic case process that shall be applied to all digital forensic cases, no matter what the evidence or circumstance, and this is defined in many textbooks as:

- acquire;
- analyse;
- evaluate;
- present.

    Or

- collection;
- examination;
- analysis;
- reporting.

    The digital evidence that is legally acceptable in the jurisdiction.
    While this is the textbook definition, FCL has adopted and adapted this to the following processes (Fig. 9.1):

A Blueprint for Implementing Best Practice Procedures in a Digital Forensic Laboratory. https://doi.org/10.1016/B978-0-12-819479-9.00016-2

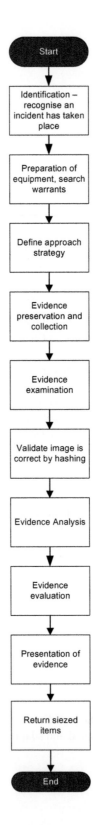

FIG. 9.1 Case processing.

While every forensic case handled will be different, they shall all go through some, if not all, of the stages of the model below:

- **identification**—recognising an incident has occurred from indicators and determining its type. This is not explicitly within the field of digital forensics, but significant because it impacts other steps. It is usually identified by the client, who will engage FCL after discovering an incident. Depending on the forensic case and the client requirements, processing the case could include:

- comparison against known data;
- extraction of data;
- recovery of deleted data files;
- keyword searching;
- password recovery;
- decryption of encrypted material;
- source code analysis;
- track and observe an intruder;
- evict an intruder and give security advice;
- examination of storage media (many types); and
- Law Enforcement support.

- **preparation**—preparing tools, techniques, Forensic Analysts, search warrants (if needed), inclusion of other agencies (if required), and monitoring authorisations and management support for any on-site first response, as defined in Chapter 8;
- **approach strategy**—dynamically formulating an approach based on potential impact on the specific technology in question and the client's staff or their clients that may be affected by the incident. The goal of the strategy shall be to maximise the collection of untainted evidence while minimising impact to the client or their clients, as defined in Chapter 8, Sections 8.4 and 8.5.4;
- **preservation**—isolating, securing, and preserving the state of physical and digital evidence. This shall include preventing people from using any of the potential evidence or allowing other electromagnetic devices to be used within the affected radius of the incident, as defined in Chapter 8, Section 8.6.2;
- **collection**—on-site recording of the physical scene and creating a duplicate image of digital evidence using standardised and accepted forensic procedures (typically done off site but may need to be done on site), as defined in Chapter 8, Sections 8.6.11, 8.6.16–8.6.18;
- **examination**—in-depth systematic search of evidence relating to the suspected incident. This shall focus on identifying and locating potential evidence, possibly within unconventional or covert locations, as defined in Section 9.10.2;
- **analysis**—determine significance of reconstructed fragments of data and draw conclusions based on evidence found. It may take several iterations of examination and analysis to support the results, as defined in Section 9.10.3;
- **evaluation**—determining the relevance of the recovered evidence, typically carried out by the Lawyers or Law Enforcement. Not only will the content of the evidence be evaluated but also the chain of custody;
- **presentation**—summarise and provide explanation of conclusions. This shall be written in a layman's terms using abstracted terminology. It must be noted that different requirements being met by forensic case processing shall have different reporting formats, and each shall be specific to case processing and client requirements. A standard incident response report template is defined in Chapter 8, Appendix 18 and a standard forensic case processing report is defined in Appendix 30. Depending on the actual work carried out, the standard template for examination of recovered evidence shall be amended to cater for the forensic case being processed;
- **returning evidence**—ensuring physical and digital property is returned to the proper owner (if the Law in the jurisdiction allows) as well as determining how and what criminal evidence shall be removed (if present). Again, not an explicit digital forensic step but shall be addressed. This step may require secure disposal, as defined in Chapter 12, Section 12.3.14.10, and all records shall be kept in line with the document retention policy, as defined in Chapter 4, Appendix 26.

9.1.3 Contractual requirements

FCL shall ensure that it meets all of the contractual requirements imposed by, and agreed with, all clients relating to processing forensic cases. All forensic case processing, of any sort, shall be subject to contract that may include a proposal or an ongoing purchase order, as defined in Chapter 6, Section 6.6. A central repository of all requirements shall be maintained and managed by the General Counsel in the ERMS to ensure compliance with all contractual requirements.

Within each jurisdiction, there will be different legislative requirements and top management shall ensure that they are both aware of them and comply with them. In addition to the legislative requirements for the jurisdiction the General Counsel shall ensure that all contractual obligations are captured and applied to the relevant forensic case or cases.

9.1.4 Work standards

As with legislation, there are different work standards for different jurisdictions. Top management shall ensure that they are aware of them and comply with them.

Work standards may be nationally or internationally recognised good or best practice or may be specific client specific requirements.

Internal procedures shall be based on recognised legislation and regulation as well as good or best practice, or International Standards as appropriate. Some of the sources of good practice used in developing FCL's forensic case processing procedures are defined in Appendix 1.

There are also any number of books, journals, articles, and blogs on digital forensics, which are too numerous and rapidly changing to list.

9.1.5 Best digital evidence principles

There are a number of generally accepted principles for processing a digital forensic case.

In the UK, the 'Association of Chief Police Officers (ACPO) Good Practice Guide for Computer-Based Electronic Evidence' describes the four key principles of handling digital evidence:

- **Principle 1**: No action taken by Law Enforcement agencies or their agents should change data held on an information processing device or storage media which may subsequently be relied upon in court;
- **Principle 2**: In circumstances where a person finds it necessary to access original data held on an information processing device or on storage media, that person must be competent to do so and be able to give evidence explaining the relevance and the implications of their actions; and
- **Principle 3**: An audit trail or other record of all processes applied to information processing device-based electronic evidence should be created and preserved. An independent third party should be able to examine those processes and achieve the same result;
- **Principle 4**: The person in charge of the investigation (the case officer) has overall responsibility for ensuring that the law and these principles are adhered to.

The G8 Proposed Principles for the Procedures Relating to Digital Evidence state:

- when dealing with digital evidence, all of the general forensic and procedural principles must be applied;
- upon seizing digital evidence, actions taken should not change that evidence;
- when it is necessary for a person to access original digital evidence, that person should be trained for the purpose;
- all activity relating to the seizure, access, storage, or transfer of digital evidence must be fully documented, preserved and available for review;
- an individual is responsible for all actions taken with respect to digital evidence while the digital evidence is in their possession; and
- any agency, which is responsible for seizing, accessing, storing or transferring digital evidence is responsible for compliance with these principles.

The International Association of Computer Investigative Specialists (IASIS) has stated that there are there are three essential requirements for the conduct of a competent digital forensic examination:

- forensically sterile examination media must be used;
- the examination must maintain the integrity of the original media; and
- printouts, copies of data, and exhibits resulting from the examination must be properly marked, controlled and transmitted.

These have been synthesised into four rules for digital forensic case processing:

1. There shall be minimal handling of any exhibit;
2. Any changes to the original media shall be accounted for;
3. The rules of evidence for the jurisdiction shall be met;
4. Forensic Analysts shall not exceed their level of competence.

The International Organisation on Computer Evidence (IOCE) has also published the 'Proposed Standards for Exchange of Digital Evidence', which suggests the following principles:

1. Upon seizing digital evidence, actions taken should not change that evidence.
2. When it is necessary for a person to access the original evidence, that person must be forensically competent.

3. All activity relating to the seizure, access, storage or transfer of digital evidence must be fully documented, preserved, and available for review.
4. An individual is responsible for all actions taken with respect to digital evidence while the digital evidence is in their possession.
5. Any agency that is responsible for seizing, accessing, storing or transferring digital evidence is responsible for compliance with these principles.

The different sets of principles and rules are broadly similar, and FCL shall ensure that it meets all of these requirements. The US National Institute of Standards and Technology (NIST) requires that disk imaging tools meet their criteria, which are:

- the tool shall make a bit-stream duplicate or an image of the original disk or partition;
- the tool shall not alter the original disk;
- the tool shall be able to verify the integrity of a disk image file;
- the tool shall provide a bit stream image or a qualified bit steam image if I/O errors are present;
- the tool shall log I/O errors;
- the tool's documentation shall be correct;
- the tool shall copy a source to a destination drive that is bigger than the source and document the parts of the disk that are not part of the copy; and
- the tool shall advise the user of a source larger than the destination.

There are also other best practice documents including the US Secret Service 'Best Practices for Seizing Electronic Evidence Pocket Guide' and the 'Sedona Principles for Electronic Document Production'.

9.1.6 Health and safety issues

Health and safety considerations are extremely important in all of the work, both inside the laboratory and on client site(s).

Full health and safety management considerations are covered in Chapter 17, but specific health and safety requirements for forensic case processing shall include, but are not limited to:

- a circuit breaker shall be provided above any forensic examination benches so that emergency power shutdown can be achieved in case of need;
- all Forensic Analysts shall be responsible for keeping their working area in a safe, clean and orderly manner;
- all employees shall be instructed in how to deal with an emergency (i.e. fire, bomb alert, etc.). These procedures, along with evacuation procedures, shall be exercised on at least an annual basis;
- antistatic devices shall be used not only to protect the Forensic Analysts but also to protect any evidence that may be corrupted by electrical discharge;
- any employees who are subject to viewing disturbing, stressful or paedophile images shall be offered counselling or psychological support from professionally qualified Counsellors competent to deal with employees exposed to these issues;
- risk assessments shall be undertaken where any equipment may be considered dangerous;
- at least one qualified First Aider shall be nominated for the laboratory. More may be needed depending on legislation, regulation or good practice in the jurisdiction. An alternate shall be nominated in case of absence of the main First Aider. This may be another employee or a suitably qualified external person. All qualifications and/or certificates shall be maintained and it is the responsibility of the Health and Safety Manager to ensure that this happens;
- if any safety equipment has been designated or required on account of a risk assessment it shall be made available to the relevant employee(s). It is their responsibility to use the equipment supplied;
- issues relating to electrical power supplied to laboratory equipment, to any seized equipment or client equipment used or processed in the laboratory;
- issues relating to the manual handling of heavy, large or awkward equipment;
- on account of the constant adding to and removing of components from forensic workstations, special care shall be taken of the risks raised by trailing cables and exposed power sources;
- regular checks for compliance with health and safety issues shall be undertaken by the Health and Safety Manager;
- the Health and Safety Manager shall ensure that all employees are subject to regular testing for the ergonomic comfort on at least an annual basis. These may be subject to legislative or regulatory requirements in the jurisdiction. Any shortfall in legislative, regulatory, good practice, or user requirements shall be addressed appropriately; and
- the use of appropriate PPE.

There may well be other health and safety issues that vary from forensic case to forensic case and incident to incident, and these shall be evaluated on a case-by-case basis and a risk assessment performed by either the Laboratory Manager and/or Health and Safety Manager.

9.1.7 Laboratory accreditation and certification

Accreditation and certification of a forensic laboratory is a management decision to be taken by each laboratory and the process is covered in Chapter 19.

All relevant certifications should be achieved in the relevant jurisdiction to maintain a competitive advantage. These certifications shall be maintained to demonstrate to the outside world the level of skill and handling that the Forensic Analysts have in managing forensic cases.

9.1.8 Caveat

While a forensic case may not start out as a case that is going to Court, the assumption that every case may follow that route, either due to evidence found or the client's wishes shall be made. On account of this, each forensic case shall be treated as if it were to be presented in Court.

9.2 Case types

There are a number of different forensic case types that may have to be investigated for a client. Some of the most common include, but are not limited to:

- inappropriate use of a system—using an information processing device and either breaking the law or an acceptable use policy;
- unauthorised access—either unauthorised external or internal threat actors attempting to gain access to information processing resources;
- malware attack—of any type; and
- denial of service attack—attempting to crash a system.

In all forensic cases, FCL shall be sensitive to the client's internal processes and procedures, and especially so if a client's systems have been used to attack or compromise another organisation's systems.

Forensic cases may be involved with requirements of different jurisdictions in many cases and have to deal with a number of different agencies, all of which must be met as part of processing the case.

9.2.1 Inappropriate use

Inappropriate use can mean many things, some of these include, but are not limited to:

- breach of the organisation's acceptable user policy;
- committing a crime;
- leaking sensitive corporate information to external parties; or
- sending inappropriate email messages or images.

The information processing equipment that is used inappropriately can vary from a server based system to a mobile device.

Some cases of inappropriate usage may result from other case types that may have occurred.

9.2.1.1 Containment

FCL is only ever called after a client discovers an incident that needs investigating as it does not provide monitoring services. Therefore, it will start at the containment stage of the incident. The procedures in Chapter 8 shall be followed for attending the incident site.

Typically, equipment shall be seized during the incident response stage and brought back to the laboratory for imaging, as defined in Section 9, and examination, as defined in Section 10, On-site imaging and remote imaging may be performed as defined in Sections 9.2 and 9.3, respectively.

There may be requirements to remove inappropriate material from a system that is not necessarily criminal (e.g. pornography in breach of the organisation's AUP) prior to returning the information processing equipment to the client. Where a criminal act has taken place the client shall be advised immediately, with a recommendation to advise the relevant Law Enforcement body, unless the client is legally required to immediately report the incident to Law Enforcement or the regulator on discovery. If this is the case, the client shall be immediately informed. Where undertaking work for Law Enforcement, they will give directions as to the requirements of handling the information processing equipment.

9.2.1.2   Gathering evidence

Evidence shall be gathered as part of the imaging process and then examination of the images produced. This shall follow the same generic framework for all case types and for all imaged devices, but the evidence required will be stored in different locations.

9.2.1.3   Follow up

After the evidence has been produced for the client, the following are typical options:

- court case;
- do nothing either as no evidence of wrongdoing was discovered or the client chooses to do nothing for some reason of their own;
- external tribunal;
- further investigation;
- improve the client's security infrastructure to prevent recurrence of the incident; and/or
- internal investigation and action.

9.2.1.4   Postincident review

A postincident review shall be undertaken to learn from the incident, as defined in Chapter 8, Section 8.9 and the agenda for the meeting is defined in Chapter 8, Appendix 19.

9.2.2   Unauthorised access

As there are so many possible different types of unauthorised access attacks that can take place when considering internal and external threat actors, it is not possible to give procedures for handling them, but rather a series of options.

9.2.2.1   Examples

Examples of unauthorised access can be from internal or external threat actors, and typical cases include, but are not limited to:

- accessing an insecure workstation in the office logged in as someone else;
- accessing and/or copying information without permission;
- accessing unsecured networks;
- attempting a root compromise;
- attempting to crack passwords by whatever means;
- running software to capture user credentials;
- theft of a laptop and using it to access the owner's account;
- undertaking a social engineering attack; or
- using a script kiddie kit to attempt to access a target.

9.2.2.2   Containment

Containment shall with the procedures for attending the incident site, as defined in Chapter 8.

Immediate response shall be performed for all unauthorised accessed incidents, especially if the access is ongoing. When dealing with unauthorised access, the immediate actions undertaken shall be to:

- disable the access method where the access method used by the threat actor can be identified;
- disable the accounts that may have been used or compromised by the attack;

- disable the affected service where the affected service can be identified;
- for internal access attacks, ensure that physical security measures are appropriate, as defined in Chapter 12, Section 12.4; and
- Isolate the affected systems, but this can be a problem unless up-to-date network maps are available.

9.2.2.3 Gathering evidence

Depending on the specifics of the incident, it may be possible for the First Response Team to:

- scan the threat actor's system to determine facts. This may be illegal within the jurisdiction and legal advice shall be sought before attempting this;
- use incident databases to see if other people have suffered similar attacks and what they did to address or remediate the incident;
- gather open source intelligence on the threat actor. Using any facts known about the attack and using search engines to see what is known about the threat actor;
- validate the threat actor's IP address. Care shall be taken that the threat actor is not alerted. Never use your own IP address. The threat actor may have used a dynamic address;
- use on-site evidence to identify the threat actor (e.g. access logs and CCTV images).

9.2.2.4 Recovery

After an attack, the threat actor usually wants to be able to return to the scene. Often a threat actor will leave a backdoor access, root kit or some other unauthorised software that may use the compromised information processing equipment as a 'bot'.

Depending on the level of access and how widespread the unauthorised access was will dictate the range of actions to be taken. Where the incident is a single computer compromised as the user left their desk and no password enabled screensaver was implemented will have a different response than a full scale network access with root or administrator access gained.

Recovery shall include, depending on the attack profile, but not be limited to:

- all passwords on the system shall be changed, in case they have been compromised;
- any system that has a trust relationship with the compromised system shall be inspected for signs of unauthorised access;
- any system that has a trust relationship with the compromised system shall have its passwords changed if it is possible that they have been compromised as well;
- the simplest method of eradication is to do a clean installation of the system from the standard build image, as none of the installed software shall be trusted in case it has been compromised;
- the method by which the system was compromised shall be addressed, typically this will involve, but is not limited to:
  - configuring the network to deny all traffic unless it is expressly permitted;
  - disable all unnecessary services and capabilities;
  - educating users on system, security, and especially social engineering attacks;
  - encrypt all desktops computers, laptops, and mobile devices;
  - enforcing password screen savers;
  - enforcing strong passwords;
  - ensure all default passwords are changed;
  - installing system protection tools such as Firewall, IDS, and IPS;
  - installing centralised log consolidation;
  - implementing host-based firewalls and personal firewalls on all hosts, critical systems and laptops;
  - patching systems;
  - placing all publicly available systems in a secure De-Militarised Zone (DMZ);
  - reviewing perimeter security and taking appropriate action to strengthen it; and
  - securing all remote connection methods.
- review the system for other vulnerabilities that could be exploited by a threat actor and mitigate them.

9.2.2.5 Postincident review

A postincident review shall be undertaken to learn from the incident.

9.2.3 Malware attack

As there are so many possible malware attacks, it is not possible to give procedures for handling them, but rather a series of options.

9.2.3.1 Examples

Malware is a term that covers many different categories of attack. These include, but are not limited to:

- blended attacks;
- cookies;
- mobile code;
- pop-ups;
- ransomware;
- Trojan hoses;
- viruses—there are a number of different types, boot sector viruses, file viruses, multipartite viruses, macro viruses, and scripting viruses;
- worms—there are two main categories of worm, network service worms and mass mailing worms.

9.2.3.2 Containment

Containment shall with the procedures for attending the incident site, as defined in Chapter 8.

By its very nature, malware will spread quickly, so immediate action is essential on the detection of a malware attack. The ideal solution shall be to disconnect any infected systems from the network, but this is not always possible, especially if the system performs a critical operation. If this is the case, then the client's top management shall make a decision based on a risk assessment whether the risk caused by taking the system down or removing it from the network outweigh the risks of leaving It connected.

Whether the system is disconnected from the network or not, there are a number of options for containing the malware outbreak and these shall include, but are not limited to:

- block specific hosts or services to which any infected systems are trying to communicate;
- configure email servers to block suspicious content, but actively manage the quarantine area in case legitimate downloads are blocked;
- configure web browsers to block suspicious content, if available;
- consider blocking services that are used by the malware, or at least suspending them until the outbreak has been contained, and recovery to a secure state is undertaken. This may have unintended consequences, as the most used propagation method for malware is email. Care shall be taken before closing down services as they may not only be essential but they may affect other services that dependent on them that may be essential;
- consider shutting down email servers where there is a serious risk to the integrity of the client's systems;
- detect nonessential programs with file transfer capabilities in accordance with the AUP;
- eliminate all open MS Windows shares;
- ensure that all open relays are closed;
- implement antimalware software if not present and run it;
- implement spam filtering software and run it;
- set scans and updates, as appropriate, for the client;
- set web browsers to prevent unauthorised downloads of mobile code; and
- update antimalware software if not up to date and run it.

9.2.3.3 Gathering evidence

It is unlikely in the extreme that a client, or the First Response Team shall be able to identify the author of a piece of malware as it is either transmitted automatically or by accident from infected users.

Disinfecting infected systems shall be carried out using antimalware software. It is recommended that more than one tool is run to identify any infected systems, as benchmarking suggests that different tools have different success rates.

The evidence of infected files and any artcfacts related to the infection shall be collated as evidence and processed accordingly.

9.2.3.4 Recovery

While antimalware software is efficient at identifying malware infections and in disinfecting or quarantining infected files, some files cannot be disinfected.

Recovery shall include, but is not limited to:

- configure software to quarantine suspicious files;
- instal file integrity checking software to detect altered files;
- ensure that antimalware software is up to date;
- patching systems to remove exploited vulnerabilities;
- rebuilding hardware from scratch;
- recovering backups to reload the system;
- re-installation of software;
- remove any MS Windows shares; and
- run two different antimalware products.

9.2.3.5 Postincident review

A postincident review hall be undertaken to learn from the incident.

9.2.4 Denial of service attack

As there are so many possible denial of service (DoS) or even Distributed DOS (DDoS) attacks, it is not possible to give procedures for handling them, but rather a series of options.

9.2.4.1 Examples

DoS/DDoS attacks can take many forms and some include, but are not limited to:

- broadcasting on the same frequency as the wireless network and rendering it unusable;
- establishing multiple login sessions so that legitimate users cannot access their systems;
- generating multiple large files to use all disk space;
- sending illegal requests to an application to crash it;
- sending malformed TCP/IP packets to crash the system;
- sending processor intensive requests to use all CPU power fully;
- using bandwidth by generating large volumes of traffic. This is not usually possible from a single attacking machine as corporate bandwidth precludes this so multiple attacking machines are used to create a distributed denial of service (DDoS) attack.

9.2.4.2 Containment

Containment shall with the procedures for attending the incident site, as defined in Chapter 8.

Containment of a DoS or DDoS incident shall usually be achieved by stopping the attack.

Options for stopping the attack shall include, but not be limited to:

- address the vulnerability being exploited. Often this is due to having unpatched systems, so patching them should eliminate a known vulnerability;
- blocking the traffic from the source. This is not usually effective as the source address is usually spoofed or uses thousands of 'Bots' to carry out the DDoS attack. Even if blocking works, the threat actor typically moves to another IP address;
- implement filtering to block the attack, however with the sophisticated hacking tools available, the attack will merely switch to another attack type. Implementing filtering can also have unintended consequences such as creating its own internal DoS in the extreme, so it should be carefully researched before being implemented;
- relocating the target is one method of overcoming the problem, but a determined threat actor will find it after it has been switched to another ISP.
- remove the host from the network whilst remedial work is carried out, but this may have a serious business impact, but some large organisations have done this in the past to protect themselves;

- turn the attack around by using tools to switch off the attack. It must be noted that the bouncing of traffic back to source may cause an innocent party to have an attack for which legal redress may be sought; and
- use the ISP to implement filtering. They will have more powerful network filtering hardware than almost all organisations and so utilise it.

9.2.4.3   Gathering evidence

Gathering evidence on DoS and DDoS attacks is a challenging and time consuming process.

Primary evidence shall come from IP addresses; however, this is usually spoofed or uses an innocent hijacked address. DDoS attacks may use thousands of hosts, each with multiple spoofed hosts. Usually, the IP addresses that are real and identified are intermediate systems that are generating the attack traffic and not the 'master' who originated it. Tracing IP addresses through multiple ISPs is fraught with difficulty as many will not cooperate without relevant legal subpoenas (or equivalent in the jurisdiction). The time taken to obtain these is usually greater than the duration of the attack and trying to trace IP addresses after an attack has ended may be impossible in many cases.

The other main source of information shall come from internal log files, but as DoS and DDoS attacks work by overwhelming the system, it follows that this shall generate excessive log traffic as well. This means that there is an excessive amount to examine and this is a time consuming process. Additionally, depending on how the logs were set up, newer log traffic may overwrite previous log traffic and therefore erase potential evidence.

9.2.4.4   Recovery

It is essential to recover systems as soon as possible in almost all cases, but they shall be secured against further attacks prior to being returned to service.

Recovery shall include, but shall not be limited to the following:

- deny any traffic that is not explicitly permitting, either into or out of the network;
- have the ISP implement filtering;
- moving to a different ISP;
- patching systems to remove exploited vulnerabilities;
- purchase and installation of additional monitoring equipment, e.g. intruder detection and prevention software;
- rebuilding hardware from scratch;
- recovering backups to reload the system;
- reinstallation of software; and
- tighten firewall rules.

9.2.4.5   Postincident review

A postincident review shall be undertaken to learn from the incident.

9.2.5   Multiple incidents

It may well be that there are multiple case types in a single incident and the processes above shall be performed in parallel. A typical scenario could be:

1. A user accesses a web site and downloads (knowingly or not) a file that is infected and the malicious code compromises a workstation.
2. The malicious code is used to infect other workstations on the system and/or other systems connected to the infected system.
3. The compromised systems are turned into 'Botnets' and used to perform a DDoS attack on another system.

In this case, all four case types defined above may possibly be present.

9.3   Precase processing

Having set up the laboratory and IT infrastructure, a number of precase processing steps independent of the type of case being processed shall be undertaken. Different types of cases to be handled are covered after this section.

9.3.1 Use of digital media in forensic cases

Types of media that this may include, but are not limited to:

- hard disk or solid state drives;
- CDs;
- DVDs;
- backup tapes;
- USB storage devices; and
- key stroke logger media.

There may be other specialised storage media used, but these are the main types used.

Each of these media may play one or more essential roles in a forensic case, and it is essential that these media shall be properly handled, tracked, and maintained throughout their working life to eventual disposal. This type of housekeeping shall reduce the chances of challenges to either the evidence itself, the chain of custody, or the forensic procedures followed.

All digital media to be used in forensic cases shall be purchased through exiting procurement channels using recognised suppliers and the process for their purchase, as defined in Chapter 6, Section 6.7.4. Where this is not possible local purchase may be authorised by the Laboratory Manager.

However, they are purchased, and they shall be recorded in the media asset register.

Note

This register is different to the asset register.

9.3.1.1 Hard or solid-state disks

On receipt of a new hard or solid-state disk, a log for the life history of the disk shall be started. The purchase order and other details to support the transaction shall be attached to the log.

The Management and Reporting System (MARS) forensic case management system shall be used to store these details before they are entered into the disk store for use. A summary of the details to be entered into MARS is defined in Appendix 3.

On receipt, each disk drive shall also be examined to determine that the manufacturers seal is present and unbroken. This fact shall be recorded in MARS. If it is necessary to break the seal to obtain the information above, this may be done, but the seal shall be resealed by applying a suitable seal that is signed and dated by employee that has opened the seal to examine the disk.

At this point, a new disk shall be given a unique local number of the form:

Disknnnn

where:

'Disk' is the identification for all hard or solid state disks;

'nnnnn' is a sequential number starting with 0001 and going to 9999 and incremented for each disk purchased.

This unique number shall stay with this particular disk for the life cycle in FCL. If the disk has been securely destroyed or passed to another agency, then no other disk shall be given this number.

All disks shall be used and stored in accordance with the manufacturer's instructions.

9.3.1.1.1 Wiping disks prior to use

Disks, once recorded and labelled, shall all be placed in a queue waiting to be low level wiped (i.e. the 7 pass process or whatever is required in the jurisdiction). This shall be carried out as an ongoing basis so that there are always 'wiped' disks available for use when they are needed.

When a disk has been wiped, a new label shall be placed on the disk to show the date it was wiped, who wiped it and with what tool. The manufacturer's tag should again be sealed with the date and the name of the person sealing it.

These details are recorded in MARS in the disk history log for the specific disk, as defined in Chapter 10, Section 10.3.5.6.4. A summary of these details is defined in Appendix 4.

Note

If the disk has previously been used, the disk wipe label is placed on top of the label showing the case to which the disk was assigned.

9.3.1.1.2 Issuing a disk for use

When one, or more, disks are required for a forensic case, then they shall be signed out from the secure disk store, noting the time, date, and person signing them out. This is recorded in the Hard Disk History Log in MARS, as defined in Chapter 10, Section 10.3.5.6.6.

If they are not to be used on a forensic case and returned then this fact is noted.

9.3.1.1.3 Disk labelling

All disks shall have their manufacturers labelling and disk details on them.

Four more labels shall be used and added to the disk:

- **wipe label**—showing when the disk was last wiped, by whom and what with (tool);
- **disk label**—this is the locally applied unique disk label that shall live with the disk for its life;
- **classification label**—this is the classification of the contents of the disk, as defined in Chapter 5, Appendix 16; and
- **ownership label**—the details of ownership of the disk (i.e. FCL), including all address and relevant contact details for the disk.

Only one of the wipe or disk labels will be visible at any one time, as disk and wipe labels will be overlaid to show the most recent action (i.e. wiping and ready for assignment or assigned to a case).

9.3.1.1.4 Disks and caddies

Hard disks shall be placed in disk caddies for use to facilitate their use and to preclude possible wear and tear on the disk leads. For this reason, once a disk has been entered into service it shall be assigned to a caddy from which it is never removed. This also facilitates storage in the fire safes and reduces the risk of accidental physical damage during storage.

The outside of the caddy shall have duplicates of the label placed on the actual disk so that this information can be easily seen without opening the caddy (but checks shall be carried out to ensure that what is on the caddy actually is the same as on the disk inside the caddy).

9.3.1.1.5 Transfer of disks

When a disk is transferred to an outside agency this fact shall also be recorded in the Hard Disk History Log in MARS.

Authority to transfer a disk shall be obtained in writing from the Laboratory Manager and be recorded in the Hard Disk History Log.

Any disks being transferred externally shall be labelled with the relevant classification level label as defined in Chapter 5, Appendix 16.

Additionally, all disks shall be clearly marked that they are the FCL's property with a contact number.

9.3.1.1.6 Disk reuse

When a disk is no longer needed for its current assignment, it shall be released back into the available pool of disks for use.

The Forensic Analyst shall ensure that any relevant backup or archival processes necessary for the forensic case are carried out as defined in Chapter 7, Section 7.7.4.

Once a disk is to be released back into the disk pool, it shall be wiped in accordance with current disk wiping procedures and labelled to show when it was wiped, by whom and with what tool.

The pool disks shall then remain in the secure storage area until needed and be reissued as required in accordance with the procedures above.

All disk movements shall be recorded in the Hard Disk History Log in MARS.

9.3.1.1.7 Forensics disk disposal

Forensic disks shall be disposed of when they become unserviceable [e.g. crashing, failing in operation or failing regular disk checking programs (if used)].

Disks for disposal shall be disposed of in one of the following ways:

- use of a specialised, vetted and approved disposal company within the jurisdiction with certificate of disposal obtained; or
- be physically destroyed by employees using a disk punch, disk shredder, sledgehammer, drill or other approved method (e.g. take the disk apart and burn it to destroy the data held on the platters).

The date and method of disposal shall be recorded on the Hard Disk History Log in MARS along with the person carrying out the task. If the disk is sent to an outside agency for disposal, then a copy of the transfer document shall be added to the relevant Hard Disk History Log. This may involve making multiple copies of the transfer note.

All Hard Disk History Logs shall be kept securely and in accordance with the retention schedule for forensic casework.

9.3.1.2 Tapes

Tapes shall be used as backup and archive media. Tapes shall not be used as primary storage for current forensic cases, as tape is more likely to fail and is more difficult to recover than disk storage.

On receipt of a new tape, a log for the life history of the tape shall be started. Attached to this shall be the purchase order and other details to support the transaction.

The MARS forensic case management system shall be used to store these details before they are entered into the disk store for. A summary of these details is defined in Appendix 5.

At this point, a new tape shall be given a unique local number of the form:

Tapennnnn

where:

'Tape' is the identification for all tapes;

'nnnnn' is a sequential number starting with 0001 and going to 9999 and incremented for each tape purchased.

This unique number shall stay with this particular tape for the life cycle of the tape. If the tape has been securely destroyed or passed to another agency, then no other tape shall be given this number.

All tapes shall be used and stored in accordance with the manufacturer's instructions.

Note

These tapes shall be used outside the normal IT backup cycle.

9.3.1.2.1 Wiping tapes prior to use

Tapes, once recorded and labelled, shall all be placed in a queue waiting to be low level wiped (i.e. degaussing or specialised secure wiping, whatever is required in the jurisdiction). This shall be carried out as an ongoing basis so that there are always 'wiped' tapes available for use when they are needed.

When a tape has been wiped, a new label shall be placed on the tape to show the date it was wiped, who wiped it and with what tool.

These details are recorded in MARS in the tape history log for the specific tape, as defined in Chapter 10, Section 10.3.5.7.4. A summary of these details is defined in Appendix 6.

Note

If the tape has previously been used, the tape wipe label shall be placed on top of the label showing the case to which the tape was assigned.

9.3.1.2.2 Issuing a tape

When one, or more, tapes are required for forensic case processing operations, then they b shall be signed out from the secure tape store, noting the time, date and person signing them out. This shall be recorded in the Tape History Log in MARS, as defined in Chapter 10, Section 10.3.5.7.6.

Tapes can be used either for general case processing backup purposes or backing up a specific set of files (e.g. a complete case to a file, a series of images for difference cases to a tape, etc.).

9.3.1.2.3 Tape labelling

All tapes shall have their manufacturers labelling and some details on them.

Four more labels shall be used and added to the tape:

- **wipe label**—showing when the tape was last wiped, by whom and what with (method or tool);
- **tape label**—this is the locally applied unique tape label that lives with the tape for its life;
- **classification label**—this is the classification of the contents of the tape; and
- **ownership label**—the details of ownership of the disk (i.e. FCL), including all address and relevant contact details for the tape.

Only one of the wipe or tape labels shall be visible at any one time, as tape and wipe labels shall be overlaid to show the most recent action (i.e. wiping and ready for assignment or assigned to a case).

9.3.1.2.4 Transfer of tapes

When a tape is transferred to an outside agency, this fact shall also be recorded in the Tape History Log in MARS.

Authority to transfer a tape shall be obtained in writing from the Laboratory Manager and be recorded in the Tape History Log.

Any tapes being transferred externally shall be labelled with the relevant classification level.

Additionally, all tapes shall be clearly marked that they are the FCL's property with a contact number.

9.3.1.2.5 Tape reuse

Once a tape is to be released back into the tape pool, it shall be wiped in accordance with current tape wiping procedures and labelled to show when it was wiped, by whom and with what tool or process.

The pool tapes shall then remain in the secure storage area until needed and be reissued as required in accordance with the procedures above.

All tape movements shall be recorded in the Tape History Log in MARS.

9.3.1.2.6 Tape disposal

Forensic tapes shall be disposed of when they become unserviceable (e.g. failing in operation or failing regular tape checking programs if used).

Tapes shall be disposed of in one of the following ways:

- use of a specialised, vetted and approved disposal company within the jurisdiction and with a certificate of disposal obtained;
- be physically destroyed by employees using an approved method (e.g. take the tape spool apart and burn the tape to destroy the data held on it—but beware of fumes given off and ensure that health and safety requirements are met.

The date and method of disposal shall be recorded on the Tape History Log in MARS along with the person carrying out the task. If the tape is sent to an outside agency for disposal, then a copy of the transfer document shall be added to the relevant Tape History Log. This may involve making multiple copies of the transfer note.

All Tape History Logs shall be kept securely and in accordance with the retention schedule for forensic casework.

9.3.1.3 Other digital media

There are often other types of digital media that can be used in laboratory and these will vary on the specific case or user requirements. It is not reasonable within this book to try to cover all different media types in detail, but some general guidelines are given below. Some common types of common digital media in use are:

- **CDs**—boot disks for clean booting, copying forensic images to or supporting a report by containing relevant files;
- **DVDs**– boot disks for clean booting, copying forensic images to or supporting a report by containing relevant files;
- **USB storage devices**—used for clean booting, copying forensic images, covert acquisitions, supporting a report by containing relevant files or general storage;
- **key loggers**—used for covert operations.

These media are collectively referred to as 'small digital media' in this book.

CDs and DVDs shall be treated as stationery and are used as required and may not all have their usage monitored in a history log.

USBs and Key Loggers used in forensic cases shall be treated as controlled items and their usage is recorded in the same way as disks and tapes in MARS, as defined in Chapter 10, Section 10.3.5.8. A summary of these details is defined in Appendix 7.

Note

Long-term storage of important data on CDs or DVDs shall be avoided if this is the only media where they are stored. Recent tests show that these media do degrade over time and are not suitable for this type of long-term storage (i.e. 5 years +).

The following shall apply to these types of media:

9.3.1.3.1 Wiping small digital media prior to use

USB and Key Loggers, once recorded and labelled, shall all be placed in a queue waiting to be low level wiped (i.e. specialised secure wiping or whatever is required in the jurisdiction). This shall be carried out as an ongoing basis so that there are always 'wiped' USBs and Key Loggers available for use when they are needed.

When a USB or Key Logger has been wiped, a new label shall be placed on the USB or Key Logger to show the date it was wiped, who wiped it and with what tool.

These details shall be recorded in MARS in the USB and Key Logger history log for the specific USB or Key Logger, as defined in Chapter 10, Section 10.3.5.8.4. A summary of these details is defined in Appendix 8.

Note

If the USB or Key Logger has previously been used, the USB or Key Logger wipe label shall be placed on top of the label showing the case to which the USB or Key Logger was assigned.

9.3.1.3.2 Issuing small digital media

When CDs or DVDs are required for forensic case processing operations, then they are removed from the stationery cupboard and used, as required.

USB and Key Logger issue shall be recorded in MARS in the small digital media log for the specific small digital media, as defined in Chapter 10, Section 10.3.5.8.6.

Note 1

All USBs and key Loggers shall be securely wiped prior to use.

Note 2

Forensic workstations that are not permitted to use these media shall have access to them restricted either by removal of reading/writing devices or software based use restriction.

9.3.1.3.3 Small digital media labelling

All CDs or DVDs used actively in operational forensic work shall be clearly labelled.

Where CDs or DVDs are used as part of a report (e.g. containing supporting materials to the case report), they shall be labelled with the following:

- case number;
- date of writing data to disk or of report;
- address and contact details of laboratory from where they were issued;
- description of contents;

- contents classification; and
- optionally, the FCL logo.

Due to size constrains, it is not always possible to affix labels to USBs and Key Loggers as if they were a disk or tape. In this case, details shall be affixed to a sealed envelope that contains these media.

Note

If possible, encrypted USBs shall be used.

9.3.1.3.4 Transfer of small digital media

When a Key Logger or USB device is transferred to an outside agency this fact shall also be recorded in the Small Device History Log in MARS, as defined in Chapter 10, Section 10.3.5.8.6.

Authority to transfer a Key Logger or USB shall be obtained in writing from the Laboratory Manager and be recorded in the Tape History Log.

Any Key Logger or USB being transferred externally shall be labelled with the relevant classification level label.

Additionally, all Key Loggers and USBs shall be clearly marked that they are the FCL's property with a contact number.

9.3.1.3.5 Small digital media reuse

Once a Key Logger or USB is to be released back into the Key Logger and USB pool it shall be wiped in accordance with current Key Logger or USB wiping procedures and labelled to show when it was wiped, by whom and with what tool or process.

The pool of Key Loggers and USBs shall then remain in the secure storage area until needed and be reissued as required in accordance with the procedures above.

All Key Logger and USB movements shall be recorded in the Small Digital Device History Log in MARS.

9.3.1.3.6 Small digital media disposal

Small electronic memory devices shall be disposed of in the following manner:

- CDs, DVDs, USBs, and Key Loggers shall be smashed into a number of pieces using a sledgehammer or if a local shredder can cope with it, they can be shredded; or
- any small digital device shall be disposed of using a specialised, vetted and approved disposal company.

9.4 Equipment maintenance

All equipment that is used to support forensic case processing shall be maintained according to the manufacturer's recommendations. An overview of equipment maintenance is defined in Chapter 7, Section 7.5.4; however, specific maintenance requirements for case processing are given below.

9.4.1 Hard disk drives

- hard disks shall be handled at initial receipt as defined above regarding checking, labelling, and wiping prior to use with records maintained in MARS;
- each time a hard drive is used, the fact shall be recorded in MARS;
- when not in use, hard disk drives that have been wiped shall be stored in the secure store in their disk caddy (if used);
- any drive that becomes unserviceable shall have the fact recorded in MARS and be securely stored until secure disposal can take place. The disposal shall be recorded in MARS along with the disposal type. Where a certificate of disposal is obtained, this shall be attached to the relevant disk record in MARS; and
- disk records shall be retained at least for as long as the case to which they refer is archived.

9.4.2 Tapes

- tapes shall be handled at initial receipt as defined above regarding checking, labelling, wiping, and formatting prior to use with records maintained in MARS;

- when not in use, tapes that have been wiped and shall be stored in the secure store;
- any tape that becomes unserviceable shall have the fact recorded in MARS and be securely stored until secure disposal can take place. The disposal shall be recorded in MARS along with the disposal type. Where a certificate of disposal is obtained, this shall be attached to the relevant record in MARS; and
- tape records shall be retained at least for as long as the case to which they refer is archived.

9.4.3   Small digital media

- small digital media shall be handled at initial receipt as defined above regarding checking, labelling, and wiping prior to use with records maintained in MARS;
- each time any small digital media is used, the fact shall be recorded in MARS;
- when not in use, small digital media that have been wiped shall be stored in the secure store;
- any small digital media that becomes unserviceable shall have the fact recorded in MARS and be securely stored until secure disposal can take place. The disposal shall be recorded in MARS along with the disposal type. Where a certificate of disposal is obtained, this shall be attached to the relevant digital media record in MARS; and
- small digital media records shall be retained at least for as long as the case to which they refer is archived.

9.4.4   Software

- a software log of all installed software shall be maintained for all forensic workstations;
- no installation shall exceed the number of permitted licences and annual audits shall be undertaken to ensure that this is so;
- all forensic software shall be maintained at the current release level after suitable testing (if deemed necessary by the Laboratory Manager). It shall be installed after going through the Change Management Process, as defined in Chapter 7, Section 7.4.3;
- operating system and application patch levels shall be monitored and applied as necessary, as defined in Chapter 7, Section 7.6.3;
- any software that is installed as part of a case (i.e. recreating a suspect's system) shall not be recorded. After recreation of a suspect machine the forensic workstation used shall be wiped and reinstalled in accordance with the anticontamination procedures, as defined in Section 9.3.1; and
- all software shall be checked to ensure that it is the correct version and that it matches any checksums or hashes, where supplied with the software.

9.4.5   Spares

The Laboratory Manager shall ensure that there are an appropriate number of spare parts and components for maintaining the forensic case processing capability is maintained.

9.4.6   Validating forensic tools

All systems used for forensic case processing shall be tested and validated to ensure that they operate correctly. The requirements for this are defined in Chapter 7, Section 7.5.5. The tests differ for various systems but in principle the standard test case shall be used and the achieved results of the standard tests shall be compared with the expected ones. If they are not the same this suggests a fault in the system set up and shall be investigated prior to using the forensic tool for case processing.

Tests shall be conducted on all new forensic systems and on existing systems including but not limited to the following circumstances:

- installation of new operating systems;
- hardware changes (e.g. motherboards);
- replacement of components directly involved in the imaging process (e.g. drive controller cards) with different components;
- software upgrades or use of new imaging software;
- use of system to image a significantly different type of media;

- doubt concerning the forensic soundness of a particular system; and
- prior to the use of new device drivers (e.g. for USB, Firewire, etc.).

Tests shall not be conducted for:
- replacement of cables, monitors, etc.

9.4.7   Forensic workstation anticontamination procedures

When the Forensic Analyst finishes working on a case and is going to load a new case on a forensic workstation, this workstation shall be wiped and the operating system re-installed to protect against any possibility of contamination of the new case being loaded and as a defence against any possibility of tainted evidence.

The Forensic Analyst shall run the anticontamination process to wipe the system disk and reinstall the operating system and instal required programs on the workstation using the standard forensic case processing image.

This process shall be recorded on the contemporaneous work record for the case in MARS. The details of the Forensic Case Work Log are defined in Appendix 9.

Note

Unless a Microsoft Site licence is in use, the continuous reinstallation of the operating system may cause problems with product key usage.

9.4.8   Hash sets

One Forensic Analyst shall be nominated as the custodian of Hash Sets and be responsible for maintaining a current list of hash sets in the ERMS for use by all Forensic Analysts in their forensic cases.

Forensic Analysts shall use hash sets to save time during case processing to identify known files by using the MD5 hashes for files. The MD5 hash is a 128 bit fingerprint of the file that should produce a unique identity for a file (or even a disk). While there is a statistical possibility that two files can create the same hash, it is mathematically insignificant as MD5 uses a 16 character hexadecimal value. So theoretically, there are 2^{128} possible MD5 hash values in existence, so if one had a file system with $2^{128} + 1$ files, it is possible to guarantee that there will be at least two different files that will generate the same hash value. As 2^{128} is approximately 340 billion billion billion billion possibilities, it can be regarded as mathematically insignificant. As a matter of interest, this is a third of a Google, which is defined as 10^{100}. Thus, known files can be identified by their MD5 hashes.

The National Software Reference Library (NSRL) is a part of NIST and maintains a list of known hashes.

- The safe hash set is a list of known good files, such as operating systems and commercial packages. This hash set shall be used to filter out known good files from a forensic case under investigation;
- The notable hash set contains hashes of known files that may be of interest to the Forensic Analyst and are worthy of further investigation. Examples of notable hash values include child pornography, malware, etc. The Forensic Analyst can also create their own hash sets if required and import them into the main case processing systems (Encase, FTK, and Cellebrite). This could be used for example for tracing the spread of confidential corporate documents throughout the organisation by creating a hash file for all relevant documents and then checking all workstations using the hash set to identify any of the documents on the workstation; and
- Hash categories are a method filtering hash values into similar groupings (e.g. Hacker tools, MS Office, Ignore, etc. depending on personal preference.

Using safe hash sets shall greatly increase the speed of a keyword search as the search tools will ignore this in the 'Ignore' hash set. A base instal hash set for all workstations shall be created then the systems are built.

Notable hash sets shall be used to identify files that may be of interest to the Forensic Analyst.

Where a Forensic Analyst creates their own hash sets, caution should be taken, as the inclusion of a 'wrong' file can cause a false positive and at best can be an irritant to the Forensic Analyst and at worst can cause serious embarrassment. The user of any in-house created hash sets relies on the experience of the hash set builder. For this reason, any in-house created hash sets shall always be reviewed and authorised by the Laboratory Manager. Where they are to be created, unique files shall be chosen for the hash set, e.g. creatmyvirus.list is unique to the tool. For example, If the file was called setup.dll and was included in the notable hash set, as part of the 'Create My Virus' set, it would also create a false positive as setup.dll is used in many commercially available software packages such as MS Office.

Note

Care shall be taken with using the NSRL hash sets as they contain known files that contain both notable hashes and safe hashes. Therefore, it shall not be used solely as a safe hash set. The NSRL hash set shall be split into a number of subcategories, and only the ones relevant to the forensic case being processed shall be loaded.

While the NSRL is one of the best hash set libraries and it is free, other sources may be used, as defined by the Laboratory Manager.

Note 2

Should the Laboratory Manager have reservations about MD 5 hashes being challenged, there is the option of using Secure Hash Algorithm SHA–256 or SHA-512, giving 2^{256} and 2^{512} possibilities, as opposed to MD5's 2^{128}. SHA was written by the National Security Agency (NSA) in the USA.

Note 3

The integrity of all software used in FCL shall be verified by use of hashing.

9.4.9 Asset register

- an asset register shall be maintained of all forensic hardware and software in use;
- invoices for all forensic hardware, software, and other associated forensic case processing equipment shall be maintained in the accounting files for the relevant period;
- a licence log of all software licences shall be maintained;
- all forensic software shall be licensed; and
- regular and at least annual audits shall be undertaken to ensure that the asset register is current and correct, as defined in Chapter 12, Section 12.3.13.2.2.1.

Note

This asset register may be a subset of the main corporate asset register or may be a separate one.

9.4.10 Previous versions

All previous versions of hardware and software shall be re-creatable and so all versions of software shall be retained with all versions of hardware to allow a standard build to be recreated for historically archived cases.

This is in case any errors or queries relating to the evidence acquisition or processing arises. It must be provable that the tools in use to process the case did not cause any issues with either the imaging or analysis of the image.

9.5 Management processes

9.5.1 Authorities

An up-to-date set of operating procedures for all digital forensic work shall be maintained. This shall be:

- authorised by the Laboratory Manager;
- approved by top management;
- reviewed on an annual basis or on influencing change, to ensure that the procedures remain suitable and effective; and
- all changes are recorded in the document control section of the procedures according to the document control procedures, as defined in Chapter 4, section 4.7.5.

9.5.2 Liaison with law enforcement

Appropriate liaison shall be maintained with the relevant Law Enforcement agencies within the jurisdiction. A single liaison point shall be nominated for general liaison, though individual Forensic Analysts will often be in regular contact with relevant Law Enforcement Officers, depending on the forensic cases being processed.

9.5.3 Other external bodies

Appropriate liaison shall be maintained with the relevant external bodies as needed within and outside the jurisdiction. A single liaison point shall be nominated for general liaison with relevant external bodies that are either relevant to general forensic case processing or specific cases. In many cases, individual Forensic Analysts will be in regular contact with such bodies, which may also include Special Interest Groups (SIGs) or other professional bodies of which they are members.

9.5.4 Service levels, priorities, and turn round times (TRTs)

9.5.4.1 Service Level Agreements

Unless set in the proposal or a purchase order for ongoing work, as defined in Chapter 6, Section 6.6, the standard default Service Level Agreement (SLA) target for the forensic case processing shall be set to:

- 2 weeks from receipt to the end of initial investigation for unencrypted cases; and
- 3 weeks from receipt to the end of initial investigation for encrypted cases.

Note

While these are targets, it is accepted that these are subject to variation for a number of reasons. Specific TRTs may be agreed that affect these targets.

9.5.4.2 Priorities

Once a request for forensic support has been approved, the Laboratory Manager shall set a priority and TRT for the case, unless the TRT has been previously agreed with the client.

This shall depend on the following:

- available resources;
- possibility of destruction of property;
- potential victims;
- children at risk;
- client or HR deadlines;
- Court or Tribunal dates;
- legal considerations;
- nature of the incident;
- possibility of death or injury based on evidence to be recovered;
- volatile nature of the evidence; and
- which exhibits have the potential to provide the most relevant information for the case.

9.5.4.3 Changing priorities and TRTs

It may well be that a case received is required to be completed faster than the current default SLAs. This shall be agreed between the Incident Manager and the Laboratory Manager. The agreement of a higher priority or fast TRT may require the re-prioritisation of case work for one or more of the Forensic Analysts.

Where this is the case, it is the responsibility of the Laboratory Manager to advise Account Managers whose client's SLAs or TRTs may be affected. Any such changes shall be recorded in the relevant case files in MARS.

9.5.5 Case monitoring

Each week, at the forensic case processing meeting, a progress report on all current forensic cases shall be carried out. The update shall include:

- all cases and their progress against TRTs;
- Court dates for the coming week;
- assigning any unassigned cases; and
- reassigning cases, where necessary.

Where TRTs are not going to be met, the Laboratory Manager shall take appropriate action, including advising the relevant Account Manager(s).

9.5.6 Audit

In addition to the quality audits undertaken as part of the ISO 9001 process, the Laboratory Manager shall carry out regular audits of work performed by the Forensic Analysts, as follows:

- an audit of all aspects of the Forensic Analyst's work (from First Responder though to Court appearances) shall be undertaken by the Laboratory Manager at least annually;
- where case files are to be audited, they shall be chosen randomly to obtain a fair representation of work carried out by the Forensic Analysts;
- records of all audits shall be retained for inspection as part of the IMS audit process, as defined in Chapter 4, Section 4.9.2. The records shall also include the requirements for any corrective actions, as defined in Chapter 4, Section 4.10; and
- all CAPAs shall be allocated to a nominated individual and shall be followed through to timely resolution by the Laboratory Manager, as defined in Chapter 4, Section 4.10.2.

9.5.7 Outsourcing

There may well be times that work that would normally be carried out by the Forensic Analysts cannot be due to any number of reasons, typically:

- staff unavailability (sick, at Court, leave, etc.);
- desire to reduce any backlog;
- urgent jobs needing to be performed; and
- lacking the specific skills in house.

The choosing of an outsourcing partner is defined in Chapter 14. All outsourcing shall be approved by the Laboratory Manager and top management, as appropriate.

9.5.8 Performance monitoring

There are a number of existing SLAs as defaults and KPIs in place as part of the ISO 9001 procedures, as defined in Appendix 10 and Chapter 6, Appendix 6, and defined TRTs for clients on a case-by-case basis. These reports shall be available from MARS and shall be published on a monthly basis to all relevant interested parties or more frequently if required.

9.5.9 Tool selection

While the core forensic case processing tools (e.g. EnCase, FTK, and Cellebrite) have been selected, a number of other tools may be used depending on the case being processed. The choice of tools to be used on a specific case shall be determined by the requirements of the forensic case, rather than slavishly following the main tools. Any new methods that are to be implemented for case processing shall be validated, as defined in Chapter 7, Section 7.5.5.

9.6 Booking exhibits in and out of the secure property store

Forensic case processing normally starts when the exhibit(s) first arrive at the laboratory, unless the First Responder Team was involved in the incident response. Incident response procedures have been covered in Chapter 8, and this chapter deals with an exhibit being processed from its arrival, through processing until either release or disposal.

These are typical processes as it is impossible, in procedures such as these, to provide specific advice for each and every situation in which a forensic laboratory may find itself.

Note

While the movement details shall be logged in MARS, paper Movement Forms that are associated with all exhibits shall be used, as defined in Chapter 8, Appendix 17. In this way a 'real' or 'wet' signature shall be captured. This also allows external transfer to external parties to be captured.

9.6.1 Booking in exhibits

When an exhibit arrives for processing, the following shall be performed (Fig. 9.2):

1. Check that items are sealed and bagged and that the contents match the manifest. If they are not then determine why this is not the case, if possible. Note the fact on the evidence Movement Record, as defined in Chapter 8, Appendix 17 and the Property Log in MARS. Consideration shall be given to rejecting the exhibit should the Laboratory Manager consider this appropriate. A sample rejection of evidence letter content is defined in Appendix 11.
2. Continuity labels shall be completed and affixed to any exhibit, unless the continuation details are integral to the exhibit, e.g. part of the Exhibit Bag. Details of information to be recorded for exhibit movements are defined in Appendix 12.
3. If this is not possible, then consideration shall be given to rejecting the exhibit should the Laboratory Manager consider this appropriate as the 'chain of custody' is incomplete. The relevant parts of MARS shall be updated, as defined in Chapter 10, Section 10.4.5.
4. The exhibit(s) shall be booked into the Secure Property Store, be recorded in the Property Log and have the Movement Log updated in MARS to reflect the movement from the person delivering the exhibit to acceptance by the Evidence Custodian. Details of information contained in the Forensic Log and exhibit Movement Forms are defined in Appendix 13 and Chapter 8, Appendix 17, respectively.
5. A new property number shall be issued to the exhibit. This shall be the next sequential exhibit number available in the Property Log. This numbering system will start at 1 and go as high as necessary. This shall be unique for each exhibit received in the Secure Property Store.
6. Consideration shall be given to rejecting the exhibit should the Laboratory Manager consider this appropriate if there is insufficient information available on the requirements of the forensic case.
7. Digital photographs shall be taken of the exhibit as it is signed into the Secure Property Store. This shall show the property from all angles, specifically showing any damage to the wrapping or contents of the Evidence Bag as well as close up photographs of the evidence label. These photographs shall be added to the case virtual file in the ERMS.
8. Any items that require special handling shall be dealt with. This typically includes any items that need the charge maintained (e.g. Mobile phones). Details of the special handling shall be recorded in the case virtual file in the ERMS. Details of any special handling procedures shall be logged in the Property Special Handling Log in MARS. Details of the Special Handling Log are defined in Appendix 15.

Note

At this point, a Case Number may not have been assigned to the case, so the Special Handling Log shall be linked to the exhibit reference number. Once a Case Number has been assigned the property reference shall be linked to the forensic case.

---

9. If the exhibit is to be rejected then the Laboratory Manager shall advise the person booking it in immediately and the reasons for rejection. It is up to the Laboratory Manager and the person booking it in to resolve the issue before the property can be accepted into the Secure Property Store.

Note

Where a property is rejected, the resolution prior to acceptance may need the involvement of other parties.

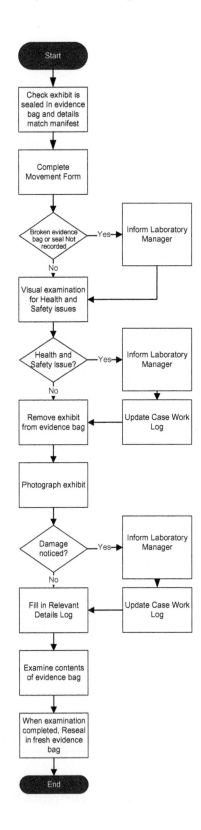

FIG. 9.2 Booking in exhibits.

10. Insurance values shall be entered to the virtual case file in the ERMS for the property placed in the Secure Property Store to ensure that there is sufficient insurance to cover them.
11. Any original documents shall be scanned prior to being added to the virtual case file in the ERMS. The originals shall be stored in the Secure Property Store.
12. Once the exhibit has been logged into the Secure Property Store, it shall be securely stored until needed for processing.
13. Confirm of receipt of the exhibit(s) shall be made to the client. The confirmation letter template is defined in Appendix 14.

9.6.2 Booking out exhibits

Once the Forensic Analyst is ready to start work on the forensic case, they shall do the following:

1. Book out the exhibit(s) from the Secure Property Store; and
2. Update the Movement Log and Property Log to show that the exhibit is currently booked out to a Forensic Analyst to work on the forensic case.

9.6.3 Returning an exhibit

The following procedures shall be carried out for returning exhibits to the Secure Property Store:

1. The Property Log and the Movement Log shall be updated to show the return of the exhibit(s) to the Secure Property Store.
2. The exhibits shall be re-sealed and the details of the exhibit(s) shall be clearly visible on the Evidence Bag. The Property Log shall be updated with the re-seal number details.
3. If the bags do not have this detail or a properly affixed seal, they should not be accepted back into the Secure Property Store, unless authorised by the Laboratory Manager, where notes covering any variation shall be entered into the Laboratory Log and also linked to the virtual forensic case file in the ERMS.

9.7 Starting a new case

Note

This is for all forensic cases processed.

9.7.1 Case numbering

Once a forensic case has been accepted, it shall be assigned a unique case number.
This file name shall be of the form:
aaa/nnnnn/yyyy
where

- aaa is the initials that identify FCL;
- nnnnn is the case number of the year
- yyyy is the year (taken from the system).

The case number is generated by MARS.
Every time that data shall be added to the case file, the virtual case file shall be saved according to the naming convention as defined in Chapter 4, Appendix 43.
Experience dictates that forensic software can crash and the reliance on a single backup forensic case file created by the software is not prudent. This process allows the Forensic Analyst to go as far back as necessary in the forensic case file for the day.

9.7.2 Assigning the case

Once the exhibit(s) for a forensic case have been booked into the Secure Store then the case shall be considered for assignment. The assignment process shall be as follows:

1. On assigning the forensic case number the 'real' case file shall be started and the relevant virtual files be created by the Laboratory Manager, as defined in Chapter 6, Section 6.6.2.2.
2. The Laboratory Manager shall set the priority level for the forensic case and the Turn Round Time (TRT) and agree them with the assigned Forensic Analyst and the client.
3. The submission forms containing the requirements of the case shall be reviewed to ensure that they are clear and complete. These may have been filled in by the client or First Responder and comprise the following forms if the exhibits were seized on site. If the exhibit was just delivered for forensic case processing, not all of the items below will be appropriate:
   - agreed proposal for the forensic case processing;

- Evidence Sought Form as defined in Appendix 16 unless this is defined in the proposal. This shall be updated as the case progresses and further evidence is sought.
- Request for Forensic Examination (from a client), as defined in Appendix 17;
- Site Summary, as defined in Chapter 8, Appendix 6;
- Seizure Summary, as defined in Chapter 8, Appendix 5;
- Seizure Forms, as defined in Chapter 8, Appendix 7;
- Movement Form.

4. Once the Laboratory Manager has confirmed that all relevant paperwork is in place and correct, any issues relating to exhibits has been resolved and any clarification of required outcomes settled, the case shall be assigned to the appropriate Forensic Analyst.
5. In this case, an appropriate Forensic Analyst is defined as one who is competent (i.e. has appropriate skills, qualifications, experience) and the workload capacity to process the forensic case.

9.7.3 Priorities and turn round times (TRTs)

1. At the same time as assigning the case to the Forensic Analyst, the Laboratory Manager shall set the priority of the case. Case Priorities shall be defined either by the default SLAs or the client agreed TRTs.
2. TRTs shall be set at this time so that the relevant Forensic Analyst knows the date that the job is expected to be completed.
3. The setting of new TRTs may impact current work, so this shall be reviewed by the Laboratory Manager and the relevant Forensic Analyst(s).
4. These instructions may be in the form of an email or be verbal. They shall be added to the virtual case file in the ERMS, as appropriate.

9.7.4 Cost revision and confirmation

If a proposal was provided for the client, then cost estimation is an integral part of that proposal and is defined in Chapter 6, Appendix 15. Where a contract exists and a quotation is required the costs shall be given on the quotation. The cost of case processing shall be checked, adjusted if necessary and the client advised accordingly. The need for this may be driven by additional requirements being set by the client, additional items being seized as part of the incident response process or any other matter that may affect the processing of the case.

The initial estimate of costs may well need to be revised, based on further requirements or on difficulties encountered (e.g. encrypted drives, etc.), and this shall require a further updated estimate to be produced. This shall also be produced using the Cost Estimating spreadsheet and sent to the instructing client with an explanation for the variation. The revised cost estimate shall be saved with the date added as part of the field name (e.g. revised cost 221,231.xls—indicating a revised cost sent on 31 December 2022);

All estimates shall be stored in the Virtual Case file in the ERMS.

9.7.5 Creating a new client paper case file

FCL has made the conscious decision to 'run' a paper-based client case file in parallel with the client's virtual case file in the ERMS.

There are a number of items of information that can only really be captured on paper, and a real signature shall be used to prove the chain of custody or to demonstrate timelines.

For all of the information captured for MARS there are hard copy forms used with 'real' or 'wet' signatures on them. The information on them shall be entered into MARS and the forms shall be scanned and added to the client's virtual forensic case file, originals being stored in the Secure Property Store.

The client's paper case file shall be maintained by the assigned Forensic Analyst for the case.

9.7.6 Creating a new client virtual forensic case file

The client's virtual forensic case file shall be created at the same time as the client's paper forensic case file. The setting up of the client virtual case file is covered in Chapter 6, Section 6.6.2.2 with the various storage areas defined in Chapter 6,

Appendix 14. MARS shall generate the forensic case number, and all information in the paper forensic case file shall be loaded into the virtual case file. The client's virtual forensic case file shall be given the name that MARS generates as the forensic case number in the format defined in Section 9.6.1.

1. Once the relevant Forensic Analyst has been assigned to the case they shall populate the client's virtual forensic case file and a client's paper forensic case file, unless this has already been done by the Laboratory Manager.
2. The Forensic Analyst shall ensure that all of the paperwork for the forensic case has been collated in the client's paper forensic case file and additionally scanned into the client's virtual case file. Additional folders shall be added to the virtual case file as the Forensic Analyst working the case sees fit.
3. The Forensic Analyst shall complete the following forms (if they have not already been completed):
   - New Case Form for cases starting at incident response, as defined in Chapter 8, Appendix 4;
   - Evidence Sought Form for exhibits delivered to the Secure Property Store; and
   - Case details.
4. All new paperwork and correspondence shall be added to the client's paper forensic case file and be scanned and added into the client's virtual forensic case file.
5. The Forensic Analyst shall then start to process the forensic case.

9.8 Preparing the forensic workstation

The procedures below are for all forensic cases whether the work is to be carried out on site using a portable forensic workstation or using a desktop workstation in the laboratory.

Any forensic workstation that is to be used to process a forensic case shall be sterile and unable to contaminate the new from case from a previous case so as to avoid any suspicion of tainting. To perform this, the following shall be carried out:

1. The operating system disk shall be wiped to erase the current operating system and any files held on the disk.
2. The standard build for the forensic workstations shall be loaded from the image held in the ERMS.
3. The wiping tool used shall be recorded on the Forensic Case Work Log.
4. Other forensic tools shall be loaded, as required for the forensic case, when needed.

One or more suitably sized sterile hard disks shall be chosen from the hard disk pool held in the Secure Property Store and assigned to the case and loaded into the forensic workstation.

9.9 Imaging

9.9.1 Physical imaging

Note

This section deals specifically with cases where the laboratory holds the actual exhibits to be imaged.

9.9.1.1 Book out the exhibit(s)

Once the Forensic Analyst has completed the paperwork, set up the sterile forensic workstation, and set up the case, the exhibit(s) should be booked out of the Secure Property Store for examination using the exhibit booking out procedures, as defined in Section 9.6.2.

9.9.1.2 External examination of exhibits

1. Each exhibit shall be examined by the Forensic Analyst. During this operation the Forensic Analyst shall wear latex or rubber gloves and other PPE, as appropriate (Fig. 9.3).
2. The Forensic Analyst shall photograph the exhibit inside the sealed Evidence Bag and ensure that the seals and seal numbers are clearly visible, as is the description box on the front of the Exhibit Bag or the exhibit label.
3. At this point, if there are any breaks to the Evidence Bag or the seals have been opened, this shall be immediately reported to the Laboratory Manager unless this has already been recorded in the Laboratory Property Log or Movement Log.

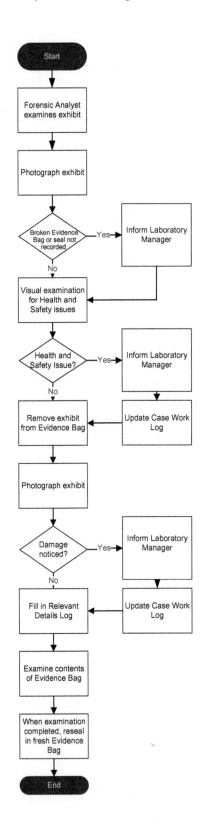

FIG. 9.3 External examination of exhibits.

4. It is at this point that a visual inspection for any Health and Safety issues shall be made, prior to opening the Exhibit Bag, and be recorded if they exist. If they exist, then the Forensic Analyst shall use their judgement whether to carry on with the inspection or not. If the examination is to be stopped, then the Laboratory Manager shall be informed and the fact recorded in the Forensic Case Work Log.

5. Once the external inspection and photographs have been carried out the equipment shall be removed from the Evidence Bag, typically by slitting the bottom of the bag, leaving the seal and the exhibit details intact. The Evidence Bag shall be retained and used to store the exhibit when it is returned to the Secure Property Store.

6. Once the equipment has been removed from the Evidence Bag it shall be photographed again. The photographs shall record any damage, unusual features, serial numbers, licences, connectors, and visible drives.

7. No physical damage should occur to any exhibit during this process, but if it does it shall be recorded on the Forensic Case Work Log and photographs of the damage shall be taken and added to the virtual forensic case file.

8. The Computer Details Log or Other Equipment Details Log shall be filled in, as appropriate. The details for both of these logs are defined in Appendix 19 and Appendix 20, respectively.

9. When the examination has been completed, and the original exhibit is no longer needed, it shall be resealed into a new Exhibit Bag, along with the original one (or seal, as appropriate) and resealed. The resealing is recorded in the Laboratory Log.

9.9.1.3 *Examination of exhibits*

1. All work on any exhibit shall be carried out on antistatic mats using antistatic wrist bands to ensure that there is not tainting of the evidence by electrical discharge;

2. All forensic workbenches shall have rubber antistatic matting under them to prevent accidental earthing;

9.9.1.3.1 Servers, PCs, and laptops

1. Servers, PCs, and laptops shall be disassembled so that the Forensic Analyst can access any hard disk drives that are to be imaged and also investigate the interior of the exhibit (Fig. 9.4).

2. Once disassembled, equipment shall be photographed internally and any 'strange' items photographed in situ, prior to removal.

3. Details of the hardware shall be recorded on the Computer Details Log.

4. Details of the hard disk shall be recorded in the Hard Disk Details Log and photographs of it shall be taken clearly showing the serial number and other similar details as well as the jumper settings.

5. If there is more than one hard disk in the exhibit then they shall be uniquely identified, e.g. using top or bottom to differential between the disks or 1, 2, 3, etc. if multiple disks are in use. The disks shall be labelled with the relevant exhibit number and also the unique identifier for the disk—e.g. FCL/00001/2022/Top—indicating that this is the top disk from exhibit FCL/00001/2022). The Forensic Case Work Log shall contain details of the numbering system used and where there are multiple hard disks, multiple Hard Disk Details Log entries shall be created to record the details of each disk. Each log entry shall be clearly marked with the relevant and unique disk drive identifier.

6. If tape drives or similar media are found in any exhibit, they shall be identified and recorded on the Other Media Details Log with suitable annotation and be uniquely identified as if they were additional hard disks. The Forensic Case Work Log shall be updated to show that these items were found. The Other Media Details Log shall be updated with details of any other media located in the exhibit.

7. All work carried out shall be recorded in the Forensic Case Work Log.

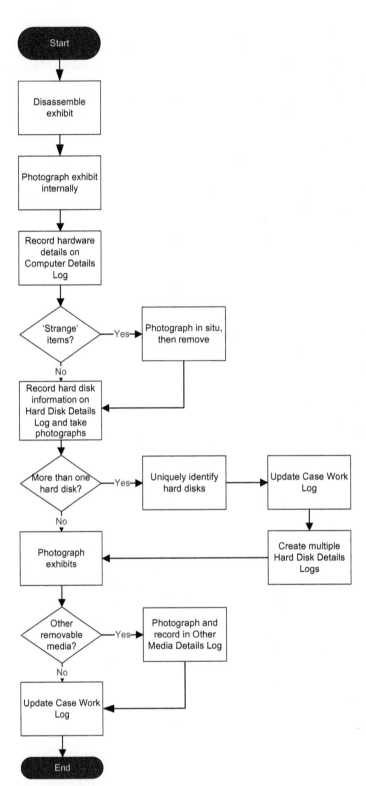

FIG. 9.4 Examination of servers, PCs, and laptops.

9.9.1.3.2 Obtaining BIOS information

BIOS information shall be obtained from servers, PCs, and laptops and recorded in the Computer Details Log. This shall be performed as below:

1. To perform a safe boot to obtain BIOS information the hard disk(s) shall be disconnected and safe boot media shall be used to boot the device.
2. Any hard disks inside shall be removed for imaging, unless imaging is to be performed in situ (i.e. through the use of a USB or Firewire Port);
3. Once the device has booted, the Forensic Analyst shall enter the BIOS Setup and record the following:
   - system date;
   - system time; and
   - boot order.

- These details shall be recorded on the Computer Details Log;
- At the same time that the system time and date are recorded, the actual time and date shall also be recorded from a known accurate time source, such as any of the atomic clocks available on the Internet. These details shall be recorded on the Computer Details Log so that the time difference can be determined between the actual time and the system time; and
- All work carried out shall be recorded in the Forensic Case Work Log.

Note

Some systems may need a password to access the BIOS data and some may require the manufacturer's boot disk to access it.

9.9.1.3.3 Tablet computers

Tablet computers refer to the range of computers that come with a touch screen and no keyboard (though an external keyboard may be attached). The tablet may have a SIM to give it access to the cellular network.

1. The tablet computer shall be photographed.
2. Details of the hardware shall be recorded on the Computer Details Log.
3. All work carried out shall be recorded in the Forensic Case Work Log.
4. Where the tablet computer has a low power level after being seized in the 'on' state, it shall be connected to a power supply so that it does not lose volatile memory until it is captured.
5. If the tablet computer was seized in the 'off' state, then the Laboratory Manager shall authorise in writing a competent Forensic Analyst to undertake the examination and perform the imaging and recovery of any evidence. This authority shall be logged on the Forensic Case Work Log and countersigned by the Laboratory Manager with the time and date of the authorisation. The power level shall be monitored and if the battery low, the procedure in Section 9.9.1.3.4, step 5 undertaken. This breaches the ACPO Principle 1, and so Principle 2 shall be relied on. This means that the requirements for competence and being able to prove it, as required in Principle 2 are even more important, as is the requirement for the audit trail in Principle 3.
6. The tablet computer shall only be taken out of its Faraday bag in a Faraday protected environment for examination and imaging.

Note

While it does not comply with ACPO principle 1, the current accepted practice is that these devices are accessed and placed in 'airplane mode.' See Chapter 20 for details.

9.9.1.3.4   Smart phones

A smart phone is a mobile phone that performs many of the functions of a tablet computer, typically having a touchscreen interface, internet access, and an operating system capable of running downloaded apps.

1. The smart phone shall be photographed.
2. Details of the hardware shall be recorded on the Smart Phone Details Log, as defined in Appendix 23.
3. All work carried out shall be recorded in the Forensic Case Work Log.
4. Where the smart phone has a low power level after being seized in the 'on' state, it shall be placed on the appropriate cradle or adaptor to charge it.
5. If the smart phone was seized in the 'off' state, then the Laboratory Manager shall authorise in writing a competent Forensic Analyst to undertake the examination and perform the imaging and recovery of any evidence. This authority shall be logged on the Forensic Case Work Log and countersigned by the Laboratory Manger with the time and date of the authorisation. The power level shall be monitored and if the battery low, the procedure in step 4 undertaken. This breaches the ACPO Principle 1, and so Principle 2 shall be relied on. The means that the requirements for competence and being able to prove it, as required in Principle 2 are even more important, as is the requirement for the audit trail in Principle 3.
6. The smart phone shall only be taken out of its Faraday Bag in a Faraday protected environment for examination and imaging.

Note

While it does not comply with ACPO principle 1, the current accepted practice is that these devices are accessed and placed in 'airplane mode.' See Chapter 20 for details.

9.9.1.3.5   Other devices

'Other devices' refers to any type of device that can be connected to an information processing device (e.g. a peripheral such as a printer, camera, MP3 player, etc.) or it may be a standalone device (e.g. a games console).

1. The device shall be photographed.
2. Details of the device shall be recorded on the Other Devices Details Log, as defined in Appendix 24.
3. All work carried out shall be recorded in the Forensic Case Work Log.
4. Where the device relies on battery power, contains volatile memory, and has a low power level after being seized in the 'on' state, it shall be charged on the appropriate cradle or adaptor so that it does not lose volatile memory until it is captured.
5. If the device was seized in the 'off' state, then the Laboratory Manager shall authorise in writing a competent Forensic Analyst to undertake the examination and perform the imaging and recovery of any evidence. This authority shall be logged on the Forensic Case Work Log and countersigned by the Laboratory Manger with the time and date of the authorisation. The power level shall be monitored and if the battery low, the procedure in step 4 undertaken. This breaches the ACPO Principle 1, and so Principle 2 shall be relied on. The means that the requirements for competence and being able to prove it, as required in Principle 2 are even more important, as is the requirement for the audit trail in Principle 3.
6. If the device has radio transmission capability, it shall only be taken out of its Faraday Bag in a Faraday protected environment for examination and imaging.

9.9.1.3.6   Other media

'Other media' refers to any type of media that is recovered and sent for forensic case processing and refers to media submitted as an exhibit rather than being located in another exhibit and discovered as part of the examination process.

1. The media shall be photographed.

2. Details of the media shall be recorded on the Other Media Details Log, as defined in Appendix 22.

3. All work carried out shall be recorded in the Forensic Case Work Log.

9.9.1.4 General forensic acquisition

1. All forensic acquisition of any media from exhibits or as standalone exhibits shall be carried out using approved write blockers wherever possible to ensure against accidental contamination or tainting of the evidence, unless the device has a write blocker built into it. Even then it is recommended that the standard write blockers are used, in case of the on board device malfunctioning.

2. If a write blocker cannot be used or is unavailable for any reason, then only a suitably trained and skilled Forensic Analyst shall undertake the acquisition, using appropriate tools.

3. Special care shall be taken with mobile devices that have radio transmitters/receivers in them that can be used to change the information held on the device or, in the extreme, wipe the device. The laboratory shall have a Faraday shielded area specifically for this purpose.

4. Acquisition shall be to a wiped disk which will be dedicated to the forensic case for the duration, as defined in Section 9.8.

5. The Forensic Analyst shall check that the time and date on the acquisition workstation is correct and shall annotate the Hard Disk Details Log to confirm this, as defined in Appendix 21.

6. The method of acquisition shall be recorded in the relevant Log with the version of the specific software used. This shall also be logged in the Forensic Case Work Log.

7. Once the image has been created, the Forensic Analyst shall be able to provide proof that it is an exact copy of the original exhibit and that this proof shall be acceptable in any proceedings that the forensic case processing supports. This shall be carried out using MD5 hashes that are normally built into digital forensic acquisition tools.

Where a disk is damaged or has multiple bad sectors, a number of acquisition tools will fail to image the disk. In this case, consideration shall be given to selecting an acquisition tool that will carry on imaging even if it finds damaged areas. Typically, these areas are overwritten with 'zeros.' These are recorded in the log file, so that the actual bad areas of the disk can be identified. This breaches the ACPO Principle 1, and so Principle 2 shall be relied on. The means that the requirements for competence and being able to prove it, as required in Principle 2 are even more important, as is the requirement for the audit trail in Principle 3. Acquiring a damaged disk can be a very time consuming process and a decision shall be made by the Laboratory Manager to use this process or not.

9.9.1.4.1 Acquiring a hard disk

1. The hard disk to be imaged shall be connected to the acquisition device via the write blocker to prevent evidence contamination, as appropriate (Fig. 9.5).

2. If the disk has jumpers, then the jumper settings may have to be changed to acquire the disk, if so the original setting and the revised setting shall be recorded on the Forensic Case Work Log.

3. The acquisition software shall be used according to the manufacturer's recommended procedures to acquire a forensic image of the hard disk.

4. Once the forensic acquisition has taken place using the chosen forensic imaging tool, the MD5 hashes of the acquisition and the original disk shall be checked to ensure that they are the same. If they are, then the bit image is exact, if they do not, then the copy is not exact and shall be re-imaged until the hashes match.

5. Experience shows that a different version of the same acquisition tool or a different acquisition tool may solve the problem.

6. Once one complete image has been taken and the hashes match a second one shall be taken, this may use the same tool or use a different one. The reason for this is that if one image corrupts, there is a fall back. This process shall require a second dedicated forensic case disk for the image.

7. Once two complete and exact images have been made, the original media shall be returned to the Secure Property Store and signed back in after being resealed.

8. Details of the acquisition process shall be recorded on the Hard Disk Details Log.

9. All work carried out shall be recorded in the Forensic Case Work Log.

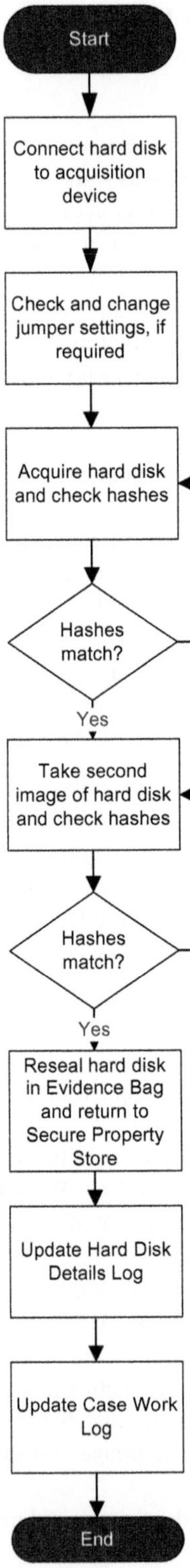

FIG. 9.5 Acquiring a hard disk.

9.9.1.4.2 Acquiring a tablet computer

1. The tablet computer to be imaged shall be connected to the acquisition device via the write blocker to prevent evidence contamination.
2. Tablet computer acquisition may require specialist software or tools and shall only be undertaken by Forensic Analysts who are competent on the specialist software or tool being used.

3. The acquisition software shall be used, according to the manufacturer's recommended procedures to acquire a forensic image of the tablet computer. Forensic software for acquiring and processing images from all tablet computers shall integrate seamlessly with its main forensic case processing software.
4. Once the forensic acquisition has taken place using the chosen forensic imaging tool, the MD5 hashes of the acquisition and the original disk shall be checked to ensure that they are the same. If they are, then the bit image is exact, if they do not, then the copy is not exact and shall be re-imaged until the hashes match.
5. Experience shows that a different version of the same acquisition tool or a different acquisition tool may solve the problem.
6. Once one complete image has been taken and the hashes match, a second one shall be taken, this may use the same tool or use a different one. The reason for this is that if one image corrupts, there is a fall back. This process shall require a second dedicated case disk for the image.
7. Once two complete and exact images have been made, the original media shall be returned to the Secure Property Store and signed back in after being resealed.
8. Details of the acquisition process shall be recorded on the Smart Phone Details Log.
9. All work carried out shall be recorded in the Forensic Case Work Log.

Note 1

To examine a tablet computer, it may be necessary to turn it on and this will make changes to it as it boots up. This breaches the ACPO Principle 1, and so Principle 2 shall be relied on. The means that the requirements for competence and being able to prove it, as required in Principle 2 are even more important, as is the requirement for the audit trail in Principle 3.

Note 2

Some tablet computer may implement screen locking after a set period and require entry of the pass code to access the tablet. Some commercial software can bypass this, but if this is not possible, then consideration should be given to making changes to the settings on the device to keep the pass code protection from activating. This breaches Principle 1 as in note 1 above, so the same proviso shall be made.

Note 3

The Forensic Analyst (or First Responder) shall avoid touching the screen as much as possible, as this may activate the tablet computer and make changes to it.

Note 4

It may be possible to disable the account with the service provider.

Note 5

The Forensic Analyst shall be aware of the possibility of the tablet computer being booby trapped or contain malware (e.g. Trojans to wipe the disk) and have a contingency plan in place if needed.

9.9.1.4.3 Acquiring smart phones

1. The smart phone to be imaged shall be connected to the acquisition device via the write blocker to prevent evidence contamination.
2. Mobile phone acquisition requires specialist software or tools and shall only be undertaken by Forensic Analysts who are competent on the specialist software or tool being used.
3. The acquisition software shall be used, according to the manufacturer's recommended procedures to acquire a forensic image of the smart phone. Forensic software for acquiring and processing images from all smart phones shall be used that integrates seamlessly with the main case processing software.
4. Once the forensic acquisition has taken place using the chosen forensic imaging tool, the MD5 hashes of the acquisition and the original shall be checked to ensure that they are the same. If they are, then the bit image is exact, if they do not, then the copy is not exact and re-imaged until the hashes match.

5. Experience shows that a different version of the same acquisition tool or a different acquisition tool may solve the problem.
6. Once one complete image has been taken and the hashes match a second one shall be taken, this may use the same tool or use a different one. The reason for this is that if one image corrupts, there is a fall back. This process shall require a second dedicated case disk for the image.
7. Once two complete and exact images have been made, the original media shall be returned to the Secure Property Store and signed back in after being resealed.
8. Details of the acquisition process shall be recorded on the Smart Phone Details Log.
9. All work carried out shall be recorded in the Forensic Case Work Log.

Note 1

To examine a smart phone, it may be necessary to turn it on and this will make changes to it as it boots up. This breaches the ACPO Principle 1, and so Principle 2 shall be relied on. The means that the requirements for competence and being able to prove it, as required in Principle 2 are even more important, as is the requirement for the audit trail in Principle 3.

Note 2

Some smart phones may implement screen locking after a set period and require entry of the pass code to access the phone. Some commercial software can bypass this, but if this is not possible, then consideration shall be given to making changes to the settings on the phone to keep the pass code protection from activating. This breaches Principle 1 as in note 1 above, so the same proviso shall be made.

Note 3

The Forensic Analyst (or First Responder) shall avoid touching the screen as much as possible, as this may activate the phone and make changes to it.

Note 4

It may be necessary to put a phone in airplane mode, again this breaches 1 as in note 1 above, so the same proviso shall be made.

Note 5

It may be possible to disable the account with the service provider.

Note 6

The Forensic Analyst shall be aware of the possibility of the smart phone being booby trapped or contain malware (e.g. Trojans to wipe the disk) and have a contingency plan in place if needed.

9.9.1.4.4 Acquiring other devices

1. Depending on the device to be acquired, specialised software shall be used that is dedicated to acquiring the device (Fig. 9.6).
2. Where the device contains a hard disk, it should, if possible, be removed and the hard disk acquired as defined in Section 9.1.4.1 above.
3. With 'difficult' devices, it may take considerable time to determine the optimum way to obtain the evidence that is required. At no time shall a Forensic Analyst be rushed into performing potentially unsafe forensic acquisition actions.
4. The device to be imaged shall be connected to the acquisition device via the write blocker to prevent evidence contamination, if at all possible.
5. Where device acquisition requires specialist software or tools it shall only be undertaken by Forensic Analysts who are competent on the specialist software or tool being used.

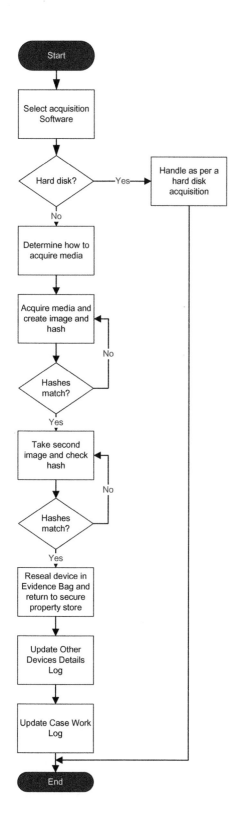

FIG. 9.6 Acquiring other devices.

6. The acquisition software shall be used, according to the manufacturer's recommended procedures to acquire a forensic image of the device.

7. Once the forensic acquisition has taken place using the chosen forensic imaging tool, the MD5 hashes of the acquisition and the original shall be checked to ensure that they are the same. If they are, then the bit image is exact, if they do not, then the copy is not exact and shall be re-imaged until the hashes match.

8. Experience shows that a different version of the same acquisition tool or a different acquisition tool may solve the problem.

9. Once one complete image has been taken and the hashes match a second one shall be taken, this may use the same tool or use a different one. The reason for this is that if one image corrupts, there is a fall back. This process shall require a second dedicated case disk for the image.
10. Once two complete and exact images have been made, the original media shall be returned to the Secure Property Store and signed back in after being resealed.
11. Details of the acquisition process shall be recorded on the Other Devices Details Log.
12. All work carried out shall be recorded in the Forensic Case Work Log.

Note 1

The Forensic Analyst shall be aware of the possibility of the device being booby trapped or contain malware (e.g. Trojans to wipe the disk) and have a contingency plan in place if needed.

9.9.1.4.5 Acquiring other media

1. The media to be imaged shall be connected to the acquisition device via the write blocker to prevent evidence contamination.
2. With 'difficult' media, it may take considerable time to determine the optimum way to obtain the evidence that is required. At no time shall a Forensic Analysts be rushed into performing potentially unsafe forensic acquisition actions.
3. Some CDs and DVDs are not easy to acquire and a variety of tools may be needed to attempt a successful acquisition. This process may preclude them from being integrated into the core forensic case processing tool(s) so these images shall be examined individually.
4. There are other devices that hold electronic media that may require specialised software, tools, and competence to extract and image or to be able to investigate. Circumstances will dictate the approach.
5. Where media acquisition requires specialist software or tools it shall only be undertaken by Forensic Analysts who are competent on the specialist software or tool being used.
6. The acquisition software shall be used in accordance with the manufacturer's recommended procedures to acquire a forensic image of the media.
7. Once the forensic acquisition has taken place using the chosen forensic imaging tool, the MD5 hashes of the acquisition and the original shall be checked to ensure that they are the same. If they are, then the bit image is exact, if they do not, then the copy is not exact shall be re-imaged until the hashes match.
8. Experience shows that a different version of the same acquisition tool or a different acquisition tool may solve the problem.
9. Once one complete image has been taken and the hashes match a second one shall be taken, this may use the same tool or use a different one. The reason for this is that if one image corrupts, there is a fall back. This process shall require a second dedicated case disk for the image.
10. Once two complete and exact images have been made, the original media shall be returned to the Secure Property Store and signed back in after being resealed.
11. Details of the acquisition process shall be recorded on the Other Media Details Log.
12. All work carried out shall be recorded in the Forensic Case Work Log.

9.9.1.4.6 Acquiring volatile memory

1. A number of devices may have volatile memory present and this will be lost when it is switched off. This lends towards on-site acquisition of volatile memory. The device may be seized and returned to the laboratory for imaging so long as power is not lost and volatile memory is not lost or the whole imaging process may be carried out on site.
2. Hardware or software acquisition may be used depending on circumstances.
3. Volatile memory acquisition requires specialist software or tools and shall only be undertaken by Forensic Analysts who are competent on the specialist software or tool being used.
4. The acquisition software or hardware shall be used, according to the manufacturer's recommended procedures to acquire a forensic image of the volatile memory.
5. Inspection of the device uptime since the last re-boot shall be used to determine whether a full volatile memory acquisition shall be undertaken. If the device has recently been rebooted, or it has been rebooted since the security incident, it may not be worth performing a full acquisition. Whatever the option chosen, the justification for it shall be documented in the Forensic Case Work Log.

6. It is not possible to run an MD5 checksum on the image, as there is no original image to compare against.
7. The evidence recovered from the acquisition will depend on the device being acquired, but some volatile evidence that may be recovered is defined in Appendix 25.
8. Details of the acquisition process shall be recorded on the Other Media Details Log.
9. All work carried out shall be recorded in the Forensic Case Work Log.

9.9.1.5   Evidence integrity

The integrity of a digital image is of paramount importance as Courts or Tribunals shall make decisions based on the presentation of forensic evidence and its integrity.

The integrity of the crime scene, where handled by the First Response Team, as defined in Chapter 8, Section 8.6, is the first step in this process. Where the scene was not secured appropriately, it may be later found that the evidence was tainted at this stage of the incident.

When handling evidence, the rules of evidence and other legislative requirements relating to the forensic case must be understood and be implemented to ensure legislative compliance within the jurisdiction(s).

Safe and secure transportation of evidence from the incident scene shall always be ensured until it is safely logged into Secure Property Store, as defined in Chapter 8, Section 8.7.

The use of sound forensic investigative methods, including the use of write blockers to ensure that evidence is not altered during the acquisition process shall be mandatory, wherever write blockers can be used.

Using forensic workstation anticontamination procedures, as defined in Section 9.4.7, shall ensure that there is no chance of cross contamination from another case.

Validation and testing of methods and tools, as defined in Chapter 7, Section 7.5.5 shall also be mandatory for all forensic case processing.

MD5 hashing shall be used to prove that the images made are the same as the original shall prove that the data is unaltered, which is standard for the imaging tools.

Copies of the exact software used in processing a forensic case shall be stored in the virtual case file. This ensures that the results are repeatable and ensures the integrity of the imaging or analysis phases as the exact software can be used to recreate any aspect of the forensic case in case of later need.

The chain of custody for all exhibits and the use of the Property Log, as defined in Chapter 8, Appendix 17, with contemporaneous Forensic Case Work Logs with the other forms and checklists in use shall demonstrate responsibility for all actions in the forensic case processing and shall provide a full end-to-end traceability of all actions taken in a forensic case,

9.9.1.6   Backing up the images

Once the exhibits have been imaged as defined in Section 9.9, they shall be backed up as follows:

1. All images shall be compressed and backed up to the image drive on the forensic server.
2. One copy of the image shall be used as the case or working disk.
3. The second copy of the image shall be placed in the Secure Property Store, marked with the case number, the contents, date and who performed the image, where it will stay according to case retention schedule, as defined in Chapter 4, Appendix 26.
4. A tape copy of the Forensic Server disk containing the images shall then be run and placed in the Secure Property Store.

9.9.1.7   Reassembly and resealing the exhibit(s)

- once the acquisition has been successfully performed the exhibit(s) shall be returned to the Secure Property Store; and
- in the case of large equipment, such as PCs or servers, consideration may be given to holding the media in the fire safe separate to the carcass of the device on space saving grounds, this shall be acceptable so long as the procedures below are followed:

9.9.1.7.1   Storing media and carcass together

Where the electronic media is to be replaced in the exhibit (or is an integral part of the exhibit) and stored in the Secure Property Store together the following procedures shall be performed:

- the exhibit shall be reassembled—BUT NOT POWERED UP;
- the exhibit shall be placed in a new Evidence Bag;

- the original Evidence Bag and seal shall be placed inside the new Evidence Bag;
- any additional peripherals associated with the exhibit shall be placed in the new Evidence Bag, if possible. If not, multiple bags shall be used;
- the Evidence Bag shall be sealed; and
- The Property Log shall be updated to show the new seal being applied to the exhibit.

9.9.1.7.2 Storing media and carcass separately

It is often the case that the carcass and the electronic media shall have to be stored separately (typically for space considerations). Where this is the case, the following procedures shall be performed:

- the exhibit shall be reassembled but without the storage media;
- the Laboratory Manager shall agree to the separation of the exhibits, and this shall be recorded in the Property Log;
- the carcass shall be placed in a new Evidence Bag;
- the original Evidence Bag and seal shall be placed inside the new Evidence Bag;
- any additional peripherals associated with the exhibit, except the electronic media, shall be placed in the new Evidence bag, if possible. If not, multiple bags shall be used;
- the Evidence Bag shall NOT be sealed;
- the storage media shall be placed in a small Evidence Bag and sealed with the relevant information about the media entered onto the Evidence Bag;
- the Property Log shall be updated to show the new seal being applied to the storage media only;
- the carcass shall be placed in a secure location as agreed with the Laboratory Manager; and
- the relevant Movement Form(s) shall be updated to show the movement of the carcass to the agreed location, as defined in Chapter 8, Appendix 17.

9.9.2 On-site imaging

Where on-site imaging has to be carried out, the Forensic Analyst shall perform the task using the portable forensic workstation.

The portable forensic workstations shall have the same software tools on them as the desktop forensic workstations. In addition, dedicated imaging hardware tools shall be carried to facilitate on-site acquisition.

The procedures for preparing the forensic workstation shall be carried out.

The procedures for imaging on-site shall be exactly the same as those above in Section 9.9.1.3.

9.9.3 Remote imaging

It may be necessary to undertake remote forensics using the chosen main case processing software if it is not possible to attend the incident scene for whatever reason.

The procedures defined in Section 9.9.1.3 shall be applied to the process of remote forensics to ensure that full documentation shall exist to cover the chain of custody and proof that the integrity of the acquired image is maintained.

There are three main methods by which a Forensic Analyst can access a remote network over a network connection:

- instructing the client's IT staff to physically attend the target device(s) and manually instal a servlet application into memory to enable network access;
- preinstalling a 'servlet' application on to all target devices so that it is constantly running in memory so access can be gained on authorised demand; or
- using 'push' technology to place a servlet application into memory on the target device(s) on demand.

While this appears to be an ideal situation, there are a number of disadvantages with the approach which is why attending the incident scene is always preferred, if possible. These include, but are not limited to:

- a number of devices may not be available (e.g. failure to have laptops connected to the network). There is also the issue of not knowing all of the possible network components;
- damaged or failing source media that requires special attention to image it;
- difficulty in ensuring continuity of evidence;
- difficulty in ensuring the integrity of evidence acquired over the internet;

- failure to access the correct network segment, even if access to the client's network is granted;
- infected target systems;
- lack of control over the incident scene;
- lack of visibility of the incident scene;
- network bandwidth;
- network unavailability;
- no matter how good the instructions to the client's IT staff are, they are not trained First Responders or forensic experts;
- proving access authority and limits of authority; and
- standalone devices are not network connected.

9.10 Examination

9.10.1 Initial examination

9.10.1.1 Loading images into the virtual case file

To start processing a forensic case, the Forensic Analyst shall load the forensic case into the forensic processing workstation:

- depending on the size of the disk, the forensic case may require the insertion of a larger disk than is currently in the disk caddy in the forensic workstation;
- the Forensic Analyst shall add relevant details to the virtual case file, as appropriate to the forensic case, in the relevant case file;
- the Forensic Analyst shall then load the images into the preferred forensic analysis software to create the digital forensic case. During this process, the required information regarding the physical case shall be entered into MARS as required and prompted for.

Once the forensic case has been set up in the relevant forensic tool it shall be processed. Hard disks and other forensically acquired images shall all be handled in generally the same way, but items such as other devices my need to be handled differently and uniquely.

9.10.1.2 Smart phones

These shall be handled in accordance with the instructions or manuals supplied with the software in use for their interrogation and investigation.

What can be recovered from these devices will vary based on such things as maintenance of charge, software in use, etc. The following contents of modern smart phones shall include but no be limited to and have value as evidence:

- IMEI;
- IMSI;
- short dial numbers;
- text messages;
- settings (language, date/time, tone/volume, etc.);
- stored audio recordings;
- stored video recordings;
- stored images;
- remote access artefacts;
- stored digital files;
- logged incoming, outgoing, and missed calls;
- apps and their associated data;
- stored calendar events;
- GPRS, WAP, and internet settings;
- browser bookmarks;
- emails;
- files in folders;
- browser URLs;
- memos

- task lists;
- key stores;
- configurations; and
- alarm settings.

Note 1

The merging of technologies of mobile devices and smart phones means that these devices will start to merge as will the evidence available from them.

Note 2

Cell site analysis can be undertaken, but this requires assistance from the phone's service provider. Powered up phones register with the nearest base stations and these registrations are stored by the service provider. Using this information and applying triangulation can allow a Forensic Analyst to make a reasonable estimation of the journey that the phone took for the period of the registration data.

9.10.1.3   Images acquired to media

While the specific software used shall dictate the exact details of using the software, there are a number of procedural steps that shall be taken at the start of any forensic case, these include, but are not limited to:

- mount the image and run at least two antimalware products against the image, the results of any malware recovered shall be recorded on the Forensic Case Log. It is advisable to run at least two tools to ensure that there was 'nothing left behind.' The recording of the findings is essential if there are later issues with the 'Trojan Defence';
- check local parameters such as date and time on the system and adjust where necessary when compared with 'actual time' from a known time source;
- set the local time zone for the exhibit;
- recover all possible deleted folders;
- view all pictures to see if there is any unlawful material—if there is then immediately stop any investigation, lock the workstation and advise the Laboratory Manager who will take appropriate action including Law Enforcement liaison;
- if running Encase, the initialise case script shall be run;
- a signature analysis and hash all of the files shall be run;
- notable files shall be identified from their hash values. If there are any notable files discovered, then they shall be examined, and if necessary, dealt with as 'unlawful material,' as defined in Section 9.19.2;
- any password protected or encrypted files or folders shall be identified;
- any Alternate Data Streams (ADS) that may be present shall be identified. This shall require specialist tools as ADS are invisible to the operating systems normal file listing commands;
- any Host Protected Areas (HPAs) and Device Configuration Overlays (DCOs) shall be identified and dealt with, as they are invisible to the operating systems and used by the manufacturer for their own purposes. However, as they are invisible to the operating system, they can be used to hide files; and
- these operations shall be recorded in the Forensic Case Work Log.

9.10.2   First stage examination

Having run the initial examination of the case image, recovery of data from the case image shall be undertaken. Some of these can be automated and others are manual processes. The following shall be carried out for all cases:

9.10.2.1   Determine appropriate method

Time spent in planning how to process a forensic case is time seldom wasted. The Forensic Analyst shall determine the optimum methods and tools to obtain the required outcomes. There is no one tool that does everything required in processing a forensic case. A variety of methods and tools shall be used to process the forensic case.

9.10.2.2 Using hash sets for first stage examinations

9.10.2.2.1 'Known' or 'safe' files

Safe or known files (identified by their hash values) shall be excluded from a forensic case and this shall substantially reduce the amount of time that is taken for searching for keywords or processing other scripts or tasks.

9.10.2.2.2 'Notable' files

As part of the first stage examination a review of all files with notable hashes shall be undertaken and if necessary, dealt with as 'unlawful material,' as defined in Section 9.19.2. Where the Forensic Analyst has created their own hash files for a specific case, as defined in Section 9.4.8, the notable files for the case using that specific set of notable files, shall be those relevant for the specific case.

9.10.2.3 Some file systems encountered

There are a number of file systems that may be encountered while processing a forensic case, these include, but are not limited to:

- APFS- Apple File System, released in 2017 and came to replace HFS+;
- BFS—BeOS;
- BREW—Various mobile /smart phones;
- CDFS—CDs;
- EFS—Amazon Extended File system;
- EROFS—Huawei Android mobiles;
- exFAT- Extended FAT file system, used for high capacity flash drives (like SDHC cards) by Windows Vista Service Pack 1, Windows 6.0 CE, and higher versions;
- Ext 2—Linux, Unix, and some mobile/smart phones;
- Ext 3—Linux and some mobile/smart phones;
- Ext 4—Linux and some mobile/smart phones;
- FAT 16—MS Dos and versions of Windows;
- FAT 32—Versions of Windows, some mobile/smart phones, iPods, and MP3 players;
- FATX—Games consoles;
- HFS and HFS+—Mac OS, iPhones;
- HPFS—OS/2 and versions of Windows;
- GFS—Linux;
- GFS2—Updated version of GFS;
- Joliet—CDs;
- NTFS—Versions of Windows
- ReFS—Windows Servers;
- RFS—Samsung Android mobiles;
- UDF—DVDs;
- UFS—UNIX file system;
- UfsBE and UfsLE—two variations of the UFS file system, used on Apple Macs and UNIX;
- VFS—Linux virtual file system;
- VMFS3—VMWare;
- YAFFS2—Android smart phones;
- ZFS—Sun systems.

A number of mobile/smart phones devices have proprietary file systems.

9.10.2.4 Automated scripts and tasks in encase

One of the core forensic tools in FCL is Encase. The following Scripts shall be run (always use the most recent version and log which versions were used and place a copy in the Virtual Case File) as appropriate to the forensic case:

- initialise case (if not already run);
- hash all files;

- signature analysis;
- info record finder—for Windows recycle bin;
- graphics file finder;
- internet history;
- HTML parser;
- link parser;
- find unique email addresses; and
- registry information—for Windows.

Other scripts can and shall be run depending on the exact requirements of the forensic case, but these are the standard set that shall be run for standard Windows forensic cases. Mobile devices shall have their own dedicated tools as well as Encase, and these shall be used, as appropriate.

Additionally, the Forensic Analyst may write an Enscript for a specific task or import one from one of the many Enscript libraries. Any new script shall be validated as defined in Chapter 7, Section 7.5.5 prior to being used for forensic case processing.

9.10.2.5 Extracting files in file structure

One of the initial manual processes shall be to extract the original file structure from the image so that it can be viewed as necessary. This can give insight into how the file structures looked in a far better manner than any tool can.

A graphical representation of the structure shall be included in the Appendix for the Forensic Case Report.

9.10.2.6 Extracting files

It is often useful to extract all of the files (by file type) as well as extracting such folders as 'my documents,' etc. to the forensic case file.

- files of a single type shall be grouped in the following folders:
  - archive or current;
  - deleted;
  - hidden; and
  - recycled.

Specific folders shall be just extracted using their own folder name.
These files shall be placed on the media that accompany the case.

9.10.2.7 Text searches

The client will typically give a number of search criteria that they want to have run against the image.
- these searches shall be run as required.

9.10.2.8 Where to find the 'smoking gun'

There is no definitive answer as to where to find the 'smoking gun' as this will vary from forensic case to forensic case, but the following should provide guidance for the areas to investigate:

- access control devices;
- access records to buildings and rooms;
- address books;
- application logs;
- audit logs;
- auto-complete memory;
- backup files;
- blogs;
- cache (temporary Internet files and other files that create caches);
- cache (memory);
- calendars and appointment books;
- smart phone call records;
- chat logs;

- comments in documents that can be recovered (e.g. using 'Final showing Markup in MS Office);
- compressed files;
- configuration files;
- content addressable memory (CAM) tables;
- cookies;
- crontab type files and other scheduled tasks;
- database files;
- desktop folder;
- documents;
- email files and headers, including deleted emails from POP, IMAP and Web mail clients;
- event logs;
- examination of source code;
- favourites folder;
- file caches;
- files embedded in other files;
- file slack space;
- free space—memory;
- hibernation files;
- hidden shares;
- identifying MAC address of author of a file;
- internet history files;
- images or graphics files;
- instant messaging;
- internet bookmarks or favourites;
- IP addresses;
- ISP records;
- last system shutdown time and date;
- last user shutdown time and date;
- layering of images;
- links to externally stored documents;
- listserve logs;
- location bar history;
- log files;
- media player file list;
- memory cache;
- metadata—though ensure that dates and times are properly reported. Examples of file system metadata is defined in Appendix 26;
- my documents folder;
- network traffic;
- newsgroups;
- open and save history;
- packet headers;
- packet payloads;
- paper based documents and other paper evidence;
- password protected files;
- peer to peer (P2P) traffic;
- p-list files;
- previous versions of web sites (www.archive.org);
- printer spool files;
- real time tracing and analysis;
- recent folder;
- recycle bin;
- registry contents;
- relational analysis;

- routing tables;
- send to folder;
- shadow files;
- shrunk images;
- slack space—disks;
- slack space—memory;
- sniffer program output;
- social media sites and communications (e.g. Facebook, Twitter, MySpace, WhatsApp, LinkedIn, etc.);
- start menu run history;
- swap files;
- syslog;
- system files;
- temporal analysis (time lining);
- temporary files;
- traffic analysis;
- trust relationships to other systems;
- unallocated clusters; and
- volume slack.

9.10.2.9 Deliberately hidden evidence

There are a number of methods of deliberately hiding files as users become more aware of technology and increasingly understand what can be recovered from a device. Some of these methods and how they can be overcome include, but are not limited to those below:

- **$boot file**—disk analysis and check contents of the attribute;
- **$bad and $BadClus**—examination of claimed bad clusters on the disk;
- **$data attribute**—check contents of the attribute;
- **additional clusters added to a file**—disk analysis;
- **alternate data streams**—specialist tools;
- **changing file attributes to make files hidden**—specialist tools;
- **deleted files and partitions**—undelete them;
- **encrypted files**—attempting to find unencrypted versions of the file, overcoming weak encryption, notification of encryption software installed, acted from the suspect's computer and if all else fails a brute force attack;
- **hidden files and directories**—unhide them;
- **HPA**—use specialised tools;
- **manually changing file system slack**—disk analysis;
- **manually changing volume slack**—disk analysis;
- **manually adding files to file slack**—analysis of slack space;
- **manually adding files to memory slack**—analysis of slack space;
- **misnamed (bad signature) files**—run signature analysis; and
- **steganography**—specialist tools and hash sets to find known steg files.

There are a number of other methods of deliberately hiding data ranging from the simple (e.g. storing data on removable media) to the very complex. For every type of data hiding, the original unencrypted file shall have existed and so there may be traces of it available.

9.10.2.10 Virtualisation

A virtual machine (VM) is a software implementation of a computer that executes programs like a physical computer—hence the name. A computer may run multiple VMs with the same or different operating systems.

The capability of virtualisation is of great benefit to the Forensic Analyst. It allows them to set up pseudo networks on their forensic workstation and suspend and freeze any sessions as required. VMs can also be used to provide sandbox facilities to allow a Forensic Analyst to investigate malicious or suspicious software in safety. It also allows a Forensic Analyst access to an operating system other than the main one they are using without the need to have dual boot capability.

One of the greatest benefits of virtualisation is that it allows a Forensic Analyst the ability to mount a system exactly as it was when used by the suspect. This can have a great benefit in presenting evidence to a judge or jury.

From a time saving point of view, VMs may be used as a VM allows a Forensic Analyst to boot an image into a virtual environment, saving a tremendous amount of time, as opposed to restoring an image to the original hardware that ran it.

From a cost perspective, VMs save money as multiple VMs can run on a single machine.

9.10.2.11   Investigating peripherals and other devices

A number of peripherals may be included in the case to be processed. These shall all be investigated for potential evidence. This may include, but not be limited to:

- access control devices;
- answering machines;
- audio recording devices;
- car engine management systems and motor vehicle event data recorders (MVEDRs);
- CCTV;
- copiers;
- digital video recorders;
- direct attached storage (DAS);
- eBook readers;
- electronic tills;
- fax machines;
- gaming consoles;
- SATNAV systems;
- household and office devices containing microchips;
- IoT (Internet of Things) devices in the home (e.g. smart meters, fridges);
- MP3 and other digital music devices;
- multifunction devices;
- network attaches storage (NAS);
- network management devices;
- pagers;
- phone systems;
- photographic recording devices;
- printers;
- radio frequency identification (RFID) devices;
- redundant array of independent disks (RAIDs);
- routers;
- scanners;
- storage area networks (SANs);
- video games devices;
- virtual machines (VMs) running multiple operating systems; and
- wireless access points.

9.10.2.12   Covert and remote investigations

Forensic Analysts undertaking covert investigations shall ensure that they are not detected by the suspect whose information processing equipment they are investigating. Some considerations shall be but not be limited to:

- breaking the investigation into a number of stages and spread them over a period of time so that the suspect is not alerted to unusual use patterns;
- ensuring that any firewalls allow relevant traffic between the Forensic Analyst's workstation and the suspect's—failure and rejection of connections or traffic may alert the suspect;
- ensuring that the investigation is strictly 'need to know' and the minimum of number of employees and other interested parties are aware of it;

- ensuring that the tools used run as a system service;
- ensuring that whatever tools are used shall leave no traces (e.g. event logs);
- ensuring that resource usage shall be minimised—i.e. do not run multiple tasks at once, as excessive resource usage may alert the suspect;
- only searching for evidence relevant to the case, this shall be strictly limited and agreed, as it is too easy to search for everything;
- using neutral naming for any remote agents or replace an innocuous name;
- ensuring that the collection process shall not impact normal operations or alert the suspect; and
- consider the best time to carry out a covert investigation—is it in the quiet hours, when it may be noticed, or during the day so it can appear as normal traffic.

9.10.2.13   Records

The following records shall be made:

- update of Forensic Case Work Log to show what has been done;
- listing of all recovered files;
- output (i.e. hard copies) of any files of note;
- a full directory listing shall be made to include folder structure, filenames, date/time stamps, logical file sizes, etc.;
- details of the installed operating systems shall be noted;
- all exhibits produced shall be recorded, as defined in Section 9.14, appropriately marked and secured;
- all tools used in a forensic case shall have a copy of the exact software used on the case placed in the virtual case file. This ensures that the results are later repeatable in case of need or challenge to evidence produced; and
- any other items in the virtual case file or the hard copy case file that shall be updated.

9.10.2.14   End of day processes

At the end of the working day, the forensic workstation and case shall be in one of two states:

1. processing instructions from the Forensic Analyst (e.g. running one or more overnight jobs); or
2. finished processing for the day.

    If the forensic workstation is processing, it shall be allowed to carry on running without interruption.
    If the forensic workstation has stopped processing for the day then:

- all of the files and folders from the forensic workstation that have been created or changed shall be copied up to the virtual case file on the Forensic server for backing up by the overnight server backup process, as defined in Chapter 7, Section 7.7.4; and
- the work disk shall be placed in the fire safe overnight until needed.

9.10.3   Second stage examination

Once the initial searches and recoveries have been done detailed investigations shall be undertaken based on either what has been recovered and is relevant to the case or to further refine what is relevant to the case.

It is at this point that the Forensic Analyst shall consider the involvement of someone intimate with the detailed requirements of the case so that together they can review the case. Typically, such a process shall lead to:

- inclusion or exclusion of search hits found to date;
- further searches to be undertaken;
- requirements for details associated with recovered files such as metadata;
- requirements for cracking passwords or encryption;
- requirements for proving that 'A' is linked to 'B' and how this can be proved (e.g. that a document was created on a specific device, the owner of the device has been identified and that they were in the office working at the time of the file creation);
- investigation of peer-to-peer packages, Instant Messaging or similar;
- recovery of printer artefacts;
- further details from the registry being recovered; and
- detailed or further requirements for files, applications or processes identified (e.g. password breaking for files, investigation of a peer to peer network, further investigation of email, etc.).

Note 1

It is not possible to give details of all possible outcomes as they will vary from forensic case to forensic case, and no two cases are ever the same.

Further and better particulars of what is required at this stage is essential to ensure that the Forensic Analyst shall recover what the client requires but also to eliminate time wasted and to determine the type, form and layout of any deliverables required (e.g. statements, depositions, reports, exhibits, etc.).

Note 2

When the results have been reported to the client, this may lead to additional requirements being identified by the client. The second stage examination shall be an iterative process that carries on until the client is satisfied with the results.

9.10.4 Best evidence

The best evidence rule is a common law rule of evidence which can be traced back at least as far as the 18th century. In Omychund v Barker (1745), Lord Harwicke stated that no evidence was admissible unless it was 'the best that the nature of the case will allow'.

'Best evidence' is therefore the best evidence that can be produced in Court. Thus, the real seized evidence is the best evidence. While in some cases, it is not possible to bring the original evidence to Court, other forms of evidence may be regarded as original evidence, but this will vary between jurisdictions. A crime scene cannot be brought into a Court room, but photographs, sketches, statements, evidence logs, etc. can be produced to illustrate the scene.

The general rule is that 'secondary' evidence (i.e. a copy of a document) will be not admissible if an original document exists, so a copy of a signed contract would not be acceptable, if the original contract exists and was available.

9.10.5 Case progress

A record of the summary of the case progress shall be held in the front of the paper case file so that it can easily be reviewed by the Laboratory Manager. The Case Progress Checklist is defined in Appendix 27.

9.10.6 Choosing an expert witness

If the case is going to a Tribunal or Court, it may be necessary to choose an Expert Witness to give 'expert testimony'. The Expert Witness may be appointed at any stage during the case processing cycle but shall have been appointed by the second stage examination.

Advice on choosing an Expert Witness is defined in Chapter 11, Section 11.4.

9.10.7 Re-hashing the image

At the end of processing the forensic case and producing the case report, the image shall be rehashed to show that during the investigation that nothing has been changed in the image. The re-hashing shall be recorded on the Forensic Case Work Log and in the report to the client. If further work is to be carried out at a later date, the image shall be re-hashed before any work is undertaken to show that no changes have occurred while it has been held in the Secure Property Store.

9.10.8 Using a forensic workstation for network investigations

When a Forensic Analyst is connected to the Internet, it must be remembered that the connection is a two way connection. If the Forensic Analyst is using an in house IP Address then their origin and IP address are revealed. This leaves the Forensic Analyst open to a possible attack.

It is for this reason that:

- no internet investigations shall be performed from a network connected forensic workstation;
- an IP address not associated with FCL shall be used for the standalone workstation being used; and
- workstations used to access the Internet shall not be Windows based, but Linux as there are also fewer malware exploits and Trojans on Linux than in Windows.

9.11   Dual tool verification

In many case that the Forensic Analysts have to deal with there shall be a quantity of evidence pointing to the guilt of the suspect.

In some cases, this may not be the case and the evidence may be a single line of text, a couple of bytes or a small file. In cases such as this, the Forensic Analyst shall verify the findings with a totally different tool.

The repeat of the examination and the findings with a second tool shall lend more reliability and credibility to the findings.

9.12   Digital time stamping

Consideration shall be given to the Forensic Analysts using a digital time stamping service to time stamp recovered documents and files as well as other documents produced in a case. Such a service would prove two facts:

- **existence**: that a file existed on a given date & time;
- **data integrity**: that the file was not altered since the time it was stamped.

These two facts are essential for a number of purposes, including but not limited to:

- gathering and registering binary data to be used as forensic evidence, such as computer files, memory dumps, packet recorder data, security analysis logs, etc.;
- electronically 'notarising' the date and time of the evidence recovered using a secure real-time clock held in tamper proof hardware;
- generating secure audit logs for recovered evidence submitted and a digitally signed time certificate identifying the files submitted; and
- the digitally signed time certificate shall provide nonrepudiated evidence of existence and integrity of the files submitted.

There are a number of organisations that provide these services, and the process is:

1. The Forensic Analyst emails a list of MD5 hashes for evidence gathered or files recovered on a given day to the digital time stamper.
2. The service returns a PGP signed message confirming receipt of the message and giving their reference number.

Whatever service is used, the service supplier shall have their time stamp device certified by an accredited certification laboratory against a known time source and provide proof of this, digitally signed by the certification laboratory.

9.13   Production of an internal case report

9.13.1   The internal report

An internal case report is a document that allows the Laboratory Manager to understand a case and determine the evidence found and how this supports or does not support the client requirements.

The Forensic Analyst shall produce a report on the case. The report shall follow the following format:

- basic case information;
- evidence sought;
- evidence found; and
- attachments and appendices.

The template for an internal report is defined in the Appendix 28.

9.13.2   Classification

All reports shall be released with appropriate security classifications placed in them either according to the classification standards, as defined in Chapter 5, Appendix 16 or the standards of the client if known. If the client's classification standards are not known then the FCL security classifications shall be used.

9.14   Creating exhibits

9.14.1   What is an exhibit?

An exhibit is real evidence that will be considered by the Court.

In forensic cases, exhibits could be:

- the seized evidence itself;
- forensically produced evidence;
- printouts of files;
- a table of file attributes (e.g. metadata);
- or anything else that is to be produced in Court or as part of the forensic investigation results.

Exhibits shall be produced and referenced in statements, depositions or reports.

A full listing of exhibits created for any forensic case processed shall be entered onto the Exhibits Created Log and produced as part of the case outputs. The details of the Exhibit Log are defined in Appendix 29.

Exhibit numbering is defined in Chapter 8, Section 8.6.10.

9.15   Producing a case report for external use

9.15.1   The report

At the end of (or even during) a forensic case, the Forensic Analyst shall be required to produce a report on the case. If the report is for internal use, as a progress report, then the Internal Case Report Template shall be used.

If the report is for an external client, then it shall follow the relevant legislative rules within the jurisdiction. Often there are differing requirements for criminal cases and civil cases in the same jurisdiction, and the Forensic Analyst must be aware of them, and shall comply with them for all reports produced.

9.15.2   Report checklist

While no two reports will ever be the same, the Report Production Checklist, as defined in Appendix 30, shall serve as a checklist along with the original requirements for the contents of any report produced by any Forensic Analyst.

It is important that the Forensic Analyst shall remember the following:

- the report shall contain facts;
- assumptions shall not be made, unless the facts back them;
- conclusions shall be backed by facts;
- leads shall not be identified. The report is for the client, and it is his or her job to identify the leads. If something important is discovered during the analysis of the exhibit or processing the case, then it shall be written up so it is obvious to the client without providing a lead;
- spell and grammar checking shall be used prior to submitting the report for peer review;
- findings shall all be checked and double checked;
- all findings shall be repeatable by any competent Forensic Analyst to produce the same results; and
- where media is provided, ensure that the media is readable and the stated fields are present and that the extraction process works.

9.15.3   Peer review

No report shall be released to a client without it having gone through a peer review process as approved by the Laboratory Manager.

The peer-review process shall not be lightly undertaken and shall be performed in a diligent manner by the reviewer(s).

There shall be a technical review that shall review the validity of any findings. The review shall seek answers to the following questions:

- are the conclusions reached appropriate?
- are the conclusions reached justified?

- are the notes complete for all examinations and searches?
- are the results achieved verified by dual tool verification, if required?
- are the results repeatable?
- does the deliverable cover all evidence submitted in the forensic case (and if not—why)?
- have all appropriate examinations been carried out?
- have the relevant procedures all been followed?
- is the deliverable (report, statements, depositions, etc.) accurate?
- is the documentation relating to all examined exhibits appropriate and complete?
- were the methods used appropriate?
- were the tools used appropriate?

A record of the technical review shall be associated with the forensic case in the client virtual forensic case file. This shall be performed as a case check, as defined in Appendix 27.

The administrative review shall cover meeting the client's requirements as well as a peer review by another Forensic Analyst and this shall form part of the document control process, as defined in Chapter 4, Section 4.7.5 and Chapter 6, Section 6.8. This shall be performed as a forensic case check.

9.15.4 Release of a case report

No case report shall be released without the authority of the Laboratory Manager, as defined in Chapter 6, Section 6.8.

9.15.5 Affidavits

Depending on the jurisdiction, there may be an affidavit included in any deliverable. It shall be the responsibility of the Laboratory Manager and the Forensic Analyst to ensure that these requirements are met.

9.16 Statements, depositions, and similar

Statements, depositions, and other similar documents, written by Forensic Analysts, shall be written in a consistent style in compliance with the requirements within the jurisdiction.

The specific requirements shall depend on the jurisdiction, the type of document to be produced and the requirements of the case itself. Most of these types of documents shall contain similar information but the exact form and structure, as well as specific content, usually differs. The consistent information shall include:

- details of the author;
- author's qualifications—this may include their CV /resume as an appendix;
- author's past and current experience relevant to the forensic case;
- background to the forensic case;
- instructions received, including who made the request, when it was submitted and what work was requested;
- proof of the chain of custody for the evidence;
- a statement of compliance with the relevant legislation, regulation or relevant forensic good practice;
- details of the work on the case;
- for each item investigated:
  - **method**—short summary of what was done with what tools;
  - **results**—what was found;
  - **technical explanations**—technical explanations of the results; and
  - **context and discussion**—context of the findings and technical points in relation to what was requested.
- summary—of the findings;
- conclusions—not always required but may be needed. These should be strongly reinforced by the factual arguments in the document; and
- appendices—as required, including:
  - list of exhibits—include summary, exhibit reference, description and origin;
  - selected Glossary.

Some documents of this type may require a question and answer process that may require detailed answers to specific questions to be recorded.

Pages shall all be numbered (x of y pages) and be signed on every page.
The purpose of a report, statement, or deposition shall be to:

- accurately describe the forensic case from start to finish;
- be able to undergo scrutiny and challenge, as appropriate;
- be created in a timely manner;
- be retained as a record of the forensic case processing undertaken;
- be understandable to the lay person;
- contain facts to support any conclusions drawn;
- contain valid conclusions, recommendations, and opinions based on the facts reported, if required; and
- not be open to misinterpretation by being unambiguous.

9.17   Forensic software tools

There are a number of forensic tools in use and the primary tools for forensic casework in FCL are Encase (OpenText), FTK (AccessData), and UFED (Cellebrite).

Other tools shall be used as required; however, it must be assured that they have been validated for use as defined in Chapter 7, Section 7.5.5, before being used to process a forensic case.

9.18   Backing up and archiving a case

Full backups shall be maintained for all stages of processing a forensic case.

9.18.1   Initial forensic case images

- a copy of each forensic case image shall be compressed and placed on the 'images' drive on the forensic server and this shall be backed up according to the standard backup cycle, as defined in Chapter 7, Section 7.7.4;
- the backup process shall ensure that a complete backup of all current forensic cases is made;
- each new forensic case image shall be added to the 'images' drive and be backed up until the drive is full; and
- when the 'images' drive is full a full backup of the drive shall be taken and the drive with the tape backup placed in the fireproof safe in the Secure Property Store with another copy placed in the Secure Offsite Backup Store.

9.18.2   Work in progress

- the work in progress on the forensic case that has been created by the Forensic Analyst shall be backed up to the forensic server on a daily basis to the relevant client's virtual forensic case folder on the 'cases' drive;
- on a weekly basis the whole of the 'cases' file drive from the forensic workstation shall be copied to the forensic server to the 'work' drive (in compressed form);
- the 'cases' drive shall be backed up every night; and
- the 'work' drive shall be backed up on a weekly basis after the compressed case files have been copied from the forensic workstation.

9.18.3   'Finished' cases

It is not easy to determine when a case is finished as there can be further requests for information, a long period of time before the Trial, Tribunal or an Appeal. The process below shall be undertaken when the case has been finally (as far as is known) handed over to the client.

- when a case has been finished (as far as can be determined), then the whole client virtual forensic case file on the forensic workstation shall be compressed and copied to the 'finished' drive;
- the forensic workstation 'work disk' shall be removed and placed in the fireproof safe in the Secure Property Store;
- a tape copy of the 'finished' drive shall be created and stored with the work disk;
- the 'finished' drive shall be backed up on a weekly basis;
- the client virtual case file on the 'cases' drive shall remain on the drive so that rapid access to important documents and files (such as reports and statements) shall be possible without having to reload a tape or decompress a case.

9.18.4 Archiving a forensic case

- once the forensic case has properly finished it shall be archived and retained according to the Retention Schedule, as defined in Chapter 4, Appendix 26;
- any hard copy case papers that have not been scanned and added to client virtual case file, shall be scanned and added to the client virtual case file;
- the client virtual case file from the forensic workstation shall be copied to another disk of similar size and hashed to ensure that the copies are exact copies;
- the copy disk shall be suitably labelled and dated;
- the two copies of the forensic workstation client virtual case file shall be sealed and placed into the fireproof safe in the Secure Property Store;
- other tape backups of the case may exist, but there shall be two copies of the final work disk as tape copies are less stable than disks;
- the hard copy forensic case file shall be held securely under control of the relevant Forensic Analyst until it is securely deposited in the Secure Property Store; and
- all archiving of the hard copy case file and the client virtual case file shall comply with the relevant legislative, regulatory, and good practice within the jurisdiction for evidence handling.

9.18.5 Recoverability of archives and backups

- every year the Laboratory Manager shall ensure that any archived and backed up cases can be recovered from their backup media. This shall be performed as a task in the business continuity plan testing as defined in Chapter 13, Section 13.6.2; and
- records of this testing shall be maintained and any failures shall be investigated, and procedures changed, where necessary, as defined in Chapter 13, Section 13.6.4.3.

9.19 Disclosure

9.19.1 The law

FCL must understand and shall comply with the legislation relating to disclosure within the jurisdiction.

Because of the possible amount of data held on a seized device, it is possible that not all of the information held on the device has been examined by a Forensic Analyst. This can lead to issues if the requirements within the jurisdiction are to list all evidence.

If some material has not been viewed, then the Forensic Analyst will not know what it contains. In this case, an entry shall be made in any report produced to that effect with the reasons why it was not viewed and confirm that 'it is not known whether it contains any data that may undermine the case or assist the defence' (or similar wording as required within the jurisdiction).

Reasons for performing a limited search shall include, but are not limited to:

- a live examination was required;
- the equipment had to be examined on site;
- the searching was limited by the search warrant or court order;
- the size of the seized data is so large that full examination was not possible; or
- the weight of evidence found is so overwhelming that further searching and investigation was not necessary.

9.19.2 'Unlawful' material

FCL must understand and shall comply with the legislation relating to production, possessing or disclosing unlawful material and what constitutes unlawful material in the jurisdiction.

The production of unlawful material from original exhibits shall be avoided at all costs if at all possible. In cases where production is required, the produced materials shall be closely supervised either by the Laboratory Manager or the named Forensic Analyst whose case they were produced from.

This Forensic Analyst shall have the responsibility of ensuring that the material does not leave their possession until returned to the laboratory for destruction, unless ordered otherwise by a Court of competent jurisdiction or an Officer of the Law.

When unlawful material is to be released either to the prosecution or defence, FCL shall comply with the legislation within the jurisdiction. There are no universal rules for this, but the following guidelines shall be used, unless there is specific legislation requiring a different course of action:

- the material shall be classified as STRICTLY CONFIDENTIAL according to the FCL data classification standards, as defined in Chapter 5, Appendix 16;
- ensure that the person receiving it has a legal right to receive it;
- ensure that the person is a suitable person to receive the material;
- ensure that that the recipient receives the material personally and signs for it;
- ensure that that the requirements placed on the recipient for security and disclosure are conveyed to the recipient;
- ensure that that the person receiving the material does not relinquish the material to any other person for any reason unless ordered otherwise by a Court of competent jurisdiction or an Officer of the Law.
- ensure that that the material released shall be suitably secured personally by the recipient;
- ensure that that the recipient shall undertake not to make any copies of the material other than for production in Court;
- ensure that that the recipient shall undertake either to return the material after use or to securely destroy it by appropriate means and provide evidence of such destruction to the Laboratory Manager; and
- these actions shall be recorded in the Forensic Case Work Log.

9.19.3 Viewing of material by defence or prosecution

FCL must understand and shall comply with the legislation relating to viewing material by the Defence or Prosecution within the jurisdiction.

9.19.4 Client attorney privileged information

During examination of an image, it is possible that the Forensic Analyst discovers that the acquisition process has acquired client attorney privileged information. If this is the case, then the Forensic Analyst is ethically and legally bound not to divulge this information. The Laboratory Manager shall be informed of the discovery and the finding logged in the Forensic Case Work Log with the date and time the Laboratory Manager was advised.

9.20 Disposal

1. Typically, when the need for holding any papers, files or items for a given forensic case has passed (i.e. the retention date has been reached) the items shall all be disposed of using secure disposal where appropriate, as defined in Chapter 12, Section 12.3.14.10.
2. Records of the date and method of disposal shall be kept, as shall details of who actually performed the disposal.
3. Media, if still usable, shall be considered by the Laboratory Manager for reuse, as should any serviceable equipment.

Appendix 1—Some international forensic good practice

There are a number of good practice guides in existence in different jurisdictions. There is no guarantee that these are relevant (some are well out of date compared with the rapid rate of change in digital forensics) and others may not be relevant to the jurisdiction. However, they give indications of good practice in working standards in addition to ISO standards.

Name	Publisher	Version/Date
Good Practice Guide for Computer-based Electronic Evidence	ACPO	V5 October 2011
First Responders Guide to Computer Forensics	CERT	March 2005
Guidelines for the Best Practice in Forensic Examination of Digital Technology	EFNSI	V 01, November 2015
Computer Forensics Part 2: Best Practices	ISFS	August 2009
Forensic Examination of Digital Evidence: A Guide for Law Enforcement	NIJ	April 2004

Continued

Name	Publisher	Version/Date
Handbook for Computer Security Incident Response Teams (CSIRTS)	SEI	April 2003
First Responder Guide to Computer Forensics: Advanced Topics	SEI	September 2005
Best Practices for Computer Forensics	SWGDE	Version 1.0, April 2018
Best Practices for Computer Forensic Acquisitions	SWGDE	Version 1.0, April 2018
Best Practices for Maintaining the Integrity of Digital Images and Digital Video	SWGIT, FBI, DoJ	April 2008
Guidelines for Digital Forensics First Responders	Interpol	Version 7, March 2021
Electronic evidence—a basic guide for First Responders	ENISA	March 2015

In addition to the above there are numerous books, journals and articles relating to digital forensics.

Appendix 2—Some international and national standards relating to digital forensics

There are a number of International (ISO) standards that relate to Digital Forensics, as well as a number of national standards. The main ISO Standards are listed below and some of the better known national standards. There is no guarantee that the national standards are still relevant (some are well out of date compared with the rapid rate of change in digital forensics).

Standard	Name	Type	Country
ISO/IEC 27037—While this is the 2012 version it was reviewed in 2018 and found to be still current	Information technology—Security techniques—Guidelines for identification, collection, acquisition and preservation of digital evidence	International	International
ISO/IEC 27041—While this is the 2015 version it was reviewed in 2021 and found to be still current	Information technology—Security techniques—Guidance on assuring suitability and adequacy of incident investigative method	International	International
ISO/IEC 27042—While this is the 2015 version it was reviewed in 2021 and found to be still current	Information technology—Security techniques—Guidelines for the analysis and interpretation of digital evidence	International	International
ISO/IEC 27043—While this is the 2015 version it was reviewed in 2020 and found to be still current	Information technology—Security techniques—Incident investigation principles and processes	International	International
ISO/IEC 30121—While this is the 2015 version it was reviewed in 2020 and found to be still current	Information technology—Governance of digital forensic risk framework	International	International
SP 800-101 Rev. 1—2014	Guidelines on Mobile Device Forensics	National	USA
SP 800-72 2004	Guidelines on PDA Forensics	National	USA
SP 800-86	Guide to Integrating Forensic Techniques into Incident Response	National	USA
SP 800-61 Rev. 2—2012	Computer Security Incident Handling Guide	NIST	USA
FSR-C-100 Issue 7, 2021	Codes of Practice and Conduct For Forensic Science Providers and Practitioners in the Criminal Justice System	Forensic Science Regulator	UK

Appendix 3—Hard disk log details

The following details in shall be recorded in MARS about all disks purchased to process forensic cases:

- make;
- model name or number;

- part number;
- serial number;
- disk type (IDE, SCSI, SATA SSD, etc.);
- size (as recorded on disk);
- cylinders (if applicable);
- heads (if applicable);
- sectors;
- tracks (if applicable);
- supplier;
- supplier reference number;
- purchase order number;
- date ordered;
- date received;
- sealed on arrival?
- checked by;
- resealed by;
- resealed date;
- unique number assigned to the disk;
- action;
- notes on assignment;
- dates assigned; and
- assigned by.

Note

It is recognised that not all of this information is always available, so what is available is entered.

Appendix 4—Disk history log

The following details shall be recorded in MARS about the history of all disks used in processing forensic cases:

- unique case number;
- action (wiped, assigned to a case (give case number), returned to store, transfer to outside agency, disposal, etc.);
- date action taken;
- action performed by;
- tool used;
- action authorised by;
- date disk resealed; and
- reseal performed by.

Note

The disk history log shall provide a complete audit trail of all disks for their complete life cycle in FCL.

Appendix 5—Tape log details

The following details shall be recorded in MARS about all tapes purchased to process forensic cases:

- make;
- model name or number;
- part number;
- serial number;
- size (as recorded on tape);

- supplier;
- supplier reference number;
- purchase order number;
- date ordered;
- date received;
- checked by;
- unique number assigned to the tape;
- action;
- purpose used for;
- date used; and
- assigned by.

Note

It is recognised that not all of this information is always available, so what is available is entered.

Appendix 6—Tape history log

The following details shall be recorded in MARS about the history of all tapes used in processing forensic cases:

- unique case number;
- action (wiped, used to back up a case, used to back up a case image, returned to store, transfer to outside agency, disposal, etc.);
- date action taken;
- action performed by;
- method or tool used; and
- action authorised by.

Note

The tape history log will give a complete audit trail of all tape for their complete life cycle in FCL.

Appendix 7—Small digital media log details

The following details shall be recoded in MARS about USBs and Key Loggers purchased to process forensic cases:

- type (USB, Key Logger, or other);
- make;
- model name or number;
- part number;
- serial number;
- size (as recorded on device);
- supplier;
- supplier reference number;
- purchase order number;
- date ordered;
- date received;
- checked by;
- unique number assigned to the device.

Note

It is recognised that not all of this information is always available, so what is available is entered.

Appendix 8—Small digital media device log

The following details shall be recorded in MARS about the history of all USBs and Key Loggers used in processing forensic cases:

- unique case number;
- action (wiped, used in a forensic case, returned to store, transfer to outside agency, disposal, etc.);
- date action taken;
- action performed by;
- method or tool used; and
- action authorised by.

Note

The small digital media device history log will give a complete audit trail of all of these devices for their complete life cycle in FCL.

Appendix 9—Forensic case work log

The following form shall be used to record all work carried out on a forensic case. It can be typed directly into MARS but can also be used as a paper based form and then scanned into the virtual case file.

- case number;
- client/case name;
- date;
- time;
- work performed;
- hours expended;
- date;
- time;
- name of Forensic Analyst;
- signature.

Each page, if using a paper copy, shall be signed and the pages numbered 'x of y pages' so that completeness can be verified.

Appendix 10—Case processing KPI's

The following case key performance indicators shall be maintained by the Laboratory Manager, with reporting carried out on a monthly basis for the year:

- feedback from clients;
- number of 'assists';
- number of successful assists;
- sentences or penalties resulting from 'assists';
- sentences or penalties resulting from processed forensic cases;
- successful cases (as a percentage of all cases);
- number of arrests;
- number of years of custodial sentence;
- number of forensic cases undertaken per year;
- number of forensic cases that failed their SLAs;
- number of forensic cases that failed their TRTs;
- number of forensic cases that met or bettered SLAs;
- number of forensic cases that met or bettered TRTs;
- number of servers examined;
- number of desktops examined;

- number of laptops examined;
- number of tablets examined;
- number of smart phones examined;
- number of other devices examined;
- number of terabytes of evidence imaged;
- requests for investigation and examination;
- training undertaken in the year for the Forensic Analysts; and
- value of assets recovered/seized.

Appendix 11—Contents of sample exhibit rejection letter

All rejection letters shall follow the same format and be produced on headed paper. Apart from the client addressing details and date, the following template shall be used for the rejection of any exhibit:

- addressee;
- date;
- case number;
- description of exhibit;
- text, e.g. The exhibit referenced above was delivered to FCL by (name) on (date).

This exhibit has been examined as part of the acceptance process into Secure Property Store. Based on this examination, the exhibit cannot be accepted, in its current state, because of the following reason(s):

Give reason(s) here. These could include, but not be limited to:

- a missing exhibit label;
- an unacceptably low level of agreement between the details on an exhibit label and those on the accompanying submission documentation;
- appropriate control samples not submitted;
- evidence of possible evidence tampering;
- illegibility in the name, identification number or any other information on an exhibit label;
- inadequate or inappropriate packaging or sealing of an exhibit that could prejudice its integrity;
- inconsistency between the details on an exhibit label and/or accompanying submission documentation and what the exhibit actually is;
- insufficient material being available for meaningful examination or analysis (e.g. incomplete or missing labelling, no bag sealed, opened Evidence Bag, etc.);
- opened exhibit packaging;
- previous handling, storage, or evidence of tampering with an exhibit that could prejudice its integrity;
- repeat of the same identification details on different exhibit labels;
- there being more than one label on an exhibit; or
- unacceptable risk in processing the exhibit;
- contact details.

Appendix 12—Sample continuity label contents

Every movement of any exhibit moved from initial seizure to return of the exhibit to the client or its originator shall be documented to maintain the chain of evidence. The following information shall be recorded on a continuity label:

- case number;
- client/case name;
- exhibit reference number;
- exhibit seal number;
- date;
- time;
- name of recipient; and
- signature.

Appendix 13—Details of the property log

The Property Log is an A3 Book, with pages numbered sequentially to counter any suggestions of page removal. It records all property (e.g. exhibits) received into, and taken out of, the Secure Property Store. It also, by default shows what exhibits should be currently in the Secure Property Store, allowing exhibit audits to be carried out.

Booking in property

- property reference number;
- date booked in;
- time booked in;
- seal number;
- client reference;
- case name;
- client name;
- property description;
- booking in name; and
- booking in signature.

On resealing property

- date resealed;
- time resealed;
- seal number;
- resealed by—name; and
- re-sealed by signature.

Booking out property

- date booked out;
- time booked out;
- reason for booking out;
- booking out name; and
- booking out signature.

Appendix 14—Contents of sample exhibit acceptance letter

All acceptance letters shall follow the same format and be produced on headed paper. Apart from the client addressing details and date, the following template shall be used for the confirmation of acceptance of one or more exhibits for forensic case processing:

- addressee;
- date;
- case number;
- text (e.g.)

  The following exhibit(s) have been received by FCL from (name) on (date).

  List the exhibit description, any of the client's exhibit number(s), if present and the exhibit numbering assigned and the Property Log number, as defined in Chapter 8, Section 8.6.10.

  The exhibit(s) have been logged into the Secure Property Store on (date) for case processing.

  Please contact the writer if you have any questions relating to these exhibits.
- contact details.

Appendix 15—Property special handling log

Where a property booked into the Secure Property Stores needs special handling, it shall be recorded in MARS. Details of what shall be recorded is defined below:

- property reference number;
- date booked in;
- time booked in;
- seal number;
- special handling processes required and undertaken;
- special handling processes undertaken by—name; and
- special handling processes undertaken by—signature.

Appendix 16—Evidence sought

The requirements from a client will vary between forensic cases, but there are a standard set of requirements for the evidence sought in a forensic case. This may change from forensic case to forensic case, as required. The standard requirements shall include:

- case reference number;
- client/case name;
- details of evidence sought and/or offences suspected;
- comments or other relevant information;
- case details completed by—name;
- case details completed by—signature;
- date; and
- time.

Appendix 17—Request for forensic examination

This form shall be completed in all forensic cases where information processing equipment is submitted for examination. Items for forensic processing shall not be accepted unless received in appropriate sealed Evidence Bags or containers and accompanied by an exhibit label signed by the person seizing or taking possession of the equipment and the person delivering the items for examination.

The following items shall be recorded:

- client reference;
- client/case name;
- for each item submitted for examination the following shall be recorded:
  - exhibit reference number;
  - description;
  - seal number;
  - insurance value.
- delivered by—name;
- delivered by—title;
- delivered by—organisation;
- delivered by—signature;
- delivery date;
- delivery time;
- accepted by—name;
- accepted by—signature;
- comments (e.g. anything relevant to the exhibit(s) being delivered);
- date entered into MARS;
- entered into MARS by—name; and
- case number (auto-generated by MARS).

Appendix 18—Client virtual case file structure

FCL uses EnCase, Forensic Tool Kit (FTK), and Cellebrite as its main forensic case processing tools, and this folder structure reflects that. Additionally, this is the base case folder structure and more folders shall be added as required depending on the actual forensic case being processed.

- case files;
- compressed files for client;
- encase images;
- files recovered in file structure;
- FTK view;
- HTML carver;
- instructions from client;
- Internet history;
- not in report to client;
- photos;
- recovered 'Documents and Settings';
- recovered 'My Documents';
- recovered attachments;
- recovered documents;
- recovered email;
- recovered HTML;
- recovered images;
- recovered of note;
- recovered presentations;
- recovered recycle bin;
- recovered spreadsheets;
- report—supporting documents;
- report;
- scanned case forms;
- schedule;
- searches;
- temp;
- text search results;
- tools used in the case;
- virus scanning; and
- working file.

Appendix 19—Computer details log

Note

In this context, 'computer' refers to servers, desktops, and laptops.

The following details shall be recorded for all computer exhibits that are to be forensically processed:

- case number;
- client/case name;
- exhibit reference number;
- Forensic Analyst undertaking examination;
- exhibit type;
- make;
- model;
- serial number:

- date;
- time;
- identifying marks or damage;
- photographs taken (Yes/No)?
- peripherals:
  - video card;
  - CD/DVD;
  - RAM strips (describe and give details);
  - SCSI card;
  - network card;
  - Modem;
  - sound card;
  - others (describe).
- BIOS settings:
  - BIOS key;
  - BIOS password;
  - boot sequence;
  - operating system;
  - system time;
  - system date;
  - actual time;
  - actual date;
- examined by:
  - full name;
  - signature;
  - date;
  - time.

Appendix 20—Other equipment details log

The following details shall be recorded for all other equipment exhibits that are to be forensically processed:

- case number;
- client/case name;
- exhibit reference number;
- equipment type;
- make;
- model;
- serial number;
- condition;
- casing type;
- identifying marks, damage or other comments;
- photographs taken (Yes/No)?
- details of the equipment;
- examined by:
  - full name;
  - signature;
  - date;
  - time.

Appendix 21—Hard disk details log

The following details shall be recorded for all hard disk exhibits that are to be forensically processed:

- case number;
- client/case name;

- exhibit reference number;
- make;
- model;
- number of partitions;
- serial number;
- size;
- cylinders (if relevant);
- heads (if relevant);
- sectors;
- controller details;
- jumper setting (if relevant);
- time and date set correctly on the acquisition machine (Y/N); and
- Imaging:
  - tool;
  - version;
  - notes
  - hard disk reference number for the image; and
  - imaged by:
    - full name;
    - signature;
    - date; and
    - time.
- backup hard drive:
  - hard disk reference number;
  - serial number;
  - capacity;
  - date wiped; and
  - image backup copy verified by:
    - full name;
    - signature;
    - date; and
    - time.

Appendix 22—Other media details log

Note

Not all of the details below are appropriate for all media (e.g. Serial No. on media or cylinders on flash media, etc.).

The following details shall be recorded for all 'other media' that are to be forensically processed:

- case number;
- client/case name;
- exhibit reference number;
- media type;
- make;
- model;
- volatile memory image taken (Yes/No)?
- number of partitions;
- serial number;
- size;
- cylinders (if relevant);
- heads (if relevant);
- sectors;

- photographs taken (Yes/No)?
- Imaging;
- software and version (Image 1);
- write blocker type used;
- software and version (Image 2);
- write blocker type used;
- notes;
- hashes image 1;
- hashes image 2;
- hash verification attached (Yes/No); and
- if hash verification not attached, location where can it be found;
  - hard disk reference number for image;
  - imaged by:
    - full name;
    - signature;
    - date; and
    - time.
- backup hard drive:
  - hard disk reference number;
  - serial number;
  - capacity;
  - date wiped; and
  - image backup copy verified by:
    - full name;
    - signature;
    - date; and
    - time.

Appendix 23—Smart phone details log

The following details shall be recorded for all smart phones that are to be forensically processed:

- case number;
- client/case name;
- exhibit reference number;
- phone type;
- make;
- model;
- the IMEI (International Mobile Station Equipment Identity);
- the IMSI (International Mobile subscriber Identity);
- the phone's serial number;
- PIN number;
- the SIM (Subscriber Identity Module);
- time displayed;
- date displayed;
- other information displayed on the screen;
- account holder name;
- account holder address;
- called parties;
- calling parties;
- SMS texts;
- account call records;
- account holder payment type data;
- SMS records;
- MMS records;

- services accessed;
- Internet Service Provider;
- access dates and times (if held);
- limited location dependent information;
- downloaded files;
- email;
- voicemail;
- address book/contacts;
- short dial number;
- calendar events
- apps loaded; and
- apps running.

Appendix 24—Other devices details log

The following details shall be recorded for all 'other devices' that are forensically processed:

- case number;
- client/case name;
- exhibit reference number;
- device type;
- make;
- model;
- time displayed, if appropriate;
- date displayed, if appropriate;
- other information displayed on the screen, if appropriate.

Note

If a device contains a hard disk, it shall be removed and treated as defined in Section 9.9.

Appendix 25—Some evidence found in volatile memory

The evidence recovered from volatile memory acquisition will vary depending on the device being acquired, but can include, but not be limited to:

- available physical memory;
- BIOS information;
- clipboard information:
- command history;
- cron jobs;
- current system uptime;
- driver information;
- hot fixes installed;
- installed applications;
- interface configurations;
- listening ports;
- local users;
- logged on users;
- malicious code that is run from memory rather than disk;
- network cards;
- network information;
- network passphrases;
- network status;

- open DLL files;
- open files and registry handles;
- open files;
- open network connections;
- operating system and version;
- pagefile location;
- passphrases and crypto keys;
- plaintext versions of encrypted material;
- process memory;
- process to port mapping;
- processes running;
- registered organisation;
- registered owner;
- remote users;
- routing information;
- service information;
- shares;
- system installation date;
- system time;
- the memory map;
- the VAD tree;
- time zone;
- total amount of physical memory;
- unsaved files;
- user IDs and passwords/passphrases.

Appendix 26—File metadata

Typical file metadata includes, but is not limited to:

- attributes;
- author;
- category;
- character count;
- child;
- comments;
- company;
- date accessed;
- date created;
- date modified;
- date printed;
- document type;
- duplicate;
- email;
- file name;
- file name and path;
- file path;
- keywords;
- last printed;
- last saved by;
- line count;
- manager;
- MD5 or SHA file hash;

- page count;
- parent;
- previous authors;
- subject;
- template used;
- title;
- total editing time;
- version; and
- word count.

Note 1

In a number of packages, the user can define their own custom metadata fields.

Note 2

Some metadata is set by the organisation, some is generated by the operating system or application and some may be entered by the document author.

Appendix 27—Case progress checklist

Note

Not all tasks are relevant to all forensic cases processed. Where a task is irrelevant, it shall be struck through.

This checklist shall be used for monitoring case progress and contains the following tasks. Where a task has been completed, the completer shall append their signature and the date of completion to the task:

- case number;
- client/case name;
- legal authority confirmed;
- exhibits received and accepted;
- exhibit rejection letter sent;
- photos of exhibits on arrival;
- case formally accepted;
- case assigned;
- insurance value reviewed;
- agreed TRT;
- paper case file set up;
- virtual case file set up;
- photos of exhibits on disassembly;
- imaged;
- image verified;
- BIOS data;
- recover files;
- malware scan;
- signature analysis;
- hash analysis;
- info record (o/n);
- graphics files (o/n);
- initialise case script;

- link parser link script;
- unique email script;
- internet history script;
- extract documents;
- extract spreadsheets;
- extract databases;
- extract images;
- extract HTML;
- extract email;
- extract files in file structure;
- 'documents and settings';
- 'recent files';
- 'favourites';
- 'my documents';
- 'desktop';
- 'temporary' files;
- HTML/Web carve;
- Artefacts;
- search 1;
- search 2;
- search 3;
- search 4;
- search 5;
- search 6;
- search 7;
- search 8;
- search 9;
- search 10;
- accounts;
- FTK view;
- metadata;
- write report draft;
- Internal technical review of report;
- Internal administrative review of report;
- agree report release;
- blow report to disk;
- sent to client;
- exhibits returned;
- backup case to disk;
- backup case to tape;
- invoiced;
- paid; and
- archived.

Appendix 28—Internal case report template

Below is a standard template for an internal forensic case report. This shall be amended as required depending on the specific forensic case requirements:

- document control;
- issue status;
- classification;
- table of contents;
- background;

- evidence required by client;
- initial examination;
- first stage investigation results;
- evidence found to date;
- appendix A—Malware reporting;
- appendix B—Encase case summary;
- Appendix C onwards—other items of note relating to the case.

Appendix 29—Exhibit log

The details of what is created as an exhibit for any case will of course vary between cases. The details below are the basic template for the log, and details shall be added to the log as appropriate to the case:

- case number;
- client/case name;
- exhibit reference number;
- description;
- created by:
  - full name;
  - signature;
  - date; and
  - time.

Appendix 30—Report production checklist

The following checklist shall be used for producing a forensic case report. It shall be used for internal and external reports and is a check on actions being performed. The checklist shall apply to the:

- hard copy case report;
- soft copy case report; and
- compressed soft copy report.

The Forensic Analyst shall determine which of the checklist items apply to which type of report media. The actions undertaken shall include:

- select correct file for report;
- print cover and spine;
- determine report classification;
- produce table of contents;
- background to the case;
- ensure evidence required by client is clearly understood;
- initial examination results;
- extract files in file structure;
- produce case FTK report;
- produce linkage analysis;
- produce internet history;
- produce HTML carve;
- recovered metadata;
- produce recovered files of note;
- produce recovered documents;
- produce recovered email;
- produce recovered HTML;
- produce recovered images;
- produce recovered PDFs;
- produce recovered spreadsheets;

- produce recovered databases;
- produce text search results;
- produce any other recovered evidence to support the case conclusions reached;
- undergo peer review;
- produce instructions for use;
- check softcopy media works properly;
- ensure that compressed files can be decompressed; and
- produce appropriate labels for each report type.

Chapter 10

Forensic case management

10.1 Overview

There is a critical need to keep control of all forensic cases that FCL processes and this need increases with growing numbers of forensic cases handled and more Forensic Analysts that need to be managed.

There are two different processes involved in managing forensic cases:

- Forensic Analysts handling their own forensic case;
- the Manager who has oversight and manages all forensic cases in the laboratory.

Each employee has different needs and these shall be met to ensure that FCL delivers quality products and services.

To achieve this, FCL uses a mix of hard copy forms and its own internally developed Forensic Case Management Database—MARS (Management and Reporting Tool).

To ensure that there was a complete chain of custody maintained and to manage and monitor Service Level Agreements (SLAs) or required Turn Round Times (TRTs) the MARS tool has been developed. The system was designed so that complete forensic case management can be undertaken for all current and historic forensic cases, as well as automated forensic case billing and also a variety of management reports can be produced to support the management of all forensic cases.

The basic system is a multiuser system for a single forensic laboratory and handles all processes that would be performed in the laboratory.

MARS has been designed to be intuitive, easy to use and minimise the need for typed input once the system had been properly set up.

All actions of any sort in MARS are logged to a secure audit trail, allowing interrogation of the audit log between two dates or times, for any forensic case or for any Forensic Analyst processing a forensic case.

10.2 Hard copy forms

FCL uses a number of hard copy forms to support forensic case processing. These can be used in a variety of situations for all stages in the processing of a forensic case.

All hard copy forms referred to in the rest of the book shall be used as required. All hard copy forms have the facility for original signatures on them and are able to be used by third parties that do not have access to MARS.

Hard copy forms, when completed, shall then be scanned and added to the client virtual forensic case file as well as being stored in the hard copy file that is securely stored in the Secure Property Store at the end of processing a forensic case.

First Responders shall always carry a full set of forensic case processing forms when they attend a client site or incident, and there shall always be hard copy forms that shall be printed from the server on an 'as required' basis.

10.3 MARS

MARS has been specifically designed for handling all aspects of forensic cases. It is a multiuser system, written in Microsoft Access.

Note 1

In the section, as the original FCL forensic laboratory was set up in the United Kingdom, all of the setup details are relating to a UK-based company (Forensic Computing Ltd.—FCL). MARS is fully configurable to any jurisdiction in the world as required.

A Blueprint for Implementing Best Practice Procedures in a Digital Forensic Laboratory. https://doi.org/10.1016/B978-0-12-819479-9.00022-8

Note 2

At the time of writing, MARS is undergoing an upgrade, so in some forensic cases the screen shots do not completely match the text. The text contains the description of the upgraded version of MARS and is the definitive one.

Note 3

This chapter shows how FCL has set up MARS, other forensic laboratories shall use their own management systems, whether paper based or as a database.

10.3.1   Initial laboratory setup

Once MARS is started for the first time, the first task to undertake is to enter the forensic laboratory organisational details. The setup screen is only shown once, so it is essential that the information entered is correct, as it cannot be later corrected. The details entered on the screen below are used for all output to screen or hard copy (Fig. 10.1).

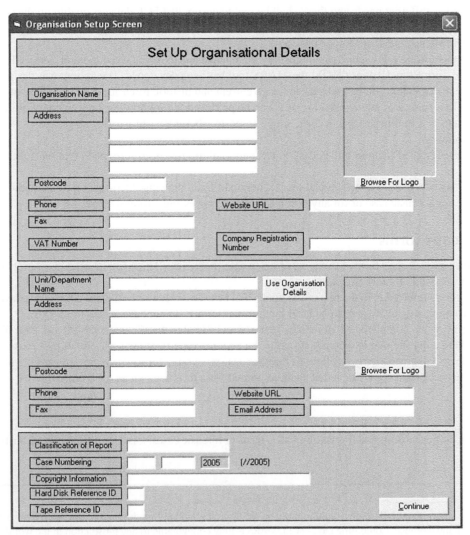

FIG. 10.1   Initial organisational details setup.

Details of the contents of all of the fields in this screen are defined in Appendix 1.

The user shall enter details as required into all of the fields on the screen.

Finally, the information entered here shall be checked to ensure it is correct as this is the only time that this information can be set up and the only time that this screen is viewed.

On pressing the 'Continue' button, the user is asked if the user is certain they want to continue and save the laboratory details with the options for 'Yes' and 'No'.

'No' allows you to return and correct any errors and omissions, 'Yes' writes the information to file and deletes the setup programme.

10.3.2   Setting up the administrator

Once MARS is installed, it shall be configured for use.

On starting MARS for the first time, it is necessary to set up the Administrator.

This is shown on the screen (Fig. 10.2).

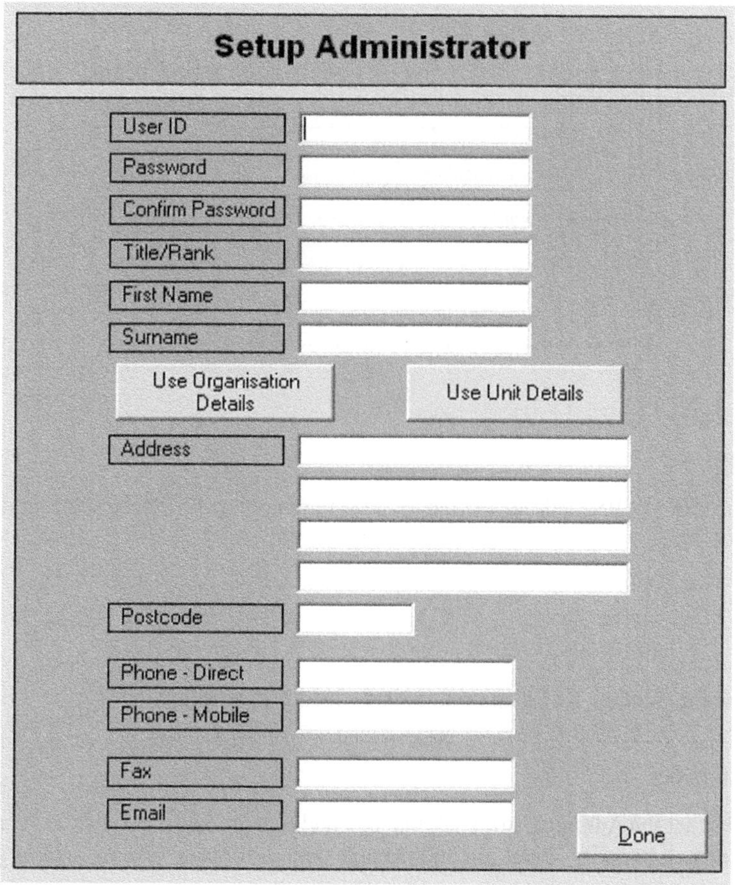

FIG. 10.2   Setting up the MARS administrator.

Details of the contents of all of the fields in this screen are defined in Appendix 2.

It is recommended that the username identifies any 'Administrators' as opposed to 'normal' users. In FCL, this is done by suffixing the User ID with the word 'admin'—e.g. 'dlwadmin' to indicate that this is the 'dlw' 'Administrator' account as opposed to the User ID 'dlw' indicating that 'dlw' 'normal user'.

MARS shall assign the Administrator the relevant 'Administrator' access rights.

Once the details are all correct, press the 'Save User' button to save the Administrator.

Note

In FCL, the Laboratory Manager is the Administrator (or their deputy).

10.3.3 MARS users

Once set up, MARS has two categories of users:

- **Administrator**—the Laboratory Manager, who has rights to manage media, forensic cases, suppliers, etc., and run a number of reports for all forensic cases and infrastructure;
- **User**—who are able to only manage their own assigned forensic cases, tasks and run reports on them. These shall be Forensic Analysts, Investigators, etc.

Once set up, users shall only have options in MARS that are related to their role and any forensic cases assigned to them.

To access MARS, any user shall have successfully been authenticated to the network using their login credentials (User ID and biometric thumbprint scan). They shall then have the MARS icon available on their desktop and access rights to use it to log into MARS, using their User ID and password as in Fig. 10.3.

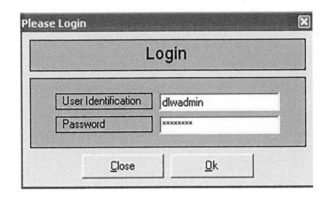

FIG. 10.3 MARS login.

10.3.4 Audit tracking

All actions taken by any user in MARS shall be written to the secure audit trail. These shall include:

- Date;
- Time;
- User ID;
- Action taken.

Audit reports are defined in Section 10.7.5 and output is defined in Appendix 3.

10.3.5 Administrator tasks

There are a number of tasks that the Administrator shall manage and that are not accessible to 'normal users'. This is setting up static information relating to laboratory operations and management of forensic cases as well as some management reports.

Note

Each of the administrator options are similar in their operation. They allow the following operations on the data:

- entry of a new record ('save and exit' option—saves a record and returns to calling menu);
- entry of a sequence of new records ('save' option—saves a record and clears screen allowing a new record to be entered);
- amendment of an existing record ('amend option'—updates record, if possible and return to calling menu);
- exits without saving ('exit'—return to calling menu without changing or updating a record);
- delete a record ('delete and exit' option—deletes a record, if possible and return to calling menu); and
- delete a sequence of records ('delete' option—deletes a record, if possible, and clears screen allowing another record to be deleted).

Note

Where the deletion of a record could affect the referential integrity of the MARS database, the system shall not permit the deletion to take place (e.g. attempted deletion of a supplier who supplied disks used in processing forensic cases, attempted deletion of a Forensic Analyst that processed a forensic case, etc.).

When the Administrator logs into the system, they are presented with a main menu, as in Fig. 10.4.

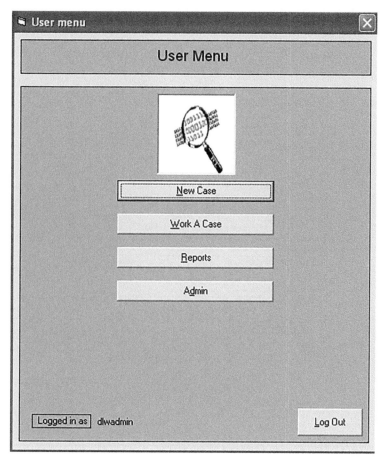

FIG. 10.4   Administrator tasks.

This shows that the current user is 'dlwadmin' (bottom left hand side of the screen next to 'Logged in as'), indicating that it is the User ID for DLW for administration purposes—not for working forensic cases.

The logo shown is the logo entered at the start up.

10.3.5.1   Manage users

The 'Manage Users' screen is shown in Fig. 10.5.

Details of the contents of all of the fields in this screen are defined in Appendix 4.

10.3.5.1.1   Add a user

The blank screen is presented and the Administrator shall populate all of the relevant fields and then save them to create a new user in MARS.

10.3.5.1.2   Amend a user

Typically, this is used where the Administrator needs to change a user's password or their contact details.

To amend a user, the user must already exist in MARS.

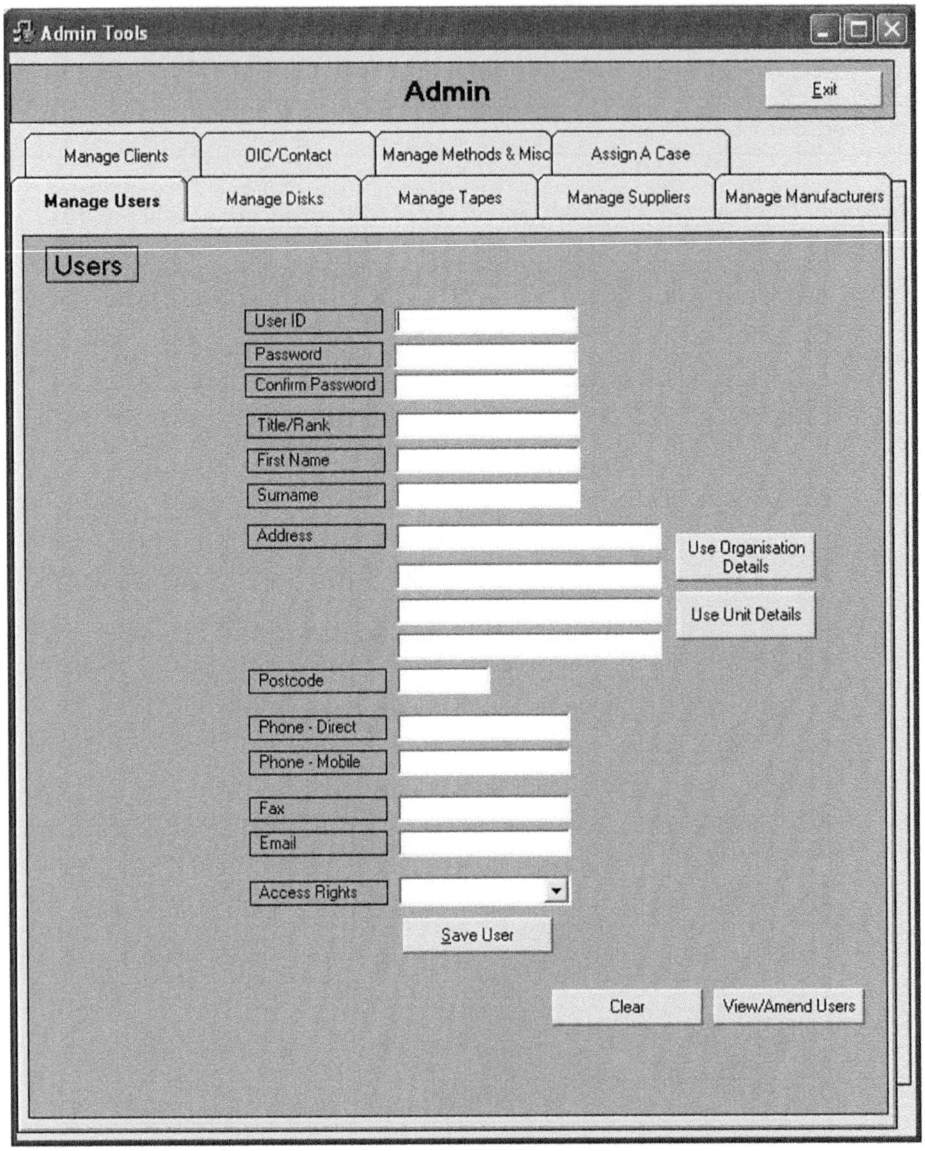

FIG. 10.5   Manage users.

Using the drop-down box for existing users, the user to have their details amended shall be selected and the screen populated with their existing details from the stored record.

The Administrator shall amend the user's data and save it, as appropriate. The Administrator shall be advised of the successful amendment and acknowledge it.

10.3.5.1.3   Delete a user

To delete a user, the user must already exist in MARS.

Using the drop-down box for existing users, the user to have their details deleted shall be selected and the screen populated with their existing details from the stored record.

It is not possible to delete a user who has been active in the MARS system, i.e. one who has been used in the system. The Administrator shall be advised that this is not possible, otherwise the Administrator shall be advised of the successful deletion of the user and acknowledge it.

10.3.5.2   Manage a manufacturer

The 'Manage Manufacturers' screen is shown in Fig. 10.6.

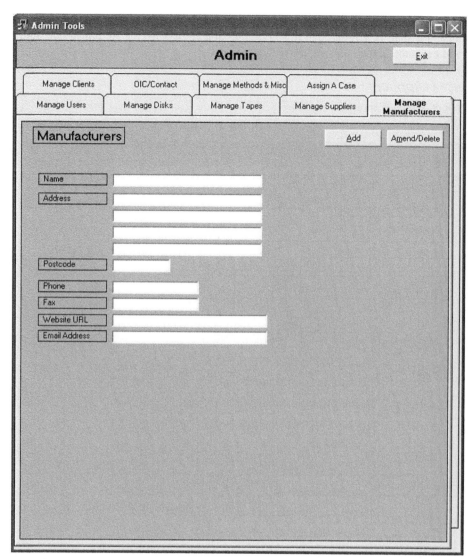

FIG. 10.6 Manage a manufacturer.

Details of the contents of all of the fields in this screen are defined in Appendix 5.

10.3.5.2.1 Add a manufacturer

The blank screen is presented and the Administrator shall populate all of the relevant fields and then save them to create a new manufacturer in MARS.

10.3.5.2.2 Amend a manufacturer

To amend a manufacturer, the manufacturer must already exist in MARS.

Using the drop-down box for existing manufacturers, the manufacturer to have their details amended shall be selected and the screen populated with their existing details from the stored record.

The Administrator shall amend the data relating to the manufacturer and save it, as appropriate. The Administrator shall be advised of the successful amendment and acknowledge it.

10.3.5.2.3 Delete a manufacturer

To delete a manufacturer, the manufacturer must already exist in MARS.

Using the drop-down box for existing manufacturers, the manufacturer to have their details deleted shall be selected and the screen populated with their existing details from the stored record.

It is not possible to delete a manufacturer who has been active in the MARS system, i.e. one who has been used in the system. The Administrator shall be advised that this is not possible, otherwise the Administrator shall be advised of the successful deletion of the manufacturer and acknowledge it.

10.3.5.3   Manage a supplier

The 'Manage Suppliers' screen is shown in Fig. 10.7.

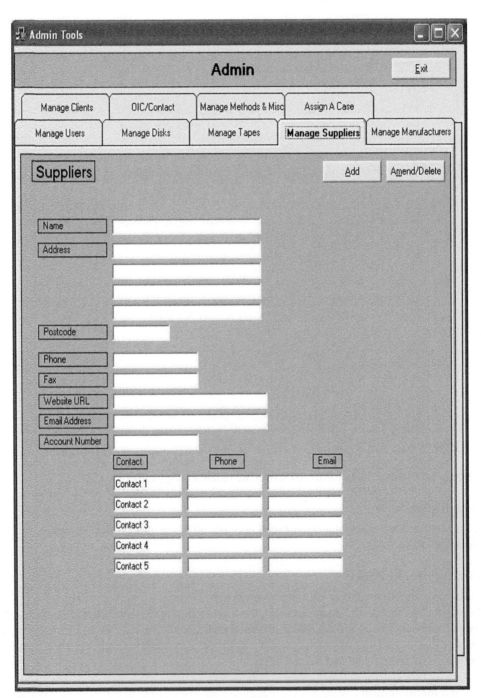

FIG. 10.7   Manage a supplier.

Details of the contents of all of the fields in this screen are defined in Appendix 6.

10.3.5.3.1 Add a supplier

The blank screen is presented and the Administrator shall populate all of the relevant fields and then save them to create a new supplier in MARS.

10.3.5.3.2 Amend a supplier

To amend a supplier, the supplier must already exist in MARS.

Using the drop-down box for existing suppliers, the supplier to have their details amended shall be selected and the screen populated with their existing details from the stored record.

The Administrator shall amend the data relating to the supplier and save it, as appropriate. The Administrator shall be advised of the successful amendment and acknowledge it.

10.3.5.3.3 Delete a supplier

To delete a supplier, the supplier must already exist in MARS.

Using the drop-down box for existing suppliers, the supplier to have their details deleted shall be selected and the screen populated with their existing details from the stored record.

It is not possible to delete a supplier who has been active in the MARS system, i.e. one who has been used in the system. The Administrator shall be advised that this is not possible, otherwise the Administrator shall be advised of the successful deletion of the supplier and acknowledge it.

10.3.5.4 *Manage a client*

The 'Manage Clients' screen is shown in Fig. 10.8.

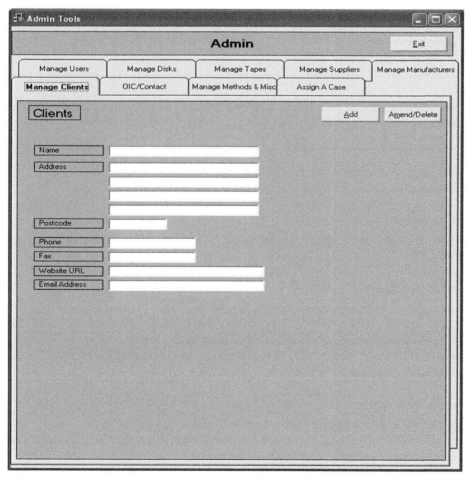

FIG. 10.8 Manage a client.

Details of the contents of all of the fields in this screen are defined in Appendix 7.

10.3.5.4.1 Add a client

The blank screen is presented and the Administrator shall populate all of the relevant fields and then save them to create a new client in MARS.

10.3.5.4.2 Amend a client

To amend a client, the client must already exist in MARS.

Using the drop-down box for existing clients, the client to have their details amended shall be selected and the screen populated with their existing details from the stored record.

The Administrator shall amend the data relating to the client and save it, as appropriate. The Administrator shall be advised of the successful update and acknowledge it.

10.3.5.4.3 Delete a client

To delete a client, the client must already exist in MARS.

Using the drop-down box for existing clients, the client to have their details deleted shall be selected and the screen populated with their existing details from the stored record.

It is not possible to delete a client who has been active in the MARS system, i.e. one who has had a forensic case processed in the system. The Administrator shall be advised that this is not possible, otherwise the Administrator shall be advised of the successful deletion of the client and acknowledge it.

10.3.5.5 Manage an investigator

Note 1

In MARS parlance, an investigator could be a corporate investigator (or Law Enforcement Officer) for the client or any other investigative contact relating to a forensic case including one of the Forensic Analysts or other employee.

Note 2

The client details can be used to populate the investigators address and contact details. If this is done, then the Administrator can still edit what is in the fields as normal—navigating by mouse or tab button. If changes to the client details are made to tailor this for the Investigator they are not reflected in the client Address or contact details—only here.

The 'Manage Investigators' screen is shown in Fig. 10.9.

Details of the contents of all of the fields in this screen are defined in Appendix 8.

10.3.5.5.1 Add an investigator

The blank screen is presented and the Administrator shall populate all of the relevant fields and then save them to create a new Investigator in MARS.

10.3.5.5.2 Amend an investigator

To amend an Investigator, the Investigator must already exist in MARS.

Using the drop-down box for existing Investigators, the Investigator to have their details amended shall be selected and the screen populated with their existing details from the stored record.

The Administrator shall amend the data relating to the Investigator and save it, as appropriate. The Administrator shall be advised of the successful update and acknowledge it.

10.3.5.5.3 Delete an investigator

To delete an Investigator, the Investigator must already exist in MARS.

Using the drop-down box for an existing Investigator, the Investigator to have their details deleted shall be selected and the screen populated with their existing details from the stored record.

It is not possible to delete an Investigator who has been active in the MARS system, i.e. one who has been used in the system. The Administrator shall be advised that this is not possible, otherwise the Administrator shall be advised of the successful deletion of the Investigator and acknowledge it.

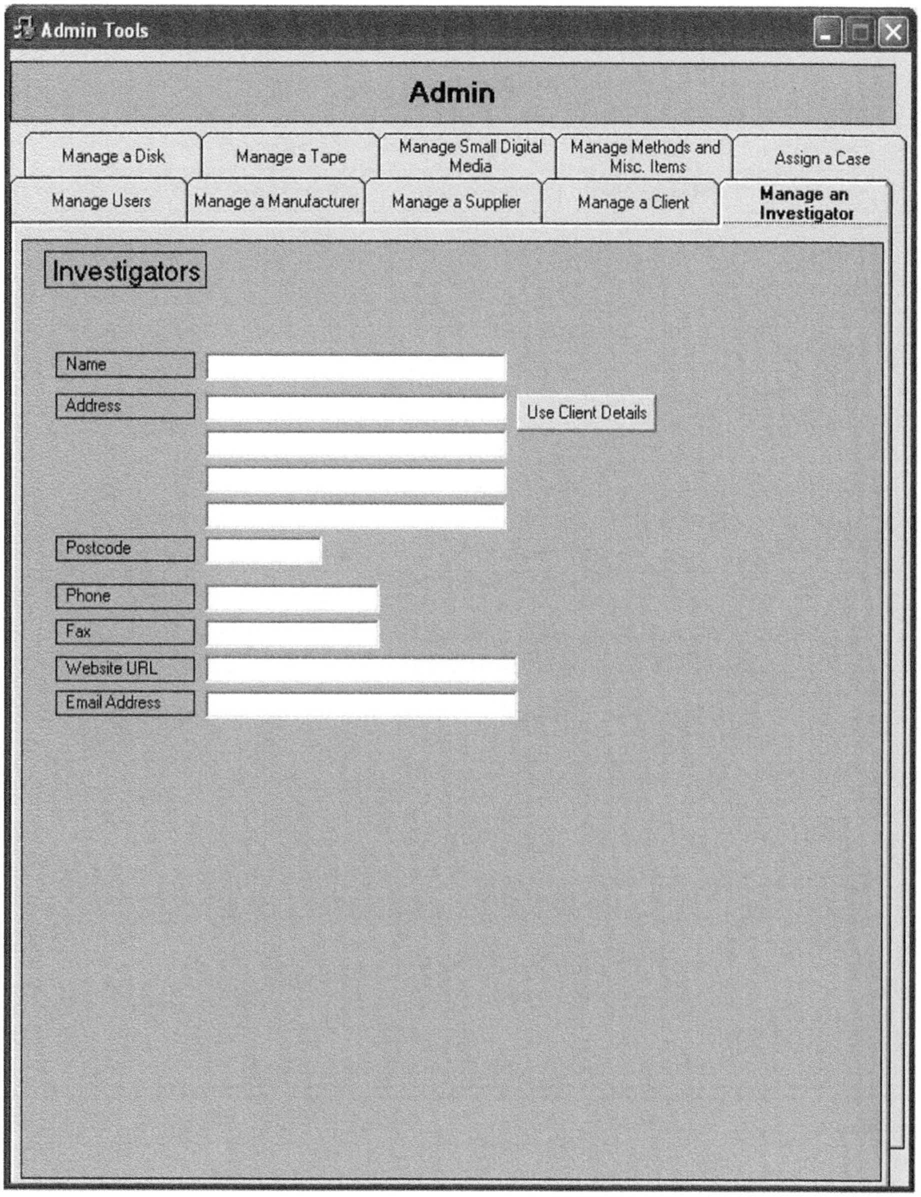

FIG. 10.9 Manage an investigator.

10.3.5.6 *Manage a disk*

Each disk used in FCL shall have its history associated with it so that a complete history of the disk shall be maintained. This shall contain the details entered on the screen and additionally a status flag indicating whether it can be assigned to a forensic case or not. The status of disks in FCL shall be as follows:

- new disks shall have a status set of 'unassigned';
- wiped disks shall have a status set of 'unassigned';
- disks that have been disposed of shall have a status set to 'disposed'; and
- disks assigned to a forensic case shall have a status set to 'assigned'.

Using this process, unassigned disks shall be assigned to current forensics forensic cases, as needed, without the risk of evidence contamination.

The 'Manage Disks' screen is shown in Fig. 10.10.

Details of the contents of all of the fields in this screen are defined in Appendix 9.

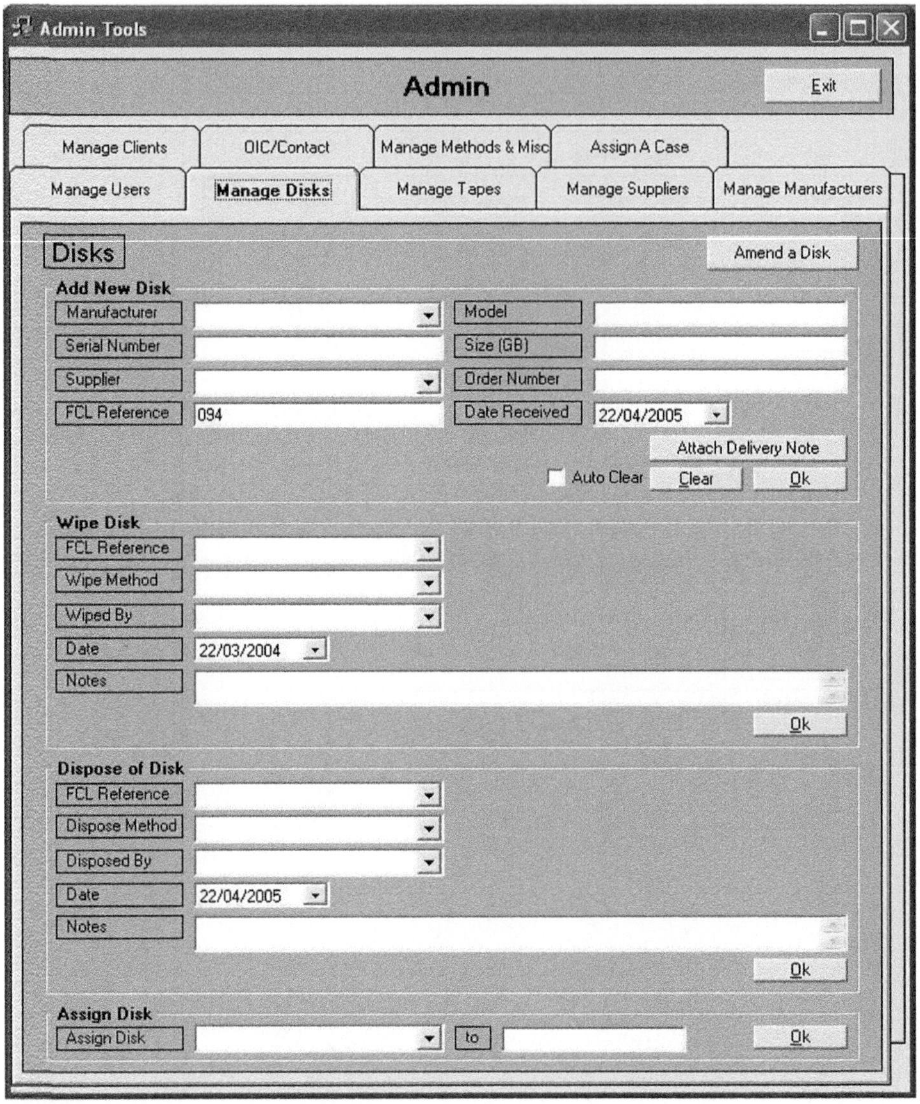

FIG. 10.10 Manage a disk.

10.3.5.6.1 Add a disk

The blank screen is presented and the Administrator shall populate all of the relevant fields and then save them to create a new disk in MARS.

10.3.5.6.2 Amend a disk

To amend the details of a disk, the disk must already exist in MARS.

Using the drop-down box for existing disks, the disk to have their details amended shall be selected and the screen populated with their existing details from the stored record.

The Administrator shall amend data relating to the disk and save it, as appropriate. The Administrator shall be advised of the successful update and acknowledge it.

10.3.5.6.3 Delete a disk

To delete a disk, the disk must already exist in MARS.

Using the drop-down box for existing disks, the disk to have its details deleted shall be selected and the screen populated with its existing details from the stored record.

It is not possible to delete a disk that is active in the MARS system, i.e. one that is still in use. The Administrator shall be advised that this is not possible, otherwise the Administrator shall be advised of the successful deletion of the disk and acknowledge it.

10.3.5.6.4 Wiping a disk

To forensically wipe a disk, the disk must already exist in MARS.

Using the drop-down box for existing disks, the disk to have its wiping details recorded in the disk's history shall be selected and the screen populated with its existing details from the stored record.

The Administrator shall enter the details of how the disk was wiped, by whom and when and add this to the disk's history log. A disk may be wiped many times during its use in FCL.

10.3.5.6.5 Disposing of a disk

To dispose of a disk, the disk must already exist in MARS.

Using the drop-down box for existing disks, the disk to have its disposal details recorded in the disk's history shall be selected and the screen populated with its existing details from the stored record.

The Administrator shall enter the details of how the disk was disposed of by whom and when and add this to the disk's history log.

A disk cannot be disposed of unless it has been forensically wiped prior to disposal unless it is a disk that has failed to operate and is being destroyed.

10.3.5.6.6 Assigning a disk

To assign a disk to a forensic case or a specific administrative task, the disk must already exist in MARS.

Using the drop-down box for existing disks, the disk to be assigned shall be selected. The disk shall have a status of unassigned and have been wiped immediately prior to assignment or reassignment.

The Administrator shall enter the details of where the disk is to be assigned.

10.3.5.7 *Manage a tape*

This process is very similar to the management of disks.

Each tape shall have a history associated with it so that a complete history of the tape shall be maintained This shall contain the details entered on the screen and additionally a status flag indicating whether it can be assigned or not.

The status for tapes in the laboratory is as follows:

- new tapes shall have a status set of 'unassigned';
- wiped tapes shall have a status set of 'unassigned';
- tapes that have been disposed of shall have a status set of 'disposed'; and
- tapes assigned to a forensic case shall have a status set of 'assigned'.

The 'Manage Tapes' screen is shown in Fig. 10.11.

Details of the contents of all of the fields in this screen are defined in Appendix 10.

10.3.5.7.1 Add a tape

The blank screen is presented and the Administrator shall populate all of the relevant fields and then save them to create a new tape in MARS.

10.3.5.7.2 Amend a tape

To amend the details of a tape, the tape must already exist in MARS.

Using the drop-down box for existing tapes, the tape to have its details amended shall be selected and the screen populated with its existing details from the stored record.

The Administrator shall amend the data relating to the tape and save it, as appropriate. The Administrator shall be advised of the successful update and acknowledge it.

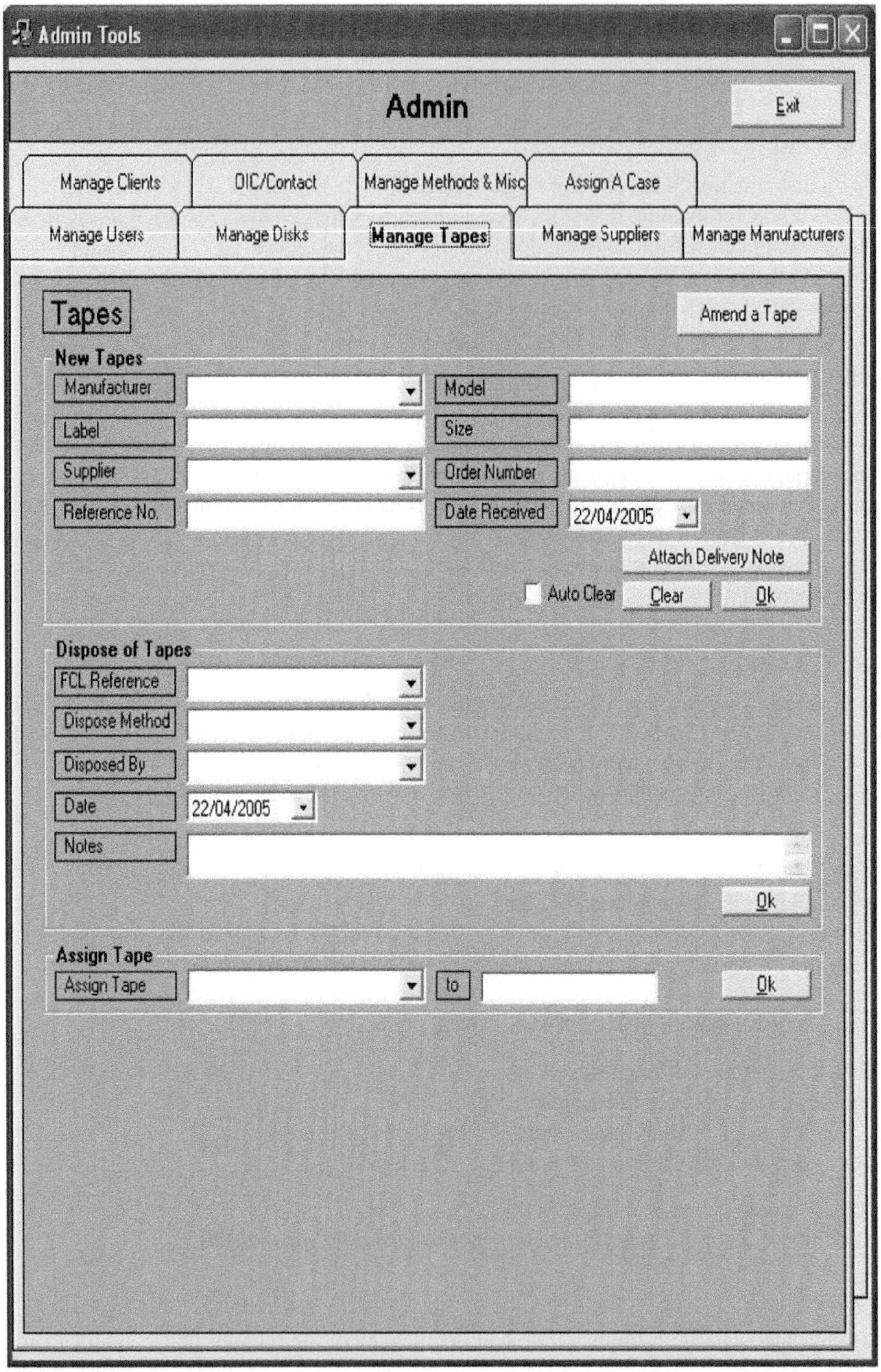

FIG. 10.11 Manage a tape.

10.3.5.7.3 Delete a tape

To delete a tape, the tape must already exist in MARS.

Using the drop-down box for existing tapes, the tape to have its details deleted shall be selected and the screen populated with its existing details from the stored record.

It is not possible to delete a tape that is active in the MARS system, i.e. one that is in use. The Administrator shall be advised that this is not possible, otherwise the Administrator shall be advised of the successful deletion of the tape and acknowledge it.

10.3.5.7.4 Wiping a tape

To forensically wipe a tape, the tape must already exist in MARS.

Using the drop-down box for existing tape, the tape to have its wiping details recorded in the tape's history shall be selected and the screen populated with their existing details from the stored record.

The Administrator shall enter the details of how the tape was wiped, by whom and when and add this to the tape's history log. A tape may be wiped many times during its use in FCL.

10.3.5.7.5 Disposing of a tape

To dispose of a tape, the tape must already exist in MARS.

Using the drop-down box for existing tape, the tape to have its disposal details recorded in the tape's history shall be selected and the screen populated with their existing details from the stored record.

The Administrator shall enter the details of how the tape was disposed of by whom and when and add this to the tape's history log.

A tape cannot be disposed of unless it has been forensically wiped in prior to disposal.

10.3.5.7.6 Assigning a tape

To assign a tape to a forensic case or a specific administrative task, the tape must already exist in MARS.

Using the drop-down box for existing tape, the tape to be assigned shall be selected. The tape shall have a status of unassigned and have been wiped immediately prior to assignment or reassignment.

The Administrator shall enter the details of where the tape is to be assigned.

10.3.5.8 Manage small digital media

This process is very similar to the management of disks.

Each item of small digital media shall have a history associated with it so that a complete history of the item of small digital media shall be maintained. This shall contain the details entered on the screen and additionally a status flag indicating whether it can be assigned or not.

The status for items of small digital media in the laboratory is as follows:

- new items of small digital media shall have a status set of 'unassigned';
- wiped items of small digital media shall have a status set of 'unassigned';
- items of small digital media that have been disposed of shall have a status set of 'disposed'; and
- items of small digital media assigned to a forensic case shall have a status set of 'assigned'.

The 'Manage Items of Small Digital Media' screen is shown in Fig. 10.12.

Details of the contents of all of the fields in this screen are defined in Appendix 11.

10.3.5.8.1 Add an item of small digital media

The blank screen is presented and the Administrator shall populate all of the relevant fields and then save them to create a new item of small digital media in MARS.

10.3.5.8.2 Amend an item of small digital media

To amend the details of item of small digital media, the item of small digital media must already exist in MARS.

Using the drop-down box for an existing item of small digital media, the item of small digital media to have their details amended shall be selected and the screen populated with their existing details from the stored record.

The Administrator shall amend data relating to the item of small digital media and save it, as appropriate. The Administrator shall be advised of the successful update and acknowledge it.

10.3.5.8.3 Delete an item of small digital media

To delete an item of small digital media, the item of small digital media must already exist in MARS.

Using the drop-down box for an existing item of small digital media, the item of small digital media to have their details deleted shall be selected and the screen populated with their existing details from the stored record.

It is not possible to delete an item of small digital media that has been active in the MARS system, i.e. one that has been used in the system. The Administrator shall be advised that this is not possible, otherwise the Administrator shall be advised of the successful deletion of the item of small digital media and acknowledge it.

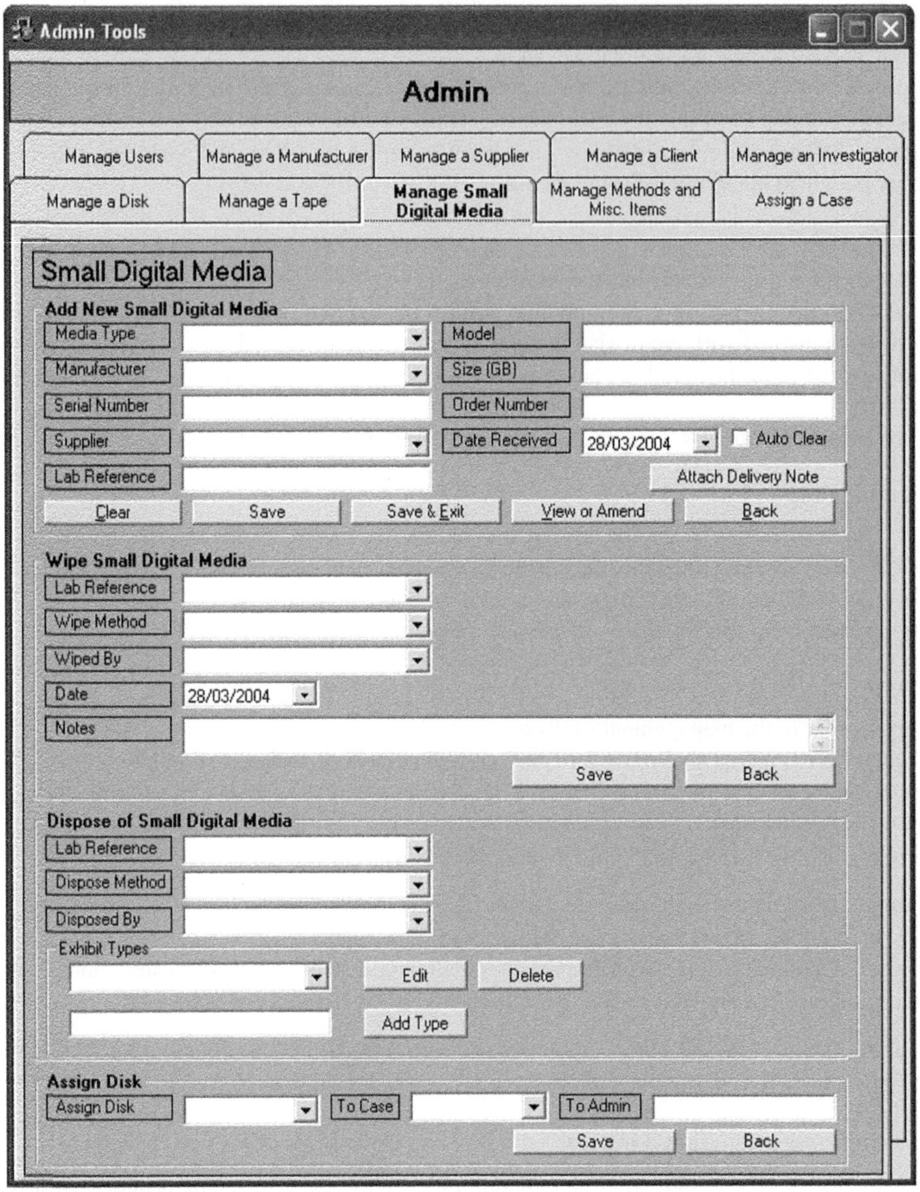

FIG. 10.12 Manage small digital media.

10.3.5.8.4 Wiping an item of small digital media

To forensically wipe an item of small digital media, the item of small digital media must already exist in MARS.

Using the drop-down box for existing items of small digital media, the item of small digital media to have its wiping details recorded in the item of small digital media's history shall be selected and the screen populated with their existing details from the stored record.

The Administrator shall then enter the details of how the item of small digital media was wiped, by whom and when and add this to the item of small digital media's history log. An item of small digital media may be wiped many times during its use.

10.3.5.8.5 Disposing of an item of small digital media

To dispose of an item of small digital media, the item of small digital media must already exist in MARS.

Using the drop-down box for existing items of small digital media, the item of small digital media to have its disposal details recorded in the item of small digital media's history shall be selected and the screen populated with their existing details from the stored record.

The Administrator shall enter the details of how the item of small digital media was disposed of, by whom and when and add this to the item of small digital media's history log.

An item of small digital media cannot be disposed of unless it has been forensically wiped prior to disposal.

10.3.5.8.6 Assigning an item of small digital media

To assign an item of small digital media to a forensic case or a specific administrative task, the item of small digital media must already exist in MARS.

Using the drop-down box for an existing item of small digital media, the item of small digital media to be assigned shall be selected. The item of small digital media shall have a status of unassigned and have been wiped immediately prior to assignment or reassignment.

The Administrator shall enter the details of where the item of small digital media is to be assigned.

10.3.5.9   Manage methods and miscellaneous items

This allows you to manage the following:

- hard disk wiping methods;
- disk and tape disposal methods;
- imaging methods;
- operating system types; and
- digital media types.

The 'Manage Methods' screen is shown in Fig. 10.13.

Details of the contents of all of the fields in this screen are defined in Appendix 11.

10.3.5.9.1   Wipe methods

10.3.5.9.1.1   Add a new wipe method A new method of wiping shall be entered into the lower of the box in the 'Wipe Methods' section of the screen. Once the method is entered, the Administrator shall confirm it.

10.3.5.9.1.2   Amend a wipe method Using the drop-down box for existing wipe methods, the wipe method to be amended shall be displayed.

The Administrator shall edit the details of the wiping method.

A wiping method cannot be edited if it has been used in MARS as this may cause problems with the chain of custody for a given disk, as all previous occurrences of the original wipe method would have been changed.

10.3.5.9.1.3   Delete a wipe method Where an existing wipe method exists, it may need to be deleted if not needed or has been incorrectly entered.

A wiping method cannot be deleted if it has been used in MARS as this may cause problems with the chain of custody for a given disk, as all previous occurrences of the original wipe method would have been changed.

Once chosen, press the 'Delete' button, as shown below.

If the wipe method has been previously used in MARS, deletion is prohibited.

10.3.5.9.2   Disposal methods

10.3.5.9.2.1   Add a new disposal method A new method of disposing of media shall be entered into the lower part of the box in the 'Dispose Methods' section of the screen. Once the method is entered, the Administrator shall confirm it.

10.3.5.9.2.2   Amend a disposal method Using the drop-down box for existing disposal methods, the disposal method to be amended shall be displayed.

The Administrator shall edit the details of the disposal method.

A disposal method cannot be edited if it has been used in MARS as this may cause problems with the chain of custody for any media disposed of using the disposal method, as all previous occurrences of the original disposal method would have been changed.

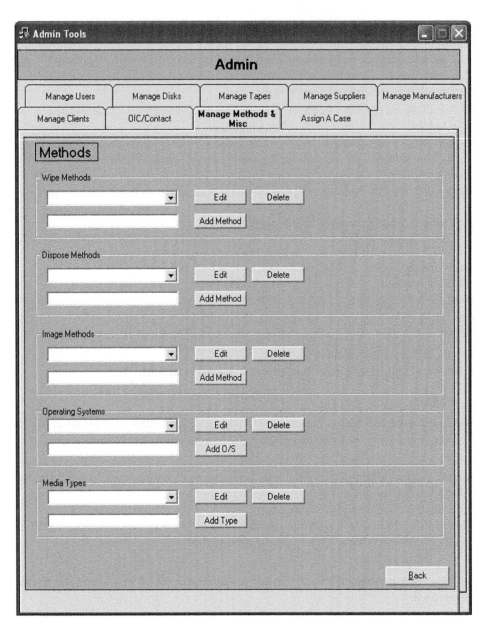

FIG. 10.13   Manage methods.

10.3.5.9.2.3   *Delete a disposal method* Where an existing disposal method exists, it may need to be deleted if not needed or has been incorrectly entered.

A disposal method cannot be deleted if it has been used in MARS as this may cause problems with the chain of custody for media disposed of using this method, as all previous occurrences of the original disposal method would have been changed.

10.3.5.9.3   Imaging methods

10.3.5.9.3.1   *Add a new imaging method* A new method of imaging media shall be entered into the lower of the box in the 'Image Methods' section of the screen. Once the method is entered, the Administrator shall confirm it.

10.3.5.9.3.2   *Amend an imaging method* Using the drop-down box for existing imaging methods, the imaging method to be amended shall be displayed.

The Administrator shall edit the details of the imaging method.

An imaging method cannot be edited if it has been used in MARS as this may cause problems with the chain of custody for any media imaged using this imaging method, as all previous occurrences of the original imaging method would have been changed.

10.3.5.9.3.3 Delete an imaging method Where an existing imaging method exists, it may need to be deleted if not needed or has been incorrectly entered.

An imaging method cannot be deleted if it has been used in MARS as this may cause problems with the chain of custody for media imaged using this method, as all previous occurrences of the original imaging method would have been changed.

10.3.5.9.4 Operating systems

10.3.5.9.4.1 Add new operating system A new operating system to be investigated shall be entered into the lower of the box in the 'Operating Systems' section of the screen. Once the method is entered, the Administrator shall confirm it.

10.3.5.9.4.2 Amend an operating system Using the drop-down box for existing operating systems, the operating system to be amended shall be displayed.

The Administrator shall edit the details of the operating system.

An operating system cannot be edited if it has been used in MARS as this may cause problems with the chain of custody for any operating system processed, as all previous occurrences of the operating system would have been changed.

10.3.5.9.4.3 Delete an operating system Where an existing operating system exists, it may need to be deleted if not needed or has been incorrectly entered.

An operating system cannot be deleted if it has been used in MARS as this may cause problems with the chain of custody for any operating system processed, as all previous occurrences of the operating system would have been changed.

10.3.5.9.5 Media types

This shall be used where media types other than hard disks and tapes are to be examined or used.

10.3.5.9.5.1 Add new media type A new media type to be examined other than a hard disk or tape and requires the media type to be added to MARS. The media type shall be entered into the lower part of the box in the 'Media Type' section of the screen. Once the media is entered, the Administrator shall confirm it.

10.3.5.9.5.2 Amend a media type Using the drop-down box for existing media types (apart from hard disks and tapes), the media type to be amended shall be displayed.

The Administrator shall amend the details of the media type.

A media type cannot be edited if it has been used in MARS as this may cause problems with the chain of custody for any media type processed, as all previous occurrences of the media type would have been changed.

10.3.5.9.5.3 Delete a media type Where a media type exists, it may need to be deleted if not needed or has been incorrectly entered.

A media type cannot be deleted if it has been used in MARS as this may cause problems with the chain of custody for any media type processed, as all previous occurrences of the media type would have been changed.

10.3.5.9.6 Exhibit types

This shall be used where exhibit types other than computer or media are to be examined.

10.3.5.9.6.1 Add new exhibit type A new exhibit type is to be examined other than a hard disk or tape and requires the exhibit type to be added to MARS. The exhibit type shall be entered into the lower part of the box in the 'Exhibit Type' section of the screen. Once the exhibit is entered, the Administrator shall confirm it.

10.3.5.9.6.2 Amend an exhibit type Using the drop-down box for existing exhibit types (apart from hard disks and tapes), the exhibit type to be amended shall be displayed.

The Administrator shall then amend the details of the exhibit type.

An exhibit type cannot be edited if it has been used in MARS as this may cause problems with the chain of custody for any exhibit type processed, as all previous occurrences of the exhibit type would have been changed.

10.3.5.9.6.3 Delete an exhibit type Where an existing exhibit type exists, it may need to be deleted if not needed or has been incorrectly entered.

An exhibit type cannot be deleted if it has been used in MARS as this may cause problems with the chain of custody for any exhibit type processed, as all previous occurrences of the exhibit type would have been changed.

10.3.5.10 Assign a case

Typically, a forensic case is assigned to a Forensic Analyst when the initial forensic case is set up or it may be assigned to a First Responder, who will typically be a Forensic Analyst or Investigator.

There are other times that a forensic case may need to be re-assigned to another Forensic Analyst, Investigator or other user and this is done here.

The 'Assign a Case' screen is shown in Fig. 10.14.

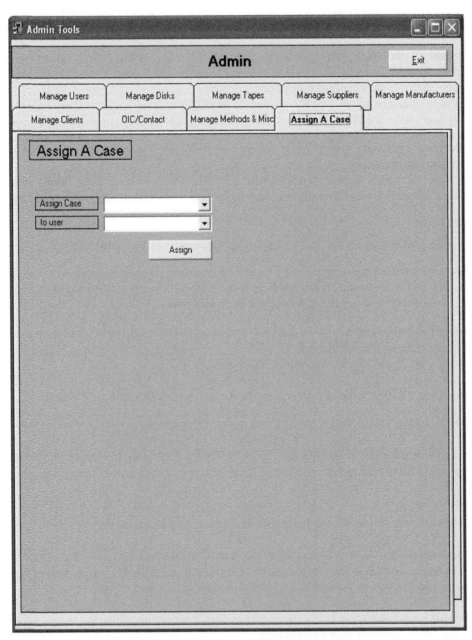

FIG. 10.14 Assign a case.

Using the drop-down box to select a forensic case, the Administrator shall select the forensic case to be assigned.

Using the drop-down box to select a Forensic Analyst to assign the forensic case to, the Administrator shall select the relevant Forensic Analyst.

Once the forensic case and the Forensic Analyst have been chosen, the Administrator shall confirm the assignment.

10.4   Setting up a new case

10.4.1   Creating a new case

Once all of the 'Static' data has been set up, it is possible to start creating forensic cases for processing. This has been made easier by entering the static data, so it can be accessed using drop-down menus, wherever possible.

The 'Add a New Case' screen is shown in Fig. 10.15.

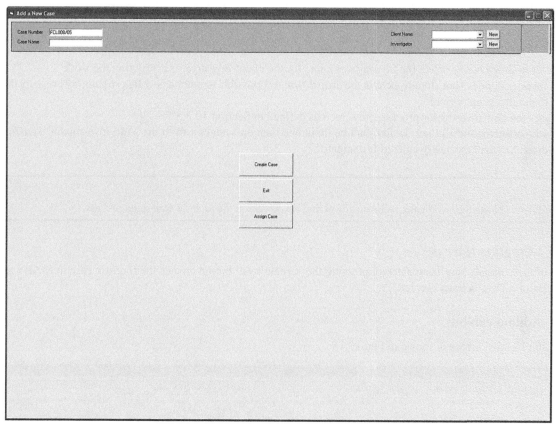

FIG. 10.15   Create a new case.

10.4.1.1   Case number

This is automatically generated and increments by 1 for each forensic case set up. This is based on the original numbering system setup when MARS was installed—it cannot be changed.

The forensic case number can never be changed once assigned to a forensic case.

10.4.1.2   Case name

A forensic case shall be called whatever is required or used to refer to the forensic case by or what the client has called it.

Note

It is possible to change the Case Name on any of the four screens in the forensic case setup process.

10.4.1.3   Client name

Using the drop-down box to select the client name for the client instructing the work, the Administrator shall select the client.

If the client does not already exist in the drop down, it is possible to enter a new client by pressing the 'New' key next to the client field.

This uses the 'Manage a client' process and screen as defined in Section 10.3.5.4.

A new client and all their details shall be input and on exiting from the 'Add client' screen, use the drop-down to select the newly entered client.

Note

It is possible to change the Client Name on any of the four screens in the forensic case setup process.

10.4.1.4 Investigator

Using the drop-down box to select the Investigator name for the client Investigator instructing the work.

If the Investigator does not already exist in the drop down, it is possible to enter a new Investigator by pressing the 'New' key next to the Investigator field.

This uses the new Investigator process and screen as defined in Section 10.3.5.5.

A new Investigator and all their details shall be input and then one can exit from the 'Add Investigator' screen and use the drop-down to select the newly entered Investigator.

Note

It is possible to change the Investigator name on any of the four screens in the forensic case setup process.

10.4.1.5 Creating the case

Once all of these details have been entered, pressing the 'Create case' button creates the forensic case in MARS and presents the 'Exhibit Details Entry' screen.

10.4.2 Adding exhibits

The 'Exhibit Details' screen is shown in Fig. 10.16.

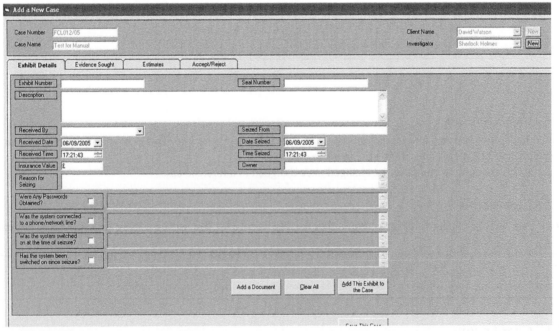

FIG. 10.16 Exhibit details.

Details of the contents of all of the fields in this screen are defined in Appendix 12.

10.4.2.1   Add an exhibit

The blank screen is presented and the Administrator shall populate all of the relevant fields and then save them to create a new exhibit in MARS.

10.4.2.2   Entering more exhibits

Once the first exhibit has been saved, none of the fields are blanked out so that a series of exhibits from the same place and the same person can be entered with the minimum of effort.

The fields that need to be changed are overwritten and the exhibit shall be saved. This process shall be repeated for all relevant exhibits.

If the details of the exhibits to be added are very different, then pressing the 'Clear All' button clears all fields apart from the two dates that are set to the current date.

Once all of the details are added for the new exhibit, the Administrator shall add the exhibit to the forensic case in MARS.

10.4.3   Evidence sought

The 'Evidence Sought' screen is shown in Fig. 10.17.

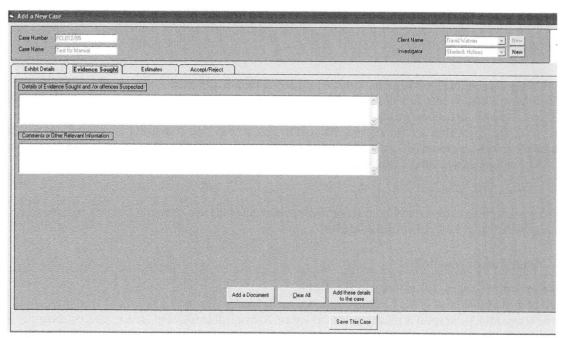

FIG. 10.17   Evidence sought.

Details of the contents of all of the fields in this screen are defined in Appendix 13.

10.4.3.1   Add details to the case

The blank screen is presented and the Administrator shall populate all of the relevant fields and then press the 'Add these details to the Case' Button to add this information to the forensic case in MARS.

10.4.3.2   Adding more information

If more information becomes available during the forensic case, it shall be added in the 'working the forensic case' part of MARS, as defined in Section 10.5.

10.4.4   Estimates

The 'Estimates' screen is shown in Fig. 10.18.

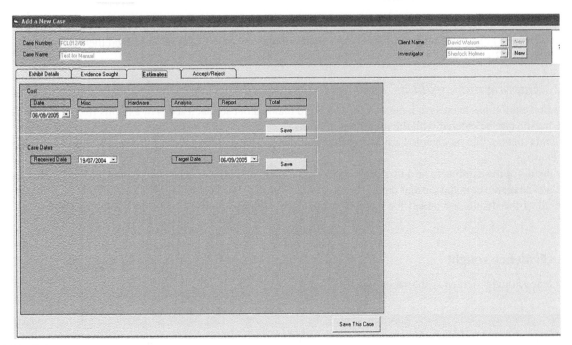

FIG. 10.18 Estimates.

Details of the contents of all of the fields in this screen are defined in Appendix 14.

Estimates of cost shall be entered at this stage of the forensic case, but this can be updated as the forensic case progresses by the Forensic Analyst (or Laboratory Manager), as defined in Section 10.5.9.

At this time, the Target Time (or Turn Round Time—TRT) for the forensic case shall be entered if known. This is the date that the client wants the results by and is used to monitor forensic case progress. If one is not known, then the internally set SLAs shall be used, as defined in Chapter 9, Section 9.5.4.1.

10.4.4.1 Add estimates to the case

The blank screen is presented and the Administrator shall populate all of the relevant fields and then press the 'Save' Button to add this information to the forensic case in MARS.

10.4.5 Accepted or rejected

The 'Accepted or Rejected' screen is shown in Fig. 10.19.

Details of the contents of all of the fields in this screen are defined in Appendix 15.

A forensic case shall be accepted or rejected using this screen. Normally forensic cases are accepted, but there may be reason the forensic case is rejected (e.g. conflict of interest, suspicion of evidence tampering, etc.), as defined in Chapter 9, Section 9.6.1.

10.4.5.1 Add case status

Once all information is added, press the 'Save this Case' button to add the status details to the forensic case.

10.4.6 Amend case details

Once the Administrator has set up a forensic case, it may be necessary to amend some details due to errors. It is possible to amend the data setup by the Administrator.

This is done from the main menu, where the Administrator shall be asked 'Which forensic case do you want to amend' and shall allow selection of the forensic case from a drop-down of all current forensic cases.

It is possible for the Administrator to amend the following:

- exhibit details;
- evidence sought; and
- accept/reject forensic case status and details.

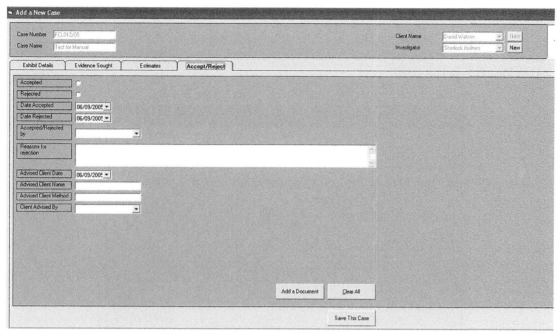

FIG. 10.19 Accepted or rejected case.

There is no need for the Administrator to update estimates, as this shall be amended by the Forensic Analyst (or Laboratory Manager) as part of the forensic casework.

10.4.6.1   Amend exhibit details

A drop-down of exhibits for this forensic case only shall be presented so the correct one can be chosen.
Any fields can be amended except the 'Exhibit Number'.
More documents can be added, as required.
If the Exhibit Number is to be changed then it shall be deleted, the new one entered and the information re-entered.

10.4.6.2   Amend evidence sought details

The details of the evidence being sought shall be amended if required.
More documents can be added, as required.

10.4.6.3   Amend accept or reject status

The accepted or rejected status of a forensic case and any supporting details shall be amended if required.
More documents can be added, as required.

10.4.7   Delete case details

The only part of the forensic case that may need to be deleted would be an exhibit assigned to the wrong forensic case or incorrectly recorded. All other changes shall be undertaken by the Administrator or the Forensic Analyst (or Laboratory Manager) working the forensic case.
An exhibit is chosen, as in amending it, and the 'Delete' button is pressed to delete it.
This will produce a confirmation box saying, 'Are you sure you want to delete <Exhibit No>?'

Note

Where the deletion of an exhibit is attempted that could affect the referential integrity of the MARS database, the system will not permit the deletion to take place, and a message stating 'This exhibit is currently in use and cannot be deleted' is displayed.

10.5 Processing a forensic case

Once a forensic case has been assigned to a Forensic Analyst by the Administrator, the Forensic Analyst shall process the forensic case, or forensic cases, assigned to them. When a Forensic Analyst logs into MARS, they are presented with a main menu (the User Menu), as in Fig. 10.20.

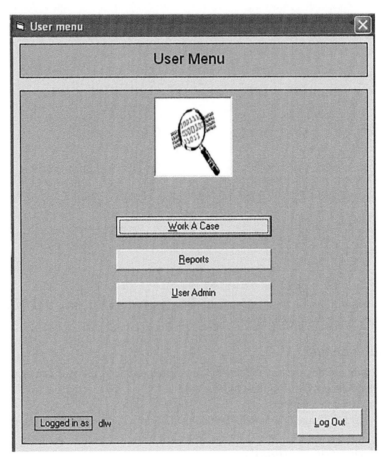

FIG. 10.20 Processing a forensic case.

This shows that the current user is 'dlw' (bottom left hand side of the screen next to 'Logged in as') indicating that it is the User ID for 'dlw' for processing forensic cases, and not performing administration tasks.

This is where the assigned Forensic Analyst actually processes the forensic case. All work that they do shall be entered through this menu.

10.5.1 Selecting a case

The 'User Menu' screen is shown in Fig. 10.21.

On taking the option to work a forensic case, the Forensic Analyst gets the option to choose any of the forensic cases that are currently assigned to them.

The Case ID drop-down box provides a list of all forensic cases that are currently assigned to the logged in Forensic Analyst. The Forensic Analyst shall select the required forensic case number and presses the 'Work Selected Case' button to work the forensic case.

This shall bring up the eight tabbed input forms as described below.

10.5.2 Movement log

The 'Movements' screen is shown in Fig. 10.22.

Details of the contents of all of the fields in this screen are defined in Appendix 16.

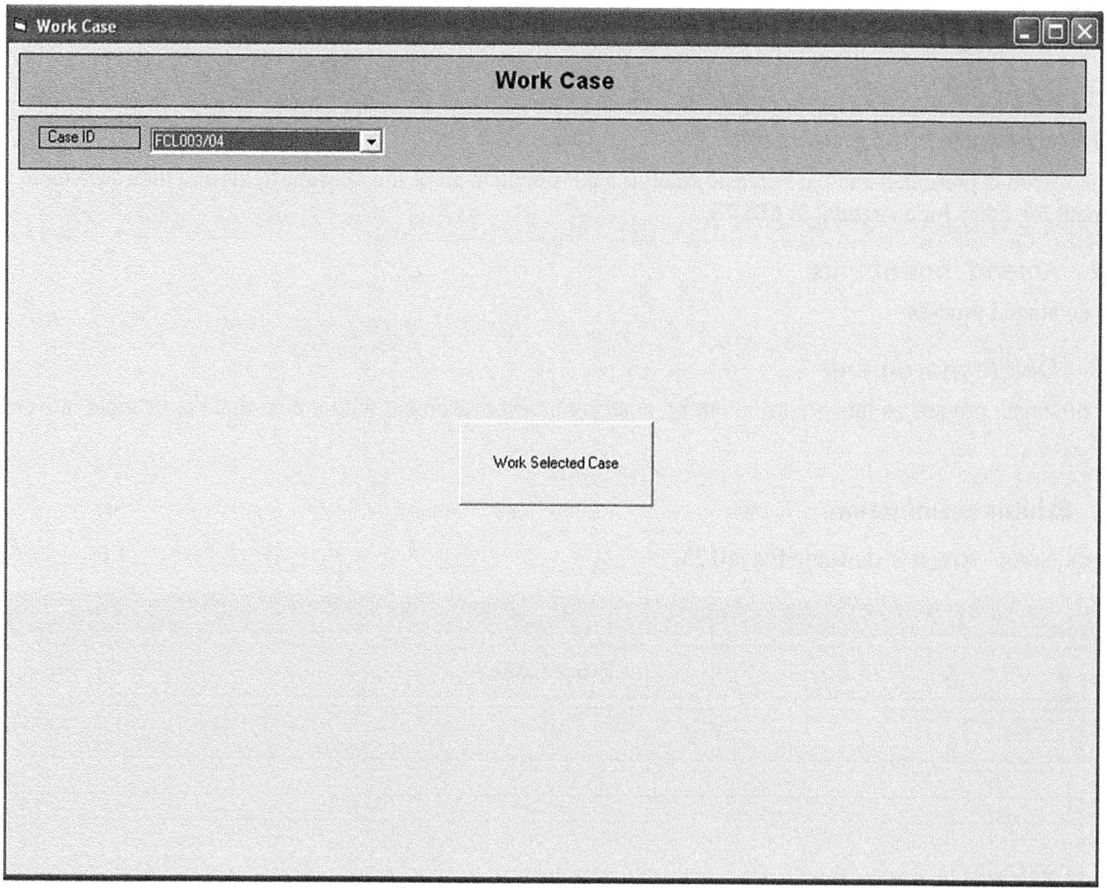

FIG. 10.21 Selecting a case.

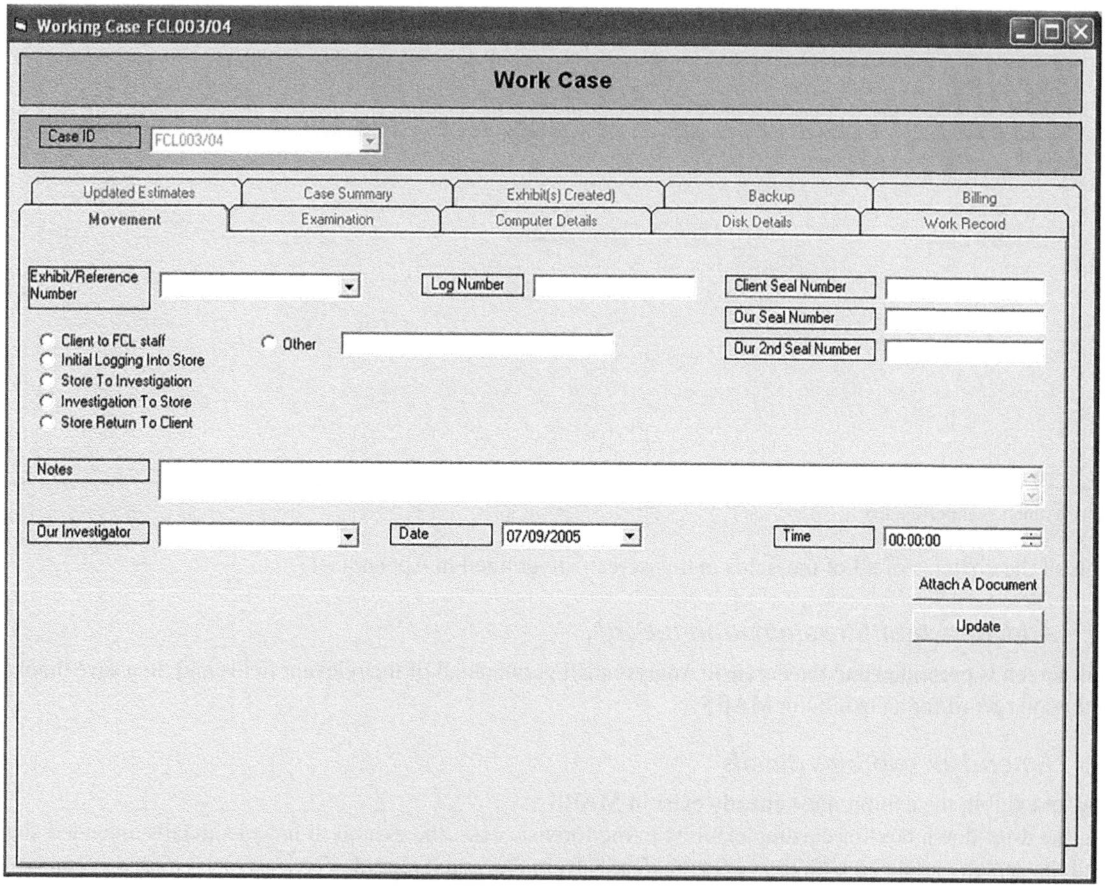

FIG. 10.22 Movement log.

10.5.2.1 Add an exhibit movement

The blank screen is presented and the Forensic Analyst shall populate all of the relevant fields and then save them to create a movement log entry for an exhibit in MARS.

10.5.2.2 Amend movements

There is no amend process.

10.5.2.3 Delete movements

There is no delete process as this is carried out by entering a new movement with a note that the original movement was incorrect.

10.5.3 Exhibit examination

The 'Examination' screen is shown in Fig. 10.23.

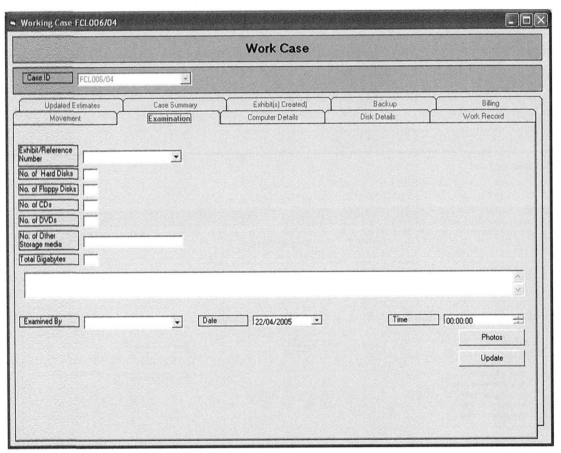

FIG. 10.23 Exhibit examination log.

Details of the contents of all of the fields in this screen are defined in Appendix 17.

10.5.3.1 Add an exhibit's examination record

The blank screen is presented and the Forensic Analyst shall populate all of the relevant fields and then save them to create an examination record for an exhibit in MARS.

10.5.3.2 Amend an exhibit's details

To amend an exhibit, the exhibit must already exist in MARS.

Using the drop-down box for existing exhibits in the forensic case, the exhibit to have its details amended shall be selected and the screen populated with their existing details from the stored record.

The Forensic Analyst shall amend the data relating to the exhibit and save it, as appropriate. The Forensic Analyst shall be advised of the successful update and acknowledge it.

10.5.3.3   Delete an exhibit

To delete an exhibit, the exhibit has to exist.

Using the drop-down box for existing exhibits in the forensic case, the exhibit to be deleted shall be selected and the screen populated with their existing details from the stored record.

It is not possible to delete an exhibit that has been active in the MARS system, i.e. one that has had its details populated in MARS. The Forensic Analyst shall be advised that this is not possible, otherwise the Forensic Analyst shall be advised of the successful deletion of the exhibit and acknowledge it.

10.5.4   Computer exhibit details

The 'Computer Details' screen is shown in Fig. 10.24.

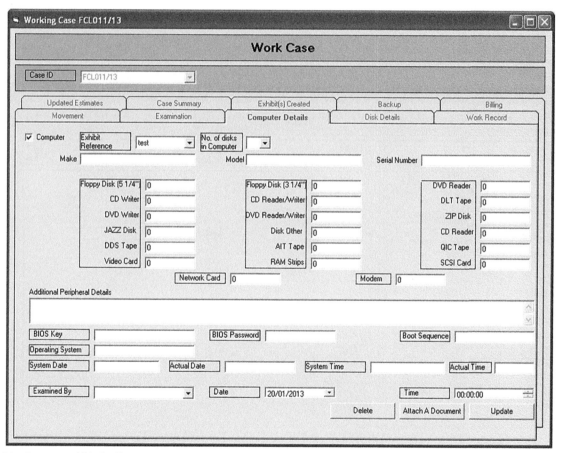

FIG. 10.24   Computer exhibit details.

Details of the contents of all of the fields in this screen are defined in Appendix 18.

Note

This screen is applicable to any information processing device, with the relevant field filled in.

10.5.4.1   Add a computer exhibit's details

The blank screen is presented and the Forensic Analyst shall populate all of the relevant fields and then save them to create the examination record for a computer exhibit in MARS.

10.5.4.2   Amend a computer's details

To amend a computer's details, the computer must already exist in MARS.

Using the drop-down box for existing exhibits in the forensic case, the computer to have its details amended shall be selected and the screen populated with their existing details from the stored record.

The Forensic Analyst shall amend the data relating to the computer and save it, as appropriate. The Forensic Analyst shall be advised of the successful update and acknowledge it.

10.5.4.3   Delete a computer exhibit

To delete a computer's details, the computer must already exist in MARS.

Using the drop-down box for existing exhibits in the forensic case, the computer to be deleted shall be selected and the screen populated with their existing details from the stored record.

It is not possible to delete a computer that has been active in the MARS system, i.e. one that has had its details populated in MARS. The Forensic Analyst shall be advised that this is not possible, otherwise the Forensic Analyst shall be advised of the successful deletion of the computer and acknowledge it.

10.5.5   Noncomputer exhibit details

The 'Non Computer Details' screen is shown in Fig. 10.25.

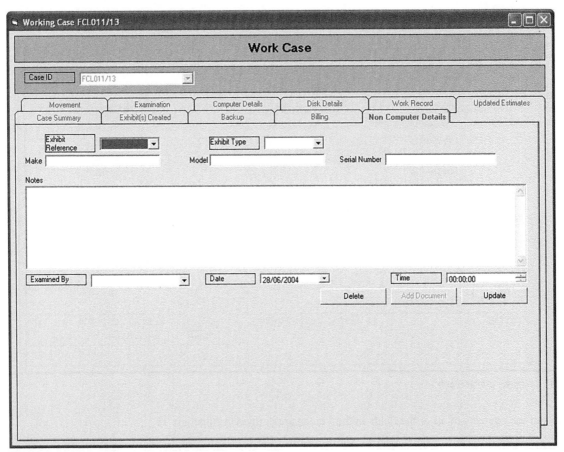

FIG. 10.25   Noncomputer exhibit details.

Details of the contents of all of the fields in this screen are defined in Appendix 19.

10.5.5.1   Add a noncomputer exhibit's details

The blank screen is presented and the Forensic Analyst shall populate all of the relevant fields and then save them to create the examination record for a Non Computer Exhibit in MARS.

If the 'Exhibit Type' does not already exist in the drop down, it is possible to enter a new Exhibit Type by pressing the 'New' key next to the Exhibit Type field.

This uses the new Exhibit Type process and screen as defined in Section 10.3.5.9.6.

A new exhibit type and all their details shall be input and then exit from the 'Add Exhibit Type' screen and use the drop-down to select the newly entered Exhibit Type.

10.5.5.2 Amend a noncomputer exhibit's details

To amend a noncomputer exhibit's details, the noncomputer exhibit must already exist in MARS.

Using the drop-down box for existing exhibits in the forensic case, the noncomputer exhibit to have its details amended shall be selected and the screen populated with their existing details from the stored record.

The Forensic Analyst shall amend the data relating to the noncomputer exhibit and save it, as appropriate. The Forensic Analyst shall be advised of the successful update and acknowledge it.

10.5.5.3 Delete a noncomputer exhibit

To delete a noncomputer exhibit's details, the noncomputer exhibit must already exist in MARS.

Using the drop-down box for existing exhibits in the forensic case, the noncomputer exhibit to be deleted shall be selected and the screen populated with their existing details from the stored record.

It is not possible to delete a noncomputer exhibit that has been active in the MARS system, i.e. one that has had its details populated in MARS. The Forensic Analyst shall be advised that this is not possible, otherwise the Forensic Analyst shall be advised of the successful deletion of the noncomputer exhibit and acknowledge it.

10.5.6 Hard disk details

The 'Hard Disk Details' screen is shown in Fig. 10.26.

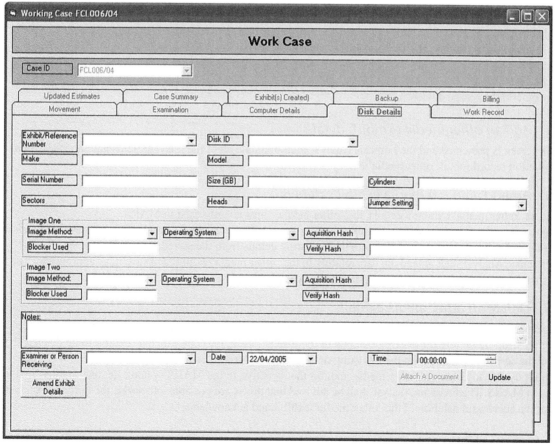

FIG. 10.26 Hard disk details.

Details of the contents of all of the fields in this screen are defined in Appendix 20.

10.5.6.1 Add a hard disk

The blank screen is presented and the Forensic Analyst shall populate all of the relevant fields and then save them to create the record for a hard disk in MARS.

10.5.6.2 Amend a hard disk's details

To amend a hard disk's details, the hard disk must already exist in MARS.

Using the drop-down boxes for existing exhibits and hard disks in the forensic case, the hard disk to have its details amended shall be selected and the screen populated with their existing details from the stored record.

The Forensic Analyst shall amend the data relating to the hard disk and save it, as appropriate. The Forensic Analyst shall be advised of the successful update and acknowledge it.

10.5.6.3 Delete a hard disk

To delete a hard disk, the hard disk must already exist in MARS.

Using the drop-down boxes for existing exhibits and hard disks in the forensic case, the hard disk to be deleted shall be selected and the screen populated with their existing details from the stored record.

It is not possible to delete a hard disk that is active in the MARS system, i.e. one that has had its details populated in MARS. The Forensic Analyst shall be advised that this is not possible, otherwise the Forensic Analyst shall be advised of the successful deletion of the hard disk and acknowledge it.

10.5.7 Other media details

Details of the contents of all of the fields in this screen are defined in Appendix 21.

In this section 'Other Media' refers to any media that can store data apart from a hard disk. This includes, but is not limited to:

- CDs/DVDs;
- mobile devices;
- other types of disks (floppy, zip, jazz, etc.);
- tapes;
- USB drives;
- or any other data storage device.

10.5.7.1 Add an other media exhibit's details

The blank screen is presented and the Forensic Analyst shall populate all of the relevant fields and then save them to create the examination record for an 'other media' exhibit in MARS.

10.5.7.2 Amend an other media exhibit's details

To amend an 'other media' exhibit's details, the 'other media' must already exist in MARS.

Using the drop-down box for existing exhibits in the forensic case, the 'other media' exhibit to have its details amended shall be selected and the screen populated with their existing details from the stored record.

The Forensic Analyst shall amend the data relating to the 'other media' exhibit and save it, as appropriate. The Forensic Analyst shall be advised of the successful update and acknowledge it.

10.5.7.3 Delete an other media exhibit

To delete an 'other media' exhibit's details, the 'other media' exhibit must already exist in MARS.

Using the drop-down box for existing exhibits in the forensic case, the 'other media' exhibit to be deleted shall be selected and the screen populated with their existing details from the stored record.

It is not possible to delete an 'other media' exhibit that is active in the MARS system, i.e. one that has had its details populated in MARS. The Forensic Analyst shall be advised that this is not possible, otherwise the Forensic Analyst shall be advised of the successful deletion of the 'other media' exhibit and acknowledge it.

10.5.8 Case work log

The 'Work Record' screen is shown in Fig. 10.27.

Details of the contents of all of the fields in this screen are defined in Appendix 22.

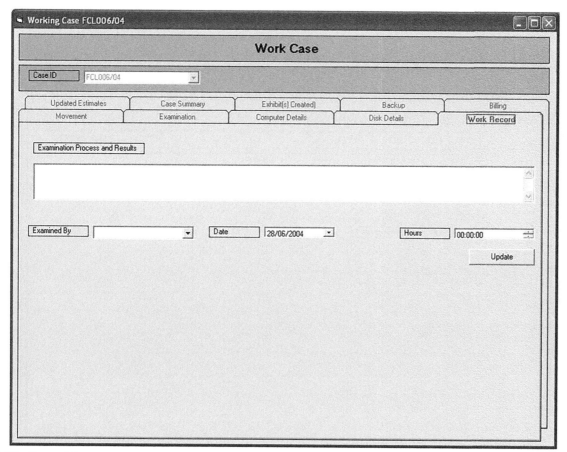

FIG. 10.27 Case work log.

10.5.8.1   Add a work record

The blank screen is presented and the Forensic Analyst shall populate all of the relevant fields and then save them to create the work record for any actions taken by the Forensic Analyst on the forensic case.

As the forensic case work log shall be used as evidence of actions taken by the Forensic Analyst, it is essential that the work record is correct before writing the record to the forensic case work log in MARS.

10.5.8.2   Amend a work record

There is no option to amend the work record for any forensic case. Any changes to be made shall be entered as another record defining what was wrong with the original record.

10.5.8.3   Delete a work record

There is no option to delete the work record for any forensic case.

10.5.9   Updated estimates

The 'Updated Estimates' screen is shown in Fig. 10.28.

Details of the contents of all of the fields in this screen are defined in Appendix 23.

This is where revised cost or target dates shall be entered along with the actual return date for the forensic case exhibits to the client.

10.5.9.1   Add estimate

The blank screen is presented and the Forensic Analyst shall populate all of the relevant fields and then save them to create an updated forensic case estimate in MARS.

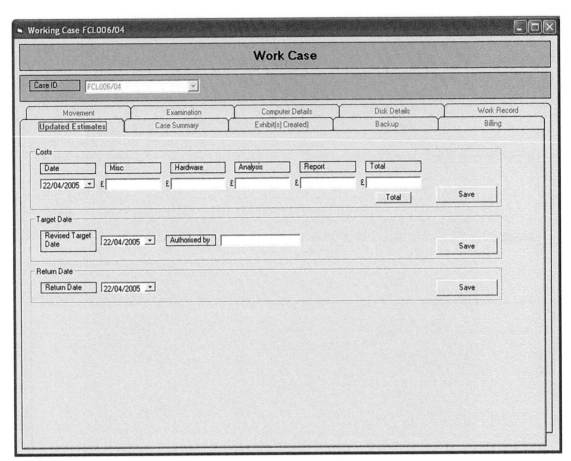

FIG. 10.28 Updated estimates.

10.5.9.2 Amend estimates

There is no amend process as new estimates shall be entered with no amending of the old ones—they are just revised and added to the forensic case file.

10.5.9.3 Delete estimates

There is no delete process as new estimates shall be entered with no deleting of the old ones—they are just revised and added to the forensic case file.

10.5.10 Exhibit(s) created

The 'Exhibits Created' screen is shown in Fig. 10.29.

Details of the contents of all of the fields in this screen are defined in Appendix 24.

This is where the Forensic Analyst shall create an exhibit. The drop-down shall only show exhibits created not the exhibits from the client brought in to be forensically examined.

10.5.10.1 Add exhibit

The blank screen is presented and the Forensic Analyst shall populate all of the relevant fields and then save them to create an exhibit in MARS. The standard for exhibit numbering shall be used, as defined in Chapter 8, Section 8.6.10.

10.5.10.2 Amend exhibit created

To amend an exhibit created, the exhibit must already exist in MARS.

Using the drop-down box for created exhibits for the forensic case, the created exhibit to have its details amended shall be selected and the screen populated with their existing details from the stored record.

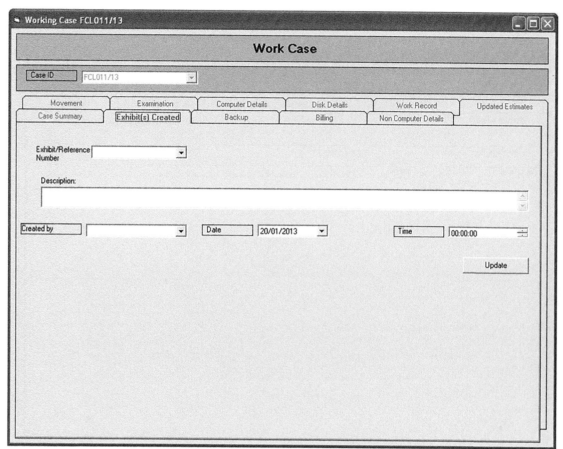

FIG. 10.29 Exhibits created.

The Forensic Analyst (or Laboratory Manager) shall amend the data relating to the exhibit created, as appropriate. The Forensic Analyst (or Laboratory Manager) shall be advised of the successful amendment and acknowledge it.

10.5.10.3 Delete exhibit created

To delete an 'exhibit created', the exhibit must already exist in MARS.

Using the drop-down box for existing exhibits created in the forensic case, the exhibit to be deleted shall be selected and the screen populated with their existing details from the stored record.

It is not possible to delete an exhibit that is active in the MARS system, i.e. one that has had its details populated in MARS. The Forensic Analyst shall be advised that this is not possible, otherwise the Forensic Analyst shall be advised of the successful deletion of the exhibit and acknowledge it.

10.5.11 Case result

The 'Case Result' screen is shown in Fig. 10.30.

Details of the contents of all of the fields in this screen are defined in Appendix 25.

One record (i.e. screen) is used for each defendant in the forensic case.

10.5.11.1 Add case result

The blank screen is presented and the Forensic Analyst (or Laboratory Manager) shall populate all of the relevant fields and then save them to create the result for each defendant in the forensic case in MARS.

10.5.11.2 Amend case result

There is no amend process.

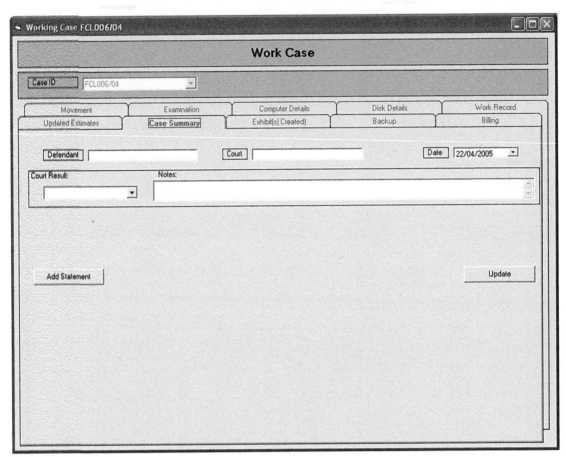

FIG. 10.30 Case result.

10.5.11.3 Delete case result

There is no delete process.

10.5.12 Case backup

The 'Backup' screen is shown in Fig. 10.31.

Details of the contents of all of the fields in this screen are defined in Appendix 26.

10.5.12.1 Add backup

The blank screen is presented and the Forensic Analyst shall populate all of the relevant fields and then save them to create an updated forensic case backup record in MARS.

10.5.12.2 Amend backups

There is no amend process as new backups shall be entered with no amending the old ones.

10.5.12.3 Delete backups

There is no delete process as new backups shall be entered with no deleting of the old ones.

10.5.13 Billing and feedback

The 'Billing and Feedback' screen is shown in Fig. 10.32.

Details of the contents of all of the fields in this screen are defined in Appendix 27.

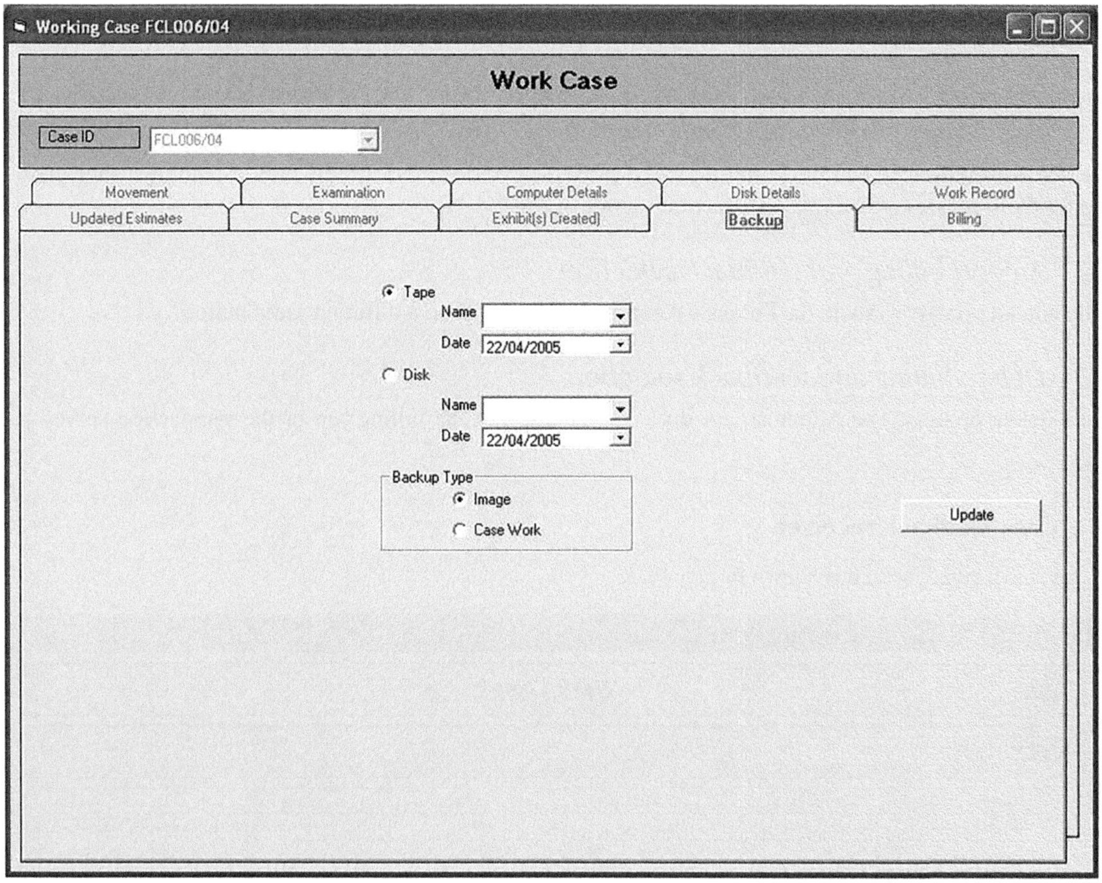

FIG. 10.31 Case backup.

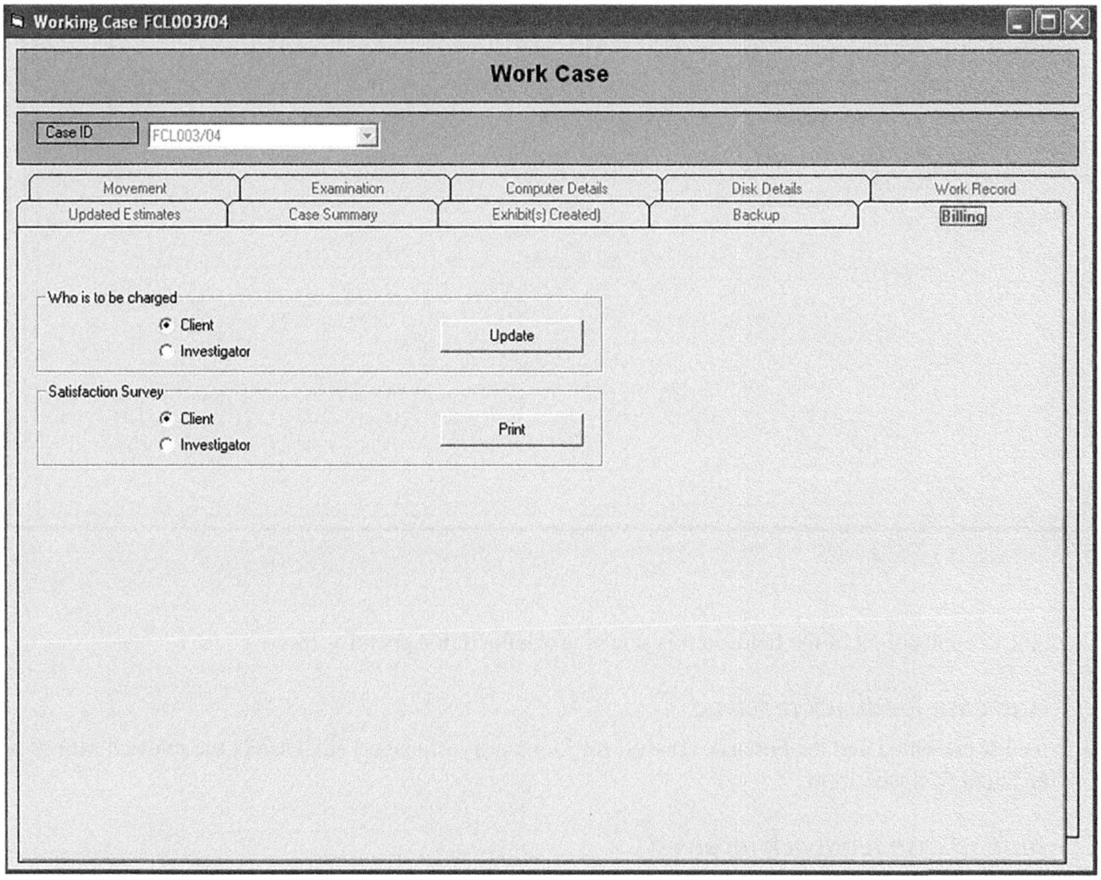

FIG. 10.32 Billing and feedback.

10.5.13.1 Add billing and feedback selection

The blank screen is presented and the Forensic Analyst shall select the relevant radio buttons and then save them to select recipients for the forensic case bill and satisfaction survey.

10.5.13.2 Amend billing and feedback selection

There is no amend process as such, the Forensic Analyst shall just choose a different radio button.

10.5.13.3 Delete billing and feedback selection

There is no delete process. The Administrator does not have to run the billing run or the satisfaction survey run, if not required.

10.5.14 Case feedback received

The 'Feedback Received' screen is shown in Fig. 10.33.

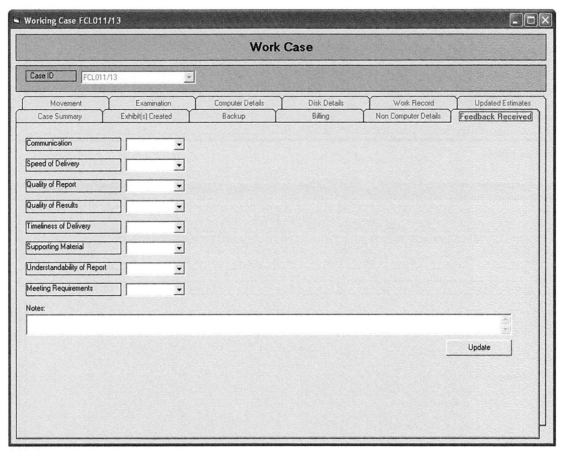

FIG. 10.33 Case feedback received.

Details of the contents of all of the fields in this screen are defined in Appendix 28.

10.5.14.1 Add case feedback received

The blank screen is presented and the Forensic Analyst (or Laboratory Manager) shall select the relevant ratings and comments from the client feedback form.

10.5.14.2 Amend case feedback received

To amend forensic case feedback received, the forensic case feedback received must already exist in MARS.

Using the drop-down box for forensic case feedback received for the forensic case, the forensic case feedback received to have its details amended shall be selected and the screen populated with their existing details from the stored record.

The Forensic Analyst is able to update data relating to the forensic case feedback received, as appropriate. The Forensic Analyst shall be advised of the successful update and acknowledge it.

10.5.14.3   Delete billing and feedback selection

There is no delete process.

10.6   Reports general

10.6.1   Report types

There are two types of reports that can be run from within MARS:

- administrator reports;
- user reports.

An Administrator can print out all reports, but a user can only print out reports relevant to the forensic cases that they are currently assigned.

10.6.2   Reporting general

For all of the reports where a selection of dates, forensic cases, etc., can be made, the following options exist:

- **forensic case**—specific forensic case number shall be selected from a drop-down box of permitted forensic cases to print or * for all forensic cases (either for the Administrator or all assigned to the user); or
- **dates**—from start date to end date.

Where a large number of reports are to be printed, they shall be printed in ascending order of the field searched on unless defined otherwise in the report.

If the search selection returns no 'hits', the user shall be advised of this otherwise the report shall be printed out using the standard attached printer.

For all (and especially) long prints, the page number being printed shall be displayed on screen so that the user shall see that something is actually happening.

10.6.3   General report layout

All reporting is set up for A4 paper.

Reports shall be either Portrait or Landscape as dictated by the output produced.

All reports shall have a number of standard elements in them. These are:

10.6.3.1   Report header

These are from the information entered in Section 10.3.1 and Appendix 1.

- Title 'Organisation Details'—top left hand side;
- Logo—top right side.

10.6.3.2   Report subheader

These are used if needed in any report.

10.6.3.3   Report footer

These are from the information entered in Section 10.3.1 and Appendix 1.

- Copyright notice—left hand side;
- Page *x* of *y* pages—centred;
- Classification—centred and below Copyright, Page '*x*' of '*y*' pages and Date. The Classification is in Bold and BLOCK CAPITALS;
- Date—bottom right side.

10.7   Administrator's reports

The Administrator Report Menu is in Fig. 10.34.

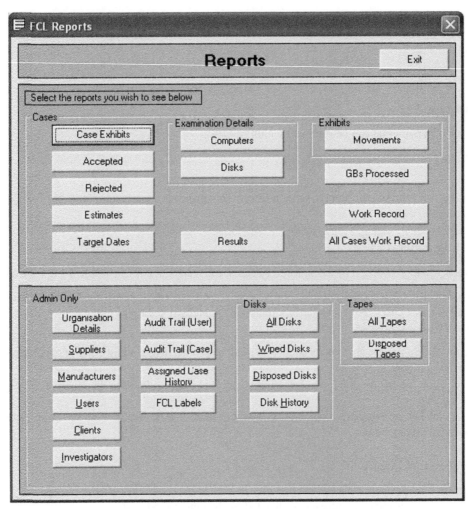

FIG. 10.34   Administrator's report.

10.7.1   Static information

10.7.1.1   Organisation

This is a one-page summary of the data entered when the system is first set up. The information produced in the report is defined in Appendix 29.

10.7.1.2   Users

This is a listing of all users setup in MARS. The information produced in the report is defined in Appendix 30.

10.7.1.3   Manufacturers

This is a report of all the Manufacturers who make the goods that are used in FCL. The information produced in the report is defined in Appendix 31.

10.7.1.4   Suppliers

This is a report of all the suppliers who supply goods to FCL. The information produced in the report is defined in Appendix 32.

10.7.1.5 Clients

This is a report of all FCL's clients, as every forensic case that is processed shall have a client associated with it. For each client listed, all the forensic cases for that client shall be listed. The information produced in the report is defined in Appendix 33.

10.7.1.6 Investigators

This is a very similar report to the client report above, but it lists forensic cases for an Investigator who is typically the Investigator in charge of the forensic case for the client. The information produced in the report is defined in Appendix 34.

10.7.1.7 Disks

10.7.1.7.1 Disks by assignment

This is a report showing all disks by the assignment of the forensic case to which they are currently assigned. The information produced in the report is defined in Appendix 35.

10.7.1.7.2 Disks by reference no.

This is a report showing all current disks in FCL in disk reference number order. The information produced in the report is defined in Appendix 36.

10.7.1.7.3 Wiped disks

This is a report showing all disks in FCL that have been wiped between two given dates. The information produced in the report is defined in Appendix 37.

10.7.1.7.4 Disposed disks

This is a report showing all disks in FCL that have been disposed of between two given dates. The information produced in the report is defined in Appendix 38.

10.7.1.7.5 Disk history

This is a report showing the actions taken on a specific disk for its life cycle in FCL. The information produced in the report is defined in Appendix 39.

10.7.1.8 Tapes

10.7.1.8.1 Tapes by assignment

This is a report showing all tapes in FCL in assignment order. The information produced in the report is defined in Appendix 40.

10.7.1.8.2 Tapes by reference no

This is a report showing all tapes in FCL in tape reference number order. The information produced in the report is defined in Appendix 41.

10.7.1.8.3 Wiped tapes

This is a report showing all tapes in FCL that have been wiped between two given dates. The information produced in the report is defined in Appendix 42.

10.7.1.8.4 Disposed tapes

This is a report showing all tapes in FCL that have been disposed of between two given dates. The information produced in the report is defined in Appendix 43.

10.7.1.8.5 Tape history

This is a report showing the actions taken on a specific tape for its life cycle. The information produced in the report is defined in Appendix 44.

10.7.1.9   Small digital media

10.7.1.9.1   Small digital media by assignment

This is a report showing all small digital media in FCL in assignment order. The information produced in the report is defined in Appendix 45.

10.7.1.9.2   Small digital media by reference no.

This is a report showing all small digital media in FCL in small digital media reference number order. The information produced in the report is defined in Appendix 46.

10.7.1.9.3   Wiped small digital media

This is a report showing all small digital media in FCL that have been wiped between two given dates. The information produced in the report is defined in Appendix 47.

10.7.1.9.4   Disposed small digital media

This is a report showing all small digital media in FCL that have been disposed of between two given dates. The information produced in the report is defined in Appendix 48.

10.7.1.9.5   Small digital media history

This is a report showing the actions taken on a specific small digital media for its life cycle. The information produced in the report is defined in Appendix 49.

10.7.1.10   Wipe methods

This is a report showing all wiping methods used for wiping media used in FCL. The information produced in the report is defined in Appendix 50.

10.7.1.11   Disposal methods

This is a report showing all disposal methods for disposing of media used in FCL. The information produced in the report is defined in Appendix 51.

10.7.1.12   Imaging methods

This is a report showing all imaging methods for imaging media in FCL. The information produced in the report is defined in Appendix 52.

10.7.1.13   Operating systems

This is a report showing all operating systems used in FCL. The information produced in the report is defined in Appendix 53.

10.7.1.14   Media types

This is a report showing all media types processed by FCL other than hard disks. The information produced in the report is defined in Appendix 54.

10.7.1.15   Exhibit types

This is a report showing all exhibit types processed by FCL other than hard disks. The information produced in the report is defined in Appendix 55.

10.7.2   Case setup information

Case setup information relates to the initial setup of a forensic case for forensic processing in FCL.

10.7.2.1   Case setup

This is a report showing all forensic cases created in FCL between two given dates or for a specific client. The information produced in the report is defined in Appendix 56.

10.7.2.2 Case movements

This is a printout of the movements of all exhibits for a forensic case or forensic cases between the dates specified. The information produced in the report is defined in Appendix 57.

10.7.2.3 Forensic case computers

This is a printout of the computers received by FCL between two dates for the examination. The information produced in the report is defined in Appendix 58.

10.7.2.4 Forensic case noncomputer evidence

This is a printout of the evidence that is not a computer received by FCL between two dates for the examination. The information produced in the report is defined in Appendix 59.

10.7.2.5 Forensic case disks received

This is a printout of the hard disks received for forensic case processing by FCL between two dates for the examination. The information produced in the report is defined in Appendix 60.

10.7.2.6 Forensic case other media received

This is a printout of the media that is not a hard disk for forensic case processing by FCL between two dates for the examination. The information produced in the report is defined in Appendix 61.

10.7.2.7 Forensic case exhibits received

This is a printout of the exhibits for selected forensic cases received by FCL between two dates for the examination. The information produced in the report is defined in Appendix 62.

10.7.2.8 Forensic case work record

This is a printout of the work performed on a given forensic case or forensic cases between two dates. The information produced in the report is defined in Appendix 63.

10.7.2.9 Forensic cases rejected

This is a printout showing all forensic cases rejected by FCL between two given dates or for a specific client. The information produced in the report is defined in Appendix 64.

10.7.2.10 Forensic cases accepted

This is a printout showing all forensic cases accepted by FCL between two given dates or for a specific client. The information produced in the report is defined in Appendix 65.

10.7.2.11 Forensic case estimates

This is a printout of all estimates for forensic cases between two dates. The information produced in the report is defined in Appendix 66.

10.7.3 Forensic case processing

10.7.3.1 Forensic cases by forensic analyst

This is a printout of the forensic cases that a Forensic Analyst has or is working on between two dates. The information produced in the report is defined in Appendix 67.

10.7.3.2 Forensic cases by client

This is a printout of the forensic cases that a client has in FCL that are currently being processed. The information produced in the report is defined in Appendix 68.

10.7.3.3 *Forensic cases by investigator*

This is a printout of the forensic cases that an Investigator has in FCL that are currently being processed. The information produced in the report is defined in Appendix 69.

10.7.3.4 *Forensic case target dates*

This is a printout of all target dates for forensic cases that are being processed by FCL. The information produced in the report is defined in Appendix 70.

10.7.3.5 *Forensic cases within 'x' days of target date*

This is a printout of the forensic cases within 'x' days of the target date currently being processed in FCL. The information produced in the report is defined in Appendix 71.

10.7.3.6 *Forensic cases past their target date*

This is a printout of the forensic cases past target date that are currently being processed in FCL. The information produced in the report is defined in Appendix 72.

10.7.3.7 *Forensic cases unassigned*

This is a printout of current forensic cases in FCL without a Forensic Analyst assigned to them. The information produced in the report is defined in Appendix 73.

10.7.3.8 *Forensic case exhibits produced*

This is a printout of the exhibits produced for the forensic case between two dates. The information produced in the report is defined in Appendix 74.

10.7.3.9 *Forensic case results*

This is a printout of the results of a given forensic case or forensic cases between two dates. The information produced in the report is defined in Appendix 75.

10.7.4 **Forensic case administration**

10.7.4.1 *Forensic case backups*

This is a printout of the backups of a forensic cases or forensic cases between two dates. The information produced in the report is defined in Appendix 76.

10.7.4.2 *Billing run*

This is a printout of the work done between two dates (the last billed date and the billing date) for each forensic case. The information produced in the report is defined in Appendix 77.

10.7.4.3 *Feedback letters*

This produces the letter asking for feedback on a given forensic case or forensic cases with the feedback form. The information produced in the report is defined in Appendix 78.

10.7.4.4 *Feedback forms printout*

This is a printout of the forms scanned into the client's virtual forensic case file that have been received from the client. The information produced in the report is defined in Appendix 79.

10.7.4.5 *Feedback reporting summary by case*

This is a report showing feedback received for forensic cases by Case No. for all forensic cases. The information produced in the report is defined in Appendix 80.

10.7.4.6 Feedback reporting summary by forensic analyst

This is a report showing feedback received for forensic cases by Case No. for each Forensic Analyst. The information produced in the report is defined in Appendix 81.

10.7.4.7 Feedback reporting summary by client

This is a report showing feedback received for forensic cases by Case No. for all forensic cases. The information produced in the report is defined in Appendix 82.

10.7.4.8 Complete forensic case report

This is a printout of a complete forensic case, with all information relating to a forensic case. The information produced in the report is defined in Appendix 83.

10.7.4.9 Forensic case processed report

This is a printout of the work done in FCL between two dates. The information produced in the report is defined in Appendix 84.

10.7.4.10 Insurance report

This is a printout of the evidence that is currently held by FCL and lists its value for insurance purposes. The information produced in the report is defined in Appendix 85.

10.7.5 Audits

10.7.5.1 Exhibit audit report

This is a printout of the evidence that is currently held by FCL. The information produced in the report is defined in Appendix 3.

10.7.5.2 Audit trail user

This is a report showing all actions taken by a user on a forensic case between two dates. The information produced in the report is defined in Appendix 3.

10.7.5.3 Audit trail case

This is a report showing all actions taken by a user on a forensic case between two dates. The information produced in the report is defined in Appendix 3.

10.7.5.4 Assigned case history

This is a report showing the assignments for a given forensic case or forensic cases. The information produced in the report is defined in Appendix 3.

10.8 User reports

The user can track their own work using the same reports as the Administrator, but only for their own assigned forensic cases.
The current user report menu is in Fig. 10.35.

10.8.1 Case setup information

The following reports are available for the Forensic Analyst to view for their own forensic cases:

- case setup;
- case movements;
- case computers;
- case noncomputer evidence;

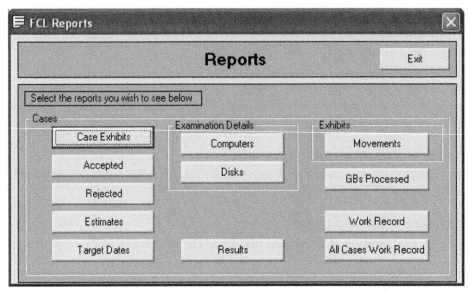

FIG. 10.35 User reports.

- case disks received;
- case other media received;
- case exhibits received;
- case work record; and
- case estimates.

10.8.2 Case processing

The following reports are available for the Forensic Analyst to view for their own forensic cases:

- cases by client;
- cases by investigator;
- case target dates;
- cases within 'x' days of target date;
- cases past their target date;
- case exhibits produced; and
- case results.

10.8.3 Case administration

The following reports are available for the Forensic Analyst to view for their own forensic cases:

- case backups;
- feedback forms printout;
- feedback reporting summary by case;
- feedback reporting summary by Forensic Analyst;
- feedback reporting summary by client;
- complete case report; and
- processed report.

10.8.4 Audits

The following reports are available for the Forensic Analyst to view for their own forensic cases:

- exhibit audit report;
- audit trail case; and
- assigned case history.

Appendix 1—Setting up organisational details

The following information is entered into setting up a forensic laboratory in MARS. Each field is described below:

Organisation name

Enter the forensic laboratory's official name here;

Address

Enter up to four lines of the forensic laboratory's official registered address here;

Postcode

Enter the forensic laboratory's postcode here (note: this is also called a Zip code in the United States);

Phone number

Enter the forensic laboratory's main phone number, typically the main switchboard.

Fax

Enter the forensic laboratory's main fax number.

Website URL

Enter the forensic laboratory's website URL.

VAT no

For laboratories in the United Kingdom, enter the forensic laboratory's VAT number, so it can be used for billing runs (in other countries other tax references may be needed and these shall be entered here).

Registered company number

Enter the forensic laboratory's Company Number, so it can be used for corporate correspondence. The use of a registered company number will vary between jurisdictions.

Logo

Enter the forensic laboratory's logo, by browsing to the relevant directory that holds it. The logo can be in BMP, JPEG, or GIF formats. It is automatically resized to be used for all output from MARS.

Unit name

Enter the forensic laboratory's unit (or department, group, etc.) that runs the forensic case processing service here.

Unit address

Where the address of the unit is the same as the forensic laboratory's address, press the 'Use Organisational Details' button that shall fill in all of the details of the Unit except the email address.

   You can overtype whatever information you want (e.g. direct phone and fax may be different from the main forensic laboratory's ones).

   If the unit address is different to the forensic laboratory's address then enter up to four lines of the address of the unit.

Unit postcode

If the unit postcode is different to the forensic laboratory's postcode, then enter the unit's postcode.

Unit phone

If the unit phone number is different to the forensic laboratory's phone number, then enter the unit's phone number.

Unit fax

If the unit fax number is different to the forensic laboratory's fax number, then enter the unit's fax number.

Unit website URL

If the unit website URL is different to the forensic laboratory's website URL, then enter the unit's website URL.

Unit email address

If the unit has its own email address, then enter the email address here.

Unit logo

If the unit has its own Logo, enter it here by browsing to the relevant directory that holds it. The logo can be in BMP, JPEG, or GIF formats. It is automatically resized to be used for all output from MARS

Classification of the reports

MARS sets up the classification level for all forensic case processing reports so that this classification appears at the bottom of all reports. This shall indicate to any user how the information in the report has to be handled in accordance with the security procedures for information classification and handling, as given in Chapter 12, Section 12.3.14.6 and Chapter 5, Appendix 16.

Case numbering

This allows FCL to set up its forensic case numbering scheme. It shall be in the format:
aaa / nnnnn / yyyy

- where aaa is the initials that identify FCL;
- nnnnn is the forensic case number of the year; and
- yyyy is the year (taken from the system)

Note 1

This shall be the first forensic case number of the unit for the current year that shall be entered into MARS.

Note 2

If historical forensic cases are to be entered, then the oldest forensic case number shall be entered. However, all forensic cases between the first one and the most recent one will have to be entered into MARS as MARS will automatically offer the next available number for the next forensic case being entered.

Note 3

Once a forensic case number has been assigned, it cannot be reassigned.

Note 4

As the first forensic case number is entered into the entry field, it shall be reflected by the details being displayed to the right of the entry box, so that the display can be checked to ensure the forensic case number is correct.

Copyright information

FCL shall always mark all of its output as a copyrighted document, and so the relevant copyright statement is entered here. It is used for all output from the MARS system.

On clicking on this field, it automatically inserts the '©' symbol followed by FCL's name.

Hard disk reference ID

Any hard disk used in FCL shall be traceable throughout its life from purchase to disposal.

Enter here the prefix to be used for identifying hard disks:

FCL shall use 'Disk' as its Hard Disk identification prefix.

Tape reference ID

Any tape used in FCL shall be traceable throughout its life from purchase to disposal.

Enter here the prefix to be used for identifying tapes:

FCL shall use 'Tape' as its Tape identification prefix.

Small digital media ID

Any small digital media used in the laboratory shall be traceable throughout its life from purchase to disposal.

Enter here the prefix to be used for identifying small digital media:

FCL shall use 'SDM' as its small digital media identification prefix.

Appendix 2—Setup the administrator

The following information is entered into setting up the Administrator in MARS. Each field is described below:

User ID

Enter the User ID of the Administrator.

Password

Enter the password for the User ID.

Confirm password

Re-enter the password for the User ID.

Title/rank

Enter the title or the rank for the Administrator.

First name

Enter the Administrator's first name.

Surname

Enter the Administrator's surname.

Address

If the Administrator is resident at FCL's address then press the 'Use Organisation Details' button and this shall fill in all of the relevant address details.

If the Administrator is resident at the unit address then press the 'Use Unit Details' button and this shall fill in all of the relevant address details.

Otherwise, enter up to four lines of the Administrator's address.

Postcode

Enter the Administrator's postcode, unless it has been already entered by pressing either of the 'Use Organisation Details' or 'Use Unit Details' buttons

Phone direct

Enter the Administrator's direct phone number.

Phone mobile

Enter the Administrator's mobile phone number.

Fax

Enter the Administrator's direct fax number.

Email

Enter the Administrator's individual email address.

Appendix 3—Audit reports

Exhibit audit report

Paper type

Portrait.

Selection criteria

None.

Sort order

Case Number then exhibit.

Report header

- Title 'Audit Listing for Exhibits'—top left hand side;
- Logo—top right hand side.

Report subheader

None.

Report contents

- Case name;
- Case ID;
- Exhibit number;
- Description;
- Forensic Analyst assigned.

Audit trail user

Paper type

Landscape.

Report description

This shall be a report showing all actions taken by a user on a forensic case between a pair of dates.

Selection criteria

Dropdown for User ID or '*' for all;

Note

If an 'Administrator' is chosen then there shall be no forensic cases available to be selected as no Administrator can 'run' a forensic case;

    If all users are chosen, then list the Administrators first;

    Usernames rather than User IDs are to be printed with the user type in brackets afterwards—see examples below;

    Dropdown for forensic case number or '*' for all;

Start date and end date. The 'start date' shall be the earliest date any action was taken on the system, the 'to date' shall be today's date. If dates are to be changed then the pop-up calendar shall be used.

Sort order

Date and time order (oldest first).

Report header

- 'Audit Trail for between "<Start Date>" and "<End Date>"'—top left hand side;
- Logo—top right hand side.

Report subheader

- User.

Report contents

- Date;
- Time;
- Case;
- Action (reporting what has been written to the audit trail).

Audit trail case

Paper type

Landscape.

Report description

This shall be a report showing all actions taken by a user on a forensic case between a pair of dates.

Selection criteria

Dropdown for forensic case number or '*' for all;

    Start date and end date. The 'start date' shall be the earliest date any action was taken on the system, the 'to date' shall be today's date. If dates are to be changed then the pop-up calendar shall be used.

Sort order

Case number (if appropriate) then by date and time;

New forensic cases to start on a new page.

Report header

- 'Audit Trail between "<Start Date>" and "<End Date>"'—top left hand side;
- Logo—top right hand side.

Report subheader

- Case number.

Report contents

- Date;
- Time;
- User—print name not User ID and user type in brackets afterwards;
- Action (reporting what has been written to the audit trail).

Assigned case history

Paper type

Portrait.

Selection criteria

Dropdown for forensic case number or '*' for all;

Start date and end date. The 'start date' shall be the earliest date any action was taken on the system, the 'to date' shall be today's date. If dates are to be changed then the pop-up calendar shall be used.

Sort order

Case number.

Report description

This shall be a report showing the assignments for a given forensic case or forensic cases.

Report header

- Title 'Case Assignment History'—top left hand side;
- Logo—top right hand side.

Report subheader

- <Case Number>—<Case Name>.

Report contents

- Date;
- Time;
- Assigned to—print name not User ID and user type in brackets afterwards;
- Assigned by—print name not User ID and user type in brackets afterwards.

Appendix 4—Manage users

The same screen is used for all actions relating to the management of users and contains the following fields:

User ID

The User ID of the User.

Password

The password for the User ID.

Confirm password

Re-entry of the password for the User ID.

When the 'Confirm' password is entered it shall be that it matches the original one entered in the field above. If it does not, it will produce an error message 'Passwords do not Match' and prompt for re-entry by blanking both password fields.

Title or rank

The title or the rank for the User.

First name

The first name for the owner of the User ID.

Surname

The surname for the owner of the User ID

Address

If the owner of the User ID is resident at FCL's main address then pressing the 'Use Organisation Details' button shall fill in all of the relevant address details.

If the owner of the User ID is resident at the unit's address then pressing the 'Use Unit Details' button and this shall fill in all of the relevant address details.

Otherwise, enter up to four lines for the address of the owner of the User ID.

Postcode

The postcode of the owner of the User ID, unless it has been already entered by pressing either of the 'Use Organisation Details' or 'Use Unit Details' buttons.

Phone direct

The direct phone number of the owner of the User ID.

Phone mobile

The mobile phone number of the owner of the User ID.

Email

The individual email address of the owner of the User ID.

Access rights

Whether this User ID is to be an 'Administrator' or a 'Normal User'.

Appendix 5—Manage manufacturers

Name

The Manufacturer's name.

Address

Up to four lines of the Manufacturer's address.

Postcode

The Manufacturer's postcode.

Phone

The Manufacturer's phone number.

Website URL

The Manufacturer's URL.

Email

The Manufacturer's email address.

Appendix 6—Manage suppliers

Name

The Supplier's name.

Address

Up to four lines of the Supplier's address.

Postcode

The Supplier's postcode.

Phone

The Supplier's phone number.

Website URL

The Supplier's URL.

Email

The Supplier's email address.

Account number

FCL's account number with the Supplier.

Contacts

Details of up to five contacts in the Supplier. Each shall have a name, phone number, and email address.

Appendix 7—Manage clients

Name

The client's name.

Address

Up to four lines of the client's address.

Postcode

The client's postcode.

Phone

The client's phone number.

Fax

The client's fax number.

Website URL

The client's URL.

Email

The client's email address.

Contacts

Details of up to five contacts in the client. Each shall have a name, phone number, and email address.

Appendix 8—Manage investigators

Name

The Investigator's name.

Address

There is a dropdown to the right of the name that allows the Administrator to select a client that the investigator works for. Once the client is found, their details shall be displayed in fields to the right of the investigator's input fields.

A button, next to the 'Address' field is available entitled 'Use client Details'. If this is pressed then the Investigator's address details are filled in automatically with the client details.

If these are wrong in any area, the Administrator shall amend them, otherwise all the address details on the left shall have to be entered manually.

If not automatically entered, then the Administrator shall be able to enter up to four lines of the Investigator's address.

Postcode

If not automatically entered, then this is the Investigator's postcode.

Phone

If not automatically entered, then this is the Investigator's phone number.

Fax

If not automatically entered, then this is the Investigator's fax number.

Website URL

If not automatically entered, then this is the Investigator's URL.

Email

If not automatically entered, then this is the Investigator's email address.

Appendix 9—Manage disks

Disk details

Manufacturer

A disk manufacturer shall be selected from the drop-down list of manufacturers entered in Section 10.3.5.2.

Serial no

The serial number of the disk.

Supplier

A supplier shall be selected from the drop-down list of suppliers entered in Section 10.3.5.3.

Disk reference

The disk reference number is auto-generated by MARS and cannot be changed. The numbering is based on the system that was entered in the organisational details when MARS was installed.

Model

The disk model name.

Size

The size of the disk in Gb.

Order no

The order number for the purchase of the disk. This number may refer to a number of different disks as a consignment.

Date received

The date that the disk was received. This uses a drop-down calendar.

Delivery note

The delivery note shall be scanned and saved to the relevant virtual file. MARS allows the Administrator to browse to the correct file and attach the scan of the delivery note to the hard disk record.

Auto clear entry

If a number of disks are to be entered and they are all from different sources then the 'auto clear' option shall be taken. Checking this box automatically clears the screen after adding each disk, apart from the system-generated disk number and today's date.

Otherwise, after entering the first disk in a series of disks from the same supplier, all of the information from the previous disk on screen (allowing bulk entry from a specific shipment of similar disks) shall remain on screen.

Wipe a disk

When a new disk arrives at FCL, it shall be immediately wiped forensically. Disks shall also be wiped forensically at a number of stages in their lifecycle in FCL. This is where the details of all wiping operations shall be entered, as they are all related to a specific disk.

Disk reference

Disks to be wiped shall be selected from the drop-down list of disks by the FCL reference number it was assigned when introduced into FCL.

Wipe method

The wipe method shall be selected from the drop-down list that was entered in Section 10.3.5.9.1.

Wiped by

The User ID of the person performing the disk wiping shall be selected from the drop-down list that was entered in Section 10.3.5.1.

Date

The date that the disk was wiped. This uses a drop-down calendar.

Notes

Any notes to be associated with this process.

Dispose of a disk

When it comes time to dispose of a disk, then the fact shall be recorded in MARS along with the disposal method.

Disk reference

Disks to be disposed of shall be selected from the drop-down list of disks by the reference number it was assigned when introduced into FCL.

Disposal method

The disposal method from the drop-down list that was entered in Section 10.3.5.9.2.

Disposed by

The User ID of the person performing the disk disposal shall be selected from the drop-down list that was entered in Section 10.3.5.1.

Date

The date that the disk was disposed of. This uses a drop-down calendar.

Notes

Any notes to be associated with this process.

Disposal certificate

Disposal certificates, where appropriate, shall be scanned in and allow the Administrator to browse to the correct file and attach the scan of the disposal certificate to the hard disk record

Assign a disk

When a disk is to be assigned to a forensic case or for a specific job, it is done here.

Disk reference

Disks to be assigned to a forensic case shall be selected from the drop-down list of disks by the reference number it was assigned when introduced into FCL.

Assign to

A disk shall be assigned to either a current forensic case or to an administrative task. Assignment shall be carried out as below:

- **forensic cases**—this has a dropdown of all forensic cases and a forensic case shall be selected to assign a disk to. The forensic case shall exist for a disk to be assigned to it and more than one disk can be assigned to a forensic case;
- **administrative purposes**—allows the Administrator to enter where this disk is being assigned if not to a forensic case. It could be for storing images, for backup, as a scratch disk, etc.

Appendix 10—Manage tapes

Tape details

Manufacturer

A tape manufacturer shall be selected from the drop-down list of manufacturers entered in Section 10.3.5.2.

Label

The label details attached to the tape.

Supplier

A supplier shall be selected from the drop-down list of suppliers entered in Section 10.3.5.3.

Tape reference

The tape reference number is auto-generated by MARS and cannot be changed. The numbering is based on the system that was entered in the organisational details when MARS was installed.

Model

The tape model name.

Size

The size of the tape in Gb.

Order no

The order number for the purchase of the tape. This number may refer to a number of different tapes as a consignment.

Date received

The date that the tape was received. This uses a drop-down calendar.

Delivery note

The delivery note shall be scanned and saved to the relevant virtual file. MARS allows the Administrator to browse to the correct file and attach the scan of the delivery note to the tape record.

Auto clear entry

If a number of tapes are to be entered and they are all from different sources then the 'auto clear' option shall be taken. Checking this box automatically clears the screen after adding each tape, apart from the system-generated tape number and today's date.

Otherwise, after entering the first tape in a series of tapes from the same supplier, all of the information from the previous tape on screen (allowing bulk entry from a specific shipment of similar tapes) shall remain on screen.

Wipe a tape

When a new tape arrives at FCL, it shall be immediately forensically wiped. Tapes shall also be forensically wiped at a number of stages in their lifecycle in FCL. This is where the details of all wiping operations shall be entered, as they are all related to a specific tape.

Tape reference

Tapes to be wiped shall be selected from the drop-down list of tapes by the reference number it was assigned when introduced to the Laboratory.

Wipe method

The wipe method shall be selected from the drop-down list that was entered in Section 10.3.5.9.1.

Wiped by

The User ID of the person performing the tape wiping shall be selected from the drop-down list that was entered in Section 10.3.5.1.

Date

The date that the tape was wiped. This uses a drop-down calendar.

Notes

Any notes to be associated with this process.

Dispose of a tape

When it comes time to dispose of a tape, then the fact shall be recorded in MARS along with the disposal method.

Tape reference

Tapes to be disposed of shall be selected from the drop-down list of tapes by the reference number it was assigned when introduced into FCL.

Disposal method

The disposal method from the drop-down list that was entered in Section 10.3.5.9.2.

Disposed by

The User ID of the person performing the tape disposal shall be selected from the drop-down list that was entered in Section 10.3.5.1.

Date

The date that the tape was disposed of. This uses a drop-down calendar.

Notes

Any notes to be associated with this process.

Disposal certificate

Disposal certificates, where appropriate, shall be scanned in and allows the Administrator to browse to the correct file and attach the scan of the disposal certificate to the tape record.

Assign a tape

When a tape is to be assigned to a forensic case or for a specific job, it shall be done here.

Tape reference

Tapes to be assigned to a forensic case shall be selected from the drop-down list of tapes by the reference number it was assigned when introduced into FCL.

Assign to

A tape shall be assigned to either a current forensic case or to an administrative task. Assignment shall be carried out as below:

- **forensic cases**—this has a dropdown of all forensic cases and a forensic case shall be selected to assign a tape to. The forensic case shall exist for a tape to be assigned to it and more than one tape can be assigned to a forensic case
- **administrative purposes**—allows the Administrator to enter where this tape is being assigned if not to a forensic case. It could be for storing images, for backup, as a scratch tape, etc.

Appendix 11—Manage small digital media

Small digital media details

Media type

A small digital media type shall be selected from the drop-down list of small digital media types entered in Section 10.3.5.8.

Manufacturer

A small digital media type manufacturer shall be selected from the drop-down list of small digital media types entered in Section 10.3.5.2.

Label

The label details attached to the small digital media type.

Supplier

A supplier shall be selected from the drop-down list of suppliers entered in Section 10.3.5.3.

Small digital media reference

The small digital media type reference number is auto-generated by MARS and cannot be changed. The numbering is based on the system that was entered in the organisational details when MARS was installed.

Model

The small digital media type model name.

Size

The size of the small digital media type in Gb.

Order no

The order number for the purchase of the small digital media type. This number may refer to a number of different small digital media types as a consignment.

Date received

The date that the small digital media type was received. This uses a drop-down calendar.

Delivery note

The delivery note shall be scanned and saved to the relevant virtual file. MARS allows the Administrator to browse to the correct file and attach the scan of the delivery note to the small digital media type record.

Auto clear entry

If a number of small digital media types are to be entered and they are all from different sources then the 'auto clear' option shall be taken. Checking this box automatically clears the screen after adding each item of small digital media, apart from the system-generated small digital media number and today's date.

Otherwise, after entering the small digital media in a series of small digital media from the same supplier, all of the information from the previous small digital media screen (allowing bulk entry from a specific shipment of similar small digital media) shall remain on screen.

Wipe a small digital media device

When a small digital media item arrives at FCL, it shall be immediately forensically wiped. Small digital media shall also be forensically wiped at a number of stages in their lifecycle in FCL. This is where the details of all wiping operations shall be entered, as they are all related to a specific small digital media.

Small digital device reference

Small digital media to be wiped shall be selected from the drop-down list of small digital media by the laboratory reference number it was assigned when introduced to the laboratory.

Wipe method

The wipe method shall be selected from the drop-down list that was entered in Section 10.3.5.8.4.

Wiped by

The User ID of the person performing the tape wiping shall be selected from the drop-down list that was entered in Section 10.3.5.1.

Date

The date that the small digital media was wiped. This uses a drop-down calendar.

Notes

Any notes to be associated with this process.

Dispose of an item of small digital media

When it comes time to dispose of an item of small digital media, then the fact shall be recorded in MARS along with the disposal method.

Small digital media reference

Small digital media to be disposed of shall be selected from the drop-down list of tapes by the reference number it was assigned when introduced into FCL.

Disposal method

The disposal method from the drop-down list that was entered in Section 10.3.5.8.5.

Disposed by

The User ID of the person performing the small digital media disposal shall be selected from the drop-down list that was entered in Section 10.3.5.1.

Date

The date that the small digital media was disposed of. This uses a drop-down calendar.

Notes

Any notes to be associated with this process.

Disposal certificate

Disposal certificates, where appropriate, shall be scanned in and allows the Administrator to browse to the correct file and attach the scan of the disposal certificate to the small digital media record.

Assign a small digital media

When an item of small digital media is to be assigned to a forensic case or for a specific job, it shall be done here.

Small digital media reference

Small digital media to be assigned to a forensic case shall be selected from the drop-down list of small digital media by the reference number it was assigned when introduced into FCL.

Assign to

A small digital media device shall be assigned to either a current forensic case or to an administrative task. Assignment shall be carried out as below:

- **forensic cases**—this has a dropdown of all forensic cases and a forensic case shall be selected to assign a tape to. The forensic case shall exist for an item of small digital media to be assigned to it and more than one item of small digital media can be assigned to a forensic case;
- **administrative purposes**—allows the Administrator to enter where this item of small digital media is being assigned if not to a forensic case. It could be for storing images, for backup, as a scratch disk, etc.

Appendix 12—Exhibit details

Exhibit number

The exhibit number of the exhibit related to the forensic case.

Seal number

The seal number of the exhibit.

Description

The description for the exhibit.

Received by

Use the drop-down box to select the User ID for the person receiving the exhibit, as defined in Section 10.3.5.1.

Seized from

From whom the exhibit was seized.

Received date

The date that the exhibit was received in FCL. This uses a drop-down calendar.

Seized date

The date that the exhibit was seized. This uses a drop-down calendar.

Received time

The time that the exhibit was received.

Time seized

The time that the exhibit was seized.

Insurance value

The insurance value of the exhibit. This is so that the total value of equipment held can be monitored to ensure that does not breach the value insured in the policy.

Owner

The owner of the exhibit.

Reason for seizing

The reason for seizing.

Checkboxes

Password?

If any passwords or PINs were obtained from the suspect or elsewhere, the checkbox shall be ticked and relevant details in the text box on the right hand side of the checkbox.

Connected?

If the exhibit was a system and it was connected to a phone or network, the checkbox shall be ticked and relevant details in the text box on the right hand side of the checkbox.

Switched on at seizure?

If the system was switched on at the time of seizure, the checkbox shall be ticked and relevant details in the text box on the right hand side of the checkbox.

Switched on after seizure?

If the system has been switched on since the time of seizure, the checkbox shall be ticked and relevant details in the text box on the right hand side of the checkbox.

Add document

If there are any documents relevant to the exhibit, their scanned imaged shall be added by pressing on the 'Add Documents' button. As many documents as required shall be added.

Appendix 13—Evidence sought

Evidence sought

The details of the evidence sought.

Comments

Any other comments or relevant information.

Add document

If there are any documents relevant to the exhibit, their scanned imaged shall be added by pressing on the 'Add Documents' button. As many documents as required shall be added.

Appendix 14—Estimates

Cost

Date

The date of the estimate. This uses a drop-down calendar.

Misc.

Any costs that are not covered elsewhere, e.g. travel and subsistence, meetings, etc.

Hardware

The costs estimated for any hardware required for the forensic case. This shall include disks, tapes, caddies, additional hardware needed to image or interrogate or analyse the forensic case.

Analysis

The estimated costs for the Forensic Analysts running the forensic case.

Report

Cost for report production, e.g. print costs, binding, etc.

Total

This is the automatically calculated total of the other fields entered.

Case dates

Date received

This defaults to the earliest date of receipt of any exhibit in the forensic case, but it can be overwritten, if required. This uses a drop-down calendar to change the date.

Target date

The date that the client wants the results delivered by (i.e. the TRT). This uses a drop-down calendar.

Appendix 15—Accept or reject case

Accepted

Check the button if the forensic case is to be accepted. If this is selected, then the date rejected and the Reason for Rejection is greyed out.

Rejected

Check the button if the forensic case is to be rejected. If this shall be selected, then the Date Accepted is greyed out.

Date accepted

The date the forensic case was accepted, the date defaults to today's date. This uses a drop-down calendar.

Date rejected

The date the forensic case was rejected, the date defaults to today's date. This uses a drop-down calendar.

Accepted or rejected by

Use the drop-down box to select the User ID for the person that accepted or rejected the forensic case.

Reason for rejection

Enter the reason for rejection. This is a freeform text box.

Date client advised

The date the client was advised of the acceptance or rejection of the forensic case, the date defaults to today's date. This uses a drop-down calendar.

Advised client name

The name of the person (in the client's Organisation) that shall be advised of the acceptance or rejection of the forensic case.

Advised client method

The method of communication that was used to advise the client could be phone, fax, face to face, or other. This is a free-form text box.

Client advised by

Use the drop-down box to select the User ID for the person that advised the client of the acceptance or rejection of the forensic case.

Add document

If there are any relevant documents to be added (e.g. copy of original signed fax or letter sent), they shall be scanned in and the scanned image be attached to the relevant forensic case by pressing the 'Add a Document' button.

Clear all

The 'Clear All' button deletes all contents of all fields to allow re-entry assuming the data has not been saved.

Appendix 16—Movement log

Exhibit or reference number

The exhibit or reference number shall be selected from the drop-down box which gives the complete listing of all exhibits assigned to the forensic case. Once the exhibit has been selected, the screen shall be populated with all details that are listed for the exhibit. All empty fields are able to be updated as required.

Log number

This shall display the Log number from the Laboratory Logbook entered when the exhibit was received into FCL.

Client seal no.

This shall display the client Seal Number entered when the exhibit was received into FCL.

FCL seal no.

If the exhibit is to be sealed by the FCL, the seal number shall be entered here.

FCL second seal no.

If the exhibit has to be resealed for any reason, then the new FCL Seal Number shall be entered here—with a note as to why a second seal was used.

Action

This is the action that was taken relating to the movements of the exhibit, using the radio buttons below.

Client to lab staff

Indicates that the exhibit was transferred from the client to FCL.

Initial logging into store

Indicates that the exhibit was logged into the Secure Property Store.

Store to investigation

Indicates that the exhibit was transferred from the Secure Property Store to a Forensic Analyst, so that work could be carried out on it.

Investigation to store

Indicates that the exhibit was transferred to the Secure Property Store from a Forensic Analyst, after work was carried out on it.

Store return to client

Indicates that the exhibit has been taken from the Secure Property Store and returned to the client.

Other

Indicates that the exhibit undergoes any other movement—e.g. pass to Law Enforcement or another authorised third party. If other is chosen, a brief description of where it has gone and why shall be entered.

Notes

Any further notes to do with this exhibit movement.

Our Forensic Analyst

Typically, this shall be the Forensic Analyst assigned to the forensic case, and this is the default inserted in the box. If another of the Forensic Analysts moved the exhibit, then this shall be recorded using the 'Our Forensic Analyst' drop-down box and selecting the relevant Forensic Analyst.

Date

The date the exhibit was moved, the date defaults to today's date. This uses a drop-down calendar to select another date, if required.

Time

The time the exhibit was moved.

Add document

If there are any relevant documents to be added (e.g. copy of original Movement Log with actual signatures), they shall be scanned in and the scanned image be attached to the relevant forensic case by pressing the 'Add a Document' button:

Appendix 17—Examination log

Exhibit reference number

The Exhibit Reference number for the exhibit to be examined shall be selected from the drop-down box of all exhibits in the selected forensic case. The exhibit to be examined shall be selected from the list and the details are entered below.

No. of hard disks

Enter the number of hard disks in the exhibit and on the same line enter the total disk size in Gb of hard disks in the exhibit.

No. of floppy disks

Enter the number of floppy disks in the exhibit and on the same line enter the total disk size in Gb of floppy disks in the exhibit.

No. of CDs

Enter the number of CDs in the exhibit and on the same line enter the total disk size in Gb of CDs in the exhibit.

No. of DVDs

Enter the number of DVDs in the exhibit and on the same line enter the total disk size in Gb of DVDs in the exhibit.

No. of other storage media

Enter the number of other storage media in the exhibit (e.g. USB sticks, Camera Chips, etc.), and on the same line enter the total disk size in Gb of other media in the exhibit

Total

The field shall automatically enter the sum of the Gb for all the items in the exhibit from the numbers entered above.

Note

The details of capacity shall all be entered in Gb.

Notes

Describe any other media and or enter any relevant details about the exhibit(s) here or any further notes to do with the examination.

Examined by

Typically, this shall be the Forensic Analyst assigned to the forensic case, and this is the default inserted in the box. If another of the Forensic Analysts undertakes any examination, then this shall be recorded using the 'Examined by' drop-down box and selecting the relevant Forensic Analyst.

Date

The date the exhibit was examined, which defaults to today's date. This uses a drop-down calendar to select another date, if required.

Time

The time the exhibit was examined.

Add photos

If there are any relevant photos of the exhibit to be added, they shall be attached to the exhibit by pressing the 'Photos' button.

Add document

If there are any relevant documents to be added, they shall be scanned in and the scanned image be attached to the relevant forensic case by pressing the 'Add Document' button.

Appendix 18—Computer hardware details

Exhibit reference

The Exhibit Reference number for the exhibit to be examined shall be selected from the drop-down box of all exhibits in the selected forensic case. The exhibit to be examined shall be selected from the list and the details are entered below.

No. of disks in computer

Enter the number of disks in the computer.

Make

Enter the computer make.

Model

Enter the model of the computer.

Serial no.

Enter the computer's serial number.

Floppy disk (5¼″)

Enter the number of 5¼″ disk drives in the computer.

Floppy disk (3½″)

Enter the number of 3½″ disk drives in the computer.

DVD reader/writer

Enter the number of DVD Readers in the computer.

CD reader/writer

Enter the number of CD Reader/Writers in the computer.

Zip disk

Enter the number of Zip Drives in the computer.

Jazz drive

Enter the number of Jazz Drives in the computer.

Disk (other)

Enter the number of other types of disk drive in the computer.

DDS tape

Enter the number of DDS Tape Backup devices in the computer.

AIT tape

Enter the number of AIT Tape Backup devices in the computer.

QIC tape

Enter the number of QIC Tape Backup devices in the computer.

Video card

Enter the number of video cards in the computer.

RAM strips

Enter the number of RAM strips in the computer.

SCSI card

Enter the number of SCSI cards in the computer.

Network card

Enter the number of network cards in the computer.

Modem

Enter the number of modem cards in the computer.

Additional peripherals details

Enter any additional details regarding any of the peripherals above for clarification or identification.

BIOS key

Enter the BIOS Key (i.e. the key sequence to get at the BIOS information).

BIOS password

Enter the BIOS Password.

Boot sequence

Enter the boot sequence.

Operating system

Enter the computer's operating system. If a new one is to be added, the 'new' button beside it shall be selected and the new operating system added. This uses the same screen as given in Section 10.3.5.9.4.

System date

The system date, this defaults to today's date. This uses a drop-down calendar to select another date, if required.

Actual date

The system date, this defaults to today's date. This uses a drop-down calendar to select another date, if required.

System time

Defaults to the current time. If this needs to be changed, the up and down arrows are used.

Actual time

Defaults to the current time. If this needs to be changed, the up and down arrows are used.

Examined by

Typically, this shall be the Forensic Analyst assigned to the forensic case, and this is the default inserted in the box. If another of the Forensic Analysts undertakes any examination, then this shall be recorded using the 'Examined by' drop-down box and selecting the relevant Forensic Analyst or employee.

Date

Defaults to today's date. This uses a drop-down calendar to select another date, if required.

Time

The time the computer was examined.

Appendix 19—Noncomputer exhibit details

Exhibit reference

The Exhibit Reference number for the exhibit to be examined shall be selected from the drop-down box of all exhibits in the selected forensic case. The exhibit to be examined shall be selected from the list and the details are entered below.

Exhibit type

Enter the exhibit type (e.g. printer, scanner, smartphone, etc.).

Make

Enter the exhibit make.

Model

Enter the model of the exhibit.

Serial no

Enter the exhibit's serial number.

Notes

Notes on the exhibit.

Add photos

If there are any relevant photos of the exhibit to be added, they shall be attached to the exhibit by pressing the 'Photos' button.

Add document

If there are any relevant documents to be added, they shall be scanned in and the scanned image be attached to the relevant forensic case by pressing the 'Add Document' button.

Examined by

Typically, this shall be the Forensic Analyst assigned to the forensic case, and this is the default inserted in the box. If another of the Forensic Analysts undertakes any examination, then this shall be recorded using the 'Examined by' drop-down box and selecting the relevant Forensic Analyst or employee.

Date

Defaults to today's date. This uses a drop-down calendar to select another date, if required.

Time

The time the computer was examined.

Appendix 20—Hard disk details

Exhibit reference

The Exhibit Reference number for the exhibit to be examined shall be selected from the drop-down box of all exhibits in the selected forensic case. The exhibit to be examined shall be selected from the list and the details are entered below.

Disk ID

The hard disk in the forensic case examined shall be selected from the drop-down box of all hard disks in the selected forensic case. The hard disk to be examined shall be selected from the list and the details are entered below.
  This shall only list the disks in the forensic case.

Make

The maker of disk drive.

Model

The model of the disk drive.

Serial number

The disk drive serial number.

Size

The size of the disk in Gb.

Cylinders

The number of cylinders on the disk where possible (if relevant).

Sectors

The number of sectors on the disk where possible (if relevant).

Heads

The number of heads on the disk where possible (if relevant).

Jumper settings

The jumper setting (if relevant). This shall come from a drop-down and the options are as shown below:

- slave;
- master or single drive;
- cable select;
- master with a non-ATA-compatible slave;
- limit drive capacity; or
- other.

Image 1

Details of the first image of the evidence.

Note

It is assumed that only two copies of the image are taken and usually this requires two tools. If only one tool is used, then just this section shall be filled in.

Image method

The imaging method shall come from the dropdown where the imaging methods have been entered in the maintenance system process.

Operating system

The operating system for the acquisition box shall come from the dropdown where the operating systems have been entered in the maintenance system process.

Blocker used

Enter the details of the write blocker used.

Acquisition hash

The acquisition hash for the exhibit.

Verify hash

The verification hash for the exhibit.

Image 2

This is where the details of the second image of the evidence are recorded if second images are taken

Image method

The imaging method shall come from the dropdown where the imaging methods have been entered in the maintenance system process.

Operating system

The operating system for the acquisition box shall come from the dropdown where the imaging methods have been entered in the maintenance system process.

Blocker used

Enter the details of the write blocker used.

Acquisition hash

The acquisition hash for the exhibit.

Verify hash

The verification hash for the exhibit.

Notes

Any notes that the examiner needs to make or thinks appropriate are entered here.

Add photos

If there are any relevant photographs of the disk to be added, they shall be scanned or downloaded from a digital camera and then added to the forensic case by pressing the 'Add Photos' button and browsing to the selected file(s) in the folder. Click 'OK' and the photographs shall be attached to the forensic case file.

Add document

If there are any relevant documents to be added, they shall be scanned in then added to the forensic case by pressing the 'Add Document' button and browsing to the selected file(s) in the folder. Click 'OK' and the document shall be attached to the forensic case file.

Examiner

Typically, this shall be the Forensic Analyst assigned to the forensic case, and this is the default inserted in the box. If another of the Forensic Analysts undertakes any examination, then this shall be recorded using the 'Examined by' drop-down box and selecting the relevant Forensic Analyst.

Date

Defaults to today's date. This uses a drop-down calendar to select another date, if required.

Time

The time the computer was examined.

Appendix 21—Other media details

Exhibit reference

The Exhibit Reference number for the exhibit to be examined shall be selected from the drop-down box of all exhibits in the selected forensic case. The exhibit to be examined shall be selected from the list and the details are entered below.

Media type

The media type for the exhibit to be examined shall be selected from the drop-down box of all media types. If the media type is not present, the 'New' button is used to add a new media type using the screen as defined in Section 10.3.5.9.5.

Make

The make of the media.

Model

The model of the media.

Serial number

The media's serial number.

Size

The size of the media in Gb.

Image 1

Details of the first image of the evidence.

Note

It is assumed that only two copies of the image are taken and usually this requires two tools. If only one tool is used, then just this section shall be filled in.

Image method

The imaging method shall come from the dropdown where the imaging methods have been entered in the maintenance system process.

Operating system

The operating system for the acquisition box shall come from the dropdown where the imaging methods have been entered in the maintenance system process.

Blocker used

Enter the details of the write blocker used.

Acquisition hash

The acquisition hash for the exhibit.

Verify hash

The verification hash for the exhibit.

Image 2

This is where the details of the second image of the evidence are recorded if second images are taken.

Image method

The imaging method shall come from the dropdown where the imaging methods have been entered in the maintenance system process.

Operating system

The operating system for the acquisition box shall come from the dropdown where the imaging methods have been entered in the maintenance system process.

Blocker used

Enter the details of the write blocker used.

Acquisition hash

The acquisition hash for the exhibit.

Verify hash

The verification hash for the exhibit.

Notes

Any notes that the examiner needs to make or thinks appropriate are entered here

Add photos

If there are any relevant photographs of the media to be added, they shall be scanned or downloaded from a digital camera and then added to the forensic case by pressing the 'Add Photos' button and browsing to the selected file(s) in the folder. Click 'OK' and the photographs shall be attached to the forensic case file.

Add document

If there are any relevant documents to be added, they shall be scanned in and then added to the forensic case by pressing the 'Add Document' button and browsing to the selected file(s) in the folder. Click 'OK' and the document shall be attached to the forensic case file.

Examiner

Typically, this shall be the Forensic Analyst assigned to the forensic case, and this is the default inserted in the box. If another of the Forensic Analysts undertakes any examination, then this shall be recorded using the 'Examined by' drop-down box and selecting the relevant Forensic Analyst.

Date

Defaults to today's date. This uses a drop-down calendar to select another date, if required.

Time

The time the media was examined.

Appendix 22—Case work record details

Examination process and results

Whatever actions are taken by the Forensic Analyst on the forensic case they shall be entered here. The record shall be regularly saved to ensure that records of action are not lost.

Add photos

If there are any relevant photographs of the work undertaken to be added, they shall be scanned or downloaded from a digital camera and then added to the forensic case by pressing the 'Add Photos' button and browsing to the selected file(s) in the folder. Click 'OK' and the photographs shall be attached to the forensic case file.

Add document

If there are any relevant documents to be added, they shall be scanned in then added to the forensic case by pressing the 'Add Document' button and browsing to the selected file(s) in the folder. Click 'OK' and the document shall be attached to the forensic case file.

Examined by

Typically, this shall be the Forensic Analyst assigned to the forensic case, and this is the default inserted in the box. If another of the Forensic Analysts undertakes any examination, then this shall be recorded using the 'Examined by' drop-down box and selecting the relevant Forensic Analyst or employee.

Date

Defaults to today's date. This uses a drop-down calendar to select another date, if required.

Hours

This is the hours spent on the tasks being written up here. The hours spent shall be used for the billing process so shall accurately reflect actual time spent working on the forensic case.

Appendix 23—Updating case estimates

Cost

Date
The date of the estimate. This uses a drop-down calendar.

Misc.
Any costs that are not covered elsewhere, e.g. travel and subsistence, meetings, etc.

Hardware
The costs estimated for any hardware required for the forensic case. This shall include disks, tapes, caddies, additional hardware needed to image or interrogate or analyse the forensic case.

Analysis
The estimated costs for the Forensic Analysts running the forensic case.

Report
Cost for report production, e.g. print costs, binding, postage and packing, etc.

Total

This is the automatically calculated total of the other fields entered.

Case dates

Target date

The date that the client wants the results delivered by (i.e. the TRT). This uses a drop-down calendar.

Revised target date

Defaults to the existing target date (or today's date if there is no date yet entered), but if another date is required then it shall be inserted. This uses a drop-down calendar to change the date.

Authorised by

Typically, this shall be the Laboratory Manager, and this shall be recorded using the 'Examined by' drop-down box and selecting the Laboratory Manager or whoever authorised the revised target date.

Return date

This is the date that the evidence is actually returned to the client.

Add photos

If there are any relevant photographs of the exhibit being returned to be added, they shall be scanned or downloaded from a digital camera and then added to the forensic case by pressing the 'Add Photos' button and browsing to the selected file(s) in the folder. Click 'OK' and the photographs shall be attached to the forensic case file.

Add document

If there are any relevant documents to be added, they shall be scanned in then added to the forensic case by pressing the 'Add Document' button and browsing to the selected file(s) in the folder. Click 'OK' and the document shall be attached to the forensic case file.

Appendix 24—Create exhibit

Exhibit reference

The dropdown shall be used to determine the existing exhibits and when a new one is to be entered it shall be typed into the box and added to the forensic case.

Description

The description of the exhibit.

Created by

Typically, this shall be the Forensic Analyst assigned to the forensic case, and this is the default entered into the box. If another of the Forensic Analysts has created an exhibit, this shall be recorded using the 'Created by' drop-down box and selecting the relevant Forensic Analyst from the list.

Date

This defaults to today's date, but if another date is required then it shall be inserted. This uses a drop-down calendar to change the date.

Appendix 25—Case result

Defendant

The name of the defendant.

Court

The name of the court where they are to appear.

Date

The date that they are in court. This defaults to today's date, but if another date is required then it shall be inserted. This uses a drop-down calendar to change the date.

Court result

The result from the court from the dropdown—either 'guilty' or 'not guilty'.

Custodial sentence

The jail term in years, months and days.

Suspended sentence

The suspended term in years, months and days.

Community service

The community service in years, months and days.

Fine

The fine in the form of the relevant local currency converted to a common base currency.

Note

FCL uses GBP for all fines.

Notes

Any notes to do with the defendant shall be entered here.

Add statement

If there are any relevant statements to be added, they shall be scanned in then added to the forensic case by pressing the 'Add Statement' button and browsing to the selected file(s) in the folder. Click 'OK' and the statement shall be attached to the forensic case file.

Appendix 26—Case backup

Tape

If a tape backup of the forensic case is to be made then the tape button shall be checked.

Tape ID

The tape shall be selected from the drop-down list of tapes available for backup next to 'name'.

Date

This defaults to today's date, but if another date is required then it shall be inserted. This uses a drop-down calendar to change the date.

Disk

Disk ID

The disk shall be selected from the dropdown of disks available for backup next to 'name'.

Date

This defaults to today's date, but if another date is required then it shall be inserted. This uses a drop-down calendar to change the date.

Backup type

The backup type shall be chosen using the relevant radio button. This shall either be a backup of the:

- forensic case image; or
- worked forensic case.

Appendix 27—Billing and feedback

Charged

This defines who is to be billed for the forensic case by using the radio button choice.

Satisfaction

This defines who is to be sent the satisfaction survey for the forensic case by using the radio button choice.

Print

This button actually prints the hard copy bill and satisfaction survey for the identified recipient(s). This can be cancelled using the print facility in MS Word, if required.

Appendix 28—Feedback received

Communication

The feedback received from the client about the forensic case (marked 1–5 using the radio buttons).

Speed of delivery

The feedback received from the client about the forensic case (marked 1–5 using the radio buttons).

Quality of report

The feedback received from the client about the forensic case (marked 1–5 using the radio buttons).

Quality of results

The feedback received from the client about the forensic case (marked 1–5 using the radio buttons).

Timeliness of delivery

The feedback received from the client about the forensic case (marked 1–5 using the radio buttons).

Supporting material

The feedback received from the client about the forensic case (marked 1–5 using the radio buttons).

Understandability of report

The feedback received from the client about the forensic case (marked 1–5 using the radio buttons).

Meeting requirements

The feedback received from the client about the forensic case (marked 1–5 using the radio buttons).

Notes

Any notes or comments from the client to be associated with this feedback form.

Appendix 29—Organisation report

Paper type

Portrait.

Selection criteria

None.

Sort order

None.

Report header

- Title 'Organisation Details'—top left hand side; and
- Logo—top right hand side.

Report subheader

Here shall be three subheaders as defined below and in the contents:

- Organisation;
- Unit or Department; and
- Miscellaneous.

Report contents

Subheader—'Organisation'

- Organisation Name;
- Address;
- Postcode;
- Phone;

- Fax;
- URL;
- Vat No;
- Company Registration; and
- Organisation Logo.

Subheader—'Unit or Department'

- Unit or Department Name;
- Address;
- Postcode;
- Phone;
- Fax;
- Email address;
- URL; and
- Unit or Department Logo.

Subheader—'Miscellaneous'

- Report Classification;
- Case numbering information (Start Number);
- Copyright Notice;
- Hard Disk Numbering Start;
- Tape Numbering Start; and
- Other Media Numbering Start.

Appendix 30—Users report

Paper type

Portrait.

Selection criteria

Dropdown for user or '*' for all.

Sort order

Username.

Report header

- Title 'Users'—top left hand side; and
- Logo—top right hand side.

Report subheader

Username (repeated for each different user).

Report contents

- User ID;
- Title;
- First Name;

- Surname;
- Address;
- Postcode;
- Phone;
- Mobile;
- Fax;
- Email; and
- Access rights (User or Administrator).

Appendix 31—Manufacturers report

Paper type

Landscape.

Selection criteria

Dropdown for manufacturer or '*' for all.

Sort order

Manufacturer name.

Report header

- 'Manufacturers'—top left hand side; and
- Logo—top right hand side.

Report subheader

Manufacturer name (repeated for each different manufacturer).

Report contents

Multiple manufacturers on a page,

- Manufacturer Name;
- Address;
- Postcode;
- Phone;
- Fax;
- URL; and
- Email address.

Appendix 32—Supplier report

Paper type

Landscape.

Selection criteria

Dropdown for supplier or '*' for all.

Sort order

Supplier Name.

Report header

- 'Suppliers'—top left hand side; and
- Logo—top right hand side.

Report subheader

Supplier name (repeated for each different supplier).

Report contents

Multiple suppliers on a page:

- Supplier Name;
- Account Number;
- Address;
- Postcode;
- Phone;
- Fax;
- URL;
- Email address; and
- Contacts 1–5 (If no details in all—leave blank).

Appendix 33—Clients report

Paper type

Landscape.

Selection criteria

Dropdown for clients or '*' for all.

Sort order

Client Name.

Report header

- 'Clients'—top left hand side; and
- Logo—top right hand side.

Report subheader

- Client; and
- Cases.

Report contents

Client subheading

- Client Name;
- Address;
- Postcode;
- Phone;

- Fax;
- URL; and
- Email address.

Cases subheading

- Case Number(s); and
- Case Name(s).

Appendix 34—Investigators report

Paper type

Landscape.

Selection criteria

Dropdown for investigators or '*' for all.

Sort order

Investigator then forensic case.

Report header

- 'Investigators'—top left hand side; and
- Logo—top right hand side.

Report subheader

- Investigator Name; and
- Cases.

Report contents

Investigator subheading

- Investigator;
- Client Name;
- Address;
- Postcode;
- Phone;
- Fax;
- URL;
- Email address;
- Case Number(s); and
- Case Name(s).

Cases subheading

- Case Number(s); and
- Case Name(s).

Appendix 35—Disks by assignment report

Paper type

Portrait.

Selection criteria

None.

Sort order

Assignment order.

Report header

- 'Disks (By Assignment)'—top left hand side; and
- Logo—top right hand side.

Report subheader

None.

Report contents

- Assigned to;
- Date assigned;
- Serial number;
- Size (Gb);
- Supplier;
- Manufacturer;
- Model;
- Disk label; and
- Order number.

Appendix 36—Disks by reference number report

Paper type

Portrait.

Selection criteria

None.

Sort order

Disk Reference number.

Report header

- 'Disks (By Reference)'—top left hand side; and
- Logo—top right hand side.

Report subheader

None.

Report contents

- Disk label;
- Date assigned;
- Assigned to;
- Serial number;
- Size (Gb);
- Supplier;
- Manufacturer;
- Model; and
- Order number.

Appendix 37—Wiped disks report

Paper type

Landscape.

Selection criteria

Start date and end date. The 'start date' shall be the earliest date any action was taken on the system, the 'to date' shall be today's date. If dates are to be changed then the pop-up calendar shall be used.

Sort order

Date order and then disk reference.

Report header

- 'Disks wiped between "<Start Date>" and "<End Date>"'—top left hand side; and.
- Logo—top right hand side.

Report subheader

None.

Report contents

- Date wiped;
- Disk label;
- Wiping method;
- Serial number;
- Size (Gb);
- Supplier;
- Manufacturer;
- Model; and
- Order number.

Appendix 38—Disposed disks report

Paper type

Landscape.

Selection criteria

Start date and end date. The 'start date' shall be the earliest date any action was taken on the system, the 'to date' shall be today's date. If dates are to be changed then the pop-up calendar shall be used.

Sort order

Date order and then disk reference.

Report header

- 'Disks disposed of between "<Start Date>" and "<End Date>"'—top left hand side; and
- Logo—top right hand side.

Report subheader

None.

Report contents

- Date disposed of;
- Disk label;
- Disposal method;
- Serial number;
- Size (Gb);
- Supplier;
- Manufacturer;
- Model; and
- Order number.

Appendix 39—Disk history report

Paper type

Landscape.

Selection criteria

Dropdown for disk number or '*' for all;
    Start date and end date. The 'start date' shall be the earliest date any action was taken on the disk the 'to date' shall be today's date. If dates are to be changed then the pop-up calendar shall be used.

Sort order

Disk number then date order if multiple disks chosen. If a single disk, then in date order.

Report header

- 'Disk history between "<Start Date>" and "<End Date>"'—top left hand side; and
- Logo—top right hand side.

Report subheader

Disk reference.

Report contents

- Date of action;
- Assignment;
- Action by (including user status—user or administrator); and
- Tools or methods for action.

Appendix 40—Tapes by assignment report

Paper type

Portrait.

Selection criteria

None.

Sort order

Assignment Order.

Report header

- Title 'Tapes by Assignment'—top left hand side; and
- Logo—top right hand side.

Report subheader

None.

Report contents

- Assigned to;
- Date assigned;
- Serial number;
- Size;
- Supplier;
- Manufacturer;
- Model;
- Reference; and
- Order No.

Appendix 41—Tapes by reference number report

Paper type

Portrait.

Selection criteria

None.

Sort order

- Reference No.

Report header

- Title 'Tapes by Reference Number'—top left hand side; and
- Logo—top right hand side.

Report subheader

None.

Report contents

- Tape reference number;
- Date assigned;
- Assigned to;
- Size;
- Supplier;
- Manufacturer;
- Model;
- Reference;
- Supplier; and
- Order No.

Appendix 42—Wiped tapes report

Paper type

Landscape.

Selection criteria

Start date and end date. The 'start date' shall be the earliest date any action was taken on the system, the 'to date' shall be today's date. If dates are to be changed then the pop-up calendar shall be used.

Sort order

Date order and then tape reference.

Report header

- 'Tapes wiped between "<Start Date>" and "<End Date>"'—top left hand side; and
- Logo—top right hand side.

Report subheader

None.

Report contents

- Date wiped;
- Tape label;
- Wiping method;
- Size (Gb);
- Supplier;
- Manufacturer;
- Model; and
- Order number.

Appendix 43—Disposed tapes report

Paper type

Landscape.

Selection criteria

Start date and end date. The 'start date' shall be the earliest date any action was taken on the system, the 'to date' shall be today's date. If dates are to be changed then the pop-up calendar shall be used.

Sort order

Date order and then tape order.

Report header

- Title 'Tapes Disposed of between "<Start Date>" and "<End Date>"'—top left hand side; and
- Logo—top right hand side.

Report subheader

None.

Report contents

- Date disposed of;
- Tape reference;
- Disposal method;
- Disposed by; and
- Notes.

Appendix 44—Tape history report

Paper type

Landscape.

Selection criteria

Dropdown for tape number or '*' for all;

Start date and end date. The 'start date' shall be the earliest date any action was taken on the disk the 'to date' shall be today's date. If dates are to be changed then the pop-up calendar shall be used.

Report header

- Title 'Tape History between "<From Date>" and "<To Date>"'—top left hand side; and
- Logo—top right hand side.

Report subheader

Tape Reference.

Report contents

- Date of action;
- Assignment;
- Action by (including user status—user or administrator); and
- Tools or methods for action.

Appendix 45—Small digital media by assignment report

Paper type

Portrait.

Selection criteria

None.

Sort order

Assignment Order.

Report header

- Title 'Small Digital Media by Assignment'—top left hand side; and
- Logo—top right hand side.

Report subheader

None.

Report contents

- Assigned to;
- Date assigned;
- Media type;
- Serial number;
- Size;
- Supplier;
- Manufacturer;
- Model;
- Reference; and
- Order No.

Appendix 46—Small digital media by reference number report

Paper type

Portrait.

Selection criteria

None.

Sort order

- Reference No.

Report header

- Title 'Small Digital Media by Reference Number'—top left hand side; and
- Logo—top right hand side.

Report subheader

None.

Report contents

- Small digital media reference number;
- Date assigned;
- Assigned to;
- Size;
- Supplier;
- Manufacturer;
- Model;
- Reference;
- Supplier; and
- Order No.

Appendix 47—Wiped small digital media report

Paper type

Landscape.

Selection criteria

Start date and end date. The 'start date' shall be the earliest date any action was taken on the system, the 'to date' shall be today's date. If dates are to be changed then the pop-up calendar shall be used.

Sort order

Date order and then tape reference.

Report header

- 'Small Digital Media wiped between "<Start Date>" and "<End Date>"'—top left hand side; and
- Logo—top right hand side.

Report subheader

None.

Report contents

- Date wiped;
- Media type;
- Small digital media label;
- Wiping method;
- Size (Gb);
- Supplier;
- Manufacturer;
- Model; and
- Order number.

Appendix 48—Disposed small digital media report

Paper type

Landscape.

Selection criteria

Start date and end date. The 'start date' shall be the earliest date any action was taken on the system, the 'to date' shall be today's date. If dates are to be changed then the pop-up calendar shall be used.

Sort order

Date order and then small digital media order.

Report header

- Title 'Small Digital Media Disposed of between "<Start Date>" and "<End Date>"'—top left hand side; and
- Logo—top right hand side.

Report subheader

None.

Report contents

- Date disposed of;
- Small digital media reference;
- Disposal method;
- Disposed by; and
- Notes.

Appendix 49—Small digital media history report

Paper type

Landscape.

Selection criteria

Dropdown for small digital media number or '*' for all.

Start date and end date. The 'start date' shall be the earliest date any action was taken on the disk the 'to date' shall be today's date. If dates are to be changed then the pop-up calendar shall be used

Report header

- Title 'Small Digital Media History between "<From Date>" and "<To Date>"'—top left hand side and
- Logo—top right hand side

Report subheader

Small digital media reference.

Report contents

- Date of action;
- Assignment;
- Action by (including user status—user or administrator); and
- Tools or methods for action.

Appendix 50—Wipe methods report

Paper type

Portrait.

Selection criteria

None.

Sort order

Wipe method (alphabetical).

Report header

- Title 'Media Wiping Methods'—top left hand side; and
- Logo—top right hand side.

Report subheader

None.

Report contents

- Wiping method.

Appendix 51—Disposal methods report

Paper type

Portrait.

Selection criteria

None.

Sort order

Disposal method (alphabetical).

Report header

- Title 'Disk Disposal Methods'—top left hand side; and
- Logo—top right hand side.

Report subheader

None.

Report contents

- Disposal method.

Appendix 52—Imaging methods report

Paper type

Portrait,

Selection criteria

None.

Sort order

Imaging method (alphabetical),

Report header

- Title 'Imaging Methods'—top left hand side; and
- Logo—top right hand side.

Report subheader

None.

Report contents

- Imaging method.

Appendix 53—Operating systems report

Paper type

Portrait.

Selection criteria

None.

Sort order

Operating system (alphabetical).

Report header

- Title 'Operating Systems'—top left hand side; and
- Logo—top right hand side.

Report subheader

None.

Report contents

Operating systems.

Appendix 54—Media types report

Paper type

Portrait.

Selection criteria

None.

Sort order

Media types (alphabetical).

Report header

- Title 'Media Types Processed'—top left hand side; and
- Logo—top right hand side.

Report subheader

None.

Report contents

- Media Types.

Appendix 55—Exhibit type report

Paper type

Portrait.

Selection criteria

None.

Sort order

Exhibit types (alphabetical).

Report header

- Title 'Exhibit Types Produced'—top left hand side; and
- Logo—top right hand side.

Report subheader

None.

Report contents

- Exhibit Types.

Appendix 56—Forensic case setup details report

Paper type

Portrait.

Selection criteria

Dropdown for forensic case number or '*' for all.

Sort order

Case Number.

Report header

- Title 'Case Setup Details'—top left hand side; and
- Logo—top right hand side.

Report subheader

- Case No;
- Requirements; and
- Exhibits.

Report contents

Case number subheading (from forensic case setup menu)

- Case Name (left hand side);

- Case Number (right hand side);
- Client and address details (left hand side);
- Investigator and address details (right hand side); and
- Any documents scanned in.

Requirements subheading (from case requirements tab)

- Evidence Sought;
- Comments Case (one under another); and
- Any documents scanned in.

Exhibits subheading (from exhibits tab)

For Each Exhibit—it has the Exhibit number as a subsubheading then followed by the details about the exhibits in exhibit order (alphabetical). This shall include:

- Exhibit number;
- Seal Number;
- Description;
- Received by;
- Seized from;
- Received Date;
- Seized Date;
- Received Time;
- Time Seized;
- Insurance Value;
- Owner;
- Reason for Seizing;
- Password(s) Recovered—give them or 'None';
- Connected—give details or 'No';
- Switched on at Seizure—give details or 'No';
- Switched on After Seizure—give details or 'No'; and
- Any documents scanned in.

Appendix 57—Forensic case movement report

Paper type

Landscape.

Selection criteria

Dropdown for forensic case number or '*' for all.

Start date and end date. The 'start date' shall be the earliest date any action was taken on the system, the 'to date' shall be today's date. If dates are to be changed then the pop-up calendar shall be used.

Sort order

Case order then date (and time if used) within forensic case.

Report header

- Title 'Exhibit Movements between "<From date>" to "<To Date>"'—top left hand side; and
- Logo—top right hand side.

Report subheader

- Case number (Case Name).

Report contents

- Date of action;
- Exhibit ID;
- Laboratory Log ID number;
- Seal number;
- Movement type; and
- User who moved the exhibit.

Appendix 58—Forensic case computers report

Paper type

Portrait.

Sort order

Case Number then exhibit number.

Selection criteria

Dropdown for forensic case number or '*' for all.

Start date and end date. The 'start date' shall be the earliest date any computer was received by the laboratory, the 'to date' shall be today's date. If dates are to be changed then the pop-up calendar shall be used.

Report header

- Title 'Computer Exhibits Received Between "<From date>" to "<To Date>"'—top left hand side; and
- Logo—top right hand side.

Report subheader

- Case Details;
- Computer Details; and
- BIOS Details.

Report contents

Each computer is printed on a separate page.

Case details subheader

- Case name;
- Exhibit number;
- Examined by; and
- Examination Date.

Computer details subheader

- Make;
- Model;

- Serial No;
- 3½ drives;
- 5¼ drives;
- Zip drives;
- CD/DVD readers/writers;
- RAM strips;
- Jazz drives;
- Graphics cards;
- AIT drives;
- DLT drives;
- QIC drives;
- SCSI cards;
- Other disk drives;
- Modem cards;
- Network cards;
- Other peripherals that exist if they are relevant; and
- Notes.

BIOS details subheader

- BIOS Key;
- BIOS Password;
- System Time;
- System Date;
- Actual Time;
- Date Difference;
- Time Difference;
- Boot Sequence;
- Operating system;
- Any photographs attached; and
- Any documents scanned in.

Appendix 59—Forensic case noncomputer evidence report

Paper type

Portrait.

Sort order

Case Number then exhibit number.

Selection criteria

Dropdown for forensic case number or '*' for all.

Start date and end date. The 'start date' shall be the earliest date any computer was received by the laboratory, the 'to date' shall be today's date. If dates are to be changed then the pop-up calendar shall be used.

Report header

- Title 'Non Computer Exhibits Received Between "<From date>" to "<To Date>"'—top left hand side; and
- Logo—top right hand side.

Report subheader

- Case Details; and
- <Exhibit Type>

Report contents

Each noncomputer exhibit starts on a separate page.

Case details subheader

- Case name;
- Exhibit number;
- Examined by; and
- Examination Date.

<Exhibit type> subheader

- Make;
- Model;
- Serial No;
- Notes;
- Any photographs attached; and
- Any documents scanned in.

Appendix 60—Forensic case disks received report

Paper type

Portrait.

Selection criteria

Dropdown for forensic case number or '*' for all.

Start date and end date. The 'start date' shall be the earliest date any computer was received by the laboratory, the 'to date' shall be today's date. If dates are to be changed then the pop-up calendar shall be used.

Sort order

Case Number then Exhibit Number.

Report header

- Title 'Details for Disks Received Between "<From date>" to "<To Date>"'—top left hand side; and
- Logo—top right hand side.

Report subheader

- Case Number;
- Computer Details; and
- Disk Exhibit Number.

Report contents

Case details subheader

- Case name;
- Case ID;
- Examined by; and
- Examination Date.

Computer details subheader

- Make;
- Model; and
- Serial No;

Hard disk details subheader

- Make;
- Model;
- Serial No;
- Heads (if relevant);
- Cylinders (if relevant);
- Sectors (if relevant);
- Size; and
- Jumper setting (if relevant).

Image 1 subsubheader—With Image 1 in Big Print

- Imaging method used;
- Blocker used;
- Operating System;
- Acquisition Hash; and
- Verification Hash.

Image 2 subsubheader

- Imaging method used;
- Blocker used;
- Operating System;
- Acquisition Hash; and
- Verification Hash.

    If there is no second imaging method used then the fields shall be blank.

- Any photographs attached; and
- Any documents scanned in.

Appendix 61—Forensic case other media received

Paper type

Portrait.

Selection criteria

Dropdown for forensic case number or '*' for all.

    Start date and end date. The 'start date' shall be the earliest date any computer was received by the laboratory, the 'to date' shall be today's date. If dates are to be changed then the pop-up calendar shall be used.

Sort order

Case Number then Exhibit Number.

Report header

- Title 'Other Media Received Between "<From date>" to "<To Date>"'—top left hand side; and
- Logo—top right hand side.

Report subheader

- Case Number; and
- Disk Exhibit Number.

Report contents

Case details subheader

- Case name;
- Case ID;
- Examined by; and
- Examination Date.

Other media details subheader

- Make;
- Model; and
- Serial No.

Other media details subheader

- Make;
- Model; and
- Serial No.

Image 1 subsubheader—With Image 1 in Big Print

- Imaging method used;
- Blocker used;
- Operating System;
- Acquisition Hash; and
- Verification Hash.

Image 2 Subsubheader

- Imaging method used;
- Blocker used;
- Operating System;
- Acquisition Hash; and
- Verification Hash.

If there is no second imaging method used then the fields shall be blank.

- Any photographs attached; and
- Any documents scanned in.

Appendix 62—Forensic case exhibits received report

Paper type

Portrait.

Selection criteria

Dropdown for forensic case number or '*' for all.

Start date and end date. The 'start date' shall be the earliest date any computer was received by the laboratory, the 'to date' shall be today's date. If dates are to be changed then the pop-up calendar shall be used.

Sort order

Case number then exhibit order.

Report description

This is a printout of the evidence received for selected forensic cases received by the laboratory between two dates for examination.

Report header

- Title 'Exhibits Received Between "<From date>" to "<To Date>"'—top left hand side; and
- Logo—top right hand side.

Report subheader

None.

Report contents

- Case ID;
- Case name;
- Exhibit number;
- Description;
- Any photographs attached; and
- Any documents scanned in.

Appendix 63—Forensic case work record

Paper type

Portrait.

Selection criteria

Dropdown for forensic case number or '*' for all.

Start date and end date. The 'start date' shall be the earliest date any exhibit was produced in the laboratory, the 'to date' shall be today's date. If dates are to be changed then the pop-up calendar shall be used.

Sort order

Case number then date.

Report description

This is a printout of the work performed on a given forensic case or forensic cases between two dates.

Report header

- Title 'Work Performed Between "<From date>" to "<To Date>"'—top left hand side; and
- Logo—top right hand side.

Report subheader

- Case ID.

Report contents

- Case ID;
- Case name;
- Date;
- Work performed;
- Username; and
- Hours.

Appendix 64—Forensic cases rejected report

Paper type

Portrait.

Selection criteria

All forensic cases where the forensic case was rejected—i.e. where the 'Rejected' box is ticked.

Start date and end date. The 'start date' shall be the earliest date any forensic case was rejected and the 'to date' shall be today's date. If dates are to be changed then the pop-up calendar shall be used.

Sort order

Case no. order.

Report header

- Title 'Cases Rejected Between "<From Date>" and "<To Date>"'—top left hand side; and
- Logo—top right hand side.

Report subheader

None.

Report contents

- Case No;
- Date rejected;
- Rejected by;
- Date client Advised;
- Who was advised;

- How they were advised;
- Reasons for rejection—if this goes over a line on the report then the output shall go into multiple lines left aligned for the field; and
- Copy of any documents scanned in.

Appendix 65—Forensic cases accepted

Paper type

Portrait.

Selection criteria

All forensic cases where the forensic case was accepted—i.e. where the 'Accepted' box is ticked.

Start date and end date. The 'start date' shall be the earliest date any forensic case was rejected and the 'to date' shall be today's date. If dates are to be changed then the pop-up calendar shall be used.

Sort order

Case No. order.

Report header

- Title 'Cases Accepted Between "<From Date>" and "<To Date>"'—top left hand side; and
- Logo—top right hand side.

Report subheader

None.

Report contents

- Case No;
- Date accepted;
- Accepted by;
- Date client Advised;
- Who was advised;
- How they were advised; and
- Copy of any documents scanned in.

Appendix 66—Forensic case estimates report

Paper type

Portrait.

Selection criteria

Dropdown for forensic case number or '*' for all.

Start date and end date. The 'start date' shall be the earliest date any action was taken on the system, the 'to date' shall be today's date. If dates are to be changed then the pop-up calendar shall be used.

Sort order

By forensic case then by date.

Report header

- Title 'Case Estimates'—top left hand side; and
- Logo—top right hand side.

Report subheader

- Case No.

Report contents

- Date;
- Misc.;
- Hardware;
- Analysis;
- Report; and
- Total.

Appendix 67—Forensic cases by forensic analyst

Paper type

Portrait.

Selection criteria

Dropdown for Forensic Analyst or '*' for all.

Start date and end date. The 'start date' shall be the earliest date any exhibit was produced in the laboratory, the 'to date' shall be today's date. If dates are to be changed then the pop-up calendar shall be used.

Sort order

Forensic Analyst then date.

Report header

- Title 'Case Assignments Between "<From date>" to "<To Date>"'—top left hand side; and
- Logo—top right hand side.

Report subheader

- <Forensic Analyst>.

Report contents

- Case name;
- Case ID;
- Date started;
- Target Date;
- Days to Target Date (if past then printed in red); and
- Status.

Appendix 68—Forensic cases by client report

Paper type

Portrait.

Selection criteria

Dropdown for client or '*' for all.

Start date and end date. The 'start date' shall be the earliest date any exhibit was produced in the laboratory, the 'to date' shall be today's date. If dates are to be changed then the pop-up calendar shall be used.

Sort order

Client then date.

Report header

- Title 'Case Assignments Between "<From date>" to "<To Date>"'—top left hand side; and
- Logo—top right hand side.

Report subheader

- Client.

Report contents

- Case name;
- Case ID;
- Date started;
- Target Date;
- Days to Target Date (if past then printed in red); and
- Status.

Appendix 69—Forensic cases by investigator report

Paper type

Portrait.

Selection criteria

Dropdown for Investigator or '*' for all.

Start date and end date. The 'start date' shall be the earliest date any exhibit was produced in the laboratory, the 'to date' shall be today's date. If dates are to be changed then the pop-up calendar shall be used.

Sort order

Investigator then date.

Report description

This is a printout of the forensic cases that an Investigator has or is working between two dates.

Report header

- Title 'Case Assignments Between "<From date>" to "<To Date>"'—top left hand side; and
- Logo—top right hand side.

Report subheader

- Investigator.

Report contents

- Case name;
- Case ID;
- Date started;
- Target Date;
- Days to Target Date (Date if past then printed in red); and
- Status.

Appendix 70—Forensic case target dates report

Paper type

Portrait.

Selection criteria

Dropdown for forensic case number or '*' for all.
    This is only for forensic cases currently open.

Sort order

Case No.

Report header

- Title 'Case Target Dates'—top left hand side; and
- Logo—top right hand side.

Report subheader

None.

Report contents

- Case No;
- User assigned;
- Date Received;
- Target date; and
- Days remaining (if past then printed in red).

Appendix 71—Forensic cases within 'x' days of target date report

Paper type

Portrait.

Selection criteria

Entry field for number of days prior to target date for report.
    This is only for forensic cases currently open.

Sort order

By days closest to Target Date.

Report header

- Title 'Case Target Dates with "*<x>*" "Days or less to Target Date"'—top left hand side; and
- Logo—top right hand side.

Report subheader

None.

Report contents

- Case No;
- User assigned;
- Date Received;
- Target date; and
- Days remaining (if past then printed in red).

Appendix 72—Forensic cases past target date report

Paper type

Portrait.

Selection criteria

This is only for forensic cases currently open.

Sort order

By days past Target Date.

Report description

This is a printout of the forensic cases past target date.

Report header

- Title 'Cases Past Target Date'—top left hand side; and
- Logo—top right hand side.

Report subheader

None.

Report contents

- Case No;
- User assigned;
- Date Received;
- Target date; and
- Days past target date.

Appendix 73—Forensic cases unassigned report

Paper type

Portrait.

Selection criteria

Any forensic case that has not got a currently assigned Forensic Analyst.

Sort order

Case number.

Report header

- Title 'Cases Currently Unassigned'—top left hand side; and
- Logo—top right hand side.

Report subheader

None.

Report contents

- Case name;
- Case ID;
- Date started;
- Target Date; and
- Days to Target Date (if past then printed in red).

Appendix 74—Forensic case exhibits produced report

Paper type

Portrait.

Selection criteria

Dropdown for forensic case number or '*' for all.

Start date and end date. The 'start date' shall be the earliest date any exhibit was produced in the laboratory, the 'to date' shall be today's date. If dates are to be changed then the pop-up calendar shall be used.

Sort order

Case number then exhibits produced.

Report header

- Title 'Exhibits Created Between "<From date>" to "<To Date>"'—top left hand side; and
- Logo—top right hand side.

Report subheader

- Case details; and
- Exhibit details.

Report contents

Case details subheader

- Case name; and
- Case ID;

Exhibit details subheader

- Exhibit number;
- Description;
- Created by;
- Any photographs attached; and
- Any documents scanned in.

Appendix 75—Forensic case results report

Paper type

Portrait.

Selection criteria

Dropdown for forensic case number or '*' for all.

Start date and end date. The 'start date' shall be the earliest date any exhibit was produced in the laboratory, the 'to date' shall be today's date. If dates are to be changed then the pop-up calendar shall be used.

Sort order

Case then Date.

Report header

- Title 'Case Results "<From date>" to "<To Date>"'—top left hand side; and
- Logo—top right hand side.

Report subheader

- Case ID; and
- Defendant(s).

Report contents

Case ID subheader

- Case name; and
- Case ID.

Defendant ID subheader

- Defendant;
- Date;
- Court;
- Jail;
- Suspended;

- Community Service;
- Fine; and
- Notes.

Appendix 76—Forensic case backups report

Paper type

Portrait.

Selection criteria

Dropdown for Case ID or '*' for all.

    Start date and end date. The 'start date' shall be the earliest date any exhibit was produced in the laboratory, the 'to date' shall be today's date. If dates are to be changed then the pop-up calendar shall be used.

Sort order

Case number order.

Report header

- Title 'Case Backups Between "<From date>" to "<To Date>"'—top left hand side; and
- Logo—top right hand side.

Report subheader

- Case ID; and
- Backups.

Report contents

Case ID subheader

- Case name; and
- Case ID.

Backups subheader

- Date;
- Backup media type (disk or tape);
- Media name (disk or type ID); and
- Backup Type (Image or Case).

Appendix 77—Forensic case billing run report

Paper type

Portrait.

Selection criteria

Dropdown for forensic case or '*' for all.

    The details recorded for the billing run shall be those from the last work billed.

    Billing date is defaulted to today's date but if dates are to be changed then the pop-up calendar shall be used. This means that the bills produced shall cover from last unbilled information to the billing date.

Sort order

None.

Report header

- Title 'Work Performed Between "<From date>" and "<To Date>"'—top left hand side; and
- Logo—top right hand side.

Report subheader

- Case ID—Case Name.

Report contents

- Date;
- Work performed;
- Username; and
- Hours.

Appendix 78—Forensic case feedback letters

Paper type

Portrait.

Selection criteria

Dropdown for forensic case number or '*' for all.

Start date and end date. The 'start date' shall be the earliest date any action was taken on the system, the 'to date' shall be today's date. If dates are to be changed then the pop-up calendar shall be used.

The forensic case shall be closed to have a feedback letter sent. This is determined by having something in the 'Court Result' filed in the 'Results' tab. If there are no letters to send out, then a message to this effect is displayed on screen rather than the page counter.

Sort order

Case No. order.

Report description

This shall be a letter asking for feedback on a given forensic case or forensic cases.

Report header

- Title 'Case Feedback Form'; and
- Logo—top right hand side.

Report subheader

None.

Report contents

- The Letter (template attached);
- The Form;

- The letter shall contain input from the following fields:
- FCL Address;
- System Date;
- Investigator Name;
- Investigator Address;
- Case name; and
- FCL reference number.

Appendix 79—Forensic case feedback forms printout

Paper type

Portrait.

Selection criteria

Dropdown for forensic case number or '*' for all.

Start date and end date. The 'start date' shall be the earliest date any action was taken on the system, the 'to date' shall be today's date. If dates are to be changed then the pop-up calendar shall be used.

Report contents

- The two pages of scanned feedback form.

Report header

- N/A.

Report footer

- N/A.

Report order

Case order.

Appendix 80—Forensic case feedback reporting summary by case

Paper type

Landscape

Selection criteria

Dropdown for forensic case number or '*' for all.

Start date and end date. The 'start date' shall be the earliest date any action was taken on the system, the 'to date' shall be today's date. If dates are to be changed then the pop-up calendar shall be used.

Sort order

Case No.

Report header

- Title 'Case Feedback Summary'; and
- Logo—top right hand side.

Report subheader

None.

Report contents

- Case No.;
- User that the forensic case is assigned to currently;
- client;
- Communication score;
- Speed Score;
- Quality Score;
- Timeliness score;
- Accompanying Material score;
- Understandability score; and
- Meeting Requirements score.

Appendix 81—Forensic case feedback reporting summary by forensic analyst

Paper type

Landscape.

Selection criteria

Dropdown for user or '*' for all.

Start date and end date. The 'start date' shall be the earliest date any action was taken on the system, the 'to date' shall be today's date. If dates are to be changed then the pop-up calendar shall be used.

Sort order

User then Case No.

Report description

This shall be a report showing feedback received for forensic cases by Case No. for each Forensic Analyst between two dates.

Report header

- Title 'Case Feedback Summary by Forensic Analyst'; and
- Logo—top right hand side.

Report subheader

Forensic Analysts name (Converted from User ID).

Report contents

Case No.;

- Client;
- Communication score;
- Speed Score;
- Quality Score;
- Timeliness score;

- Accompanying Material score;
- Understandability score; and.
- Meeting Requirements score.

Appendix 82—Forensic case feedback reporting summary by client

Paper type

Landscape.

Selection criteria

Dropdown for a client or '*' for all.

Start date and end date. The 'start date' shall be the earliest date any action was taken on the system, the 'to date' shall be today's date. If dates are to be changed then the pop-up calendar shall be used.

Sort order

client then Case No.

Report header

- Title 'Case Feedback Summary'; and
- Logo—top right hand side.

Report subheader

- Client name.

Report contents

- Case No.;
- User forensic case is assigned to currently;
- Communication score;
- Speed Score;
- Quality Score;
- Timeliness score;
- Accompanying Material score;
- Understandability score; and
- Meeting Requirements score.

Appendix 83—Complete forensic case report

Paper type

Portrait and portrait where appropriate.

Selection criteria

Dropdown for Case ID or '*' for all.

Report description

This is a printout of the complete forensic case.

It shall be made up of previous reports that are defined above.

Report header

- Title 'Complete Case Report for "<Case ID>"'—top left hand side; and
- Logo—top right hand side.

Report subheader

- Each of the titles of the previous reports with their subheaders included.

Report contents

The contents of the following reports (already defined in the text)

- Case requirements;
- Case movements;
- Computer details;
- Other media details;
- Disk details;
- Other media details;
- Work record;
- Exhibits produced;
- Case results;
- Case feedback; and
- Case backups.

Appendix 84—Items processed report

Paper type

Portrait.

Selection criteria

Dropdown for Examiner or '*' for all.

Start date and end date. The 'start date' shall be the earliest date for the media processed in the laboratory, the 'to date' shall be today's date. If dates are to be changed then the pop-up calendar shall be used.

Report header

- Title 'Work Performed Between "<From date>" to "<To Date>"'—top left hand side; and
- Logo—top right hand side.

Report subheader

- Exhibits processed;
- Media processed;
- Hours worked; and
- Court results.

Report contents

Exhibits processed subheader
- List of exhibits.

Media processed subheader
- Disks; and
- Other media.

Hours worked subheader
- Hours worked.

Court results subheader
Court results.

Appendix 85—Insurance report

Paper type

Portrait.

Selection criteria

None.

Sort order

Case number then evidence number.

Report header

- Title 'Insurance Listing for Exhibits'—top left hand side; and
- Logo—top right hand side.

Report contents

- Case name;
- Case ID;
- Exhibit number;
- Description;
- Value. and
- Automatic total of values.

Report order

Exhibit order within forensic cases.

Chapter 11

Forensic case evidence presentation

11.1 Overview

Note

This is not an attempt at providing legal guidance, but the experiences that the authors have had in testimony in Courts of Law and Tribunals. This is purely as seen from the author's view of presentation of evidence, reports, and testimony and studiously attempts to avoid any legal issues as these are left to the Lawyers in the Legal Team on any forensic case.

After completing the processing of a forensic case, the Forensic Analyst will have to present their findings to the client. This is usually in the form of a report but can require attendance in a Court of Law or Tribunal.

The Forensic Analyst may, depending on their qualifications and the jurisdiction, be regarded as an 'Expert Witness'.

Other employees may have to give evidence if they have been involved in the case (e.g. a First Responder, the Imager, and the Forensic Analyst undertaking the analysis of the evidence if they are different people, and possibly the Laboratory Manager to testify about tool validation).

It is essential that the processing of a forensic case is not let down by the evidence presentation.

Whatever presentation is required by the client, it shall be based on sound (and best) evidence, as defined in Chapter 8, Section 8.2, Chapter 9, Sections 9.1.5 and 9.10.4. This is why it is essential to ensure that all actions regarding the evidence are recorded and the Forensic Analysts are competent.

All Forensic Analysts shall be taught to believe that credibility is believability and that FCL's reputation depends on this so they shall all be competent in presenting their testimony.

11.2 Notes

During forensic case processing, all those involved in the processing the forensic case will make a number of notes, these can include, but not be limited to:

- draft report outlines;
- drawings;
- filling in checklists;
- filling in forms;
- personal notebooks (contemporaneous notes);
- photographs; and
- sketches.

Notes are made for a variety of different reasons. Some examples of the different types of notes and their selected audiences are given below.

11.2.1 Notes for the forensic analyst

These are typically notes made by a Forensic Analyst that record their own actions during processing a forensic case. These are made contemporaneously and shall be used to provide records of actions, as defined in Chapter 4, Section 4.7.5. These are primarily used by the Forensic Analyst as the basis for writing reports, statements, and depositions, as they record actions taken at the time. They are also used for refreshing memory, and where permitted, when giving testimony or at meetings with other Forensic Experts as part of the forensic case.

11.2.2 Notes for colleagues

These are the same as those for the Forensic Analyst, but their purpose is different. These notes are there so that any report produced by the Forensic Analyst can be peer reviewed by other employees or external Forensic Experts/Expert Witnesses to ensure that the opinions given or conclusions reached are sound and based on the processing of the case. These are also used if a new Forensic Analyst needs to take over processing a case where the original Forensic Analyst is not available for any reason.

11.2.3 Notes for the case

These are the same as those for the Forensic Analyst, but their purpose is different. These are to record the actions taken by the Forensic Analyst so that the 'other side' can see what actions were taken and be able to repeat the actions and produce the same results. It is also necessary for all involved in the case to understand why any opinions are formed or conclusions were reached. It also allows anyone involved in the forensic case to see exactly what actions were taken and also what actions were omitted.

11.2.4 Note taking

The taking of notes in forensic case processing is a personal matter for the Forensic Analyst, but within the structure set by the procedures, notes shall:

- be available to back up any reports, statements or depositions made as well as opinions made or conclusions reached;
- be made contemporaneously;
- be signed and dated by the employee making them; and
- be readable.

These notes are there so that any report produced can be backed up by contemporaneous notes.

11.3 Evidence

The rules for admissibility of evidence are governed by the laws of the jurisdiction of the Court of Law or Tribunal where the evidence is to be introduced. For this reason, amongst others, it is essential that all employees connected to a forensic case are fully familiar with these requirements and comply with them.

The rules are typically defined as 'The Rules of Evidence' for the jurisdiction. These vary between jurisdictions and types of Court of Law or Tribunal.

11.3.1 Rules of evidence

The Rules of Evidence will vary with the jurisdiction and as such, only generic advice can be given here. There are, however, some widely accepted standards and norms that are used, for example, the Daubert standard which is a rule of evidence regarding the admissibility of an Expert Witnesses' testimony during US federal legal proceedings, as defined in Chapter 1, Section 1.1.6. The Daubert standard looks at the scientific 'soundness' of the processes and procedures that have been used in the case to determine whether they are acceptable.

Some different Rules of Evidence include:

- Australia—Federal Court Rules;
- UK—Criminal Procedure Rules (2020);
- UK—Civil Evidence Act (1995)—specifically S 8 and 9;
- UK Civil Procedure Rules; and
- USA—Federal Rules of Evidence (FRE)—specifically Article V11, Sections 701–706.

It is of note that in the USA there are the FRE, but many States have adopted their own sets of rules, some of which differ from, and some of which are identical to, the FRE.

The Rules of Evidence cover such matters as:

- basis of opinion testimony;
- contents of reports;

- Court powers over Experts;
- different types of Expert and their duties;
- disclosure;
- discussion between Experts;
- qualifications of Experts; and
- testimony.

11.3.2 Authenticity of evidence

In general terms, all evidence presented for a forensic case shall be authenticated, which typically means that a Witness testifies to its authenticity either in the form of a statement or deposition and/or by giving oral testimony. This could be from:

- the First Responder, who seized it;
- the Evidence Custodian, who logged it in and out;
- the Forensic Analyst that imaged it;
- the Forensic Analyst that analysed it;
- anyone else that was involved in the 'Chain of Custody' or processing the forensic case, including the owner of the seized equipment or data.

In some cases, it is not necessary to authenticate evidence as it is accepted as being authentic according to the Rules of Evidence in force for the jurisdiction or both sides agree to accept it as authentic. It will vary between jurisdictions as to what is accepted without the need for authentication through testimony.

It is essential when preparing for any Court of Law or Tribunal hearing that the relevant Witnesses are able to testify to the existence and validity of the evidence produced, describe how it was discovered, maintain its 'Chain of Custody', and verify that it has not been tampered with or contaminated.

11.3.3 Evidence handling

Different jurisdictions have different requirements for digital evidence handling procedures. In Europe, the Budapest Convention on Cybercrime was the first international treaty seeking to address computer crime and Internet crimes by harmonising national laws, improving investigative techniques, and increasing cooperation amongst nations. This has met with success and whilst it is a European initiative, a number of other nations have ratified it, and as at the time of writing, these are defined in Appendix 1.

11.3.4 Admissibility of evidence

Again, this will depend on the jurisdiction and the Court of Law or Tribunal and so it is essential that FCL understands these requirements and complies with them.

They generally include the requirements for the evidence to be:

- **credible**—believable within the confines of the case;
- **material**—it substantiates an issue that may be in question relating to the case;
- **obtained legally**—the issue of fruits of the poisonous tree is defined in Chapter 8, Section 8.1.2.;
- **relevant**—proving a point in the case; and
- **reliable**—showing that the source of the evidence makes it reliable, including ensuring the Chain of custody;

Whilst the Rules of Evidence vary in different jurisdictions, FCL shall always strive to, not only meet the requirements but exceed them. This approach reduces the chance of any evidence being ruled as 'inadmissible' and also demonstrates professional competence. As defined in Chapter 9, Section 9.1.5, FCL shall meet the requirements of ACPO, IASIS, G8, and IOCE.

Evidence derived from the original evidence seized or supplied (e.g. a printout, display, or product of the imaging and analysis) that becomes an exhibit, as defined in Chapter 9, Section 9.14, shall also have a 'Chain of Custody' associated with it. The Forensic Analyst that produces it in the Court of Law or Tribunal shall formally produce the exhibit and give testimony to support its admissibility.

Depending on the jurisdiction, 'hearsay' evidence may be admitted, but care shall be taken with this.

11.3.5 Types of evidence

There are a number of different types of evidence that can be produced at a Court of Law or Tribunal and the Rules of Evidence apply to them all. FCL shall ensure that it knows the Rules of Evidence for them all and complies with them for the jurisdiction. Types of evidence from processing a forensic case can include, but are not limited to:

- **derived**—a representation of 'Best Evidence' that can be used to illustrate how opinions may be derived and conclusions drawn. This can use number of different media and shall meet the Rules of Evidence in the jurisdiction. Some examples are defined in Section 3.1.
- **documents**—a business record that can be authenticated and produced in admissible evidence;
- **evidentiary**—statements of fact from an employee who has been involved in a forensic case, but is not an Expert Witness;
- **expert**—opinions and conclusions of an Expert Witness;
- **real**—an actual physical piece of evidence that can be produced and examined in the Court of Law or Tribunal, typically 'Best Evidence'; and
- **testimony**—the contemporaneous recollections of a Witness to some action that is relevant to the case;

11.3.6 Weight of evidence

Once the admissibility of evidence has been addressed, its weight can be considered. Weight of evidence relates to the value that the evidence brings to the case, and it is accepted that this is a subjective measure, especially when dealing with a Jury.

The relevant attributes of evidence include, but are not limited to:

- **accurate**—based on facts that are demonstrable, including forensic case processing procedures that are explainable by an employee. This may also require details of the validation of the methods or tools used, as defined in Chapter 7, Section 7.5.5;
- **authenticity**—specifically linked to the case; and
- **complete**—in as much as it tells the complete 'history' of an item of evidence.

11.3.7 Evidential continuity

This is also known as the 'Chain of Custody' and has been defined in Chapter 8, Section 8.6.4. It is essential that FCL shall be able to accurately state everything that has happened to the exhibit from its original acquisition to it being exhibited in the Court of Law or Tribunal, and who was accountable and responsible for it during that time. This shall entail statements, checklists, pocketbooks, photographs, etc., from, as appropriate:

- the First Responder seizing it;
- the First Responder taking pictures of, and sketching, the incident scene;
- the on-site Exhibit Custodian;
- the First Responder transporting it back to the Secure Property Store;
- the Evidence Custodian at the Secure Property Store signing the exhibit(s) in and out;
- the Forensic Analyst(s) carrying out the initial examination;
- the Forensic Analyst(s) performing the imaging;
- the Forensic Analyst(s) undertaking the first stage examination;
- the Forensic Analyst(s) undertaking the second stage and subsequent examinations;
- the Forensic Analyst(s) conveying the exhibit(s) to the Court or Tribunal;
- the Evidence Custodian at the Court of Law or Tribunal who safely stores it;
- the Forensic Analyst(s) who create exhibits derived from the original evidence, as defined in Chapter 10, Section 10.4; and
- any other person who has had custody of the exhibit or handled it for any reason or even the Forensic Analyst who validated the tool or method as defined in Chapter 7, Section 7.5.5.

The whole 'Chain of Custody' process is designed to ensure the integrity of the evidence and reduce the opportunity of contamination.

11.3.8 Issues with digital evidence

There are different issues with digital evidence to other types of physical evidence that are encountered when processing a forensic case. Issues relating to evidence volatility have been covered in Chapter 8, Section 8.6.18.2. Other challenges facing the Forensic Analysts processing cases for their clients are defined in Chapter 20.

11.4 Types of witness

In whatever way the Forensic Analyst has to present the evidence from processing a forensic case, the physical and intangible evidence shall be supported by some testimony, whether it is written or oral.

All forensic cases handled by FCL shall always be regarded as a possible criminal case and the relevant rules for criminal evidence production shall be followed.

Note

A Forensic Analyst may be an Evidentiary Witness or an Expert Witness, depending on the client's requirements and the Court of Law or Tribunal's acceptance of the evidence.

11.4.1 An evidentiary witness

An 'Evidentiary Witness' (depending on the jurisdiction) is someone who has direct knowledge of a forensic case processed by FCL. Evidentiary Witnesses can only report on, or testify, to what they saw, heard, or did (i.e. facts). They are often referred to as Witnesses of Fact. They cannot give authoritative opinions or draw conclusions from what they observed or did (e.g. a Forensic Analyst who only imaged a disk cannot give an opinion on the evidence contained on it, only how the imaging was done and the image was verified).

In some jurisdictions, this is called a 'Non Testifying Expert Consultant', but advice shall be taken to ascertain the status of all claimed Experts within the jurisdiction.

11.4.2 An expert witness

An 'Expert Witness' is different from an Evidentiary Witness in that they can give opinions or draw conclusions about a forensic case processed by FCL. The interesting thing about an Expert Witness is that they may have had no involvement in the processing of the forensic case but they have a special technical expertise or knowledge that qualifies them to draw conclusions or give opinions on technical matters. Often, an Expert Witness can prepare a report on their opinions and conclusions, giving reasons for those opinions and conclusions.

An Expert Witness can be an employee (typically the Forensic Analyst processing the case) or may be an external Expert Witness chosen specifically for the case, as defined in Chapter 9, Section 9.10.6.

Where an external Expert Witness is to be selected, careful consideration of their suitability shall be undertaken, some guidance is defined in Appendix 2 for the selection of an external Expert Witness. Obviously, the same standards will apply, as appropriate, to employees that perform an Expert Witness role.

Within FCL, a code of conduct for employees acting as Expert Witnesses has been developed and has been implemented and this is defined in Appendix 3.

Note

Within some jurisdictions, an Expert Witness can act as an Advocate and in others this is not permitted. A thorough understanding of the legislative and procedural requirements of the jurisdiction is essential and shall be complied with.

11.4.3 Single joint expert witnesses

In some cases, a Single Joint Expert Witness may be appointed. A Single Joint Expert Witness represents both parties, rather than each party having their own appointed Expert Witness(es). A Single Joint Expert Witness shall show transparency and fairness to both or all, parties that they represent.

11.4.4 Court appointed expert witnesses

In some cases, a Judge will direct an Expert Witness to act for the parties. Typically, the Expert Witness will be drawn from a list of suitable candidates. The reasons for this vary but may include situations where the party's Expert Witnesses are in dispute and a single authoritative view is required of the interpretation of the evidence.

11.4.5 Experts not acting as expert witnesses

There are times that a Forensic Analyst, or other employee, may be required to act as an expert, but not act as an Expert or Evidentiary Witness. In these cases, they are asked to perform tasks such as explaining technical aspects of a case in plain language, reviewing statements and evidence presented to identify any anomalies, and suggest questions relating to them. In situations like this, the expert is used more as a Consultant and, as they never provide sworn evidence, are generally unknown to a Court of Law or Tribunal.

In other cases, the Expert may be present in a Court of Law or Tribunal and provide information on the evidence that a Witness provides as part of their testimony or suggest questions that may be asked as part of the cross-examination process, but not give formal testimony.

11.4.6 Over-riding duty

The over-riding duty of an Expert Witness is to assist the Court of Law or Tribunal in the interpretation of the evidence and not the party that pays or instructs them.

11.4.7 Codes of conduct for expert witnesses

Different jurisdictions will have different requirements for their Expert Witnesses, and typically professional bodies for Expert Witnesses will have their own Codes of Conduct. However, these are not always consistent and not directly relevant to the presentation of digital evidence. The FCL Code of Conduct has been developed and shall be applied to any employee giving evidence, in any form.

11.4.8 Code of conduct for evidentiary witnesses

The Code of Practice for Expert Witnesses, referred to above, is also applied to Evidentiary Witnesses apart from those parts not relevant (i.e. giving opinions and drawing conclusions).

11.4.9 Different jurisdictions

Different jurisdictions will treat all types of Witnesses in accordance with their own Rules of Evidence and procedures and any Witness shall be aware of these requirements before giving evidence.

11.5 Reports

11.5.1 General

The writing of the report is one of the most important tasks that is undertaken in FCL. This may seem a strong statement to make, but in reality, the quality of the reports that are produced by FCL and its Forensic Analysts are not only the 'shop window' to the work that is done but are also fundamental in representing all of the forensic processing that has taken place in the forensic case. The report represents a written statement of the findings of the Forensic Analyst(s) processing the forensic case.

The process for producing a report is defined Chapter 4, Section 4.7.5 and for external reports is defined in Chapter 9, Section 9.15 with a standard template for report production defined in Chapter 6, Appendix 28. Different jurisdictions may have specific requirements for report production and these shall be understood and met.

Whatever the specific requirements for report production, a good report shall be clear, well organised, concise, and accurate, it shall be:

- **admissible**—the report shall be written in the format that may be prescribed within the jurisdiction or shall follow good practice;
- **concise**—the report shall tell the complete story in as few words as possible. After preparing the first draft of the report, it will be revised, probably a number of times, to eliminate redundant or unnecessary material and add additional findings. This process is defined in Chapter 4, Section 4.7.5.4.3;

- **accurate**—the report shall clearly record or reference all of the relevant findings and observations. Information obtained during forensic case processing shall be validated through the use of as many sources as are necessary. All of the material presented in the report shall be able to be substantiated from the evidence available. The report shall not contain any opinions or views of the Forensic Analyst, unless they are acting as an Expert Witness for the case and recognised as such by the Court of Law or Tribunal;
- **understandable**—the report shall be understandable to decision-makers and as far as possible, written in terms that are easily understood;
- **complete**—the report shall contain all of the information required to explain any opinions given or conclusions reached, as appropriate. This means that it should include exculpatory material as well as the inculpatory;
- **believable**—the report shall be believable to the intended audience. This means that not only does it have to be written in language that can be understood by the audience, but also that there shall be an adequate level of explanation and detail for the audience to be able to believe the material presented.

FCL shall produce reports that meet the requirements of ISO/IEC 17025, as defined in Chapter 6, Appendix 27, though it shall be able to meet any report production requirements for the jurisdiction as required by the Court of Law or tribunal and the relevant Rules of Evidence.

The main purpose of a report is to assist the Court of Law or Tribunal in evaluating the admissibility, and weight, of any evidence found on the digital devices and media that were examined for the case by FCL.

11.5.2 Audience identification

Note

A report should 'stand on its own' in as much as it contains all the relevant information regarding the subject so that no external resources need to be referenced.

Fundamental to the production of any report is an understanding of the purpose for which it is to be written and the audience for whom it is intended. For a Forensic Analyst, it is very easy to produce a technically detailed and very complete report that will be unusable for the audience for whom it is intended. This is not advocating that the technical detail should not be included, but it may well be that the most suitable place for this is in the Appendices with the main body of the report being in plain language that the layperson can understand it. Reports that are to be viewed by a Jury shall be 'Jury friendly' and not open to misinterpretation.

By identifying the intended audience from the start, the report shall be written and structured in the most suitable manner.

The document review process defined in Chapter 4, Section 4.7.5.4.3, Chapter 6, Section 6.8, and Chapter 9, Section 9.15 for all reports ensures that a proper peer review process has taken place and this shall ensure that the report is 'fit for purpose'.

11.5.3 Types of report

There are five main types of report that are likely to be produced by a Forensic Analyst in FCL. Three of these report types are similar in the processes that are involved, but differ in the legal restrictions, the type of digital evidence, and the structure of the report. The main types of report are:

11.5.3.1 Forensic reports for criminal cases

This is probably the oldest and best known of the reports and comes under the remit of Law Enforcement (or agents and agencies working on their behalf). Forensic reports for criminal cases are normally intended to facilitate an investigation and to be entered as evidence before the Court of Law. It is important that these reports use simple terms that the layperson will be able to understand. Either the relevant Rules of Evidence or the client shall define the specific reporting requirements.

11.5.3.2 Electronic discovery or eDiscovery

This type of report is similar to the forensic report for a criminal case but relates to civil litigation. The processes are exactly the same as for criminal cases, but there are legal limitations and restrictions such as the scope of the investigation, human rights and privacy, which relate to eDiscovery. Either the relevant Rules of Evidence or the client shall define the specific reporting requirements.

11.5.3.3 Industrial disciplinary tribunals

This type of report is again similar to the forensic report for a criminal case but relates to the relevant rules, policies, and procedures within an organisation. This type of report is produced for internal disciplinary proceedings to deal with inappropriate activity by employees. Whilst they do not normally require the same level of detail as a criminal report, it shall be borne in mind that an investigation that starts off as a 'computer misuse' may discover evidence of criminal activity, so the same duty of care shall be taken in the handling of the evidence and preparation of the report. As has been stated in Chapter 8, Section 8.6.9, FCL shall always adopt this approach. Either the relevant Rules of Evidence or the client shall define the specific reporting requirements.

11.5.3.4 Intrusion investigations

This type of report is different from the previous three. An intrusion investigation report is produced as a result of a network intrusion which may have been a hacker trying to steal corporate information or access corporate resources. The aim of this report is to identify the entry point of the attack, the degree of and scope of the penetration, and to highlight the measures that can be taken to mitigate the effects of the attack. Again, this could result in a criminal trial, if the perpetrator can be identified, so the same duty of care shall be taken in the handling of the evidence and preparation of the report, as if it were a criminal case at the outset. Either the relevant Rules of Evidence or the client shall define the specific reporting requirements.

11.5.3.5 Intelligence gathering

This type of report is produced to provide intelligence to help track, stop, or identify illegal or unauthorised activity. This activity may be criminal in nature or nation sponsored espionage. This type of report does not require that the evidence has been collected in a forensically sound manner as it will normally not be taken to Court of Law or Tribunal. The aim of this report is to understand what has happened, what tools and techniques were used, and who may have been responsible.

11.5.3.6 Statements and depositions

Statements and depositions have been covered in Chapter 9, Section 9.16.

11.5.3.7 Report checklists

There is a report production checklist defined in Chapter 9, Appendix 31, and the procedures within FCL for document production are defined in Chapter 4, Section 4.7.5. However, the checklist that is used for all forensic reports produced by FCL is defined in Appendix 4, and for statements and depositions in Appendix 5.

11.5.4 Level of detail in reports

The level of detail that is included in the report will depend on the type of report and the intended audience. There are increasing constraints on the level of effort that can be invested in any forensic case, although of course this will vary with the importance and priority of the forensic case. With the increasing size of the storage media that is in use and the potential volume of information that is available, the report shall be written in a way that provides a complete picture of the evidence, but which provides detail on the relevant areas, otherwise reports will become larger and the relevant evidence will become obscured in irrelevant detail.

11.5.5 Duty of care

One of the issues that is often overlooked is that of ensuring the quality of the report itself. The report represents the efforts that FCL, and its Forensic Analysts, have made in all of the previous phases of processing the forensic case, and no matter how well they have been carried out, a poorly presented report may cause a forensic case to fail. The use of the report checklist, as defined in Chapter 9, Section 9.15.2 and the review of deliverables as defined in Chapter 6, Section 6.8 all go towards improving the quality of reports produced by FCL. Underlying this, reports shall meet the criteria defined in Section 11.5.1.

The process of continuous improvement as defined in Chapter 4, Section 4.10, eliciting feedback from clients as defined in Chapter 6, Appendix 20, and the handling of complaints as defined in Chapter 6, Section 6.14 ensures the quality of product realisation in FCL (i.e. the results of forensic case processing).

11.5.6 Duty to the client

The Forensic Analyst who produces the report shall fulfil their commitment to the duty of care by ensuring that the report meets the criteria defined by the client in the agreed proposal or other instruction documents as well as those defined in the relevant Rules of Evidence or similar.

The report shall meet the requirement that was specified in the tasking from the client.

11.5.7 Duty to the court of law or tribunal

The Forensic Analyst who produces the report has an over-riding duty to assist the Court of Law or Tribunal in the discovery of facts. This will be interpreted differently from jurisdiction to jurisdiction and shall also depend on the legal system in place, but the duty to the Court of Law or Tribunal is perhaps well summed up in the preamble to the Code of Ethics of the California Association of Criminalists which states that:

"It is the duty of any person practicing the profession of criminalistics to serve the interests of justice to the best of his ability at all times. In fulfilling this duty, he will use all of the scientific means at his command to ascertain all of the significant physical facts relative to the matters under investigation. Having made factual determinations, the criminalist shall then interpret and evaluate his findings. In this, he will be guided by experience and knowledge which, coupled with a serious consideration of his analytical findings and the application of sound judgment, may enable him to arrive at opinions and conclusions pertaining to the matters under study. These findings of fact and his conclusions and opinions should then be reported, with all the accuracy and skill of which the criminalist is capable, to the end that all may fully understand and be able to place the findings in their proper relationship to the problem at issue. In carrying out these functions, the criminalist will be guided by those practices and procedures which are generally recognised within the profession to be consistent with a high level of professional ethics. The motives, methods, and actions of the criminalist shall at all times be above reproach, in good taste, and consistent with proper moral conduct."

11.6 Testimony in court

Experience has shown that the majority of forensic cases are resolved prior to trial; however, a number of them require Forensic Analysts to testify in Court of Law or at a Tribunal. Presentation of case evidence can be an unnerving prospect and experience, and so FCL shall ensure that all of its employees that may be required to give evidence are appropriately trained and prepared.

11.6.1 Teamwork

When being presented in a Court of Law, it is important that the evidence presented is able to withstand cross-examination. For this to happen, the report shall meet the conditions given above, but also the person presenting it shall be experienced and fully aware of the contents of the report and the collection and analysis processes that were used to extract the facts. This requires the Forensic Analyst(s) that processed the forensic case and the client's Legal Team to work as a team so that poor presentation or understanding of the forensic case by the Legal Team does not undermine the work carried out by FCL and the Forensic Analyst(s) that processed the forensic case. If the Legal Team are not able to 'speak the same language' relating to the forensic case, it is essential that the Forensic Analyst(s) 'educate' the Legal Team so that they have a full understanding of all aspects of the forensic case, the evidence processed, the exhibits produced, the opinions given and the conclusions drawn as well as the reasons for them. The other side of this coin is that the Forensic Analyst(s) shall also understand how best to present their findings in the correct form of testimony in the Court of Law or Tribunal.

For these reasons, FCL shall try to ensure that the client's Legal Team and the Forensic Analyst(s) who processed the forensic case undertake joint training and so that the outcome of this is that they can work as an effective and efficient team.

11.6.2 Pretrial meetings

It is essential that prior to the trial itself, the client's Legal Team and the Forensic Analyst(s) shall have met an appropriate number of times to ensure that they both understand the requirements for presenting the forensic case effectively and undergoing cross-examination. The scope and limitations of the evidence produced shall also be clearly understood by the Legal Team as well as the Forensic Analyst(s).

Pretrial meetings shall also try to determine how the 'other side' will present their case and to have answers to questions that they are likely to raise. A good example of this is a child pornography case where the defence often used is that 'someone else put a Trojan Horse on my computer, and it downloaded these pictures'. The Forensic Analyst may state that their standard operating procedures ensure that two different antimalware products are run on acquired images to determine if any malware, including Trojan Horses, was found, as defined in Chapter 9, Section 9.10.1.3.

11.6.3 Reviewing case notes and reports

It is essential that the Forensic Analyst(s) going to testify in a Court of Law or Tribunal shall fully refresh their memory of all aspects of the forensic case, the evidence processed, the exhibits produced, the opinions given and the conclusions drawn as well as the reasons for them. A Forensic Analyst who has not done this can find themselves and the forensic case seriously disadvantaged.

11.6.4 First impressions count

To paraphrase Samuel Johnson, 'you never get a second chance to make a first impression'. Whilst this has little to do with the processing of a forensic case, the first impression that any Witness makes will affect their credibility. Unfair as this may seem, it is a part of human nature and so shall be understood and addressed.

First impressions to consider include, but are not limited to:

- **attitude**—a confident attitude is essential;
- **body language**—nonverbal communication can give a different impression to the actual words spoken;
- **clothing**—conservative dress is essential as it portrays confidence and trustworthiness, even if every day dress is jeans and a tee shirt;
- **entry**—entry into the Witness Box or stand should be confident without swaggering;
- **eye contact**—with the Judge and individual members, if present, of the Jury is essential. Looking someone in the eye portrays nonverbal communication which has been shown to indicate that the speaker is trustworthy, honest, and sincere. Those unable to look someone in the eye are often thought of as shifty and untrustworthy. Eye contact, or rather lack of it can also undermine the credibility of a Witness;
- **grooming**—is as important as clothing. A dishevelled Witness trying to claim that they processed a forensic case responsibly and followed the required procedures may be undermined by appearances;
- **spoken language**—testimony shall be in terms the Judge and Jury can understand without using complex technical jargon, multiple or repeated filler words; and
- **stance**—when giving testimony stood up, stance is important, especially if the testimony is to be 'given' to the Judge. Training in presentation for Court of Law or Tribunal etiquette shall be undertaken for all employees who shall give evidence;

The Witness giving testimony is trying to impress on the Judge and the Jury that they are responsible and credible, and the way in which they present themselves will say a lot about these qualities.

There are a number of nervous habits, gestures, and other nonverbal communications that can undermine the credibility of a Witness and distract the audience. Some of these, to be avoided at all costs, are defined in Appendix 6.

Whilst etiquette is often overlooked, and may these days be largely unwritten, there are often definite expected rules of etiquette in a Court of Law or Tribunal. Some of the most important points are defined in Appendix 7.

11.6.5 Being an effective witness

One of the most challenging aspects of presenting the report in a Court of Law or Tribunal is that the technical complexity of the material that is being presented will often far exceed the knowledge of the Judge or the Jury. Consideration shall be given to how complex computer terms can be explained in terms that can be understood. The Forensic Analyst presenting the report shall never forget that it is known for the defence, if they cannot undermine the confidence of the Court of Law or Tribunal in the report itself and the processes used to produce it, may attempt to undermine the credibility of the Witness presenting it.

There is no substitute for being well prepared for giving testimony in a Court of Law or Tribunal. Time spent in effective preparation is never wasted. Within FCL, the Laboratory Manager shall ensure that all Forensic Analysts who are going to give testimony are properly prepared and shall often attend pretrial meetings to review progress. Being unprepared is usually be seen as being unprofessional and can seriously undermine the credibility of the testimony and the Witness.

The Forensic Analyst(s) giving testimony will be required to provide details of their:

- educational qualifications;
- forensic certifications;
- training received that is relevant to the case;
- details of experience in similar cases; and
- details of previous testimony given.

One of the basic rules of testifying is to listen to the question carefully and give consideration to the response and then answer the question as fully as possible. A rushed answer can cause problems.

Another basic rule is to only answer the question asked and not volunteer any information that was not asked. This may seem obvious, but the more that is given to 'the other side' affords the possibility of more questions to be asked.

Whilst it can be frustrating when testifying and the 'other side' are able to make the Forensic Analyst lose their temper or become overly sarcastic the Forensic Analyst's credibility can be seriously damaged.

Any testimony given shall be unbiased, independent, based on facts and clearly presented. The weight of the testimony given depends on the credibility of the Witness.

11.6.6   Using visual aids

The old adage of 'a picture is worth a thousand words' really is true. Where necessary, and permitted by the Court of Law or Tribunal, consideration should be given to using visual aids to clarify and points that may be difficult for the Judge and/ or Jury to understand.

Some visual aids that can be used include, but are not limited to:

- animation;
- charts;
- diagrams;
- photographs; and
- sketches.

Linking testimony to a visual aid can create a lasting image of understanding the point being explained.

Live on-line demonstrations can be very effective so long as they work. It cannot be over-stressed that these shall be rehearsed so that any possible 'glitches' are overcome and there is a plan in place if any live demonstration does not work properly, as this can seriously undermine the credibility of the testimony.

As well as rehearsing any live demonstrations, ensure that there is adequate setup time in the Court of Law or Tribunal. This can include power, internet connections, and other relevant issues relating to the demonstration. Ensure that there is a sanitised forensic workstation being used and that the Judge, Jury, or others cannot see details of any other case. As this is an exhibit, it shall be treated as such and have a full Chain of Custody available.

The Witness shall determine from the Legal Team whether any visual aids need to be disclosed pretrial.

11.6.7   Using feedback

During and after giving testimony, the Forensic Analyst(s) shall receive feedback as follows:

11.6.7.1   During testimony

Whilst giving evidence, it is essential to be able to look the Judge and Jury in the eye and hold eye contact (but do not stare or glower!), as it is possible to determine how testimony is being received by the audience. They will be making nonverbal responses about how the testimony is received. By understanding this feedback and reacting to it, the Witness can keep their audience engaged and not send them to sleep.

11.6.7.2   Posttrial review

After a trial, all employees who gave testimony will have their performance assessed as part of the continuous improvement process. The Laboratory Manager shall detail an experienced Expert Witness to examine the presentation and provide feedback, as well as requesting feedback from the client on the Forensic Analyst's presentation of testimony. The form used for this is defined in Appendix 8.

11.7 Why a forensic case may fail

Forensic cases may fail at any point in the process and for a whole range of reasons but the most common causes are:

- **chain of custody issues**—This is one of the easiest avenues for a defence to attack and a significant number of forensic cases have failed as a result of the chain of custody not being maintained. This is addressed by use of the movement log, as defined in Chapter 8, Appendix 17 and Chapter 9, Section 9.6.1, respectively, with contemporaneous case work logs, as defined in Chapter 9, Appendix 9 with the other forms and checklists in use shows responsibility for all actions and full end-to-end traceability of all actions taken in a forensic case;
- **legality of the seizure of the evidence**—Forensic cases may fail because of a challenge to the legality of the way in which the evidence was seized. This is addressed by ensuring all legislative requirements are met for the case, as defined in Chapter 9, Section 9.9.1.5;
- **the scope of the investigation was too narrow, and as a result, the evidence presented was not complete**—This is addressed by ensuring the client's required outcomes are properly defined and agreed by reviewing and agreeing the proposal as defined in Chapter 6, Section 6.6.2.4;
- **failure to convince the Judge or Jury of what took place**—This is most common in complex forensic cases such as fraud but can affect any forensic case where the evidence is very technical or in a specialist area that the Jury may not have a good knowledge of the subject. This is addressed by ensuring that reports are properly reviewed for completeness and understanding in plain language as defined in Section 11.5.1; and
- **disputable interpretation of the evidence**—The meaning of the evidence that is presented can be interpreted in more than one way. This is addressed by the peer review process to determine that opinions given and conclusions drawn are based on sound scientific principles and are complete, as defined in Chapter 9, Section 9.15.3.

Appendix 1—Nations ratifying the Budapest convention[a]

Members of Council of Europe

Nation	Signed	Ratified	Entry into force
Albania	23/11/2001	20/06/2002	01/07/2004
Andorra	23/04/2013	16/11/2016	01/03/2017
Armenia	23/11/2001	12/10/2006	01/02/2007
Austria	23/11/2001	13/06/2012	01/10/2012
Azerbaijan	30/06/2008	15/03/2010	01/07/2010
Belgium	23/11/2001	20/08/2012	01/12/2012
Bosnia and Herzegovina	09/02/2005	19/05/2006	01/09/2006
Bulgaria	23/11/2001	07/04/2005	01/08/2005
Croatia	23/11/2001	17/10/2002	01/07/2004
Cyprus	23/11/2001	19/01/2005	01/05/2005
Czech Republic	09/02/2005	22/08/2013	01/12/2013
Denmark	22/04/2003	21/06/2005	01/10/2005
Estonia	23/11/2001	12/05/2003	01/07/2004
Finland	23/11/2001	24/05/2007	01/09/2007
France	23/11/2001	10/01/2006	01/05/2006
Georgia	01/04/2008	06/06/2012	01/10/2012
Germany	23/11/2001	09/03/2009	01/07/2009

a. http://conventions.coe.int/Treaty/Commun/ChercheSig.asp?NT=185&CM=8&DF=&CL=ENG.

Nation	Signed	Ratified	Entry into force
Greece	23/11/2001	25/01/2017	01/05/2017
Hungary	23/11/2001	04/12/2003	01/07/2004
Iceland	30/11/2001	29/01/2007	01/05/2007
Ireland	28/02/2002		
Italy	23/11/2001	05/06/2008	01/10/2008
Latvia	05/05/2004	14/02/2007	01/06/2007
Liechtenstein	17/11/2008	27/01/2016	01/05/2016
Lithuania	23/06/2003	18/03/2004	01/07/2004
Luxembourg	28/01/2003	16/10/2014	01/02/2015
Malta	17/01/2002	12/04/2012	01/08/2012
Monaco	02/05/2013	17/03/2017	01/07/2017
Montenegro	07/04/2005	03/03/2010	01/07/2010
Netherlands	23/11/2001	16/11/2006	01/03/2007
North Macedonia	23/11/2001	15/09/2004	01/01/2005
Norway	23/11/2001	30/06/2006	01/10/2006
Poland	23/11/2001	20/02/2015	01/06/2015
Portugal	23/11/2001	24/03/2010	01/07/2010
Republic of Moldova	23/11/2001	12/05/2009	01/09/2009
Romania	23/11/2001	12/05/2004	01/09/2004
San Marino	17/03/2017	08/03/2019	01/07/2019
Serbia	07/04/2005	14/04/2009	01/08/2009
Slovak Republic	04/02/2005	08/01/2008	01/05/2008
Slovenia	24/07/2002	08/09/2004	01/01/2005
Spain	23/11/2001	03/06/2010	01/10/2010
Sweden	23/11/2001	28/04/2021	01/08/2021
Switzerland	23/11/2001	21/09/2011	01/01/2012
Turkey	10/11/2010	29/09/2014	01/01/2015
Ukraine	23/11/2001	10/03/2006	01/07/2006
UK	23/11/2001	25/05/2011	01/09/2011

Nonmembers of Council of Europe

Nation	Signed	Ratified	Entry into Force
Argentina	05/06/2018 a	01/10/2018	
Australia		30/11/2012 a	01/03/2013
Benin		a	
Brazil		a	
Burkina Faso		a	
Cabo Verde		19/06/2018 a	01/10/2018

Continued

Nation	Signed	Ratified	Entry into Force
Canada	23/11/2001	08/07/2015	01/11/2015
Chile		20/04/2017 a	01/08/2017
Colombia		16/03/2020a	01/07/2020
Costa Rica		22/09/2017 a	01/01/2018
Cote d'Ivoire		a	
Dominican Republic		07/02/2013 a	01/06/2013
Ecuador		a	
Fiji		a	
Ghana		03/12/2018 a	01/04/2019
Guatemala		a	
Israel		09/05/2016 a	01/09/2016
Japan	23/11/2001	03/07/2012	01/11/2012
Mauritius		15/11/2013 a	01/03/2014
Mexico		a	
Morocco		29/06/2018 a	01/10/2018
Niger		a	
Nigeria		06/07/2022 a	10/11/2022
Panama		05/03/2014 a	01/07/2014
Paraguay		30/07/2018 a	01/11/2018
Peru		26/08/2018 a	01/12/2019
Philippines		28/03/2018 a	01/07/2018
Senegal		16/12/2016 a	01/04/2017
South Africa	23/11/2001		
Sri Lanka		29/05/2015 a	01/09/2015
Tonga		09/05/2017 a	01/09/2017
Trinidad and Tobago		a	
Tunisia		a	
USA	23/11/2001	29/09/2006	01/01/2007
Vanuatu		a	

Note: 'a' indicates 'Accession.

Appendix 2—Criteria for selection an expert witness

There are few qualifications available for any Expert Witness in digital forensics today, but this will change. Anyone can put 'Digital Forensic Expert Witness' on their business card but choosing the 'right' one is a matter that is of utmost importance, as it could win or lose the forensic case, no matter how good the Forensic Analyst's examination and analysis has been.

FCL has identified a number of criteria that shall be used in selecting an Expert Witness (and the same generally applies to outsourcing suppliers, as covered in Chapter 14).

The criteria used are subjective, but the criteria and the reasons shall be documented and form a record on the client's virtual case file stored in the ERMS.

For any Expert Witness to be considered, FCL shall consider, but is not limited to, have they:

- any credentials from a Law Enforcement organisation?
- any Law Enforcement organisation or investigations experience?
- formal ongoing and recorded training (CPD/CPE)?
- past performance in the field required?
- recommendations from recognised professional digital forensic bodies?
- understood the process not the tool?
- a CV and references supplied that pass scrutiny?
- published articles in journals or books?
- experience in the hardware in the case?
- experience in the operating system in the case?
- experience in the tools used in the case?
- been actually performing forensic examination for a considerable time/when did they start their digital forensic career?
- determined how long will it take to process the forensic case?
- determined that their cost is acceptable?
- a confidentiality agreement in place?
- an appropriate level of security vetting in the jurisdiction that matches the forensic case requirements?
- appropriate professional qualifications relating to digital forensics?
- expertise and competence on the tools used in the forensic case?
- been trained by a recognised digital forensic expert/organisation?
- dedicated to the case or will it be one of many handled by the Expert Witness?

Appendix 3—Code of conduct for expert witnesses

Whilst a forensic laboratory will need to develop its own Code of Conduct for Expert Witnesses, it should be recognised that legislation, procedures, and accepted practices may, in some jurisdictions, conflict with this Code of Conduct. In cases such as this, the legislation, procedures, and accepted practices shall be followed. The FCL Expert Witness Code of Conduct is that Expert Witnesses shall:

- tell the truth under oath and not commit perjury;
- have a duty to impartially serve the Court of Law or Tribunal;
- have a secondary duty to serve the best interests of the instructing party;
- depending on the jurisdiction, may or may not be able to act as an Advocate;
- ensure the client's requirements are clearly understood and clarify any areas of uncertainty;
- not be paid, depending on the outcome of a forensic case (as this may affect the Expert Witness' objectivity);
- ensure that their terms of engagement are clearly stated, including their limit of liability in their engagement letter;
- be able to display competence in their technical duties;
- continually maintain and update their skills and provide proof of this through Continuing Professional Development (CPD) or Continual Professional Education (CPE) submitted and audited by the relevant professional bodies to which they belong;
- gain qualifications and certifications relevant to their work that are generally accepted as appropriate and good practice for their work;
- be able to demonstrate the required duty of care for the case;
- avoid conflicts of interest, as defined in the Conflict of Interest Policy Chapter 3, Appendix 3;
- immediately report to the Laboratory Manager if they feel that their work is being compromised by undue influence or by not being permitted to perform tests or investigations that they feel are appropriate to the forensic case;
- be scrupulously honest and forthright in their dealings with all involved in a forensic case;
- be honest about their limitations and not accept instructions outside their limitations;
- not discriminate against anyone based on any grounds, whatsoever;
- maintain confidentiality during and after the forensic case has completed;
- ensure safe custody of all exhibits and other materials relating to the forensic case whilst in their custody;
- ensure, through the Laboratory Manager, that appropriate insurance is in place to protect them as Expert Witnesses, in case of need;
- use necessary visual aids and explanations, as permitted in the Court of Law or Tribunal to help explain complex of technical matters;

- obtain best evidence, where available, relating to the forensic case so that reliance on assumptions is minimised and opinions and conclusions are based on verifiable fact;
- clearly state any assumptions and the reasons for them;
- consider all possible options, opinions, and theories relating to the forensic case, before forming their own opinions and conclusions;
- produce reports and testimony as required for the relevant legislation, procedures, or accepted practices for the Court of Law or Tribunal;
- bring to the immediate attention of the Laboratory Manager, and the client, any change to any opinion given or conclusion drawn during the forensic case after submitting their report. This may involve production of a supplemental report that also clearly states the reasons for the revised opinion given and/or conclusion drawn;
- endeavour to reach agreement with other Expert Witnesses on material facts in the forensic case;
- where appropriate, provide a list of matters that are agreed between the Expert Witnesses, and those not agreed with the reason for them. This is usually a joint report from the Expert Witnesses involved; and
- comply with all directions from the Court of Law or Tribunal.

Appendix 4—Report writing checklist

Does the report:

Preparation and planning

- address intended audience (who)?
- clearly identify requirements and research (how)?
- identify where the report refers to (where)?
- clearly define the purpose of the report and met it (why)?
- the relevant facts are present (what)? and
- times and dates are clearly stated (when)?

Content and structure

- answer the key questions?
- contain an opinion or range of opinions or conclusions—as appropriate?
- correctly use appendices?
- 'standalone'?
- ensure chain of custody throughout?
- ensure that facts are clearly separated from opinions and conclusions?
- include a glossary of terms and acronyms used?
- identify all of the facts relevant to the forensic case?
- identify further information—if required?
- identify the issues clearly and identifies them based on the client's required outcomes?
- identify the key questions to be answered?
- include facts to support the opinions given and conclusions drawn?
- meet the requirements of ISO 17025 as defined in Chapter 6, Appendix 27, and
- use of key checklists and internal forms?

Layout

- use appropriate classification of the report?
- use consistent language?
- use the standard template and font (Ariel 12)?
- use headers and footers correctly?
- use headings and subheadings correctly?
- use diagrams appropriately?

- ensure correct pagination?
- use correct paragraph numbering (and line numbering—if required)?
- use photographs appropriately?
- use sketches appropriately? and
- ensure 'white space' present?

Language used

- use 1st person—if appropriate?
- accurately reflect the findings and opinions?
- provide clear and understandable content?
- provide a concise report?
- ensure it is grammatically correct?
- has logical structure? and
- uses short sentences and is accurate?

Presentation and language

Some of these are only applicable to hard copy deliverable and not a PDF file:

- have appropriate binding?
- has had its grammar checked?
- use appropriate layout and structure?
- have the right look and feel?
- has the appropriate overall view?
- use the right paper—appropriate paper weight?

Final presentation

- pass peer review?

Appendix 5—Statement and deposition writing checklist

The requirements of statements and depositions do vary between jurisdictions and the generic checklist below is that which shall be used:

Author's details

- name;
- address—FCL or personal—as required; and
- occupation.

Layout and language

- as per requirement in the jurisdiction;
- classification as used for the jurisdiction;
- concise language;
- grammar correct;
- manually checked for mistakes—not just computer spell checked;
- margins;
- meets requirements of in-house reports;
- figures and diagrams numbered;
- page numbered 'x of y', in appropriate place;
- peer reviewed;

- punctuation correct;
- short sentences;
- spelling correct;
- structure tells a story;
- tone appropriate; and
- white space.

Content

- consistent with other case documents;
- consistent with proposed oral testimony;
- consistent with the exhibits;
- contents logically sequenced;
- dealt with any weaknesses in the case;
- exhibits kept separate;
- exhibits properly labelled;
- facts separated from assumptions, opinions, beliefs, and conclusions;
- glossary of terms;
- identifies the facts to support the issues;
- identifies the issues;
- include all strengths of case;
- introduction;
- list of documents referenced;
- list of exhibits referenced;
- professional opinion based on fact;
- signed and dated;
- statement of truth, if required in jurisdiction;
- structure; and
- where possible, does not make assumptions or inferences.

Appendix 6—Nonverbal communication to avoid

There are a number of nonverbal communications that should be avoided as they can undermine the credibility of a Witness by distracting the Judge and/or Jury from the testimony being given. These include, but are not limited to:

- allowing a pager or mobile device to ring;
- arrogant or condescending tone;
- being late;
- biting the lip or nails;
- clicking the top of a pen;
- cracking knuckles;
- drumming fingers;
- fidgeting;
- folding arms across the body;
- inappropriate communication that the Judge/Jury does not understand;
- jingling keys or change in pockets;
- leaning on hands and rocking backwards and forwards;
- overuse of 'fillers';
- picking at the body, especially the nose;
- poor posture;
- playing with items of clothing;
- pointing at the Judge or Jury;
- rolling the eyes;

- rubbing the eyes;
- scratching any part of the body;
- slouching, if sitting; and
- twiddling thumbs.

Appendix 7—Etiquette in Court

This section could be called 'No—No's'!

Different Courts of Law and Tribunals in different Jurisdictions will have different expected levels of etiquette; however, the following shall be used by FCL as a minimum level of acceptable standards of etiquette in any Court of Law or Tribunal, anywhere;

- answer questions asked fully and honestly, but do not volunteer too much information;
- avoid 'taboo' subjects;
- be on time;
- be respectful, polite, and courteous to everyone, from the front desk staff to the Judge and Jury, and the 'other side';
- be well prepared;
- do not upset the Judge;
- it is acceptable to say, 'I do not understand the question' and ask for a rephrasing;
- no matter what—a Witness of any type shall not lose their temper with anyone questioning them;
- remain focussed;
- be respectful and sincere;
- the Witness shall be aware of questions that may leave them in a disadvantaged position (e.g. questions that are like 'is it possible that …' often it is possible, but no answer should be given that detracts from the evidence presented, the opinions given and the conclusions drawn); and
- turn your mobile devices off (in some jurisdictions this is regarded as 'contempt of Court' and an offence.

Appendix 8—Testimony feedback form

Case details

- case number;
- client/case name;
- defendant;
- Court of Law or Tribunal location;
- Court of Law or Tribunal type;
- Forensic Analyst giving testimony;
- date(s) of testimony.

Feedback

Feedback on the following aspects of the testimony shall be obtained:

Personal impressions

- ability to respond to feedback;
- attitude;
- dress;
- entry to the Witness Box;
- eye contact;
- nonverbal communication;
- personal appearance;
- understanding of Court of Law or Tribunal Etiquette; and
- voice (volume, tone, and understandability).

Delivery of testimony

- ability to explain complex issues;
- ability to use appropriate language;
- clarity of delivery;
- conciseness of delivery;
- confidence level;
- decline to answer questions that required knowledge outside their experience and competence;
- knowledge level relating to the case and the case processing tools and methods used;
- level of preparation;
- remain within the scope of their experience and competence;
- response to questions; and
- use of visual aids.

The above are all marked as follows:

1—Very Poor;
2—Poor;
3—Good;
4—Very Good;
5—Excellent.
N/A—Not Applicable.

Length of testimony

- evidence in chief; and
- cross-examination.

Case result

What was the result of the forensic case/investigation that this testimony was used to support (Did the testimony play a pivotal role)?

Corrective actions recommended

Any corrective actions needed to improve the Forensic Analyst's testimony presentation.

Sign off

- signed;
- date; and
- name.

Chapter 12

Secure working practices

12.1 Introduction

Information is now globally accepted as being a vital asset for most, if not all, organisations and businesses and FCL is no exception. Information may be printed or written on paper, stored electronically, transmitted by post or email, shown on films, or spoken in conversation. Whatever the form that information takes, FCL shall have processes and procedures to protect it.

Information security can be characterised as the preservation of:

- **Confidentiality**—ensuring that access to information is appropriately authorised;
- **Integrity**—safeguarding the accuracy and completeness of information and processing methods; and
- **Availability**—ensuring that authorised users have access to information when they need it.

ISO/IEC 27001 is a specification for the management of Information Security (ISO/IEC 27001 is the specification and ISO/IEC 27002 is the Code of Practice). It is applicable to all sectors of industry and commerce and not confined to information held on computers. It addresses the security of information in whatever form it is held, and this shall be applied throughout FCL.

As such, the confidentiality, integrity, and availability of FCL and client information are essential to maintain competitive edge, deliverability to clients, legal compliance, and commercial image. ISO/IEC 27001 supports this. It is easy to imagine the consequences for FCL if FCL's or its client information was lost, destroyed, corrupted, or misused.

In adopting ISO/IEC 27001, FCL is not immune from security breaches but shall make these breaches less likely to occur and reduce the consequential impact in terms of cost and disruption if they do occur. It shall also demonstrate that:

- FCL has addressed, implemented, and controlled the security of its information and client information entrusted to it;
- it provides reassurance to clients, employees, trading partners, and interested parties that FCL has implemented secure systems based on the perceived risk;
- it demonstrates credibility and trust;
- it confirms that relevant legislation and regulations within the jurisdiction are being met; and
- it ensures that a commitment to information security exists at all levels throughout FCL.

The Information Security Policy is defined in Chapter 4, Appendix 20.

FCL has chosen not to achieve certification to ISO/IEC 27001 by an Accredited Certification Body, but to be compliant to it. This ensures that there is a mature Information Security Management System (ISMS) in place that can easily gain a certificate of registration should this be a client or business requirement.

Within FCL the requirements of ISO/IEC 27001 using the Statement of Applicability (SoA) as defined in Appendix 1. Whilst it shall choose its controls from ISO/IEC 27001, Annex A, it is free to choose other controls if they are indicated by the risk assessment undertaken on the assets in the scope of the ISMS. It has used ISO/IEC 27001 as a baseline and selected other controls as required from other sources or the risk assessment output.

12.2 Principles of information security within FCL

There are nine 'Generally Accepted Information Security Principles' (GAISP—Version 3.0) that provide guidance in the security of information. This was written in January 2004 and published by ISSA—the Information System Security Association—but is still valid as principles, in the opinion of FCL. Whilst FCL does not want to achieve ISO/IEC 27001 certification, these principles are adjudged to be appropriate as well. How they are met is defined in Appendix 2.

These principles are:

12.2.1 Accountability principle

Information security accountability and responsibility must be clearly defined and acknowledged.

A Blueprint for Implementing Best Practice Procedures in a Digital Forensic Laboratory. https://doi.org/10.1016/B978-0-12-819479-9.00020-4

12.2.2 Awareness principle

All parties, including but not limited to information owners and information security practitioners, with a need to know, should have access to applied or available principles, standards, conventions, or mechanisms for the security of information and information systems, and should be informed of applicable threats to the security of information.

12.2.3 Ethics principle

Information should be used, and the administration of information security should be executed, in an ethical manner.

12.2.4 Multidisciplinary principle

Principles, standards, conventions, and mechanisms for the security of information and information systems should address the considerations and viewpoints of all interested parties.

12.2.5 Proportionality principle

Information security controls should be proportionate to the risks of modification, denial of use, or disclosure of the information.

12.2.6 Integration principle

Principles, standards, conventions, and mechanisms for the security of information should be coordinated and integrated with each other and with the organisation's policies and procedures to create and maintain security throughout an information system.

12.2.7 Timeliness principle

All accountable parties should act in a timely, coordinated manner to prevent or respond to breaches of, and threats to, the security of information and information systems.

12.2.8 Assessment principle

The risks to information and information systems should be assessed periodically.

12.2.9 Equity principle

Management shall respect the rights and dignity of individuals when setting policy and when selecting, implementing, and enforcing security measures.

12.2.10 NIST principles and practices for securing IT systems

It is of note that the National Institute of Standards and Technology (NIST) produced NIST 800-14—'Generally Accepted Principles and practices for Security Information Technology Systems' in September 1996. These principles are much more aligned to supporting the business and are more aligned to CObIT 2019 than any straightforward information security standards and so they are reproduced below and have also been adopted as business and risk-driven information security principles within FCL.

- Computer security supports the mission of the organisation;
- Computer security is an integral element of sound management;
- Computer security should be cost-effective;
- Systems Owners have security responsibilities outside their own organisations;
- Computer security responsibilities and accountability should be made explicit;
- Computer security requires a comprehensive and integrated approach;
- Computer security should be periodically reassessed; and
- Computer security is constrained by societal factors.

12.3 Managing information security in FCL

Whilst GAISP and NIST 800-14 define principles for information security and there are a number of national and international standards for information security, FCL has adopted ISO/IEC 27001 and the supporting standards within the ISO 270xx series of standards with others as required from a variety of sources. Some of these are defined in Appendix 2.

12.3.1 Managing organisational security

FCL shall adopt a multidisciplinary approach to information security that involves the co-operation and collaboration of managers, users, administration staff, auditors, security staff, and specialist skills in areas such as insurance and risk management. External third-party suppliers and other interested parties shall also be involved.

FCL shall manage the implementation of information security through:

- an Information Security Committee;
- allocation of information security responsibilities;
- authorisation for new information processing facilities;
- provision for specialist information security advice; and
- independent reviews of the information security systems implemented in FCL.

12.3.1.1 The information security committee

Information security is a business responsibility shared by all employees. To ensure that information security is properly incorporated into FCL business activities, a management board shall be created to promote information security and this is called the Information Security Committee. Its terms of reference are defined in Chapter 4, Appendix 11. There are a number of other management committees set up to manage various other aspects of FCL, and these are all listed in Chapter 4.

12.3.1.2 Allocation of information security responsibilities

FCL shall ensure that the responsibilities for the protection of individual assets and for carrying out specific information security processes are clearly defined.

Responsibilities shall be defined as follows:

- The information security policy shall provide general guidance on the allocation of security roles and responsibilities within FCL;
- the Information Security Manager (ISM) shall have overall responsibility for the development and implementation of security, and to support the identification of controls. The ISM's job description is defined in Appendix 16;
- generic responsibilities are defined in the scope statement for the Integrated Management System (IMS), as defined in Chapter 5, Appendix 11;
- defined responsibilities for all other aspects of information security are contained within the documents of this ISMS or in their specific job descriptions; and
- all employees have specific job descriptions that include the requirements for information security.

12.3.1.3 Authorisation for new information processing facilities

FCL shall ensure that all new information processing facilities are authorised before implementation is allowed. This authorisation is detailed within the relevant documents of this ISMS and shall include:

- business approval via the Business Owner and the Business Risk Owner (if different people);
- the ISM approval to ensure that all relevant security policies and requirements are met and that all relevant risks have been identified and treated as appropriate;
- hardware and software testing to ensure that new information processing facilities are compatible with other system components; and
- information protection approval for processing personal information to meet current data protection and privacy legislation.

All new information processing facilities shall only be allowed into the live environment via the Change Management Process, as defined in Chapter 7, Section 7.4.3.

12.3.1.4 Provision for specialist security advice

Initial specialist information security advice is in the first instance provided by the ISM. Where additional or specialised advice is required, it shall be sought from:

- vendors;
- other security professionals;
- Special Interest Groups (SIGs) and specialist professional bodies; and
- local or national authorities.

The ISM shall coordinate the use of these sources of advice.

The ISM shall provide access to external specialist security advice on an as needed basis. The assessment of security threats and the level of internal knowledge provide indicators for whether external security advice is required.

The ISM and other relevant employees shall be encouraged to join/attend appropriate information security bodies and maintain contacts with law enforcement authorities, regulatory bodies, information service providers, and telecommunications operators. All employees shall be reminded to be discrete when discussing FCL issues with nonemployees and shall never divulge confidential information to employees who are not authorised to have access to that information. Nondisclosure Agreements (NDAs) shall be used where FCL information is passed to a third party unless a contract (with an appropriate confidentiality clause) has been executed between FCL and the third party.

The types of threat intelligence information gained can include details of specific attacks, methods that attackers are using, and types of attacks that are current. This shall provide awareness of the threat environment so that appropriate risk treatment and mitigation can be implemented, managed, and monitored.

12.3.1.5 Independent review of the information security system

The implementation of FCL's information security system shall be reviewed independently at least once each year, or on influencing change, to provide assurance that practices implemented properly reflect the policy, and that it is feasible and effective.

This review shall be carried out either by independent internal staff trained in a security audit function or (at the discretion of the ISM) by a third-party specialist auditing company. This is in addition to any penetration testing or other technical or management testing or exercising undertaken by internal or external resources and the annual Certification Body audits.

The process for undertaking internal audits is defined in Chapter 4, Section 4.9.2.

12.3.2 Educating and training employees in information security

FCL shall undertake educating and training of employees to ensure that standards are implemented to ensure continued employee awareness of their information security responsibilities.

This requirement applies to all employees that have access to FCL and/or client information or information processing systems.

This shall include:

- security awareness:
  - educating new employees (induction training);
  - guidelines for educating new employees; and
  - maintaining employee awareness.
- specialised ongoing security training (e.g. mobile device security training, annual refresher training, etc.).

12.3.2.1 Security awareness

Awareness of securing information requirements shall be an important responsibility of every employee on a daily basis. Loss of information could result in a loss of the work hours spent creating information, as well as more work hours trying to recover. Information lost outside the work environment could result in the violation of customer confidentiality, a contractual or legislative breach.

It is ultimately the responsibility of FCL management to ensure that all employees and any others with access to FCL and/or client information and information processing systems understand the key elements of information security, why it is needed, and their personal information security responsibilities.

Awareness of information security shall be maintained via effective awareness and training programmes for all employees. All employees shall undertake the security awareness and training programme. They shall be provided with guidance to help them understand information security, the importance of complying with FCL's internal policies, procedures, and standards, and to be aware of their own personal responsibilities. It is HR's responsibility, in cooperation with the ISM, to promote security awareness and training to all employees on a continuous basis.

FCL shall follow these guidelines to promote awareness of information security amongst all of its employees to ensure that:

- formal awareness and training sessions shall be run using specialised awareness material;
- all training sessions shall be kept up to date with current practices;
- all training sessions shall be attended by all employees; and
- security awareness training sessions shall be reviewed annually by the ISM for continued relevance and updated as appropriate.

12.3.2.1.1 Educating new employees

Upon permanent or contract employment at FCL:

1. All employees shall be briefed, as part of their induction, on the application of information security policies, procedures and standards within FCL, as defined in Chapter 6, Appendix 8.
2. A written summary of the basic information security measures shall be available in the Information Security Policy, which is supplied to all employees at induction. A signed copy is to be kept in the employee's personnel file in case of later need.
3. New employees shall have access to the ISMS and supporting policies and procedures.
4. New employees shall be able to:
   - understand their responsibilities as a user of FCL and client information and FCL's information processing systems;
   - identify information security resources;
   - identify examples of sensitive and/or confidential information in their department; and
   - understand the impact of information security violations and other information security incidents.

12.3.2.1.2 Guidelines for educating new employees

The following aspects of information security shall be included when educating all new employees:

- user ID and passphrase requirements;
- information security, including malware protection, malware reporting, and malware elimination;
- the appropriate handling (and destruction) of information of different classifications;
- awareness of social engineering techniques employed by threat actors;
- information backup guidelines;
- business continuity and disaster recovery;
- FCL's information security programme;
- internet access;
- email use;
- information security monitoring processes that are in use;
- use of information processing equipment and information outside the office;
- incident reporting; and
- who to contact for additional information.

12.3.2.1.3 Maintaining awareness

FCL recognises that retention and applicable knowledge of employees increases considerably when the matter is subject to revision and refreshment. To assist with this:

- all FCL employees shall be re-briefed on information security annually by the ISM; and
- the ISM shall develop and implement a security awareness programme, which addresses periodic information security awareness update requirements. A written summary of the basic information security measures shall be made available for each employee and relevant third parties.

Some of the issues covered by the periodic security updates may include:

- how FCL deals with users who do not comply with security policies and procedures;
- success of security policies;
- problems or difficulties experienced by users;
- changes to security policies;
- incident reporting;
- security metrics;
- learning from incidents and issues affecting FCL; and
- malicious software discovered.

12.3.2.2 Security training

Education and training shall be provided to all employees who are involved in controlling, using, running, developing, and securing information and information processing systems.

Security training shall provide all employees with the knowledge they require to assess security requirements, propose security controls, and to ensure that controls function effectively.

The objective of security training at FCL shall be to ensure that:

- security controls are applied correctly to FCL information processing systems;
- all employees understand their responsibilities; and
- the IT Department develops systems in a disciplined manner.

The ISM and HR are responsible for ensuring that all employees obtain adequate training via:

- advising employees of available courses;
- encouraging certification and qualifications, where applicable;
- ensuring knowledge transfer from third-party suppliers and other interested parties to employees, where appropriate; and
- maintenance of individual employee's training records.

The following shall be the points of focus for security training:

- all users shall choose quality passphrases following the passphrase standard;
- passphrases and user IDs shall be kept confidential;
- access cards or other security mechanisms shall not be shared by anyone, and shall immediately be reported if lost or stolen;
- users shall be encouraged to contact the ISM when unusual situations occur;
- building security shall be alerted whenever a user's access card or key has been compromised;
- users shall protect portable information processing devices by using encryption, physical locks, locking away sensitive media and documentation and to log off, if leaving them unattended;
- users shall be trained not to provide information to anyone representing himself or herself as a member of the IT Department (i.e. social engineering) that could allow that person to gain access to classified or client information; and
- all documents received regarding security issues shall be read carefully.

12.3.3 Managing information security for employees

It is essential that good information security practices are implemented in FCL and that all employees understand these from their initial employment. This shall include:

- a policy for screening applicants during recruitment, as defined in Chapter 18, Section 18.1.3.7 and Appendix 2; and
- policies for promoting information security for employees—which covers:
  - job descriptions;
  - confidentiality agreements;
  - terms and conditions of employment.

The implementation and maintenance of information security policies and procedures with respect to employees are HR's responsibility, based on recommendations provided by the ISM.

12.3.3.1   Promoting information security for employees

FCL shall pursue an active policy of encouraging and promoting awareness of information security issues for all employees. To assist with information security awareness FCL shall implement the following:

- defining security roles in job descriptions;
- issuing confidentiality agreements; and
- issuing terms and conditions of employment.

12.3.3.2   Defining security roles in job descriptions

The FCL policy for defining security roles in job definitions shall be that:

- all new job applicants shall be provided with a job description when applying for employment;
- job descriptions for all existing employees shall be available on request from HR;
- all job descriptions shall include a responsibility for handling FCL and client information in accordance with the ISMS, and a reference to the information security policy; and
- employment roles with specific information security tasks or activities shall be listed in the relevant job description.

12.3.3.3   Issuing confidentiality agreements

Confidentiality agreements help reinforce FCL's commitment to information security by reinforcing employee attitudes that all FCL and client information that they handle during the course of their work shall be treated on a confidential basis according to its classification, as defined in Chapter 5, Appendix 16.

Responsibility for managing Confidentiality Agreements lies with HR in association with General Counsel.

FCL policy for issuing confidentiality agreements shall be that:

1. All employees shall be issued with and sign a Confidentiality Agreement (agreements are normally issued at time of recruitment and form a part of the contract of employment).
2. Confidentiality Agreements shall define the undertakings to which an employee agrees with respect to the maintenance of confidentiality and information security during and postemployment.

The Confidentiality Agreement shall be subject to periodic reviews by Legal Counsel as follows:

- reviews shall be conducted following changes to:
  - job roles;
  - legislation;
  - Information Security Policy or any relevant supporting documents.
- any changes to the Confidentiality Agreement shall be implemented by HR after review and updating by General Counsel or specialised external legal sources.

12.3.3.4   Issuing terms and conditions of employment

Terms and conditions of employment shall be stated in an employee contract which shall be issued to each employee and specify the particulars of the employment relationship between FCL and the employee. The issue of information security shall be expressly addressed.

Responsibility for managing employee contracts lies with HR with suitable input from General Counsel or specialised external legal sources.

The policy for issuing terms and conditions of employment is that:

- all employees shall be issued with terms and conditions of employment; and
- no employee should be allowed access to FCL or client information or information processing facilities without signing the terms and conditions of employment or an appropriate NDA.

The terms and conditions of employment shall outline:

- the need for employees to comply with current statutory legislation and regulations;
- the security responsibilities of employees outside the workplace and whilst working away (e.g. on business trips or working away from the office);

- the disciplinary procedures or contractual sanctions which would be applied if information security policies or procedures are breached; and
- confirmation that it is FCL's responsibility to provide appropriate training and education in the subject of information security.

Note

HR shall be responsible for taking disciplinary action against employees who breach the terms and conditions of their employment. Legal Counsel shall be responsible for taking action against third-party suppliers and their employees who breach the terms and conditions of their employment.

12.3.4 Termination or change of employment

HR shall ensure that all employees who change employment or leave FCL for any reason are appropriately processed. This shall ensure that there is a clean break and that all such employees are reminded of their contractual responsibilities in their postemployment phase.

To assist in the process, FCL shall ensure that the following areas are covered with the relevant staff:

- termination responsibilities;
- return of assets; and
- removal of access rights.

These are defined in Chapter 18, Section 18.3.

12.3.5 Segregation of IT duties

FCL shall implement a number of controls for maintaining and enforcing segregation of IT duties to:

- reduce security risks via accidental or deliberate misuse of FCL or clients information or information processing systems; and
- reduce opportunities for unauthorised access or modification of services or information.

Segregation of duties within the IT Department helps ensure that information assets are safeguarded by segregating duties. This ensures that access to computer, production information, software, documentation, and operating systems and utilities are limited (and potential damage from the actions of any 'rogue' employee(s) are reduced). All employees shall be organised to achieve adequate segregation of duties, to the greatest extent possible.

Note 1

Whilst FCL is a relatively small organisation and where segregation of duties is not always achievable, compensatory controls shall be used, for example audit trails and management supervision.

Note 2

Other forensic laboratories may adopt this or a different approach.

Daily management of the policy of segregation of duties is the responsibility of all Team Leaders and Managers. Formal maintenance of these guidelines is the responsibility of the ISM (in association with other key management staff).

Where possible, the following IT duties shall be performed by separate groups/employees:

- access control;
- IT management;
- network management;
- programme migration;
- Service Desk;
- software development; and
- systems operations/daily administration.

Account creation and maintenance shall ensure that elements of segregation are automatically performed (i.e. HR and Line Managers shall authorise account changes and the IT Department shall implement them).

User profiles shall be developed taking into consideration segregation of duties. These user profiles shall be reviewed periodically and it is the responsibility of the Line Managers to report any changes to the Service Desk and the ISM to record any changes.

12.3.6 Segregation of other duties

Not only shall FCL implement segregation for IT duties, but also ensure that no one person is able to control a whole process and that there is always external oversight.

Risk assessments shall be carried out to ensure that the risks of segregation failures are understood and appropriate controls implemented to reduce the risks as far as practical.

Some of processes shall have segregation enforced in addition to IT access segregation:

- raising payment requests and paying them;
- acquiring and disposing of assets; and
- managing the employee database and paying salaries.

This is not a complete list but indicative of types of process that shall require segregation control, specific processes shall be identified by risk assessment.

12.3.7 Electronic mail

FCL shall adopt a number of security measures for email users, that cover:

- email accounts;
- protection of email;
- acceptable use of email; and
- unacceptable use of email.

12.3.7.1 Email accounts

Email accounts shall be provided to employees following completion of an official account request from the employee's Business Unit or Department Manager.

An email account shall be strictly confidential and shall be for the exclusive use of the employee for whom it has been created. In addition, email passphrases shall not be shared under any circumstances between employees.

The size of each email user's mailbox is limited according to the standard currently defined by the IT Department.

No email accounts shall be deleted when an employee is terminated, they shall be archived in case of future need but only for emails that relate to forensic case processing in case of appeal or the need to revisit the case. Deletion of personal email shall be carried out as defined in Retention Schedule and meet current data protection and privacy legislation and regulation.

12.3.7.2 Protection of email

Measures shall include:

- email messages containing confidential information shall only be sent to recipients who have the right to know the confidential information;
- email messages containing confidential information shall have suitable controls implemented to protect against unauthorised access, modification, or disclosure during transmission; and
- sending options, privacy markings, and expiry options shall be set if available within email client application, as appropriate within FCL. The use of internal settings is not as strong as using a dedicated encryption solution.

12.3.7.3 Acceptable use of email

Note

Acceptable use of FCL's information processing facilities is fully covered in the Acceptable Use Policy (AUP) in Chapter 4, Appendix 35.

Acceptable use of FCL email system shall include, but not be limited to:

- communication between employees and external parties for business purposes only;
- transmission of information related to FCL operations (financial information, statistical information, newsletters, reports) that are essential for the accomplishment of an employee's daily job;
- sending and receiving official internal memos;
- to inform employees of new policies and procedures that have been adopted;
- to inform employees of products and services provided by FCL; and
- sending and receiving messages containing information in relation to recent developments in a particular area of business, which assist with knowledge improvement.

12.3.7.4 Unacceptable use of email

Note

Unacceptable use of FCL's information processing facilities is fully covered in the Acceptable Use Policy (AUP) in Chapter 4, Appendix 35.

The following activities shall be considered unacceptable use of FCL email system:

- transmission of confidential information either belonging to FCL or a client without prior authorisation/approval;
- copying, transmission, or acceptance of material that is copyright protected;
- transmission or acceptance of any material that may be reasonably considered offensive, disruptive, defamatory, or derogatory, including but not limited to sexual comments or images, racial slurs, or other comments or images that would offend someone on the basis of his/her race, national origin, gender, sexual orientation, religious or political beliefs, disability or on any other basis;
- transmission or acceptance of any information which may lead to any illegal or criminal activity, or breach of local, national, or international laws;
- transmission or acceptance of any marketing material that has no relationship with FCL's products and services;
- sending of messages to external 'newsgroups' or bulletin boards without it being expressly defined in the employee's job responsibilities;
- deliberate transmission or acceptance of malicious code such as viruses, phishing attacks, ransomware emails, Trojan horses into the network;
- subscription to Internet mailing lists is prohibited without prior approval from the employee's Line Manager;
- attempts to gain unauthorised access to email accounts;
- unauthorised cracking or decryption attempts in relation to passphrases or encrypted files;
- disclosure of the personal user passphrases to unauthorised third parties;
- attempts to alter the sender's identity during the transmission of electronic messages; and
- activities involving gambling, speculative, illegal, or other such activities.

12.3.8 Leaving equipment unattended

Note

Chapter 7, Section 7.3.4 gives details of the controls that FCL uses to control the business and security risks associated with the physical location of electronic office systems (e.g. photocopiers, fax machines, printers, scanners, projectors, and video machines).

FCL shall implement a number of controls to ensure that information processing and communication systems are adequately protected if users need to leave equipment such as information processing devices unattended;

- employees shall always protect easily portable information processing devices against theft by locking items in secure areas when they are unattended;
- sensitive media and documentation shall always be securely stored when not in use; and

- computers that are left temporarily unattended shall have access temporarily blocked using either of the following:
  - a manual, passphrase-protected keyboard lock facility initiated by a user before leaving the computer;
  - an automatic, passphrase-protected screen saver which is activated after 15 min of inactivity.
  - terminate active sessions when finished, unless the device is secured using an appropriate locking mechanism, e.g. a passphrase-protected screen saver; and
  - protect removable storage media (e.g. USBs, CDs, disks, flash memory, and tapes) against theft or copying, by complying with Clear Screen and Clear Desk Policy, as defined in Chapter 4, Appendix 23.

12.3.9   Mobile computing

Note

In FCL, mobile computing includes all information processing devices that can be used independently of the FCL network but can establish a connection to the network.

FCL shall implement a number of policies and procedures to protect their mobile computing facilities. These shall include, but not be limited to:

- general policy on mobile computing;
- responsibilities of users;
- responsibilities of the IT Department; and
- using mobile information processing devices of any type.

12.3.9.1   General policy on mobile computing

The policy on Mobile Computing is defined in Chapter 4, Appendix 28.

12.3.9.2   User's responsibilities

User responsibilities shall include, but not be limited to:

1. Accepting the conditions of use contained within the mobile computing policy, and all other relevant FCL policies;
2. Not attaching unauthorised equipment to the information processing network;
3. Ensuring that users have specific authorisation from the IT Department before they can connect to the network using a mobile processing device;
4. Not explicitly setting up a mobile device to be a specific function server (e.g. file server or email server);
5. Not transferring network settings or host identities from one machine to another (whether already registered or not);
6. Ensuring that any equipment connected to the network is in good working condition; and
7. Backing up any business information held locally on a mobile device.

12.3.9.3   IT Department responsibilities

IT Department responsibilities shall include, but not be limited to:

1. Developing, maintaining, and updating the mobile computing policy and supporting security standards in conjunction with the ISM.
2. Maintaining details of all networks and access points.
3. Resolving mobile communication problems.
4. Setting up mobile connections to the network following a request from a business manager for one of their employees.
5. Monitoring performance and security where necessary.
6. Monitoring the development of new mobile computing technology and evaluate network technology enhancements.
7. Providing support to mobile computer users.
8. Safeguarding the security of FCL and client information and information processing facilities.
9. Ensuring that systems administrators and users understand the security implications and performance limitations of mobile computing technology.

12.3.9.4   Using mobile computers

FCL mobile computing users shall follow these guidelines:

1. All users shall exercise particular care when using mobile computers in public places to:
   * avoid unauthorised access to FCL network;
   * avoid disclosure or information stored locally on a mobile computer, or which may be accessed via the FCL network;
   * avoid overlooking by unauthorised persons;
   * ensure the physical protection of mobile computing equipment (including risks from theft, and leaving equipment unattended).
2. No business-critical information shall be only stored locally on a mobile computer.
3. Ensure that the access control mechanisms (which are maintained by the IT Department) shall only allow a mobile computer to access the FCL network following successful identification and authentication.
4. Use the FCL Virtual Private Network (VPN) for all access.

12.3.10   Securing IT assets off-site

FCL shall implement a number of policies and procedures to control the security of IT assets and information in terms of off-site use to minimise loss and damage to the business. It shall cover:

* general guidelines for securing IT assets off-site;
* securing all types of mobile computers off-site; and
* securing IT assets for maintenance off-site.

All IT assets which are used outside of FCL premises shall be subject to rigorous controls to accommodate the security risks of working outside the office.

12.3.10.1   General guidelines for securing IT assets off-site

The following guidelines shall govern securing of IT assets off-site:

* IT assets shall only be supplied to employees based on a justified business need;
* employees shall obtain the approval of their Line Manager before the IT Department shall grant a request for use of off-site equipment;
* employees who are approved for off-site working shall attend specialised training from the ISM relating to the risks of off-site working and controls required to be implemented;
* employees who are approved to telework shall receive a risk assessment of their home prior to being granted approval for teleworking, if appropriate in the jurisdiction;
* all information processing devices shall be returned to the IT Department when a business justification is no longer valid;
* all employees shall abide by hardware and software licence agreements and acknowledge that software programmes are subject to copyright and patent laws as defined in the licence agreements; and
* all employees shall make every effort to secure FCL and client information and information processing equipment when out of the office and in their own homes.

12.3.10.2   Securing mobile computers off-site

The following guidelines shall govern the use of mobile devices off-site:

* only FCL authorised mobile computers using standard hardened build configurations shall be authorised for use outside the office;
* security features in all mobile computers, where available, shall be enable as part of the secure hardened build;
* personal mobile computers shall not be permitted to connect to any FCL network. FCL does not subscribe to the Bring Your Own Device (BYOD) culture;
* mission-critical information shall never be permanently stored on a mobile computer. All FCL and client information shall be uploaded regularly into the ERMS;
* proprietary information shall only be loaded onto a mobile computer following appropriate authorisation;

- strong authentication devices shall be used to protect mobile computers, where appropriate and possible. If this is not possible, the strongest possible authentication process shall be used. If this is not acceptable for the business risk involved, the device shall not be used;
- unauthorised software shall not be loaded onto a mobile computer, this includes software downloaded from the Internet; and
- mobile computers shall be locked away at all times, when not in use, and shall never be left on view in a motor vehicle or left in hotel rooms.

12.3.10.3   Securing tablets, mobile, and smartphones off-site

As mobile and smartphones become increasingly powerful and are used to connect to corporate networks, they pose an increasing risk if they are compromised in any way. Whilst the definition of mobile computing within this book covers mobile and smartphones, there are specific requirements that shall be implemented to protect them as opposed to laptops.

The following guidelines shall govern the use of tablets, mobile and smartphones off-site:

- employees shall report any loss or damage to a FCL tablet, mobile or smartphone to the Service Desk and the service provider as soon as possible;
- any loss of a FCL tablet, mobile or smartphone shall be reported to the ISM immediately after the service provider has been notified, so that a risk assessment of the loss of the information it contained may be undertaken;
- the Service Desk shall ensure that the service provider has blocked the line of a lost tablet, mobile or smartphone as soon as possible, and also record the loss in the Asset Register;
- where possible, remote 'kill switches', remote wiping, and mobile phone tracking applications shall be utilised;
- PIN codes or biometric access controls shall be used to protect all FCL tablets, mobile and smartphones;
- only FCL issued tablets, mobile and smartphones shall be used for FCL business; and
- tablets, mobile and smartphones shall never be used as a means to connect a networked PC directly to the Internet unless the use of the device to provide VPN access is more secure than other means of access.

12.3.10.4   Securing IT assets sent for maintenance off-site

In the case of IT assets that are sent off-site for maintenance:

- FCL assets shall only be sent for off-site maintenance to an approved and authorised third party;
- where possible, all maintenance shall be carried out on-site;
- any information held in any IT asset that is sent off-site shall be removed or made inaccessible. This includes removing hard disks, encrypting information, securely erasing it, or other measures; and
- all maintenance shall be carried out with an appropriate contract in place with a suitable confidentiality clause, as defined in Chapter 14, Sections 14.8 and 14.9.

12.3.11   Retaining documents

FCL shall implement a number of policies and procedures to control the record retention and disposition process. The Retention Schedule is defined in Chapter 4, Appendix 26.

To prevent unauthorised or accidental disclosure of the information, it is essential that care shall be exercised in the information disposal, including protecting its security and confidentiality during storage, transportation, handling, and destruction.

12.3.12   Handling and securing storage media

FCL shall implement a number of policies and procedures to manage how it controls and physically protects its storage media which covers information processing media (e.g. USB devices, disks, tapes) and system documentation.

The objective of these controls is to prevent damage to FCL assets or interruption to FCL business activities.

It covers:

- guidelines for handling media;
- securing media in transit; and
- managing removable computer media.

12.3.12.1 Guidelines for handling media

The following guidelines shall govern handling of media:

- FCL and client information shall only be generated in hard copy or stored on computer media to the extent necessary to complete normal business operations or forensic case processing;
- copies of information shall be kept to a minimum to better facilitate control and distribution. All records, and especially vital records, shall be managed and controlled by the ERMS;
- when not in use, confidential and forensic case file information shall be stored in locked drawers, cabinets, or rooms specifically designated for the purpose (and which are accessible only by authorised individuals). Original paper records shall be stored in the Document Registry in the Secure Property Store and only scanned electronic copies be used;
- physical access to storage media and the Document Registry shall be restricted to employees who require access for authorised business purposes;
- authorisation lists shall be regarded as confidential information;
- FCL or client information or any media sent via interoffice mail, courier, or other means, shall be clearly labelled with the appropriate recipient information (i.e. name, position, company or department name, address, etc.) A return address shall also be provided, in case of need.

12.3.12.2 Securing media in transit

Media items are vulnerable to unauthorised access, misuse, or corruption whilst being transported and therefore distribution of media items shall be kept to a minimum. When transporting physical or electronic records between FCL and non-FCL Laboratory sites:

- All media shall be secured in accordance with its classification level, and this includes:
  - printer spools on systems;
  - printed materials awaiting distribution;
  - printed materials awaiting pick-up for external delivery services; and
  - media items, such as back-up tapes awaiting pickup for off-site storage.
- only authorised courier and delivery service companies shall be used;
- Information Owners shall maintain a formal record within the ERMS which provides evidence of removals and recipients of documents or computer media (to provide an audit trail should retrieval of such information be required);
- any information sent by postal service or courier shall be protected from unauthorised access, misuse, or corruption. Employees shall ensure packaging for information, and the media it is stored on, is sufficient to protect contents from physical damage or tampering and, where applicable, in accordance with the manufacturers' specifications and its classification;
- for confidential information, the following shall be used
  - locked containers;
  - tamper resistant packaging;
  - delivery by hand; and
  - delivery upon signature.

  Minimum requirements for handling all assets of any classification are defined in Section 12.3.14.
- where computer media is provided to/from third parties, provisions shall be made for malicious software checks of information media both before dispatching and at the time of receipt.

12.3.12.3 Management of removable media

The following controls shall be in place:

- no information processing equipment in FCL shall contain removable hard disks (unless specifically authorised, this includes servers with removable disks and tapes under the control of the IT Department and forensic case processing equipment, where each forensic case is held on its own removable hard disk);
- a register of all requests and installations of removable storage devices shall be maintained by the Service Desk;
- all employees shall be made aware of FCL's protection measures in relation to removable storage media (e.g. USB devices, disks, CD/DVDs, and tapes), through induction and appropriate awareness and training programmes. This shall include physical security to prevent theft, and environmental controls to prevent media degradation;

- employees shall limit the use of removable computer media (e.g. USB devices, CD/DVDs, and tapes to store sensitive information files and every effort shall be made to store all electronic records and documents in the ERMS);
- manufacturing specifications shall be met when storing any electronic records and documents on media items such as tapes, hard drives, or optical media;
- if the contents of re-usable media are no longer required, it shall be securely erased; and
- all disposition records shall be authorised as defined in Section 12.3.14.10.3.2.

Note

If FCL servers use removable media for backup, the policies and procedures for backing up servers is defined in Chapter 7, Section 7.7.4.

12.3.13 Managing compliance

FCL shall implement a number of policies and procedures to ensure that it complies with all legal, regulatory, contractual, and system technical requirements. It covers:

- complying with legal and regulatory requirements within the jurisdiction of operations;
- complying with all client contractual obligations;
- reviewing the information security system; and
- reviewing system technical compliance.

12.3.13.1 Complying with legal and regulatory requirements

FCL information systems shall comply with all required legal and regulatory requirements by implementing the following processes and procedures:

- identifying applicable legislation and regulation within the jurisdiction and complying with it;
- identifying contractual obligations from clients;
- protecting intellectual property rights within the jurisdiction;
- safeguarding forensic case processing and general business records;
- information protection and privacy of personal information;
- preventing misuse of information systems;
- collecting evidence for compliance; and
- regulation of cryptographic controls within the jurisdiction.

12.3.13.1.1 Identifying applicable legislation

All relevant statutory, regulatory, and contractual requirements shall be defined in various documentation in the IMS including policies, standards, procedures, contracts, and project documentation.

A list of these shall be maintained by the ISM in the Statement of Applicability document, as defined in Appendix 1, and by the General Counsel for all contractual obligations that shall be met, specifically in the areas of information security and Service Level Agreements (SLAs).

Changes to this list shall be maintained by the Information Security Committee, where the General Counsel is a member.

12.3.13.1.2 Protecting intellectual property rights

FCL shall ensure that it meets all legislative and licensing requirements for all intellectual property rights for any third-party suppliers (e.g. Software Developers as well as publishers of printed or electronic documents). In this context 'Software' means computer instructions or information that are stored electronically. FCL shall have contracts and licences with software vendors which enables the use of their software by specific groups of computer users, or for specified applications. These contracts acknowledge the ownership of the copyright in the software. The use of such software outside the terms of the contracts is prohibited and may be unlawful.

As well as respecting the rights of third-party supplier whose copyright material FCL uses, it shall ensure that any third party that uses its copyright material also respects those rights.

The following controls shall be in place for using third-party copyright material:

- all software and other intellectual products shall only be purchased from reputable sources;
- unless authorised by the copyright Owner, software shall not be copied to another location;
- software shall not be loaned for use outside FCL for whom it is licensed;
- software manuals and other documentation may only be copied in accordance with the provisions of the licence agreement;
- books and journals are usually subject to copyright legislation and this shall also be met. The requirements vary between jurisdictions, and FCL shall ensure that it meets the relevant requirements;
- FCL funds shall not be used to purchase software that has been copied without approval of the copyright Owner (i.e. pirated software);
- illegally copied software from any source shall not be run on any FCL information processing device; and
- 'shareware' shall also be used only in compliance with the shareware agreement accompanying the software.

A software register shall be maintained by the IT Department to ensure that FCL complies with their legal requirements in relationship to its Intellectual Property Rights (IPR) obligations. The register shall include details of site-licensed software, Original Equipment Manufacturer (OEM) software, and software acquired from authorised sources. Software licence management software shall also be used to audit software installation throughout FCL.

The minimum level of information required for each software application is defined in Appendix 4.

FCL shall regularly perform audits on software to ensure that no unauthorised software is installed and used on its information processing equipment. The process for this is:

1. Each year the IT Department Manager shall authorise a software audit on a randomly selected sample of information processing devices or all devices, as appropriate.
2. the ISM shall perform the audit and compare the results with the asset register.
3. The IT Department Manager and the ISM shall investigate any discrepancies.
4. Discrepancies shall be raised as incidents.
5. Where discrepancies are found, discussion with the relevant individuals and/or Departmental Managers shall be undertaken and, where a justifiable business requirement is identified, the Finance Department shall be authorised to purchase additional licences to ensure compliance.
6. If there is no business justification identified, disciplinary action shall be considered against the employee who has installed the software.
7. Software found on information processing equipment for which no evidence of purchase can be found shall be removed immediately, unless it is validated through purchase of new licence(s);

12.3.13.1.3 Safeguarding records

FCL shall have a number of controls and processes in place to protect physical and electronic records against loss, destruction, and falsification.

The following controls shall be considered:

- record retention periods shall be determined by the legislative, regulatory, and contractual requirements;
- all records shall be categorised into specific record types, with each type having its own retention period;
- storage and handling procedures shall be managed using the ERMS;
- original physical records shall all be stored in the document registry, with scanned copies being placed in the relevant virtual case or business file held in the ERMS. The ERMS shall be regularly backed up to prevent information loss;
- all electronic records shall be subject to the in-house file naming conventions, as defined in Chapter 4, Appendix 43; and
- record disposition shall take place according to the procedures in Section 12.3.14.10.3.2.

Note

Chapter 15 covers the process of 'Effective Records Management'.

12.3.13.1.4 Data protection and the security of personal data

FCL shall ensure compliance to all legislative, regulatory, and contractual requirements relating to the privacy and security of personal data.

Personal data is defined in the EU General Data Protection Regulation (GDPR) as 'any information relating to an identified or identifiable natural person ("data subject"); an identifiable natural person is one who can be identified, directly or indirectly, in particular by reference to an identifier such as a name, an identification number, location data, an online identifier or to one or more factors specific to the physical, physiological, genetic, mental, economic, cultural or social identity of that natural person'.

Personal information includes information such as client contact details, forensic case records, and employment records—in fact, all the types of personal data which needs to be collected, processed, and retained during the normal course of FCL business.

Personal data can be found in electronic format, such as voice, text, and number information stored on a phone or information on information processing devices (including email). It may also be retained in physical records, such as filing systems, diaries, card indexes, and even photographs.

Different jurisdictions have different requirements for personal data and the protection of personal data and FCL shall ensure that these are met.

12.3.13.1.5 Preventing misuse of information systems

FCL's information processing facilities have been provided for business use only. Limited personal use of Internet facilities may be permitted, but not from forensic case processing equipment. The use of any FCL information processing facility for nonbusiness purposes shall be kept to a minimum. Excessive activity and specific activity shall be regularly monitored to detect and prevent abuse of the privilege. The following controls shall be in place:

- all employees shall be provided with business-specific accounts related solely to their role in FCL;
- when an employee logs on, a message shall be displayed on the screen, stating that this is a FCL-owned system and unauthorised access is not permitted—the employee shall accept the message on the screen to continue with the log-on process. The FCL log-on banner is defined in Appendix 5; and
- usage monitoring shall be performed on all FCL information processing facilities, including Internet and email facilities.

12.3.13.1.6 Collecting evidence for compliance

FCL shall have a number of controls in place for collecting evidence of compliance if a problem arises with legal implications. Evidence shall be collected to ensure that any action taken against an employee or any third party follows the appropriate procedures.

Note

The responsibility for defining the evidence-gathering processes lies with the following:

- General Counsel;
- IT Manager; and
- Laboratory Manager;
- Other business managers whose operations may be affected by the evidence collection process.
- The HR Manager;
- The ISM;

HR shall be the lead department for employee disciplinary matters.

In general terms, the incident response procedures used shall be followed, as defined in Chapter 7, Section 7.4.1 and in Chapter 8.

The following controls shall be in place:

- all evidence collection shall conform to the rules for evidence laid down in the relevant law, or in the rules of the specific Court in the jurisdiction;
- all evidence collected shall comply with the following rules:
  - **admissibility of evidence**—information systems shall comply with all published standards and codes of practice for the production of admissible evidence so that it can be used in a Court of Law or Tribunal;
  - **weight of evidence**—information systems shall be designed so that a trail of evidence can be followed for both physical and electronic records independent of the media on which it is held; and
  - **adequate evidence**—information systems shall have controls so that storage and processing of information are consistent throughout the period that evidence can be recovered.

12.3.13.1.7 Regulation of cryptographic controls

FCL shall ensure that the use of cryptographic controls complies with all legal requirements for the jurisdiction. All cryptographic controls shall be purchased and licensed from reputable sources.

12.3.13.2 Reviewing the information security system compliance

FCL shall undertake a programme of security reviews of their information security systems to ensure compliance with security policies and standards to:

- validate that all employees are conforming to documented requirements;
- determine if security activities are performing as expected;
- determine, using agreed metrics, that the agreed security objectives have been met, as defined in Appendix 6;
- determine actions that need to be taken to resolve any nonconformities identified, using the CAPA process.

12.3.13.2.1 Responsibilities

Line Managers shall ensure that all security procedures within their area of responsibility are carried out correctly to achieve compliance with security policies and standards.

The ISM shall be responsible for planning and commissioning all forms of information security compliance checking.

12.3.13.2.2 Review framework

All reviews of information security system compliance shall be carried out according to the IMS Calendar agreed by the Information Security Committee and approved by the Management Review. The IMS Calendar is defined in Appendix 7.

12.3.13.2.2.1 Internal audits Internal audits shall be carried out using the procedures defined in Chapter 4, Section 4.9.2, and the IMS Calendar.

12.3.13.2.2.2 Internal BCP exercises and tests All BCP tests shall be carried out using the procedures defined in Chapter 13, Section 13.6.

12.3.13.2.2.3 Internal technical testing The following procedures shall be undertaken for penetration testing:

1. The ISM shall agree the scope and frequency of technical testing for:
    - firewall audits;
    - open port scanning;
    - account reviews;
    - vulnerability scanning;
    - patch testing; and
    - workstation scans.
   with the IT Manager. This shall be performed by automated and noninvasive specialised tools, wherever possible.
2. The IT Manager shall provide IT Department resources to produce the relevant reports.
3. The results shall be examined by the ISM, and any discrepancies or other anomalies shall be investigated by the ISM.
4. Firewall audits shall be reviewed for appropriateness, and where needed, permissions shall be changed.
5. Any open ports (incoming or outgoing) that are not authorised shall be immediately closed.
6. Access rights shall be reviewed with the relevant Asset Owner for continued business need. Where there is no justified need, the rights are removed by the IT Department immediately.
7. Where missing patches are identified, they shall be reviewed for appropriateness and risk by the ISM and the IT Manager.
8. If any workstation scan shows unauthorised activity, it shall be investigated and appropriate action taken, including disciplinary action if required.
9. Where appropriate remedial action shall be taken and tracked through the CAPA process, as defined in Chapter 4, Section 4.10.
10. All changes to the IT infrastructure shall be addressed through FCL Change Management Process.

Note

All system access to review compliance shall be monitored and logged to ensure that an adequate audit trail is created. Any tools used during the audit shall be protected from unauthorised use.

12.3.13.2.2.4 External audits A number of third parties may undertake audits of FCL. These typically include clients (or third parties acting on their behalf), Insurers, or Regulators. Each shall have its own specific audit procedures, but they shall have a consistent theme that shall be similar to the internal audit process, as defined in Chapter 4, Section 4.9.2.

12.3.13.2.2.5 External technical testing External technical testing shall be carried out at least once a year to validate the internal technical testing and shall be carried out by specialised third-party suppliers. Some of the testing may be invasive, and so it shall be handled by the following process:

1. the ISM shall identify an area of the information security system that requires a technical compliance review (e.g. penetration testing, vulnerability scanning, or any other relevant technical test).
2. the ISM shall appoint a suitably qualified third-party supplier to plan and perform the review.
3. The ISM shall plan the compliance review as follows:
   - define the objectives and scope of the review;
   - identify the inputs to the review:
   - information systems (hardware and software) in scope;
   - reviewing system documentation;
   - identifying Owners of information and information assets;
   - identifying users; and
   - Identifying a suitable date and time for the review.
4. The third-party supplier shall prepare a brief outline review plan describing the above details. The plan shall be issued to all employees involved in the testing (who may comment on the plan and suitable arrangements shall then be made to conduct the review).
5. Any contractual matters shall be agreed, including any 'hold harmless agreements'.
6. The third-party supplier shall undertake the review.
7. The IT Manager and the ISM with relevant employees shall review the technical compliance of the information systems reviewed in the scope.
8. Nonconformity with information security standards shall be identified.
9. CAPAs shall be raised as appropriate using the CAPA process, as defined in Chapter 4, Section 4.10.
10. All changes required shall be managed through FCL Change Management Process.

Note

All system access to review compliance shall be monitored and logged to ensure that an adequate audit trail is created. Any tools used during the audit shall be protected from unauthorised use.

12.3.14 Managing assets in FCL

All assets within FCL shall be handled in a standard, consistent, and appropriate manner according to their classification. This is a specific requirement for information assets, but other assets shall also be managed appropriately (e.g. fixed assets).

During their life cycle in FCL, physical assets shall go through a number of phases before eventual disposal. These phases typically may include:

- a new asset is purchased and shall be added to the asset database in the Finance Department with Ownership details;
- an asset is reassigned to a new Asset Owner and the asset information database shall be updated with the new Asset Owner details. This may be to an individual being an Asset Owner or an interdepartmental transfer, so the asset is owned by the Departmental Asset Owner;
- an asset is upgraded or updated, where the asset register shall be updated with the relevant details and Ownership details remain unchanged, unless a transfer is also part of the upgrade process; and
- disposal of an asset.

12.3.14.1 Establishing accountability of assets

FCL shall establish accountability of assets in terms of the fixed assets register, the IT Service Desk Asset Register, and Ownership for tangible as well as intangible assets (e.g. electronic files and reputation).

The following controls are implemented:

- an asset is defined as an element or component of a system. It could be hardware or software, information files, transaction profiles, terminals, terminal input/output, disk/tape volumes, business information, etc.;

- an Asset Owner is FCL employee who has responsibility for a predetermined set of assets and who is, therefore, accountable for the integrity, availability, and confidentiality of the asset. An Owner is also accountable for the consequences of the actions of users of these assets;
- all assets shall have an agreed Asset Owner. Normally business information shall be owned by the business user at Top Management level;
- Asset Owners may delegate all or part of their administrative responsibilities and authority to a Custodian. However, irrespective of any such delegation, overall accountability and responsibility for the asset is retained by the Asset Owner; and
- a Custodian is normally at the Management level within the IT Department but may be a third-party supplier.

12.3.14.2 Purchasing assets

All capital and IT assets shall be purchased through official procedures to ensure accountability of the purchaser and the asset itself, as defined in Chapter 6, Section 6.7.4.

A simplified flowchart of the purchase process is (Fig. 12.1):

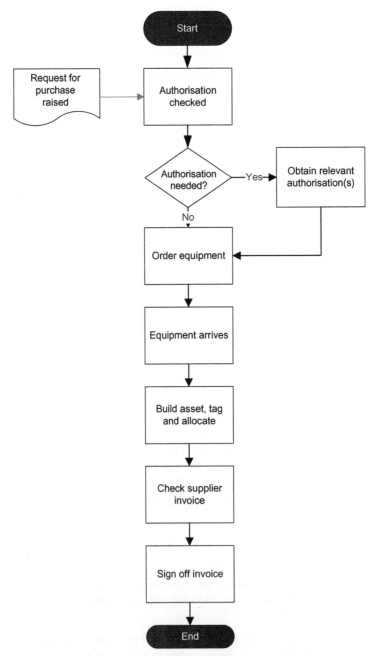

FIG. 12.1 Purchasing process.

12.3.14.2.1   Roles and responsibilities

12.3.14.2.1.1   Individual departments

1. A FCL Laboratory employee identifies a need for an asset that they do not have and discusses the requirement with their Line Manager.
2. The purchase may be for a specific case, a specific project, or an upgrade to existing services.
3. The Line Manager discusses this with the employee and either agrees to the purchase or rejects it.
4. Assuming the Line Manager agrees the purchase, they shall check for budgetary approval and obtain any necessary approvals for the purchase.
5. The Line Manager (now the Requestor) shall then raise a purchase order in association with the Finance Department.
6. If the required asset has not been received by the contracted or agreed time, the Finance Department shall be advised.
7. When the asset is delivered to FCL, the Requestor shall check the delivery for completeness and that it is fit for purpose.
8. The Requestor shall advise the Finance Department accordingly.

12.3.14.2.1.2   Finance department

1. The Finance Department shall assist the Requestor in raising a purchase order.
2. The Finance Department shall check to ensure that budgetary approval is in place.
3. A Finance Department order number for large purchases or projects shall be obtained.
4. A check on the current suppliers shall be undertaken to determine whether a suitable supplier already has a contract in place with FCL. If so, the purchase shall be placed with the supplier.
5. If no existing supplier is able to supply the required asset, an alternate supplier shall be sourced. This could be a recommendation from the Requestor or a supplier agreed after a search of the market for the required asset.
6. Once the supplier is identified, the Finance Department shall place the order with the supplier.
7. If the required asset has not been received from the supplier in the specified time, they shall contact the supplier to expedite delivery.
8. When the Finance Department has been advised of the delivery of the asset, they:
   - shall contact the supplier if the asset is damaged, not fit for purpose, or is rejected for some other reason. They shall either request a replacement or cancel the order; and
   - shall implement the payment process if the Requestor has accepted the asset.
9. Add the asset to the Finance Department asset register and add an asset tag, if appropriate.
10. Add the asset to the IT Department asset register in the Service Desk and add an asset tag, if appropriate.
11. Register any warranty details with the supplier or manufacturer, if appropriate, and add these to the relevant asset register.

12.3.14.2.1.3   IT Department

1. The IT Department shall check to see if there is a suitable asset that meets the Requestor's needs held in stock in the IT Department store.
2. If there is, the asset shall be issued to the Requestor and:
   - the Service Desk database shall be updated with the issue details;
   - the Finance Department shall be advised, if appropriate;
   - the IT Department shall commission the asset(s) for the Requestor, using the Change Management Process, if required; and
   - any required training shall be given to the Requestor on the new asset.
3. If not, the IT Department shall:
   - assist the Requestor in selection of an appropriate asset to meet the Requestor's needs;
   - assist the Requestor in the selection of a suitable supplier;
   - check all IT assets on arrival;
   - reconcile all accounting codes to relevant projects;
   - add the asset to the Service Desk application;
   - undertake IT Department asset tagging, if applicable;
   - register any warranty details with the supplier or manufacturer, if appropriate, and add these to the asset register;
   - place the asset in the IT Department Stores;
   - issue the asset to the Requestor as described above.

Note

For all assets in the Service Desk Asset Register, the minimum information to be recorded is defined in Appendix 8.

12.3.14.3   Physical asset transfer

There are a number of times where a physical asset may be transferred in FCL, each is dealt with below:

12.3.14.3.1   Asset transfer between individuals

Note

This is not applicable to information processing assets (see below).

1. FCL employee who wants to transfer a physical asset to another employee shall fill in an asset transfer form.
2. FCL employee to receive the asset and become the new Asset Owner shall countersign the asset transfer form, accepting the transfer of the asset and the responsibilities and accountabilities for that asset.
3. The asset transfer form shall be sent to the Finance Department, so that the asset register can be updated with the new Asset Owner details.

12.3.14.3.2   Asset transfer from storage to an individual

Note

This is not applicable to information processing assets (see below).

1. Where an asset is to be issued to an employee from store, it shall be issued from the store which shall fill in an asset transfer form.
2. The employee to receive the asset and become the new Asset Owner shall countersign the asset transfer form, accepting the transfer of the asset and the responsibilities and accountabilities for that asset.
3. The asset transfer form shall be sent to the Finance Department, so that the asset register can be updated with the new Asset Owner details.

12.3.14.3.3   Asset transfer between departments

Note

This is not applicable to information processing assets (see below)

1. The Departmental Asset Owner that wants to transfer a physical asset to another department shall fill in an asset transfer form.
2. The Departmental Asset Owner to receive the asset and become the new Asset Owner shall countersign the asset transfer form, accepting the transfer of the asset and the responsibilities and accountabilities for that asset.
3. The asset transfer form shall be sent to the Finance Department, so that the asset register can be updated with the new Asset Owner details.

12.3.14.3.4   Issue of an IT asset

Note

All IT Assets shall be issued via the IT Department and shall not be transferred directly between individual employees. This allows the IT Department to check them prior to issue or reissue. All IT assets are issued from the IT Department Store and shall be:

- placed there on purchase, prior to initial issue;
- recovered there on employee termination; and
- recovered there when no longer needed by their current Owner.

12.3.14.3.4.1 New IT assets

1. A new asset shall be received into FCL, as described above.
2. The asset shall be built to the relevant standard hardened build prior to issue.
3. The asset shall be tested to ensure that it meets its defined need, including testing all applications and connections.
4. The IT Department shall fill in their part of the asset transfer form.
5. The asset transfer form shall be countersigned by the new Asset Owner and the asset issued to them. Appropriate training may be undertaken at this stage, as defined in Section 12.3.2.2 for security training and as defined in Chapter 18, Section 18.2.1 for general usage training.
6. The Service Desk asset register shall be updated with the new Asset Owner details.

12.3.14.3.4.2 Reissued IT assets

1. When an IT Asset is received back into the IT Stores it shall be checked to ensure that it is still fit for purpose.
2. If the asset is capable of processing and storing information it is ensured that the information on it shall be backed up either to the ERMS or main backup (e.g. case file information from forensic case processing, business information from business area workstations or configuration information from network components).
3. Once the backups have been carried out, and verified, all information shall then be securely erased from the IT asset.
4. A new build shall be carried out using the current build to the relevant standard hardened build.
5. Issue shall then be carried out as for new assets above.

All physical and IT assets shall be audited on an annual basis to ensure that they are still accounted for; otherwise, an incident shall be raised. These audits shall be carried out by the ISM using the internal auditing process defined in Chapter 4, Section 4.9.2.

Note

If an asset is lost or stolen, an incident shall be raised and the relevant asset register updated to reflect the asset's status.

12.3.14.4 Removing assets from FCL premises

FCL shall implement controls for the removal of assets to reduce security risks by loss of assets and to secure FCL and client information and information processing devices:

- employees shall never remove assets from FCL premises without prior authorisation of an appropriate Manager, unless personally issued to them (e.g. a mobile computer) and recorded on the asset register, this includes:
  - Information processing devices and their software;
  - electronic office hardware and equipment (e.g. audio–visual equipment, etc.); and
  - information on any medium.
- all authorised assets that are removed from FCL business premises that are not personally issued to the employee shall be logged out and logged back in, when returned; and
- all employees shall be made aware during induction that spot checks may be made by FCL security staff.

12.3.14.4.1 Asset removals procedure

The procedure by which FCL shall authorise and track all assets which are removed from FCL premises shall be as below. This ensures that asset removals obtain adequate removal justification and approval and that continual controls are implemented.

If a need is identified to remove an asset from FCL premises, for example:

- a temporary off-site loan for project work;
- loan of equipment to a third party; or
- teleworking needs.

The procedure for removing and returning assets shall be:

1. The employee (the Requestor) shall seek authorisation from the Asset Owner to remove the asset. The information that shall be included in the request is defined in Appendix 9.
2. The Asset Owner shall consider the request including:
   - the impact on the business;
   - the risk to the business;
   - the physical security of the asset during transit and in use; and
   - the issues concerning the security of the information which may be held on the asset (and actions which may need to be taken to safeguard or remove that information prior to the removal of the asset).
3. If the request is rejected, the Asset Owner shall provide the Requestor with formal notification (e.g. via an email), and no further action is taken.
4. If the request is approved, the Asset Owner shall provide the Requestor with formal authorisation (e.g. via an email), and any terms under which the asset is to be removed, for example:
   - the dates and limiting timescales;
   - the issues concerning physical security when off premises; and
   - the actions concerning the safeguarding of the asset and information (e.g. transport arrangements, removal of information, etc.) during the period off premises.
5. The Requestor shall submit a request form to the Service Desk. (This forms the basis of an asset control list and acts as an audit trail for all authorised asset removals from the premises).
6. The Service Desk shall raise a ticket to track the asset removal, and details of the request shall be updated in the asset register in accordance with the procedures for Managing the Asset Register, as defined in Section 12.3.14.
7. The asset shall be removed from the premises in accordance with the agreed terms.
8. On return of the asset to the premises, the Requestor who required the asset shall:
   - arrange for inspection of the asset by the Asset Owner, who authorises any appropriate action in the event that there is a problem;
   - notify the Service Desk that the asset has been returned.

Note

In the event that an asset is not returned on the due date, the Service Desk shall escalate the matter in accordance with the process for managing incidents.

---

9. The service desk shall update the asset register and close the asset removal notification ticket in the service desk system.

12.3.14.5 Managing information assets

Information assets are the lifeblood of FCL and they shall be protected according to relevant legislative and regulatory requirements in the jurisdiction as well as recognised good practice and contractual requirements. Once all of the information assets have been identified, they shall be classified and appropriate decisions regarding the level of security to be applied to them shall be identified to protect them.

Additionally, FCL shall also decide about the level of information redundancy that is necessary (e.g. keeping an extra copy of the information on an extra hot standby server); however, any redundancy must also meet relevant personal data privacy legislation.

FCL shall classify information assets into four categories as follows:

12.3.14.5.1 Created information assets

This is FCL information. This is information that has been collected, classified, organised, and stored in the ERMS. It shall include:

- **Databases and other structured information**: Information about customers, personnel, production, sales, marketing, finances held in the ERMS. This information is critical for the business. Its confidentiality, integrity, and availability are of utmost importance.

- **Information files**: Transactional information giving up-to-date information about each event, also typically held in the ERMS, but may be held elsewhere.
- **Operational and support procedures**: These have been developed over the years and provide detailed instructions on how to perform various activities and are held in the IMS (and also backed up into the ERMS).
- **Archived information**: Old records that may be required to be maintained by legislation, regulation, good practice, or contractual requirements. Typically, these are held in the ERMS.
- **Continuity plans and fallback arrangements**: These are developed to overcome any disaster and maintain the continuity of business. The absence of these may lead to ad hoc decisions in a crisis. They are held in the ERMS as well as on the secure corporate website.
- **Unstructured information**: Typically, user-created office documents and email.

12.3.14.5.2 Software assets

Software assets shall include:

- **Application software**: Application software implements business rules within FCL. Creation of application software is a time-consuming task. Integrity of application software is essential. Any flaw in the application software could impact the business adversely. All forensic tools shall be validated in accordance with Chapter 7. Section 7.5.5; and
- **System software**: Packaged software programmes, e.g. operating systems, DBMS, development tools and utilities, software packages, office productivity suites, etc. Most of the software under this category would be available off the shelf unless the software is obsolete or nonstandard.

12.3.14.5.3 Physical assets

Physical assets shall include:

- **Computer equipment**: Servers, desktops, and mobile computers;
- **Mobile devices**: Smartphones, tablets;
- **Communication and network equipment**: Modems, routers, switches, and PABXs;
- **Storage media**: Magnetic tapes, hard disks, all types of removable media, DLTs and DATs; and
- **Technical equipment**: Power supplies, air conditioners, UPS, generators.

12.3.14.5.4 Services

These are essential services required for running the office and include, but are not limited to:

- **communication services**: voice communication, information communication, value-added services, wide area network, etc.; and
- **environmental conditioning services**: heating, lighting, air conditioning, and power.

12.3.14.6 Classification of assets

Note

Asset classification typically refers to information but shall also refer to the infrastructure on which the information is actually stored and processed. Examples of this include:

- information processing devices holding sensitive forensic case files;
- systems containing information that may need to be physically and logically isolated to implement appropriate information security;
- other situations where classified information (either classified by FCL or a client) shall be handled according to its classification;
- assets can include physical media, e.g. paper, recordings, magnetic or paper tapes, disks, and microfilms; and

- data held in other forms such as shorthand notebooks shall also be classified. This classification process shall also include information from any third party that has been entrusted to FCL, in the course of normal business dealings.

  Within FCL, the following shall be adopted as the schema with the reasons given for the adoption. If the reasoning or types of information held change, the schema shall be reviewed.
- **Confidentiality**—this shall be applicable to FCL as all forensic case files are classified as 'Confidential' as is most internally produced information and records. Access rights to all information shall be based on justified business need and reflected in the Access Control Policy, as defined in Chapter 4, Appendix 21. Access rights shall be granted to named employees or defined groups of employees;

Not included are:

- **Value**—as FCL does not process any payments that are of high value (i.e. it is not a financial institution);
- **Time**—timeliness is not an issue within FCL (e.g. release of company financial results prior to official release). All information held in the ERMS shall be subject to regular review and this, combined with legislative, regulatory, and contractual requirements is seen as appropriate without additional levels of information classification.

Confidentiality classifications in use shall be:

- Public;
- Internal Use Only;
- Confidential; and
- Strictly Confidential.

Note

Other classifications from clients may differ from these classifications and they shall either be assigned to the required FCL classification or a specific set of handling procedures be defined according to the client's contractual requirements.

12.3.14.7 Duties of information owners and custodians

Information Owners, and Custodians on their behalf, shall be responsible for:

1. Classifying information, functions, and systems according to the classifications in use in FCL, as defined in Chapter 5, Section 5.5.6.6.
2. Ensuring that risk management is applied to the processes carried out on their information, as defined in Chapter 5.
3. Ensuring that adequate and cost-effective measures are employed to minimise the risks to the integrity, availability, and confidentiality of their information.
4. Agreeing the level of security to be applied to the creation, reading, updating, execution, and deleting of information, and authorising any changes to these levels.
5. Ensuring that the level of auditing available is in line with these standards.
6. Ensuring that adequate recovery procedures are in place for all situations for their information and that these meet the requirements of client SLAs, if appropriate.
7. Regularly exercising or testing recovery procedures to ensure that recovery processes do work and meet SLAs.
8. Agreeing access levels for all employees to 'their' information.
9. Reviewing, on a regular basis, with the ISM, that all access to their information is based on current justified business needs.
10. Establishing a local security administration function that has responsibility for the access control and monitoring procedures to be applied to the resources. The responsibilities of this function shall consist of coordinating, monitoring, and administration and these responsibilities should be performed by different people to provide segregation of duties. In all cases, the monitoring and administration functions shall be separate.
11. The IT Department shall have the responsibility to ensure that production information files under their control are only updated, deleted, or otherwise changed by authorised programmes operating within the Change Management Process.
12. Ensuring that all operations involving personal information comply with any relevant personal data privacy legislation.
13. Defining the backup requirements for their information. The IT Department shall ensure that this is performed according to the Owner's requirements and that it is restorable.

12.3.14.8 Labelling assets

Note

Whilst the Asset Owner is responsible for classification of all of their assets, labelling is usually performed by the Custodian.

The Asset Owner shall ensure that all of 'their' assets are classified and labelled according to the classification scheme in place. Output from systems containing classified information shall also be classified to the same level as the system processing the information.

Items for consideration shall include, but not be limited to:

- information processing systems;
- printed reports;
- screen displays;
- recorded media (e.g. hard disks, tapes, all types of removable media);
- electronic messages (e.g. email, before, during, and after transmission);
- file transfers (before, during, and after transmission); and
- system output (whilst in the system as well as having been output from the system).

For each classification level, handling procedures including the secure processing, storage, transmission, declassification, and destruction have been defined in this section.

Labelling and secure handling of classified information is a key requirement for information-sharing arrangements. Physical labels are a common form of labelling. However, some information assets, such as documents in electronic form, cannot be physically labelled and electronic means of labelling shall be used.

12.3.14.8.1 Documents

All documents shall be marked with their classification in the footer on every page, according to the document control requirements defined in Chapter 4, Section 4.7.5, and appropriate appendices.

12.3.14.8.2 Physical assets

All physical assets shall have a self-adhesive sticker showing the asset number and the asset's classification securely attached to it.

12.3.14.8.3 Information assets

Where labelling is not feasible, other means of designating the asset number of the information may be applied, e.g. via procedures or metainformation.

12.3.14.9 Handling classified assets

All classified assets in FCL shall be handled according to their classification.

Assets shall only be handled by those who have a need to know and a justified business need to access them according to the Access Control Policy.

Where a client entrusts its classified information to FCL, it shall be handled in line with the most appropriate FCL classification. Ideally, this shall be agreed in writing with the client so that there is no misunderstanding.

It should also be noted that FCL requires that the:

- storage of any media shall be in accordance with manufacturers' specifications; and
- the distribution of classified material shall be kept to a minimum.

These procedures shall apply to information in documents, information processing systems, networks, mobile computers, email, voice mail, voice communications in general, multimedia, postal services/facilities, use of facsimile machines, and any other sensitive items, e.g. blank cheques and invoices.

The current handling procedures in use are the default ones, unless overridden by the client, and are defined in, Appendix 10.

12.3.14.10   Disposing of assets

There are two types of asset in FCL that may need to be disposed of, in addition to electronic and physical record disposal. Assets can be disposed of by employees or a specialised third-party service provider can be used. Generic requirements for third-party suppliers are defined in Chapter 14, but specific requirements for third-party service providers for IT asset disposal are given below.

12.3.14.10.1   Asset disposal by third-party service providers

Asset disposal of physical assets that contain no sensitive material (e.g. furniture) shall be carried out by any third-party service provider or even a charity if appropriate. However, when disposing of IT assets extreme caution shall be undertaken. The procedures for preparation for disposal shall be the same as those for maintenance, as defined in Chapter 7, Section 7.5.1.1. If FCL is going to ship media that has not been securely wiped or the media removed from the device to a third-party service provider for disposal then additional safeguards shall be in place. The procedures for using a third-party service provider for disposal shall be:

1. A need is identified for the disposal of one or more IT Assets. The IT Manager selects an approved third-party service provider for disposal from the list of approved third-party service providers and contacts them to arrange collection of the asset(s).
2. The asset(s) shall be stored in the secure holding area, to await disposal.
3. The asset register shall be updated to show the disposal and the details required for this are defined in Appendix 11.
4. The third-party service provider shall collect the asset(s) for disposal. Destruction may be performed at their location or on-site at FCL premises. It is essential that the vehicle used to either perform the destruction or to convey the asset(s) to their premises shall be fit for purpose and able to provide appropriate levels of security.
5. The method of disposal and/or destruction shall be agreed with the IT manager, based on the classification or sensitivity of the data held on the asset(s).
6. The third-party service provider shall supply a destruction certificate, as appropriate, to the IT Manager, who shall scan it and associate it with the asset's records in the Service Desk Asset Register.
7. Where appropriate, the IT Manager shall advise the Finance Department.

Note 1

The loading and unloading area shall be covered by CCTV, if possible.

Note 2

Where practical, all assets shall be appropriately recycled as part of FCL's commitment to the environment.

Note 3

The ISM shall undertake random checks of the disposal process.

12.3.14.10.2   Physical assets

These procedures apply to any non-IT capital asset to be disposed of within FCL and would typically involve fixtures and fittings. The Asset Owner shall determine, in association with the Finance Department, that an asset is to be disposed of.

12.3.14.10.3   IT assets

The following controls shall be in place to prevent careless disposal of IT assets and unauthorised disclosure of sensitive information:

- all media items are disposed of in a manner commensurate with the classification of information stored within them and using one of the acceptable methods of disposal;
- waste or recycling bins are not appropriate means of disposal for media items containing sensitive information. It is the responsibility of all Information Owners, Custodians or holders of classified information ensure that appropriate disposal occurs.

- The following are acceptable methods of disposal:
  - **crosscut shredders**: these are available throughout the office and they shall be used to dispose of all documents, and media that can be shredded;
  - **secure wiping of computer media**: all information stored on hard disks shall be removed by wiping that securely erases all data from the hard disks;

Note

Normal formatting does not securely erase information on media.

- **hard disk destroyers**: hard disks that cannot be wiped successfully shall be physically destroyed using a hard disk destroyer under the control of the ISM;
- other methods of disposal may be used with the authorisation of the ISM.

Note

Only the IT Manager is authorised to dispose of IT assets.

A simplified flowchart of the disposal process is (Fig. 12.2):

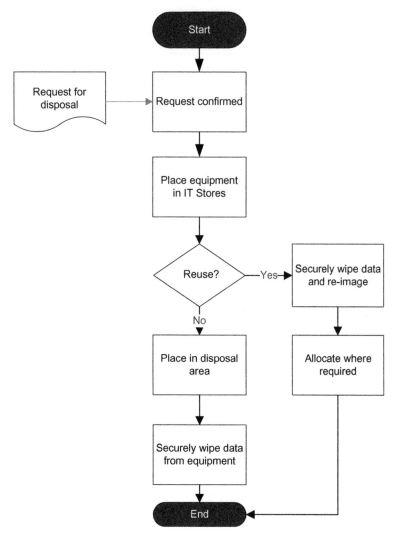

FIG. 12.2 Disposal of IT assets.

12.3.14.10.3.1 IT Department roles and responsibilities The IT Manager shall be the central authority for all IT asset disposals.

The IT Department, via the Service Desk, shall be the first point of contact for all employees who want to dispose of an IT asset. The responsibilities of this role include:

- maintaining the Secure IT Store;
- reallocating IT equipment;
- erasing information from equipment;
- logging disposal certificates; and
- updating the asset register.

12.3.14.10.3.2 Disposing of an IT asset procedure
1. An employee shall email the IT Department and request a change to their IT equipment that causes a piece of equipment to be removed or reports a fault to the Service Desk that shall result in an IT asset disposal;

Note 1

The employee shall have discussed the proposed disposal with the registered Asset Owner of the IT asset before contacting the Service Desk, where appropriate.

Note 2

Only equipment that requires replacement based on a business need/justification or is confirmed to be faulty shall be replaced.

---

2. The Service Desk shall log the request and the IT Department shall perform a brief investigation into whether the equipment needs replacing or is faulty. If the equipment needs replacing or is faulty, the IT Department shall confirm this and arrange for delivery/collection of the redundant equipment.

If the equipment is to be replaced it shall be delivered to/collected by the IT Department and then placed into the IT Department stores. When a request for new equipment is made at the Service Desk, the IT Department store shall be checked to see whether the equipment can be reused. If it can be reused it shall be assigned to the relevant user and the Asset Register shall be updated. All internal storage media (e.g. disks, etc.) shall be securely erased and then re-imaged before use.

Note

All unallocated equipment details shall be changed in the Asset Register to 'IT spares'.

If the equipment cannot be reused due to a fault or the equipment is too outdated to be of any use it shall be disposed of.

3. The IT Department shall place the equipment for disposal into the disposal area.
4. An authorised member of the IT Department shall perform the disposal of the equipment.
5. The Service Desk and the Finance Department shall record the disposal details against the asset.

12.4 Physical security in FCL

The first layer of security in FCL is physical security. These are general controls that are reinforced for secure areas within FCL and for IT areas.

All physical security measures shall be managed by the building Facilities Department, and are in place to help prevent unauthorised access, damage, and interference to FCL's business operations.

There are four different areas for increased physical security over and above the standard office security in place:

- secure IT areas, which include:
  - the server rooms ('the Data Centre');
  - wiring closets;
  - the Secure IT Store (for incoming stores and those waiting disposal).
- secure delivery storage area;
- the laboratory where forensic case processing is performed; and
- the Secure Property Store.

Similar processes are in place for all of these areas, but typically the authoriser(s) for these areas are the relevant Managers who 'own' the areas.

Secure area access is defined in Section 12.4.4 and is defined in the Physical Security Policy in Chapter 2, Appendix 2.

12.4.1 Physical controls

The following physical security controls are in place in FCL:

1. FCL shall not have signage stating what activities are carried out on-site.
2. Access to FCL shall be through a staffed reception area. All visitors and service engineers shall be required to report to this reception area before being granted access, as defined in Section 12.4.2.
3. The reception area shall be staffed at all times. During the working day, at least one employee shall be present at the reception desk, so that they can manage phone calls, visitors and deliveries.
4. All emergency exits shall only be operable from inside using break glass locks and shall be alarmed.
5. CCTV shall cover the entrance and all exits, as well as all secure areas (as defined above) and the loading bay. The use of CCTV is defined in Section 4.5 and how it is managed is defined in Chapter 7, Section 7.5.3.
6. All access to FCL shall be via access control cards with associated PIN numbers. This shall be for employees as well as visitors and service engineers.
7. Access to secure areas shall be as above but reinforced with biometric fingerprint readers.
8. Full burglar alarms shall be in place throughout FCL for both perimeter and internal detection. The alarm system shall be connected to a 24/7 staffed site.
9. Full fire detection and quenching shall be in place throughout FCL and connected to a 24/7 staffed site. Fire quenching shall be provided using a variety of quenching mechanisms, from fire blankets in the kitchens through handheld quenching devices in the office to FM 200 suppression in the Data Centre.
10. Where a secure area has been defined, it shall be secured from real floor to real ceiling, rather than just using internal partition walling.

Specific procedures to support physical security access control are defined in the following sections:

12.4.2 Hosting visitors

Note

FCL defines anyone not under a contract of employment as a 'Visitor'.

FCL is likely to experience visitors for a number of reasons, this includes, but is not limited to:

- client visits;
- interviews;
- forensic case viewing;
- meetings;
- equipment maintenance; and
- equipment or service support.

Visitors to FCL, unless properly managed and controlled, can pose great risks to FCL, its information or information processing facilities.

12.4.2.1 Definitions

The following definitions are in use in FCL:

Term	Meaning
Visitor	An individual, not an employee, who visits FCL premises for any reason (this includes visitors who attend for training, interviews, maintenance visits, meetings, etc.) Visitors may also visit the Data Centre or the Disaster Recovery (DR) site, but they are subject to additional requirements for these locations in addition to those for 'normal' Visitors to the office
Host	An employee who sponsors a visitor
Escort	An employee who accompanies a visitor during their time on FCL premises

12.4.2.2 General

This procedure shall apply to all visitors to FCL, the host, and escort for those visitors.

FCL takes seriously the security of its visitors, its own assets, and those entrusted to them by clients and shall ensure that all are appropriately protected.

These procedures shall be implemented to prevent unauthorised access, damage, and interference to critical or sensitive business information as well as provide appropriate protection to employees and visitors.

12.4.2.3 Levels of access

There are four levels of access granted to all FCL facilities, including the Data Centre and the Disaster Recovery (DR) site. These are defined below:

12.4.2.3.1 Normal access

This is access granted to employees who, as part of their job role, have a business need to access a specific area of FCL. Their access cards or other access credentials enable the permitted access.

12.4.2.3.2 Access authoriser

This is access granted to specific employees who, as part of their job role, are permitted to authorise other employees or visitors to access specific areas of FCL temporarily or permanently as defined in Section 12.4.4.1 below.

12.4.2.3.3 Escorted access

This is the standard access level granted to visitors. Visitors shall be continuously monitored by their escort during their time on FCL premises. All visitors shall have a current Visitor and Visit Checklist Form filled in for them as defined in Appendix 12.

12.4.2.3.4 Unescorted access

This is access granted to maintenance engineers and others who work for third-party suppliers that have a business need to visit FCL and are covered by existing Nondisclosure Agreements (NDAs) or contracts containing a confidentiality agreement and who have had a current Visitor and Visit Checklist filled in for them.

Unescorted access visitors shall still have to sign into, and out of, the Data Centre and are subject to the Rules of the Data Centre as defined in Appendix 13.

12.4.2.4 The visit life cycle

The swim lane diagram below outlines the life cycle of a visit to FCL (Fig. 12.3).

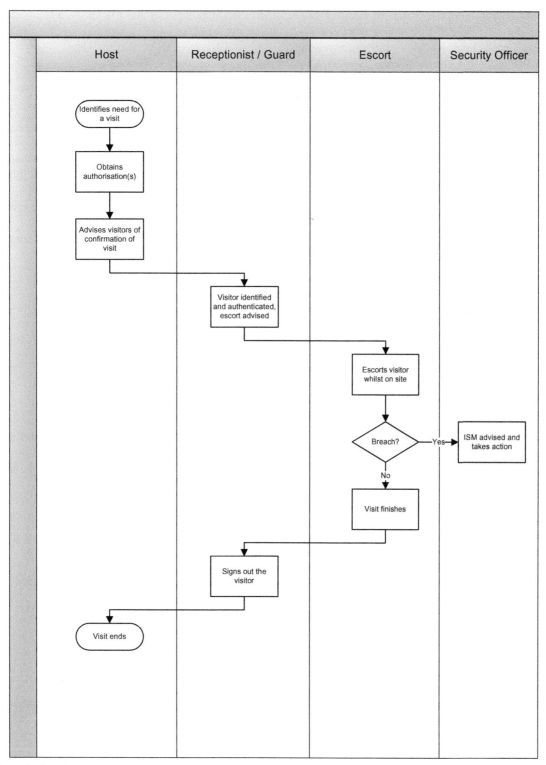

FIG. 12.3   Visit life cycle.

12.4.2.4.1   Prior to the visit

All visits to FCL shall be scheduled in advance, preferably with at least a day's notice, and the following shall be undertaken before the visit:

1. A requirement for a visit is identified.
2. The employee who is hosting the visit (the 'host') is identified.

3. The host obtains from the visitor the information required to facilitate the visit and fills in the relevant parts of the Visitor and Visit Checklist.
4. The host obtains relevant authorisation(s), as required.
5. The host checks to determine if an existing NDA or contract is in place to cover the visit.
6. The host confirms the visit details with the visitor and advises them to report to Reception.
7. The host advises the Building Facilities Manager of visit.
8. The Building Facilities Manager advises the Receptionists of the visit.
9. The host ensures that they are available for the visit, or that they have appointed someone else who shall be present, to be the host/escort for the visit.
10. Where the visit is for training purposes or a meeting, rather than an individual visitor, the host shall provide a roster of expected attendees to the Receptionists. The host shall have been expected to set up the facilities for training (e.g. classroom, equipment, etc.) or a meeting (meeting room, etc.).
11. Typically, visitors shall arrive during the working day, but if an emergency call-out is required (e.g. hardware or maintenance engineers), then these shall be handled by the night security guards.
12. Personal visits are not permitted except in an emergency. In this case, the procedure below is followed, but the host is the subject of the emergency visit.

12.4.2.4.2 On arrival

Note

The host and the escort may be the same person or may be different people. For simplicity, the term 'escort' has been used in this section to identify the employee escorting the visitor.

When the visitor arrives, the following procedures shall be carried out:

1. The visitor shall report to Reception, who checks their offered ID, if appropriate, and issues them their personal visitor pass.
2. The Receptionist shall contact the escort, their nominated deputy, or someone in the same business area if neither are available and advises them of the visitor's arrival and places the visitor into the reception area.
3. The escort shall arrive and greet the visitor. They shall then undertake the visitor briefing as defined on the Visitor and Visit Checklist.
4. All relevant actions shall be undertaken and the Visitor and Visit Checklist shall be retained by the escort (or their nominated deputy) as a record when completed, with associated signed forms, and given to the ISM who shall retain it as a record for later audit.
5. The escort shall ensure that the visitor swipes into the office and wears their visitor badge.
6. The escort shall then accompany the visitor for their visit and shall be responsible and accountable for the visitor whilst on-site. This shall include ensuring they wear their visitor badge, complying with local procedures and requirements, returning their badges at the end of the visit, and swiping out when leaving.

12.4.2.4.3 During the visit

During the visit, the following procedures shall apply:

1. The escort shall escort the visitor into the appropriate area(s).
2. During the visit, the visitor shall be monitored at all times where practical. Visitors shall never be left unattended, as far as is practical for office visits. Where a visit is to a secure area, they shall be accompanied at all times.
3. Where the visitor is a 'known' visitor (i.e. one that is subject to relevant nondisclosure or contractual agreements that are current and in force), this requirement is not necessary (e.g. plant watering, maintenance engineers, etc.). These visitors shall wear visitor badges and optionally their own company ones at all times whilst on-site.
4. During a visit, if the escort notices that the visitor is in breach of any mandated security or safety requirements or any other inappropriate activity, they shall advise the visitor. If the visitor does not amend their behaviour, the escort shall immediately raise an incident and advise the ISM, by appropriate means, for action.
5. Should the visitor be required to leave the office at ISM's request, the escort shall ensure that this is done immediately.

6. The only exception to these requirements is where emergency access is required for emergency service or emergency building work access. This shall be treated as an information security incident and an information security incident report raised. Appropriate retrospective authorities shall be recorded on the information security incident report.

12.4.2.4.4 Accessing secure areas

Within FCL, there are four secure areas, which are identified in Section 12.4 (above). These areas have a higher requirement for security in place than the rest of the office on account of the information, assets, or the resources they contain.

Where a visitor is also going to access one of these secure areas, the following additional procedures shall be followed:

1. Any visitor requiring access to a secure area shall declare this in advance of their visit, otherwise access may not be permitted.
2. The host shall ensure that the visitor swipes into the secure area after the host has authenticated themselves with their access card and their biometrics.
3. The host shall advise the visitor of any relevant rules for the secure area and this briefing shall be recorded on the Visitor and Visit Checklist.
4. The visitor shall only be permitted access to those secure areas authorised on Visitor and Visit Checklist.
5. Should the visitor be required to leave a secure area at the ISM's request, the host shall ensure that this is done immediately (and also the building if required).
6. Where the visitor is a maintenance engineer or similar, the supplier shall, where practicable, provide a list of authorised engineers to FCL so that these may be recorded on the 'known' visitor access list for the secure area.
7. Where an arriving engineer, or similar, is not on the 'known' visitor list, their credentials shall be checked, according to the Visitor and Visit Checklist, prior to permitting access.
8. No unauthorised visitor or employee shall be permitted access to any secure area.
9. The relevant authorising Manager shall have the right to refuse admission to anyone or to terminate a visit should they feel it appropriate. In this case, an incident report shall be raised.
10. The only exception to these requirements is where emergency access is required for emergency service or emergency building work access. This shall be treated as an information security incident and an information security incident report raised. Appropriate retrospective authorities shall be recorded on the information security incident report.

12.4.2.4.5 Ending the visit

12.4.2.4.5.1 Office
1. When the visit is complete, the escort shall escort the visitor to the Reception desk.
2. The visitor shall swipe out and return their visitor card.
3. The visitor leaves.

12.4.2.4.5.2 Secure areas In addition to the above, the escort shall ensure that the visitor swipes out of any secure area to which they were authorised access.

12.4.2.5 End-of-day procedures

At the end of the day, the Receptionists shall:

1. Reconcile the visitor passes to ensure they have all been returned.
2. Ensure that they hold no ID for any visitors.
3. Ensure that the Visitor Log is properly completed and sign it off as a true and accurate record.
4. Alert the ISM of any issues during the day, including visitor passes not returned.

12.4.2.5.1 Unwanted visitors

The following actions shall be performed to handle unwanted visitors:

1. If it is a simple situation, the Receptionists shall refuse entry to the premises or call for assistance, as appropriate.
2. If the visitor is already inside the premises, then appropriate action should be taken, including calling the Police, if necessary. This shall be a management decision and typically taken by the senior person on-site at the time.

12.4.3 Managing deliveries

FCL will normally have a number of deliveries and collections during the WORKING day. All deliveries shall be made to the Receptionists at the front desk who have access to the incoming secure delivery storage area. The following controls shall be in place to protect deliveries from unauthorised access, removal, destruction, or loss:

- all deliveries to FCL shall be held in the designated and secure delivery storage area at reception;
- only designated employees shall have access to the secure holding area;
- all incoming deliveries shall be registered before being moved to the secure delivery storage area or directly to the intended recipient;
- all deliveries shall be inspected, prior to acceptance for potential hazards; and
- removal from the secure delivery storage area shall only be undertaken by designated employees, and the removal documented and added to the ERMS.

12.4.3.1 Procedure for receiving deliveries

FCL shall follow this procedure to receive deliveries and therefore maintain isolation of environments between Reception and the information processing areas (Fig. 12.4).

1. An employee (usually the one mentioned in the delivery note) receives notification of a delivery. They advise the Building Facilities Manager to:
   - make the Receptionists aware of the delivery so that they can be advised of the arrival or to manage it if they are not available and place it in the secure delivery storage area;
   - request that the Receptionists advise them on arrival so that they can personally receive their delivery.
2. Often deliveries are attempted without prior notification. In this case, the Receptionists shall attempt to contact the intended recipient so they can collect in person. If they are not available, the Receptionists shall receive the delivery on their behalf and place it into the secure delivery storage area.
3. Whether the delivery is to be received by the intended recipient or the Receptionists, it shall be subject to a routine initial inspection to ensure that no dangerous items are brought onto the premises.
4. If the delivery is rejected for any reason, the delivery company shall be advised of the reason and the delivery not accepted. The paperwork from the delivery company shall be completed and a copy of it retained and added to the ERMS and the Finance Department advised.
5. After the initial inspection is carried out and the delivery accepted, it shall either be either taken by the intended recipient or placed in the secure delivery storage area by the Receptionists. The paperwork from the delivery company shall be completed and a copy of it shall be retained and later added to the ERMS and the Finance Department advised.
6. If the delivery has to go into the secure delivery storage area or is collected by the intended recipient, the following information is logged and the Finance Department advised:
   - date and time of delivery;
   - delivery by (courier or other details);
   - item description;
   - delivery inspection results;
   - received by;
   - date and time of transfer into the secure delivery storage area, if applicable;
   - name of the person who transferred it to the secure delivery storage area;
   - location of the items in the secure delivery storage area, if required;
   - intended recipient, if known;
   - date and time of transfer from the secure delivery storage area, if applicable;
   - name of the person who transferred it from the secure delivery storage area; and
   - any other relevant information (as required).
7. If the delivery goes into the secure delivery storage area, the Receptionists shall advise the intended recipient and arrange a suitable time for its collection.
8. When the delivery is collected by the intended recipient, the details above are updated accordingly.
9. When the delivery is finally received by the intended recipient (either on delivery or via the secure delivery storage area), and the following checks undertaken on unpacking:
   - the delivery shall be validated as being the correct/expected item(s);
   - the delivery shall be verified as complete; and
   - an inspection shall be made for any potential hazards.

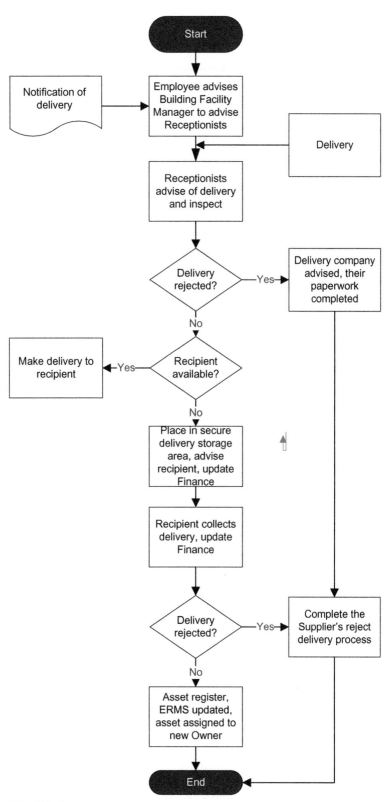

FIG. 12.4 Procedure for receiving deliveries.

In the event that after unpacking, an item is not acceptable for any reason, it should be rejected by the supplier's delivery rejection process and the Finance Department advised accordingly.

Note

Care shall be taken to ensure that any rejection of a delivery takes place within the period defined for this process by the supplier.

---

10. Where the delivery is finally accepted by the recipient the relevant asset register(s) shall be updated and the asset assigned to its relevant Owner.

12.4.4　Managing access control

Logical access control is the second layer of security in the defence in-depth model. This shall be implemented, to differing levels depending on whether users are the general office or secure areas as defined in Section 12.4.

12.4.4.1　Authorisations

Different Managers shall be responsible for authorising access to areas. These are (Table 12.1):

TABLE 12.1 Access authorisation table.

Area	Relevant authorising manager
The office[a]	HR Manager ISM
Secure IT areas	IT Manager ISM
Secure delivery store	Building Facilities Manager ISM
Forensic case processing area	Laboratory Manager ISM
Secure property store	Laboratory Manager ISM

[a] This is the basic entry level to the office and all additional accesses to 'secure areas' require this basic access authority.

Note 1

The ISM shall be a co-signature to the authorisations to ensure that there is no one person that authorises access.

Note 2

Where the term 'Relevant Manager' is used below, it refers to those defined in the table above.

12.4.4.2　Working in secure areas

All areas shall be secured, not only those areas defined as 'secure areas'. These controls shall be implemented to prevent unauthorised access to, modification of, erasure, loss, abuse of FCL or client information or other assets:

- physical access to a secure area shall be secured on entry and when leaving the area;
- unauthorised employees or visitors shall not be allowed access to a secure area except where authorised access is required (e.g. by a service engineer, third-party service provider staff, or clients);
- permission from the Relevant Managers shall always be obtained when entry to a secure area is required;
- visitors shall never be left unattended or unsupervised in a secure area;
- other guidelines that shall be considered for access to secure areas include:
  - photographic or audio recording equipment shall not be permitted in any secure area;
  - eating and drinking shall not be allowed in the Data Centre.

12.4.4.3 Managing access to secure areas

Access control to the secure areas shall be implemented to prevent unauthorised access, damage to, and interference with any FCL or client assets in secure areas.

Access to secure areas shall be restricted to authorised employees. Access rights to secure areas shall be reviewed as follows:

- access requirements to secure areas shall be changed regularly (e.g. periodic changes of PIN codes) and in particular when an employee is terminated, for those areas where they had authorised access; and
- all access requirements and rights to secure areas shall be reviewed on a quarterly basis and updated (as appropriate) by the Relevant Managers, or more frequently in the event of a security breach or other influencing change.

The process by which FCL manages access to secure areas is (Fig. 12.5):

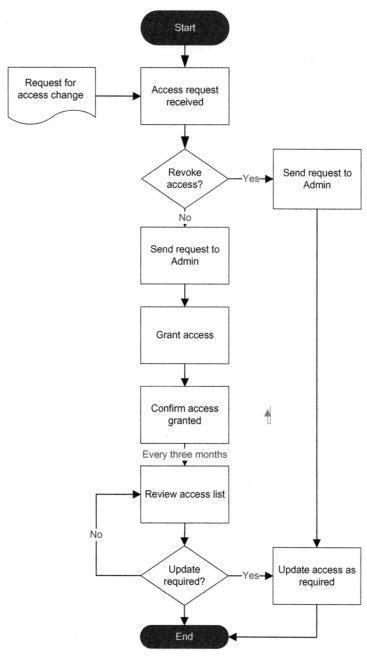

FIG. 12.5 Access process for access to secure areas.

12.4.4.3.1 Roles and responsibilities

The following roles and responsibilities are defined for controlling access to secure areas:

12.4.4.3.1.1 Building Facilities Manager The Building Facilities Manager shall be responsible for the following processes:

- applying authorised access requests to the physical access controls, and ensuring that access is granted;
- managing the Receptionists and the secure delivery storage area;
- applying authorised access revocations from the physical access controls, and ensuring access is removed;
- maintaining a secure physical environment;
- performing periodic reviews of the secure delivery storage area access rights and physical security controls with other Relevant Managers;
- assessing requests for access to secure areas with the Relevant Managers;
- confirming that access to a secure IT area is granted or revoked in accordance with a specific business justified request; and
- monitoring the close circuit television (CCTV) recording system, the staffed security guards, and the office access control system.

12.4.4.3.1.2 IT Manager The IT Manager shall be responsible for:

- performing periodic reviews of the physical controls to secure IT areas;
- performing periodic reviews of access rights to secure IT areas with other Relevant Managers and Asset Owners;
- technical support for the CCTV recording system, and the access control system;
- authorising requests for access to Data Centre; and
- maintaining a secure physical environment for secure IT areas.

12.4.4.3.1.3 ISM The ISM shall be responsible for:

- providing assistance to other Relevant Managers and other interested parties as required;
- being a co-signatory on all access authorisation requires, to provide segregation of duties for all authorisation requests; and
- undertaking access rights audits, as appropriate.

12.4.4.3.2 Granting access to IT secure areas

Access to secure areas shall only be granted on a temporary basis to authorised employees, and all access rights shall be reviewed every 3 months.

This means that access to secure areas is under continuous review.

The following actions shall be performed to grant access:

1. The Requester sends the Access Request Form to the Service Desk, who logs the request in the Service Desk System.
2. The Relevant Manager(s) validate the request and determine whether access to a secure area is required by the employee, according to their job role. For example:
   - some IT Department employees may require access to certain secure areas for server or network management and cabling (e.g. Data Centre and Wiring Closets);
   - some third-party service providers working for FCL (or for their clients) may require access for specific purposes (e.g. third-party support engineers for server management in the Data Centre);
   - come Service Desk employees may require access to particular area for access to IT equipment (e.g. the Secure IT Store);
   - clients' employees may require access to view forensic case material.

Note

Some IT Department employees may not be granted access to a secure IT area and may instead be hosted by another employee, who has authorised access.

---

3. The Building Facilities Manager shall ensure that a pass with the required access rights is available, as required.
4. The host shall check that their access is valid on the day required, and then confirms this with the Service Desk to close the Service Desk request.

12.4.4.3.3 Revoking access rights to secure areas

Where access to secure areas is to be revoked, for whatever reason, the following actions shall be performed to revoke access:

1. The Relevant Manager shall determine that access to a secure area is no longer required by an employee or visitor. Typically, this is when:
   - the employee is terminated;
   - the visitor is no longer required on-site;
   - a project requiring the employee to use the area has finished;
   - the employee is subject to disciplinary measures involving a secure area; and
   - an access rights review has determined that access is no longer justified.
2. The Relevant Manager sends a request to the Service Desk to create a Service Desk request for revoking the access. The request shall contain the following details:
   - access removal authorisation;
   - name of the employee or visitor for which access is to be removed; and
   - date on which access is to be removed.
3. The Building Facilities Manager shall be advised of the details of the revocation requirement.
4. The Building Facilities Manager shall confirm that access to the secure area is removed on the day required, advising relevant interested parties, and then confirm this with the Service Desk to close the Service Desk request.

Note

No prior warning is needed for access rights revocation to be performed immediately by the Building Facilities Manager on request.

12.4.4.3.4 Reviewing access to secure areas

Access to all Secure Areas shall be regularly reviewed to ensure that all access to them is based on a current justified business need.

The following actions are performed to review access:

1. Every 3 months the ISM shall obtain a list from Building Facilities Manager of all employees who have access to the various secure areas.
2. the ISM shall meet with Relevant Managers and work through the lists to determine if there is a justified and continued business need for the access to continue.
3. If access is still required to a secure area, no further action shall be taken and the employee remains on the access list.
4. If access is no longer required, the procedure to revoke access to a secure area shall be followed.
5. Records of all access rights reviews shall be added to the ERMS.

12.4.5 CCTV

Where allowed within the jurisdiction, a CCTV system shall be installed to cover, at least:

- all entrances;
- all exits;
- all secure areas in the office;
- the area immediately outside the office;
- the delivery and collection area;
- the loading bay;
- the perimeter of the office; and
- the reception area.

The exact legislative requirements in the jurisdiction for using CCTV shall be understood, as defined in Section 12.3.13.1.1. These requirements shall be met.

Roles and responsibilities for managing the CCTV system have been defined in Chapter 7, Section 7.5.3.1.

CCTV shall be used primarily to record events taking place, but also as a deterrent.

Professional installers shall be used to plan, instal and service the CCTV system and provide training to the IT Department who shall maintain it internally.

If the CCTV system is not connected to the network, the system time shall be regularly reviewed and updated. This may be done manually against a known time source and a log retained of the date of the check and any time drift since the last check. If it is network connected, then it shall be possible to automatically perform this task, as defined in Chapter 7, Section 7.7.5. If this is not possible the manual approach shall be undertaken.

Where CCTV evidence is required for retrieval the procedures for this are defined in Chapter 7, Section 7.5.3.3. If this is to be used as evidence, then the rules of evidence for the jurisdiction shall be followed to produce it as an exhibit and the chain of custody maintained as defined in Chapter 8, Section 8.6.4.

12.4.6 Reviewing physical access controls

All physical access controls to FCL shall be reviewed to ensure that they remain appropriate and fit for purpose. These shall be reviewed at least quarterly, after any major incident or any influencing control by the ISM, the IT Manager, Health and Safety Manager, and the Building Facilities Manager, with input from Top Management if appropriate.

Items discussed shall include, but not be limited to:

- adequacy of existing physical access controls to areas and specifically those defined as 'secure areas';
- new access controls that may be required;
- changes required to existing physical controls and supporting systems;
- adequacy of existing procedures relating to physical security;
- updates of risk assessments;
- any incidents relating to physical security breaches; and
- any CAPAs raised after reviews, audits, or tests that relate to physical security.

Any changes agreed to be implemented shall be managed through the CAPA process, and the Change Management Process, if applicable. There shall be different responsibilities for these changes, depending on where they are to be implemented.

12.5 Managing service delivery

IT operations are essential to the deliverability of products and services to internal and external clients. Operational procedures are detailed below:

Service delivery to either internal departments or from any third-party supplier shall include the agreed security arrangements, service definitions, and aspects of service management. In case of third-party service provider arrangements, FCL shall plan the necessary transitions (of information, information processing facilities, and anything else that needs to be moved), and shall ensure that security is maintained throughout the transition period. This process shall be overseen by the ISM, the Service Delivery Manager, and the IT Manager. This applies to transfers from and to FCL.

FCL shall ensure that the third-party service provider shall maintain sufficient service capability together with workable plans designed to ensure that agreed service continuity levels are maintained following major service failures or a disruptive event that requires invocation of one or more Business Continuity Plans.

SLAs shall be agreed with all third-party service providers, suppliers, and clients so that FCL can measure deliverability of third-party service providers and suppliers as well as the services they deliver to their internal and external clients.

FCL shall monitor and review all third-party supplier services, to ensure that the information security terms and conditions of the agreements are being adhered to, and that information security incidents and problems are managed properly. Regular second-party audits shall be undertaken as defined in Chapter 4, Section 4.9.2.

This shall involve a service management relationship and process between FCL and relevant third-party service providers and suppliers. It shall cover:

- monitoring service performance levels to check adherence to the agreements;
- reviewing service reports produced by all third parties and arrange regular progress meetings as required by the agreements;
- providing information about information security incidents and review of this information as required by the agreements and any supporting guidelines and procedures;
- reviewing all third-party audit trails and records of security events, operational problems, failures, tracing of faults and disruptions related to the service(s) delivered; and

- resolving and managing any identified deficiencies.

FCL shall ensure that they take appropriate action when deficiencies in the service delivery are observed.

FCL shall, through the ISM, ensure that they maintain sufficient overall control and visibility into all security aspects for sensitive or critical information or information processing facilities accessed, processed, or managed by any third party.

FCL shall, through the ISM, ensure that they control all security activities including, but not limited to:

- change management;
- identification and treatment of identified vulnerabilities;
- identification and management of threat intelligence;
- information security incident reporting/response through a clearly defined reporting process, format, and structure;
- access control and review; and
- risk management.

The ISM shall be responsible for any auditing or compliance requirements for all third parties of any type, where possible.

In all cases of using any type of third-party service provider, the ultimate responsibility for service provision shall remain with FCL and is owned by the relevant FCL Owner.

12.6 Managing system access

To enforce the Access Control Policy, FCL shall manage access to all systems for which they have responsibility.

This policy defines the principles, standards, guidelines, and responsibilities related to accessing FCL information processing systems. This policy supports information security by preventing unauthorised access to information processing facilities and information.

New technologies and more automation are increasing opportunities for information sharing. Therefore, FCL shall seek a balance between the need to protect information resources and allowing greater access to information and applications. Several factors affect how FCL controls access to its information processing facilities and information—this includes revised calculation of risk and consequences of unauthorised access.

Whilst forcing regular password changes is still common, practice experience shows that this often leads to weaker passwords being chosen as users run out of new ideas.

Within FCL, a conscious decision has been made to have passphrases that are strong and do not expire, where the risk is acceptable. For these systems, the ISM shall regularly run password/passphrase cracking software to identify weak passphrases. When found, the passphrase owner shall be advised of procedures for strong passphrases and how to implement them.

12.6.1 Access control rules for users and user groups

All users and user groups that need to access FCL and client information shall have specific, predetermined access rights to information, operating systems, and applications that conform to, and are restricted by, the Access Control Policy.

12.6.1.1 Introduction to user groups

User groups shall be used in FCL on all platforms and in all applications where possible. Good security practice is not to assign permissions of any kind to an individual user, but rather assigning all permissions on a group basis, and then assigning a user to a user group:

- user groups shall provide access to shared resources;
- information asset owners shall manage user groups to ensure that they have the correct level and type of access and that this is subject to regular review;
- user groups shall be defined by respective team or function; and
- each departmental Manager shall have authority over access to their department's shared folder.

12.6.1.2 Roles and responsibilities

12.6.1.2.1 IT Manager

The IT Manager shall be responsible for:

- creating, documenting, and maintaining user group profiles that meet the requirements of the Access Control Policy; and
- ensuring that adequate user group controls are in place.

12.6.1.2.2 ISM

The ISM shall be responsible for reviewing user group profiles and user group membership with the relevant information Asset Owner.

12.6.1.2.3 Departmental managers

Each Departmental Manager shall be the central authority for the department's user groups. The responsibilities of this role shall include liaising with relevant resource Owners about changes to critical servers or changes that have a major impact on services.

12.6.1.2.4 Service desk

The Service Desk shall act as first-line support for user group maintenance. The responsibilities of this role shall include:

- logging the requests for adding, amending, or removing users within user groups in the Service Desk ticketing system;
- assigning users to, or removing them from, user groups via the Service Desk ticketing system; and
- creating new user groups via the Service Desk ticketing system.

12.6.1.2.5 Application administrators

Application Administrators shall be responsible for:

- requesting the Service desk to create, maintain or delete user groups; and
- adding and removing users within user groups.

12.6.1.3 Reviewing user groups

1. At least quarterly, or at any time when required for operational reasons, the IT Manager and the ISM shall list out all user groups, and their access rights with their members.
2. the ISM shall meet with each of the user group Owners and review the access rights and the membership of the groups.
3. Where a group has inappropriate rights, the ISM shall obtain the correct access rights for the group from the user group Owner and then advise the Service Desk of the required changes.
4. If a user group is deemed redundant, the ISM shall confirm this with the user group Owner and they advise the Service Desk of the required changes.
5. The Service Desk shall advise the ISM and the user group Owner of the completion of the changes and the new rights assigned.

12.6.2 Managing privileged user accounts

The use of special privileged user access accounts shall be tightly restricted by the IT Department and the ISM so that special privileged user access shall be granted on a need-to-have basis. Such privileges shall only be assigned to specific system administrators.

User registration and de-registration procedures shall also apply to the management of privileged users access.

However, additional measures shall be applied to system-wide privileges (such as the Administrator account in Windows and root in Unix-type systems) that enable the user to access powerful utilities and bypass system or application controls.

Third parties shall not be allowed to use privileged accounts. Instead, emergency user IDs and passphrases shall be used. For maintenance purposes, third parties needing privileged access shall be assigned privileged maintenance user ID, which shall be activated upon commencement of maintenance work. Upon completion of the maintenance work, the third-party user ID shall be de-activated. All actions performed by third parties shall be logged from the activation to deactivation period.

12.6.3   Maintaining server passphrases

The relevant members of the IT Department that provide server support all know their own passphrases and user IDs and these shall permit access to FCL servers.

The exception to this is any server that is classed as secure, for whatever reason (e.g. client requirement, Information classification, or need to know principle). Procedures for accessing secure servers are given below.

12.6.3.1   Guidelines for securing server passphrases

1. Passphrases for 'standard' servers that provide day-to-day services for authorised users shall be provided via a normal user login with IT Department employees placed in the administrator user group.
2. All access to all servers shall also be supplemented by 2-factor authentication biometric scanners;
3. Passphrases for secure servers shall be generated and recorded and then stored in the IT Manager's passphrase safe.
4. A passphrase for an individual secure server shall be maintained in a passphrase safe such as Keepass and a backup of the Keepass database stored on removable media and stored in the safe.
5. Secure server passphrases shall only be removed from the passphrase safe by the following:
   - IT Manager;
   - ISM; or
   - Top management.
6. A note shall be made in the passphrase log each time a passphrase is retrieved from the safe.

12.6.3.2   IT Manager role and responsibilities

The IT Manager shall be the central authority for server passphrase changes. The responsibilities of this role shall include, but not be limited to:

- ensuring that adequate server passphrase controls are in place;
- changing passphrases for secure servers when required;
- recording changed passphrases and storing them in their safe; and
- retrieving passphrases from their safe.

12.6.3.3   Retrieving a secure server passphrase

1. An authorised member of the IT Department requests access to a secure server for operational purposes.
2. The IT Manager shall confirm that access is required and retrieves the required passphrase from the safe. The IT Manager shall record the retrieval in the passphrase logbook which is also kept in the safe.
3. The envelope for the relevant server shall be passed to the IT Department member requesting it, who shall open it and use it to access the server, or the password safe (Keepass or similar) will be accessed and the passphrase retrieved.
4. In the case of hardcopy, the envelope and the passphrase shall be securely disposed of by immediate shredding.
5. After the work is completed, the process for changing a secure passphrase shall be followed.
6. The new passphrase shall be placed in a sealed envelope or the password safe as above.
7. The IT Manager shall place the envelope back in the safe and record its return in the logbook.

12.6.3.4   Changing a secure server passphrase

Note

All secure server passphrases **SHALL** be changed when a member of the IT Department with administrator rights or access to service accounts leaves FCL, for whatever reason. For operational reasons, these changes may not be performed immediately.

---

1. The IT Manager shall retrieve the relevant secure server passphrase(s) from the safe.
2. The IT Manager shall record the retrieval in the passphrase logbook which is also kept in the safe.
3. The IT Manager shall generate new passphrase(s) for the secure server(s) using FCL passphrase standard.
4. The IT Manager shall change the passphrase(s) on the relevant secure server(s) and then place the written copy of the passphrases back in the relevant envelopes or update the password safe (Keepass or similar).
5. The IT Manager shall place the envelope(s) back in the safe and record the return of the envelope in the logbook. The previous hard copy of the passphrases shall be securely destroyed by shredding.

12.6.4 Maintaining user accounts

Everyday use of FCL information processing equipment shall be achieved using user IDs and passphrases, with additional 2-factor authentication biometric scanners for some users.

Note

Third-party employees working for FCL or that require access to information and information processing facilities shall be treated in the same manner as employees for this process but the responsibility for them shall lie with their Line Manager.

12.6.4.1 An overview of user accounts

All employees and authorised third parties working for FCL shall be provided with user accounts to enable them to access their workstation and network resources, and with application, accounts to enable them to access specific applications.

1. User accounts shall only be created and maintained by the Service Desk on receipt of appropriately authorised requests.
2. The Service Desk shall unlock locked accounts and reset passphrases on receipt of an authorised and verified request.
3. All requests for new user accounts shall be provided to the Service Desk by the user's authorised Line Manager and where necessary countersigned by the relevant Information Owner or HR for new hires. (Ideally, requests should be made at least 2 days before the account is required). The requirements for the User Account Maintenance Form are defined in Appendix 14.
4. All requests for user account amendments shall be provided to the Service Desk by the user's authorised Line Manager and where necessary countersigned by the relevant information Owner.
5. Requests for user account deletions shall be sent from HR or an authorised Line Manager to the Service Desk.

12.6.4.2 Roles and responsibilities

12.6.4.2.1 Service desk

The Service Desk shall act as a first point of contact for all account management. The responsibilities of this role shall include:

- recording and tracking all requests via the Service Desk system;
- acting as the first point of contact for the creation, maintenance, and deletion of all user accounts of any type; and
- ensuring all requests for account maintenance are only accepted from an appropriately authorised employee.

12.6.4.2.2 Management

Management are the people who request new accounts and changes to existing accounts. The responsibilities of this role shall include:

- properly authorise the creation or amendment of a user account of any type;
- submit a request for the creation or amendment of an account to the Service Desk;
- supply the Service Desk with all the necessary information that they require for administering a user account; and
- notifying the Service Desk of the requirement for an account suspension or deletion (requests for account suspensions and deletions can only be accepted from a relevant Line Manager or HR).

12.6.4.2.3 HR

HR coordinates leavers and starters. The responsibilities of this role shall include:

- notifying the ISM, the Service Desk, and the employees' Line Manager of starters and leavers on a regular basis;
- notifying the relevant Line Manager and the IT Manager in the event of an urgent requirement for account modification or deletion; and
- advising the IT Department of any account management issues.

12.6.4.3 Creating a new user account

New user accounts are created for users to provide them with access to their workstation and network resources.

A simplified flowchart of the account creation process is (Fig. 12.6):

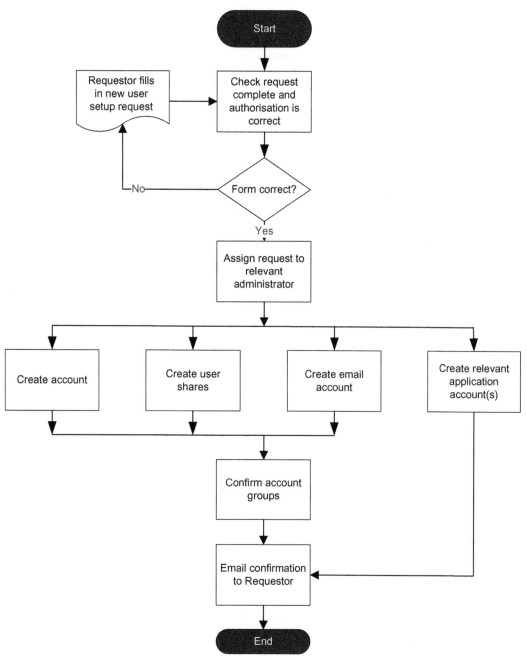

FIG. 12.6   Creating a new user account.

The process to create a new account is as follows:

1. HR and the Line Manager of the new employee shall complete a User Account Maintenance Form.
2. This shall be used to set up an account and other requirements for the user, as required by their job function.
3. The Service Desk shall log the request in the Service Desk system and check that the authorisation is correct using the Outlook address book to confirm management responsibility.
4. The Service Desk shall check that the User Account Management Form has been correctly completed and authorised as follows:
   - checks the requested user details; and
   - checks the services required.

If some details are missing, the Service Desk shall contact the Requestor to obtain the missing details.

5. If all the details required are present, the Service Desk shall assign the case to the relevant administrator to create or manage the account.

6. The administrator shall create the user's account. This can include:
   - user group settings;
   - full user details as required by the account set up process;
   - enter an initial passphrase to be changed on first access; and
   - other details as required by the operating system, applications requested, or other details on the account set-up form.

7. The Service Desk shall advise the Requestor of successful setup and close the ticket.

12.6.4.4 Creating a new application user account

New application user accounts are created for employees to provide them with access to specific applications that run on any operating system that require an additional login account.

A simplified flowchart of the account creation process is (Fig. 12.7):

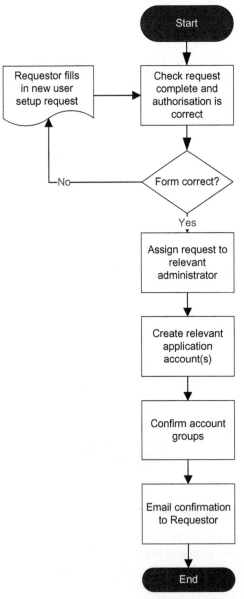

FIG. 12.7 Creating a new application user account.

The process to create a new account is as follows.

1. The employee's Line Manager shall complete a User Account Maintenance Form.
2. This shall be used to set up an application account and other requirements for the user, as required by their job function.

Note

If a request for a new account is received directly from a user and is not properly authorised, the Service Desk shall respond to indicate that the request is invalid and must come from the user's Line Manager or HR with the appropriate authorisation.

---

3. The Service Desk shall log the request in the Service Desk system and checks that the authorisation is correct using the Outlook address book to confirm management responsibility.
4. The Service Desk shall check that the User Account Management Form has been correctly completed and authorised as follows:
   - checks the requested user details; and
   - checks the services required.
5. If some details are missing, the Service Desk shall contact the Requestor to obtain the missing details.
6. If all the details required are present, the Service Desk shall assign the case to the relevant application administrator to create or manage the account.
7. The relevant administrator shall set up the new application account with the default passphrase, to be changed on first access, if possible and appropriate.
8. The Service Desk advises the Requestor of the successful setup and closes the ticket.

12.6.4.5   Amending an existing user account

The process to amend an existing user account is as follows:

1. The employee's Line Manager shall Manager shall complete a User Account Maintenance Form.
2. This shall be used to amend the user's account.

Note

If a request for an account change is received directly from a user and is not properly authorised, the Service Desk shall respond to indicate that the request is invalid and must come from the user's Line Manager or HR with the appropriate authorisation.

---

3. The Service Desk shall log the request in the Service Desk system and checks that the authorisation is correct using the Outlook address book to confirm management responsibility.
4. The Service Desk shall check that the User Account Management Form has been correctly completed and authorised as follows:
   - checks the requested user details; and
   - checks the services required.
5. If some details are missing, the Service Desk shall contact the Requestor to obtain the missing details.
6. The Service Desk assigns it to the relevant administrator(s).
7. The relevant amendments are made.
8. The administrator(s) shall confirm that the user's details have been amended by emailing the summary to the Requestor and the account holder and close the ticket

12.6.4.6   Suspending an existing user account

Accounts shall be suspended when a user is temporarily absent from the office (e.g. on parental leave or on secondment) or when a user is terminated. The suspension for a terminated user shall be for a period of 3 months subject to review by the user's Line Manager who may wish to extend the period.

The process to suspend an existing user account operating systems and applications is as follows:

1. HR or the employee's Line Manager shall complete a User Account Maintenance Form.
2. This shall be used to amend the user's account.

3. The Service Desk shall log the request in the Service Desk system and check that the authorisation is correct using the Outlook address book to confirm management responsibility.
4. The Service Desk shall check that the User Account Management Form has been correctly completed and authorised as follows:
   - checks the requested user details; and
   - checks the services required.
5. If some details are missing, the Service Desk shall contact the Requestor to obtain the missing details.
6. The Service Desk assigns it to the relevant administrator(s).
7. The Service Desk shall confirm that the user's account has been suspended by emailing the confirmation to the Requestor and close the ticket.

Note

Accounts suspended in the production environment shall also be suspended in the following environments, where appropriate:

- development;
- test;
- Disaster Recovery (DR) site.

12.6.4.7 Deleting an existing user account

Accounts are deleted when a user's account is no longer needed at the end of the suspension period.

Note 1

When a user's Windows account is deleted, all their information on shared drives is also deleted. If some of the information is important, the user's Line Manager shall ensure that it has been safely backed up or stored elsewhere whilst the account is suspended and before it is deleted.

Note 2

User accounts may also be deleted during periodic reviews of access rights if they are no longer required.

Note 3

There are some applications, particularly financial, that require full transaction histories. For these applications, a user shall not be deleted but shall suspended permanently.

Note 4

No user shall be deleted from MARS in case of a later challenge to a forensic case.

Note 5

In urgent cases, HR or relevant Line Manager may immediately email the Service Desk to inform them of the requirement of an immediate deletion because a member of staff is leaving, and that the account requires immediate deletion.

Note 6

Accounts deleted in the production environment shall also be deleted in the following environments, where appropriate:

- development;
- test; and
- Disaster Recovery (DR) site.

The process to delete an existing user account is as follows:

1. HR or the employee's Line Manager shall complete a User Account Maintenance Form.
2. This shall be used to delete a suspended user's account.
3. The Service Desk shall log the request in the Service Desk system and check that the authorisation is correct using the Outlook address book to confirm management responsibility.
4. The Service Desk shall check that the User Account Management Form has been correctly completed and authorised as follows:
   - checks the requested user details; and
   - checks the services required.
5. If some details are missing, the Service Desk shall contact the Requestor to obtain the missing details.
6. The Service Desk assigns it to the relevant administrator(s).
7. The Service Desk shall confirm that the user's account has been deleted by emailing the confirmation to the Requestor and close the ticket.

Note

Where possible, all backup copies shall also be deleted, but this may not always be possible.

12.6.5   Managing application access control

Any software that is not an operating system is defined within FCL as an 'Application'. FCL shall prevent unauthorised access to information in applications which is held in FCL information processing systems.

The Access Control Policy restricts access to the capabilities of applications and associated information only to authorised users, and to enforce strict user access controls. Application access privileges shall be restricted to privileges required by each user to perform their job. User access privileges shall be granted in accordance with user account registration and approved by the HR, the User's Line Manager, relevant application, or information Owners.

For applications that are developed in-house, specific access control mechanisms shall be incorporated in the design.

12.6.5.1   Restricting access to information

The following controls and guidelines shall be in place to restrict access to information via applications:

1. User profiles shall be used to define specific access rights to programmes and files (e.g. read, write, delete, run, etc.).
2. All access shall be restricted unless explicitly permitted.
3. Menus should be used to restrict access to application capabilities, where appropriate.
4. Restrictive application menus shall be used to stop users gaining access to system prompts or command lines.
5. Knowledge and information shall be restricted on a 'need to know' basis, and publication of application content and functionality (e.g. through editing of user documentation).
6. All access shall comply with user ID, authentication standards.
7. The need for special access privileges shall be minimised.
8. Outputs from applications handling sensitive information shall be controlled to ensure that:
   - only relevant information is released;
   - all output is classified and labelled accordingly; and
   - information is only released to authorised users and/or locations.

12.6.6   Managing operating system access control

Restricting access to information and information processing systems is easiest at the operating system level. FCL shall ensure that operating system access control is implemented by implementing the following controls, where applicable.

12.6.6.1 Automatic terminal identification

Terminal or workstation identification shall be used to automatically authenticate connections initiated from a specific location or computer equipment, where technically feasible. An identifier in or attached to, the workstation is checked by the system to indicate whether the session request shall be allowed. Users can therefore be restricted to a set of specific terminals for logging into a specific system, e.g. only terminals in HR can access the personnel or payroll application. To ensure the effectiveness of this control, physical access control to the workstation shall also be implemented based on the classification or value of the information being processed. Multifactor authentication shall be used for workstations that can process 'sensitive' information.

12.6.6.2 Managing logon

Access to information and information processing facilities shall be through a secure log-on procedure to minimise the risk of unauthorised access. The approval of the IT Manager and the ISM shall be obtained before any important features of the log-on process are bypassed, disabled, or changed.

The following guidelines shall be implemented, as a minimum and may change as technology evolves:

1. Where technically feasible, identification of FCL, the network, the location, or any details of the host shall not be visible prior to a successful login.
2. Before being given the opportunity to log into any FCL information processing system, users shall be presented with a login banner which:
   - provides users with a chance to terminate the login before accessing a system that they are not authorised; and
   - provides FCL with legal grounds to prosecute unauthorised access.
3. The logon banner shall indicate:
   - that the system is to be used only by authorised users;
   - by continuing to use the system, a user represents that he/she is an authorised user; and
   - use of the system is for business purposes only and constitutes consent to monitoring.
4. No FCL system shall facilitate a log-on procedure via help messages, which could aid an unauthorised user.
5. There shall be maximum and minimum time restrictions for the logon process (if logon time is exceeded, the system shall terminate the logon where possible).
6. Three consecutive authentication failures shall lock users out of the resource to which they are attempting to gain access (in which case they shall have to have their account manually reset) after being authenticated by the Service Desk.
7. Systems shall be configured not to provide any information following an unsuccessful logon (this includes identifying which portion of login sequence (user ID or passphrase) was incorrect).
8. Logon mechanisms shall not store authentication details in clear text, such as in scripts, macros, or cache memory.
9. Logon screens for production systems or applications shall be different to logon screen for systems or applications in the development environment (e.g. include a notification that the application is in the development environment), if possible.

12.6.6.3 User identification and authorisation

In the production environment, all FCL information processing system users shall have a unique user ID, with the exception of service accounts or other privileged accounts whose details must be shared.

In the development environment, a user may be assigned more than one user ID, provided that it is done so in a controlled and authorised manner and remains accountable to the user.

12.6.6.4 Managing user passphrases

Prior to being granted access to any FCL information processing systems, users shall be required to enter a valid user ID and passphrase. This is the minimum acceptable level of authentication, which is applicable to all FCL information processing systems and users, including the IT Department (except in the case of privileged users and those processing forensic cases, where a higher level of authentication method shall be required).

To ensure passphrases are properly controlled, these minimum standards have been developed for FCL (which shall be applied and enforced on all systems):

- passphrase shall consist of three 6 (or more) character concatenated words;
- at least one of each of numeric, special, and upper- and lower-case characters is mandated either as part of the passphrase or appended to it;

- a passphrase history shall be maintained so that previous passphrases cannot be used after being changed;
- the minimum passphrase history shall be 3 generations;
- maximum logon attempts before lockout shall be 3;
- users shall have to log on to change their passphrase; and
- no passphrases shall be displayed on logon screens.

12.6.6.5 Use of system utilities

Operating systems often have utilities that can circumvent system and application controls. It is FCL's policy that use of these utilities shall be restricted and controlled so that:

1. Only authorised staff (system administrators, IT operations staff, etc.) shall have access to such utilities (i.e. those with a justified business need to access and use them).
2. Use of system utilities shall be granted in accordance with FCL's privileged user registration standards.
3. Use of system utilities shall be monitored and logged.
4. Utilities shall be removed from the system when not required as part of the hardened build.

12.6.6.6 Terminal timeouts

Use of timeout facilities in operating systems shall be used to clear the terminal screen, and either close down or not close down application and network sessions after a terminal has been inactive for a specified period of time. This automatic facility prevents access by unauthorised persons to, in particular, inactive terminals in sensitive areas or those operating high-risk systems.

The following standards shall be employed in FCL:

1. Any sessions that are not active for 30 min shall be automatically terminated (except if justifiable by business case e.g. for performing end-of-day activities).
2. Systems that cannot automatically terminate connections shall have passphrase-protected screen savers or terminal locks that shall be activated in accordance with the Clear Screen Policy.
3. Users shall not attempt to circumvent the use of these controls.
4. All information processing devices (when applicable) shall be configured with a passphrase-protected screensaver (the screensaver shall require the entry of a passphrase after 15 min of inactivity).
5. Where possible, in addition to passphrase-protected screen savers, systems shall force users off after a predetermined period of inactivity (except if justifiable by business case e.g. for performing end-of-day activities). The user shall have to log back into the system.

12.6.6.7 Limiting connection times

Limiting connection times allows FCL to provide additional security for systems that are considered high-risk. Time restrictions should be imposed for particular processes such as batch processing, file transmissions, and for sensitive computer applications, particularly those with terminals installed in high-risk locations. Limiting the time for user access narrows the window of opportunity for unauthorised access. However, due to working constraints, this control shall be implemented with care so as not to preclude users working nonstandard hours.

12.6.7 Monitoring and reviewing system access and use

To ensure individual accountability and to enable incidents such as access violations to be investigated and resolved, all access and use of information and/or systems shall be logged. Access events that shall be logged (including sign-on and files accessed) and the review process that is followed (including frequency and responsibility) shall be determined between the ISM and relevant system and information Owners. Whilst physical access to areas is covered in Section 12.4.4.3.4, a similar process shall be carried out for logical access control, with the frequencies of reviews stated in the IMS Calendar.

To assist with monitoring network access, FCL shall use automated event logging for purposes of recording exceptions and other security-related events.

To undertake a system access review, the ISM shall follow the procedure below:

1. The ISM shall check the IMS Calendar to determine when the next review is to take place.
2. Consideration shall be given to the planned review cycle and if there are any areas suffering unauthorised access incidents.

3. At every review, all of the administrator accounts shall be checked, along with any high-risk applications.
4. the ISM shall specify the requirements for the review and have the relevant reports run. These shall include:
   - group membership;
   - access rights for the group;
   - any members of the group with rights in addition to the standard group rights;
   - any account not used for 30 days;
   - review of disabled accounts;
   - review of suspended accounts;
   - any directly assigned rights that the user has;
   - any accounts that are locked out; and
   - any accounts that do not meet FCL account policy.
5. All rights shall be reviewed by the ISM with the relevant system or information Owner, who shall formally approve that the rights assigned are correct and appropriate for the user.
6. Any anomalies found shall be investigated by the ISM, the IT Manager, and the relevant information or system Owner.
7. The outcome of the investigation may lead to:
   - removal of current rights granted; or
   - revision of current rights granted.
8. Any changes shall be raised as a CAPA and managed through the CAPA process.

12.6.8 Implementing enforced paths

FCL prevents users from selecting routes outside of the approved routes between their user workstation and the services that they are authorised to access (i.e. user roaming).

Enforced paths of access shall be implemented via:

1. Allocation of dedicated lines or telephone numbers.
2. Separation of networks, depending on the information system's criticality, to increase the level of security provided during information transport/storage.
3. Use of security gateways or proxy servers to control allowed access to communications.
4. Configuration of network devices.
5. Implementation of traffic filtering controls.

12.6.9 Enabling teleworking for users

FCL shall implement a number of controls for teleworking for employees who work remotely from a fixed location outside the office (these controls shall apply to employees who may be—or plan to be—working from home).

This became a business need for a large number of employees as a part of their protection during the COVID-19 lockdowns.

Note

Teleworking is defined as 'the action or practice of working from home, making use of the internet, email, and the telephone'. This is different from mobile working where work can be performed from hotels, on-site, on a train, etc.

12.6.9.1 Obtaining approval for teleworking

A formal request shall be submitted to the Service Desk by an authorised Line Manager for approval so that employees can use remote access to FCL information processing and communication systems.

The process for approving teleworking shall be:

1. An authorised Line Manager (the Requestor) shall submit a formal request to Service Desk for teleworking approval and opens a ticket with the Service Desk, the Teleworking Request Form contents are defined in Appendix 15. Details shall include:
   - name of the user;
   - description of the business need;

- location and description of teleworking environment;
- equipment to be used; and
- access required to information processing systems.

2. The request shall be reviewed by the IT Manager, the ISM, and the relevant information and application Owners. The following risks shall be considered when reviewing a teleworking request:
   - physical security of the proposed teleworking site;
   - security requirements for communications with FCL networks, and access to FCL information processing systems; and
   - potential threats from unauthorised access to systems.
3. The proposed teleworking location shall be visited by the IT Manager and the ISM who shall undertake a risk assessment and audit of the site, using the procedures defined in Chapter 4, Section 4.9.2.

Note

In the case of a large number of users needing to work from home (e.g. in a Pandemic), this may not be possible so other alternatives shall be used. These shall include self-assessment forms with sample visits (if possible), a generic risk assessment, or other processes agreed by Top Management and the ISM.

---

4. The IT Manager shall provide the Requestor with approval (or in the event that the request is considered high risk, alternative arrangements may be put to the relevant Business Manager for further discussion).
5. Any appropriate corrective action shall be undertaken at the proposed location, and the Teleworker shall undertake relevant training.
6. After approval is issued, the IT Department performs the following:
   - issue the user with details of the work permitted, the remote connection(s) permitted, FCL systems which the user is allowed to access remotely, and levels of access which are permitted; and
   - enable the required connections.

12.6.10   Securing teleworking environments

The following controls shall be implemented for securing teleworking environments where remote access is required to FCL information processing and communication systems:

1. All users shall comply with the teleworking and other appropriate controls when working remotely from the FCL Office.
2. Users shall be responsible for backing up any business information which may be stored locally (business information shall not be permanently stored locally on mobile or teleworking computers).
3. Users shall be responsible for the physical security of the teleworking location, and shall exercise particular care to:
   - avoid unauthorised access to the FCL network;
   - avoid disclosure of information;
   - avoid overlooking by unauthorised persons, including family and visitors; and
   - ensure the physical protection of all FCL equipment (including risks from theft and leaving equipment unattended).
4. The IT Department shall be responsible for providing support services for teleworking issues associated with remote access to FCL's information processing and communications systems.
5. Remote connections to FCL information processing and communications systems shall be monitored for security and audit purposes.
6. The IT Department shall revoke rights of remote access to information processing and communications systems when:
   - a user fails to comply with any information security guideline, policy, or procedure;
   - the ISM requests termination of teleworking authority based on information security concerns;
   - teleworking activities cease to exist; and
   - HR or the relevant Line Manager indicates that teleworking is no longer appropriate for the user.

12.7   Managing information on public systems

FCL has a formal approval process before the information is made publicly available.

FCL shall manage publicly accessed web server hardware and software to minimise risks that may arise as a result of unauthorised information being made generally available through web technologies.

Note

Many potential problems that are associated with web servers can be mitigated by either completely separating the web server from the private networks via a strong DMZ, or having it completely off-site, and managed by a third party under contract. (i.e. a web hosting service).

In general, FCL shall ensure that:

1. Security risks to FCL caused by poorly managed and maintained web servers shall be mitigated by extensive testing and remediation of weaknesses, vulnerabilities, and any other risks prior to deployment.
2. Hardened builds shall be used for all public-facing systems that shall be reinforced by extensive vulnerability scanning (and remediation), penetration testing, code reviews, and other such testing that the ISM sees fit.
3. Web servers connected to the network shall be managed in such a way that FCL presents an image of reliability.
4. Web facilities handled and managed by third parties shall comply with all FCL information security requirements, including change and incident management processes.
5. Material related to FCL shall only be published on the formal FCL web server(s)—though FCL has little control over information copied and posted on other websites or back linkages from other websites.
6. All FCL material shall be formally approved by the 'business' prior to publication on any websites. This shall include any social media postings made in FCL's name.
7. the approval process for any externally published documents is defined in Chapter 4, Section 4.7.
8. Records of the review and approval process shall be stored in the ERMS.

12.7.1 Hardware and software standards

The following standards shall apply to ensure that configuration standards are maintained for systems containing publicly available information:

1. Web servers shall conform to standards for configuration that represent current best practice. Specifics of configuration for hardware, server operating systems, web server software, and any other relevant software shall be reviewed and updated on regular basis.
2. Hardened builds shall be used for all public-facing systems and regularly scanned against the hardened build requirements with any deficiencies managed through the CAPA process.
3. All systems shall be patched to manufacturer-recommended levels at all times.
4. All server applications shall be patched to manufacturer-recommended levels at all times.
5. The control of technical vulnerabilities and patching are defined in Chapter 7, Section 7.6.2 and 7.6.3, respectively.

12.7.2 Information security standards

The following information security standards shall apply to ensure that information security standards are maintained for systems containing publicly available information:

1. The requirements of the Information Security Policy shall be met at all times.
2. Industry best practice and accepted standards for information security shall be applied to web server configuration and management shall be implemented and followed at all times.
3. Information security requirements shall be reviewed regularly to ensure that they meet with current legislation, regulation, contractual obligations, and good practice. Remediation shall be undertaken where these requirements are not met though FCL CAPA process.

12.7.3 Published information guidelines

The following guidelines shall apply to ensure that material published on publicly available systems is suitable for release:

1. The document management process shall be responsible for checking information before publication to a web server.
2. Once internally checked, it shall be submitted to the CAB for document change control approval. Attendance at that CAB shall be mandatory for all interested parties that may be affected by any published information.

3. The IT Department shall provide tools to enable the authorised departments to publish information to the web server, but only after formal approval for publishing has been granted

4. The IT Department shall enable designated and authorised employees to access web servers based on business need only.

12.7.4 Server management

The following standards shall apply to ensure that servers containing publicly available information are managed appropriately:

1. Web servers shall only be accessed by designated and authorised IT Department employees.
2. Web servers shall be managed to assure maximum availability, balanced with appropriate security for the content, based on a risk assessment undertaken by the ISM and the relevant content Owner(s).
3. Down-time shall be scheduled well in advance to ensure that viewers have advance notice of the work and is timed to coincide with periods of minimum usage.
4. The IT Department shall regularly check web servers to determine that all hardware and software is correct including versions and patches installed.
5. The IT Department shall regularly review server and other logs for publicly available systems to determine, and then recommend appropriate remedial action for situations that occur, including but not limited to:
   - the number of times that security on web servers has been compromised or there are compromise attempts detected;
   - the total time a registered web server is not available to respond to http requests; and
   - the number of instances of information published without the correct approvals.
6. Where web servers are managed or hosted by third parties the above shall apply and formal reports of monitoring shall be submitted to the IT Manager and the ISM.

12.7.5 Reviewing security for public systems

The process by which FCL manages and reviews information on public systems shall be as follows:

1. The IT Department shall be responsible for web server security aspects review, and they may receive requests from business users to change aspects. The assessment shall cover the following areas:
   - hardware and software standards;
   - information security standards;
   - published information; and
   - server management.
2. The IT Department in association with the ISM shall assess the requirements from a security perspective, taking particular notice of changes in configuration settings, access by employees and external partners.
3. The IT Department shall send an email outlining their findings to the IT Manager, and the ISM together with any recommendations as appropriate.
4. The IT Manager shall check the findings and determines whether the requirements can be approved. Additional discussions shall be held with the ISM and any other interested parties to clarify any of the findings or recommendations.
5. The IT Manager shall confirm the decisions as follows:
   - If approved, the IT Manager shall send an email to the ISM confirming that the request can be implemented (subject to any changes to the configuration, etc., that are recommended).

Note

The request shall not be granted on a permanent basis. A review of the request shall be scheduled by the IT Manager and the ISM within 12 months to ensure that the request remains valid.

   - If rejected, the IT Manager shall send an email to the ISM outlining the reasons for rejection.
6. The IT Department shall implement the changes to the public server system.
7. At the appointed time according to the review schedule, the public servers shall be assessed again to check whether the changes remain valid using the above procedure.

12.8   Securely managing IT systems

As well as managing the IT infrastructure, the IT Department shall securely manage IT operations on behalf of their internal and external clients. These are typically day-to-day operational issues.

12.8.1   Accepting new systems

When FCL accepts a new system, it shall ensure that it has been subjected to rigorous testing and checking prior to their implementation in the live environment.

All changes to FCL information systems shall be undertaken in accordance with the Change Management Process.

12.8.1.1   Guidelines for system acceptance

Acceptance criteria for new systems shall be:

- all security assessments shall have been performed, and security controls developed, tested, documented, and signed off by the ISM;
- all performance and capacity requirements shall be fulfilled;
- all development problems shall be successfully resolved;
- testing proves there shall be no adverse effect on existing live systems;
- all specifications shall be met;
- the system shall be able to be supported by the IT Department on a continuing basis (for example via the Service Desk);
- roll-back arrangements shall be in place in the event of the changes failing to function as intended (all rollbacks shall be performed in accordance with the Change Management Process);
- sign-off shall have been obtained from the key interested parties (for example the business unit, System Administrator(s), Application Owner, etc.);
- error recovery and restart procedures shall have been established, and business continuity plans have been developed or updated and exercised/tested;
- system operating procedures shall have been tested, with remediation applied as appropriate; and
- users shall be educated in the use of the system, and the IT Department are trained to run the system correctly.

In addition, the following checks shall be observed when accepting a new system:

- old and unsupported software, procedures, and documentation shall be discontinued—but archived in case of later need;
- acceptance checks, change control, release, and configuration management processes shall ensure that only tested and approved versions of software are accepted into the live environment; and
- responsibility shall be transferred to system operators after installation is complete.

12.8.1.2   Procedures for assessing and accepting a new system

The process by which FCL shall accept new systems is as follows:

1. Appropriate members of the IT Department under the supervision of the IT Manager shall assess the system and send the assessment reports to the ISM to determine whether any changes and enhancements shall be required to meet the required security standards. A report shall be produced outlining the changes.
2. The IT Manager and the ISM shall review the report and then send it to relevant interested parties for comment. Follow-up discussions shall be held with the developers to clarify any areas needing clarification.
3. Appropriate members of the IT Department, with input from the ISM shall develop security, test, and acceptance procedures that act as the basis for testing a beta version of the system, where it is developed in-house or a trial version if it is a COTS product.
4. Later in the development cycle the developers shall release a beta version of the system for testing purposes.
5. The test team shall instal the beta or trial version of the system and perform security checks on it according to test and acceptance procedures in test environment.
6. For Forensic Tools, Validation Testing shall be carried out, as defined in Chapter 7, Section 7.5.5.
7. The results of the testing and all security recommendations shall be documented in a report and sent to the ISM.
8. The ISM shall check the results and security recommendations and pass on those that require action to the development team or the third-party service provider or supplier. The development team, third-party service provider, or the supplier, as appropriate, shall implement the security recommendations and sign-off the work with the ISM and other relevant interested parties through additional testing and formal approval at the CAB.

12.8.2   Securing business information systems

The following security standards shall be in place at FCL to control the business and security risks associated with business information systems such as accounting systems, photo copiers, printers, scanners, projectors, and video machines.

12.8.2.1   Roles and responsibilities

12.8.2.1.1   FCL laboratory information security manager

The ISM shall be responsible for risk assessments.

12.8.2.1.2   IT Manager

The IT Manager shall be responsible for configuration and management of the information processing systems.

12.8.2.1.3   Information system owners

The Owner of the information system shall have specific responsibilities for the classification of assets, as defined in Section 12.3.14.6. In addition to those responsibilities, they shall be responsible for:

- undertaking a risk assessment to take into account all known vulnerabilities in all the administrative and forensic case processing systems and particularly in terms of physical access and connection with due regard for the access control, as defined in Chapter 5;
- any special considerations to known vulnerabilities in the administrative and forensic case processing systems where information is shared between different users or departments/units within FCL;
- full consideration of the vulnerabilities of information in business communication systems, e.g. recording voice calls or conference calls, confidentiality of calls, opening mail, distribution of mail should be considered;
- policy and appropriate controls to manage information sharing;
- information processing systems (especially output devices) shall only be installed in areas which are not freely accessible and to which access is controlled;
- where possible, information processing and devices handling classified or sensitive information shall only be installed in rooms or areas which are constantly occupied or are otherwise secured;
- where possible, entry to areas containing information processing systems shall be controlled, and usage of those systems and all peripherals connected to them restricted to appropriate and authorised business needs of users;
- printers shall be sited in accordance with the sensitivity of the information that is being printed;
- processing output which is spooled shall be controlled via secure configuration of print servers to prevent reports from being accidentally selected from different print spool queues, and/or directed to a different printer;
- printers and copiers shall not be left unattended by employees if Confidential or Strictly Confidential information is being printed or copied;
- all waste generated in the course of copying, printing, and faxing Confidential or Strictly Confidential information shall be destroyed in accordance with the procedure for disposal of media, as defined in Section 12.3.14.10;
- excluding categories of sensitive business information and classified documents if any system does not provide an appropriate level of protection for that information;
- restricting access to diary information relating to selected individuals, e.g. personnel working on sensitive projects or cases;
- ensuring that the access control policy of the information processing system is appropriate for its intended and authorised business use, including users allowed to use the system and the locations from which it may be accessed;
- restricting selected system and administrative facilities to specific categories of user;
- identifying the status of information processing system users, e.g. employees in directories and by user naming convention of all accounts for the benefit of other users;
- retention and back-up of the information held on the system, as defined in Chapter 4, Appendix 26; and
- business continuity arrangements, as defined in Chapter 13.

12.8.3   Ensuring correct data processing

It is FCL's policy to ensure that all information input, processing, and output shall be validated to ensure that the output from the system meets the expectations defined. All validation tests shall be recorded and securely maintained, forensic tool validation is defined in Chapter 7, Section 7.5.5 but normal validation is covered below.

To do this, FCL shall check that information has not been modified by any unauthorised process during its life cycle. Testing is carried out at the following stages:

- data input;
- data processing; and
- data output.

12.8.3.1 Security during data input

FCL shall implement the following controls during information input to ensure that information is validated as correct and appropriate:

- data input requirements shall be fully validated during system development, testing, and user acceptance;
- data input shall be subject to full validation checks such as out-of-range values, invalid characters, and missing or incomplete information; and
- users shall regularly check information input into systems.

12.8.3.2 Security during data processing

FCL shall implement the following controls during information processing to ensure that information is not corrupted:

- data processing requirements shall be validated during system development, testing, and user acceptance;
- programmes and batch systems shall be run in the correct order;
- users shall regularly check processing systems to ensure that operations are running properly; and
- message authentication shall be performed on systems where integrity of the message is paramount, such as systems with credit card information and sensitive emails.

12.8.3.3 Security during data output

FCL shall implement the following controls during information output to ensure that information is validated as correct and appropriate:

- data output requirements shall be validated during system development, testing, and user acceptance;
- data output shall be subject to validation checks such as out-of-range values, invalid characters, and missing or incomplete information;
- users shall regularly check information output from systems; and
- input is followed through the processing life cycle to ensure that the actual output produced is as expected from the test packs and test cases.

12.8.3.4 Types of testing

FCL shall implement the following types of testing prior to submission of any system upgrade or before a new system is submitted to the Change Management Process:

- integration testing;
- link testing;
- performance testing;
- regression testing to ensure that no new change corrupts a previous working change;
- unit testing; and
- User Acceptance Testing (UAT).

Within FCL, standard test cases and test packs shall be used with automated testing tools to ensure completeness and consistency of testing, rather than relying on any human bias.

12.8.3.5 Test records

FCL shall maintain full records of all testing for later audits. These test packs, with the results, shall be submitted to the Change Management Process.

12.8.4 Information exchange

FCL shall ensure that formal exchange policies, procedures, and controls are in place to protect the exchange of any information through the use of all types of communication facilities.

Information exchange may occur through the use of a number of different types of communication facilities, including electronic mail, voice, facsimile, video, and other forms of electronic media.

Software exchange may occur through a number of different mediums, including downloading from the Internet and acquired from vendors selling COTS products.

The business, legal, and security implications associated with electronic information interchange, electronic communications, and the requirements for controls shall be considered and their risks assessed and appropriately treated before information exchange is undertaken.

Information could be compromised due to lack of awareness of policy or procedures on the use of information exchange facilities, (e.g. being overheard on a mobile phone in a public place, misdirection of an electronic mail message, answering machines being overheard or unauthorised access to dial-in voice-mail systems).

Business operations could be disrupted and information could be compromised if communications facilities fail, are overloaded, or interrupted.

Information could be compromised if accessed by unauthorised users.

12.8.4.1 Information exchange procedures and controls

1. Procedures shall be designed and implemented to protect exchanged information from interception, copying, modification, misrouting, and destruction.
2. Procedures shall be designed and implemented for the detection of, and protection against, malicious code that may be transmitted through the use of electronic communications, as defined in Chapter 7, Section 7.6.1.
3. Procedures shall be designed and implemented for protecting communicated sensitive electronic information that is in the form of an email attachment.
4. Policy and procedures shall be designed and implemented for the acceptable use of electronic communication facilities.
5. Employee's shall not compromise FCL, (e.g. through defamation, harassment, impersonation, forwarding of chain letters, unauthorised purchasing, entering unauthorised contracts, etc.).
6. Cryptographic techniques shall be used to protect the confidentiality, integrity, and authenticity of information and provide nonrepudiation services.
7. Retention and disposal procedures for all business correspondence including messages, shall be implemented in accordance with relevant national and local legislation and regulations as defined in Chapter 4, Appendix 16.
8. Sensitive or critical information shall not be left on printing facilities, (e.g. copiers and printers, as these may be accessed by unauthorised personnel).
9. Controls and restrictions shall be implemented to restrict the forwarding of communication facilities, (e.g. automatic forwarding of electronic mail to external mail addresses).
10. Employees shall be reminded that they should take appropriate precautions, e.g. not to reveal sensitive information to avoid being overheard or intercepted when making a phone call by:
    - being aware of people in their immediate vicinity particularly when using mobile phones; and
    - being aware of wiretapping, and other forms of eavesdropping through physical access to the phone handset or the phone line or using scanning receivers; or people at the recipient's end.
11. Messages containing sensitive information shall not be left on answering machines since these may be replayed by unauthorised persons, stored on communal systems or stored incorrectly as a result of misdialling.
12. Employees shall be reminded not to register demographic information, such as the email address or other personal information, in any software to avoid collection for unauthorised use.
13. Employees shall be reminded that modern photocopiers have page caches and store pages in case of a paper fault, which can print the pages once the fault is cleared.

In addition, all employees shall be reminded that they should not have confidential conversations in public places or open offices and meeting places with nonsound proofed walls.

12.8.4.2 Exchange agreements

FCL shall ensure that formal and legally binding exchange agreements are established, where appropriate, for the exchange of information and software between themselves and any external parties.

Exchange agreements shall include the following security conditions:

- management responsibilities for controlling and notifying of transmission and receipt;
- procedures for notifying sender of transmission and receipt;
- procedures to ensure traceability and nonrepudiation;
- minimum technical standards for packaging and transmission;
- courier identification standards, if appropriate;
- responsibilities and liabilities in the event of information security incidents, such as loss of information;
- use of an agreed labelling system for sensitive or critical information, ensuring that the meaning of the labels is immediately understood and that the information is appropriately protected, as defined in Sections 12.3.14.8 and 12.3.14.9.
- Ownership and responsibilities for information protection, copyright, software licence compliance and similar considerations;
- technical standards for recording and reading information and software; and
- any special controls that may be required to protect sensitive items, such as cryptographic keys.

Policies, procedures, and standards shall be established and maintained to protect information and physical media in transit and shall be referenced in such exchange agreements.

The security content of any agreement shall reflect the sensitivity of the business information involved.

12.8.5 Cryptographic controls

For secure communication, digital certificates shall be required for some systems, depending on the information classification and client requirements.

The Policy for Cryptographic Controls is defined in Chapter 4, Appendix 25.

12.8.5.1 Guidelines for key management

The IT Manager shall be responsible for the management of cryptographic keys, where appropriate. The tasks that shall be performed are:

1. Cryptographic keys shall be generated directly by the IT Manager—no copy of the key shall be taken for storage.
2. Cryptographic keys shall become part of the device configuration and are subsequently backed up when the configuration is saved.
3. If any compromise of a cryptographic key is detected, the IT Manager shall change the cryptographic key directly on the device. This may require the requesting of a new cryptographic key and distributing it to all relevant users.
4. If any compromise occurs, the ISM shall be alerted and an incident shall be raised at the Service Desk.
5. All changes to keys shall be noted within the Service Desk system against the asset record.

Note

Some one-time key pads may need to be generated and written down for devices such as routers. If this is the case, then the key shall be stored securely with server passphrases as defined in Section 12.6.3.1.

12.8.5.2 Managing keys procedures

The process by which FCL shall manage device keys is as follows:

1. The IT Manager shall assess the requirements for a new key:
   - when the existing key is suspected to be compromised;
   - when a new device is installed; or
   - when devices are relocated.
2. The IT Manager shall open a ticket within the Service Desk.
3. The IT Manager shall access the device and generates the key. A note is made of the key details.
4. The IT Manager shall record the details of the key against the device information.
5. The ticket is closed.

12.9 Information systems development and maintenance

Information systems in FCL shall include operating systems, infrastructure, business applications, off-the-shelf products, services, and user-developed applications.

12.9.1 System development life cycle

The following policies shall apply to the system development life cycle:

1. All projects shall have security considered at every point in the development life cycle. This means adopting a secure software/system development life cycle (SSDLC).
2. the ISM shall have the power to halt the implementation or commissioning of any project that has insufficient security controls built into it.
3. the ISM shall be one of the mandatory signatures at all 'gate' reviews.
4. No project shall be implemented that may prejudice FCL information on account of security failures (if the system were installed).

12.9.2 Programme specification

All projects shall have the requirements for security considered and specified from the start of the project. The requirements for controls shall depend on the classification of the information handled or accessed by the system, client requirements, and the appropriate risk assessment.

All new programmes, projects, or upgrades to existing programmes and projects shall formally have their security measures approved and their residual risks accepted by the information Owner and the ISM. This shall be formally recorded and be available for audit, forming part of the project documentation, and be available for the CAB to consider.

12.9.3 Security of system files

12.9.3.1 Control of operational software

The following procedures shall apply to control operational software:

1. All operational software (whether live or still in development) shall be fully controlled.
2. Only executable code shall be held on operational systems (source code shall be retained securely in appropriate system development areas).
3. All access to programme source code and associated files shall be audited, and access regularly reviewed by the ISM.
4. Updated or new source code shall not be released into the live environment without first undergoing and passing appropriate tests and being approved by the CAB.

12.9.3.2 Protection of system test data

The following procedures apply to protection of system test information:

1. All test information shall be protected against unauthorised access, erasure, modification, and disclosure.
2. There shall be a separate authorisation each time any test information is copied to a test system.
3. Where test information contains personal information, the requirements of the data protection and privacy legislation within the jurisdiction shall be met.
4. Ideally, personal information shall be sanitised to prevent real names being divulged. This shall include pseudonymisation and data masking.
5. Where test information is used from operational data, it shall be authorised at each use and immediately removed securely after use from the test environment;
6. After use, the test information shall be securely stored so that it can be reused for regression testing, if required, or securely deleted.
7. Where possible, no operational data shall be used for testing purposes. Where personal data is to be used it shall be:
   - Pseudonymised;
   - Masked; or
   - Otherwise protected to ensure that it cannot be reverse engineer o identify the data subject.
8. Any hard copy output from the testing process shall be securely disposed of, preferably by shredding, but according to the procedure defined in Section 12.3.14.10.

12.9.3.3 Access to programme source library

The following procedures shall apply to access to programme source libraries:

1. Access to programme source libraries shall be fully controlled, authorised, and subject to regular review for continued business need.
2. Programme source libraries shall not be held in operational systems.
3. Old versions of code shall be archived.

12.9.4 Security in development and support processes

12.9.4.1 Packaged solution use

Where FCL uses a packaged (or COTS) solution, it shall be maintained at a level supported by the manufacturer. Any changes to a packaged solution shall be submitted to the Change Management Process after full testing before promotion to the live environment.

12.9.4.2 Fixes and service packs

The ISM and the IT Manager, where appropriate, shall subscribe to all relevant sources of information and threat intelligence to ensure that all patches required to address published vulnerabilities are implemented. Vendor-issued amendments to software shall be fully tested and passed by the Change Management Process before being applied to existing software in the production environment.

12.9.4.2.1 Change control process

All changes to live systems shall be controlled via the Change Management Process.

12.9.4.2.2 Technical review of operating system changes

Application systems shall be reviewed and tested when changes occur.

12.9.4.2.3 Restrictions on changes to software packages

Modifications to software packages shall be discouraged and essential changes strictly controlled. All changes shall be controlled via the Change Management Process.

12.9.4.2.4 Covert channels and Trojan code

The purchase, use, and modification of software shall be controlled and checked to protect against possible covert channels and malicious code.

12.9.4.2.5 Outsourced software development

Where software is developed by a third party, it shall be subject to contractual terms that ensure that the development meets all requirements, is of appropriate quality, and is fully tested by the third party prior to submission to FCL.

All software developed by third parties shall be fully tested by FCL before acceptance and shall only be implemented in the live environment via the Change Management Process.

Where this involves a forensic tool, it shall be subject either to external Validation testing by a competent laboratory, or internal validation as defined in Chapter 7, Section 7.5.5.

12.9.5 Developing software applications

The process that controls how code is accessed and worked with shall be the same for all applications developed within FCL.

All access to source code shall be controlled at the file level by the use of user groups for the relevant developers' group. Employees who are employed to develop or maintain software shall be included in the group as part of the user account creation process.

Note

No development shall be performed on source code unless the development or changes required have been approved via the Change Management Process.

A simplified flowchart of the software development process is (Fig. 12.8):

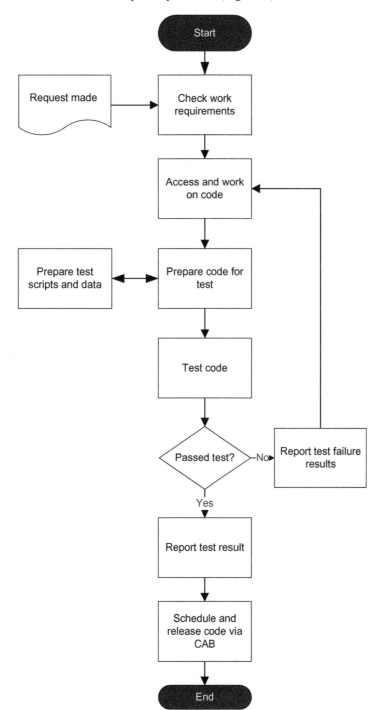

FIG. 12.8 Developing software applications.

12.9.5.1 *Roles and responsibilities*

12.9.5.1.1 Software developer

The Software Developer is the person who creates and maintains software application(s) within the IT Department. The responsibilities of this role shall include:

1. Checking development requirements.
2. Developing the code.
3. Pretesting code prior to formal testing.

4. Preparing the code for formal testing.
5. Submitting changes through the Change Management Process.

12.9.5.1.2 Quality assurance

The Quality Assurance function shall test any in-house developed software (as well as any externally sourced software). The responsibilities of this role shall include:

1. Checking the test criteria.
2. Performing a test against the agreed test criteria.
3. Reporting the results of a test to the Software Developer.

12.9.5.1.3 IT Manager

The IT Manager shall be the central authority for system development. The responsibilities of this role shall include ensuring that adequate system development controls are in place.

12.9.5.2 Developing the code

To develop the code, a Software Developer shall perform the following tasks:

1. Check the requirements for the work. This is normally on a development specification or a change request but can also be on an email.
2. Prepare a change request for the implementation of the software and put this request through the Change Management Process
3. Access a copy of the live source code using the appropriate development tools.
    WARNING: No development work shall be performed on the live source code.
4. Work shall be carried out by the relevant member of the IT Department on the source code using the appropriate development tools and standards.

12.9.5.3 Testing the code

FCL shall apply the following processes to code testing:

1. All FCL systems shall be fully tested before being submitted for release via the Change Management Process. Full testing shall mean unit, functional, system, performance, and integration testing, as well as user acceptance and regression testing (where appropriate).
2. All test results shall be recorded and securely maintained for later audit.
3. Confirm the test criteria and prepare any test packs and information that are required for the test.
4. Send an email to the assigned testers and confirm the test requirements.
5. The tester(s) shall perform the tests against the specified criteria using any supplied test scripts and information. The results shall be recorded in an email that is sent back to the relevant developers, the IT Manager, and the ISM.
6. If any changes are required to the code following testing, the relevant developer(s) shall implement them and then generate a further set of tests as above.
7. If no changes are required to the code, it shall be released to the Change Management Process for review with the specification, test criteria, and test pack results.

12.9.5.4 Releasing the code

To release the code to the production environment a Software Developer shall perform the following tasks:

1. Confirm that the testing has been successfully completed against the test criteria and that it has been approved by the CAB.
2. File all of the documentation relating to the release in the ERMS.
3. Make a live version of the source code.
4. Advise the Release Manager of the proposed release so it can be scheduled.

    The Release Manager shall:

1. Schedule the update to the live software application;
2. Confirm the release of the software application to relevant users and the timetable for release.

Note

The job description for the Release Manager is defined in Chapter 7, Appendix 16.

12.9.6 Security in systems development

These controls shall be used within the context of the Secure System Development Life Cycle (SSDLC). They are designed as a checklist to ensure that proper attention shall be given to all aspects relevant to the security of developed software.

An SSDLC methodology shall be implemented to consider security issues in all phases so that:

1. All information security concerns shall be addressed at every stage of the development project from business case to postimplementation maintenance.
2. Test criteria shall all be met prior to the implementation of operational software.
3. Change Management Processes for all operational software shall be implemented.

Note

FCL does not perform development or modification on purchased software packages.

12.9.6.1 Systems development projects

FCL Software Developers shall consider the following aspects of information security on system development projects:

1. A security specialist shall be appointed to provide security advice for the project—this is usually the ISM.
2. Any employee that is involved in software development shall have the appropriate training, experience, and qualifications for the required development work.
3. The IT Manager, ISM, and other interested parties as appropriate shall review the completion of major phases of the system, and provide formal signoffs that make them personally liable and accountable for the development. These shall be recorded in the ERMS.
4. Audits shall be performed internally within IT to monitor development progress.
5. Project management methods shall be used to control the development process.

12.9.6.2 Systems development methods

The IT Department shall follow these guidelines for system development methods:

1. All system development shall be planned and approved.
2. All systems shall be documented to a formal standard.
3. Users shall be consulted in all stages of system development.
4. The security issues for a development shall be identified by a formal risk analysis.
5. The ISM shall ensure that the required security features are included in the system.
6. A configuration management system shall be implemented during development and implementation. The configuration management process is defined in Chapter 7, Section 7.4.5.

12.9.6.3 System design

FCL shall follow these information security controls during system design:

1. All changes to a system shall be formally controlled via the Change Management Process.
2. All change requests shall be authorised before they take place.
3. Techniques for error prevention, error detection, and system recovery shall be part of design standards.
4. Testing standards shall be developed and implemented including:
   - user acceptance testing;
   - parallel and/or pilot running of systems;
   - independent testing of software changes prior to implementation.
5. Security mechanisms shall be independently tested and proved to work as claimed in system documentation.
6. All system design shall be reviewed and signed-off.
7. A full test strategy shall be agreed and documented.
8. System test of programme changes shall, wherever possible, not include live information—note that the relevant business Owner shall approve this and care shall be taken in handling output if the information includes sensitive financial, personally identifiable information, or other classified or sensitive information.

9. All remediation of detected test failures or errors shall be fully tested to ensure that the test failures have been eliminated as part of the regression testing process, and that no new ones have been introduced.

12.9.6.4 Development environment

The IT Department shall follow these information security controls during the preparation of the systems development environment:

1. Effective control mechanisms shall be implemented to control multiple versions of software.
2. There shall be adequate back-up procedures.
3. There shall be adequate procedures to govern 'emergency fixes' (but in general this shall only be used for emergencies).
4. No utilities shall be used that could bypass control measures.

12.9.6.5 Software testing

The IT Department shall follow these information security controls for software testing:

1. Results of software testing shall be documented and approved by the IT Manager, the ISM, and the relevant Owner(s).
2. Those who undertake testing shall be made aware of the need to observe confidentiality of the information used in the testing process.
3. Software testing shall take place in a specialised testing environment and should test the full functionality of the system (the Test Environment).
4. Only authorised employees shall perform software tests.
5. Output of software tests shall be considered as confidential information.
6. Security of the existing system shall not be decreased whilst system testing is taking place.
7. Tests shall prove that the system complies with all design specifications and any required information security measures.
8. System tests shall take place in the Test Environment.

12.9.7 System implementation

During the process of bringing developed software into operational use (the implementation process), many activities need to be performed, which can have influence on the security of information systems. These controls shall ensure that during the process of bringing the software into operational use, the security of the information system shall comply with the defined security requirements.

FCL shall follow these information security controls during the implementation process:

1. The ISM shall be involved in all system developments and implementations and be a signatory at all review stages for system approval.
2. New system working procedures shall fulfil the required security levels.
3. System authorisations given to users shall not exceed the required system authorisation to compete their tasks.
4. There shall be control facilities to check that no user can exceed their given system access authorisations.
5. Security measures implemented for a system shall be part of the user training.
6. Only authorised employees shall change and modify information on any information processing system.
7. System users shall be trained on how to use all systems and their security features.
8. The security of existing systems shall not be endangered during the training of users.
9. Transfer of software and information from the Test Environment into the Production Environment shall be controlled in an appropriate manner, using the Change Management Process.
10. Transfer of information and software between the Test and Production Environments shall be undertaken securely as defined in Chapter 7, Section 7.4.4.
11. During the period of transfer, information, and software shall not be made available to unauthorised users.

12.9.8 Security for third-party systems development

These controls shall be used within the context of the project management framework which FCL adopts for systems development by third parties. They are designed as a checklist to ensure that proper attention shall be given to all aspects which are relevant to the secure implementation of software that is developed on behalf of FCL by a third party.

All project work for third-party system development shall be conducted in accordance with FCL's policies and procedures on systems development projects.

12.9.8.1 Developing system specifications/requirements

The IT Department shall consider the following aspects of information security when developing a specification or requirements for a system that is to be developed by a third party:

1. The IT Department shall appoint a security specialist to provide information security advice and be responsible for all aspects of information security throughout the development project (this is usually the ISM).
2. All information security requirements shall be formally documented in a system specification or requirements document.
3. Specific information security requirements that shall be addressed in a system specification or requirements document shall include, but not be limited to:
   - information security requirements for each phase of the development life cycle, including development, testing, and implementation;
   - information security requirements/considerations for the third party that is to develop the system;
   - licensing arrangements, code Ownership, escrow, and copyright issues (where applicable); and
   - methods by which the IT Department shall certify the quality and accuracy of the work which is performed.
4. Rights of access for the IT Department and the ISM to audit the quality and accuracy of the work done
5. Contractual requirements for quality of code.

12.9.8.2 Requests for proposals and quotations

The IT Department shall consider the following aspects of information security during requests for proposals and quotations for a system that is to be developed by a third party:

1. All information security issues which are outlined in the system specification or requirements document shall be addressed and formally agreed.
2. Issues of code ownership and copyright throughout the development life cycle shall be formally agreed by FCL and the third party.

12.9.8.3 System development

The IT Department shall consider the following aspects of information security during the development of a system by a third party:

1. Any systems development work which is carried out on FCL's premises shall be performed in accordance with the relevant FCL policies and procedures and specifically the IT Department's policies on systems development design, methods, and environment.
2. Periodic reviews shall be conducted to ensure that third parties meet contractual requirements for quality of code, and quality and accuracy of work performed.

12.9.8.4 System testing

The IT Department shall consider the following aspects of information security during the testing of systems that are developed by a third party:

1. Testing shall be carried out in accordance with FCL's systems testing procedures, as defined in Sections 12.9.5.3 and 12.9.6.5.
2. Testing shall be carried out according to an agreed testing plan.
3. Testing shall provide a certification of the quality and accuracy of the work carried out to the satisfaction of the security specialist appointed to the project.
4. Testing shall be performed for the detection of malicious and Trojan code and to detect known vulnerabilities, especially for web-based applications.
5. Testing shall prove that the system complies with any required security measures.

12.9.8.5 System implementation and sign-off

The IT Department shall consider the following aspects of information security when implementing systems that are developed by a third party:

1. Implementation shall be carried out in accordance with the IT Department's policies and procedures on systems implementation through the Change Management and Release Management Processes.
2. Implementation shall comply with the defined security requirements.

3. The ISM (or security specialist appointed to the project) shall be involved in system implementation at each stage and be a sign-off at each stage.
4. Sign-off with the third party shall only take place following completed and successful system testing and implementation.

12.9.9 Reviewing application systems

FCL shall perform a technical review of application systems when changes occur to ensure that there is no adverse impact on operational security.

This framework by which the ISM performs a technical review shall be:

1. A member of the IT Department identifies an update or change to an application system and shall contact the IT Manager to discuss details.
2. The IT Manager and the ISM shall identify and assign a suitably qualified member of the IT Department to perform a technical review and schedule it.

Note

FCL shall ensure that any relevant specialist technical expertise is used during technical review including the appropriate software tools that generate technical reports for subsequent interpretation by a technical specialist.

---

3. The appointed member of the IT Department shall perform a full technical review including:
   - assessing the changes to the application system;
   - checking the application control and integrity procedures to ensure that they shall not be compromised by the operating system changes.
4. The appointed member of the IT Department shall discuss the findings with the IT Manager and the ISM. The IT Manager shall determine whether a rollout of the application is feasible. If so the appointed member of the IT Department shall perform further investigation work as follows:
   - designing an annual support plan and budget to cover future reviews and system testing resulting from operating system changes;
   - highlighting changes required to Business Continuity and Disaster Recovery Plans.
5. The ISM or the appointed member of the IT Department shall discuss the additional details with the IT Manager. The IT Manager shall confirm whether the application is to be rolled out. If rollout is approved, the work shall be scheduled.

12.9.10 Separating development, test, and production environments

The development, test, and production environments shall be separated to reduce the risk of unauthorised access or change to the Production Environment.

There are a number of controls in the IT Department that shall control the segregation of the IT environments.

Formal implementation and maintenance shall be the responsibility of the IT Manager.

12.9.10.1 Development, test, and production environments separation controls

The following controls shall be implemented:

1. Separate controlled environments shall exist for:
   - development and production of source and executable code;
   - testing source and executable code; and
   - the Production Environment for the operation of executable code, applications, and IT systems.
2. Only the relevant IT Department employees shall have authorised access to the Development Environment (Software Developers for development purposes plus library management, other employees, where necessary, for administrative purposes).
3. Compilers or other system development tools shall never be installed on production machines.
4. All code shall be compiled into an executable format before promotion to the Production Environment.

5. Software shall only be transferred from the Test Environment to the Production Environment after completion of the system testing required by the Change Management Process and authorisation from the CAB.
6. The test environment shall mirror the operational environment.
7. Where possible, different log-on screens shall be displayed to indicate the environment in which an application is running—for example, the login screen for a production system or application shall include a notification that it is in the Production Environment.

ISO/IEC 27001 certification

A forensic laboratory may aspire to hold a Certificate of Registration to ISO/IEC 27001 from an Accredited Certification Body to provide third-party assurance of meeting the information security requirements.

This is up to each forensic laboratory to determine.

Appendix 1—FCL statement of applicability (SOA)

ISO 27001: 2022 section	Control	Include	Exclude	Risk assessment	Notes
Organisational controls					
A.5.1	Policies for information security	✓		✓	Chapter 4, Appendix 20
A.5.2	Information security roles and responsibilities	✓		✓	Various job descriptions in the chapters Chapter 18, Section 18.1.2.1
A.5.3	Segregation of duties	✓		✓	Sections 12.3.5 and 12.3.6
A.5.4	Management responsibilities	✓		✓	Various job descriptions Chapter 4, Section 4.7.1
A.5.5	Contact with authorities	✓		✓	Various job descriptions Section 12.3.1.4 Section 12.9.4.2
A.5.6	Contact with special interest groups	✓		✓	Section 12.3.1.4 Section 12.9.4.2
A.5.7	Threat intelligence	✓		✓	Section 12.3.14 Section 12.5 Section 12.9.4.2
A.5.8	Information security in project management	✓		✓	Section 12.9.6
A.5.9	Inventory of information and other associated assets	✓		✓	Section 12.3.14 Section 12.3.14.7
A.5.10	Acceptable use of information and other associated assets	✓		✓	Chapter 4, Appendix 35 Sections 12.3.7.3, 12.8.4.1
A.5.11	Return of assets	✓		✓	Section 12.3.14.4
A.5.12	Classification of information	✓		✓	Chapter 5, Appendix 16 Section 12.3.14.6
A.5.13	Labelling of information	✓		✓	Sections 12.3.12, 12.3.14.8, 12.3.14.9 and Appendix 8
A.5.14	Information transfer policies and procedures	✓		✓	Chapter 4, Appendix 26 Sections 12.3.7, 12.7, 12.8.4 Chapter 14, Section 14.2
A.5.15	Access control	✓		✓	Chapter 4, Appendix 21

Continued

ISO 27001: 2022 section	Control	Include	Exclude	Risk assessment	Notes
A.5.16	Identity management	✓		✓	Chapter 4, Appendix 19 Section 12.6
A.5.17	Authentication information	✓		✓	Sections 12.6.3 and 12.6.6
A.5.18	Access rights	✓		✓	Sections 12.3.4, 12.4.6, 12.6.1.3, 12.6.7
A.5.19	Information security in supplier relationships	✓		✓	Chapter 14, Section 14.3.3
A.5.20	Addressing security within supplier agreements	✓		✓	Chapter 14, Section 14.3.3
A.5.21	Managing information security in the ICT supply chain	✓		✓	Chapter 14, Section 14.3.3
A.5.22	Monitoring and review of supplier services	✓		✓	Chapter 7, Section 7.4.3 Section 12.5 Chapter 14, Sections 14.3.3 and 14.8.2
A.5.23	Information security for use of cloud services	✓		✓	Chapter 14
A.5.24	Information security incident management planning and preparation	✓		✓	Chapter 7, Section 7.4.1.3
A.5.25	Assessment and decision of information security events	✓		✓	Chapter 7 Chapter 8
A.5.26	Response to information security incidents	✓		✓	Chapter 7 Chapter 8
A.5.27	Learning from information security incidents	✓		✓	Chapter 8, Appendix 18 Chapter 7, Section 7.4.1.6
A.5.28	Collection of evidence	✓		✓	Chapter 7, Section 7.4.1.7 Chapter 8 Section 12.3.13.1.6
A.5.29	Information security during disruption	✓		✓	Chapter 13 Section 13.5 Chapter 13, Section 13.6
A.5.30	ICT readiness for business continuity	✓		✓	Chapter 13, Section 13.6.2
A.5.31	Legal, statutory, regulatory and contractual requirements	✓		✓	Chapter 4, Appendix 25 Sections 12.3.13.1.1 and 12.3.13.1.7
A.5.32	Intellectual property rights (IPR)	✓		✓	Section 12.3.13.1.2
A.5.33	Protection of Records	✓		✓	Section 12.3.13.1.3
A.5.34	Privacy and protection of PII	✓		✓	Section 12.3.13.1.4
A.5.35	Independent review of information security	✓		✓	Sections 12.3.1.5 and 12.3.13.2
A.5.36	Compliance with policies, rules and standards for information security	✓		✓	Chapter 4, Section 4.9.2 Section 12.3.13
A.5.37	Documented operating procedures	✓		✓	This book

ISO 27001: 2022 section	Control	Include	Exclude	Risk assessment	Notes
People controls					
A.6.1	Screening	✓		✓	Chapter 4, Appendix 20 Section 12.3.3 Chapter 18, Section 18.1.3
A.6.2	Terms and conditions of employment	✓		✓	Chapter 18, Section 18.3.1.5
A.6.3	Information security awareness, education and training	✓		✓	Chapter 4, Section 4.7.3 Section 12.3.2
A.6.4	Disciplinary process	✓		✓	Section 12.3.3
A.6.5	Responsibilities after termination or change of employment	✓		✓	Chapter 4, Appendix 22 Section 12.3.4
A.6.6	Confidentiality or nondisclosure agreements	✓		✓	Section 12.3.1.4 Chapter 18, Section 18.1.4
A.6.7	Remote working	✓		✓	Section 12.6.9
A.6.8	Information security event reporting	✓		✓	Chapter 7, Section 7.4.1.4
A.6.8	Reporting information security weaknesses	✓		✓	Chapter 7, Section 7.4.1.4
Physical controls					
A.7.1	Physical security perimeter	✓		✓	Chapter 2, Section 2.4
A.7.2	Physical entry	✓		✓	Chapter 2, Sections 2.4.1, 2.4.3, 2.4.4, and 2.4.5 Sections 12.4.1 12.4.3, and 12.4.4
A.7.3	Securing office, room, and facilities	✓		✓	Chapter 2, Section 2.4.4
A.7.4	Physical security monitoring	✓		✓	Section 12.4.6
A.7.5	Protecting against external end environmental threats	✓		✓	Chapter 2, Sections 2.3, 2.4.1 and 2.4.2
A.7.6	Working in secure areas	✓		✓	Section 12.4.1
A.7.7	Clear desk and clear screen policy	✓		✓	Chapter 4, Appendix 23
A.7.8	Equipment siting and protection	✓		✓	Chapter 2, Sections 2.4 and 2.5 Chapter 7, Section 7.3.4
A.7.9	Security of assets off-premises	✓		✓	Chapter 4, Appendix 28 Section 12.3.10
A.7.10	Storage media	✓		✓	Chapter 7 Section 7.7 This chapter Sections 12.3.12.2, 12.3.14.10
A.7.11	Supporting utilities	✓		✓	Chapter 2, Section 2.3
A.7.12	Cabling security	✓		✓	Chapter 2, Section 2.3.1 Chapter 7, Section 7.3.2.1 Section 12.4.4.3.2
A.7.13	Equipment maintenance	✓		✓	Chapter 7, Section 7.5.4

Continued

ISO 27001: 2022 section	Control	Include	Exclude	Risk assessment	Notes
A.7.14	Security disposal or reuse of equipment	✓		✓	Section 12.3.14.10
Technological controls					
A.8.1	User endpoint devices	✓		✓	Chapter 4, Appendix 13 and 18 Section 12.3.8
A.8.2	Privileged access rights	✓		✓	Sections 12.6.2, 12.6.4 and 12.6.5
A.8.3	Information access restriction	✓		✓	Section 12.6
A.8.4	Access to source code	✓		✓	Section 12.9
A.8.5	Secure authentication	✓		✓	Section 12.6.6.2, 12.6.6.6 and 12.6.6.7
A.8.6	Capacity management	✓		✓	Chapter 7, Section 7.4.6
A.8.7	Protection against malware	✓		✓	Chapter 7 Section 7.6.1
A.8.8	Management of technical vulnerabilities	✓		✓	Chapter 7, Section 7.6.2 Chapter 4, Section 4.9.3 Section 12.3.13.2.2.5
A.8.9	Configuration management	✓		✓	Chapter 7, Section 7.6.2 Section 12.3.10.2 Section 12.3.13 Section 12.3.14 Section 12.6.6.5 Section 12.7.1
A.8.10	Information deletion	✓		✓	Section 12.3.11 Section 12.3.13.1.3
A.8.11	Data masking	✓		✓	Section 12.9.3.2
A.8.12	Data leakage prevention	✓		✓	Section 12.3.13.2 Section 12.7
A.8.13	Information backup	✓		✓	Chapter 7 Section 7.7.4
A.8.14	Redundancy of information processing facilities	✓		✓	Chapter 13
A.8.15	Logging	✓		✓	Chapter 7, Sections 7.4.3, 7.4.6, 7.4.7, 7.4.10, 7.7.1.1 Section 12.6.7
A.8.16	Monitoring activities	✓		✓	Sections 12.3.2.1.2 Section 12.6
A.8.17	Clock synchronisation	✓		✓	Chapter 7, Section 7.5
A.8.18	Use of privileged utility programmes	✓		✓	Section 12.6.4 Section 12.6.6.5
A.8.19	Installation of software on operational systems	✓		✓	Chapter 7, Section 7.6
A.8.20	Networks security	✓		✓	Chapter 7 Section 7.7
A.8.21	Security of network services	✓		✓	Chapter 7 Sections 7.3 and 7.7 Sections 12.3.5 and 12.3.6
A.8.22	Segregation of networks	✓		✓	Section 12.9.10
A.8.23	Web filtering	✓		✓	Chapter 7, Section 7.7

ISO 27001: 2022 section	Control	Include	Exclude	Risk assessment	Notes
A.8.24	Use of cryptography	✓		✓	Chapter 4, Appendix 25 Section 12.8.5
A.8.25	Secure development life cycle	✓		✓	Sections 9.1, 9.8.1 and 9.8.2
A.8.26	Application security requirements		✓	✓	Section 12.7
A.8.27	Secure system architecture and engineering principles	✓		✓	Chapter 7, Section 7.6.2 Section 12.3.10.2 Section 12.3.13 Section 12.3.14 Section 12.6.6.5 Section 12.7.1
A.8.28	Secure coding	✓		✓	Section 12.9
A.8.29	Security testing in development and acceptance	✓		✓	Chapter 7 Section 7.4.4
A.8.30	Outsourced development	✓		✓	Section 12.9.8
A.8.31	Separation of development, test, and operational environments	✓		✓	Section 12.9.10
A.8.32	Change management	✓		✓	Chapter 7 Section 7.4.3 Section 12.3.13.2.2
A.8.33	Test information	✓		✓	Section 12.9
A.8.34	Protection of information systems during audit testing	✓		✓	Chapter 4, Section 4.9.2

Appendix 2—ISO/IEC 27002 attributes

ISO/IEC 27002:2022 has now included a number of attributes to create different views of the controls in the standard. These are defined below:

Control type

#Preventive;
#Detective; and
#Corrective.

Information security properties

#Confidentiality;
#Integrity; and
#Availability.

Cyber security concepts

These are taken from the NIST Cyber Security Framework (NCSF).
#Identify;
#Protect;
#Detect;
#Respond; and
#Recover.

Operational capabilities

These are mappable back to the controls from ISO/IEC 27001:2013
#Governance;
#Asset_management;
#Information_protection;
#Human_resource_security;
#Physical_security;
#System_and_network_security;
#Application_security;
#Secure_configuration;
#Identity_and_access_management;
#Threat_and_vulnerability;
#Continuity;
#Supplier_relationships_security;
#Legal_and_compliance;
#Information_security_event_management; and
#Information_security_assurance.

Security domains

#Governance_and_Ecosystem;
#Protection;
#Defence; and
#Resilience.

Appendix 3—Some information/cyber security standards adopted by FCL

Listed below are some of the international and national standards that have been considered for information security input to FCL's ISMS:

- ISO/IEC 20000-x: Service management;
- ISO/IEC 27001: Information technology—Security techniques—Information security management systems—Requirements;
- ISO/IEC 27002: Information technology—Security techniques—Code of practice for information security controls;
- ISO/IEC 27003: Information technology—Security techniques—Information security management system implementation guidance;
- ISO/IEC 27004: Information technology—Security techniques—Information security management—Monitoring, measurement, analysis, and evaluation;
- ISO/IEC 27005: Information technology—Security techniques—Information security risk management;
- ISO/IEC 27006: Information technology—Security techniques—Requirements for bodies providing audit and certification of information security management systems;
- ISO/IEC 27007: Information technology—Security techniques—Guidelines for information security management systems auditing;
- ISO/IEC TR 27008: Information technology—Security techniques—Guidelines for auditors on information security controls;
- ISO/IEC 27010: Information technology—Security techniques—Information security management for intersector and interorganisational communications;
- ISO/IEC 27013 Information technology—Security techniques—Guidance on the integrated implementation of ISO/IEC 27001 and ISO/IEC 20000-1;
- ISO/IEC 27014 Information technology—Security techniques—Governance of information security;
- ISO/IEC TR 27015 Information technology—Security techniques—Information security management guidelines for financial services;

- ISO/IEC TR 27016: Information technology—Security techniques—Information security management—Organisational economics;
- ISO/IEC 27017: Information technology—Security techniques—Code of practice for information security controls based on ISO/IEC 27002 for cloud services;
- ISO/IEC 27018: Information technology—Security techniques—Code of practice for protection of personally identifiable information (PII) in public clouds acting as PII processors.
- ISO/IEC 27019: Information technology—Security techniques—Information security controls for the energy utility industry;
- ISO/IEC 27021: Information technology—Security techniques—Competence requirements for information security management systems professionals;
- ISO/IEC 27022: Information technology—Security techniques—Guidance on ISMS processes;
- ISO/IEC 27030: Information technology—Security techniques—Guidelines for security and privacy in Internet of Things (IoT)
- ISO/IEC 27031: Information technology—Security techniques—Guidelines for information and communication technology readiness for business continuity.
- ISO/IEC 27032 Information technology—Security techniques—Guidelines for cybersecurity;
- ISO/IEC 27033-x: Information technology—Security techniques—Network security
- ISO/IEC 27034-x: Information technology—Security techniques—Application security;
- ISO/IEC 27035-x: Information technology—Security techniques—Information security incident management;
- ISO/IEC 27036-x: Information technology—Security techniques—Information security for supplier relationships;
- ISO/IEC 27037: Information technology—Security techniques—Guidelines for identification, collection, acquisition, and preservation of digital evidence;
- ISO/IEC 27038: Information technology—Security techniques—Specification for digital redaction;
- ISO/IEC 27039: Information technology—Security techniques—Selection, deployment, and operations of intrusion detection systems (IDPS);
- ISO/IEC 27040: Information technology—Security techniques—Storage security;
- ISO/IEC 27041: Information technology—Security techniques—Guidance on assuring suitability and adequacy of incident investigative methods.;
- ISO/IEC 27042: Information technology—Security techniques—Guidelines for the analysis and interpretation of digital evidence.
- ISO/IEC 27043: Information technology—Information technology—Security techniques—Incident investigation principles and processes;
- ISO/IEC 27045 Information technology—Big data security and privacy—Processes;
- ISO/IEC 27050-x: Information technology—Security techniques—Electronic discovery;
- ISO/IEC 27070 Information technology—Security techniques—Requirements for establishing virtualised roots of trust;
- ISO/IEC TS 27101: Information technology—Security techniques—Cybersecurity—Framework development guidelines;
- ISO/IEC 27102: Information security management—Guidelines for cyber-insurance;
- ISO/IEC TR 27103 Information technology—Security techniques—Cybersecurity and ISO and IEC standards;
- ISO/IEC TR 27550 Information technology—Security techniques—Privacy engineering for system life cycle processes;
- ISO/IEC 27551 Information technology—Security techniques—Requirements for attribute-based unlinkable entity authentication
- ISO/IEC 27552 (1st edition)—Security techniques—Extension to ISO/IEC 27001 and ISO/IEC 27002 for privacy information management—Requirements and guidelines;
- ISO/IEC 27553—Information Technology—Security Techniques—Security requirements for authentication using biometrics on mobile devices
- ISO/IEC 27701: Information technology—Security techniques—Enhancement to ISO/IEC 27001 for privacy management—Requirements;
- ISO 22301: Societal security—Business continuity management systems—Requirements;
- ISO 22311: Societal security—Video-surveillance—Export interoperability;
- ISO 22313: Societal security—Business continuity management systems—Guidance;
- ISO 22315: Societal security—Mass evacuation—Guidelines for planning;

- ISO 22316 Security and resilience—Guidelines for organisational resilience;
- ISO/DTS 22317 Societal security—Business continuity management systems—Business impact analysis;
- ISO/DTS 22318 Societal security—Business continuity management—Guidance on supply chain continuity;
- ISO 22320: Societal security—Emergency management—Requirements for incident response;
- ISO 22322: Societal security—Emergency management—Guidelines for public warning;
- ISO 22324: Societal security—Emergency management—Guidelines for colour-coded alert;
- ISO 22397: Societal security—Guidelines for establishing partnering arrangements;
- ISO 22398:2013 Societal security—Guidelines for exercises;
- ISO 2800×: Specification for security management systems for the supply chain;
- ISO/IEC 29100: Information technology—Security techniques—Privacy framework;
- ISO/IEC 29101: Information technology—Security techniques—Privacy architecture framework;
- ISO/IEC 29119 Software and systems engineering—Software testing;
- ISO 29134—Information technology—Security techniques—Guidelines for privacy impact assessment— Techniques;
- ISO/IEC 29151: Information technology—Security techniques—Code of practice for personally identifiable information protection;
- ISO 31000: Risk management—Guidelines;
- ISO 37500: Guidance on outsourcing;
- ISO/IEC 3850×: Information technology—Governance of IT for the organisation;
- CobIT 2019;
- NIST 800-14;
- NIST 800-53;
- MIST 800-171; and
- NIST Cyber Security Framework.

Appendix 4—Software licence database information held

The following details shall be recorded for all software installations:

- product name
- product version;
- vendor;
- manufacturer;
- number of licences purchased;
- date purchased;
- locations where installed (i.e. user and computer details);
- number of licences in use;
- patches installed;
- updates installed;
- licence type;
- licence renewal date;
- proof of licence;
- software key(s);
- registration details; and
- date retired.

Appendix 5—Logon banner

The following banner shall be used on all FCL information processing equipment, where possible:

This is a private information processing system for authorised users performing authorised functions only.
Unauthorised use is prohibited and may constitute a criminal offence under the <state legislation>.
Unauthorised use by authorised users shall result in disciplinary or legislative action to the full extent permitted.

Press OK below to accept these terms of use.

Note

The relevant legislation for the jurisdiction shall be stated above. Specific legal advice should be sought for the relevant jurisdiction, as this book does not claim to provide legal advice.

Appendix 6—FCL's security objectives

ISO/IEC 27001 requires FCL to set security objectives (Clause 6.2) for the ISMS. These are business-driven objectives that the ISMS shall achieve.

Security objectives are driven by legislative, regulatory, client, and internal requirements.

FCL has agreed the security objectives below as meeting its current requirements and these shall be regularly reviewed at each Management Review meeting or on any influencing change that may affect them.

ISO/IEC 27001 requires that employees shall understand the Information Security Objectives, why they are important, and what they can do to help FCL achieve them. These are defined below, having been agreed by Top Management:

- increase client base because of ISO/IEC 27001 compliance;
- increase client satisfaction with improved information security requirements;
- commit sufficient resources to information security to maintain appropriate information security levels;
- continuously review and improve FCL's information security implementation;
- ensure that all employees know their security roles and responsibilities;
- ensure that all FCL assets, and assets held by FCL on behalf of any third party, are appropriately protected against loss, disclosure, unauthorised modification, or deletion;
- ensure that FCL is appropriately protected through contractual means when dealing with any third party, including measurement of services delivered against SLAs;
- ensure the physical security of FCL's offices shall be protected against unauthorised access;
- ensure that the IT Department securely deliver the services required by internal and external clients;
- ensure that the IT services are continuously monitored and corrective action is taken, if needed;
- ensure that all access to information is based on a documented business need, and that this is regularly reviewed for continued business need;
- ensure that any development undertaken, or products purchased by FCL, have appropriate information security in place, based on perceived risk and/or client requirements. This includes complete testing against predefined criteria prior to purchase or implementation;
- minimise the number of security incidents that may affect delivery of FCL's services, and learn from any incident to prevent recurrence;
- ensure that in case of any incident that requires invocation of Business Continuity Plans that there is minimal impact on the delivery of FCL's services to clients;
- meet all legislative and contractual requirements for information security.

These are derived from existing documentation within FCL, implied contractual terms, and good information security practice.

The ISM shall produce quarterly reports showing how these security objectives are met by use of the defined metrics, as defined in Chapter 16, Section 16.2.4. A report, showing year-on-year trending shall be presented to the annual Management Review by the ISM.

Appendix 7—IMS calendar

The calendar below is a summary of FCL's IMS Compliance Calendar.

Month	Standard	Action
January	All standards	2nd Party (Supplier) Audit 1st Party (Internal) Audit
January	ISO/IEC 27001	Vulnerability Assessment for all servers Perimeter scan for open ports Workstation scan Firewall audit
February	All standards	2nd Party (Supplier) Audit 1st Party (Internal) Audit Refresher Training for all management standards implemented
February	ISO/IEC 27001	Perimeter scan for open ports Workstation scan Account Rights Review Firewall audit
March	All standards	2nd Party (Supplier) Audit 1st Party (Internal) Audit Refresher Training for all management standards implemented
March	ISO/IEC 27001	Vulnerability Assessment for all servers Perimeter scan for open ports Workstation scan Firewall audit UPS Test Produce Metrics for Security Objectives
April	All standards	2nd Party (Supplier) Audit 1st Party (Internal) Audit Refresher Training for all management standards implemented
April	ISO/IEC 27001	Vulnerability Assessment for all servers Perimeter scan for open ports Workstation scan Firewall audit
May	All standards	2nd Party (Supplier) Audit 1st Party (Internal) Audit Refresher Training for all management standards implemented
May	ISO/IEC 27001	Vulnerability Assessment for all servers Account Rights Review Perimeter scan for open ports Workstation scan Firewall audit
June	ISO 22301	BCP test Update BCP, as appropriate
June	ISO/IEC 27001	Vulnerability Assessment for all servers Perimeter scan for open ports Workstation scan Firewall audit UPS Test Asset Audit—Finance and IT Produce Metrics for Security Objectives

Month	Standard	Action
June	All standards	2nd Party (Supplier) Audit 1st Party (Internal) Audit Refresher Training for all management standards implemented Collate information for integrated Management Review (ISO 9001, ISO 22301, ISO/IEC 27001 and ISO 45001).
July	ISO/IEC 27001	Vulnerability Assessment for all servers Perimeter scan for open ports Workstation scan Firewall audit
July	All standards	2nd Party (Supplier) Audit 1st Party (Internal) Audit Refresher Training for all management standards implemented Management Review
August	ISO/IEC 27001	Vulnerability Assessment for all servers Account Rights Review Perimeter scan for open ports Workstation scan Firewall audit
August	All standards	2nd Party (Supplier) Audit 1st Party (Internal) Audit Refresher Training for all management standards implemented
September	ISO/IEC 27001	Vulnerability Assessment for all servers Account Rights Review Perimeter scan for open ports Workstation scan Firewall audit External technical testing UPS Test
September	All standards	2nd Party (Supplier) Audit 1st Party (Internal) Audit Refresher Training for all management standards implemented
October	ISO/IEC 27001	Vulnerability Assessment for all servers Perimeter scan for open ports Workstation scan Firewall audit Software audit
October	All standards	2nd Party (Supplier) Audit 1st Party (Internal) Audit Refresher Training for all management standards implemented
November	ISO/IEC 27001	Vulnerability Assessment for all servers Account Rights Review Perimeter scan for open ports Workstation scan Firewall audit
November	All standards	2nd Party (Supplier) Audit 1st Party (Internal) Audit
December	ISO/IEC 27001	Vulnerability Assessment for all servers Account Rights Review Perimeter scan for open ports Workstation scan Firewall audit UPS Test
December	All standards	2nd Party (Supplier) Audit 1st Party (Internal) Audit Refresher Training for all management standards implemented

---

Note

All 1st party (Internal) and 2nd Party (Supplier) audits shall be integrated for the relevant management standards so that only one audit is carried out on each business area or supplier. Audit work programmes shall be specifically defined for each target audit.

Appendix 8—Asset details to be recorded in the asset register

The following are the minimum details to be recorded for any asset in the IT Department Asset Register, in addition to the disposal details defined in Appendix 11:

Asset details

- asset description;
- barcode;
- asset number;
- manufacturer;
- asset type;
- model number;
- serial number; and
- date last audited.

Current owner details

- name;
- location;
- phone;
- email;
- classification, if appropriate; and
- date assigned.

Validation and maintenance details

- date last validated;
- validation interval;
- warranty details;
- date of warranty expiry;
- maintenance details;
- date of last maintenance visit;
- date of next planned maintenance visit;
- manufacturer's documentation location;
- results of last validation test; and
- Reference of validation testing identifier.

Updated by

- asset register updated by, name;
- asset register updated, date;
- ERMS updated by, name;
- ERMS updated, date.

Appendix 9—Details required for removal of an asset

The following details are required for removal of an asset from FCL's premises:

- name of Requestor;
- Requestor's contact details;
- date of request;
- item to be removed;
- asset number;
- purpose/justification of the asset removal;
- intended location of asset;
- intended removal date;
- transportation details, if appropriate;
- intended return date;
- Asset Owner's name;
- Asset Owner's contact details;
- authorisation signature;
- date asset register updated;
- asset register updated by;
- date asset returned;
- date asset register updated; and
- asset register updated by.

Appendix 10—Handling classified assets

The table below shows the minimum requirements for how assets are to be handled in FCL. These procedures are mandatory for all classified assets and are summarised below:

Requirement	Public	Internal use	Confidential	Strictly confidential
Page numbering 'x of y pages'			✓	✓
Numbered copies			✓	✓
Classification in footer of each page	✓	✓	✓	✓
Strict access control lists applied for assets			✓	✓
Standard FCL document control table required	✓	✓	✓	✓
Movement of document to be held in a register				✓
Permission to copy required and to be recorded			✓	✓
To be held in secure containers when not in use			✓	✓
Can be sent by unencrypted email	✓	✓		
Only to be sent by encrypted email			✓	✓
Disposal to be by crosscut shredder[a]			✓	✓
Disposal shall be recorded in the register			✓	✓
Can be carried and handed over by hand[b]	✓	✓	✓	✓
Can be sent in a sealed single envelope internally or externally	✓	✓		
Can be sent internally or externally in a tamper-proof envelope or container			✓	✓
Delivery receipt required				✓

[a] If a crosscut shredder is not appropriate (e.g., for a hard disk or non-paper asset), then a suitable alternative shall be used. Advice on alternate methods of disposal shall be obtained from the ISM.

[b] By a known and trusted employee or a trusted and bonded courier service who has a suitable contract in place.

Appendix 11—Asset disposal form

The contents of FCL Asset Disposal form are defined below:

Form

- asset description;
- barcode;
- asset number;
- location;
- condition;
- reason for disposal;
- method of disposal;
- age of asset;
- expected date of disposal;
- written down value, if appropriate;
- sold to, if appropriate;
- sale price, if appropriate;
- donated to, if appropriate;
- asset owner name;
- asset owner signature;
- Finance Department authoriser name;
- Finance Department authoriser signature;
- date of authorisation;
- asset register updated by, name;
- asset register updated, date;
- ERMS updated by, name; and
- ERMS updated, date.

Within the form, the following codes are used:

Condition codes

The following condition codes are used in the asset disposal process:

- P—poor;
- F—fair;
- G—good; and
- E—excellent.

Reason for disposal

- B—beyond economic repair;
- D—damaged and no longer fit for purpose;
- O—obsolete;
- R—replaced by upgrade;
- S—surplus to requirements; and
- T—theft or loss.

Method of disposal

- C—computer recycle scheme;
- D—donated;
- I—already scrapped without approval;

- P—used for parts;
- S—scrapped;
- So—sold; and
- TI—traded in.

Appendix 12—Visitor checklist

FCL shall capture the following information for all visitors to any site:

Visitor details

- name;
- employer;
- mobile no;
- office no;
- reason for visit:
  - meeting;
  - service visit;
  - case progress review;
  - other (describe).
- describe visit details and justification if information centre or DR site visit.

Host details

- name;
- mobile no; and
- office no.

Escort details

- name;
- mobile no;
- office no;
- alternate contact details:
  - name;
  - mobile no; and
  - office no.

Visit details

- date;
- time;
- access authority to the following needed;
  - office;
  - information centre;
  - forensic laboratory;
  - DR site;
  - other (describe).
- authoriser name(s);
- signature(s); and
- date(s).

Checklist

- subject to existing contract with confidentiality clause (Date);
- subject to existing NDA (Date);
- new NDA signed (Date);
- information security policy received;
- Visitor briefing received (including emergency procedures); and
- rules of the Data Centre received.

For each of the above, the date they were actioned and the signature of employee performing the action shall be recorded.

Signatures

Signatures to confirm the above details and to comply with their requirements shall be obtained from the visitor and the host/escort.

New NDAs

If a new NDA is executed, a copy shall be given to the visitor and one retained by the ISM.

Appendix 13—Rules of the data centre

- all visitors shall be preapproved by the IT Manager, or his nominee, and escorted at all times;
- The IT Manager's word is final on all authorisations for access to the Data Centre;
- all visitors to the Data Centre shall register their access and egress using their visitor badge;
- the Data Centre main door shall be kept closed and secured all the time;
- all Data Centre hardware changes including additions, removals, and/or reconfigurations shall follow the Change Management Process, and shall be coordinated with, and approved by, the IT Manager;
- all cables connected to any device in the Data Centre shall be maintained in a safe, orderly and documented fashion;
- no material is to be stored on top of any server rack, and a minimum of 18 in. (45 cm) clearance between racks and the ceiling shall be maintained;
- all packing materials, cardboard, boxes, plastic, etc., shall be removed from the premises (including the Tape Vault) when work is complete;
- any nonessential or personal item left in the Data Centre may be confiscated;
- all cabinet doors shall be closed, or locked if appropriate, after work completion;
- all employees with access to the Data Centre shall acquire familiarity with the installed fire quenching system;
- the following items are prohibited in the Data Centre:
  - explosives;
  - weapons;
  - hazardous materials;
  - alcohol, illegal drugs or other toxicants;
  - electromagnetic devices that may interfere with any information processing equipment;
  - radioactive materials;
  - photographic or recording equipment (other than authorised media backup devices);
  - visitor's mobile phones; and
  - food and drink.

Any violations of the above rules shall be reported to the IT Manager as an information security incident and dealt with by the ISM/HR, as appropriate.

Appendix 14—User account management form contents

One form shall be used for the management of all user accounts. This shall cover the processes of:

- creation;
- modification; and
- deletion.

Account owner details

- name;
- forename;
- employer;
- position;
- room number;
- phone;
- email address;
- start date;
- status (permanent, part time, direct contractor, third party. Other); and
- end date (for fixed term contracts and known end dates only).

Authorised requestor details

- name;
- forename;
- position;
- room number;
- phone;
- email address; and
- signature.

Request type

- new user;
- account modification; and
- account deletion.

Hardware required

- desktop;
- forensic workstation (Windows);
- forensic workstation (Unix and variants);
- Apple Mac;
- laptop;
- desk phone—define type;
- other specialised forensic case processing hardware; and
- secureID.

Mobile devices required

- Android phone;
- iPhone; and
- other mobile device—define.

Communications accounts

- corporate email;
- email distribution lists—define;
- outlook calendars—define;
- groups to be a member of—define;

- internet access;
- Teams, Skype, WhatsApp, etc.; and
- other.

Drive access

- standard forensic laboratory shared drive;
- standard department shared drive;
- personal home drive; and
- others—define.

Software required

- FCL Laboratory standard desktop;
- FCL Laboratory standard forensic toolkit; and
- other—define.

Information access

- ERMS;
- finance system;
- human resources system;
- forensic case processing; and
- others—define.

Note

For each application or information to be accessed, each application or information database shall be authorised by the application or information Owner. This authorisation can be by signature on the form or by email associated to the application.

Forensic case processing

For each forensic case, specific access rights are assigned so that only named employees shall have access to the case:
- define case number.

Setup details

- name;
- forename;
- position;
- room number;
- phone;
- email address;
- date actions completed;
- date user advised (email); and
- signature.

Appendix 15—Teleworking request form contents

The form to authorise teleworking shall be used in conjunction with the Account Management Form, as defined in Appendix 14, for managing teleworkers.

Proposed teleworker details

- name;
- forename;
- employer;
- position;
- phone;
- email address; and
- status (permanent, part time, direct contractor, third party. Other);

Proposed teleworker location

- address;
- description of the site;
- details of security controls currently in place; and
- other people having access to the site.

Authorised requestor details

- name;
- forename;
- position;
- room number;
- phone;
- email address; and
- signature.

Business justification

- details of the business justification.

Duration of teleworking

- proposed start date;
- frequency of review for continued business need; and
- proposed end date (if known).

Communication method

- define secure communications method;
- defined strong authentication to be used;
- risk assessment carried out by;
- risk assessment carried out on;
- frequency of risk assessment update; and
- approved by the ISM on.

Teleworking additional measures required

- define any teleworking equipment needed for a secure home office—e.g. secure storage, shredder, etc.
- additional controls required by the risk assessment and agreed by the ISM;
- frequency of audit for teleworking site to be audited, and added to the IMS Calendar, as defined in Appendix 7.

Legislative requirements

- have all relevant legislative requirements been identified (e.g. Health and Safety, Personal data and privacy requirements);
- have all relevant legislative requirements been met?
- is appropriate insurance cover in place?
- has the teleworking site been audited prior to operations commencing?
- Auditor name;
- audit date; and
- nonconformities raised are on the relevant audit report, as defined in Chapter 4, Section 4.9.2, and are dealt with through the CAPA process.

Training

- date teleworking training undertaken;
- teleworking training undertaken by; and
- frequency of training update.

Authority and approval

- formal approval signed by;
- formal approval signed on;
- terms and conditions accepted by the Teleworker on; and
- copy lodged with Human Resources department on.

Note

Authority for teleworking is not permitted until all CAPAs are cleared.

Appendix 16—Information security manager (ISM), job description

Objective and role

The Information Security Manager (ISM) shall be responsible for establishing and monitoring adherence to ISO/IEC 27001 information security standards in FCL. Information security covers information on any media that is owned by FCL or is entrusted to their care.

Information security is defined as having the following aspects:

- confidentiality;
- integrity;
- availability;
- accountability;
- auditability;
- nonrepudiation; and
- authenticity.

Problems and challenges

The primary challenge for the ISM is establishing a good working relationship with all employees that encourage cooperation and teamwork to ensure that effective information security is in place. The ISM shall balance the needs of providing appropriate information security countermeasures against the problems of possibly stifling innovation and implementing draconian countermeasures that employees may resent and try to circumvent.

Principal responsibilities

The ISM shall:

- develop, maintain, and implement the information security policy;
- develop, maintain, and implement all relevant information security procedures supporting the information security policy;
- undertake appropriate training for all employees, clients, and visitors, as appropriate. This shall include induction training, ongoing information security awareness training, and specialised training;
- provide project management and operational responsibility for the administration, coordination, and implementation of information security policies and procedures across all information processing systems throughout FCL;
- assist the Business Continuity Manager in developing, implementing, exercising, and testing response plans;
- perform periodic information security risk assessments including disaster recovery and business contingency planning with the Business Continuity Manager, and coordinate internal audits to ensure that appropriate access to information assets is maintained;
- identify and implement information security controls, based on risk assessments, as appropriate;
- serve as a central repository for information security-related issues and performance indicators;
- assess changes to the information processing infrastructure for information security issues;
- review ongoing and update threat analysis, vulnerability alerts, and other issues and take appropriate action;
- function, when necessary, as an approval authority for platform and/or application security and coordinate efforts to educate all employees in good information security practices;
- maintain a broad understanding of laws relating to information security and privacy, security policies, industry best practices, exposures, and their application to FCL's information processing environment;
- make recommendations for short and long-range security planning in response to future systems, new technology, and new organisational challenges;
- undertake a rolling programme of information security audits and tests, as appropriate;
- provide regular reports on how FCL meets its information security objectives;
- ensure that all access to all information, including information held by FCL for its clients, is subject to agreed access levels, contractual agreements, and relevant legislation;
- act as an advocate for security and privacy on internal and external committees as necessary;
- develop plans for migration of information security policies and procedures to support FCL's future directions;
- develop FCL's long-range information security strategy;
- participate in international, national, and local SIG presentations, and may publish articles describing FCL's information security initiatives and how they relate to the business;
- develop and manage effective working relationships with all appropriate internal and external stakeholders;
- maintain external links to other companies in the industry to gain competitive assessments and share information, where appropriate;
- identify the emerging information technologies to be assimilated, integrated, and introduced within FCL, which could significantly impact FCL's ability to maintain a secure working environment;
- interface with external industrial and academic organisations to maintain state-of-the-art knowledge in emerging information security issues and to enhance FCL's image as a first-class solution provider utilising the latest thinking in this field;
- adhere to established FCL policies, standards, and procedures;
- performs all responsibilities in accordance with, or in excess of, the requirements of the FCL Compliance Management System.

Authority

The ISM shall have the authority to:

- set FCL's information security requirements;
- monitor production service offerings for adherence to FCL's information security standards;
- monitor FCL's internal processes and procedures for adherence to FCL's information security standards;
- identify and implement appropriate controls, based on business risk assessments to protect FCL's service offerings;
- enforce FCLs information security requirements.

Contacts

Internal

Contacts within FCL shall be throughout the whole business. Reporting shall be outside the line management areas that are being reported on

The ISM shall have a dotted line report to the relevant management committees.

External

Those external to FCL will be with appropriate Special Interest Groups (SIGs), other Information Security professionals, and organisations such as the British Computer Society (BCS), Information Systems Audit and Control Association (ISACA), International Information Systems Security Certifications Consortium (ISC2), etc.

Reports to

The ISM shall report to:
- Top Management.

Chapter 13

Ensuring continuity of operations

13.1 Business justification for ensuring continuity of operations

13.1.1 General

Business continuity is essential to all businesses and FCL is no exception. FCL has a number of Service Level Agreements (SLAs) and Turn Round Times (TRTs) in place for clients. FCL is contractually obliged to meet these requirements, as well as Court dates. Any disruptive event that affects case processing in FCL shall have one or more business continuity plans (BCPs) in place to address this and ensure continuity of operations.

FCL shall have in place processes and procedures to protect against, reduce the likelihood of occurrence of, prepare for, respond to, and recover from any disruptive events that may occur that affect forensic case processing.

ISO 22301:2019 Security and resilience—Business Continuity Management Systems (BCMSs)—provides the method of implementing FCL's BCMS. This is supported by ISO 22313: 2020 Security and resilience—BCMSs—Guidance on the use of ISO 22301 and other standards in the ISO 230xx series of standards.

As is common with ISO Standards, ISO 22301 is based on the Plan-Do-Check-Act or Deming cycle, as defined in Chapter 4, Section 4.3.

Note

Clauses A.5.29 (Information security during disruptions) and A.5.30 (ICT readiness for business continuity) of ISO/IEC 27001 and ISO 27002 also provides guidance on business continuity as do a number of other ISO[a] and national standards. This section of the book is based on ISO 22301.

13.1.2 PDCA applied to the BCMS

Applying PDCA to the BCMS gives the following stages:

- **Plan**—establish the Business Continuity Policy, as defined in Chapter 4, Appendix 19, defining targets, objectives, processes, and procedures to continuously improve FCL's business continuity capability;
- **Do**—implement and operate the processes and procedures defined in the 'Plan' stage;
- **Check**—monitor the implementation of the processes and procedures and review performance against targets and objectives defined at the 'Plan' stage, reporting the results of these reviews to management for preventive or corrective action, as appropriate;
- **Act**—undertaking the corrective and preventive actions based on the performance review in the 'Check' stage, using the CAPA process, as defined in Chapter 4, Section 4.9.

13.1.3 BCMS scope and purpose

The scope of the BCMS implemented in FCL is to provide resilience for its critical business activities through the implementation of controls that minimise the impact of a disruptive event on its business products, services, employees, and infrastructure located in FCL.

---

a. These include but are not limited to: ISO 27031 Information technology—Security techniques—Guidelines for communication technology readiness for business continuity, CSA Z1600: Standard on emergency management and business continuity (Canada); SI 24001: Security and Continuity Management Systems (Israel), BS 65000 Organisational resilience. Code of practice UK) and NFPA 1600 Standard on disaster/recovery management systems (USA).

A Blueprint for Implementing Best Practice Procedures in a Digital Forensic Laboratory. https://doi.org/10.1016/B978-0-12-819479-9.00011-3

- the scope of the IMS and so the BCMS, is defined in Chapter 5, Appendix 11;
- risk reduction shall be implemented by the implementation of controls identified in the ISO/IEC 27001 Statement of Applicability and is defined in Chapter 5. FCL's risk appetite has been defined in Chapter 5, Appendix 14;
- generic outsourcing and supplier agreements relating to premises and IT operations are defined in the IMS scope (e.g. gas, water, electricity, telephone, internet, other services and suppliers). All forensic supplier agreements of any type shall be subject to individual contracts with SLAs;
- products and services within FCL are defined simply as forensic case processing and this includes all of the activities outlined in this book;
- it is acknowledged that FCL is highly dependent on its supply chain for delivery of its products and services, however, there is little ability to manage some of these (e.g. electricity, water, internet access, etc.). These risks shall be recorded in the risk register and shall be managed as appropriate.
- Information security objectives have been defined in Chapter 12, Appendix 6; business continuity objectives have been defined in Section 13.1.5;
- suppliers shall be approved from a financial probity perspective as well as from an information security and resilience perspective including the supply chain risk and their own contingency arrangements. Details to be held about suppliers as defined in Appendix 1. The headings of the financial and security questionnaire are defined in Appendix 2. The key suppliers shall be subject to second-party audits, as defined in the IMS Calendar in Chapter 4, Appendix 46 on a risk-based approach;
- client details shall be maintained in MARS in the ERMS; and
- the BCMS shall be owned by the Business Continuity Manager (BCM), with a job description as defined in Appendix 3.

13.1.4 Requirements

FCL shall identify its own requirements based on legislative, regulatory, and contractual obligations as defined in Chapter 12, Sections 12.3.13.1 and 13.1.7.

- business continuity arrangements shall be implemented and exercised to support FCL's key business operations and ensure that these operations continue to operate in the event of a disruptive event;
- the high-level FCL business activities that are covered by these arrangements shall be:
  - client contracts and client management activities;
  - specifications, development and management activities;
  - case processing activities;
  - case testing and reviewing activities;
  - case delivery activities;
  - financial management activities; and
  - supporting infrastructure activities including:
    - IT systems;
    - employees;
    - building facilities; and
    - contracted third parties.

13.1.5 Organisational BCP objectives

The FCL business continuity objectives shall be to:

- identify business activities that are critical FCL's operations;
- reduce risk to an acceptable level in line with FCL's risk appetite, as defined in Chapter 5, Section 5.5.9.1;
- ensure that all employees know their responsibilities;
- provide a planned and regularly exercised and tested response to business disruptive events;
- successfully manage any disruptive events that affect business operations;
- be measurable, in line with the business continuity objectives and information security objectives, using the ISO/IEC 27001 Clauses A.5.29 and A.5.30. Other specific measurable objectives shall be developed as needed based on changing legislative, regulatory and client requirements;
- regularly exercise and test plans to ensure they are effective;
- provide regular training to ensure employees are competent in business continuity matters; and
- continuously improve response to incidents and learn from them.

13.1.6 Acceptable level of risk

FCL recognises that not all risks can be mitigated fully and that a level of residual risk shall remain and that this has to be knowingly accepted and regularly monitored using the risk register, as defined in Chapter 5, Appendix 17.

The BCMS has been designed to support FCL's critical business activities once assessed through risk management and Business Impact Assessment (BIA) exercises. The contents of the BIA forms are defined in Appendix 4.

The main processes that support the business shall be identified in the business risk assessment process, as defined in Chapter 5. Risk reduction shall be effected by the implementation of controls identified in the ISO/IEC 27001 Statement of Applicability (SoA) as defined in Chapter 12, Appendix 1.

FCL has identified its acceptable levels of risk and how to evaluate this in Chapter 5, with the FCL risk appetite as defined in Chapter 5, Appendix 14.

FCL shall knowingly accept the residual risk and actively manage the risks through its risk register and risk processes. FCL management shall regularly review the risks to company activities and agree appropriate risk treatment.

Note

Often it is wrongly thought that risk is always a negative outcome, but this is not always true. The positive side of risk is called an opportunity, and opportunities also require a business continuity response if adopted by FCL.

As part of FCL's risk management process, a business risk workshop shall always be undertaken, usually driven by the BIA that shall identify the relevant business processes to be evaluated. The process shall be as follows:

- after undertaking the BIA, a clear picture of business processes in FCL shall be presented with all internal and external linkages, this shall include any outsourcing risks, as defined in Chapter 14, Section 14.14.8.1.2;
- once these processes and their linkages have been agreed by the relevant Business Owner, a business risk assessment shall be carried out on the processes identified. Whilst this is part of the risk assessment process within FCL, it is an outcome of the BIA process but it shall be used to populate the Statement of Applicability and the Corporate Risk Register;
- the advantage of this approach is that all relevant Business Owners are present with Top Management. Where individual interviews are on a 'one-on-one' basis this can provide a biased and skewed perception based on the respondent's views, a workshop shall allow all views to be challenged and have Top Management make objective decisions, rather than respondent's possibly subjective ones;
- based on the results of the BIA from all relevant Business Owners, the top-level business processes shall be identified within FCL with internal and external linkages and also they shall be agreed;
- once agreed, the risks shall be identified. This shall always be undertaken in business terms facilitated by the Information Security Manager (ISM) and the BCM, who shall then turn business-driven results into terms of required information / cyber security controls; and
- using the risk management process the risks identified in this process shall be evaluated and added to the SoA and the Corporate Risk Register, as appropriate, after consensual agreement between the relevant business Owners and Top Management.

13.1.7 Statutory, regulatory, and contractual obligations

FCL shall ensure that all applicable statutory, regulatory, and contractual obligations are included in the BCMS as appropriate.

There will be different legislative and regulatory requirements in different jurisdictions and these shall be identified, both as part of the ISO/IEC 27001 implementation process, as defined in Chapter 12, Section 3.13.1 or as part of the contractual obligations for operating FCL's business.

Contracts with clients and suppliers shall identify any business continuity-related contractual requirements.

13.1.8 Interests of key interested parties

The BCMS shall ensure that the interests of interested parties are identified and incorporated into the BCMS. The interested parties defined by FCL include, but are not limited to:

- **employees**—people who work on FCL products and services;
- **clients**—organisations that use or purchase FCL products and services;

- **suppliers**—organisations or third-party consultants who provide services or products to FCL; and
- **investors**—organisations and people who provide finance and support to FCL business activities as defined in Chapter 4 Section 4.4.1.1.

13.2 Management commitment

Management commitment to the BCMS shall be demonstrable in FCL by all management and employees. Additionally, Top Management shall demonstrate this level of commitment and leadership by:

- establishing, approving, and communicating the Business Continuity Policy, as defined in Chapter 4, Appendix 19 to all employees;
- identifying FCL's objectives for its BCMS and business continuity response capability, as defined in Section 13.1.5;
- embedding business continuity and the BCMS into the IMS, which is used as the main business management tool by all employees, as defined in Section 13.8;
- providing appropriate resources for operating and continuously improvement of FCL's business continuity capability, as defined in Section 13.2.1;
- ensuring that induction and information security training cover the requirements of business continuity and the importance of each employee's input to the process, as defined in Section 13.3;
- developing a range of disruptive event scenarios appropriate to FCL and identifying business continuity strategies that address them, as defined in Section 13.4;
- developing an appropriate business continuity response appropriate for FCL, as defined in Section 13.5;
- undertaking regular exercising and testing of BCPs, as defined in Section 13.6; and
- continuously improving the IMS as defined in Chapter 4, Section 4.10 and the BCMS in particular as defined in Section 13.7.

13.2.1 Provision of resources

FCL is committed to ensuring that appropriate resources have been assigned to the business continuity process and the IMS generally, as defined in Chapter 4, Section 4.7.1 and for the BCMS, specifically in this section.

FCL shall appoint a BCM to oversee the business continuity process.

When setting up the BCMS, resources shall be ring-fenced for the project to ensure implementation occurs effectively. The high-level project plan for this is defined in Appendix 5.

Resources shall be made available for ongoing development, exercising, testing and continuously improving FCL's business continuity response.

Information, data, and communication channels shall be available as required as soon after the invocation of any BCP to relevant employees.

An alternate forensic case processing environment, in case the main office is unavailable, shall be available in case of need. This may be a dedicated hot work site owned by FCL, through a commercially available warm site down to teleworking and client site working. Whatever is required shall be available to ensure ongoing forensic case processing. Wherever forensic case processing is to be carried out in a business continuity environment, the Forensic Analysts and other employees shall have the relevant facilities, equipment, consumables, etc., to undertake forensic case processing as defined by the BIA for reduced working.

Additional to forensic case processing requirements are peripheral services that support forensic case processing and these include human resources, finance, facilities, physical security, etc. Peripheral resources shall also include those resources outside FCL's direct control (e.g. suppliers, outsourcing partners, service providers, etc).

As an output of the risk management process undertaken, relevant controls shall be identified, implemented, resourced, and continuously monitored to reduce risk to an acceptable level.

All employees shall undergo appropriate training for their role in the business continuity response capability.

First-party (internal) audits of the business continuity capability as well as second party (supplier) audits of key suppliers shall be undertaken, as defined in Chapter 4, Section 4.9.2.

The BCMS and other management systems implemented in FCL shall be subject to regular Management Reviews, as defined in Chapter 4, Section 4.9.3, with corrective and preventive actions being tracked through the CAPA system to completion.

13.3 Training and competence

FCL shall develop and implement policies and procedures for recruiting employees, to ensure that:

- all employees shall have the necessary technical and interpersonal skills that are required for attaining all of FCL's management system objectives;
- employees shall have the necessary training, skills, and personal development to fully contribute to the design, development, production, and support of FCL's products and services on recruitment;
- those employees that need additional training shall have this identified as part of their annual appraisal process using the Training Needs Analysis (TNA) process, as defined in Chapter 18, Section 18.2.2; and
- ongoing training and awareness updates are a critical part of employee development and shall be completed as planned.

FCL shall have policies for promoting business continuity awareness and training for employees to ensure that business continuity forms part of FCL's core values, that business continuity shall be effectively managed throughout FCL, and that all employees shall be aware of, and shall be adequately trained to fulfil, their business continuity responsibilities. This shall specifically cover:

- roles and responsibilities;
- recruitment;
- introducing new employees;
- managing business continuity awareness and education;
- managing skills training for business continuity response;
- training records; and
- performing employee appraisals.

13.3.1 Roles and responsibilities

13.3.1.1 Business Continuity Manager (BCM)

The BCM shall be responsible and accountable for all aspects of developing, implementing, maintaining, exercising, and testing FCL's BCPs.

13.3.1.2 Management

Management are executives or other management-level employees who are responsible for the following with regard to business continuity aspects of employee recruitment and training:

- recruiting employees in accordance with the relevant FCL recruitment procedures;
- defining requirement specifications for new employees, especially those with a business continuity element in their job role;
- ensuring that all employees have the necessary skill sets and personal qualities to perform their role in attainment of FCL's, and specifically the business continuity, objectives;
- assigning appropriate team mentors to new employees;
- ensuring that employees observe appropriate FCL policies and procedures as defined in the IMS and specifically the BCMS;
- performing employee appraisals, and determining/initiating action based on the findings of appraisals;
- identifying opportunities for employee business continuity training, and determining requirements for the ongoing employee development; and
- providing authorisation for employee business continuity training.

Specific Managers shall have individual job descriptions for their delegated roles, and these have been defined in various chapters throughout this book and are centrally defined in Chapter 18, Section18.1.5.

13.3.1.3 Employees

Employees shall be responsible and accountable for complying with all policies, standards, and procedures, in the IMS and specifically the BCMS.

Some employees will be part of the various recovery teams supporting BCPs and shall have to perform the defined role, as appropriate.

Employees shall be educated to understand their contribution to the business continuity process.

13.3.2 Managing business continuity awareness and education

Note

This section is in addition to the general promotion of awareness of management systems that shall be given to new employees at induction as defined in Chapter 6, Appendix 8.

13.3.2.1 Overview

Awareness of business continuity is an essential aspect of business continuity management in FCL. Employees shall be made aware of and understand that business continuity is an ongoing commitment that has the full demonstrable support of Top Management, and which provides a framework for ensuring the resilience of critical activities in the event of a disruptive event.

It is ultimately the responsibility of Top Management to ensure that all employees understand the key elements of business continuity, the approach, why it is needed, and their personal business continuity responsibilities. It shall be the responsibility of the BCM to promote business continuity awareness to all employees on a continuous basis.

Awareness of business continuity shall be delivered via an ongoing business continuity education and information/cyber security programme where employees are provided with information and guidance to help them understand business continuity and its importance to the business.

FCL shall follow these guidelines to promote awareness of business continuity:

1. A business continuity management education and training programme shall be run on a regular basis to promote and enhance business continuity management awareness.
2. All employees shall be kept up to date with current business continuity management activities via information updates from the BCM (e.g. email updates following a business continuity management exercise, test, or invocation).
3. Business continuity management awareness needs shall be reviewed on an ongoing basis to identify new awareness requirements, to evaluate the effectiveness of their delivery, and to identify improvements to the awareness programme.

13.3.2.2 Guidelines for educating new employees in business continuity

1. In addition to the 'normal' induction training, when joining all employees:
   - shall be briefed on the culture of business continuity within FCL, and as a minimum include the following:
     - the importance business continuity;
     - business continuity and recovery objectives;
     - FCL's business continuity management education and information programme; and
     - who to contact for additional information.
   - shall be directed to the BCMS element of the IMS and shall be able to:
     - understand they have responsibilities with regard to business continuity;
     - identify business continuity resources (the BCMS part of the IMS and any plans which they involved with); and
     - understand they have a role to play in helping FCL successfully operate and improve business continuity.
2. As part of the induction process, new employees shall be made aware of the IMS with supporting management system policies and objectives, with the following points of focus:
   - the IMS shall exist to ensure promotion of quality, information security, resilience, health and safety, Corporate Social Responsibility (CSR), and Environmental, Social and Governance (ESG) throughout the design, development, production, and support of FCL products and services;
   - FCL shall have specific measurable objectives with regard to obtaining quality in the design, development, production, and support of their products and services;
   - all employees shall be responsible for applying IMS procedures and policies within FCL and shall play a key role in the attainment of quality, information security, resilience and health and safety objectives;
   - all FCL products and services shall be developed in accordance with the requirements of the IMS;

- the IMS includes the BCMS which shall describe policies and procedures by which FCL shall ensure that critical business activities are resumed in the event of a disruptive event in FCL;
- the IMS shall include a number of separate management systems that have been integrated which describe policies, procedures, and controls which FCL shall employ for the promotion of quality, information security, resilience, health and safety, CSR and ESG throughout the design, development, production, and support of FCL products and services; and
- System Management Managers shall be responsible for their management systems and shall outline their contribution to FCL and the employee's role and responsibilities.

13.3.2.3   Business continuity management education and information programme

1. FCL shall implement a business continuity education and information programme, the purpose of which is to:
   - build a culture of business continuity within FCL;
   - embed business continuity management in all FCL products and services;
   - enhance awareness and understanding of business continuity amongst all employees;
   - communicate business continuity objectives to all employees;
   - instil confidence in employees' ability to deal with disruptive events that affect FCL; and
   - ensure that all employees are aware of their individual importance and contribution to FCL's business continuity objectives, and in maintaining the delivery of FCL's products and services.
2. The business continuity education and information programme shall be the responsibility of the BCM with the support of Top Management and shall be delivered on a regular basis (at least once a year), and additionally, on as-needed basis as determined by the BCM (e.g. following a business continuity management exercise, test or innovation, an audit nonconformity being raised, or any other influencing change).
3. The business continuity management education and information programme shall be delivered by the BCM in a workshop format and shall be attended by **all** employees. If considered appropriate, the BCM may invite representatives from suppliers (with the approval of Top Management).
4. Issues covered during a business continuity education and information programme workshop vary, but shall include, but not be limited to:
   - the status of business continuity within FCL;
   - planned developments for business continuity within FCL (improvements, emerging/changing business activities, their likely impact, etc.);
   - changes to FCL's business continuity processes, BCPs, etc.;
   - problems or difficulties experienced by employees;
   - employee's training requirements for business continuity;
   - employee's feedback on all aspects of business continuity management in FCL (including learning from disruptive events); and
   - internal and external BCMS audits.

13.3.2.4   Reviewing and improving business continuity awareness

1. The review, evaluation, and improvement of business continuity awareness in FCL is an ongoing, internal process that shall:
   - identify new requirements for business continuity management awareness amongst employees;
   - provide a means for delivering awareness requirements;
   - confirm that objectives for business continuity management awareness amongst employees are being met; and
   - improve business continuity management awareness and its delivery throughout FCL.
2. The BCM shall perform these reviews and they shall be performed:
   - on an ongoing basis (as part of the BCM' role);
   - following a full-scale business continuity management exercise or an invocation of a BCP in the event of a disruptive event;
   - during internal audits of the BCMS to examine compliance with the ISO 22301 standard; and
   - following a business continuity management education and information programme session.
3. The process by which FCL shall review and improve business continuity awareness shall be:
   - the BCM identifies areas of business continuity awareness that require review based on:
     - lack of employees understanding or performance with regard to business continuity;
     - issues identified at business continuity management education and information sessions;

      ○ operational, performance, or understanding issues arising from a BCP, exercise or invocation; and
      ○ audits performed on the BCMS to confirm its compliance with the ISO 22301 standard.
- the BCM shall perform the review and:
  - ○ determine the current level of awareness;
  - ○ confirm the desired level of awareness;
  - ○ identify gaps in employee's awareness;
  - ○ evaluate how business continuity awareness activities are performing, (e.g. the business continuity management education and information sessions and in particular whether any activities are not performing as expected); and
  - ○ identify possible improvements to business continuity awareness delivery.
- the BCM shall produce a brief report that documents the findings of the review. The report shall cover:
  - ○ objectives and scope of the review;
  - ○ recommendations for improvements to business continuity awareness (if any improvements are identified); and
  - ○ recommendations on how improvements are to be implemented (if any improvements are identified).

4. The report shall be distributed to Top Management.
5. The BCM and Top Management shall review the identified improvements and:
   - agree the proposed improvements;
   - obtain approval for implementing improvements;
   - seek consultation with other employees as necessary on how improvements can be delivered; and
   - agree on how to deliver the necessary improvements.
6. The agreed improvements shall be implemented as corrective or preventive actions using the CAPA process.

13.3.3 Managing skills training for business continuity management

13.3.3.1 Overview for managing skills training for business continuity management

1. Appropriate education and skills training shall be provided to all employees who are involved in planning, implementing, exercising, maintaining, and improving business continuity.
2. Training shall be provided for Top Management and Line Managers so they have the knowledge and skills that they require to manage the business continuity management programme, perform risk and threat assessments, perform BIAs, develop and implement BCPs, and to run business continuity tests, exercises, and invocations.
3. Training shall be provided for all employees, so that they have the knowledge and skills that they require to undertake their nominated roles during a disruptive event.
4. The BCM and the HR shall be responsible for ensuring that employees obtain adequate training to perform their business continuity roles via:
   - identification of employee's skills and competences for business continuity management;
   - advising employees of available courses as part of the TNA process and encouraging certification where applicable;
   - ensuring knowledge transfer between employees, as appropriate;
   - maintenance of individual personnel training records; and
   - active participation in business continuity management planning, implementation, exercising, testing, maintenance, and improvement.

13.3.3.2 Identifying employees' skills and competences for business continuity

1. FCL shall ensure that all employees are adequately trained to perform their assigned business continuity management tasks, to enhance the professional and personal development of individuals and to ensure that all employees can fully contribute towards achievement of business continuity objectives.
2. Training and development needs for all employees shall be identified in FCL using the following methods:
   - at least once a year Managers or Team Leaders meet with their employees to perform appraisals aimed at evaluating the skill set of their employees, and determining whether additional training may be required to:
   - enhance the skills of the employee; or
   - aid personal development.
3. After the appraisal is performed, employee's records shall be updated with the date and outcome of the review.
   - at the planning stage of a new project or case, Line Managers or employees may identify specific training which is required to enable them to be assigned to a particular project, aspect of a project or case;

- an employee identifies training that they would like to receive, and seeks approval from their Line Manager to attend a course; and
- the BCM or an employee identifies a skills or competency gap for which remedial action is required to enable them to perform a particular business continuity role.

13.3.3.3 Reviewing training outcomes

All employee training which is performed to improve the skills and competences of employees for business continuity purposes shall be reviewed to:

- evaluate the effectiveness of the training; and
- determine if the training was adequate.

13.3.4 Training records

FCL shall maintain training records for all employees undertaking business continuity management and disaster recovery training.

13.4 Determining the business continuity strategy

In order to determine the correct strategy(ies) for business continuity within FCL, it is necessary to ensure that all of FCL's requirements are captured, including legislative and regulatory requirements within the jurisdiction as well as any relevant contractual obligations.

Note

This shall also include any outsourcing that may be undertaken by FCL and all critical third-party suppliers.

To determine the business continuity strategy, a number of issues shall be examined before an appropriate strategy (or set of strategies) is defined and agreed.

13.4.1 Overall activity strategy

This is a review of the overall strategy for the business continuity response activity within FCL to be considered in the review shall include:

- maximum tolerable period of disruption (MTPoD) for the affected business activity(ies);
- Recovery time objectives (RTOs) for the affected business activity(ies);
- Recovery point objectives (RPOs) for the affected business activity(ies);
- costs of implementing a business continuity strategy for the business activity to address disruptive events in a timely manner according to contractual or other business drivers; and
- consequences of failing to implement a business continuity strategy for the business activity.

The outcomes shall be documented by the BCM and sent to Top Management for review and action.

13.4.2 Key products and services

FCL has the following high-level key company products and services that support FCL's objectives. It is the BCM's job to either agree these products and services or to amend the list to accurately reflect FCL's requirements. It is these products and services that shall be included within the BCMS:

- acquire clients;
- maintain clients;
- process invoices;
- supplier process;
- process cases;

- internal procedures (non-IT);
- deliver client's requirements; and
- internal IT Management.

The key is that the FCL business processes shall have had their risks assessed in the relevant BIA, as defined in Appendix 4, and in the Business Risk Workshops as defined in Section 13.1.6.

13.4.3 Business continuity policy

FCL shall develop and implement a Business Continuity Policy that sets the high-level requirements for business continuity within the business. This shall be approved by Top Management and is defined in Chapter 4, Appendix 19.

13.4.4 The approach

The approach to determining a business continuity strategy for FCL shall be:

- identifying critical business activities using the BIA process;
- performing the risk assessments on all business activities;
- implementing appropriate controls as defined in the ISO/IEC 27001 SoA;
- determining residual risk and how to treat it, as defined in Chapter 5, Sections 5.6 and 5.8; and
- determining the approach to business continuity, based on the findings.

Once the approach to business continuity has been determined, the appropriate strategies shall be selected for development into the relevant BCPs for FCL.

1. The basis for FCL's business continuity response shall be determined by a regular review of business activities in the BIAs by the BCM at least once each year and also when new business systems, products, or services are introduced or changed. Risk assessments shall be performed on those activities identified as critical.
2. In addition to this, business-driven risk workshops and infrastructure risk assessments shall be performed in conjunction with the BIA, as required. This shall enable FCL to identify their critical activities, and the resources needed to support them, their dependencies and to understand the threats to them.
3. The implementation of controls identified by the risk assessment and treatment process shall reduce the likelihood, but not necessarily the severity, of any threat that may exploit a vulnerability to become an information security incident or disruptive event and need to be treated as such.
4. Residual risks shall be knowingly accepted by the Risk Owner or as a blanket acceptance by Top Management as acceptable after risk treatment. This shall be subject to regular review at the Management Review and formally approved with records retained of this according to the requirements of ISO/IEC 27001, Clause 6.1.3f).
5. The criticalities shall be included in the BCP with the MTPODs, RTOs and RPOs. From this, FCL shall choose appropriate risk treatments and determine an appropriate business continuity strategy or strategies that shall ensure that:
   - MTPoDs are not breached, RTOs and RPOs are met;
   - appropriate resources are available for resumption of critical and key activities;
   - third-party suppliers of any type are not single points of failure for resumption purposes;
   - all dependencies have been identified for key business processes and activities;
   - recovery has been prioritised according to business need; and
   - minimum levels of service that can be tolerated are in place.

13.4.4.1 Reviewing employee resource options

This is a review and identification of strategies to ensure that core skills and knowledge shall be maintained by employees so that FCL is protected against loss or absence of key employees. Strategies considered in the review shall include:

- development of process documentation that allows employees to undertake roles with which they are unfamiliar;
- multiskill training and cross-training of employees to spread skills across a number of employees;
- succession planning to develop employees' skills and knowledge;
- use of permanent or occasional external support reinforced by contractual agreements; and
- knowledge management programmes supported by off-site storage for protection of data.

The selected strategies for each critical business activity shall be documented by the BCM.

13.4.4.2 *Reviewing work location and buildings options*

This is a review and identification of strategies to reduce the impact of the unavailability of the offices—or parts of them—so that employees can relocate to continue working.

Note

The review shall make estimates on the timescale for unavailability—the RTO. An RTO of less than a day may mean no action is required, whereas an RTO of a few days or several months means that employees shall relocate to continue work.

Strategies considered in the review shall include:

- increase in office density to accommodate more employees in specific areas of the building;
- displacement of employees performing less urgent business processes (to enable employees performing a higher priority activity to continue work);
- remote working from alternative sites (such as home, client or other nonoffice locations);
- reciprocal arrangements with other organisations. These shall be approached with extreme care and FCL has determined that it is not prepared to accept the risk of reciprocal arrangements;
- third-party alternative sites from a commercial or service company including dedicated or syndicated space and mobile facilities; and
- resilient operations to provide a continuously available solution.

The selected strategies for each critical business activity shall be documented by the BCM.

13.4.5 Reviewing supporting technology options

This is a review and identification of strategies to reduce the impact of the unavailability of supporting technology that underpins a critical business activity.

Note

Supporting technology covers any provision from within FCL as well as products or services contracted by FCL from third-party suppliers of any type.

Strategies considered in the review shall include:

- storage of older or unused equipment for spares or emergency use;
- provision of duplicate technology at an alternative site in advance of, or postdisruptive event (e.g. failover or dark site);
- provision of ship-in contracts to include equipment in the event of a disruptive event;
- planned temporary redirection of telecommunications services; and
- provision of remote working.

The selected strategies for each critical business activity shall be documented by the BCM.

13.4.6 Reviewing information and other data options

This is a review and identification of strategies to ensure that information and data required by FCL in both hardcopy and electronic formats are protected and recoverable within the required timescale.

Strategies considered in the review shall include:

- provision for confidentiality of information so that the required level of confidentiality shall be maintained during a disruptive event;
- provision for integrity of information so that information restored is accurate;
- provision for availability of information is available at the time needed;
- provision for currency of information for replication across systems without hampering employees' ability to resume operations; and

- remote storage of records including off-site managed document stores and optical copies for hardcopy records and data vaulting for electronic records.

The selected strategies for each critical business activity shall be documented by the BCM.

13.4.7 Reviewing supplies and equipment options

This is a review and identification of strategies to ensure that the business supplies required by FCL are available to support its critical business activities.

Strategies considered in the review shall include:

- storage of supplies at an alternative location;
- arrangements with third parties for delivery of supplies or stock at short notice;
- transfer of some operations to an alternate location either in-house, to a third party, or to a client;
- storage of older or unused equipment for spares or emergency use; and
- risk mitigation for unique or long lead-time equipment through a planned programme of replacement.

The selected strategies for each critical business activity shall be documented by the BCM.

Note

Where FCL has a single source of supply that relates to a critical business activity, potential alternative supplies shall be identified, wherever possible, or workarounds implementable, to ensure continuity of supply, in case of need.

13.4.8 Reviewing interested party's options

This is a review and identification of strategies to ensure that the requirements of interested parties are understood and managed during response actions by FCL.

Strategies considered in the review shall include:

- provision of requirements for interested parties as part of overall response actions;
- protection of interested parties; and
- understanding of arrangements with civil emergency responders.

The selected strategies for each critical business activity shall be documented in a report by the BCM and circulated to the Top Management for comment.

Note

For some strategies, it may be appropriate to use the services of a third-party supplier. The arrangements to obtain information from a third-party supplier about a service or to contract business continuity services to a third-party supplier shall be performed by the BCM in consultation with other relevant Managers. Agreements with third-party suppliers shall be governed by strict contractual obligations to ensure confidentiality, assurance and resilience.

Top Management shall meet with the BCM to review the report, to confirm that the continuity strategies have been properly undertaken, and to address the likely causes and effects of disruption or an adverse event to FCL's critical business activities. Top Management shall sign off the report assuming they agree, otherwise the report shall be reworked and resubmitted until there is agreement.

13.4.9 Reviewing business continuity strategy

FCL shall select the appropriate strategies to meet its business continuity objectives for critical business activities identified in the BIAs and the business-driven workshops. This shall allow FCL to provide a level of confidence that critical business activities will remain operational in the event of a disruptive event.

Through the selection of appropriate strategies, FCL shall ensure that it:

- has a fit-for-purpose, predefined, and documented information/cyber security incident response structure to provide effective response and recovery from disruptive events (including BCPs);

- understands how it recovers each critical business activity within the agreed timeframe; and
- understands the relationships between employees and third-party suppliers, and how these relationships shall be managed during recovery activities.

Note 1

For those critical business activities that have not been added to the business continuity strategy (i.e. business activities for which risks have been accepted), no further assessment is performed.

For each critical business activity identified during a BIA and which has been added to the business continuity strategy, a review of the appropriate strategy/strategies shall cover the following:

- implementation of the appropriate measures to reduce the likelihood of a disruptive event occurring and/or reduce their potential effects;
- resilience and mitigation measures;
- continuity for critical activities during and following a disruptive event; and
- account for those activities that have not been identified as critical.

Note 2

For some strategies, it may be appropriate to use the services of a third-party supplier. The arrangements to obtain information from a third-party supplier about a service or to contract business continuity services to a third-party supplier shall be performed by the BCM in consultation with other relevant Managers. Agreements with third-party suppliers shall be governed by strict rules to ensure confidentiality, assurance, and resilience.

The selected business continuity strategies shall be documented and then signed off by Top Management.
The process by which FCL selects appropriate business continuity strategies shall be:

- The BCM, together with the appropriate employees, shall meet to review the signed-off approach to business continuity.

13.4.10   Agreeing a strategy or strategies

Once a strategy or strategies has been developed, it/they shall be reviewed, amended as necessary until agreed. Then:

- the strategy or strategies shall be agreed;
- Top Management shall formally approve the strategy or strategies; and
- the strategy or strategies shall be used as the basis for developing a business continuity management response appropriate for FCL.

13.5   Developing and implementing a business continuity management response

13.5.1   BCMS structure

The BCMS structure used in FCL shall be as below:

1. The BCMS development and ongoing management shall be performed by the BCM.
2. The development of the BCMS shall be performed in-house. A project timeline for the development of a BCMS shall be developed and implemented for FCL as defined in Appendix 5.
3. A set of BCMS documentation shall be developed that encompasses:
   - an overview of the BCMS;
   - incident scenarios, as defined in Appendix 6;
   - BIAs for all business areas, as defined in Appendix 4;
   - BCP Strategy Options, as defined in Section 13.4 and defined in Appendix 7;
   - BCPs for each business area, as defined in Section 13.5.4;
   - BCP exercising and testing scenarios, as defined in Section 13.6 and in Appendix 6;
   - BCP exercise and test results and any corrective action; and
   - supporting material (e.g. forms, templates, and checklists).

4. Responsibility for the maintenance of specific sections within the BCMS shall be allocated to the BCM, but some areas shall be assigned or delegated to Business Process Owners.
5. The BCMS shall be produced in the IMS as a series of HTML, Excel, PowerPoint, Access, Word, or PDF documents accessed via an HTML front end for viewing using a browser. All the FCL computers shall have an internet browser installed.
6. All BCMS documents shall follow the requirements of document control.
7. All BCMS documents produced shall be retained in accordance with the document retention policy and schedule, as defined in Chapter 4, Appendix 26;
8. Responding to, and resolving, hardware, software, and service interruptions is crucial for the provision of information processing systems and services for internal and external business clients. If disruptive events cannot be resolved quickly and efficiently with the MTPoD or RTO, employees cannot perform their assigned tasks for clients. This, in turn, can potentially impact delivery of products and services, for clients, partners, and the ability of FCL to conduct their normal business operations. Timely recovery of critical business activities is essential.
9. The initial response is critical and FCL has three discrete processes that interlink to address this:
   - incident management;
   - business continuity management response; and
   - reviewing and continuously improving the BCPs implemented in FCL.

13.5.2 Information security incident management

This is a well-tried and trusted process and is part of the ISO/IEC 27001 process (A.5.26 and A.5.27), and is defined in Chapter 7, Section 7.4.1.

This process covers internal and external incidents reported to the Service Desk as well as any international or national incidents that may occur that are advised through national or international reporting channels or threat intelligence.

13.5.3 Business continuity response

There are many different types of plans that can be developed and fall into one of two groups of plans:

- **Incident management plan (IMP)**—describes the key management tasks required for managing an information security incident. This plan is followed whilst Top Management obtain an understanding of the information security incident and then organise full response actions; and
- **Business continuity plan (BCP)**—describes all the planned activities to enable the FCL to recover or maintain its critical business activities in the event of a disruptive event that affects normal business operations. This type of plan is invoked in whole or part and at any stage of the response to a disruptive event.

IMPs (including Crisis Management Plans (CMPs) where appropriate) and BCPs (including Disaster Recovery Plans (DRPs) where appropriate) shall be produced to ensure that all the critical business activities identified in the business continuity strategy have an appropriate managed response to a disruptive event.

Note 1

A specific plan does not have to contain the same headings or items, but all the plans shall collectively address the full requirements defined for FCL.

Note 2

Depending on a forensic laboratory's size, response actions to a disruptive event may be contained within one BCP. As it expands, additional requirements for incident response and business continuity may mean the division of activities into a number of specific IMPs, CMPs, BCPs, and/or DRPs.

Note 3

For simplicity, these plans have been referred to as BCPs as that is what is implemented in FCL.

13.5.4 Developing a business continuity plan (BCP)

Production of a BCP is a key stage in the development of an appropriate response to disruptive events identified by FCL to its critical business activities.

The main purpose of a BCP is to document the activities that are required to respond to a disruptive event that affects normal business operations, the recovery activities required to resume operations, the ways in which these activities are managed to restore operations within the required timeframe and the roles and responsibilities involved in the process.

Note 1

BCPs are developed to be 'living' documents and shall be maintained so that they reflect FCL's current circumstances.

Note 2

This process applies to any BCP.

The process by which FCL shall develop a BCP is:

1. The BCM, together with the other appropriate relevant Managers and employees, shall meet to review the signed-off approach to business continuity, the identified threats to critical business activities, and to obtain a clear understanding of the requirements for the BCP.
2. Any existing BCPs shall be reviewed to determine the level of integration with the new BCP requirements. If an update to an existing BCP is required instead of a new BCP then it shall follow the BCP updating and approval process.
3. A clear communication plan shall be agreed for pre and postinvocation of the BCP. This shall be regularly exercised, tested, and maintained to ensure it remains current.
4. The BCM shall produce a draft of the new or revised BCP. The minimum requirements for the contents of a BCP are defined in Appendix 8.
5. Where a third-party supplier is involved in response activities, details of the activities performed by the third-party supplier shall be obtained and incorporated into the BCP. The BCM shall make arrangements for this material to be obtained from the relevant third-party supplier.
6. The BCM shall produce the BCP according to the procedures for document production, as defined in Chapter 4, Section 4.7.5.
7. Once agreed, each BCP shall then be:
   - classified as a confidential document and subject to full document handling protection and control;
   - stored both on-site and off-site in hardcopy and electronic formats ready for use during a disruptive event; and
   - issued to the relevant third-party suppliers and interested parties in reduced but relevant form subject to confidentiality agreements (e.g. removing the elements not performed by the third party but retaining key communications and reporting information).

13.5.5 Updating and approving a BCP

As FCL, and its business expands, its requirements for business continuity will inevitably change, which will undoubtably affect the existing BCPs for responding to a disruptive event.

When changes are identified to the agreed critical business activities, all BCPs shall be reviewed and updated to reflect FCL's current requirements.

The process by which FCL shall update a BCP is:

1. The BCM, together with the appropriate employees, shall meet to review FCL's changing business requirements as identified in a revised approach to business continuity, the updated threats to critical business activities, and to obtain a clear understanding of the revised requirements

---

Note

Any changes to FCL's business means that revised risk assessments and BIAs shall be undertaken and used as input to strategies before a BCP can be updated. This should be one of the outcomes of the Change Management process.

---

2. Minor changes to a BCP, such as changes to employee's contact details shall normally be updated directly by the BCM without peer review and approval. In FCL's BCP(s), the volatile information shall be contained in the Appendix to the BCP. The table of contents for the Appendix to FCL's BCPs is defined in Appendix 9.

3. The outcome of the meeting shall be a detailed and documented list of the required changes to existing BCP(s) and potential new BCP(s). This shall be passed to the Top Management for review and the list of details for changes as defined in Appendix 10.

4. The Change Advisory Board (CAB) shall review the list of changes required to the BCP and confirm:
   - changes that are acceptable and can be implemented; or
   - changes which are not acceptable and which need to be further discussed.

   If the changes are not accepted, the BCM shall clarify the changes that have not been approved and shall resubmit information as required. The change management process is defined in Chapter 7, Section 7.4.3.

5. The BCM shall revise the existing BCP(s) (and draft a new BCP if one needs to be developed), according to the document control procedures defined in Chapter 4, Section 4.7.5.

6. The amended, or new, BCP(s) shall be reviewed according to FCL's document control standards.

7. Once agreed, each new or revised BCP shall then be:
   - classified as a confidential document and subject to full document handling protection and control, as defined in Chapter 12, Section 12.3.14.9;
   - stored both on-site and off-site in hardcopy and electronic formats ready for use during a disruptive event; and
   - issued to the relevant third parties and relevant interested parties in reduced but relevant form subject to confidentiality agreements (e.g. removing the elements not performed by the third party but retaining key communications and reporting information).

Note

Minor changes to a BCP do not normally need a major release update and can be issued as an incremental release, e.g. 1.1, 1.2, etc.

---

8. The BCM shall ensure that all issued hardcopies and electronic copies of the previous version of the BCP are collected and securely destroyed. At least one copy shall be retained for archive purposes.

13.5.6 Reviewing and improving the BCP development process

Review and continual improvement of FCL's process to create and update BCPs shall be an ongoing, internal process which seeks to confirm that the correct objectives are being met. The purpose of a review shall be to:

- determine whether the BCP development activities (people and methods) are occurring as expected;
- examine the process with a view to improvement of work methods; and
- identify improvements to the process.

   Reviews shall be the responsibility of the BCM, and shall be performed:

- on an ongoing basis (as part of the BCM's role);
- following a full-scale BCP exercise or an invocation of a BCP in the event of a disruptive event; and
- during internal audits of the BCMS to examine compliance with the ISO 22301 management system.

   The process by which FCL shall review and improve the BCP development process is:

1. The BCM shall identify areas of the BCP development process that require review based on:
   - aspects of the process which are not performing as expected;
   - matters arising from BCP exercises, tests, or invocations; and
   - audits performed on the process to confirm compliance with ISO 22301 and the BCMS.

2. The BCM shall review the process, and determine:
   - how BCP development activities are performing (in particular whether any activities are not performing as expected);
   - the effectiveness of the process;
   - the effectiveness of any previous improvements to the process; and
   - possible new improvements to the process and methodology.

3. The BCM shall produce a brief report that documents the findings of the review. The report shall cover:
- objectives and scope of the review;
- recommendations for new improvements to the process and methodology (if any improvements are identified); and
- recommendations on how improvements are to be implemented (if any improvements are identified).

The report shall be distributed to the relevant interested parties, including Top Management, for review.

4. The BCM shall review the identified improvements with Top Management and:
- outline the proposed improvements;
- obtain approval for implementing improvements;
- seek consultation with other employees as necessary on how improvements to the process can be implemented; and
- agree on how to implement the necessary improvements.

5. The agreed process and methodology improvements shall be implemented by the BCM.

13.5.7 Reviewing and improving BCP implementation

Review and continual improvement of FCL's processes to assess the business continuity requirements and then select appropriate continuity strategies shall be an ongoing, internal process which shall confirm that the correct objectives are being met. The review shall:

- determine whether assessment activities (people, technology, and/or methodology) are occurring as expected;
- examine the process with a view to improvement of work methods, the assessment and selection methodologies used; and
- identify improvements to the business continuity implementation process and methodology.

Reviews shall be the responsibility of the BCM, and shall be performed:

- on an ongoing basis (as part of the BCM's role);
- following a full-scale BCP exercise, test, or an invocation of a BCP in the event of a disruption; and
- during internal audits of the business continuity management system to examine compliance with the ISO 22301 management system.

The process by which FCL shall review and improve the business continuity implementation process is:

1. The BCM shall identify areas of the business continuity implementation process that require review based on:
- aspects of the process which are not performing as expected;
- matters arising from BCP exercises or invocations; and
- audits performed on the process to confirm compliance with the ISO 22301 BCMS.

2. The BCM shall review the process, and determine:
- how business continuity implementation activities are performing (in particular whether any activities are not performing as expected);
- the effectiveness of the risk assessment and BIA methodologies;
- the effectiveness of the risk treatment process;
- the effectiveness of any previous improvements to the process and methodology; and
- possible new improvements to the process and methodology.

3. The BCM shall produce a brief report that documents the findings of the review. The report shall cover:
- objectives and scope of the review;
- recommendations for new improvements to the process and methodology (if any improvements are identified); and
- recommendations on how improvements are to be implemented (if any improvements are identified).

The table of contents for the review is defined in Appendix 12.

4. The report shall be distributed to Top Management for review.

5. The BCM shall review the identified improvements with Top Management and:
- outline the proposed improvements;
- obtain approval for implementing improvements;
- seek consultation with other employees as necessary on how improvements to the process can be implemented; and
- agree on how to implement the necessary improvements.

6. The agreed process and methodology improvements shall be implemented by the BCM.

13.6 Exercising, maintaining and reviewing business continuity arrangements

FCL shall plan and implement business continuity exercising to verify the effectiveness of the business continuity arrangements and to identify areas of BCPs that require amendment.

13.6.1 Roles and responsibilities

13.6.1.1 Business Continuity Manager (BCM)

The BCM is the person who has responsibility for the management of the business continuity exercising and testing. In addition to the job responsibilities for the role, the BCM shall specifically be responsible for:

- maintaining the business continuity exercise and test programme;
- planning business continuity exercises and tests;
- drafting business continuity exercise and test plans;
- taking part in business continuity exercises and tests;
- appointing facilitators and/or observers for the business continuity exercises and tests;
- collating information from completed business continuity exercises and tests;
- generating reports on the outcome of a business continuity exercise and/or test;
- analysing completed business continuity exercises and tests;
- identifying and agreeing action points and improvements arising from business continuity exercise and test reviews; and
- implementing improvements arising from business continuity exercise and test reviews, if required.

13.6.1.2 Top management responsibilities

Top Management shall be responsible for providing management support to the BCM during BCP exercising and testing. In addition to the job responsibilities for their specific role, they shall be responsible for:

- supporting the BCM in all aspects of business continuity exercise and test management as required;
- ensuring appropriate resources are made available for the exercise or test;
- taking part in the exercise or test, as appropriate;
- providing input to the revision and approval of the business continuity exercise and test programme;
- providing sign-off for business continuity exercise and test plans; and
- agreeing action points and improvements to business continuity arrangements following an analysis of a business continuity exercise or test.

13.6.2 Business continuity exercise and test exercises

Business continuity exercises and tests shall validate the effectiveness of FCL's business continuity arrangements by exercising and testing the BCPs, procedures, and employees in a controlled manner.

The purpose of performing business continuity exercises and tests shall be to:

- test the effectiveness of the business continuity arrangements;
- validate the technical, logistical, and administrative aspects of BCPs;
- validate the recovery infrastructure;
- practise the ability to recover from a disruptive event;
- evaluate the current business continuity competence;
- develop teamwork and raise awareness of business continuity; and
- identify shortcomings and implement improvements to business continuity readiness.

Business continuity exercises and tests shall be governed by an exercise or scenario plan. Whilst each individual exercise or test may evaluate a specific plan or element of a plan, the range of exercises performed over a year shall validate the overall the business continuity arrangements. The template for scenario plans used is defined in Appendix 11.

Business continuity exercises and tests shall be performed on one of three levels:

- **simple**—typically a short and uncomplicated exercise—typically a desk check;
- **medium**—typically a walk-through of a plan or a part of a plan, a simulation, or an exercise of critical activities only (e.g. a critical server rebuild from backups, a ransomware attack, loss of a key person, testing the UPS, etc.); and
- **full**—typically a complex exercise that is a full test run of a plan.

Each business continuity exercise and/or test shall have three distinct phases:

- **preparing a plan**—to cover the exercise or test to ensure that all resources are available, the level of exercise or test is valid and the objectives of the exercise or test are clear;
- **performing the exercise or test**—in a controlled manner to check the validity of the BCP element(s) that is being exercised or tested; and
- **reviewing the exercise**—to analyse the actions and outcomes and determine whether the exercise or test objectives were achieved and adopt the lessons learned.

13.6.3 Maintaining the business continuity exercise and test programme

Exercising and testing the BCPs is a key business continuity activity that allows FCL to validate the effectiveness of its business continuity arrangements by exercising and testing BCPs, their supporting procedures and employee's understanding of them.

To ensure that all aspects of business continuity exercises and tests have been fully considered, FCL shall maintain a programme that covers the frequency and type of exercises and tests. This ensures that the business continuity arrangements as a whole shall be validated at least once each year, as in the IMS Calendar, as defined in Chapter 4, Appendix 46.

The exercise and test programme shall be assessed and updated at least once every 6 months and shall be the responsibility of the BCM. The programme shall be approved by Top Management.

The process by which FCL shall maintain the business continuity exercise and test programme is:

1. The BCM shall assess the business continuity exercise and test requirements for the next 6-month period and determine whether any changes are required to suit business needs. Generally:
   - business continuity exercises and tests shall be prioritised to meet business continuity needs and recovery objectives;
   - an exercise or test of FCL's overall business continuity capability shall be programmed to take place at least once every 12 months; and
   - the exercises and tests added to the programme shall be exercised or tested and be appropriate to FCL's recovery objectives.

Note

Where third-party suppliers have activities within a plan, suitable arrangements shall be made to exercise or test these activities as part of the programme by either involving the third-party supplier in an exercise or test or enabling the activities of the third-party supplier to be performed separately.

A review shall also take place on an ad hoc basis if events trigger a revision of the programme (e.g. a significant change in the external business environment or an internal change to processes, employees, technology, or business activities).

2. The BCM shall meet with Top Management to discuss the programme with a view to its revision and shall cover the following key aspects:
   - the current programme;
   - requirements and priorities for business continuity validation, exercising and testing;
   - outcomes from previous business continuity exercises and tests (e.g. a need to re-run an exercise or test, any relevant corrective and preventive actions);
   - timescales and resource availability; and
   - the levels of exercising and testing required (these may vary in complexity from a simple desk exercise or walk-through of options to a selected set of recovery activities or a full test of a BCP for total recovery).
3. Top Management shall approve the revised programme including:
   - a list of business continuity exercises and tests required;
   - scheduling of each business continuity exercise and test; and
   - levels of testing required for each exercise and test.
4. The approved programme in the IMS Calendar shall be updated by the BCM and issued to all relevant employees and other interested parties.
5. The issue of the programme may lead to a revision of the business continuity awareness programme to ensure that all employees are aware of when exercises will be held.

13.6.4 Performing business continuity exercises and tests

All business continuity exercises and tests shall be designed to exercise or test BCPs, and FCL shall adopt a positive attitude towards this exercising and testing to ensure that business continuity competence strengths are acknowledged and to allow weaknesses to be seen as opportunities for improvement rather than criticism.

Business continuity exercises and tests shall be an ongoing process in FCL that is conducted in accordance with the business continuity exercise and test programme (maintained by the BCM). There are three distinct phases to complete a business continuity exercise and/or test, as defined above.

13.6.4.1 Planning a business continuity exercise or test

All business continuity exercises and tests shall be fully planned to ensure that specific objectives for an exercise or test are agreed. The level of detail in an exercise or test plan will vary depending on the scope and level of the exercise or test selected.

The BCM shall ensure that business continuity exercise and test plans contain enough detail to allow the employees who are responsible for conducting, monitoring, and reviewing a business continuity exercise or test to fully assess requirements from a business continuity perspective, and to conduct and review an exercise or test.

The process by which FCL shall plan a business continuity exercise or test is:

1. The BCM, together with appropriate employees, shall meet to plan a business continuity exercise or test. This discussion may be spread over several sessions and can include requirement-gathering sessions with key interested parties, other employees and others who may need to be involved the exercise (e.g. third-party suppliers, or local authorities), or who need to develop information that is required for the exercise (e.g. scenarios).
   Items for consideration shall include:
   * reports/outcomes/reviews from previous business continuity exercises, tests and invocations;
   * current business activities and the effect the exercise or test may have on those activities (e.g. interdependencies of business activities and technologies);
   * exercise scope (what is included, what is not included);
   * aims and objectives;
   * exercise or test level;
   * development of scenarios and sets of assumptions to put the exercise or test in context (which should be suitably realistic and detailed);
   * roles and responsibilities;
   * timings, duration, and resources; and
   * reporting requirements.

Note

Exercises and tests shall be planned so as to minimise risks from information/cyber security incidents occurring as a result of the exercise or test. In the event that a business continuity exercise or test is considered to pose a risk to business activities, the BCM, in association with the ISM, shall conduct a risk assessment of the exercise (if a risk assessment is deemed appropriate) to assess the risk consequences of the exercise or test on business operations.

---

2. The BCM shall draft an exercise or test plan. The plan shall include the following:
   * exercise or test overview, aims, and objectives;
   * scope of the exercise or test (what is included and what is not included);
   * exercise or test level (simple, medium, or complex)—and details of how the exercise or test is to be conducted;
   * exercise or test scenario and assumptions—date, time, current business workloads, political and economic conditions, seasonal issues, etc., as required;
   * timescales;
   * relevant BCPs (or sections of BCPs);
   * required exercise or test participants (this may include representatives from third-party suppliers, or local authorities, if relevant);
   * roles and responsibilities for employees involved in the exercise or test;
   * notification and awareness requirements to employees, third-party suppliers and other relevant interested parties, where required; and
   * postexercise or test review and reporting arrangements.

Additionally, a business continuity exercise or test plan may detail:

- any risks identified and how these risks are to be mitigated; and
- budget requirements, if appropriate.

The draft exercise or test plan shall be circulated for review to Top Management and other interested parties, where required.

3. Top Management shall review the exercise or test plan and provide suitable feedback.
4. The BCM shall implement changes to the draft exercise or test plan as required.

Where changes are to be implemented, the exercise plan shall be re-issued for additional review and feedback. Where no further changes are required, the revised exercise or test plan shall be issued as version 1.0, as defined in Chapter 4, Section 4.7.5. This is the version of the exercise or test plan that shall be used to prepare for and run the exercise.

6. Top Management shall sign off the exercise plan.
7. The BCM shall distribute the signed-off exercise or test plan ready for the exercise.

Note

Where appropriate, a business continuity education and information session shall be convened to make employees aware of the forthcoming exercise.

The business continuity exercise or test shall then be conducted in accordance with the plan, and the results/outcomes documented.

13.6.4.2 Performing a business continuity exercise or test exercise

Business continuity exercises or tests shall be performed according to the signed-off exercise plan and managed by the BCM using the procedures for exercising and testing BCPs.

Before the exercise or test begins, the BCM shall ensure:

- all equipment, employees and resources are available, including any third parties if required;
- copies and the business continuity exercises or test plans and the appropriate BCP are available to all involved in the exercise or test, including any external interested parties; and
- employees are aware that a business continuity exercise or test is to be performed.

Note

There may be occasions where an exercise or test occurs where no warning is given to employees shall be considered by Top Management. This shall be carried out at a time where there is little operational impact on account of the test being performed.

The process by which a business continuity exercise or test shall be performed is:

1. The BCM shall start the exercise.
2. Relevant employees and third-party suppliers, as required, shall complete their activities according to the BCP specified in the exercise or test plan.
3. The BCM, and additional Facilitators, if required, shall facilitate the exercise or test;
4. The BCM and additional Observers, if required, shall monitor the exercise or test through observations and progress reports provided by employees.

Where issues arise that may affect the conduct of the exercise, these shall be escalated to the BCM for determination.

Note

The BCM may also have activities to perform during the exercise.

---

5. When the exercise finishes, the BCM shall declare the exercise or test over.

13.6.4.3 Reviewing a business continuity exercise or test

Reviews of business continuity exercises or tests shall be performed as soon as possible after an exercise or test is completed to analyse the exercise or test outcome, and to determine if exercise or test objectives were achieved and identify lessons learned.

A report of the business continuity exercise or test results shall be produced by the BCM as part of the review and sent to Top Management for comment.

Note

The review of a business continuity exercise or test shall also include a review of the business continuity exercise or test processes to determine whether the business continuity exercise or test activities (people and methods) are occurring as expected. Updates to the processes shall be considered.

The process by which FCL shall review a business continuity exercise or test is:

1. The BCM shall review the evidence from the exercise or test and generate a 'review report' based on its outcome.

   This evidence shall include the results of exercise and/or test activities, feedback from participants, Facilitators and Observers and also questionnaire results from selected participants to capture any lessons they may have learned, if appropriate.

   The report template used is defined in Appendix 12.

2. The report shall be circulated to Top Management, participants in the exercise or test and other relevant interested parties, as required.

3. The BCM and Top Management shall meet to discuss the report, analyse the exercise or test, identify and agree action points and improvements.

   Possible action points or improvements identified may include:

   - updates to BCPs, for example, a revision of a plan's approach to recovery or updates to details of specific tasks, actions, responsibilities, etc.;
   - changes to FCL's overall business continuity strategy;
   - changes to business continuity operating procedures;
   - a re-run of an exercise or test that has shown serious deficiencies after remediation or updating the plan;
   - changes to the business continuity exercise or test programme;
   - feedback to participants on the outcome of an exercise or test, and the lessons learned (e.g. via a business continuity education and information session); and
   - recommendations for improvements to the process and methodology.

4. Corrective action and improvements shall be agreed at the meeting, noted in the minutes, actioned through the CAPA process.

5. The BCM shall manage the implementation of the agreed action points through the CAPA process, undertaking a Post-Implementation Review (PIR) to ensure that the corrective action and improvement have been effective.

13.7 Maintaining and improving the BCMS

FCL is committed to a programme of continuous improvement of their IMS and other management subsystems, including the BCMS. This process is defined for the IMS in Chapter 4, Section 4.10. FCL shall perform regular audits and reviews of the IMS, as defined in Chapter 4, Section 4.9.1, with a view to continuous improvement, and shall focus on:

- how business activities are performing (in particular whether any activities are not performing as expected);
- the effectiveness of system controls and policies;
- the level of risk to FCL, based on changes to technology, business objectives and processes;
- the scope of the BCMS, and whether it requires changing; and
- potential improvements to processes and procedures in the BCMS;

For reviews of the BCMS arrangements, this review shall additionally focus on:

- ensuring that all FCL products and services are included in the business continuity strategy;
- ensuring that all policies and strategies, plans, etc., reflect FCL's priorities and requirements;

- confirming that FCL business continuity capability is effective, fit-for-purpose, and appropriate to the level of risk;
- considering the effectiveness and outcomes from ongoing business continuity capability maintenance, exercising and testing programmes; and
- evaluating business continuity training, awareness, and communication amongst employees, as appropriate.

The outcome of this review process can include:

- corrective action; or
- preventive action.

13.8 Embedding business continuity in FCL processes

To ensure that business continuity is implemented, managed and embedded effectively within FCL, a business continuity awareness programme shall be developed, implemented and maintained to define and manage this.

The business continuity programme shall be the BCM's responsibility, with assistance provided by Top Management. The programme shall cover the following items:

- a high-level plan that shall describe the design, build, and implementation of the programme which is defined in the business justification for implementing business continuity in FCL;
- assigning the responsibilities for business continuity at a senior management level, these responsibilities shall be documented in the BCMS and reviewed each year during the BCMS audit and also as part of the annual appraisal process as defined in Chapter 18, Section 18.2.4;
- reviewing employee skills and training requirements to meet the business continuity objectives as part of the annual Management Review as defined in Chapter 4, Section 4.9.3;
- raising the awareness of business continuity—to provide for greater levels of understanding by employees and relevant third parties about how they contribute to business continuity through workshops, training, and documentation such as quick reference material and presentations, as defined in Section 13.3;
- developing and maintaining the relevant BCPs and incident management plans to manage and resolve business disruptions and adverse events, as defined in Section 13.5.4;
- performing exercises and tests on the business continuity capability to ensure that it remains effective and fit-for-purpose, as defined in Section 13.6;
- reviewing and updating the BCMS documentation to ensure that it remains effective and reflects the processes in place;
- reviewing and updating the risk assessments and the BIAs to ensure that the business continuity objectives remain current, as defined in Chapter 5; and
- reviewing and updating FCL's business continuity arrangements through a self-assessment of the BCMS to ensure that these arrangements remain suitable, adequate and effective.

13.9 BCMS documentation and records—General

FCL shall produce a document set to support the BCMS in operation. This shall include documentation and records as below:

13.9.1 Documentation

The following documentation shall be created:

- scope and objectives, as defined in Chapter 5, Appendix 11 and Section 13.1.3;
- the business continuity management policy, as defined in Chapter 4, Appendix 19;
- provision of resources, as defined in Chapter 4, Section 4.7.1 and Section 13.2.1;
- competency of FCL employees, as defined in Chapter 4, Section 4.7.3 and Section 13.3;
- risk assessment, management and treatment process, as defined in Chapter 5;
- business continuity strategy, as defined in Section 13.4;
- incident response plans, as defined in Chapter 7, Section 7.4.1 and Chapter 8;
- business continuity management response, as defined in Section 13.5;
- exercising and testing procedures, as defined in Section 13.6;

- internal auditing procedures, as defined in Chapter 4, Section 4.9.2;
- Management Review procedures, as defined in Chapter 4, Section 4.9.3; and
- continuous improvement procedures, as defined in Chapter 4, Section 4.10;

13.9.2   Records

The following records shall exist:

- training records;
- results of BIAs and risk assessments, as defined in Section 13.4.4 and Chapter 5;
- BCP(s), as defined in Section 13.5.4, and Section 13.5.5;
- incident management plan(s), as defined in Chapter 7, Section 7.4.1;
- results of business continuity exercises and tests, as defined in Section 13.6;
- internal audit results and responses, as defined in Chapter 4, Section 4.9.2;
- management review results, as defined in Chapter 4, Section 4.9.3; and
- corrective and preventive actions, as defined in Chapter 4, Section 4.10;

13.9.3   Control of documents and records

Documents and records shall be managed according to FCL's document and record management procedures, as defined in Chapter 4, Sections 4.7.5 Section 4.7.6, respectively.

Appendix 1—Supplier details held

FCL shall hold the following information on its suppliers, apart from transaction, correspondence and payment details:

- supplier name;
- key supplier (Y/N)?
- financial status—credited rating;
- supplier address;
- supplier phone;
- supplier fax;
- supplier URL;
- supplier legal status and business registration details;
- supplier account number in FCL;
- date supplier returned financial and security due diligence checklist;
- approved as a supplier on date;
- approved by;
- last audit date;
- last audit result;
- next audit date;
- products and/or services provided;
- SLA in force;
- date of last SLA review;
- results of last SLA review;
- date of next SLA review;
- supplier risk category; and
- supplier contacts:
- name;
- email;
- phone;
- mobile phone; and
- fax.

Appendix 2—Headings for financial and security due diligence questionnaire

Whilst this is the standard form, some details shall be left out, as appropriate. It is not appropriate for detailed financial information to be obtained for the company watering the plants in the office, but certainly parts of the information security section will be required as their staff will have access to FCL premises. Likewise, a hosting service shall be required to provide all details completed as financial stability is critical and they will have access to FCL and client information and information processing systems. The Finance Department, Information Security Manager, Quality Manager and the BCM shall determine the sections to be used and may add additional questions, as needed.

Finance

- financial status.

Management systems

- management systems implemented;
- certifications and accreditations held, including copies of certificates; and
- management responsibility for management systems.

Information security

- information security policy;
- organisational setup;
- organisational assets;
- human resources security;
- physical and environmental security;
- operational security;
- identity, authentication and system access;
- system acquisition, development and maintenance;
- information security incident handling;
- business continuity status; and
- compliance and governance.

Quality

- the quality system.

Appendix 3—Business continuity manager (BCM), job description

Objective and role

The BCM shall be responsible for managing the business continuity process, developing the BCPs to support the process, exercising and testing the BCPs, maintaining them and continuously improving them.

In addition, during a disruptive event, the BCM shall be responsible for the continued operation of the business' infrastructure. The BCM is also responsible for long-range disaster recovery planning to provide the highest level of protection possible for FCL's clients.

The scope of responsibility includes all business processes and IT functions, including the third-party suppliers supporting them.

The main objective is to ensure that FCL's product and service offerings to their clients are resumed within required and agreed timescales.

Problems and challenges

Business continuity is an absolutely critical function for FCL's everyday business operations. For this responsibility, there is no substitute for advanced planning.

The BCM faces the challenge of developing ever-current BCPs and managing a recovery in an efficient and effective manner.

The BCPs shall be reviewed, exercised, tested, and updated on a regular basis, in association with clients, third-party service providers, and other relevant interested parties.

Principal accountabilities

The BCM shall:

- plan and chart the direction for the BCP process;
- establish procedures and priorities for the business continuity process;
- perform or facilitate BIAs for all services and systems;
- ensure the development and maintenance of all BCPs needed by the business for their clients;
- perform risk assessments and implement risk management in association with the ISM to reduce risk to an acceptable level to reduce the likelihood of service interruptions, where practical and cost-justifiable;
- maintain a comprehensive exercising and testing schedule for all BCPs, in line with business requirements and after every significant change in products and services offered to clients. The exercising and testing process shall cover not only BCPs but also communication with all relevant interested parties, no matter what the actual disruptive event is;
- undertake regular reviews, at least annually or on influencing change, with the relevant process or system Owner, to ensure that the BCPs accurately reflect business need;
- undertake regular reviews of training and awareness materials used to ensure that they are still appropriate and fit for purpose;
- provide regular reports to Top Management on all business continuity management activities;
- monitor national and international threat intelligence and advisory systems and update BCPs accordingly;
- ensure that an appropriate communication plan is in place for all employees, for all matters relating to business continuity response and planning. Communication shall cover training, awareness sessions, meetings and formal communication plans as defined in Chapter 5, Appendix 1;
- assess changes submitted to the Change Advisory Board (CAB) for impact on the BCP plans and recovery processes;
- attend the CAB, as appropriate;
- reviews all insurance coverage in the event of a disruptive event to ensure that they are appropriate. A review of relevant coverage amounts should be performed at 3-month intervals to ensure optimal coverage in the event of a disruptive event and amendments to cover made, as needed;
- secure the scene of a disruptive event and ensure that all movement of equipment into and out of the scene is authorised and recorded;
- Coordinate and manage all recovery activities during the business continuity process;
- coordinate and supervise all special projects relating to business continuity and capacity;
- develop plans for migration of BCPs, the business continuity and recovery process policies and procedures to support FCL's future directions;
- maintain the BCMS' compliance with ISO 22301;
- develop long-range business continuity and business recovery strategy;
- define direction of in-house technical training seminars to improve overall employee awareness, response time, and ability to look into future business continuity and business recovery requirements;
- participate in international, national, and local SIG presentations, and publishes articles describing FCL's activities and assessments of business continuity and business recovery and how they relate to the business;
- develop and manage effective working relationships with all appropriate internal and external interested parties;
- maintain external links to other companies in the industry to gain competitive assessments and share information, where appropriate;
- identify the emerging information technologies to be assimilated, integrated and introduced within FCL, which could significantly impact FCL's business continuity and business recovery ability;
- interface with external industrial and academic organisations to maintain state-of-the-art knowledge in emerging business continuity and business recovery issues and to enhance FCL's image as a first-class solution provider utilising the latest thinking in this field;
- adheres to established policies, standards, and procedures; and
- perform all responsibilities in accordance with, or in excess of, the requirements of the Integrated Management System (IMS).

Authority

The BCM shall have the authority to:

- attend the CAB and commenting on proposed changes;
- develop, maintain, and implement, where necessary, the BCPs; and
- supervising the entire recovery process during a disruption, adverse event, exercise or test.

Contacts

Internal

This position requires contact with all levels of FCL employees to:

- determine recovery requirements;
- perform BIAs;
- perform risk assessments; and
- maintain, exercise and test BCPs.

External

Externally, the BCM shall maintain contacts with suppliers, other third parties and interested parties, as required. Additionally, contact shall be maintained with FCL's clients to determine their requirements as well as FCL's insurers to ensure that insurance coverage is appropriate.

Reports to

The BCM reports to:
- Top Management.

Appendix 4—Contents of the BIA form

The following is captured during the BIA process:

- date of BIA;
- name of respondent;
- respondent contact details;
- respondent title;
- number of staff reporting to respondent;
- respondent responsibilities;
- key functions and tasks undertaken;
- definition and quantification of risks to these functions and tasks;
- criticality of failure to provide these functions and tasks over a range of times (2 h, 4 h, 1 day, 2 days, 1 week, 2 weeks, a month, more than 3 months);
- financial loss of failure to provide these functions and tasks over a range of times (2 h, 4 h, 1 day, 2 days, 1 week, 2 weeks, a month, more than 3 months);
- maximum outage for these functions and tasks sustainable;
- recovery time objectives (RTOs) for each function;
- recovery point objectives (RPOs) for each function;
- maximum tolerable periods of disruption (MTPoDs) for each function;
- impact of disruptions to these functions and tasks in terms of Strategy, Finance, Customer Relationship, Supplier Relationship, Legal or Regulatory, Personnel, Operations, etc.;
- input and outputs for each of these functions and tasks;
- minimum numbers of staff to perform each of these functions and tasks;
- minimum equipment to perform each of these functions and tasks;
- how functions and tasks would be performed in case of unavailability of FCL's offices; and
- any other relevant comments.

Where quantifications are needed, the following is used: 0—no impact/not applicable, 1—little impact, 2—some impact, 3—Significant impact, 4—severe impact, 5—catastrophic impact. The consequences table given in Chapter 5, Appendix 5 is used to assist with the quantification process.

Appendix 5—Proposed BCMS development timescales

Initial BCMS development and compliance targets are as follows:

Task 1: Business continuity process lifecycle development, scope confirmation, and required documents identified.

- Duration 2 weeks.

Task 2: Management systems production, including BIAs and development of BCPs:

- Duration: 24 weeks.

Task 3: Management systems training:

- Duration: 1 week.

Task 4: Exercising and testing BCPs, updating where necessary and undertaking the Management Review

- Duration: 8 weeks.

Appendix 6—Incident scenarios

Any number of scenarios shall be developed based on the perceived risks that FCL faces, management opinions, and threat intelligence. These shall include, but not be limited to:

- **partial interruption of computer services** (e.g. critical server, multiple hard disk failure, with no available mirrored drives. The impact obviously will depend on the number of disks affected, the number of mirrored disks, the level of RAID and the type of server, and spares held);
- **telecommunications failure** (e.g. failure of the communications switch or the internet during the working day. This affects all communications that are serviced through them);
- **email failure** (e.g. loss of either the mail server, ISP or a third-party service provider failure);
- **power or other utility failure** (e.g. loss of electricity, water, etc., for a varying period);
- **temporary interruption of office occupation** (e.g. bomb or fire in the vicinity precludes access to the office for a period of up to 1 week, occurrence outside office hours. There is no damage to any equipment or office;
- **short to medium interruption of office occupation** (e.g. bomb or fire in the vicinity precludes access to the office for a period of a month whilst rebuilding and refurbishing takes place. Minimal damage to office and contents, occurrence outside office hours. Time period—up to a month;
- **office destroyed or very seriously damaged** (e.g. bomb explosion or fire in the close vicinity that structurally affects the office and destroys most of the contents. The off-site store is not affected. The damage precludes access to the office for salvage for a considerable time, and the building needs rebuilding and complete renovation, occurrence outside office hours);
- **loss of key employees** (e.g. one or more key employees is either seriously injured, killed in the scenarios above, or leaves FCL for whatever reason. This would obviously depend on who the 'key member' of staff actually was);
- **Pandemic, adverse weather or other event precluding access to the office** (e.g. Avian flu, COVID-type pandemics, hurricane, snow or transport issues);
- **Ransomware attack** (e.g. encryption of FCL's main data stores for ransom);
- **Malware attack** (e.g. Virus, worm, Trojan Horse, or similar attack); and
- **Personal data breach** (e.g. breach of legislative requirements for protection of personal data including mandated reporting processes to be met).

In each scenario above, or any others that are developed by FCL, the following shall be considered as essential high-level phases of the recovery process:

- initial response;
- communications (internal to employees and external to clients, other interested parties, suppliers, the press, etc.);
- implementing the relevant BCP;
- relocating staff;
- setting up alternate premises as the office for forensic case processing;
- working at the alternate premises; and
- final recovery either back to the original office or a new one—depending on the damage.

The point of these scenarios is to try, based on the BIA results, to determine the possible scenarios that shall be considered as appropriate. The high-level stages of the response and recovery process shall be considered with possible elapsed time and impact on the delivery of FCL's products and services to clients.

Appendix 7—Strategy options

There are a number of strategic options that shall be considered based on the risks that FCL faces and the relevant scenarios that it has developed. Options include, at a high level, the following:

- hot standby;
- cold standby;
- reciprocal arrangements;
- finding an office to rent;
- home working and client site working;
- a hybrid solution; and
- do nothing.

Each option shall have pros and cons associated with it, and these shall be considered in line with FCL's legislative, regulatory and contractual obligations to determine one or more appropriate strategies for a given scenario. The choice of strategy will also depend on the expected duration of the outage and FCL shall consider the following time scales in business continuity planning:

- short term (less than 1 day);
- short to medium term (2–5 days);
- medium term (5–10 days); or
- medium to long term (more than 10 days).

Appendix 8—Standard BCP contents

The FCL's BCPs shall contain the following items:

- a purpose and scope;
- recovery objectives and timescales; and
- a named plan owner.

The following items do not need to be in each and every BCP, but all of the BCPs combined shall collectively contain:

- lines of communications;
- key tasks and reference information;
- roles and responsibilities for employees and teams having authority during and following a disruptive event;
- guidelines and criteria regarding who has the authority to invoke each BCP and under what circumstances;
- method by which the BCP is invoked and implemented;
- meeting locations with alternatives, and up-to-date contact and mobilisation details for any third-party supplier or any other external resource (e.g. local authority, emergency services, etc.) that might be required to support the response, including relevant interested parties;
- internal and external communications processes;
- resource requirements for all stages of the recovery process;
- process for standing down once the disruptive event is over;
- reference to the essential contact details for all key interested parties;
- details to manage the immediate consequences of a disruptive event giving due regard to:
- welfare of all employees;
- strategic and operational options for responding to the disruptive event; and
- prevention of further loss or unavailability of critical activities.
- details for managing a disruptive event including:
  - provision for managing issues during a disruptive event;
  - processes to enable continuity and recovery of critical activities.
- details on how and under what circumstances FCL shall communicate with employees and their relatives, interested parties and emergency contacts;

- details on FCL's media response following a disruptive event:
  - the communications strategy;
  - preferred interface with the media;
  - guideline or template for drafting a statement for the media; and
  - appropriate spokespeople.
- method for recording key information about a disruptive event, actions taken and decisions made;
- details of actions and tasks that need to be performed;
- details of the resources required for business continuity business recovery at different points in time; and
- prioritised objectives in terms of the critical activities to be recovered, the timescales in which they are to be recovered, and the recovery levels needed for each critical activity.

Appendix 9—Table of contents to the appendix to a BCP

BCPs will have volatile information associated with them and this is placed in the Appendix to a BCP, so that changes in the volatile information (e.g. a mobile phone number change) do not mean that the whole BCP needs to be reissued to all relevant employees and other interested parties.

BCP Appendices shall include, but not be limited to the following information, where appropriate:

- alternate premises details;
- alternate premises requirements;
- backup and recovery overview;
- building contacts;
- emergency notification list;
- employee contact details;
- employees to travel to the recovery site;
- equipment needed for inspection of incident scene;
- equipment to be brought from the off-site store;
- equipment to be brought to the recovery site;
- evacuation assembly points;
- fire wardens;
- first aiders;
- hardware failure details;
- health and safety regulations;
- identified services and applications to be recovered;
- identified services and applications;
- impact of disruption to key tasks and functions;
- information to obtain from a caller (for anonymous calls including bomb threats or similar);
- insurance policy details;
- key task and function criticality;
- key tasks and functions identified;
- management succession list;
- materials source;
- membership of the Readiness Team;
- minimum staff required for recovery operations;
- off-site recovery procedures;
- off-site store details;
- office key holders;
- organogram;
- overview of business processes;
- press release recipients;
- recovery site details;
- recovery team details;
- recovery team responsibilities;

- sample press release;
- software failure details;
- sources of government advice;
- sources of industry advice;
- supplier details;
- telecoms failure details;
- Top Management permitted to talk to the press; and
- training.

Appendix 10—BCP change list contents

The following shall be considered for inclusion in the formal BCP change list:

- Date;
- Summary of review;
  - Required change;
  - Reason for change;
  - Accept/Reject?
  - By; and
  - Date.

Each change shall be put through the Change Management Process so it can be reviewed by all interested parties prior to implementation.

Appendix 11—BCP scenario plan contents

The following shall be considered for inclusion in the BCP Scenario Plan:

- Scenario rules;
- The event:
  - Issues;
  - Objective;
  - Scope;
  - Roles and responsibilities;
  - Actions; and
  - Timings, duration and resources.
- Reporting requirements.

Appendix 12—BCP review report template contents

The template for a BCP review plan shall be:

- management summary;
- re-assertion of the exercise or test aims, objectives, and scope;
- results and outcomes;
- exercise or test highlights and successes;
- shortcomings and lessons learned;
- issues for further investigation and action;
- recommendations for action and improvement (if any action points and improvements have been identified); and
- process of implementation of changes:
  - timeline;
  - resources;
  - integration to current systems;
  - related CAPAs; and
  - related requests for change.

Appendix 13—Mapping IMS procedures to ISO 22301

This appendix contains the mapping of ISO 22301 to the procedures developed to implement the standard.

ISO 22301 clause	Control	Procedure
4	Context of the organisation	
4.1	Understanding of the organisation and its context	Chapter 5, Section 5.3.2
		Chapter 5, Appendix 11
		Chapter 5, Appendix 14
		Section 13.1
		Section 13.4.2
4.2	Understanding the needs and expectations of interested parties	Section 13.1.7
		Section 13.1.8
4.3	Determining the scope of the business continuity management system	Chapter 5, Appendix 11
		Section 13.1.3
		Section 13.1.5
		Section 13.1.8
4.4	Business continuity management system	The Integrated Management System (IMS)
5	Leadership	
5.1	Leadership and commitment	Chapter 4, Section 4.5.1
		Chapter 4, Appendix 8
		Section 13.2
		Section 13.3.1
		Section 13.6.1
		Section 13.7
		Appendix 3
5.2	Policy	Chapter 4, Appendix 19
5.4	Roles, responsibilities and authorities	Section 13.3.1
		Chapter 18, Section 18.1.2.1.1
6	Planning	
6.1	Actions to address risks and opportunities	Chapter 5
		Section 13.1.6
6.2	Business continuity objectives and plans to achieve them	Chapter 4, Section 4.10
		Section 13.1.5
6.3	Planning changes to the business continuity management system	Chapter 7, Section 7.4.3
7	Support	
7.1	Resources	Chapter 4, Section 4.7.1
		Section 13.2.1
7.2	Competence	Chapter 4, Section 4.7.2
		Section 13.3

ISO 22301 clause	Control	Procedure
7.3	Awareness	Chapter 3, Section 3.1.12
		Chapter 4, Section 4.7.3
		Section 13.3.2
		Chapter 18, Section 18.2.1
7.4	Communication	Chapter 4, Section 4.7.4
		The Integrated Management System (IMS)
7.5	Documented information	Chapter 4, Section 4.7.5
		The Integrated Management System (IMS)
8	Operation	
8.1	Operational planning and control	Section 13.4
8.2	Business impact analysis and risk assessment	Chapter 3, Section 3.1.13.2
		Chapter 5
		Section 13.1.6
		Section 13.1.7
		Appendix 4
8.3	Business continuity strategies and solutions	Chapter 5
		Section 13.4
8.4	Business continuity plans and procedures	Chapter 7, Section 7.4.1
		Section 13.5
		Appendix 8
8.5	Exercise programme	Section 13.6
8.6	Evaluation of business continuity documentation and capabilities	Chapter 4, Section 4.9.2
		Section 13.6
		Section 13.7
9	Performance evaluation	
9.1	Monitoring, measurement, analysis and evaluation	Chapter 4, Section 4.9.1
9.2	Internal audit	Chapter 4, Section 4.9.2
9.3	Management review	Chapter 4, Section 4.9.3
10	Improvement	
10.1	Nonconformity and corrective action	Chapter 4, Section 4.10
10.2	Continual improvement	Chapter 4, Section 4.10

Chapter 14

Managing business relationships

14.1 The need for third parties

All organisations need to have clients and suppliers of some type, and FCL is no exception. FCL considers the following category of business relationships as being relevant:

- clients, for whom they undertake forensic case processing;
- suppliers of office and IT equipment (e.g. IT suppliers, office furniture, etc.);
- suppliers of IT services (e.g. ISPs, hardware maintenance, etc.);
- suppliers of office services (e.g. cleaners, plant watering, service engineers);
- utility service providers (e.g. communications, water, electricity, gas, etc.);
- individual consultants engaged on case processing (e.g. Expert Witnesses or experts in an area of forensic case processing that is not available, for any reason, in FCL); and
- outsourcing providers for IT services (e.g. outsourcing of email, telephony services up to full-scale date centre outsourcing);

Note 1

Some IT suppliers are responsible for providing warranty cover or maintenance contracts for the products or services they supply.

Note 2

Each category has its own issues and risks relating to the products or services they provide and how one of their disruptive events can affect FCL.

Note 3

This chapter is not intended as legal advice but just how FCL manages their business relationships. It is recommended that any legal issues are taken up with legal experts in the relevant jurisdiction.

Note 4

This chapter is not intended to be a treatise on client, supplier, or outsourcing management, merely the processes and procedures that are implemented in FCL to meet relevant IMS requirements and adapted to specific circumstances relating to legislation, regulation of contractual obligations in the jurisdiction(s) of operations.

Note 5

FCL has a Relationship Management Policy in force for clients and all types of suppliers, as defined in Chapter 4, Appendix 31.

Note 6

This chapter does not relate to provision of IT services to employees, merely support for forensic case processing. In this case, the IT Department is viewed as a supplier to FCL for case processing.

A Blueprint for Implementing Best Practice Procedures in a Digital Forensic Laboratory. https://doi.org/10.1016/B978-0-12-819479-9.00023-X

Note 7

FCL may employ temporary workers, interns, or students on placement. In these cases, they shall be treated as employees if they are not involved in any forensic case processing, or if they are, they shall be considered as individual consultants providing case processing expertise and subject to the screening requirements defined in Chapter 18, Section 18.1.3.

FCL shall manage these 3risks from the very outset, during the service or product provision, and as long as required after the termination of business relationships between the parties.

14.2   Clients

FCL shall ensure that the management of client relations is implemented by following approved processes and guidelines.

First-class client relationships are at the heart of FCL's business, and the management of relationships is a strategy that FCL shall adopt to understand more about their clients' needs and behaviour, to develop stronger working relationships, and to enhance the services that are provided.

14.2.1   Forensic laboratory mechanisms for managing customer relations

The following mechanisms shall be implemented to ensure that the management of client relations complies with the Relationship Management Policy.

14.2.1.1   Identification of clients, products, services, and interested parties

FCL clients, products, services, and interested parties shall be identified via contracts, service-level agreements (SLAs), or Turn Round Times (TRTs), as follows:

- all clients of FCL products and services shall be identified in SLAs or TRTs, as defined in the proposal or call-off contract as defined in Chapter 6, Section 6.6.2.3 and its review in Chapter 6, Section 6.6.2.4;
- each SLA or TRT shall describe one or more product or service that is provided by FCL to a particular client for forensic case processing;
- one SLA or TRT shall be in place for each client or specific case; and
- each SLA or TRT shall identify:
- the product or service provided by FCL;
- the client;
- the agreed service level or TRT for the client;
- service level reporting requirements;
- handling of breaches of SLAs or TRTs; and
- all interested parties.

Note

Where SLAs or TRTs do not exist for a client or a supplier they shall be developed, as defined in Section 14.4.

14.2.1.2   Client service monitoring and review

The following mechanisms shall be implemented to ensure that client products and services are continually monitored and reviewed by FCL (Fig. 14.1):

1. A formal review of all FCL products and services shall be performed at least once each year, as agreed between the parties or after any incident or influencing change.
2. Any changes arising from the annual service review shall be performed in accordance with FCL Change Management Process as defined in Chapter 7, Section 7.4.3, and tracked through the CAPA process, as defined in Chapter 4, Section 4.10.
3. Interim monitoring and review of client products and services shall be performed via the Account Manager for the client and the formal meetings that they have with the client.
4. These meetings shall review products and services provided by FCL to each client and:
   - focus on the business aspects of products and services delivered;
   - act as the FCL contact point for regular monitoring and review of the operational aspect of their products and services; and
   - act as FCL forum for monitoring SLAs and TRTs for clients.

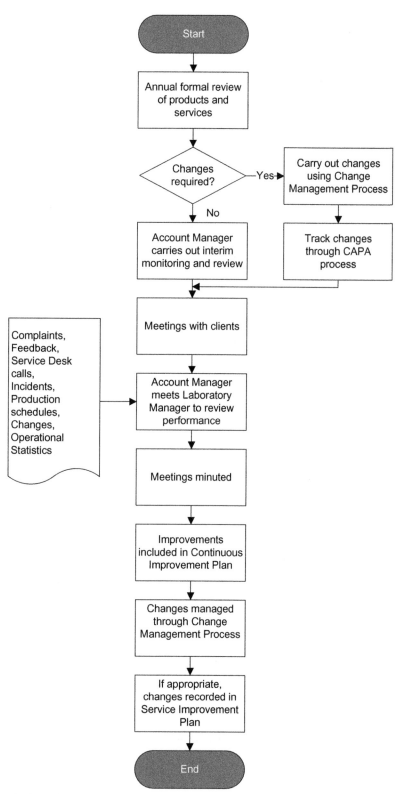

FIG. 14.1 Client service monitoring and review.

5. After meeting a client, the Account Manager shall schedule a meeting with the Laboratory Manager to review the performance for the client, and this shall cover, but not be limited to:
   - performance and achievements against SLAs and/or TRTs;
   - client and service requirements;
   - service changes and action plans; and
   - awareness of business needs.

Inputs shall include, but are not limited to:
   - client complaints, if any, as defined in Chapter 6, Section 6.14;
   - client feedback forms returned for each case processed, as defined in Chapter 6, Appendix 17;
   - client calls to the Service Desk indicating support levels needed and provided;
   - any incidents or disruptive event involving the client;
   - production schedules;
   - system change schedules;
   - operational statistics from MARS reports, as defined in Chapter 10, Section 10.7.3; and
   - for internal clients, other operational statistics shall be covered, as appropriate.

6. All meetings between the Account Manager and the Laboratory Manager, with other employees as needed, shall be minuted and added to the relevant virtual case file.
7. All recommendations for improvement shall be included in the Contract Improvement Plan (CIP) and followed through to completion using the CAPA process.
8. All changes shall be managed through Change Management Process.
9. Where appropriate they will be recorded in the Service Improvement Plan (SIP), as defined in Chapter 7, Appendix 10.

14.2.1.3 Client complaints

The client complaint process has been defined in Chapter 6, Section 6.14.

14.2.1.4 Client feedback

The client feedback forms shall be used as input into the review process defined Section 14.2.1.2.

14.2.1.5 Service desk

The Service Desk shall provide monthly, and 'on demand' reports, relating to client contact with the Service Desk, again, this shall be used as input into the review process.

14.2.2 Managing products and services

FCL must change with the times and changes in technology as required by their clients, and so products and services shall be updated to reflect changes in these requirements. This shall cover:

- creating a new product or service;
- implementing a new product or service;
- changing an existing product or service; and
- terminating an existing product or service.

14.2.2.1 Creating a new product or service

To ensure that products and services are planned and implemented effectively within FCL, the Laboratory Manager with relevant managers and with other employees as required, shall define and produce one or more Service Plans. These plans shall cover all the required aspects of implementing a new product or service (Fig. 14.2).

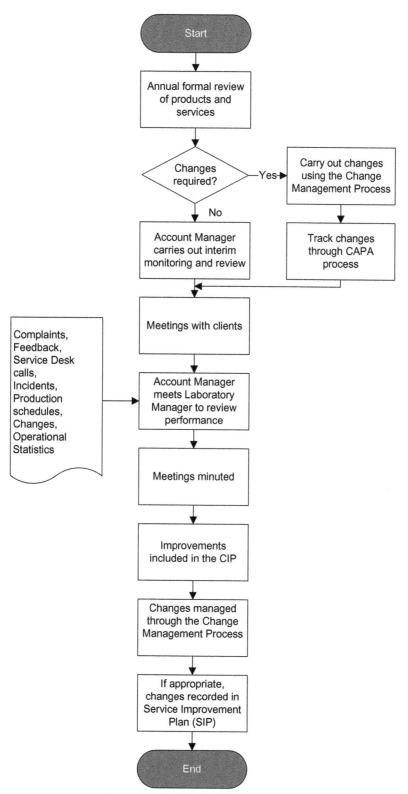

FIG. 14.2 Creating a product or service.

1. A client identifies a new product or service that they would like implemented by FCL.
2. The Account Manager shall meet with the client to ascertain the specific requirements of a new product or service required.
3. The Account Manager shall meet with the Laboratory Manager, and other Subject Matter Experts as required, to discuss the new requirements.
4. An initial feasibility study shall be carried out by the Laboratory Manager and any other required employees, and an initial report produced as to:
   - whether the product or service is one that can potentially be provided by FCL;
   - whether there are competent Forensic Analysts available or they require training to achieve competence;
   - whether the required tools are available, or if not, the implications of their acquisition;
   - whether the client can make any funds available for putting the product or service in place;
   - The Laboratory Manager shall discuss the initial feasibility report with the Account Manager.
5. Assuming it is approved, the Account Manager shall submit a formal request for the new product or service to be implemented, using Change Management Process. This shall cover:
   - product or service requirements and service levels;
   - budgets;
   - staff resources;
   - SLAs and other targets or service commitments; and
   - service management processes, procedures, and documentation.
6. If the request is for a product or service that is very simple to implement, the Laboratory Manager shall confirm to the Account Manager that it shall be provided. If the requested service is not simple or is potentially costly the further investigation process is undertaken, as defined in Step 8 below.
7. The Laboratory Manager shall appoint a suitable Forensic Analyst to prepare a draught Service Plan. This plan shall reflect the client requirements and also the capability of FCL to provide the required product or services as set out in step 6 above.
8. The Laboratory Manager shall circulate the Service Plan to the Account Manager and other relevant employees for comment.
9. The recipients shall review the Service Plan and ensure that all items raised are satisfactory from FCL's perspective. All comments shall be passed back to the Laboratory Manager, who shall review them, and implement appropriate changes. A copy of the finalised plan shall be sent to the Account Manager.
10. The Laboratory Manager and the Account Manager shall meet to discuss the Service Plan. They shall negotiate to determine the final product or service based upon the details within the Service Plan. At the end of these negotiations, the Service Plan shall be agreed in principle subject to confirmation in a service-level agreement (SLA).
11. Once agreed, the product or service shall be implemented.

14.2.2.2 Implementing a product or service

Once a Service Plan has been agreed, the next stage is to implement the provisions of the Service Plan to provide the new product or service to the client's requirements (Fig. 14.3).

1. The Laboratory Manager shall arrange a meeting with all affected employees and request that they review the Service Plan and prepare further details for input to the meeting.
2. The Laboratory Manager and the affected employees shall meet to discuss the implementation of the product or service. The following details shall be confirmed during the discussion:
   - allocation of funds and budgets for each aspect of the Service Plan;
   - allocation of roles and responsibilities for the implementation of the new or changed product or service;
   - provision for documenting and maintaining the policies, plans, and procedures that are affected by the new or changed product or service;
   - the identification and management of risks to the new or changed product or service defined in the Service Plan;
   - procedures for validating the product or service;
   - the identification of the managing team(s) for the new or changed product or service, including the possible need of recruitment of new employees;
   - the management of the team(s) supporting the new or changed product or service including the Service Desk;
   - training relating to the new or changed product or service, where required (e.g. new tools or methods); and
   - communicating details about the new product or service to FCL's clients and any suitable prospective clients.

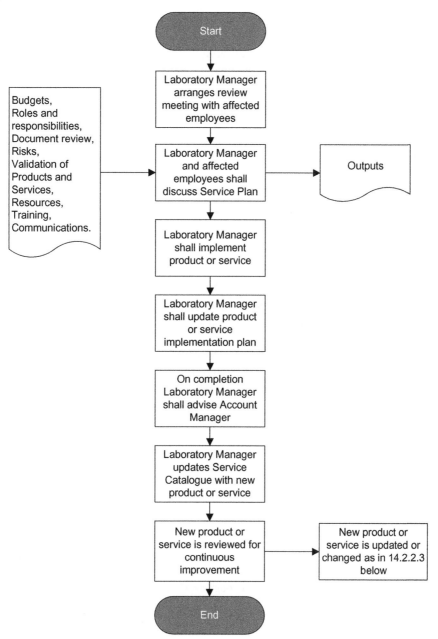

FIG. 14.3 Implementing a product or service.

3. The Laboratory Manager shall be responsible for implementing the new product or service and implements it according to the agreed Service Plan. The new product or service shall be implemented in accordance with Change Management Process.
4. The Laboratory Manager shall regularly produce updates of the implementation progress of the new product or service to interested parties.
5. When implementation is complete, and the new product or service available for clients, the Laboratory Manager shall advise all Account Managers that the new product or service is now successfully running.
6. The Laboratory Manager shall update the Service Catalogue with details of the new product or service and ensure that product or service metrics information is being collected.
7. The review and improvement of the new product or service shall now be performed within the framework of service management, as defined in Chapter 7, Section 7.4.7 to review the outcome of implementing the new product or service against the Service Implementation Plan (SIP).

14.2.2.3   Changing an existing product or service

A product or service can be changed at the request of either a client or from within FCL itself as part of its continuous improvement process. The process to change a product or service is generally the same as the process for creating a new product or service (although not all steps may need to be followed depending upon the change required). As a minimum, the process for changing a product or service involves:

- identifying and agreeing the details of the change with the client or internally with relevant employees;
- ensuring that all resources are available;
- planning the implementation of the change; and
- implementing the change and confirming its success.

Note

A formal change to a product or service is different from improving a product or service through the continuous improvement process.

14.2.2.4   Terminating a product or service

A product or service shall be terminated if there is no longer any demand for it (Fig. 14.4).

1. The Laboratory Manager and relevant Account Manager(s) shall meet to discuss the requirement for terminating a product or service. The Account Manager(s) shall confirm that the product or service is no longer required, and when it is to be terminated.

   If a similar product or service is required, this shall be treated as a request for a new product or service and the procedure for creating a product or service, as defined in Section 14.2.2.1 above, shall be followed.
2. The Laboratory Manager and relevant Account Managers shall meet to discuss the termination of a product or service. The following details shall be confirmed during the discussion:
   - confirmation of the termination of the product and service due to lack of demand from clients;
   - the re-allocation of roles and responsibilities away from the product or service;
   - the impact of the termination of the product or service on existing employees and operations generally;
   - impact on FCL and any associated SLAs;
   - provision for updating policies, plans, and procedures that are affected by the termination of the product or service, including the service catalogue;
   - the identification and management of risks to FCL on termination of the product or service; and
   - communicating details about the termination of the product or service to FCL and clients.

Note

The termination of a product or service shall be processed through the Change Management Process.

---

3. The Laboratory Manager shall draw up a Termination Plan which shall be reviewed by the relevant Account Manager(s) and any other affected parties.
4. FCL shall terminate the product or service at the scheduled time. All documents associated with the product or service shall be withdrawn by the Laboratory Manager and archived in the ERMS, as appropriate.
5. The Laboratory Manager shall update the Service Catalogue and remove the product or service from it. No further metrics information shall be collected.
6. The Laboratory Manager shall conduct a review of the product or service termination and review the outcome against the Termination Plan.

14.3   Third parties accessing FCL and client information

14.3.1   General

Whilst FCL has internal processes and procedures for handling client information entrusted to it, based on agreements in force, internal handling procedures, or the classification of the information, a similar process shall be put in place for third parties (e.g. suppliers, Consultants under contract to FCL, or outsourcing partners). The levels of security of any FCL or client information shall not be reduced by the introduction of third-party products or services.

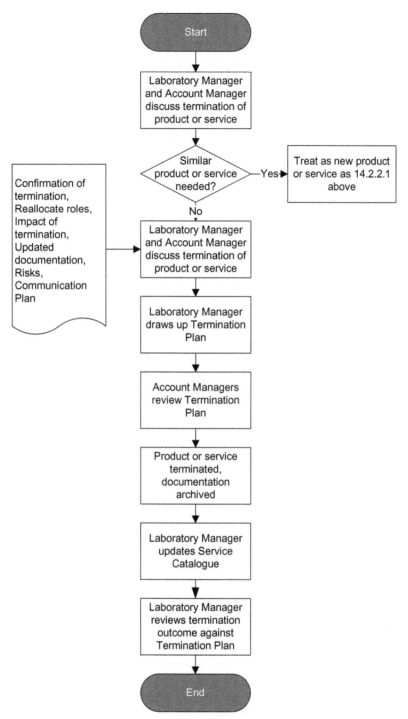

FIG. 14.4 Terminating a product or service.

Where any third party of the type defined in Section 14.1 has access to FCL or client information and information processing systems, a risk assessment shall be undertaken, as defined in Chapter 5. This shall determine the risks associated with the product or service being provided, and the controls needed to reduce the risk to an acceptable level, as defined in Chapter 5, Appendix 15, and be subject to regular risk reviews using the corporate risk register, as defined in Chapter 5, Appendix 17.

Any control requirements identified shall be agreed between the parties, made part of the contract, and the key suppliers subject to second-party audits as defined in Chapter 4, Section 4.9 and defined in the IMS Calendar, as defined in Chapter 4, Appendix 46.

14.3.2 Identification of third-party risks

Some of the issues to be considered for third-party risk assessments have been defined in Appendix 2.

Once the risk assessment has been undertaken, it shall be subject to a formal report to the Risk Committee, as defined in Chapter 4, Appendix 13, if the risk level, information classification, or the level of access to FCL and client information warrants it. The Risk Committee shall consider the report, the risks to be managed and the recommended controls, and shall make a final decision on the third party having access to FCL information processing systems, on what basis, and additional controls to be put in place to reduce the risks identified to an acceptable level.

No access by a third party to any FCL information processing systems shall be permitted until appropriate controls are in place. Depending on access types and levels, this can include, but not be limited to:

- signing confidentiality agreements or Non-Disclosure Agreements (NDAs), as defined in Chapter 12, Section 12.3.1.4;
- signed contracts specifying the required information security controls and service levels to be provided, as defined in Chapter 9, Section 9.1.3; this chapter, Section 14.5; and Chapter 18, Section 18.1.4;
- implementation of any required additional security controls indicated by the risk assessment and agreed by the Risk Committee; and
- appropriate training for any third-party employees relating to induction training, specialised security or project training, and other training as appropriate.

14.3.3 Third-party contractual terms relating to information security

---

Note

This does not constitute legal advice but is the checklist that FCL shall use with its General Counsel for agreements covering third-party access to FCL information processing systems.

Whether a confidentiality agreement, NDA, or full contract is executed between the parties, it shall clearly define each party's obligations, responsibilities, and liabilities involved in accessing, processing, communicating, or managing information and information processing facilities. The execution of the relevant agreement shall signify acceptance of these obligations, responsibilities, and liabilities.

Whilst confidentiality agreements and NDAs are typically standard, contracts can vary greatly depending on the specific circumstances and level of access required by the third party and will depend on information and information processing systems accessed. FCL shall ensure that all relevant clauses are in place to protect their information, client information, and information processing systems against unauthorised access, erasure, modification, or disclosure of information.

For information security issues only, FCL has produced the checklist for discussion with the Legal Counsel in drafting appropriate contractual terms for any third party, as defined in Section 14.1.

The agreement shall ensure that there is no misunderstanding between FCL and the third party and that if issues do arise, they have been contractually covered.

Wherever possible, FCL shall use its own agreements with all third parties but recognises that there are occasions when the third party's agreement must be used. In cases such as this, careful consideration shall be given to the contractual terms to ensure that FCL information security is not prejudiced and that it can meet the requirements in the contract. FCL shall decide, based on a risk assessment whether to undertake any forensic case processing or supply of products and services if the contract terms do not meet FCL's requirements.

14.4 Managing service-level agreements

At the heart of service delivery are service-level agreements (SLAs). These agreements document the full details for a product or service to be provided together with the corresponding service-level targets and workload characteristics.

14.4.1 Creating an SLA

SLAs are created in conjunction with Account Managers for a specific product or service (Fig. 14.5).

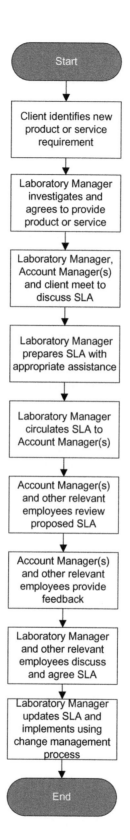

FIG. 14.5 Create an SLA.

1. A client identifies a new product or service that they would like implemented by FCL. The Laboratory Manager investigates the feasibility of the product or service and then agrees to provide it as defined in Section 14.2.2.1.

   To confirm the product or service details and have measurable targets, an SLA shall be confirmed between FCL and the client.

2. The Laboratory Manager and the relevant Account Manager (and optionally a client representative) shall attend a service-level meeting which outlines the details to be included in the SLA for the required product or service. The minutes of the meeting shall form the terms of reference for the proposed SLA.

   The client's business needs and budget shall be the basis for the content, structure, and targets of the SLA. The targets, against which the delivered product or service is to be measured, shall be clearly stated and match the client's needs.

Note

Only the key targets shall be included in the SLA to ensure that the correct business focus is identified for the product or service.

---

3. The Laboratory Manager shall prepare an SLA with the assistance of the relevant Account Manager(s), other relevant employees, and, optionally, the relevant client(s). The SLA template that shall be used is defined in Appendix 4. This shall be amended as appropriate for the product or service being provided.

4. The Laboratory Manager shall circulate the SLA to the relevant Account Manager(s) and/or employees for comment.

5. The relevant Account Manager(s), and other relevant employees, shall review the SLA, and ensure that all items raised are satisfactory from the product or service delivery perspective. All comments shall be passed back to the Laboratory Manager. The SLA shall be updated in accordance with the procedures defined in Chapter 4, Section 4.7.5. A copy of the finalised SLA shall be sent to the relevant Account Manager(s).

6. The Laboratory Manager shall meet with the Account Manager(s), and optionally the relevant client(s) representatives, to discuss the SLA.

7. All relevant parties shall negotiate to determine the final product or service SLA based upon the details within the draught SLA. At the end of these negotiations, the SLA shall be agreed.

8. The Laboratory Manager shall update the SLA with the agreed details and then submit it to Change Management Process, for approval and implementation.

14.4.2 Monitoring and reviewing an SLA

The monitoring and reviewing of SLAs shall be performed on a regular basis to ensure that the targets are being met.

A formal review shall be performed at least each year, or when a significant change is required to the SLA. The review shall determine whether the SLA remains effective.

1. On a monthly basis, the Laboratory Manager shall collect performance information for product and service delivery. This information shall come from a variety of sources:
   - internal reporting from MARS;
   - Service Desk calls relating to a product or service;
   - client complaints;
   - client feedback forms on case processing;
   - feedback from meetings with the Account Managers; and
   - other input, as appropriate.

2. The Laboratory Manager shall prepare a service report that documents the current service levels and shall circulate this to the relevant Account Manager(s). The report shall detail:
   - current service levels against targets;
   - trends in service levels;
   - explanations to support problem areas; and
   - identification of improvements, where required.

3. If any clarification on the report is required by an Account Manager, the Laboratory Manager shall provide this.

4. If any improvements to the product or service are identified, these shall be processed as appropriate.

Note

Any changes to an SLA shall be processed through the Change Management Process.

14.5 Suppliers of office and IT products and services

FCL shall ensure that management of office and IT supplier relations is implemented across the whole of the organisation by following the processes and guidelines that comply with Policy for Relationship Management.

Managing relations with office and IT suppliers shall allow FCL to manage its interactions with the organisations that supply these products and services. Within FCL, the goal of office and IT supplier relationship management is to streamline and make more effective the processes between FCL and its office and IT product and service suppliers (in the same way that the client relationship management strategy streamlines and make more effective the processes between FCL and its clients).

By implementing a series of guidelines and processes for managing their office and IT suppliers (and making them aware of these), FCL shall create a common frame of reference that enables effective communication with office and IT suppliers who use different business practices and terminology.

The generic high-level process for purchasing is defined in Chapter 6, Section 6.7.4 with handling of purchased assets in Chapter 12, Section 12.3.14.

14.5.1 Selecting a new supplier of office and IT equipment

The Finance Department shall maintain an approved supplier list. Any purchases for the office shall use this list of approved and vetted suppliers, wherever possible, as defined in Chapter 12, Section 12.3.14.2.1.2. The details of suppliers on the approved supplier list are defined in Chapter 13, Appendix 1.

Where a product or service is not available for any reason from the approved supplier list, authority may be given by the Finance Department for a local purchase if the need is urgent.

If the need is not urgent, then a suitable supplier shall be identified with the Requestor and shall undergo the supplier approval process as defined in Chapter 13, Section 13.1.3 and the checklist defined in Chapter 13, Appendix 2.

The process for selecting a new supplier and placing them on the approved supplier list is shown below (Fig. 14.6):

1. A need is identified to add a supplier of a product or service to the approved supplier list.
2. The Requestor and the Finance Department shall agree the specific products(s) or service(es) required.
3. The Finance Department shall contact the supplier to determine whether they can supply the product or service and the terms and conditions for it. This may take the form of a simple purchase order process or be a full Request for Information (RFI), Request for Quotation (RFQ), or a Request for Proposal (RFP) depending on what product or service is to be supplied. There are a number of other 'Request for…' (RFx) procurement processes. A description of these is defined in Appendix 5. The template for the preparation of all RFx documents is defined in Appendix 6.
4. If an RFx document is to be issued, then the Finance Department, with the Requestor, shall undertake the following:
   - define scope of work;
   - create evaluation criteria; and
   - create RFx document using the RFx template.
5. The RFx document and the financial and security checklist shall be sent to selected potential suppliers with the anticipated timeframe for the evaluation and selection process. The steps in this process used in FCL are defined in Appendix 7.
6. The Evaluation Team shall be identified and trained, if required.
7. Receive back results of the RFx submissions.
8. If the RFx was an RFI, then the RFP, RFQ, or RFT shall be developed and steps 5–7 repeated above for the RFx.
9. The responses shall be evaluated from a technical and business perspective using the defined evaluation criteria.
10. The successful supplier shall be identified.
11. Appropriate unsuccessful bidder letters shall be sent, as appropriate.
12. References shall be taken up and site visits may be required
13. The contract negotiation stage shall now be undertaken.
14. Once negotiation is completed the contract shall be agreed and signed.
15. The provision of product(s) or service(s) shall start.

14.5.2 Requirements for office and IT supplier contracts

All new contracts that are established between FCL and any supplier of office and IT products and services shall be executed between the parties prior to starting product or service delivery or allowing access to any FCL premises (unless as a hosted visitor, as defined in Chapter 12, Section 12.4.2), information or information processing facilities.

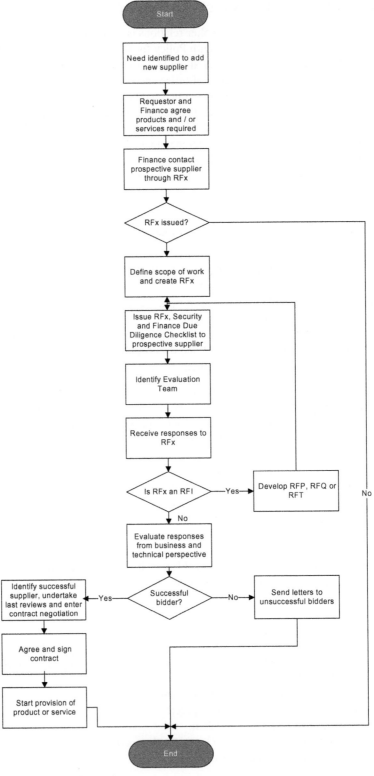

FIG. 14.6 Selecting a new supplier of office and IT equipment.

Where appropriate, SLAs set up with suppliers of office and IT products and services, shall include details as defined in Appendix 4.

14.5.3   Monitoring supplier service performance

FCL shall operate continuous monitoring of products and services provided by suppliers to:

- measure service performance against agreed SLAs;
- help identify and correct potential problems with suppliers and/or their products and/or services; and
- develop actions for service improvement, as defined in Chapter 7, Section 7.4.8.

The monitoring process is (Fig. 14.7):

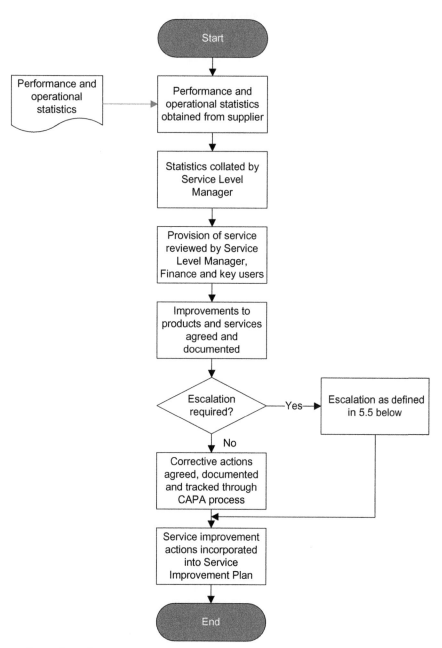

FIG. 14.7   Monitoring supplier service performance.

1. Performance and operational statistics for a supplier product or service shall be obtained from the supplier in accordance with:
   - agreements reached regarding the provision of product or service statistics during contract negotiation;
   - supplier commitments for statistics provision (as documented in the SLA); and
   - performance statistics for supplier services that shall be provided to the Service-Level Manager.
2. The statistics shall be collated by the Service-Level Manager (and additional performance information from FCL sources shall be included, as appropriate).
3. The performance of the service shall be reviewed by the Service-Level Manager, the Finance Department, key users of the product or service, and the supplier, as appropriate. Additional items which may be discussed include but are not limited to:
   - changes to the service scope; and
   - changes to the product or service delivered and business requirements.
4. Any agreed actions concerning the possible improvement of the service shall be agreed and documented.
5. If the performance of the service is business-critical, the issue shall be escalated, as defined in Section 14.5.5.
6. Corrective actions shall be determined and agreed between FCL and the supplier as appropriate. They shall be tracked to satisfactory resolution using the CAPA process and a Post-Implementation Review (PIR) shall be carried out to determine that the corrective action is efficiently completed.
7. Any other suggested actions for service improvement shall be incorporated into SIP and for discussion during the annual review of supplier contracts.

14.5.4   Reviewing supplier contracts

FCL shall undertake a formal review of all contracts with suppliers of its products and services. This review shall be performed on an annual basis and is the responsibility of the Finance Manager. The review meeting shall comprise the Finance Manager, the Service-Level Manager, the Laboratory Manager, and other relevant Managers affected by the provision of the products and/or services. There may be a number of meetings undertaken for different products and services (Fig. 14.8).

The process is:

1. The Finance Manager shall gather information on each supplier contract requiring review. Inputs shall include, but not be limited to:
   - existing contracts;
   - SLAs for supplier products and services;
   - the SIP;
   - feedback from service level reporting;
   - feedback from the complaints process;
   - feedback from the Service Desk;
   - any other relevant feedback for the supplier(s) under discussion.
2. The performance and requirements of each supplier contract shall be evaluated, with assistance from relevant Managers, as required. Items for consideration shall include, but not be limited to:
   - validation of supplier's contractual obligations;
   - affirmation of the service adequacy for defined business requirements;
   - product availability and performance;
   - service availability and performance;
   - supplier availability and performance;
   - funds and budgets;
   - contract disputes;
   - planned changes to the scope of required products and/or services;
   - future business requirements;
   - planned changes to infrastructure;
   - the overall FCL strategy for provision of services in the SIP.
3. The Finance Manager, in association with relevant Managers, shall draught a supplier CIP which shall cover the resources, communications, and documentation needed to implement the required improvements.

   New targets for improvements in quality, costs, and resource utilisation shall be included, in addition to details on the predicted improvement measures to assess the effectiveness of the change (if required).
4. The CIP and the SIP shall be circulated to relevant Managers for comment, as appropriate. Any comments from employees shall be incorporated into the CIP and the SIP.
5. FCL shall perform the relevant actions detailed in the CIP and the SIP. Where necessary, the Finance Manager shall renegotiate the contract terms with a supplier.
6. Outcomes shall be reported to the relevant Managers, as required.

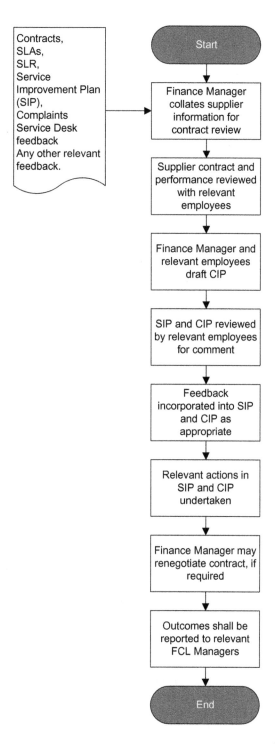

FIG. 14.8 Reviewing supplier contracts.

14.5.5   Resolving contractual disputes with suppliers

FCL shall follow this process in the event that a contractual dispute arises between FCL and a contracted supplier of products and/or services.

Complaints and disputes may originate for a wide variety of reasons, real or perceived, and they reflect negatively on the integrity of a product or service. In such circumstances, FCL shall work vigorously to identify root causes and implement solutions to address these. Ideally, this shall be accomplished through a collaborative, interest-based process that seeks mutual gain by establishing a solution, building trust, and promoting open and clear communications with the supplier.

FCL shall make every effort to prevent disputes from arising with a supplier by being as clear as possible when communicating its needs and requirements during contract negotiation, and SLA determination. FCL's policy shall be to:

- adopt a nonconfrontational approach to enhance or preserve good supplier relationships; and
- resolve concerns in a manner which is timely and which provides options and satisfactory results to both parties.

The process is (Fig. 14.9):

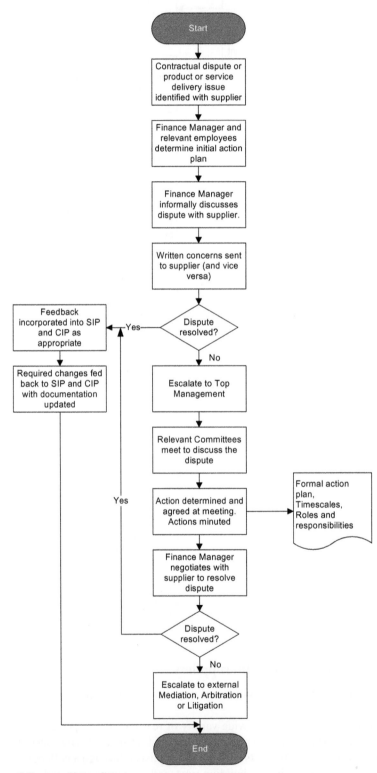

FIG. 14.9   Resolving contractual disputes with suppliers.

1. A contractual dispute or issue with the provision of a product or services from a supplier is identified.
2. The relevant Manager(s) and the Finance Manager shall discuss the dispute internally to determine an initial action plan.
3. The Finance Manager shall discuss the dispute informally with the supplier contact (to attempt to reach a resolution before escalating the matter to higher management). During this stage, both parties shall provide written concerns to each other.

   If the dispute is successfully resolved in this informal manner, the resolution shall be documented, and relevant Managers shall be informed of the outcome. Changes shall be fed back into the SIP, CIP, and policies and procedures for the management of services suppliers, as appropriate.

   If the process is not successful, the dispute shall be escalated to Top Management.

Note

Only the Finance Director shall be permitted to discuss a contract dispute with a supplier after a dispute has been escalated to Top Management.

---

4. If escalated, the dispute shall be discussed by Top Management and this may include:
   - Risk Committee meetings;
   - Service Delivery Committee meetings, as defined in Chapter 4, Appendix 14; and/or
   - special meetings convened by Top Management to discuss the dispute.
5. Action shall be determined and agreed between the attendees at the relevant meeting(s), the minutes of which shall be documented and retained as records, as defined in Chapter 4, Section 4.7.6 and stored in the ERMS. Outputs shall include:
   - a formal action plan;
   - roles and responsibilities; and
   - timescales.
6. The Finance Director shall negotiate with the supplier to resolve the dispute. Options may include:
   - renegotiation of contract terms;
   - redefinition of SLAs; or
   - termination of contract in line with the guidelines for Managing Termination of a Supplier Service, as defined in Section 14.5.6.

   If the dispute is successfully resolved, the resolution is documented, and relevant Managers shall be informed of the outcome. Changes shall be fed back into the SIP, CIP, and policies and procedures for the management of services suppliers, as appropriate.

   If the process is not successful, the dispute shall be further escalated.
7. If the dispute is further escalated, options may include external resolution processes:
   - mediation by a neutral third party to reach a mutually agreeable resolution;
   - arbitration by a neutral Arbitrator (selected by the parties) in a more formalised proceeding where evidence and arguments for each side are presented to the Arbitrator to reach a final determination imposed on the parties; and
   - litigation—where a settlement cannot be agreed.

Note

The dispute resolution process, including Alternate Dispute Resolution (ADR) and the jurisdiction, shall have been agreed in the contract.

If the dispute is successfully resolved in this informal manner, the resolution shall be documented, and relevant Managers shall be informed of the outcome. Changes shall be fed back into the SIP, CIP, and policies and procedures for the management of services suppliers, as appropriate.

14.5.6 Managing termination of supplier services

All contracts or SLAs between FCL and suppliers for products and/or services to FCL shall include details of:

- expected end of product or service provision;
- outline arrangements or responsibilities in the event of an early end to product or service provision; and
- outline arrangements or responsibilities for transfer of service (if appropriate).

When supplier services are terminated, FCL shall always consider:

- the impact on the provision of products or services to FCL and its clients; and
- alternative arrangements for product or service provision to FCL and their clients.

14.6 Utility service providers

In a number of jurisdictions, a forensic laboratory has no choice on the selection of utility service providers as they are the national suppliers. Situations such as this are the provision of:

- electricity;
- gas;
- local infrastructure services; and
- water and sewage.

In cases such as this where there is a monopoly, a forensic laboratory has little option but to accept the terms and conditions for the supply of those services. However, alternate support or sourcing shall be considered as part of the risk assessment process as defined in Chapter 5.

Where a monopoly does not exist, utility service providers shall be treated as suppliers of office and IT products and services as defined in Section 14.5.

14.7 Contracted forensic consultants and expert witnesses

Within FCL, there are occasions when external resources are needed in forensic case processing, these are typically:

- the need for an Expert Witness;
- covering a shortfall in staffing for any reason; and
- the need for a specific skill not present in FCL.

As the digital forensic world is rather small, it is likely that any required Expert Witness or Forensic Analyst is known to FCL; however, a selection process that stands up to due diligence shall be followed in all cases.

Note 1

Consultants such as these shall be regarded as 'Subcontractors' within the IMS.

Note 2

In some jurisdictions, some forensic case processing is preferred to be carried out by Law Enforcement primarily, their appointed suppliers secondarily, and not by subsubcontractors. FCL shall be aware of these constraints and any legal ramifications of the use of subcontractors in these types of cases.

The criteria for selecting an Expert Witness are defined in Chapter 11, Appendix 2. The same criteria shall apply for Forensic Consultants apart from the fact that their experience is primarily in case processing with specific tools and methods but may also require Expert Witness work (Fig. 14.10).

1. FCL identifies a need for a Forensic Consultant that has skills not currently available within the laboratory.
2. The requirements for the role are identified and agreed.
3. A search of 'known' Forensic Consultants shall be undertaken. If there is already one under contract to FCL, they are approached for the task.
4. If there is no 'known' availability, then a search shall be undertaken, using appropriate resources, for a competent Forensic Consultant to meet the requirement.
5. The role of the Forensic Consultant will typically include:
   - providing FCL with the skills, knowledge, and/or equipment that is required to undertake the task;
   - communicating with all relevant employees, at all levels, who are involved with the task;
   - assisting FCL in the effective planning, operation, control, and delivery of the task.

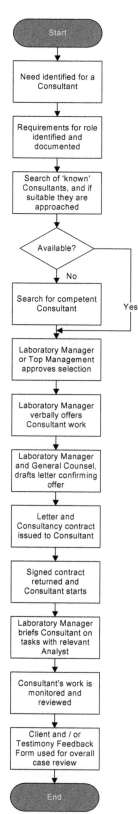

FIG. 14.10 Contracted forensic consultants and expert witnesses.

6. The Forensic Consultant, as well as demonstrating competence, shall be able to demonstrate ethical behaviour, compliance with the rules of evidence in the jurisdiction, and appropriate personal attributes, as defined in Appendix 8.
7. The employment of a Forensic Consultant shall be approved by the Laboratory Manager, and where appropriate, by Top Management.
8. The Laboratory Manager shall verbally offer the Forensic Consultant the work when terms are agreed.
9. The Laboratory Manager, with input from General Counsel, shall draught an offer letter to the Forensic Consultant for the work within the terms verbally agreed. The letter shall contain at least the following information:
   - brief summary of the case or project;
   - charges and invoicing arrangements for the work;
   - period of the work;
   - start date of the work;
   - estimated end date of the work;
   - roles and responsibilities;
   - contractual obligations; and
   - request to confirm acceptance of the offer in writing.
10. The letter shall be sent with a copy of a Consultancy Contract that the Laboratory Manager and Forensic Consultant shall sign before the Forensic Consultant can start work. Terms may be sent via an email. The exact contents of the Consultancy Contract will depend on custom, practice, and legislative requirements for the jurisdiction as well as the following, where appropriate:
    - agreed contract objectives that are SMART, as defined in Chapter 3, Section 3.1.17;
    - a defined contract plan with milestones and deliverables defined; and
    - defining a process to confirm that the contract terms have been met.
11. Under no circumstances shall a contract Forensic Consultant start work on processing a forensic case if a signed contract has not been received. It is the responsibility of the Laboratory Manager to ensure that a signed contract shall be received within a reasonable timescale to enable work to commence promptly.
12. The Laboratory Manager shall arrange a briefing between the contract Forensic Consultant and the relevant Forensic Analysts for the specific case.
13. Once employed, their work shall be monitored and reviewed in the same way as a supplier as defined in Sections 14.5.3–14.5.6.

The client signoff and feedback form shall be used for overall case processing, whilst the testimony feedback forms shall be used for Expert Witnesses, as defined in Chapter 11, Appendix 8.

Note

The Forensic Consultant may have to be security cleared according to the requirements of the jurisdiction to undertake some forensic case processing.

14.8 Outsourcing

Note 1

In this context, within FCL, outsourcing refers to the outsourcing of IT services. Forensic case processing shall never be outsourced but may have contract Forensic Consultants working on a case, as defined in Section 14.7.

Note 2

FCL shall manage all of its IT capability in house, but should this change, the following processes and procedures shall be used.

A quote from BS 7799—the precursor to ISO/IEC 270xx:

The use of an external contractor to manage computer or network facilities may introduce a number of potential security exposures, such as the possibility of compromise, damage, or loss of data at the contractor's site. These risks should be identified in advance, and appropriate security measures agreed with the contractor, and incorporated into the contract.

If any aspect of FCL's IT service provision is outsourced, the agreements shall address how the outsourcer shall guarantee that adequate security, as defined by the risk assessment, shall be maintained, and how security shall be adapted to identify and deal with changes to risks.

Some of the differences between outsourcing and the other forms of third-party service provision include the question of liability, planning the transition period and potential disruption of operations during this period, contingency planning arrangements and due diligence reviews, and collection and management of information on security incidents. Therefore, FCL shall plan and manage the transition to an outsourced arrangement and have suitable processes in place to manage changes and the renegotiation/termination of agreements.

Note

This book is not about the technical side of IT outsourcing, it is only focussing on the security of forensic case processing if outsourcing of IT operations is implemented for some or all of the IT operations undertaken in FCL.

Where outsourcing takes place, FCL shall ensure that it maintains control over the provision of any outsourced services through the following requirements:

- a continuous process of feedback for these services, including complaints and service-level failures;
- a process of continuous improvement;
- a process of ongoing internal audits (also of the outsource service provider itself—i.e. second-party audits), as defined in Chapter 4, Section 4.9.2;
- addressing security and control in dealings with third parties, as defined by the risk assessment and treatment process defined in Chapter 5; and
- addressing security and control in third-party contracts, as defined in Appendix 3.

14.8.1 Determining objectives of outsourcing

The first step in the outsourcing process is to determine the objective of outsourcing for some or all of FCL's IT operations and the required outcomes. Without this essential step, any outsourcing will not deliver the required or expected benefits and outcomes.

14.8.1.1 Benefits of outsourcing

Marketing material is full of the benefits of outsourcing IT operations, but FCL (and any other forensic laboratory considering outsourcing) shall define its own benefits and required outcomes, rather than rely on marketing material. Some of the claimed benefits include:

- the ability of the organisation to concentrate on core functions, rather than IT (Peter Drucker—'Do what you do best—and outsource the rest');
- acquiring innovative ideas from the outsource provider;
- control of expenses;
- delegation of responsibilities of difficult to manage functions to an outsource provider, whilst still reaping the benefits of the functions;
- faster setup of a new function or service;
- freeing up internal resources to concentrate on core processes;
- gain access to skills and competencies not available in house;
- gain high-quality IT staff;
- gain market access and business opportunities through the outsource provider's network;
- gain the benefits of re-engineering;
- generate cash by transferring assets to the outsource provider;
- greater ability to control delivery dates (e.g. via penalty clauses);
- greater flexibility and ability to define the requisite service;
- increase commitment and energy in noncore areas;
- increase flexibility to meet changing business conditions;
- less dependency upon internal resources;

- lower costs due to economies of scale;
- lower ongoing investment required for internal infrastructure;
- minimise technology risk;
- purchase of industry best practise;
- specific outsource service provider benefits, depending on the specific outsource provider's skills; and
- turn fixed costs into variable costs.

14.8.1.2 Risks of outsourcing

The flipside of the claimed benefits of outsourcing is the risks that outsourcing can introduce to FCL (or any other forensic laboratory considering outsourcing). As has been said before, FCL shall never outsource its forensic case processing, but may use contract Forensic Consultants, so these risks are for mainstream IT operations outsourcing and can include.

- availability of resources when needed (e.g. BCP invocation);
- being 'locked in' to a specific outsource service provider and their preferred technology;
- different approaches and commitments to information security relating to FCL and client information and information processing systems;
- different outcome requirements. FCL can define its required outcomes, but at the end of the day, the outsource service provider is only really interested in making a profit from the relationship;
- difficulty of undertaking forensic incident response;
- IPR ownership may be an issue, where the outsourcing provider develops processes, procedures, methods, or tools during the duration of the contract unless clearly resolved in the contract;
- even if the IPR is covered in the outsourcing contract, there is nothing to stop an unscrupulous outsourcer, or a member of their staff, in IPR theft for later reuse;
- failure to 'go the extra mile' as employees would;
- hidden costs, where anything outside strict contractual terms will require an additional fee—which may not have been agreed in advance;
- impact on employee morale;
- inappropriate contract terms;
- lack of control over security of FCL and client information, including access to it;
- lack of organisational culture and commitment;
- legislative differences relating to IPR and privacy if offshoring;
- legislative issues relating to where data may be stored for privacy concerns, especially if using the 'cloud';
- liability issues so that in the case of an information security breach, the client(s) whose information has been compromised will have to take legal action against FCL as they are the contracting party, then FCL will have to act against the outsourcing service provider;
- linguistic issues if outsourcing is really offshoring;
- loss of management control over operational issues;
- loss of the team spirit or personal touch within FCL between the outsource service provider's employees and FCL employees;
- not complying with intangible aspects of the contract (e.g. FCL culture, ethos, and ethics);
- physical and logical security processes and procedures, especially if offshoring, are not necessarily to the same level as those required by FCL;
- problems with auditing the outsource provider, especially if offshoring;
- problems with terminating the outsourcing contract if documentation is not accurate and current;
- problems with terminating the outsourcing contract if proprietary systems are used;
- proprietary systems are used that are not understood in house or by the next outsourcing provider;
- reliance on an unrelated third party is an often overlooked issue in outsourcing. The outsource service provider may go bankrupt, merge, or be taken over, and FCL has little or no control over these processes;
- sacrifice of quality is a strong possibility as the outsource service provider is motivated by profit. As the price in the contract is fixed, the only way of increasing profit is to reduce costs. In effect this means, from experience, that the outsource service provider will do the minimum to meet contractual requirements and charge for anything not covered by the contract and this will almost certainly affect the quality of deliverables to FCL and so to the client;
- some IT functions are not easy to outsource;
- unequal contracting parties—outsourcing service providers are experts at outsourcing contracts, whereas FCL has never undertaken an outsourcing contact; and
- unknown contingency capabilities.

14.8.2 Selecting an outsourcing service provider

Should FCL ever consider outsourcing some parts of its IT operations, then it shall be necessary to select an appropriate outsourcing service provider. If there is no list of outsource service providers on the approved suppliers list maintained by the Finance Department an outsourcing service provider will have to be selected.

The process for selecting an outsourcing service provider is similar to that for selecting a supplier, as defined in Section 14.5.1, but with a number of significant differences, and is shown below (Fig. 14.11):

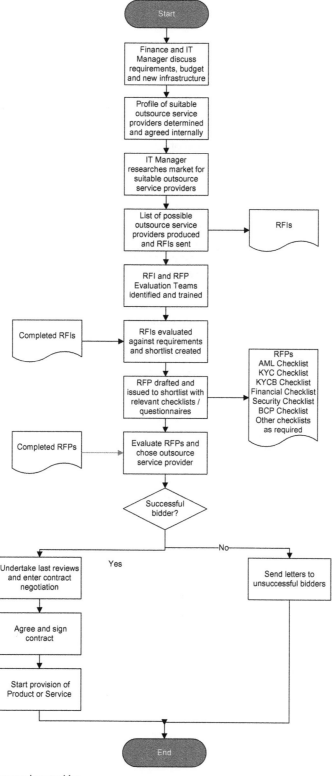

FIG. 14.11 Selecting an outsourcing service provider.

1. FCL makes a Top Management decision to outsource some or all of its IT operations. The areas to be outsourced shall be defined and the objectives of outsourcing shall be agreed. A business case for this shall be produced.
2. The IT Manager and the Finance Manager shall meet to discuss requirements, plan a budget, and determine the new structure after outsourcing is implemented.
3. The IT Manager shall research the market for possible outsource service providers that may meet FCL's agreed requirements. The building of this list can come from a variety of sources, including:
   - experiences of colleagues;
   - professional and trade bodies or shows;
   - Internet searches;
   - advertising and marketing material;
   - etc.
4. The profile of a potential outsource service provider shall be defined and agreed internally.
5. Once a list of possible outsource providers has been produced, a full Request for Information (RFI) shall be used to obtain detailed information about outsource service providers and their service offerings. The template for the preparation of an RFI shall be used.
6. An RFI shall be specifically tailored to the selection of an outsourcing service provider for all or part of IT systems. This shall include, but not be limited to:
   - define scope of work;
   - create evaluation criteria; and
   - process for completing the RFI.
7. The RFI shall be issued to outsource service providers based on the list of key issues that FCL requires information on. These shall be prioritised and weighted for the evaluation criteria.
8. The RFI Evaluation Team shall be identified and trained, required.
9. RFI submissions shall be received and the responses evaluated, based on the specific requirements stated. This shall produce a clear picture of the market and its trends, and where various outsource service provider offerings fit into the marketplace. After evaluation, there shall be clear information to be able to:
   - draught a comprehensive RFP to meet FCL's stated objectives; and
   - produce a list of no more than 3–5 possible candidates to receive the RFP.
10. The RFP shall be issued with the financial, Know Your Customer (KYC), Know Your Customer's Business (KYCB), Anti-Money Laundering (AML), business continuity, and information/cyber security checklists to selected potential outsource service providers, the anticipated timeframe for the evaluation and selection process.
11. Identify the RFP evaluation team and train them if required.
12. Receive back results of the RFP submissions.
13. Evaluate the responses from a technical and business perspective using the defined evaluation criteria. Some other tips for selecting an appropriate outsourcing service provider are defined in Appendix 9.
14. Identify the successful outsource service provider.
15. Send appropriate unsuccessful bidder letters, as appropriate.
16. Undergo site visits and take up references.
17. Enter contract negotiation stage.
18. Agree best and final offer (BAFO).
19. Agree and sign contract.
20. Start provision of outsource service provision transition process.

14.8.2.1 Requirements for outsourcing contracts

Outsourcing contracts are not like any other supplier contract, and it is likely, if not certain, that the outsourcing service provider will have more experience than FCL in outsourcing contracts, so expert advice shall be needed. An experienced outsourcing Lawyer shall be appointed for this as it is outside the competence of in-house Legal Counsel. Whilst not competent to provide legal advice, FCL has defined a number of areas that shall be addressed in any outsourcing contract, these are defined in Appendix 10.

14.8.2.2   Monitoring outsourcing service supplier performance

FCL shall operate continuous monitoring of outsourced products and services provided by the outsource service provider to:

- measure service performance against agreed SLAs;
- help identify and correct potential problems with the outsource service provider and/or their products and/or services; and
- develop actions for service improvement, as defined in Chapter 7, Section 7.4.8.

The monitoring process is (Fig. 14.12):

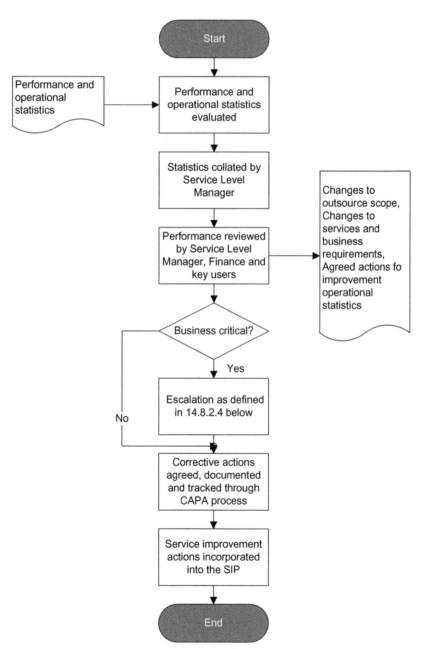

FIG. 14.12   Monitoring outsourcing service supplier performance.

1. Performance and operational statistics for any outsourced service shall be obtained from the outsource service provider in accordance with:
   - agreements reached regarding the provision of service statistics during contract negotiation;
   - supplier commitments for statistics provision (as documented in the SLA); and
   - performance statistics for supplier services shall be provided to the Service-Level Manager.
2. The outsource service provider's performance shall be reviewed by the Service-Level Manager, the Finance Department, key users of the product or service, and the outsource service provider on a regular basis (at least monthly), with formal reporting in place. Additional items which may be discussed include, but are not limited to:
   - changes to the outsource service scope; and
   - changes to the service and business requirements.
3. Any agreed actions concerning the possible improvement of the outsource service shall be agreed and documented.
4. If the performance of the outsource service is business-critical, the issue shall be escalated, as defined in Section 14.8.2.4.
5. Corrective actions shall be determined and agreed between the parties and the outsource service provider's own processes, as appropriate. They shall be tracked to satisfactory resolution using the CAPA process and a PIR is carried out to determine that the corrective action is completed effectively.
6. Any other suggested actions for outsourced service improvement shall be incorporated into the SIP, and for discussion during the review of the outsource service provider's contract as defined in Section 14.8.2.3.

14.8.2.3 Reviewing the outsourcing contract

FCL shall undertake a formal review of the outsourcing contract on the terms agreed in the contract, which shall be at least annually. Performance shall be reviewed on an ongoing monthly (or more frequently if needed) basis with formal records of the meetings and actions being tracked through the SLR process with any corrective actions processed through the CAPA process.

The review shall be the responsibility of the Finance Director. The review meeting shall comprise the Finance Director, the Service-Level Manager, the Laboratory Manager, and other relevant Managers with the outsource service provider's management team.

The process is (Fig. 14.13):

1. The Finance Director gathers information on the provision of the services provided by the outsource service provider. Inputs shall include:
   - the existing contract;
   - the SLA for the provision of the outsources services;
   - the SIP;
   - feedback from service level reporting;
   - feedback from the complaints process;
   - feedback from the Service Desk; and
   - any other relevant feedback relating to the outsourced service provision.
2. The performance requirements of the outsource service provider shall be evaluated, with assistance from relevant Managers, as required. Items for consideration shall include:
   - validation of outsource service provider's contractual obligations;
   - affirmation of the service adequacy for defined business requirements;
   - service availability and performance;
   - funds and budgets;
   - contract disputes;
   - planned changes to the scope of required outsource service;
   - future business requirements;
   - planned changes to infrastructure; and
   - the overall strategy for provision of services in the SIP.
3. The Finance Director, in association with relevant Managers, shall draught a CIP which covers the resources, communications, and documentation needed to implement the required improvements.
4. New targets for improvements in quality, costs, and resource utilisation shall be included, in addition to details on the predicted improvement measures to assess the effectiveness of the change (if required).

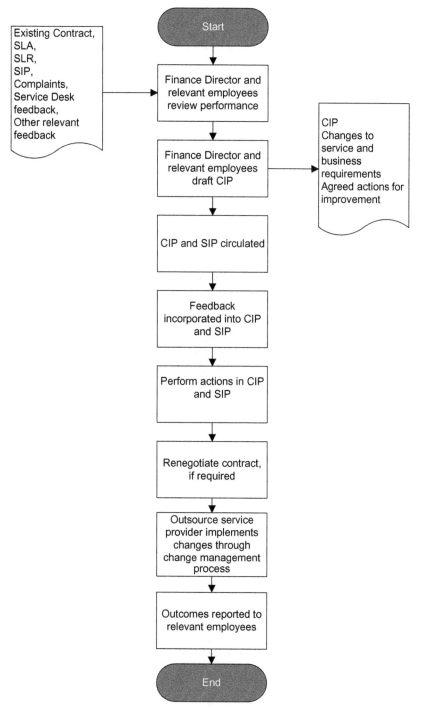

FIG. 14.13 Reviewing the outsourcing contract.

5. The CIP and the SIP shall be circulated to relevant Managers for comment, as appropriate. Any comments shall be incorporated into the CIP and the SIP.
6. The relevant actions detailed in the CIP and the SIP are performed. Where necessary, the Finance Director shall renegotiate the contract terms with the outsource service provider.
7. The outsource service provider shall implement any relevant changes through the Change Management Process.
8. Outcomes shall be reported to the relevant Managers, as required.

14.8.2.4 Resolving contractual disputes with an outsource service provider

FCL shall follow this process in the event that a contractual dispute arises between FCL and the outsource service provider which is similar to that for suppliers as defined in Section 14.5.5 above.

The process is (Fig. 14.14):

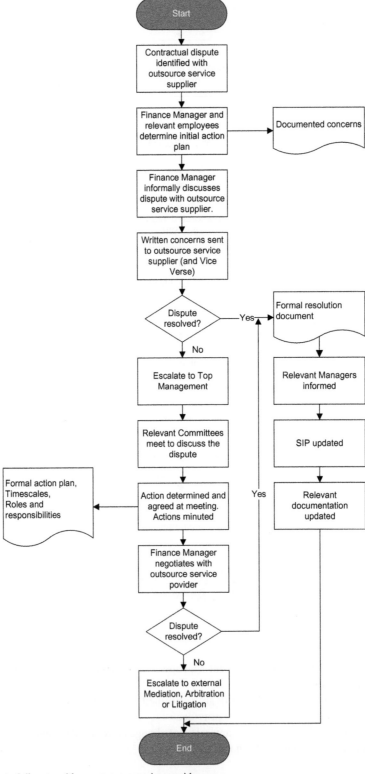

FIG. 14.14 Resolving contractual disputes with an outsource service provider.

1. A contractual dispute or issue with the provision of service from the outsource service provider is identified.
2. The Finance Director and relevant Manager(s) shall discuss the dispute internally to determine an initial action plan.
3. The Finance Director shall discuss the dispute informally with the outsource service provider contact (to attempt to reach a resolution before escalating the matter to higher management). During this stage, both parties shall provide written concerns to each other.

   If the dispute is successfully resolved in this informal manner, the resolution shall be documented, and relevant Managers shall be informed of the outcome. Changes shall be fed back into the SIP, CIP, and policies and procedures for the management of services suppliers, as appropriate.

   If the process is not successful, the dispute shall be escalated to Top Management.

Note

Only the Finance Director is permitted to discuss a contract dispute with the outsource service provider.

---

4. If escalated, the dispute is taken by the Finance Director to the rest of FCL Top Management, this may include:
   - Risk Committee meetings;
   - Service Delivery Committee meetings; and/or
   - special meetings convened by Top Management to discuss the dispute.
5. Action shall be determined and agreed between the attendees at the relevant meeting, the minutes of which shall be documented and retained as records, as defined in Chapter 4, Appendix 13 and stored in the ERMS. Outputs shall include:
   - a formal action plan;
   - roles and responsibilities; and
   - timescales.
6. The Finance Director shall negotiate with the outsource service provider to resolve the dispute. Options may include:
   - renegotiation of contract terms;
   - redefinition of SLAs; or
   - termination of contract in line with the guidelines for Managing termination of a outsource service provider, as defined in Section 14.8.2.4.

   If the dispute is successfully resolved, the resolution is documented, and relevant Managers are informed of the outcome. Changes may be fed back into the SIP and also relevant policies and procedures for the management of services and suppliers.

   If the process is not successful, the dispute shall be escalated.
7. If the dispute is escalated, options may include external resolution processes:
   - mediation by a neutral third party to reach a mutually agreeable resolution;
   - arbitration by a neutral Arbitrator (selected by the parties) in a more formalised proceeding where evidence and arguments for each side is presented to the Arbitrator to reach a final determination imposed on the parties; or
   - litigation—where a settlement cannot be agreed.

Note

The dispute resolution process, including Alternate Dispute Resolution (ADR) and the jurisdiction, shall be agreed in the contract.

When the dispute is successfully resolved, the resolution shall be documented, and relevant Managers informed of the outcome. Changes shall be fed back into the SIP, CIP, and policies and procedures, as appropriate.

14.8.2.5 *Managing termination of an outsourcing contract*

Any outsourcing agreement shall include details of:

- expected end service provision;
- outline arrangements or responsibilities in the event of an early end to service provision; and
- outline arrangements or responsibilities for transfer of service, information, and IPR back to FCL or another outsource service provider.

When outsourcing services are terminated, FCL shall always consider:

- the impact on the provision of the outsourced services to FCL and its clients; and
- alternative arrangements for outsourced service provision to FCL and their clients.

14.9 Use of subcontractors

14.9.1 By FCL

FCL uses Forensic Consultants on contract as subcontractors on occasion for a specific purpose. Purposes range from:

- requirement of a specific tool for a case where there is no in-house expertise;
- covering for unexpected demand on caseload;
- clearing any backlog of cases;
- covering for staff shortages—e.g. illness and holiday issues; and
- the need for an Expert Witness.

In every case where a subcontractor is to be used the client shall be advised of the identity and qualifications of the Forensic Consultant to be used. The client shall be requested to confirm that they accept the Forensic Consultant to work on processing their case.

All forensic cases to be processed that may involve sensitive or classified information shall be processed by employees and not a contracted Forensic Consultant, wherever possible. Where not possible, the client shall be consulted.

FCL shall maintain a list of 'known and trusted' Forensic Consultants. This shall include qualification, certifications, and areas of expertise to assist in selection of a Forensic Consultant for a specific requirement.

Only the Laboratory Manager shall authorise the use of a Forensic Consultant. In some sensitive cases, it may be necessary to obtain Top management approval as well.

FCL shall be accountable and responsible to the client for the delivery and quality of any subcontracted forensic case processing. The exception to this rule shall be where a client requests a specific subcontractor to work on their case.

When the case has been processed by the Forensic Consultant, all exhibits relating to the case and any work product shall be returned to FCL for storage in the Secure Property Store and in the ERMS in the client virtual file as appropriate. Movement Forms, as defined in Chapter 8, Appendix 17 shall be used to maintain the chain of custody.

14.9.2 By suppliers or outsourcing service providers

FCL shall not permit this, unless agreed at the contract negotiation stage. Due diligence shall be undertaken relating to the use of any subcontractor and they shall be required to complete the financial, Know Your Customer (KYC), Know Your Customer's Business (KYCB), Anti-Money Laundering (AML), business continuity, and security checklists and security questionnaire, as defined in Chapter 13, Appendix 2.

The supplier or outsource service provider shall be accountable for the work of any subcontractors they engage. FCL shall have the right to perform second-party audits, as defined in Chapter 4, Section 4.9.2 on any suppliers or outsource service providers and subcontractors they engage and the right to demand termination of their use, if appropriate (e.g. client complaints, substandard work, conflict of interest, etc.).

14.10 Managing complaints

The receipt of a complaint is a serious issue within FCL.

FCL process and procedures for managing client complaints are defined in Chapter 6, Section 6.14.

Complaints that FCL may have with its suppliers are covered in Section 14.5.5 and its outsource service providers (if they ever use them) in Section 14.8.2.4.

14.11 Some reasons for outsourcing failure

There are a wide range of causes for the failure of outsourcing arrangements. Detailed below are some of the potential failure points that may arise during an outsourcing process:

- **Failure to define requirements**—too often requirements are poorly defined and when the outsource service provider meets them, they are not what is required, even if it is what was requested;
- **Failure to understand and comply with the SLA**—Even if well structured, it is not uncommon for SLAs to be misunderstood or not complied with. It is essential to monitor the performance of the conduct of the outsourced task to ensure that both parties understand and follow the terms of the SLA;

- **Failure to understand the potential costs and savings**—If cost is one of the factors in the outsourcing decision, both parties must have a clear understanding the financial aims of the outsourced function. The aims shall be stated and the way in which they will be monitored shall be clearly stated. The SLA shall define and report on what is expected to be delivered by both parties;
- **Ineffective contract management**—If the contract management process is not efficient or not efficiently implemented, there is an increasing risk that if the outsourcing arrangement is not well designed, managed, and executed there will be a failure in the contract;
- **Outsourcer attitudes**—experience dictates there is the possibility of an 'us' and 'them' approach. The client wants lots of work, often in addition to the contract, carried out as part of the work to be performed. The outsource service provider will stick to the contract, unlike the situation where the client's employees were carrying out the work;
- **Outsourcing for the wrong reason**—often an organisation sees that the solution to a problem is to outsource the problem. This gives the illusion of a 'fix' but often ends up with a worse situation as the organisation now has less control over the problem. The other main reason for outsourcing is financial. Whilst this brings short term benefits in many cases, the organisation loses in-house skills that are essential, especially when the outsourcing contract is terminated for any reason. The outsource service provider may not adopt and adapt to the same cultural values and dedication that permanent employees have;
- **Poor contract drafting**—in general, Lawyers are not expert IT specialists and IT specialists are not Lawyers. Unless both parties work together, there can be problems with contract drafting relating to required outcomes and how to measure them;
- **Poor SLAs defined**—if the SLAs defined are inappropriate, then there is little chance of outcomes being met or continuous improvement being achieved;
- **Risk assessment is not carried out**—If the risks relating to the outsourcing of the task are not clearly researched and understood before the outsourcing process is initiated, then poor decisions may be made;
- **The outsourcing of a function or process that is not efficient**—If a process or function that does not work well within a forensic laboratory it may be tempting to outsource it to another organisation—to outsource the problem. This should be avoided because if the business requirements cannot be adequately communicated and managed within the forensic laboratory, it is unlikely to be successfully outsourced. The process or function should be fixed before it can be outsourced.

There are numerous other reasons for failure and many books have been written about this.

Appendix 1—Contents of a service plan

The Service Plan template includes, but is not limited to:

- the roles and responsibilities for implementing, operating, and maintaining the service;
- activities to be performed by clients and third-party suppliers (where required);
- changes to the existing service management framework and services (where required);
- communication plan for all interested parties;
- contracts and agreements to align with the changes in business need;
- workforce and recruitment requirements;
- skills and training requirements, e.g. end users, technical support;
- processes, measures, methods, and tools to be used in connection with the service;
- budgets and timescales;
- service acceptance criteria; and
- the expected outcomes from operating the service expressed in measurable terms.

Appendix 2—Risks to consider with third parties

Whilst different third parties will have different risks associated with the products and services they provide to FCL, the following template shall be used, as a basis and amended as needed, for consideration of risks:

- information processing facilities that the third party will be able to access;
- the information that is located on those information processing facilities;
- the type of access the third party will have to information processing facilities, and this includes:

- physical access (e.g. to offices, data centres, wiring closets, other areas of risk);
- logical access (e.g. what access, and level of access they have to information processing facilities holding information);
- network connectivity between FCL and the third party, including identification and authentication mechanisms and protection of transmitted data;
- methods of access in place (e.g. dedicated line, remote roving access on mobile devices, etc.); and
- type of access (e.g. on-site or remote to the office).
- existing controls in place;
- additional controls required by the risk assessment to adequately protect information and information processing systems;
- the criticality of the information processing systems that the third party can access;
- the level of vetting and screening of the third-party employees that can access information and information processing systems;
- contractual and insurance measures in place against unauthorised access, modification, disclosure, or erasure of information by a third-party employee;
- how identification authorisation is achieved, especially for remote connections by third parties;
- how frequently remote access needs to be reconfirmed, both during a session and on an ongoing basis;
- the controls that the third party has in place to demonstrate that they are appropriate to store FCL and client information and guard against unauthorised access, modification, disclosure, or erasure;
- the controls that the third party has in place to demonstrate that they are appropriate for transmission or exchange of FCL and client information to guard against unauthorised access, modification, disclosure, or erasure;
- how effectively these controls are implemented, with regular metrics reporting and second-party audits;
- impact of data corruption of data during transmission and controls to mitigate this risk;
- certifications and accreditations held and their value;
- the impact of the third party not being able to access information processing systems for a variety of times, using the scenarios defined in Chapter 13, Appendix 6;
- status of the third party's business continuity response and its effectiveness;
- impact of the third party being unavailable to undertake their contracted role for a variety of times;
- how information security incidents are handled by the third party, and the process for reporting them in a timely manner;
- how conflicts of interest are handled by the third party;
- identification of any possible conflicts of interest; and
- legal, regulatory, and client requirements.

Note

This is not a complete list and the ISM shall amend it as appropriate for any third party to be assessed.

Appendix 3—Contract checklist for information security issues

All identified security requirements shall be addressed before giving any third-party access to FCL's premises, assets, information, or information processing systems.

The following checklist shall be used to address security and information/cyber security specifically, in any contractual terms. Not all items are relevant to all contracts and this will depend on the type and extent of access given, the information classification, and the information processing systems to be used:

Product or service description

- scope of service provided (and if necessary, what is NOT covered);
- description of the product or service to be provided;
- a description of the information to be accessed in the product or service and its classification, as defined in Chapter 5, Appendix 16, or the third party's classification and definition so it can be mapped to FCL classification system;
- the target level of service and unacceptable levels of service, as defined in the SLA;
- the definition of verifiable performance criteria (i.e. metrics against the SLA);
- a formal, documented procedure by which the supplier or outsource service provider manages product or service delivery;
- maintenance arrangements (if relevant); and
- expected end of service.

Roles and responsibilities

- for FCL;
- for the supplier or outsource service provider;
- for responsibilities regarding hardware and software installation and maintenance; and
- for commitment for provision of statistics to/from the supplier or outsource service provider for service level reporting about the product or service provided, as defined in Chapter 7, Section 7.4.9.

Communications and reporting between the parties

- a clear reporting structure and agreed reporting formats, including:
  - contact points;
  - Account Manager responsible for the contract for the product or service provided;
  - mechanisms of interaction (including procedures/methods for review of services, and escalation of service issues); and
  - formats and requirements for service level reporting.
- arrangements for reporting, notification, and investigation of information security incidents and security breaches, as well as violations of the requirements stated in the contract between the parties.

Information/cyber security controls required

- information/cyber security requirements for each element of a product or service provided before access to premises, information, or information processing systems;
- commitment to information/cyber security to protect all information and information processing systems against unauthorised access, modification, erasure, or disclosure of information and information processing systems;
- Information Security Policy, as defined in Chapter 4, Appendix 20;
- the risk management process in place;
- asset protection, including:
  - physical and logical processes and procedures to protect assets, including premises, information, information processing systems, and software, including management of known vulnerabilities, as defined in Chapter 7, Section 7.6;
  - integrity requirements;
  - confidentiality requirements;
  - availability requirements;
  - authenticity requirements;
  - auditability requirements;
  - accountability requirements;
  - restrictions on copying and disclosing information; and
  - controls to ensure the return, or destruction, of information and assets at the end of, or at an agreed point in time during, the contract.
- processes and procedures for ensuring human resources security, including screening of employees and the right to review screening of employees who can access premises, information, and information processing systems with the right to refuse access if appropriate;
- access control policy, covering:
  - a process for revoking access rights or interrupting the connection between systems;
  - a requirement to maintain a list of individuals authorised to use the product or service being made available, what their rights and privileges are with respect to such use, and a commitment to provide timely updates to the access list;
  - a statement that all access that is not explicitly authorised is forbidden;
  - an authorisation process for user access and privileges;
  - permitted access methods, and the control and use of unique identifiers such as user IDs, passphrases, and multifactor authentication;
  - the different reasons, requirements, and benefits that make the access by the third party necessary; and
  - the right to monitor, and revoke, any activity related to FCL's information or information processing systems.
- user and administrator training in methods, procedures, and security;
- ensuring user awareness for information security responsibilities and issues;
- a clear and specified incident management process, as defined in Chapter 7, Section 7.4.1;

- a clear and specified problem management process, as defined in Chapter 7, Section 7.4.2;
- a clear and specified Change Management Process;
- a clear and specified release management process, as defined in Chapter 7, Section 7.4.4;
- a clear and specified configuration management process, as defined in Chapter 7, Section 7.4.5;
- a clear and specified capacity management process, as defined in Chapter 7, Section 7.4.6;
- a clear and specified service management process, as defined in Chapter 7, Section 7.4.7;
- a clear and specified service improvement process, as defined in Chapter 7, Section 7.4.8;
- a clear and specified service reporting process, as defined in Chapter 7, Section 7.4.9;
- the establishment of an escalation process for every process;
- the right to audit responsibilities defined in the contract, to have those audits carried out by a third party, and to enforce the statutory rights of auditors; and
- business continuity processes in place with results of exercises and tests being provided, as appropriate, on a timely basis.

Legal matters

- the respective liabilities and responsibilities with respect to legal matters and how it is ensured that the legal requirements are met (e.g. privacy legislation, computer-related legislation, etc.);
- intellectual property rights, licencing and copyright assignment, and protection of any collaborative or outsourced work; and
- escrow arrangements in the event of failure of the supplier or outsource service provider.

Miscellaneous

- provision for the transfer of personnel, where appropriate; and
- involvement of FCL, the supplier or outsource service provider with subcontractors, and the security controls these subcontractors shall implement and the process for advising of, and receiving authorisation for, the use of subcontractors.

Contract termination and renegotiation

- conditions for renegotiation/termination of agreements:
  - a contingency plan shall be in place in case either party wishes to terminate the relationship before the end of the contract; and
  - renegotiation of the contract if the risk profile or security requirements of either party change or any other influencing change.

Note 1

This can be used for clients and suppliers.

Note 2

This is not a complete checklist and other items shall be added as required.

Appendix 4—SLA template for products and services for clients

As a minimum, the SLA shall have the following information included or directly referenced (in other documents):

- brief product or service description;
- validity period and/or SLA change control mechanism;
- product or service authorisation details;
- brief description of communications relating to the product or services, including reporting mechanisms and frequencies;
- contact details for both parties authorised to act in emergencies, to participate in incident and problem management, recovery, or workaround, as defined in Chapter 7, Section 7.4.1;
- the service hours (e.g. 09:00 to 17:00 h, date exceptions (e.g. weekends, public holidays), critical business periods and out of hours cover, etc.), where appropriate;
- scheduled and agreed interruptions, including notice to be given, number per period;
- client responsibilities (e.g. security, reporting, instructions, etc.);
- service provider liability and obligations (e.g. security, reporting, instructions, etc.);
- impact and priority guidelines;

- escalation and notification process;
- complaints procedure, as defined in Chapter 6, Section 6.14;
- service targets;
- upper and lower workload limits (e.g. the ability of the product or service to support the expected volume of work or system throughput);
- high-level financial management details relating to the product or service;
- action to be taken in the event of a product or service interruption, based in the incident management procedures, but specifically for the product or service;
- housekeeping procedures;
- glossary of terms relating to the product or service, as required;
- supporting and/or related products and services; and
- any exceptions to the terms defined in the SLA.

Appendix 5—RFx descriptions

There are a number of different documents in the RFx family and a number of others that are used in the Contract Management Process. There are a number of textbooks that describe the process in detail, but below is given the summary of the RFx documents used in FCL.

RFI—Request for information

RFIs are primarily used as a planning tool to gather information to be used as input to a detailed procurement document (e.g. an RFP). They shall be used where there is not adequate information about a product or service to be sourced to create a meaningful and detailed procurement document. A large number of possible suppliers or outsource service providers (more than 10 perhaps) shall be identified and sent RFIs. This is a coarse filter to reduce the number of potential suppliers or outsource service providers to fewer than five who receive the detailed procurement document. This process shall produce information about:

- suppliers and their details (finance, location, capacity, etc.);
- state of the market;
- market trends;
- contact details;
- delivery criteria;
- pricing information;
- product and service offerings;
- product and service plans;
- supplier competition; and
- supplier focus (current and future).

Note

More details may well be collected than the above, but this is a minimum set.

RFQ—Request for quotation

RFQs (quotations) are used where it is possible to tightly define the product or service required. There may be the requirement for a fixed price, a range of prices based on quantity, or some other agreed pricing structure.

RFQ—Request for qualification

RFQs (qualifications) are typically used for obtaining professional service consultancy and evaluation is solely based on the supplier's qualification and price is not considered until after selection. This is a 'get the best and worry about price afterwards' approach which may occasionally be appropriate where competency of the supplier or outsource service provider is paramount.

RFP—Request for proposal

RFPs are used where a solution is needed but it cannot be clearly and concisely defined so there are few objective criteria for evaluation available or there are criteria other than price to be considered. These are often based on the results of an RFI response. The supplier or outsource service provider is expected to use its best efforts to state how the requirement will be met and use their competence and innovation to propose a solution. Different suppliers will propose different approaches, tools, and methods to be evaluated. The RFP usually results in a creative or collaborative partnership being formed between the supplier or outsource service provider and FCL. It is essential that the RFP is a quality document that captures all requirements and outcomes in as much detail as possible, as this shall clearly define the required deliverables. A poorly defined RFP will inevitably result in a poorly performing deliverable if it meets the requirements at all.

RFT—Request for tender

RFTs are used where there is a strict requirement for quality, quantity, and delivery schedules, as opposed to a request being sent to potential suppliers or outsource service providers. These are often based on feedback from an RFI, and typically ask for a fixed price. RFTs must be tightly defined and where it is possible to be concise and explicit on the product or service definition.

Appendix 6—RFx template checklist

The following template shall be used, as appropriate, for all RFx's produced in FCL by choosing the appropriate clauses from the list or adding specific ones relating to the product or service being sourced. It is no particular order:

- RFx title;
- RFx reference number;
- RFx date;
- FCL details;
- FCL overview;
- addressee;
- applicable FCL policies and procedures—which have to be accepted as part of the contract;
- bankruptcy information (corporate and Top Management);
- business continuity capability;
- business requirements;
- communication processes;
- confidentiality agreement/NDA;
- conflict of interest declaration;
- contact details for any queries;
- contract management process including service reporting;
- contract monitoring, including second-party audits;
- contract period;
- contract variance;
- cost/pricing structure;
- delivery criteria;
- delivery schedule;
- description of solutions including appropriate supporting material;
- detailed information on the product or service required;
- draught contract;
- due date;
- evaluation criteria;
- implementation schedule;
- incident management processes;
- information;
- innovative ideas;
- inspection of products or services and acceptance/rejection process;
- instructions on how to reply to the RFx;

- insurance coverage;
- legal status;
- legislative, regulatory, or other requirements;
- maintenance-related issues;
- outstanding complaints, litigation relating to the supplier and/or the products or services to be supplied;
- past performance;
- performance measures;
- presubmission conference, if applicable;
- privacy and security measures in place;
- procurement process schedule;
- quality requirements;
- quantities or volumes;
- references;
- relationship with any partners or subcontractors in the response for provision of products or services;
- relevant experience;
- relevant qualifications (certifications, accreditations, and personal qualifications), including copies where appropriate;
- response format;
- RFx timeline;
- scope of work;
- solutions;
- staffing and competencies;
- supplier's corporate information and profile;
- support available;
- technical proposal evaluation process;
- terms and conditions;
- the supplier selection process; and
- training required.

Appendix 7—RFx timeline for response, evaluation, and selection

The following template shall be used for defining the timeline for the submission, evaluation, and selection of an RFx document:

Stage	Due date
Issue RFI	<Define date>
Questions for RFI due by	<Define date>
Responses for RFIs due	<Define date>
Supplier demonstrations	<Define date>
Shortlist defined for receipt of RFP	<Define date>
Issue RFP	<Define date>
Questions for RFP due by	<Define date>
Responses for RFPs due	<Define date>
Supplier demonstrations	<Define date>
Shortlist defined	<Define date>
Site visits and reference taken	<Define date>
Contract negotiations	<Define date>
Contract signed	<Define date>
Service commences	<Define date>

Appendix 8—Forensic consultant's personal attributes

Personal attributes for any Forensic Consultant are essential. FCL shall recruit Forensic Consultants who have the following personal attributes, as well as other criteria:

- **accountable**—able to take responsibility for his/her own actions;
- **communicative**—able to listen to, and effectively interface with all levels of both FCL and client employees, confidently and with sensitivity relating to the forensic case being processed and any other relevant matters;
- **decisive**—capable of reaching timely conclusions and opinions based on logical reasoning and analysis of evidence recovered;
- **discrete**—ensuring that any forensic case processing and any other FCL or client matters are kept confidential, as defined in Chapter 12, Section 12.3.3.3 or their contract of employment, as applicable;
- **ethical**—agree to ethical practices and follow relevant codes of conduct/practice/ethics;
- **fair**—in all dealings giving a balanced view;
- **meticulous**—in record keeping and report production;
- **observant**—constantly and actively aware of FCL's culture and values;
- **perceptive**—aware of, and able to understand, the need for excellence in forensic case processing and the need for continuous improvement;
- **practical**—realistic and flexible with good time management;
- **self-reliant**—able to act and function independently whilst interacting effectively with other employees;
- **tenacious**—persistent, focused on achieving objectives;
- **truthful**—in all aspects of forensic case processing; and
- **versatile**—able to adapt to different situations in forensic cases and provide alternative and creative solutions to forensic case processing situations.

Appendix 9—Some tips for selecting an outsourcing service provider

This is to find out more about the potential outsource service provider's culture, business model, employees, management, technology, solutions, success, and security. It shall be determined at the outset whether any proposed outsource service provider is right for FCL's needs. Whilst the evaluation criteria will provide quantitative and repeatable scores for the selection process, some qualitative criteria that shall be considered include, but not be limited to:

- a commitment to retaining control of operations and services by FCL;
- a guarantee of not being locked into either particular hardware or proprietary software;
- a proven track record in the operations and services required by FCL;
- a sustainable business model;
- agreements relating to any IPR created in the outsourcing relationship;
- an appropriate technology refresh cycle;
- appropriate management systems and experience that match FCL's requirements;
- appropriate references relating to similar outsourcing being provided to FCL and not just proposed products and services—but mature ones;
- assured continuity of the outsourcing team, so that the initial team in the transfer process is the team for the duration of the outsourcing contract;
- broad experience of the required operations and service;
- business profile being appropriate for FCL's needs;
- details of undertaking the knowledge transfer process;
- declaration of the use of subcontractors;
- demonstrable and appropriate information security in place to protect all information and information processing systems against unauthorised access, modification, erasure, or disclosure;
- details of the last technology upgrade undertaken;
- escalation procedures that meet the requirements defined in FCL's IMS;
- evidence of a quality management system in place, preferably certification to ISO 9001;
- experience in effective handling human resources issues relating to the transition;
- good if not outstanding reference for the provision of the operations and services to be provided across a range of industry sectors;

- guaranteed quantifiable cost savings;
- guarantees that there are no conflicts of interest with any of their, or FCL's, clients;
- other recognised international or national accreditations and/or certifications (e.g. ISO/IEC 27001, 27002, 27017, 27018, 27035, 27036, 27701, and ISO 22301, or relevant national ones according to the jurisdiction);
- project management processes that match the ones in use in FCL; and
- proof of the current and ongoing competence of the outsource service provider's employees (including CPE/CPD).

Appendix 10—Areas to consider for outsourcing contracts

The following does not constitute legal advice, but are the areas where FCL shall ensure that appropriate terms are in an outsourcing contract from an information security viewpoint, not the whole legal contract—which is the domain of lawyers:

- agree ownership of physical assets;
- agree ownership of software assets;
- define Change Management Process;
- define information security (and other) incident process;
- define SLAs and SLA reporting process;
- determine review dates and checkpoints;
- determine, if appropriate, a pilot with stop/go clauses;
- explicitly define monitoring and reporting processes;
- explicitly define responsibilities;
- explicitly define staffing requirements;
- explicitly define the IPR terms including escrow;
- explicitly define the outsourcing requirement scope;
- explicitly define the re-negotiation process;
- explicitly define the termination process;
- explicitly define the transition process;
- explicitly define what is outside the outsourcing scope;
- penalties for nonconformity; and
- understand completely the terms of the contract offered. This is even more important if offshoring.

Chapter 15

Effective records management

15.1 Introduction

Every organisation has the ability to improve its efficiency and the products and services it delivers to its clients, and FCL is no exception. As FCL creates documents and records as the majority of its work products, it is essential that these shall be suitably protected throughout their lifecycle.

The proper management of records is essential in upholding FCL's reputation as a provider of forensic case processing and digital evidence. It ensures that FCL can satisfy the scrutiny of other digital forensic experts, as well as the relevant legislative and regulatory processes. Records held by FCL are needed as evidence to support the conclusions that the Forensic Analysts make in their processing of all cases.

An inability to provide records, of known provenance, is likely to be a major failure in the accountability and transparency of the decision-making process supporting the digital evidence provided and the conclusions drawn from it.

The systematic creation and capture of records supporting activity on any case processed by FCL into its recordkeeping systems is fundamental to the efficient and effective management of all cases.

The systematic management of records ensures that FCL shall be able to:

- conduct all of its business is a structured, orderly, efficient, accountable, and transparent manner, especially forensic case processing;
- meet identified legislative and regulatory requirements in the jurisdiction as well as relevant codes of practice and contractual requirements;
- protect client and other interested party's interests;
- provide continuity of operations in the case of any disruptive event that could affect normal business operations; and
- support and document all decision-making, conclusions reached, and opinions given.

All records shall be kept for varying periods of time according to legislation within the jurisdiction, contractual requirements, established good practice, and internal business requirements. The default retention periods in FCL are defined in Chapter 4, Appendix 26. Records shall be disposed only in accordance with officially approved disposal procedures and records made of all disposals, as defined in Chapter 12, Section 12.3.14.10.

There are a number of schemes that describe requirements of storage and management of records, and these include:

- ISO 15489—Information and documentation—Records management;
- ISO 13008—Information and documentation—Digital records conversion and migration process;
- ISO 16175—Information and documentation—Processes and functional requirements for software for managing records;
- ISO 17068—Information and documentation—Trusted third-party repository for digital records;
- ISO 19005—Document management—Electronic document file format for long-term preservation;
- ISO 23081—Information and documentation—Records management processes—Metadata for records;
- ISO 30300—Information and documentation—Records management—Core concepts and vocabulary;
- ISO 30301—Information and documentation—Management systems for records—Requirements;
- ISO 30302—Information and documentation—Management systems for records—Guidelines for implementation;
- ISO/TR 13028—Information and documentation—Implementation guidelines for digitisation of records;
- ISO/TR 18128—Information and documentation—Risk assessment for records processes and systems;
- ISO/TR 21946—Information and documentation—Appraisal for managing records;
- ISO/TR 21965—Information and documentation—Records management in enterprise architecture;
- ISO/TR 22428—Managing records in cloud computing environments;
- BS 10008—Evidential Weight and Legal Admissibility of Electronic Information;

- Model Requirements for the Management of Electronic Records Version 2010 (MoReq2010). Whilst this is called MoReq2010, it was actually released in May 2011. Details of functional requirements for MoReq2010 are defined in Appendix 1;
- Open Archival Information and Systems Reference Model (OAIS). This has been ratified now as ISO 14721;
- Designing and Implementing Recordkeeping Systems (DIRKS);
- International Standard Archival Authority Record for Corporate Bodies, Persons and Families, ISAAR (CPF); and
- Electronic Records Management Software Applications Design Criteria Standard—US DoD 5015.02-STD.

FCL has adopted ISO 15489 as its preferred records management standard and has implemented this as part of its Integrated Management System (IMS). Mapping of ISO 15489 Part 1 to FCL Procedures in the IMS is defined in Appendix 2.

To understand the concept of 'Records Management', some basic definitions and concepts need to be understood.

15.1.1   What is a record?

ISO 15489 defines a record as: 'information created, received, and maintained as evidence and as an asset by an organisation or person, in pursuit of legal obligations or in the transaction of business'.

Records consist of information recorded in any medium or form, including hardcopy correspondence, spreadsheets, email, databases, documents, content appearing on websites, plans, publications, photographs, registers, diaries, film, handwritten notes, and maps. Records are maintained as evidence any activity relating to a forensic case being processed by FCL.

Examples of records within FCL include:

- case instructions,
- case notes;
- complaints;
- computer generated evidence (e.g. as audit logs);
- evidence recovered;
- exhibits;
- filled in case forms;
- forensic images;
- meeting minutes;
- recovery scene documentation, including photographs, drawings, and handwritten notes;
- reports;
- statements or depositions; and
- etc.

Records of all types within FCL are regarded as 'assets' within FCL, as defined in Chapter 12, Section 12.3.14, throughout their life cycle.

When evaluating records, FCL shall determine what physical records are to be converted into electronic records, with appropriate linkages. Scanned images shall ensure that records are complete, with all linkages correctly in place after migration to the electronic records management system (ERMS).

After scanning of physical record, FCL shall determine what happens to the original source records according to the retention schedule. This shall be based on client contracts, legislative and regulatory requirements, and other relevant drivers.

Note

FCL has implemented BS 10008 to ensure that the scanned images are legally admissible as evidence under Sections 8 and 9 of the UK's Civil Evidence Act 1995.

15.1.2   What is a vital record?

FCL defines 'Vital Records' as those records without which FCL could not continue to operate. These records are those, which in the event of a disruptive event, are essential for continued operations and are those that contain the information needed to re-establish FCL in case of a disruptive event. These are the records that protect FCL's interests and those assets and interests of all other interested parties, including clients.

Vital records shall always be identified as such. With physical records, they shall be physically marked on every page according to the FCL Classification and Labelling procedures as defined in Chapter 5. Section 5.5.6.6 and Chapter 5, Appendix 16. The marking shall not affect the admissibility of hard copy evidence, so in the case of photographs or other similar physical records they shall be housed in plastic see-through housings that are marked appropriately. Electronic records shall be marked with their embedded metadata annotated appropriately. All records in the ERMS shall be classified and labelled appropriately.

Whilst all records within FCL have some importance, all of the forensic case records and some general business records shall be defined as 'Vital Records'.

15.1.3   What is a document?

Whilst a record is evidence of an activity, a document is formatted information that can be used by any employee, typically in electronic, digital, or paper format. They serve to convey information to other recipients of the documents. Examples of documents include, but are not limited to:

- agendas;
- blank forms waiting to be filled in;
- policies;
- procedures;
- books or instruction manuals for equipment; and
- checklists.

Note 1

Agendas are not records, they are the intention of the meeting, and the minutes produced are the records.

Note 2

Blank forms become records when they are filled in (e.g. an exhibit movement form, as defined in Chapter 8, Appendix 17).

15.1.4   What is records management?

Records Management is a logical and organised approach to the creation, maintenance, use, and disposition of records, as defined in Chapter 4, Appendix 26, Chapter 12, Section 12.3.14.10. Records management ensures that FCL can control the quality and quantity of information that it creates or receives and ensures it shall be able to meet the requirements of its interested parties and its legislative, regulatory and other business requirements.

15.1.5   What is a recordkeeping system?

A recordkeeping system is 'an information system that captures, maintains, and provides access to records over time'. This can be a manual system that will typically store paper records (e.g. filing cabinets and files and the contents of the secure property store for paper records) or an electronic system (e.g. a database or an ERMS).

15.1.6   Records life cycle

Records all go through a common life cycle, as above, and this is (Fig. 15.1):

- creation;
- use;
- retention; and
- disposal.

Between the creation and use stages, records shall be defined as being 'current', i.e. they are used to carry out day-to-day work.

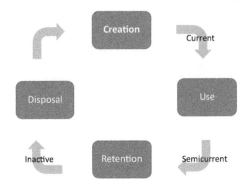

FIG. 15.1 Record life cycle.

Between the use and retention stages, the records shall be defined as 'semicurrent', i.e. they only need to be referred to occasionally or shall be retained for legal, regulatory, contractual, or other business reasons.

Between the retention and disposal stages, the records shall be defined as 'inactive', i.e. a decision has to be made whether to keep them or dispose of them.

15.1.7 Why records must be managed

Correct record management in FCL underpins the whole of the forensic case processing and associated administrative processes. It is essential if FCL is to uphold its reputation as a transparent, competent, and accountable forensic service provider. The need to properly manage records shall be evidenced by the crucial role that they play in all aspects of a forensic case. Only too often are cases lost as the evidence is tainted due to failures in record management, typically, evidence movement.

15.1.8 Benefits of effective records management

There are numerous benefits to be gained by embracing best practice for records management. These include:

- allowing rapid identification and recovery of records;
- conducting business in an orderly, efficient, and accountable manner;
- defining authorities and responsibilities and various job descriptions as defined in Chapter 18;
- defining consistent procedures for managing records throughout FCL;
- delivering products and services in a consistent and equitable manner;
- ensuring continuity whenever employees move employment;
- facilitating finding records requested through legal processes, e.g. discovery orders, or similar;
- improving quality of information by providing employees with reliable and up to date records;
- increasing efficiency by ensuring records are readily identifiable and available;
- maintaining corporate, personal, and collective memory;
- meeting legislative and regulatory requirements including archival, audit, and oversight activities;
- preventing the illegal, arbitrary, and premature destruction of records, thereby protecting FCL's corporate memory and ensuring it is kept available for future reference;
- promoting administrative efficiencies by ensuring that employees have timely access to relevant and complete records;
- promoting informed decision-making;
- protecting FCL's interests and the rights of employees, clients and present and future interested parties;
- providing consistency, continuity, and productivity in management and administration;
- providing continuity in the event of a disruptive event;
- providing evidence of business and personal decisions and actions on forensic cases processed;
- providing protection and support in defending decisions made by FCL in all forensic case processing;
- saving space by preventing records from being held longer than necessary and meeting legislative requirements (e.g. GDPR); and
- underpinning accountability and transparency by ensuring that its case processing processes can stand up to external scrutiny, if required.

15.1.9   Stakeholders in FCL's recordkeeping process

FCL is accountable to a number of interested parties who all have an interest in FCL's effective and efficient management of its records. These include, but are not limited to:

- management;
- employees;
- clients;
- Courts;
- Law Enforcement;
- Lawyers;
- other digital forensic experts;
- Regulators, where appropriate;
- Auditors.

15.2   Legislative, regulatory, and other requirements

15.2.1   Legislative, regulatory requirements, and codes of practice

A forensic laboratory, depending on its location and relevant jurisdiction, is subject to a number of legislative, regulatory, and other requirements that affect digital forensic case processing operations and also the requirements to undertake record management. It is essential that any forensic laboratory understands these requirements in its records management policies and procedures and is able to evidence this.

These include:

- legislation;
- regulation;
- contractual requirements;
- mandatory standards of practice; and
- voluntary codes of conduct and ethics—both organisationally and individually.

There are a number of pieces of legislation that specifically cover recordkeeping. Whilst these will vary between jurisdictions, a generic set of legislation and regulation that can affect a forensic laboratory has been identified and is defined in Appendix 3.

Typically, these will have requirements in them for:

- definitions of a 'record' and record types;
- requirements for a recordkeeping plan defined;
- how records are handled during the record life cycle;
- security of data, especially personal data;
- retention periods;
- disposal methods;
- responsibilities and accountabilities;
- requirements for training;
- requirements for auditing and other monitoring activities; and
- offences and penalties for compliance failure.

15.2.2   Principles of record management within FCL

Records, within FCL, are created or received, accessed, and stored during processing of forensic cases as well as day-to-day business activities.

To comply with the relevant legislative, contractual, and business requirements, as well as providing appropriate traceability, accountability, and transparency, FCL has implemented a recordkeeping process. This has been developed and implemented to create and maintain authentic, reliable, and useable records, and protect the integrity of those records, for as long as required.

To implement the recordkeeping system, FCL has undertaken a process that determines what records should be created, managed, and retained in each process relating to either forensic case processing or normal business activities. This includes, but is not limited to:

- assessing the risks of failure to have authentic and reliable records, as defined in Chapter 5;
- complying with relevant legislative, contractual, and business requirements as well as internal processes, procedures and work instructions, as defined in Chapter 12, Section 12.3.13.1;
- deciding how to organise records so as to support requirements for use;
- determining requirements for retrieving, using, and securely transmitting records between business processes and other users;
- ensuring that all records are secured according to their classification and any other relevant requirements, specifically legislative ones, as defined in Chapter 5, Appendix 16;
- ensuring that records are retained according to the Record Retention schedule, as defined in Chapter 4, Appendix 26;
- deciding how metadata will be persistently linked and managed;
- identification of the metadata that should be created with the record and through record processing;
- identifying and evaluating opportunities for continued improvement of the effectiveness, efficiency, or quality of the recordkeeping processes;
- preserving records and making them available to authorised employees according to legitimate business needs; and
- deciding the form and structure of records that should be created and managed.

15.3 Record characteristics

15.3.1 General requirements

Within FCL, all records shall be able to show that they accurately reflect the message of the record, be that actions taken, decisions made or instructions or material communicated. All records shall have to be able to support the business in its defined needs for those records and provide a transparent, accountable audit trail for the record's life cycle.

As well as the record itself, the integral metadata (for electronic records having such a facility) or the associated metadata (for paper records and electronic records that do not have appropriate integral metadata) shall be permanently and irrevocably linked to the record by the appropriate means to fully document any business transaction involving the record.

In FCL, the metadata used shall define the following functions:

- the business context in which the record was created, received, and used should be apparent in the record, whether it be for a forensic case or in general business transactions;
- the links between any documents that may be combined to either from a whole or part of a record (e.g. manuals or checklists used to create a specific piece of evidence);
- the links between the record and other records that may combine to create a whole forensic case; and
- the structure of the record (i.e. record structure and relationships between the elements that make up the record itself, to ensure that the record remains intact and of known integrity).

The records management processes and procedures shall be used to produce records with the following attributes, where much of this is achieved using the procedures defined in Chapter 4, Section 4.7.5.

15.3.1.1 Record authenticity

Record authenticity is essential, for the records created and used by employees in forensic cases.

FCL defines an authentic record as one where it can be proved that it:

- has been created or sent at the time purported (i.e. non-repudiation of time, typically by digital time stamping);
- has been created or sent by the person who claims to have created or sent it (i.e. non-repudiation or origin); and
- is what it claims to be.

FCL has implemented procedures for information handling and information security that ensure that all users:

- shall not be permitted to use accounts that do not provide accountability (e.g. Administrator, root, etc.) unless appropriate compensating controls are in place, as defined Chapter 12, Section 12.6;
- shall be uniquely identified; as defined Chapter 12, Section 12.6.4;

- shall have a full user account registration history available;
- shall have their access rights regularly reviewed for continued business need, as defined Chapter 12, Section 12.6.7; and
- shall have their access rights set by the relevant information, system, process, or business owners, as defined Chapter 12, Section 12.6.1;

In addition to the management of all user accounts, FCL uses mixture of organisational and technical controls to ensure that records are protected against:

- unauthorised access;
- unauthorised disclosure;
- unauthorised destruction;
- unauthorised modification; and
- unauthorised use.

and that during a record's life cycle, using organisational or technical measures, the following processes are controlled:

- record creation;
- record receipt;
- record use;
- record maintenance;
- record transfer; and
- record disposition.

15.3.1.2   Record reliability

Record reliability is essential, as the records created and used by employees are used in forensic cases.

All records shall be able to stand internal and external scrutiny and be depended on as a full and accurate representation of the transaction(s), activity(ies), or fact(s) to which they provide evidence.

In most cases, records shall be created contemporaneously by the person undertaking the transaction or activity to which the record relates. If not contemporaneous, procedures shall mandate the creation of records immediately afterwards, as soon as is reasonably practicable.

Where records are received from a third party, FCL has no direct control over their reliability. However, they shall:

- be logged into the recordkeeping system on receipt;
- be handled in accordance with contractual requirements, information security classifications, or other instructions accompanying them, as defined in Chapter 12, Section 12.3.14;
- be securely stored in the Document Registry and retained in the Secure Property Store, if appropriate;
- ensure that all movements of the record are tracked, as appropriate, for internal movement or disposition, using the movement sheet;
- have a full evidence trail for the complete time whilst in FCL's possession.

15.3.1.3   Record integrity

Record integrity is essential, as the records created and used by employees are used in forensic cases at various Courts and Tribunals.

Integrity, when dealing with any records, refers to the record being complete and unaltered by any unauthorised process. Authorised processes and procedures can be used for either updating or annotating an existing record, but these will all have an audit trail associated with them.

Record updating or annotation shall only be undertaken by employees who are specifically authorised to perform these tasks in accordance with their user access rights to the record, as defined in Chapter 12, Section 12.6.5.1.

The audit trail of any record shall show, as a minimum, the following:

- the identity of person (or process) making the update or annotation;
- the date of update or annotation;
- the time of annotation; and
- the update or annotation made.

Depending on the system in use, the following may also be recorded:

- IP address of machine used; and
- machine identity of machine used.

15.3.1.4 Record usability

There is no point in having records that are not fit for purpose and useable.

A usable record is defined as one that can be:

- assured to be reliable;
- easily and fully retrieved from the recordkeeping system;
- easily located in the recordkeeping system;
- interpreted by both employees as well as any relevant external parties (e.g. other Forensic Experts, Lawyers, Law Enforcement, or a Court of competent jurisdiction);
- of assured integrity;
- only created by an authorised user;
- presented in a meaningful manner to its intended audience or recipients;
- securely stored in the recordkeeping system;
- shown to be directly related to the transaction(s), activity(ies) or fact(s) to which it provides evidence;
- shown to have all appropriate linkages to other related documents, records, or sequence steps;
- shown to identify the processes and procedures that created it; and
- shown to identify the relevant context (business or forensic case), with appropriate details.

15.4 A records management policy

15.4.1 Why a recordkeeping policy?

FCL is accountable for all of its actions relating to the forensic cases it processes and this is typically evidenced through the existence and maintenance of good recordkeeping allowing traceable fact-based decision taking to be demonstrated.

A policy is the key component of any 'leg' of good corporate governance, including management standards, and it sets the scene for an appropriate direction and cultural requirement within FCL.

ISO 15489 also asserts the importance of corporate control structures by stipulating policy as a requirement for compliance to the standard. 'An organisation seeking to conform to this part of ISO 15489 should establish, document, maintain, and promulgate policies, procedures, and practices for records management to ensure that its business need for evidence, accountability, and information about its activities is met'.

Within FCL, it demonstrates its commitment to undertake recordkeeping in an effective, efficient, diligent, and accountable manner. It shall also be used to:

- show that it applies to all relevant records regardless of format, including electronic records;
- communicate this commitment clearly and effectively to all employees;
- define the recordkeeping responsibilities of all employees;
- demonstrate commitment to comply with recordkeeping standards and guidelines;
- demonstrate top management commitment through the authorisation of the policy;
- identify any legislation which affects recordkeeping requirements within the jurisdiction; and
- promote good recordkeeping practices.

15.4.2 Key components of a recordkeeping policy

In keeping with other policies, a recordkeeping policy is a brief set of statements that provides a broad picture of how FCL creates and manages its records to satisfy legislative, regulatory, business, and relevant interested party's expectations.

Typically, the following headings are used:

- purpose'
- policy statement;

- scope;
- policy context;
- legislation, regulation, and standards;
- recordkeeping systems;
- responsibilities;
- monitoring and review;
- authorisation; and
- policy review.

The Record Management Policy is defined in Appendix 4.

15.5 Defining records management requirements

15.5.1 General

In defining an appropriate Electronic Record Management System (ERMS) for FCL, a project was set up to identify the optimum system to be implemented for the way that FCL actually works.

15.5.2 Objectives

Prior to starting to define requirements for records management in FCL, Top Management had to identify and agree the objectives to be met by the new system. After a number of workshops, Top Management agreed to the objectives, which are defined in Appendix 5.

15.5.3 Choosing a design and implementation methodology

FCL uses the standard System Development Life Cycle (SDLC) process to manage the design and implementation of its records management system. This has the traditional eight steps:

- initiation;
- feasibility;
- analysis;
- design;
- development;
- testing;
- implementation; and
- postimplementation review.

15.5.3.1 Initiation

Top Management supported the project and were the project sponsors appointing an experienced project manager to oversee the project. A team of subject matter experts (SMEs) was assembled to evaluate the feasibility of the project.

Resources throughout FCL for undertaking the project were identified and protected to ensure that they were available for the project. This was assisted by using a 'responsibilities chart' clearly showing roles, boundaries, timescales, budgets, and targets.

15.5.3.2 Feasibility study

The team carried out preliminary investigations to produce a business case for the implementation of an appropriate records management system. Information was collected using the following methods:

- competitive evaluation;
- examination of documentation;
- interviews;
- observation;
- sampling; and
- workshops.

In order to determine FCL's:

- business drivers;
- contractual drivers;
- critical success factors (CSFs);
- legislative drivers;
- political drivers;
- regulatory drivers;
- requirements to meet good practice; and
- specific roles and functions.

and define the ideal requirements for a suitable record management system. This was compared and contrasted against the existing records management system and the gaps and weaknesses identified. The business case was based on these findings, resource requirements, and associated costings.

The business case was presented to Top Management for approval based on the business case. The template for a business case is defined in Appendix 6. The outline of the ERMS project is defined in Appendix 7.

15.5.3.3 Business analysis

Once the project has been approved, it was essential to determine the detailed requirements for each business process or function to determine the information flows within and between different business functions. It was essential that FCL was evaluated as a whole entity rather than on a department by department basis. Experience shows that often a departmental strategy will be ideal for that department alone and not fit into an organisation wide strategy.

The method of collection of this information was the same as the initial feasibility but using specialised questionnaires and forms for the workshops.

It was essential to determine what records were to be kept and why and how they fit into the overall record retention schedule. Only too often, it is discovered that records are held 'just in case' and this is wasteful of resources and in some cases is actually illegal. Retention limits, as well as archiving requirements and purging functions were included in defining records to be retained, and what shall be destroyed.

For each business activity, whether part of forensic case processing or operating the business, each business function, activity, and transaction was examined to establish a hierarchy of them, their interactions, and document the flow of business processes and the transactions which comprise them. Failure to do this leads to the risks of not having appropriate records in place or the risks of failing to have an appropriate ERMS in place based on the drivers established in the Feasibility Stage.

15.5.3.4 Existing records management system evaluation

Once the ideal record management system for FCL had been defined using the results of the stages above, the existing records management system was evaluated to determine how well these requirements are met. This was carried out by evaluating all of the specific requirements of the ideal system against the existing system and producing a 'Gap Analysis'. The Gap Analysis also evaluated the risks of failure of compliance with the ideal requirements.

15.5.3.5 Resolution strategies

The gaps between the existing records management system and the ideal records management system were evaluated, and a number of strategies were considered to address the gap. These included:

- do nothing;
- change existing policies and procedures;
- apply different strategies to physical records and electronic records;
- amend the existing ERMS to cover new requirements;
- convert all physical records to electronic records and purchase a new ERMS;
- convert all physical records to electronic records and amend the existing ERMS to cover new requirements;
- purchase a new ERMS that handles electronic records as required but allows registration of physical records as well and allows all records in FCL to be handled in a consistent manner. This meant that two systems will have to be run in parallel, the ERMS as well as the physical record registry.

Each of the strategies was evaluated. Consideration of the risk, costs, feasibility of implementation in a timely manner, user acceptance, and other criteria was undertaken to finally choose an appropriate strategy.

15.5.3.6   Selection of an ERMS

Once the decision as to which strategy had been taken, products in the marketplace were evaluated for those that meet the specific defined requirements.

This was carried out by the traditional Request for Information (RFI) and Request for Proposal (RFP) process against a large number of suppliers. The criteria used for selecting products are defined in Appendix 8.

A short list was produced and RFPs sent to them. These were evaluated and a selection made.

15.5.3.7   Pilot implementation and testing

The Implementation Stage was carried out with assistance from the Supplier and a 'Pilot Exercise' was set up to see how the system would work, and check that the Supplier's claims are valid.

A variety of different records in both physical and electronic format were loaded into the ERMS for testing purposes. At the same time, a new document registry was built for the pilot and the physical records stored in the Document Registry and retained in the Secure Property Store. As well as the ERMS being implemented a variety of documentation was produced and included:

- policies;
- procedures;
- work instructions;
- forms;
- checklists;
- test packs and expected test results; and
- training.

Once the proof of concept was satisfactorily demonstrated, a strategy was defined to migrate all of the records to the new ERMS.

All interested parties were signatories at all gates in the project, so collective responsibility was assured and that any risks were knowingly accepted. This was formally approved at the CAB, using the Change Management Process defined in Chapter 7, Section 7.4.3.

The project, including the pilot, was run using standard project management processes from the Project Management Institute (PMI).

15.5.3.8   Full implementation and record migration

The full implementation was a phased process, migrating function by function. As a fallback, the new and old systems were run in parallel for a number of months, where possible and practicable. This identified any variations with the full migration to the new system. Full testing was carried out as defined in Chapter 12, Section 12.8.3.

Once full migration was achieved, all electronic records from the old system were retained, according to the record retention schedule, as an archive and retaining their authenticity, reliability, integrity, and usability, in case of need. The archive shall be maintained with relevant hardware, operating system software, and application software retained in case of the need to fallback.

As part of the implementation process, all users of the ERMS shall receive appropriate training, as defined in Section 15.8.1.1 which shall be recorded on all personnel files, as defined in Chapter 4, Section 4.7.5.3. Specific and detailed training shall also be given to the Service Desk as they will be providing first and second-line support.

15.5.3.9   Decommissioning the old ERMS

Where the old ERMS was to be decommissioned no more records were added to it, even though the existing records were accessible. During parallel running, they were both online, but once the new ERMS was fully accepted, the old ERMS was archived, including all relevant hardware and software, so that it could be re-commissioned if needed. The decision to perform disposal and disposition on the archived system shall depend on requirements.

The archived system shall still be able to prove that all records held in it have retained their authenticity, reliability, integrity, and usability, as defined in Section 15.3.1.

15.5.3.10   Postimplementation review

A postimplementation review (PIR) was carried out as a multiple-phase PIR for the ERMS, as it is so critical to the services and products provided by FCL. The initial PIR was carried out after a month of 'go live' and consisted of a questionnaire to all users to obtain subjective qualitative and quantitative feedback about the new ERMS.

Details of the user questionnaire are defined in Appendix 9.

After 3 months, a full system PIR shall be undertaken as there will be enough system records available (including the Service Desk) and user familiarity with the system. The PIR shall be evaluated against the criteria defined in the RFI.

After the PIR has been completed, regular reviews of the ERMS shall be undertaken and reported on at the Management Reviews, as defined in Chapter 4, Section 4.9.3, with trending information. Any shortfall or non-conformity identified shall then be raised and tracked through the CAPA system as defined in Chapter 4, Section 4.10.

15.6 Determining records to be managed by the ERMS

15.6.1 General

One of the most important decisions in records management is to ensure that the correct records are retained. There are two types of record held in FCL:

- forensic case records and
- general business records.

As has been noted above, some records fall into both categories (e.g. financial records relating to case billing).

15.6.2 Forensic case records

Forensic case records to be managed by FCL can be identified by:

- legislative and regulatory requirements;
- accountability requirements for case processing within the jurisdiction;
- good practice;
- existing procedures in place for case processing; and
- the risk of not being able to produce records as part of a forensic case during its life cycle.

In practical terms, this actually means that for any case, including quotations and estimates for cases not processed by FCL, all records from initial contact to case disposition shall be retained in the ERMS.

Forensic case records that are stored on digital media shall have metadata that can be attached to the record. A list of metadata in use in FCL for Microsoft Office Documents and Email is defined in Appendix 10 and Appendix 11, respectively.

There are other packages that can also store metadata and shall be used as required. One example of metadata in another program is the use of Exchangeable Image File (Exif) format. Exif is a standard that specifies the formats for images, sound, and ancillary tags used by digital cameras (including smartphones), scanners, and other hardware handling recorded image and sound files.

The metadata tags defined in the Exif standard cover a broad spectrum of information such as:

- artist (camera owner)*;
- camera settings (e.g. the camera model and make, and information that varies with each image such as orientation (rotation), aperture, shutter speed, focal length, metering mode, and ISO speed information);
- copyright information;
- date and time a picture was taken*;
- descriptions (of the image); and
- thumbnail preview of the image on the camera's LCD screen, in file managers, or in photo manipulation software.

Note 1

The list above is not complete, for a full description of Exif data in use is in the current standard V2.32 (May 2019).

Note 2

Those items marked with an '*' are only accurate if the camera has had these details set, otherwise their default is 'null'.

Note 3

There are also specifications for .jpeg files and .wav files.

Note 4

Another common form of metadata is XMP in Adobe products.

Care shall be exercised when using Exif data or relying on it for the following reasons:

- Exif does not store time zone-related information with the image, resulting in time recorded for the image being made of dubious provenance;
- Exif is not a maintained standard;
- Exif is very often used in images created by scanners, but the standard makes no provisions for any scanner-specific information;
- Exif only specifies a format for .tiff and .jpeg files;
- Exif standard has no provision for video files;
- Exif uses file offset pointers that can become easily corrupted; and
- Some manufacturers use camera settings not defined in the Exif standard.

It is for the reasons above that FCL shall enter metadata manually with such images or audio files, treating them as paper records in the ERMS.

Paper records shall have their metadata entered with an image of the record into the ERMS, the original record being deposited in the document registry in the secure store.

A list of some of the forensic case records stored by FCL is defined in Appendix 12.

15.6.3 General business records

The FCL approach to physical records is to scan all physical records, retaining originals where necessary in the Document Registry and they will be retained in the Secure Property Store. Scanned records shall then be registered in the ERMS and copied to the relevant case file or general business file.

Having scanned and digitised all physical records, linked them to the ERMS, they shall be easily located and accessed.

General business records to be retained shall depend on a variety of factors. As this book is about digital forensics, these records have been ignored, and what is included in FCL shall be a matter of choice for the Top Management. However, they will be subject to many of the requirements and controls below for forensic case processing records.

15.6.4 Document retention

Business records and forensic case records shall be retained for set periods of time according to the requirements defined a variety of sources. Record retention within FCL shall:

- meet current legislative and regulatory requirements, though consideration of changes to legislation and regulation that may become effective need to be considered during the life cycle of a forensic case;
- meet current and future needs of all interested parties for all forensic cases. This shall include all of the interests of interested parties for a forensic case. This can include Law Enforcement, Lawyers, the Courts, other Forensic Experts, etc.;
- meet current and future internal business needs for forensic case processing. This shall include decisions and activities relating to forensic case processing as part of FCL's corporate memory in case of future need. As well as maintaining FCL's corporate memory it shall allow traceability, transparency, and accountability to be assured, whilst disposing of records when they are no longer required through an authorised process, as defined in Chapter 12, Section 12.3.14.10.3. This process shall also ensure that the record's reliability and authenticity can be assured by future users, even on changes of technology, so long as the record transfer has been carried out according to FCL record transfer procedures; and
- consider the risk of not being able to produce records as part of a forensic case during its life cycle.

In practical terms, this actually means that for any forensic case, including quotations and estimates for cases not processed by FCL, all records from initial contact to case disposition shall be retained in the ERMS.

Forensic case disposition can be either transferred from FCL to a third party authorised to receive them or secure destruction at the end of the relevant retention time period for the case type. The Record Retention Policy is defined in Chapter 4, Appendix 26.

15.7 Using metadata in FCL

Recordkeeping metadata can be defined as data describing the context, content, and structure of records and their management over their complete lifecycle. In essence, metadata facilitates the record management process by giving context to the content of the record and facilitates record management according to good recordkeeping principles.

Depending on the record type and jurisdiction, there may be legislative or other requirements for the application and use of metadata.

Using metadata considerably facilitates the accessibility to, and management of, records. It enables records to be found whenever they are needed by providing different search methods for the efficient location of relevant records, and it allows tight control to be exercised over access to confidential and sensitive information.

The use of metadata to control access to information is extremely important, especially where there are confidentiality or privacy implications. This shall include all forensic case records as well as internal administrative records such as HR records.

The audit trail provided by metadata can be crucial in giving assurances about a record's authenticity by authoritatively demonstrating who created the record, when it was accessed, modified, or when it is to be disposed of. The use of metadata shall also help to ensure that records are retained for their appropriate retention period before any disposal action can be undertaken.

The systematic and consistent application of metadata shall be used in FCL to assist in the recordkeeping process and to ensure that FCL's records can be relied upon to support all of their operations relating to forensic case processing and internal operations.

15.7.1 The benefits of creating and using metadata

It is essential that records that have been captured into FCL's ERMS can be efficiently retrieved whenever needed. Furthermore, records require sufficient contextual and descriptive metadata to ensure they are meaningful and can be properly managed over time.

Accordingly, the creation and use metadata shall provide the following benefits:

- enabling access to confidential records, or those subject to privacy requirements, to be effectively controlled by assigning relevant access/security levels at the time of creation and/or registration into the ERMS;
- enabling records required for a specific forensic case or investigation to be readily identified;
- enabling the efficient searching for records by utilising various search criteria including search by title, keywords, dates, and location;
- ensuring that records are retained for their minimum retention period;
- facilitating compliance with legislative, regulatory, contractual, business, and good practice requirements;
- facilitating efficient and timely disposition of records;
- facilitating the migration of records through successive upgrades of hardware and software and provides evidence of these activities;
- providing audit trails that shows evidence of who has accessed a record and when;
- providing evidence of disposition actions; and
- supporting accountability, auditing processes, and transparency of processes relating to record use within FCL.

From the benefits above, it is easy to see why metadata for recordkeeping purposes shall be an integral component of records management within FCL.

There are two main standards for metadata, these are:

- Dublin Core Data Initiative (DCMI), since adopted by ISO as ISO 15386. Information and documentation—The Dublin Core Metadata Element Set. There are 15 core elements of the Dublin Core Metadata Standard, and these are defined in Appendix 13;
- National Archives of Australia Metadata Standard, which captures up to 25 different elements, and these are defined in Appendix 14.

15.7.2 Responsibilities

The general roles and responsibilities for recordkeeping in FCL are defined in the Records Management Policy, defined in Appendix 4.

Generic requirements are defined in Appendix 15 with specific requirements being defined in Chapter 18 in specific job descriptions.

15.7.3 Recordkeeping metadata needed

Note

Different ERMSs may contain, use, and process different metadata, and this is a generic approach for both the ERMS and office applications. Readers will need to tailor this section to their own specific requirements and the ERMS is use.

15.7.3.1 Microsoft office suite

All of FCL case processing and business processes are underpinned by the Microsoft Office Suite. Using Microsoft Office Suite shall require the input of metadata in the following packages, at least:

- Access;
- Excel;
- PowerPoint; and
- Word.

Outlook (email) has a different set of rules and the relevant metadata for email shall be used.

All employees shall comply with the requirement to create minimum metadata for the records they create using Microsoft Office applications.

The automatically entered metadata, which is shown under 'Properties' in each of the Microsoft Office application suite, includes, but is not limited to:

- size;
- pages;
- words;
- total editing time;
- template;
- company (if set up when Office installed);
- last modified;
- created;
- last printed;
- author;
- last modified by; and
- open file location.

Whilst documents are created in Microsoft Office, some of the metadata is automatically created; however, this shall be checked to ensure that it is correct, it will also need input for such fields as 'keywords', etc.

Other metadata shall be manually entered under 'Properties'. This includes the:

- title;
- tags (keywords);
- comments;
- status;
- category;
- subject;
- hyperlink base; and
- manager.

15.7.3.2   Email

Corporate email transmissions are official FCL records within the meaning of the law and are therefore subject to the same recordkeeping requirements as records created or registered as part of forensic case processing or everyday business operations.

As with any record, all email messages, together with any attachments, shall be included in ERMS system, and securely retained according to relevant legislative, regulatory, contractual, and business requirements. Without recordkeeping metadata, email messages cannot be accepted as authentic and reliable evidence of the business activity it purports to support.

It is essential that associated metadata shall be captured and stored with each email record. Without this metadata, the context, meaning, and value of the email as an authentic record are considerably devalued.

In many court cases, email evidence, and its authenticity, is frequently challenged. In FCL, using the ERMS, it shall be possible to prove:

* that an email message was sent through a certain server(s);
* the date and time it was sent to the recipient;
* the date and time it was delivered to the recipient; and
* the date and time it was read by the recipient.

Automatically generated metadata such as the sender, recipient, date, and time is tagged to email transmissions. To facilitate the correct classification of the email record, employees shall always include a title in the subject heading.

15.7.3.3   Hard copy records on-site

There are a number of occasions when hard copy records are either created or received by employees. These shall be tracked like electronic records. Within FCL, all hard copy records shall be assigned a record number.

Metadata is then recorded against the record in the ERMS against the record number.

15.7.3.4   Hard copy records sent off-site

Records of hard copy records that are sent off-site shall also be maintained (e.g. off-site secure archive stores). Whilst it is not possible to attach metadata to hard copy records in the same way as it is with electronic records, it is possible to assign them in the ERMS.

The data used in the ERMS within FCL is defined in Appendix 16.

15.7.3.5   Retaining metadata

Recordkeeping metadata is essentially a record in itself and, as such, shall be treated as a record. Where electronic records are created (e.g. Microsoft Word), then the record's metadata is integral to the record itself and both are treated as one record. In some cases, the metadata for a record is retained separately from the record (e.g. a paper record where the record-keeping metadata has been entered into the ERMS).

In general, most recordkeeping metadata associated with a record shall be retained for at least as long as the retention period of the record to which it relates. In some cases, the recordkeeping metadata shall be retained for a longer retention period.

Retaining some recordkeeping metadata elements past the life of a record to which they are linked is an integral part of demonstrating accountability and transparency. It shall provide, for example, auditable evidence of FCL's record disposal authority and actions.

FCL shall retain the following in the ERMS after disposal of any record:

* record number;
* record title;
* date created;
* date of disposal;
* method of disposal;
* disposal authority; and
* event log of the record.

The retention of this metadata shall provide evidence about how records have been used in FCL and managed over time by providing an audit trail of all actions undertaken on the records and their associated metadata.

15.8 Record management procedures

Within FCL, the ERMS manages general business records as well as dictating how a forensic case progresses. As the ERMS was built to ensure that forensic cases were properly managed, as well as manage business records, this shall be the case. Within the life cycle of a record, there are a number of phases, and each is covered below:

15.8.1 Common processes

There are a number of common processes and procedures for general business records and forensic case processing, and these are covered below:

15.8.1.1 Training

All employees shall undergo appropriate training for their job role, including the use of the ERMS.

Training records shall be maintained in individual personnel files, as defined in Chapter 4, Section 4.7.5.3.

All training shall be carried out in accordance with the procedures in Chapter 4, Section 4.7.3.

Needs for training shall be identified during the Training Needs Analysis (TNA) process at the annual appraisal process as defined in Chapter 18, Section 18.2.2.

All employees shall be trained to understand their roles and responsibilities for records management responsibilities for records management are defined in Section 15.7.2 and defined in Appendix 4.

15.8.1.2 General

When records are stored in the ERMS, they shall always be stored on media where their reliability, usability, authenticity, and preservation for the duration of the forensic case life cycle are assured. Once they have been archived, they shall still need to retain these properties.

All electronic records shall be backed up according to the backup procedures in place, as defined in Chapter 7, Section 7.7.4. This includes long-term archiving. Physical records shall always be retained in fireproof safes and never removed after they have been scanned, unless for a specific reason, otherwise electronic scanned images shall be used.

Where electronic records are to be migrated from one ERMS to another, the process defined in Section 15.5.3.8 shall be followed to ensure that the migration is complete and of assured integrity. As a backup, FCL shall always retain the hardware, software, manuals, data, backups, and other components of the old ERMS so that it can be accessed if needed. As part of this process, a regular schedule of testing that the past ERMSs can actually be restored with their records accessed shall be undertaken.

Where physical and electronic records are transferred to an authorised third party, they shall be subject to the checking of the authorisation and a full log of records transferred on the appropriate movement sheet and Property Log as defined in Chapter 9, Appendix 13. Physical records shall be transferred in their 'native' format and electronic records in whatever format that the third party requires, assuming FCL has the technology to provide the required format. If the required format is not currently possible, either FCL shall need to obtain the necessary technology to produce the required format or agree an alternative format that they can produce.

15.8.1.3 Record capture

Record capture is the process of entering records into the ERMS to establish the relationship between the record and its constituent parts (i.e. its context, the record creator), and any linkages to other records and/or documents.

This process shall use metadata either embedded into the record itself, or metadata added into the ERMS and permanently associated with the record.

All forensic case processing records in the ERMS shall be linked by the common forensic case number that is uniquely assigned to each case, whether it is completed or not. Details of the forensic case numbering system that is used in FCL are defined in Chapter 9, Section 9.7.1. Exhibit numbering is defined in Chapter 8, Section 8.6.10.

Access rights and security settings for forensic cases shall be set on a per case basis and shall be set up at the point of record capture in the ERMS. General business record access control shall be dependent on job roles.

At the same time as the record capture process is undertaken, default values or settings shall be entered (e.g. disposition, retention periods, etc.).

General business records can come in many forms, physical and electronic. Where information that comprises a record is captured (or copied, converted, or moved) from an external source to the ERMS, there is the potential of information loss.

Information loss refers to the record in the ERMS not exactly matching the original source document. This can be due to a number of reasons, including but not limited to:

- human error in the scanning or copying processing that results in information loss;
- loss of metadata on conversion between different application formats;
- physical destruction of the original physical record, which may be of critical importance (e.g. latent prints, paper type, type impressions from a typewriter, etc.); or
- resolution loss on scanning where legibility may be lost.

Careful consideration shall be made of the possible loss of information, especially in forensic case processing, which is why original physical records are all stored for the duration of the forensic case life cycle in the Document Registry and retained in the Secure Property Store. The decision to retain original business records is a matter for the relevant business manager that owns them to determine, typically based on experience and consideration of the cost of storage matched against the cost of failure to have the original document. In some cases, originals shall be retained no matter what (e.g. legal contracts).

When creating or importing documents into the ERMS, their authenticity, integrity, and reliability for later scrutiny are of paramount importance as is their usability, as defined in Section 15.3.1. Whilst this is under FCL's control for records it creates, it has little control over those that are produced by a third party, so it is essential that checks are carried out to ensure they have not been tampered with and that the originator is verifiable. The level of checking for documents from third parties shall depend on their business criticality. In the case of exhibits, these shall all be accompanied by a movement sheet to demonstrate the chain of custody.

Where documents are converted from one format to another, it is essential to ensure that all metadata is also captured so the context of the captured record is properly understood.

Where records are scanned, appropriate detailed work instructions shall be in place to handle the preparation of documents for scanning. These cover:

- physical examination of documents prior to scanning and undertaking any necessary risk assessment and evaluation of possible scanning problems;
- oversized documents that may need to be photo-reduced or have multiple copies made of parts of them and then scan the constituent composite parts;
- removal of binding mechanisms (e.g. comb binding, staples, etc.);
- procedures for dealing with attachments (e.g. post it notes) affixed to the document;
- dealing with photocopies, rather than original documents, including their marking as such;
- integrity of multi-page documents to overcome possible human error in the scanning process (e.g. missing a page due to paper misfeed that is not immediately noticed);
- checking the integrity of the output against the original source document;
- dealing with faint or low-resolution source material;
- dealing with delicate documents (e.g. the need to photocopy first, in case of damage by the scanning process, use of document wallets, etc.);
- the scanner type to be used (e.g. single sheet, batch, colour, or black and white);
- output format (e.g. single or double sided and paper size). All forensic case processing notes for use in the client virtual case file shall be scanned as single sided. This allows the 'back of the previous page' to be used for notes directly related to the right-hand page. This facilitates the 'page turning' syndrome where information may be missed or it causes difficulty in page turning;
- the use of photographic capture as opposed to scanning;
- requirements for scanning resolution for different types of document;
- postscanning image enhancement, in case it affects the original document, in which case the original shall be retained;
- protection of source documents (e.g. the content of some fax paper may deteriorate over time);
- regular validation of the scanning process (a test pack of documents of different types shall be used and the validation process carried out with records of the results retained in the similar way that forensic tools are validated as defined in Chapter 7, Section 7.5.5. The Records Manager shall undertake this task with other relevant employees, as required; and
- data extraction from documents using processes such as optical character recognition (OCR), intelligent character recognition (ICR), optical mark reading (OMR), bar codes, QR Codes or direct manual keyboard entry, and the quality of the results. Extreme care shall be exercised if used for forensic case processing, as manipulation may be regarded as 'tampering' with the evidence.

ERMS, record registration shall be carried out at the same time as record capture. Registration is the formal recognition of record capture into the ERMS. At the point of registration, a known trusted time source shall be used for recording the identity of a document, using its hash value to prove that:

- a file existed on a defined date & time; and
- the file was not altered since the time it was stamped.

The procedures for this are defined in Chapter 9, Section 9.12.

15.8.1.4 Indexing

Indexing is a vital part of record management as it allows for easy retrieval of a record or series of records. If indexing information is corrupted or unavailable for any reason, the record may also be unavailable or only be found after additional manual searching.

Business records are automatically indexed, whereas all forensic case file information shall be manually indexed by the relevant Forensic Analyst(s) processing the case. As the records for a forensic case are all held in the client virtual case file, the use of manual indexing is not an overly onerous task.

All changes to the indexes are subject to audit for their lifetime clearly showing a 'before and after image'. Index databases often require the index to be rebuilt to improve performance, as is common with all database systems, and the manufacturer's recommendations shall be followed.

15.8.1.5 Records stored in FCL

FCL two general types of records relating to forensic casework. Each is handled differently, but both are captured and registered in the ERMS. The two types are:

- physical records; and
- electronic records.

15.8.1.5.1 Physical records

A number of records relating to forensic cases are created or received as physical records. These may be:

- audio or video recordings (e.g. Dictaphone records, cassettes, answer phone tapes, non-digital video);
- microfiche;
- paper records; and
- photographs.

FCL has decided that all physical records are to be converted to an electronic form for entry into the ERMS, if possible, with the original physical records being placed into the Document Registry and retained in the Secure Property Store, where appropriate.

Once a physical record has been converted into an electronic one, the appropriate metadata shall be associated with it when it is captured into the ERMS.

Only electronic copies of the records shall be used in any forensic case unless there is a need to revert to original source material. In any case, a record of all accesses to any original physical record and a Movement Form shall be filled in for any movements to or from the Document Registry.

15.8.1.5.2 Electronic records

Electronic records often have the ability to associate metadata with them within the record, where this is not possible, the relevant metadata shall be associated with the record in the ERMS, as defined in Section 15.7.

15.8.1.6 Record classification

For all forensic cases, the records are classified as 'Vital Records'. General business records are normally classified according to the classification system in Appendix 17.

The classification of all forensic case records as 'Vital Records' shall be a conscious decision as all forensic cases are of a similar type.

All records entered into the ERMS shall have a consistent naming standard as defined in Chapter 4, Appendix 43, and all completed forms and records shall contain a unique forensic case reference number, as defined in Chapter 9, Section 9.7.1.

However, records for a case shall be classified for sensitivity and confidentiality requirements as defined in Chapter 5, Section 5.5.6.6. This classification process shall set the requirements for information security for the case.

15.8.1.7 Document control

As well as using the naming conventions, all records created shall be subject to document and version control. Using a rigid document and version control process shall allow recovery to any version of a document on a defined day by using version control procedures as defined in Chapter 4, Section 4.7.5.

15.8.1.8 Secure storage

Secure storage shall be required for physical as well as electronic records.

15.8.1.8.1 Physical record storage

All physical records shall be stored in the Document Registry in the Secure Property Store and recorded in the ERMS with associated metadata. The registry shall be managed by the Record Registrar, who shall be accountable and responsible for the safeguarding of all physical forensic case records.

The Record Registrar shall be responsible for ensuring that all physical records are captured and registered into the ERMS against the appropriate forensic case virtual case file, as defined in Chapter 9, Section 9.7.6. Once captured, the physical record shall be copied into appropriate electronic format and transferred to the appropriate Forensic Analyst for the case. The transfer shall be recorded in the ERMS and the original record securely stored.

Any transfer of the original physical record shall be authorised and the transfer recorded in the ERMS according to the records transfer procedure using the Movement Form.

15.8.1.8.2 Electronic record storage

All electronic records shall be stored in the ERMS with associated metadata. Where these have been received from a third party, they will typically require metadata to be associated with them prior to storage in the ERMS.

Where electronic records are created in FCL, they shall all have metadata added to them, where possible, so that it is embedded in the document. If this is not possible, then appropriate metadata shall be associated with the record in the ERMS.

Any transfer of the electronic record shall be authorised and the transfer recorded in the ERMS according to the records transfer procedure.

Note 1

The server(s) and media—including archival and backup drives—shall also be physically secured to the appropriate level as defined by its classification as defined in Chapter 12, Section 12.4 and optionally the risk management process as defined in Chapter 5.

Note 2

Electronic records shall be compressed to save space, either for storage or transmission.

Note 3

Encryption shall be used in FCL for confidentiality, integrity, and non-repudiation purposes.

15.8.1.9 Access to records

Access to all records shall be according to the Access Control Policy in force as defined in Chapter 4, Appendix 21. This gives group access rights as well as specific access rights per forensic case. In some cases, these shall also be confirmed in the metadata of the records in the ERMS.

In general terms, the only employees access a forensic case shall be as follows:

- write access—the Forensic Analyst(s) actively working on the case; and

- read access—the Forensic Analyst(s) who have oversight of the case (e.g. Case Managers) or those that need read access for quality assurance purposes (e.g. Quality Assurance Manager, Audit Manager). Where a client requires access to a live case that is in the ERMS, they may be granted temporary 'read only' access under controlled conditions. Visitors shall have their access controlled and monitored according to the procedures in defined in Chapter 12, Section 12.4.2. All access rights shall be regularly reviewed to ensure that authorisation is appropriate according to business need as defined in Chapter 12, Section 12.4.6 for physical security and Chapter 12, Section 12.6.2 for logical access. Records of all authorities for access shall be recorded in the Service Desk system as defined in Chapter 12, Sections 12.6.1 and 12.6.2.

All output (e.g. printouts or output on magnetic or digital media) shall be securely disposed of according to the classification of the record as defined in Chapter 12, Section 12.3.14.10.

15.8.1.10   Output

Output from the ERMS shall meet the requirements for authenticity, integrity, reliability, and usability as defined in Section 15.3.1. In addition to this, a known trusted time source shall be for recording the identity of a document, using its hash value to prove that:

- a file existed on a defined date and time; and
- the file was not altered since the time it was time stamped.

The procedures for this are defined in Chapter 9, Section 9.12.

The procedures for ensuring that all clocks in information processing equipment shall be accurately set are defined in Chapter 7, Section 7.7.5.

Output shall also meet the rules of evidence for the jurisdiction.

Output formats will vary. Obviously scanned images shall be reproduced as a facsimile image, supported by the original, where appropriate. The output from MARS has been defined by FCL to suit its purposes for reporting, as defined in Chapter 10, Sections 10.6–10.8.

15.8.1.11   Transmission

Records, and any documents transmitted to and from FCL, shall be subject to the data handling rules depending on the classification of the record or document, as defined in Chapter 12, Sections 12.3.12 and 12.3.14.9.

Digital signatures shall be used by all Forensic Analysts.

For forensic case processing, secure transmission methods shall be agreed as part of the proposal process, as defined in Chapter 6, Sections 6.6.2.3 and 6.6.2.4. Remote secure connections to and from FCL are covered in Chapter 7, Section 7.7.3.

Where a physical exhibit is being transmitted, the chain of custody shall be maintained using the exhibit movement forms.

15.8.1.12   Retention

Record and document retention shall be defined by legislative, regulatory, good practice, and client contractual requirements. The record retention schedule is defined in Chapter 4, Appendix 26.

15.8.1.13   Record review

On an annual basis, or on influencing change, the Record Manager shall review all records in the ERMS with their owners (typically the relevant Forensic Analyst for a forensic case and relevant business unit managers) to determine whether the records should be considered for disposition.

Record reviews shall be undertaken to ensure that records in primary storage are not held there for longer than necessary. Primary storage is an expensive medium to manage, both in terms of space requirements and dedicated employees to manage both physical and electronic records.

Where appropriate, records that do not need to remain in primary storage shall be considered for transfer to archive storage.

Where transfer to archive storage is authorised, transfer shall be undertaken using the procedures for transfer of records.

Record reviews shall always be carried out to ensure compliance with relevant legislation.

15.8.1.14   Disposal and disposition

Record disposition, whether for physical or electronic records shall only be carried out as a controlled and authorised process, but. This may be dictated by the client's policies and procedures. Disposition requests shall be carefully evaluated prior to authority being granted for one of the following disposition actions:

- immediate physical destruction of the record (this shall include electronic destruction processes such as secure overwriting and deletion of a record), as defined in Chapter 12, Section 12.3.14.10;
- migration from one internal system to another;
- transfer of records to another employee; or
- transfer of records to an authorised third party.

The record disposition authorisation form is defined in Appendix 18.

Note

Record disposition (typically disposal or transfer) may also be the result of an annual review of records held.

15.8.1.15   Audit trails and tracking

All actions taken on any forensic case shall have an audit trail associated with the action, clearly showing:

- who did what;
- when;
- where it was carried out;
- why; and
- how it was done.

This process is defined in Section 15.3.1.3.

The audit trail shall be either a secure audit trail within a computer system (e.g. operating system audit trails, application system audit trails, the ERMS audit trail, specialised tool audit trails) or it can be the use of the physical movement and the Property Log.

Where a record is booked out to an authorised recipient, it shall have actions associated with it for completion recorded in the ERMS as a form of workflow. This facilitates ensuring that required actions have been carried out in the timescale proscribed in the ERMS by the employee to whom the record is assigned. Reporting shall be carried out for all actions past their 'due by date' as well as providing reporting on the efficiency of actions and meeting TRTs agreed with the client, as defined in Chapter 6, Section 6.6 at the proposal stage and in Chapter 9, Section 9.5.4 if they need to be adjusted.

Regular auditing and monitoring of all record movements and accesses shall be undertaken. These shall primarily be internal (First Party) audits, as defined in Chapter 4, Section 4.9.2.

In addition to auditing, customer satisfaction surveys shall be undertaken at the end of each forensic case. The customer satisfaction survey template is defined in Chapter 6, Appendix 17.

Any complaints raised against FCL for its forensic case processing shall be investigated. Procedures for this are defined in Chapter 6, Section 6.14.

Any complaints and all feedback received shall be reviewed at the regular Management Review meetings, as defined in Chapter 4, Section 4.9.3.

The process for internal auditing is defined in Chapter 4, Section 4.9.3. For auditing FCL Record Management System, the following areas of internal audit shall include, but not be limited to:

- records inventory;
- creation and receipt of records;
- storage of records;
- disposition of records;
- electronic records;
- security and confidentiality of records;

- reliability of records;
- records management policy; and
- records management training.

15.8.1.16 Backup

Backup of the ERMS is covered in Chapter 7, Section 7.7.4.

15.8.1.17 Business continuity

Business continuity is covered in Chapter 13.

15.8.1.18 ERMS maintenance

Maintenance of all hardware and software is covered in Chapter 7, Section 7.5.4.

15.8.1.19 Change management

Change Management Procedures for managing changes to the ERMS and documents are defined in Chapter 7, Section 7.4.3.

15.8.1.20 Securely managing the ERMS

The risks to the ERMS are defined in Chapter 5.
  Procedures for managing the IT infrastructure which underpins the ERMS are defined in Chapter 7.
  Secure working procedures are defined in Chapter 12.

15.8.1.21 Third parties

The use of third parties for any part of processing any document or record (business or forensic case file) is defined in Chapter 14.

15.8.2 Forensic case processing

As well as meeting the general requirements identified in Section 15.8.1 above, the creation of a client virtual case file is different from normal business records as it has its own creation and naming processes, as defined below.

15.8.2.1 Case creation

The first step in records management is the creation of a record within the ERMS. This process is as follows (Fig. 15.2):

1. A requirement for a new case is identified. This could be the result of any type of communication from a prospective client.
2. The recipient of the communication shall contact the Records Manager with details of the communication.
3. If the communication has any hard copy records associated with it (e.g. a letter), they shall be sent to the Records Manager, who will scan them and add to the virtual case file, as defined in Chapter 9, Section 9.7.6 and the structure defined in Chapter 9, Appendix 18. The original physical record shall be added to the case file in the document registry.
4. The Records Manager shall assign a case number to the incoming communication and advises the Requestor of the case number.
5. All relevant metadata shall be added, whether by the Records Manager or the Forensic Analyst;
6. The Records Manager shall assign access rights to the virtual case file to the Requestor as read/write and their Manager as read-only. Other employees shall be granted access to the virtual case file according to the Access Control Policy.
7. The new case shall be automatically backed up as part of the overnight backup process, as defined in Chapter 7, Section 7.7.4.
8. All access to the virtual case file shall be written to the audit trail. The new case form, used for setting up a new virtual case file is defined in Chapter 8, Appendix 4.

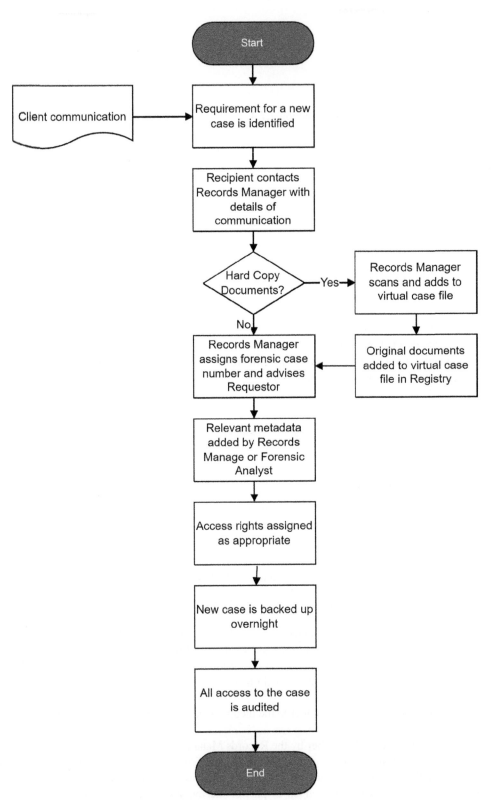

FIG. 15.2   Case creation.

15.8.2.2 *Adding records to the virtual case file*

Once the virtual case file has been set up, the relevant Forensic Analyst(s) shall add records to the case for the duration of the case life cycle.

1. If the communication has any hard copy records associated with it (e.g. a letter, filled-in form, pocket-book records, etc.), they shall be sent to the Records Manager, who will scan them and add to the virtual case file. The original physical record shall be added to the case file in the Document Registry held in the Secure Property Store.
2. If electronic records are created, then these shall be added to the relevant virtual case file. The ERMS shall ensure that all documents created have appropriate metadata added to them as part of the record creation.
3. All document naming is as defined in the records control procedure, as defined in Chapter 4, Section 4.7.5. This ensures that for any document the previous version is available.
4. All access to the virtual case file shall be written to the audit trail.

15.8.3 Record disposition

This has been covered in Section 15.6.2.

15.9 Business continuity

FCL has a business continuity plan in place that also addresses the requirements of recordkeeping. This is defined in Chapter 13 and is based on ISO 22301.

FCL shall undertake a specific risk assessment to determine the effects of the loss of the ERMS. How to undertake a risk assessment is defined in Chapter 5.

A Business Impact Analysis (BIA) shall be undertaken to determine the Recovery Time Objectives (RTOs) and Maximum Tolerable Periods of Disruption (MTPoDs), as defined in Chapter 13, Section 13.4.2 and Chapter 13, Appendix 4.

The results of the risk assessment shall be used to create a Statement of Applicability (SoA) for ISO/IEC 27001, as defined in Chapter 12, Appendix 19. This shall indicate the controls to be implemented to reduce the risk of a disruptive event occurring. Additionally, the incident management process, as defined in Chapter 7, Section 7.4.1 shall ensure that timely action is taken on discovery of any disruptive event which may require the invocation of the BCP.

There may be a number of specific facilities needed over and above the standard BCP for records management. These include the requirements for physical record recovery defined in Appendix 19 and Appendix 20.

Appendix 1—MOReq2010 requirements

A MoReq2010 Compliant Records System (MCRS) must implement the functionality of:

- a user and group service;
- a role service;
- a classification service;
- a record service;
- a metadata service;
- a disposal scheduling service;
- a disposal holding service;
- a searching and reporting service; and
- an export service.

  Other non-functional requirements include:

- performance;
- scalability;
- manageability;
- portability;
- security;

- privacy;
- usability;
- accessibility;
- availability;
- reliability;
- recoverability;
- maintainability;
- supported;
- warranted; and
- compliance.

Appendix 2—Mapping of ISO 15489 part 1 to FCL procedures

ISO 15489: 1 clause	Control	IMS procedure
4	Principles for managing records	Chapter 4, Section 4.7.5 Section 15.2.2 and Appendix 5
5	Records and records systems	
5.1	General	Chapter 4, Section 4.7.5 Sections 15.6 and 15.5.1
5.2	Records	Section 15.3
5.2.1	General	Section 15.3.1
5.2.2	Characteristics of authoritative records	Section 15.3
5.2.3	Metadata for records	Section 15.7 and Appendices 10, 11, 13, 14, and 16
5.3	Records systems	Sections 15.5 and 15.8
5.3.1	General	Section 15.5
5.3.2	Characteristics of records systems	Section 15.3
6	Policies and responsibilities	
6.1	General	The Integrated Management System (IMS) and the Electronic Records Management System (ERMS)
6.2	Policies	Sections 15.4 and 15.7.2 and Appendices 4, 15, and 18
6.3	Responsibilities	Section 15.8 Appendix 15 Appendix 18 Various job descriptions in Chapter 18
6.4	Monitoring and evaluation	Chapter 4, Section 4.9.1 Section 15.8.1.13 Chapter 16.6.2.1
6.5	Competence and training	Chapter 4, Section 4.7.3 Section 15.8.1.1
7	Appraisal	
7.1	General	Section 15.8.1.2
7.2	Scope of appraisal	
7.3	Understanding the business	Section 15.5
7.4	Determining records requirements	Section 15.5

ISO 15489: 1 clause	Control	IMS procedure
7.5	Implementing records requirements	Section 15.8
8	Records controls	15.8.1.13
8.1	General	Section 15.8.1.7
8.2	Metadata schemas for records	Section 15.7
8.3	Business classification schemes	Section 15.8.1.6
8.4	Access and permissions rules	Chapter 12, Section 12.6 Section 15.8.1.9
8.5	Disposition authorities	Chapter 4, Appendix 26 Chapter 12, Section 12. 3.14.10 Section 15.6.4 Section 15.8.1.2 Section 15.8.1.4 Section 15.8.1.14 Appendix 18
9	Processes for creating, capturing and managing records	
9.1	General	Chapter 10, Sections 10.3, 10.4, and 10.5 Sections 15.5, 15.6, and 15.8, Section 15.8.1.2
9.2	Creating records	Section 15.8.1.3
9.3	Capturing records	Section 15.8.1.3
9.4	Records classification and indexing	Chapter 5, Appendix 16 Chapter 12, Section 12.3.14.6 Section 15.6 Section 15.8.1.4 Section 15.8.1.6
9.5	Access control	Sections 15.8.1.7 and 15.8.1.9
9.6	Storing records	Section 15.8.1.8
9.7	Use and reuse	Not used in FCL
9.8	Migrating and converting records	Chapter 4, Appendix 41 Chapter 8, Section 8.6.10 Chapter 10, Section 10.4.1.1
9.9	Disposition	Chapter 4, Appendix 26 Chapter 12, Section 12.3.14.10 Section 15.6.4 Section 15.8.1.2 Section 15.8.1.4 Section 15.8.1.14 Appendix 18

Appendix 3—Types of legislation and regulation that will affect recordkeeping

The list below gives subject areas and is the checklist used to identify specific legislation or regulation in the jurisdiction that may affect recordkeeping. It is not meant to be a complete list.

- access to information;
- business focussed legislation;
- computer use and misuse;

- copyright, designs and patents;
- criminal;
- data protection;
- defence and homeland security;
- emergency planning and business resumption;
- evidence;
- financial information;
- health and medical information;
- health and safety;
- human resources;
- human rights;
- identity theft and identity protection;
- information management;
- information security;
- insurance;
- privacy; and
- workplace and workforce.

Appendix 4—Record management policy

The Record Management Policy is reproduced below. It has been modified to make it jurisdiction neutral.

Purpose

The purpose of this policy is to establish a framework for the creation and management of records. FCL is committed to establishing and maintaining recordkeeping processes and supporting procedures that meet, or exceed, its business needs, accountability requirements, and relevant interested party's expectations.

Policy statement

Records are an organisation's 'corporate memory', and as such are a vital asset for ongoing operations, providing valuable evidence of forensic case processing and business transactions.

FCL recognises its legislative, regulatory, contractual, and internal business requirements and is committed to the principles and practices set out in the ISO 15489 (Information and documentation—Records management). FCL is also committed to implementing the best available recordkeeping processes and procedures, with supporting systems, to ensure the creation, maintenance, and protection of accurate and reliable records. All recordkeeping activities shall comply with this policy and its supporting procedures.

Scope

This policy applies to all employees and:

- all aspects of FCL's operations;
- all records created during forensic case processing and any business transactions. This shall include any computer applications and operating systems used to create records including, but not limited to:
- database applications;
- email,
- internet access;
- operating system and application audit logs; and
- specialised software.

This policy provides the overarching framework for any other record management policies, procedures, or work instructions.

Policy context

FCL's recordkeeping policies, procedures, and work instructions are tightly integrated with other policies, procedures, and work instructions in the Integrated Management System.

The Record Manager shall be responsible for developing, implementing, and maintaining all recordkeeping strategies with supporting policies, procedures, and work instructions.

Legislation, regulation, and standards

FCL has identified the following legislation that applies to records and information processed as part of ongoing operations:

- <relevant legislation for the jurisdiction defined here>

FCL has identified the following regulations that apply to records and information processed as part of ongoing operations:

- <relevant legislation for the jurisdiction defined here>

FCL shall develop recordkeeping systems that capture and maintain records with appropriate evidential characteristics in accordance with its obligations under the legislation and regulations identified above.

FCL is committed to current best practice in recordkeeping, and shall develop recordkeeping policies, procedures, systems, and work instructions consistent with ISO 15489.

Record management systems

The record management system is a hybrid ERMS and paper records. Whilst copies of paper records may be scanned into the ERMS, the originals shall be securely retained, even if captured in accordance with the admissibility of electronic evidence within the jurisdiction.

The recordkeeping systems are dedicated to the creation and maintenance of authentic, reliable, and usable records for as long as they are required to support forensic case processing or any business activities effectively and efficiently.

The recordkeeping systems shall manage the following processes:

- the creation or capture of records within the recordkeeping system;
- the storage of records;
- the protection of record integrity and authenticity;
- the security of records;
- access to, and accessibility of, records; and
- the disposal of records according to relevant legislative, regulatory, contractual, or business requirements.

Responsibilities

This policy has been authorised by Top Management.

Line Managers shall be responsible for the implementation of this policy through resource allocation, demonstrable commitment, and other management support.

The Records Manager shall be responsible for overseeing the design, implementation, and maintenance of this record management policy, as well as monitoring compliance.

System administrators shall be responsible for maintaining the technology for all recordkeeping systems, including responsibility for maintaining the integrity and authenticity of records and audit trails.

System designers shall be responsible for designing IT and other systems that comply with the requirements of this policy.

The Information Security Manager shall be responsible for ensuring that appropriate information security has been implemented and managed to ensure security of records during their life cycle. This shall be confirmed by internal audit.

All employees shall be responsible for the creation of accurate and reliable records of their activities as defined by this policy and complying with its requirements.

All responsibilities for recordkeeping shall be defined in the relevant job descriptions.

Monitor and review

This policy shall be scheduled for review at least on an annual basis, unless an incident or other influencing change necessitates review.

Appendix 5—Record management system objectives

Top Management has defined the following objectives for the records management system to be implemented in FCL.

- to continuously improve the records management processes by an ongoing process of performance assessment and corrective or preventive action where needed;
- to develop a formal training program, with supporting processes and procedures, on Records Management that is appropriate to all employees;
- to ensure that full and accurate records are made, captured into, maintained by, accessible in the ERMS;
- to ensure that records within the ERMS are retained, managed, and disposed of in accordance with relevant legislation, regulation, good practice within the jurisdiction, as well as client's contractual requirements;
- to exploit current and emerging technology to assist in the management of case processing and general business records;
- to have demonstrable Top Management support to implement an appropriate ERMS, with appropriate resources to support its ongoing operations;
- to have the ERMS able that can record and monitor the various stages of action of all types of correspondence (including forensic case processing) from initiation to closure.
- to have the ERMS that will capture, store, index, and make available to all authorised users details of forensic case processing and general business records; and
- to have the ERMS that will provide efficient tracking and retrieval of logical and physical records using metadata and other keyword searches.

Appendix 6—Business case template

The business case for the implementation of ERMS shall contain the following sections:

- synopsis of the current situation and how the project will improve the management of records and information in FCL;
- business benefits of implementing an ERMS, including the impact and effect the system will have on the business immediately after implementation and beyond;
- business options and recommendations;
- objectives and business drivers;
- key performance indicators;
- project budget;
- plans for interested party's involvement;
- implementation plan;
- risk-mitigation strategies; and
- change management initiatives.

Appendix 7—Outline of the ERMS project

The ERMS project shall have three main phases with a number of subphases as shown below:

Initiation phase

- initial analysis;
- developing the business case;
- seek and gain approval from project sponsor; and
- draft technical and functional requirements.

Implementation phase

- analyse business needs and processes;
- work with interested parties to identify process improvements, including use of workflow;
- develop a communications strategy for implementation;
- develop training material;
- analyse impact of new ERMS on existing IT infrastructure and need for changes;
- ensure IT infrastructure ready for deployment;
- develop records migration strategy for existing records;
- develop administration model to manage ERMS;
- develop and gain approval from all interested parties for records security model;
- develop and gain approval for business rules relating to record management for the ERMS and Document Registry;
- develop, or update, the record classification scheme;
- review and update the technical and functional requirements to incorporate any changes identified to date;
- procurement phase (to include RFI, RFP, evaluation of proposals, and entry into contract with chosen service provider);
- develop implementation and rollout strategy and plan;
- implement the pilot and configure it for the defined needs;
- review the pilot and make adjustments as needed until the ERMS meets the defined needs;
- develop a full rollout and implementation plan;
- develop a support model for the implementation and rollout;
- operate phased implementation and rollout by departments;
- collect feedback as rollout and implementation progresses and adjust as needed;
- train all ERMS users according to their roles and responsibilities; and
- act on feedback as feedback is obtained.

Postimplementation phase (PIR)

- develop PIR plan;
- undertake PIR;
- raise appropriate CAPAs based on PIR;
- implement required changes through change control; and
- ensure continuous improvement through ongoing auditing after the PIR.

Appendix 8—Selection criteria for an ERMS

As part of the ERMS package evaluation process from the RFI exercise, all packages shall be compared against a set of criteria. These are reproduced below:

Criteria	Requirement
Authenticity	As defined in Section 15.3.1.1 This may have an additional login to the ERMS with access rights definable and shall have a fully secure audit trail
Reliability	As defined in Section 15.3.1.2 Additionally: • the ERMS shall be able to capture all records in the scope of the business activities in scope; • organise captured records in a logical and understandable manner that reflects the current business structures; • be capable of being used as the prime record repository with no issues about the reliability of the records produced; and • provide easy and intuitive access to records, as defined by the user's access rights, as well as any associated metadata or linked records and documents

Continued

Criteria	Requirement
Integrity	As defined in Section 15.3.1.3 Additionally: • maintain record integrity during any transfer into or out of the ERMS; • provide processes for user account monitoring down to individual users; • provide user Identification and Access Management (IAM) processes, including two-factor authentication (various technologies); • provide appropriate security based on the perceived risks to the system, as defined in Chapter 5; • permit authorised actions only (specifically destruction or transfer), based on authorised access rights, as defined in Chapter 12, Section 12.6.5.1; and • provide full audit trail facilities with configurable reporting capabilities **Note:** These will be in addition to those facilities provided by the operating system as it cannot provide this level of granularity
Usability	As defined in Section 15.3.1.4
Compliance	The ERMS shall be compliant with all legislation, regulation, codes of practice, and good practice within the jurisdiction where it is operated Where appropriate, certification should be provided.
Completeness	The ERMS shall capture and securely store all records in complete form (including linkages, related documents, other records, and all other elements that comprise the record) within the defined scope
Retention periods	The ERMS shall be able to set different retention periods for different records or record types, as defined in Chapter 4, Appendix 26
Distributed management	Whilst FCL is located in one location currently, this may change with other offices opening in different jurisdictions. The ERMS shall be able to support distributed management of records between multiple offices, in different jurisdictions. There will be one office nominated as the main data centre, but others will be nominated as fallback sites in case of a disruptive event. Different offices will retain ownership of their own records, even if stored at another site, and this shall be facilitated through the ERMS. The main data centre will be responsible for all issues relating to day-to-day operations, including backups
User interface	A GUI shall be provided and this may be a web interface
Transfers and migrations	Where transfers or migrations are undertaken, the ERMS shall ensure the authenticity, integrity, reliability, usability, and security of all existing records for their entire life cycle. A full audit trail shall show all actions taken on all records, including transfers and migrations
Accessibility	The ERMS shall provide a timely, intuitive, and efficient process for locating, retrieving, and using records according to business need and access rights for the user Audit trails of all access attempts (successful or not) shall be maintained securely and provide configurable reports of audit activity as required, as defined in Section 15.3.1.3
Disposition	As defined in retention periods, the ERMS shall be able to implement appropriate record disposition according to the retention schedule, with an appropriate secure audit trail Disposition shall only be possible by authorised users as defined in Chapter 12, Section 12.6.5.1

Appendix 9—Initial ERMS FEEDBACK questionnaire

Users shall be asked the following subjective questions and to score them as below using the standard feedback scoring process:

- overall experience;
- new ERMS overall;
- creating new records;
- registering records;
- locating records;
- retrieving records;
- record linkage to documents or other records;
- metadata use for searching;
- printing and scanning;
- audit trail use;
- documentation supplied was of great assistance;

- training received was of great assistance;
- Service Desk support was of great assistance;
- I felt involved in the process and listened to
- implementation was well handled; and
- my expectations were met.

The following rankings shall be used:

1. totally dissatisfied;
2. somewhat dissatisfied;
3. neither satisfied nor dissatisfied
4. somewhat satisfied;
5. very satisfied.

In addition to these qualitative questions, the following four qualitative questions shall be asked:

- What I like most about the new ERMS? (Please explain);
- What I like least about the new ERMS? (Please explain);
- What can be done to improve its ERMS? (Please explain)
- Any other comments or clarifications of answers above? (Please enter below).

Appendix 10—Metadata required in the ERMS

The following metadata shall be used:

Note

Note: 'M/O' refers to whether the entry of the field is mandatory or optional.

Field	M/O?	Purpose	Comments
Record number	M	Allocates a unique number to identify any record in the ERMS	All record numbers shall be entered in accordance with the numbering system in the ERMS. No records shall be entered into the ERMS without a valid record number
Title	M	The text used to name the subject of each record	Facilitates searching and retrieval of records by searching on a record's official title or words contained in the title
Creator (also sometimes called Author)	M	The unique identity of the creator of the record	This may be an employee or an external creator
Date created	M	The date the record was created	Dates may be automatically generated by the ERMS or manually input (over-riding automatically created ones)
Date registered	M	The date and time a record is captured into the ERMS	Automatically set by the ERMS as opposed to the date of creation.
Date closed	M	The date the record was closed	Automatically generated by the ERMS when a file is closed
Notes	O	Allows for additional descriptive information to be associated with a record	Use of the notes field should be used if the record title does not provide sufficient information to permit effective searching
Retention period	M	The period for which the record shall be retained for legislative, regulatory, contractual, or business reasons	This shall define the period and the reason

Continued

Field	M/O?	Purpose	Comments
Disposition method	M	The method of disposition required	How the record is to be dispositioned
Disposition date	M	The date of disposition	A trigger for starting the relevant disposition process
Audit trail	M	An audit trail of all actions taken on the record from creation/registration to disposition	This will show a complete history of all actions on the record, including sign in and out and changes made
Access rights	M	Access rights for the record	Defining who can have access to the record—linked to Active Directory for Microsoft systems
Movements	M	Recording the actions taken on the record	This is a record, like the audit trail, that records all employees' activity relating to the record. This specifically applies to the signing in and out of the record
Location	M	Where the record is located	This may be an electronic or hard copy record location. Where an electronic record in the ERMS, this is automatically generated by the ERMS
Record type	M	Defining the type of record to which the metadata refers	A number of predefined records are used to identify record types
Related records	M	Identifies links between different records and identifies the linkages between them	This shall be automatically generated by the ERMS for some records, but may need manual input to the 'Notes' field
Keywords	M	The keywords relating to the record	These are free text entries and are left to the creator to define

Appendix 11—Sample email metadata

Field	M/O?	Purpose	Comments
Bcc	M	Recipients of the email message but whose names are not visible to other recipients of the email	Manually entered
Cc	M	Recipients other than the primary recipient of the email message	Manually entered
Date received	M	Shows the time when a message was received by the intended recipient	Auto generated
Date sent	M	Date and time message sent	Auto generated
From	M	Sender's identity	Auto generated
Message ID	M	A unique identification code assigned by the email client to each message. This may be important when authenticating email	System generated
Message options	O	These permit the sender to attach importance and sensitivity levels to messages	When these options are selected the importance and sensitivity level shall be displayed in both electronic and hardcopy
Security settings	O	The contents and attachments of confidential messages can be encrypted (scrambled) by using the security settings. The option of adding a digital signature to an email is also available	
Subject	M	The subject/title of the email message	Entered manually
To	M	The recipient(s) of the email transmission	Manually entered

Appendix 12—Forensic case records stored in the ERMS

The following are some of the records or record types stored for a forensic case.

Where an estimate or quotation is produced and the case does not proceed, the records to the point of abandonment shall be entered into the ERMS.

FCL uses Encase, FTK, and Cellebrite as its main forensic tools but has a variety of specialised tools in use.

Where the evidence is hardware or media other than a PC, appropriate records relating to the exhibit shall be taken.

Note

Those defined below are intended to be representative of a case.

Where received in FCL

- initial contact details (fax, letter, email, or records of visit or phone call);
- instructions from the client;
- case summary from the client;
- supplementary information from the client;
- any correspondence between the client and FCL;
- initial quotation/estimate to client;
- client contact details (phone, fax, mobile, email, address);
- client case reference;
- case reference number assigned;
- internal forms used during forensic case processing;
- exhibits received and accepted;
- movement records;
- rejection notice (if applicable);
- updated insurance schedule;
- case acceptance letter;
- case assignment details;
- agreed Turn Round Times (TRTs);
- case file;
- virtual case file;
- notes on exhibits;
- photographs of exhibits;
- image(s) created;
- evidence of verification of imaging process;
- details of initial examination of exhibits;
- details of the BIOS and time offset;
- details of any relevant metadata, if present;
- work instructions made contemporaneously by the assigned Forensic Analyst;
- details of files recovered from the image;
- a copy of the file structure of the exhibits;
- results of malware scanning;
- results of any signature analysis for the image;
- results of the analysis of the image;
- the extracted info record;
- results of recovery of all graphics files;
- the 'initialise Case' report from Encase;
- the link parser report;
- extracts of all unique email addresses;
- internet history report;
- extracted documents;

- extracted spreadsheets;
- extracted databases;
- extracted images;
- extracted html files;
- extracted email;
- extracted 'Favourites';
- extracted 'My Documents';
- extracted 'Recent';
- extracted 'Documents and Settings';
- extracted 'Desktop';
- extracted temporary files;
- internet file carves from Encase;
- other artefacts;
- the FTK view of the case;
- results of all searches;
- statements or reports as required;
- authority for release of statements or reports;
- iterations of statements or reports between the client and FCL;
- handover of final report and any supporting exhibits to the client;
- records backup of case to disk, tape, or the Cloud; and
- case archived.

Note

Some of these records may require iterated discussion with the client (also entered into the ERMS) based on the results found (e.g. search results indicate the need for additional searches).

Where an on-site seizure is undertaken

Where on-site seizure is undertaken, as defined in Chapter 8, (whether a 'friendly' seizure or not) the following additional records shall be entered into the ERMS:

- health and safety briefing notes;
- briefing notes for the location of seizure;
- details of others to be present;
- details of what is to be seized;
- evidence log;
- details of evidence bags used;
- identity of the exhibit custodian;
- photos of the seizure site;
- diagrams of the seizure site;
- handover paperwork, if appropriate;
- photos of the equipment to be seized, including the labelled leads;
- notebooks and other contemporaneous notes;
- details of how the exhibits were transported to the Secure Property Store; and
- movement forms.

General

In addition to the records above, all records of any actions taken by anyone to do with the case shall be treated as a record and entered into the ERMS.

Where different exhibits are to be examined, the records above shall be amended, or added to, to accommodate the exhibits being seized or examined.

Appendix 13—Dublin core metadata elements

Number	Element
1	Contributor—an entity responsible for making contributions to the content of the resource
2	Coverage—the extent or scope of the content of the resource
3	Creator—an entity primarily responsible for making the content of the resource
4	Date—date of an event in the life cycle of the resource
5	Description—an account of the content of the resource
6	Format—the physical or logical manifestation of the resource
7	Identifier—an unambiguous reference to the resource within a defined context
8	Language—the language of the intellectual content of the resource
9	Publisher—the entity responsible for making the resource available
10	Relation—a reference to a related resource
11	Rights—details of the rights held in and over the resource
12	Source—a reference to the resource from which the present resource is derived
13	Subject—the topic of the content of the resource
14	Title—a name defined to the resource
15	Type—the nature or genre of the content of the resource

Appendix 14—National archives of Australia metadata standard

The minimum metadata set is cumulative and arranged in three levels:

- **core**—all records in system, including high volume, low-value information in transactional systems;
- **additional**—higher value and long-term records; and
- **transfer**—business information of archival value or records to be transferred between systems or agencies.

Level	Property	Purpose
Core	Identifier	The Identifier is a string of characters, numbers or letters, or a combination thereof, that uniquely identifies a record within a given domain. It acts as an access point to find an information asset within a system
Core	Creator	The Creator is the individual, work group, or agency that created a record. It is essential to: • show ownership for evidence and context purposes • identify the creator of the record • support user searching, allowing information to be filtered
Core	Date created	The Date Created property records the date a record first came into existence. It does not represent the date on which the content was finalised, or the date of digitisation. It provides evidence that the record is authentic, and is required for applying disposal actions, sentencing, and transfer to the National Archives of Australia

Continued

Level	Property	Purpose
Additional	Title	The Title of a record describes its content. Its purpose is to: • enable information search and discovery • facilitate user choice • provide additional context
Additional	Protective marking	The Protective Marking property denotes the security status of a record
Additional	Disposal Class	The Disposal Class is a number string that identifies the specific disposal class authorising the retention or destruction of a record. It can also indicate its function or subject
Additional	Format	The Format property provides information about the format of a record to determine preservation, storage, migration, and other management actions. It only applies to digital records
Transfer	Rights	The Rights property must be used if there are non-security related restrictions or policies affecting the access to or use of a record
Transfer	Integrity Check	The purpose of the Integrity Check property is to prove the authenticity of records by: • verifying if a record has been altered in an undocumented or unauthorised way • ensuring the integrity of the original record over time An Integrity Check works by generating a message digest (AGRkMS 22.2) commonly referred to as a 'checksum' using an integrity algorithm (AGRkMS 22.1, Hash Function), based on the unique sequence of bits within a digital record. Comparing this value over time can determine whether the bits that make up a record have been changed in the course of transmission or storage. This process helps to check whether the integrity or 'fixity' of the record remains intact. Preservation strategies may be required to restore the record if an issue is identified This property only applies to digital records

Appendix 15—Responsibilities for records management

Specific roles and responsibilities for all employees shall be defined in their detailed job descriptions. However, some high-level and general roles and responsibilities are defined below:

Top management

Shall:

- recognise the importance of a robust records management system in the Forensic laboratory;
- demonstrate commitment to the records management process;
- provide appropriate resources (tools, training, and ring-fenced employees) to manage the records management system;
- support and endorse the records management policy;
- ensure that a robust and effective records management program is established and maintained;
- ensure that all types of records are managed by the ERMS (i.e. physical and electronic records);
- ensure that regular auditing of the ERMS is undertaken and corrective or preventive action is undertaken, where appropriate; and
- include ERMS performance in the Management Review.

Line managers

Shall:

- familiarise themselves with and follow the records management procedures;
- ensure that their staff understand and follow the procedures;
- identify records, and specifically vital records, within their areas of responsibility for capture in the ERMS;
- ensure that there is an up-to-date inventory maintained of all records that they own;
- review, on an ongoing basis, the records that they own for completeness, reliability, and relevance within the ERMS;

- ensure that, where necessary, employees have appropriate security clearances to undertake their work;
- undertake annual appraisals, with assistance from the Human Resources Department, and identify any training needs for their reports;
- provide input to the disposition requirements of all records within their area of responsibility; and
- undertake peer reviews of their report's work.

Employees

Shall:

- ensure that records are properly created and managed. This includes the responsibility to ensure that appropriate metadata shall be manually included with the records they create or receive, where applicable. This shall include ensuring that:
  - all mandatory recordkeeping metadata is systematically and consistently applied to all records created, or registered, as part of all forensic case processing as well as everyday business activities;
  - all records are entered into FCL ERMS on creation or registration;
  - mandatory recordkeeping metadata is systematically and consistently applied to all records created, where the software permits this. The main application suite for business applications is Microsoft Office;
  - mandatory recordkeeping metadata is systematically and consistently applied to all hardcopy records;
  - recordkeeping metadata is securely retained for as long as required by legislative, regulatory, contractual, or preservation requirements; and
  - the integrity and authenticity of records are assured by ensuring that FCL recordkeeping system guarantees against any unauthorised modification of a records metadata and that a full audit trail of record access and movement is maintained.
- follow the records management procedures;
- ensure that they dispose of hard copy output appropriately; and
- report any suspicious activity or faults according to the Service Desk and not try to 'prove' a weakness in systems or procedures.

Records management team

Shall:

- establish implement, manage, maintain, and continuously improve the records management policy and procedures;
- update the records management policy and procedures, as needed;
- support the record management system users;
- issue records management guidance;
- develop and undertake training to all users, as appropriate;
- ensure that the ERMS is functioning correctly;
- create and maintain access rights for all records according to authorised business needs; and
- administer the ERMS and Registry as required.

Audit manager

Shall:
- undertake audits of the ERMS according to the IMS calendar or on an as-required basis according to the internal audit procedures.

Quality manager

Shall:

- undertake quality audits and reviews of all samples of work products and services relating to forensic casework as well as general business operations; and
- provide regular management reports relating to ISO 9001 procedures and agreed quality objectives.

Appendix 16—Metadata for records stored off-site

Note

A 'carton' is a box containing one or more record.

Field	M/O?	Purpose	Comments
Borrowed date	M	The date the file/carton was signed out	
Borrower	M	Identity of anyone 'borrowing the carton'—for whatever reason	
Box number	M	The unique ID of the carton containing the record	
Date sent offsite	M	The date when a carton is collected and taken to the off-site storage facility	
Destroy year	M	The date when records in a specific carton are to be destroyed in accordance with record retention schedule	
Destroyed	M	The 'marker' to show when written authorisation has been provided to the off-site storage provider confirming the destruction of cartons listed in the periodic disposal report	
Recall barcode number	M	The unique barcode number provided by the off-site storage provider that is provided to each of the cartons that they are managing	
Record number	M	Allocates a unique number to identify any record in the ERMS	All record numbers shall be entered in accordance with the numbering system in the ERMS. No records shall be entered into the ERMS without a valid record number
Returned date	M	The date the file/carton was returned	
Returner	M	Identity of person returning the carton or file	

Appendix 17—Records classification system

FCL shall use a four-level classification system for records within the ERMS.
These are as follows:

Classification	Description	Some examples
Business critical	Records without which FCL could not continue to operate. Records that give evidence of status and protect FCL and its clients **Irreplaceable**	• Legal documents; • Contracts; • Accounts; • All forensic case records
Important	Important to FCL's continued operations. Could be reproduced from a variety of source documents, from clients/suppliers, or backups. **Replaceable**	• Procedures; • Non-essential business records;
Useful	Loss would cause temporary inconvenience **Replaceable**	• Most regular business correspondence
Nonessential	No value beyond either the time limits of the life cycle of the record or records/documents for public consumption **Replaceable**	• Advertising material; • Published articles

Appendix 18—Disposition authorisation

The same form shall be used for the requesting authority for disposition, authorising disposition, and recording disposition method. It shall contain:

- date;
- requestor;
- address;
- office phone;
- mobile email;
- description of record(s) for which disposition is required;
- location of record(s);
- forensic case file number, if appropriate;
- retention expiry date;
- signature and name of requestor;
- disposition authorised; and
- disposition method agreed:
- physical or logical destruction;
- retain for a further period;
- archive and retain for a further period; and
- transfer to a named third party.
- authorised by and date;
- date of disposition;
- disposition effected by name and signature;
- destruction method, if appropriate;
- certificate of destruction, if appropriate;
- confirmation of retention for a further period;
- confirmation of archival in-house and retention for a further period;
- details of third party to receive it;
- movement sheet completed, if appropriate; and
- property log updated, if appropriate.

Appendix 19—Additional requirements for physical record recovery

Whilst the standard BCP allows recovery of IT systems and electronic records as well as specific business functions, the requirements for physical record (e.g. paper documents, photographs, etc.) are not covered. Some of the specific requirements are defined below for record management recovery, in case of need:

- has consideration of fire preplanning been undertaken specifically for physical records with the local fire service?
- are the physical records covered by non-water fire quenching systems (e.g. Halon or FM 200)?
- are specialised document recovery specialists identified in the BCP?
- if records are wet as part of fire quenching, where can they be laid out to dry and sort?
- whilst wet records can be recovered and burned records not, has it been ensured that there will always space available for records to be dried and sorted?
- if the original accommodation is unavailable for any reason, where will the refurbished records be located?
- whilst records recovery specialists may advise that movement of physical records after a fire, with ensuing water damage, may cause irreparable damage, immediate action may be required.
- have the Records Management Team been trained in how to safely and securely undertake immediate actions that will not overly damage the physical records?
- is there someone who can undertake a risk assessment of the area for records recovery and make recommendations according to local health and safety requirements?
- is there a process for handling burnt records;
- is there a process for 'hoovering up' material relating to physical records?
- how will microfilms be recovered, if applicable?
- have specialist equipment suppliers for records management been identified and documented?

- have specialists for records management been identified and documented?
- have specialist checklists been created for records recovery?
- are appropriate forms in use for record recovery?

Appendix 20—Specialised equipment needed for inspection and recovery of damaged records

Equipment

The following equipment shall be stored off-site and be used if inspection and recovery of the damaged physical records are required.

- adhesive tape (clear);
- blotting paper (archival);
- brooms;
- building plans;
- camera (Digital or Polaroid) and films (or video camera);
- cling film;
- clipboards;
- crates;
- dehumidifiers to prevent the onset of mould;
- Dictaphones or smartphones that can record conversations;
- dry wipe boards;
- entry signs (prohibiting entry, smoking, etc.)
- first aid kit;
- flip charts;
- hazard tape;
- medical supplies;
- mops and buckets;
- newsprint (plain);
- packing materials and crates for record recovery (these may be water-draining packing crates, but these also have a downside);
- paper clips;
- pens (multi-coloured);
- plastic sheeting to protect the damaged area;
- plastic wallets (A4 and larger);
- polythene freezer bags;
- record register;
- rubbish bags;
- scissors;
- sponges;
- squeegees;
- string;
- tape for securing a variety of items;
- tie on labels;
- torches and batteries;
- ventilators to draw spores away from the Records Management Team—the area shall be well ventilated;
- wax crayons (water resistant);
- wrapping paper; and
- writing pads.

Clothing

Before touching any physical records, personal protective equipment (PPE) should be issued to the Records Management Team. The team shall have received training how to use any PPE issued, as defined in Chapter 18.

The following should be used, as a minimum:

- stout shoes or boots;
- hard hats;
- protective eyewear;
- protective gloves;
- coveralls or overalls; and
- respirators.

Chapter 16

Performance assessment

16.1 Overview

Every organisation has the ability to improve its efficiency and the services it delivers to its clients, and FCL is no exception.

To ensure that FCL is able to continuously improve its management systems, associated procedures, and products and services that it delivers to its clients, it shall monitor and measure how well the applicable requirements from those systems are being met. This shall be carried out using the following processes:

- monitoring and measurement;
- SLAs and TRTs;
- evaluation of compliance;
- security metrics;
- internal audit;
- client feedback;
- complaints management;
- handling of nonconformities; and
- Management Review.

Each of these processes is covered in different parts of this book but is summarised below for ease of reference.

16.2 Performance assessment

16.2.1 Monitoring and measurement

FCL shall carry out monitoring and measurement of its management systems and other internal processes to determine the extent to which their requirements are met. This shall be carried out using a mix of the following:

- trend analysis, as defined in Chapter 6, Section 6.13.4, Chapter 7, Section 7.4.1.3.4, Chapter 7, Section 7.4.1.6, Chapter 7, Section 7.4.6.4, Chapter 7, Section 7.4.8.1, Chapter 7, Section 7.4.10.4 and Chapter 14, Section 14.4.2;
- internal audits, as defined in Chapter 4, Section 4.9.2, Chapter 6, Section 6.13.3, Chapter 7, Section 7.4.5.7, Chapter 12, Section 12.3.13.2.2.1 and Section 16.2.5;
- external audits, as defined in Chapter 12, Section 12.3.13.2.2.4;
- Management Review, as defined in Chapter 4, Section 4.9.3 and Section 16.2.9;
- Business continuity plan (BCP) exercise and test feedback, as defined in Chapter 13, Sections 13.6 and 13.7;
- penetration testing as defined in Chapter 12, Section 12.3.13.2.2.3;
- self-assessments, as defined in Chapter 13, Section 13.8;
- examination of complaints, as defined in Chapter 6, Section 6.14, Chapter 6, Appendices 18–20, Chapter 14, Section 14.2.1.3 and Chapter 14, Section 14.10;
- examination of incident reports, as defined in Chapter 7, Section 7.4.1;
- examination of fault logs, as defined in Chapter 7, Section 7.4.1;
- examination of problem reports, as defined in Chapter 7, Section 7.4.2;
- such other processes as management sees fit.

The scope, frequency, aims and objectives of these tests and reviews shall be defined and agreed with the Audit Committee. Records of these monitoring and measurement processes shall be maintained with associated corrective action requests.

The results of these exercises and tests and any associated corrective action requests shall be communicated to relevant interested parties, as appropriate.

A Blueprint for Implementing Best Practice Procedures in a Digital Forensic Laboratory. https://doi.org/10.1016/B978-0-12-819479-9.00013-7

16.2.2   SLAs and TRTs

The TRTs required by a client and the SLAs defined by the Laboratory Manager and agreed with the client, as defined in Chapter 9, Section 9.5.4, shall be under constant review, these include:

- requests for investigation and examination;
- number of jobs (or cases) undertaken per year;
- number of terabytes of evidence imaged;
- number of computers examined;
- number of mobile devices examined;
- number of other devices examined;
- training undertaken in the year for employees;
- successful cases (as a percentage of all cases);
- sentences or penalties resulting from forensic cases;
- number of 'assists';
- number of 'successful assists';
- sentences or penalties resulting from 'assists';
- numbers of jobs that met or bettered TRTs;
- number of jobs that failed their TRTs;
- numbers of jobs that met or bettered SLAs;
- number of jobs that failed their SLAs; and
- feedback from clients (using the client feedback forms).

16.2.3   Evaluation of maturity

The results of the monitoring and measurement processes above shall be used to evaluate the level of maturity that FCL has achieved for the aims and objectives of its management systems, other governing processes and legislative requirements.

A formal report of these evaluations shall be maintained and presented, with their supporting records, to the relevant oversight committees:

- ISO 9001—Quality Committee, as defined in Chapter 4, Appendix 12;
- ISO 45001—Health and Safety Committee, as defined in Chapter 4, Appendix 10;
- ISO 22301—Business Continuity Committee as defined in Chapter 4, Appendix 8;
- ISO/IEC 27001—Information Security Committee, as defined in Chapter 4, Appendix 11;
- Audit Committee, as defined in Chapter 4, Appendix 7;
- Risk Committee, as defined in Chapter 4, Appendix 13.

At a high level, metrics are quantifiable measurements of some aspect of a management system. For a management system, there are some identifiable attributes that collectively characterise the level of compliance of the management system. This is a quantitative measure of how much of that attribute the management system contains and can be built from lower-level physical measures that are the outcome of monitoring and measurement.

Typically, the following types of metrics shall be identified and studied:

- **Process metrics**—Specific metrics that shall serve as quantitative or qualitative evidence of the level of maturity for a particular management system that could serve as a binary indication of the presence or absence of a mature process;
- **Management system metrics**—A measurable attribute of the result of a capability maturity process, that shall serve as evidence of its effectiveness. A metric may be objective or subjective, and quantitative or qualitative.

The first type of metric shall provide information about the processes themselves. The second type of metric shall provide information on the results of those processes and what they can tell the interested parties about how effective use of the processes has been in achieving an acceptable security outcome. FCL shall tailor their own metrics program to measure their progress against defined and agree objectives.

There are a number of capability maturity models that can be used in a forensic laboratory to evaluate compliance levels and that are recognised worldwide. These include, but are not limited to the following:

16.2.3.1   Analytics

- Big data maturity models (BDMM); and
- Business intelligence (BI) maturity model.

16.2.3.2   Business process management

- Business process maturity model (BPMM); and
- BPM-maturity model EDEN e.V.

16.2.3.3   Change management

- Change management maturity model (Prosci).

16.2.3.4   Continuous delivery

- Continuous delivery maturity model.

16.2.3.5   Health and safety

- Capability maturity model for health and safety.

16.2.3.6   Human resources

- People capability maturity model (PCMM); and
- Virtual team maturity model (VTMM).

16.2.3.7   Information security management

- Capability maturity model for business continuity;
- Capability maturity model for system security engineering (this has since become ISO/IEC 21827);
- Capability maturity model for information security; and
- Building in security maturity model.

16.2.3.8   Information technology

- CERT resilience management model (capability model focused on operational resilience, i.e., cybersecurity, service continuity, IT operations);
- Capability maturity model (CMM, focusing on software development);
- open source maturity model (for open-source software development);
- Service integration maturity model (for SOA);
- The SharePoint maturity model;
- ITIL maturity model; and
- ISO/IEC 15504 (for process maturity).

16.2.3.9   Learning

- E-learning maturity model (eMM); and
- Learning maturity model.

16.2.3.10   Project management

- Organisational project management maturity model (OPM3);
- Portfolio, programme and project management maturity model (P3M3).

16.2.3.11   Quality management

- Quality management maturity grid (QMMG);
- Quality maturity model (QMM).

16.2.3.12   Supply chain

- Supply chain maturity model (Gartner and others);
- Capability maturity model for quality.

Whilst these are specific maturity models covering a variety of topics, there is no specific capability maturity mode for the operation of forensic laboratories at the time of writing.

Note 1

Not all of the above are used in FCL.

Note 2

A forensic laboratory should adopt and adapt a number of these for its own use and develop their own forensic capability maturity model based on the metrics that they collect.

16.2.4   Information security metrics

Security metrics shall be measured on a regular basis.

16.2.5   Internal audit

Internal audits shall be carried out on a regular basis to cover all aspects of operations in FCL.

16.2.6   Client feedback

Client feedback is essential as it allows clients to provide comment on the products and services they receive from FCL. It is closely linked to 'Complaints' but allows any feedback to be provided in a structured manner rather than a complaint being some dissatisfaction with the products and services provided.

Client feedback can be:

- in person;
- by telephone;
- in writing by letter;
- online by completing the Complaints form or the feedback form.

Unstructured feedback that provides qualitative feedback shall be provided by the following feedback processes:

- in person;
- by telephone;
- in writing by letter;
- online by completing the Complaints form.

These forms of feedback allow free-form communication, whereas a feedback form 'scores' the service offering and allows quantitative measurements to be made.

The forensic case processing feedback process is defined in Chapter 14, Section 14.2.1.4 and the contents of the feedback form are defined in Chapter 6, Appendix 17.

The testimony feedback form is defined in Chapter 11, Appendix 8.

16.2.7   Managing client complaints

The procedures for managing client complaints are defined in Chapter 6, Section 6.14.

16.2.8   Handling of nonconformities

Where nonconformities have been identified either from:

- **Internal audit finding**—Any discrepancy in the management system found and reported by Internal Auditors;
- **External audit finding**—Any discrepancy in the management system found and reported by External Auditors;

- **Management review finding**—Any discrepancy in the management system found and reported by a management review of the relevant management systems that comprise the integrated management system (IMS);
- **Incident**—any incident identified and reported that affects the expected outcome of the management system and may lead to corrective action.

They shall be reviewed to determine action to be taken, as defined in Chapter 4, Section 4.10.

The review shall be in the form of a formal response to the audit report or incident.

FCL shall also use trend analysis for the identification of persistent nonconformities or incidents or faults.

In some cases, a response to the audit report shall suffice, but if action is needed it shall be raised as a CAPA and communicated to all relevant interested parties, as appropriate.

Corrective action is often derived from the above and agreed with the person raising it. The raising and agreeing of a corrective action plan shall derive the required agreed corrective action.

Depending on the nature and severity of the nonconformity, it shall be discussed at the next relevant management system meeting. In exceptional circumstances, an emergency meeting shall be called. It is essential to:

- determine the root cause of the nonconformity; and
- evaluate the corrective action needed to be taken to ensure that the nonconformity does not recur.

16.2.9 Management reviews

Management Reviews are defined in Chapter 4, Section 4.9.3.

Chapter 17

Occupational health and safety (OH&S) procedures

17.1 General

17.1.1 The importance of people and a safe workplace

No organisation can function without people, who are an organisation's most important asset. Work can make a positive or negative impact on an individual employee's mental and physical health. They can be affected if the employee is exposed to harm as part of their everyday duties (e.g. an unsafe work environment, violence in the workplace, or unsafe working practices). However, with a safe and secure workplace where employees are interested in their job, feel safe, and know they are using safe working practices, then job satisfaction can increase and improvements in the employee's personal health and well-being can result.

Organisations that successfully manage health and safety in the workplace recognise the relationship between risk management, employee health, and its relationship with the business itself. A good health and safety policy is aligned with all other Human Resources (HR) policies and other policies designed to demonstrate Top Management commitment to ensuring a safe and secure working environment for all employees. Increasingly, employees are undertaking mobile and teleworking, and these risks must also be managed.

The aim of implementing appropriate health and safety policies is to improve the health and safety performance within all operational areas so that accidents and ill health are substantially reduced, if not totally eliminated, and that work is a satisfying experience for all employees.

Organisations must recognise the relationship between the health and safety of its employees, HR, and the very core of its business as they recognise that its employees are the key resource. Like other ethical and responsible organisations, FCL shall:

- recognise the benefits of a fit, healthy, enthusiastic, competent, and committed workforce;
- realise that good HR policies can be undermined by poor or weak health and safety policies and procedures;
- visibly demonstrate that they are not concerned with 'paying lip service' to health and safety issues, relevant legislation, and regulation within the jurisdiction but are genuinely committed to continuously improving the workplace for their employees; and
- promote a positive healthy and safe workplace for all of its employees.

Accidents, ill health, and safety-related incidents are seldom random events but are usually due to some failure in control or process and often involve multiple contributory factors and events. The immediate cause may well be a human one, but the root cause is more often a management failure. This is why, for each incident or accident, organisations must establish the root cause and continuously improve their health and safety performance. Health and safety must start with visible and demonstrable commitment from Top Management as without this, experience shows that the implementation will fail.

The ultimate goal is to improve health and safety performance so that accidents, injuries, work-related health issues, and 'near misses' are either eliminated or reduced to an acceptable level. FCL's risk appetite is defined in Chapter 5, Section 5.5.9.1 and Chapter 5, Appendix 14. Work should be part of a satisfying lifestyle for all employees.

FCL shall adopt a total loss approach concentrating on effective prevention of operational health and safety (OH&S) incidents, identifying and eliminating (where possible) root causes of incidents, as defined in Chapter 4, Appendix 49. The traditional organisational approach has been to manage issues at the end of the process or when an incident occurs. This is costly, inefficient, and ineffective in all areas. FCL shall build in OH&S and ensure that it is embedded from the start, just like quality, information security, etc. FCL shall adopt a process-based approach where excellent business processes are designed 'in' rather than having IMS failures detected by inspection, auditing, or other means and then addressed after an OH&S failure.

A Blueprint for Implementing Best Practice Procedures in a Digital Forensic Laboratory. https://doi.org/10.1016/B978-0-12-819479-9.00017-4
Copyright © 2024 Elsevier Inc. All rights reserved.

17.1.2 Management requirements

FCL is committed the provision of a safe working environment as a key element of their goal of achieving quality in every aspect of its operations. In addition, around the world, there are a number of different legislative and regulatory requirements may need to be addressed and prove demonstrable compliance when processing forensic cases in different jurisdictions.

The Occupational Health and Safety Management Systems ISO 45001 standard uses the Annex L approach for management system standards that facilitate OH&S being integrated into the FCL Integrated Management System (IMS). ISO 45001 follows the traditional Plan-Do-Check-Act process, as defined in Chapter 4, Section 4.3.1. Specifically, in OH&S, this means:

- **Plan**: determine and assess OH&S risks, OH&S opportunities, and other risks and other opportunities, establish OH&S objectives and processes necessary to deliver results in accordance with the OH&S policy;
- **Do**: implement the processes as planned;
- **Check**: monitor and measure activities and processes with regard to the OH&S policy and OH&S objectives, and report the results; and
- **Act**: take actions to continually improve the OH&S performance to achieve the intended outcomes as defined in Chapter 4, Section 4.10.

There are three main areas where OH&S is applicable in FCL. These are:

1. The working environment (in the office, laboratory, teleworking, or mobile working).
2. On undertaking First Responder or similar duties at a location remote to the normal workplace and collecting evidence for return to the working environment.
3. Processing evidence as part of forensic case processing in the working environment.

To achieve the above, FCL has established, documented, implemented, maintained, monitored, and continuously improved its Occupational Health and Safety Management System (OHSMS) for the defined scope, as defined in Chapter 5, Appendix 11. This has been integrated into the IMS so that economies of scale and management system integration can be implemented, reducing duplication of effort across the different implemented management systems.

17.1.3 Benefits

17.1.3.1 Direct benefits

The direct benefits of an effective OHSMS integrated into the IMS shall include, but are not limited to:

- an OH&S system that is specifically tailored organisational requirements as it is risk driven;
- less money spent for overtime benefits;
- less time lost due to OH&S incidents;
- lower costs for job accommodations for injured employees;
- lower employee's compensation insurance costs;
- lower expenditures for return-to-work programmes;
- lower medical expenditures;
- legislative compliance is easier to attain and prove with appropriate records;
- provides a manageable method for continuous improvement of OH&S;
- demonstrates visible Top Management commitment;
- is a part of corporate governance;
- demonstrates corporate social responsibility;
- provides reassurance to enforcement authorities;
- provides an emergency preparedness capability; and
- has a process-based systematic risk management process.

17.1.3.2 Indirect benefits

OH&S shall provide benefits in indirect costs, due to:

- better employee relations;
- better use of human resources;

- higher quality work products;
- increased morale;
- increased productivity; and
- reduced employee turnover.

17.1.3.3 Family benefits

Employees and their families shall also benefit from safety and health because

- their incomes are protected;
- their family lives are not hindered by injury; and
- their level of stress is not increased.

OH&S adds value to the business, workplaces, and the lives of their employees and is in the best interests of the employees.

17.2 Leadership and worker participation

17.2.1 Leadership and commitment

Top Management shall demonstrate leadership and commitment with respect to the OHSMS by:

- taking overall responsibility and accountability for the prevention of work-related injury and ill health, as well as the provision of safe and healthy workplaces and activities;
- ensuring that the OH&S policy and related OH&S objectives are established and are compatible with FCL's strategic direction and objectives;
- ensuring the integration of the OHSMS requirements into the IMS;
- ensuring that the resources needed to establish, implement, maintain, and improve the OHSMS are available and ring-fenced;
- communicating the importance of an effective OHSMS and of conforming to the OHSMS requirements to all employees;
- ensuring that the OHSMS achieves its intended outcome(s);
- directing and supporting employees to contribute to the effectiveness of the OHSMS;
- ensuring and promoting continual improvement;
- supporting other relevant management roles and integration to other management systems to demonstrate their leadership as it applies to their areas of responsibility;
- developing, leading, and promoting a culture that supports the intended outcomes of the OHSMS as an integral part of the IMS;
- protecting employees from reprisals when reporting incidents, hazards, risks, and opportunity—commonly called whistleblowing protection;
- ensuring consultation and participation of workers; and
- supporting the establishment and functioning of health and safety committees.

17.2.2 The OH&S policy

The OH&S policy shall be defined to be appropriate to FCL's specific setup, its operation, and the legislative requirements in the jurisdiction(s) where it is operation.

Note

This may cause different policies to be adopted for different forensic laboratories in different jurisdictions, even if part of the same organisation.

The OH&S policy shall ensure that it gives a commitment to the prevention of accidents, ill health due to work, safety incidents and that all relevant legislation and regulations within the jurisdiction are at least met, or preferably exceeded.

As with other management frameworks in the IMS, the OH&S framework shall be populated with appropriate documents, be implemented, maintained, monitored, and continuously improved. Education and awareness shall be undertaken from induction time and refresher training undertaken, especially if an accident or incident occurs, as defined in Chapter 4, Section 4.7.3 and the checklist defined in Chapter 6, Appendix 23 to termination of employment.

Top Management shall enforce the OH&S policy, as with all other policies, starting at the top and reaching every employee, as well as ensuring that the OH&S policy is regularly reviewed. This shall happen at least annually at the Management Review, as defied in Chapter 4, Section 4.9, after an incident or accident or any other influencing change.

A checklist for developing an OH&S policy is defined in Appendix 1.

The FCL OH&S policy as implemented is defined in Appendix 2.

17.2.3   Organisational roles, responsibilities, and authorities

Top Management shall ensure that the responsibilities and authorities for relevant roles within the OHSMS are assigned and communicated and maintained as documented information.

Employees shall assume responsibility for those aspects of the OHSMS over which they have control.

Top Management shall assign the responsibility and authority for:

- ensuring that the OHSMS conforms to the requirements of this document; and
- reporting on the performance of the OHSMS to Top Management.

17.2.3.1   Responsibilities

Within the OH&S process, there shall be a number of responsibilities at every level in the organisation. These include:

17.2.3.1.1   Top management

Top Management's responsibilities shall include, but are not limited to:

- agreeing and authorising the OH&S policy;
- reviewing OH&S performance;
- setting direction for OH&S;
- ensuring that appropriate resources are available to support the OH&S policy;
- ensuring there is demonstrable Top Management support for the OH&S policy;
- keeping up with relevant legislation and regulation within the jurisdiction; and
- planning for OH&S issues.

17.2.3.1.2   Health and safety manager

The Health and Safety Manager's responsibilities shall include, but are not limited to:

- developing and maintaining a suitable and relevant OH&S policy, processes and procedures;
- undertaking risk assessments, as appropriate, for the working environment;
- being a competent person to provide advice and guidance on all OH&S issues;
- ensuring that appropriate controls are in place to reduce OH&S risks to acceptable levels;
- delivering training, as required, for all employees in OH&S;
- undertaking auditing and monitoring activities for the OH&S system, including any remediation required, on behalf of Top Management; and
- keeping up to date with legislative and regulatory changes in OH&S within their jurisdiction.

17.2.3.1.3   Line managers

Line manager's responsibilities shall include, but are not limited to:

- complying with all OH&S policy requirements, including supporting procedures;
- taking care of their own OH&S and that of others who may be affected by their work;
- implementing the OH&S policy in their areas of responsibility;
- ensuring that the appropriate controls are in place in their area of responsibility;
- liaising with the Health and Safety Manager, including advising of any change in working procedures that may require risks to be reassessed;

- communicating the requirements of the IMS, and specifically the OHSMS, to their staff;
- monitoring the effectiveness of controls in their area of responsibility; and
- setting an example for their reports in the area of OH&S.

17.2.3.1.4 FCL

FCL has a duty of care to their employees to provide a safe working environment, as far as is reasonably practicable. This shall include, but is not limited to the provision and maintenance of

- safe access and egress to the office;
- safe systems of work;
- safe plant and equipment for use anywhere in the laboratory;
- provision of appropriate Personal Protective Equipment (PPE); and
- a safe location where any employees may work, including teleworking, mobile working, and on-site working.

17.2.3.1.5 Employees

All employees' responsibilities shall include, but are not limited to

- complying with all OH&S policy requirements, including supporting procedures;
- taking reasonable care of their own OH&S and that of others who may be affected by their work;
- maintaining clean and tidy individual work areas;
- co-operating with Line Managers in all OH&S matters;
- not intentionally, or recklessly, interfering with any plant, equipment, or material relating to case processing;
- correctly using any OH&S equipment or Personal Protective Equipment (PPE) that they are required to use as part of their job role;
- knowing where to find, and use, any safe system of working procedures;
- informing their Line Manager of any change of condition that may affect their work performance (e.g. pregnancy) that may affect existing risk assessments or working practices and procedures; and
- reporting any OH&S incidents, accidents, or health issues to their line managers.

17.2.4 Consultation and participation of employees

FCL shall establish, implement, and maintain a process(es) for consultation and participation of employees at all applicable levels in FCL in the development, planning, implementation, performance evaluation, and actions for improvement of the OH&S management system (OHSMS). This shall include:

- providing mechanisms, time, training, and resources necessary for consultation and participation with all employees for compliance with the IMS;
- providing timely access to clear, understandable, and relevant information about the OHSMS;
- determining and removing obstacles or barriers to participation and minimise those that cannot be removed;

Note

Obstacles and barriers can include failure to respond to employee's inputs or suggestions, language or literacy barriers, reprisals or threats of reprisals, and policies or practices that discourage or penalise employee participation.

- emphasising the consultation of all employees on the following:
  - determining the needs and expectations of interested parties;
  - establishing the OH&S policy;
  - assigning organisational roles, responsibilities, and authorities, as applicable;
  - determining how to fulfil legal and other requirements;
  - establishing OH&S objectives and planning to achieve them;
  - determining applicable controls for outsourcing, procurement, and contractors;
  - determining what needs to be monitored, measured, and evaluated;

- planning, establishing, implementing, and maintaining an audit programme(s); and
- ensuring continual improvement.
- emphasise the participation all employees in the following:
  - determining the mechanisms for their consultation and participation;
  - identifying hazards and assessing risks and opportunities;
  - determining actions to eliminate hazards and reduce OH&S risks;
  - determining competence requirements, training needs, training, and evaluating training;
  - determining what needs to be communicated and how this will be done;
  - determining control measures and their effective implementation and use; and
  - investigating incidents and nonconformities and determining corrective actions.

17.3 Planning for OH&S

17.3.1 Actions to address risks and opportunities

This is the first stage in the PDCA cycle for implementing a robust OHSMS.

The reduction of, and response to, OH&S incidents is part of the OHSMS which shall address the types of incidents, accidents, and health hazards that could happen in a forensic laboratory to:

- give assurance that the OHSMS can achieve its intended outcome(s);
- prevent, or reduce undesired effects; and
- achieve continual improvement.

When determining the risks and opportunities for the OHSMS and its intended outcomes that need to be addressed, the following shall be taken into account:

- hazards;
- OH&S risks and other risks;
- opportunities and other opportunities; and
- legal and other requirements.

17.3.2 Planning for hazard identification

It is essential that Top Management ensures that appropriate plans are put in place to develop and implement the OHSMS. Plans shall cover all operations whether in the office or at any location remote to it (e.g. on-site working).

17.3.2.1 General workplace hazard identification

It is Top Management's responsibility to identify hazards that may affect their employees. A hazard is defined as 'the potential for harm to an employee'.

These can happen in everyday tasks or be related to an occasional specific task (e.g. forensic evidence seizure).

A list of common hazards that may be found in a forensic laboratory is defined in Appendix 6.

Inspection of the workplace shall be carried out to identify hazards present, or likely to be present, by Top Management and/or the Health and Safety Manager. This is one of the major components of the OHSMS and demonstrates management commitment. This process shall identify existing and potential hazards in the workplace, wherever it happens to be. Whilst hazard identification is the first step in the process, the likelihood of the risk happening shall also be calculated and controls put in place to reduce the risk to an acceptable level. If hazards are identified and not treated, then the OHSMS and Top Management's commitment to it will lose credibility with the employees.

Whilst there are a number of hazards that can be identified in the workplace and employees work, jobs for hazard identification shall be prioritised as follows:

- jobs with highest incident or 'near miss' rate;
- jobs with the potential to cause serious incidents, even if there is no previous history of incidents;
- jobs that are new or have recently changed; and
- all other jobs.

Hazard identification shall also be reviewed on a regular basis, at least annually, after any incident, 'near miss', or on influencing change to the jobs undertaken by any employee.

17.3.2.2 Performing the hazard analysis

The first task to be undertaken is a review of the OH&S incident history. This process shall also assist in prioritisation of the jobs to be examined for hazards.

When undertaking workplace hazard identification, all employees shall be involved in the process. They have a unique understanding of how they perform their job, and this is invaluable for the identification of hazards. Involving all employees will help to minimise any omissions and demonstrates management commitment to the employees as well as obtaining their 'buy in' to the process. They will also feel involved in the process and will 'own' the results for their own specific workplace.

As part of the process, all employees shall be involved in discussions as to what they perceive as hazards in their job. They may also have ideas for likelihood of occurrence and methods for reducing them to acceptable levels. If there are any hazards identified that pose an immediate danger, they shall be immediately treated to reduce the risk to an acceptable level, according to FCL's the risk appetite.

Once all of the jobs have been identified, they shall be prioritised for inspection and hazard analysis. Part of the inspection process shall be to break jobs down into component tasks or steps, where appropriate, to facilitate the hazard analysis process. All relevant employees shall be involved in this process to ensure that the work breakdown is correct.

The goal of the inspection of the employee's workplace and discussions shall be to identify:

- what can go wrong (i.e. the hazard);
- the consequences for the employee;
- who else may be affected (e.g. members of the public, visitors, etc.);
- whether a specific class of employees are at risk (e.g. pregnant employees, disabled employees, First Responders, etc.);
- circumstances in which the hazard can occur; and
- any other factors that may contribute to the hazard occurring.

A consistent approach to documenting the findings shall be adopted using Hazard Identification Forms. The contents of the Hazard Identification form are defined in Appendix 7.

Rarely will a hazard have a single root cause and a single effect, more likely it will be the result of a number of factors happening together. This is where the employee's knowledge about their job is invaluable.

Some areas of that should be examined are defined in Appendix 8.

17.3.3 Risk assessment

Once all of the possible hazards have been identified for each job and tasks, the level of risk attached to each shall be determined. OH&S risk assessments are simply a careful examination of the likelihood of the hazard occurring and its potential impact. The risk assessment process that shall be used is defined in Chapter 5. The risks shall be managed using the Corporate Risk Register, as defined in Chapter 5, Appendix 17.

Again, much of the input to this process will come from discussion with the employees themselves and a review of past accidents or near misses, if available. Some inputs to the risk assessment processes used are defined in Appendix 9.

The purpose of risk assessment is to rate the hazards or risks in terms of harm they can cause. Ideally, all hazards shall be eliminated, but often this is not possible and they have to be reduced to an acceptable level. Different levels of health and safety consequences are defined in Appendix 10 and these shall be used in combination with the consequences table defined in Chapter 5, Appendix 5, specifically the following columns:

- value;
- embarrassment level;
- published outside organisation; and
- financial cost of disruption to activities.

Note

The 'value' values in Appendix 10 and Chapter 5, Appendix 5 are mapped directly to each other.

There are a number of different approaches to reducing, or eliminating, OH&S risks. These include the following approaches:

- using a less risky option of working;
- preventing access to the hazard source;

- organising work to reduce the exposure to the hazard;
- ensure that all employees have appropriate Personal Protective Equipment (PPE) to reduce the risk of the hazard occurring; and
- ensure that there are recovery facilities available in case the risk crystallises (e.g. first aid facilities).

The controls chosen should not have a major financial impact, and ideally they should be low-cost solutions.

Risk assessments shall be regularly reviewed, at least annually, after any incident and on any influencing change (e.g. legislative change or change in personal medical circumstances for an employee such as a disability, injury, or pregnancy).

Any change in working practices shall have an OH&S risk assessment carried out on the changed, or new, process, and all OH&S issues shall be considered and addressed prior to the implementation of the change. Any changes shall use the Change Management Process, as defined in Chapter 7, Section 7.4.3, and ensure that the risks are all identified, recorded, and managed to either eliminate the risk or reduce it to an acceptable level.

17.3.4 Control selection

After carrying out the risk assessment and hazard identification, the risks shall be prioritised and treated appropriately using a variety of controls. These can be additional to existing controls or totally new ones. The hierarchy for implementing controls to reduce the risks shall be as follows:

- elimination of the risk;
- reduction to within the risk appetite;
- implementation of engineering controls;
- administrative or procedural controls including signage; and
- using Personal Protective Equipment (PPE).

There are a number of basic OH&S precautions that can be taken as a basic set of controls for employees. These include specific situations as well as generic laboratory controls, and these shall include, but not be limited to:

17.3.4.1 General controls

17.3.4.1.1 Electrical hazards

- all electrical equipment used shall be maintained in accordance with the manufacturers' recommendations;
- all electrical equipment used shall be regularly inspected to ensure that it has no defects. If defects are found they shall be immediately dealt with and unsafe electrical equipment shall be taken out of service until they are made safe. Hazards to check for include, but are not limited to:
  - damaged electrical outlets or plugs;
  - equipment that is overheating (e.g. feels hot), smells (e.g. sparking, smoke, or electrical smell);
  - frayed power leads;
  - gives off electrical shocks;
  - has loose connections and is sparking or arcing; or
  - other tell-tale signs of defective electrical equipment that is not maintained in accordance with the manufacturers' recommendations.
- ensure that any employees that use personally owned equipment have it tested in accordance with jurisdictional requirements and that it is regularly tested;
- ensure that all electric leads are routed to reduce the likelihood of them causing any hazard. Ideally, specifically designed trunking shall be used;
- ensure that power sockets are not overloaded or that employees have not 'daisy-chained' numerous extension leads, specifically multisocket extensions;
- where floor sockets are in use, ensure that appropriate covers are used to ensure that they do not become a hazard and that walkways are routed to avoid them (or they are not used if in a walkway);
- ensure that all employees know what types of fire extinguisher are to be used on electrical fires (i.e. Carbon Dioxide and Powder), how to recognise them and ensure that they are clearly marked; and
- ensure that where an employee identifies a possible electrical defect they immediately report it and await instructions rather than attempt to rectify it themselves.

17.3.4.1.2 Falls

- ensure that all equipment or other materials used are stored properly to prevent falls;
- ensure that all employees are trained appropriately so that the risk of falls is minimised in their work;
- ensure that all employees know how to stack materials and equipment to minimise the risk of falls;
- steps and dedicated stepping devices shall be used to reach high shelves and not use inappropriate devices (e.g. a chair);
- ensure that all employees using stepping devices (e.g. step ladders) know how to use them properly, including having assistance to secure it and hold it firmly;
- promptly report any storage materials that appear damaged or broken; and
- ensure that employees know that heavier items should be stored closer to floor level, rather than on higher shelves.

17.3.4.1.3 Fire and other emergencies

- detailed emergency procedures shall be developed to cover fire and other emergencies, including evacuation plans and assembly points;
- evacuation drills shall be practiced at least once a year for all employees;
- an appropriate number of Fire Wardens shall be appointed and trained in their duties;
- ensure that all employees know the location of emergency equipment (e.g. first aid kits, etc.) and how to use them;
- ensure that all employees know the location of all fire call points, fire extinguishers, and fire blankets and how to use them;
- ensure that all employees know escape routes and assembly point(s); and
- ensure that all employees know the sound(s) and the meaning of any alarms.

17.3.4.1.4 First aid and accident reporting

- ensure that all employees know how to report any accident or 'near miss', even if they do not result in an incident relating to an employee or visitor;
- ensure that all accidents and near misses are reported via Line Managers;
- ensure that there is a process for anonymous reporting of incidents (or suspected incidents) and that it is available to all employees;
- ensure that trained first aiders are available, as per legislative requirements, and that their qualifications/certifications are maintained;
- ensure that appropriate first aid equipment is available as required;
- ensure that First Aid provision is adequate and appropriate;
- where appropriate, all relevant legislation and regulations within the jurisdiction are met;
- ensure that there are sufficient 'First Aiders' available as required either by internal procedures or the legislation within the jurisdiction;
- ensure that First Aid is applied wherever a person is subject to an incident, where life needs to be preserved or the consequences of the incident are minimised or controlled until appropriate professional help is available. First Aid should also be administered where injuries are minor and need no external medical health (e.g. treatment does not need to be administered by a healthcare professional);
- ensure that all employees know both who their 'First Aiders' are and how to contact them, as well as the location of any first aid facilities;
- the level of First Aid provision shall be determined by risk assessment, which will in turn be determined by such factors as:
  - workplace hazards and risks;
  - incident history;
  - the work and disposition of employees;
  - the needs of lone workers;
  - the needs of teleworkers;
  - the needs of mobile workers;
  - the needs of employees of other organisations that are working with employees; and
  - annual leave and other absences of First Aiders.
- ensure that only competent First Aiders undertake First Aider tasks and that their competence is maintained;

- appropriate First Aid equipment shall be held by relevant employees. Equipment locations shall be identified by signage appropriate to the requirements of the legislation and regulation within the jurisdiction. For individual employees, they shall hold either the minimum required first aid equipment defined by the legislation and regulation within the jurisdiction or agreed internal requirements based on relevant risk assessments;
- ensure that all employees know what incidents need to be reported according to the legislation and regulations within the jurisdiction and how to report them, as defined in Chapter 7, Section 7.4.1; and
- ensure that employees, when assisting an injured colleague, do not place themselves in danger. They shall protect an injured colleague from further harm from the source of the danger, assuming it is safe so to do.

17.3.4.1.5 Hand tools—Powered

- there will be occasions where employees will need to use powered hand tools (e.g. Electric Screwdrivers or other small tools in the laboratory necessary for performing their job). All employees shall be trained in their safe use, prior to being allowed to operate them. In some jurisdictions, it may be necessary to undertake certificated training as a prerequisite prior to use;
- where appropriate, PPE shall be used; and
- ensure that employees actually use the correct tool for the job.

17.3.4.1.6 Housekeeping

- all employees shall ensure that they maintain a tidy workplace and eliminate any hazards due to untidy or unsafe working practices;
- ensure that all walkways and corridors are kept clear of obstructions;
- ensure all that rubbish (whether confidential or not) is disposed of in the proper bins, including recycling for environmental or other purposes, as appropriate. All bins shall be regularly emptied to prevent risks of either overflow or information leakage;
- all sharp edges on equipment, furniture, buildings, or even sharp items of equipment themselves (e.g. knives) shall be appropriately protected to prevent employees injuring themselves; and
- ensure that any equipment used in a case that is being used at the employee's desk is securely stored.

17.3.4.1.7 Lone working

Lone working occurs when an employee is engaging any work-related activity where there is no other employee present to take any action needed to assist in case of need.

- lone working should be avoided as far as possible;
- any employee that is required to perform lone working shall be provided with the facility to summon emergency or other assistance if it is required (e.g. medical emergency, intruders, etc.);
- employees shall minimise the risk to their well-being whilst lone working;
- consideration shall be given to the provision of personal alarms to a manned station;
- some tasks may be prohibited whilst lone working is being undertaken; and
- separate risk assessments shall be undertaken for individuals undertaking lone working, especially for anyone who may have health-related issues.

17.3.4.1.8 Manual handling

- all employees that may be involved in manual handling shall be appropriately trained before performing such operations. Refresher training shall also be undertaken in accordance with the Training Needs Assessment requirements, as defined in Chapter 18, Section 18.2.2. Failure to provide appropriate training may leave employees open to injury and possible injury claims;
- appropriate aids shall be provided to facilitate handling large, heavy, or awkward equipment. These will include trolleys and other wheeled equipment;
- where aids to manual handling are to be used, risk assessments shall be undertaken to ensure that these aids do not themselves introduce new hazards;
- all employees shall avoid attempting to lift or move equipment or other items that they cannot easily manage on their own. Assistance shall always be sought if required and no employee shall attempt operations beyond their own capability;

- all employees shall be taught good manual handling techniques if they are likely to be handling loads that are bulky, heavy, awkward, have sharp edges, or any other relevant hazards. Records of all training undertaken shall be maintained by HR, as defined in Chapter 4, Section 4.7.5;
- where heavy, large, or awkward loads are to be moved, the journey shall be planned. All possible hazards that may affect the journey shall be removed or the hazard minimised. This includes being able to see any hazards as they occur on the journey;
- any employee identifying a hazardous situation relating to manual handling shall report this to their Line Manager or the Health and Safety Manager; and
- all employees shall ensure that their actions in manual handling do not put other employees at risk and follow appropriate procedures or work instructions related to manual handling as part of their work.

17.3.4.1.9   Personal protective equipment (PPE)—General

- there will be some occasions where routine laboratory tasks may require the use of PPE. Where this is a requirement, all employees shall undergo appropriate training and use the PPE provided in the correct manner to reduce the risk of injury, with records of the training maintained; and
- employees shall be educated to safely store their PPE and replace it if it becomes damaged.

17.3.4.1.10   Safety signage

- there may be a variety of different sign types (e.g. colour, shape, and meanings), and employees shall be educated to understand the difference between them. Some are advisory (e.g. Fire Exit), others provide warnings for risks that are present (e.g. slippery floors), others are prohibitory (e.g. No Smoking), others are related to first aid or firefighting (e.g. location of a first aid kit or fire extinguisher).

17.3.4.1.11   Slips and trips

- ensure that all areas have appropriate lighting so that employees can see the floor space and steps;
- ensure that there are no areas that become wet or slippery;
- ensure that appropriate footwear is worn, where appropriate;
- ensure that there are no holes or worn areas in carpets or floors that could contribute to a fall or slip;
- ensure that employees do not run or move too fast in the office, whilst teleworking, or when on site;
- ensure that employees are familiar with manual handling techniques including the safe carrying of loads, to ensure that vision is not impaired leading to a slip or trip; and
- ensure that drawers are not opened so that a risk occurs either from an employee walking into an unexpected hazard or that a chest of drawers or a cabinet overbalances.

17.3.4.1.12   Smoking, alcohol, and drug use

- there shall be a smoking policy in place that defines where and when smoking is permitted. Typically, this will depend on the legislation within the jurisdiction;
- where smoking is permitted, all employees shall be trained to ensure that they dispose of cigarette ends and other smoking materials responsibly and minimise the risk of fire;
- there shall be an alcohol policy in place that defines where and if alcohol consumption is permitted in the office (e.g. a formal office function). In general terms, alcohol consumption shall be strictly prohibited in the laboratory itself. Rules for employees who appear under the influence of alcohol in the workplace shall be defined by HR; and
- there shall be a drug use/abuse policy in place that defines what action an employee is to take if they are taking prescription medication that may affect their work. Illegal drugs shall be strictly prohibited. Rules for employees who appear under the influence of drugs in the workplace shall be defined by HR.

17.3.4.1.13   Stress

- stress in the workplace can be of major concern to employees. Stress can be due to a number of reasons (e.g. work pressure, workplace bullying, cases being worked—e.g. paedophilia, etc.);
- during times of increased work pressure (e.g. tight Turn Round Times) FCL shall ensure that the OH&S of all employees is not put at increased risk;

- risk assessments shall identify all work-related stressors and appropriate action be taken to reduce them. Where appropriate, close monitoring of the situation shall be undertaken;
- a confidential counselling service shall be provided for any employee suffering stress that is related to their role, or from external factors that affects their work;
- Line Managers shall monitor workloads to ensure that no employee is subject to work overload. This shall also include monitoring of working hours and overtime worked;
- eliminate, as far as reasonably practicable, any workplace harassment or bullying of any type;
- HR shall regularly monitor absence statistics to identify any significant trends; and
- preventative action to reduce stress is more effective that trying to find a cure and all employees should be encouraged to advise HR, the OH&S Manager, or their Line Manager(s) of any concerns at the earliest opportunity. Any identified preventive action agreed to be implemented, shall be implemented using the procedures defined in Chapter 4, Section 4.10.

17.3.4.1.14 Waste disposal (general)

- The principles of good waste management are:
  - reduction;
  - recycling;
  - recovery; and
  - responsible for safe disposal.
- all employees have a duty of care to ensure that they only purchase minimum quantities of materials through the approved purchasing process, as defined in Chapter 6, Section 6.7.4 and Chapter 14, Section 14.5;
- all materials shall be recycled wherever possible in line with local recycling schemes. However, care shall be taken to ensure that confidential material (paper, storage media, etc.) is not subject to unauthorised access, modification, or disclosure;
- specific procedures shall be put in place for handling and disposing of confidential materials of all types, as defined in Chapter 12, Section 12.3.14.10; and
- only authorised waste disposal companies shall be used. There shall be traceability of all material being disposed of and the ISM shall retain all disposal certificates.

17.3.4.2   Incident response controls

Whilst the controls above are relevant for an office or laboratory, a number of them will be relevant for incident response situations where employees are required to attend a client site to recover forensic evidence, provide First Responder services or other services as required, as defined in Chapter 8. Whilst all incident response situations may be different, the controls above shall form the basis of good OH&S practices for incident response. Part of the planning process for any incident response activities shall include a Health and Safety Briefing, either carried out by the First Response Team Leader (or their designate) or the instructing client, as defined in Chapter 8, Section 8.1.4 and Chapter 8, Section 8.6.3. The First Response Team Leader shall be responsible for ensuring all health and safety issues at the incident are identified, documented, and treated accordingly, including but not limited to:

- the prime task of the First Response Team Leader shall be to ensure the health and safety of all persons at the incident site;
- if possible, a health and safety briefing shall be carried out prior to any move to the incident site;
- consideration shall be given to unfamiliar equipment that may pose an electrical hazard to the First Response Team;
- some electrical equipment may hold an electric charge after unplugging;
- consideration shall be given to unfamiliar equipment that may pose a manual handling hazard, have sharp edges or that may cause any other injury;
- if imaging on site, consideration shall be given to the safe handling of all equipment and ensure that employees do not void any manufacturer's warranties;
- some equipment may give out radio waves that may be dangerous (e.g. microwave transmissions);
- some equipment may have lasers attached that may damage eyesight;
- travel and subsistence issues shall be dealt with for any employee travelling to and from an incident scene, as appropriate;
- any controls put in place shall not affect the evidence or its secure recovery;
- unfamiliar chemicals and liquids may be present at the incident site; and
- on arrival at the incident site, the First Response Team Leader shall scan the incident site for sights, sounds, smells, or anything else that does not 'seem right'. This may require the incident risk assessment to be revised with appropriate additional risk treatment put in place.

17.3.4.3 Work controls for forensic case processing

Most OH&S hazards and risks are the same for forensic case processing as those in the office environment but with some additional ones. The following additional risks may apply:

- a large percentage of forensic cases today deal with paedophile material. Mandatory counselling for all those involved in paedophile cases shall be undertaken on a regular basis;
- counselling and evaluation shall take place for all new employees prior to them working on any paedophile or other possibly distressing cases;
- when an employee stops working on forensic cases and is deployed on other duties, a final counselling session should take place;
- records of counselling shall be maintained on the employee's HR records;
- Line Managers shall be trained to detect any possible signs of distress amongst their employees relating to any case work (or other external factors). If detected, the Line Manager shall consult with HR to determine the treatment to reduce the effect of the hazard;
- all forensic workstations shall have rubber mats located under and around the workbenches to prevent earthing;
- no employee shall be unnecessarily exposed to disturbing images of any type;
- circuit breakers shall be provided to cut power to all equipment locally and for the whole laboratory in case of accident; and
- antistatic flooring and wristbands shall be provided to protect employees, as well as volatile evidence.

17.3.4.4 Teleworking controls

- teleworking is defined as an employee who spends a significant amount of their work time working from their home or some other nonoffice location. It is different from mobile working as it is from a fixed location remote from FCL's remises.
- depending on the legislation within the jurisdiction, there may be a legal requirement to provide a safe and secure working environment for Teleworkers in their own home or other remote site and be legally liable for its provision and maintenance. They may also be liable for any equipment they provide to the Teleworker but usually not for equipment and facilities provided by the Teleworker;
- all Teleworkers shall have risk assessments carried out on their working environments, wherever they are, and not be permitted to undertake any teleworking until the risk assessment has been carried out and appropriate risk treatment is put in place;
- for those teleworking from home, the risks are not only to the employee, but also to their families, visitors to their home, etc., and these cannot be overstated, especially if there are young children present;
- all FCL supplied equipment that a teleworking employee uses shall be regularly checked to ensure that it is properly maintained in accordance with manufacturer's recommendations and is not in any condition that may cause harm to the employee or their family;
- anyone providing training for safe working to a Teleworker shall be competent to provide such training. All records of such training shall be recorded by HR in line with the procedures defined in Chapter 4, Section 4.7.5; and
- in general terms, the teleworking employee's home shall be regarded as an extension of the office and all OH&S risks are treated as if they were in the office.

17.3.4.5 Mobile working controls

Mobile working is where any employee uses an information processing device of any type whilst travelling outside the office. This is different from Teleworking, which is from a fixed remote location, as it can be from any location anywhere in the world.

- all mobile workers shall be trained in issues relating to mobile working, both from a security and health and safety viewpoint. All records of such training shall be recorded by HR;
- all FCL supplied equipment that a mobile employee uses shall be regularly checked to ensure that it is properly maintained in accordance with manufacturer's recommendations and is not in any condition that may cause harm to the employee; and
- in general terms, any mobile working location should be regarded as an extension of the office and all OH&S risks treated as if they were in the office.

17.3.4.6 Display screen equipment (DSE)

DSE refers to any equipment that is used to present information to a user from an information processing device. These can include Visual Display Units (VDUs), Visual Display Terminals (VDTs), Cathode Ray Tubes (CRTs), Liquid Display Crystal (LCD) screens, or any other similar technology. These can be attached to servers, desktop computers, laptops or notebooks, or mobile information processing devices. Health problems can be caused by poor design of the employee's workspace, and careful design can substantially reduce or even eliminate the risk of any DSE-related health risks:

- all FCL employees use information processing devices and so shall use some form of DSE. This will also include teleworkers and mobile workers. Compliance with any relevant DSE legislation or regulation within the relevant jurisdiction shall be undertaken, this may include a definition as to whom the legislation or regulation applies;
- most issues related to DSE, health, and safety have little to do with the DSE itself, but its use. All DSE shall be used appropriately and not negatively impact the health and safety of FCL employees;
- typical issues relating to DSE use are Upper Limb Disorders (ULDs). These are typified by pains in the hands, wrists, neck, shoulders, or back. Other issues can be stress and temporary eye strain (but not eye damage). Many issues can be avoided by adopting simple measures. Additionally, prolonged use of DSE can lead to tired eyes and may affect eyesight;
- all employees shall be protected from issues relating to DSE hazards according to the legislation and regulations within the jurisdiction;
- the initial stage of assessment of any hazards within the employee's workplace is for the employee to fill in an initial DSE assessment checklist. This primarily relates to the use of desktop and laptop computers as well as other mobile devices. The DSE Assessment Checklist used is defined in Appendix 11;
- all employees shall undertake eyesight tests on at least an annual basis and obtain suitable glasses for DSE work. FCL shall contribute to those according to legislation within the jurisdiction or as defined by local working practices;
- DSE use can induce stress in employees, but this is usually due to work pressure and not the physical use of DSE. The risk assessments shall ensure that when DSE risk is evaluated, the level of work and work pressure is included;
- all DSE shall be ergonomically situated to ensure that the hazardous effect of its use is minimised and that they meet the legislation or regulations in the jurisdiction;
- workplace lighting shall be appropriate for prolonged DSE use;
- all employees shall be educated that prolonged and uninterrupted DSE use may be harmful and that regular breaks should be taken. In some jurisdictions, this is recommended or mandated. The training syllabus used for training employees about risks from DSE is defined in Appendix 12;
- where a DSE user is pregnant, has just given birth, or is breastfeeding, a regular risk assessment shall be undertaken to ensure that any risks of hazards are minimised or avoided. The same shall apply to any employee with any disabilities or medical issues;
- where mobile devices are used, they may have smaller screens or keyboards and employees shall be advised that these may not be appropriate for prolonged use. Alternative communication devices, or devices such as docking stations, shall be used wherever possible, especially if the employee has raised an issue with the use of a small screen or keyboard;
- wherever possible, aids to assist mouse or pointing devices shall be used. These include mouse pads with wrist rests, dedicated wrist rests, other types of pointing devices such as tracker balls, etc.;
- one of the most important factors to reduce, if not eliminate, ULD is the proper evaluation of the workplace (whether in the office or for teleworkers and others) from an optimum ergonomic viewpoint. These shall be regularly carried out with their results documented and retained with the employee's personnel records held by HR. This is more important if the employee is pregnant, just given birth, breastfeeding or has some medical complaint that affects their work;
- appropriate furniture shall be supplied to all employees to reduce the likelihood of ULD. This includes adjustable seating, appropriate lighting, alternative input devices, document holders, footrests, glare avoidance measures (e.g. location away from windows or blinds), etc.;
- when using DSE, employees shall understand the requirements to have a clean screen, have fonts that are 'easy on the eyes', ensure that text is large enough to read, that the screen does not flicker, etc.;
- where issues (incidents) have been reported relating to DSE, the most serious risks shall be addressed first, and prioritise all other issues;
- all DSE assessors (and others involved in determining controls) shall be aware of possible exaggeration of claims that may be made by employees, obtain objective evidence to support claims, and take appropriate action;
- all employees shall fill in a DSE Assessment Checklist themselves for each DSE that they use;
- the DSE Assessor shall evaluate the filled-in DSE Assessment Checklists and consider further controls for treating the risks and hazards identified. The forms for this are defined in Appendix 13;

- all employees shall be educated to ensure that they report any persistent pain/discomfort that they experience from DSE use. In some jurisdictions, this shall be formally reported in the mandatory 'Accident Book' where required by the legislation or regulation within the jurisdiction. Where this is not mandated, it shall be reported to the Health and Safety Manager, their Line Manager, or the Service Desk. It shall be treated as an incident as defined in Chapter 7, Section 7.4.1;
- any legislative or regulatory requirements for eye tests relating to DSE use shall be complied with for the jurisdiction of operations. This may include regular eye tests for employees during employment;
- where any change of equipment, working practice, or employee tasking occurs, consideration of a revised risk assessment shall be undertaken; and
- ensure that all employees are made aware of the measures taken to protect them and their own personal responsibilities to report any influencing changes or incident.

Note

It may be possible to carry out a baseline assessment for all employees and an additional one for those deemed specifically at risk (e.g. pregnancy, disability, etc.), rather than an individual risk assessment for each employee.

17.3.4.7 Pregnancy controls

- employees who are pregnant, just given birth or breastfeeding have additional OH&S needs above other employees, and these may be covered by specific legislation within the jurisdiction of operations. They shall have additional risk assessments performed for them as soon as they advise HR that they are pregnant;
- as with normal risk assessments, any hazards shall be identified that are specific to the situation (i.e. pregnancy), their possible harm shall be calculated, the hazard reduced or eliminated by application of one or more controls and the situation monitored regularly. This will be relative to unborn children, newly born children, or breastfed children;
- regular risk assessments shall be undertaken during the pregnancy, after birth, and during breastfeeding as this is a dynamic process not a static one. Different risks may be present at different times during the pregnancy, immediately after birth, and during breastfeeding;
- where this process does not reduce the hazard risk to an acceptable level, adjustment of working patterns or conditions of work shall be considered for relevant employees. This situation may be covered in legislation within the jurisdiction (e.g. prolonged maternity leave);
- where working at night is undertaken by an employee who is pregnant, just given birth, or breastfeeding, this shall require an additional risk assessment to consider these specific risks;
- if the risk assessment identifies additional risks to any employee who is pregnant, just given birth, or breastfeeding, they shall be advised of it and also any measures that is being taking to reduce or avoid the risks. This process may involve a consultation process between the employee and HR and/or the Health and Safety Manager;
- employees who are pregnant, just given birth, or breastfeeding shall also have a duty of care to themselves to protect themselves as well as any controls that FCL may put in place;
- whilst pregnant, just given birth, or breastfeeding, some substances that would not normally be hazardous (e.g. chemical cleaning materials) may well prove to be. These shall be risk assessed for the specific situation. Many chemical products already carry identification and warning labels relating to toxicity, though these may vary between different jurisdictions;
- whilst there is not a great deal of reliable empirical evidence linking chemicals with genetic disorders, a precautionary stance shall be undertaken with regard to dealing with any chemicals that could be linked to possible reproductive disorders;
- during pregnancy, the body changes shape and this will affect body posture and can often affect working practices. Ongoing risk assessments shall be undertaken and steps taken to reduce any effects that the pregnancy may bring. This is especially relevant in seating, manual handling, use of PPE, and use of information processing devices of all types;
- whilst an employee is pregnant, just giving birth, or is breastfeeding, the provision of a safe and secure location for resting and breastfeeding to take place shall be considered, as well as easy access to toilet (and associated hygiene) facilities;
- where emergency evacuation is needed (e.g. a fire alarm), any employee that is pregnant, just given birth, or breastfeeding shall have an appointed 'buddy' to assist them in the evacuation process;

- disclosure to HR of a pregnancy, or any information relating to it, shall be treated in the strictest confidence and not divulged if the mother to be does not wish the fact to be known; and
- all legislation within the jurisdiction relating to pregnancy and maternity/paternity rights shall be met.

17.3.5 Creating the risk register

Once the risk assessment has been carried out, the results shall be documented and managed using the Corporate Risk Register.

17.3.6 Legal, regulatory, and other requirements

It is essential that all relevant legal and regulatory requirements for OH&S within the jurisdiction are identified and that these shall all be taken into consideration when the OHSMS is being implemented and operated. This is defined in Chapter 12, Section 12.3.13.

Within many jurisdictions, there are different legislative and regulatory OH&S requirements. They may have different requirements in performing tasks such as risk assessments or to provide protection for different people (e.g. employees, members of the public, etc.). Top Management shall ensure that they are aware of such differences, and it is imperative that a competent external resource is used to provide specialist advice.

Top Management shall also ensure that they maintain the list of applicable legislation and regulations and that their OH&S Management System is updated to ensure compliance with any relevant changes.

Some examples of drivers for OH&S are defined in Appendix 4.

All employees shall be made aware of these requirements.

17.3.7 Objectives

An OHSMS shall be established in FCL, implemented, monitored, and maintained with supporting framework to achieve defined OH&S objectives.

These objectives shall take into account:

- the results of the assessment of risks and opportunities;
- applicable legislation, regulation, and good practice; and
- the results of consultation with employees and, where applicable, their representatives.

And be defined, agreed and documented. They shall be aligned to the OH&S policy and be relevant to operations carried out in the workplace. The SMART (Specific, Measurable, Achievable, Relevant, Time-bound) approach shall be used to evaluate OH&S objectives, as defined in Chapter 3, Section 3.1.17;

The OH&S objectives have been defined in Appendix 5. Appropriate metrics shall be defined and be measurable so that performance against the objectives can be measured, analysed with corrective action taken where appropriate.

OH&S responsibilities for OH&S shall be established and communicated to all levels of employees. This shall be reinforced at induction and refresher training, as defined in Chapter 6, Section 6.12.5. Where additional training is required for those with specific responsibilities (e.g. OH&S Manager, DSE Assessor, etc.), it shall be incorporated into training plans after being identified by relevant TNA reviews, as defined in Chapter 18, Section 18.2.2.

The Management Review shall ensure that at least annually the OH&S objectives are reviewed, adjusted as necessary, and ensure continuously improvement of the OHSMS, as defined in Chapter 4, Section 4.10.

17.3.8 Planning to achieve OH&S objectives

When planning how to achieve its OH&S objectives, the following shall be determined:

- what metrics shall be used to provide evidence of meeting objectives;
- what resources will be required (people, financial, equipment, and infrastructure);
- who will be responsible for evaluating results;
- frequency of reporting;
- how the results will be evaluated, including indicators for monitoring; and
- how the actions to achieve OH&S objectives shall be embedded in business processes.

17.4 Support for the OHSMS

Once all of the planning for the OHSMS has been completed and the risk treatment agreed, the relevant controls shall be implemented and maintained. To ensure that the controls are properly implemented and continuously improved, the following shall be carried out:

17.4.1 Resource provision

- Top Management shall take visible and demonstrable ownership and final accountability for the OHSMS;
- a Health and Safety Manager shall be appointed by Top Management to specifically manage the OHSMS on a day-to-day basis. This may be one of a number of roles that the employee fulfils or may be a dedicated role;
- Top Management shall ensure that there are sufficient competent resources appointed and in place to effectively implement, manage, monitor, and continuously improve the OHSMS;
- Top Management shall ensure that there is sufficient budget allocated to implement, manage, monitor, and continuously improve the OHSMS;
- Top Management shall ensure that there is sufficient technology to implement, manage, monitor, and continuously improve the OHSMS. This includes office and laboratory equipment as well as PPE;
- the OHSMS policies, procedures, and supporting infrastructure shall be fully documented and made available to all employees;
- regular reports relating to the operation of the OHSMS shall be produced for the Management Review and continuous improvement, as defined in Chapter 4. Sections 4.9 and 4.10 respectively; and
- Health and Safety posters shall be clearly displayed, as required by the legislation and regulation within the jurisdiction. This shall include the location and identity of key OH&S-appointed employees.

17.4.2 Some operational responsibilities and accountabilities

Specific OH&S responsibilities shall be contained in individual job descriptions and agreed between the employee, their Line Manager, and HR. However, an overview of generic operational responsibilities is defined below:

17.4.2.1 Top management

Note

This is a role for a nominated member of Top Management, rather than a collective responsibility for day-to-day operations.

- Top Management shall own OH&S;
- Top Management shall approve the Health and Safety Policy;
- Top Management shall appoint an employee (the Health and Safety Manager), with appropriate authority, to develop, implement, manage, monitor, and continuously improve the OH&S Management System; and
- Top Management shall attend the Management Review and approve the changes necessary, as decided at the review.

17.4.2.2 Health and safety manager

A full job description for the Health and Safety Manager is defined in Appendix 3.

17.4.2.3 Line management

In addition to the responsibilities above, Line Management shall have the following responsibilities:

- making an official record of risk assessment findings;
- addressing the risks found in the office, laboratory, or on site to eliminate them or reduce them to an acceptable level;
- ensure that appropriate training and awareness are provided to all employees, appropriate to their job roles;
- provide a safe and secure workplace for all employees (wherever that is);
- ensure that all equipment (including any plant and machinery) is safe to use, that safe working practices are set up and followed, and that employees receive appropriate training to use it;

- provide adequate first aid facilities, including trained First Aiders;
- set up emergency response plans, maintain them, and ensure that they are regularly exercised and tested, as defined in Chapter 13;
- advise all employees of any potential hazards in any of the work that they undertake as part of their role. This can include hazards from working in the laboratory, office, or on site as well as any hazards present in any equipment or materials in use in any location;
- ensure that all premises meet requirements in the jurisdiction for ventilation, temperature, lighting, washing, and resting facilities, as appropriate;
- ensure that the correct equipment is used for all tasks and that it is properly maintained according to the manufacturer's specifications, as defined in Chapter 7, Section 7.5.4;
- prevent or control exposure to any hazards that may affect an employee's health and welfare;
- provide appropriate PPE for all employees, as needed;
- ensure that appropriate signage is located throughout the premises to advise of Health and Safety issues, as required in the jurisdiction; and
- maintain records of any OH&S incidents or 'near misses' and reporting them to appropriate authorities as required in the jurisdiction.

17.4.2.4 Employees

As well as the management responsibilities for OH&S, each employee shall have the responsibilities as well as rights, and these shall include:

- taking reasonable care of their own health and safety whilst at work, wherever that may be;
- taking reasonable care not to put fellow employees, visitors, third-party employees, or members of the public at risk during the performance of their role;
- cooperate with the management in all OH&S matters, including reporting incidents, 'near misses', using PPE when required, and undertaking training as required;
- advising management, as appropriate, of any health issues that may affect their work or require a risk assessment to be revised (e.g. becoming pregnant, are taking any medication, or have any disability or injury that may affect their work, etc.);
- advise management of any OH&S concerns that they may have; and
- use all equipment in the correct manner.

17.4.3 Competence, training, and awareness

All employees shall be deemed competent in the area of OH&S by ensuring that they undertake appropriate training and attend mandatory awareness sessions with records of training and awareness maintained by HR.

All training needs in the area of OH&S shall be identified in the Training Needs Analysis process undertaken at least on an annual basis as part of the employee's performance assessment, as defined in Chapter 18, Section 18.2.1.8.

As in common with other management systems implemented in the IMS (e.g. ISO 9001, ISO/IEC 27001, etc.), all employees shall be made aware of their contribution to the continuous improvement of the OHSMS as well as the possible consequences of failure to comply with the requirements of the OHSMS.

Levels of training required shall depend on the specific responsibilities and accountabilities of the employee and the OH&S risk(s) that they face in their specific job role.

17.4.4 Communications

Top Management shall establish an appropriate process for communication of the OH&S policy and supporting procedures to all employees, relevant interested parties, and visitors.

Effective communication of the OH&S message relies on:

- incoming information;
- internal information flows; and
- outward information transmission.

Incoming information that shall consist of legislative or regulatory requirements as well as developments within OH&S management practice and risk control.

Internal information flow shall include the whole range of OH&S information from the OH&S policy through to lessons learned and incident reporting and corrective action as part of the Management Review process.

For employees, this shall consist of the online OHSMS and regular awareness and training sessions as well as regular practice of relevant procedures (e.g. evacuation). Employees shall also be encouraged to be involved in the identification and reporting of hazards and the selection of appropriate controls to eliminate them or at least reduce the risk to an acceptable level. This shall apply to current as well as planned working practices. Where appropriate, they shall be involved in the investigation of any incident or 'near miss' that affects them.

For visitors, they shall all be given an OH&S briefing and records of this shall be held in the visitor's book.

Where an external organisation requests information about the OH&S policy and procedures, records of this shall be maintained by the Health and Safety Manager.

17.4.5   OH&S documentation

Within the IMS, the OH&S documentation shall include the following:

- the OH&S policy and its scope;
- the measurable OH&S objectives (or KPIs) set by management;
- procedures, work instructions, and forms used to support the OH&S policy; and
- relevant records to provide objective evidence of the conformity to the requirements of the OHSMS and ISO 45001 that was used to develop it.

All documents and records shall be controlled in accordance with the document and record control procedures, as defined in Chapter 4, Sections 4.7.5.

17.5   Operational planning and control

Operational planning and control of the processes shall be established and implemented as necessary to enhance OH&S, by eliminating hazards or, if not practicable, by reducing the OH&S risks to levels as low as reasonably practicable for operational areas and activities.

Examples of operational control of the processes shall include:

- the use of documented procedures and systems of work;
- ensuring employee competence;
- establishing preventive or predictive maintenance and inspection programmes;
- specifications for the procurement of goods and services;
- application of legal requirements and other requirements, or manufacturers' instructions for equipment; and
- engineering and administrative controls.

17.5.1   Eliminating hazards and reducing OH&S risks

Once the hazard and risk analysis has been undertaken, it shall be necessary to implement a number of controls to either eliminate the hazard or reduce its impact to an acceptable level.

The order of precedence and effectiveness of control implementation is:

- elimination;
- substitution;
- engineering controls;
- administrative controls; and
- PPE.

In an ideal world, all controls would be engineering ones but this is impractical, so a mix of all five types of control shall be used.

17.5.1.1   Elimination

This is removing the hazard. Examples include:

- stopping using hazardous chemicals;

- applying ergonomics approaches when planning new workplaces; and
- eliminating monotonous work or work that causes negative stress.

17.5.1.2 Substitution

This is replacing the hazardous with less hazardous. Examples include:

- changing to answering customer complaints with online guidance;
- combating OH&S risks at source;
- adapting to technical progress;
- changing slippery floor material; and
- lowering voltage requirements for equipment.

17.5.1.3 Engineering controls

These are controls that eliminate the hazard or reduce it to an acceptable level, including but not limited to:

- designing the premises, process, or operation to eliminate the hazard or reduce it to an acceptable level;
- enclosing the hazard by use of appropriate controls;
- isolating the hazard by using appropriate controls; and
- removal or redirection of the hazard.

17.5.1.4 Administrative controls

These are controls that eliminate the hazard or reduce it to an acceptable level, including but not limited to:

- developing and implementing administrative procedures, work instructions, and safe working practices for all locations where employees may work;
- monitoring and controlling exposure to hazardous situations or materials;
- use of alarms, signs, and warning notices; and
- training, awareness, and developing competencies appropriate to job roles.

17.5.1.5 Personal protective equipment (PPE)

These are controls that eliminate the hazard or reduce it to an acceptable level, including but not limited to the following situations:

- where engineering or administrative controls either do not eliminate the hazard or reduce it to an acceptable level;
- whilst engineering or administrative controls are being developed or are not fully implemented;
- where implemented engineering or administrative controls do not provide sufficient protection against the identified hazards or risks; and
- during situations where engineering or administrative controls are not feasible or appropriate (e.g. incident response off site).

17.5.2 Implementing controls

Each of the above categories of controls has its place on the OHSMS.

17.5.2.1 Some generic controls

There are a number of generic controls that can be implemented in office and laboratory environments. Different locations may have specific requirements, but this is a generic list:

All employees shall:

- ensure that their actions do not cause a hazard, accident, or injury to fellow employees or visitors to the office or laboratory by following stated working practices and procedures;
- maintain a clean and tidy workspace;
- replace all material (equipment, evidence, and files) in their correct location after use and not leave them out in the incorrect storage area;

- return all equipment in a condition fit for the next user, reporting any identified defects to the appropriate reporting point and labelling the equipment appropriately;
- never block or obstruct a fire escape route;
- never allow combustible materials to build up and cause a possible fire hazard;
- ensure that when using any chemical (including cleaning materials, correction fluids, or other chemicals that may pose a hazard if used incorrectly) is used that it is used in accordance with manufacturer's instructions;
- where there are options available for cleaning equipment or offices, that the safer option is used (e.g. wipes rather than sprays, etc.);
- where chemicals have been used, that hands are washed;
- not take exhibits into the office area but only allow them to be located in the secure property store or laboratory;
- not eat in the laboratory;
- report any potential hazard that they identify to their Line Manager or Health and Safety Manager;
- wear appropriate PPE, as required;
- know where first aid kits are located and the identity of First Aiders;
- know and regularly practice the emergency evacuation procedure;
- ensure that all waste from the laboratory and office is disposed of appropriately, as defined in Chapter 12, Section 12.3.14.10. This includes recycling, if appropriate, and secure disposal of confidential material as well as anything else that may cause a hazard; and
- ensure that antistatic devices are used in the laboratory.

17.5.3 Management of change

Where changes are made or new processes and procedures implemented in working processes, a risk assessment of the change shall be undertaken. Where the change is to be implemented, the Change Management Process shall be followed, as defined in Chapter 7, Section 7.4.3.

All existing and new procedures and work instructions relating to operations shall be integrated into the IMS. This shall include:

- policies;
- operational procedures;
- work instructions; and
- records, as appropriate.

The objective of the management of change process is to enhance OH&S at work, by minimising the introduction of new hazards and OH&S risks into the work environment as changes occur (e.g. with technology, equipment, facilities, work practices and procedures, design specifications, raw materials, staffing, standards, or regulations).

17.5.4 Procurement

17.5.4.1 General

Procurement process(es) shall be used to determine, assess, and eliminate hazards, and to reduce OH&S risks associated with new products, services, equipment, or working practices before their introduction into the workplace. This shall include verification that all with new products, services, equipment, or working practices are safe to use by ensuring:

- products, services, and equipment shall be delivered according to specification and shall be tested to ensure they work as intended;
- installations shall be commissioned to ensure they function as designed; and
- any usage requirements, precautions, or other protective measures shall be communicated to relevant employees and made available.

17.5.4.2 Contractors

Contractor activities and operations within a forensic laboratory can include, but not be limited to:

- cleaning;
- construction;

- consultants;
- maintenance;
- operations; and
- physical security.

or other specialists in administrative, accounting, and other functions as required for operations.

Contractors' activities shall be managed using appropriate contracts that clearly define the responsibilities of the parties involved. Contracts shall include, but not be limited to:

- controlling access to hazardous areas;
- integration of the contractor's OH&S processes into the IMS;
- procedures to follow in emergencies; and
- the requirements for hazard reporting.

Contractors shall be evaluated to ensure that they are competent to perform their contractual tasks before being allowed to proceed with their contractual obligations. This shall be performed by:

- ensuring the contractor's OH&S performance records are up to date and satisfactory;
- ensuring that employees who are going to perform the contractual obligations have appropriate qualifications, experience, and competence; and
- resources, equipment, and work preparations are adequate and ready for the work to proceed.

17.5.4.3   Outsourcing

Outsourcing shall be controlled to achieve the intended outcome(s) of the OHSMS.

Note

Outsourcing does not eliminate an organisation's responsibility for OH&S for employees.

Control over outsourced function(s) or process(es) shall be based upon factors such as:

- the ability of the outsourcer to meet the OHSMS requirements;
- the technical competence of the outsourcer to define appropriate controls or assess the adequacy of controls;
- the potential effect the outsourced process or function will have on the ability to achieve the intended outcome(s) of the OHSMS;
- the extent to which the outsourced process or function is shared;
- the capability of the outsourcer to achieve the necessary control through the application of its procurement process; and
- opportunities for improvement.

In some countries, legal and regulatory requirements address outsourced functions or processes.

17.5.5   Emergency preparedness and response

Procedures shall be established and maintained for incident response. These will be for a variety of different reasons including OH&S ones as well as other possible incidents that require an emergency response, as defined in Chapter 8.

Emergency response equipment shall be maintained in line with any legislative or regulatory requirements and good practice for the jurisdiction;

Every incident shall be reported and handled according to the Incident Management Procedures, as defined in Chapter 7, Section 7.4.1.

Each situation shall be judged on its merits and the risks it poses and Emergency and Business Continuity Plans shall be regularly exercised and tested as defined in Chapter 13, Section 13.6.4.

17.6   Performance evaluation

17.6.1   Monitoring, measurement, analysis, and performance evaluation

17.6.1.1   General

To achieve the OHSMS' intended outcomes, the processes that comprise it shall be monitored, measured, and analysed.

The following shall be monitored and measured include, but are not limited to:

- occupational health complaints, employee health (through surveillance), and work environment;
- work-related incidents, injuries and ill health, and complaints, including trends;
- the effectiveness of operational controls and emergency exercises, or the need to modify or introduce new controls; and
- competence.

The following shall be monitored and measured to evaluate the fulfilment of legal requirements include, but are not limited to:

- identified legal requirements (e.g. whether all legal requirements have been determined, and whether the documented register of them is kept up to date);
- collective agreements (when legally binding); and
- the status of identified gaps in compliance.

The following shall be monitored and measured to evaluate the fulfilment of other requirements include, but are not limited to:

- collective agreements (when not legally binding);
- standards and codes;
- corporate and other policies, rules, and regulations; and
- insurance requirements.

Criteria are what shall be used to compare performance against by benchmarking:

- other organisations;
- standards and codes;
- internal objectives; and
- OH&S statistics.

17.6.1.2 Monitoring

Monitoring shall involve continual checking, supervising, critically observing, or determining the status to identify change from the performance level required or expected. Monitoring can be applied to the OHSMS, to processes, or to controls.

17.6.1.2.1 Active monitoring systems

An active monitoring system shall be embedded in operations as part of the IMS so that it has feedback on OH&S issues **before** an incident occurs. It shall include monitoring and management, through the OHSMS, of specific OH&S objectives as well as meeting relevant legislative and regulatory requirements. This shall then provide a solid basis for factual-based decision-making by Top Management. The main advantage of active monitoring is that it is in 'real time' and can reinforce positive achievement in OH&S by publicising and rewarding 'good' OH&S work rather than penalising failures after the event (i.e. an OH&S incident). This can have a serious impact on employee motivation.

Active Monitoring systems shall:

- undertake routine monitoring against defined OH&S objectives;
- check that the OH&S system is operating effectively and efficiently;
- ensure that all employees have appropriate job descriptions, including OH&S responsibilities;
- undertake systematic inspection of all premises for all OH&S risks;
- ongoing monitoring and management of OH&S to ensure that it is effective;
- ongoing audit (and other similar processes, e.g. self-assessments, tests, etc.) to ensure continuous improvement;
- ensure that Top Management continuously improves the OHSMS;
- ensure that preventive and corrective action is taken, as needed;
- ensure remedial action is taken in a timely manner;
- ensure that effective OH&S controls are implemented and managed according to risk exposure; and
- regular monitoring shall be carried out according to the published IMS Calendar, after an incident or after an influencing change.

17.6.1.2.2 Reactive monitoring systems

A reactive OH&S monitoring system shall be implemented that answers the following questions relating to injuries, ill health related to work, losses, or near misses:

- are they occurring?
- how serious are they?
- is OH&S performance getting better or worse?
- what are the costs (not just financial)?
- what are the potential consequences?
- what controls were in place?
- what is the nature of the root cause?
- what remedial (corrective or preventive) action is needed?
- where are they occurring?

17.6.1.3 Performance measurement

Performance measurement shall be carried out by appropriate means and this can include:

- audits;
- direct observation;
- examination of monitoring devices;
- examination of records;
- self-assessments; and
- talking to employees.

These shall be used individually or in combination, as appropriate.

Measurement generally involves the assignment of numbers to objects or events. It is the basis for quantitative data and is generally associated with the performance evaluation of safety programmes and health surveillance.

17.6.1.4 Analysis

Analysis is the process of examining data to reveal relationships, patterns, and trends. This can mean the use of statistical operations, including information from other similar organisations, to help draw conclusions from the data. This process is most often associated with measurement activities.

17.6.2 Evaluation of compliance

The frequency and timing of compliance or performance evaluations can vary depending on the importance of the requirement, variations in operating conditions, changes in legal requirements and other requirements, and FCL's past performance. A variety of methods shall be used to maintain its knowledge and understanding of its compliance status.

One or more procedures shall be established, implemented, and maintained to monitor and measure OH&S performance and compliance. This shall be consistent with the processes of the other management systems implemented in the IMS shall use the SMARTER (Specific, Meaningful, Achievable, Relevant, Time Bound, Evaluate, Readjust) process.

- this process, for OH&S, shall ensure that the measurements are appropriate;
- the measurement and monitoring process is in line, and reports against, the Health and Safety Objectives (using KPIs or metrics);
- measures the effectiveness of the controls implemented are for health as well as safety;
- ensures that any issues identified within the OHSMS are completely resolved using the continuous improvement process, as defined in Chapter 4, Section 4.10; and
- ensure that appropriate records are available for all internal audits, self-assessments, external audits, or other assessments as appropriate within the jurisdiction, as defined in Chapter 4, Section 4.7.5

Monitoring and measurement of compliance shall include legislative, regulatory, and Management System requirements. The reporting of monitoring and measurement of compliance shall depend on the requirements of legislative, regulatory, and Management System requirements depending on the jurisdiction.

The following questions shall be answered:

- are controls in place to minimise the hazard or to eliminate it?
- do these controls comply with at least the minimum legislation within the jurisdiction?
- do they operate effectively?

Measurement is a key step in any management process and with the CAPA process and shall form the basis of continuous improvement. If measurement is not carried out correctly, the effectiveness of the OH&S system cannot be validated, which in turn undermines the effective control of health and safety risks. Typically, health and safety statistics rely on the reporting of injuries or incidents, or lack of them. This is a measure of failure and this shall not be used as a single measure of health and safety effectiveness, but a basket of positive and negative measures shall be used to show effectiveness of its controls.

The reasons for this are that the reporting of injury or incident rates alone has a number of inherent problems:

- a low injury rate can lead to complacency;
- an organisation can have what appears to be a low injury rate on account of low numbers of employees exposed to the hazard or sheer luck;
- employees may stay off work for reasons that are not directly linked with the severity of their injury or the incident;
- injury or incident rates do not measure the severity of the incident or injury;
- injury or incident rates reflect outcomes, not the root cause of the incident or injury;
- just using incident or injury rates can lead to underreporting to maintain a 'good' result, especially if linked to a reward system;
- to have a statistic, it requires a control to fail for the incident or injury to take place; and
- when an incident or injury occurs, it is as a consequence of the hazard not being under control and the risk crystallising rather than an indication that the hazard was properly controlled.

The measurement of OH&S success used is defined in Appendix 14.

17.6.3 Audits

Regular OH&S audits shall be undertaken according to the IMS Calendar, as defined in Chapter 4, Appendix 46. This shall include the following types of audits:

- external (3rd Party) audits;
- internal (1st Party) audits;
- self-assessments (1st Party Audits); and
- supplier (2nd Party) audits.

The purpose of the audits is to evaluate and continuously improve the OHSMS implemented and ensure that:

- the implementation conforms to the requirements of ISO 45001;
- has been properly implemented and maintained;
- is effective in meeting the defined OH&S objectives;
- is monitored appropriately;
- produces timely and useful management reports for Top Management action;
- has any corrective and preventive OH&S action effectively implemented and either eliminate the hazard or reduces the risk to an acceptable level; and
- Auditors are independent of the area being audited.

All 1st and 2nd party audits performed shall be conducted in line with the Internal Audit procedures, as defined in Chapter 4, Section 4.9.

17.6.4 Management review

Top Management shall review the OHSMS at regular intervals, at least annually, on influencing change or after any incident. As the OHSMS is integrated into the IMS, OH&S issues shall be dealt with at the common Management Review process, as defined in Chapter 4, Section 4.9.3 unless a specific alternative requirement is identified.

The agenda for the inclusion of OH&S matters is defined in Chapter 4, Appendix 46.

Records of all decisions made at Management Reviews shall be documented and retained as records, as defined in Chapter 4, Section 4.7.5. This is the main review point of all OH&S objectives, performance, and compliance reviews and is the primary point for reviewing and adjusting the objectives or deciding any corrective or preventive action. The Management Review may use the inputs from any other OH&S meetings or incident reports, or action may be taken after these without the need to call for a Management Review. Records of any such actions shall be taken and managed through the CAPA process.

The Mapping between the IMS and ISO 45001 is defined in Appendix 18.

17.7   Improvement

17.7.1   General

FCL shall consider the results from analysis and evaluation of OH&S performance, evaluation of compliance, internal audits, and management review when taking action to improve.

Examples of improvement include corrective action, continual improvement, breakthrough change, innovation, and re-organisation.

17.7.2   Incident reporting, investigation, and management

The immediate purpose of incident reporting (including 'near misses') is to identify immediate and underlying causes, so that the reoccurrence of the incident is minimised if not eliminated. All employees and visitors shall be required to report any incidents, injuries, or near misses so that appropriate preventive or corrective action may be taken. Whilst individual employees may be occasionally reluctant to report an incident, injury, or 'near miss', Line Managers shall be encouraged to generate a positive OH&S culture where the emphasis is on continuous improvement and not a 'blame' culture.

The process for reporting information security incidents shall be followed, as defined in Chapter 7, Section 7.4.1, but for OH&S incidents rather than information security incidents. This has the advantage of using a common incident reporting process and a single incident database held by the Service Desk.

Details of what shall be recorded on an incident report are the main information defined in Chapter 7, Section 7.4.1.4 relating the identity and details of the employee reporting the incident. Additionally, there is some OH&S-specific information required and this is defined in Appendix 15.

Wherever there is an incident, including any injury or near miss, it shall be investigated. A procedure shall be developed, implemented, and maintained to investigate the OH&S incident or near miss in a timely manner. This shall include:

- identification of the underlying failure of either implemented controls, or lack of controls, that caused or contributed to the incident;
- analysing the incident to determine the root cause, as defined in Chapter 4, Appendix 53;
- updating any relevant risk assessments, if appropriate;
- identifying any appropriate corrective action;
- identifying any preventive action;
- identifying any other opportunities for continual improvement;
- implementing relevant action through the continuous improvement process, as defined in Chapter 4, Section 4.10;
- updating any relevant procedures;
- communicating the results of the investigation and any updated procedures and/or work instructions;
- undertaking a PIR to ensure that the controls implemented have eliminated the hazard, or at least reduced it to an acceptable level or risk, as defined in the Continuous Improvement Policy defined in Chapter 4, Appendix 24; and
- creating a record of the investigation and all actions taken.

The implementation of the incident management process is essential to ensure that all OH&S (and any other incidents) are managed in a consistent and effective manner. The OH&S Incident Investigation checklist and form is defined in Appendix 16.

Whilst the OH&S Incident Investigation checklist and form may be filled in by the Health and Safety Manager, it may be carried out by another employee. The completed forms shall be reviewed by the Health and Safety Manager, and Top Management, if appropriate (e.g. when a member of public is involved, or cases of serious injury or death). The Incident Review Form contents are defined in Appendix 17.

Note

There may be specific reporting requirements specified within legislation and/or regulations within the jurisdiction of a forensic laboratory's operations for the reporting of incidents (e.g. types, reporting formats, reporting timescales, etc.).

17.7.3 Nonconformity and corrective action

Nonconformity typically comes from performance evaluation and is classified as defined in Chapter 4, Section 4.9.2.5.

Where a nonconformity is raised, it shall be addressed using the CAPA process.

Reviewing the effectiveness of corrective actions by using a PIR shall determine to the extent to which the implemented corrective actions adequately address the root cause(s).

17.7.4 Continual improvement

Continuous improvement in the OH&S context shall include, but not be limited to:

- adopting new technology;
- adopting updated good practices, as available;
- adopting suggestions and recommendations from interested parties;
- gaining and adopting new knowledge and understanding of OH&S-related issues;
- using new or improved tools and processes;
- updating competence; and
- achieving improved performance with fewer resources (i.e. simplification, streamlining, etc.).

Appendix 1—OH&S policy checklist

Top Management shall define and authorise the OH&S policy and ensure that within the defined scope of its OHSMS, it:

- has demonstrable Top Management commitment;
- has appropriate financial and physical resources committed to maintain and improve OH&S, as defined in Chapter 4, Section 4.7.1, and Section 17.4.1;
- includes the commitment to at least comply with applicable legislative and regulatory requirement within the jurisdiction of operations, as defined in Chapter 12, Section 12.3.13.1 and Section 17.3.6;
- is appropriate to the nature and scale of the risks faced in all of its operations, as defined in Chapter 5 and Sections 17.3.3 and 17.3.5;
- appoints competent employees to assist in the implementation of the OH&S policy, as defined in Chapter 4, Section 4.5.3, and elsewhere for specific management systems and job descriptions;
- ensures that a proper and effective risk assessment system identifies hazards, as defined in Chapter 5 and Section 17.3.2;
- assesses the risks and implements measures to remove, reduce, or control the risks so far as is reasonably practicable; as defined in Chapter 5 and Sections 17.3.3 and 17.3.4;
- reassesses risks where new processes are implemented;
- that employee training is undertaken on these changes, as defined in Chapter 4, Sections 4.7.2 and 4.7.3, and Section 17.4.3;
- includes a commitment to the prevention of any OH&S incident, accident, or illness;
- has a framework that establishes the overall direction and realistic and achievable objectives for OH&S, as defined in the IMS;
- has the OH&S framework implemented within the IMS which is consistent with all other policies, processes, and procedures;
- is documented, implemented, and maintained;
- has its OH&S performance measured and monitored;
- ensures that all equipment used is suitable for its intended purpose and that it is maintained in a safe condition;
- establishes arrangements for use, handling, transportation, and storage of any items that are used as part of the employee's duties;
- has any accident, illness, and safety incident fully investigated to determine its root cause, as defined in Chapter 4, Appendix 53, and Section 17.7.2;
- is committed to continuous improvement of its OHSMS, as defined in Chapter 4, Section 4.10, and Section 17.7;

- is communicated to all employees, ensuring that they all are made aware of their personal accountabilities and responsibilities, as defined in Section 17.4.4; and
- is regularly reviewed, at least annually, after any incident or accident or on influencing change to ensure that it remains appropriate.

Appendix 2—The OH&S policy

Implementation and maintenance of this policy shall provide a safe and healthy working environment in accordance with the Occupational Health and Safety legislation and regulations in force in the jurisdiction.

The responsibility for health, safety, and welfare is placed with Top Management. At the heart of this commitment to health and safety are the seven core safety principles that all employees shall be required to embrace and which facilitate this commitment to continual improvement of health and safety performance. These are:

1. All injuries can be prevented.
2. For all employees, involvement and consultation are essential.
3. Top and Line Management shall be responsible for preventing injuries.
4. Working safely and contributing to safety improvements shall be a condition of employment.
5. All operating exposures shall be safeguarded.
6. Training employees to work safely is essential.
7. Prevention of personal injury makes good business sense.

Top Management, through the various management system committees and line management, ensure that all employees shall fulfil these commitments by:

- pursuing the deployment of the safety strategy and the goal of zero injuries, accidents, or health and safety incidents;
- ensuring that arrangements and resources exist to support this policy;
- effective management of OH&S;
- recognising the risks inherent in a consultancy and service management organisation;
- conducting and maintaining risk assessments and safe systems of work;
- meeting the requirements of ISO 45001, the Health and Safety Management specification[a];
- continue to invest in health and safety improvements on a progressive basis, setting objectives and targets in its annual health and safety programmes; and
- engaging and involving all employees in creating and maintaining a safe working environment.

This policy is issued and maintained by the Health and Safety Manager, who also provides advice and guidance on its implementation and ensures compliance.

All employees shall comply with this policy.

Appendix 3—Health and safety manager job description

Objective and role

The Health and Safety Manager is responsible for initiating, developing, and maintaining the culture of health and safety management.

Problems and challenges

The Health and Safety Manager is challenged with balancing the health and safety requirements for providing a safe and secure working environment for employees without stifling innovation and development of product and service offerings.

Principal accountabilities

The Health and Safety Manager shall:

- develop and maintain a suitable and relevant health and safety policy;

---

a. ISO 45001 has now replaced the previous OHSAS 18001 standard.

- provide employees with a safe workplace without risk to health;
- provide employees with a workplace that satisfies health, safety, and welfare requirements for ventilation, temperature, lighting, sanitary, washing, and rest facilities, as defined within the jurisdiction;
- provide employees with safe plant and machinery, and safe movement, storage, and use of articles and substances;
- provide employees with adequate provision of first aid and welfare facilities and support;
- provide employees and visitors with suitable and current information and supervision concerning health and safety policies and practices;
- undertake proper and timely assessment of risks to health and safety, and implementation of measures and arrangements identified as necessary from the assessments;
- provide employees with emergency procedures, first-aid facilities, safety signs, relevant protective clothing and equipment, and incident reporting to the relevant authorities;
- liaises as necessary, with other organisations and relevant authorities, and provides assistance and cooperation concerning audits and remedial actions;
- prevent exposure to, and adequate protection from, hazardous substances, and danger from flammable, explosive, electrical, noise, radiation, and manual handling risks;
- report on health and safety practices and systems;
- develop the health and safety strategy;
- define the direction of in-house technical training seminars to improve overall employee awareness of health and safety issues;
- participate in international, national, and local SIG presentations, and publishes articles describing the health and safety systems and how they relate to the business;
- develop and manage effective working relationships with all appropriate internal and external stakeholders;
- maintain external links to other companies in the industry to gain competitive assessments and share information, where appropriate;
- identify the emerging information technologies to be assimilated, integrated, and introduced within the IMS, which could significantly impact health and safety compliance;
- interface with external industrial and academic organisations to maintain state-of-the-art knowledge in emerging health and safety issues and to enhance FCL's image as a responsible employer;
- adhere to established policies, standards, and procedures; and
- performs all responsibilities in accordance with, or in excess of, the requirements of the IMS.

Authority

The Health and Safety Manager has the authority to:

- develop long-range budget estimation for health and safety issues;
- provide input to acquisition and use of facilities and resources;
- perform risk assessments for health and safety, as required;
- audit the implementation of health and safety;
- establish and make decisions about health and safety reporting methods, and outputs; and
- determines preventive and corrective action to ensure a safe and legally compliant working environment is present.

Contacts
Internal

Contacts are throughout the whole business.

External

Those external contacts will be with appropriate Special Interest Groups (SIGs), other Health and Safety professionals and organisations, as appropriate.

Reports to

The Health and Safety Manager shall report to:
- Top Management.

Appendix 4—Examples of OH&S drivers

There are a number of legislative, regulatory, or other drivers that affect the OHSMS and its supporting procedures. These include, but are not limited to:

- agreements with employees, including employment contracts;
- agreements with local or national authorities;
- agreements with trade or similar unions, if appropriate;
- codes of practice or conduct;
- contractual conditions from clients;
- corporate governance requirements;
- corporate social responsibility;
- good practice;
- judgements or rulings affecting health and safety within the jurisdiction of operations;
- legislation and regulations within the jurisdiction; and
- permits, licences, or any forms of authorisation to operate.

Appendix 5—The forensic laboratory OH&S objectives

There is no such thing as a definitive list of OH&S objectives, below are some that shall be used as a baseline by FCL for inclusion in the OHSMS:

- to reduce the number of OH&S incidents by x% be the end of the year;
- identify any trends in incidents and implement corrective or preventive action as appropriate;
- ensure that 100% of employees have received OHSMS and other relevant health and safety training on an annual basis (either at induction or as refresher training);
- review all risk assessments during the year to ensure that they are still effective and appropriate;
- undertake regular DSE assessments for all employees on a regular basis or influencing change;
- reduce workplace stress;
- encourage all employees to report all OH&S incidents and 'near misses';
- ensure that 100% of reported OH&S incidents and 'near misses' are investigated to determine their root cause, and implement corrective or preventive action as appropriate;
- where OH&S audits indicate a shortfall in implemented processes and procedures, to implement corrective or preventive action as appropriate;
- to ensure that all employees who are working on 'stressful' cases or situations have access as required to appropriate forms of counselling;
- to comply with 100% of legislative and regulatory requirements applicable in the jurisdiction of operations;
- to undertake risk assessments for 100% of cases where employees have to act as First Responders on a client site;
- to ensure that all First Responders are equipped with appropriate Personal Protective Equipment (PPE) for the duties that they are required to undertake;
- to ensure that 100% maintenance of all equipment in accordance with the manufacturers recommendations is undertaken; and
- review the whole OH&S Management System on at least an annual basis at the Management Review, after an OH&S Incident or on influencing change to support continuous improvement.

Appendix 6—Common hazards in a forensic laboratory

The following are a sample list of possible hazards that may be found in a forensic laboratory. It is not meant to be a complete list, as each location or forensic laboratory may have its own specific hazards.

Hazard	Description
Bullying	Possible intimidation of employees, whether in the laboratory or out on site (e.g. working with a third party or recovering evidence)
Chemical (corrosive)	A chemical that, when it comes into contact with metal, an employee's skin, or other materials will cause damage to the material it contacts

Hazard	Description
Chemical (flammable)	A chemical that, when exposed to a heat ignition source, results in combustion
Chemical (toxic)	A chemical that may be encountered by an employee typically by absorption through the skin or inhalation. The amount of chemical involved is critical in the determination of effect
Electrical (fire)	Where an electrical power source causes a fire due to overheating, arcing, or similar
Electrical (loss of power)	Where the electrical power supply fails and this causes equipment failure or data loss
Electrical (shock)	Where an employee is exposed to an electrical current that may cause injury or death to the employee
Electrical (static damage)	Where volatile memory or media is damaged by a static electrical discharge
Ergonomics	Employee injury due to incorrect working environment or repetitive strain (e.g. incorrect positioning of workplace environment whilst using computers)
Fire	Where the workplace is susceptible to a fire
Health	Where an employee suffers from some health issue that may affect the performance of their duties (e.g. a permanent physical or mental disability or a temporary one such as pregnancy of injury)
Mechanical failure	Where equipment used can fail due to poor maintenance or where the equipment is used contrary to the manufacturer's recommended limits
Noise	Where the workplace is subject to noise levels in excess of the permitted limits.
Trip or stumble	Where an employee has a fall whilst walking on normal surfaces. This could be due to a slippery surface or a hazard placed on a floor (e.g. a trailing cable)
Visibility	Where the workplace is insufficiently lit and this impacts the employee's sight and ability to perform their duties safely
Weather	Where inclement weather, of any type, can affect operations.
Workload	Where the employee has an excessive workload or is subject to disturbing images in a forensic case
Workplace specific	Where the employee is working in a specific workplace that has its own specific hazards (e.g. mobile working, teleworking, or attending the scene of an incident)
Workplace violence	Possible violence in the forensic laboratory premises or out on site (e.g. working with a third party or recovering evidence)

Appendix 7—Hazard identification form

The following details shall be recorded on the Hazard Identification Forms for each hazard identified:

- job title;
- job location;
- Hazard Analyst;
- date;
- risk level (1–25), as defined in Chapter 5, Appendix 14;
- task description;
- hazard description;
- any past incidents relating to the hazard identified;
- persons at risk (e.g. employees, members of the public, etc.);
- consequence;
- current controls implemented;
- effectiveness of current controls implemented;
- controls recommended;
- comments;
- additional controls implemented;
- date of proposed implementation;
- owner of the implementation;
- CAPA number;

- date PIR carried out;
- PIR carried out by; and
- signature of employee carrying out PIR.

Appendix 8—Some areas for inspection for hazards

Some areas for inspection for OH&S hazards include, but are not limited to:

- **buildings**—floors, walls, ceilings, entrances, exits, stairs, laboratories, viewing areas, external areas surrounding the office, loading bays;
- **electricity supply**—equipment, switches, breakers, cabling, insulation, extensions, cables, electrically powered tools, electrical grounding, national electric code compliance;
- **evacuation plan**—established procedures for an emergency evacuation, last test results, as defined in Chapter 13;
- **fire prevention**—extinguishers, alarms, sprinklers, smoking rules, fire exits, employees assigned as Fire Wardens, separation of flammable materials and dangerous operations, training of personnel;
- **first-aid system**—medical care facilities, accessible first aid kits, first aid trained employees;
- **hand and power tools**—inspection prior to use, storage, repair, maintenance, grounding, training, use, and handling;
- **heating and ventilation**—type, effectiveness, temperature, humidity, controls, natural and artificial ventilation, national lighting code compliance;
- **laboratory housekeeping**—confidential waste disposal, tools used in the forensic process, cleaning methods, local work areas, remote work areas, storage areas;
- **lighting**—type, intensity, controls, conditions, diffusion, location, glare, and shadow control;
- **maintenance**—provide regular and preventive maintenance on all equipment used, maintaining records of all maintenance undertaken, and training personnel on the correct use and servicing of equipment for which they are responsible;
- **personnel**—training, including hazard identification training; experience; PPE for use in incident response and in the workplace;
- **PPE**—type, size, maintenance, repair, age, storage, training in care and use, rules of use, especially when working off site;
- **processing a case**—specific problems with any equipment, finding unexpected items in seized material; manual handling;
- **shipping seized material**—manual handling, training;
- **storage of seized material**—manual handling, safe storage heights, packaging;
- **transportation**—motor vehicle safety, seat belts, vehicle maintenance, safe driver programmes, recovery of evidence from site.

Note

This is just the checklist used and not a definitive statement of what is mandatory for a forensic laboratory in various jurisdictions of operations.

Appendix 9—Inputs to the risk assessment process

Inputs to the risk assessment can include, but are not limited to:

- any emergency procedures in place;
- any environmental conditions that may affect the task being undertaken;
- details of any PPE in place;
- details of any specific manufacturers' instructions for operating any equipment;
- employee competences;
- incident and near miss data;
- legislative and regulatory requirements within the jurisdiction;
- levels of employee training (work specific as well as OH&S specific) using training records as defined in Chapter 4, Section 4.7.5;
- details of the location where the task is performed;

- OH&S statistics;
- results of any OH&S monitoring activities;
- results of any past risk assessments;
- safety arrangements and controls in place;
- security arrangements in place;
- skill and experience of the person undertaking the risk assessment and hazard analysis;
- the effect of 'knock-on' failures;
- the impact of any disruption to services or utilities;
- the impact of any equipment failure;
- work instructions; and
- work procedures.

Appendix 10—OH&S risk rating

Value	Level of effect	Personal safety implication
1	Insignificant	Minor injury to individual
2	Minor	Minor injury to several people
3	Significant	Major injury to individual
4	Major	Major injury to several people or death of individual
5	Acute	Death of several people

Appendix 11—DSE initial workstation self-assessment checklist

This checklist provides a generic aid to risk assessment for DSE use but may need to be adjusted to meet the specific requirements of legislation or regulation within a specific jurisdiction. Local advice shall be sought to ensure that it is correct and comprehensive; however, some thoughts for a self-assessment checklist to be filled in by the employee include, but are not limited to:

- name of assessor;
- job title;
- workstation location (one form shall be used for each information processing device where the user has more than one);
- asset number;
- employee being assessed;
- date of assessment; and
- further action required? (Yes / No).[b]

Chair

- is the chair comfortable?
- is the chair adjustable (height, tilt, etc.)?
- does the employee know how to adjust their chair?
- do the employee's feet fit flat on the floor without effort when working?

Desk and workplace

- is there enough room for all of the employee's equipment to be close at hand (i.e. on the desk or other furniture around the desk)?
- is there enough room to change position when using DSE?

---

b. This should be raised as a CAPA and followed through using the continuous improvement process, as defined in Chapter 4, Section 4.10.

- is all equipment and other essential job items within easy reach?
- is there sufficient storage space available for secure storage if needed, as well as for normal storage?
- is there enough space to allow wrists and hands to rest for easy use of the keyboard, mouse, or any other devices?
- does the employee have a wrist rest?

Display screens

- are the characters clear and readable?
- is the screen clean and are cleaning materials made available to the employee?
- do the text and background colours work well together?[c]
- is the text size comfortable to read?
- is the image stable? (i.e. free of flicker or other movement);
- is the screen's specification suitable for its intended use?
- is brightness and/or contrast adjustable?
- can the screen swivel and tilt?
- is the screen free from glare and reflections[d]?
- where there is a risk of glare from external sources, are adjustable window coverings provided and in adequate condition?

Keyboards

- is the keyboard separate from the screen?
- does the keyboard tilt?
- is it possible to find a comfortable keying position?
- does the employee have a wrist wrest or mouse mat with a wrist rest?
- do the employees have good keyboard techniques?
- are the characters on the keys easily readable[e]?

Pointing devices

- is the device suitable for the tasks it is used for?
- is the device close enough to the employee to facilitate easy use?
- is there support for the employee's wrist and forearm?
- does the device work smoothly at a speed that suits the employee?
- does the employee know how to maintain the device (e.g. cleaning)?
- is the surface that the employee is using the device on appropriate?
- Has the employee been trained in how to adjust the setting on their screens, pointing devices, and furniture to minimise the hazards present?

Software

- is the software suitable for the task that the employee is performing?
- have there been any usability issues with the software?

Furniture

- is the working environment appropriate for the tasks carried out by the employee (e.g. work surface large enough to perform expected tasks)?
- can the employee comfortably reach all the equipment and papers they need to use in the execution of their job role?

c. Consider the W3 requirements (http://www.w3.org/) or others as appropriate.
d. This may vary between different times of day, locations (if a Teleworker or mobile worker) or other situations and these shall be taken into account.
e. Some handheld devices have very small screens and keys that are difficult to use for employees with large fingers.

- are surfaces free from glare and reflection, either from external or internal sources?
- is the employee's chair suitable for their job roles? (This may include backrests, armrests, or even footstools);

General working environment

- is there enough room to change position and vary movement?
- does the employee take regular breaks from using their computer (give approximate length and frequency of breaks)?
- is the lighting suitable, e.g. not too bright or too dim to work comfortably?
- does the environment (heat, airflow, etc.) feel comfortable?
- are temperature and humidity levels comfortable?
- are levels of noise comfortable?
- has the employee been trained in using DSE equipment so that they are aware of the risks and can adjust their general working environment?
- does the employee have to work to tight deadlines and Turn Round Times (TRTs)?

Health concerns

- does the employee suffer from any discomfort or other symptoms when using DSE?
- specify, if appropriate:
  - hands;
  - arms;
  - shoulders;
  - neck;
  - lower back;
  - other part of the body;
  - tired or sore eyes after using any DSE?

Note 1

Remember this assessment is completed by the employee (the DSE user) and is used to evaluate risks by a DSE Assessor. It is their perception of how they are exposed to any hazards as part of their work with DSE only and not their larger working environment.

Appendix 12—DSE training syllabus

This is the training syllabus used for educating employees about the risks of, and controls to be implemented for, DSE use. Other requirements may be mandated depending on the legislation and/or regulations in the jurisdiction: The list below is for DSE users:

- the risks from using DSE;
- the importance of good posture, changing position, and regular breaks;
- how to adjust furniture (chairs, keyboards, mice or other pointing devices, desks, lights, etc.) to help avoid risks. This should also include space under the desk as well as equipment on the desktop and the local environment;
- organising the workplace to avoid awkward or frequently repeated stretching movements;
- avoiding reflections and glare on or around the screen;
- the importance of adjusting and cleaning the screen;
- who to contact for help and to report problems or symptoms of DSE health issues;
- understanding and carrying out the DSE risk self-assessment process.

Additional training for DSE Assessors includes:

- how to undertake risk assessments for DSE;
- how to review the DSE self-assessment checklists that employees have filled in;
- identification of obvious (and less obvious) hazards;
- identification of hazards in specific situations (e.g. pregnancy);

- understanding where additional information and help are needed, and knowing sources of such guidance within the jurisdiction;
- understanding filled-in risk assessment and self-assessment questionnaires and being able to identify controls to reduce the risk to an acceptable level;
- how to maintain appropriate records for the lifecycle of a risk according to the requirements of the legislation or regulation within the jurisdiction;
- how to advise employees at risk as to controls that need to be put in place to reduce the risk to an acceptable level;
- being able to communicate the risk level of DSE use to all levels of employee;
- the need for appropriate resources to ensure that appropriate controls are implemented to reduce the risks relating to DSE to an acceptable level.

Types of training that are used include, but are not limited to:

- online training;
- wall charts;
- seminars (internal or external led); and
- professionally arranged external courses.

Note 1

A number of organisations produce DSE training materials.

Note 2

A mixture of the above shall be used, as appropriate.

Appendix 13—DSE assessors checklist

This checklist provides a detailed DSE checklist for a competent DSE Assessor and shall be used to obtain further and better details where the initial self-assessment performed by an employee may indicate a possible risk. It also includes items to consider and actions to be taken. It is generic and may need to be adjusted to meet the specific requirements of legislation or regulation within a specific jurisdiction. Local advice shall be sought to ensure that it is correct and comprehensive. The DSE assessment checklist below shall be filled in by the DSE Assessor:

- name of assessor;
- job title;
- employee being assessed (the DSE User);
- employee's signature;
- job title;
- workstation location (one form shall be used for each information processing device where the user has more than one);
- asset number;
- date of assessment;
- date of review to be undertaken;
- action required?
- CAPA number;
- date action completed.

Chair

Risk factor	Things to consider
Is the chair comfortable?	Consider replacing the chair or using a support
Is the chair adjustable (height, tilt, etc.)	If it is not, consider replacing it or using a support, if appropriate Ensure that the lower back is properly supported

Risk factor	Things to consider
Does the employee know how to adjust their chair?	If not—train them how to adjust it for optimum comfort Ensure that the chair is adjusted to suit the employee Train the employee in how to adjust their posture Consider using chairs that are fully adjustable and that have armrests Ensure that the employee's back is supported with relaxed shoulders Ensure the armrests are also properly adjusted **Note:** Adjustment may also include adjustments to the DSE itself
Do the employee's feet fit flat on the floor without effort when working?	If not, consider adjusting the chair or providing a footrest of appropriate height

Desk and workplace

Risk factor	Things to consider
Is there enough room for all of the employee' equipment to be close at hand (i.e. on the desk or other furniture around the desk)?	Consider a larger desk or other working surface if there is not enough space Create more room by removing printers and/or scanners from the employee's desk Create more room by removing infrequently used materials (e.g. reference material) from the desk and storing it elsewhere Consideration of additional power sockets may be needed to relocate equipment There should be the ability to have flexibility in the employee's workspace to permit optimal comfort and usability
Is there enough room to change position when using DSE?	Space is needed by all employees to stretch and fidget Consider rearranging the employee's workplace to permit optimum movement Remove any obstructions and any materials or equipment stored under the desk, wherever possible Ensure all cables are tidily stored so they do not present a trip or snag hazard
Is all equipment and other essential job items within easy reach?	Consider rearranging all DSE equipment, materials, etc. to bring frequently used items in easy reach Consider using document holders to minimise uncomfortable head or eye movements
Is there sufficient storage space available for secure storage if needed, as well as for normal storage?	Ensure that secure storage is provided Ensure that other storage facilities are available as close as possible to the employee, but not so close that it restricts their ability to move freely
Is there enough space to allow wrists and hands to rest for easy use of the keyboard, mouse, or any other devices?	Consider rearranging the desk to ensure that this is possible
Does the employee have a wrist rest?	Consider providing wrist rests

Display screens

Risk factor	Things to consider
Are the characters clear and readable?	Ensure that the screen is clean and cleaning materials are available Check that the text and background colours work well together, and if not adjust them for optimum use, if possible Consider implementing the W3 requirements—undertake a 'Bobby Test'
Is the screen clean and cleaning materials are made available to the employee?	Ensure that the screen is clean and cleaning materials are available
Do the text and background colours work well together?	Check that the text and background colours work well together, and if not adjust them for optimum use, if possible Consider implementing the W3 requirements—undertake a 'Bobby Test'
Is the text size comfortable to read?	Software or hardware settings may need to be adjusted to change text size, if possible Consider implementing the W3 requirements—undertake a 'Bobby Test'
Is the image stable? (i.e. free of flicker or other movement).	Consider using different screen colours to reduce flicker Consider altering the screen refresh rate Consider the power supply and whether it is stable Consider replacing the screen

Continued

Risk factor	Things to consider
Is the screen's specification suitable for its intended use?	Ensure that the screen type suits the applications in use (e.g. intensive graphic work may require attention to detail that requires a large screen with high resolution and definition) Consider all employees for having multiple screens off their main workstation
Is brightness and/or contrast adjustable?	Separate controls should be available for all screens. However, so long as the employee can read the screen easily at all times they are not really necessary
Can the screen swivel and tilt?	Not all screens can swivel and tilt. However, consideration of purchasing a separate swivel and tilt mechanism should be undertaken Replacement of the screen should be considered if the existing swivel and/or tilt mechanism is inappropriate or does not function properly or the employee has problems getting the screen into a comfortable working position Consideration may also be given to a monitor stand if the screen height is uncomfortable for the employee
Is the screen free from glare and reflections?	Identify any source of reflections that affect the employee Reduce the effect of any reflections by moving the screen or even the employee's desk. Consideration may be given to providing a suitable screen to stop the reflection or glare Consideration may be given to changing the font and background colours. Dark backgrounds and light fonts are less prone to glare and reflections A number of controls may be needed to reduce the effect of glare and reflections
Where there is a risk of glare from external sources, are adjustable window coverings provided and in adequate condition?	Check that all blinds and curtains are in good working order and if not repair or replace them If this does not fix the problem, consider antiglare screen filters

Keyboards

Risk factor	Things to consider
Is the keyboard separate from the screen?	This is a requirement for being able to adjust the working environment, but in some cases may not be possible (e.g. a laptop). Where this is not possible, an external keyboard should be considered
Does the keyboard tilt?	A keyboard stand should be considered.
Is it possible to find a comfortable keying position?	Consider pushing the screen further back on the desk to gain more space for wrists and hands Try a mixture of all of the 'things to consider' defined in this appendix to provide a comfortable position
Does the employee have a wrist wrest or mouse mat with a wrist rest?	Consider provision of wrist rests or mouse pads with wrist rests
Does the employee have good keyboard techniques?	Consider training the employee in good keyboard techniques, these include, but are not limited to • Setting up the workspace properly (screen keyboard, desk, chair, etc.) • Not overstretching • Not hitting the keys too hard • Ensuring that the wrist is comfortable' • Etc.
Are the characters on the keys easily readable?	Keyboards should be kept clean If the keys cannot be read, after cleaning, consider replacing the keyboard Always ensure that keyboards are matt to reduce the chance of glare or reflection

Pointing devices

Risk factor	Things to consider
Is the device suitable for the tasks it is used for?	Ensure that the device being used is appropriate for the task Ensure that the device has been properly set up for the user. This may require resetting some of the user settings If the employee has a problem with one type of device, consider trying another (e.g. Tracker ball instead of a mouse)

Risk factor	Things to consider
Is the device close enough to the employee to facilitate easy use?	Most devices are best located as close to the user, screen, and keyboard as possible. Ensure that this is the case Consider training for the employee specifically for their pointing device including all of the items considered in this appendix to ensure maximum comfort
Is there support for the employee's wrist and forearm?	Support may be gained from the desktop itself. If this is not appropriate for the employee then a specific wrist or arm support should be considered. Typically, these are foam or gel filled. Gel-filled ones mould themselves to the employee's wrist or arm
Does the device work smoothly at a speed that suits the user?	All pointing devices with moving parts should be regularly cleaned (e.g. tracker ball in a mouse) Cleaning materials should be made available for all employees Ensure that the surface on which the pointing device is used is appropriate for the device. Consideration should be given to providing appropriate mouse mats or similar Ensure that the employee is aware how to change the setting on their pointing device and clean it
Does the employee know how to maintain the device (e.g. cleaning)?	All pointing devices with moving parts should be regularly cleaned (e.g. tracker ball in a mouse) Cleaning materials should be made available for all employees
Is the surface that the employee is using the device on appropriate?	Ensure that the surface on which the pointing device is used is appropriate for the device Consideration should be given to providing appropriate mouse mats or similar
Have employees been trained in how to adjust the setting on their screens, pointing devices, and furniture to minimise the hazards present?	Ensure all employees have been trained in all aspects of their information processing equipment that they use to the required levels and in line with the manufacturer's recommendations

Software

Risk factor	Things to consider
Is the software suitable for the task that the employee is performing?	Software should assist the employee to do their job, minimise stress and make them more effective and productive Ensure that all employees have been given appropriate training in any software that they use and that their records of training are maintained by HR
Have there been any usability issues with the software?	Review fault and incident logs and take appropriate action

Furniture

Risk factor	Things to consider
Is the working environment appropriate for the tasks carried out by the employee (e.g. work surface large enough to perform expected tasks)?	Consider a larger desk or other working surface if there is not enough space Create more room by removing printers and/or scanners from the main desk Create more room by removing infrequently used materials (e.g. reference material) from the desk and storing it elsewhere Consideration of additional power sockets may be needed to relocate equipment There should be the ability to have flexibility in the employee's workspace to permit optimal comfort and usability
Can the employee comfortably reach all the equipment and papers they need to use in the execution of their job role?	Consider rearranging all equipment, materials, etc., to bring frequently used items in easy reach Consider using document holders to minimise uncomfortable head or eye movements
Are surfaces free from glare and reflection, either from external or internal sources?	Identify any source of reflections that affect the employee Reduce the effect of any reflections by moving the screen and other equipment or even the employee's desk Consideration may be given to providing a suitable screen to stop the reflection or glare Consideration may be given to changing the font and background colours. Dark backgrounds and light fonts are less prone to glare and reflections A number of controls may be needed to reduce the effect of glare and reflections
Is the employee's chair suitable for their job roles? (This may include backrests, armrests, or even footstools)	See section of chairs above

General working environment

Risk factor	Things to consider
Is there enough room to change position and vary movement?	Space is needed by all employees to stretch and fidget Consider rearranging the employee's workspace to permit optimum movement Remove any obstructions and any materials or equipment stored under the desk, wherever possible Ensure all cables are tidily stored so they do not present a trip or snag hazard
Does the employee take regular breaks from using their computer (give approximate length and frequency of breaks)?	Determine breaks taken and advise on optimising this
Is the lighting suitable, e.g. not too bright or too dim to work comfortably?	Employees should be able to control their own lighting levels, whether it is from overhead lights, desk lamps, or natural light from windows Ensure that the employee can control their own lighting environment Consider using shades or other local light sources if needed—but ensure that the light sources provided do not themselves cause glare and reflection
Does the environment (heat, airflow, etc.) feel comfortable?	Information processing equipment may affect the environment Consider the circulation of fresh air Consider green plants as they increase moisture in the air Consider humidifiers, if appropriate. Consider how the office/laboratory environment controls work and are set
Are temperature and humidity levels comfortable?	Information processing equipment may affect the environment Consider the circulation of fresh air Consider green plants as they increase moisture in the air Consider humidifiers, if appropriate Consider how the office/laboratory environment controls work and are set
Are levels of noise comfortable?	Consider the source of the level of noise and consider moving it away from the employee (e.g. printers) If this does not work to reduce to an acceptable level consider putting equipment in a soundproof environment (e.g. box, container, or room)
Has the employee been trained in using DSE equipment so that you are aware of the risks and can adjust your general working environment?	Ensure all employees have been trained to the level that their job roles require and that records of such training are maintained by the Human Resources function
Does the employee have to work to tight deadlines and Turn Round Times (TRTs)?	Consider the effect of tight deadlines on the employee's environment

Health concerns

Risk factor	Things to consider
Discomfort—hands	Specific issues relating to DSE use and hands
Discomfort—arms	Specific issues relating to DSE use and arms
Discomfort—shoulders	Specific issues relating to DSE use and shoulders
Discomfort—neck	Specific issues relating to DSE use and the neck
Discomfort—lower back	Specific issues relating to DSE use and the lower back
Discomfort—other parts of the body	Specific issues relating to DSE use and other parts of the body
Discomfort—eyes	Specific issues relating to DSE use and eyes

Appendix 14—Measurement of OH&S success

The checklist below identifies the main areas which shall be reviewed and measured where possible. The checklist shall be used for measurement purposes as well as an input to operational internal audits.

Management commitment

- do all levels of management demonstrate that OH&S is an embedded part of their job?
- does Top Management demonstrably show that they visibly support the OHSMS?
- does Top Management ensure that OH&S is not compromised in pursuit of other corporate goals?
- does Top Management ensure that regular reviews and audits of OH&S are undertaken?
- does Top Management provide appropriate resources to effectively implement, maintain, measure, and monitor the OHSMS?
- does Top Management receive regular reports on OH&S status?
- does Top Management regularly review OH&S performance against other similar organisations?
- does Top Management take appropriate remedial action when it is identified?
- has Top Management endorsed the OH&S policy?
- is the OH&S policy prominently displayed in all working locations?
- is the OH&S policy regularly reviewed?

Organisational and operational requirements

- are there clear OH&S objectives set with realistic targets?
- do all employees understand that they are personally accountable for OH&S issues within their areas of control?
- do job descriptions for all employees specify OH&S responsibilities?
- does the Health and Safety Manager have direct access to Top Management on OH&S issues?
- is there an effective OH&S Management System in place?
- is there an incident and injury reporting system in place (including near misses)?

Competence, awareness, and training

- are OH&S training records maintained by HR?
- do all employees receive annual OH&S awareness sessions?
- do all employees receive appropriate OH&S training when they start work or change jobs?
- is competent OH&S advice available to Top Management either from internal or external sources?
- is OH&S covered at induction for all employees?
- is there a process for defining competencies for all roles?
- is there a process for measuring the effectiveness of any OH&S training that employees undertake?
- is there a Training Needs Analysis (TNA) process in place for all employees following changes to equipment, standards, processes, or procedures to ensure that effective training is implemented in a timely manner?
- is there a follow-up process for new employees to ensure that they have received appropriate OH&S training?
- where 'on the job training' is carried out, that it is carried out in a consistent, reliable, and measurable manner?

Operational processes

- are operational procedures and work instructions available to all employees in a clear and easily readable format?
- are PPE requirements rigorously enforced?
- are procedures and work instructions regularly reviewed and updated as needed?
- are there clearly documented procedures and work instructions for all work undertaken by employees?
- is conformity to operational procedures regularly monitored and measured?
- is the OHSMS effective?
- is there a consistent process in place for identifying hazards and measuring OH&S risks?

- is there a procedure in place to ensure that safe working practices are defined, documented, followed, and updated as appropriate?
- are Personal Protective Equipment (PPE) requirements identified for all employees in all locations where they work?

Emergency and incident response

- are lessons learned from an invocation of the plans and procedures or tests used for updating the plans and procedures?
- are postimplementation reviews (PIRs) undertaken to ensure that the hazard has been eliminated or reduced to an acceptable level?
- are the procedures and plans easily understandable?
- are the procedures and plans well communicated and understood by all employees?
- are there effective emergency and incident response plans?
- do all employees understand their own responsibilities?
- how frequently are they tested?
- are they regularly reviewed, and updated as required?
- is remedial action implemented using the CAPA process?
- is root cause analysis undertaken?
- is there a documented emergency response procedure?
- is there a formal incident or injury investigation process in place?

Audit

- are the auditors independent of the areas that they are auditing?
- how are audit recommendations followed up?
- how do the auditors demonstrate that they are competent?
- is the IMS Calendar followed?
- is the audit work programme comprehensive?
- is there an annual IMS Calendar published that covers all operations?

Communicating the OH&S message

- are there regular OH&S meetings, with records, involving relevant interested parties?
- are there regular updates of the OH&S message to all employees?
- do all employees, including Top Management, attend OH&S awareness training sessions?
- is frank two-way communication possible on OH&S issues?
- is OH&S covered at induction for all employees?
- is there a clearly defined process for communicating the OH&S message?
- is there an easy-to-use and effective system for reporting hazards, including feedback to the reportee?
- is there an easy-to-use system in place to elicit OH&S suggestions and ideas?
- is there clear communication of organisational as well as individual conformity with the OHSMS?
- is there communication and consultation on OH&S objectives and measurable targets?

Appendix 15—Specific OH&S incident reporting requirements

Whilst there may be legislative or regulatory requirements in the specific jurisdiction where a forensic laboratory is located, the following is a generic list of details that shall be recorded on an incident report that covers actual accidents, injuries, ill health that is due to a work-related cause or a 'near miss'.

This shall be filled in as soon as possible after the incident and no later than 7 days after its occurrence unless the injured employee is not well enough/incapable of doing it. In this case, a witness shall fill it in, if possible. Completed forms shall be sent securely to the Health and Safety Manager, the Service Desk for recording the incident and the Line Manager with supervisory responsibility for the area where the incident occurred:

- name of person(s)[f] involved in the incident;
- address of person(s) involved in the incident (including phone numbers and email address);
- date(s) of birth;
- sex (es);
- job title(s) if an employee;
- experience in their role if an employee;
- status of each person involved in the incident (employee, visitor, member of the public, etc.);
- location of incident;
- date of incident;
- time of incident;
- nature of incident (define fully—even if a 'near miss');
- other relevant information as deemed appropriate; and
- date of incident report.

Note

Where an accident is 'serious' (e.g. loss of life, injury requiring medical care rather than on-site first aid, etc.), a telephone report of the incident shall be made immediately to the Health and Safety Manager and the formal report submitted as above.

Appendix 16—OH&S investigation checklist and form contents

Whilst there may be legislative or regulatory requirements in the specific jurisdiction where a forensic laboratory is located, the following is a generic list of details that shall be recorded on an OH&S incident investigation report that covers actual accidents, injuries, ill health that is due to a work-related cause or a 'near miss'.

This shall be filled in as soon as possible after the incident report is received and no later than 7 days after its occurrence, by the employee with supervisory responsibility for the area where the incident occurred.

Completed forms shall be sent securely to the Health and Safety Manager and the Service Desk for incident record updating:

- incident number;
- name of person(s)[f] involved in the incident;
- address of person(s) involved in the incident (including phone numbers and email address);
- date(s) of birth;
- sex(es);
- job title(s) if an employee;
- experience in their role if an employee;
- status of each person involved in the incident (employee, visitor, member of the public, etc.);
- location of incident;
- date of incident;
- time of incident;
- nature of incident (define fully—even if a 'near miss');
- other relevant information as deemed appropriate;
- worst consequences of incident;
- what stopped incident reaching worst-case scenario?
- whether first aid was administered, and if so what?
- whether an ambulance attended or not?
- ambulance incident log number;
- were any of the people involved in the incident hospitalised for more than 24 h?
- weather conditions;
- type of lighting in place and effectiveness of it;
- floor or ground conditions;

---

f. The person(s) involved in the incident may not be an employee.

- were the person(s) involved in the incident under supervision, and is so whose (name, title);
- details of any PPE being worn or that should have been worn that was not being worn;
- details of any procedures that should have been followed for the task being carried out or the area where the incident took place;
- whether a risk assessment had been undertaken for the task being carried out or the area where the incident took place;
- the date of the last review of the risk assessment;
- whether any similar incidents had occurred in the same task or area where the incident took place, and if appropriate, their incident reference numbers;
- controls that were in place or should have been in place to either eliminate the risk or reduce it to an acceptable level;
- number of days absent from work (for employees) or incapacitated and unable to fully follow their normal lives (nonemployees);
- immediate cause (e.g. unsafe working conditions, unfamiliar equipment being examined, etc.);
- root cause (e.g. no risk assessment undertaken or reviewed, lack of training, etc.);
- immediate action taken;
- further corrective action or preventive action taken to prevent recurrence of the incident;
- CAPA number;
- target date for completion of CAPA;
- name of any witnesses to the incident;
- address of any witnesses to the incident (including phone numbers and email address);
- name of employee having supervisory control where the incident took place;
- job title of the employee having supervisory control where the incident took place;
- contact details of the employee having supervisory control where the incident took place;
- signature of the employee having supervisory control where the incident took place;
- date of investigation report;
- name of investigating employee;
- title of investigating employee; and
- signature of investigating employee.

Note

Not all items above will be relevant to an incident, and if not, they should be marked as 'Not Applicable'.

Appendix 17—OH&S incident review

Whilst there may be legislative or regulatory requirements in the specific jurisdiction where the laboratory is located, the following is a generic list of details that shall be recorded on an incident review report that covers actual accidents, injuries, ill health that is due to a work-related cause or a 'near miss'.

The results of the review shall be discussed and agreed with the appropriate level of management to agree actions to be taken. The results of this meeting shall be formally recorded in the OH&S Incident Log and reviewed at the Management Review meeting.

- incident number;
- name of person(s) involved in the incident;
- comments on the investigation report;
- comments on proposed CAPA;
- confirmation that the PIR shows that the risk has been eliminated or reduced to an acceptable level;
- details of the revised risk assessment carried out;
- other relevant information as deemed appropriate;
- date of investigation review;
- name of Health and Safety Manager;
- signature of Health and Safety Manager;
- name of Top Management representative, if appropriate; and
- countersignature of Top Management representative, if appropriate.

Appendix 18—ISO 45,001 mapping to IMS procedures

ISO 45001 clause	Control	IMS procedure
4	Context of the organisation	
4.1	Understanding the organisation and its context	Chapter 4, Section 4.4
4.2	Understanding the needs and expectations of workers and other interested parties	Chapter 4, Section 4.4.2
4.3	Determining the scope of the OH&S management system	Chapter 4, Section 4.4.3
4.4	OH&S management system	The Integrated Management System (IMS) Chapter 5, Appendix 11
5	Leadership and worker participation	
5.1	Leadership and commitment	Chapter 4, Section 4.5
5.2	OH&S policy	Chapter 4, Section 4.5.2, and Appendix 17 Section 1.3
5.3	Organisational roles, responsibilities, and authorities	Chapter 4, Section 4.5.3 Section 17.4.2
5.4	Consultation and participation of workers	Chapter 5, Appendix 1 Section 17.2.4
6	Planning	
6.1	Actions to address risks and opportunities	Chapter 4, Section 4.6.1 Section 17.3.1
6.1.1	General	
6.1.2	Hazard identification and assessment of risks and opportunities	Chapter 5 and Appendix 17 Sections 17.3.2 and 17.3.3
6.1.3	Determination of legal requirements and other requirements	Chapter 12, Section 12.3.13.1 Section 17.3.6
6.1.4	Planning action	Section 17.3.4
6.2	OH&S objectives and planning to achieve them	Section 17.3.7
6.2.1	OH&S objectives	Chapter 3, Section 3.1.17 Section 17.3.7 and Appendix 5
6.2.2	Planning to achieve OH&S objectives	Section 17.3.8
7	Support	
7.1	Resources	Chapter 4, Section 4.7.1 Section 17.4.1
7.2	Competence	Chapter 4, Section 4.7.2 Section 17.4.3 Chapter 18, Section 18.2
7.3	Awareness	Chapter 4, Section 4.7.3 Section 17.4.3 Chapter 18, Section 18.2
7.4	Communication	Chapter 5, Appendix 1 Chapter 12, Section 4.2 Section 17.4.4
7.4.1	General	Chapter 5, Appendix 1 Chapter 12, Section 4.2 Section 17.4.4

ISO 45001 clause	Control	IMS procedure
7.4.2	Internal communication	Chapter 5, Appendix 1 Chapter 12, Section 4.2 Section 17.4.4
7.4.3	External communication	Chapter 5, Appendix 1 Chapter 12, Section 4.2 Section 17.4.4
7.5	Documented information	The Integrated Management System (IMS) Section 17.3.5
7.5.1	General	Chapter 4, Section 4.7.5.1
7.5.2	Creating and updating	Chapter 4, Section 4.7.5.4
7.5.3	Control of documented information	Chapter 4, Section 4.7.5.3
8	Operation	
8.1	Operational planning and control	Chapter 4, Section 4.8
8.1.1	General	Chapter 4, Section 4.8
8.1.2	Eliminating hazards and reducing OH&S risks	Sections 17.5.1 and 17.5.2
8.1.3	Management of change	Section 17.5.3
8.1.4	Procurement	Section 17.5.4
8.2	Emergency preparedness and response	Chapter 13 Section 17.5.5
9	Performance evaluation	Chapter 16
9.1	Monitoring, measurement, analysis, and performance evaluation	Section 17.6.1
9.1.1	General	Section 17.6.1
9.1.2	Evaluation of compliance	Chapter 4, Section 4.9 Section 17.6.2 and Appendix 14
9.2	Internal audit	Chapter 4, Section 4.9.2 Section 17.6.3
9.2.1	General	Chapter 4, Section 4.9.2 Section 17.6.3
9.2.2	Internal audit programme	Chapter 4, Section 4.9.2 Section 17.6.3
9.3	Management review	Chapter 4, Section 4.9.3, and Appendix 40 Section 17.6.4
10	Improvement	
10.1	General	Chapter 4, Section 4.10
10.2	Incident, nonconformity, and corrective action	Chapter 4, Sections 4.10.1, 4.10.2, 4.10.3, 4.10.4, and 4.10.5 and Appendix 49 Chapter 6, Sections 6.8 and 6.14 Chapter 7, Section 7.4.1 Sections 17.7.2, 17.7.3, and Appendices 15, 16, and 17
10.3	Continual improvement	Chapter 4, Section 4.10 Section 17.7.4

Chapter 18

Human resources

18.1 Employee development

Note

This chapter is not intended to be a Human Resources (HR) manual, but to merely identify areas of information security that must be considered if a certificate of registration or compliance to ISO/IEC 27001 is sought. These are also regarded as good practice and should be present in some form or other in any forensic laboratory.

18.1.1 Overview of employee development

For a forensic laboratory to succeed, it needs competent employees and third parties that can use appropriate tools to acquire, preserve, analyse, and present the evidence recovered for a specific forensic case as well as other duties as required.

In line with the Deming Cycle,[a] as defined in Chapter 4, Section 4.3, FCL shall continuously improve its employee's competence and, for the same reason, improving its own deliverability skills for its clients.

FCL shall integrate its HR processes into its Integrated Management System (IMS) so that they can be managed in line with the requirements of the relevant management standards that have been implemented.

FCL has recognised that properly developed and managed employees are critical for ongoing business development and continuous improvement, as defined in Chapter 4, Section 4.10.

HR shall be integrated into the PDCA cycle as shown in the four principles below:

- **Commitment**—making a commitment to develop all employees to help them achieve the business objectives of FCL, as defined in Chapter 3, Section 3.1.17, Chapter 6, Section 6.2.2.1 and Chapter 6, Appendix 9;
- **Planning**—regularly review the needs and plans for the training and development of employees;
- **Action**—take action to train and develop employees to enable them to competently perform their roles; and
- **Evaluation**—evaluate the investment in employee training and to assess achievement and improve its effectiveness through a process of continuous improvement.

Whilst these four principles remain the guiding processes for HR, it is readily accepted that there are numerous HR processes or generic HR requirements within the various jurisdictions within which a forensic laboratory may reside and operate, as well as other appropriate international or national standards.

Each of the principles is expanded below:

18.1.1.1 Commitment

Commitment to these principles shall be demonstrated by integrating them into the IMS.

Top Management shall demonstrably recognise that properly developed and managed employees are critical for ongoing business development and continuous improvement. They shall ensure that there are appropriate competent resources to perform the tasks that FCL has committed to deliver. The use of the IMS for all employees, where policies, procedures, forms, and checklists can be referenced, has been introduced as part of induction training as defined in Chapter 6, Appendix 8.

All employees shall be committed to personal development plans to improve their competence.

Job descriptions, with well-defined roles and responsibilities, shall be agreed between all employees and Top Management.

---

a. Not all management systems now require compliance with the W Edwards Deming (Plan-Do-Check-Act) cycle (e.g. ISO/IEC 27001) but FCL has implemented this as part of the IMS and continues to use it.

A Blueprint for Implementing Best Practice Procedures in a Digital Forensic Laboratory. https://doi.org/10.1016/B978-0-12-819479-9.00007-1

18.1.1.2 Planning

FCL shall ensure that there is a continuous programme of training and awareness for its employees. This is essential to develop the full potential of those employees and further the business objectives.

18.1.1.3 Action

FCL shall ensure that it appropriately develops and trains its employees. It shall do this by:

- identifying forthcoming business requirements, as defined in Chapter 3, Section 3.1.13;
- performing a Training Needs Analysis (TNA), as defined in Section 18.2.2;
- undertaking training, awareness, and development for relevant employees, as defined in Chapter 4, Section 4.7.3 and Section 18.2.1;
- creating and maintaining records of training undertaken, as defined in Chapter 4, Section 4.7.5;
- recording continuous professional development and continuous professional education credits; and
- 'bringing employees on' from the moment that they join FCL.

18.1.1.4 Evaluation

FCL shall ensure that any investment in its employees is evaluated to ensure that it:

- is appropriate;
- is effective;
- provides value for money;
- supports personal objectives; and
- supports the business objectives.

   This shall be carried out by:

- reviewing staff performance as defined in Section 18.2.4; and
- reviewing training, awareness, and competence as defined in Section 18.2.4 and Appendix 1.

18.1.2 Recruitment overview

FCL needs to attract and recruit employees with the necessary skills and experience that will help FCL to improve the quality of the products and services which it provides to its clients. This process shall be applied to all employees.

1. A Manager (at any level from Top Management downwards) identifies a possible requirement for a new employee to:
   - fill a vacancy, for example when an employee leaves; or
   - address employee shortages, skills gaps, and new competency requirements.
2. When identifying a requirement for a new employee, the Manager shall consider:
   - reasons for recruiting;
   - possible alternatives to recruitment;
   - competence profile required by the role;
   - timescales—when is the employee with the competence profile to start work; and
   - implications and possible options if it is not possible to recruit appropriate employees.
3. The Manager shall develop a requirement specification that includes details on:
   - skill sets and competence profile required of the new employee;
   - how the recruitment is to be performed/managed (e.g. referrals from existing employees, a recruitment agency, etc.); and
   - outline of costs of employment.
4. Requirements specifications shall be developed in consultation with other Managers and HR, as required. The Manager shall present the requirement specification to their line management, if appropriate.
   - if a requirement specification is approved, authorisation to proceed with the recruitment process shall be granted;

- if a requirement specification is rejected, it may be amended and re-presented, or the recruitment process terminated; and
- if changes and updates are required to the recruitment profile, the requirement specification shall be amended (and then reissued for review as required).

5. The Manager shall arrange the appropriate recruitment advertising via HR or directly, for example by:
   - engagement of an appropriate recruitment agency;
   - placement of advertisements in the relevant press or online; and
   - advertisement internally to current employees.

6. The recruiting Manager shall receive applications from candidates, either directly or via the HR, who may do an initial 'sift' of candidates. Where FCL is managing the advertising, the recruiting Manager shall notify all candidates of receipt of their application. Different recruitment agencies will have their own internal procedures.

7. The recruiting Manager shall present suitable applications to their management, if appropriate, with a view to selection of candidates for interview based upon matching of available competencies to the requirement specification.

8. The recruiting Manager or HR shall contact candidates or the recruitment agency, if used, to either:
   - arrange an interview for successful candidates, or
   - notify unsuccessful candidates that their application is not being progressed further.

9. Interviews shall be conducted using the 'grandfather' principle where:
   - the recruiting Manager or HR conducts interviews with each candidate to obtain a view on their competence and suitability—in some cases, a standard interview test may be conducted as part of this interview to help assess candidate suitability; and
   - the line manager of the recruiting Manager interviews candidates who are selected and approved by the recruiting Manager.

10. The interviewer(s) shall meet to review the candidates and:
    - a candidate may be invited back for a further interview, if required and where appropriate, either with the same or a different interviewer;
    - a candidate is recommended for employment (and a salary offer decision made), subject to successful employee screening as defined in Section 18.1.3 and other checks as appropriate; or
    - unsuitable candidates are rejected.

11. If a candidate accepts the offer (in writing or verbally) a start date shall be agreed and confirmed in writing, together with a draft contract and job description for the new employee.

12. HR shall create a personnel folder for the employee and file all documentation relating to the employee's recruitment, where appropriate.

Note

Consistent recruitment processes, including employee screening, shall be undertaken for any employee—regardless of seniority of the position or employment type. This may have serious consequences if the employee is not subject to the appropriate employee screening process.

18.1.2.1   *Employees roles and responsibilities*

18.1.2.1.1   Roles and responsibility definitions for job applicants

- where FCL is recruiting employees, a clear statement of the security roles and responsibilities for that role shall be included as part of the job advertisement; and
- during the interview process for all candidates, the interviewer shall assure themselves that the potential recruit understands these responsibilities clearly.

18.1.2.1.2   General roles and responsibilities

General roles and responsibilities for all employees are defined in:

- Scope Statement for the IMS;
- Information Security, Acceptable Use, and other relevant Policies; and
- Employment Handbook.

18.1.2.1.3 Specific roles and responsibilities

Specific roles and responsibilities for jobs and tasks shall be defined in:

- duties of Owners and Custodians; and
- specific job descriptions as defined in Section 18.1.5.

18.1.2.1.4 Roles and responsibilities for third-party employees

Where third parties (e.g. contractors and Consultants) are employed to perform specific tasks they shall be advised of their specific responsibilities by the same sorts of documents as above and also their contracts of employment.

18.1.2.2 Management responsibilities

There are a number of management responsibilities for Managers to ensure that all employees are aware of their responsibilities in information security and the requirements of the IMS. This covers ensuring that all employees shall have ongoing updating of their specific responsibilities, including information security, legislative and regulatory requirements, throughout their employment life cycle. This is achieved at a number of stages in the employment cycle and uses a variety of different media and methods.

18.1.2.2.1 Prior to employment

Prior to employment, at the recruitment stage, all prospective employees shall be advised of the roles and responsibilities with regard to information security, legislative and regulatory requirements for the post for which they are applying.

This shall be agreed between HR and the Manager to whom they will report. This information shall be available at the preemployment stage to the applicant.

The applicant shall be made aware of these responsibilities and the interviewer shall satisfy themselves that the interviewee understands them.

18.1.2.2.2 New employees

When a new employee starts employment, they shall undergo the standard induction process, which shall cover, but not be limited to, the following:

- Handbook of Employment;
- various FCL policies as defined in Section 18.1.8; and
- information security and other relevant online training.

Note

No employee shall be permitted to access any information processing facilities, organisational or client data until they have undertaken the induction process and undergone and passed the relevant training courses.

As well as the induction process covering the policies above, the employee shall be handed the job description for their role, as defined in Section 18.1.5. Each job description shall contain specific details for the information security responsibilities for their role.

The new employee shall be encouraged to ask any questions relating to their job and information security responsibilities.

The induction checklist is defined in Chapter 6, Appendix 8.

Records of the induction process shall be retained for later audit.

18.1.2.2.3 During employment

Annually, there shall be mandatory refresher training for all employees and records of the training shall be retained in personnel files, as defined in Chapter 4, Section 4.6.7.5.

Additional training may be undertaken after an incident for either specific employees or all employees if the incident warrants it.

For employees being issued with specific information processing equipment (e.g. mobile devices) or undertaking a new process (e.g. mobile working or teleworking), specific and relevant training shall be undertaken.

18.1.3   Employee screening

18.1.3.1   Definitions

There are a number of definitions that need to be clearly understood for their specific use, and these are defined here. These are;

- **ancillary employees**—employees involved in ancillary activities such as administration, personnel, building maintenance and cleaning;
- **provisional employment**—the initial period of employment for a new employee during which security screening is continuing, if FCL chooses to employ the individual prior to the completion of screening;
- **confirmed employment**—employment (beyond the period of provisional employment, if any) granted upon successful completion of security screening and any additional criteria applied by FCL;
- **relevant employment**—employment which involves, or may involve, the acquisition of, or access to, information or equipment, the improper use of which could involve FCL, any of their clients, in a security incident or other risk that may negatively impact FCL;
- **screening controller**—the individual in FCL responsible for security screening; and
- **security screening period**—the period of years immediately prior to the commencement of relevant employment or transfer to relevant employment, or back to the school leaving age, if deemed appropriate.

18.1.3.2   Overview

Different levels of screening shall be carried out in different jurisdictions, where there are different requirements. The level of screening shall vary for different roles based on their access to information and its sensitivity.

This brings together the requirements for verifying:

- identity;
- residential address(es);
- the right to work in the jurisdiction;
- employment history;
- qualifications;
- criminal records; and
- financial status.

Additionally, the following shall be obtained:

- personal character reference(s); and
- other references for applicants in specific situations.

Whilst some of the above requirements may be internal, some (e.g. right to work in a defined jurisdiction) are usually legal requirements, as defined in Chapter 12, Section 12.3.13.1.1.

18.1.3.3   General requirements

FCL shall:

- not offer employment to any applicant whose career or history indicates that they would be unlikely to resist the opportunities for illicit personal gain, the possibilities of being compromised, or the opportunities for creating any other breach of security, which such employment might offer;
- not offer employment to any potential recruit who, where required, cannot produce a valid work permit, visa, or worker registration card within the timescales required by law in the relevant jurisdiction;
- make clear to all employees employed in employee security screening, and to those with authority to offer provisional or confirmed employment, that FCL requires that the highest standards of honesty and integrity shall be maintained in view of the special circumstances of the environment in which they are employed;
- obtain consent from the applicant to undertake security screening;
- carry out employee security screening prior to any engagement for relevant employment or to employees being transferred to relevant employment from other duties for which they have not previously been subjected to employee security screening. However, provisional employment may be offered in some cases, based on a risk assessment on current employee screening status;

- ensure that employee security screening has been carried out on all individuals, at every level in FCL, including those already employed;
- inform applicants and employees being screened that their personal data will be used for the purposes of employee security screening and that any documents presented to establish identity and proof of residence may be checked using an ultraviolet scanner or other method to deter identity theft and fraud. FCL shall also inform the applicant or employee that any original identity documents that appear to be forgeries will be reported to the relevant authority;
- create an employee screening policy and procedures and embed them into the recruitment process. The checklist for an employment screening policy is defined in Appendix 2; and
- ensure that employee security screening is applied to all levels of employees, including Top Management.

Successful completion of employee security screening is one criterion upon which the decision to grant confirmed employment shall be based.

18.1.3.4 Involvement in the employee screening process

The size and structure of FCL and the level and role of the applicant's position shall be used to determine which departments should be involved in the employee security screening process. This includes, but may not be limited to:

- **HR**—HR shall be used to conduct or commission employee security screening. It is essential that HR has a thorough understanding of the screening process and the applicable legislation and regulations within the employment jurisdiction;
- **Information and physical security**—The Information Security Manager (ISM) is responsible for assisting HR in the employee security screening process. The ISM shall be responsible for dealing with security concerns that emerge from the screening checks, as well as advising on the levels of checks that are required for required for different posts;
- **Management**—Managers play a significant role in recruitment. They shall be involved in the recruitment and interview process, and they should look for information which may influence the direction of the employee security screening process;
- **Legal Counsel**—Employee security screening processes shall comply with the relevant legislation and regulations in the jurisdiction. The Legal Counsel, whether internal or external, plays a critical role in the development of the employee security screening processes. They shall be consulted in the production of all documents or forms that are to be used for the employee security screening process, where appropriate; and
- **Others**—Other functions that may be involved include procurement and Auditors—Those responsible for confirming that any contractors are adequately screening their employees.

Within FCL, there is only one single Owner of the employee security screening process (the Screening Controller) who shall be accountable and responsible for it. The Screening Controller shall ensure that the screening process is robust and is consistently applied across FCL and to all prospective employees. If the screening process is to be performed internally, then the Screening Controller shall ensure that there are an appropriate number of properly trained employees to undertake employee security screening.

Third parties—Where FCL chooses to use an external employee security screening agency or a recruitment agency, the Screening Controller shall ensure that the third party understands how their products and services fit into the recruitment and screening process. The Screening Controller shall ensure that roles and responsibilities of both parties are both understood and communicated to all relevant parties. Additionally, where a third party is responsible for making employee security screening decisions that affect the applicant, they shall follow a documented and repeatable decision-making process. By repeatable, it means that any competent person having the same information would come to the same conclusions if they followed the agreed employee security screening procedures.

Even if the decision-making process is outsourced, FCL shall still remain responsible and accountable for the effective implementation of the employee security screening process. This is especially true where contractors and Consultants are recruited, as they sometimes do not go through the same screening processes as full-time or part-time staff.

18.1.3.5 Application forms

Using an appropriate application form is considered to be good practice as the applicant receives a standardised application form that shall define the information that is required for any specific post. The use of an application form shall ensure that the applicant confirms the information by signature that the information supplied is correct.

The application form used by FCL provides the majority, if not all, of the information required for the employee screening process. The employee application form is defined in Appendix 3, with the supporting notes for completion of the form defined in Appendix 4.

It may be necessary to customise the application form depending on the post for which the application form is being used. For example, educational qualifications may not be required for a semiskilled staff role (e.g. drivers, or cleaners), but additional information may be required for senior or specialised posts. Applicants should be clear what information is required, and information that is irrelevant to the post shall not be requested.

The form highlights the fact that employee security screening shall take place and that the applicant shall provide their consent for checks to be undertaken. It also includes a clear statement that lies or omissions are grounds to terminate the recruitment process or employment, no matter when they are discovered. This is important legally but anecdotal reporting suggests that it can also have significant deterrent value. The actual wording of the application form, the consents, the information required and the screening process shall be checked by Legal Counsel to ensure that they meet all of the relevant legal requirements in the jurisdiction where they are used.

Note

Depending on the jurisdiction, there may be specific requirements for explicit consent to process some personal data. In all cases, Legal Counsel shall be involved to ensure that all legislative requirements relating to the recruitment and employee security screening process are met. Where consent forms are used, in addition to the Reference Authorisation defined in Appendix 9, they shall be associated with the applicant's or employees file as appropriate (e.g. Medical Consent forms, processing sensitive or special categories of personal data, etc.). These documents shall be held securely by HR and their disposition is defined in the Document Retention Schedule, as defined in Chapter 4, Appendix 26. Appropriate disposal methods are defined in Chapter 12, Section 12.3.14.10.

18.1.3.6   Employment screening levels

One of the most important aspects of any screening strategy is deciding what preemployment checks to perform for each post advertised. FCL shall not perform the same employee security screening checks for all applicants, regardless of the post, as this can add unnecessary cost and delays to the recruitment process and may not be the most efficient employee security screening strategy. The employee security screening process shall be tailored according to the post advertised and the risks that the post presents. In all cases, full employee security screening shall be carried out.

The opportunity to cause harm or damage shall be a key consideration in any employee security risk assessment and an important factor in determining the level of employee security screening checks that are required.

Note

There are three general levels of employee security screening used, as shown below, but a specific level may be introduced for a specific post, based on the levels shown below.

18.1.3.6.1   Minimum level of employee security screening

As a minimum all new employees shall:

- verify identity (either a birth certificate, current passport, or photo ID driving licence);
- verify address (normally by bank statements or letters from government departments or utilities);
- confirm right to work in the country; and
- complete self-declaration criminal record form.

The Screening Controller shall be satisfied about a prospective employee's identity (because of the risks of identity fraud), their address, that the applicant has a right to work in the country. Failure to do so may lead to subsequent civil and criminal liabilities. On account of the work that FCL carries out, the applicant shall declare any criminal record that they have according to the relevant criminal record declaration legislation for the jurisdiction.

18.1.3.6.2   Medium level of employee security screening

The medium level of screening shall cover the minimum requirements above and:

- most recent academic qualifications;
- relevant professional qualifications;

- most recent employment references (at least 3 years, preferably 5 years); and
- basic confirmation with the past employer's HR Department of the applicant's employment history (e.g. dates, post, and reason for leaving).

18.1.3.6.3 High level of employee security screening

The high level of screening shall cover the requirements above and:

- all academic qualifications;
- all professional qualifications;
- employment references to cover at least 5 years (preferably 10–15 years).
- basic confirmation with the past employer's HR Department of the applicant's employment history (e.g. dates, post, and reason for leaving) and preferably past Line Manager's references, if possible;
- financial status;
- interviews with Reference Givers, if appropriate; and
- interviews with residential neighbours, if appropriate.

18.1.3.7 Security screening procedures

18.1.3.7.1 The employment screening plan and records

FCL has developed an employee security screening plan that meets its requirements with clear steps and time constraints for the process.

It is also essential that the Screening Controller shall ensure that there is a screening file for each applicant that contains all of the information for each applicant so that there is an audit trail, records and that any gaps and omissions are identified.

18.1.3.7.2 Verifying identity

Identity is the most fundamental employee security screening check. It shall, therefore, be the first part of the employee security screening process and no other checks shall be carried out until the applicant's identity has been established and satisfactorily proven.

There are three elements to an identity:

- **biometric identity**—The attributes that are biologically determined and unique to an individual (e.g. fingerprints, voice, retina, facial structure, DNA profile);
- **attributed identity**—The components of an applicant's identity that they are defined at their birth, including their name, place of birth, parents' names and addresses; and
- **biographical identity**—An individual's personal history, including, but not limited to:
  o registration of birth;
  o education and qualifications;
  o details of taxes and benefits paid by, or to, the individual;
  o employment history;
  o registration of marriage/civil partnership;
  o mortgage account details;
  o insurance policies; and
  o interactions with banks, utilities, etc.

The objectives of verifying identity are to relate the applicant to the information they have defined about themselves by:

- determining that the claimed identity is genuine and relates to the applicant or employee; and
- establishing that the applicant or employee owns and is rightfully using that identity.

The traditional method of determining an identity is to have the applicant present documents to the corroboration of the applicant's or employee's:

- full name—forenames and last name;
- signature; and
- date of birth.

Applicants shall be required to provide, with their application form, the following:

- a document containing the individual's photograph, such as a passport, government identity document, or photographic driving licence.

The level of assurance about the applicant's identity will increase with the number and quality of the documents received. It is important to stress that documents do not have equal value. The ideal document:

- is issued by a trustworthy and reliable source;
- is difficult to forge;
- is dated and current;
- contains the applicant or employee's name, photograph, and signature; and
- requires evidence of identity before being issued.

Copies may be submitted with an application, but unless they are certified by a Notary Public or similar, the originals should be produced at the interview stage. Some document types that may be considered for verifying identity are defined in Appendix 5.

Government documents may have a number of characteristics that make them difficult to forge. These will vary from document to document and from issuing body to issuing body in different jurisdictions, but some of the checks that may be considered are defined in Appendix 6.

18.1.3.7.3   Verifying address

This check confirms that the address actually exists, relates to a real property, and establishes that the applicant or employee either permanently resides there or has previously resided at the address.

Verifying the address given by the applicant or employee is important because it affirms that some other information provided is correct (e.g. an address on a driving licence or official correspondence). An applicant or employee may wish to omit their current or a former address to conceal adverse information, such as a poor credit rating or criminal convictions. The Screening Controller, in association with other interested parties in the employee security screening process, shall determine the level of address confirmation that is required. The requirement for address verification for a cleaner or driver will be less than that for a Finance Director. In the latter case, a full disclosure of all recent addresses shall be judged necessary.

The applicant or employee shall provide documentation to prove residence at the address(es) they have provided. Providing documentation for previous addresses may be difficult for the applicant or employee if the verification checking covers a long time period. Where this is the case, the applicant or employee may have gaps in proving residency for which they are unable to account. Whilst there may be perfectly plausible explanations for these gaps (e.g. foreign residence, travel, loss of documentation, etc.,) there may also be an attempt to conceal information that may be prejudicial to their application (e.g. criminal conviction, etc.,).

If there are gaps in the applicant's address verification, the following process shall be undertaken:

1. Request further documentation to cover the gap(s).
2. Consider the length of the gap(s). If it is less than 3 months and the level of employee screening is low or medium, the Screening Controller may consider that the effort to confirm the gap(s) based on the risk is not appropriate. This shall be part of the agreed procedures for employee security screening.
3. Where the gap(s) are discovered whilst using a third-party employee security screening service provider, a process for handling this shall also be part of the agreed employee screening procedures. How the third-party handles this shall be well understood prior to their engagement and subject to second-party audits;
4. Where the gap(s) are for claimed foreign travel, then a cross reference to the applicant's or employee's passport may indicate entry and exit stamps for the claimed period. However, this is not always the case as travel between some countries, depending on nationality, may not require the passport to be stamped. In this case, alternative proof shall be sought to cover the period of foreign travel claimed;
5. If the applicant was actually working abroad, they may have other documentation to prove their foreign residence (e.g. contract of employment, rental agreement for living accommodation, bank statements, etc.).

If FCL is unable to obtain satisfactory explanations for gaps and/or inconsistencies in the addresses the applicant or employee provides, the decision may be made to not to employ the applicant.

Some document types that may be considered for verifying address(es) are defined in Appendix 7.

18.1.3.7.4   Verifying the right to work

FCL shall ensure that its employees have the right to work in the jurisdiction where FCL is located. In some jurisdictions, an employer who is negligent or not sufficiently diligent in establishing the applicant's, or employee's, right to work in the jurisdiction may be liable for criminal and/or civil action. In some jurisdictions, an employer who knowingly employs an illegal worker will face more severe penalties. Additionally, some jurisdictions have penalties per illegal worker.

Once the applicant has been employed, FCL has an ongoing duty in most jurisdictions, to ensure that the employee has the right to remain employed (i.e., work permits, visas, etc.).

In some jurisdictions, it is possible to have a 'statutory defence' so long as the organisation has undertaken appropriate employee security screening and aftercare. It will be usually necessary for the organisation to provide records to prove that this process has been diligently carried out.

Different jurisdictions will have different requirements for proving the right to work, and FCL shall understand these, as defined in Chapter 12, Section 12.3.13.1.1, and use them in their employee security screening checks for confirming the right to work.

The standard questions used for verifying the right to work are defined in Appendix 8.

FCL shall ensure that:

- the applicant produces the relevant documents to prove the right to work in the jurisdiction;
- the applicant is the rightful owner of the documents produced;
- the documents produced permit the work the applicant will be performing;
- they check, as far as they are able, that the documentation produced is consistent with the claims made and with each other (e.g. validity, dates, and other details match, etc.);
- they check, as far as they are able that the documentation produced has not been tampered with in any way;
- where inconsistent documentation is produced, the applicant shall be requested to provide further documentation to support their application for employment;
- they retain copies (photocopies or digital scans, as acceptable within the jurisdiction) for all documentation supplied in the employee security screening process. For passports and similar, only relevant pages should be copied (e.g. front cover, data page, and pages with relevant visas, permits, etc.)[b]; and
- they retain documents securely according to legislative requirements for the jurisdiction, including document retention and data privacy requirements.

18.1.3.7.5   Verifying employment history

Employment history checks involve verifying an applicant's employment history as stated on their application form, in terms of:

- dates of employment;
- position;
- duties and responsibilities;
- salary; and
- reason for leaving.

The applicant's current employer shall not normally be contacted without prior written permission from the applicant.

The length of the period of previous employer's checks will depend on the role for which the applicant is being considered and the level of employee security screening applied to the post. Obviously, the more of the applicant's employment history that is checked the better, so a complete picture is built about the applicant's past employment history.

A Line Manager's reference is not, strictly speaking, part of the employee security screening process as it does not verify factual information but is opinion evidence. It is also open to abuse by exaggerating claims about the applicant, either positively or detrimentally. However, it can help assess the applicant's personality, etc.

Some jurisdictions have privacy laws that may restrict the information that can be supplied as a past employer's reference and some employers do not allow references to come from anyone other than HR. Additionally, there is an increasing reluctance on the part of many employers to provide frank and timely comments on an individual's character because they are concerned about claims for defamation or breach of contract. On account of this, an employer's reference may add little more than confirmation of employment, dates employed and position held.

---

b. In some jurisdictions, government documents are copyrighted, so care shall be made to fully comply with this legislative requirement, where it exists.

FCL shall use a standardised reference form for all written employer references. This has the advantage of identification of relevant information required about the applicant and shall be presented in such a way that it makes is reasonably easy for the employer to respond. The Employer Reference Form used for this is defined in Appendix 11.

Where an oral reference has been taken from an employer, this shall also be verified. The form used for this is defined in Appendix 12 and shall be filled in by the Reference Taker who takes the oral reference. Once the oral reference has been taken, a letter of confirmation shall be sent to the Reference Giver to confirm what was recorded as the oral reference. The letter for this is defined in Appendix 13 and a copy of the oral reference record (i.e., the filled-in Oral Reference Form as defined in Appendix 12) and the Reference Authorisation shall be enclosed with the letter.

18.1.3.7.6 Verifying qualifications

Qualification checks involve verifying an applicant's claimed qualifications as stated on their application form or curriculum vitae (resume) for educational or professional qualifications, in terms of

- educational establishment attended;
- course dates (from and to);
- title of the course;
- grade/mark awarded;
- qualification achieved (educational or professional); and
- being in good standing (professional qualifications).

As part of the profile for each post, the educational and professional qualifications required for it shall be defined as part of the job advertising process. For some posts (e.g. cleaners, etc.), it may not be necessary to request qualifications; however, all technical and management posts shall be required to provide claimed qualifications.

Original copies of qualifications shall be requested, but certified copies are acceptable if certified by a Notary Public or similar professional permitted to certify documents within the jurisdiction. If a plain photocopy is provided, it shall be verified with the issuing organisation.

The applicant's supplied qualifications shall be checked to ensure that they are genuine and that the claimed qualifications match the application form and the applicant's curriculum vitae (resume). The standard checklist used for this is defined in Appendix 14.

18.1.3.7.7 Verifying criminal records

For all posts in FCL, any prior criminal convictions, or similar may preclude any applicant from employment, bearing in mind the work that is to be performed. As this is the case, it is essential that FCL obtains details of any applicant's criminal record. In many jurisdictions, 'spent' convictions do not have to be declared, but the law relating to this will vary between different jurisdictions, and FCL must be aware of, and understand, the implications of the relevant legislation. Professional legal advice shall be sought. There are usually exemptions from not disclosing spent convictions for certain categories of jobs and it is almost certain that FCL will be covered by the exemption to uphold and support law and order, but this is not certain for all jurisdictions.

There are a number of ways of obtaining and verifying any criminal activity associated with an applicant and these are:

18.1.3.7.7.1 *A criminal record declaration* A Criminal Record Declaration that the applicant fills in and submits with their application form. The form used is defined in Appendix 15.

The Declaration requires the applicant to give details of any criminal convictions or Courts Martial. This relies on the honesty of the individual and any declaration shall be verified to ensure that it is complete and correct. The form states that verification shall take place.

The criteria for determining whether a conviction, whether spent or unspent, is a bar to employment shall be clearly defined in FCL's employee security screening policy and supporting procedures and be compliant with the legislation within the jurisdiction. The following guidance shall be considered:

- the age of the applicant when the offence was committed;
- the length of time since the offence was committed;
- the nature and the background of the offence;
- the seriousness of the offence;
- whether there were a number of offences or just a single offence;

- whether the offence casts doubt on the applicant's integrity;
- whether the offence could cast doubt on FCL's reputation, especially as employees may well have to give testimony in court;
- whether the offence is relevant to the post for which the applicant is applying (e.g. a fraud conviction would affect the decision to appoint the applicant to a Finance Department post, but it may not be relevant to a post where there is no interaction with money); and
- whether the offence would affect the applicant's ability to fulfil the requirements of their role.

18.1.3.7.7.2 Verifying the criminal record declaration How the verification process is performed through the relevant government agencies will vary from jurisdiction to jurisdiction, but in most jurisdictions, it is possible to verify the declaration.

It may also be possible to use a specialised third-party screening service provider to perform this verification process that is familiar with the requirements of the jurisdiction. This applies to both 'home' declarations as well as those from overseas.

18.1.3.7.8 Verifying financial status

Financial status checks involve verifying an applicant's financial status and may well be seen as essential in some roles within the organisation. Interpretation of the results of financial status checks is not a straightforward matter and like personal references, is not necessarily seen as a core aspect of employee security screening.

Financial checks can provide details about many different aspects of an applicant's financial background. Types of checks shall include, depending on the jurisdiction:

- **credit information**—listed at the applicant's current and previous addresses. This sort of information can include court matters, bankruptcies, etc.
- **credit history**—a report from a local or international credit reference agency; and
- **Company Officer's search**—using the national company register or other organisations that maintain such information, to ascertain whether the applicant has been or currently is, an Officer or Director of a company, or equivalent in the jurisdiction and whether they have ever been disqualified from being a Company Officer.

For sensitive positions, and particularly those that involve handling money, additional questions regarding previous handling of money and related issues shall be asked.

Financial enquiries shall be conducted in a number of ways including:

- as part of online searches, specialised databases shall be used and it is possible to undertake a number of different searches. These shall be cross referenced against paper evidence provided by the applicant;
- various national and international credit reference agencies shall be used to provide financial details on individuals. Again, these shall be cross referenced against paper evidence provided by the applicant;
- specialist, third-party employee security screening service providers financial reporting services. In these cases, FCL shall evaluate their service offering to ensure it meets their specific requirements.

FCL shall then evaluate the reports it receives about the applicant, from whatever source, assuming that a financial employee security screening report is required for the post. This requires judgement calls to be made as the reports may not provide clear-cut answers to the financial health of the applicant. Guidance on how to interpret the results forms part of the screening process and procedures. The procedures shall be clear and unambiguous to allow the process to be repeatable and consistent if challenged.

18.1.3.7.9 Personal character reference(s)

A personal character reference is similar to a Line Manager's reference in that it is not, strictly speaking, part of the employee security screening process as it does not verify factual information but is opinion evidence. It is also open to abuse by exaggerating claims about the applicant, either positively or detrimentally. No applicant will knowingly choose a referee that will give them a bad reference.

When considering the value of the reference, the credibility of the Reference Giver shall be considered. Given the above, the personal character reference can also help in making a further assessment of the applicant's personality, etc., from a different viewpoint than the Line Manager's, assuming one was submitted.

The Personal Reference Form used for this is defined in Appendix 16.

Where an oral reference has been taken for a personal reference, just as with oral references from an employer, this shall also be verified. The form used for this is defined in Appendix 17 and shall be filled in by the Reference Taker who takes the oral reference. Once the oral reference has been taken, a letter of confirmation shall be sent to the Reference Giver to confirm what was recorded as the oral reference. The letter for this is defined in Appendix 13 and a copy of the oral reference record (i.e. the filled-in Oral Reference Form) and the Reference Authorisation shall be enclosed with the letter.

18.1.3.7.10 Other reference(s)

The applicant may present preprepared references, either from an employer or a personal character reference. Where this is the case, FCL shall satisfy itself that the reference is genuine or disregard it and request a replacement reference directly from the Reference Giver.

If the reference is to be accepted, an audit trail of the steps taken to ensure the reference(s) are genuine shall be retained on the screening file. Such checks shall include:

- telephonic verification of the reference from the Reference Giver, the relevant oral reference record, and the Reference Authorisation, though a supplied phone number from the applicant should not be relied upon; and
- checking that the employer actually exists by reference to paper or electronic records (e.g. National Company Register, business directories, Chamber of Commerce, etc.).

Where a reference for a period of self-employment is claimed it shall come from a relevant government department (e.g. Tax Office), a professional adviser to the business (e.g. a banker, accountant, or solicitor) to confirm that the applicant's business was properly conducted and was terminated in a satisfactory manner.

Depending on the applicant's individual circumstances, other or additional references may also be required. If, for example:

- the applicant claims to have been working overseas for a period of three or more months consecutively, every effort should be made to obtain a reference from the employer;
- an employer's reference is not available (e.g. the employer has ceased trading), a reference shall be attempted to be obtained from an Officer or Line Manager from the employers' staff;
- the applicant claims to have been in full-time education, a reference from the academic institute shall be obtained in lieu of an employer's reference; and
- the applicant claims military service, a reference should be obtained from the relevant unit Commanding Officer.

Where an oral reference has been taken for a personal reference, just as with oral references from an employer, this shall also be verified. The form used for this shall be filled in by the Reference Taker who takes the oral reference. Once the oral reference has been taken, a letter of confirmation is sent to the Reference Giver to confirm what was recorded as the oral reference. The letter and a copy of the oral reference record (i.e. the filled-in Oral Reference Form) and the Reference Authorisation shall be enclosed with the letter.

18.1.3.7.11 Interviews

Interviews provide a unique opportunity to evaluate the applicant using two-way dialogue and observation. In addition to this, the interviewer shall request additional or missing information, as well as attempt to resolve any apparent inconsistencies in the information provided or when combined with the results of online searches of the reports from specialised third-party screening service providers or other sources. If an applicant knows that they shall be subject of one or more interviews, it has been suggested that this encourages them to be honest in the whole application process.

The interview shall allow the applicant and the interviewer to assess each other first-hand, and the feedback from the applicant can also give pointers towards the applicant's integrity and reliability.

Clear guidelines for interviewers for dealing with situations where either the evidence supplied by the applicant, or discovered as part of associated checks, reveals inconsistencies or raises concerns shall be documented. Whilst this may not automatically indicate some level of attempting to subvert information, there may well be a perfectly reasonable explanation for it. Situations such as these shall be carefully and sensitively handled during the interview, though clear guidance shall be provided to the interviewer for determining when the authorities or police should be involved (e.g. suspected forged documents).

All employment interviews shall be undertaken by HR in association with the relevant Line Manager(s).

18.1.3.7.12   The employment decision

The employee security screening strategy shall clearly set out how to deal with the results of all checks carried out, particularly where the results produce potentially adverse or conflicting information.

It shall not be necessary to complete the screening process, if initial checks indicate that an applicant has provided inaccurate information or that there are significant doubts raised initially about an applicant's honesty, integrity of reliability.

Most of the screening checks do not require interpretation; the information provided is either true or false. However, where checks requiring a judgement call to be made are performed, there shall be clear guidelines for interpretation of the results and determining what is acceptable and what is not. The method of determining what is acceptable or not shall be by setting thresholds for specific roles for the different areas of the employee security screening process.

Depending on the urgency of the requirement, employment may commence after completion of limited security screening by this stage. Such employment is deemed to be 'provisional employment' and limited security screening has been carried out. This shall, as a minimum, include the following for each applicant undergoing the employee security screening process.

- establishment of a screening file, as defined in Appendix 20;
- a signed application form declaration; and
- all the information requested to have been supplied (e.g. through a fully completed application form) and a full review of the information provided to confirm that there is nothing to suggest that the individual shall be unlikely to complete security screening satisfactorily;

Under no circumstances shall provisional employment commence until limited security screening as identified above has been completed. During the period of provisional employment, the individual shall be classed as employed, subject to satisfactory completion of security screening.

Note

Where it is imperative that an applicant starts employment with FCL prior to the completion of the employee security screening process, this may be done after the risk has been assessed and knowingly accepted by Top Management using the Top Management Acceptance of Employment Risk Form, as defined in Appendix 21.

18.1.3.7.13   Electronically cross-checking information provided

The traditional, paper-based approach is cheaper than the electronic approach. Also, it allows original documentation to be closely examined. If necessary, this shall include the use of an ultra-violet (UV) light source and magnifying glass to increase the prospect of identifying any basic forgeries against the checklist for detecting forged documents. However, just relying on a paper-based approach has a number of disadvantages, some of which include:

- documents can easily be forged;
- false or stolen documents can easily be purchased;
- starting with one key forged document can allow other genuine documents to be procured from the production of the original forged or purchased document.
- with good forgeries or stolen/purchased documents, only an expert may be able to identify them; and
- document verification can be labour intensive and time-consuming process.

The method that shall be used in FCL to undertake the employee security screening process is to combine the traditional paper-based approach with online checks against the paper documents held. There are a number of online databases that can be searched, some are free, whilst others require a payment for their use. Using online searching capabilities shall build a 'picture' of the applicant and corroborate the paper base evidence provided or the applicant's claims.

By searching relevant databases for records associated with the name, date of birth, and address(es) provided by an individual, it is possible to build a picture of that individual's past and current life. A long history of varied transactions and events indicates that the identity is more likely to be genuine. A history that lacks detail and/or depth may indicate that the identity is false.

There is a problem in as much as online checks only confirm what is present, they do not necessarily confirm that the applicant is the rightful owner of the identity that they claim. The interview process shall be used to assure the interviewer that the applicant is providing appropriate documentation.

Note 1

One of the issues that shall be understood is that the quality and accuracy of the data in the online databases or other online sources may be questionable.

Note 2

The quality and quantity of information in online databases vary between different jurisdictions, and total reliance on online databases in some jurisdictions is not recommended.

18.1.3.8   Using a third-party screening service provider

There are occasions when it is better to use a third-party screening service provider. This may be a specialist company or a service provided by a recruitment agency. If this option is chosen, FCL shall ensure that they understand the range of services being offered. There are a number of advantages of this approach, and these include:

- compliance with government, regulatory and legislative requirements;
- innovative technology;
- flexibility in services used;
- global reach, with the larger service providers;
- reduced setup and training costs; and
- typically, faster results as they service providers are specialists;

Where at third-party service provider is used, FCL shall ensure that the security of the applicant's data is assured. A checklist for selecting a third-party screening service provider is defined in Appendix 22.

18.1.3.9   Employing third parties

FCL employs third parties from time to time, these may be individuals on a contract or a service provider providing a variety of essential services. Whichever the case, any third party permitted access to information processing resources and the information that they process, shall have these screening procedures successfully applied to them prior to employment. However, as has been stated in Section 18.1.3.7.12, Top Management may choose to knowingly accept the risk of incomplete employee security screening.

The level of screening required shall depend on the third party's levels of access to information processing systems and confidential information. All third parties shall have a nominated and accountable owner of the relationship to ensure that the correct level of employment security screening is undertaken. Ideally, this will be the Screening Controller, but all employees wanting to employ a third party shall ensure that the Screening Controller is made aware of the employment of all third parties.

Where a recruitment consultancy is engaged to supply applicants for a specific role, the contracts between the parties shall clearly define the responsibilities for security screening of applicants.

FCL may accept the fact that a third party has undertaken appropriate employment screening that meets those requirements. If they cannot demonstrate this, FCL shall undertake the screening process themselves or engage an appropriate specialist employee security screening service provider.

18.1.3.10   Individuals employed in the screening process

The Screening Controller and all of those employees carrying out the employee security screening process, shall themselves be subject to employee security screening in accordance with these procedures. However, the process of segregation of duties shall be adhered to so that no one can be involved in their own employee security screening process.

The Screening Controller and all of those employees carrying out the employee security screening process shall individually sign a confidentiality agreement relating to the disclosure of confidential information and/or material with respect to an applicant or employee's past, present, and future.

Where the tasks of interviewing, employee security screening, and deciding whether to employ or to terminate employment are carried out, attention shall be given to the division of functions and authority for internal control purposes. Again, this reinforces the principle of segregation of duties, as defined in Chapter 12, Sections 12.3.5 and 12.3.6.

For example, where an employee has been engaged on a provisional basis, any subsequent offer of confirmed employment shall be authorised only by someone other than the individual who authorised the provisional employment, and the individual authorising confirmed employment shall see and review the employee's file in each case.

18.1.3.11 Employee security screening training

The Screening Controller and all employees carrying out the employee security screening process of applicants or employees shall be fully trained to perform their duties. This training shall be regularly reviewed and updated as required (e.g. on a time-elapsed process or changes of legislation, regulation, or standards relating to the employee security screening process within the jurisdiction).

The relevant employee's HR training record shall be updated and the contents used for input to their TNA.

18.1.3.12 Employee screening records

All employee screening records shall be maintained and stored securely in the relevant screening file and measures shall be put in place to prevent unauthorised access, disclosure modification, or erasure. These requirements shall be met by the implementation of ISO/IEC 27001 including:

- a separate file for each applicant to undergo employee security screening shall be maintained. This includes every employee from Top Management down to the newest recruit. The files of all employees currently employed on a provisional basis shall be identified separately from other employee files;
- details of all occasions where Top Management (or other management) discretion shall be used to accept any risks for gaps or inconsistencies in the employee screening file for an applicant or employee and offer employment shall be documented and placed in the relevant screening file using the Top Management Acceptance of Employment Risk Form; and
- updated Employee Security Screening files for all applicants and employees.

All screening files shall clearly indicate, where applicable, that an applicant is employed on a provisional basis, showing prominently the dates on which provisional employment commenced and is to cease; the latter shall be not later than 'n'[c] weeks after the date of commencement of provisional employment.

The full screening file shall be retained during the applicant's employment by the Screening Controller, with a copy held on the applicant's personnel file held by HR.

Where employment is ceased for whatever reason, the full screening file shall be retained according to the document retention schedule. In jurisdictions where there is privacy legislation for personal data, the legislation shall define handling, retention, and security requirements. These requirements shall be complied with to ensure that they protect the contents of the screening file (and other personal data) against unauthorised access, disclosure, modification, or erasure.

18.1.4 Contracts, confidentiality, and nondisclosure agreements (NDAs)

To address the need to protect confidential information, all employees shall be subject to a confidentiality agreement or clause in their employment contracts. Additionally, any third party that may have access for legitimate reasons to confidential data shall be subject to execution of an NDA prior to having access to that data, as defined in Chapter 14, Section 14.3.3. Confidentiality clauses shall be constructed with appropriate legal advice and be legally enforceable within the relevant jurisdiction(s). It is also necessary to determine their specific business requirements for such agreements, and this shall include consideration of at least the following:

- a legal definition of the information to be protected (i.e., what constitutes the confidential information to be protected);
- the expected duration of the agreement, this may be a period of time or may need to be indefinitely;
- actions to be taken at the termination of the agreement (employment contract, confidentiality agreement, or NDA);
- the responsibilities of the parties to the agreement during the term of the agreement;
- ownership of information created as part of employment, where appropriate;
- permitted uses of any confidential information covered by the agreement;
- right to audit or monitor any activities that involve the use or processing of confidential information covered by the agreement;

---

c. The period of provisional employment without finishing the employee screening process will vary between posts.

- the process for advising the owner of the confidential information in the case of any incident, unauthorised disclosure, or security breach relating to the confidential information;
- process for return, or disposal, of any confidential information covered by the agreement at the termination of the agreement, including proof of secure disposal; and
- action expected to be taken, and possible penalties, in the case of a breach of the agreement.

FCL has a number of different standard forms and types of contract for different situations or jurisdictions. These are in addition to specific contracts that are created for nonstandard situations. All agreements in use shall be subject to regular review.

Requirements for confidentiality clauses in employment contracts, confidentiality agreements, and NDAs shall be regularly reviewed for continued business need or when business, regulatory, or legislative changes occur that may affect the requirements for protecting confidential information.

All employment contracts shall be held centrally by HR. Confidentiality agreement and NDAs shall also be centrally held by Legal Counsel and a register of them shall be maintained. They shall be regularly audited to ensure that they are all present and current.

No employee shall sign any confidentiality agreement or NDA that may legally bind FCL without the authority of the Legal Counsel.

18.1.5 Job descriptions

All employees shall have up to date job descriptions relevant to their role(s).

The job description has four main uses:

- **organisational position**—it defines where the job is positioned in the organisation structure and shows reporting lines;
- **recruitment**—it provides essential information to applicants so they can see if they meet the requirements of the role. At the same time, it provides information to the recruiter for evaluation of the applicants and to determine an applicant's suitability and competence for a job;
- **legal**—a job description forms part of the legally binding contract of employment. Other elements include the contract of employment itself as well as the employee handbook and other documents depending on legal requirements within the jurisdiction; and
- **performance appraisal**—individual objectives can be set based on the job description for use at the appraisal process.

Job descriptions shall all follow the same format, as a minimum:

- job title;
- objective and role;
- problems and challenges;
- principal accountabilities;
- authority;
- contacts (internal and external); and
- reporting line(s).

All job descriptions shall contain a requirement to comply with all legislation, regulations, organisational policies, and procedures.

Job descriptions shall be used as the basis of the employee's appraisal and need to be regularly reviewed to ensure that they remain appropriate.

Whilst not all job descriptions are shown below, those with specific information security requirements are:

- ISM, as defined in Chapter 12, Appendix 11;
- Quality Manager, as defined in Chapter 6, Appendix 4;
- Laboratory Manager, as defined in Chapter 6, Appendix 21;
- Forensic Analyst, as defined in Chapter 6, Appendix 22;
- Service Desk Manager, as defined in Chapter 7, Appendix 4;
- Incident Manager, as defined in Chapter 7, Appendix 5;
- Problem Manager, as defined in Chapter 7, Appendix 9;
- Change Manager, as defined in Chapter 7, Appendix 12;
- Release Manager, as defined in Chapter 7, Appendix 16;

- Configuration Manager, as defined in Chapter 7, Appendix 19;
- Capacity Manager, as defined in Chapter 7, Appendix 21;
- Service Level Manager, as defined in Chapter 7, Appendix 24;
- Business Continuity Manager, as defined in Chapter 13, Appendix 3;
- Health and Safety Manager, as defined in Chapter 17, Appendix 3;
- Investigation Manager, as defined in Appendix 24;
- System Administrator, as defined in Appendix 25;
- Employees, as defined in Appendix 26.

18.1.6 Competence on arrival

All new employees shall have their competence evaluated during the recruitment process and so most should be competent to perform their role from initial employment. However, there will be times that an employee (e.g. a new entrant or an employee on transfer or promotion) may not have all of the competences required for their role, and part of their job shall include initial training. During the recruitment process, a competence assessment shall be carried out, matching the applicant against the requirements of the job description. The results of this evaluation can be used as input to the TNA process, as defined in Section 18.2.2.

Psychometric testing shall be used as part of the recruitment process. There are a number of different tests that can be used and these fall generally into two broad categories:

- interest and personality tests; and
- aptitude and ability tests.

These shall only be administered by competent testers who can interpret the results correctly. Results of psychometric testing shall be added to the applicant's personnel file.

18.1.7 Induction

All new employees shall be assigned a 'mentor' who is personally responsible for:

- inducting the new employee to working methods, practises, and the work environment;
- induction the new employee into their team;
- acting as a focal point for any issues; and
- ensuring that an appropriate workplace is available to the employee when they start work (workstation, keys, security codes, access to IT facilities, etc.).

The procedure for this shall be:

1. HR performs the first part of the induction process which ensures that all personal information is collated and that generic documentation is both issued and received. The induction checklist used is defined in Chapter 6, Appendix 8.
2. The relevant Line Manager introduces the new employee to the existing team members (and other employees, as appropriate), and then performs the second part of the induction that describes working practices (this task may be delegated to another employee, as necessary).
3. The Line Manager continues with the induction programme and describes the new employee's role, their area of work, and introduces them to their assigned mentor.
4. The Line Manager continues and describes the site facilities, and ensures that the new employee is provided with the relevant building keys, security access codes, and alarm codes as appropriate;
5. Any equipment necessary for performing their role is issued to the new employee;
6. Each of the Management System Owners outlines their part of the IMS, as appropriate. This shall focus on;
   - that the IMS exists to ensure promotion of quality, security, continuity, environmental responsibility, health and safety, and legislative compliance throughout the design, development, production, and support of all products and services. Specific information security requirements are defined in Chapter 12, Section 12.3.2.1;
   - the specific measurable objectives with regard to obtaining quality in the design, development, production, and support of all products and services;
   - the all employees shall be responsible for applying the IMS procedures and policies and play a key role in the attainment of the IMS objectives;
   - all products and services shall be developed in accordance with the requirements of the IMS;

- all new employees shall understand their responsibilities with regard to attainment of IMS objectives and how their contribution affects this, positively or negatively; and
- all new employees shall understand the impact of violating the IMS procedures and policies.

7. The employee's induction form, as defined in Chapter 6, Appendix 8, shall be completed and then filed with the employee's other HR records. The employee's training record shall be updated to show that they have undertaken Induction Training.

18.1.8 Policies and procedures

There are a number of policies and procedures in place in the IMS, these include, but are not limited to:

- acceptable use policy, as defined in Chapter 4, Appendix 35;
- access control policy, as defined in Chapter 4, Appendix 21;
- business continuity policy, as defined in Chapter 4, Appendix 19;
- change or termination policy, as defined in Chapter 4, Appendix 22.
- clear desk and clear screen policy, as defined in Chapter 4, Appendix 23;
- conflict of interest policy, as defined in Chapter 3, Appendix 3;
- continuous improvement policy, as defined in Chapter 4, Appendix 24;
- document retention policy, as defined in Chapter 4, Appendix 26.
- employment screening policy, as defined in Chapter 4, Appendix 30;
- environment policy, as defined in Chapter 4, Appendix 16;
- health and safety policy, as defined in Chapter 4, Appendix 17;
- information security policy, as defined in Chapter 4, Appendix 20;
- mobile computing policy, as defined in Chapter 4, Appendix 28;
- network services policy, as defined in Chapter 4, Appendix 29;
- quality policy, as defined in Chapter 3, Appendix 4.

Supporting procedures for all of these policies, along with relevant forms and checklists, are located in the IMS.

Records of issues to all employees shall be maintained so that updates may be provided on publication to ensure that all recipients have current copies.

18.2 Development

18.2.1 Ongoing training

After induction training has been undertaken, as defined in Section 18.1.7, all employees shall embark on a schedule of specific forensic training as well as ongoing organisation-based training. Generic training requirements are defined in Chapter 4, Section 4.7.3. Ongoing organisation training shall include annual updates for the IMS system and training for specific issues as required.

Note

The specific requirements for information security awareness training are defined in Chapter 12, Section 12.3.2.

18.2.1.1 *Promotion of IMS awareness*

Awareness of IMS objectives is an important responsibility of every employee on a daily basis. The objective of IMS awareness is to:

- ensure that all employees are aware of the IMS in operation, their importance to the attainment of the IMS objectives for the design, development, and production of all products and services;
- explain why the management systems are needed for the different standards implemented and why a top-level IMS has been implemented to incorporate all of the common requirements of the different standards in IMS rather than replicating them for each standard implemented;
- ensure that all employees are aware of their personal responsibilities and follow correct policies, procedures, and work instructions to ensure attainment of the IMS objectives; and

- ensure that all employees design, develop and produce products and services, as well as manage and maintain them, in an appropriate and disciplined manner, in accordance with the requirements of the IMS.

The relevant Management System Owner shall be responsible for promoting awareness of their management system amongst employees, including:

- awareness sessions shall be performed by the relevant Management Systems Owners for all new employees to ensure they are aware of the IMS, and their contribution towards the successful attainment of IMS objectives;
- all employees shall be kept up to date with changing and current IMS practices and objectives; and
- the IMS awareness programme and its effectiveness shall be reviewed at least annually by the Management System Owners as part of the IMS audit and Management Review process, using the Training Feedback Form. Where improvements to the programme are proposed to Top Management that they are agreed and implemented using the continuous improvement process, as defined in Chapter 4, Section 4.10.

To promote ongoing awareness the relevant Management System Owner shall periodically re-brief all employees on their management system and the attainment of current IMS objectives Some of the issues covered by periodic updates shall include:

- the internal audit programme, as defined in the IMS Calendar, defined in Chapter 4, Appendix 46;
- the ongoing success of the IMS;
- improvements to the IMS and attainment of the IMS objectives;
- how improvements to the IMS affect working practises;
- making changes to IMS policies, procedures, and work instructions;
- understanding problems or difficulties experienced by employees whilst using the IMS; and
- how employees who do not comply with IMS policies, procedure, and work instructions are to be dealt with.

18.2.1.2 Maintaining employee IMS awareness

FCL recognises that retention and applicable knowledge of employees increase considerably when the matter is subject to revision. To assist with this:

- all employees shall be re-briefed on all parts of the IMS annually, or on influencing change by the relevant Management System Owner;
- the relevant Management System Owner shall develop and implement an awareness programme for their management system, which addresses periodic IMS awareness update requirements;
- some of the issues covered by the periodic management system updates shall include:
  - success of implementation and use of the IMS, its policies, procedures and work instructions;
  - problems or difficulties experienced with the IMS, its policies, procedures, and work instructions;
  - any changes to the IMS, its policies, procedures, and work instructions; and
  - breaches and incidents relating to the IMS.

18.2.1.3 Other business-related training

There are a variety of business-type training sessions for a variety of specific subjects that shall be applicable to employees. Some will be applicable to all employees, others will be applicable to specific employees doing a specific task (e.g. mobile device security, teleworking) and others will be indicated by the annual appraisal process and the employee's TNA. Generic requirements for all types of training are defined in Chapter 4, Section 4.7.3.

18.2.1.4 Information security training

Awareness of information security requirements relating to information is an essential responsibility of every employee on a daily basis. Unauthorised access, disclosure, modification, or erasure of information could result in a loss of work hours spent creating information, as well as more work hours trying to recover it and possible severe reputational loss or financial penalties. Information compromise inside or outside the work environment could result in the violation of client confidentiality or relevant privacy legislation in the jurisdiction. This could lead to criminal charges or civil litigation.

It is ultimately the responsibility of Top Management to ensure that all employees with access to information processing resources and information shall understand the key elements of information security, why it is needed, and their personal information security responsibilities.

All employees shall participate in the security awareness and training program, as defined in Chapter 12, Section 12.3.2.

All employees shall be provided with guidance to help them understand information security, the importance of complying with the relevant policies, procedures and work instructions relating to information security, and to be aware of their own personal responsibilities. It is the responsibility of Line Managers, in cooperation with the ISM, to promote security awareness and training to all employees on a continuous basis.

FCL shall follow these guidelines to promote awareness of information security amongst all employees with access to information processing resources and information:

- formal awareness and training sessions shall be run using specialised awareness material;
- all training sessions shall be kept up to date with current practices and the evolving threat landscape;
- training sessions shall be attended by all employees, including Top Management; and
- feedback from the information security awareness training sessions shall be regularly reviewed by the ISM to ensure continuous improvement is in place.

The objective of security training is to ensure that:

- appropriate risk management techniques and tools shall be used to choose appropriate security controls;
- information security controls shall be applied correctly to information processing systems and information; and
- products and services shall be developed, and cases processed, in a disciplined and secure manner.

The HR Manager and relevant Management System Owners shall be responsible for ensuring that all employees obtain adequate training via:

- advising employees of available courses and seminars that are appropriate to their needs;
- encouraging membership of suitable professional bodies;
- encouraging personal certification, where applicable;
- ensuring knowledge transfer from third parties employees, where appropriate;
- identifying online training resources and encouraging employees to use them;
- implementing a learning management system (LMS) with learning reinforcement that is part of the annual awareness update process. Those employees that do not pass the marking threshold shall have to retake the training until they do pass.

18.2.1.5 Technical training for employees

All employees involved in case processing shall be technically trained in a number of different areas of digital forensics. A list of areas of some required knowledge is defined in Appendix 27.

18.2.1.6 Training development

It is essential that all employees who handle forensic cases are properly trained, but because this is a relatively new field, few mature competency frameworks currently exist that can be relied upon to authenticate training.

Often it is tempting to send employees who handle forensic cases to product-specific training before a clear understanding of the underlying principles of computer operations and general forensic procedures are clearly understood, to make employees who handle cases productive as soon as possible. However, without basic understanding of the hardware and general forensic procedures, employees who handle cases and have only product-specific knowledge will produce work that may be of little use as any evidence found cannot be supported by the knowledge of how it got there. The framework for initial development for overcoming this issue is defined in Chapter 6, Appendix 23.

18.2.1.7 Individual certification or not?

As well as undertaking general training and role-specific training, all employees shall be encouraged to enhance their professional and personal development. Individual certification lends gravitas to employees when they are giving evidence either orally or in writing. As part of the certification process, individual employees usually have to undertake reporting requirements for Continuing Professional Development (CPD) or Continuing Professional Education (CPE), and these records shall be associated with the employee's training records.

Whilst individual certification is not a prerequisite, it is a matter for the employee and their Line Managers to determine whether certification should be sought or not, and if so, what certifications should be pursued.

A list of some existing security and forensic certifications that could be considered is defined in Chapter 6, Appendix 24.

Note

This list is expanding rapidly and current certifications should be researched to determine the optimum ones for an employee.

As well as certifications, membership of professional bodies should also be considered. There are a variety of national and international professional bodies that can be considered. Some of the better-known ones are listed in Appendix 28.

18.2.1.8 Training records

All employees shall have full training records maintained as part of their HR file. This shall also contain the employee's training and development plan based on feedback from the TNA process.

Copies of the following training records or certificates shall be retained on an employee's personnel file:

- academic qualifications;
- awareness sessions attended;
- certifications gained;
- continual professional development (CPD) logs;
- continual professional education (CPE) logs;
- external courses attended;
- internal course attended;
- other accolades or commendations achieved as part of the training process;
- professional qualifications; and
- remedial action as part of the TNA process.

After training or gaining a new or updated qualification, all employees shall complete and submit a training evaluation form, to HR to both provide feedback and allow their training records to be updated.

18.2.2 Training needs analysis (TNA)

The whole process of TNA starts off with identifying the needs of the business. After all, if there is no justifiable business need for undertaking some specific training why should it be undertaken?

There are two specific types of business needs:

Planned—this is where there are either environmental needs to be met (e.g. planned legislative changes) or business needs to be met that align with the business strategy and objectives. FCL shall ensure that it is constantly aware of environmental changes on the horizon that may affect it, as well as evaluating (and constantly re-evaluating) its business strategy and objectives and managing the business to meet them;

Unplanned—this occurs when some event that was not planned for occurs (e.g. a flurry of complaints from clients, a major case collapsing on account of a failure in forensic case processing procedures, etc.) that needs to be urgently fixed and where training appears to be the solution. However, care shall be taken not to rush into this solution as it can be costly and not always be effective in solving the underlying root cause of the problem.

18.2.2.1 Identifying training needs

Having identified the business needs, whether they are planned or unplanned, they shall be turned into training needs. There are three different levels of training needs that FCL considers:

- **organisational**—this is where a training need is identified for all employees and is typically a new initiative or a legislative change;
- **group**—this is where a specific group, or groups, of employees have a specific training need identified that relates only to them (e.g. a new tool or process to be used in their specific work area);
- **individual**—this will typically be derived from the employee appraisal process and will include any remediation training, training according to the employee's training plan, or could be an un-planned event (e.g. a promotion requiring management training).

FCL uses five tools to assist in this process and these are:

- **HR planning**—which includes how resourcing shall be carried out to align to the business strategy and objectives as well as employee appraisals;

- **succession planning**—which is a subset of HR planning but ensures that there shall be cover for any specific role. Whilst this typically refers planning for management succession, it can also refer to a specialist role and often covers issues like cross training employees so there are always at least two employees with a specific skill;
- **critical incidents**—which are typically 'one off' incidents that can affect credibility or reputation in the marketplace (e.g. a loss of a major client, audit failure, etc.). The root cause of any such incident shall be determined, as defined in Chapter 4, Section 4.10.1 and Chapter 4, Appendix 53, and then consideration defined as to whether training is actually the correct solution;
- **management information systems**—which uses monitoring and analysis of a variety of key performance indicators or quality objectives to determine areas of performance that may need improvement. This is a performance management process and may also indicate a need for additional training;
- **performance appraisals**—which is the individual employee's annual appraisal that identifies weaknesses in the employee's performance that can be resolved by training or as part of the employee's training plan.

Whilst training may be a solution to an identified problem, careful determination of the root cause of the problem may indicate other solutions that are more effective. These could include:

- better use of technology;
- improving procedures;
- employee rotation or changes; and
- redesign of job roles.

18.2.2.2 Specifying training needs

Having identified that a training need exists, it is necessary to specify the requirement precisely. A gap analysis approach shall identify the key tasks, deliverables, and competencies for a specific role and the employee's performance, whether this is for an individual employee or a group of them. The gap analysis shall be carried out using a combination of data-gathering approaches and may include, but not be limited to:

- critical incident reviews;
- desk research or competitor analysis;
- direct observation of the employee's performance;
- interviews;
- psychometric assessments; and
- self-assessment questionnaires.

18.2.2.3 Turning training needs into action

Once the decision that a training solution is appropriate has been agreed, then the type of training to be used shall be determined. Training can be divided into formal and informal training as defined below:

18.2.2.3.1 Formal training

This is defined as classroom training with the tutor 'teaching' the participants. Heavy trainer input is usually required for knowledge transfer, with less being required for skill and attitude training where the trainer becomes more of a 'facilitator'. However, there are a number of alternatives to classroom training and they can use a number of different training media. The choice of these will depend on training material availability, budget, cultural fit, etc.

Some options include:

18.2.2.3.1.1 Out of doors training For management, leadership, and teambuilding training, this is often used and usually comprises a number of practical tasks to be performed, either on an individual basis or as teams. This may include competitions to build bridges or overcome obstacles, assault courses, paintball competitions, or confidence exercises such as zip lines and high-level bridges.

18.2.2.3.1.2 Online training This type of training is typically used for knowledge-based competencies. The advent of multimedia training and virtual online classrooms has made this form of training both affordable and a real contender to replace formal classroom training in a number of areas, including internal training and awareness courses. Though it does have the disadvantage that face-to-face interaction is limited so a mix of traditional classroom and virtual online training may be needed.

18.2.2.3.1.3 Distance learning There are a wide range of distance learning programmes available for a variety of training. Often, they include tutor and classroom sessions as part of the training and typically will have assessments and/or examination(s). Distance learning can deliver very straightforward and highly focussed training up to a full degree or beyond.

18.2.2.3.1.4 Job rotation This is a formal process where a preplanned sequence of different role experiences is undertaken by an employee. This is used at the start of employment for employees to gain a full understanding of different processes that make up the whole organisational structure, as appropriate to their role.

18.2.2.3.1.5 Job shadowing This is another formal process, often used with other types of training, which involves the employee observing or working alongside relevant post holders to gain experience a particular task or skill.

18.2.2.3.2 Informal training

Whilst there are a number of formal training methods used, as defined above, there are a number of very useful informal ones that can be used.

These are often seen as a cheap option when compared against formal training, but this type of training shall be used when:

- it is being used for developing a skill (rather than learning a new one);
- there is a need for specific training tailored to the specific work environment;
- an individual employee responds better to this type of training than any other;
- there are no formal training courses available;
- there is a limited training budget; or
- there is a time constraint in that there is no formal training available within the required time frame.

Coaching

Coaching shall be undertaken either by a Line Manager or an external consultant whilst the employee being coached can be anyone who wants to get better at their work.

Coaching is a collaborative process to manage the employee to deliver better results in their role. In the process, the Coach shall be responsible for keeping the coaching focussed on a clearly defined goal and the employee being coached to generate ideas, options, and methods for achieving a goal, acting to achieve it, and reporting the progress towards the goal. One of the most common reasons for coaching to fail is to get these roles confused.

The process that FCL shall use is the 'GROW' model:

- **goal**—defining the required outcome;
- **reality**—identifying the current situation and future trends;
- **options**—identifying new ideas for achieving the goal; and
- **what/who/when**—deciding on the plan of action to achieve this.

As can be seen, again this is a variation of W Edwards Deming's PDCA cycle.

18.2.2.3.2.1 Mentoring Mentoring is similar to coaching. The Mentor can be part of a formal or informal training process. A Mentor can play a number of roles, these can range from:

- acting as the 'buddy' for new employee to assist them settle into their role;
- a 'listening ear' to any level of employee and they do not even have to be other employees but may be outsiders. If they are external, care shall be taken to ensure that there is no leakage of confidential information or that if confidential information may be discussed that appropriate Confidentiality Agreements or NDAs have been put in place;
- acting as a 'sounding board' for new ideas, again care shall be taken about disclosure of confidential information; or
- taking a proactive role in another employee's development.

18.2.2.4 The training specification

The training specification is a blueprint for the training to be undertaken to meet the gap in performance identified and to measure its effectiveness. The exact form of a training specification will vary between different types of training undertaken. The training specification is defined in Appendix 29.

It is essential that any training that is undertaken meets the stated training objectives (often referred to as 'learning' objectives). These are descriptions of the performance and/or behaviours that the employees are expected to exhibit at the end of the training. It is essential that these shall be clearly and precisely defined as they shall be the basis of the evaluation of the effectiveness of the training. The SMARTER approach for evaluation training shall be adopted to evaluate training objectives:

- **S**pecific—avoiding poorly defined training objectives;
- **M**easurable—ensuring that it is possible to measure the training objective when complete and to know if it was achieved;
- **A**ttainable—not using a training objective that can never be achieved;
- **R**ealistic—ensuring that the employee is capable of achieving the objective;
- **T**imelines—ensuring each objective has written within it a timeline (date) for completion;
- **E**xtending—the task should stretch the employee's capabilities;
- **R**ewarding—ensuring that the employee is rewarded for delivery in an appropriate manner.

Note

This is a variation on the SMART approach used for measurements of Management System objectives, as defined in Chapter 3, Section 3.1.17.

Whilst it may appear an onerous task to create a training specification for each training course for each employee, sometimes a shorter specification can be used. Where the course is for only one or two employees it may be that this is not required, but for some specialised or management positions, it is essential.

The creation of the training specification shall ensure that the requirements are clearly thought through, allow commercial offerings to be compared against them in detail and provide the basis for the all-important step of evaluation of the training.

18.2.2.4.1 Develop or purchase?

Having developed the training specification, the decision to be made shall be to either develop a course to meet the training objectives or find a commercial offering that meets them.

Note

There may be other options available such as amending an existing course or reusing modules from other courses.

The 'develop or buy?' decision shall be influenced by five main factors:

- **number of employees to be trained**—it is cheaper to develop a course if there are a large number of employees to be trained;
- **the competencies to be trained**—if the competencies are specific and tailored it is better to develop a course;
- **the time constraints**—if a course is not needed immediately, it may be better to develop a course;
- **the skills required of the trainer**—if the required skills of the trainer do not exist externally then they may be no choice but to develop a course internally; and
- **the learning experience required**—if there is a need to train employees together then it may be better to develop a course.

18.2.2.4.2 Choosing a supplier

If developing or purchasing a course, it is essential that the supplier meets the training objectives set for their training: The process used is similar to that of the tendering process that exists for any service, as defined in Chapter 14, Section 14.5, and shall follow the specific steps below for choosing a training supplier, as opposed to any other office product or service:

- research the market to find suitable suppliers;
- create a shortlist of five or six that seem to be the closest match to the training requirements;
- ask the shortlist to submit a training RFP based on the agreed training specification. A checklist for evaluation training proposals is defined in Appendix 30;

- evaluate the proposals against the training specification and based on the responses select a shortlist of two or three;
- invite them for interview, if deemed appropriate A checklist for evaluation at interview is defined in Appendix 31;
- follow up with the supplier's client references, if required; and
- based on the responses to all of the above, select a supplier.

If purchasing an existing course, then the following shall be considered:

- create a shortlist of five or six that seem to be the closest match to the training requirements and then determine:
  - how well the course content and learning objectives meet the defined training objectives;
  - the quality of the course based on feedback;
  - the costs of the course;
  - the timing of the course; and
  - the location of the course, which can have a cost implication and also a staff unavailability issue if the course is held at a distant location.
- based on the responses to all of the above, select a supplier.

18.2.2.5 Planning the training

Having determined the training needs from a number of sources, the training to be delivered shall be planned in terms of:

- what training should be included based on a variety of constraints;
- the order for carrying out training on an organisational, group, and employee level;
- what training can be postponed without impacting the ability to deliver quality products and services; and
- fallback plans in case of changing requirements or supplier failure.

Whilst it is possible to plan for most training, often training needs are unplanned and so there shall be a great degree of flexibility in the training plans.

18.2.2.6 Training evaluation

Training evaluation shall be carried out for three main reasons:

- to continuously improve training content and delivery quality;
- to assess the effectiveness of the course in meeting the defined training objectives; and
- to justify the course by proving the benefits outweigh the costs.

For each of these reasons, hard empirical data shall be collected.
The evaluation is at four different levels:

- **reaction level**—what the employee thought of the training;
- **immediate level**—what the employee learned from the training;
- **intermediate level**—the effect the training had on the employee's job performance;
- **ultimate level**—the effect the training had on organisational performance;

The main methods of collecting data are:

- questionnaires;
- interviews;
- observation; and
- desk research.

A mixture of all of these methods shall be used, as appropriate, as each has its advantages and disadvantages.

18.2.2.6.1 Reaction level evaluation

This form of evaluation is usually undertaken using forms that the employee has filled in either at the end of the course or on their return to the office by HR or the employee's Line Manager using the form defined in Appendix 32. They are used to evaluate the training and are stored with the employee's personnel records.

18.2.2.6.1.1   Immediate level evaluation This form of evaluation is aimed and determining how much the employee has actually learned on the course. Typically, this is done using quizzes or and exam at the end of the course that is based specifically on the content of the course. There are three main methods of obtaining immediate-level evaluation:

- simple 'Yes'/'No'/'Don't Know' or 'True'/'False'/'Don't Know' type answers to multiple questions covering the course content;
- multiple choice questions where the employee is offered a number of possible answers and has to choose the correct answer(s); and
- open-ended questions that require free-form essay style answers to the question asked.

The first two are useful for testing simple knowledge retention and the last one is mainly used for determining the employees understanding and application of the concepts learned and applying them to real situations.

18.2.2.6.1.2   Intermediate level evaluation Intermediate-level evaluation determines how well the employee has assimilated the knowledge or skills learned to improve their job performance. This is the most essential level of evaluation and if the TNA has been properly carried out, the training undertaken shall close any employee's performance gap. When combined with the immediate level evaluation, this can be a clear indicator of how good the training actually was for the employee(s). If the results for both are poor for one or two employees, where many are attending, this can indicate a specific issue with the specific employee(s) performing poorly. Where there are multiple poor results, it can indicate that the training was possibly inappropriate for the employees or that the training and how the material was delivered was poor. These two evaluation levels shall be carefully examined to determine the effectiveness of the training being undertaken. Wherever results are poor for one or more employee, the reason for the poor results shall be determined and appropriate action taken to address the root cause.

A range of tools can be used to evaluate intermediate-level evaluation, these include:

- independent assessment;
- management review;
- observation;
- peer review; and
- self-assessment questionnaires.

An appropriate 'mix and match' of the tools above shall be used to evaluate the effectiveness of all employee training undertaken.

18.2.2.6.1.2.1   Ultimate level evaluation. In some ways, this is the most difficult level to evaluate as the method of measuring performance may not be easy to implement or measure. There are a number of reasons for this:

- there are often no direct or obvious performance measures (e.g. the management or leadership training);
- many factors apart from the training undertaken can affect performance (e.g. economic conditions can affect sales even if a sales training course was world class); and
- often performance measures are measured for a whole department, and it is not possible to identify the effects of the training unless all members of the department attended the training.

The optimum measurement process uses the SMARTER approach, and has a six-stage approach:

1. Identify the key performance indicators that shall be used for performance measurement;
2. Ensure that the performance figures are available in the right form prior to the training being undertaken;
3. Determine how long it will be before the training has made the optimum impact on operations;
4. Determine the new performance figures from the period immediately after training was undertaken to the point determined above;
5. Identify any other factors that may affect performance on operations; and
6. Compare the results of the 'before' and 'after' training'.

Appropriate key performance indicators (or Quality Objectives in ISO 9001 terms) shall be developed for measuring the effectiveness of training. Some examples that are easy to measure include:

- absenteeism levels;
- level of orders or sales;
- meeting case Turn Round Times (TRTs);
- number of successful case outcomes;
- reduction in customer complaints; and
- increasing referrals from existing customers.

18.2.3 Monitoring and reviewing

Suitable monitoring systems shall be implemented to evaluate the performance of products and services, this is in addition to technical IT performance monitoring and review. Examples of this are defined in Chapter 4, Section 4.9.1, Chapter 5, Section 5.7.1.5, Chapter 6, Section 6.13.1, Chapter 9, Sections 9.5.5 and 9.5.9, Chapter 14, Sections 14.4.2, 14.5.3, and 14.8.2.2, and Chapter 16 in addition to Continuous Improvement and Management Review, defined in Chapter 4, Sections 4.9.3 and 4.10, respectively.

This shall include reviewing employee performance and development requirements. Generally, monitoring shall be an ongoing process and reviewing shall also be performed at the end of a project or case, during a project or case review.

Monitoring systems shall capture performance measures on an ongoing basis, using computer as well as manual systems. System use shall also be monitored to ensure that they are used in accordance with the acceptable use and other policies in force.

Reviews shall be performed by Top Management, Line Managers, or Account Managers, as appropriate, on a particular process, project, or case. Reviews shall be formal or informal and can cover the following:

- client and employee liaison;
- compliance with IMS procedures and suggestions for procedure improvement;
- identification of training gaps;
- innovation and ideas generation;
- problems resolved;
- research and information gathering techniques;
- review of a process, project, or case;
- suggestions for personal improvement and setting of objectives; and
- writing and editing performance and client feedback.

The review shall be documented in the form of a report and filed in the client's virtual case file in the ERMS and the relevant employee's HR file as appropriate. Following a review, notes and revisions may be required in the following areas:

- First Responder procedures;
- quality procedures;
- security procedures;
- other procedures; or
- employee training and development plans.

18.2.4 Employee appraisals

All employees shall undergo annual appraisals where training needs and performance are analysed. The appraisal process shall be carried out in line with the human resources good practice for the jurisdiction.

Note

This is not intended to replace the standard HR approach, but ensures that TNA, continuous improvement, and all IMS issues are covered at appraisal time.

To ensure the ongoing and continuing development periodic appraisals of all employees shall be undertaken to:

- evaluate the competence of employees;
- determine if training is required;

- assess the need for any personal development; and
- determine any other requirements for ongoing employee development.

Appraisals shall be performed for all employees at least once a year, or more if deemed necessary, and are the responsibility of Line Managers at all levels in association with HR.

The employee appraisal process shall be as follows:

1. A Line Manager shall arrange an appraisal with a member of their team at the appropriate time with HR.
2. The Line Manager and the HR employee conducting the appraisal, reviews the employee's training records contained in their personnel file.
3. The Line Manager and the HR shall conduct the appraisal with the employee. Activities may include, but not be limited to:
   - assessment of the performance of the employee with regard to their work competences, evaluation of qualifications and skill sets;
   - review of project and case processing work completed;
   - identification of key competences and skills for future development;
   - identification of requirements for training or personal development;
   - review and evaluation of any training and personal development which has been undertaken since the last appraisal; and
   - review and evaluation of any training undertaken to carry out system management and business process.

For appraisals of Line Managers, appraisal activities shall additionally cover:

- review and evaluation of employee management skills;
- review and evaluation of project management skills (task management, schedule management, risk management, etc.,);
- evaluation of team leadership qualities; and
- identification of requirements for management skills development and/or training.

4. The Line Manager and the HR employee conducting the appraisal agree any further action which is required with the Line Manager.

If training is required this may be performed by internal or external resources and as formal or informal training. Management approval shall be required for all types of training and may be arranged either by an employee (with the authorisation of their Line Manager), or by a Line Manager on behalf of the employee via HR.

The relevant Management System Owner shall approve specific management system training.

18.2.5 Competence

Competence is checking that the individual employee is able to conduct a specific task.

Whilst employees shall have a planned schedule of training and awareness according to internal procedures and the results of the employee's appraisals and resulting TNA, this does not guarantee competence, all employees shall be evaluated to demonstrate competence on a regular basis. Where competence is found to be not present, corrective action shall be taken as defined in Chapter 4, Section 4.10 and Section 18.2.2.3.

Individual employees' competence shall be evaluated using the following techniques and these are used as input to the appraisal process. if a serious concern is raised, a meeting with the employee, HR, and relevant Line Managers shall be called when needed.

- **formal observation**—Line Managers and the Laboratory Manager shall observe the progress made by the employee and make recommendations to improve performance, where appropriate;
- **case reviews**—at the end of a forensic case, the case and its processing shall always be reviewed and any lessons learned shall be used as part of the continuous improvement process, as defined in Chapter 4, Section 4.10;
- **client feedback**—as defined in Chapter 6, Appendix 17;
- **client complaints**—as defined in Chapter 6, Section 6.14;
- **testimony feedback**—as defined in Chapter 11, Appendix 8;
- **gaining of additional qualifications**;
- **other relevant forms of observation**.

Note

A number of forensic laboratories have their own requirements for competency testing. Where appropriate, these would be used.

18.2.6 Proficiency

Proficiency is where an employee has attained a series of competences that demonstrate proficiency in a specific discipline, as opposed to competence in a specific task.

Annual proficiency testing shall be undertaken and used to confirm that employees are qualified to continue performing their role, irrespective of specific competencies, qualifications, or certifications.

Where proficiency is found to be not present, corrective action shall be taken.

The following procedures shall be used to test an individual Forensic Analyst's proficiency:

1. The Laboratory Manager shall create a mock case evidence pack, containing the evidence to be recovered, processed, and presented that are to be used to test the Forensic Analysts proficiency.
2. The Laboratory Manager shall test the case and obtain the results required as the mark for the proficiency testing.
3. Relevant Forensic Analyst(s) shall be issued the mock case evidence pack and undertake the proficiency test;
4. Evaluate the results obtained by the Forensic Analyst(s) undertaking the test;
5. Compare the results obtained with the master marking sheet;
6. Update the Forensic Analyst's Proficiency Record with the scores from the test;
7. Discuss the results with the relevant Forensic Analyst(s);
8. Plan and agree any corrective action with the relevant Forensic Analyst(s), if appropriate.
9. Redeploy any Forensic Analyst if there are concerns about proficiency until the matters are resolved.
10. Ensure that the corrective action is carried out, if appropriate.
11. Retest the Forensic Analyst after corrective action, if appropriate.
12. Review the mock case test pack to see that it meets its intended purpose and undertake any corrective or preventive action identified from the test feedback.

Note

There shall be a number of different mock case scenario packs used to test different proficiencies.

18.2.7 Code of ethics

The Code of Ethics for all forensic case processing is defined in Appendix 33.

This is in addition to any personal Codes of Ethics that employees may have due to their professional organisation memberships or personally held certifications.

The Code of Ethics has been created so that there is no conflict of interest between the varying Codes of Ethics in place.

18.3 Termination

When an employee changes employment or is terminated for any reason, it is essential that the appropriate process for ensuring a clean break is undertaken. To do this the following parties have defined responsibilities that shall be carried out and documented, with records available for audit:

- all responsibilities in the termination process shall be explicitly defined; and
- all termination procedures shall be documented and comply with current legislation within the jurisdiction.

Note

Special care shall be taken if the termination concerns a possible disgruntled (or soon-to-be disgruntled) employee.

18.3.1 Permanent employee terminations

Where permanent employees are terminated, the following responsibilities shall exist.

18.3.1.1 HR Department

The HR Department procedure shall be:

1. To ensure that the employee is reminded of their obligations under their confidentiality agreement;

2. To ensure that all termination paperwork is finalised and correct and that HR records are updated to reflect the termination and its associated procedures;
3. To obtain a list of all assets held by the employee from the Finance Department and/or the IT Department.
4. To ensure that all assets held by the employee are returned.
5. Where assets (e.g. information) are held on the employees own personal equipment, procedures shall be in place to ensure that this information is returned and is securely erased from the employee's hardware.
6. Where assets (e.g. information) are held by the employee and not held in a documented form, procedures shall be in place to ensure that this information is transferred in an appropriate form (e.g. readable form or knowledge transfer).
7. Ensure that the IT Department is advised of the forthcoming termination and the date of it. It may be necessary to ensure that this information is kept confidential if the employee does not know of the termination.
8. Ensure that the employee termination checklist, as defined in Appendix 34, is completed and countersigned by the terminated employee.

Note

It may be that the ISM is required to perform any security debriefing, including reminders about confidential information, where the risk assessment warrants it.

18.3.1.2   Finance Department

The Finance Department has the responsibility:

1. To provide a list of all assets held by the employee when asked by HR in a timely manner.
2. To recover the assets from the employee via HR and update the current status of the assets recovered in the Asset Register.

18.3.1.3   IT Department

The IT Department has the responsibility:

1. To provide a list of all assets held by the employee when asked by HR in a timely manner.
2. To recover the assets from the employee via HR and update the current status of the assets recovered in the IT Asset Database.
3. To disable the employee's account(s), but not to delete them, as defined in the Termination Checklist.
4. To change all passwords that the employee may have known if the accounts or services still exist after the employee has been terminated. A risk assessment of this may need to be undertaken. This should be done in association with the relevant Asset Owner and the ISM.

18.3.1.4   Employee's Line Manger

The Line Manager has the responsibility to assist HR and the IT Department where appropriate to facilitate the termination process.

The Line Manager shall be responsible for informing relevant clients, contractors, or third-party users of changes in responsibilities and of employee changes and new operating arrangements.

18.3.1.5   Employee

The employee has the responsibility:

1. To return all assets held when asked by HR in a timely basis;
2. To return all documents and other assets whether they are recorded in the Asset Register or the IT Asset Database or not, in a timely manner;
3. To comply with the terms and conditions of employment for the period after termination;
4. To confirm compliance with the termination procedures and the requirements within them in writing, so that a record can be made available for later auditing, as defined in the Termination Checklist.

18.3.2 Other employee terminations

This covers temporary or contract employees and employees of authorised third-party service providers who are terminated, and the following responsibilities exist.

The same process as that defined in Section 18.3.1 shall be followed, with the addition of the requirements below:

18.3.2.1 Agency or Outsourcing Partner

The Agency or Outsourcing Partner has the responsibility:

1. To ensure that the temporary, contract, or third-party employee shall comply with all termination requirements.
2. To ensure that any information or documentation is either returned or disposed of in accordance with contractual requirements.
3. To delete all FCL information or their clients, from their information processing systems and warrant that this is performed, unless a justified and documented legal reason for retention is present, which shall be documented with the proposed deletion date.

18.3.3 Change of employee responsibilities

Change of employment shall use the same procedures as those defined in Section 18.3.1, where applicable. Changes of responsibility or employment shall be managed as the termination of the respective responsibility or employment, and the new responsibility or employment shall be controlled as if the employee was a new hire.

Note

It is essential that access rights are updated immediately on change of employment so that the employee does not continue to hold inappropriate access rights.

18.3.4 Removal of access rights

On termination or change of employment, all of the employee's access rights shall be reviewed.

18.3.4.1 Termination

Where an employee has terminated all access rights that they had shall be removed and all access rights that they had access to as part of their duties that are a group or shared access rights shall be immediately changed. Where the termination is planned, consideration should be defined as to whether or not the employee should still have any access to information processing systems during the notice period. It may be that restricted access is considered but a risk assessment shall be undertaken of the risks posed by the employee still having access. The following shall be considered in making this decision:

- who initiated the termination;
- the reason for the termination;
- the employee's role and current access rights;
- any relevant human resources or disciplinary issues that are currently in progress;
- the value of the assets the employee can access;
- the possible reputational risk that the employee could inflict;
- the employee's technical competence;
- consideration of disgruntled employee's (or soon-to-be ex-employees) is a major risk factor that shall be carefully considered. Emergency access right removal shall be undertaken, if needed; and
- employee activity shall be monitored as theft of corporate information is a simple matter with the current media capacity available at the desktop.

18.3.4.2 Employment change

Where an employee changes roles, HR and the relevant Line Manager(s) shall ensure that all of the employee's access rights are changed when they change jobs or roles to reflect their new responsibilities.

It is essential that employees that move jobs or roles do not retain inappropriate access rights. Access rights of this type include, but are not limited to:

- physical and logical access;
- keys;
- identification cards;
- information processing resource access;
- subscriptions;
- corporate memberships;
- corporate schemes; and
- representation as a member of FCL on any committee, etc.

18.3.5 Return of assets

When an employee leaves, it is essential that they return all assets that they have been issued with during their employment.

Where an employee has used their own computer equipment, this shall be recorded on the authorisation for use. These employees shall be required to bring any equipment used into the office so that the ISM can ascertain that there is no FCL or client still remaining on it.

Where necessary, an appropriate secure wiping process shall be used for computers and mobile devices. Consideration shall be given to the swapping of an employee's storage media on a 'like for like' basis rather than performing a secure erasure. Assets of this type include, but are not limited to:

- hard disks;
- external disks;
- CDs;
- DVDs;
- backup tape; and
- USB/Firewire type storage devices.

Note

These media may not be recorded on the asset register.

Where an employee has essential or critical knowledge for a project a process of knowledge transfer to at least one other employee shall be undertaken unless this has already been documented and a formal handover has taken place.

Should any assets not be handed back at this point, their contract of employment, the associated Handbook of Employment, and the issuing paperwork for the asset all require that the asset shall be returned on demand and specifically at the termination of employment. If this is the case, appropriate action shall be taken against the employee in consultation with Legal Counsel.

Appendix 1—Training feedback form

The form below shall be used to collect feedback from all employees for all internal and external training undertaken. It provides qualitative as well as quantitative feedback.

- name;
- course title;
- training provider;
- date of the course;
- instructor name (mandatory if internal training);
- training feedback:
  - the objectives of the training were clearly defined;
  - participation and interaction were encouraged;
  - the topics covered were relevant to me;
  - I can use the product(s) or service(s) more effectively than I could before I attended the training;

- the content was organised and easy to follow;
- the materials distributed were helpful;
- this training experience will be useful in my work;
- the trainer was knowledgeable about the training topics;
- the trainer was well prepared;
- the trainer answered questions effectively;
- my training objectives were met;
- the time allotted for the training was sufficient;
- if trained via the internet, the interface technology was easy to use and an effective way for me to receive training;
- the accommodation and facilities were adequate and comfortable, if applicable.
- Each of the points above is graded or scored as follows:
  - 0—Not applicable.
  - 1—Strongly disagree.
  - 2—Disagree.
  - 3—Neutral.
  - 4—Agree.
  - 5—Strongly agree.
- Additionally:
  - what did you like most about this training?
  - what did you like least about this training?
  - what aspects of the training could be improved?
  - how do you hope to change your working practices as a result of this training?
  - would you recommend this training to other employees and if not explain why?
- any other comments;
- date;
- signature.

Appendix 2—Employee security screening policy checklist

The following shall be considered for including in an employee security screening policy:

- acknowledgement by the applicant that misrepresentation, or failure to disclose material facts, either during the application or throughout employment may constitute grounds for immediate dismissal and/or legal action;
- define criteria for failing/rejecting an applicant;
- embed the employee security screening process into the recruitment process;
- ensure that applicant gives consent for the employee security screening process to meet legal requirements in the jurisdiction for the whole process, including further checks;
- ensure the whole recruitment process, including the employee security screening process and supporting forms, are legally compliant for the jurisdiction;
- ensure those performing employee security screening have appropriate resources, including training and budget;
- have a process for dealing with fakes or forged supporting documentation;
- identify the Screening Controller;
- inform applicants that confirmed employment is conditional on satisfactory completion of the employee security screening process, even if provisional employment is offered;
- involve all relevant stakeholders in the employee security screening process and ensure that they all communicate effectively for the employee security screening process;
- maintain a list of employee security screening service providers for specialist tasks; and
- undertake employee security screening for all employees;

Maintain a screening file as part of the HR process for the applicant or employee.

Appendix 3—Employment application form

The following shall be included on the employment application form:

- post applied for;
- surname;

- other surnames if the applicant has changed their surname for any reason (e.g. marriage or other legitimate reasons for changing their surname;
- alias—if appropriate (e.g. stage name)
- forenames;
- title;
- address(es) for last 'n'^{d} years;
- contact details;
- date of birth;
- place of birth:
- nationality;
- proof of identity;
- proof of address;
- whether a work permit is required or not;
- current employer and current role information;
- past employment for last 'n'^{e} years;
- education history and qualifications;
- professional qualifications and certifications;
- training courses undertaken with results;
- reasons for applying for the post;
- other information that may be relevant (e.g. details of disabilities, driving licence holder);
- personal and employer reference details;
- any other information required by the legislation in the jurisdiction of employment; and
- a declaration of completeness and truth that is signed and dated.

The form shall contain a clear statement that employee security screening will take place. Applicants shall provide their consent to undergo employment security screening. This may be internal or a third-party screening service provider, as appropriate.

Applicants shall also affirm whether their current employer can be contacted for a reference. If not agreed at the point of a conditional job offer for temporary employment, then an agreement that permanent employment is conditional (or not) on a satisfactory reference from the immediate past employer.

In addition to this form, there shall be additional forms to cover:

- criminal history declaration meeting the legal requirements in the jurisdiction of employment;
- consent for employee security screening; and
- other requirements, as appropriate for the post applied for.

There may be additions information required for specific roles, which will be defined by the role.

Appendix 4—Employment application form notes

Notes to assist an applicant filling in the form shall be supplied to the applicant, as defined below:

The application form

- the application form plays an important part in the selection process;
- decisions to shortlist candidates for interview are based solely upon the information you supply on your form and the form provides a basis for the interview itself;
- Curriculum Vitaes (CVs) alone will not be accepted. However, CVs will be accepted *in addition* to a fully completed application form; and
- you may complete the form on a word processor but please use the appropriate headings and format.

---

d. The period of addresses to be disclosed will vary between posts.

e. The period of past employment to be disclosed will vary between posts.

Section 1: Personal details

- Please give your surname and forenames and title. If you have another other name you would like to be called (should you be called for an interview), you may at your discretion enter those details. Two forms of proof identity shall be required with one proof of address.

Section 2: Education and professional qualifications

- Please list academic qualifications, membership of professional institutes, in-house courses, and professional qualifications if applicable. Essential qualifications will be checked on appointment to a post.

Section 3: Present post

- please provide brief information in respect of responsibilities including reporting and management duties. This section should not be left blank unless the position you are applying for is your first job; and
- should you be selected for the role 'your reason for leaving or wishing to leave' may be verified if we take references per Section 7 below.

Section 4: Previous employment

- do not simply list the duties of your jobs. Please give a brief explanation of the main duties of your previous jobs; and
- whilst you are not required to provide dates in relation to previous jobs it is important you confirm whether or not you have had material gaps in your employment. If you have, it would be helpful if you could provide relevant details.

Section 5: Relevant skills, abilities, knowledge, and experience

- this section is vital;
- think about what evidence you can provide to demonstrate you have the necessary skills, ability, knowledge, experience, and competence required;
- you may have acquired these in a variety of ways e.g.; through work, running a home, voluntary work, hobbies, etc.; and
- address each of the criteria separately and briefly outline how you meet each one, providing specific examples.

Section 6: Other information

- a simple list will suffice unless positions are held and the skills/experience attained are directly relevant to the position for which you are applying.

Section 7: References

- should you be selected for interview we will want to take up referees as outlined below. However, if possible, we would like to do this earlier in the process;
- *employment references*—please provide referee details to cover recent relevant employment;
- *academic references*—if you are a school leaver or graduate entrant and do not have any previous employment history, please supply the details of a school/college tutor;
- *personal references*—if you have no previous employment please give details of someone who can provide a character reference; and
- we reserve the right to take up references from any previous employer.

Section 8: Declaration

- This section shall be signed by you, the applicant. It is a declaration of the validity of the information in the application and confirms that misleading information would be sufficient grounds for terminating of employment.

Appendix 5—Verifying identity

The following document types shall be considered for verifying an identity and supplied as appropriate with the application form:

- adoption certificate;
- Armed Forces identity card;
- current photo card driving licence;
- current signed full passport,
- full birth certificate;
- marriage/civil partnership certificate;
- National Identity Card;
- other valid documentation relating to immigration status or permits to work; and
- Police registration document.

Note

It shall be understood that a government cannot give an individual an identity that is only something the individual can do. Of the examples above the only one that really proves identity is a birth certificate, but it is difficult to link a paper birth certificate to an individual applicant. A passport is only a travel document, a driving licence is only a permit to drive, etc.

Multiple copies of the above all verifying the claimed identity do strengthen the verification process.

Appendix 6—Document authenticity checklist

Some items that shall be checked on officially issued documents include, but are not limited to:

- font used;
- holograms;
- lamination of photographs;
- number of pages, if applicable (e.g. a passport);
- numbering sequence;
- paper type;
- perforations and indentations, if applicable;
- size;
- stamps applied;
- UV reaction;
- validity; and
- watermarks.

Appendix 7—Verifying addresses

The following document types shall be considered for verifying an address and supplied as appropriate with the application form:

- utility bill, but not a mobile phone bill;
- bank statement;
- rental or tenancy agreement;
- letter from a recognised government department; or
- mortgage statement from a recognised lender.

Where such documentation is provided, it shall relate to the period claimed.

Appendix 8—Verifying right to work checklist

The following shall be used for making a declaration relating to nationality and immigration status declaration for the right to work in the jurisdiction:

- advice that if the applicant is employed, corroboration of answers defined on the form shall be sought to confirm answers defined;

- surname/family name;
- forenames;
- any aliases/other names used;
- full current address;
- date of birth;
- nationality at birth;
- nationality now (if different);
- whether the applicant has held any other nationality. If so, give details;
- whether the applicant is subject to immigration control.[f] If so, give details;
- whether the applicant is lawfully resident in the country;
- whether there are any restrictions on the applicant's continued residence in the country. If so, give details;
- whether there are any restrictions on the applicant's ability to take up the type of work being offered to the applicant. If so, give details;
- a declaration that the information on the form is true, accurate, and complete to the best of the applicant's knowledge and that if they have made a false declaration it may prejudice their hiring or continued employment;
- a declaration that should the information contained on the form at the start of employment change during the applicant's employment that the applicant shall advise either HR or the Screening Controller;
- signature;
- date;
- a declaration that FCL will hold this information in the strictest confidence and that all relevant privacy legislation covering the information and documents supplied will be met; and
- The declaration should ensure that the applicant is giving explicit (and not implicit) consent for holding and processing this personal data in line with the employee security screening process.

Appendix 9—Reference authorisation

Note

The wording used for the reference authorisation shall be checked to ensure that it is appropriate for the jurisdiction and meets the requirements of the relevant legislation.

Please read this carefully before signing the declaration.

I understand that employment is subject to satisfactory references and employee security screening in accordance with good practice within the jurisdiction.

I undertake to cooperate in providing any additional information required to meet these criteria.

I authorise FCL and/or its nominated agent(s) to approach previous employers, schools/colleges, character referees, or Government Agencies to verify that the information I have provided is correct.

I authorise FCL to make a consumer information search with a credit reference agency, which will keep a record of that search and may share that information with other credit reference agencies.

I understand that some of the information I have provided in this application shall be held on a computer and some or all will be held in manual records.

I consent to reasonable processing of any sensitive or special categories of personal information obtained for the purposes of establishing my medical condition and future fitness to perform my duties. I accept that I may be required to undergo a medical examination where requested.

Subject to the legislation relating to medical records in the jurisdiction, I consent to the results of such examinations to be disclosed to HR.

I understand and agree that if so, required I will make a Statutory Declaration in accordance with the provisions of the relevant legislation relating to Statutory Declarations (or equivalent), in confirmation of previous employment or unemployment. A copy of the Statutory Declaration used is defined in Appendix 10.

---

f. Immigration Control is where the applicant requires permission (or 'leave') to enter or remain in a country but do not have it or where the applicant has leave to enter or remain but is subject to a formal undertaking. A formal undertaking is typically where the applicant's sponsor makes a formal legal undertaking that they will support the applicant during their period of residence in the country.

I hereby certify that, to the best of my knowledge, the details I have defined in this application form are complete and correct. I understand that any false statement or omission may render me liable to dismissal without notice.

Signature

Printed Name

Witness signature

Witness printed name

Witness Address

Date

Appendix 10—Statutory declaration

Note

The use of Statutory Declarations is not universal, and the form of the Declaration may well vary between jurisdictions, so Legal Advice shall be taken to ensure that the Declaration, if used, is appropriate to the relevant legislation.

I [full name] of [address]

DO SOLEMNLY AND SINCERELY DECLARE as follows:

[See below for matter to declare]

and I make this solemn Declaration conscientiously believing the same to be true and by virtue of the provisions of the [state the relevant legislation]

SIGNED []

DECLARED at [].
in the County of [].
on this [] day, the [] of [] 20[].
Before me [].
Lawyer/Solicitor/Commissioner for Oaths/Judge.

Matter to declare (examples):

- that I was self-employed as a [job title] for the period(s) from [date] to [date];
- that I was registered as unemployed for the period(s) from/date] to [date];
- that I was employed as a [job title] for the period(s) from [date] to [date] by [name of employer] of [address];
- that I was not employed from [date] to [date] because [state reason]; or
- that I was known as [state previous name] for the period from [date] to [date].

Appendix 11—Employer reference form

The form used for employer references is defined below:

Employee or applicant

- full name of the subject of the reference;

Previous employer

- name;
- location;
- contact;
- phone; and
- email.

Employment details

- dates of employment—confirmed by employer;
- their title; and
- what did their duties involve?

Miscellaneous

- are you related to the subject?—if so, please state your relationship;
- do you consider the subject to be strictly honest, conscientious, reliable, and discreet?
- are you aware of any factor(s) concerning the subject that may affect his fitness to be employed?—if so please explain; and
- would you be content to employ the individual again?

Declaration

- a declaration that the information on the form is true, accurate, and complete to the best of the Reference Giver's knowledge and belief;
- name;
- signature;
- position in the organisation;
- date;
- phone;
- email; and
- company detail and company stamp (if applicable).

A declaration this information shall be held in the strictest confidence and that all relevant privacy legislation covering the information and documents supplied shall be met.

Note

It may well be corporate policy of the Reference Giver's organisation that some of this information may not be disclosed and only periods of work and job titles given.

Appendix 12—Employer's oral reference form

The following information shall be transcribed onto an Oral Reference Form by the Reference Taker with input from the Reference Giver:

The form used for employer references is defined below:

Employee or applicant

- full name of the subject of the reference;

Previous employer

- name;
- location;
- contact;
- phone; and
- email.

Employment details

- dates of employment—claimed by employee or applicant;
- dates of employment—confirmed by employer;
- their title; and
- what did their duties involve?

Miscellaneous

- are you related to the subject?—if so, please state your relationship;
- do you consider the subject to be strictly honest, conscientious, reliable, and discreet?
- are you aware of any factor(s) concerning the subject that may affect his fitness to be employed by FCL?—if so please explain; and
- would you be content to employ the individual again?

Declaration

- name of Reference Taker;
- signature;
- title or position in specialised third-party employee security screening organisation
- employer;
- date;
- phone;
- email;
- Screening Controller's name;
- countersigned by the Screening Controller; and
- a declaration this information shall be held in the strictest confidence and that all relevant privacy legislation covering the information and documents supplied shall be met.

Note

If response indicates that applicant is NOT suitable for proposed employment, this shall be brought to the immediate attention of Screening Controller.

Appendix 13—Confirmation of an oral reference letter

Note

This letter shall be sent on headed stationery (paper or emailed as a secured PDF) to the Reference Giver to confirm their information. The Screening Controller shall sign it.

[Name]
[Address]
[Date]

We refer to our conversation with you on [date] about [title and name] connection with the application made to us by the above-named for employment as [specify].

Details of the information which you supplied to us orally are enclosed and we would be obliged if you would kindly confirm these details fairly reflect the information you supplied.

Due to the nature of our business, it is vitally important that we employ only individuals of integrity who are likely to be able to resist the opportunities for improper personal gain or other information security breaches which such employment might offer and who are responsible and conscientious.

Our internal procedures based on our ISO 9001 and ISO/IEC 27001 certifications, require us to obtain written confirmation of all references, we receive in connection with applicants for employment.

A copy of a Form of Authority signed by the applicant is enclosed and also a stamped addressed envelope for the favour of your reply.

Yours Faithfully.

[Name]
[Title]
[Specify Enclosures]

Appendix 14—Verifying qualifications checklist

The following shall be considered for checking paper certificates of educational and professional qualifications:

- matching names on all documents or explanation for change (marriage, etc.);
- matching dates from documents to application forms;
- logo is correct;
- no evidence of tampering;
- quality of the paper;
- watermarks (if present); and
- embossing (if present).

Each establishment that has issued the certificate presented shall be contacted to ascertain the validity of the document produced, if possible and practical.

Appendix 15—Criminal record declaration checklist

Note

Depending on the jurisdiction, the terminology may need to be changed to reflect the requirements of the legislation within the jurisdiction.

The following shall be used for making a declaration relating to a criminal record declaration:

- advice that if the applicant is employed, corroboration of answers defined on the form will be sought to confirm answers defined;
- surname/Family Name;
- forenames;
- full current address;
- date of birth;
- a declaration whether the applicant has ever been convicted or found guilty by a Court of Competent Jurisdiction of any offence in any country (excluding parking but including all motoring offences even where a spot fine has been administered by the Police) or absolutely/conditionally discharged or whether there is there any current action pending;
- a declaration whether the applicant has ever been convicted by a Court Martial, sentenced to detention, or dismissed from service in any county's armed services;
- a declaration whether the applicant is aware of any other matters in their background that may affect their suitability or reliability for the post for which they are applying;
- a note to say that 'Spent' convictions, according to the legislation in the jurisdiction, need not be declared;
- for each of the three questions above, a 'Yes'/'No' reply box is used for this and if the answer is 'Yes', the applicant is required to give further details;
- a declaration that the information on the form is true, accurate, and complete to the best of the applicant's knowledge and that if they have made a false declaration it may prejudice their hiring or continued employment;
- signature;
- date;
- a declaration that this information shall be held in the strictest confidence and that all relevant privacy legislation covering the information and documents supplied shall be met; and
- the declaration shall ensure that the applicant is giving explicit (and not implicit) consent for holding and processing this data in line with the employee security screening process.

Appendix 16—Personal reference form

The form used for personal references is defined below:

Employee or applicant

- full name of the subject of the reference.

The Reference Giver

- name;
- location;
- contact
- phone; and
- email.

Relationship details

- over what period have you known [name]
- how would you define your relationship with [name]; and
- are you related to [name]?—if so, please state your relationship.

Miscellaneous

- do you consider the subject to be strictly honest, conscientious, reliable, and discreet?
- are you aware of any factor(s) concerning the subject that may affect his fitness to be employed by FCL?—if so please explain.

Declaration

- a declaration that the information on the form is true, accurate, and complete to the best of the Reference Giver's knowledge and belief;
- name;
- signature;
- date;
- phone; and
- email.

A declaration that this information shall be held in the strictest confidence and that all relevant privacy legislation covering the information and documents supplied shall be met.

Appendix 17—Personal oral reference form

The following information shall be transcribed onto an Oral Reference Form by the Reference Taker with input from the Reference Giver:

The form used for personal references is defined below:

Employee or applicant

- full name of the subject of the reference.

The Reference Giver

- name;
- location;
- contact;
- phone; and
- email.

Relationship details

- over what period have you known [name]
- how would you define your relationship with [name]; an
- are you related to [name]?—if so, please state your relationship;

Miscellaneous

- do you consider the subject to be strictly honest, conscientious, reliable, and discreet?
- are you aware of any factor(s) concerning the subject that may affect his fitness to be employed?—if so please explain;

Declaration

- name of Reference Taker;
- signature;
- title or position in specialised third-party employee security screening organisation
- employer;
- date;
- phone;
- email;
- Screening Controller's name; and
- Countersigned by the Screening Controller.

A declaration that this information shall be held in the strictest confidence and that all relevant privacy legislation covering the information and documents supplied shall be met.

Note

If response indicates that the applicant is NOT suitable for proposed employment, this shall be brought to the immediate attention of Screening Controller.

Appendix 18—Other reference form

Note

This form is used where it is inappropriate to use either the Employer Reference Form or the Personal Reference Form. Situations where this is relevant can include, but are not limited to:

- Living abroad;
- Periods of unemployment;
- A 'trade' reference;
- Education confirmation;
- Military service confirmation; or
- Where an employer no longer exists and a past employee provides a reference.

The form used for other references is defined below:

Employee or applicant

- full name of the subject of the reference.

The Reference Giver

- name;
- location;
- contact;
- phone; and
- email.

Details required

- [define exactly what is required];
- over what period have you known [name];
- how would you define your relationship with [name]; and
- are you related to [name]?—if so, please state your relationship.

Miscellaneous

- do you consider the subject to be strictly honest, conscientious, reliable, and discreet?
- are you aware of any factor(s) concerning the subject that may affect his fitness to be employed by FCL?—if so please explain;

Declaration

- a declaration that the information on the form is true, accurate, and complete to the best of the Reference Giver's knowledge and belief;
- name;
- signature;
- date;
- phone; and
- email.

A declaration that this information shall be held in the strictest confidence and that all relevant privacy legislation covering the information and documents supplied shall be met.

Appendix 19—Other reference oral reference form

Note

This is the oral version of the Other Reference Form and is used for the reasons defined in Appendix 18.

The following information shall be transcribed onto an Oral Reference Form by the Reference Taker with input from the Reference Giver:

The form used for other references is defined below:

Employee or applicant

- full name of the subject of the reference.

The Reference Giver

- name;
- location;
- contact;
- phone; and
- email.

Details

- [define exactly what is required];
- over what period have you known [name];
- how would you define your relationship with [name]; and
- are you related to [name]?—if so, please state your relationship.

Miscellaneous

- do you consider the subject to be strictly honest, conscientious, reliable, and discreet?
- are you aware of any factor(s) concerning the subject that may affect his fitness to be employed by FCL?—if so please explain;

Declaration

- name of Reference Taker;
- signature;
- title or position in specialised third-party employee security screening organisation
- employer;
- date;
- phone;
- email;
- Screening Controller's name; and
- countersigned by the Screening Controller.

A declaration that this information shall be held in the strictest confidence and that all relevant privacy legislation covering the information and documents supplied shall be met.

Note

If response indicates that applicant is NOT suitable for proposed employment, this shall be brought to the immediate attention of Screening Controller.

Appendix 20—Employee security screening file

Any job applicant shall have their own employee security screening file. In some cases, this shall be updated during employment (e.g. an internal move to a post with a higher security clearance requirement). The contents of the employee security screening file are defined below:

Applicant details

- surname;
- forenames;
- address;
- phone;
- date of birth;
- place of birth:
- nationality;
- former or dual nationality: (with dates if applicable);
- employee ID Number (if applicable);
- tax ID or other government ID (if applicable);
- date Employment Commenced;
- date Employment Terminated; and
- screening period.

Information given by the applicant

- dates employed (from and to);
- employer;
- other information;
- code (see below);

- request sent;
- confirmation of facts; and
- audited by name;
- title; and
- date.

Codes in use

- AR—Accountant's Reference;
- CL—Chaser Letter;
- CR—Character Reference;
- DR—Documentation Request;
- ER—Education Reference;
- FI—Further Information Request;
- GR—Government Department Request;
- LR—Lawyer's Reference;
- OR—Other Request (Define);
- SDR—Statutory Declaration Request
- TR—Trade Reference; and
- WR—Work (Employer) Reference.

Documents seen

Note

These are just tick boxes with comments if appropriate and a copy shall also be retained on the applicant's employee file. Ideally, original documents are presented but if a copy, comments shall be made on it.

- The following have been inspected:
- work registration card;
- birth certificate.
- current passport;
- military or Service Discharge Certificate;
- photo driving licence.
- marriage or civil partnership certificate;
- proof of address;
- work permit, if applicable;
- visa, if applicable; and
- educational qualifications;
- There shall be a note to check whether the documents seen are originals or copies or not available. Where copies are provided or they are not available, comment shall be made on this; and
- The documents seen shall be subject to audit.

Processes undertaken

Note 1

A number of processes shall be undertaken and these shall be tracked through to completion:

- financial checks;
- reference requests;
- follow-ups after oral references; and
- other processes as required.

Note 2

The dates of requests and receipt shall be recorded for each process with notes as appropriate. The processes shall be subject to audit.

Certification of identity

For each document listed, its date of issue shall be recorded, if there is one present.

- document 1;
- document 2;
- document 3
- document 4; and
- document 5;

References

At least one work reference is required and at least on personal one.
  For each Referee, the following shall be listed:

- surname;
- forenames;
- address:
- phone;
- email;
- relationship; and
- length of association.

Authorisation

Note

This section of the file shall record the employment authorisation (or not) and shall contain:

- authorisation of acceptance of employment risk by Top Management;
- authoriser name, signature, and date;
- authorisation date for provisional employment;
- authoriser name, signature and date;
- authorisation date for confirmed employment;
- authorisation for employment declined; and
- decliner name, signature, and date.

Certification

The file shall contain a statement from the Screening Controller or the employee that carried out the verification checks, for each time something new is added to the file, to state that they have verified the documents presented and updated the file.

- name;
- title;
- phone;
- email;
- signature; and
- date.

  Each file shall contain the documents that have been referred to in the summary sheet above.

Appendix 21—Top management acceptance of employment risk

Note 1

Risks identified during the employee security screening process may be signed off by Top Management, as acceptable, if the applicant is to be employed in the new post where the employee security screening process has not been completed but the risks are deemed acceptable.

- surname;
- forenames;
- position;
- date commenced provisional employment:
- items requiring acceptance of risk (define);
- Screening Controller name;
- Signature;
- Date;
- Top Management Declaration:

The above-named applicant's employee security screening file has been reviewed and I have accepted this applicant as being appropriate for offering provisional employment and accept the risk of incomplete employee security screening.

- name;
- signature;
- position; and
- date.

Note 2

The Top Management providing signoff shall be independent the screening process.

Note 3

If the risks are not accepted, then the form is not signed by Top Management as they do not accept the risks.

Appendix 22—Third-party employee security screening provider checklist

The following issues shall be considered when selecting a third-party screening service provider:

- are their screening processes transparent;
- are they as good as they claim—obtain references from existing clients;
- are they subject to any current litigation?
- can they meet all of the defined needs?
- does their contract give the right to audit the employee security screening process?
- how do their costs and service levels compare with other employee security screening service providers?
- how do they deal with incomplete or conflicting information?
- how many complaints have they had in the last year?
- how will personal data and special categories of personal data collected as part of the screening process be secured against unauthorised access, modification, disclosure, or erasure?
- is their work repeatable by a competent alternative?
- what access to overseas information do they have?
- what information can they access?
- what is their continuous improvement process?
- what is typical Turn Round Times for a full screening report in jurisdictions of interest?
- what level of reporting do they provide?

- what level of employee security screening do the screening service provider's employees undergo?
- what quality processes do they have in place?
- what certifications do they hold relevant to their products and services?
- what services do they provide?
- will they make employment recommendations based on the results of the screening process or leave it to HR or Top Management to make the final decision based on their findings?

Appendix 23—Recruitment agency contract checklist

The following items shall be considered for inclusion in any contract with a recruitment consultancy for all types of employment:

- details of the employee security screening requirements for different posts;
- a statement that there is the right to audit the recruitment agency's employee security screening process and details of applicants at any time;
- statement that the recruitment agency shall advise if any applicant supplied by the recruitment agency is undergoing any disciplinary procedures, has been arrested or similar;
- a statement that the recruitment agency shall be liable for financial penalties if they have not performed the level of employee security screening required according to contractual requirements; and
- a statement to the effect that the recruitment agency shall not be paid for any applicant that has not undergone security screening according to contractual requirements.

Note

There may be issues that arise if the applicant does not tell the truth or omits prejudicial information on their application forms and this is not picked up by the recruitment agency.

Appendix 24—Investigation manager, job description

Objective and role

The Investigation Manager is responsible for all aspects of investigations carried out. This covers the long- and medium-term planning as well as the day-to-day conduct of investigations.

The main objectives are to ensure that investigations are conducted in a manner that is compliant with relevant legislation, regulations, and standards within the jurisdiction and that products and services offered to clients are available, when required, at an acceptable cost and of superior quality.

Problems and challenges

The efficient conduct of an investigation is only achieved by ensuring that all aspects of the investigation are planned and managed well. The Investigation Manager faces the challenge of ensuring the development, maintenance, and implementation of all relevant policies and procedures.

The Investigation Manager shall ensure that the required resources are available and working efficiently and that all tasks are carried out to meet the defined quality standards. The Investigation Manager shall liaise with the Laboratory Manager to manage resources.

Principal accountabilities

The Investigation Manager shall:

- have an in-depth understanding of data collection and preservation principles;
- have an in-depth understanding of investigative procedures;
- have an in-depth understanding of investigative legislation, regulation, standards, and good practice within the jurisdiction;
- have a good understanding of the client's needs in digital forensic investigation management;

- conduct and lead digital forensic investigation tasks from beginning to end, including task acceptance, the processing of digital media through to report production and billing;
- lead the Request for Proposal (RFP) process or quotation process for client engagements, including the production of budget estimates, in association with the Laboratory Manager and the relevant Account Manager;
- maintain regular contact, through the relevant Account Manager with clients to help ensure client satisfaction and that their expectations are properly managed. This shall include progress reports, both internally and externally, where required;
- conduct client and internal team meetings to document client requirements, with the relevant Account Manager, whilst making recommendations and determining the best solutions;
- ensure that IMS procedures are followed for all investigations carried out;
- ensure work quality is of a consistently high standard;
- manage a range of priorities and tasks on a daily basis;
- manage employee development by conducting annual employee appraisals and TNA in association with HR;
- brief the Laboratory Manager on the progress of investigations;
- maintain investigation training and awareness for all employees involved in investigations and forensic case processing on the importance and impact of maintaining stringent controls;
- manage the case review process;
- participate in international, national, and local SIG presentations;
- develop and manages effective working relationships with all appropriate internal and external stakeholders;
- maintain external links to other companies in the industry to gain competitive assessments and share information, where appropriate;
- identify the emerging information technologies to be assimilated, integrated, and introduced, which could significantly improve the investigation management processes;
- interface with external industrial and academic organisations to maintain state-of-the-art knowledge in emerging investigation management issues and to enhance FCL's image as a first-class solution provider utilising the latest thinking in this field;
- adhere to the established policies, standards, and procedures; and
- perform all responsibilities in accordance with, or in excess of, the requirements of the IMS.

Authority

The Investigation Manager shall have the authority to:

- plan and implement investigations; and
- supervise the conduct of digital forensic investigations;

Contacts

Internal

This position requires contact with all levels of employees, and specifically the Laboratory Manager, for the day-to-day conduct of investigations, to ensure the maintenance and implementation of procedures.

External

Externally, the Investigation Manager shall maintain contacts with Suppliers and Vendors, as required. Additionally, contact shall be maintained with clients to determine their requirements in association with the relevant Account Manager.

Reports to

The Investigation Manager shall report to:

Top Management.

Appendix 25—Forensic laboratory system administrator, job description

---

Note

The Forensic Laboratory System Administrator is a different role to the System Administrator for the remainder of the IT systems, who reports to the IT Manager.

Objective and role

The Forensic Laboratory System Administrator shall be responsible for the effective provisioning, installation/configuration, operation, and maintenance of system hardware and software and related infrastructure within the forensic laboratory.

The Forensic Laboratory System Administrator shall also undertake technical research and development to enable continuing innovation within the forensic laboratory infrastructure. This individual ensures that system hardware, operating systems, software systems adhere to the relevant FCL procedures.

Problems and challenges

Efficiency in FCL is only achieved by ensuring that all aspects of the information systems that are used within the forensic laboratory operate efficiently and are managed in a professional manner, following the laid down procedures, and to an acceptable quality standard. The Forensic Laboratory System Administrator shall ensure that all information processing systems used forensic case processing adheres to all of the relevant policies and procedures in the IMS.

Principal accountabilities

The Forensic Laboratory System Administrator shall:

- instal new and/or rebuild existing systems and configure hardware, peripherals, services, settings, directories, and storage in accordance with FCL's standards and procedures;
- develop and maintain installation and configuration procedures and records;
- contribute to and maintain system standards;
- research and recommend innovative and, where possible, automated approaches for system administration tasks;
- perform regular system monitoring, to verify the integrity and availability of all hardware, systems, and key processes, monitor system and application logs, and control regular scheduled tasks such as backups;
- perform regular security monitoring to identify possible misuse of information processing resources;
- perform regular file archiving and purging as required;
- create, modify, and delete user accounts as required;
- investigate and troubleshoot faults, incidents, problems, and other issues that may affect the delivery of products and services to clients that are reliant on the forensic laboratory IT infrastructure and services;
- restore and recover systems after hardware or software failures. Coordinates and communicates with departments that have been affected;
- apply system patches and upgrades on a regular basis;
- upgrade administrative tools and utilities and configure/add new services as necessary;
- produce periodic performance reports to Top Management on IT performance in the forensic laboratory';
- carry out ongoing performance tuning, hardware upgrades, and resource optimisation as required;
- manage employee development by conducting annual employee appraisals and TNA in association with HR;
- maintain IT training and awareness for all employees on the importance and impact of maintaining stringent controls for forensic case processing using the IT infrastructure and services, in association with the ISM;
- manage the information security incident Post Implementation Review (PIR) process for incidents affecting the forensic laboratory IT infrastructure;
- participate in international, national, and local SIG presentations;
- develop and manage effective working relationships with all appropriate internal and external interested parties;
- maintain external links to other companies in the industry to gain competitive assessments and share information, where appropriate;
- identify the emerging information technologies to be assimilated, integrated, and introduced which could significantly improve forensic case processing using the forensic laboratory IT infrastructure;
- interface with external industrial and academic organisations to maintain state-of-the-art knowledge in emerging investigation management issues and to enhance FCL's image as a first-class solution provider utilising the latest thinking in this field;
- adhere to the established policies, standards, and procedures; and
- perform all responsibilities in accordance with, or in excess of, the requirements of the IMS.

Authority

The System Administrator/Operator shall have the authority to:
- manage and maintain the forensic laboratory information processing systems.

Contacts

Internal

This position requires contact with all levels of employees, and specifically the Laboratory Manager, for the day-to-day operation of the information systems to support forensic case processing.

External

Externally, the Systems Administrator shall maintain contacts with Suppliers and Vendors, as required.

Reports to

The System Administrator shall report to:
- The Laboratory Manager.

Appendix 26—Employee, job description

Objective and role

Employees shall be responsible for delivering products and services to clients.

Problems and challenges

Day-to-day issues, as met, during working with clients and internal processes.

Principal accountabilities

Employees shall:

- understand their responsibilities as an employee with regard to attainment of management system objectives in the design, development, production, and support of products and services to be delivered to internal and external clients;
- deliver solutions to internal and external clients on time and on budget;
- Identify opportunities for further training and personal development (and seeking appropriate authorisation from their Line Manager or HR;
- co-operate with their Line Manager when an appraisal is performed to ensure that the appraisal is conducted effectively;
- develop and manage effective working relationships with all appropriate internal and external interested parties;
- adhere to the established IMS policies, standards, and procedures;
- perform all responsibilities in accordance with, or in excess of, the requirements of the IMS.

Reports to

Employees shall report to:
- relevant Line Managers.

Appendix 27—Areas of technical competence

All Forensic Analysts and their Line Management shall know, but not be limited to, the following:

- the Law:
    - know specific legal system and relevant legislation for the jurisdiction of operations;
    - what is permissible and what is not in all aspects of forensic case processing?

- basic computer knowledge:
  - blockchain:
  - cloud computing;
  - data interface technology;
  - diagnosing and troubleshooting systems;
  - different types of storage and their characteristics;
  - dynamic/static IP—addressing;
  - e-commerce, digital signatures;
  - encryption/compressed files;
  - file sharing and peer-to-peer concepts;
  - file systems and logical/physical—slack space, etc.;
  - hardware and peripherals;
  - hidden files/flags/rename/steganography;
  - image capturing devices, including write blockers;
  - installing, configuring, and maintaining computer systems;
  - internet protocols (TCP, IP);
  - Internet of Things (IoT) devices and technologies
  - internet services: web, www, chat, file transfer protocol (FTP), newsgroups, voice over IP;
  - network operating systems;
  - network protocols;
  - network-specific devices (e.g. switches, firewalls, routers, etc.);
  - network topologies;
  - operating systems (i.e., Windows, Unix, and variants as well as mobile device operating systems (e.g. iOS and Android, etc.);
  - social media of all types;
  - software—forensic as well as nonforensic software;
  - system time and file timestamps;
  - the TOR project: and
  - time critical/perishable data (i.e., log files, email on servers, memory dumps).
- identification and preservation of digital evidence at the scene
  - computer/digital devices;
  - equipment/systems/software/infrastructure.
  - evidence handling;
  - first response requirements; and
  - investigative techniques.
- collecting digital evidence:
  - First Responder procedures;
  - ability to recognise potential sources of evidence;
  - chain of custody (evidence).
  - computer hardware;
  - network infrastructure;
  - operating systems;
  - packaging and transport evidence;
  - types of storage media;
  - volatile data;
  - image capture;
  - image storage; and
  - image transfer.
- image processing:
  - anticontamination procedures;
  - setting up a client virtual case file;
  - processing a case using in-house agreed procedures and tools; and
  - need for contemporaneous notes.
- product based training:

- there are a number of tools in use in the forensic laboratory and Forensic Analysts using them shall be qualified to use them by attending the manufacturer's own (or authorised) training courses. These include:
- OpenText (Guidance) Software;
- Access Data (FTK);
- Paraben;
- XRY
- Cellebrite (UFED);
- Oxygen.

These are the main suppliers of tools used for processing forensic cases, however, there are a number of other tools in use, and many of these either do not need or have certified training programs.

The following vendors that are used have product certification programs, and these include, but are not limited to:

- Access Data;
- Check Point;
- Cisco;
- OpenText (Guidance) Software;
- Microsoft;
- Paraben.

forensic skills required:

- adhere to backup, archiving, and retention policy;
- adhere to the continuity of evidential chain procedures;
- advise relevant interested parties as to the evidential weight of recovered data;
- assist in interviews of suspects, where relevant;
- comply with the relevant IMS policies and procedures for forensic case processing;
- documentation of case notes on contemporaneous basis;
- engage in peer review to ensure quality, impartiality, and good practice;
- ensure currency of knowledge of relevant legislation and case law for the relevant jurisdiction(s);
- ensure intelligence is correctly recorded within appropriate systems;
- ensure that all equipment is maintained/replaced/updated to ensure optimum efficiency;
- ensure the security and continuity chain of custody of exhibits;
- keep up to date with current forensic computing techniques and tools;
- keep up to date with the advances in computer technology;
- keep up to date with the technology of digital media and its use;
- liaise with Prosecution and Defence representatives in an impartial manner;
- maintain a full contemporaneous work log for each forensic examination undertaken;
- prepare reports and briefings on relevant new legislation and its effect in the area of forensic case processing; and
- produce and present training and awareness lectures/talks for employees and external bodies, where appropriate.

report writing and testifying:

- description of evidentiary procedures for digital capture;
- mock court role playing;
- presentation of credentials;
- rehearsals and preparation;
- writing expert reports; and
- writing statements according to legislative requirements in the jurisdiction.

Appendix 28—Some professional forensic and security organisations

Note 1

Most jurisdictions will have its own specific organisations or Chapters of an international organisation.

Note 2

Some of these organisations offer certifications, others do not.

Note 3

It is impossible to list these all, so a selection of better-known international ones has been defined and these are ones that employees are members of, are aware of, or hold certifications from:

Specific Forensic Organisations

- AAFS—American Academy of Forensic Sciences—http://www.aafs.org/;
- ADFSL—The Association of Digital Forensics, Security and Law—https://www.adfsl.org/;
- CDFS—Consortium of Digital Forensic Specialists—http://www.cdfs.org/index.php;
- DFA—Digital Forensics Association—http://www.digitalforensicsassociation.org/;
- F3—First Forensic Forum www.f3.org.uk/;
- CSFS—Chartered Society of Forensic Sciences—https://www.csofs.org/;
- HTCI—High Tech Crime Institute—http://www.gohtci.com/;
- HTCIA—High Technology Crime Investigation Association—https://htcia.org;
- HTCN—High Tech Crime Network—www.htcn.org;
- IACIS—International Association of Computer Investigative Specialists—www.iacis.com;
- ISFCE—International Society of Forensic Computer Examiners—www.isfce.com;

Information Security Organisations

- ACFE—Association of Certified Fraud Examiners—www.acfe.com;
- APWG—Anti Phishing Working Group—www.antiphishing.org;
- ASIS—American Society for Industrial Security—www.asisonline.org;
- BCS—British Computer Society—www.bcs.org/;
- FBI InfraGard—www.infragard.org;
- IEEE—Institute of Electrical and Electronic Engineers—www.ieee-security.org;
- IIA—Institute of Internal Auditors—www.theiia.org;
- ISACA—Information Systems Audit and Control Association—www.isaca.org;
- ISC2—International Information Systems Security Certification Consortium—www.isc2.org;
- ISSA—Information Systems Security Association—www.issa.org
- SANS—System Administration, Networking, and Security Institute—www.sans.org;

Appendix 29—Training specification template

The following template shall be used for the development of a training specification:

- background to the business need that has given rise to the training need;
- identification of the employee(s) that require the training;
- overall aim of the training and details how the business need has been met;
- the objective(s) of the training;
- training methods and style to be used;
- the required skills of the trainer;
- the method of evaluation of the training;
- timescale for delivery of the training;
- the proposed venue (in-house or external); and
- any other relevant details.

Appendix 30—Training proposal evaluation checklist

The following evaluation checklist shall be used for evaluating a training proposal based on a supplied training specification RFP:

- a well-written and concise response to the training specification RFP;
- a clear description of how the supplier will meet the defined training objectives;
- ensuring that the training methods are appropriate to the defined needs;
- full details of the proposed trainers, including their qualifications, relevant experience, and experience of training similar or the same courses;
- experience of the supplier providing the same or similar courses;
- a realistic timetable for delivery;
- a full breakdown of costs;
- sample client references; and
- any other material that may be considered relevant.

Appendix 31—Training supplier interview and presentation checklist

The following checklist shall be used for evaluating a training supplier's interview performance and presentation based on a supplied training specification RFP:

Note

Some of these may have been covered in the Training Proposal Checklist or the response to the RFP but may require clarification.

Interviews

An interview gives the opportunity to probe or clarify any of the answers defined in the formal training RFP response submitted. Some issues that shall be considered include:

- what is the structure of the training?
- how will it meet the training objectives?
- how will the training methods assist in meeting the training objectives;
- who will actually deliver the training?
- what are the competencies of the trainer for the subject matter of the training course;
- what are the qualifications and competencies of anyone involved in developing a new course (if appropriate);
- what is their professional reputation, based on feedback, for the subject matter they are going to develop/teach?
- what complaints for training have they received in the past year?
- have they received any training awards that are nationally, industry wide, or internationally recognised?
- how will they evaluate their success for the delivery?
- confirmation that they will be able to meet both the required timescales and volume of employees;
- confirmation of costs;
- confirmation of any other contractual details; and
- any other information that may be relevant.

Presentation

The following shall be considered in evaluating the prospective supplier's presentation:

- a good opening—if they cannot manage that, how will they hold the attention of employees attending their training courses?
- good presentation and communication style;
- a clear structure, with all relevant areas covered in a logical and concise manner—again a possible indicator of how they run their courses;

- good timekeeping for the stated length of the presentation;
- a good close with a concise summary and conclusions; and
- professional handling of any questions raised.

Appendix 32—Training reaction level questionnaire

The following form shall be used as their training reaction level questionnaire:

General

- course title;
- course date;
- course supplier;
- name of the employee; and
- job title.

Precourse briefing

whether a precourse briefing was defined and if it was:

- were the learning objectives of the course explained;
- why the course was appropriate to the employee; and
- understanding how the course related to the employee's job role.

Training objectives

- define up to five of the employee's training objectives that were met by the course and their level of relevance; and
- how relevant did the employee think the course was to their job role (scale of 1–5);

Training methods

- for each of the training methods used in the course evaluate their usefulness to the employee (scale of 1–5 or not applicable—see Marking Scheme below);
- methods of training could include, but not be limited to:
  - breakout sessions;
  - case studies;
  - classroom training;
  - extra sessions with the tutor/coaching;
  - group discussion;
  - handouts;
  - practicals;
  - quizzes;
  - role play;
  - syndicate work;
  - videos; and
  - virtual presentations and demonstrations carried out remotely.

Trainers

For each trainer, rate their performance (scale of 1–5):

- ability to relate the subject to the employees;
- appropriate course pace;

- engaging with the class;
- knowledge; and
- practical experience.

Facilities and administration

- for each item below, evaluate the quality, facilities, and administration for the course (scale of 1–5 or not applicable);
  - audiovisual equipment;
  - breakout rooms;
  - catering;
  - clarity of joining instructions;
  - convenience of location;
  - handling of queries;
  - timeliness of joining instructions; and
  - training room(s).

Other comments

Allow any other comments that the employee wants to put in.

Marking scheme

The marking scheme that shall be used is:
   0—Not applicable;
   1—Very Poor;
   2—Poor;
   3—Neutral;
   4—Good;
   5—Very Good.

Appendix 33—Code of ethics

This is FCL's own Code of Ethics. It has been designed to meet not only FCL's own requirements but also to incorporate other known Codes of Ethics from other forensic and security organisations that publish them.

Where an inconsistency is discovered between FCL's Code of Ethics and other published ones, the discrepancy shall be investigated and FCL's Code of Ethics be amended, if appropriate.

- act in all dealings with honesty, objectivity, and impartiality;
- admit to mistakes and errors and continuously improve;
- be able to demonstrate due care;
- be able to report a possible miscarriage of justice to an appropriate person without fear of recrimination;
- be able to terminate their engagement if they feel undue pressure is being applied to them;
- be honest about skills and limitations and rely on other qualified experts when needed;
- be honest and forthright in dealing with others;
- be open minded and not discriminatory on any grounds;
- be paid for their work and not a desired outcome that may influence their objectivity;
- be prepared to revisit forensic casework if any new evidence is discovered that may impact findings to date;
- be professional and perform all work in a competent, accurate, timely, and cost-effective manner;
- be respectful of intellectual property rights;
- charge reasonable fees and expenses as agreed between the parties and in line with good practice;
- credit other people's work;
- declare any conflicts of interest as soon as they are identified;
- ensure security of all case processing exhibits at all times whilst in their possession;

- establish the integrity and continuity of any exhibits as soon as they are received and maintain the chain of custody whilst in the Forensic Analyst's possession;
- have open communications with the client and keep the client informed of any major developments;
- maintain and update technical and other relevant skills;
- maintain professional competence;
- maintain the highest standards of professionalism and ethical conduct;
- only use validated methods, unless preparing a new method for validation. Even then, the method shall not be used until validated;
- only work and provide evidence within the limits of professional competence;
- preserve confidentiality unless otherwise ordered by a Court of competent jurisdiction or explicitly by the instructing client;
- remember that their overriding duty to serve the Court or Tribunal, and that that their secondary duty is to the client instructing them, as appropriate in the jurisdiction;
- report any reportable offence to the proper legal authorities as required by law in the jurisdiction;
- respect confidentiality relating to all matters relating to forensic case processing; and
- strive to ensure the integrity and repeatability of the work carried out.

Appendix 34—Termination checklist

The following checklist shall be used for employee terminations. Where the employee is undertaking an internal move or promotion, those parts of the form that are irrelevant shall be omitted.

Employee details

- employee name;
- employee ID number;
- employee position; and
- period of service (from and to dates);

General questions

1. Please identify the reason(s) for initially seeking and accepting a position with FCL:
   - compensation;
   - fringe benefits;
   - location;
   - FCL's reputation;
   - career change;
   - job responsibilities;
   - technical challenges;
   - other

Note 1

These are tick boxes and allows comments to be added.

---

2. Have your feelings changed?

Note 2

This is a 'Yes/No' question and allows comments to be added.

---

3. Did you understand the job expectations when you were hired?

Note 3

This is a 'Yes/No' question and allows comments to be added.

---

4. Did you receive sufficient training to meet those expectations?

Note 4

This is a 'Yes/No' question and allows comments to be added.

---

5. Did you know how or where to get information you needed to succeed in your job?

Note 5

This is a 'Yes/No' question and allows comments to be added.

---

6. What did you find to be the most satisfying and enjoyable about your experience with FCL?

Note 6

This is a free-form answer and allows comments to be added.

---

7. What did you find to be least satisfying and enjoyable about your experience with FCL?

Note 7

This is a free-form answer and allows comments to be added.

Job specific questions

This section attempts to rate aspects of the employee's 'employment experience' using quantitative and qualitative feedback. The following scoring shall be used for aspects of employment:

1—Very Poor;
2—Poor;
3—Neutral;
4—Good;
5—Very Good.

The aspects to be evaluated shall be:

1. opportunity for advancement;
2. performance appraisals;
3. physical working conditions;
4. technical challenges;
5. your salary;
6. vacation/holidays;
7. other company benefits;
8. feeling of belonging;
9. work/home life balance;

10. internal communications;
11. access to appropriate resources;
12. please provide any constructive feedback you feel would be beneficial towards improving the effectiveness of FCL as an employer;

Note 8

This is a free-form answer and allows comments to be added.

---

13. what would make you interested in returning to work at FCL?

Note 9

This is a free-form answer and allows comments to be added.

---

14. Do you feel that your particular job was important to the overall operational success of FCL?

Note 10

This is a 'Yes/No' question and allows comments to be added.

Evaluation of management

This section attempts to rate aspects of the employee's 'perception of their Line Manager using quantitative and qualitative feedback. The following scoring shall be used for aspects of employment.

The following scoring is used for aspects of employment:

1—Very Poor;
2—Poor;
3—Neutral;
4—Good;
5—Very Good.

The aspects to be evaluated shall be:

1. demonstrates fair and equal treatment;
2. provides appropriate recognition;
3. resolves complaints/difficulties in timely fashion;
4. follows FCL policy and procedures;
5. informs employee of matters relating to work in a timely manner;
6. encourages feedback;
7. is knowledgeable in own job;
8. expresses instructions clearly;
9. develops cooperation;
10. provides assistance, training, and mentoring as needed;
11. if you came back to work for the Company would you work for the same Line Manager?

Note 11

This is a 'Yes/No' question and allows comments to be added.

---

12. how would you rate your own performance on the job?

Note 2

This question uses the rankings above and allows comments to be added.

New role

This section attempts to determine details of reasons for leaving and the new role to which the employee is moving:

1. Which of the following methods did you use to search for a new position?
   - advertisements;
   - recruitment consultants;
   - personal contacts;
   - client contact and;
   - Other

Note 13

This is a tick box answer and allows comments to be added.

2. Are you leaving for a similar job?

Note 14

This is a 'Yes/No' question and allows comments to be added.

3. How is your new job different from your old one?

Note 15

This is a free-form text answer.

4. Are you staying in the same industry?

Note 16

This is a 'Yes/No' question and allows comments to be added.

5. What part does salary play in your decision to leave?

Note 17

This is a free-form text answer.

6. What made you begin looking for another position, or if appropriate what made you listen to the offer to interview for another position?

Note 18

This is a free-form text answer.

7. What is your primary reason for leaving?

- compensation;
- Fringe benefits;
- location;
- supervision;
- career change;
- job fit;
- other:

Note 19

This is a tick box answer and allows comments to be added.

---

8. If you used recruitment consultants, which ones did you find the most useful?

Note 20

This is a free-form text answer.

---

9. What could FCL have done to prevent you from leaving?

Note 21

This is a free-form text answer.

---

10. What does the job you are going to offer you that your job here did not?

Note 22

This is a free-form text answer.

---

11. Any Other Feedback/Comments/Suggestions?

Note 23

This is a free-form text answer.

The form is then signed and dated by the employee and the HR employee conduction the exit interview.

Return of assets

This section is a checklist of items that have been issued to the employee as part of their job role that shall be returned on termination. The list comes from the Finance or IT asset register listing and shall record anything that the employee hands over at the exit interview:

- access card;
- all information—on any media;
- car and keys;
- credit card;
- laptop;
- media returned;
- mobile device (phone, tablet, etc');
- office keys;
- other IT equipment; and
- other (define).

Note 24

This is a tick box answer and allows comments to be added.

The form is then signed and dated by the employee and the HR employee conduction the exit interview.

IT Department actions

This section is a checklist of tasks that shall be performed by the IT Department as part of the termination process.

Each item shall have a date and the name and signature of the person carrying out each task.

Not all tasks will be relevant to each employee being terminated so they are stated as 'Not done' dated and signed. The tasks are:

- all employee accounts disabled;
- Administration/root passwords changed (define);
- other 'shared' passwords changed (define);
- removed from access list (physical);
- removed from access list (logical);
- email archived;
- PIN numbers and access codes changed (define);
- voicemail a diverted to Line Manager;
- voice mail access code changed;
- mobile phone either reassigned or terminated;
- Check all IT equipment returned via HR; and
- Other tasks required (define).

Chapter 19

Accreditation and Certification for a digital forensic laboratory

19.1 Accreditation and Certification

19.1.1 Definitions

The terms 'Accreditation' and 'Certification' are often used interchangeably by those that do not understand what they mean. They have different meanings and should be used correctly. Their definitions are given below:

ISO/IEC 17011:2017 defines Accreditation as:

Third party attestation related to a Conformity Assessment Body conveying formal demonstration of its competence to carry out specific conformity assessment tasks.

Accreditation is a formal, third-party recognition of competence to perform specific tasks. It provides a means to identify a proven, competent evaluator so that the selection of a Conformity Assessment Body (Laboratory, Inspection, or Conformance assessment body) is an informed choice.

ISO/IEC 17000:2004 defines Certification as:

Third party attestation related to products, processes, systems or persons.

Certification is a formal procedure by which an accredited or authorised person or agency assesses and verifies (and attests in writing by issuing a certificate) the attributes, characteristics, quality, qualification, or status of individuals or organisations, goods or services, procedures or processes, or events or situations, conforms with established requirements or standards.

Note

Certification of a Management System is sometimes called Registration and the organisation gains a 'Certificate of Registration'. To simplify matters, 'Certification' rather than 'gaining a Certificate of Registration' has been used in the book.

19.1.2 The International Accreditation Forum

Accreditation Bodies (ABs) can apply to join the International Accreditation Forum (IAF). When they have been evaluated by their peers as competent, they sign arrangements that enhance the acceptance of products and services across national borders.

The purpose of the arrangement, the IAF Multilateral Recognition Arrangement (MLA), is to ensure mutual recognition of Accredited Certification between signatories to the MLA, and subsequently acceptance of Accredited Certification in many markets based on one Accreditation.

Accreditations granted by IAF MLA signatories are recognised worldwide based on their equivalent Accreditation programmes, therefore, reducing costs and adding value to business and consumers. This creates a framework to support international trade through the removal of technical barriers.

AB members of IAF are admitted to the MLA only after stringent evaluation of their operations by a peer evaluation team.

These arrangements are managed by the IAF, in the fields of Management Systems, products, services, personnel, and other similar programmes of Conformity Assessment, and the International Laboratory Accreditation Cooperation (ILAC), in the field of laboratory and inspection Accreditation. Both organisations, ILAC and IAF, work together and coordinate their efforts to enhance the Accreditation and the Conformity Assessment processes worldwide.

A Blueprint for Implementing Best Practice Procedures in a Digital Forensic Laboratory. https://doi.org/10.1016/B978-0-12-819479-9.00001-0

19.1.3   The hierarchy of ISO standards for Accreditation and Certification

There is a distinct hierarchy for Accreditation and Certification within ISO standards.

At the top level is the AB that will Accredit Conformity Assessment Bodies (CABs), who in turn will Certify or Register clients.

Note

CABs are also referred to as Certification Bodies (CBs) and to simplify matters, 'Certification Body' rather than 'Conformance Assessment Body' has been used in the book.

19.1.3.1   Accreditation Bodies

The following ISO Standards are applicable to ABs:

- ISO/IEC 17011:2017 Conformity assessment—General requirements for Accreditation bodies accrediting conformity assessment bodies.

  ABs are recognised/peer evaluated by the IAF.
  ABs have been established in many countries with the primary purpose of ensuring that CBs in their country are subject to oversight by an authoritative body.

19.1.3.2   Certification Bodies

The following ISO Standards are applicable to CBs:

- ISO/IEC 17020:2012 Conformity assessment—Requirements for the operation of various types of bodies performing inspection (This relates to Inspection Bodies). This was reviewed and confirmed in 2017—so this version remains current.
- ISO/IEC 17021-1:2015 Conformity assessment—Requirements for bodies providing audit and certification of Management Systems (This relates to Certification Bodies and typically relates to Management Systems) (this replaced ISO/IEC Guide 62:1996 General requirements for bodies operating assessment and Certification/registration of quality systems and ISO/IEC Guide 66:1999 General requirements for bodies operating assessment and Certification/registration of environmental Management Systems (EMS)). This was reviewed and confirmed in 2020—so this version remains current.
- ISO/IEC 17024:2012 Conformity assessment—General requirements for bodies operating certification of persons (This relates to Individuals). This was reviewed and confirmed in 2018—so this version remains current.
- ISO/IEC 17043:2010 Conformity assessment—General requirements for proficiency testing (this replaced ISO Guide 43 ISO/IEC Guide 43-1:1997 Proficiency testing by interlaboratory comparisons—Part 1: Development and operation of proficiency testing schemes and Part 2: Selection and use of proficiency testing schemes by laboratory Accreditation Bodies). This is under review at the time of writing and is at Draft International Standard (DIS) state.
- ISO/IEC 17065:2012 Conformity assessment—Requirements for bodies certifying products, processes, and services (this is replacing ISO/IEC Guide 65:1996 General requirements for bodies operating product Certification systems). This was reviewed and confirmed in 2018—so this version remains current.

  CBs are assessed and Accredited by the relevant AB.

Note

Whilst the release dates are given above for the relevant standards, these are dropped in the text as references will relate to these versions.

Whilst these are the ISO Standards relevant to Accreditation and Certification, a number of organisations throughout the world have adopted and adapted them to suit their own specific requirements.

A number of these relate to forensic laboratories, three of the main ABs offering ISO/IEC 17025 'plus' are:

The American Society of Crime Laboratory Directors/Laboratory Accreditation Board (ASCLD/LAB). However, the ASCLD/LAB has now signed an affiliation agreement and merged with the ANSI-ASQ National Accreditation Board (ANAB) https://www.anab.org/forensic-accreditation.

The American Association for Laboratory Accreditation (A2LA)—https://www.a2la.org/accreditation.

Laboratory Accreditation Bureau (L-A-B). However, in 2016 the L-A-B merged with the ANSI-ASQ National Accreditation Board (ANAB). https://www.anab.org/forensic-accreditation.

19.1.4 Standards and regulations applicable to a forensic laboratory

To gain either Accredited or Certified status, a digital forensic laboratory (referred to throughout as a forensic laboratory) shall choose the standards it wishes to meet and demonstrate to a third party that it meets those requirements.

These are typically:

- International Standards;
- National Standards.

Note 1

This book has applied the requirements of the standards below to FCL, but FCL has not sought Accreditation or Certification, merely the ability to prove conformity if audited.

Note 2

Therefore, this is general guidance for any forensic laboratory that wants to be Accredited or Certified.

19.1.4.1 Accreditation

The following Accreditations are addressed with the procedures in this book:

- ISO/IEC 17025 General requirements for the competence of testing and calibration laboratories;
- ISO/IEC 17020:2012 Conformity assessment—Requirements for the operation of various types of bodies performing inspection. This is now recognised as being 'the standard for crime scene investigation' and Bedfordshire Police were the first British police force to gain this November 2020.

Note 1

It is not possible to list all of the specific variations on ISO/IEC 17025 Accreditation, so the generic ISO/IEC 17025 Management System has been chosen as a 'vanilla' Accreditation. The different variations of ISO/IEC 17025 are always based on ISO/IEC 17025 with extra requirements over and above the 'vanilla' ISO/IEC 17025.

Note 2

A forensic laboratory is regarded as a 'Testing' Laboratory in ISO/IEC 17025 terms, rather than a 'Calibration Laboratory'.

Note 3

ISO/IEC 17025 is now the mandatory standard in the United Kingdom for some types of digital forensic laboratories as of October 2017. Any forensic laboratory in the United Kingdom which is not ISO/IEC 17025 certified will be required to declare itself as 'noncompliant' on each issued report. In their annual report, the Forensic Science Regulator (FSR) stated that 'failure to comply with the Regulator's standards could significantly detract from the credibility of a forensic science professional, particularly when acting as an expert witness, and/or have a bearing on reliability'.

Note 4

In the United States, a number of States have mandated that Crime Laboratories are Accredited. Similar requirements may exist, or be planned, for other countries.

19.1.4.2 Certifications

The following Certifications are addressed with the procedures in this book:

- ISO 22301:2019 Societal Security—Business Continuity Management Systems;
- ISO 3310:2018 Risk management, guidelines;
- ISO 15489:2016 Information and documentation—Records management—Part 1: Concepts and principles;
- ISO 45001:2018 Occupational health and safety Management Systems—Requirements with guidance for use;
- ISO 9001:2015 Quality Management Systems—Requirements; and
- ISO/IEC 27001:2022 Information technology—Security techniques—Information security Management Systems—Requirements.

Note

Whilst the release dates are given above for the relevant standards, these are dropped in the text as references will relate to these versions.

19.1.4.3 Compliance

The following standards are used in this book and procedures implemented are compliant with them as there are no processes for Certification or Accreditation for them:

- BS 7858:2019 Security screening of individuals employed in a security environment. Code of practice;
- ISO 10002:2018 Quality management—Customer satisfaction—Guidelines for complaints handling in organisations;
- ISO 10003:2018 Quality management—Customer satisfaction—Guidelines for dispute resolution external to organisations.

Note 1

Whilst the release dates are given above for the relevant standards, these are dropped in the text as references will relate to these versions.

Note 2

Previously, PAS 99:2012 Specification of common Management System requirements as a framework for integration was used. However, with the common use of 'Annex L' in management standards which provides a common framework, this has been used where appropriate.

19.1.4.4 Regulations and legislation

In a number of jurisdictions, there are emerging a number of Forensic Regulators, who are implementing forensic regulations within their jurisdiction.

In the United Kingdom, the function of the Forensic Science Regulator (FSR) is to ensure that the provision of forensic science services across the criminal justice system is subject to an appropriate regime of scientific quality standards. The current version of the FSR's 'Codes of Practice and Conduct for forensic science providers and practitioners in the Criminal Justice System' is V 7 and was issued in 2021.

19.1.4.5 Guidance

The International Laboratory Accreditation Cooperation (ILAC) has produced 'ILAC G19:06/2022 Modules in a Forensic Science Process'.

This document is intended to provide guidance for forensic science units involved in examination and testing in the forensic science process by providing the application of ISO/IEC 17025 and ISO/IEC 17020.

19.1.4.6 ISO 9001, ISO/IEC 17025, and ISO/IEC 17020

ISO/IEC 17025 covers a number of technical competence requirements that are not covered in ISO 9001.

Certification against ISO 9001 does not, in itself, demonstrate the competence of a forensic Laboratory to produce technically valid data and results.

In effect, a forensic laboratory must decide if it requires being Accredited to ISO/IEC 17025, or Certified to ISO 9001, or both. Accreditation and Certification are two separate processes. No forensic laboratory that claims ISO/IEC 17025 Accreditation can also automatically claim ISO 9001 Certification and likewise ISO 9001 Certification does not provide ISO/IEC 17025 Accreditation status.

ISO/IEC 17020 is a standalone standard.

19.1.5 Benefits of Accreditation and Certification for a forensic laboratory

19.1.5.1 Accreditation

Formal recognition of competence of a forensic laboratory by an AB in accordance with international criteria has many advantages:

- a competent workforce performing tasks within the forensic laboratory;
- a positive reputation for the forensic laboratory for having achieved ISO/IEC 17025 or 17020 Accreditation and in the United Kingdom does not have to provide a 'noncompliance' statement in each report it produces;
- a public statement that the forensic laboratory has met the highest operational requirements;
- assurance of the accuracy and integrity of the forensic laboratory's processes and outputs;
- demonstrable compliance verified by a third-party AB;
- increased confidence in reports issued by the forensic laboratory;
- international recognition for the forensic laboratory;
- marketing advantage;
- potential increase in business due to enhanced customer confidence and satisfaction;
- processes and procedures for the operation of the forensic laboratory are documented and tested;
- quality assurance of test and calibration data;
- rigorous quality processes that equate to fewer failures and errors;
- savings in terms of time and money due to reduction or elimination of the need for rework;
- suitability, calibration, and maintenance of test equipment;
- the forensic laboratory has better control of operations and feedback to ascertain whether they have a sound quality assurance system and are assessed as technically competent; and
- traceability of measurements and calibrations to international standards.

19.1.5.2 Certification

If the forensic laboratory gains Certification (where applicable) and conformity to the standards referred to in the book, then it will have the following advantages:

- allows the forensic laboratory to seek new markets where they may have been precluded, if they had not gained the relevant Certification(s);
- assures management and customers of the forensic laboratory's information security, quality, business continuity, and health and safety measures in place;
- builds team spirit as the Integrated Management System (IMS) requires a team, not an individual, approach;
- creates an organisational structure to ensure that roles and responsibilities are clearly defined;
- demonstrates conformity with the relevant standards verified by a third-party CB, where a Certification process exists;
- demonstrates legal and regulatory compliance;
- demonstrates that the forensic laboratory is continually improving and refining their Management Systems by achieving and maintaining their Certification(s);
- demonstrates to relevant interested parties, through a third party, that the forensic laboratory uses industry-respected standards and good practices;
- demonstrates to relevant interested parties that the forensic laboratory is run effectively and continuously improves its processes;
- detects defects that do occur earlier and they are corrected at a lower cost;
- develops a Statement of Applicability (SoA) that identifies controls to be implemented to address the risks relating to information security identified in the forensic laboratory;
- ensures corrective action is taken whenever defects in products and services occur;
- ensures that a commitment to the components in the IMS (e.g. ISMS, BCMS, QMS, etc.) exists at all levels throughout the forensic laboratory;
- ensures that an appropriate incident management process is in place;

- ensures that there is an ongoing compliance and monitoring mechanism in place;
- identifies, evaluates, and treats risks in the forensic laboratory, in a timely manner, in line with their risk appetite;
- improves the forensic laboratory's image and builds a better reputation;
- improves management control and reporting, ensuring improved and fact-based decision-making;
- improves staff responsibility, commitment, and motivation through ongoing Assessment;
- increases customer confidence in the forensic laboratory's products and services;
- integrates information security, quality, business continuity, and health and safety into a common IMS to exploit synchronicity between standards with similar management requirements;
- makes a public statement that the forensic laboratory has addressed its own information security needs, as well as those of clients who entrust their information to them;
- makes it easier for new employees 'get up to speed' by following documented procedures;
- potentially reduced insurance premiums;
- provides a positive health and safety track record;
- reduces the risk of accidents and therefore lower employee absence; and
- reduces operational costs.

19.1.6   Establishing the need for Accreditation and/or Certification

The common requirements for a forensic laboratory for Accreditation and/or Certification include:

- improving the quality of products and services provided to its clients;
- adopting, developing, and maintaining processes and procedures which may be used to assess its level of conformity to relevant standards;
- providing an independent, impartial, and objective process of Accreditation and Certification by which it benefits from a total operational review on a regular basis;
- offering to the general public and to its clients a means of identifying that it has demonstrated conformity with established standards and allows possible clients to make informed choices; and
- in some cases, Accreditation, Certification, or compliance with Codes of Conduct is mandated.

19.1.7   Requirements for Accreditation and/or Certification

To achieve Accreditation or Certification, a forensic laboratory shall demonstrate to a competent third party that it meets the requirements of the standard(s) against which it is being assessed.

Once the need for an Accreditation or Certification has been agreed and identified, it is necessary to determine which ABs or CBs can offer the services required. This may involve an AB or CB from within the jurisdiction or may require a specific service to be procured from outside the jurisdiction.

19.2   Accreditation for a forensic laboratory

Note

In this book, 'audit' refers to first and second-party (internal and supplier, respectively) audits undertaken by a forensic laboratory, and 'assessment' is used for third-party audits (by a CB or AB).

The process for gaining Accreditation is broadly similar for any standard throughout the world. However, different ABs may have different requirements based on their scopes or on the jurisdiction within which they operate.

The generic approach is shown below, but when Accreditation is sought, the specific AB requirements shall be met.

Whichever process for Accreditation is taken, a forensic laboratory shall undergo similar processes as defined below.

19.2.1   Self-evaluation prior to application

Whilst it may not be a mandatory requirement for Accreditation, it is a sensible approach to perform a self-assessment as preparation for the Accreditation process. This should determine whether a forensic laboratory's processes, procedures, and records meet the requirements of the Accreditation sought.

This may require the:

- purchase of a number of standards;
- completion of self-assessment forms for use prior to seeking Accreditation and undertake any identified Corrective Actions or Preventive Actions (CAPAs) arising from the self-assessment process.

Note 1

Some standards still use 'Preventive Actions' but ISO/IEC 27001 has stopped using the term; however, the term CAPA is still used in this book.

Note 2

A forensic laboratory may choose to undertake the self-assessment in-house or contract a third-party service provider to perform the task on their behalf.

19.2.2 Selecting an Accreditation Body

Once the achieving the required Accreditation has been agreed, a forensic laboratory shall:

1. research the market to see what ABs provide the required Accreditation services;
2. obtain marketing materials from each of the possible ABs to determine the range of services that they provide;
3. research other forensic laboratories to determine the ABs that they have used and their opinion of the services provided;
4. create a shortlist of three possible ABs from whom to obtain quotations for the Accreditation required, if possible. It may well be that there is only one AB operating in the jurisdiction or that the use of the national AB is mandated.

Note

Where a forensic laboratory already has a relationship with an AB, the first approach should be made to that AB for additional services if they can provide them. This will have the benefit of reduced costs for integrated audits and the fact that the AB already 'knows' their client's business.

19.2.3 Accreditation information to be made available

To assist in selection of an AB, all ABs shall make publicly available, and update at adequate intervals, the following:

- detailed information about the AB's Assessment and Accreditation processes, including arrangements for granting, maintaining, extending, reducing, suspending, and withdrawing Accreditation;
- documentation containing the requirements for Accreditation, including technical requirements specific to each field of Accreditation, that the AB offers;
- general information about the fees relating to the accreditation;
- a description of the rights and obligations of ABs;
- information on the CBs that the AB has accredited in a publicly available register;
- information on procedures for lodging and handling complaints and appeals;
- information about the authority under which the Accreditation programme operates;
- a description of its rights and duties;
- general information about the means by which it obtains financial support; and
- information about its activities and stated limitations under which it operates.

From this information, an informed choice of AB can be made by a forensic laboratory.

19.2.4 Appointing an AB

Once the quotation(s) from the shortlist of ABs for the provision of Accreditation services have been received by the forensic laboratory with the range of services offered, the forensic laboratory is in the position to make an informed choice about the selection of an appropriate AB.

19.2.5 Application

Once the AB has been selected for the provision of Accreditation, the forensic laboratory shall initiate the Accreditation process. To initiate the Accreditation process, the forensic laboratory shall:

1. obtain the relevant application forms from the selected AB (often called the 'Application Pack').
2. fill in relevant application forms and return them to the relevant AB.
3. provide a copy of the forensic laboratory's Quality Manual.
4. provide proof of legal status.
5. pay the relevant fees.
6. execute the relevant contracts.

Whilst application forms will vary between ABs, the application process will typically require the forensic laboratory to provide the following information on the application forms:

- the legal name and full address of the forensic laboratory;
- the ownership and legal status of the forensic laboratory;
- the forensic laboratory's Authorised Representative's name and contact information;
- an organisational chart defining relationships that are relevant to performing testing covered in the Accreditation request;
- a general description of the forensic laboratory, including its facilities and scope of operation;
- declarations relevant to the application; and
- the requested Scope of Accreditation.

By signing the application, the forensic laboratory's Authorised Representative commits the forensic laboratory to fulfil the conditions for Accreditation. Whilst these will vary between ABs, a typical set of conditions for Accreditation is defined in Appendix 1.

The forensic laboratory's Authorised Representative shall review all documents provided with the application package and become familiar the requirements and how the forensic laboratory meets them, before signing the application.

19.2.6 Scope of Accreditation

The form and definition of the Scope of Accreditation will depend on the forensic laboratory's requirements.

ABs will have forms and guidance to assist the forensic laboratory in defining their scope for Accreditation.

Typically, the AB works closely with a forensic laboratory to define the Scope of Accreditation to ensure that the forensic laboratory's clients are provided with an accurate and unambiguous description of the range of calibration/tests covered by a forensic laboratory's Accreditation.

This is the reason that the forensic laboratory is required to list, on its application form, the standard specifications or other methods or procedures relevant to the calibration or tests for which accreditation is sought, and the major items of laboratory equipment used to conduct those calibrations/tests.

In some cases, as the Assessment proceeds, it may become clear that the forensic laboratory is not in a position to achieve Accreditation for certain areas within the proposed scope. In cases such as this, the AB's Lead Assessor may be able to recommend Accreditation for a suitably reduced or redefined schedule.

The Scope of Accreditation for the forensic laboratory is regarded as being in the public domain, as ABs are required to maintain a public register of organisations that they have Accredited.

19.2.7 Fees for Accreditation

Fees will vary for each specific part of the Assessment between ABs in different jurisdictions and may even be for different standards.

Additionally, fees will normally change over time.

For this reason, no details of fees are given.

19.2.8 Processing applications

Upon receipt of a forensic laboratory's application for accreditation, the AB will:

- log the application;
- acknowledge the receipt of the application in writing (typically email these days) to the forensic laboratory;

- confirm payment of fees;
- review the forensic laboratory's application, to ensure that:
  - the application is complete; and
  - correct fees are paid.

Note

Where the application is unclear or incomplete, the AB shall request further clarification or documents until they are satisfied that the application is complete.

Additionally, the AB shall check to see that they:

- have fully understood the forensic laboratory's requirements;
- can arrange Assessment Teams with all the necessary expertise and competence; and
- can make realistic estimates of the timescales and costs involved.

The AB shall review the forensic laboratory Quality Manual and any supporting documentation supplied by the forensic laboratory and determine the apparent conformity of the documents submitted for the relevant Standard. The AB can then recommend whether:

- a preassessment visit should take place;
- exceptionally, plans for the forensic laboratory's Assessment to the relevant standard to proceed without any preassessment visit (this would typically be following discussions between the forensic laboratory and the AB); and
- the forensic laboratory is not in a position to proceed to preassessment.

Proper completion and submission of records and documents are required before the Assessment process can start.

19.2.9 Assigning the Lead Assessor

After reviewing a forensic laboratory's application and determining that it is complete, the AB shall assign a Lead Assessor to manage the application. (This is often also referred to as the Assessment Manager.) The Lead Assessor shall have an understanding of the area of calibration, testing, or sampling concerned, and will be able to discuss with the forensic laboratory's Authorised Representative any matters that may arise during the processing of the application, as far as possible.

Most ABs try to ensure that the Lead Assessor is responsible for processing the forensic laboratory's application through the Accreditation life cycle for at least the first full 3-year cycle.

The Lead Assessor shall perform the contract review and is responsible for selecting and appointing the Assessment Team.

19.2.10 Appointing the Assessment Team

The Assessment Team comprises a Lead Assessor and as many Technical Assessors or Experts as are necessary to provide the technical expertise adequately to assess the forensic laboratory's competence.

Technical Assessors and Experts shall be selected on the basis of their professional and academic achievements, experience in the field of testing or calibration, management experience, training, technical knowledge, and communications skills. They evaluate all information collected from the forensic laboratory to conduct the Assessment at the forensic laboratory and any other sites where activities to be covered by the Scope of Accreditation are performed.

Assessors shall be assigned to conduct an on-site Assessment of the forensic laboratory on the basis of how well their experience matches the type of testing or calibration to be assessed, as well as the absence of conflicts of interest.

A forensic laboratory has the right to object to the appointment of any Technical Assessor(s) or Expert(s) and, in such cases, the AB will endeavour to offer an alternative. In the event that a suitable alternative cannot be identified, or the grounds for objection are considered to be unreasonable, the AB will typically reserve the right to appoint the original Technical Assessor(s) and Expert(s) to the Assessment Team.

19.2.11 Document review

The Lead Assessor assigned to assess the forensic laboratory's application shall review the Quality Manual and related Management System documentation submitted with the application to ensure they cover all aspects of the Management System related to the requirements of the Scope of Accreditation sought.

The Lead Assessor may ask for additional Management System documents and/or records to facilitate the document review.

The Lead Assessor may identify nonconformities in the documentation during the Document Review.

Any nonconformity identified during the Document Review shall be discussed with the Authorised Representative and the forensic laboratory is given the opportunity to address them prior to progressing to the next stage in the Accreditation process.

Based on the Document Review, the AB may require the forensic laboratory to address any identified nonconformities before any on-site assessment is scheduled.

In these cases, the Lead Assessor shall provide a list of the nonconformities to the forensic laboratory in writing. If the Management System documentation requires significant revision, the AB may require the forensic laboratory to improve its documentation and re-submit it for further review prior to proceeding with the Accreditation process.

If the nonconformities are serious enough, the Lead Assessor can 'suspend' the Accreditation process until the gaps have been satisfactorily been addressed.

If a nonconformity is found, it will be marked as to its severity, and the forensic laboratory advised of it.

Different ABs use different terminologies for assessing conformity to the requirements of the Management Systems, and a standard one is defined in Chapter 4, Section 4.9.

If any nonconformities are identified, the forensic laboratory shall be required to formally respond to the audit report and state how they are going to address any nonconformities raised. This is performed by the raising of a CAPA, though some organisations call them CARs (Corrective Action Requests).

A typical response for an audit report is defined in Appendix 2.

The Document Review is usually carried out on-site, but may be performed off-site, if required.

19.2.12   Preassessment visit

Note 1

Some ABs may require preassessment visits and others leave them as optional. A forensic laboratory should always take advantage of a preassessment visit for Accreditation, if offered.

Note 2

A forensic laboratory may, if the ABs permit it, request a longer preassessment visit.

The preassessment visit is usually carried out by the Lead Assessor (accompanied by a Technical Assessor where appropriate) and is usually completed in 1 day.

The preassessment visit allows discussion with the forensic laboratory's Top Management on the extent to which the forensic laboratory's Management System, Quality Manual, and operating procedures fulfil the requirements for Accreditation to the relevant Standard.

The preassessment visit is structured so that the Assessment Team can ascertain that the essential components of the forensic laboratory's Management System for quality, administrative, and technical operation are present. The Assessment Team shall establish whether the forensic laboratory has defined responsibilities and the means of meeting each of the requirements of the relevant Standard.

As well as examining the documented Management System prepared by the forensic laboratory, the Assessment Team will usually take the opportunity to discuss the proposed Scope of Accreditation and to carry out a brief examination of the forensic laboratory's facilities.

As part of the examination, the Assessment Team may discuss any documented in-house methods used for activities that form part of the Scope of Accreditation and any in-house calibrations and/or tests used in support of accredited measurement activities.

This should provide evidence to the Assessment Team that such methods have been validated, as defined in Chapter 7, Section 7.5.5, and to allow any changes necessary to be made to the systems or procedures prior to the initial assessment. Also covered during the preassessment visit shall be the forensic laboratory's policy and procedures for estimating uncertainty of measurement, as defined in Chapter 7, Appendix 27.

During the preassessment visit, the Assessment Team may raise nonconformities where they identify any areas that appear to require attention to fulfil the requirements for Accreditation.

The forensic laboratory will be reminded that the preassessment visit is not a full assessment and will be advised of the structure and scope of the full assessment visit.

At the end of the preassessment visit, the Assessment Team shall make a report of their visit and its findings, including any nonconformities, to the AB. The report shall indicate:

- whether a further preassessment visit is recommended;
- whether plans for initial assessment of the forensic laboratory can proceed;
- specific reasons why plans cannot proceed; and
- whether an interlaboratory comparison (e.g. measurement audit) is needed.

A copy of the report of the preassessment visit shall be passed on to the forensic laboratory. At the same time, the Assessment Team will discuss timescales for the full assessment visit and may provisionally agree dates for it.

After the preassessment visit, the Lead Assessor shall determine:

- the composition of the full Assessment Team; and
- the effort (in man days) required for the initial assessment visit including time for preparation and standard postvisit activities.

This shall take into account all factors necessary to enable a reliable assessment of the forensic laboratory's competence to perform the full range of activities proposed for inclusion in its Scope of Accreditation, including;

- whether it is necessary to assess all activities, or if a representative sample can be selected;
- the need to assess all key activities; and
- handling of multisite locations, where necessary, to ensure all key activities are assessed.

This forms part of the ABs Contract Review procedure and shall be agreed and approved by an independent decision maker.

Preassessment visits are strictly prohibited from performing any consultancy services. This includes giving any advice on selecting any Corrective Actions or Preventive Actions (CAPAs) but can include discussing the appropriateness and sufficiency of a proposed CAPA.

19.2.13 Scheduling the initial on-site assessment

Once any outstanding CAPAs from the preassessment visit have been closed out, a forensic laboratory is ready, and able, to proceed to the Initial Assessment.

If a date has been provisionally agreed and it is still feasible, then this date will be confirmed, if it is not, another mutually agreed date shall be confirmed. If the scheduled date needs to be changed for any reason by the forensic laboratory, then it shall contact the AB and request an alternate date. The forensic laboratory is responsible for any costs associated with the date change.

An assessment usually takes between 1 and 5 days, depending on the size of the forensic laboratory being assessed and its Scope of Accreditation. Every effort is made to conduct all Assessments with as little disruption as possible to the forensic laboratory's normal operations.

A detailed visit plan shall be prepared indicating the section/activities/location(s) to be assessed by each Assessor and specify the calibrations/testing/sampling that each Assessor must witness during the visit, including any on-site activities and in-house calibrations, as necessary.

Copies of the visit plan shall be distributed to the forensic laboratory and to all of the Assessment Team; allowing all parties to raise any issues with the visit plan.

The assessment visit cannot be scheduled until all outstanding nonconformities have been addressed.

19.2.14 Logistics of the initial on-site assessment

Once the Assessment Team has been appointed and the date of the assessment visit agreed, the logistics of planning the visit shall be undertaken.

Typically, an AB shall make its own travel and accommodation arrangements, but assistance from the forensic laboratory may be required.

In addition to having the operations defined in the Scope of Accreditation ready for the assessment, the forensic laboratory shall arrange:

- a secure room or working area for the Assessment Team;
- all employees on the agenda for assessment to be available, or their alternates;
- refreshments, including lunch; and
- one or more 'Guides' appointed to ensure that the Assessment Team can get to the right places in the forensic laboratory at the right time and facilitate any requests for information.

Prior to arrival on-site, any other specific needs shall be advised to the forensic laboratory.

19.2.15   Opening meeting

At the beginning of all Assessments, an opening meeting is conducted. This is attended by the Assessment Team and relevant Top Management from the forensic laboratory.

This meeting is held at the start of the Assessment to:

- enable the Assessment Team and the forensic laboratory's Top Management and nominated representatives to become acquainted;
- to confirm the purpose of the Assessment;
- to remind the forensic laboratory of what is expected during the assessment;
- confirm Guides for the duration of the visit; and
- allow for any last-minute changes to the schedule (e.g. unavailability of an Auditee and replacement, security briefing—if not already carried out, health and safety briefing—if not already carried out, etc.).

It sets the scene for the Assessment and is chaired by the Lead Assessor and any questions about what is to occur during the on-site assessment should be resolved at this meeting.

The forensic laboratory shall ensure that the Assessment Team are taken on a brief tour of the forensic laboratory to familiarise the Assessment Team with the facility and to introduce them to the relevant employees in their work environment, if appropriate.

A typical Opening Meeting Agenda is defined in Chapter 4, Appendix 50.

19.2.16   Other meetings

When appropriate, or when requested by the forensic laboratory or the Assessment Team, a meeting shall be set up between the Assessment Team and the forensic laboratory nominated staff.

19.2.17   The Assessment

Following the opening meeting and tour, the Assessment Team shall start the Assessment.

The on-site Assessment is conducted at all forensic laboratory location(s) where work is performed that is in scope, or if not, a representative sample of them.

Witnessing of the testing and sampling activities carried out by the forensic laboratory form the most important part of the Assessment. Although the Assessment shall, as far as possible, assess current work being performed, the AB may request the forensic laboratory to provide a demonstration of some activities that are not currently being performed, to cover the range of tests for which the Scope of Accreditation is sought.

The Assessment Team shall use checklists provided by the AB to ensure that there are consistent assessments across all forensic laboratories being assessed.

Typically, the Lead Assessor shall examine the forensic laboratory's Management System and quality documentation with the forensic laboratory Quality Manager and any other appropriate staff, to verify that it meets the requirements of the relevant standard.

The Technical Assessors shall proceed according to the agreed agenda and examine the forensic laboratory's Management System in operation and the competence of the employees to perform specific activities. All components of the Management System involved shall be assessed. This will typically involve the following:

- examination of the Management System in action;
- reviews of quality and technical records;

- examination of equipment and facilities;
- interviews with staff;
- observing demonstrations of testing and work performed; and
- examination of tests and work performed.

They shall determine whether the treatment of measurement uncertainty is in accordance with international criteria and the specific requirements of the AB. It may not always be necessary to examine every procedure in operation in a forensic laboratory because of the similarities between some activities; however, the Technical Assessors shall verify the implementation of the working procedures listed in the Assessment Agenda.

They shall typically ask to see the equipment involved, the manufacturer's manuals, validation of testing, and establish the state of calibration of the equipment, where appropriate. They shall examine documentation concerning working procedures and testing in progress and will review associated records and reports/certificates.

During the Assessment, the Technical Assessors shall examine the processes for establishing traceability of measurements including any in-house calibrations and the results from participation in appropriate proficiency testing schemes and other quality control and quality assessment procedures. They shall also assess procedures used to establish the validity of methods used.

As well as examining equipment and processes, the Technical Assessors shall also assess the competence of the forensic laboratory employees performing the processes. The Technical Assessors shall require access to HR records for relevant forensic laboratory employees who routinely perform or affect the quality of the testing or calibration for which accreditation is sought. This may include:

- resumes;
- job descriptions of key personnel;
- training plans and records;
- copies of relevant certifications;
- competency evaluations; and
- proficiency evaluations.

The forensic laboratory shall ensure that it only provides information relevant to the Scope of Accreditation and does not divulge information that may violate the individual employee's rights to privacy.

The objective of on-site Assessment is to establish, by observation and examination, whether the forensic laboratory's work product meets the requirements of the relevant standard. Observations made shall be based on objective evidence and shall be recorded and verified with the relevant forensic laboratory employee.

19.2.18 Recording Assessment findings

As the Assessment progresses, each Assessor or Expert shall record their findings, these records shall provide objective evidence on which the Lead Assessor will base the recommendations for Accreditation to the AB. All ABs have forms for handwritten or electronically produced findings. Nonconformities shall be recorded on a Non-Conformity Report (NCR) or a Corrective Action Request (CAR), and the contents of a typical CAR are defined in Chapter 4, Appendix 49.

After the Assessment Team have completed their individual assignments, they shall meet to produce a coordinated view of the forensic laboratory's work. The Lead Assessor shall then compile the Assessment Report form based on the findings recorded by the individual Assessors. All nonconformities shall be graded and have objective evidence to support the finding. Different ABs use varying terms for grading of nonconformities, and an example is defined in Chapter 4, Section 4.10, though different ABs may use different terminology.[a] Examples for each category are defined in Appendix 3.

All Assessments shall have a formal Assessment Report produced before the Closing Meeting, or a short whilst after the end of the Assessment if agreed with the forensic laboratory. The Assessment Report shall:

- summarise the Assessors' findings;
- indicate key areas needing corrective or improvement action; and
- contain the Lead Assessor's recommendations about Accreditation.

The recommendation may be for:

- an unconditional offer of Accreditation;

---

a. ILAC-G20:2002, Guidelines on Grading of Non-Conformities gives details of the grading process.

- a conditional offer (e.g. subject to the satisfactory clearance of nonconformities); and
- a refusal for Accreditation.

In some cases, it may be appropriate to recommend that an offer of Accreditation be made for a reduced scope.

Report formats vary between ABs, but a typical Assessment Report contents is defined in Chapter 4, Appendix 52.

The Assessment Report may be left with the forensic laboratory at the Closing Meeting or may be produced within a fixed time period after the end of the Assessment. This process varies between ABs and is often subject to agreement between the parties. In some cases, a provisional report is produced and a final report is produced after closing out all of the nonconformities raised.

19.2.19 Factors affecting the recommendation

In deciding the recommendation for Accreditation, the Lead Assessor shall take into account the extent of competence and conformity within the forensic laboratory to the relevant standard found during the assessment.

if there are no nonconformities found, the Lead Assessor normally recommends that Accreditation be offered immediately to the forensic laboratory.

If there are some nonconformities found, the Lead Assessor normally recommends that Accreditation is offered subject to satisfactory action being taken by the forensic laboratory to address the nonconformities raised.

If there are one or more areas in which the extent of competence or conformity is not acceptable, but there are no overall major systems failures, the Lead Assessor may recommend accreditation for an appropriately reduced scope.

If the number and seriousness of the nonconformities are such that the forensic laboratory's Management System and organisation fails to demonstrate competence or conformity with the requirements of the relevant standard, the Lead Assessor's recommendation will be that Accreditation is refused, and that the forensic laboratory will be advised to discuss future actions with the AB.

19.2.20 Closing Meeting

The Accreditation Assessment concludes with a Closing Meeting held by the Lead Assessor and the Assessment Team and relevant forensic laboratory employees.

The purpose of the Closing Meeting is to formally present the Assessment conclusions, including any documented nonconformities.

The Lead Assessor shall present a summary of the results of the Assessment and informs the forensic laboratory Top Management of the recommendation that will be made to the AB regarding the granting of Accreditation.

The Lead Assessor chairs the Closing Meeting.

Depending on the ABs, an Assessment Report may be left with the forensic laboratory; otherwise, the report shall be sent within an agreed timescale to the forensic laboratory.

Whenever the report is produced, it shall list any nonconformities identified.

A typical Closing Meeting Agenda is defined in Chapter 4, Appendix 51.

On return to their office, the Lead Assessor shall submit the Assessment Report, with the recommendation for Accreditation to the AB.

19.2.21 Quality assurance of the Assessment Report

The AB shall undertake a quality review of the Assessment Report, including any nonconformities or comments documented by the Assessment Team.

The quality review of the Assessment Team's findings is an important element of the AB's internal quality control.

The purposes of the quality review shall include considering consistency of interpretations, appropriate relationships between the nonconformity(s) raised and the clause(s) to which the nonconformity is assigned, and to consider the recommended level assigned to each nonconformity raised by the Assessment Team.

If there are any changes to the Lead Auditor's recommendation already provided to the forensic laboratory, this shall be notified to them with the justification for the revision.

19.2.22 Addressing nonconformities

The forensic laboratory shall respond in writing to the AB within the specified period after the date of the on-site Assessment Report, on how it will address all documented nonconformities. A Corrective Action Plan shall include a list of actions, target completion dates, and names of persons responsible for discharging those actions.

When creating the Corrective Action Plan, the forensic laboratory shall reference each nonconformity by the item number shown on the on-site Assessment Report. There is no set standard form for a Corrective Action Plan. Corrective Action plans are derived from the formal audit response, and then have appropriate CAPAs raised as defined in Chapter 4, Section 4.10.

The forensic laboratory may ask for clarification of a nonconformity from either the Assessor (who raised it) at the Closing Meeting or from that AB at any time after the Closing Meeting.

The forensic laboratory may also challenge the validity of a nonconformity by writing to the Lead Assessor at the AB.

Where nonconformities have been raised, they shall be satisfactorily resolved before Accreditation can be granted.

Should close out take longer than the agreed time, the forensic laboratory may submit a revised Corrective Action Plan, providing evidence of resolved actions and a revised timescale for planned actions. The granting of an extension shall be at the AB's discretion. Typical close-out periods are defined in Appendix 4.

Where there are a substantial number of nonconformities raised, the AB may require an additional on-site assessment, at additional cost to the forensic laboratory, prior to granting Accreditation.

19.2.23 The Accreditation decision

Contrary to opinion, it is not the Lead Assessor that grants Accreditation status, but the AB, based on the recommendation of the Lead Assessor. The AB's Top Management is responsible for all Accreditation actions, including granting, renewing, suspending, and revoking any AB Accreditation.

The Accreditation decision is based on their review of information gathered during the Accreditation Assessment and a determination by the Lead Assessor as to whether, or not, all requirements for Accreditation have been fulfilled.

The evaluation process shall consider the forensic laboratory's record as a whole, including:

- information provided on the application;
- results of Management System documentation review;
- on-site assessment reports;
- actions taken by the forensic laboratory to correct nonconformities, where raised; and
- results of proficiency testing, if required.

Based on this evaluation, the AB shall determine whether or not the forensic laboratory should be Accredited. If the evaluation reveals nonconformities beyond those identified in the Assessment process, the AB shall inform the forensic laboratory in writing of the nonconformities. In this case, the forensic laboratory shall respond to the AB as if it were the outcome of the Assessment Report.

All nonconformities shall be resolved to the AB's satisfaction before Accreditation can be granted.

Once the decision to grant Accreditation has been taken (whether in full or in reduced scope). The AB shall advise the forensic laboratory in writing with the proposed Accreditation details. This will include the Scope of Accreditation and the Schedule. The forensic laboratory shall formally agree, in writing, to this prior to the granting of Accreditation.

19.2.24 Accreditation certificate

Once the forensic laboratory has been approved for Accreditation, it shall receive a communication granting of Accreditation and the Accreditation certificate.

The certificate shall:

- bear a unique certificate number;
- identify the forensic laboratory and the address(es) to which the Scope of Accreditation refers;
- date when the Accreditation was granted; and
- the date of expiration of Accreditation.

In addition to a Certificate of Accreditation, the forensic laboratory shall receive a corresponding Scope of Accreditation document. The scope document will specify the discipline(s) and each category in which the forensic laboratory is accredited.

Although presented to the forensic laboratory, each Accreditation Certificate and Scope of Accreditation document remains the property of the AB. Failure to remain compliant with Accreditation standards could result in the revocation of Accreditation and the return of the certificate to the AB.

Some ABs encourage the publicising of Accreditations gained and actively support a presentation ceremony with attendant media interest.

19.2.25 The Accreditation cycle

To maintain Accreditation, the forensic laboratory shall comply with the AB's requirements for maintaining Accreditation, and this may vary between ABs.

Accreditation is granted for a renewable period defined by the AB provided that the forensic laboratory:

- continues to meet all applicable Management System standards;
- continues to meet all applicable AB requirements; and
- submits to scheduled on-site Surveillance Assessments.

Once the forensic laboratory has achieved Accreditation, it is necessary for it to continue to meet the requirement of the standard(s) under which it was Accredited for the duration of the Accreditation cycle.

The forensic laboratory shall be advised by its AB of the dates for planned Surveillance or Re-Assessment Assessments. However, some ABs may reserve the right to make an unannounced visit at any time.

19.2.26 Surveillance visits

All ABs have an established and documented programme for carrying out periodic surveillance activities and surveillance visits at sufficiently close intervals to ensure that the forensic laboratory continues to comply with all Accreditation criteria.

The forensic laboratory shall be subject to a cycle of surveillance visits, typically at yearly intervals, though the first one after initial Accreditation may have a shorter interval. This interval is shorter than other surveillance intervals to avoid a commonly occurring problem that, after the initial Assessment, there is a decrease in quality awareness post granting the Accreditation Certificate. The second and subsequent surveillance visits will typically be on a 12-month cycle and certainly no longer than 18 months.

In deciding on the interval of the surveillance visits and related activities for the forensic laboratory, the AB may take into account the forensic laboratory's performance at previous surveillance visits. A minimum of three consecutive visits with good performance may lead to fewer surveillance visits in the future. Conversely, if the forensic laboratory's performance deteriorates, the frequency of surveillance activities (and visits) may be increased.

An AB may decide to conduct the surveillance visits without prior notice or with short notice only (less than 2 weeks) as a mechanism to lower the frequency of visits.

Surveillance visits shall include such activities as:

- enquiries from the AB to the forensic laboratory on aspects concerning its Accreditation;
- declarations by the forensic laboratory with respect to their operations;
- requests to the forensic laboratory to provide documents and records, including updates from Quality Manuals;
- assessing the forensic laboratory's performance; and
- other means of monitoring the forensic laboratory's performance.

The purpose of a surveillance visit is to determine whether or not the forensic laboratory is continuing to fulfil the requirements for Accreditation.

At the Opening Meeting, the Lead Assessor shall establish whether all significant changes in the forensic laboratory's status or operations have been notified to the AB and shall confirm that there are no outstanding CAPAs from the previous visit.

If the surveillance visit reveals that there have been significant changes in the forensic laboratory's operations, e.g. to employees, equipment, or the range of services available, the Lead Assessor shall record these matters. Assessors shall check that the changes have not lessened the forensic laboratory's capabilities and that they have already been fully notified to the AB.

During a Surveillance Visit, the Assessors will not check the whole operational system, as they did on the Initial Assessment, but a representative sample so that the entire forensic laboratory is covered during the Accreditation cycle. The scope of surveillance visits is planned based on the outcome of previous visits. The Lead Assessor shall normally include an assessment of Management Review, Audits, and Complaint Records at each Surveillance Visit.

At the conclusion of a Surveillance Visit, the Lead Assessor shall produce an Assessment Report and make a recommendation to the AB on the forensic laboratory's continuing Accreditation. Where a number of nonconformities are found and that the forensic laboratory is not able to demonstrate that it is conforming with the requirements of the relevant standard, then sanctions shall be recommended.

19.2.27   Re-assessments

Unlike a surveillance visit, a re-assessment visit shall involve a comprehensive re-examination of the forensic laboratory's Management System and testing activities and will be similar in format and detail to the Initial Assessment.

All ABs have a documented process for performing re-assessments, including the time interval between the initial assessment and re-assessment and between re-assessments.

This time period should not exceed 5 years, but different ABs may use shorter time periods. Shorter time periods are typically used if the AB does not perform surveillance visits, but just performs re-assessments.

The process for undertaking the Initial Assessment is followed for re-assessments.

At the end of the re-assessment visit, the Lead Assessor (as with an Initial Assessment) shall make a recommendation to the AB on the continuing Accreditation of the forensic laboratory.

Sanctions shall be recommended where the number and seriousness of the nonconformities identified in the forensic laboratory's Management System indicate that it is not able to demonstrate that the requirements of the relevant standard continue to be met.

19.2.28   Proficiency Testing

There are a number of different Proficiency Testing programmes in place throughout the world. Some are Accredited, some are not, and each will have its own rules and specific requirements.

Proficiency testing is a component of the Surveillance process, but it cannot replace surveillance visits as it usually only covers a small part of the scope for which the forensic laboratory is Accredited, and therefore cannot reflect the overall performance of the forensic laboratory and its quality system.

As part of ISO/IEC 17025 Accreditation, a forensic laboratory is expected to select appropriate schemes, and implement them.

In addition to this, interlaboratory comparisons shall be carried out, where appropriate. However, the forensic laboratory must ensure that they do not breach any client confidentiality agreements or Non-Disclosure Agreements in this process.

19.2.29   Changes to the scope

The forensic laboratory can request a change to its scope of Accreditation. This can be to increase or decrease scope or temporarily suspend some part of the Accreditation.

Especially in the case of extensions of scope, the forensic laboratory shall give advance warning to the AB of the intention to increase the scope. It is recommended that, on cost grounds and minimising business interruption, extension to the scope is assessed as part of the ongoing surveillance or re-assessment visits.

All ABs have forms for this and will require specific documentation to be produced for extensions of scope.

Any extension to the Scope of Accreditation may require the AB to check to determine any additional technical expertise required for the visit that handles the scope extension.

If the change of scope is urgent, then an AB can arrange a special interim visit to address this issue.

All requests for changing scope shall be made in writing to the AB.

19.2.30   Special Interim Assessments

If an AB receives any written claims or complaints creating doubts concerning the forensic laboratory's conformity with the relevant standards, then it shall carry out surveillance activities (inquiries) or even a Special Interim Assessment as soon as possible after it becomes aware of the issue. The AB shall decide the required action.

Where a Special Interim Assessment is undertaken, the scope of the Assessment shall be determined by the AB, based on the nature of the issue(s) brought to their attention.

The forensic laboratory may be required to provide relevant documentation to the AB prior to their visit. The findings of the Assessment Team shall be reported to the forensic laboratory's Top Management, as normal, and also to the AB for consideration.

The forensic laboratory Top Management shall be notified of any sanctions under consideration for the nonconformity and shall have the right to make representations in person at any subsequent meeting in which the forensic laboratory's alleged nonconformity is considered. The AB shall decide what, if any, sanction will be imposed. Sanctions are defined in Section 19.2.33.

There may be some occasions when the forensic laboratory itself requests a Special Interim Assessment, reasons for this could include:

- extensions of scope not carried out at Surveillance Visit time;
- laboratory relocation; or
- other management needs.

19.2.31 Conformity records

The forensic laboratory shall generate and maintain appropriate records of conformity with all applicable requirements of the Accreditation programme throughout each Accreditation Cycle.

Once the forensic laboratory becomes Accredited, it shall maintain records to demonstrate conformity with the relevant standard's requirements, as defined in Chapter 4, Section 4.7.5.

Record retention requirements are defined by the AB, relevant standards, as well as legislation, regulation, and good business practice that ensure availability of records for Assessment purposes and the ability to dispose of out-of-date records.

19.2.32 Disclosure of nonconformity

Once the forensic laboratory becomes Accredited, it is required to remain conformant to the requirements of the Accreditation programme through each Accreditation cycle.

The forensic laboratory is required to disclose to the AB all substantive occurrences of nonconformity within a defined period after determining that the nonconformity has occurred.

Disclosure of such occurrences shall be in writing to the AB and include a summary of the occurrence(s) and a statement of actions taken or being taken by the forensic laboratory to:

- determine the root cause of the nonconformity;
- determine who may have been impacted by the occurrence(s);
- notify those who are potentially impacted by the occurrence(s); and
- appropriately correct and/or eliminate the cause of the occurrence(s).

Where a nonconformity occurs, it shall be handled using the forensic laboratory's Incident Management procedures, raising one or more a CAPAs.

The AB may undertake a Special Interim Assessment to further investigate the nonconformities and/or impose sanctions as appropriate to the nonconformity.

19.2.33 Sanctions

ABs recognise that unforeseen circumstances may cause a forensic laboratory to experience temporary nonconformity with some of the requirements.

When it is recognised that a forensic laboratory is experiencing, or has experienced, a period of nonconformity, it shall take appropriate corrective action(s) to return to conformity.

Failure to take timely, appropriate, and required corrective actions regarding nonconformity may result in any of the following sanctions:

- **Probation** for a specified time during which the forensic laboratory shall comply with specified requirements and/or conditions;
- **Suspension** for a specified time during which the forensic laboratory shall demonstrate that the issue/problem has been remediated.
- **Revocation (also called Withdrawal in some cases)** for a specified time during which the forensic laboratory shall address any nonconformities and after which it must pass an Assessment prior to being re-instated.

If any of these sanctions are applied by the AB, the forensic laboratory shall be advised as to their practical implications. This may include the prohibiting of displaying or advertising the AB's Logo or Accreditations Marks.

The AB may require the forensic laboratory to return of its Accreditation Certificate or Scope of Accreditation/Schedule documents at this stage.

19.2.33.1 Appeal of sanction

If the AB classifies the forensic laboratory's Accreditation status as probationary, suspended, or revoked, they may appeal against the sanction imposed. Typically, the forensic laboratory Top Management would do this.

Written reasons for appeal shall be filed with the AB within a set period of the decision to apply a sanction. Usually, the forensic laboratory Top Management will have the right to appear in person before the AB to make representations.

19.2.33.2 Removal of sanction

Probation and suspension sanctions shall be removed when the forensic laboratory can demonstrate to the satisfaction of the AB that the nonconformities which resulted in probation or suspension have been corrected.

This may require a Special Interim Assessment or other measures defined by the AB.

If the forensic laboratory has had its Accreditation revoked, it may need to re-apply for Accreditation and re-submit to the entire Assessment and Accreditation process again.

19.2.34 Voluntary termination of Accreditation

The forensic laboratory may at any time terminate its Accredited status by advising the AB in writing of their desire so to do.

When the AB receives the forensic laboratory's request for termination, it shall:

- terminate their Accreditation;
- formally notify the forensic laboratory that its Accreditation has been terminated;
- instruct the forensic laboratory to return its Certificate and Scope of Accreditation;
- instruct the forensic laboratory to remove any related Accreditation logos or marks from any forensic laboratory material; and
- remove the forensic laboratory from its register of Accredited Laboratories and any other tasks it is required to undertake to terminate the Accreditation.

If the forensic laboratory wishes to reapply for Accreditation, it will reapply as above.

19.2.35 Appeals

The forensic laboratory has the right to appeal at any time during any Assessment process. An appeals process is present in all ABs, and this process shall be followed. This will vary between ABs.

19.2.36 Obligations of Accredited Laboratories

As a condition of Accreditation, a forensic laboratory shall inform the AB within a defined period of any significant changes relevant to the forensic laboratory's Accreditation, in any aspect of its status or operation relating to:

- its legal, commercial, ownership, or organisational status;
- the organisation, top management, and key personnel;
- main policies;
- resources and premises;
- Scope of Accreditation; and
- other such matters that may affect the ability of the forensic laboratory to fulfil requirements for Accreditation.

A forensic laboratory's obligations shall also, depending on the AB, include:

- a commitment to fulfil continually the requirements for Accreditation within the forensic laboratory's Scope of Accreditation, including an agreement to adapt to changes in the requirements in accordance with schedules adopted by the AB;
- affording such accommodation and cooperation as is necessary to enable the AB to verify fulfilment of requirements for Accreditation;
- providing access to information, documents, and records as necessary for inspections or Assessments and maintenance of Accreditation;
- where applicable, providing access to documents or other information that provides insight into the level of independence and impartiality of the forensic laboratory from any related body;

- arranging the witnessing of the forensic laboratory services when requested by the AB;
- claiming Accreditation only with respect to the scope for which the forensic laboratory has been granted Accreditation; and
- not using its Accreditation in such a manner as to bring the AB into disrepute.

19.2.37 Obligations of the AB

The AB shall make publicly available information about the current status of the Accreditations that it has granted. This shall be maintained to ensure that it is correct and current. The following information shall be published:

- name and address of each Accredited organisation;
- dates of granting Accreditation and expiry dates, as applicable; and
- Scope of Accreditation.

  The AB shall:

- provide the Accredited organisations with information about suitable ways to obtain traceability of measurement results in relation to the scope for which Accreditation is provided;
- provide information about international arrangements in which it is involved, where applicable; and
- give due notice of any changes to its requirements for Accreditation. It shall take account of views expressed by interested parties before deciding on the precise form and effective date of the changes. Following a decision on, and publication of, the changed requirements, it shall verify that each of their Accredited organisations carry out any necessary adjustments.

19.2.38 Use of the AB's logos and marks

Every AB, as the owner of the Accreditation logos and marks that are intended for use by the AB's Accredited organisations, will have rules for their use. These may vary between different ABs, and compliance with the rules for use of the logos and marks shall be a requirement for a forensic laboratory's continued Accreditation. Failure to comply with these conditions may result in suspension or revocation of their Accreditation. These will include requirements such as:

- the ability to use the AB's logos and marks is granted to the forensic laboratory for the limited purpose of announcing their Accredited status, and for use on reports that describe only activities within the Scope of Accreditation;
- when a forensic laboratory has applied for Accreditation, but not yet achieved it may make reference to its applicant status. At this time, a forensic laboratory shall not use the AB's logos or marks in a manner that implies Accreditation;
- a forensic laboratory shall have a policy and procedure for controlling the use of the AB's Logos and Marks, based on the requirements of the AB;
- the AB's logos and marks shall not be used in a manner that brings the AB into disrepute or misrepresents a forensic laboratory's Scope of Accreditation or Accredited status;
- when the AB's logos and marks are used to reference a forensic laboratory's Accredited status, they shall be used only in accordance with the AB's rules governing the use of their logo and mark, including and associated captions;
- the terms *certified* or *registered* shall not be used when referencing their AB Accreditation or conformity to a standard. The correct term is ***Accredited***;
- a forensic laboratory shall not use the AB's logo or mark in any way that the AB may consider misleading or unauthorised; and
- a forensic laboratory must cease to use the AB's logo mark if they are under a sanction or have withdrawn from the AB's Accreditation scheme.

19.2.39 Misuse of the AB's logo and mark

19.2.39.1 By an Accredited Laboratory

Misuse of marks and logos may be identified when the Assessment Team perform one of the Assessments in the Accreditation cycle.

If this is the case, then the circumstance of the misuse shall be recorded in the Assessment Report, and the Lead Assessor shall advise the forensic laboratory of the misuse at the time of the Assessment, and this will be raised as a nonconformity, requiring corrective action to be taken.

Alternatively, the AB may receive correspondence about alleged logo or mark misuse. In this case, the AB shall investigate the allegation. If the AB determines that the forensic laboratory is misusing its logo or mark, it will take such action as it considers appropriate. This may include:

- requests for corrective action;
- suspension of Accreditation;
- revocation of Accreditation; and
- legal action.

Continued or persistent mark or logo misuse may lead to permanent revocation of the Certificate of Accreditation.

19.2.39.2 By nonclients

Alternatively, the AB may receive correspondence about alleged logo or mark misuse by a nonclient. The AB shall investigate and take the appropriate action; however, this will not include the sanctions possible if the alleged offender was one of their Accredited forensic laboratories. Typical recourse will include direct resolution with the alleged offender.

If that fails, recourse to the appropriate bodies shall be undertaken (e.g. Legal action, etc.).

19.3 Certification for a forensic laboratory

There are a number of different ISO Standard certifications that a forensic laboratory can achieve and the ones addressed in this book are those defined in Section 19.1.4.2.

Like Accreditation, the process of gaining Certification for any of these standards is broadly similar for any standard using any CB throughout the world. However, different CBs may have different requirements based on their scopes or on the jurisdiction within which they operate.

This is a generic approach below.

19.3.1 Self-evaluation prior to application

Whilst it may not be a mandatory requirement for Certification, it is a sensible approach to perform a self-assessment as preparation for the Certification process. This shall determine whether a forensic laboratory's processes, procedures, and records meet the requirements of the Certification sought.

This may require the:

- purchase of a number of standards; and
- completion of self-assessment forms for use prior to seeking Certification and undertake any identified CAPAs arising from the self-evaluation process.

A forensic laboratory may choose to undertake the self-assessment in-house or contract a third-party service provider to perform the task on their behalf.

19.3.2 Selecting a CB

Once the required Certification(s) have been agreed, the forensic laboratory shall:

1. research the market to see what CBs provide the required Certification services.
2. obtain marketing materials from each of the possible CBs to determine the range of services that they provide.
3. research other forensic laboratories and other organisations to determine the CBs that they have used and their opinion of the services provided.
4. create a shortlist of three possible CBs from whom to obtain quotations for the Certification(s) required.
5. if possible, a CB that provides all of the required Certification services required shall be chosen. This will allow integrated Certification Audits to be carried out, with associated cost savings and a CB who knows all aspects of the forensic laboratory's business.

Note

Where a forensic laboratory already has a relationship with a CB, the first approach should be made to that CB for additional services if they can provide them. This will have the benefit of reduced costs for integrated audits and the fact that the CB already 'knows' their client's business.

19.3.3 Certification information to be made available

To assist in selection of a CB, all CBs shall make publicly available, and update at adequate intervals, the following:

- a detailed description of the initial and continuing Certification activity, including the application, initial audits, surveillance audits, and the process for granting, maintaining, reducing, extending, suspending, withdrawing Certification and Re-Certification;
- the normative requirements for certification;
- information about the fees for application, initial Certification, and continuing Certification;
- the CB's requirements for prospective clients;
  - to comply with Certification requirements;
  - to make all necessary arrangements for the conduct of the audits, including provision for examining documentation and the access to all processes and areas, records, and personnel for the purposes of initial certification, surveillance, recertification, and resolution of complaints; and
  - to make provisions, where applicable, to accommodate the presence of observers (e.g. Certification Auditors, Accreditation Service Observers, or Trainee Auditors).
- documents describing the rights and duties of Certified clients, including requirements, when making reference to its Certification in communication of any kind in line with the CB's Rules and Regulations for Logo and Mark Usage;
- information on procedures for handling complaints and appeals;
- a description of the rights and obligations of a CB's clients; and
- information on the clients that the CB has certified in a publicly available register.

From this information, an informed choice of CB can be made by a forensic laboratory.

19.3.4 Appointing a CB

Once the quotation(s) from the shortlist of CBs for the provision of Certification services have been received by a forensic laboratory with the range of services offered, the forensic laboratory shall be in the position to make an informed choice about the selection of an appropriate CB.

19.3.5 Scope of Certification

The form and definition of the Scope of Certification shall depend on the Certification(s) sought by the forensic laboratory.

It is up to the applicant (i.e. the forensic laboratory) to define the scope in their own words to meet the requirements for defining the Scope of Certification in line with the requirements of the relevant standard(s).

19.3.6 Application

The CB requires the forensic laboratory's Authorised Representative to provide the necessary information to enable it to establish the following:

- the desired Scope of Certification;
- the forensic laboratory's general features, including:
  - its legal name;
  - the address(es) of its physical location(s) in the scope;
  - significant aspects of its process and operations; and
  - any relevant legal obligations.
- general information, about the forensic laboratory relevant to its scope for Certification(s) being sought; and
- the standard(s) for which the forensic laboratory is seeking Certification.

19.3.7 Fees for Certification

Fees will vary for each specific part of the Assessment between CBs in different jurisdictions and may even be for different standards.

Additionally, fees will normally change over time.

For this reason, no details of fees are given.

19.3.8   Processing applications

Upon receipt of the forensic laboratory's application for Certification, the CB will:

- log the application;
- acknowledge the receipt of the application in writing (typically email these days) to the forensic laboratory;
- confirm payment of fees;
- review the forensic laboratory's application, to ensure that:
  - the application is complete;
  - correct fees are paid.

Note

Where the application is unclear or incomplete, the CB shall request further clarification or documents until they are satisfied that the application is complete.

Additionally, the CB will check to see that they have fully understood the forensic laboratory's requirements.

19.3.9   Assigning the Lead Assessor

Note

For all Management System Assessments, the application of ISO 19011—Guidelines for auditing Management Systems—is used.

After reviewing the forensic laboratory's application and determining that it is complete, the CB shall assign a Lead Assessor to manage the application (this is often also referred to as the Assessment Manager). The Lead Assessor shall have an understanding of the forensic laboratory and their operations and shall be able to discuss with the forensic laboratory's Authorised Representative any matters that may arise during the processing of the application.

Most CBs try to ensure that the Lead Assessor is responsible for processing the forensic laboratory's application through the Certification life cycle for at least the first full cycle.

The Lead Assessor Shall perform the contract review and is responsible, for selecting and appointing the Assessment Team.

19.3.10   Review of the application

Before proceeding with the Assessment, the Lead Assessor will review the application. This will check that the information supplied by the forensic laboratory and its Management System is sufficient for the conduct of the Assessment and that:

- the requirements for the forensic laboratory's Certification(s) are clearly defined and documented;
- any known difference in understanding between the CB and the forensic laboratory is resolved;
- the CB has the competence and ability to perform the required certification activities;
- the Scope of Certification(s) sought, the location(s) of the applicant organisation's operations, time required to complete Assessments, and any other issues influencing the certification activities shall be taken into account (language, safety conditions, threats to impartiality, etc.); and
- records of the justification for the decision to undertake the Assessment are maintained.

Based on this review, the CB shall determine the competences it needs to include in its Assessment Team and for the Certification decision.

19.3.11   Appointing the Assessment Team

The Assessment Team comprises a Lead Assessor and as many Assessors or Experts as are necessary to provide the technical expertise to assess the forensic laboratory's conformity with the relevant standard(s) for which it wants to gain Certification.

Technical Assessors and Experts shall be selected on the basis of their professional and academic achievements, experience in digital forensics, experience in the relevant standards and communications skills. They shall evaluate all information collected from the forensic laboratory and to conduct the Assessment at the forensic laboratory and any other sites where activities to be covered by the Scope of Certification are performed.

Assessors shall be assigned to conduct an on-site Assessment of the forensic laboratory on the basis of how well their experience matches requirements of the standards for which Certification is sought.

The forensic laboratory has the right to object to the appointment of any Assessor(s) or Expert(s) and, in such cases, the CB shall endeavour to offer an alternative. In the event that a suitable alternative cannot be identified, or the grounds for objection are considered to be unreasonable, the CB will typically reserve the right to appoint the original Assessor(s) and Expert(s) to the Assessment Team.

19.3.12 Assessment duration

As part of the Assessment Plan that the CB sends to the forensic laboratory, the CB shall determine the time needed to complete the forensic laboratory's Assessment cycle. This shall be derived from consideration of:

- the requirements of the relevant Management System standard;
- the forensic laboratory's size and complexity;
- the technological and regulatory context in which the forensic laboratory operates;
- any outsourcing of any activities included in the scope of the forensic laboratory's Management System(s);
- the results of any prior assessments; and
- number of sites and multisite considerations, assuming the forensic laboratory has more than one site in Scope of Certification.

In the case of ISO/IEC 27001, guidance is given in ISO/IEC 27006: Information technology—Security techniques—Requirements for bodies providing audit and Certification of information security Management Systems. ISO 27006 Annex C gives details of these time requirements that may be used.

Once the Assessment Plan has been defined, it shall be sent to the forensic laboratory in advance of any Assessment so that the forensic laboratory can meet the requirements of the plan.

19.3.13 Optional preassessment visits

Note

Whilst not a part of the formal assessment, the forensic laboratory can request a short preassessment visit if they choose. These visits are usually to review and discuss any specific concerns that the forensic laboratory may have about their current conformity status. They are also called 'Gap Analysis Assessments' by some CBs.

The preassessment visit is usually carried out by the Lead Assessor (accompanied by one or more Assessors where appropriate) and is usually completed in 1 day.

The preassessment visit allows discussion with the forensic laboratory's Top Management on the extent to which the forensic laboratory's Management Systems appear to fulfil the requirements for Certification to the relevant Standard(s).

In ISO 27001, it could be used for ensuring that the ISMS is appropriate, prior to undertaking a full document review (Stage 1 audit). Other ISO management standards can also use preassessment visits as a 'gap analysis' of their current processes.

As well as examining the documented Management System(s) prepared by the forensic laboratory, the Assessment Team shall take the opportunity to discuss the proposed Scope of Certification and to carry out a brief examination of the forensic laboratory's facilities.

During the preassessment visit, the Assessment Team may raise nonconformities where there are any areas that appear to require attention to fulfil the requirements for Certification.

The forensic laboratory shall be reminded that the preassessment visit is not a full assessment and advised of the structure and scope of the Stage 1 Assessment visit.

At the end of the preassessment visit, the Assessment Team shall make a report of their visit and its findings, including any nonconformities, to the CB. The report shall indicate:

- whether a further preassessment visit is recommended;
- whether plans for the Stage 1 Assessment for the forensic laboratory can proceed; or
- specific reasons why plans cannot proceed.

A copy of the report of the preassessment visit shall be passed on to the forensic laboratory, this is usually in the standard form for Stage 1 and Stage 2 Audits, as defined in Chapter 4, Appendix 52. At the same time, the Assessment Team shall discuss timescales for the Stage 1 Assessment visit and may provisionally agree dates for it.

After the preassessment visit, the Lead Assessor will determine:

- the composition of the full Assessment Team; and
- the effort (in man days) required for the Stage 1 Assessment visit including time for preparation and standard postvisit activities.

This shall take into account all factors necessary to enable a reliable Assessment of the forensic laboratory's competence to perform the full range of activities proposed for inclusion in its Scope of Certification, including,

- whether it is necessary to assess all activities, or if a representative sample can be selected;
- the need to assess all key activities; and
- handling of multisite locations, where necessary, to ensure all key activities are assessed.

Preassessment visits are strictly prohibited from performing any consultancy services. This includes giving any advice on selecting any CAPAs but can include discussing the appropriateness and sufficiency of a proposed CAPA.

19.3.14 Scheduling the Stage 1 Assessment

Once any outstanding CAPAs from the preassessment visit (if raised and the visit has taken place) have been closed out, the forensic laboratory is ready, and able, to proceed to the Stage 1 Assessment.

If a date has been provisionally agreed and it is still feasible, then this date shall be confirmed, if it is not, another mutually agreed date shall be confirmed. If the scheduled date needs to be changed for any reason by the forensic laboratory, then it shall contact the CB and request an alternate date. The forensic laboratory shall be responsible for any costs associated with the date change.

The Stage 1 Assessment can take place off-site or on-site.

A Stage 1 Assessment for a single standard usually takes between 1 and 5 days, this will depend on the:

- size of the forensic laboratory being assessed;
- Scope of Certification; and
- number of standards against which Certification is sought.

Every effort shall be made to conduct all Assessment with as little disruption as possible to the forensic laboratory's normal operations.

A detailed visit plan shall be prepared indicating the section/activities/location(s) to be assessed by each Assessor and specify the activities that each Assessor shall want to witness during the visit.

Copies of the visit plan to the forensic laboratory shall be distributed to the forensic laboratory and to all of the Assessment Team; allowing all parties to raise any issues with the visit plan.

The Stage 1 Assessment visit shall not be scheduled until all outstanding nonconformities have been addressed.

19.3.15 Logistics of the Stage 1 Assessment

Once the Assessment Team has been appointed and the date of the Assessment visit agreed, the logistics of planning the visit shall be undertaken.

Typically, a CB makes its own travel and accommodation arrangements, but assistance from the forensic laboratory may be required.

In addition to having the operations defined in the Scope of Certification ready for the Assessment, the forensic laboratory shall arrange:

- a secure room or working area for the Assessment Team;
- all employees on the agenda for assessment to be available, or their alternates;
- refreshments, including lunch; and
- one or more 'Guides' appointed to ensure that the Assessment Team can get to the right places in the forensic laboratory at the right time and facilitate any requests for information.

Prior to arrival on site, any other specific needs shall be advised to the forensic laboratory.

Where the Stage 1 Assessment is to be carried out remotely at the CB's offices, the logistics will be much simpler.

19.3.16 Opening meeting

At the beginning of all Assessments, an opening meeting shall be conducted. This shall be attended by the Assessment Team and relevant Top Management from the forensic laboratory.

This meeting shall be held at the start of the Assessment to:

- enable the Assessment Team and the forensic laboratory's Top Management and nominated representatives to become acquainted;
- to confirm the purpose of the Assessment;
- to remind the forensic laboratory of what is expected during the assessment;
- confirm Guides for the duration of the visit; and
- allow for any last-minute changes to the schedule (e.g. unavailability of an Auditee and replacement, security briefing— if not already carried out, health and safety briefing—if not already carried out, etc.).

It sets the scene for the Assessment and is chaired by the Lead Assessor and any questions about what is to occur during the on-site Assessment shall be resolved at this meeting.

The forensic laboratory shall ensure that the Assessment Team are taken on a brief tour of the laboratory to familiarise the Assessment team with the facility and to introduce them to the forensic laboratory employees.

19.3.17 Other meetings

When appropriate, or when requested by the forensic laboratory, a meeting can be set up between the Assessment Team and the forensic laboratory nominated employees.

19.3.18 Stage 1 Assessment

Note

These are often referred to as Documentation or Initial Audits.

The process for carrying out a Stage 1 Assessment should be consistent across all CBs. Its purpose is to:

- assess the forensic laboratory's Integrated Management System documentation;
- evaluate the forensic laboratory's location and site-specific conditions and to undertake discussions with their authorised employees to determine their preparedness for the Stage 2 Assessment;
- review the forensic laboratory's status and understanding regarding requirements of the standard(s) for which Certification is sought, in particular with respect to the identification of key performance or significant aspects, processes, objectives, and operation of the forensic laboratory's Integrated Management System;
- collect necessary information regarding the forensic laboratory's Scope of the Management System(s), processes, and location(s), with related statutory and regulatory aspects and compliance requirements (e.g. quality, environmental, legal, associated risks, etc.);
- review the allocation of resources for the Stage 2 Assessment and agree with the forensic laboratory about the details of the Stage 2 Assessment;
- provide a focus for planning for the Stage 2 Assessment by gaining a sufficient understanding of the forensic laboratory's Management System(s) and on-site operations in the context of possible significant aspects; and
- evaluate if the Internal Audits and Management Review are being planned and performed, and that the level of implementation of the Management System(s) substantiates that the forensic laboratory is ready for the Stage 2 Assessment.

19.3.19 Recording Stage 1 Assessment findings

As the Assessment progresses, each Assessor, assuming there are more than one for the Stage 1 Assessment, shall record their findings and these records shall provide objective evidence on which the Lead Assessor will base the recommendations for Certification to the CB.

After the Assessment Team has completed their individual assignments, they meet to produce a coordinated view of the forensic laboratory's work. The Lead Assessor shall compile the Assessment Report form based on the findings recorded by the individual Assessors. All nonconformities shall be graded and have objective evidence to support the finding. Different CBs may use varying terms for grading of nonconformities, and an example is defined in Chapter 4, Section 4.10.

All Assessments shall have a formal Assessment Report produced before the Closing Meeting or a short whilst after the end of the Assessment if agreed with the forensic laboratory. The Assessment Report shall:

- summarise the Assessors' findings;
- indicate key areas needing corrective or improvement action; and
- contain the Lead Assessor's recommendations about Certification.

Report formats may vary between CBs, but a typical Assessment Report content is defined in Chapter 4, Appendix 52.

The Assessment Report may be left with the forensic laboratory at the Closing Meeting or may be produced within a fixed time period after the end of the Assessment. This process varies between CBs and is often subject to agreement between the parties. In some cases, a provisional report shall be produced and a final report shall be produced after closing out all of the nonconformities raised.

19.3.20   Joint Assessments

Where the forensic laboratory is seeking more than one Certification or wishes to add an additional one to those that they already have, they can, if the CB agrees, combine Assessments for more than one Management System.

Where more than one Management System is to undergo Certification, it may be that the Stage 1 and Stage 2 Assessments can be combined as well as for the Surveillance or Triennial Review Assessments.

Joint Assessments require more planning and logistical support unless a single Assessor is carrying out the Joint Assessment.

19.3.21   Factors affecting the recommendation for a Stage 2 Assessment

In deciding the recommendation for progressing to Stage 2 Assessment, the Lead Assessor shall take into account the extent of competence and conformity within the forensic laboratory to the standard(s) to which they are applying for Certification against.

Where there are some Major Non-Conformities found, the Lead Assessor normally recommends that progress to a Stage 2 Assessment is delayed until the Major Non-Conformities are addressed. Any agreed CAPAs to address any nonconformities raised at the Stage 1 Assessment will be automatically reviewed and checked during the Stage 2 Assessment.

19.3.22   Closing Meeting

The Stage 1 Assessment concludes with a Closing Meeting held by the Lead Assessor and the Assessment Team and relevant forensic laboratory Top Management and employees.

The purpose of the Closing Meeting is to formally present the assessment conclusions, including any documented nonconformities.

The Lead Assessor shall present a summary of the results of the Assessment and informs the forensic laboratory Top Management of the recommendation that will be made to the CB.

Depending on the CB, an Assessment Report may be left with the forensic laboratory; otherwise, the report will be sent within an agreed timescale to the forensic laboratory.

Whatever report is produced, it will list any nonconformities identified.

A typical Closing Meeting Agenda is defined in Chapter 4, Appendix 51.

Immediately after the Closing Meeting, the Lead Assessor shall submit the Assessment Report to the CB, with the recommendation for either progressing to a Stage 2 Assessment or delaying it until all outstanding nonconformities are closed out.

19.3.23   Quality assurance of the Assessment Report

The CB shall undertake a quality review of all Assessment Reports, including any nonconformities or comments documented by the Assessment Team.

The quality review of the Assessment Team's findings is an important element of the CB's internal quality control.

The purposes of the quality review shall include considering consistency of interpretations, appropriate relationships between the nonconformity(s) raised and the clause(s) to which the nonconformity is assigned, and to consider the recommended level assigned to each nonconformity raised by the Assessment Team.

If there are any changes to the Lead Auditor's recommendation already provided to the forensic laboratory, this shall be notified to the forensic laboratory with the justification for the revision.

19.3.24 Addressing nonconformities

The forensic laboratory shall be informed of any nonconformities raised by the Assessment Team during the Stage 1 Assessment, and these nonconformities shall be documented in the Stage 1 Assessment Report.

The forensic laboratory shall respond in writing to the CB within the specified period after the date of the Stage 1 Assessment Report, addressing all documented nonconformities. A Corrective Action Plan shall include a list of actions, target completion dates, and names of persons responsible for discharging those actions.

When creating the Corrective Action Plan, the forensic laboratory shall reference each nonconformity by the item number shown on the on-site Stage 1 Assessment Report. There is no set standard form for a Corrective Action Plan, they shall be derived from the formal audit response and then have appropriate CAPAs raised as defined in Chapter 4, Section 4.10.

The forensic laboratory may ask for clarification of a nonconformity from either the Assessor (who raised it) at the Closing Meeting or from that CB at any time after the Closing Meeting.

The forensic laboratory may also challenge the validity of a nonconformity by writing to the Lead Assessor at the CB.

The forensic laboratory shall analyse the cause of the nonconformities and describe the specific correction and corrective actions taken, or planned to be taken, to eliminate detected nonconformities, within a defined time.

The forensic laboratory shall submit their corrections and corrective actions to the CB for review and to determine if they are acceptable.

Should close out take longer than the agreed time, the forensic laboratory may submit a revised Corrective Action Plan, providing evidence of resolved actions and a revised timescale for planned actions. This process will be at the CB's discretion.

Depending on the number and seriousness of the nonconformities raised, the CB may require them to:

- undergo an additional full assessment;
- undergo an additional limited Assessment; or
- provide documented evidence (to be confirmed during future surveillance audits).

To verify effective correction and corrective actions.

19.3.25 Scheduling the Stage 2 Assessment

Once any outstanding CAPAs from the Stage 1 Assessment visit have been closed out, the forensic laboratory is ready, and able, to proceed to the Stage 2 Assessment.

If a date has been provisionally agreed and it is still feasible, then this date shall be confirmed, if it is not, another mutually agreed date shall be confirmed. If the scheduled date needs to be changed for any reason by the forensic laboratory, then it shall contact the CB and request an alternate date. The forensic laboratory shall be responsible for any costs associated with the date change.

The Stage 2 shall take place on-site.

A Stage 2 Assessment usually takes between 1 and 5 days per standard, this will depend on the:

- size of the forensic laboratory being assessed;
- scope of Certification; and
- number of standards against which Certification is sought.

Every effort shall be made to conduct all Assessments with as little disruption as possible to the forensic laboratory' normal operations.

A detailed visit plan shall be prepared indicating the section/activities/location(s) to be assessed by each Assessor and specify the activities that each Assessor shall witness during the visit.

Copies of the visit plan to the forensic laboratory shall be distributed to the forensic laboratory and to all of the Assessment Team allowing all parties to raise any issues with the visit plan.

The Stage 2 Assessment visit shall not be scheduled until all outstanding nonconformities have been addressed from the Stage 1 Assessment.

19.3.26 Logistics of the Stage 2 Assessment

These will be similar to those from the Stage 1 Assessment.

19.3.27 Opening meeting

The opening meeting will be similar to that from the Stage 1 Assessment.

19.3.28 Stage 2 Assessment

Note

These are often referred to as Certification or Registration Assessments.

The purpose of a Stage 2 Assessment is to evaluate the implementation, including effectiveness, of the forensic laboratory's Integrated Management System and the relevant Management System for which Certification is being sought.

Whilst the Stage 1 Assessment may take place at the forensic laboratory, or remotely, the Stage 2 Assessment shall take place at the forensic laboratory. The Stage 2 Assessment shall include, but not be limited to, the following:

- information and evidence about conformity to all requirements of the applicable Management System Standard(s) or other normative document;
- performance monitoring, measuring, reporting, and reviewing against key performance objectives and targets (consistent with the expectations in the applicable Management System Standard(s) or other normative document);
- the forensic laboratory's Management System(s) and performance as regards legal compliance;
- operational control of the forensic laboratory's processes;
- internal audits undertaken, their results, and how any nonconformities raised were addressed;
- the results of the Management Review(s) of the Management System(s) implemented;
- management responsibility for the forensic laboratory's implemented policies; and
- the links between the normative requirements, policy, performance objectives, and targets (consistent with the expectations in the applicable Management System Standard or other normative document), any applicable legislative requirements, responsibilities, competence of personnel, operations, procedures.

19.3.29 Recording Stage 2 Assessment findings

These will be similar to those from the Stage 1 Assessment.

19.3.30 Factors affecting the recommendation

In deciding the recommendation for Certification, the Lead Assessor shall consider the extent of competence and conformity within the forensic laboratory of the implementation of the Management System(s) to the standard(s) to which Certification is sought. This shall involve:

- analysis of all information and objective evidence gathered during the Stage 1 and Stage 2 Assessments;
- reviewing of all of the findings; and
- agreeing on the audit conclusions.

If there are no nonconformities found, the Lead Assessor recommends that Certification is offered immediately.

If there are Major Non-Conformities found, the Lead Assessor normally recommends that Certification is delayed until all nonconformities are addressed.

If a small number of minor nonconformities are found, the Lead Assessor may recommend Certification after the Corrective Action Plan has been agreed.

19.3.31 Closing Meeting

The Closing Meeting will be similar to that from the Stage 1 Assessment; however, the conclusion shall be about the recommendation for Certification, rather than proceeding to the Stage 2 Assessment.

19.3.32 Quality assurance of the Assessment report

The quality assurance process for a Stage 2 Assessment report is the same as the Stage 1 process.

19.3.33 Addressing nonconformities

Nonconformities raised at the Stage 2 Assessment shall be dealt with in the same way as those raised at the Stage 1 Assessment.

However, failure to close them out may affect the granting of Certification for the relevant Management System Standard(s).

19.3.34 Granting initial Certification

When the Lead Assessor makes a recommendation for Certification for a Management System Standard, the following information, as a minimum, shall be sent the CB to enable the Certification decision to be made:

- the Assessment Reports;
- comments on the nonconformities raised and, where applicable, the correction actions taken by the forensic laboratory;
- confirmation of the information provided by the forensic laboratory to the CB in support of its application for Certification; and
- a recommendation whether or not to grant Certification, together with any conditions or observations.

The CB shall make the Certification decision on the basis of an evaluation of the Assessment findings and conclusions and any other relevant information that is appropriate.

19.3.35 Confidentiality of the Assessment process

CBs require all participants in the Assessment and Certification process to recognise and respect the confidentiality of information relating to the forensic laboratory.

CBs use Non-Disclosure Agreements (NDAs) or confidentiality agreements, either stand-alone or as part of the engagement contract, to ensure confidentiality of the forensic laboratory's information. Assessors shall not take documentation belonging to the forensic laboratory off-site unless they are performing an off-site document review.

19.3.36 Certification certificates

Once the CB has granted Certification status, the forensic laboratory shall be issued with the Certificate for the appropriate standard(s).

The Certificate shall show the Standard to which it applies, the name of the applicant, the defined Scope of Certification, the issue, and the expiry dates.

The defined Scope Statement shall be agreed between the Lead Assessor and the applicant as part of the Assessment process.

19.3.37 Obligations of Certified organisations

There may be slightly differing obligations between different CBs, but a typical set of these is:

- a duty to inform the CB of changes in circumstances—the forensic laboratory shall inform the CB immediately in writing of any changes that may occur to the forensic laboratory's circumstances that are reasonably likely to affect the compliance of the forensic laboratory's Management System(s) to the standard(s) used for their Certification. This may include, but not be limited to, changes in:
  - the legal, commercial, organisational status or ownership,
  - organisation and management (e.g. key managerial, decision-making, or technical staff),
  - contact address and sites,
  - scope of operations under the certified Management System(s), and
  - major changes to the Management System(s) and processes.
- to make no misleading statements—the forensic laboratory shall not make any misleading statement concerning their application for, or achievement of, Certification to anyone. This shall include the statements that they make in their advertising brochures (whether for internal or external use);
- to ensure no harm is caused to the CB's name—the forensic laboratory shall not say or do anything that could be reasonably believed to have the effect of harming the CB's name or putting them into ill repute. This includes anything that may cause any person to question the authenticity or merit of the forensic laboratory's Certification;

- to fulfil all of the obligations for gaining and maintaining Certified status;
- to assist in the assessment process by providing the appropriate resources (i.e. all records, documentation, work areas, and personnel relevant to the scope of Certification). The information provided shall be in sufficient detail to enable the Lead Assessor to draw reasonable conclusions from it;
- the Certification certificate and the relevant Certification Mark(s) may be displayed, but this must be done in compliance with the contractual terms agreed; and
- to promptly pay fees due.

19.3.38 Postassessment evaluation

All CBs seek feedback from those undergoing Assessment for Certification as to the effectiveness and performance of their staff during the Assessment process.

Evaluations can be formal and completed online or on paper, or informally as an unsolicited email or other communication.

These are important Quality Objectives or Key Performance Indicators and provide invaluable feedback on services offered and possible problem areas or opportunities for improvement.

19.3.39 Certification cycle

Management System Certification is granted for a period of 3 years provided that the forensic laboratory:

- continues to meet all applicable Management System standards;
- continues to meet all applicable CB requirements; and
- submits to scheduled on-site Surveillance Assessments and Triennial Assessments.

Note

A forensic laboratory does not need to submit a new application for Certification, the Surveillance and Triennial Assessments are a continuation of the certification cycle. The dates and timing of the Triennial Assessment shall be agreed with the forensic laboratory at the Surveillance Assessment immediately prior to the Triennial Assessment.

19.3.40 Extending the Scope of Certification

Where the forensic laboratory wants to extend the scope of its Management System Certification(s), it shall discuss this with its CB.

The scope extension may be incorporated into the next Surveillance Assessment if the scope extension has a minor impact on the current Certification. If the change has a significant impact, then a visit with an additional Surveillance Assessment may be required. This will depend on the CB's specific requirements.

19.3.41 Surveillance activities

There are two main Assessment processes for monitoring conformity in Management Systems. These are:

- Surveillance Assessments; and
- Triennial Assessments.

19.3.41.1 Surveillance Assessments

Details for Surveillance Assessments shall be agreed at the Assessment prior to the Surveillance Assessment itself including the agenda.

Surveillance Assessments can be regarded as interim Assessments and are part of the required Certification cycle and are typically carried out during:

- Year 1—Surveillance Assessment;
- Year 2—Surveillance Assessment; and
- Year 3—Re-Certification—called the Triennial Assessment (on or about the third anniversary of the granting of the first Certificate).

However, different CBs may use different time periods between successive Assessments, but they shall be conducted at least once a year.

It may also be that the first Assessment is closer to the Stage 2 Assessment than a year. This typically happens if the forensic laboratory was regarded as a high-risk applicant or had a number of Minor Non-Conformities that needed proof of being satisfactorily closed out. Surveillance Assessments shall be on-site assessments, but not necessarily full assessments of the forensic laboratory's Scope of Certification(s).

During a Surveillance Assessment, the following, as a minimum, shall be evaluated:

- continued conformity with the controls in the relevant standard that are implemented;
- results of internal audits and the Management Review(s);
- a review of actions taken on nonconformities identified during any previous audits or assessments;
- the treatment of complaints;
- the effectiveness of the Management System(s) with regard to achieving the forensic laboratory's objectives;
- the progress of planned activities aimed at continual improvement;
- continuing operational control;
- the use of marks, logos, and/or any other reference to Certification;
- a selection of controls in the relevant standard(s);
- any changes in the forensic laboratory's organisational infrastructure or working practices; and
- where the forensic laboratory has more than one site, ensure that all sites are visited at least once in the Assessment cycle, if possible.

As with Stage 1 and Stage 2 Assessments, each assessment shall have an agenda prepared and agreed prior to the Assessment.

The Assessment, reporting, and raising of nonconformities shall be carried out in the same manner as a Stage 2 Assessment.

19.3.41.2 Triennial Assessment

The Triennial Assessment is a full Conformity Assessment performed at the end of the 3-year Assessment Cycle.

The duration is typically shorter than the Stage 2 Assessment as there should be fewer nonconformities found as the forensic laboratory has been subjected to the previous 3 years' worth of Assessments in the Assessment Cycle and the Conformance assessment body has now 'known' the forensic laboratory for 3 years.

The Triennial Assessment shall cover the following:

- changes in working practice or technology since the last audit (to determine whether relevant controls are in place and effective);
- the effectiveness of the relevant Management System(s) in its entirety in the light of internal and external changes and its continued relevance and applicability to the scope of Certification;
- the demonstrated Top Management commitment to maintain the effectiveness and improvement of the Management System(s) to enhance overall performance;
- whether the operation of the Certified Management System(s) contributes to the achievement of the forensic laboratory's policy and objectives;
- any outstanding CAPAs;
- all mandatory controls;
- any controls in the standard that have not yet been covered in the 3-year Assessment cycle; and
- any sites in the Scope of Certification that have not been covered within the 3-year Assessment cycle, if appropriate and practical.

As with Stage 1 and Stage 2 Assessments, each assessment shall have an agenda prepared and agreed prior to the Assessment.

Additionally, at the Triennial Assessment, the Lead Assessor shall consider the following in determining the outcome of the Triennial Assessment:

- number of nonconformities over the last 3 years;
- repeated occurrences of nonconformities against the same controls in the relevant standard(s); and
- failures to implement adequate and effective countermeasures against any nonconformity(s) raised in a timely manner.

The Assessment, reporting, and raising of nonconformities shall be carried out in the same manner as a Stage 2 Assessment.

19.3.42   Maintaining Certification

The CB shall maintain the forensic laboratory's Certification(s) based on demonstration that it continues to satisfy the requirements of the relevant Management System standard(s). It shall maintain the forensic laboratory's Certification(s) based on a positive conclusion by the Lead Assessor following assessment.

19.3.43   Joint Assessments

It is possible to undertake Joint Assessments, where more than one standard is assessed either at the Surveillance Assessment or the Triennial Audit in the same manner as a Joint Assessment for Stage 1 or Stage 2 Assessments.

19.3.44   Other means of monitoring performance

A CB shall retain the right to monitor the forensic laboratory's ongoing performance through all other reasonable means available to them, in addition to on-site assessments, the following surveillance activities may include:

- enquiries from the CB to the forensic laboratory on any aspects of Certification;
- reviewing any of the forensic laboratory's statements with respect to its operations (e.g. promotional material, website);
- requests to the forensic laboratory to provide documents and records (on paper or electronic media);
- investigation of any complaints received; and
- other means of monitoring the forensic laboratory's performance.

19.3.45   Sanctions

Where the forensic laboratory fails to meet the requirements of ongoing Certification, the CB shall require corrective action to be taken to address the nonconformity. Where the forensic laboratory does not take appropriate timely action or fails to take appropriate action to meet their Certification obligations, a number of sanctions can be imposed, these include:

19.3.45.1   Suspension of a Certificate

The forensic laboratory's Certificate(s) shall be suspended if they:

- advise the CB of significant changes to the organisation that render the existing Certificate invalid;
- fails to take corrective action in a specific period;
- misuse the Certificate, the CB trademark, or Certification mark; or
- does not meet its obligations to the CB body.

The reasons for suspending the Certificate(s) shall be recorded and advised to the forensic laboratory in writing.

The forensic laboratory's name shall be removed from any lists of Certified organisations that the CB holds or lists maintained by a third party based on the granting of a Certificate.

The CB shall have to be satisfied that the forensic laboratory is complying with all the requirements of Certification prior to re-awarding (or un-suspending) the Certificate.

When the forensic laboratory has complied with the requirements of the certification process and the Certificate is re-awarded, the re-awarding of the Certificate shall be transmitted to all interested parties.

19.3.45.2   Withdrawal of Certificates

The forensic laboratory's Certificate shall be withdrawn if they:

- after suspension, have taken no, or insufficient, corrective action within the required period;
- persistent misuse the Certification or Registration Mark(s);
- breach of the CB's regulations (e.g. refusal to permit the CB to perform its duties); and
- breach of other CB requirements.

The reasons for withdrawing the Certificate(s) shall be recorded and advised to the forensic laboratory in writing.

The forensic laboratory's name shall be removed from any lists of Certified organisations that the CB holds or lists maintained by a third party based on the granting of a Certificate.

The CB shall have to be satisfied that the forensic laboratory is complying with all the requirements of Certification prior to re-awarding the Certificate.

When the forensic laboratory has complied with the requirements of the Certification process and the Certificate is re-awarded, the re-awarding of the Certificate shall be transmitted to all interested parties.

19.3.45.3 Cancelling the Certificate

The forensic laboratory's Certificate shall be cancelled if they terminate their business arrangement with the CB.

The reasons for cancelling the Certificate shall be recorded and advised to the forensic laboratory in writing.

The forensic laboratory's name shall be removed from any lists of Certified organisations that the CB holds or lists maintained by a third party based on the granting of a Certificate.

19.3.46 Appeals and complaints

Differing CBs may have slightly different appeals and complaints processes, but the generic process is that appeals and complaints shall be made to the normal contact (e.g. the Certification Manager). Once an appeal or complaint is received, the internal procedure for the CB shall be used.

19.3.47 Obligations of the CB

The CB shall maintain and make publicly accessible, or provide upon request, information describing its audit processes and certification processes for granting, maintaining, extending, renewing, reducing, suspending, or withdrawing certification, about the certification activities, types of Management Systems, and geographical areas in which it operates. This information shall be accurate and not misleading.

In addition, it shall make publicly accessible information about suspended, withdrawn, or cancelled Certificates as well as validating any Certificate, on request.

Where there is a change in the requirement for certification, the CB shall advise the forensic laboratory of the change and verify that the forensic laboratory complies with any new requirements.

19.3.48 Use of the CB's logos and marks

The rules governing the use of a CB's Logos and marks are similar to those of an AB, which are covered above.

Appendix 1—Typical conditions of Accreditation

To gain and maintain Accreditation, a forensic laboratory shall agree in writing to comply with the ABs conditions for accreditation.

A forensic laboratory's Authorised Representative, when signing the application forms, shall attest that the information in the application is correct and to commit the forensic laboratory to fulfil the conditions for gaining and maintaining Accreditation, which shall include, but not be limited to:

- complying at all times with the AB's requirements for Accreditation as defined in the relevant technical documents, terms and conditions, and contractual requirements for Accreditation;
- fulfilling the Accreditation procedure, especially to:
  - receiving and assisting the Assessment Team in their duty;
  - paying the fees due to the AB whatever the result of the Assessment may be, and to accept and pay the charges relating to the process of maintaining Accreditation;
  - participating in proficiency testing, as required;
  - following the rules and regulations for AB logo use and for referencing Accreditation status; and
  - resolving all nonconformities in a timely manner.
- reporting to the AB within the specified time period of any major changes that affect the forensic laboratory's:
  - legal, commercial, organisational, or ownership status;
  - organisation and management; e.g. key managerial staff;
  - policies or procedures, where appropriate;
  - location;
  - personnel, equipment, facilities, working environment, or other resources, where significant;
  - Authorised Representative or Approved Signatories; and
  - other matters that may affect the forensic laboratory's capability, scope of Accredited activities, or compliance with the AB's requirements for Accreditation.

Appendix 2—Contents of an audit response

An audit response template shall include the following:

- details of the audit report being responded to;
- reference;
- nonconformity details;
- nonconformity type;
- corrective action required;
- comments on finding;
- proposed CAPA response;
- date by which remediation is to be completed; and
- person responsible for carrying out the remediation.

Appendix 3—Management system assessment nonconformity examples

A nonconformity shall be recorded whenever the Assessor discovers that the documented procedures are inadequate to prevent breaches of the system requirements, or they are adequate but are not being followed correctly. Some examples to illustrate the definitions defined in Chapter 4, Section 4.7.5 are defined below:

Major Non-Conformity

Examples

Some examples could include:

- after previous warnings, the forensic laboratory is still using the AB or CB's logo and/or marks in contravention of the AB or CB's Rules and Regulations for their use;
- ongoing and systematic breaches of the requirements have been found;
- some of the procedures for document control, and record control are incomplete or are not being followed;
- the forensic laboratory has lost its key technical manager(s) for particular work and no longer has competent employees doing that work. They continue to perform work that needs competent employees and did not advise the AB or CB of this;
- the forensic laboratory has no records of the training plans for the past year, any evidence of appraisals and Training Needs Analysis being undertaken;
- the Management Review for the current year has not been done;
- there are a number of outstanding CAPAs and no evidence of them having been closed out;
- there is no procedure for control of nonconforming work (or recall of incorrect reports); and
- there is significant evidence that the Management System(s) is seriously failing and there are no records of any internal audits being carried out.

Obviously, Major Non-Conformities will depend on the Assessment Team's findings and the Lead Assessor's evaluation of the finding.

Minor Non-Conformity

Examples

Some examples could include:

- a hard copy of an obsolete procedure was found;
- one customer complaint had been acted upon but not been closed out;
- one employee had not got an up-to-date job description;
- the document control procedure requires specific reviewers to review all procedures before implementation. Records show that a document has not gone through this process but has been released; and
- the forensic laboratory Exhibits Log has one or two incomplete entries.

Obviously, Minor Non-Conformities will depend on the Assessment Team's findings and the Lead Assessor's evaluation of the finding.

It should be noted, however, that a number of Minor Non-Conformities in the same area can be symptomatic of a system breakdown and could therefore be compounded into a Major Non-Conformity.

Opportunity for improvement (OFIs)

Additionally, whilst not a nonconformity marking an Assessor may identify an area of the Management System(s) that could be improved, but is still conformant. The Assessor has to ensure that this is an objective comment and does not constitute consulting.

Appendix 4—Typical close-out periods

Different ABs and CBs may have different periods permissible for close out of nonconformities, and in some cases, these will be agreed with a client on a case-by-case basis. However, the ones listed below are typical closeout periods.

Assessment type	Period allowed for providing evidence of close out after a Corrective Action Plan is agreed
Initial	Normally, no more than 3 months
Surveillance	Normally 1 month, exceptionally 3 months
Re-assessment	Normally 1 month, exceptionally 3 months
Extension to scope	Normally, no more than 3 months

Chapter 20

Emerging issues

20.1   Introduction

Digital forensics is a relatively new discipline in forensic science, the first cases being in the late 1970s and early 1980s. In those days, there were no established procedures and no specialized tools, just hex editors. As has been stated in Chapter 1, Section 1.1.7, there is a need to have appropriate, scientifically robust, and repeatable procedures that meet the legislative requirements for the jurisdiction.

With the ongoing rapid changes in technology available, and its use, digital forensics will always be playing catch-up as new technology appears and the ways it is used for both legal and illegal purposes develop. The processing of a forensic case in a forensic laboratory follows the following steps, as defined in Chapter 1, Section 1.1.2:

- preserving the evidence;
- identifying the evidence;
- extracting the evidence;
- documenting the evidence recovered and how it was recovered;
- interpreting the evidence; and
- presenting the evidence (either to the client or a Court).

Some of the problems with digital evidence generally were defined in Chapter 1, Section 1.1.8.

However, as digital forensics is ever evolving, different jurisdictions will have updated requirements. These include, but are not limited to, in the UK, since the new draft of the second edition was started:

'Digital Forensic Science Strategy', July 2020, National Police Chiefs' Council (NPCC) (Formerly ACPO);
'Digital Forensics, An Inspection into how well the police and other agencies use digital forensics in their investigations' His Majesty's Inspectorate of Constabulary and Fire & Rescue Services, December 2022;
Extraction of Information from electronic devices, code of practice, HMG, October 2022.

Much of the newly published documentation applies to Law Enforcement and the requirements shall be advised to a forensic laboratory as part of the engagement.

This chapter looks at the specific current and future challenges, such as those highlighted in the Digital Forensic Science Strategy that a forensic laboratory and its employees face when processing forensic cases.

20.2   Specific challenges

20.2.1   Legislative issues

20.2.1.1   Changing laws

Laws are constantly being changed to keep pace with developments in technology and the potential sources of evidence that this creates and also the way in which the new technologies are exploited by criminals.

20.2.1.2   Time to enact legislation

New legislation needs to be carefully crafted to address issues of digital evidence and computer crime and this takes time. Rushed or 'knee jerk' legislation can cause legislative nightmares unless it is appropriate for the task in hand. This often means that the technology has moved on since the legislative drafting process started and means that the legislation may be inappropriate, flawed or need major revision to make it effective.

A Blueprint for Implementing Best Practice Procedures in a Digital Forensic Laboratory. https://doi.org/10.1016/B978-0-12-819479-9.00003-4

20.2.1.3 Following legislative procedures

It is essential that the legislative procedures for seizing evidence are followed exactly in the jurisdiction to ensure that any seizure is legal. This also means that the exact scope of what is to be seized has to be clearly and properly defined. The tools and techniques also have to meet the requirements of the legislation and be validated.

20.2.1.4 Evidence in different jurisdictions

Given the Internet and global connectivity, it is often the case that evidence for a case can be located in more than one jurisdiction, or even that the actual location of the evidence is not known (e.g. cloud computing). This can cause a logistical nightmare for seizure as well as knowing the relevant legislation for the final jurisdiction where the case will be heard and how this will interact with the other jurisdictions. As has been found in the past, what is illegal in one jurisdiction may be legal (or not illegal) in another jurisdiction for any number of reasons. This does not always mean that the different jurisdictions are different countries, but where different states have different legislations in the same country.

20.2.1.5 Spoliation

Spoliation can be the result of a deliberate act or negligence. Claims of spoliation may be made if appropriate and a forensic laboratory must be able to respond to any challenge of spoliation. This will depend on fully documented cases and having repeatable processes undertaken by competent Forensic Analysts. Depending on the jurisdiction, this may be a criminal offence where the act is intentional. Again, the importance of having appropriately validated tools, techniques, and procedures in place, that these are followed and that there are contemporaneous records to support all stages of the processing of the case is essential.

20.2.1.6 Privacy issues

Individual privacy and the needs of the Forensic Analyst will frequently be in conflict. This has become an increasingly relevant issue with the wider use of cloud computing.

20.2.1.7 Judicial decisions

In a Court of Law, of any type, the Judge is rarely a digital forensic expert. A Judge is an expert in the law and its interpretation. The digital forensic evidence provided is normally only part of the evidence produced to the Judge for decision-making. The Judge is there to come to a conclusion based on the relevant tests applicable to the Court under the law in the jurisdiction. Ensuring that the Judge understands the evidence presented is therefore essential.

20.2.1.8 Common language

There is no common language in use that is accepted in digital forensic cases across multiple jurisdictions. Many different universities and commercial providers have 'jumped on the bandwagon' and provide digital forensic courses, but they do not have a common and universally accepted level of academic standards. This leads to a number of 'qualified' experts throughout the world, all having differing levels of competence.

20.2.2 Technology issues

20.2.2.1 Rapid changes in technology

Rapid changes in technology are driving the need for the development of new tools, techniques and procedures to process forensic cases that involve the new technologies deployed. This is a classic case of digital forensics having to play 'catch-up'. New tools, techniques and procedures all need to be validated prior to use, as defined in Chapter 7, Sections 7.5.5 and 20.2.12.2.

The best practice for examining electronic devices in situ has evolved over the past decade driven largely by changes in technology. This has given rise to the traditional best practice approach versus a modern best practice.

Generally speaking, operational computer systems can be classified as being in one of the following three states,

- when computer is off;
- when computer is on; or
- when computer is in hibernation (sleep) mode.

Traditionally, when a computer was located in a powered-off state the best practice was to leave it powered off. This was achieved by unplugging the power directly from the back of the computer (not from the wall socket). The traditional approach required the examiner to ensure the system was truly off, not just appearing to be off as the system could be in hibernation or sleep mode. The best practice to do this was to either move the mouse or hit the shift key on the keyboard.

The rationale behind leaving the computer off was the fact that turning the computer system on would introduce changes to the data. These changes could be in the form of last shutdown time, last logged-on time, etc. The rationale behind the traditional approach remains relevant today. However, changes in technology have forced a rethink of this approach. The traditional golden rules of computer forensics best practice are now changing as it comes down to what the investigation team is after, or if legislation allows investigator to do that action.

The table below summarises common changes in best practice dealing with computer devices:

Traditional best practice	New best practice
If the computer is off, leave it off	If the computer is off, turn it on
If the computer is on, leave it on	If the computer is on, leave it on AND
If the computer is on, leave it on AND Determine if the powered-on system has any destructive processes running. Any wiping utility or formatting utility that may be running may be a deliberate attempt to destroy data	Determine if the powered-on system has any destructive processes running. Any wiping utility or formatting utility that may be running may be a deliberate attempt to destroy data Check if the system is connected to a network Check Cloud storage Visual inspection of the screen and any proprietary software used on the computer Check encrypted container, if identified, acquire recovery key Conduct RAM capture Check system date and time Take photographs of what is on the screen, taskbar
PC—Hard shutdown Unplug the power directly from the back of the computer (not from the wall socket) **Server—Normal shutdown** When it comes to a business server, hard shutdown may not be acceptable as this action could severely damage the system and/or render data unrecoverable. Also, this could disrupt legitimate business operation and create a potential liability issue. (Especially when the business is not a target offender, we want the business to continue to operate.) When it comes to a server or business computers, a proper shutdown (normal shutdown, using windows button and shutdown menu) is required	Both personal PCs and business computers—normal shutdown And shutdown while pressing SHIFT key (for laptop computers)
Do not introduce any changes	With the introduction of default full disk encryption, e.g. BitLocker, Forensic specialists now operate in an environment where harvesting original evidence without minimal alteration is often unavoidable A simple triage procedure causing minimal system changes may be used to detect these encryption schemes while encrypted evidence is mounted When changes are performed, document all actions The minimum changes that are listed in this table are very minimal and are viewed as acceptable in the current forensic environment if evidence is to be obtained Keep moving mouse to awake the computer system if you are already in the system. Do not let the system power down or go into sleep mode as this will eliminate the examiner's opportunity to get the encryption recovery key

Continued

Traditional best practice	New best practice
Best practice is always acquiring Physical hard drives	Physical acquisition is still preferable unless situation dictates otherwise

Exceptions:

The easiest way to recover the encrypted data is to image

the machine while it is live is conduct logical acquisition

Server (when the business is not the target offender) |
| Rely on passwords provided by the person of interest | Be sure to ask for more than just the password. The suspect may have both a user and an administrative password for the BIOS boot-up; there may be multiple passwords for different email

accounts, encrypted files, and a different password for their system login. By obtaining this information, hours or days of forensic processing could be saved

Rather than rely on what the suspect provides to you, you can extract passwords saved on their web browser while their system is ON |

The recommended best practice when dealing with a computer that is important to the case and is found in a powered-off or hibernation state is to turn it on. There are a number of factors that will determine if a computer is considered important to the case. These will depend on the circumstances at that time. Examples are if the computer is used by the person of interest or if the computer is considered the only source of specific data relevant to the investigation.

When a computer is turned on, the exact time should be documented together with the reason. The purpose of powering on the computer is to carry out an onsite triage. The onsite triage will be made up of the following tasks:

- confirm that the username and password provided are correct;
- check for any destructive processes running;
- perform RAM capture;
- determine if full disk or volume encryption is active and take appropriate action to mitigate;
- check the system time and date settings and is accurate;
- record through photographs and notes what is on the desktop and taskbar;
- record what processes are running;
- check for proprietary applications running on the system;
- check for a connection to a local area network and for the existence of network storage; and
- check for any active cloud storage and the sync status of the cloud account.

20.2.2.2 Disk encryption

The computer should be assessed to determine if there is any encryption such as BitLocker running on the device.

If the computer is on, photograph what is on the screen as a means of capturing what the suspect may have been doing prior to the seizure. At this point, the trained First Responder will want to consult with a skilled examiner and have them respond or conduct a minimally invasive triage procedure.

20.2.2.3 Wireless connectivity

The problem of the ever-wider use of wireless connectivity, coupled with the increasing ranges for connectivity that are being achieved continue to cause increasing problems for the Investigator. The initial problem at the crime scene will be to determine what devices are relevant to the investigation. At any location, there are likely to be a number of access points and the density of these is likely to continue to increase with greater use of wireless connectivity. The next problem is that if the suspect is skilled they may be using a wireless channel that is not in the standard range and which could easily be overlooked. Another problem will be keeping the wireless device isolated during the collection and analysis phases.

20.2.2.4 Cloud computing

While there is nothing new in the elements that make up cloud computing (Software as a Service, Platform as a Service, Infrastructure as a Service), the developing implementations of cloud-based systems for document storage and data management, such as Google Docs, Microsoft 365, and others, are being increasingly used by a large number of organizations. With this move to cloud computing, there is an increasing need for a wide range of digital forensics from criminal investigation to e-discovery.

One of the issues that will continue to develop as a result of this will be the requirement to effectively deal with large volumes of cloud-based data. The problem with cloud computing and forensics is that the organization's information is no longer under their control, breaking all of the conventional rules of information security and personal ownership.

Due to the elasticity of the cloud and the potential for data to be accessed from anywhere and possibly moved or destroyed, it is of the utmost importance and urgency to preserve and obtain the evidentiary data as soon as practicable. It is, therefore, the 'Best Practice' in relation to cloud-based data to access and download it during the course of the execution of the search warrant, before removing devices for forensic copying off-site.

This means that, at the place of the search warrant, a trained electronic Forensic Examiner will need to access the cloud-based platforms using a computer that has been located and seized at the place. The Forensic Examiner will access the various user accounts for cloud data using the credentials of the user. He/she will then download each set of cloud data to a storage device connected to that personal computer.

The Forensic Examiner will ensure that the data is collected in a manner that is as reasonably forensically sound as possible.

A clear contract between the user and the cloud supplier is needed to ensure that appropriate legislative and business requirements are met, and while cloud computing is now well established, consideration will still have to be given to ensure that services are 'forensically ready'.

The 'cloud' is borderless and data can potentially be stored anywhere in the world. Some regions such as the European Union have taken steps such as the EU-US Privacy Shield Framework, which replaced the previous Safe Harbor agreement to try to control where data is stored, but this is the exception rather than the rule. The problem with not knowing where the data is stored is that it may be stored in a jurisdiction that makes it difficult to recover. Laws are defined within jurisdictions while cloud data is borderless. In many jurisdictions, law enforcement agencies are waiting for case law to guide the best practices; however, some countries are starting to discuss the issue of cloud in their legal systems.

Other issues with cloud computing include the fact that the law has not adjusted for the complexities that cloud evidence contains as it has become a mainstream practice. Depending on the service provider, the steps that need to be taken for acquisition could be different for each cloud service provider. In most cases, acquisition requires user credentials, username and password, and most of times 2FA code or use Tokens (if they have legal authority) that are extracted from mobile/computer devices.

Digital forensics has continued to evolve from the scientific method, which requires a repeatable, reproducible method. With cloud, exact replication of an acquisition is statistically not possible. Tracking metadata is also different from traditional forensics (e.g. trace URL request).

20.2.2.5 Mobile devices

The digital forensics of mobile devices is an everyday problem for all digital forensic laboratories. The type of device will dictate the procedures that need to be followed during a forensic investigation. Mobile devices can be divided into a number of categories which are:

- standard mass-market phones (iPhone, Samsung, LG, etc.);
- Blackberry devices;
- Android devices;
- iPads;
- Other tablets;
- Chinese mobile phones.

The examination of mobile devices such as smartphones and tablets will differ from the traditional computer forensic process. This is due to the nature of the devices involved and the storage within a phone cannot be easily removed and examined. Examination of mobile devices requires the use of forensic software, which communicates directly with the phone and extracts data from it.

Generally speaking, mobile device examination does not produce a forensic clone (unless the image was acquired by chip-off method) of the phone but rather a forensic report with files that have been extracted. Therefore, the term 'Clone' does not apply for mobile devices unless the chip-off operation is conducted.

Traditional best practice	New best practice
Do not browse through user data unless exigency exists	Remains the same
Obtain the Passcode: PIN, password, pattern, knock code from the user	Remains the same
If the phone is OFF, leave it off	Obviously having a device power itself on without being in a controlled environment is a bad thing. The experienced electronic forensic examiner needs to make a judgment call and turn it on when the risk is minimum, and document everything!
	Turn it ON:
	1. To verify the passcode, PIN, password or pattern lock is correct. This may be the only chance to ensure you can access the phone data later on. No passcode could mean no data can be extracted
	2. To obtain 2FA verification code for cloud data acquisition
	3. To conduct sample check
	4. To photograph user accounts, settings, IMEI number (s) and the phone number
	5. To obtain saved password(s)
If it is ON, leave it ON	Remains the same. Also DO NOT ALLOW POWER OFF (For AFU—After First Unlock extraction)
	Connect the phone to power charger
Do not change any settings	It is still important to keep the change in minimum. For example, browsing through text messages can change unread message flags to read. These alterations within the evidence cannot be changed back. Viewing photographs will often update their last accessed date and potentially create new thumbnail images
	Some changes need to be made for the purpose of extracting data from mobile devices:
	• Change language settings if required • Set Screenlock to Never or select the longest time • For android devices: Enable developer option and USB debugging while the phone is connected to the network (while executing search warrant). Some android mobile phones will not allow user to change this setting if the phone is not connected to the network Document all setting changes or phone manipulation in the report
Disable security lock	Disable security lock or remove and document
Set phone to Airplane Mode	Set phone to Airplane Mode *PLUS* make sure Wi-Fi and Bluetooth are OFF
	(Apple iOS device will now remember user behaviour. If the user turns on Airplane Mode, then activates Wi-Fi or Bluetooth, the device will remember. The next time the device is placed into Airplane Mode, those wireless or Bluetooth will remain on. It is important to verify all wireless connectivity has been turned off.)
Transport and to Secure Storage location and put the device into a faraday isolation bag	Remains the same. In regard to the Faraday isolation bag—only required if it is not possible to isolate such a device through Airplane Mode

20.2.2.5.1   Standard mass market phones

The forensics of standard phones has well-established processes and procedures. The main problem that will be encountered in the future is the number of new models and the increasing number of data cable and power cables that a forensic laboratory will need to maintain to deal with them. A secondary issue will be with the isolation of these devices. There is currently increasing evidence that Faraday bags may not be as effective as previously thought and additional effort and testing will be required to prove their efficacy. Future issues will include the increasing availability of functionality for encryption and remote wiping. On the positive side, there is an increasing use of the Joint Test Action Group (JTAG) interface on mobile phones. The JTAG interface was originally designed to test circuit boards in processors and memory chips. The use of the JTAG interface could provide direct access to the processors and memory. This means that the use of the operating system is avoided. This approach is still developing as it relies on knowledge of the architecture of the device.

20.2.2.5.2 Blackberry devices

While the Blackberry device has gone through a major change and now uses the Android operating system, there are still a large number of legacy devices in use. The Blackberry is in a permanent state of 'push messaging', and for this reason, they need to be contained in a Radio Frequency shielded container until they can be taken to a safe, shielded location where they can be examined. The encryption of Blackberry devices will continue to be an issue for Forensic Analysts and Investigators, and the remote wipe functionality will be a problem if the device is not isolated. While the market share of Blackberry has declined there are still a significant number of these devices in circulation.

20.2.2.5.3 Android devices

Although there has been a rapid evolution of android-based devices, in the form of phones, tablets, netbooks and laptops, these devices are now well understood and there are well-established processes and procedures for dealing with them.

20.2.2.5.4 iPads

The iPad is currently available in a number of offerings and the iPad mini is now available and there have been a large number of software versions released. There are currently no solutions for the physical extraction of the iPad unless the device is jailbroken. The rapid pace of software releases for the iPad will mean that there is a constant battle to update knowledge and tools to be able to image these devices.

20.2.2.5.5 Other tablets

The advent of the Tablet has been widely adopted, and most of the major manufacturers and Chinese manufacturers are all producing their own versions. There are a wide range of operating systems being used for Tablet computers including Windows, Android, and OSX. Having the correct data and power connectors will continue to be an issue, and Tablets will also be affected by many of the issues that are found in mobile phones.

20.2.2.5.6 Chinese mobile phones

While there are a wide range of Chinese mobile phones, Huawei has become a mainstream, high-end device supplier that has gained significant market share in the West. Many of these devices cause major challenges for Forensic Analysts as the manufacturers of these devices do not follow standards and as a result, the way in which the device operates cannot be predicted. Other issues with these devices will continue to be the nonstandard operating systems, data cables, and power cables. The issue with power cables may lead to the battery becoming depleted with a resultant loss of volatile data.

20.2.2.6 Large disks

Larger and larger electro-mechanical and solid-state hard drives will continue to be an issue in static digital forensics. This is because there is a physical limitation to the speed that data can be transferred. The time taken to image a disk and the storage capacity required within a forensic laboratory will continue to increase as the size of disks increases. The volume of data that the disks will potentially contain will also mean that additional time will be required to index and analyse the massive volumes of data. Three terabyte disks are already in common use even in the home environment and the speed of increase in storage volumes is not likely to reduce at any time in the near future.

20.2.2.7 Alternative technologies—The Internet of Things (IoT)

There is an increasing diversity of computer processors in use in all aspects of our lives. Cars have engine management systems, and satellite navigation systems and household devices such as TVs, refrigerators and washing machines now increasingly have network connectivity and computer processors to enable them to download data or be remotely operated. The extraction of potential evidence from these devices means that there is a requirement for new tools, techniques and knowledge of the architecture of the processor and any digital storage media in the device.

20.2.2.8 Smart environments

With the development of the smart home and smart cities, there is an increasing use of interconnections between devices from the PC to devices that perform functions such as the heating system controller and sensors. All of these devices produce data but there is no standardisation of the operating systems, the formats of the data that they generate or the volatility of the data. All could potentially be producing data of evidential value, but there is a significant gap in the availability of tools to collect and analyse this data and there is an increasing knowledge gap for the investigators as these environments are more widely used.

20.2.2.9 Game consoles

The number of gaming consoles that are in use and their increasing storage and processing capability mean that they can also be a digital forensic problem. These devices are similar in most aspects to computers and can be used for internet browsing and also email. There have been cases where game consoles were used for storing paedophile material, and standard forensic tools are not necessarily currently able to process them.

20.2.2.10 Proprietary operating systems

The development of new proprietary operating systems for both alternative and conventional technologies will continue to cause digital forensic issues. With each new operating system, there is a need for new tools, techniques, and procedures. There is also a need for the acquisition of skills by the Forensic Analyst on new operating systems. This causes an issue of a diversification of the range of skills that are required within a forensic laboratory.

20.2.2.11 Noncompliant hardware

The proliferation of noncompliant hardware means that there is a need for device-specific data and/or power connectors and the development of new tools, techniques, and procedures for the examination of these devices.

20.2.2.12 Solid-state devices

The use of solid-state storage is now well established and they are rapidly replacing the electromechanical disk in many environments. These devices utilise a system for wear levelling, which is used to maximize the lifetime of the flash memory as it can only be written and erased a certain number of times. Wear levelling utilizes both software and hardware means to ensure that all areas of the memory are used an equal number of times. Solid-state devices have a purge routine that functions after a device has been 'quick formatted'. This is a function that is required before new data can be written to the storage; however, there is a problem that once the storage media is connected to a power supply, even if it has been interrupted, this process will resume as the device can initiate the routine independent of a computer.

20.2.2.13 Detection tools and fitness for forensic purpose

There are a number of detection tools in place in the normal IT Infrastructure (e.g. monitoring systems, Intruder Detection Systems, Intruder Prevention Systems, etc.) that can identify activity that causes incidents and breaches. While these have been designed to perform these tasks, few have been designed with the identification and preservation of digital evidence for later analysis in mind.

20.2.2.14 Network forensic issues

While early digital forensic cases dealt with a single computer, most of today's cases will involve network forensics at some level. Network forensics has matured and is now almost as well understood as the forensic analysis of a single stand-alone computer. Some of the challenges faced in network forensics include, but are not limited to:

- analysing encrypted network traffic;
- consistent analysis of network traffic and protocols;
- handling different devices (types and makes) of network devices;
- preservation of large volumes of network traffic;
- proving integrity of network traffic;
- secured networked applications (e.g. Skype);
- the accurate capture of real-time traffic in high-speed networks;
- time issues across different networks;
- the visual display of network traffic; and
- the volatile nature of network traffic.

20.2.3   Human issues

20.2.3.1   Training

As technology continues to change at a rapid pace, there is an ongoing need to undertake training on new tools, techniques, and procedures. This has an impact on the cost of training and the time that the Forensic Analyst has to spend away from case processing. It also means that Forensic Analysts have to be familiar with more and more different tools, techniques, and procedures. This also causes an issue of a diversification of the range of skills that are required within a forensic laboratory.

20.2.3.2   Competence and proficiency

Forensic Analysts have to prove their competence and proficiency regularly as defined in Chapter 18, Sections 18.2.5 and 18.2.6, respectively. Should they fail any competence or proficiency testing, they will be unable to undertake relevant parts of forensic case processing until they have proved their competence and/or proficiency.

20.2.3.3   Maintaining records

Records ideally should be contemporaneous to reflect what was happening at the time or what actions were carried out at the time. Unless the Forensic Analyst or First Responder is always diligent in this task, it is too easy to 'leave it till later' and documentation and record failures occur. This can become a real problem later in the case where critical records have been overlooked (e.g. breaking the chain of custody).

20.2.3.4   Complying with procedures

A forensic laboratory shall have defined procedures for all stages of case processing, and all Forensic Analysts and First Responders are mandated to follow these. If it can be proved that they did not follow in-house procedures, then the evidence that they produce is open to challenge. This is why it is essential that all Forensic Analysts and First Responders follow the relevant procedures in a forensic laboratory and the jurisdiction.

20.2.3.5   Going beyond the safety zone

There are occasions when a Forensic Analyst starts a case that they are competent to process and that as the case progresses, they are no longer competent or proficient to proceed with new requirements. It is at this point that the Forensic Analyst should declare the problem to their Line Manager or the Laboratory Manager, but sadly sometimes they struggle on. When challenged on their evidence, their lacking competence or proficiency can then have a detrimental effect on the outcome of the case. The worst possible situation is where a Forensic Analyst starts a case, knowing that they are neither competent nor proficient to process the case.

20.2.3.6   Standard procedures

There is a lack of standard procedures for forensic case processing throughout a jurisdiction as different Forensic Analysts may follow different internal procedures.

20.2.4   Preserving the evidence

20.2.4.1   Volume of data

The volume of data to be captured is growing rapidly based on the rapidly increasing sizes of all forms of storage media. If on-site imaging is to be carried out, this can create a problem not only of size of data to be captured but also the time taken to capture the image(s). It is essential for First Responders that they have suitable media for capturing possibly huge amounts of data and also tools to do this accurately and with optimum speed.

20.2.4.2   Challenging the chain of custody

The chain of custody is often attacked at this stage and, sadly, this is often successful, especially where a number of different people have been involved in a major case. The more people seizing the evidence and handling it till it is received in the secure property store the more likely it is that failures occur at this stage. This is often compounded by having members of the seizure teams working for different organizations that have different procedures.

20.2.4.3 Changes made during preservation

During the preservation stage, it may be that the original evidence may be changed by the process, though the ideal situation is that the copy of the evidence worked on during the case processing is an exact copy of the original. If unavoidable changes have been made (e.g. live capture), then unless the Forensic Analyst is competent and can accurately and convincingly explain the changes to the evidence and why they were unavoidable, then the evidence may be challenged. This is enshrined in the ACPO Guidelines as principle 2, as defined in Chapter 1, Section 1.1.9.

20.2.5 Identifying the evidence

20.2.5.1 Numbers of systems

As computing has become more pervasive, the potential evidence that is sought is no longer found on a single PC or server but can be spread across multiple systems and devices. This means that multiple systems and devices may need to be imaged and investigated. Combined with the increasing volume of data issues, as defined in Sections 20.2.2.5 and 20.2.7.1, the possible multiple jurisdictional issues, as defined in Section 20.2.1.4, this will increase the cost of case processing, as defined in Section 20.2.12.4. An additional dimension to this is that different computers, systems and devices can often be under the control of a number of different organizations.

20.2.5.2 At the scene

Where a seizure is undertaken, it must be legal for any evidence seized. This can cause problems if the scope of the potential evidence is not known and 'seizure creep' occurs making some of the evidence seized an illegal seizure. There is rarely a second chance to return to the scene to undertake a second seizure, so it is essential that the seizure paperwork is correct and covers all relevant and required evidence. This can cause problems in defining in the actual scope for seizure.

20.2.5.3 During processing

The identification phase can be attacked if the connection between the evidence obtained and the incident to which it refers can be challenged. Any evidence found must be able to link the evidence to the incident, to enable conclusions and opinions that are repeatable, to be drawn. If this is not provable, then it is possibly subject to challenge. It must be remembered the evidence that is collected must not only include evidence that can prove the suspect's actions (inculpatory) but also evidence that could prove their innocence (exculpatory).

20.2.6 Collecting the evidence

20.2.6.1 Completeness of evidence seized

The collection phase can be attacked if the completeness of the data that is being collected can be challenged or the tools, techniques, procedures, and competence of the Forensic Analyst processing the case can be called into question.

20.2.6.2 Transporting the evidence

Where evidence is seized at the scene and transferred to another location for examination and analysis, the issue of its transportation from the site of seizure to a forensic laboratory can cause issues. The methods of transportation should be safe and secure and protect the evidence from any unauthorized modification or tampering. If this cannot be proven, then it is possible to challenge the transportation process. This is especially the case with mobile devices that may have a remote wipe capability or batteries that can become exhausted and lose volatile memory.

20.2.7 Extracting the evidence

20.2.7.1 Volume of data

The volume of data to be searched is still growing rapidly and the time taken to undertake comprehensive searching is a factor of the number, type, and complexity of searches to be undertaken. The use of specialist tools is essential to recover all of the evidence relevant to the case, and this is a time-consuming process, which also affects the costs of processing the case. All tools, techniques, and procedures for extracting the evidence must be validated and, in some cases, will require dual tool verification and if this is not the case, the evidence may be challenged.

20.2.7.2 Speed of searching

With increasing volumes of data to be searched and the number, type, and complexity of searches to be undertaken, the speed of searching can be seriously impacted, which also affects the costs of processing the case. Depending on the time-table for the case to be processed (either for client or Court requirements), full extraction of all evidence may not be possible. Either the delivery date (TRT or Court date) may have to be amended, if possible, or incomplete extraction may occur. In the latter case, a challenge may well be made to the recovered evidence and its completeness for producing inculpatory evidence as well as exculpatory evidence.

20.2.7.3 Completeness of extracting

It is infeasible that every case has been thorough and completely finished as a case could actually be investigated for years to exhaust every possible avenue of enquiry. There comes a point where the investigation of a forensic case must come to an end and it is usually a function of cost of case processing, time constraints, or the Officer in the Case deciding that 'enough is enough'. At this point, there may still be inculpatory evidence as well as exculpatory evidence that has not been discovered, and this may leave the case processing open to challenge.

20.2.8 Documenting how it was recovered

20.2.8.1 Chain of custody

Only too often is the chain of custody broken and doubt cast on the authenticity and legal acceptance. This is one of the most common methods of undermining a case, and in theory, the creation and maintenance of the chain of custody should be a simple process to maintain.

20.2.9 Interpreting the evidence

20.2.9.1 Difference of interpretation opinions

The interpretation of the evidence can be attacked by calling into question as there are always multiple ways of interpreting evidence that is recovered during case processing. The 'other side' will always put their interpretation on the evidence recovered and this leads to challenges of interpretation of the evidence by either side in a forensic case.

20.2.9.2 Time issues

When trying to determine the timeline of a forensic case, this can prove problematic as time can be a major issue if clocks are amended or different correlating logs are using different time zones or are in different jurisdictions. While timestamps that are generated are usually reliable, the sources that they come from, unless proven to be accurate, can themselves be unreliable and therefore pass on an unreliable time. There are also differences between operating systems where universal time is used as opposed to the government-mandated time (i.e. including daylight saving hours).

It is also possible for a user to tamper with the time on a PC and change it forward or backward as required and create transactions or documents on the new (amended and tampered with time). This can affect trying to reverse timelines as well as taking them forward and is a common area of challenge.

20.2.9.3 Consistency

Given a forensic image, it is possible that a number of Forensic Analysts will interpret the evidence available differently. There are no international standards for interpretation of evidence and all Forensic Analysts will interpret evidence according to their own competencies.

20.2.10 Presenting the evidence (either to the client or a court)

20.2.10.1 Lack of visibility

Digital evidence cannot be seen and may be volatile, unlike some other forms of evidence. On account of this, it is often a major challenge to explain digital evidence and digital case processing of the evidence to a nontechnologist and link the results produced to the original evidence in a form that they can readily comprehend. This problem is applicable to the judiciary that are involved in prosecuting, defending or judging a case as well as the general public who may serve on juries, or a client.

20.2.10.2 Method of presentation

The method of presentation must be appropriate to the audience (either the client or a Court) so that the audiences understand the evidence being presented and that this links the evidence to the incident and allows repeatable and justifiable conclusions to be drawn or opinions presented. The evidence and conclusions drawn from it must be convincing to the intended audience. The wrong method of presentation, actions supporting it, or failure to convince the intended audience can seriously affect the intended outcome of the evidence presentation and so affect the outcome of the case. Some methods of presentation may require the Forensic Analyst to obtain outside assistance for creating convincing presentations.

20.2.10.3 Completeness of the presentation

The presentation phase can be challenged by attacking the reliability and completeness of reports that the Forensic Analyst has produced. This is why it is essential that all work products in the case are peer reviewed by a competent reviewer to ensure their completeness, that the results are repeatable, and that they are fit for purpose. If this is not the case, then they will be subject to challenge, which in turn can lead to challenges relating to the Forensic Analyst's competence and proficiency.

20.2.11 Antiforensics and counter-forensics

Antiforensics are the measures that are taken to prevent digital forensic case processing from being carried out while counter-forensics measures are those taken to inhibit or undermine a digital forensic investigation.

The term antiforensics was originally used by the hacking community and was first used in around 2006. Dr. Marc Rogers from Purdue University has defined antiforensics as 'Attempts to negatively affect the existence, amount and/or quality of evidence from a crime scene or make the analysis and examination of evidence difficult or impossible to conduct'. However, this description encompasses both antiforensics and counter-forensics and the terms are often used interchangeably. The methods described below encompass both antiforensics and counter-forensics. Antiforensic and counter-forensic methods include:

20.2.11.1 Encryption

The use of encryption does not necessarily mean that it is for the purpose of antiforensics although in some ways, it is the perfect antiforensics tool. In the majority of cases where encryption is used, it will be for the purpose of ensuring privacy and confidentiality. The use of encryption is one of the most difficult for the Forensic Analyst to overcome unless they gain access to the encryption keys that have been used. The probability of cracking even a medium grade of encryption is extremely remote with the level of resources that are available to the average digital forensics laboratory.

The use of encryption is becoming increasingly common and the number of freely available and easy-to-use encryption tools is becoming more widespread. New operating systems such as Windows 10 have the BitLocker Drive Encryption feature included and there are other disks and file encryption tools such as AxCrypt, GNU Privacy Guard and VeraCrypt. Applications such as WinZip, Microsoft Office, and Adobe Acrobat provide the ability for the password protection of individual files and groups of files. At the network level, the Secure Sockets Layer and the use of Virtual Private Networks make the collection of network traffic extremely difficult.

20.2.11.2 Data hiding

There are a number of ways to hide data, at least from cursory searches. Data can be hidden in the slack and unallocated spaces on computer hard drives and in the metadata of many types of files. Data can also be hidden in closed sessions on compact disks or on other peoples' systems that have been hijacked. Some of the main methods used for hiding data include Steganography, Covert Channels, and trail obfuscation.

20.2.11.2.1 Steganography

Steganography has been around for more than two millennia and early examples include the tattooing of messages on the courier's scalp and hiding it by letting the hair grow. Modern Steganography is the hiding of information within digital files. Data may be hidden in most types of files including image, audio, video and executable files, and given the wide range of tools and methods that can be used to hide data within files its use is very difficult to detect. While encryption protects the contents of a communication but does not hide the path taken (who was the sender and who was the recipient), Steganography can be used to hide not only the data but also the recipient (if it is posted in an image on a website, it could be accessed by a large number of people, but only the person it was intended for would know that it was there).

20.2.11.2.2 Covert channels

A covert data channel is a communication channel that is hidden inside a legitimate communication channel. An example of this is the Transmission Control Protocol/Internet Protocol (TCP/IP) suite, which has a number of weaknesses that can be exploited to enable covert communications. An example of this is the covert channels that are based on modification of network protocol header values. In a 1985 US Department of Defense publication 'Trusted Computer System Evaluation' defined a covert channel as: '*Any communication channel that can be exploited by a process to transfer information in a manner that violates the system's security policy*'.

This chapter goes on to describe two separate categories of covert channels: storage channels and timing channels. It defines them as '*Covert storage channels include all vehicles that would allow the direct or indirect writing of a storage location by one process and the direct or indirect reading of it by another. Covert timing channels include all vehicles that would allow one process to signal information to another process by modulating its own use of system resources in such a way that the change in response time observed by the second process would provide information*'.

20.2.11.2.3 Trail obfuscation

Trail obfuscation has been an issue for almost as long as there have been publicly accessible computers. It can be achieved by logon spoofing, IP spoofing (often used for Distributed Denial of Service attacks) and Media Access Control (MAC) address spoofing. Other methods of trail obfuscation such as email and Web anonymizers provide privacy services or the wiping or modification of server log files or the changing of file dates.

20.2.11.2.4 Disk and file wiping

There are a number of tools available that can wipe either whole disk drives or files. Commonly available tools including programs such as Blancco, BC Wipe and Eraser can erase either the whole contents of a disk or individual data files. This is normally achieved by overwriting the target a number of times with random data strings. Other tools such as Evidence Eraser can be used to remove temporary files, Internet history, cache files, and wipe both slack and unallocated spaces.

20.2.11.2.5 Physical destruction

The physical destruction of the media is an extremely effective method of preventing any evidence that the media contained from being recovered and has the advantage of being visible and checkable. However, while disk and file wiping tools are freely available and either freeware or very cost-effective, the physical destruction of the media requires either specific tools or the application of considerable force and may not be achievable at short notice.

20.2.11.2.6 Attacks on digital forensics tools

Direct attacks on the digital forensics process are one form of antiforensics. While all other antiforensic techniques are passive, the direct attack on the process is an active measure. All six of the phases of the digital forensic process, Identification, Preservation, Collection, Examination, Analysis and Presentation are potentially liable to attack, as shown above.

There have already been a number of attacks on several of the main digital forensics tools, including Computer Online Forensic Evidence Extractor (COFEE), EnCase, FTK and SleuthKit. An example of this is the application called DECAF that was released by hackers to undermine the Microsoft forensic toolkit, COFEE, which is only available to law enforcement agencies.

20.2.12 Miscellaneous

20.2.12.1 Accreditation and certification

There is a growing demand for the certification of both individual digital forensics practitioners and laboratories to be certified and accredited. This is in part driven by the growing maturity of the science of digital forensics and in part as a result of the growing understanding of the range of skills and knowledge that are needed to conduct effective digital forensic investigations. In the UK, the quality standard required by the Home Office Forensic Science Regulator (FSR) of all government and law enforcement digital forensic laboratories is the current version of ISO/IEC 17025, the Forensic Science Regulators Codes of Practice and Conduct for forensic science providers and practitioners in the Criminal Justice System.

In the USA, there has been an ongoing discussion as to whether Digital Forensic Investigators should be required to carry a Private Investigator's license and in addition, there are the US Department of Justice regulations that govern computer forensics, and the best practices employed by the International Association of Computer Investigative Specialists. In addition, the US National Commission for Forensic Science has published a number of documents regarding proficiency testing and accreditation of forensic practitioners and laboratories.

20.2.12.2   Testing and validation

The testing and validation of tools is an increasing problem with the increasing diversity of tools that will be required. With the increasing diversity of hardware and operating systems as well as the new technologies that are coming into use, there is a requirement for more tools. The life cycle of software and many of the technologies is short, but the testing and validation of the tools required to carry out a forensic investigation of the tools are lengthy. No tool, process, or procedure should ever be used that has not been validated; however, the use of two independent tools (dual tool verification) is one option that can be used to ensure that the evidence produced can be replicated.

20.2.12.3   Key dependence of digital evidence

Frequently, digital evidence is vital to the success of any case.

20.2.12.4   Growth in the need for digital forensics

Increasingly, what was seen as traditional crime now has some element of information processing systems associated with it (e.g. mobile devices) and these devices need to be processed in the prosecution of the crime. This has an impact on the cost of processing a forensic case, as well as the time to prepare the evidence needed to prosecute the case. This leads to the situation where a decision may be made that the costs of the prosecution of the case mean that it is not followed up, as the overhead of forensic case processing makes it impractical to pursue.

20.2.12.5   Training

As has been stated above, there are a variety of academic (or other) courses available. Many of these courses are taught by academics (or others) who have never actually processed a forensic case and so are totally unaware of what this entails. Many academic institutes and commercial training providers seem to have seen this subject as a 'cash cow' and are not particularly worried about the outcome so long as they have fee-paying students to fill the course. This problem is exacerbated by the lack of standard processes and procedures for many aspects of the digital forensic process.

20.2.13   Focus

Typically, digital forensic tools have been created to solve issues where evidence is on a computer or a device. They were not developed to detect and resolve crimes against an information processing system.

Glossary

Throughout this book, the 'terms and definitions' of the relevant standards referenced in this book shall be used. However, there are some that do not fit the relevant standards or may be different from those used in the standards. These are defined herein.

Case Any investigation carried out by a forensic laboratory that uses the processes and disciplines of 'digital forensics'.

Disruptive event An occurrence or change that interrupts planned activities, operations, or functions, whether anticipated or unanticipated (ISO 28000).

> **Note:** A disruptive event can be the result of an information security incident, but not all information security incidents will become a disruptive event (e.g. not complying with a clear desk policy, loss of a backed-up and encrypted mobile device, etc.)

Employee Anyone employed by the Forensic Computing Ltd. Forensic Laboratory (FCL) in any capacity, including but not limited to:

- contractors;
- consultants;
- expert witnesses;
- former members of staff;
- interns;
- members of staff;
- part-time staff;
- prospective members of staff;
- secondees;
- third-party employees.

> **Note:** ISO 45001 uses the term 'worker', but in the book we have used employee rather than this term.

Escort A forensic laboratory employee who accompanies a Visitor during their time on the forensic laboratory premises.

FCL Forensic Computing Ltd.

First Responder A person who is first on the scene after an incident or the first Forensic Analyst or investigator on the scene of an incident.

Forensic Analyst A person responsible for performing forensic work on a case in a forensic laboratory.

Forensic case For the purposes of this book, any reference to a forensic case is to a digital forensic case, i.e. the recovery of digital evidence.

Forensic Team One or more Forensic Analysts deployed on a given case.

Host A forensic laboratory employee who sponsors a Visitor.

IMS Integrated Management System.

Incident Manager The person managing an incident irrespective of what organisation they are from.

Information processing system Any system capable of processing digital information. This covers computers of all types (e.g. desktops, laptops, tablets and servers as well as mobile phones and other devices, and other computer-related peripherals). However, this definition can also include nontypical devices that may contain a computer chip and these can include, but are not limited to:

- a car's engine management system;
- a smart fridge, freezer, microwave, or similar;
- a shop till;
- games consoles; and
- any system with an embedded chip (e.g. Internet of Things (IoT) and Operational Technology (OT)).

Information security For the purposes of this book, the term cyber security has not been used and information security has been used. Cyber security by its definition, rather than marketing speak, is a subset of information security being an attack over cyberspace. Therefore 'Information security' has been used to encompass all forms of protection of 'information' in any form unless otherwise defined.

Investigator A person working with the Forensic Analyst to investigate the case, which may also be the Forensic Analyst.

ISMS Information Security Management System.

Laboratory Manager The person in operational charge of a forensic laboratory.

LE Law Enforcement.

Lead Forensic Analyst The person who is in charge of a team of Forensic Analysts. Where there is only one Forensic Analyst in the Forensic Team, he or she is the Lead Forensic Analyst for the case.

Mobile Device In the context of this book, a 'Mobile Device' is any portable information processing device including, but not limited to Laptops, Tablets, Smart Phones, wearable smart devices, etc.

Noncompliance The failure to adhere to an Act or its Regulations.

Nonconformance Same as nonconformity, but ISO has deprecated the term nonconformance in favour of nonconformity.

Nonconformity The failure to comply with a requirement.

> **Note:** For simplicity, the term 'nonconformity' has been used rather than including both terms. The definition of the nonconformity raised will show if it is a nonconformity or noncompliance.

Officer in the Case Also known as the 'Case Officer'—the lead investigator in a case, typically a Police Officer or similar.

OHSMS Occupational Health and Safety Management System.

QMS Quality Management System.

Third-party An entity (organisation or person) that is not directly involved in the legal interactions between the involved parties but may affect it or be influenced by it.

Visitor An individual, not an employee, who visits the forensic laboratory premises for any reason.

> **Note:** There are times when a person may have more than one role (e.g. a single Forensic Analyst going out on-site to deal with a search and seizure and being appointed the Lead (and only) Forensic Analyst for the case would be the Forensic Team, First Responder, Lead Forensic Analyst, Forensic Analyst, and may be the Laboratory Manager as well).

Index

Note: Page numbers followed by *f* indicate figures and *t* indicate tables.

Printed and bound by CPI Group (UK) Ltd, Croydon, CR0 4YY

03/10/2024

01040322-0014